World Guide

to

Abbreviations of Organizations

Sixth Edition

F. A. BUTTRESS

Leonard Hill

Published by
Leonard Hill
A division of
The Blackie Publishing Group
Bishopbriggs, Glasgow G64 2NZ, and
Furnival House, 14-18 High Holborn, London WC1V 6BX

First Edition	*1954*
Second Edition	*1960*
Third Edition	*1966*
Fourth Edition	*1971*
Fifth Edition	*1974*
This Edition	*1981*

British Library Cataloguing in Publication Data

Buttress, Frederick Arthur
World guide to abbreviations of organizations. — 6th ed.

1. Associations, institutions, etc. — Abbreviations
I. Title
060′.1′48   AS 8

ISBN 0-249-44159-4

Printed in Great Britain

Introduction

Modern times have seen a bewildering proliferation of abbreviations, presenting the reader with a considerable problem of identification. This difficulty is increased, and much of the advantage of abbreviation is lost, when a reader is obliged to search a large publication for definitions inconveniently placed, or, as often happens, when editors fail to record the full meaning of an acronym at least once.

The World Guide offers a wide-ranging and up-to-date summary of the abbreviated titles of organizations and their definitions. This new edition has been expanded from 18 000 to over 27 500 entries. Apart from British, North, Central and South American and international bodies, Common Market countries account for 7 500 entries, and African states for over 1 500. Where the country of origin is not stated, it is assumed to correspond to the language of the entry, except in the case of international and continental areas. This worldwide coverage can be augmented if necessary at a more local level by reference to works dealing exclusively with British or American abbreviations, in which the addresses of many of the organizations can also be found. For a selection of these, the reader is referred to the bibliography (p. vi). An additional bibliography (p. vii) contains sources of Russian and Eastern European abbreviations not covered by the present work.

Grateful acknowledgment is made to the staff of the Library of the Department of Applied Biology, Cambridge; the Cambridge University Library; the Scientific Periodicals Library, Cambridge; the Department of Land Economy Library, Cambridge; the Cambridge Public Library, and the Food and Agricultural Organization Library, Rome. I am also especially indebted to Mr. I. G. Anderson, G. P. Henderson and S. P. A. Henderson of CBD Research Ltd., and finally to those readers who have so kindly pointed out errors and omissions.

F.A.B.

Bibliography

A. Excluding Russia and Eastern Europe

Abbreviations used by FAO for International Organizations, Congresses, Commissions, Committees etc. Terminology Bulletin no.27. 1st revision, Rome, 1976.

Abkürzungen, Abréviations, Abbreviations. Swiss Bank Corporation, London, 1964.

Acronyms, Initialisms and Abbreviations Dictionary. 5th ed. Gale Research Co., Detroit, 1976. (Mainly for USA).

ANDERSON, I.G. (Ed.) *Directory of European Associations. Part 1. National Industrial, Trade and Professional Associations.* 2nd ed. CBD Research Ltd, Beckenham, 1976.

ANDERSON, I.G. (Ed.) *Directory of European Associations. Part 2. National Learned, Scientific and Technical Societies.* CBD Research Ltd, Beckenham, 1975.

ANDERSON, I.G. (Ed.) *Marketing and Management. A World Register of Organisations.* CBD Research Publication. Beckenham, 1969.

COPE, S.T. *Glossary of Abbreviations with Particular Reference to the Telecommunications Industry.* Marconi Co., Chelmsford, 1955.

Directory of Scientific Institutes, Organizations and Services. Scientific Council for Africa South of the Sahara. Publication no.14. London, 1954.

Directory of Scientific Research Organizations in South Africa. CSIR, Pretoria, 1975.

Directory of Scientific and Technical Societies in South Africa. CSIR, Pretoria, 1975.

Encyclopedia of Associations. Vol. 1. National Organizations of the United States. 12th ed. Gale Research Co., Detroit, 1978.

Europa Year Book; a World Survey. 2 vols. London, 1977–8.

European Community Directory and Diary, 1974. Institute of Public Administration, Dublin, 1973.

FANG, J.R. and SONGE, A.H. *International Guide to Library, Archival and Information Science Associations.* Bowker, New York, 1976.

Federation of British Industries Register of British Manufacturers. London, 1965.

GALRÃO, M.J. and ARBOLEDA-SEPÚLVEDA, O. *Directorio de Siglas en Ciencias Agrícolas.* 2nd ed. IICA, Turrialba, Costa Rica, 1971.

Glossary of Symbols and Abbreviations. OEEC, Paris, 1956.

GURNETT, J.W. and KYTE, C.H.J. *Cassell's Dictionary of Abbreviations.* 2nd ed. London, 1972.

Handbook of Commonwealth Organisations. Methuen, London, 1965.

HENDERSON, G.P. and S.P.A. (Eds) *Directory of British Associations.* 5th ed. CBD Research Ltd, Beckenham, 1977–8.

Industrial Research Laboratories of the United States. 13th ed. Bowker Co., New York, 1970.

International Initialese. 2nd ed. Publication no.182. Union of International Associations, Brussels, 1963. 1st Supplement. Publication no.193. 2nd Supplement, 1973.

International Register of Organisations Undertaking Africanist Research in the Social Sciences and Humanities. International African Institute, London, 1971.

International Scientific Organisations. Library of Congress, Washington, 1962.

International Scientific Organisations. OECD, Paris, 1965.

Landbouwgids (Annual). Utrecht. (For the Netherlands).

LANDI, G. *Initials and Acronyms of Bodies, Activities and Projects concerned with Fisheries and Aquatic Sciences.* FAO Fisheries Circular no.110. 2nd revision. Rome, 1975.

MILLARD, P. *Trade Associations and Professional Bodies of the United Kingdom.* 5th ed. Letchworth, 1971.

NATO Handbook. Brussels, 1973.

OECD–ICVA Directory. Development Aid of Non-Governmental Non-Profit Organisations. Paris, 1967.

PUGH, E. *A Dictionary of Acronyms and Abbreviations.* 2nd ed. London, 1970.

PUGH, E. *Second Dictionary of Acronyms and Abbreviations.* London, 1974.

PUGH, E. *Third Dictionary of Acronyms and Abbreviations.* London, 1977.

Register of International Organisations that have Formal Relations with FAO. Rome, 1972.

ROTH, N. *Förkortnings-Lexicon.* 2nd ed. Wahlstrom & Widstrand, Stockholm, 1967.

Scientific and Learned Societies of Great Britain. Allen & Unwin, London, 1964.

Scientific, Technical and Related Societies of the United States. 9th ed. National Academy of Sciences, Washington, 1971.

Sigles Agricoles. Organisations d'Interêt Agricole à Cadre Nationale. Répertoire Alphabétique. Assemblée Permanente des Présidents des Chambres d'Agriculture, Paris, 1965.

Sociétés et Fournisseurs d'Afrique Noire et de Madagascar. 24th ed. Guide Économique NORIA. Paris, 1974.

SPILLNER, P. *Internationales Wörterbuch der Abkürzungen von Organisationen*. 2nd ed. 3 vols. Verlag Dokumentation, München–Pullach, 1970–72.

Tuinbouwgids (Annual). Den Haag. (For the Netherlands).

Whitaker's Almanack. London (Annual).

WILKES, I. *British Initials and Abbreviations*. 3rd ed. International Textbook Co., London, 1971.

WILLIAMS, M. *Directory of Trade Unions in the European Economic Community*. London, 1974.

World Airline Directory. Flight International. Special Issue, 18 May 1972.

World Directory of Social Science Institutions. UNESCO, Paris, 1977.

World Guide to Scientific Associations. 1st ed. Verlag Dokumentation, München–Pullach, 1974.

World Guide to Technical Information and Documentation Services. 2nd ed. UNESCO, Paris, 1975.

World Guide to Trade Associations. 1st ed. Part 1. Europe. Verlag Dokumentation. München–Pullach, 1973.

World Guide to Trade Associations. 1st ed. Part 2. Africa, America, Asia, Oceania. Verlag Dokumentation. München–Pullach, 1974.

World of Learning. Europa Publications, London (latest edition).

Yearbook of International Organizations. 17th ed. Union of International Associations. Brussels, 1979.

B.   Russia and Eastern Europe

BAKO, E. *Hungarian Abbreviations, A Selective List*. Library of Congress, Washington, 1961.

Dictionary of Yugoslav Abbreviations. Medunarodna Politika, Belgrade, 1971.

FURNESS, K.Z. *Bulgarian Abbreviations, A Selective List*. Library of Congress, Washington, 1961.

Glossary of Russian Abbreviations and Acronyms. Library of Congress, Washington, 1967.

HORECKY, P.L. *Czech and Slovak Abbreviations, A Selective List*. Library of Congress, Washington, 1956.

KORITSKII, B.F. (Ed.) *Dictionary of Abbreviations of the Russian Language* (Russian text). State Publishing House, Moscow, 1963.

PATRICK, G.Z. *A List Of Abbreviations Commonly Used in the U.S.S.R.* University of California, Berkeley, 1937.

PLAMENATZ, I.P. *Yugoslav Abbreviations, A Selective List*. 2nd ed. Library of Congress, Washington, 1962.

ROSENBERG, A. *Russian Abbreviations, A Selective List*. 2nd ed. Library of Congress, Washington, 1957.

WOJCICKA, J. *Polish Abbreviations, A Selective List*. 2nd ed. Library of Congress, Washington, 1957.

ZALUCKI, H. *Dictionary of Russian Technical and Scientific Abbreviations*. Elsevier, London, 1968.

A

AA	Advertising Association
AA	Akademisk Arkitektforening
AA	Alcoholics Anonymous
AA	Architectural Association
AA	Automobile Association
AA	Avisenes Arbeidsgiverforening
AAA	Agricultural Adjustment Administration (U.S.A.)
AAA	Allied Artists of America
AAA	Amateur Athletic Association
AAA	American Academy of Advertising
AAA	American Academy of Allergy
AAA	American Accounting Association
AAA	American Airship Association
AAA	American Angus Association
AAA	American Arbitration Association
AAA	American Association of Anatomists
AAA	American Anthropological Association
AAA	American Automobile Association
AAA	Anglo-American Associates (U.S.A.)
AAA	Architectural Aluminium Association
AAA	Association of Attenders and Alumni of the Hague Academy of International Law
AAAA	American Association for Advancement of Atheism
AAAA	American Association of Advertising Agencies
AAAA	American Association of Audio Analgesia
AAAA	Asian Amateur Athletic Association
AAAA	Asociación Argentina 'Amigos de la Astronomia'
AAAA	Association of Accredited Advertising Agencies of New Zealand
AAAA	Australian Association of Advertising Agencies
AAAC	Alliance Atlantique des Anciens Combattants
AAACC	Association of Asian-American Chambers of Commerce

AAACE	American Association of Agricultural College Editors
AAAE	American Association of Airport Executives
AAAEENAA	Association Amicale des Anciens Élèves de l'École National Agronomique d'Alger (*formerly* AAEIAA)
AAAEINA	Association Amicale des Anciens Élèves de l'Institut National Agronomique
AAAF	Association Aéronautique et Astronautique de France
AAAI	Advertising Agencies Association of India
AAAI	Affiliated Advertising Agencies International (U.S.A.)
AAAJ	Association Afro-Asiatique des Journalistes
AAAL	American Academy of Arts and Letters
AAALAC	American Association for Accreditation of Laboratory Animal Care
AAAM	American Association of Aircraft Manufacturers
AAAM	American Association for Automotive Medicine
AAAN	American Academy of Applied Nutrition
AAAS	American Academy of Asian Studies
AAAS	American Academy of Arts and Sciences
AAAS	American Association for the Advancement of Science
AAASA	Association for the Advancement of Agricultural Sciences in Africa
AAASS	American Association for the Advancement of Slavic Studies
AAB	Alliance Agricole Belge
AAB	American Association of Bioanalysts
AAB	Association of Applied Biologists
AABA	Associação Atletica Brasil Açucareiro
AABB	American Association of Blood Banks
AABB	Association des Archivistes et Bibliothécaires de Belgique
AABC	American Association of Bible Colleges
AABDF	Allied Association of Bleachers, Printers, Dyers and Finishers
AABE	Asian Association for Biology Education
AABEVK	Arbeitsgemeinschaft für das Archiv- und Bibliothekswesen in der Evangelischen Kirche
AABGA	American Association of Botanical Gardens and Arboretums

AABL	Associated Australasian Banks in London	**AACK**	Asociación Argentina Criadores de Karakul
AABM	American Association of Battery Manufacturers	**AACL**	Association of American Correspondents in London
AABM	Australian Association of British Manufacturers	**AACLA**	Association of American Chambers of Commerce in Latin America
AABP	Australian Association of Business Relations	**AACM**	American Academy of Compensation Medicine
AAC	Acadèmia Argentina de Cirugía		
AAC	Affärsarbetsgivarnas Centralförbund	**AACMA**	All-Africa Church Music Association
AAC	Agrarische Adviescommissie (of NIBEM)	**AACNP**	Asociación Argentina de Ciéncias Naturáles 'Physis'
AAC	Agricultural Advisory Council for England and Wales	**AACO**	Arab Air Carriers Organization
AAC	Anglo American Corporation	**AACOBS**	Australian Advisory Council on Bibliographical Services
AAC	Association of American Colleges	**AACP**	American Academy for Cerebral Palsy
AAC	Australian Agricultural Council	**AACP**	American Academy of Child Psychiatry
AAC	Austrian Alpine Club	**AACP**	American Association of Colleges of Pharmacy
AACB	Aeronautics and Astronautics Coordinating Board (U.S.A.)	**AACP**	American Association of Commerce Publications
AACB	Association of African Central Banks	**AACP**	American Association of Correctional Psychologists
AACC	Airport Associations Coordinating Council	**AACP**	Anglo-American Council for Productivity
AACC	All Africa Conference of Churches	**AACP**	Association des Agences Conseils en Publicité
AACC	American Association of Cereal Chemists		
AACC	American Association of Clinical Chemists	**AACPS**	American Association of Clinic Physicians and Surgeons
AACC	American Association of Commercial Colleges	**AACR**	American Association for Cancer Research
AACC	American Association for Contamination Control	**AACR**	American Association of Clinical Research
AACC	American Automatic Control Council	**AACR**	Association for the Advancement of Civil Rights (Gibraltar)
AACC	Arab Air Carriers Organization		
AACC	Asociación Argentina de Criadores de Caprinos	**AACREA**	Asociación Argentina de Consorcios Regionales de Experimentación Agrícola
AACC	Asociación Argentina de Criadores de Cebú	**AACSL**	American Association for the Comparative Study of Law
AACC	Asociación Argentina de Criadores de Cerdos	**AACT**	American Association of Clinical Toxicology
AACC	Asociación Argentina de Criadores de Corriedale	**AACTE**	American Association of Colleges for Teacher Education
AACCH	American Association for Child Care in Hospital	**AACU**	American Association of Clinical Urologists
AACCH	Asociación Argentina Criadores de Charolais	**AAD**	American Academy of Dermatology
AACE	African Association for Correspondence Education	**AADE**	American Academy of Dental Electrosurgery
		AADE	American Association of Dental Editors
AACE	American Association for Cancer Education	**AADFI**	Association of African Development Finance Institutions
AACE	American Association of Cost Engineers		
AACG	American Association for Crystal Growth	**AADM**	American Academy of Dental Medicine
AACI	American Association for Conservation Information	**AADR**	American Academy of Dental Radiology
		AADS	American Academy of Dermatology and Syphilology
AACIA	American Association for Clinical Immunity		

AAE	Agrupación Astronautica Española
AAE	American Association of Endodontists
AAE	American Association of Engineers
AAE	Asociación Argentina de Electrotécnicos
AAEA	African Adult Education Association (Nigeria)
AAEA	American Agricultural Economics Association
AAEA	American Agricultural Editors Association
AAEC	Association Africaine pour l'Enseignement par Correspondence
AAEC	Australian Atomic Energy Commission
AAEE	American Association of Economic Entomologists
AAEE	American Association of Electromyography and Electrodiagnosis
AAEE	Association pour l'Accueil des Étudiants Étrangers
AAEIAA	Association des Anciens Élèves de l'Institut Agricole d'Algérie et de l'École Nationale d'Agriculture d'Alger (*now* AAAEENAA)
AAES	Australian Agricultural Economics Society
AAESU	Allgemeine Arabische Eisen und Stahl Union
AAF	Académie d'Agriculture de France
AAF	Agricultural Aids Foundation (U.S.A.)
AAF	American Advertising Federation
AAF	American Architectural Foundation
AAF	American Astronautical Federation
AAF	Asociatia Artiştilor Fotografi din Republica Socialista România
AAFA	Anglo-American Families Association
AAFCO	Association of American Fertiliser Control Officials
AAFE	Asociación Argentina de Fomento Equiño
AAFI	Association des Anciens Fonctionnaires Internationaux
AAFM	American Association of Feed Microscopists
AAFRA	Association of African Airlines
AAFS	American Academy of Forensic Sciences
AAFU	All African Farmers Union
AAG	Afdeling Agrarische Geschiedenis
AAG	Association of American Geographers
AAGBA	American Angora Goat Breeders' Association
AAGG	Asociación Argentina de Geofisicos y Geodestas
AÄGP	Allgemeine Ärztliche Gesellschaft für Psychotherapie
AAGREF	Association Amicale de Genie Rural des Eaux et des Forêts
AAGS	Association of African Geological Surveys
AAGUS	American Association of Genito-Urinary Surgeons
AAHA	American Association of Handwriting Analysts
AAHD	American Academy of the History of Dentistry
AAHE	American Association for Higher Education
AAHM	American Association for the History of Medicine
AAHO	Afro-Asian Housing Organisation (Egypt)
AAHPER	American Association for Health, Physical Education, and Recreation
AAHRA	Asian and Australasian Hotel and Restaurant Association (Singapore)
AAHS	American Aviation Historical Society
AAI	Académie des Affaires Internationales (U.S.A.)
AAI	African-American Institute (U.S.A.)
AAI	Agricultural Ammonia Institute (U.S.A.)
AAI	American Association of Immunologists
AAI	Architectural Association of Ireland
AAI	Association Actuarielle Internationale
AAI	Association of Advertisers in Ireland
AAI	Association of Art Institutions
AAIA	Association on American Indian Affairs
AAID	American Association of Industrial Dentists
AAIE	American Association of Industrial Editors
AAIE	American Association of Industrial Engineers
AAIH	Association Amicale des Ingénieurs Horticoles et des Élèves de l'École Nationale d'Horticulture de Versailles
AAIN	American Association of Industrial Nurses
AAIO	Afro-Asian Islamic Organization
AAIPS	American Association of Industrial Physicians and Surgeons
AAJR	American Academy for Jewish Research
AAL	Académia Argentina de Létras
AAL	Association of Assistant Librarians
AALAS	American Association for Laboratory Animal Science

AALDI	Association of Agricultural Librarians and Documentalists of India	**AANS**	American Academy of Neurological Surgery
AALGCSU	American Association of Land Grant Colleges and State Universities	**AANS**	American Agricultural News Service
AALL	American Association for Labour Legislation	**AAO**	American Academy of Osteopathy
AALL	American Association of Law Libraries	**AAO**	American Association of Ophthalmology
AALS	American Association of Library Schools	**AAO**	American Association of Orthodontists
AALS	Association of American Law Schools	**AAO**	Arbeitsgemeinschaft der Altphilologen Österreichs
AAM	American Academy of Microbiology	**AAODC**	American Association of Oilwell Drilling Contractors
AAM	Anti-Apartheid Movement	**AAOEC**	Afro-Asian Organization for Economic Cooperation
AAM	Asociación Argentina de Marketing	**AAOGAS**	American Association of Obstetricians, Gynecologists and Abdominal Surgeons
AAM	Automobile Association of Malaysia	**AAOM**	American Academy of Occupational Medicine
AAMA	American Academy of Medical Administration	**AAOM**	American Academy of Oral Medicine
AAMA	American Apparel Manufacturers Association	**AAOMD**	American Association on Mental Deficiency
AAMA	Automotive Accessories Manufacturers of America	**AAOO**	American Academy of Ophthalmology and Otolaryngology
AAMC	Association of American Medical Colleges	**AAOP**	American Academy of Oral Pathology
AAMCH	American Association for Maternal and Child Health	**AAOS**	American Academy of Orthopaedic Surgery
AAMD	American Association on Mental Deficiency	**AAOT**	American Association of Orthoptic Technicians
AAMF	Association Aéromédicale de France	**AAP**	American Academy of Pediatrics
AAMI	Association for the Advancement of Medical Instrumentation (U.S.A.)	**AAP**	American Academy of Periodontology
AAMMC	American Association of Medical Milk Commissions	**AAP**	Art Association of the Philippines
AAMOA	Afro-American Music Opportunities Association	**AAP**	Association for the Advancement of Psychoanalysis (U.S.A.)
AAMOCIOS	Conseil International pour l'Organisation Scientifique Regional Committee Asia	**AAP**	Association for the Advancement of Psychotherapy (U.S.A.)
AAMPR	American Association of Medico-Physical Research	**AAP**	Association of American Physicians
AAMR	American Academy on Mental Retardation	**AAP**	Association of American Publishers
AAMRL	American Association of Medical Record Librarians	**AAP**	Australian Associated Press
AAMS	American Air Mail Society	**AAPA**	Advertising Agency Production Association
AAMS	Associated African and Malagasy States	**AAPA**	American Association of Port Authorities
AAMSW	American Association of Medical Social Workers	**AAPA**	Asociación Argentina de Producción Animal
AAMVA	American Association of Motor Vehicle Administrators	**AAPA**	Asociación Argentina de Productores Agrícolas
AAN	American Association of Neuropathologists	**AAPA**	Association of Accredited Practitioners in Advertising (South Africa)
AANA	Australian Association of National Advertisers	**AAPA**	Australian Asphalt Pavement Association
AANO	Albanian-American National Organisation	**AAPB**	American Association of Pathologists and Bacteriologists
AANP	American Association of Neuropathologists	**AAPC**	All African Peoples' Conference
		AAPC	Asociación Argentina para el Progreso de las Ciencias

AAPCC	American Association of Poison Control Centres	**AARF**	Australian Accounting Research Foundation
AAPCO	Association of American Pesticide Control Officials	**AAROI**	Associazione Anestesisti Rianimatori Ospedalieri Italiani
AAPD	American Academy of Physiologic Dentistry	**AARP**	American Association of Retired Persons
AAPG	American Association of Petroleum Geologists	**AARRO**	Afro-Asian Rural Reconstruction Organisation
AAPI	Associazione Aziende Pubblicitarie Italiane	**AARS**	American Association of Railway Surgeons
AAPL	Afro-American Patrolmen's League	**AARS**	Awassa Agricultural Research Station (Ethiopia)
AAPM	American Association of Physicists in Medicine	**AART**	American Association for Rehabilitation Therapy
AAPM	Asian Association of Personnel Management	**AARU**	Association of Arab Universities (Egypt)
AAPMR	American Academy of Physical Medicine and Rehabilitation	**AAS**	American Antiquarian Society
		AAS	American Astronomical Society
AAPO	All African Peoples' Organisation	**AAS**	Archaeology Abroad Service
AAPOR	American Association for Public Opinion Research	**AAS**	Association of Architects and Surveyors
		AAS	Association des Archivistes Suisses
AAPPP	American Association of Planned Parenthood Physicians	**AAS**	Association for Asia Studies (U.S.A.)
AAPRO	Asociación Argentina de la Productividad	**AAS**	Auckland Astronomical Society (N.Z.)
AAPS	African Association of Political Science (Tanzania)	**AASA**	American Association of School Administrators
AAPS	American Association of Plastic Surgeons	**AASA**	Australian Association of Social Anthropologists
AAPS	American Association for the Promotion of Science	**AASB**	American Association of Small Businesses
AAPS	Asian Association of Pediatric Surgeons	**AASCW**	American Association of Scientific Workers
AAPS	Association of American Physicians and Surgeons	**AASE**	Australian Associated Stock Exchanges
		AASG	Association of American State Geologists
AAPSC	Afro-Asian Peoples Solidarity Council	**AASHTO**	American Association of State Highway and Transportation Officials
AAPSC	American Association of Psychiatric Services for Children	**AASL**	American Association of School Librarians
AAPSE	American Association of Professors in Sanitary Engineering	**AASL**	American Association of State Libraries
		AASM	Associated African States and Madagascar
AAPSO	Afro-Asian Peoples Solidarity Organisation (Egypt)	**AASND**	American Association for Study of Neoplastic Diseases
AAPSS	American Academy of Political and Social Sciences	**AASP**	American Association of Stratigraphic Palynologists
AAPT	American Association of Physics Teachers	**AASP**	American Association of Swine Practitioners
AAPTS & R	Australian Association for Predetermined Time Standards and Research	**AASP**	Association d'Agences Suisses de Publicité
		AASS	American Association for Social Security
AAR	Association of American Railroads	**AASSREC**	Association of Asian Social Science Research Councils (India)
AARC	Asociación de Agricultores del Rio Caulicán (Mexico)	**AAST**	American Association for the Surgery of Trauma
AARDES	Association Algérienne pour la Recherche Démographique Économique et Sociale	**AASU**	All-African Students Union (Tanzania)
AARDS	Australian Advertising Rate and Data Service	**AATA**	Anglo-American Tourist Association

AATCA	Austrian Air Traffic Controllers Association
AATCC	American Association of Textile Chemists and Colorists
AATM	American Academy of Tropical Medicine
AATNU	Administration de l'Assistance Technique des Nations Unies
AATP	American Academy of Tuberculosis Physicians
AATRAA	Association Argentina de Tecnicos de Refrigeración y Acondiciónamiento de Aire
AATS	American Association for Thoracic Surgery
AATS	Committee on the Application of Aerospace Technology to Society (*of* AIAA)
AATSEEL	American Association of Teachers of Slavic and East European Languages
AATT	American Association for Textile Technology
AATTA	Arab Association of Tourism and Travel Agents
AATUF	All-African Trade Union Federation
AAU	Amateur Athletic Union of Eire
AAU	Amateur Athletic Union of the United States
AAU	Association of American Universities
AAUN	American Association for the United Nations
AAUP	American Association of University Presses
AAUP	American Association of University Professors
AAUW	American Association of University Women
AAV	Nederlandse Vereniging van Algemene Aansprakelijk heids-Verzekeraars
AAVA	American Association of Veterinary Anatomists
AAVIM	American Association for Vocational Instructional Materials
AAVN	American Association of Veterinary Nutrition
AAVP	American Association of Veterinary Parasitologists
AAVSC	American Association of Volunteer Services Coordinators
AAVSO	American Association of Variable Star Observers
AAVT	Association of Audio-Visual Technicians (U.S.A.)
AAWE	Association of American Wives of Europeans
AAWSA	Addis Ababa Water and Sewerage Authority (Ethiopia)
AAYPL	Atlantic Association of Young Political Leaders
AAZPA	American Association of Zoological Parks and Aquariums
AB	Alliance Balkanique
ABA	Amateur Boxing Association
ABA	American Bankers Association
ABA	American Bakers' Association
ABA	American Booksellers' Association
ABA	Antiquarian Booksellers Association
ABA	Association Belge des Aerosols
ABA	Association of British Archaeologists
ABAA	Antiquarian Booksellers Association of America
ABAA	Association of British Adoption Agencies
ABAC	Association of British Aero Clubs
ABAC	Association of British Aviation Consultants
ABADCAM	Association des Bibliothécaires, Archivistes, Documentalistes et Muséographers du Cameroun
ABAFA	Association of British Adoption and Fostering Agencies
ABAH	Asociación de Bibliotecarios y Archiveros de Honduras
ABAM	Association of Bee Appliance Manufacturers
ABAM	Association Belge des Assureurs Maritimes
ABAN	Algemene Bond van Autorijsschoolhouders in Nederland
ABAP	Associação Brasileira de Agencias de Propaganda
ABAPE	Associaçao Brasileira de Administraçao de Pessoal
ABAPSTAS	Association of Blind and Partially Sighted Teachers
ABAS	Amateur Basketball Association of Scotland
ABB	American Board of Bioanalysis
ABB	Association Belge des Banques
ABB	Asociación Boliviana de Bibliotecarios
ABBA	Amateur Basket Ball Association
ABBF	Association of Bronze and Brass Founders
ABBL	Association des Banques et Banquiers Luxembourg
ABBMM	Association of British Brush Machinery Manufacturers
ABC	Academia Brasileira de Ciencias
ABC	Africa Bibliographic Centre (Tanzania)
ABC	American Bibliographical Centre
ABC	Asian Badminton Confederation

ABC	Asian Basketball Confederation	ABDP	Association of British Directory Publishers
ABC	Asian Benevolent Corps (U.S.A.)	ABDSA	Association of British Dental Surgery Assistants
ABC	Asian Billiards Confederation (Japan)		
ABC	Associação Brasileira de Criadores	ABE	Asociação Brasileira de Exportadores
ABC	Audit Bureau of Circulations of South Africa Ltd	ABEAS	Association Belge des Entreprises d'Alimentation à Succursales
ABC	Audit Bureau of Circulations (U.S.A.)	ABEAS	Associação Brasileira de Educação Agrícola Superior
ABC	Australian Broadcasting Commission	ABEBD	Associação Brasileira de Escolas de Biblioteconomia e Documentação
ABCA	American Business Communication Association		
ABCA	Association des Banques Centrales Africaines	ABEC	Asociación Boliviana de Educación Catolica
		ABEDA	Arab Bank for Economic Development in Africa
ABCA	Association Belge des Chefs d'Approvisionnement	ABEF	Association des Bibliothèques Ecclésiastiques de France
ABCAR	Asociación Brasilena de Crédito y Asistensia Rural	ABELF	Association Belge des Éditeurs de Langue Française
ABCB	American Bottlers of Carbonated Beverages	ABEM	Association Belge pour l'Étude, l'Essai et l'Emploi des Matériaux
ABCC	Association of British Chambers of Commerce		
ABCC	Association of British Correspondence Colleges	ABES	Asociación de Bibliotecarios de El Salvador
		ABETA	Associação Brasileira de Estudos Técnicos de Agricultura
ABCD	Art, Copy and Design Association of Sweden		
ABCD	Association Belge de la Chaussure au Détail (France)	ABEX	Association Belge des Experts
		ABF	Aerosolindustriens Brancheforening
ABCFM	American Board of Commissioners for Foreign Missions	ABF	American Beekeeping Federation
		ABF	Arbetarnas Bildningsförbund
ABCI	Amis Belges de la Cooperation Internationale	ABF	Asian Baptist Fellowship
ABCM	Association of British Chemical Manufacturers	ABF	Association des Bibliothécaires Français
		ABF	Den Danske Antikvarboghandlerforening
ABCO	Association of British Conference Organisers	ABFACD	Association Belge des Fabricants d'Appareils de Chauffage et de Cuisine Domestiques
ABCOOP	Aliança Brasileira de Cooperativas		
ABCP	Asian Buddhist Conference for Peace (Japan)	ABFL	Association of British Foam Laminators
ABCP	Associação Técnica Brasileira de Celulose e Papel	ABFM	American Board of Foreign Missions
		ABG	Association of British Geodesists
ABCPA	Alberta Beef Cattle Performance Association (Canada)	ABG	Associazione Italiana fra gli Industriali delle Acque e Bevande
ABCT	Association Belgo-Zairoise du Textile	ABGRA	Asociación de Bibliotecarios Graduados de la República Argentina
ABD	Association Belge des Detectives		
ABD	Association Belge du Diabète	ABH	Association Belge des Hôpitaux
ABD	Association Belge de Documentation	ABH	Association of British Hairdressers
ABD	Association of British Detectives	ABHM	Association of Builders Hardware Manufacturers
ABDA	Arbeitsgemeinschaft der Berufsvertretungen Deutscher Apotheker		
		ABI	American Butter Institute
ABDI	Asociação Brasileira de Desenho Industrial	ABI	Asociación de Bienestar Infantil (Guatemala)
		ABI	Association des Bibliothèques Internationales
ABDIB	Associação Brasileira para o Desenvolvimento das Industrias de Base	ABI	Associazione Bancaria Italiana

ABIA	Associação Brasileira das Industrias da Alimentação
ABIC	Association Belge de l'Industrie du Caoutchouc
ABICIT	Association Belge d'Ingénieurs-Conseils Diplomés Ingénieurs Techniciens
ABICTIC	Association Belge des Ingénieurs, des Chimistres et des Techniciens des Industries du Cuir
ABIEAS	Asociación Boliviana de Instituciones de Educación Agrícola Superior
ABIISE	Agrupación de Bibliotecas para la Integración de la Información Socio-Económica (Peru)
ABIM	American Board of International Missions
ABIM	Association of British Insecticide Manufacturers
ABIPAR	Asociación de Bibliotecarios del Paraguay
ABIR	Associação Brasileira de Informação Rural
ABIS	Association of Burglary Insurance Surveyors
ABITA	Association Belge des Ingénieurs et Technicians de l'Aéronautique et de l'Astronautique
ABJ	Association of Brewers of Japan
ABJA	Association Belge des Journalistes Agricoles
ABJPAA	Association Belge des Journalistes Professionnels de l'Aéronautique et de l'Astronautique
ABL	Association Belge des Logopèdes
ABLC	Association of British Launderers and Cleaners
ABLGPL	Association Belgo-Luxembourgeoise des Gaz de Pétrole Liquefiés
ABLISS	Association of British Library and Information Studies Schools
ABLS	Association of British Library Schools
ABM	Associação Brasileira de Matais
ABM	Association Belge du Moulinage
ABM	Association of British Maltsters
ABM	Australian Board of Missions
ABMA	American Boiler Manufacturers Association
ABMAC	American Bureau for Medical Aid to China
ABMAC	Association of British Manufacturers of Agricultural Chemicals (*now* BAA)
ABMEX	Association of British Mining Equipment Exporters
ABMP	Association Belge des Matières Plastiques
ABMPM	Association of British Manufacturers of Printers Machinery
ABMS	American Bureau of Metal Statistics
ABMS	Associação Brasileira de Mecanica dos Solos
ABN	Algemene Nederlandse Bond van Natuursteen-bewerkende Bedrijven
ABNEI	Association Belge des Négociants Exportateurs et Importateurs
ABNT	Associaçao Brasiliera de Normas Técnicas
ABO	American Board of Ophthalmology
ABO	American Board of Otolaryngology
ABO	Associaçao Brasileira de Odontologia
ABOCF	Association of British Organic and Compound Fertilisers
ABOI	Association of British Oceanological Industries
ABOP	Algemene Bond van Onderwijzend Personeel
ABP	Association Belge des Paralysés
ABPA	Australian Book Publishers Association
ABPC	American Book Publishers Council
ABPC	Associated British Picture Corporation
ABPC	Association Belge de Photographie et de Cinématographie
ABPC	Association of British Packing Contractors
ABPE	Association Belgo-Luxembourgeoise de la Presse d'Entreprise
ABPI	Association of the British Pharmaceutical Industry
ABPM	American Board of Preventive Medicine
ABPN	American Board of Psychiatry and Neurology
ABPN	Association of British Paediatric Nurses
ABPNL	Association Belge des Pilotes et Navigateurs de Ligne
ABPVM	Association of British Plywood and Veneer Manufacturers
ABQ	Associação Brasileira de Quimica
ABRA	Asociação Brasileira de Reforma Agraria
ABRACE	Associação Brasileira de Computadores Electronicos
ABRAPEC	Associação Brasileira de Orientação Agro Pecuária
ABRAVA	Associação Brasileira de Refrigeração, Ar-Condicionado, Ventilação e Aquecimento
ABRFM	Association of British Roofing Felt Manufacturers

ABRO	Animal Breeding Research Organization	**ABYA**	Association of British Yacht Agents
ABRP	Association of British Rose Producers	**ABZ**	Association of British Zoologists
ABRRM	Association of British Reclaimed Rubber Manufacturers	**AC**	Affärsarbetsgivarnas Centralförbund
		ACA	Acoustic Corporation of America
ABRS	Association of British Riding Schools	**ACA**	Advertisement Contractors Association
ABS	American Bible Association	**ACA**	Agence Camerounaise d'Assurances
ABS	American Bureau of Shipping	**ACA**	Agence Congolaise d'Assurances
ABS	Association des Bibliothécaires Suisses	**ACA**	Agricultural Co-operative Association (*now* ACMS)
ABS	Association of British Spectroscopists		
ABS	Association of Broadcasting Staffs	**ACA**	American College of Apothecaries
ABS	Auckland Botanical Society (N.Z.)	**ACA**	American Composers Alliance
ABSI	Association of the Boot and Shoe Industry	**ACA**	Asociación Centro-americana de Anatomia
ABSM	Association of British Sterilizer Manufacturers	**ACA**	Asociación Colombiana de Apicultores
		ACA	Association of Canadian Advertisers
ABSTECH	American Bureau of Shipping Worldwide Technical Services	**ACA**	Association des Compagnies d'Assurances Agréés au Grand-Duché de Luxembourg
ABSW	Association of British Science Writers	**ACA**	Australian Consumers Association
ABT	Association of Building Technicians	**ACA**	Australian Council for Aeronautics
ABTA	Allied Brewery Trader's Association	**ACAAI**	Air Cargo Agents Association of India
ABTA	Association of British Travel Agents	**ACABQ**	Advisory Committee on Administrative and Budgetary Questions (UN)
ABTA	Australian British Trade Association		
ABTAC	Australian Book Trade Advisory Committee	**ACACC**	Asian Conference on Agricultural Credit and Cooperatives
ABTAPL	Association of British Theological and Philosophical Libraries	**ACADEVIR**	Collège Academique International de l'Environnement
ABTB	Aartsdiocesane Roomskatholieke Boeren-en Tuindersbond	**ACADI**	Association des Cadres Dirigeants de l'Industrie pour le Progrès Sociale et Économique
ABTCM	Association of British Textured Coating Manufacturers		
		ACAE	Ateliers et Chantiers de l'Afrique Equatoriale
ABTICS	Abstract and Book Title Index Card Service	**ACAHN**	Asociación Centro-Americano de Historia Natural (Guatemala)
ABTL	Association Belge des Technologues de Laboratoire		
		ACAI	Accademia Archeologica Italiana
ABTM	Association of British Transport Museums	**ACAI**	Associazione fra i Costruttori in Acciaio Italiani
ABTSA	Association of British Tree Surgeons and Arborists		
		ACAI	Associazione Cristiana Artigiani Italiani
ABTT	Association of British Theatre Technicians	**ACAIT**	Asociación Centroamericana de Industrias Textiles (Guatemala)
ABTUC	All-Burma Trade Union Congress		
ABU	Alliance Biblique Universelle	**ACAM**	Association des Compagnies d'Assurances Moyennes
ABU	Asian Broadcasting Union		
ABUEN	Asociación de Bibliotecas Universitarias y Especializadas de Nicaragua	**ACAMAR**	Asociación Centroamericana de Armadores (Guatemala)
ABV	Algemeen Belgisch Vlasverbond	**ACAP**	Asociación Colombiana de Agencias de Publicidad
ABWAK	Association of British Wild Animal Keepers		
ABWARC	Australian Baptist World Aid and Relief Committee	**ACAPA**	American Concrete Agricultural Pipe Association
ABWE	Association of Baptists for World Evangelism (U.S.A)	**ACAR**	Associacão de Credito e Assistencia Rural (Brazil)

ACARPESC Serviço de Extensão de Santa Catarina

ACAS Advisory Conciliation and Arbitration Service

ACAS Association Centrale des Assistants Sociaux (Belgium)

ACAST *see* ACASTD

ACASTD Advisory Committee on the Application of Science and Technology to Development (*of* UNO)

ACATS Association of Civil Aviation Technical Staffs

ACAUP Associazione Capi Aziende Pubblicitarie

ACAV American Committee on Arthropod-borne Viruses

ACB Asociación Costarricense de Bibliotecarios

ACB Association Canadienne des Bibliothèques

ACBCC Advisory Committee to the Board and to the Committee on Commodities (UNCTAD)

ACBCU Association Canadienne des Bibliothèques de Collège et d'Université

ACBD Association Canadienne des Bibliothèques de Droit

ACBI Agricultural Cooperatives Bank of Iran

ACBLF Association Canadienne des Bibliothécaires de Langue Française (*now* ASTED)

ACBM Association Canadienne des Bibliothèques Musicales

ACC Administrative Committee on Co-ordination (ECOSOC)

ACC Agricultural Credit Corporation Ltd

ACC Asian Coconut Community

ACC Associated Communications Corporation

ACCA American Clinical and Climatological Association

ACCA American Cotton Cooperative Association

ACCA Associated Chambers of Commerce of Australia

ACCA Association of Certified and Corporate Accountants

ACCAST Advisory Committee on Colonial Colleges of Arts, Science and Technology (*now* COCAST)

ACC & CE Association of Consulting Chemists and Chemical Engineers (U.S.A.)

ACCCI American Coke and Coal Chemicals Institute

ACCEC Australian Chambers of Commerce Export Council

ACCEFN Academia Colombiana de Ciencias Exactas Físicas y Naturales

ACCET Asian Centre for Comparative Education (Iran)

ACCF Agence Centrafricaine des Communications Fluviales

ACCFA Agricultural Credit and Co-operative Financing Administration (Philippines)

ACCG American Committee for Crystal Growth

ACCHAN Allied Command Channel

ACCI Association of Chambers of Commerce of Ireland

ACCL American Council of Commercial Laboratories

ACCMLRI Association des Caisses de Crédit Mutuel Libres à Responsabilité Illimitée

ACCN Académia Chilena de Ciências Naturales

ACCO Algemene Classificatiecommissie voor de Overheidsadministratie

ACCO Association of Child Care Officers

ACCOR Associated Chambers of Commerce of Rhodesia

ACCP American College of Chest Physicians

ACCS Associazione del Commercio dei Cereali e Semi

ACCT Agence de Coopération Culturelle et Technique

ACCTI American Chamber of Commerce for Trade with Italy

ACCU Asian Confederation of Credit Unions

ACDA Asian Centre for Development Administration (Malaysia)

ACDA United States Arms Control and Disarmament Agency

ACDB Association du Catalogue Documentaire du Bâtiment

ACDE Asociación Cristiana de Dirigentes de Empresa (Uruguay)

ACDI Agence Canadienne de Développement International

ACDI Agricultural Cooperative Development International (U.S.A.)

ACDO Association of Civil Defence Officers

ACDRI CSIR Advisory Committee on the Development of Research for Industry (South Africa)

ACDS Anglo Continental Dental Society

ACDTPN	Association pour le Controle de la Descendance des Taureaux Pie Noirs	**ACFAS**	Association Canadienne Française pour l'Avancement des Sciences
ACE	Académia de Ciéncias Económicas (Argentina)	**ACFB**	Associations Culturelles Franco-Brésiliennes (Brazil)
ACE	Advisory Centre for Education	**ACFFTU**	All-Ceylon Federation of Free Trade Unions
ACE	Allied Command Europe	**ACFHE**	Association of Colleges for Further and Higher Education
ACE	Americans for Childrens Relief		
ACE	American Council on Education	**ACFMO**	Alliance de Constructeurs Français de Machines-Outils
ACE	Amitiés Chrétiennes Européennes		
ACE	Association of Conference Executives	**ACFOA**	Australian Council for Overseas Aid
ACE	Association of Consulting Engineers	**ACFOD**	Asian Cultural Forum on Development (Thailand)
ACE	Association des Conseillers Européens	**ACFRA**	Assureurs Conseils Franco-Africains
ACE	Athens Centre of Ekistiks (Greece)	**ACGB**	Aircraft Corporation of Great Britain
ACE	Australian Christian Endeavour Union	**ACGB**	Arts Council of Great Britain
ACEA	Asociación Costarricense de Economistas Agrícolas (Costa Rico)	**ACGBI**	Automobile Club of Great Britain and Ireland
		ACGF	Australian Citrus Growing Federation
ACEA	Canadian Association of African Studies	**ACGR**	Associate Committee on Geotechnical Research (Canada)
ACEAR	Atelier Central d'Études d'Aménagement Rural		
		ACH	Academia Colombiana de Historia
ACEB	Association Canadienne des Écoles de Bibliothécaires	**ACHA**	American College of Hospital Administration
ACEC	Advisory Council on Energy Conservation	**ACHA**	Asociación Criadores de Holando Argentino
ACEC	Associazione Cattolica Esercenti Cinema	**ACHAC**	Association des Centres pour Handicapés de l'Afrique Centrale
ACEC	Ateliers de Constructions Électriques de Charleroi	**ACHAP**	Asociación Chilena de Agencias de Publicidad
ACEHI	Association of Canadian Educators of the Hearing-Impaired	**ACHCN**	Academia Chilena de Ciencias Naturales
ACEI	Association for Childhood Education International (U.S.A.)	**ACHIF**	Asociación Chilena de Ingenieros Forestales
		ACHM	Asociación Chilena Microbiología
ACEIB	Association des Centrales Électriques Industrielles de Belgique	**ACHTR**	Advisory Committee for Humid Tropics Research (of UNESCO)
ACEID	Asian Centre of Educational Innovation for Development (Thailand)	**ACI**	African Cultural Institute (Senegal)
		ACI	Algemene Vereniging voor de Centrale Verwarmings- en Luchtbehandelingsindustrie
ACEN	Assembly of Captive European Nations		
ACENZ	Association of Consultant Engineers of New Zealand	**ACI**	Alliance Coopérative Internationale
		ACI	American Concrete Institute
ACEO	Association of Chief Education Officers	**ACI**	Association Cartographique Internationale
ACEP	Advisory Committee on Export Policy (U.S.A.)	**ACI**	Association of Chambers of Commerce of Ireland
ACER	Australian Council for Educational Research	**ACI**	Automobile Club d'Italia
ACERP	Asociación Cubana de Ejecutivos de Relaciones Públicas	**ACIA**	Asociación Centroamericana de Informaciones Agrícolas
ACF	Académie Canadienne Française	**ACIA**	Asociación Colombiana de Ingenieros Agrónomos
ACF	Agricultural Co-operative Federation		
ACF	Australian Conservation Foundation	**ACIA**	Association of the Corporation of Insurance Agents
ACF	Automobile Club de France		

11

ACIAA	Australian Commercial and Industrial Artists Association
ACIC	Aeronautical Charting and Information Centre (U.S.A.)
ACICAFE	Association du Commerce et de l'Industrie du Café dans la CEE
ACID	Advisory Committee on Industrial Development (S. Rhodesia)
ACID	Association of Canadian Industrial Designers
ACIEAS	Asociación Colombiana de Instituciones de Educación Agrícola Superior
ACIEL	Coordinating Action of Free Institutions of Commerce and Trade (Argentine)
ACIEMP	Association Catholique Internationale d'Études Médico-Psychologiques
ACIESTI	Association Catholique Internationale des Enseignants et Chercheurs en Sciences et Techniques de l'Information
ACIF	Asociación Colombiana de Ingenieros Forestales
ACIFA	Auxiliare Commerciale Immobilière Franco-Africaine
ACIL	American Council of Independent Laboratories
ACILECE	Association Cooperative Intersyndicale de Librairie et d'Édition du Corps Enseignant
ACIM	American Committee on Italian Migration
ACIMALL	Associazione Costruttori Italiani Macchine e Accessori per la Lavorazione del Legno
ACIMGA	Associazione Costruttori Italiani Macchine Grafiche e Affini
ACIMIT	Associazione Costruttori Italiani di Macchinario per l'Industria Tessile
ACINDECO	Action Internationale de Développement Coopératif
ACIOPJF	Association Catholique Internationale des Oeuvres de Protection de la Jeune Fille
ACIS	American Committee for Irish Studies
ACISJF	Association Catholique Internationale des Services de la Jeunesse Féminine
ACIT	Académie Internationale du Tourisme
ACIT	Association des Chimistes de l'Industrie Textile
ACIVS	Association Internationale pour la Lutte contre la Violence Associée au Sport
ACIWLP	American Committee for International Wild Life Protection
ACJ	Alianz Mundial de Asociaciones Christianas de Jóvenes
ACL	Académia Carioca de Létras (Brazil)
ACL	Academia Chilena de la Lengua
ACL	Academia das Ciéncias de Lisboa
ACL	Atlantic Container Line Ltd
ACLALS	Association for Commonwealth Literature and Language Studies (Canada)
ACLAM	American College of Laboratory Animal Medicine
ACLANT	Allied Command Atlantic
ACLS	American Council of Learned Societies
ACLU	American Civil Liberties Union
ACM	Arab Common Market
ACM	Association for Computing Machines (U.S.A.)
ACM	Association of Crane Makers (*now* FMCEC)
ACM	Ateliers et Chantiers du Mali
ACMA	Agricultural Co-operative Managers Association
ACMA	Asbestos Cement Manufacturers Association
ACMA	Asphalt Coated Macadam Association
ACMA	Associated Chambers of Manufacturers of Australia
ACMC	Association of Canadian Medical Colleges
ACME	Advisory Council on Medical Education (U.S.A.)
ACME	Association of Consulting Management Engineers (U.S.A.)
ACMET	Advisory Council on Middle East Trade
ACMF	American Corn Millers Federation
ACML	Anti-Common Market League
ACML	Association of Canadian Map Libraries
ACMRR	Advisory Committee on Marine Resources Research (FAO)
ACMS	Agricultural Co-operation and Marketing Services
ACMS	Australasian Conference on the Mechanics of Structures and Materials
ACNA	Aziende Colori Nazionali Affini Spa
ACNUR	United Nations High Commissioner for Refugees
ACOA	American Committee on Africa
ACODEX	Asociación Colombiana de Exportadores
ACOEXA	Asociación Colombiana de Expertos Agrícolas

ACOFAL	Asociación Colombiana de Fabricantes de Alimentos para Animales	**ACPF**	Asociación del Congreso Panamericano de Ferrocarrilles (Argentina)
ACOG	American College of Obstetricians and Gynecologists	**ACPI**	Associazione Consulenti Pubblicitari Italiani
ACOGE	Asociación Colombiana de Geógrafos	**ACPM**	American College of Preventive Medicine
ACOH	Advisory Committee for Operational Hydrology (WMO)	**ACPM**	American Congress on Physical Medicine
ACOMEX	Asociación Colombiana de Comercio Exterior	**ACPM**	Association of Corrugated Paper Makers
		ACPO	Asian Committee for People's Organization (Philippines)
ACOMR	Advisory Committee on Oceanic Meteorological Research (*of* WMO)	**ACPO**	Association of Chief Police Officers of England and Wales
ACOOG	American College of Osteopathic Obstetricians and Gynecologists	**ACPS**	Arab Company for Petroleum Services (*of* OAPEC)
ACOPI	Asociación Colombiana de Pequeños Industriales	**AC & R**	American Cable and Radio Corporation
ACORBAT	Association for Co-operation in Banana Research in the Caribbean and Tropical America	**ACR**	American College of Radiology
		ACR	Australian Catholic Relief
		ACRC	Academia de Ciencias de la República de Cuba
ACORD	Advisory Council on Research and Development	**ACRI**	American Cocoa Research Institute
ACORD	Agency for Cooperation in Rural Development (Switzerland)	**ACRI**	Associazione fra le Casse di Risparmio Italiano
ACOSCA	Africa Cooperative Savings and Credit Association	**ACRILIS**	Australian Centre for Research in Library and Information Science
ACOSA	Aluminium Company of South Africa	**ACRL**	Association of College and Reference Libraries (U.S.A.)
ACP	African, Caribbean and Pacific Countries associated with the European Economic Community	**ACROA**	Australian Council for Overseas Aid
		ACRPP	Association pour la Conservation et la Reproduction Photographique de la Presse (France)
ACP	American College of Physicians		
ACP	Association of Canadian Publishers	**ACRR**	American Council on Race Relations
ACP	Associated Church Press of the Western Hemisphere (U.S.A.)	**ACRS**	Advisory Committee on Reactor Safeguards (U.S.A.)
ACP	Association of Circus Proprietors of Great Britain	**ACS**	American Cancer Society
		ACS	American Ceramic Society
ACP	Association of Clinical Pathologists	**ACS**	American Chemical Society
ACP Group	Groupe des États d'Afrique, des Caraïbes et du Pacifique	**ACS**	American College of Surgeons
		ACS	Association of Commonwealth Students
ACPA	American Capon Producers Association	**ACS**	Australian Computer Society
ACPA	American Concrete Paving Association	**ACS**	Automobil Club der Schweiz
ACPA	Association des Chefs de Publicité d'Annonceurs de Belgique	**ACSA**	Aerocarga SA (Mexico)
ACPA	Asociación Costarricense de Productores de Algodon (Costa Rico)	**ACSA**	Allied Communications Security Agency (*of* NATO)
ACPC	Asian Christian Peace Conference (India)	**ACSA**	American Cotton Shippers Association
ACPCC	American Council of Polish Cultural Clubs	**ACSAD**	Arab Centre for the Studies of Arid Zones and Dry Lands (Syria)
ACPE	Agrupación National Sindical de Constructores Promotores de Edificios Urbanos	**ACSE**	Association of Consulting Structural Engineers (Australia)

ACSEDIA	Association pour le Controle Sanitaire, l'Étude et le Développement de l'Insémination Artificielle
ACSI	Association Canadienne des Sciences de l'Information
ACSIL	Admiralty Centre for Scientific Information and Liaison
ACSP	Advisory Council on Scientific Policy
ACSP	Association Canadienne de Science Politique
ACSPA	Australian Council of Salaried and Professional Associations
ACSPFT	Asian Committee for Standardisation of Physical Fitness Tests
ACSR	Association Cinématographique Suisse Romande
ACSSM	Associate Committee on Soil and Snow Mechanics (Canada)
ACST *see* ACASTD	
ACSUS	Association for Canadian Studies in the United States (U.S.A.)
ACT	Agricultural Central Trading
ACT	Australian Capital Territory
ACTA	Association des Commissionaires de Transports Aériens (Switzerland)
ACTA	Association de Coordination Technique Agricole (of FNSEA)
ACTIS	Auckland Commercial and Technical Information Service (N.Z.)
ACTRA	Association of Canadian Television and Radio Artists
ACTT	Association of Cinematograph, Television and Allied Technicians
ACTU	Australian Council of Trade Unions
ACU	Asian Clearing Union
ACU	Association of Commonwealth Universities
ACU	Association of Cricket Umpires
ACUA	Association of Cambridge University Assistants
ACUP	Association of Canadian University Presses
ACURIL	Association of Caribbean University and Research Libraries
ACV	Algemeen Christelijk Vakverbond (Belgium)
ACV	Association Centrale des Vétérinaires
ACV	Stichting Afnemers Controle op Veevoeder
ACVAFS	American Council of Voluntary Agencies for Foreign Service

ACVPF	Association des Createurs de Variétés Potagères et Florales
ACWW	Associated Countrywomen of the World
ACYPL	Atlantic Association of Young Political Leaders
ADA	Agence Dahoméenne d'Assurances
ADA	Agricultural Development Association
ADA	Aluminium Development Association
ADA	American Dairy Association
ADA	American Dehydration Association
ADA	American Dental Association
ADA	American Diabetes Association
ADA	American Dietetic Association
ADA	Associazione Direttori Albergo
ADA	Atomic Development Authority (U.S.A.)
ADA	Australian Dental Association
ADAA	Australian Development Assistance Agency
ADACI	Associazione degli Approvvigionatori e Compratori Italiani
ADAF	Arbeitskreis Deutscher Afrika-Forschungsstellen
ADAGP	Association pour la Diffusion des Arts Graphiques et Plastiques
ADAI	Associazione degli Approvvigionatori Italiani
ADAM	Association Dauphinoise pour l'Aménagement de la Montagne
ADAPSO	Association of Data Processing Organisations (U.S.A.)
ADAS	African Demonstration Centre on Sampling Agricultural Surveys (*of* CCTA and FAO)
ADAS	Agricultural Development and Advisory Service (*formerly* NAAS)
	Army Dependants Assurance Trust
ADATIG	Anglo-Dutch African Textiles Investigation Group
ADB	African Bank for Development
ADB	Asian Development Bank (Philippines)
ADBACI	Association pour le Développement de la Documentation, des Bibliothèques et Archives de la Côte d'Ivoire
ADBP	Agricultural Development Bank of Pakistan
ADBPA	Association pour le Développement Bibliothèques Publiques en Afrique
ADBS	Association Française des Documentalistes et des Bibliothécaires Spécialisés
ADC	Agricultural Development Council (*formerly* CECA) (U.S.A.)

ADC	Andean Development Corporation
ADC	Arsenic Development Committee (France)
ADC	Asian Development Centre (Philippines)
ADC	Asociación Demografica Costarricense (Costa Rica)
ADCCK	Association for the Development of Commonwealth Knowledge (Canada)
ADCF	Association pour le Développement de la Culture Fourragère (Switzerland)
ADCO	Andean Development Company (Ecuador)
ADD	Arbeitsgemeinschaft Deutscher Detektive
ADDE	Association des Dépôts Dentaires Européens
ADEAC	Association d'Entrepôts en Afrique Centrale
ADEARTA	Association pour le Développement de l'Équipement des Ateliers de Réparation des Tracteurs Agricoles
ADEB	Association des Entrepreneurs Belges de Travaux de Génie Civil
ADEC	Association pour le Développement de la Cooperation Agricole
ADECO	Programa de Adiestramiento de Extensionistas en Comunicaciones, Latinoamérica
ADEE	Association for Dental Education in Europe (Netherlands)
ADEKRA	Arbeitsgemeinschaft Deutscher Kraftwagen-Spediteure
ADELA	Atlantic Community Development Group for Latin America
ADELF	Association des Écrivains de Langue Française
ADEPA	Association pour le Développement de la Production Automatique
ADES	Association of Directors of Education in Scotland
ADESPE	Association pour le Développement de la Science Politique Européenne
ADETEM	Association pour le Développement des Techniques d'Exécution et de l'Exploitation des Études de Marché
ADETIM	Association pour le Développement des Techniques des Industries Mécaniques
ADETOM	Association pour le Développement de l'Enseignement Technique Outre-Mer
ADEVIA	Associación de Editoras para Deficientes Visuales de Ibero-América
ADEXA	Association pour le Développement des Exportations Agricoles

ADEZ	Association pour le Développement des Études Zootechniques (Belgium)
ADEZ	Association des Entrepreneurs du Zaire
ADF	Aerosolinteressenters Förening
ADF	Arbeitsgemeinschaft Deutscher Filztuchfabriken
ADF	Association Dentaire Française
ADFA	Australian Dried Fruits Association
ADGA	American Dairy Goat Association
ADGLC	Abu Dhabi Gas Liquefaction Company
ADH	Association of Dental Hospitals of Great Britain and Northern Ireland
ADI	Agrupación de Diseñadores Industriales
ADI	American Documentation Institute
ADI	Association pour le Développement International
ADI	Associazione Detectives Italiani
ADI	Associazione Dietetica Italiana
ADI	Associazione per il Disegno Industriale
ADIA	Academy of Diplomacy and International Affairs (Germany)
ADIBBEL	Association des Dirigeants des Instituts de Beauté de Belgique
ADIC	Association des Dirigeants et Cadres Chrétiens
ADICEP	Associacion des Directeurs des Centres des Matières Plastiques
ADIN	Asociación de Industrias Náuticas
ADIP	Association Nationale de Défense de Élevage et du Commerce Rural Interprofessionnel
ADIP	Associazione Italiana dei Direttori del Personale
ADIRI	Association de Droit International et de Relations Internationales (Romania)
ADK	Arbeitgeberverband der Deutschen Kautschukindustrie
ADKPZ	Arbeitskreis Deutscher Klein- und Pelztier-Züchter
ADL	Verband für Informationsverarbeitung
ADLAF	Arbeitsgemeinschaft Deutsche Lateinamerika-Forschung
ADLP	Australian Democratic Labour Party
ADLRI	Arthur D. Little Research Institute
ADM	Arbeitkreis Deutscher Marktforschungsinstitut
ADM	Asociación Dental Mexicana

ADM	Association pour le Développement du Droit Mondial	**ADSCAT**	Associations of Distributors to the Self-Service and Coin-Operated Laundry and Allied Trades
ADMA	American Drug Manufacturers' Association	**ADSE**	American Dental Society of Europe
ADMA	Association of Dance and Mime Artists	**ADSI**	Agricultural Development Service, Inc. (Philippines)
ADMARC	Agricultural Development and Marketing Corporation (Malawi)	**ADSOC**	Administrative Support Operations Centre (U.S.A.)
ADMI	American Dry Milk Institute		
ADMSt	Arbeitsgemeinschaft Deutscher Messerschmiede und Stahlwarenhändler	**ADSRI**	Animal and Dairy Science Research Institute (South Africa)
ADMT	Association of Dental Manufacturers and Traders of the United Kingdom	**ADSS**	Association of Direct Speech Suppliers
ADN	Allgemeines Deutsches Nachrichtenbüro	**ADSS**	Australian Defence Scientific Service
ADNOC	Abu Dhabi National Oil Company	**ADSSA**	Association pour le Développement des Sciences Sociales Appliquées
ADO	Association of Dispensing Opticians	**ADTA**	American Dental Trade Association
ADO	Avdelningen för Driftsorganisation	**ADTC**	Anglo-Dutch Trade Council
ADP	Association of Database Producers	**ADTCB**	Association des Directeurs de Théatres Cinématographiques de Belgique
ADP	Association for Dental Prosthesis		
ADPBA	Association Internationale pour le Développement des Bibliothèques en Afrique	**ADTM**	Association pour le Diffusion des Technique Ménagères
ADPC	Abu Dhabi Petroleum Company	**ADTV**	Allgemeiner Deutscher Tanzlehrerverband
ADPI	Association Internationale d'Études pour la Protection des Investissements	**ADV**	Addressenverleger- und Direktwerbe-Unternehmerverband
ADPSO	Association of Data Processing Service Organizations	**ADV**	Arbeitsgemeinschaft für Datenverarbeiten
ADR	Arbeitsgemeinschaft Deutscher Rinderzüchter	**ADV**	Arbeitsgemeinschaft Deutscher Verkerksflughäfen
ADR	Association pour le Développement de la Recherche	**ADVB**	Associação dos Diretores de Vendas do Brasil
ADRA	Animal Disease Research Association	**ADW**	Verband Deutscher Werbeagenturen und Werbemittlungen
ADRAO	Association pour le Développement du Riz en Afrique Occidentale	**ADWA**	Atlantic Deeper Waterways Association (U.S.A.)
ADRDI	Abra Diocesan Rural Development Inc. (Philippines)	**AEA**	Agence Européenne d'Approvisionneme
ADRI-PECHE	Armement Dakarois pour le Regroupement de l'Industrie de la Pêche	**AEA**	Agricultural Education Association
		AEA	Agricultural Engineers' Association
ADRIS	Association for the Development of Religious Information Systems	**AEA**	American Economic Association
		AEA	Association d'Entreprises d'Affichage (Belgium)
ADS	Arbeitsgemeinschaft Deutscher Schafzüchter	**AEA**	Association of European Airlines
ADS	Arbeitsgemeinschaft Deutscher Schweinezüchter	**AEA**	Association Européenne de l'Asphalte
		AEA	Atomic Energy Authority
ADSA	American Dairy Science Association	**AEAA**	Asociación de Escritores y Artistas Americanos (Cuba)
ADSADLT	Association de Défense des Sociétés Agricoles Dépossédées par la Loi Tunisienne du 12 Mai, 1964	**AEAC**	Asociación Española de Amigos de los Castillos
ADSATIS	Australian Defence Science and Technology Information Service	**AEAFM**	Association d'Entraide des Agriculteurs Français du Maroc

AEANC	Association des Éclaireurs de l'Armée Nationale Congolaise	**AEDF**	Asian Economic Development Fund
AEB	American Ethnology Bureau	**AEDIPE**	Asociación Española de Directores Jefes de Personal
AEB	Asociación Ecuatoriana de Bibliotecarios	**AEDP**	Association Européenne pour la Direction de Personnel
AEB	Atomic Energy Bureau (Japan)		
AEBU	Asociación de Bancarios del Uruguay	**AEDT**	Association Européenne des Organisations Nationales des Commerçants Détaillants en Textiles
AEC	Algemene Emigratie Centrale		
AEC	American Engineering Council		
AEC	Asociación Española de la Carretera	**AEE**	Asociacion Electrónica Española
AEC	Association Européenne des Enducteurs, Calandreurs et Fabricants de Revêtements de Sols Plastiques et Synthétiques	**AEE**	Atomic Energy Establishment
		AEEC	Airlines Electronic Engineering Committee (International)
AEC	Associação Educação Católica (Brazil)	**AEED**	Association Européenne des Enseignants Dentaires
AEC	Association Européenne de Céramique		
AEC	Association Européenne pour la Coopération	**AEEF**	Association Européenne des Exploitations Frigorifiques
AEC	Associazione Europea per la Cooperazione		
AEC	Atomic Energy Commission (U.S.A.)	**AEEN**	Agence Européenne pour l'Energie Nucléaire
AECA	Anglican and Eastern Churches Association	**AEEP**	Associação das Enfermeiras e dos Enfermeiros Portugueses
AECA	Association Européenne des Centres d'Audiophonologie		
		AEEP	Association of European Engineering Periodicals
AECB	Associação de Educação Católica do Brasil	**AEEPA**	Association d'Études Européennes de Presse Agricole
AECB	Association for the Export of Canadian Books		
AECC	Asociación Espanola para el Control de la Calida	**AEEPJ**	Association Européenne des Publications pour la Jeunesse
		AEESA	Asociación Española de Economía y Sociología Agrarias
AECC	Association des Éclaireurs Catholiques du Congo		
AECD	Asian Ecumenical Conference on Development	**AEET**	Atomic Energy Establishment Trombay (India)
		AEEW	Atomic Energy Establishment Winfrith
AECF	Association des Exploitants de Cinéma et des Distributeurs de Films du Grand Duché de Luxembourg	**AEEZ**	Association des Entreprises de l'Est du Zaire
		AEF	Africa Evangelical Fellowship
	African Explosives and Chemical Industries	**AEF**	American Economic Foundation
AECL	Atomic Energy of Canada Ltd	**AEF**	Asfaltentreprenørenes Forening
AECM	Association of Exhibitors and Conference Managers	**AEF**	Asociación Española de Financiadores
		AEF	Centre d'Action Européenne Fédéraliste
AECMA	Association Européenne de Constructeurs de Matériel Aérospatial (*formerly* AICMA)	**AEFM**	Association Européenne des Festivals de Musique
	Aero Club der Schweiz	**AEFS**	Association des Éleveurs Française de Southdown
AECS	Australia Europe Container Services		
	Association of Engineering Distributors	**AEFTOP**	Agrupación Española de Fabricantes de Transmisiones Oleo-Hidraulicas y Pneumaticas
AEDA	Asociación Española de Aerosoles		
	Association Européenne pour le Droit de l'Alimentation	**AEG**	Allgemeine Elektrizitäts Gesellschaft
		AEGC	Association Européenne de Genie Civil
AEDE	Association Européenne des Enseignants		
AEDEMO	Asociación Española de Estudios de Mercado y de Opinion Comercial	**AEGIS**	Aid for the Elderly in Government Institutions

AEGM	Anglican Evangelical Group Movement	**AEN**	Agence de l'UCDE pour l'Energie Nucléaire
AEGPL	Association Européenne des Gaz de Pétrole Liquéfiés	**AENA**	All-England Netball Association
AEI	Associated Electrical Industries	**AENSB**	Association de l'École Nationale Supérieure de Bibliothécaires
AEI	Association des Écoles Internationales	**AEO**	Arbeitsgemeinschaft für Elektronenoptik
AEI	Associazione Educatrice Italiana	**AEOM**	Association of European Open Air Museums
AEI	Associazione Ellettrotecnica ed Elletronica Italiana	**AEOZ**	Association des Entreprises de l'Ouest du Zaire
AEI	Associazione Enotecnici Italiani	**AEP**	Agence Européenne de Productivité (*of* OECE)
AEI	Auto Enthusiasts International (U.S.A.)		
AEIA	Asociación Escuela Ingenieria Agronomica (Ecuador)	**AEPB**	Association pour l'Emploi des Plastiques dans le Bâtiment
AEIAAF	Association Européenne de l'Industrie des Aliments pour Animaux Familiers	**AEPC**	Asociación Española para el Progreso de las Ciencias
AEID	European Association of Development Research Institutions	**AEPCO**	Association of Economic Poisons Control Officials (U.S.A.)
AEIDC	Arctic Environmental Information and Data Centre	**AEPE**	Asociación Establecimientos Privados de Enseñanza (Costa Rica)
AEIH	Association Européenne des Industries de l'Habillement	**AEPE**	Association pour l'Étude des Problèmes de l'Europe
AEIL	American Export Isbrandtsen Lines	**AEPE**	Association Européenne des Professeurs d'Espagnol
AEIOU	Agenzia Editoriale Internazionale Organizzazioni	**AEPIF**	Association pour l'Étude et de Progrès de l'Irrigation Fertilisante
AEIOU	Association Européenne pour une Interaction entre les Organismes Universitaires	**AEPT**	Asociación Española de Prensa Tecnica
AEJI	Association of European Jute Industries	**AEQCT**	Asociación Española de Quimicos y Coloristas Textiles
AEKPC	Association Européenne des Kinesitherapeutes Photographes et Cinéastes	**AER**	Association for Education by Radio (U.S.A.)
AELE	Association Européenne de Libre-Echange	**AER**	Association Européenne pour l'Étude du Probleme des Réfugiés
AELFA	Asociación Española de Logopedia, Foniatria y Audiologia	**AER**	Association Européenne de Radiologie
AELI	Asociación Europea de Libre Intercambio	**AERA**	American Educational Research Association
AELLA	Association des Entrepreneurs Luxembourgeois des Lignes d'Autobus	**AERA**	Association pour l'Étude et la Recherche Astronautique et Cosmique
AELTC	All England Lawn Tennis Club	**AERAC**	Association Auxiliaire pour l'Enseignement Supérieur et la Recherche Agronomique en Coopération
AEM	Asociación Española de Marketing		
AEMB	Association des Entrepreneurs de Montage de Belgique	**AERALL**	Association d'Études et de Recherches sur les Aéronefs Allégés
AEMDA	Alliance Européenne des Associations de Myopathes	**AERD**	Atomic Energy Research Department (U.S.A.)
AEMIE	Association Européenne de Médecine Interne d'Ensemble	**AERE**	Atomic Energy Research Establishment
AEMP	Association of European Management Publishers	**AERI**	Agricultural Economics Research Institute
AEMT	Association of Electrical Machinery Trades	**AERO**	Association of Electronic Reserve Officers (U.S.A.)
AEMTM	Association of European Machine Tool Merchants	**AERO-ARCTIC**	International Study Society for the Exploration of Arctic Regions by Airship

AERP	Agrupación Española de Relaciones Publicas
AERP	Association Européenne pour la Recherche sur le Pomme de Terre
AERTEL	Association Européenne Rubans, Tresses, Tissus Elastiques
AERZAP	Association pour les Études et Recherches de Zoologie Appliquée et de Phytopathologie (Belgium)
AES	Agricultural Economics Society
AES	American Electrochemical Society
AES	American Electroencephalographic Society
AES	American Electroplaters' Society
AES	American Entomological Society
AES	American Epidemiological Society
AES	American Epilepsy Society
AES	American Ethnological Society
AES	American Eugenics Society
AES	Asian Environmental Society (Philippines)
AES	Audio Engineering Society (U.S.A.)
AESA	Aerolines et Salvador SA
AESA	Agricultural Engineering Society (Australia)
AESA	Association pour l'Enseignement Social en Afrique (Ethiopia)
AESC	American Engineering Standards Committee
AESE	Association of Earth Science Editors (U.S.A.)
AESED	Association Européenne de Sociétés d'Études pour le Développement
AESF	Association des Écrivains Scientifiques de France
AESGP	Association Européenne des Spécialités Grand Public
AESIMP	Association pour l'Étude de la Stérilité et la Médecine Périnatale
AESN	Association of Export Subscription Newsagents
AESOR	Association Européenne de Sous-officiers de Réserve
AESU	Arabische Eisen und Stahl Union
AET	Association of Auto-Electrical Technicians
AET	Association Européenne de Thanatologie
AETFAT	Association pour l'Étude Taxonomique de la Flore d'Afrique Tropicale (Belgium)
AEU	Amalgamated Engineering Union (*now* AUEW)
AEU	American Ethical Union
AEU	Asia Electronics Union (Japan)
AEV	Arbeitsgemeinschaft Erdölgewinnung und Verarbeitung (Germany)
AEVII	Federación de Veterinarios Europeos de la Industria y la Investigación
AEWHA	All England Women's Hockey Association
AEWLA	All England Women's Lacrosse Association
AF	Angpanneföreningen
AFA	Allergy Foundation of America
AFA	Amateur Fencing Association
AFA	Amateur Football Alliance
AFA	American Federation of Arts
AFA	American Federation of Astrologers
AFA	American Forensic Society
AFA	American Forestry Association
AFA	American Foundrymen's Association
AFA	Asociación Física Argentina
AFA	Association Française d'Astronomie
AFAA	Association of Faculties of Agriculture in Africa
AFAA	Australian Federation of Advertising Agencies
AFAB	Association Française d'Agriculture Biologique
AFABA	Association of African Basketball Federations
AFACO	Association Française des Amateurs Constructeurs l'Ordinateurs
AFACPG	Association Française des Amateurs de Cactées et de Plantes Grasses
AFAD	Association of Fatty Acid Distillers
AFAL	Association Francophone d'Accueil et de Liaison
AFAP	Association Française pour l'Accroissement de la Productivité
AFAQ	Association Française pour l'Expansion des Produits Agricoles de Qualité Garantie
AFAR	Asociación Feminia de Acción Rural (Argentina)
AFAS	American Fine Arts Society
AFAS	Association Française pour l'Avancement des Sciences
AFASE	Association for Applied Solar Energy (U.S.A.)
AFASIC	Association for all Speech Impaired Children
AFASTOF	Afro-Asian Federation for Tobacco Producers and Manufacturers

AFB	Arbeitsgemeinschaft Fachärztlicher Berufsverbände
AFBA	Asociación Farmacéutica y Bioquímica Argentina
AFBF	American Farm Bureau Federation
AFBS	American and Foreign Bible Society
AFC	African Football Confederation
AFC	African Forestry Commission
AFC	Asian Football Confederation
AFC	Association Française de Chimiurgie
AFC	Association Française de Cristallographie
AFC	Association France-Containers
AFC	Latin-American Forestry Commission (*of* FAO)
AFCA	Association pour la Formation des Cadres de l'Industrie et de l'Administration en Langue Française
AFCA	Association Française pour la Communauté Atlantique
AFCA	Association Professionelle des Fabricants de Compléments pour l'Alimentation Animale
AFCAC	African Civil Aviation Commission
AFCALTI	Association Française de Calcul et de Traitement de l'Information
AFCASOL	Association des Fabricants de Café Soluble des Pays de la CEE
AFCAT	Association Française de Calorimétrie et d'Analyse Thermique
AFCC	Association Française du Commerce des Cacaos
AFCET	Association Française de Cybernétique Économique et Technique
AFCIMAT	Asociación de Fabricantes de Conjuntos Importantes para la Mecanización del Agro y el Transporte (Argentina)
AFCIQ	Association Française pour le Contrôle Industriel de Qualité
AFCL	African Container Line
AFCMA	Aluminium Foil Container Manufacturers Association
AFCMA	Australian Fibreboard Containers Manufacturers Association
AFCOA	Australian Council for Overseas Aid
AFCOD	Association Française des Conseilleurs de Direction
AFCODI	Africaine Commerciale de Diffusion
AFCOFEL	Association Française Comités Économiques Agricoles de Fruits et Légumes
AFCOM	Africaine de Constructions Mécaniques (Ivory Coast)
AFCOS	Association Française des Conseils en Organisation Scientifique
AFCOT	Association Française Cotonnière
AFCR	American Federation for Clinical Research
AFCU	American and Foreign Christian Union
AFD	African Development Fund
AFDAC	Association Française de Documentation Automatique en Chimie
AfDB	African Development Bank
AFDBS	Association Française des Documentaires et des Bibliothécaires Specialisés
AFDC	Agriculture and Fishery Development Corporation (Korea)
AFDI	Association Française des Déménageurs Internationaux
AFDIN	Association Française de Documentation et d'Information
AFDOUS	Association of Food and Drug Officials of the United States
AFE	Asociación de Forestales del Ecuador
AFEA	American Farm Economic Association
AFEC	Association Française pour le Contrôle de la Qualité des Hormones Désherbantes
AFEC	Association Francophone d'Education Comparée
AFECI	Association des Fabricants Européens de Chauffebains et Chauff-eau Instantanés au Gaz
AFECOGAZ	Association de Fabricants Européens d'Appareils de Contrôle pour le Gaz et l'Huile
AFEDES	Association Française pour l'Étude et le Développement des Applications de l'Énergie Solaire
AFEE	Association Française pour l'Étude des Eaux
AFEI	Association Française pour l'Étiquetage d'Information
AFEID	Association Française pour l'Étude des Irrigations et du Drainage
AFEP	Association Française de l'École Paysanne (*now* CAEVR)
AFEQ	Association Française pour l'Étude du Quaternaire
AFERA	Association des Fabricants Européens des Rubans Auto-adhésifs

AFERO	Asia and the Far East Regional Office (FAO)
AFES	Association Française pour l'Étude du Sol
AFESA	Agrupación de Almacenistas de Ferretaria de España
AFESD	Arab Fund for Economic and Social Development
AFF	Affischeringsföretagens Forening
AFF	Association Française du Froid
AFF	Australian Farmers' Federation
AFFCO	Alaska Forest Fire Council
AFFCOD	Association Française des Firmes de Conseillers de Direction
AFFHC	Australian Freedom from Hunger Campaign
AFFI	American Frozen Food Institute
AFFW	Arab Federation of Food Workers
AFG	Association des Fabricants de Glucose de la CEE
AFG	Association Française de Gemmologie
AFGC	American Forage and Grassland Council
AFGE	American Federation of Government Employees
AFGM	American Federation of Grain Millers
AFGR	Association Française de Génie Rural
AFH	American Foundation for Homeopathy
AFI	American Film Industry
AFI	Associazione Farmacisti dell'Industria
AFI	Associazione dei Fonografici Italiani
AFI	Les Auxiliaires Féminines Internationales
AFIA	American Foreign Insurance Association
AFIA	Apparel and Fashion Industry's Association of Great Britain
AFIA	Association Française Interprofessionelle des Agrumes
AFICAU	Association de Fomento del Intercambio Comercial Anglo-Uruguayo
AFICE	Association Française des Ingenieurs et Chefs d'Entretien
AFICEP	Association Française des Ingenieurs du Caoutchouc et des Plastiques
AFICS	Association of Former International Civil Servants
AFICTIC	Association Française des Ingénieurs, Chimistes et Techniciens des Industries du Cuir
AFIEM	Association Française pour l'Information en Économie Ménagère
AFIF	Association Suisse des Fournisseurs de l'Industrie pour la Ferraille
AFII	American Federation of International Institutes
AFIMAC	Association des Fabricants et Importateurs de Matériel à Air Comprimé (Belgium)
AFIMIN	Association Française des Fabricants et Importateurs de Matériels et de Produits pour l'Industrie du Nettoyage
AFINE	Association Française pour l'Industrie Nucléaire d'Équipement
AFIP	Association Française des Indépendants du Pétrole
AFIP	Associazione Fotografi Italiani Professionisti
AFIPS	American Federation of Information Processing Societies
AFIREC	Association Financière Internationale de l'Océan Indien
AFIRO	Association Française d'Informatique et de Recherche Opérationnelle
AFIS	Amministrazione Fiduciaria Italiana della Somalia
AFISA	Aero Fletes Internationales SA (Panama)
AFISAC	Associazione Fabbricanti Italiani e Staniere di Macchinari e Apparecchiature ad Aria Compressa
AFITAE	Association Française des Ingénieurs et Techniciens de l'Aéronautique et de l'Espace
AFJA	Association Française des Journalistes Agricoles
AFJET	Association Française de Journalistes et Écrivains du Tourisme
AfK	Arbeitsgemeinschaft für Kommunikationsforschung
AFL	American Federation of Labor
AFL	Association Française Laitière
AFLA	American Foreign Law Association
AFLA	Asian Federation of the Library Association
AFL-CIO	American Federation of Labor and Congress of Industrial Organizations
AFM	Asociación Española de Fabricantes de Maquinas-Herramienta
AFM	Aussenhandelsverband für Mineralöl
AFMA	American Feed Manufacturers Association
AFMA	American Footwear Manufacturers Association
AFMA	Artificial Flower Manufacturers Association of Great Britain

AFME	American Friends of the Middle East
AFMH	American Foundation for Mental Hygiene
AFMM	Association of Fish Meal Manufacturers
AFMO	Association Française de Constructeurs de Machines-Outils
AFMR	American Foundation for Management Research
AFMR	Association pour la Formation en Milieu Rural
AFMS	American Federation of Mineralogical Societies
AFN	Aerosolforbundet Norge
AFN	American Forces Network
AFNIL	Agence Francophone pour la Numération Internationale du Livre
AFNOR	Association Française de Normalisation
AFOB	American Foundation for Overseas Blind
AFOCA	Association Nationale pour la Formation Professionnelle suivant les Techniques de l'Industrie du Caoutchouc
AFOCEL	Association Forêts – Cellulose
AFOG	Asian Federation of Obstetrics and Gynaecology
AFOMJ	Association of Fats and Oil Manufacturers of Japan
AFOSR	Air Force Office of Scientific Research (U.S.A.)
AFP	Agence France Presse
AFP	Asociación Forestal del Perú
AFPA	Association de Formation et Perfectionnement Agricole (France)
AFPA	Association pour la Formation Professionnelle des Adultes
AFPA	Australian Fire Protection Association
AFPE	American Foundation for Pharmaceutical Education
AFPE	American Foundation for Political Education
AFPEP	Association Française des Producteurs Exportateurs de Pommes
AFPF	Association Française pour la Production Fourragère
AFPP	Association Française de Producteurs de Plantes à Protéines Legumineuses à Grosses Graines
AFPPT	Association pour la Formation et le Perfectionnement des Planteurs de Tabac
AfPU	African Postal Union

AFPU	Association Française pour la Paix Universelle
AFPW	Association Française du Poney Welsh
AFQ	Association Forestière Québecoise (Canada)
AFR	Auktoriserade Fastighetsmäklares Riksförbund
AFRA	American Farm Research Association
AFRAA	African Airlines Association
AFRACA	African Regional Agricultural Credit Association
AFRAN	Association Française pour la Recherche de l'Alimentation Normale
AFRASEC	Afro-Asian Organisation for Economic Co-operation (Egypt)
AFRAT	Association pour la Formation des Ruraux aux Activités du Tourisme
AFREC	Association Française pour les Recherches et les Études Camerounaises
AFREM	Association Française de Recherches et d'Essais sur les Matériaux et les Constructions
AFREP	Association Française des Relations Publiques
AFRESCO	Association Française de Recherches et Études Statistiques Commerciales
AFRIC	Société Africaine Française de Representations Industrielles et Commerciales
AFRIC	Agence Française de Representation et d'Industries au Cameroun
AFRICA-PLAST	Industrie Africaine des Plastiques
AFRIMEX-CI	Africaine Import-Export Côte d'Ivoire
AFROFED-OP	African Regional Organization of the Public Services and Teachers
AFROLIT	Society for the Promotion of Adult Literacy in Africa
AFRP	American Foundation of Religion and Psychiatry
AFS	American Fisheries Society
AFS	Atlantic Ferry Service
AFSA	Association des Fabricants Suisses d'Accumulateurs
AFSBO	American Federation of Small Business Organizations
AFSBO	Association des Fabricants Suisses de Bijouterie et d'Orfèvrerie

AFSC	American Friends Service Committee	**AGA**	American Goiter Association
AFSCA	Amalgamated Flying Saucer Clubs of America	**AGA**	Arbeitgeberverband Gross- und Aussenhandel
AFSE	Association Française de Science Économique	**AGA**	Architectural Granite Association
AFSEuropa	European Federation for Intercultural Learning	**AGA**	Asociación General de Agricultores (Guatemala)
AFSP	Association Française des Sciences Politiques	**AGA**	Association des Entreprises de Gros en Alimentation Générale (Belgium)
AFST	Association of Food Scientists and Technologists (India)	**AGA**	Australian Gas Association
AFT	American Federation of Teachers	**AGAAC**	Acuerdo General sobre Aranceles Aduaneros y Comercio (GATT)
AFTA	Arab Fund for Technical Assistance to Arab and African Countries (Egypt)	**AGAC**	American Guild of Authors and Composers
AFTA	Atlantic Free Trade Area	**AGADU**	Asociación General de Autores del Uruguay
AFTAA	Association Française des Techniciens de l'Alimentation Animale	**AGAF**	Associazione Nazionale fra i Grossisti di Articoli Fotografici
AFTE	American Federation of Technical Engineers	**AGANAPA**	Asociación de Ganaderos y Agricultores de la Panamericana (Venezuela)
AFTIM	Association Française des Techniciens et Ingénieurs de Sécurité et des Médecins du Travail	**AGARD**	Advisory Group for Aerospace Research and Development (NATO)
AFTM	American Foundation for Tropical Medicine	**AGASAL**	Association des Grossistes en Appareils Sanitaires du Luxembourg
AFTN	Aeronautical Fixed Telecommunication Network (U.K.)	**AGB**	Arbeitskreis Ganzheitliches Bauen
AFTP	Association Française des Techniciens du Pétrole	**AGC**	African Groundnut Council
		AGC	American Grassland Council
AFTPV	Association Française des Techniciens des Peintures, Vernis, Encres d'Imprimerie, Colles et Adhésifs	**AGC**	Ashanti Goldfields Corporation (Ghana)
		AGCC	American Guernsey Cattle Club
AFTRI	Association Française des Transporteurs Routiers Internationaux	**AGCD**	Administration Générale Belge de la Coopération au Développement
AFTS	Aeronautical Fixed Telecommunications Service	**AGCD**	Association of Green Crop Driers
		AGCI	Associazione Generale delle Cooperative Italiane
AFTW	Arab Federation of Transport Workers	**AGCM**	Association of Glass Container Manufacturers
AFUCA	Asian Federation of Unesco Clubs and Associations	**AGDT**	Advisory Group on Data Transmission (*of* NEDO)
AFULE	Australian Federated Union of Locomotive Enginemen	**AGDW**	Arbeitsgemeinschaft Deutscher Waldbesitzerverbände
AFVP	Association Française des Volontaires du Progrès	**AGE**	Asian Information Centre for Geotechnical Engineering (Thailand)
AfW	Arbeitskreis für Wehrforschung	**AGEAM**	Association pour la Gérance des Écoles d'Apprentissage Maritime
AFZ	Association Française de Zootechnie		
AG	Action Group (Nigeria)	**AGEC**	Arbeitsgemeinschaft Europäischer Chorverbände
AG	Actuarieël Genootschap	**AGECO**	Agences Générales d'Exchanges Commerciaux
AGA	Agricola Ganadera Antelana		
AGA	American Gas Association	**AGECOOP**	Agency for Cultural and Technical Cooperation (France)
AGA	American Gastroenterological Association		
AGA	American Genetic Association		

AGED	Association des Grandes Entreprises de Distribution de Belgique	**AGNIB**	Union of the Internal Timber Trade Associations of the EEC
AGEHR	American Guild of English Handbell Ringers	**AGNVH**	Association of Growers of the New Varieties of Hops
AGEI	Associazione Gerontologica Italiana		
AGELAF	Association des Groupes Nationaux d'Éducation Nouvelle de Langue Française	**AGO**	Arbeitsgemeinschaft der Ordenshochschulen
		AGÖ	Arbeitsgemeinschaft Österreicherischer Organisationsberater
AGEMI	Association des Groupements d'Engraisseurs de Moutons d'Importation	**AGOD**	International Association on the Genesis of Ore Deposits
AGEMOS	Associazione Nazionale Gestori di Magazzini di Vendita Generi Monopoli di Stato	**AGOF**	Arbeitsgemeinschaft Österreichischer Friedensvereine
AGET	Advisory Group on Electron Tubes (U.S.A.)		
AGF	Akademische Gesellschaft für Finanzwirtschaft	**AGOR**	Advisory Group on Ocean Research (*of* WMO)
AGF	Arbeitsgemeinschaft Getreideforschung	**AGPB**	Association Générale des Producteurs de Blé et autres Céréales (France)
AGF	Asian Games Federation		
AGFF	Arbeitsgemeinschaft zur Förderung des Futterbaues (Switzerland)	**AGP-CNO**	Assemblée Générale Permanente des Comités Nationaux Olympiques
AGFI	Assemblée Générale des Fédérations Internationales	**AGPD**	Allgemeine Gesellschaft für Philosophie in Deutschland
AGGS	Allgemeine Geschichtforschende Gesellschaft der Schweiz	**AGPH**	Association Générale des Producteurs de Houblon
AGHTM	Association Générale des Hygiénistes et Techniciens Municipaux	**AGPL**	Association Générale des Producteurs de Lin
AGI	Alliance Graphique Internationale	**AGPM**	Association Générale des Producteurs de Maïs
AGI	American Geological Institute	**AGPO**	Association Générale des Producteurs d'Oléagineux
AGI	Arbeitsgemeinschaft Industriebau		
AGI	Associazione Genetica Italiana	**AGPV**	Association Générale des Producteurs de Viande
AGI	Associazione Geofisica Italiana		
AGID	Association of Geoscientists for International Development	**Agra-Presse**	Agency Générale de Renseignements Agricoles
AGIF	Automobilgummi-Importørernes Forening	**AGREE**	Advisory Group for Reliability of Electronic Equipment (U.S.A.)
AGIFORS	Airline Group International Federation of Operational Research Societies	**AGRF**	American Geriatric Research Foundation
AGIM	Association Générale de l'Industrie du Médicament (Belgium)	**AGRI-PECHE-IVOIRE**	Société Ivoiro Sénégalaise d'Agriculture et de Pêche
AGIP	Agenzia Generale Italiana Petroli		
AGIS	Associazione Generale Italiana dello Spettacolo	**AGRIS**	International Formation System for the Agricultural Sciences and Technology (Italy)
AGK	Arbeitsgemeinschaft Korrosion	**AGROLAC**	Association des Groupements de Producteurs de Lait de Chèvre
AGLINET	Agricultural Libraries and Documentation Centres Network		
AGMA	American Gear Manufacturers' Association	**AGROMAS**	International Association for Vine-, Fruit- and Vegetable-growing Mechanization
AGMA	American Guild of Musical Artists	**AGROSEM**	Trustul pentru Asigurarea Productiei si Valorificarea Semintelor Agricole (Roumania)
AGMB	Association Générale des Meuniers Belges		
AGMÖ	Arbeitsgemeinschaft der Musikerzieher Österreichs	**AGRR**	Association Générale de Retraite par Reparition
AGMS	Arbeitsgemeinschaft Massenspektroskopie		

AGRUSA	Agricultores Unidos S.A.
AGS	American Geographical Society
AGS	American Geriatrics Society
AGS	American Goat Society
AGS	American Gynecological Society
AGS	Appalachian Geological Society (U.S.A.)
AGSG	Akademische Gesellschaft Schweizerischer Germanisten
AGSRO	Association of Government Supervisors and Radio Officers
AGT	Arbeitsgeververband Schweizerischer Transportunternehmungen
AGT	Association of Geology Teachers (U.S.A.)
AGTA	Agence Générale de Transit en Afrique (Congo)
AGU	American Geophysical Union
AGU	Arbeitsgemeinschaft für Umweltfragen
AGV	Aachener Geschichtsverein
AGV	Arbeitsgemeinschaft der Verbraucher
AGVA	American Guild of Variety Artists
AGVS	Autogewerbeverband der Schweiz
AGW	Anthropologische Gesellschaft in Wien (Austria)
AGW	Arbeitsgemeinschaft der Werbefachverbände
AHA	American Heart Association
AHA	American Hereford Association
AHA	American Historical Association
AHA	American Hospital Association
AHA	American Humane Association
AHA	American Hypnotherapy Association
AHBA	Association of Hotel Booking Agents
AHC	American Horticultural Council
AHD	Arbeitsgemeinschaft für Hochschuldidaktik
AHDRI	Animal Husbandry and Dairy Research Institute (South Africa)
AHE	Association for Higher Education (U.S.A.)
AHEA	American Home Economics Association
AHEM	Association of Hydraulic Equipment Manufacturers
AHF	Allmänna Handelslagsförbundet
AHFITB	Agricultural, Horticultural and Forestry Training Board (*now* ATB)
AHIOI	Association Historique Internationale de l'Océan Indien
AHIRS	Australian Health Information and Research Service
AHITI	Animal Health and Industry Training Institute (Kenya)
AHM	Ateneo de Historia de la Medicina (Argentina)
AHMCA	Asociación de Hombres de Mercadeo de Centro América (Guatemala)
AHPMB	Alberta Hog Producers Marketing Board
AHS	Agricultural History Society (U.S.A.)
AHS	American Horticultural Society
AHS	American Hypnodontic Society
AHSA	American Hampshire Sheep Association
AHSA	American Horse Shows Association
AHSA	Art, Historical and Scientific Association (Canada)
AHSD	Authority Health and Safety Division
AHSPM	Association of Health Service Personnel Managers
AHSR	Association des Horticulteurs de la Suisse Romande
AHT	Animal Health Trust
AHWA	Association of Hospital and Welfare Administrators
AI	Asphalt Institute (U.S.A.)
AIA	Abrasive Industries Association
AIA	Aerospace Industries Association of America
AIA	American Institute of Architects
AIA	American International Association for Economic and Social Development
AIA	Anglo-Indian Association
AIA	Anglo-Israel Association
AIA	Archeological Institute of America
AIA	Artists International Association
AIA	Asociación de Ingenieros Aeronáuticos
AIA	Associación de Ingenieros Agronomos (Uruguay)
AIA	Association for Industrial Archaeology
AIA	Association of International Accountants
AIA	Association Internationale des Allergistes
AIA	Associazione Italiana Aerosol
AIA	Associazione Italiana Allevatori
AIA	Associazione Italiana delle Industrie Aerospaziali
AIA	Aviation Industry Association (N.Z.)
AIAA	Aircraft Industries Association of America
AIAA	American Institute of Aeronautics and Astronautics

AIAA	Association Interprofessionnelle de l'Aviation Agricole	**AIBA**	Association Internationale de Boxe Amateur
AIAB	Association Internationale des Anthropobiologistes	**AIBA**	Association Interprofessionnelle des Producteurs de Betteraves et d'Alcool de Betteraves
AIAC	Air Industries Association of Canada	**AIBA**	Association of International Border Agencies (U.S.A.)
AIAC	Association des Ingénieurs en Anticorrosion		
AIAC	Association Internationale d'Archeologie Classique	**AIBA**	Associazione Italiana Brokers di Assicurazioni
AIAC	Associazione Italiana Agenti di Cambio	**AIBANIC**	Asociación de Instituciones Bancarias de Nicaragua
AIACE	Association Internationale des Anciens des Communautés Européennes	**AIBC**	Architectural Institute of British Columbia
AIAESD	American International Association for Economics and Social Development	**AIBCM**	Association of Industrialized Building Component Manufacturers
AIAF	Association de l'Industrie et de l'Agriculture Française	**AIBD**	Association of International Bond Dealers
AIAF	Associazione Italiana degli Analisti Finanziari	**AIBDA**	Asociación Interamericana de Bibliotecarios y Documentalistas Agrícolas
AIAFD	Association des Institutions Africaines de Financement du Développement	**AIBGA**	All Island Banana Growers Association (Jamaica)
AIAG	Aluminium Industrie Aktien Gesellschaft (Switzerland)	**AIBI**	International Association of the Bread Industry
AIAG	Association Internationale des Assureurs contre la Grêle	**AIBM**	Association Internationale des Bibliothèques Musicales
AIAMA	Association Internationale pour l'Art et les Moyens Audio-Visuels	**AIBS**	American Institute of Biological Sciences
AIAP	Association Internationale des Arts Plastiques	**AIC**	Académie Internationale de la Céramique
		AIC	Agricultural Improvement Council
AIAREF	Association Internationale des Anesthésistes-Réanimateurs	**AIC**	Agricultural Institute of Canada
		AIC	American Institute of Chemists
AIAS	Australian Institute of Aboriginal Studies	**AIC**	American Institute of Cooperation
AIAS	Australian Institute of Agricultural Science	**AIC**	Arab Investment Company (Saudi Arabia)
AIASR	Association des Ingenieurs Agronomes de la Suisse Romande	**AIC**	Asbestos Information Committee
		AIC	Association Internationale de la Couleur
AIAT	Association Internationale pour le Développement Économique et l'Aide Technique	**AIC**	Association Internationale Cybernétique
		AIC	Associazione Italiana di Cartografia
AIB	Academy of International Business (U.S.A.)	**AICA**	American International Charolais Association
AIB	Aerosol Industrien Brancheforening	**AICA**	Association Internationale pour Calcul Analogique
AIB	American Institute of Baking		
AIB	American Institute of Banking	**AICA**	Association Internationale des Critiques d'Art
AIB	Associate of the Institute of Bankers	**AICA**	Associazione degli Industriali delle Conserve Animali
AIB	Association des Industries de Belgique		
AIB	Association of Insurance Brokers	**AICA**	Associazione Italiana per il Calcolo Automatico
AIB	Associazione Italiana Biblioteca	**AICAR**	Association Internationale de Co-opération et d'Animation Régionales
AIBA	American Industrial Bankers Association		
AIBA	Asociación Interamericana de Bibliotecarios Agrícolas	**AICB**	Association Internationale de Lutte contre le Bruit
		AICC	All India Congress Committee

AICC   Association Internationale de Chimie Céréalière

AICC   Groupe des Chambres Syndicales et Unions Professionnelles d'Agents Independants, Courtiers et Concessionnaires du Commerce et de l'Industrie (Belgium)

AICCF   Association Internationale du Congrès de Chemins de Fer (Belgium)

AICD   Association Internationale des Compagnies de Dragage

AICD   International Association of Dredging Companies

AICDT   International Advisory Committee on Documentation and Terminology in Pure and Applied Science

AICE   American Institute of Chemical Engineers

AICE   American Institute of Consulting Engineers

AICE   American Institute of Crop Ecology

AICF   Ambassador International Cultural Foundation (U.S.A.)

AICF   American-Israel Cultural Foundation

AICFO   Asociación Internacional para las Ciencias Físicas del Océano

AICH   Asociación Internacional de Hidrología Científica

AICHE   American Institute of Chemical Engineers

AICI   Associazione Ingegneri Consulenti Italiani

AICK   Association Internationale pour la Conscience de Krishna

AICL   Association Internationale des Critiques Littéraires

AICMA   Association Internationale des Constructeurs de Matériel Aérospatial (*now* AECMA)

AICMES   Association Interprofessionelle des Constructeurs de Matériel d'Équipement Scientifiques

AICMR   Association Internationale des Constructeurs de Matériel Roulant

AICPA   American Institute of Certified Public Accountants

AICPA   Associazione Italiana Concessionari Produzione Automobilistica

AICQ   Associazione Italiana per il Controllo della Qualita

AICRIP   All India Coordinated Rice Improvement Project

AICS   Association Internationale du Cinéma Scientifique

AICT   Association Internationale des Critiques de Théâtre

AICTC   Associazione Italiana di Chimica Tessile e Coloristica

AICU   All India Cooperative Union

AICVF   Association des Ingénieurs de Chauffage et de Ventilation de France

AICVP   Association Internationale des Charités de St-Vincent

AID   Agency for International Development (*formerly* ICA)

AID   Agricultural Information Division (Philippines)

AID   Algemene Inspectiedienst

AID   Alliance Internationale de la Diffusion par Fil

AID   American Institute of Decorators

AID   Association Internationale pour le Développement

AID   Association Internationale des Documentalistes et Techniciens de l'Information

AID   Land- und Hauswirtschaftlicher Auswertungs- und Informationsdienst

AIDA   Asociación Internacional de Derecha de Aguas

AIDA   Association Internationale de la Distribution des Produits Alimentaires

AIDA   Association Internationale de Droit Africain

AIDA   Association Internationale du Droit de l'Assurance

AIDA   Associazione Industrie Dolciarie Italiane

AIDA   Associazione Italiana di Aerotecnica

AIDAA   Associazione Italiana di Aeronautica e Astronautica

AIDBA   Association Internationale pour le Développement de la Documentation, des Bibliothéques et des Archives en Afrique

AIDC   American Industrial Development Council

AIDC   Asian Industrial Development Council

AIDD   American Institute for Design and Drafting

AIDE   Asociación Interamericana de Educación

AIDE   Association Internationale de Distribution d'Eau

AIDE   Association Internationale du Droit des Eaux

AIDEC   Association for European Industrial Development and Economic Co-operation (Netherlands)

AIDEC	Association Internationale d'Expertise Chimique
AIDELA	Association Internationale d'Éditeurs pour la Linguistique Appliquée
AIDEM	Associazione Italiana degli Editori di Musica
AIDEP	Association Interentreprises pour le Développement de l'Enseignement Programmé
AIDI	Associazione Industrie Dolciarie Italiane
AIDI	Associazione Italiana per la Documentazione e Informazione
AIDI	Associazione Italiana di Illuminazione
AIDIC	Associazione Italiana di Ingegneria Chimico
AIDIS	Association Inter-Americaine de Genie Sanitaire
AIDIS	Associazione Italiana di Ingeneria Sismica
AIDL	Asociación Interamericana pro Democracia y Libertad
AIDL	Auckland Industrial Development Laboratory (N.Z.)
AIDLCM	Association Internationale pour la Defense des Langues et Cultures Menacées
AIDN	Associazione Internazionale Diritt Nucleare
AIDP	Association Internationale de Droit Pénal
AIDR	Association de Développement Rural d'Outre-mer
AIDR	Association Internationale de Développement Rural
AIDS	Australian Institute of Aboriginal Studies
AIDSEGA	Amitié Internationale des Scouts et Guides Adultes
AIDT	Association Interparlementaire du Tourisme
AIDUM	Association Internationale pour le Développement des Universités Internationales et Mondiales
AIE	Agence Internationale de l'Énergie
AIE	Associazione Italiana Editori
AIEA	L'Agence Internationale de l'Énergie Atomique
AIEA	Association Internationale des Économistes Agronomiques
AIEA	Association Internationale des Étudiants en Agriculture
AIECE	Association d'Instituts Européens de Conjoncture Économique
AIED	Association Internationale d'Entreprises de Dragage
AIED	Association Internationale des Étudiants Dentaires
AIEDP	Asian Institute for Economic Development and Planning (Thailand)
AIEE	American Institute of Electrical Engineers (*now* IEEE)
AIEE	Association des Instituts d'Études Européennes
AIEF	Association Internationale des Études Françaises
AIEGL	Association Internationale d'Epigraphie Grecque et Latine (France)
AIEI	Association of Indian Engineering Industry
AIEID	Asociación Internacional de Estudio Integral del Deporte (Argentina)
AIEJI	Association Internationale des Éducateurs de Jeunes Inadaptés
AIEL	Asociación Internacional de Estructuras Laminares
AIEL	Association Internationale d'Epigraphie Latine
AIEM	Association Internationale d'Études sur la Mécanographie et l'Informatique
AIEMA	Association Internationale pour l'Étude de la Mosaïque Antique
AIENSAN	Association des Ingénieurs de l'École Nationale Supérieure Agronomique de Nancy (France)
AIEP	Association des Importateurs d'Essence et Pétroles
AIEP	Association Internationale d'Études Patristiques
AIEP	Association Internationale des Usagers d'Embranchements Particuliers
AIEPD	African Institute for Economic Planning and Development
AIEPE	Association Internationale des Écoles Privées Européennes
AIEPM	Association Internationale des Educateurs pour la Paix Mondiale
AIER	American Institute of Economic Research
AIERI	Association Internationale d'Études et Recherches sur l'Information
AIES	Association Internationale d'Essais de Semences
AIESEC	Association Internationale des Étudiants en Sciences Économiques et Commerciales
AIESEE	Association Internationale d'Études du Sud-est Européen

AIESEP	Association Internationale des Écoles ou Instituts Supérieurs d'Éducation Physique et Sportive
AIESS	Association Internationale des Écoles du Service Social
AIEST	Association International d'Experts Scientifiques du Tourisme
AIF	Alliance Internationale des Femmes
AIF	Arbeitsgemeinschaft Industrieller Forschungsvereinigungen
AIF	Asociación Internacional de Fomento
AIF	Association des Industriels de France contre les Accidents du Travail
AIF	Association Internationale Futuribles
AIF	Associazione Italiana del Franchising
AIFA	Asociación Internacional de Fabricantes de Aceites
AIFE	Association Internationale des Femmes Ecrivains
AIFEA	All Indian Federation of Educational Association (India)
AIFL	Anglo-Israel Friendship League
AIFLD	American Institute for Free Labor Development
AIFM	Association Internationale des Femmes Médecins
AIFOB	Association Internationale des Sylviculteurs et des Utilisateurs de Produits de la Forêt et du Bois
AIFRB	American Institute of Fishery Research Biologists
AIFRO	Association Internationale Francophone de Recherche Odontologique
AIFS	African Improved Farming Scheme
AIFS	American Institute for Foreign Study
AIFS	Association Internationale des Fabricants de Superphosphate
AIFSPR	Associazione Italiana di Fisica Sanitaria e di Protezione contro le Radiazioni
AIFST	Australian Institute of Food Science and Technology
AIFT	American Institute for Foreign Trade
AIG	Association pour l'Information de Gestion
AIG	Association Internationale de Géodésie
AIGA	American Institute of Graphic Arts
AIGA	Association Internationale de Géomagnétisme et d'Aéronomie
AIGE	Asociación Interamericana de Gastroenterologia
AIGI	Association Internationale de Géologie de l'Ingénieur
AIGM	Association Internationale de Grands Magasins
AIGMF	All India Glass Manufacturers Federation
AIGREF	Association des Ingénieurs du Génie Rural, des Eaux et des Forêts
AIGSL	Alleanza Internazionale dei Giornalisti e Scrittori Latini
AIGT	Association for the Improvement of Geometrical Teaching
AIGYPFB	Asociación de Ingenieros y Geólogos de Yacimientos Petrolíferos Fiscales Bolivianos
AIH	Academie Internationale d'Heraldique
AIH	American Institute of Homeopathy
AIH	Asociación Internacional de Hispanists
AIH	Association of Independent Hospitals
AIH	Association des Ingénieurs Horticoles
AIH	Association Internationale de l'Hôtellerie
AIH	Association Internationale des Hydrogéologues
AIHA	American Industrial Hygiene Association
AIHDI	Association Internationale d'Histoire du Droit et des Institutions
AIHE	International Economic History Association (Switzerland)
AIHP	American Institute of the History of Pharmacy
AIHS	Académie Internationale d'Histoire des Sciences (France)
AIHS	American Irish Historical Society
AIHS	Association Internationale d'Hydrologie Scientifique
AII	Associazione Italiana degli Inventori
AIIA	Association of International Insurance Agents
AIIA	Atlantic Institute for International Affairs (France)
AIIA	Australian Institute of International Affairs
AIIAA	Association des Ingénieurs des Industries Agricoles et Alimentaires
AIIC	Association Internationale des Interprètes de Conférence
AIICA	Asociación Internacional para las Investigaciones sobre Contaminación de las Aguas

AIIE	American Institute of Industrial Engineers
AIIG	Associazione Italiana degli Insegnanti di Geografia
AIIH	Asociación Internacional de Investigaciones Hidráulicas
AIIHPH	All-India Institute of Hygiene and Public Health
AIIMB	Associazione Italiana di Ingegneria Medica e Biologica
AIIMS	All-Indian Institute of Medical Sciences
AIIPA	Associazione Italiana Industriali Prodotti Alimentari
AIIPC	American International Institute for the Protection of Childhood
AIIRM	Association Internationale des Intérêts Radio-Maritimes
AIIS	American Institute for Imported Steel
AIIS	American Institute of Indian Studies
AIIS	Asian Institute of International Studies (Philippines)
AIISA	Association des Ingénieurs de l'Institut Supérieur d'Agriculture
AIISP	Associazione Italiana per l'Igiene e la Sanita Pubblica
AIISUP	Association Internationale d'Information Scolaire, Universitaire et Professionnelle
AIIT	Association Internationale de l'Inspection du Travail
AIJA	Association Internationale des Jeunes Avocats
AIJD	Association Internationale des Juristes Démocrates
AIJE	Association des Industries du Jute Européennes
AIJE	Association Internationale des Juges des Enfants
AIJE	Association Internationale des Magistrats de la Jeunesse
AIJLF	Association Internationale des Journalistes de Langue Française
AIJP	Association Internationale des Journalistes Philateliques
AIJPF	Association Internationale des Journalistes de la Presse Féminine et Familiale
AIL	Association of International Libraries
AIL	Association Internationale de Limnologie Théorique et Appliquée
AILA	Agenzia Internazionale Letteraria Artistica
AILA	Agrupación Ibero- Latinoamericana para el Estudio Cientifico de la Deficiencia Mental
AILA	Asociación de Industriales Latino-Americanos
AILA	Association Internationale de Linguistique Appliquée
AILC	Association Internationale de Littérature Comparée
AILE	Association Internationale des Loteries d'Etat
AIM	American Indian Movement
AIM	American Institute of Management
AIM	American Institute for Microminiaturization
AIM	Arbeitsgemeinschaft Information Meeresforschung und Meerestechnik
AIM	Association pour les Applications de l'Informatique à la Médecine
AIM	Association of Industrial Machinery Merchants
AIM	Association Internationale de Metéorologie
AIM	Association Internationale de la Mutualité
AIM	Associazione Italiana di Metallurgia
AIM	Atlantic International Marketing Committee
AIM	Australian Institute of Management
AIMA	All India Management Association
AIMA	Azienda di Stato per gli Inteventi nel Mercato Agricolo
AIMAS	Académie Internationale de Médecine Aéronautique et Spatiale
AIMAS	Associazione Italiana di Medicina Aeronautica e Spaziale
AIMAV	Association Internationale pour la Recherche et la Diffusion des Méthodes Audio-visuelles et Structuro-globales
AIMBE	Association Internationale de Médecine et de Biologie de l'Environnement
AIMC	American Institute of Medical Climatology
AIMC	Associazione Italiana Maestri Cattolici
AIME	American Institute of Mining and Metallurgical Engineers
AIME	Asociación de Investigación para la Mejora de la Alfalfa
AIMEA	Association Internationale des Métiers et Enseignements d'Art
AIMETA	Associazione Italiana di Meccanica Teorica e Applicata
AIMFA	Asociación Internacional de Meteorología y Física Atmosférica

AIMFR	Association Internationale des Maisons Familiales Rurales
AIMH	Academy of International Military History (U.S.A.)
AIMI	Association Internationale de Meditation Transcendentale
AIMIC	Association of Insurance Managers in Industry and Commerce (*now* AIRMIC)
AIMJ	Association Internationale des Magistrats de la Jeunesse
AIMM	Association Internationale des Musées Médicaux
AIMM	Australian Institute of Mining and Metallurgy
AIMMPE	American Institute of Mining, Metallurgical and Petroleum Engineers
AIMO	Accademia Italiana di Medicina Omeopatica
AIMO	All-India Manufacturers Organisation
AIMO	Association of Industrial Medical Officers
AIMP	Associação da Indústria de Malte Portuguesa
AIMPA	Association Internationale de Météorologie et de Physique de l'Atmosphère
AIMPE	Australian Institute of Marine and Power Engineers
AIMPES	Associazione Italiana Manufatturieri Pelli Cuoio e Succedonei
AIMS	American Institute of Merchant Shipping
AIMS	American International Marchigiana Society
AIMS	Association for Improving Moral Standards
AIMS	Association for International Medical Study
AIMS	Australian Institute of Marine Science
AIN	American Institute of Nutrition
AINA	Arctic Institute of North America (Canada)
AINDT	Australian Institute for Non-Destructive Testing
AINEC	All-India Newspaper Editors Conference
AINP	Association Internationale des Numismates Professionnels
AIOA	Aviation Insurance Officers Association
AIOB	Association Internationale d'Océanografie Biologique
AIOCC	Association Internationale des Organisateurs de Courses Cyclistes
AIOP	Association Internationale d'Océanographie Physique
AIOP	Association Internationale d'Orientation Professionnelle
AIOPI	Association of Information Officers in the Pharmaceutical Industry
AIOSP	Association Internationale d'Orientation Scolaire et Professionnelle
AIP	American Institute of Physics
AIP	American Institute of Planners
AIP	Asociación Interamericana de Productividad
AIP	Associação Industrial Portuguesa
AIP	Association Internationale de Papyrologues
AIP	Association Internationale de Pédiatrie
AIP	Association Internationale de Photobiologie
AIP	Association Internationale de Psychotechnique
AIP	Associazione Italiana della Pellicceria
AIP	Associazione Italiana Prefabbricazione per l'Edilizia Industrializzata
AIPA	Association Internationale de la Psychologie Adlérienne
AIPA	Association Internationale de Psychologie Analytique
AIPA	Association Internationale de Psychologie Appliquée
AIPA	Associazione Italiana Planificazione Aziendale
AIPA	Associazione Italiana per lo Studio della Psicologia Analitica
AIPC	Association Internationale des Palais des Congrès
AIPC	Association Internationale des Ponts et Charpentes
AIPC	Association Internationale de Prophylaxie de la Cécité
AIPCEE	Association des Industries du Poisson de la CEE
AIPCN	Association Internationale Permanente des Congrès de Navigation
AIPCR	Association Internationale Permanente des Congrès de la Route
AIPE	American Institute of Plant Engineers
AIPE	Association de l'Industrie des Produits d'Entretien (Belgium)
AIPE	Association Internationale de la Presse Echiquéenne
AIPEA	Association Internationale pour l'Étude des Argiles (*formerly* CIPEA)
AIPELF	Association Internationale de Pédagogie Expérimentale de Langue Française
AIPEPO	Association Internationale de Presse pour l'Étude des Problèmes d'Outre-Mer
AIPEU	American Institute on Problems of European Unity

AIPH	Association Internationale des Producteurs de l'Horticulture		**AIRE**	Association Internationale des Ressources en Eau
AIPI	Association Internationale des Professeurs d'Italien		**AIRE**	Associazione Italiana per la Promozione degli e delle Richerche per l'Edilizia
AIPLF	Association Internationale des Parlementaires de Langue Française		**AIRG**	Agency for Intellectual Relief in Germany
AIPMA	All-India Plastics Manufacturers Association		**AIRH**	Association Internationale de Recherches Hydrauliques
AIPPI	Association Internationale pour la Protection de la Propriété Industrielle		**AIRI**	Animal Industry Research Institute (Australia)
AIPPL	Association Internationale des Professeurs de Philosophie		**AIRIT**	Association Internationale de Recherche en Informatique Toxicologique
AIPR	American Institute of Pacific Relations		**AIRMA**	All-India Radio Manufacturers Association
AIPRC	Associazione Italiana per la Promozione delle Ricerche sul Cancro		**AIRMEC**	Association Internationale pour la Recherche Médicale et les Echanges Culturels
AIPS	Association Internationale de la Presse Sportive		**AIRMIC**	Association of Insurance and Risk Managers in Industry and Commerce
AIPS	Association Internationale pour la Prévention du Suicide		**AIRO**	Associazione Italiana di Recerca Operativa
AIPS	Association Internationale pour le Progrès Social		**AIRP**	Association Internationale de Relations Professionnelles
AIPS	Australian Institute of Political Science		**AIRP**	Associazione Italiana per le Relazioni Pubbliche
AIPSA	Agro Industrias Peruanas S.A.		**AIRP**	Associazione Italiana Ricostruttori Pneumatici
AIPULF	Association Internationale des Presses Universitaires de Langue Français		**AIRPE**	Association Internationale de Recherche sur la Pollution de l'Eau
AIR	All-India Radio		**AIRXRS**	American Industrial Radium and X-Ray Society
AIR	American Institute of Refrigeration		**AIS**	Association Internationale de la Savonnerie et de la Détergence
AIR	American Institute for Research			
AIR	American Institutes for Research in the Behavioural Sciences		**AIS**	Association Internationale de Sociologie
AIR	Association des Instituteurs Réunis du Grande-Duché de Luxembourg		**AIS**	Association Internationale de la Soie
			AIS	Associazione Italiana Sociologi
AIR	Associazione Italiana Ragioneri		**AIS**	Australian Iron and Steel Pty
AIR	Autorité Internationale de la Ruhr		**AISA**	Agricultural Information Society for Asia
AIR	Inter-American Broadcasting Association		**AISA**	Association Internationale pour la Sécurité Aérienne
AIRAH	Australian Institute of Refrigeration, Air Conditioning and Heating		**AISAM**	Association Internationale des Sociétés d'Assurance Mutuelle
AIRAPT	Association Internationale pour l'Avancement de la Recherche et de la Technologie aux Hautes Pressions		**AISB**	Association Internationale de Standardisation Biologique
AIRBM	Associazione Italiana di Radiobiologia Medica		**AISC**	American Institute of Steel Construction
			AISC	Année Internationale du Soleil Calme
AIRBO	Association Internationale pour les Recherches au Bas Fourneau d'Ougrée		**AISC**	Assistenza Internazionale Servici di Congresso
AIRBR	Association Internationale du Registre des Bateaux du Rhin		**AISC**	Association Internationale des Skal Clubs
AIRCAT	Association Internationale des Régies et Commissions des Accidents du Travail		**AISC**	Associazione Italiana Santa Cecilia per la Musica Sacra

AISE	Association Internationale des Sciences de l'Éducation
AISE	Association Internationale des Sciences Économiques
AISE	Association of Iron and Steel Engineers (U.S.A.)
AISF	Association Internationale de Solidarité Francophone
AISFO	Associazione Italiana Sviluppo Foraggere
AISH	Association Internationale des Sciences Hydrologiques
AISI	Association Internationale des Syndicats d'Initiative et Groupements Similaires
AISI	American Iron and Steel Institute
AISJ	Association Internationale des Sciences Juridiques
AISL	Association Internationale de l'Hôpital Schweitzer de Lambaréné
AISL	Associazione Italiana di Studio del Lavoro
AISLF	Association Internationale des Sociologues de Langue Française
AISM	Association Internationale de Signalisation Maritime
AISM	Association Internationale des Sociétés de Microbiologie
AISM	Associazione Italiana per gli Studi di Mercato
AISÖ	Arbeitsgemeinschaft Internationaler Strassenverkehrsunternehmer Österreichs
AISP	Académie Internationale des Sciences Politiques
AISP	Association Internationale de Science Politique
AISP	Associazione delle Imprese Svizzere di Perforazione
AISPA	Associazione Italiana Selezionatori Produttori Avicoli di Milano
AISPIT	Association Internationale de Seismologie et de Physique de l'Interieur de la Terre
AISPO	Association Internationale des Sciences Physiques de l'Océan
AISRU	Association Internationale pour la Statistique Regionale et Urbaine
AISS	Association Internationale de la Science du Sol
AISS	Association Internationale de la Sécurité Sociale
AISS	Associazione Italiana Selezionatori Sementi e Costitutori Razze
AIST	Agenzia Italiana Spettacolo e Turismo
AIST	Arbeitsgemeinschaft zur Förderung und Entwicklung des Internationalen Strassenverkehrs in der Deutschen Demokratischen Republik
AISTS	Associazione Italiana della Stampa Tecnica Scientifica e Periodica
AISU	Arab Iron and Steel Union
AIT	Alliance Internationale de Tourisme
AIT	Asian Institute of Technology (Thailand)
AIT	Association of H.M. Inspectors of Taxes
AITA	Association Internationale du Théâtre d'Amateurs
AITA	Association Internationale des Transports Aériens
AITB	Associazione Italiana dei Tecnici Birrari
AITC	American Institute for Timber Construction
AITC	Association Internationale des Traducteurs de Conférence
AITE	Asociación de Industrias Textiles del Ecuador
AITEC	Association Internationale de Technologie des Conférences
AITEC	Associazione Italiana Tecnico Economica del Cemento
AITEL	Associazione Italiana Tecnici del Latte
AITFA	Association des Ingénieurs et Techniciens Française des Aéroglisseurs
AITha	Association Internationale de Thalassothérapie
AITI	Associazione Italiana Traduttori ed Interpreti
AITIM	Asociación de Investigación Técnica de las Industrias de la Madera y Corcho
AITIT	Association Internationale de la Teinture et de l'Impression Textiles (*formerly* AITT)
AITIVA	Associazione Italiana Tecnici Industrie Vernici e Affini
AITPCI	Association des Ingénieurs, Techniciens et Professionels du Contrôle Industrielle
AITT	Association Internationale de la Teinture Textile (*now* AITIT)
AIU	Alliance Israelite Universelle
AIU	Association Internationale des Universités
AIU	Association Internationale des Urbanistes
AIUFFAS	Association Internationale des Utilisateurs de Filés de Fibres Artificielles et Synthétiques
AIUM	American Institute of Ultrasound in Medicine (U.S.A.)

AIV	Association Internationale de Volcanologie	**AJV**	Algemene Juweliers Vereniging
AIV	Associazione Italiana del Vuoto	**AKA**	British Amateur Karate Association
AIVCIT	Association Internationale de Volcanologie et de Chimie de l'Intérieur de la Terre	**AKAVA**	Akateemisten Järjestöjen Keskuselin
		AKB	Association des Kinésithérapeutes de Belgique
AIVM	Association Internationale pour les Voiles Minces et les Voiles Spatiaux	**AKEB**	Aktiengesellschaft für Kernenergie Beteiligungen (Switzerland)
AIVPA	Association Internationale Vétérinaire de Production Animale	**AKEL**	Progressive Party of Working People (Cyprus)
AIW	Arbeitkreis Fachagenturen und Berater für Industrie-Werbung	**AKEW**	Arbeitsgemeinschaft Kernkraftwerk der Elektrizitätswirtschaft (Austria)
AIW	Arbeitsgemeinschaft Industrieöfenbau- und Wärmeanlagen	**AKF**	American-Korean Foundation
AIW	International Union of Allied Industrial Workers of America	**AKI**	Arbeitsgemeinschaft Deutsche Kunstoffindustrie
AIWC	All India Women's Conference	**AKI**	Arbeitsgemeinschaft Keramische Industrie
AIWFC	All India Women's Food Council	**AKL**	Autoalan Keskusliitto
AIWM	American Institute of Weights and Measures	**AKOR**	Gesellschaft für Operations Research in Wirtschaft und Verwaltung
AIWO	Agudas Israel World Organisation		
AJA	Amateur Judo Association of Great Britain	**AKU**	Algemene Kunstzijde Unie NV
AJA	Australian Journalists Association	**ALA**	Afghan Library Association
AJBD	Arbeitsgemeinschaft für Juristisches Bibliotheks- und Dokumentationswesen	**ALA**	American Landrace Association
		ALA	American Library Association
AJC	Alianza Mundial de Asociaciones Cristianas de Jóvenes	**ALA**	Arbeitsgemeinschaft der Schweizerischen Aluminiumwaren-Fabrikanten
AJC	Asociación Judicial de Chile	**ALA**	Asociación de Líneas Aéreas
AJC	Association des Journalistes de la Consommation	**ALA**	Austral Lineas Aereas (Argentina)
AJC	Australian Jockey Club	**ALACF**	Asociación Latinoamericana de Ciencias Fisiológicas
AJCC	American Jersey Cattle Club	**ALAD**	Arid Lands Agricultural Development Program (Middle East)
AJCOR	Australian Joint Council for Operational Research		
AJDC	American Joint Distribution Committee	**ALADA**	Asociación Latinoamericana del Algodon (Venezuela)
AJE	Association des Journalistes Européens	**ALAE**	Asociación Latinoamericana de Entomología
AJE	Association des Juristes Européens	**ALAF**	Asociación Latino-Americana de Ferrocarriles
AJEF	Association des Jeunes Européens Fédéralistes		
AJEF	Association des Journalistes Économiques et Financiers	**ALAF**	Asociación Latinoamericana de Fitotecnia
		ALAFAR	Association Latino-Américaine des Matières Refractaires
AJEX	Association of Jewish Ex-Servicemen and Women	**ALAFO**	Asociación Latinoamericana de Facultades de Odontologia
AJH	Association des Journalistes de l'Horticulture	**ALAI**	Association Littéraire et Artistique Internationale
AJPAA	Association des Journalistes Professionnels de l'Aéronautique et de l'Astronautique		
AJPBE	Association des Journalistes Périodiques Belges et Étrangers	**ALAIH**	Asociación Latino-Americano de Ictiologos y Herpetologos
AJPF	Association Internationale des Journalistes de la Presse Féminine et Familiale	**ALALC**	Asociación Latinoamericana de Libre Comercio

ALALE	Association Latino-Américaine de Libre Echange	**ALEC**	Algemeen Landbouw Emigratie-Comité (Netherlands)
ALAM	Asociación Latinoamericana de Malezas	**ALEC**	Asian Labour Education Centre (Philippines)
ALAM	Association of Lightweight Aggregate Manufacturers	**ALECSO**	Arab League Educational, Cultural and Scientific Organization
ALAMAR	Asociación Latinoamericana de Armadores	**ALEGEO**	Latin American Association of Editors in the Earth Sciences (Venezuela)
ALAP	Agricultural Librarians Association of the Philippines	**ALEJ**	Association Luxembourgeoise des Éditeurs de Journaux
ALAP	Association Latino-Américaine d'Administration Publique	**ALENCA**	Alena Enterprises of Canada
ALAR	Association of Light Alloy Refiners	**ALER**	Asociación Latinoamericana de Educación Radiofónica (Argentina)
ALARS	Association of Light Alloy Refiners and Smelters	**ALERB**	Asociación Latinoamericana de Redactores de Revistas Biológicas (Mexico)
ALAS	Asociación Argentina de Sociologia	**ALERT**	All-Africa Leprosy and Rehabilitation Training Centre (Ethiopia)
ALAS	Asociación Latinoamericana del Suelo	**ALES**	American Labour Education Service
ALASBIMN	Association Latino-Américaine des Sociétés de Biologie et Médecine Nucléaires	**ALF**	Arbeitsgemeinschaft der Lebensmittel-Filialbetriebe
ALATAC	Asociación Latinoamericana del Transporte Automotor por Carreteras	**ALF**	Asociación Latinoamericana de Fitopatología (Colombia)
ALB	Arbeitkreis Ladenbau im HDH	**ALF**	Association Laitière Française pour le Développement de la Production et des Industries du Lait
ALB	Arbeitsgemeinschaft Landwirtschaftliches Bauen		
ALC	Agricultural Land Commission	**ALF**	Azania Liberation Front
ALC	Alberta Livestock Co-operative (Canada)	**ALFAL**	Asociación de Lingüística y Filogia de América Latina
ALCA	American Leather Chemists Association		
ALCA	Asociación Latinoamericana de Ciencias Agrícolas	**ALFE**	Association Linguistique Franco-Européenne
ALCAN	Aluminium Company of Canada	**ALFEDIAM**	Association de Langue Française pour l'Étude du Diabète et des Maladies Métaboliques
ALCATEL	Société Alsacienne de Constructions Atomiques, de Telecommunications et d'Électronique		
		ALGES	Association of Local Government Engineers and Surveyors
ALCL	Association of London Chief Librarians	**ALGFO**	Association of Local Government Financial Officers
ALCOA	Aluminium Company of America		
ALDA	American Land Development Association	**ALGÖ**	Arbeitsgemeinschaft Landwirtschaftlicher Geflügelzüchter Österreichs
ALDEC	Asociación Latinoamericana de Derecho Constitucional		
		ALGO	Association des Livres Généalogiques Ovins
ALDEV	African Land Development Board (Kenya)	**ALGU**	Association of Land Grant Colleges and Universities (U.S.A.)
ALEA	Air Line Employees Association International		
		ALI	Alfa-Laval International (Sweden)
ALEAS	Asociación Latinoamericana de Educación Agrícola	**ALI**	American Library Institute
		ALI	Association Luxembourgeoise des Ingénieurs
ALEASS	Association Latino-Américaine des Écoles de Service Social	**ALI**	Associazione Librai Italiani
		ALI	Latin American Exchange Association
ALEBCI	Asociación Latinoamericana de Biblioteconomía y Ciencias de la Información	**ALIA**	American Life Insurance Association
ALEBCI	Latin American Association of Schools of Library and Information Sciences (Brazil)	**ALIAZO**	Alianca Angolana des Originarios do Zombo

ALICA	Asociación Latinoamericana de Industrias de Conservas Alimenticias
ALIDE	Asociación Latinoamericana de Instituciones Financieras de Desarrollo (Peru)
ALII	Association Luxembourgeoise des Ingénieurs et Industriels
ALIMDA	Association of Life Insurance Medical Directors of America
ALJE	Association Luxembourgeoise des Juristes Européens
ALJHE	Association of Libraries of Judaica and Hebraica in Europe
ALJP	Association Luxembourgeoise des Journalistes Professionnels
ALKD	Association Luxembourgeoise des Kinésithérapeutes Diplomés
ALLA	Allied Long Lines Agency (of NATO)
ALM	Antillaanse Luchtvaart Maatschappij (Netherlands Antilles)
ALM	Asociación Latinoamericana de Microbiología
ALMA	Katholieke Academische Actie voor Internationale Samenwerking
ALMER-COM	European Chambers of Commerce Group for Trade with Latin America
ALMO	African Livestock Marketing Organisation
ALN	Armée de Libération Nationale (Algeria)
ALO	Asian Labour Organisation
ALOSEV	Asamblea Latinoamerica de Organizaciones de Servicio Voluntario
ALP	Afdeling Arbeidsfysiologie v. h. Laboratorium v. Fysiologie d. Dieren
ALP	Australian Labour Party
ALPA	Asociación Latinoamericana de Producción Animal
ALPAI	Air Line Pilots Association International
ALPAR	Association Luxembourgeoise pour l'Alimentation et l'Hygiene Rationnelles
ALPDS	Association des Laboratoires de Prothèse Dentaire de Suisse
ALFP	Algemeen Landbouw Pensioenfonds (Indonesia)
ALPL	Association Luxembourgeoise des Pilotes de Ligne
ALPO	Association of Land and Property Owners
ALPO	Association of Lunar and Planetary Observers
ALPRO	Alianza para el Progresso (of OAS)

ALPSP	Association of Learned and Professional Society Publishers
ALR	Société Luxembourgeoise de Radiologie
ALRA	Abortion Law Reform Association
ALRA	Adult Literacy Resource Agency
ALRC	Anti-Locust Research Centre
ALROS	American Laryngological, Rhinological and Otological Society
ALS	Agricultural Land Service (now ADAS)
ALS	Algemeen Landbouw Syndicaat (Indonesia)
ALSATEX	Société Alsacienne d'Étude et d'Exploitation
ALSPI	Société Alsacienne de Participations Industrielles
ALT	Association of Law Teachers
ALTA	American Library Trustee Association
ALTU	Association of Liberal Trade Unionists
ALUPA	Association Luxembourgeoise pour l'Utilisation Pacifique de l'Énergie Atomique
ALUS	African Land Utilisation and Settlement Board
ALVAO	Association des Langues Vivantes pour l'Afrique Occidentale
ALWIC	Anti Leprosy World Information Centre
AMA	Accumulator Makers Association
AMA	Adhesive Manufacturers Association (now BAMA)
AMA	Agricultural Marketing Administration (U.S.A.)
AMA	American Machinery Association
AMA	American Management Association
AMA	American Maritime Association
AMA	American Medical Association
AMA	American Meteor Association
AMA	Architectural Metalwork Association
AMA	Asociación Médica Argentina
AMA	Association Centrale des Moniteurs d'Auto-Écoles (Switzerland)
AMA	Association of Manufacturers Allied to the Electrical and Electronic Industry
AMA	Auckland Mathematical Association (N.Z.)
AMA	Australian Medical Association
AMA	Australian Musical Association
AMA	Automobile Manufacturers' Associations (U.S.A.)
AMADE	Association Mondiale des Amis de l'Enfance
AMAE	Associação Mineira de Administração Escolar (Brazil)

AMAPROP	Anglo American Properties Ltd
AMAS	Association Mondiale d'Aviculture Scientifique
AMASC	Association Mondiale des Anciennes Élèves du Sacré Coeur
AMAT	Association des Musées de l'Afrique Tropicale
AMAUS	Aero Medical Association of the United States
AMAX	American Metal Climax Inc.
AMBAC	Asociación Mexicana de Bibliotecarios
AMBES	Association of Metropolitan Borough Engineers and Surveyors
AMBMO	Asociación Mediterránea de Biología Marina y Oceanografía
AMC	Agricultural Mortgage Corporation
AMC	American Mining Congress
AMC	Association of Municipal Corporations
AMCA	Academia Mexicana de Ciencias Agrícolas
AMCA	Academia Mexicana de Ciencias Avícola
AMCA	Amateur Motor-Cycle Association
AMCA	American Mosquito Control Association
AMCAN	Anglo American Corporation of Canada Ltd
AMCC	Association Mondiale pour la Communication Chrétienne
AMCCW	Association of Manufacturers of Chilled Car Wheels (U.S.A.)
AMCHAM	American Chamber of Commerce in the Netherlands
AMCL	Association of Metropolitan Chief Librarians
AMCOR	African Metals Corporation Ltd
AMD	Asociación Médica Dominicana
AMDB	Agricultural Machinery Development Board
AMDEA	Association of Manufacturers of Domestic Electrical Appliances
AMDEC	Agricultural Marketing Development Executive Committee
AMDEC	Associated Manufacturers of Domestic Electric Cookers
AMDEL	Australian Mineral Development Laboratories
AMDI	Associazione Medici Dentisti Italiani
AME	Accord Monetaire Européen
AMEB	Agrupación Mundial de Ex-Boxeadores
AMECEA	Association of Member Episcopal Conferences in Eastern Africa
AMECUSD	Association of Manufacturers and Exporters of Concentrated and Unconcentrated Soft Drinks
AMEE	Association of Managerial Electrical Executives
AMEME	Association of Mining, Electrical and Mechanical Engineers
AMES	Air Ministry Experimental Station
AMES	Association of Marine Engineering Schools
AMEU	Association of Municipal Electricity Undertakings of Southern Africa
AMEWA	Associated Manufacturers of Electric Wiring Accessories
AMEX	American Stock Exchange
AMFIE	Association of Mutual Fire Insurance Engineers (U.S.A.)
AMFORT	Association Mondiale pour la Formation Professionelle Touristique
AMGE	Association Mondiale des Guides et des Éclaireuses
AMGI	Associazione Medici Geriatri Italiani
AMGP	Asociación Mexicana de Geólogos Petroleros
AMGRA	American Milk Goat Record Association
AMGSR	Association des Marchands Grainiers de la Suisse Romande
AMHS	American Material Handling Society
AMI	American Meat Institute
AMI	Apostolat Militaire International
AMI	Arbeitsgemeinschaft Mahlkorkverarbeitender Industrie
AMI	Assistance Médicale Internationale (Canada)
AMI	Association Maçonnique Internationale
AMI	Association of Meat Inspectors
AMI	Association Montessori Internationale
AMI	Associazione Medica Italiana
AMIA	American Metal Importers Association
AMIA	Association Mondiale pour l'Union du Troisième Age (Switzerland)
AMIC	Anglo American Industrial Corporation Ltd
AMIC	Asian Mass Communications Research and Information Centre, Singapore (Malaysia)
AMICEE	Asociación Mexicana de Ingenieros en Comunicaciónes Electricas y Electronicas
AMICI	Association Mondiale des Interprètes de Conférences Internationales
AMIEV	Association Médicale Internationale pour l'Étude des Conditions de Vie et de la Santé

AMIF	American Meat Institute Federation	**AMP**	Australian Mycological Panel
AMII	Association of Musical Instrument Industries	**AMPA**	Agricultural Machinery Parts Association
AMINA	Association Mondiale des Inventeurs (Belgium)	**AMPA**	American Manganese Producers' Association
AMISLA	Comité Organisateur de l'Académie Musulmane Internationale des Sciences des Lettres et des Beaux-Arts	**AMPA**	American Medical Publishers Association
		AMPA	Asociación Mexicana de Producción Animal
AMJ	Assemblée Mondiale de la Jeunesse	**AMPA**	Centro Nazionale Applicazioni Materie Plastiche Agricoltura
AMK	Arbeitsgemeinschaft Die Moderne Küche	**AMPAS**	Academy of Motion Picture Arts and Sciences (U.S.A.)
AML	American Mail Line Ltd		
AML	Applied Mathematics Laboratory (DSIR) (N.Z.)	**AMPFAC**	Asociación Mexicana de Profesionistas Forestales
AMLAR	Asociación Médico Latino-Americano de Rehabilitacion	**AMPM**	Association of Malt Products Manufacturers
AMLATFE-DOP	Latin American Federation of Employees in Public Service	**AMPrA**	Association Nationale pour les Mutations Professionnelles en Agriculture
		AMPTC	Arab Maritime Petroleum Transport Company
AMLC	Australian Meat and Livestock Corporation		
AMLF	Association des Microbiologistes de Langue Française	**AMQUA**	American Quaternary Association
		AMR	Année Mondiale de Réfugié
AMLFC	Association des Médecins de Langue Française du Canada	**AMR**	Association de Médicine Rurale
		AMRA	American Metal Repair Association
AMM	Asociación Mexicana de Microbiología	**AMRA**	Ancient Mediterranean Research Association
AMM	Association of Manipulative Medicine	**AMRA**	Associationi Belge des Maisons de Réforme Alimentaire
AMM	Association Médicale Mondiale		
AMMA	Assistant Masters and Mistresses Association	**AMRC**	Abadina Media Resource Centre (Nigeria)
		AMRC	Australian Meat Research Committee
AMMA	Associazione Industriali Metallurgici Meccanici Affini	**AMRCB**	Annales du Musée Royal du Congo Belge
		AMRF	African Medical and Research Foundation
AMMFI	Austrian Man-Made Fibres Institute	**AMRO**	Association of Medical Record Officers
AMMI	American Merchant Marine Institute	**AMROP**	Association Mondiale pour l'Étude de l'Opinion Publique
AMMP	Association of Manufacturers of Medicinal Preparations		
		AMS	Agricultural Marketing Service (U.S.A.)
AMMRA	Arbeitsgemeinschaft Mittelständischer Mineralölraffinerien	**AMS**	American Mathematical Society (U.S.A.)
		AMS	American Meteorological Society
AMNH	American Museum of Natural History	**AMS**	American Microchemical Society
AMÖ	Arbeitsgemeinschaft Möbeltransport Bundesverband	**AMS**	American Microscopical Society
		AMS	Army Map Service (U.S.A.)
AMOC	American Miscellaneous Society	**AMS**	Association of Metal Sprayers
AMONO	Agricultural Machinery Operation and Management Office (China)	**AMS**	Association des Musiciens Suisses
		AMSA	American Meat Science Association
AMOP	Association of Mail Order Publishers	**AMSA**	Association of Medical Schools in Africa
AMORC	Ordre Rosicrucien (U.S.A.)	**AMSA**	Association Mondiale des Sciences Agricoles
AMP	Associated Master Plumbers and Domestic Engineers	**AMSA**	Australian Marine Sciences Association
		AMSAC	American Society of African Culture
AMP	Association Méditerranéenne de Psychiatrie	**AMSAT**	Radio Amateur Satellite Corporation
AMP	Australian Mutual Provident Society		

AMSC	American Marine Standards Committee
AMSE	Australian Mining and Smelting Europe Ltd
AMSGA	Association of Manufacturers and Suppliers for the Graphic Arts
AMSH	Association for Moral and Social Hygiene
AMSO	Association of Market Survey Organisations
AMSS	American Milking Shorthorn Society
AMSUS	Association of Military Surgeons of the United States
AMT	Academy of Medicine Toronto (Canada)
AMT	Ateliers Metallurgiques Togolais
AMTCL	Association for Machine Translation and Computational Linguistics (U.S.A.) (*now* Association for Computational Linguistics)
AMTDA	Agricultural Machinery and Tractor Dealers' Association
AMTDA	American Machine Tool Distributors Association
AMTDS	Agricultural Machinery Training Development Society
AMTEC	Australian Meat Trades Export Group
AMTU	Agence Mondiale pour les Problèmes de Circulation en Milieu Urbain
AMTV	Allgemeiner Möbeltransportverband (Austria)
AMU	Associated Metalworkers Union
AMU	Association de Médecine Urbaine
AMUFOC	Association des Établissements Multi-plicateurs de Semences Fourragères des Communautés Européennes
AMV	Association du Mérite Viticole
AMV	Association Mondiale Vétérinaire
AMVES	Asociación de Médicos Veterinarios de El Salvador
AMVMI	Association Mondiale des Vétérinaires Microbiologistes, Immunologistes et Spécialistes des Maladies Infectieuses
AMVR	Asociación Mundial de Vivienda Rural
AMVZ	Asociación de Médicos Veterinarios Zootecnistas (Colombia)
AMWG	American Movement for World Government
AMZ	Association Mondiale de Zootechnie
ANA	Agence Nigérienne d'Assurances
ANA	Accademia Nazionale di Agricoltura
ANA	All Nippon Airways (Japan)
ANA	American Nature Association
ANA	American Neurological Association
ANA	American Numismatic Association
ANA	Asociación Nacional de Agricultores
ANA	Associazione Nationale fra gli Agenti di Assicurazione
ANA	Australian National Airways
ANAAS	Australian and New Zealand Society for the Advancement of Science
ANAB	Algemene Nederlandse Agrarische Bedrijfsbond
ANABA	Asociación Nacional de Bibliotecarios, Archiveros y Arqueólogos
ANABADS	Association Nationale des Bibliothécaires, Archivistes et Documentalistes Sénégalais
ANABIC	Associazione Nazionale Allevatori Bestiame Italiano da Carne
ANAC	Associazione Nazionale Autoservizi in Concessione
ANAC	Auckland Nuclear Accessory Co. (New Zealand)
ANACAFE	Asociación Nacional del Café (Guatemala)
ANACAP	Associazione Nazionale Aziende Concessionarie Affissioni e Pubblicità
ANACH	Asociación Nacional de Campesinos de Honduras
ANACNA	Associazione Nazionale Assistenti e Controllori della Navigazione Aerea
ANADISME	Associazione Nazionale Aziende Distributrici Specialità-Medicinali e Prodotti Chimico-Farmaceutici
ANAF	Association Nationale des Avocats de France
ANAGINA	Associazione Nazionale Agenti General Istituto Nazionale delle Assicurazione e le Assicurazione d'Italia
ANAGSA	Aseguradora Nacional Agrícola y Ganadera (Mexico)
ANAH	Association Nationale des Agronomes Haitiens
ANAHPS	Association Nationale Agricole et Horticole de Promotion Sociale
ANAI	Associazione Nazionale Archivistica Italiana
ANAIP	Asociación Nacional Autónoma de Industriales de Plásticos
ANALAC	Asociación Nacional de Productores e Industriales Lácteos (Colombia)
ANALJA	Asociación Nacional de la Industria del Jabón (Colombia)

ANALPES	Asociación Nacional de Productores de Pesticidas (Colombia)	**ANCAR**	Assoc. Nordestina de Credito e Assistencia Rural (Brazil)
ANALTIR	Association Nationale des Entreprises Albanaises des Transports Routiers	**ANCAR**	Australian National Committee for Antarctic Research
ANAMSO	Association Nationale des Agriculteurs Multiplicateurs de Semences Oléagineuses	**ANCB**	Association Nationale de Comptables de Belgique
ANAOA	Association Nationale des Appellations d'Origine Agricole	**ANCC**	Associazione Nazionale per il Controllo della Combustione (Italy)
ANAP	Asociación Nacional de Agricultores Pequeños (Cuba)	**ANCCR**	Association Nationale des Chanteurs et des Conteurs Ruraux
ANAP	Associazione Nazionale Agenti di Pubblicità	**ANCE**	Assemblé des Nations Captives d'Europe
ANAPO	Alianza Nacional Popular (Colombia)	**ANCE**	Associazione Nazionale del Commercio con l'Estero
ANARE	Australian National Antarctic Research Expeditions	**ANCE**	Associazione Nazionale Costruttori Edili
ANARLEP	Association Nationale des Animateurs Ruraux de Loisirs et d'Éducation Populaire	**ANCEFN**	Académia Naciónal de Ciéncias Exactas, Fisicas y Naturáles (Argentina)
ANAS	Association Nationale des Assistantes Sociales et Assistants Sociaux	**ANCI**	Associazione Nazionale Calzaturifici Italiani
ANAS	Associazione Nazionale Agenzie Stampa	**ANCI**	Associazione Nazionale dei Comuni Italiani
ANASED	Associazione Nazionale Aziende Servizi Elaborazione Dati	**ANCI**	Ateliers Navals de Côte-d'Ivoire
ANATO	Asociación Colombiana de Agencias de Turismo	**ANCIA**	Association Nationale des Centres d'Insemination Artificielle
ANAV	Academia Nacional de Agronomía y Veterinaria (Argentina)	**ANCIC**	Associazione Nazionale Case di Informazioni Commerciali
ANB	Associazione Nazionale Bieticoltori Italiani	**ANCLI**	Associazione Nazionale fra le Centrali del Latte d'Italia
ANBE	Asociación Nacional de Bananeros del Ecuador	**ANCMA**	Associazione Nazionale del Ciclo, Motociclo ed Accessori
ANBEF	Association Nationale des Bibliothécaires d'Expression Française	**ANCO**	Asociación Nacional de Criadores de Ovejas (Ecuador)
ANBOS	Algemene Nederlandse Bond van Schoonheidsinstituten	**ANCO**	Associazione Nazionale dei Consorzi dell' Ortoflorofrutticoltura
ANBP	Algemene Nederlandse Bond van Postorderbedrijven	**ANCOGAS**	Associazione Nazionale Commercianti Gas Liquefatti
ANC	Academia Nacional de Ciencias (Mexico)	**ANCOL**	Associated Newsagents Co-operative Ltd (Australia)
ANC	African National Congress (Zambia)	**ANCOM**	Agrupación Nacional Sindical Autonoma de Constructores de Maquinaria
ANC	African National Council		
ANC	Australian Newspaper Council	**ANCOM**	Andean Common Market
ANCA	Allied Naval Communications Agency (*of* NATO)	**ANCOMAG**	Associazione Nazionale Commercianti Macchine Grafiche Cartarie e Affini
ANCA	American National Cattlemen's Association	**ANCORA**	Association Nationale pour la Coordination la Compensation des Restraites Complementaires
ANCA	Asociación Nacional Cultivadores de Algodón (Venezuela)		
ANCAD	Associazione Nazionale Commercianti Articoli Dentari	**ANCPEP**	Association Nationale de Contrôle des Performances Porcines
ANCAP	Administración Nacional de Combustiles, Alcohol y Portland (Uruguay)	**ANCPI**	Association des Négociateurs-Conseils en Propriété Industrielle (Germany)

ANCRA Associazione Nazionale Commercianti Radio, Televisione, Elettrodomestici ed Affini

ANCRIGAP Asociación Nacional de Criadores de Ganado Porcino (Venezuela)

ANCS Association Nationale des Clubs Scientifiques

ANCUN Australian National Committee for the United Nations

ANDA Administración Nacional de Acueductos y Alcantarillados (Salvador)

ANDA Associação Nacional para Difusão de Adubos (Brazil)

ANDA Associação Nordestina do Desenvolvimento Agrícola (Brazil)

ANDA Association Nationale pour le Développement Agricole

ANDB Air Navigation Development Board (U.S.A.)

ANDB Algemene Nederlandse Drogistenbond

ANDBP Association Nationale pour le Développement des Bibliothèques Publiques

ANDCP Association Nationale des Directeurs et Chefs de Personnel (France)

ANDCS Académia Nacionál de Derécho y Ciéncias Sociales (Argentina)

ANDE Asociación Nacional de Educadores (Costa Rica)

ANDE Asociación Nacional de Empresarios (Ecuador)

ANDEC Acerías Nacionales del Ecuador

ANDECE Agrupación Nacional de los Derivados del Cemento

ANDESA Asociación Nacional de Directores de la Escuelas Superiores de Agricultura (Mexico)

ANDESE Association Nationale des Docteurs ès Sciences Économiques

ANDI Asociación Nacional de Industriales (Colombia)

ANDI Associazione Nazionale degli Inventori

ANDIL Associazione Nazionale degli Industriali dei Laterizi

ANDIMA Asociación Nacional de Industriales Madereros (Venezuela)

ANDIN Associazione Nazionale di Ingegneria Nucleare

ANDIS Associazione Nazionale di Ingegneria Sanitaria

ANDSCJR Association Nationale pour le Developpement Social et Culturel de la Jeunesse Rurale

ANE Asociación Numismatica Española

ANE Associação Nacional dos Exportadores (Brazil)

ANEC Asociación Nacional de Enfermeras de Colombia

ANEC Associação Nacional dos Exportadores de Cereais (Brazil)

ANEC Association Nationale des Éleveurs de Chinchillas

ANEC Associazione Nazionale Esercenti Cinema

ANECEA Association Nationale d'Élevage du Cheval, d'Équitation et d'Agriculture

ANEDA Association Nationale d'Études pour la Documentation Automatique

ANEF Associazione Nazionale di Educazioni Fisica

ANEFPR Association Nationale d'Enseignement et de Formation Professionnelle Rurale

ANEM Association Nationale d'Études Municipales pour la Promotion de la Fonction Communale

ANENA Association Nationale pour l'Étude de la Neige et des Avalanches

ANEP Asociación Nacional de Ex-Parlamentarios (Peru)

ANESV Associazione Nazionale Esercenti Spettacoli Viaggianti

ANET Associazione Nazionale Esercenti Teatri

ANEVEI Algemene Nederlandse Vereniging van Eierhandelaren

ANF Académia Nacionál de Farmácia (Brazil)

ANFAC Agrupación Nacional de Fabricantes de Automóviles y Camiones

ANFAC Asociación Colombiana de Fabricantes de Articulos de Caucho (Colombia)

ANFACI Association Nationale des Fabricants de Colles Industrielles

ANFAMA Agrupación Nacional de Fabricantes de Maquinaria Agrícola

ANFAO Associazione Nazionale Fabbricanti Articoli di Occhialeria

ANFE Asociación Nacional de Fomento Económico (Costa Rica)

ANFIA Associazione Nazionale fra Industrie Automobilistiche

ANFIMA Associazione Nazionale fra i Fabbricanti di Imballagi Metallici ed Affini

ANFMA Associátion Nationale pour la Formation des Moniteurs Agricoles

ANFOPAR	Association Nationale pour la Formation et le Perfectionnement Professionnel des Adultes Ruraux
ANFP	Associação dos Fabricantes de Papel (Brazil)
ANFRUT	Asociación Nacional de Fruticultores (Venezuela)
ANG	Academia Nacional de Geografía (Argentina)
ANGA	Associazione Nazionale Giovani Agricoltori
ANGAISA	Associazione Nazionale Grossisti Apparecchi Igienco-Sanitari
ANGAU	Australian New Guinea Administrative Unit
ANGIP	Associazione Nazionale Grossisti Italiani Profumeria
ANGO	Association du Négoce des Graisses Oléagineuses, Huiles et Graisses Animales et Végétales et leurs Dérivés de la CEE
ANGPVCC	Association Nationale des Groupements de Producteurs (Vins de Consommation Courante)
ANGR	Association Nationale des Grossistes Répartiteurs en Spécialités Pharmaceutiques
ANGRO	Associazione Nazionale Italiana Grossisti Orologiai
ANGV	Asociación Nacional de Ganaderos de Venezuela
ANHG	Academia Nacional de Historia y Geografía (Mexico)
ANHSA	Aerovias Nacionales de Honduras SA
ANHUL	Australian National Humanities Library
ANI	Academia de Negocios Internacionales (U.S.A.)
ANIA	Asociación Nacional de Ingenieros Agronomos
ANIA	Associazione Nazionale fra le Imprese Assicuratrici
ANIAA	Association Nationale des Industries Agricoles et Alimentaires
ANIAI	Associazione Nazionale Ingegneri e Architetti Italiani
ANICA	Associazione Nazionale Instituti di Credito Agrario
ANICAF	Asociación Nacional de Industriales del Café (Venezuela)
ANICAV	Associazione Nazionale fra gli Industriali delle Conserve Alimentari Vegetali
ANICC	Association Nationale Interprofessionnelle du Champignon de Couché
ANICO-BECA	Associazione Nazionale Importatori e Commercianti di Bestiame e Carne
ANICTA	Associazione Nazionale Imprenditori Coibentazioni Termoacustiche
ANID	Associazione Nazionale Insegnanti di Disegno
ANIDECOL	Federazione Nazionale Importatori Caffè, Coloniali e Droghe
ANIE	Associazione Nazionale Industrie Elettrotecniche ed Elettroniche
ANIEM	Unione Nazionale Industrie Edili Minori
ANIERM	Asociación Nacional de Importadores y Exportadores de la República Mexicana
ANIEST	Associazione Nazionale Italiana Esperti Scientifici del Turismo
ANIFRMO	Association National Interprofessionnelle pour la Formation Rationnelle de la Main-d'Oeuvre
ANIG	Associazione Nazionale Industriali Gas
ANILEC	Association Nationale Interprofessionnelle des Légumes de Conserve (France) (*formerly* UNILEC)
ANILS	Associazione Nazionale Insegnanti di Lingue Straniere
ANIM	Asociación Nacional de Industriales Madereros (Venezuela)
ANIMA	Associazione Nazionale Industria Meccanica Varia ed Affine
ANIMeM	Associazione Nazionale Industriali Metalmeccanici Minori
ANIMPEC	Associazione Nazionale Industriali Manufatturieri delle Pelli e del Cuoio
ANIPESCA	Associazione Nazionale Importatori Prodotti della Pesca Conservati
ANIPLA	Associazione Nazionale Italiana per l'Automazione
ANIR	Associazione Nazionale Industrie Refrattari
ANIT	Associazione Nazionale Imprese Teatrais e Similares
ANITA	Associazione Nazionale Imprese dei Trasporti Automobilistici
ANITPAT	Associazione Nazionale Incegnanti Tecnico-Pratici e di Applicazioni Tecniche
ANJIM	Association Nationale des Journalistes d'Information Médicale
ANKO	Algemene Nederlandse Kappersorganisatie
ANL	Argonne National Laboratory (U.S.A.)
ANL	Australian National Line

ANM	Acadêmia Nacionál de Medicína (Brazil)
ANM	Associazione Nazionale Magistrati
ANMA	Association Nationale des Maitres Agricoles et des Maitresses Ménagères
ANMA	Associazione Nazionale Meccanizzazione Agraria
ANMB	Algemene Nederlandse Molenaarsbond
ANMC	American National Metric Council (*of* ANSI)
ANMER	L'Association Nationale de Migration et d'Établissement Ruraux
ANMF	Association Nationale de la Meunerie Française
ANMRC	Australian Numerical Meteorology Research Centre
ANNF	Association Nazionale de la Navigation Fluviale
ANOF	Algemene Nederlandse Onderwijzers Federatie
ANOFPR	Association Nationale Ouvrière pour la Formation Professionnelle Rurale
ANP	United Nations Applied Nutrition Programme
ANP	Australian Nationalist Party
ANPA	American Newspaper Publishers' Association
ANPA	Asociación Nacional de Productores de Arroz (Peru)
ANPAC	Associazione Nazionale Piloti Aviazione Commerciale
ANPAG	Associazione Nazionale Piloti Aviazione Generale
ANPAN	Associazione Nazionale Provveditori e Appaltatori Navali
ANPAT	Association Nationale pour la Prévention des Accidents du Travail (Belgium)
ANPC	Association Nationale des Promoteurs de Constructions
ANPCC	Asociación Nacional de Productores de Coco y Copra (Venezuela)
ANPE	Association Nationale des Producteurs d'Endives
ANPEA	Association Nationale pour le Développement de l'Utilisation des Engrais et Amendements
ANPEB	Association Nationale des Patrons Électriciens de Belgique
ANPES	Associação Nacional de Programação Economica e Social (Brazil)
ANPI	Association Nationale pour la Protection contre l'Incendie (Belgium)
ANPIHF	Association Nationale des Planteurs Independants de Houblons Français
ANPL	Assistencia Nestle dos Produtores de Leite (Brazil)
ANPLC	Association Nationale des Producteurs de Legumes Conservés
ANPM	Association of Name Plate Manufacturers
ANPPDOS-HR	Association Nationale Professionnelle des Personnels de Direction des Organismes Spécialisés d'Habitat Rural
ANPPSA	Association Nationale pour la Promotion Professionnelle des Salaries de l'Agriculture
ANPRDPP	Association Nationale des Proprietaires Ruraux et Défenseurs de la Propriété Privée
ANPROSE	Asociación Nacional de Productores de Semillas Certificadas (Venezuela)
ANPS	Asociación Nacional de Producción de Semillas (Chile, Colombia)
ANPSCAH	Association Nationale de Promotion Socio-Culturelle en Agriculture et en Horticulture
ANPUEP	Association Nationale des Propriétaires et Usagers d'Embranchements Particuliers
ANPUR	Associazione Nazionale Professori Universitari di Ruolo
ANPV	Algemene Nederlandse Pluimveeteeltvereniging
ANQUE	Asociación Nacional de Quimicos de España
ANR	Association Nationale de Révision de la Coopération Agricole
ANR	Association Nationale de Révision (des Coopératives)
ANRC	American National Red Cross
ANRC	Animal Nutrition Research Council (U.S.A.)
ANRC	Australian National Research Council
ANRCA	Association Nationale de Revision de la Coopération Agricole
ANRFVCN-ER	Association Nationale des Ruches Familiales de Vacances de la Confédération Nationale de la Famille Rurale
ANRPC	Association of Natural Rubber Producing Countries
ANRT	Association Nationale de la Recherche Technique ·
ANS	Algemene Nederlandse Slagersbond
ANS	American Name Society
ANS	American Nuclear Society

ANS	American Nutrition Society
ANSA	Agenzia Nazionale Stampa Associazione
ANSA	Aktiebolaget Nordiske Skinnauktioner
ANSA	Association Nationale des Sociétés par Action
ANSDHA	Association Nationale pour le Développement des Sciences Humaines Appliquées
ANSEAU	Association Nationale des Services d'Eau (Belgium)
ANSI	American National Standards Institute
ANSL	Australian National Standards Laboratory
ANSMO	Association des Négociants Suisses en Machines et Outils
ANSOL	Australian National Social Sciences Library
ANSP	Australian National Socialist Party
ANSS	American Nature Study Society
ANSSMFE	Australian National Society of Soil Mechanics and Foundation Engineering
ANSTEL	Australian National Scientific and Technological Library
ANT	Administracion Nacional de Telecomunicacións (Paraguay)
ANTA	American National Theatre and Academy
ANTAI	Associazione Nazionale Tappezzieri e Arredatorie Italiani
ANTAV	Association Nationale Technique pour l'Amelioration de la Viticulture (*formerly* ATAV)
ANTeL	Associazione Nazionale Tecnici di Laboratorio
ANTI	Associazione Nazionale Tributaristi Italiani
ANTL	Association Nationale des Tisseurs de Lin (Belgium)
ANTO	Antarctic Treaty Organization
ANTOR	Association of National Tourist Office Representatives in Great Britain
ANTSAL	Association Nationale des Techniciens Supérieurs Agricoles de Laiterie
ANTSH	Association Nationale des Techniciens Supérieurs Horticoles
ANTZA	Associazione Nazionale fra i Tecnici dello Zucchero e dell' Alcole
ANU	Australian National University
ANUCAG	Asociación Nacional de Uniones de Crédito Agricola y Ganadero (Mexico)
ANUDE	Administration des Nations Unies pour le Développement Économique
ANUEG	Association des Usagers de l'Électricité et du Gaz
ANUGA	Allgemeine Nahrungs und Genussmittel-Ausstellung
ANUIES	Asociación Nacional de Universidades e Institutos de Enseñanza Superior (Mexico)
ANV	Asociación Nacional de Vitivinicultores (Mexico)
ANVAR	Agence Nationale pour la Valorization de la Recherche
ANVC	Algemene Nederlandse Vereniging van Contactlenzenspecialisten
ANVEC	Associazione Nazionale fra Aziende di Vendita per Corrispondenza
ANVR	Algemene Nederlandse Vereniging van Reisbureaus
ANVS	Algemene Nederlandse Vereniging van Speelgoedhandelaren
ANVSG	Algemene Nederlandse Vereniging voor Sociale Geneeskunde
ANVUMA	Association Nationale de Vulgarisation du Machinisme Agricole
ANVV	Algemene Nederlandse Vereniging voor Vreemdelingenverkeer
ANVW	Algemene Nederlandse Vereniging voor Wijsbegeerte
ANZ	Algemene Nederlandse Zuivelbond
ANZA	Association of New Zealand Advertisers
ANZAAS	Australian and New Zealand Association for the Advancement of Science
ANZAME	Australian and New Zealand Association for Medical Education
ANZAMRS	Australian and New Zealand Association for Medieval and Renaissance Studies
ANZASA	Australian and New Zealand American Studies Association
ANZDEC	Asian-New Zealand Development Corporation
ANZEFA	Australia and New Zealand Emigrants and Families Association
ANZHES	Australian and New Zealand History of Education Society
ANZM & S	Australian and New Zealand Merchants and Shippers Association
ANZSRLO	Australian and New Zealand Scientific Research Liaison Office

ANZUS	Australia, New Zealand, United States Pact	**AOMA**	American Occupational Medical Association
AO	Aide Olympique	**AOO**	American Oceanic Organisation
AOA	American Optometric Association	**AOP**	Association of Optical Practitioners
AOA	American Orthopsychiatric Association	**AOPA**	Aircraft Owners' and Pilots Association (International)
AOA	American Osteopathic Association	**AOPEC**	Arab Organisation of Petroleum Exporting Countries
AOA	Army Ordnance Association (U.S.A.)		
AOA	Asociación Odontológica Argentina	**AOPI**	Associazione Orticola Professionale Italiana
AOA	Association of Official Architects		
AOAC	Association of Official Analytical Chemists (U.S.A.)	**AOPU**	Asian-Oceanic Postal Union
		AORG	Army Operational Research Group
AOAI	American Organist Association International	**AOS**	American Ophthalmological Society
AOAO	American Osteopathic Academy of Orthopedics	**AOS**	American Otological Society
		AOS	Apostleship of the Sea
AOAS	Arab Organization for Administrative Sciences (Egypt)	**AOSA**	Association of Official Seed Analysts (U.S.A.)
AOAS	American Osteopathic Academy of Sclerotherapy	**AOSCA**	Association of Official Seed Certifying Agencies (U.S.A.)
AOAS	Arab Organization for Administrative Sciences (Egypt)	**AOTA**	American Occupational Therapy Association
AÖB	Arbeitsgemeinschaft Österreichischer Bausparkassen	**AOU**	American Ornithologists' Union
		AOUD	Alliance Universelle des Ouvriers Diamantaires
AOB	Association Ornithologique de Belgique		
AOC	American Orthoptic Council	**AP**	Alliance for Progress (of OAS)
AOC	Associated Overseas Countries (of EEC)	**APA**	All Parties Administration (Australia)
AOCI	Airport Operators Council International	**APA**	American Pharmaceutical Association
AOCP	Asia Oceania Congress of Perinatology (Singapore)	**APA**	American Philological Association
		APA	American Physicists Association
AOCS	American Oil Chemists' Society	**APA**	American Plywood Association
AOCTL	Association of Oriental Carpet Traders	**APA**	American Poultry Association
AODC	Argentine Oceanographic Data Centre	**APA**	American Press Association
AODRA	American Oxford Down Record Association	**APA**	American Protestant Association
AODT	Association Européenne des Organisations Nationales de Commerçants Détaillants en Textiles	**APA**	American Psychiatric Association
		APA	American Psychological Association
		APA	Asociación Peruana de Avicultura (Peru)
AÖE	Arbeitsgemeinschaft Österreichischer Entomologen	**APA**	Association of Preventive Medicine
		APA	Association of Public Analysts
AOEC	Airways Operations Evaluation Centre (U.S.A.)	**APA**	Australian Physiotherapy Association
		APA	Austria Presse Agentur
AOF	Afrique Occidentale Française	**APAC**	Appointment and Promotion Advisory Committee (FAO)
AOIP	Association des Ouvriers en Instruments de Précision		
ÄOL	Äidinkielen Opettajain Liitto	**APAC**	Asociación Peruana para el Avance de la Ciencia
AÖM	Arbeitsgemeinschaft Österreichischer Musikverleger	**APACL**	Asian Peoples Anti-Communist League
AOM	Overseas States, Territories and Departments associated with EEC	**APADA**	Asociación de Productores Agrarios del Delta Argentino

APAE	Association of Public Address Engineers	**APCMF**	Assemblée des Présidents des Chambres de Métiers de France
APAIS	Australian Public Affairs Information Service	**APCO**	Asian Parasite Control Organization (Japan)
APAM	Association Populaire des Amis des Musées	**APCOL**	All-Pakistan Confederation of Labour
APAN	Administración de los Parques Nacionales (Venezuela)	**APCS**	Association de la Presse Cinématographique Suisse
APAR	Association Parlementaire Agricole et Rurale (France)	**APD**	Associazione Aziende Italiane Pubblicità Diretta
APAS	Association Paritaire d'Action Sociale du Bâtiment et des Travaux Publiques	**APDC**	Apple and Pear Development Council
APASP	Association pour le Perfectionnement des Approvisionnements dans les Services Publiques	**APDCP**	Associação Portuguesa dos Directores e Chefes de Pessoal
		APDILA	Association des Pharmaciens Directeurs de Laboratoires d'Analyses Biologiques
APAVIT	Asociación Peruana de Agencias de Viajes y Turismo	**APDSA**	Asian Pacific Dental Student Association
APB	Association Pharmaceutique Belge	**APE**	Assemblée Parlementaire Européenne
APBC	American Book Publishers Council	**APEA**	Asociación Peruana de Economistas Agrícolas (Peru)
APBD	Association Professionnelle de Bibliothécaires et Documentalistes (Belgium)	**APEA**	Association des Producteurs Européens d'Azote
APBF	Accredited Poultry Breeders Federation	**APEA**	Association of Professional Engineers of Alberta (Canada)
APBGPL	Association Professionnelle Belge des Gaz de Pétrole Liquefiés	**APEA**	Australian Petroleum Exploration Association
APBS	Accredited Poultry Breeding Stations Scheme		
APC	African Groundnut (Peanut) Council	**APEAI**	Alliance pour l'Expansion de l'Apiculture et ses Industries
APC	All People's Congress (Sierra Leone)	**APEC**	Asociación de Industriales de Puerto Rico
APC	Atomic Power Constructions	**APEC**	Asociación Paraguaya Enseñanza Católica
APCA	Air Pollution Control Association (U.S.A.)	**APEC**	Atlantic Provinces Economic Council (Canada)
APCA	Anglo-Polish Catholic Association		
APCA	Assemblée Permanente des Chambres d'Agriculture (formerly APPCA)	**APECCO**	Association Européenne des Promoteurs de Centres Commerciaux
APCADEC	Associação Portuguesa dos Chefes de Aprovisionamento e de Compras (Portugal)	**APECITA**	Association pour l'Emploi des Cadres, Ingénieurs et Techniciens de l'Agriculture
APCB	Associação Paulista de Criadores de Bovinos (Brazil)	**APECS**	Association des Propriétaires et Éleveurs de Chevaux de Selle
APCC	Agricultural Planning and Coordinating Committee (of MOEA, Taiwan)	**APEDE**	Asociación Panamena de Ejecutivos de Empresas (Panama)
APCC	Asian and Pacific Coconut Community	**APEE**	Association for Pediatric Education in Europe (France)
APCC	Assemblée des Présidents des Chambres de Commerce	**APEF**	Association des Pays Exportateurs de Minerai de Fer (India)
APCCI	Assemblée Permanente des Chambres de Commerce et l'Industrie	**APEF**	Association Professionnelle des Établissements Financiers
APCEI	Association pour le Perfectionnement Pratique des Cadres des Entreprises Industrielles	**APEID**	Asian Programme of Educational Innovation for Development
APCK	Association for Promoting Christian Knowledge		
APCM	Assemblée Permanente des Chambres de Métiers	**APEL**	Associação Portuguesa dos Editores e Livreiros

APEL	Societé pour le Développement des Applications de l'Électricité (France)	**APHB**	Association Patronale Horlogère (Switzerland)
APELUX	Association des Patrons-Électriciens du Grand-Duché de Luxembourg	**APHCA**	Regional Animal Production and Health Commission for Asia, the Far East and the South-West Pacific (FAO)
APEPA	Association pour l'Encouragement de la Productivité Agricole	**APHF**	American Poultry and Hatchery Federation
APEPM	Association of Professional Engineers of the Province of Manitoba (Canada)	**APHI**	Association of Public Health Inspectors
APEPNB	Association of Professional Engineers of the Province of New Brunswick (Canada)	**APHIA**	Association for the Promotion of Humour in International Affairs (France)
APEPO	Association of Professional Engineers of the Province of Ontario (Canada)	**APHS**	American Poultry Historical Society
APER	Association of Publishers Educational Representatives	**APHV**	Bundesverband des Deutschen Briefmarkenhandels
APERU	Asociación pro Enseñanza Rural Universitaria (Argentina)	**API**	American Paper Institute
APES	Association of Professional Engineers of Saskatchewan (Canada)	**API**	American Petroleum Institute
		API	American Potash Institute
APESCA	Asociación Colombiana de Pescadores e Industriales de Pesca	**API**	Association Phonétique Internationale
APESS	Association des Professeurs de l'Enseignement Secondaire Supérieur du Grand-Duché de Luxembourg	**API**	Associazione Pedagogica Italiana
		API	Associazione Piscicoltori Italiani
APETI	Asociación Profesional Española de Traductores e Intérpretes	**APIA**	Arkansas Poultry Improvement Association (U.S.A.)
APEX	Association of Professional Executive, Clerical and Computer Staff	**APIA**	Asociación Peruana de Ingenieros Agrónomos (Peru)
APF	Asian Packaging Federation Philippines	**APIA**	Association pour la Promotion de l'Information Agricole
APF	Associação Portuguesa de Fundição	**APIC**	Asian Packaging Information Centre (Hong Kong)
APF	Associazione per il Promuovimento della Foraggicoltura (Switzerland)	**APICE**	Asociación Panamericana de Instituciones de Crédito Educativo (Colombia)
APF	Pontifical Association for the Propagation of the Faith	**APICE**	Associazione fra Produttori Italiani di Calcestruzzi per l'Edilizia (Italy)
APFA	Associated Poultry Farmers of Australia	**APICP**	Association for the Promotion of the International Circulation of the Press
APFAV	Association des Producteurs Suisses de Films et de Production Audio-visuelle	**APICS**	American Production and Inventory Control Society
APFC	American Plant Food Council	**APIDC**	Andra Pradesh Industrial Development Corporation (India)
APFC	Asia-Pacific Forestry Commission	**APIEAS**	Asociacion Peruana de Instituciones de Agrícola Superior
APFIRO	Association des Producteurs de Femelles issues de Béliers Finnois ou Romanov	**APIIPP**	Association Professionnelle des Importateurs Indépendants des Produits du Pétrole
APFS	African Peasant Farming Scheme		
APG	Arbeitskreis Pharmazeutischer Grosshandelsverbände	**APIMO**	Associazione Professionale Italiana Medici Oculisti
APHA	American Polled Hereford Association	**APIMOND-IA**	Fédération Internationale des Associations d'Apiculture
APHA	American Printing History Association		
APHA	American Public Health Association	**APIS**	Architectural and Planning Information Service (N. Ireland)
APHA	Australian Pneumatic and Hydraulic Association	**APIS**	Army Photographic Intelligence Service

APJBF	Association des Producteurs de Jeunes Bovins de France	**APPA**	Association de Propagande pour les Produits Agricoles
APJT	Association Professionnelle des Journalistes du Tourisme	**APPC**	Associação Portuguesa para o Progresso das Ciências
APL	Association of Photographic Laboratories	**APPCA**	Assemblée Permanente des Présidents des Chambres d'Agriculture (*now* APCA)
APLA	American Patent Law Association		
APLC	Association of Patent Licensing Consultants (Germany)	**APPCB**	Association Professionnelle de la Presse Cinématographique Belge
APLE	Association of Public Lighting Engineers	**APPI**	Association Internationale d'Études pour la Promotion et la Protection des Investissements Privés en Territoires Étrangers
APLET	Association for Programmed Learning and Educational Technology		
APLIC	Association for Population/Family Planning Libraries (U.S.A.)	**APPITA**	Australian Pulp and Paper Industry Technical Association
APLICI	Association for Population, Family Planning Libraries and Information Centers International (U.S.A.)	**APPMSA**	American Pulp and Paper Mills Superintendents' Association
		APPS	Australian Plant Pathology Society
APLS	American Plant Life Society	**APPU**	Australian Primary Producers' Union
APLV	Association des Professeurs de Langues Vivantes de l'Enseignement Publique	**APQI**	Associação Portuguesa para a Qualidade Industrial
APMA	American Pharmaceutical Manufacturers' Association	**APRA**	Air Public Relations Association
APMBFP	Association de la Petite et Moyenne Brasserie Familiale de Belgique	**APRA**	American Petroleum Refiners Association
		APRA	American Public Relations Association
APMC	Allied Political and Military Commission	**APRA**	Australian Plastics Research Association
APMC	Andra Pradesh Mining Corporation (India)	**APRACA**	Asian and Pacific Regional Agricultural Credit Association
APME	Associated Press Managing Editors Association (U.S.A.)	**APRAGA**	Association des Propriétaires de Récipients à Gaz Comprimés (Belgium)
APMEP	Association des Professeurs de Mathématiques de l'Enseignement	**APREA**	American Peanut Research and Education Association
APO	African People's Organisation		
APO	Asian Productivity Organisation	**APRIA**	Association pour la Promotion Industrie-Agriculture
APO	Australian Purchasing Officers Association	**APRL**	Association for the Preservation of Rural Life
APOA	Arctic Petroleum Operators Association	**APRO**	Aerial Phenomena Research Organization (U.S.A.)
APOB	Association Professionnelle des Opticiens de Belgique		
		APROBA	Association Professionelle pour l'Accroissement de la Productivité dans l'Industrie du Bâtiment
APOS	Association Professionnelle des Opticiens Suisses de Formation Supérieure		
		APROSC	Agricultural Projects Services Centre (Nepal)
APPA	American Psychopathological Association	**APRR**	Association for Planning and Regional Reconstruction
APPA	American Public Power Association		
APPA	American Pulp and Paper Association	**APRS**	Arab Public Relations Society (UAR)
APPA	Associação Brasileira de Pesquisas sobre Plantas Aromaticas e Oleos Essenciaias	**APRS**	Association for the Preservation of Rural Scotland
APPA	Association des Pilotes et Propriétaires d'Aéronefs	**APS**	American Peace Society
		APS	American Philatelic Society
APPA	Association pour la Prévention de la Pollution Atmosphérique	**APS**	American Philosophical Society

APS	American Physical Society
APS	American Physiological Society
APS	American Phytopathological Society
APS	American Polar Society
APS	American Prosthodontic Society
APS	American Psychosomatic Society
APS	Association Patronale des Serigraphes (Switzerland)
APS	Association de la Presse Suisse
APS	Associazione Pubblicità Stampa
APS	Australian Photogrammetric Society
APS	Australian Psychological Society
APSA	Aerolineas Peruanas S.A.
APSA	American Political Science Association
APSA	Australian Political Studies Association
APSAI	Assemblée Plénière des Sociétiés d'Assurances contre l'Incendie
APSC	Asian-Pacific Society of Cardiology
APSC	Association des Producteurs de Semence du Canada
APSIB	Association Professionelle des Sociétiés Immobilières en Belgique
APSO	Afro-Asian Peoples' Solidarity Organisation
APSO	Asia-Pacific Socialist Organization
APSSEAR	Association of Pediatric Societies of the Southeast Asian Region
APSTC	Andra Pradesh State Road Transport Corporation (India)
APTA	American Physical Therapy Association
APTA	American Public Transit Association
APTA	Asian Pineapple Traders Association
APTA	Asociación de la Prensa Técnica Argentina
APTI	Association of Principals of Technical Institutions
APTI	Associazione Produttori Tabacchi Italiani
APTIC	African Pyrethrum Technical Information Centre
APTO	Association of Psychiatric Treatment of Offenders
APTU	African Postal and Telecommunications Union
APU	Arab Postal Union
APU	Asia Parliamentarians Union
APUC	Association for Promoting the Unity of Christendom

APUMAG	Asociación de Profesionales Universitarios del Ministerio de Agricultura y Ganadería de la Nación (Argentina)
APV	Arbeitsgemeinschaft für Pharmazeutische Verfahrenstechnik
APV	Association de Propagande pour le Vin
APV	Associazione Italiana Promozione Vendite e Pubblicità Punto Vendite
APWA	All Pakistan Women's Association
APWA	American Public Works Association
APWSS	Asian-Pacific Weed Science Society
AQA	Asociación Quimica Argentina
AQS	Association des Quincailliers Suisses
AQTE	Association Québécoise des Techniques de l'Eau (Canada)
ARA	Aerial Ropeways Association
ARA	Agricultural Research Administration (U.S.A.)
ARA	Aircraft Research Association
ARA	Amateur Rowing Association
ARA	American Rheumatism Association
ARA	Association of River Authorities
ARAB	Association Royale des Actuaires Belges
ARAMCO	Arabian-American Oil Company
ARAN	Association for the Reduction of Aircraft Noise
ARB	Air Registration Board
ARBA	American Rabbit Breeders Association
ARBA	American Road Builders Association
ARBE	Académie Royale des Beaux-Arts et École Supérieure d'Architecture de Bruxelles
ARBICA	Arab Regional Branch of the International Council on Archives
ARBIT	Arbeitsgemeinschaft der Bitumen-Industrie
ARBM	Association of Radio Battery Manufacturers
ARC	Action for Renewal of the Church (Trinidad)
ARC	Aeronautical Research Council
ARC	Agricultural Research Council
ARC	Anthropological Research Club
ARC	Arthritis and Rheumatism Council for Research in Great Britain and the Commonwealth
ARC	Association Romande des Conseils en Publicité (Switzerland)
ARC	Asthma Research Council
ARC	Regional Conference for Africa (FAO)

ARCCA	Agricultural Research Council of Central Africa	**ARENA**	Aliança Renovadora Nacional (Brazil)
		ARER	Association Régionale d'Économie Rurale
ARCESP	Associação Brasileira de Vendedores	**ARERS**	Association Régionale pour l'Étude et la Recherche Scientifiques
ARCI	Atelier de Rectification de Côte-d'Ivoire		
ARCN	Agricultural Research Council of Norway	**ARESA**	Association pour le Recherche sur l'Énergie Solaire en Algérie
ARCOA	Asociación Rosarina de Criadores de Ovejeros Alemanes (Argentina)	**ARETO**	Arab Republic of Egypt Telecommunications Organization
ARCOS	Anglo-Russian Co-operative Society		
ARCRAN	Agricultural Research Council of Rhodesia and Nyasaland	**ARF**	Advertising Research Foundation (U.S.A.)
		ARF	Association of Rehabilitation Facilities (U.S.A.)
ARCRL	Agricultural Research Council Radiobiological Laboratory	**ARF**	Autoriserte Reklambyåers Forening
ARCUK	Architects Registration Council of the United Kingdom	**ARFA**	Allied Radio Frequency Agency (*of* NATO)
		ARGA	American Personal and Guidance Association
ARD	Arbeitsgemeinschaft der Offentlich-Rechtlichen Rundfunkanstalten der Bundesrepublik Deutschland	**ARGB**	Association Royale des Gaziers Belges
		ARGCA	American Rice Growers Cooperative Association
ARDA	Agricultural and Rural Development Act (Canada)	**ARGCI**	Agence de Representation Générale en Côte-d'Ivoire
ARDA	American Railway Development Association		
ARDC	Agricultural Refinance and Development Corporation (India)	**ARGE**	Arbeitsgemeinschaft der Europäischen Schloss- und Beschlag-industrie
ARDC	Agricultural and Rural Development Corporation (Burma)	**ARGF**	Automobildel- og Rekvisita-Grossistenes Forening
ARDC	U.S. Air Research and Development Command	**ARGR**	Association for Research in Growth Relationships (U.S.A.)
ARDE	Armament Research and Development Establishment	**ARHS**	Australian Railway Historical Society
ARDE	Associazione Romano di Entomologia	**ARI**	Agricultural Research Institute and Agricultural Board (U.S.A.)
ARDECO	Aluminium Resources Development Co. (Japan)	**ARI**	Aluminium Research Institute (U.S.A.)
		ARI	American Refractories Institute
ARDES	Association pour la Recherche Démographique, Économique et Sociale (Algeria)	**ARI**	Association of Rhodesian Industries
		ARIAC	Agricultural Research Institute and Agricultural College, Glen (South Africa)
ARDI	Association of Registered Driving Instructors	**ARICN**	Asian Regional Communication Network (U.S.A.)
ARDOI	Association of Institutes for Research and Development in the Indian Ocean (Mauritius)		
		ARIEL	Asociación Reformista Independiente de Estudiantes de Letras (Peru)
ARE	Association for Religious Education		
AREA	Aerovias Ecuatorianas, CA	**ARINC**	Aeronautical Radio Incorporated (U.S.A.)
AREA	American Railway Engineering Association	**ARIP**	Association pour la Recherche et l'Intervention Psychosociologiques
AREC	Agricultural Research and Educational Centre (Lebanon)	**ARISBR**	Asian Regional Institute for School Building Research
AREC	Amitié Rurale des Étudiants Catholiques	**ARJA**	Association Suisse Romande des Journalistes de l'Aéronautique et de l'Astronautique
ARELAP	Asociación Regional Latinoamericana de Puertos de Pacifico		
ARELS	Association of Recognized English Language Schools	**ARJORA**	Association des Réalisateurs de Journaux Ruraux Africains

ARL	Admiralty Research Laboratory
ARL	Aeronautical Research Laboratories (Australia)
ARL	Akademie für Raumsforschung und Landesplanung
ARL	Autonrengasliitto
ARLIF	Académie Royale de Langue et de Littérature Françaises
ARLO	Arab Literacy and Adult Education Organization
ARM	Alliance Reformée Mondiale
ARMA	American Records Management Association
ARMA	American Registry of Medical Assistants
ARMA	Australian Rubber Manufacturers Association
ARMALIB-ERI	Associazione Armatori Liberi
ARMB	Académie Royale de Médécine de Belgique
ARMEF	Association pour la Rationalisation et la Mécanisation de l'Exploitation Forestière
ARMO	Servicio Nacional de Adiestramiento Rápido de la Mano de Obra en la Industria (Mexico)
ARMSA	Asian Regional Medical Student Association
ARN	Association pour la Renovation de la Noyeraie
ARnI	Association of Rhodesian Industries
ARO	Army Research Office (U.S.A.)
ARO	Asian Regional Organisation of ICFTU
AROMA	Groupement des Fabricants d'Essences, Huiles Essentielles, Extraits, Produits Chimiques, Aromatiques et Colorants (Belgium)
AROMAR	Rumanian Marketing Association
AROW	Association of Retailer Owned Wholesalers in Foodstuffs (Belgium)
ARP	Australian Republican Party
ARPA	Advanced Research Projects Agency (U.S.A.)
ARPA	Association pour les Recherches sur les Parodontopathies (Switzerland) (ceased)
ARPAC	Agricultural Research Policy Advisory Committee (U.S.A.)
ARPEL	Asociación de Asistencia Reciproca Petrolera Estatal Latino-Americano
ARPF	Agricultural Research Program and Facilities Subcommittee (U.S.A.)
ARPLOE	Association des Rééducateurs de la Parole et du Langage Oral et Écrit
ARPS	Association of Railway Preservation Societies
ARPS	Australian Royal Photographic Society
ARR	Association for Radiation Research
ARRB	Australian Road Research Board
ARRL	American Radio Relay League
ARS	American Radium Society
ARS	American Rhinologic Society
ARS	American Rocket Society
ARSAP	Agricultural Requisites Scheme for Asia and the Pacific
ARSBA	American Rambouillet Sheep Breeders Association
ARSC	Académie Royale des Sciences Coloniales (Belgium)
ARSO	African Regional Organization for Standardization
ARSO	Autorité pour l'Aménagement de la Région du Sud-Ouest (Ivory Coast)
ARSOM	Académie Royale des Sciences d'Outremer (Belgium)
ARSUBA	Société Française d'Archéologie Sub-Aquatique
ARTEMAT	Chambre Syndicale Belge des Détaillants Specialisés en Matériel pour le Dessin, les Beaux-Arts, les Arts Appliqués
ARTFP	Association de Recherche sur les Techniques de Forage et de Production
ARTSM	Association of Road Traffic Sign Makers
ARU	American Railway Union
ARU	Asociación Rural del Uruguay
ASA	Acoustical Society of America
ASA	Advertising Standards Authority
ASA	African Studies Association (U.S.A.)
ASA	Amateur Swimming Association
ASA	American Society of Agronomy
ASA	American Sociological Association
ASA	American Society of Anesthesiologists
ASA	American Soybean Association
ASA	American Standards Association
ASA	American Statistical Association
ASA	American Stockyards Association
ASA	American Surgical Association
ASA	Arbeitsgemeinschaft der Schweizerischen Altstoffwirtschaft
ASA	Army Signal Association (U.S.A.)

ASA	Asian Students Association (Hong Kong)	**ASB**	Afrikaans Studentebond
ASA	Asociación Salvadorena Agropecuaria (Salvador)	**ASB**	Arbeitsgemeinschaft für Wirtschaftliche Betriebsführung und Soziale Betriebsgestaltung
ASA	Asociación Semilleros Argentinos		
ASA	Association der Schweizerischen Aerosolindustrie	**ASB**	Association of Southeastern Biologists (U.S.A.)
ASA	Association of South-East Asia	**ASBA**	American Shorthorn Breeders Association
ASA	Association des Statisticiens Agricoles	**ASBA**	American Southdown Breeders' Association
ASA	Association Suisse des Annonceurs	**ASBAH**	Association for Spina Bifida and Hydrocephalus
ASA	Associazione per le Scienze Astronautiche	**ASBC**	American Society of Biological Chemists
ASA	Atomic Scientists Association	**ASBC**	American Society of Biophysics and Cosmology
ASA	Avicultural Society of America		
ASAB	Association for the Study of Animal Behaviour	**ASBC**	American Society of Brewing Chemists
ASAE	American Society of Agricultural Engineers	**ASBE**	American Society of Bakery Engineers
ASAE	American Society of Association Executives	**ASBI**	Advisory Service for the Building Industry
ASAE	Association Suisse pour l'Aménagement des Eaux	**ASBMT**	Annales de la Société Belge de Médecine Tropicale
ASAF	Association Suisse des Analystes Financiers	**ASBPA**	American Shore and Beach Preservation Association
ASAIHL	Association of South-East Asian Institutions of Higher Learning	**ASBS**	Association of Social and Behavioral Scientists (U.S.A.)
ASAIO	American Society for Artificial Internal Organs	**ASBU**	Arab States Broadcasting Union
ASAJA	Asociación Sudamericana de Jueces de Atletismo	**ASC**	Aardappel Studie Centrum
		ASC	American Society of Cinematographers
ASAM	American Society for Abrasive Methods	**ASC**	American Society of Cybernetics
ASAO	Association for Social Anthropology in Oceania (Hawaii)	**ASC**	American Society of Cytology
		ASC	Association Suisse des Entreprises de Transport à Câbles
ASAP	American Society of Animal Production		
ASAP	Arab Socialist Action Party	**ASC**	Associazione Svizzera dei Critici Cinematografica
ASAP	Australian Society of Animal Production		
ASAS	American Society of Abdominal Surgery	**ASC**	Conferencia Socialista Asiatica
ASAS	American Society of Agricultural Sciences	**ASCA**	Association for Science Cooperation in Asia
ASAS	American Society of Animal Science	**ASCAN**	Asociación Canaria para Defensa de la Naturaleza (Canary Islands)
ASAS	Association of South-East Asian States		
ASAS	Association Suisse des Assistants Sociaux	**ASCAP**	American Society of Composers, Authors and Publishers
ASATA	Associazione Svizzera per le Attrezzature Tecniche Agricole	**ASCAP**	Association Suisse pour le Commerce et l'Art Photographique
ASATOM	Association pour les Stages et l'Accueil des Techniciens d'Outre-Mer	**ASCAR**	Anglo-Soviet Co-operation on Agricultural Research
ASAUK	African Studies Association of the United Kingdom	**ASCAR**	Associaçao Sulina de Crédito e Assistência Rural (Brazil)
ASAVPA	Association de Salariés de l'Agriculture pour la Vulgarisation du Progrès Agricole	**ASCATEP**	Arab States Centre for Educational Planning and Administration
ASAWI	African Studies Association of the West Indies (Jamaica)	**ASCBF**	Association pour la Sélection et la Création de Betteraves Fourragères

ASCC	Australian Society of Cosmetic Chemists
ASCDH	Association Scientifique pour la Culture et le Développement de l'Hydroponique
ASCE	American Society of Civil Engineers
ASCE	Asian Society for Comparative Education (Iran)
ASCEA	American Society of Civil Engineers and Architects
ASCHIMICI	Associazione Nazionale dell' Industria Chimica
ASCI	American Society for Clinical Investigation
ASCIM	Association of Casing Importers
ASCL	American Sugar Cane League of the U.S.A.
ASCM	Association of Ships Compositions Manufacturers
ASCM	Association of Steel Conduit Manufacturers
ASCN	American Society for Clinical Nutrition
ASCN	Association Suisse des Constructeurs Navals
ASCO	American Society on Contemporary Ophthalmology
ASCO	Association Suisse des Conseils en Organisation et Gestion
ASCO	Association Suisse des Tenaciers de Cafés – Concerts
ASCOBEL	Association Belge des Conseils en Organisation et Gestion
ASCOFAM	Association Mondiale de Lutte Contre la Faim
ASCOLBI	Asociación Colombiana de Bibliotecarios
ASCOLPA	Asociación Colombiana de Cultivadores de Papa
ASCOLSI	Asociación Colombiana de Sistemas
AsCoMA	Associazione Nazionale Commercianti di Macchine Agricole
ASCOMACE	Association des Constructeurs de Machines à Coudre de la CEE
ASCP	American Society of Clinical Pathologists
ASCP	American Society of Consultant Pharmacists
ASCPI	Association Suisse des Conseils en Propriété Industrielle
ASCREMON	Association Professionnelle des Créateurs Belge et Monopolistes de Créateurs Étrangers de Variétés de Plantes
ASCTA	Association of Short-Circuit Testing Authorities
ASCUN	Asociación Colombiana de Universidades

ASCV	Association Suisse des Entreprises de Chauffage et de Ventilation
AScW	Association of Scientific Workers (now ASTMS)
ASCWSA	Association of Scientific Workers of South Africa
ASD	Association Suisse de Documentation
ASD	Association Suisse des Droguistes
ASDA	Association Suisse de Droit Aérien et Spatial
ASDAN	Association Suisse de la Diététique et de l'Alimentation
ASDAR	Association pour la Selection et le Développement des Animaux de Race
ASDB	Asian Development Bank
ASDBAM	Association Sénégalaise pour le Développement de la Documentation, des Bibliothèques, des Archives et des Musées
ASDIC	Allied Submarine-Detection Investigation Committee
ASDSFB	Association of Scottish District Salmon Fishery Boards
ASDT	Association Suisse des Détaillants en Textiles
ASE	Admiralty Signal Establishment
ASE	Agence Spatiale Européenne
ASE	Amalgamated Society of Engineers
ASE	American Society of Enologists
ASE	Association for Science Education
ASE	Association Suisse des Électriciens
ASE	Association Suisse des Ergothérapeutes
ASE	Association Suisse des Experts – Comptables
ASE	Astronomical Society of Edinburgh
ASEA	Allmänna Svenska Elektriska Aktiobolaget
ASEA	American Society of Engineers and Architects
ASEA	Association Suisse des Électriciens sur Automobiles
ASEA	Associazione Svizzera di Economia delle Acque (Switzerland)
ASEA	Australian Society for Education through Art
ASEAI	Association Suisse des Experts Automobiles Indépendants
ASEAN	Association of South East Asian Nations (Thailand)
ASEAP	Association of South East Asian Publishers
ASEAS	Association Suisse pour l'Essai et l'Approvisionnement en Semenceaux des Pommes de Terre

ASECNA	Agence pour la Sécurité de la Navigation Aérienne en Afrique et Madagascar	**ASF**	Association des Selectionneurs Français
ASECOLDA	Asociación Colombiana de Compañias de Seguros	**ASF**	Association Suisse des Fonderies de Fer
ASEE	American Society for Engineering Education	**ASFA**	American Science Film Association
ASEE	Association of Supervisory and Executive Engineers	**ASFAC**	Regional Centre for Functional Literacy in Rural Areas in the Arab States
ASEF	Association Suisse d'Économie Forestière	**ASFAID**	American Association for Artificial Internal Organs
ASEF	Association Suisse des Entreprises de Forage	**ASFALEC**	Association des Fabricants de Laits de Conserve des Pays de la CEE
ASEG	Association Suisse des Entrepreneurs Généraux	**ASFB**	Australian Society for Fish Biology
ASEG	Associazione Svizzera degli Editori di Giornali	**ASFBT**	Association Suisse des Fabricants de Briques et Juiles
ASEIB	Asociación de Egresados de la Escuela Interamericana de Bibliotecologia (Colombia)	**ASFC**	Association Suisse des Fabricants de Cigarettes
ASEJ	Association Suisse des Éditeurs de Journaux	**ASFD**	Azienda di Stato per le Foreste Demaniali
ASELCA	Spanish Association Against Air Pollution	**ASFEC**	Arab States Fundamental Education Centre (Egypt)
ASELF	Asociación Española de Lucha Contra et Fuego	**ASFFI**	Association des Sociétés et Fonds Françaises d'Investissement
ASELT	European Association for the Exchange of Technical Literature in the Field of Ferrous Metallurgy	**ASFIL-COTON**	Association Belge des Filateurs de Coton et de Fibres Connexes
ASEMOLP-RO	Asociación Nacional de Molineros de Arroz (Colombia)	**ASFIS**	Aquatic Sciences and Fisheries Information System (FAO/IOC)
ASEN	Association Suisse des Entrepreneurs en Nettoyage	**ASFPH**	Association Suisse des Fabricants de Pierres d'Horlogerie et Scientifiques
ASEO	Associazion Svizra per l'Economia de las Ovas	**ASFSE**	American Swiss Foundation for Scientific Exchange
ASEP	American Society of Electroplated Plastics	**ASG**	Agrarsoziale Gesellschaft
ASEP	American Society for Experimental Pathology	**ASG**	Arbeitsgemeinschaft Schweizerischer Grafiker
ASEPD	Association Suisse pour l'Étude des Problèmes Démographiques	**ASG**	Association Suisse des Gravières
ASEPELT	European Association for Medium and Long Term Economic Forecasting	**ASGA**	Association des Services Géologiques Africains
ASERJ	Association Sénégalaise d'Études et de Recherches Juridiques (Senegal)	**ASGB**	Adlerian Society of Great Britain
		ASGB	Aeronautical Society of Great Britain
ASET	Association Suisse pour l'Étude des Transports	**ASGB**	Anthroposophical Society in Great Britain
ASET	Association Suisse pour l'Étude du Travail	**ASGBI**	Anatomical Society of Great Britain and Ireland
ASETA	Asociación de Empresas Estatales de Telecommunicaciones del Acuerdo Sub Regional Andino (Ecuador)	**ASGC**	Associazione Svizzera dei Grossisti di Carta
		ASGE	American Society for Gastrointestinal Endoscopy
ASETA	Association Suisse pour l'Équipement Technique de l'Agriculture	**ASGP**	Association Suisse des Grossistes en Papier
		ASGROW	Associated Seed Growers, Inc. (U.S.A.)
ASF	Albatros Superfosfaat-fabrieken N.V. te Utrecht	**ASH**	Action on Smoking and Health
		ASH	American Society of Haematology
		ASH	Association Suisse des Horlogers

ASH	Association Suisse des Horticulteurs
ASHA	American School Health Association
ASHA	American Social Hygiene Association
ASHBA	American Saddle Horse Breeders Association
ASHG	American Society of Human Genetics
ASHRAE	American Society of Heating, Refrigerating and Air-conditioning Engineers
ASHR	Association Suisse des Ateliers d'Héliographie et de Reprographie
ASHS	American Society for Horticultural Science
ASHVE	American Society of Heating and Ventilating Engineers
ASI	Air Service Ivoirien
ASI	Asian Statistical Institute
ASI	Association Soroptimiste Internationale
ASI	Association Stomatologique Internationale
ASI	Association Suisse des Inventeurs et des Détenteurs de Brevets
ASIA	Airlines Staff International Association
ASIA	Association Scientifique Internationale d'Auriculothérapie
ASIA	Association Suisse de l'Industrie Aéronautique
ASIAG	Association Interprofessionnelle de l'Aviation Agricole
ASIAT	Association Suisse des Ingénieurs Agronomes et des Ingénieurs en Technologie Alimentaire
ASIB	Association Suisse de l'Industrie du Bois
ASIC	Association Scientifique Internationale du Café
ASIC	Association Suisse des Ingénieurs-Conseils
ASICA	Association Internationale pour le Calcul Analogique
ASICH	Confederación Cristiana de Trabajadores de Chile
ASID	American Society of Industrial Designers
ASID	Association Suisse des Infirmières et Infirmiers Diplomés
ASIDIC	Association of Scientific Information Dissemination Centers (U.S.A.)
ASIE	American Society of International Executives
ASIF	Amateur Swimming International Federation
ASIFA	Association Internationale du Film d'Animation
ASIH	American Society of Ichthyologists and Herpetologists
ASIHG	Association Suisse des Importateurs d'Huiles de Graissage
ASII	American Science Information Institute
ASIIA	Adlai Stevenson Institute of International Affairs (U.S.A.)
ASIL	American Society of International Law
ASIL	Associazione Italiana di Studio del Lavoro
ASILP	Associazione Svizzera degli Impresari di Lavori Pubblica e del Genio Civile (Switzerland)
ASILS	Association of Student International Law Societies (U.S.A.)
ASIM	American Society of Internal Medicine
ASINAPLA	Agrupación Sindical Nacional de Plaguicidas
ASIO	Australian Security and Intelligence Organisation
ASIP	Asociación Interamericana de Presupuesto Publico (Venezuela)
ASIPI	Association Interaméricaine de Propriété Industrielle
ASIPLA	Asociación de Industrias Plasticas (Chile)
ASIRA	Associazione Svizzera delle Imprese di Riscaldamento e di Aerazione
ASIRC	Aquatic Sciences Information Retrieval Center (U.S.A.)
ASIS	American Society for Information Science
ASIS	Asociación Internacional de la Sintesis
ASIS	Association for the Study of Internal Secretions (U.S.A.)
ASIT	Asociatia Stiintifica a Inginerilor si Tehnicienilor (Roumania)
ASJA	Association Suisse des Journalistes Agricoles
ASJLP	Association Suisse de Journalists Libres Professionnels
ASJS	Association Suisse des Journalistes Sportifs
ASKI	Arbeitsgemeinschaft der Schweizerischen Kunststoff-Industrie
ASL	Association Suisse des Entreprises de Linoleum et des Sols Spéciaux
ASL	Australian Society for Limnology
ASL	Avelsföreningen för Svensk Låglandsboskap
ASLA	American Society of Landscape Architects
ASLA	Australian School Library Association
ASLE	American Society of Lubrication Engineers
ASLEC	Association of Street Lighting Erection Contractors
ASLEF	Associated Society of Locomotive Engineers and Firemen

ASLEP	Asociación de Sociólogos de Lengua Española y Portuguesa
ASLIB	Association of Special Libraries and Information Bureaux
ASLIC	Indian Association of Special Libraries and Documentation Centres
ASLO	American Society of Limnology and Oceanography
ASLO	Australian Scientific Liaison Office
ASLP	Amalgamated Society of Lithographic Printers
ASLP	Association of Special Libraries of the Philippines
ASLW	Amalgamated Society of Leather Workers
ASM	Aktionsgemeinschaft Soziale Marktwirtschaft
ASM	American Society of Mammalogists
ASM	American Society for Microbiology
ASM	American Society for Metals
ASM	Arbeitgeberverband Schweizerischer Maschinen-und Metall-Industrieller
ASM	Association for Systems Management (U.S.A.)
ASMA	Arizona State Medical Association (U.S.A.)
ASMA	Association de Médecine Aéronautique et Spatiale
ASMAF	Association Scientifique des Médecins Acupuncteurs de France
ASMAP	Association of Soviet International Road Carriers
ASMAS	Association Suisse des Magasins d'Articles de Sport
ASMC	Association Suisse des Maîtres Coiffeurs
ASMC	Association Suisse des Maîtres Couvreurs
ASMCBO	Association Suisse des Maîtres-Cordonniers et Bottiers-Orthopédistes
ASME	American Society of Mechanical Engineers
ASME	Association for the Study of Medical Education
ASME	Association Suisse des Marchands d'Engrais
ASMECCA-NICA	Associazione Nazionale di Meccanica
ASMET	Arbeitsgemeinschaft Schweizerischer Metallmöbelfabrikanten
ASMEVEZ	Asociación Nacional de Médicos Veterinarios Zootecnistas (Colombia)
ASMFA	Association Suisse des Maîtres Ferblantiers et Appareilleurs
ASMFC	Atlantic States Marine Fisheries Commission
ASMFE	International Association of Soil Mechanics and Foundation Engineering
ASMG	Association Suisse des Marchands-Grainiers
ASMH	Association Suisse des Manufactures d'Horlogerie
ASMI	Associazione Stampa Medica Italiana
ASMIC	Association pour l'Organisation des Missions de Cooperation Technique
ASMM	Associazione Svizzera dei Maestri Meccanici
ASMMA	American Supply and Machinery Manufacturers Association
ASMMB	Association Suisse des Marchands de Machines à Ecrire et de Bureau
ASMMC	Association Suisse des Marchands de Matériaux de Construction
ASMO	Arab Organisation for Standardisation and Metrology
ASMP	American Society of Magazine Photographers
ASMP	Association Suisse des Marchands de Poissons
ASMPP	Association Suisse des Maîtres Plâtriers-Peintres
ASMS	American Society of Maxillofacial Surgeons
ASMS	American-Soviet Medical Society
ASMT	American Society of Medical Technologists
ASMT	Association Suisse des Maîtres Tapissiers-Décorateurs, Revêtements de Sols et des Maisons d'Ameublements
ASMT	Association Suisse de Microtechnique
ASN	American Society of Naturalists
ASNE	American Society of Naval Engineers
ASNE	American Society of Newspaper Editors
ASNEF	Agrupación Sindical Nacional de Empresas de Financiación de Ventas a Plazos
ASNEMGE	Association des Sociétés Nationales Européennes et Méditerranéennes de Gastroentérologie
ASNF	Association Suisse des Négociants en Fourrage
ASNIBI	Asociación Nicaragüense de Bibliotecarios
ASNIP	Associazione Sindacale Nazionale dell'Industria Petrolifera
ASNK	Association Suisse des Négociants de Kiosques

ASNP	Association Suisse de Négociants en Timbres-Poste
ASO	American Society for Oceanography
ASO	Association Suisse des Opticians
ASOCANA	Asociación Nacional de Cultivadores de Caña de Azúcar (Colombia)
ASOCESAR	Association of Cotton Growers of Cesar (Colombia)
ASODOBI	Asociación Dominicana de Bibliotecarios
ASOM	Académie des Sciences d'Outre-Mer
ASOMER	Association des Salaries des Organismes de Migration et d'Establissement Ruraux
ASONIDA	Asociación Nacional de Industriales del Arroz (Venezuela)
ASOS	Association Suisse d'Organisation Scientifique
ASOSP	Association Suisse pour l'Orientation Scolaire et Professionnelle
ASOVAC	Asociación Venezolana para el Avance de la Ciencia
ASP	American Society of Parasitologists
ASP	American Society of Pharmacognosy
ASP	American Society of Photogrammetry
ASP	Association Professionnelle Suisse des Commerçants en Peinture
ASP	Association Scientifique de la Précontrainte
ASP	Association of Self-Employed Persons
ASP	Association Suisse des Pédicures
ASP	Association Suisse du Pneu
ASP	Association Suisse de Publicité
ASP	Astronomical Society of the Pacific (U.S.A.)
ASPA	American Society for Personnel Administration
ASPA	American Society for Public Administration
ASPA	Association Suisse des Propriétaires d'Autocamions
ASPA	Australian Sugar Producers' Association
ASPA	Syndicat National des Fabricants d'Agents de Surface et Produits Auxiliaires Industriels
ASPAC	Asian and Pacific Council
ASPACA	Asian and Pacific Cultural Association (Korea)
ASPADS	Associated Sheep, Police and Army Dog Society
ASPAM	Association des Producteurs d'Agrumes du Maroc

ASPAN	Association Suisse pour le Plan d'Aménagement National (Switzerland)
ASPAU	African Scholarship Program of American Universities
ASPB	Algemene Schoorsteenvegers Patroonsbond
ASPB	American Society of Professional Biologists
ASPB	Asian Student Press Bureau
ASPB	Arbeitsgemeinschaft der Spezialbibliotheken
ASPBAE	Asian-South Pacific Bureau of Adult Education (India)
ASPC	American Sheep Producers Council
ASPC	Association Suisse des Philologues Classiques
ASPCA	American Society for the Prevention of Cruelty to Animals
ASPE	Association des Firmes représentant en Suisse des Spécialités Pharmaceutiques Étrangères à Marques Déposées
ASPEA	Association Suisse pour l'Énergie Atomique
ASPEC	Association pour la Prévention et l'Étude de la Contamination
ASPEE	Association Suisse des Professionnels de l'Épuration des Eaux
ASPESCA	Asociación Colombiana de Pescadores
ASPET	American Society for Pharmacology and Experimental Therapeutics
ASPF	Australian Society of Perfumers and Flavourists
ASPFAV	Associazione Svizzera dei Produttori di Films e Audiovisivi
ASPHER	Association of Schools of Public Health in the European Region
ASPI	Arbeitgeberverband Schweizerischer Papier-Industrieller
ASPI	Asociación Publicitaria Internacional (Honduras)
ASPLA	Agrupacion Sindical de Pilotes de Líneas Aéreas
ASPM	Association of Surgeons and Physicians of Malta
ASPO	American Society of Planning Officials
ASPO	American Society for Psychoprophylaxis in Obstetrics
ASPP	American Society of Plant Physiologists
ASPP	Association Suisse de Photographes de Presse
ASPPR	Association of Sugar Producers of Puerto Rico

ASPQ	Association Suisse pour la Promotion de la Qualité
ASPR	American Society for Psychical Research
ASPRAM	Association des Producteurs d'Agrumes du Maroc
ASPRS	American Society of Plastic and Reconstructive Surgery
ASPS	African Succulent Plant Society
ASPT	American Society of Plant Taxonomists
ASQ	Deutsche Gesellschaft für Qualität
ASQC	American Society for Quality Control
ASR	Arbeitskreis Freier Sanitär-Röhrenhändler
ASR	Association Suisse des Romanistes
ASRA	American Shropshire Registry Association
ASRC	Atmospheric Sciences Research Center (U.S.A.)
ASRCT	Applied Scientific Research Corporation of Thailand
ASRD	Astronomy, Space and Radio Division (*of* SRC)
ASRE	American Society of Refrigerating Engineers
ASRI	Academy of Sciences Research Institute (Ghana)
ASRLO	Australian Scientific Research Liaison Office
ASRM	American Association of Range Management
ASRO	Association Suisse de Recherche Opérationnelle
ASRT	Atlantic Salmon Research Trust
ASRZB	Annales de la Société Royale Zoologiques de Belgique
ASS	Asociación Salvadoreña de Sociologia
ASS	Association Suisse des Selectionneurs
ASSA	American Society for the Study of Arteriosclerosis
ASSA	Association for Sociology in Southern Africa (South Africa)
ASSA	Astronomical Association of South Africa
ASSA	Astronomical Society of South Australia
ASSALZOO	Associazione Nazionale fra i Produttori di Alimenti Zootecnici
ASSBRA	Association Belge des Brasseries
ASSBT	American Association of Sugar Beet Technologists
ASSCO	Associazione fra Società e Studi di Consulenza Organizzativa
ASSE	American Society of Safety Engineers
ASSE	American Society of Sanitary Engineering
ASSE	American Society of Swedish Engineers
ASSEDIC-COOP-AGRI	Association pour l'Emploi dans les Coopératives Agricoles
ASSELECTO	Association des Multiplicateurs de Graines Selectionées de Tomates
ASSET	Association of Supervisory Staffs, Executives and Technicians
ASSETERIE	Associazione Italiana Fabbricanti Seterie
ASSGB	Association of Ski Schools in Great Britain
ASSH	American Society for Surgery of the Hand
ASSICREDITO	Associazione Sindicale fra le Aziende del Credito
ASSIDER	Associazione Industrie Siderurgiche Italiana
ASSIFONTE	Association de l'Industrie de la Fonte de Fromage de la CEE
ASSILEC	Association de l'Industrie Laitière de la Communauté Européenne
ASSINFORM	Associazione Costruttori Macchine, Attrezzature per Ufficio e per il Trattamento delle Informazione
ASSINSEL	Association Internationale des Sélectionneurs Professionels pour la Protection des Obtentions Végétales
ASSISTAL	Associazione Nazionale Installatori d'Impianti Termici e di Ventilazione, Idrici, Sanitari, Elettrici, Telefonici ed Affini
ASSITEJ	Association Internationale du Théâtre pour l'Enfance et la Jeunesse
ASSITOL	Associazione Italiana dell'Industria Olearia
ASSL	Associazione Svizzera per lo Studio del Lavoro
ASSMB	Association des Sociétés Scientifiques Médicales Belges
ASSNAS	Associazione Nazionale Assistenti Sociali
ASSOBAF	Société d'Intérêt CollectifAgricole (Guadeloupe)
ASSOBEST-IAME	Associazione Nazionale Commercianti Grossisti Esportatori Importatori di Bestiame e Carni
ASSOCARTA	Associazione Italiana fra gli Industriali della Carta, Cartoni e Paste per Carta
ASSOCASEARI	Associazione Nazionale Stagionatori e Grossisti di Prodotti Caseari
ASSOCDETERGENZA	Associazione Nationale dell'Industria della Saponeria, della Detergenza e dei Prodotti d'Igiene

ASSOCE-MENTO Associazione dell'Industria Italiana del Cemento, dell'Amiantocemento, della Calce e del Gesso

ASSOCHAM Associated Chambers of Commerce and Industry (India)

ASSOCO-MAPLAST Associazione Nazionale Costruttori Macchine per Materie Plastiche e Gomma

ASSOFAR-MA Associazione fra Industrie Chimico-Farmaceutiche

ASSOFER-MET Associazione Nationale dei Commercianti in Ferro e Acciai, Metalli non Ferrosi, Ferramenta e Affini, Rottami

ASSOFLUID Associazione dei Costruttori Italiani di Apparecchiature Oleodrauliche e Pneumatiche

ASSOFOND Associazione Nazionale delle Fonderie

ASSOGIO-CATTOLI Associazione Nazionale Fabbricanti Giocattoli

ASSOGOM-MA Associazione Nazionale fra le Industrie della Gomma, Cavi Elettrici ed Affini

ASSO-GRASSI Associazione Nationale Grassi Animali

ASSOITAL-PELLI Associazione Italiana fra i Commercianti di Pelli Grezze

ASSO-LAMPADE Associazione Nazionale Fabbricanti Lampade Elettriche, Valvole Termoioniche, Tubi Luminscenti, Bottiglie Isolanti, Apparecchi Termostatici

ASSO-LATTE Associazione Italiana Lattiero-Casearia

ASSOLIOS-EMI Associazione Nazionale fra gli Industriali degli Olii da Semi

ASSO-MARMI Associazione dell'Industria Marmifera Italiana e delle Industrie Affini

ASSOMET Associazione Nazionale Industrie Metalli non Ferrosi

ASSOMINE-RARIA Associazione Mineraria Italiana

ASSONAVE Associazione Nazionale fra Costruttori di Navi d'Alto Mare

ASSONIME Associazione Società Italiane per Azione

ASSONOT-AI Associazione Nazionale dei Notai

ASSO-PETROLI Associazione Nationale Commercio Petroli

ASSOPIAS-TRELLE Associazione Nationale dei Produttori di Piastrelle di Ceramica

ASSO-POMAC Association of Common Market Potato Breeders (Germany)

ASSO-POTER Associazione Nazionale Industriali Porcellane e Terraglie

ASSOSPAZ-ZOLE Associazione Nazionale Fabbricanti Spazzole, Pennelli e Preparatori Relative Materie Prime

ASSOSPORT Associazione Nazionale Produttori Articoli Sportivi

ASSOTTICA Associazione Nationale Industriali dell'Ottica, Meccanica Fine e di Precisione

ASSOUOVA Associazione Nazionale fra Commercianti Grossisti Esportatori Importatori di Uova, Pollame e Affini

ASSP Association Suisse de Science Politique

ASSPA Association Suisse pour l'Automatisme

ASSPA Associaziun Svizra dils Specialists dalla Purificaziun d'Aqua

ASSPLV Association des Sociétés Suisses des Professeurs de Langues Vivantes

ASSS American Society for the Study of Sterility

ASSS American Suffolk Sheep Society

ASST American Society for Steel Treating

ASST Associazione Svizzera per lo Studio degli Trasporti

ASSUC Association des Organisations Professionnelles du Commerce des Sucres pour les Pays de la CEE

AST Association Suisse des Marchands de Tapis

AST Association Suisse de Thanatologie

AST Astronomical Society of Tasmania

ASTA American Seed Trade Association

ASTA American Spice Trade Association

ASTA American Society of Travel Agents

ASTA American Surgical Trade Association

ASTA Auckland Science Teachers Association

ASTC Administrative Section for Technical Cooperation (UNO)

ASTC Associazione Svizzera dei Tecnici-Catastali

ASTD American Society for Training and Development

ASTE American Society of Tool Engineers

ASTE Association pour le Développement des Sciences et Techniques de l'Environnement

ASTE Association for Study of Soviet-Type Economics (U.S.A.)

ASTEA Associazione Svizzera Tecnici Epurazione Acque

ASTED	Association pour l'Avancement des Sciences et des Techniques de la Documentation (Canada)	**ASW**	Allianz Schweizerischer Werbeberater
		ASWEA	Association for Social Work Education in Africa (Ethiopia)
ASTEF	Association pour l'Organisation des Stages en France	**ASXRT**	American Society of X-Ray Technicians
		ASYBEL	Syndicat Belge de l'Acide Sulfurique
ASTEL	Association de Spécialistes de Techniques d'Enseignement du Langage	**ASZ**	American Society of Zoologists
		AT	Autotuojat
ASTEM	Association Scientifique et Technique pour l'Exploitation des Mers	**ATA**	Advertising Typographers Association of America
ASTEO	Association Scientifique et Technique pour l'Exploitation des Océans	**ATA**	Air Transport Association of America
ASTG	Association Suisse des Techniciens-Géomètres	**ATA**	Air Transport Association
		ATA	American Translators Association
ASTI	Association Suisse des Traducteurs et Interprètes	**ATA**	American Transport Association
		ATA	American Transit Association
ASTIA	Armed Services Technical Information Agency (U.S.A.)	**ATA**	American Tree Association
		ATA	American Trucking Association
ASTIC	Agrupación Sindical del Transporte Internacional por Carretera	**ATA**	Animal Technicians Association
		ATA	Associazione Tecnica dell'Automobile
ASTM	American Society for Testing and Materials	**ATA**	Atlantic Treaty Association
ASTM	American Society of Tropical Medicine	**ATAB**	Association des Détaillants en Tabacs (Belgium)
ASTM	Association of Sanitary Towel Manufacturers	**ATABW**	American Trade Association for British Woollens
ASTME	American Society of Tool Manufacturing Engineers	**ATAC**	Air Transport Advisory Council
ASTMH	American Society of Tropical Medicine and Hygiene	**ATAC**	Air Transport Association of Canada
		ATAC	Asociación de Tecnicos Azucareros de Cuba
ASTMS	Association of Scientific, Technical and Managerial Staffs	**ATAF**	Association Internationale de Transporteurs Aériens
ASTP	Association des Entrepreneurs Suisses de Travaux Publics	**ATAFEG**	Austria Tabakeinlöse und Fermentionsgesellschaft
ASTRID	Association Scientifique et Technique pour la Recherche en Informatique Documentaire (Belgium)	**ATALA**	Association pour l'Étude et le Développement de la Traduction Automatique et de la Linguistique Appliquée
ASTS	Association Suisse pour la Technique du Soudage	**ATAM**	Asociación de Técnicos en Alimentos de México
ASTUC	Anglo-Soviet Trades Union Committee	**ATAM**	Association of Teaching Aids in Mathematics
ASU	Arbeitsgemeinschaft Selbständiger Unternehmer	**ATAR**	Association des Transporteurs Aériens Régionaux
ASUA	Amateur Swimming Union of the Americas		
ASV	Arbeitsgemeinschaft Schweizer Volkstanzkreise	**ATAV**	Association Technique pour l'Amelioration de la Viticulture (*now* ANTAV)
ASVILMET	Associazione Italiani per lo Sviluppo degli Studi Sperimentali sulla Lavorazione dei Metalli	**ATAVE**	Asociación de Técnicos Azucareros de Venezuela
		ATB	Agricultural Training Board
ASVPP	American Society of Veterinary Physiologists and Pharmacologists	**ATB**	Arbeidertoeristenbond
		ATB	Association of Tropical Biology (Costa Rica)
ASVS	Anotera Scholi Viomichanikon Spouden	**ATC**	African Timber Company

ATC	Agence Transcongolaise des Communications
ATC	Association Européenne des Cadres Commerciaux et Technico-commerciaux
ATC	Vereniging van Automobieltechnici
ATCAS	African Training Centre for Agricultural Statistics (*of* FAO) (Nigeria)
ATCC	American Type Culture Collection
ATCDE	Association of Teachers in College and Departments of Education
ATCEU	Air Traffic Control Experimental Unit
ATCP	Asociación Mexicana de Técnicos de las Industrias de la Celulosa y del Papel
ATD	Association of Tar Distillers
ATD	Association Tunisienne des Documentalistes, Bibliothécaires et Archivistes
ATDA	Australian Telecommunications Development Association
ATDC	Asociacion Técnica de Derivados del Cemento
ATE	Automatic Telephone and Electric Company
ATEA	American Technical Education Association
ATeAC	Associazione Tecnica dell'Acciaio per Costruzioni Civili
ATEC	Agence Transequatoriale de Communications (Central Africa)
ATEC	Air Transport Electronics Council
ATECMA	Agrupación Técnica Española de Constructores de Material Aeroespacial
ATEFI	Associazione Tecnica delle Società Finanziarie
ATEFL	Association of Teachers of English and Foreign Languages (*now* IATEFL)
ATEG	Asociación Técnica Española de Galvanización
ATEGIP	Association Technique pour l'Étude de la Gestion des Institutions Publiques et des Entreprises Privées
ATEN	Association Technique pour l'Énergie Nucléaire
ATF	Association Technique de Fonderie
ATFB	Association Technique de Fonderie de Belgique
ATFS	Association of Track and Field Statisticians
ATG	Association Technique de l'industrie du Gaz en France
ATI	American Television Incorporated

ATI	Association of Technical Institutions (*now* ACFHE)
ATI	Associazione Trafiliere Italiani
ATI	Azienda Tabacchi Italiani
ATIBT	Association Technique pour l'Importation des Bois Tropicaux
ATIC	Associação Tecnica da Indústria do Cimento (Portugal)
ATIC	Association Technique pour l'Importation du Charbon en France
ATIC	Association Technique de l'Industrie du Chauffage de la Ventilation et des Branches Connexes (Belgium)
ATIC	Associazione Tecnica Italiana per la Cinematografia
ATIC	Australian Tin Information Centre
ATICELCA	Associazione Tecnica Italiana per la Cellulosa e per la Carta
ATICPA	Asociación de Tecnicos de la Industria Papelara e Celulosa Argentina
ATIFAS	Associazione Tessiture Italiana Fibre Artificiali e Sintetiche
ATIP	Association Technique de l'Industrie Papetière
ATIPCA	Asociación de Técnicos de la Industria Papelera y Celulósica Argentina
ATIPIC	Association des Technicians de l'Industrie des Peintures et des Industries Connexes
ATIRA	Ahmedabad Textile Industry's Research Association (India)
ATISEA	Associazione Tappezzori in Stoffa e Affini
ATL	American Tariff League
ATL	Autoriserte Trafikkskolers Landsforbund
ATLAS	Agrupacion de Trabajordes Latinoamericanos Sindicalistes
ATLB	Air Transport Licensing Board
ATLF	Association des Traducteurs Littéraires de France
ATLIS	Army Technical Libraries and Information Systems (U.S.A.)
ATM	Association of Teachers of Management
ATMA	Adhesive Tape Manufacturers Association
ATMA	American Textile Machinery Association
ATMA	American Textile Manufacturers Association
ATMA	Association Technique, Maritime et Aéronautique

ATME	Association International pour la Promotion des Techniques Modernes d'Enseignement
ATMI	American Textile Manufacturers Institute
ATO	African Telecommunications Union
ATO	Antarctic Treaty Organization
ATO	Arbeitskreis Topinambur
ATOA	American Tung Oil Association
ATOCI	Association de Traducteurs et Réviseurs des Organisations et Conférences Intergouvernementales
ATOI	Alliance Touristique de l'Océan Indien
ATOM	Association d'Aide aux Travailleurs d'Outre-Mer
ATONU	Assistance Technique de l'Organisation des Nations Unies
ATP	Association of Tennis Professionals
ATP	Association for Transpersonal Psychology (U.S.A.)
ATPAS	Association of Teachers of Printing and Allied Subjects
ATPI	American Textbook Publishers Institute
ATPUL	Association Technique pour la Production et l'Utilisation du Lin et Autres Fibres Liberiennes
ATR	Association Technique de la Route
ATREM	Association Technique de la Refrigération et de l'Équipement Ménager
ATRIH	Association des Transporteurs Routiers Internationaux en Hongrie (Hungary)
ATS	Agence Télégraphique Suisse
ATS	American Television Society
ATS	American Thoracic Society
ATS	American Therapeutic Society
ATS	American Thyroid Society
ATS	American Travel Service
ATS	Association Technique de la Sidérurgie Française
ATS	Atomtekniska Sällskapet i Finland
ATS	Suomen Atomiteknillinen Seura
ATSA	Aero Transportes, South America
ATSA	Association des Techniciens Supérieurs Agricoles
AT & T	American Telephone and Telegraph Company
ATTA	American Tin Trade Association

ATTI	Association of Teachers in Technical Institutions
ATU	African Telecommunication Union
ATU	Arab Tourism Union (Jordan)
ATUC	African Trade Union Confederation
ATV	Abwassertechnische Vereinigung
ATV	Agence de Transit et de Voyages (Central Africa)
ATV	Akademiet for de Tekniske Videnskaber
ATV	Associated Television Corporation
ATVF	Association Technique pour la Vulgarisation Forestière
ATWA	Association of Third World Affairs (U.S.A.)
ATYPI	Association Typographique Internationale
AUA	American Unitarian Association
AUA	American Urological Association
AUA	Associated Unions of America
AUA	Association des Universités Africaines
AUA	Austrian Airlines
AUALPA	Austrian Airline Pilots Association
AUAW	Amalgamated Union of Asphalt Workers
AUB	American University of Beirut
AUBC	Association of Universities of the British Commonwealth
AUBTW	Amalgamated Union of Building Trade Workers (*now* UCATT)
AUC	Auckland University College (N.Z.)
AUCC	Association of Universities and Colleges of Canada
AUCCTU	All-Union Central Council of Trade Unions (U.S.S.R.)
AUDAVI	Asociación Uruguaya de Agencias de Viajes Internacionales
AUDECAM	Association Universitaire pour le Développement de l'Enseignement et de la Culture en Afrique et à Madagascar
AUDI	Société Internationale d'Audiologie
AUDIVIR	Conseil International pour l'Application des Moyens Audio-Visuels à l'Environnement
AUE	Association des Universitaires d'Europe
AUEW	Amalgamated Union of Engineering and Foundry Workers
AUFM	Asociación Universal de Federalistas Mundiales
AUFS	American Universities Field Staff
AUFW	Amalgamated Union of Foundry Workers (*now* AUEW)

AUGB	Association of Ukrainians in Great Britain Ltd.	**AVARD**	Association of Voluntary Agencies for Rural Development (India)
AUI	Action d'Urgence Internationale	**AVAS**	Association of Voluntary Action Scholars (U.S.A.)
AUI	Associated Universities, Inc. (U.S.A.)		
AULA	Arab University Library Association	**AVASS**	Association of Voluntary Aided Secondary Schools
AULLA	Australasian Universities Language and Literature Association	**AVB**	Afdeling Agrarische Vertegenwoordiging Buitenland
AUMA	Ausstellungs- und Messe-Ausschuss der Deutschen Wirtschaft	**AVB**	Autorité pour l'Aménagement de la Vallée du Bandama (Ivory Coast)
AUMLA	Australian Universities Modern Language Association (*now* AULLA)	**AVBB**	Algemeen Verbond Bouwbedrijft
AUO	African Unity Organisation	**AVC**	Asociación Venezolana de Caficultores (Venezuela)
AUOD	Alliance Universelle des Ouvriers Diamantaires	**AVC**	Association of Vitamin Chemists (U.S.A.)
AUPELF	Association des Universités Partiellement ou Entièrement de Langue Française (Canada)	**AVCFOM**	Association des Villages Communautaires de France d'Outre-Mer
AURA	Association of Universities for Research in Astronomy (U.S.A.)	**AFCGC**	Asociación Venezolana de Criadores de Ganada Cebú (Venezuela)
AUREG	Association de Recherches Géographiques et Cartographiques	**AVCZ**	Algemeen Verbond der Cooperatieve Zuivelfabrieken (Belgium)
AURP	American Universities Research Program	**AVDA**	American Venereal Disease Association
AUSPICE	Association of University Staff to Promote Inter-University Cooperation in Europe (France)	**AVDA**	Asociación Venezolana de Derecho Agrario
		AVDBAD	Association Voltaique pour le Développement des Bibliothèques, des Archives et de la Documentation
AUT	Association of University Teachers		
AUTEC	Atlantic Underwater Test Evaluation Centre	**AVE**	Asociación Venezolana de Ejecutivos
AUTIG	Auto-Tilbehørs Grossist-Foreningen	**AVE**	Association for Volunteer Service in Europe
AUTOVIA	Autotransport-Gewerbeverband der Schweiz	**AVE**	Aussenhandelsvereinigung des Deutschen Einzelhandels
AUWE	Admiralty Underwater Weapons Establishment	**AVEC**	Asociación Venezolana Educación Católica
AUXIMAD	Société Auxiliaire Maritime de Madagascar	**AVEC**	Association des Centres d'Abbatage de Volailles et du Commerce d'Importation et d'Exportation de Volailles des Pays de la EEC
AVA	Aan en Verkoopbureau van Akkerbouwproducten	**AVEN-CULTA**	Asociación Venezolana de Cultivadores de Tabaco
AVA	Academy of Visual Arts	**AVENEX-CAF**	Asociación Venezolana de Exportadores de Café
AVA	Alberta Veterinary Association (Canada)		
AVA	Algemene Vereniging voor de Nederlandse Aardewerken Glasindustrie	**AVENSA**	Aerovias Venezonalas, South America
AVA	Amateur Volleyball Association (*now* EVA)	**AVEX**	Asociación Venezolana de Exportadores
AVA	American Vocational Association	**AVF**	Académie Vétérinaire de France
AVA	Asociación Vitivinícola Argentina	**AVG**	Asociación Venezolana de Ganaderos
AVA	Atlantic Visitors Association (Belgium)	**AVGI**	Algemene Vereniging van de Geneesmiddelenindustrie (Belgium)
AVA	Australian Veterinary Association	**AVGMP**	Asociación Venezolana de Geología, Minas y Petróleo
AVAB	Automatic Vending Association of Britain		
AVAL	Association pour les Ventes dans Alimentation	**AVHA**	Association Vétérinaire d'Hygiène Alimentaire

AVI	Arbeitsgemeinschaft der Eisen- und Metallverarbeitenden Industrie
AVI	Association Universelle d'Aviculture Scientifique
AVIANCA	Aerovías Nacionales de Colombia
AVIEAS	Asociación Venezolana de Instituciones de Educación Agrícola Superior
AVIEM	Asociación Venezolana de Ingeneiria Eléctrica y Mécanica
AVIFIA	Congrès International sur les Applications Nouvelles du Vide et du Froid dans les Industries Alimentaires
AVIJ	Algemene Vereniging voor de Ijzerhandel
AvJ	Arbeitsgemeinschaft von Jugendbuchvelegern in der Bundesrepublik Deutschland
AVK	Arbeitsgemeinschaft Verstärke Kunststoffe
AVLA	Audio Visual Language Association
AVM	Algemene Vereeniging voor Melkvoorziening
AVM	Association des Fabricants de Verres de Montres (Switzerland)
AVMA	American Veterinary Medical Association
AVMA	Automatic Vending Machine Association
AVMD	Algemene Vereniging van Leraren bij Voorbereidend Wetenschappelijk en Algemeen Voortgezet Onderwijs
AVNEG	Algemene Vereniging van Nederlandse Gieterijen
AVPA	Asociación Venezolana de Peritos Agropecuarios
AVPC	Asociación Venezolana de Productores de Cacao
AVRA	Audio-Visual Research Foundation (U.S.A.)
AVRAC	Agricultural and Veterinary Research Advisory Committee (East Africa)
AVRDC	Asian Vegetable Research and Development Centre, Taipei
AVRO	Algemene Vereniging Radio-Omroep
AVRS	American Veterinary Radiology Society
AVS	American Vacuum Society
AVS	Association of Veterinary Students of Great Britain and Ireland
AVS	Autovermieter-Verband der Schweiz
AVTRW	Association of Veterinary Teachers and Research Workers
AVV	L'Autorité d'Aménagement des Vallées des Volta (Upper Volta)
AVVE	Assemblee der Versklavten Völker Europas
AVVL	Algemeen Verbond van Leerkrachten (Belgium)
AVVN	Algemene Vereniging van Naaimachinenhandelaren
AVWV	Antilliaans Verbond van Werknemers Verenigingen
AVZ	Algemene Vereniging voor de Teelt en Handel in Zaaizaad en Pootgoed (Netherlands)
AWA	Amalgamated Wireless (Australasia)
AWAM	Association of West African Merchants
AWAS	Australian Womens Army Service
AWB	Agricultural Wages Board
AWB	Australian Wool Board
AWBA	American World's Boxing Association
AWC	American Wool Council
AWCU	Association of World Colleges and Universities (U.S.A.)
AWE	Association for World Education (U.S.A.)
AWES	Association of Western Europe Shipbuilders
AWF	American Wildlife Foundation
AWF	Asian Weightlifting Federation
AWF	Ausschuss für Wirtschaftliche Fertigung
AWGC	Australian Woolgrowers and Graziers Council
AWHA	Australian Womens Home Army
AWIS	Association for Women in Science (U.S.A.)
AWIU	Aluminium Workers International Union (U.S.A.)
AWLA	Association of Welsh Local Authorities
AWLLA	All Wales Ladies Lacrosse Association
AWMF	Arbeitsgemeinschaft Wissenschaftlich-Medizinische Fachgesellschaften
AWMM	Arbeitsgemeinschaft für Werbung, Markt- und Meinungsforschung (Switzerland)
AWMPF	Australian Wool and Meat Producers Federation
AWN	Archaeologische Werkgemeenschap voor Nederland
AWNL	Australian Womens National League
AWPA	American Wood-Preservers' Association
AWR	Arbeitsgemeinschaft der Deutschen Werksredakteure
AWR	Association for the Study of the World Refugee Problem
AWRA	American Water Resources Association

AWRA	Australian Welding Research Association
AWRA	Australian Wool Realisation Agency
AWRBIAC	Arkansas-White-Red Basins Inter-Agency Committee
AWRC	Australian Water Resources Council
AWRC	Australian Wool Realisation Commission
AWRE	Atomic Weapons Research Establishment
AWS	Agricultural Wholesale Society
AWS	Algemene Werksgeversorganisatie Schoonmaakbedrijven
AWS	American Welding Society
AWST	Association of Women Science Teachers (*now* ASE)
AWT	Arbeitsgemeinschaft für Wärmebehandlung und Werkstoff-Technik
AWT	Arbeitsgemeinschaft für Wirkstoffe in der Tierernährung
AWTA	Association for World Travel Exchange
AWTCE	Association of World Trade Chamber Executives (U.S.A.)
AWU	Agricultural Workers Union (South Africa)
AWU	Australian Workers Union
AWV	Algemene Werkgevers-Vereniging
AWV	Amalgamated Wireless Valve Co. (Australia)
AWV	Ausschuss Wirtschaftliche Verwaltung
AWWA	American Water-Works Association
AWWM	Association of Wholesale Woollen Merchants Ltd
AWWV	Arbeitsgemeinschaft der Wasserwirtschafsverbande
AYF	Arab Youth Federation (Egypt)
AYH	Academia Yucateca de Historia (Mexico)
AYRS	Amateur Yacht Research Society
AZABDO	Association Zairoise des Archivistes, Bibliothécaires et Documentalistes
AZRC	Arid Zone Research Centre (Australia)
AZRI	Arid Zone Research in Iraq
AZU	Aktionszentrum Umweltschutz
AZV	Autofahrlehrer-Zentralverband (Switzerland)

B

BA	Booksellers Association of Great Britain and Ireland
BA	British Association for the Advancement of Science
BAA	Booking Agents Association of Great Britain Ltd
BAA	British Acetylene Association (*now* BCGA)
BAA	British Agrochemicals Association
BAA	British Aikido Association
BAA	British Alsatian Association
BAA	British Anodising Association
BAA	British Archaeological Association
BAA	British Astronomical Association
BAA & A	British Association of Accountants and Auditors
BAAB	British Amateur Athletic Board
BAAC	Bank for Agriculture and Agricultural Co-operatives (Thailand)
BAAL	British Association of Applied Linguistics
BAALPE	British Association of Advisers in Physical Education
BAAS	British Association for the Advancement of Science
BAAS	British Association for American Studies
BAAT	British Association of Art Therapists
BAB	Berufsverband Freischaffender Architekten und Bauingenieure
BAB	Bond van Aannemers in de Bouwnijverheid
BAB	British Airways Board
BABEX	Bond van Aannemers met Bevoegdheid voor Explosieven
BABF	British Amateur Baseball Federation
BABS	British Aluminium Building Service
BABS	British Association for Brazing and Soldering
BABW	Beratender Ausschuss für Bildungs- und Wissenschaftspolitik
BAC	Biblioteca Agropecuaria de Colombia
BAC	Block Advisory Committee (India)
BAC	Bois Africaines Contreplaques (Gabon)
BAC	British Aircraft Corporation
BAC	British Association of Chemists
BAC	British Atlantic Committee
BAC	British Automatic Company
BAC	Brouwtechnische Adviescommissie
BAC	Bureau Agricole Commun pour l'Etude de Conjoncture Economique
BACA	British Agricultural Contractors' Association

BACAAO	Banque Centrale des Etats de l'Afrique Occidentale	**BAF**	British Air Ferries Ltd
BACAH	British Association of Consultants in Agriculture and Horticulture (*now* BIAC)	**BAF**	Bundesarbeitsgemeinschaft der Fruchtimportmärkte
BACAN	British Association for the Control of Aircraft Noise	**BÄF**	Byggnadsämnesförbundet
		BAFA	British Animated Film Association
BACC	British American Chamber of Commerce (U.S.A.)	**BAFA**	British Arts Festivals Association
		BAfD	Banque Africaine de Développement
BACE	British Association of Corrosion Engineers	**BAFM**	British Association of Forensic Medicine
BACE	Bureau of Agricultural Chemistry and Engineering (U.S.A.)	**BAFM**	British Association of Friends of Museums
		BAFMA	British and Foreign Maritime Agencies
BACEA	British Airport Construction and Equipment Association	**BAFOG**	Bureau Agricole et Forestier Guyanais
		BAFRA	British Aluminium Foil Rollers Association
BACG	British Association of Crystal Growth	**BAFS**	Banque Americano-Franco-Suisse
BACI	British Association of Caving Instructors	**BAFS**	British Academy of Forensic Sciences
BACIE	British Association for Commercial and Industrial Education	**BAFSC**	British Association of Field and Sports Contractors
BACM	British Association of Colliery Management	**BAFSM**	British Association of Feed Supplement Manufacturers
BACMA	British Aromatic Compound Manufacturers Association	**BAFTA**	British Academy of Film and Television Arts
BACMA	British Artists' Colour Manufacturers' Association	**BAFTM**	British Association of Fishing Tackle Makers
		BAG	British Animation Group (*now* BAFA)
BACR	British Association for Cancer Research	**BAG**	Bundesarbeitsgemeinschaft für das Schlacht- und Viehhofswesen
BACT	British Association of Conference Towns		
BACTA	British Amusement Catering Trades Association	**BAGA**	British Amateur Gymnastic Association
		BAGB	Baseball Association of Great Britain
BACTE	British Association for Commercial and Technical Education	**BAGB**	Bicycle Association of Great Britain
		BAGCD	British Association of Green Crop Driers
BAD	Associação Portuguesa de Bibliotecarios, Arquivistas e Documentalistes	**BAGDA**	British Advertising Gift Distributors Association
BAD	Banque Africaine de Développement	**BAGMA**	British Agricultural and Garden Machinery Association
BADA	British Amateur Dancers Association		
BADA	British Antique Dealers' Association Ltd	**BAH**	Biologische Anstalt Helgoland
BAE	Badminton Association of England	**BAH**	British Airways Helicopters
BAE	Belfast Association of Engineers	**BAHO**	British Association of Helicopter Operators
BAE	Bureau of Agricultural Economics (U.S.A.)	**BAHOH**	British Association of the Hard of Hearing
BAEA	British Actors Equity Association	**BAHPA**	British Agricultural and Horticultural Plastics Association
BAEC	British Agricultural Export Council		
BAECE	British Association of Early Childhood Education	**BAHS**	British Agricultural History Society
		BAI	Bundesverband der Agraringenieure
BAECON	Bureau of Agricultural Economics (Philippines)	**BAI**	Bureau des Affaires Indigènes
		BAI	Bureau of Animal Industry (U.S.A.)
BAED	British Airways European Division	**BAIC**	Bureau of Agricultural and Industrial Chemistry (U.S.A.)
BAEF	Belgian-American Educational Foundation		
BAEng	Bureau of Agricultural Engineering (U.S.A.)	**BAIE**	British Association of Industrial Editors
BAEQ	Bureau d'Aménagement de l'Est du Québec (Canada)	**BAIF**	Bharatiya Agro-Industries Foundation (India)

BAK	Bundesgemeinschaft der Architektenkammern	**BAOM**	Bibliothèque d'Afrique et d'Outre-Mer
BAK	Bundesapothekerkammer	**BAOS**	British Association of Oral Surgeons
BALI	British Association of Landscape Industries	**BAOT**	British Association of Occupational Therapists
BALPA	British Air Line Pilots' Association	**BAPA**	British Air Pilots Association
BAM	Brothers to All Men	**BAPA**	British Amateur Press Association
BAM	Bundesanstalt für Materialprüfung	**BAPAL**	British Adult Publications Association Ltd
BAMA	British Adhesive Manufacturers Association	**BAPC**	British Aircraft Preservation Council
BAMA	British Aerosol Manufacturers Association	**BAPCO**	Bahrain Petroleum Company
BAMA	British Amsterdam Maritime Agencies	**BAPIP**	British Association of Palestine-Israel Philatelists
BAMA	British Army Motoring Association	**BAPM & R**	British Association of Physical Medicine and Rheumatology (*now* BARR)
BAMB	Bureau of Administrative Management and Budget (UNDP)	**BAPP**	British Association of Pig Producers
BAMDO	British Agricultural Marketing Development Organisation	**BAPS**	British Association of Paediatric Surgeons
BAMES	Banque Malagasy d'Escompte et de Crédit	**BAPS**	British Association of Plastic Surgeons
BAMEX	British Art Metal Manufacturers Export Group	**BAPSA**	Budget Annexe des Prestations Sociales Agricoles
BAMM	British Association of Manipulative Medicine	**BAPSC**	Badeku Agricultural Production and Supply Company (Nigeria)
BAMMATA	British Animal Medicine Makers' and Allied Traders' Association	**BAPT**	Incorporated British Association for Physical Training
BAMRG	British Agricultural Marketing Research Group	**BAQ**	Bundesanstalt für Qualitätsforschung Pflanzlicher Erzeugnisse
BAMS	British Air Mail Society	**BAR**	British Association of Removers
BAMTM	British Association of Machine Tool Merchants (*now* AEMTM)	**BAR**	Bundesarbeitsgemeinschaft für Rehabilitation
BAMW	British Association of Meat Wholesalers	**BARB**	British Association of Rose Breeders
BAN	British Association of Neurologists	**BARC**	Bhabha Atomic Research Centre (India)
BANC	Biblioteca Agrícola Nacional de Colombia	**BARC**	British Automobile Racing Club
BANC	British Association of National Coaches	**BARD**	Bangladesh Academy for Rural Development
BANDECO	Banana Development Corporation of Costa Rica	**BARMA**	Boiler and Radiator Manufacturers Association
BANDESCO	Banco del Desarrollo Economico Espanol	**BARMA**	Bureau pour l'Application des Renseignements Météorologiques aux Activités Économiques et Agricoles
BANFAIC	Banco de Fomento Agrícola e Industrial de Cuba	**BARP**	British Association of Retired Persons
BANS	British Association of Numismatic Societies	**BARR**	Board on Agricultural and Renewable Resources (U.S.A.)
BANSDOC	Bangladesh National Scientific and Documentation Centre	**BARR**	British Association for Rheumatology and Rehabilitation
BANZARE	British-Australian-New Zealand Antarctic Research Expedition	**BARS**	British Association of Residential Settlements
BAO	British Association of Orthodontists	**BARTO**	British Association of Resort Tourist Officers
BAO	British Association of Otolaryngologists	**BAS**	British Acoustical Society
BAOD	British Airways Overseas Division	**BAS**	British Antarctic Survey
BAOFR	British Association of Overseas Furniture Removers	**BAS**	British Association of Settlements
BAOLPE	British Association of Organisers and Lecturers in Physical Education		

BASA	British Architectural Students' Association	**BAUA**	Business Aircraft Users' Association
BASA	British Association of Seed Analysts	**BAUS**	British Association of Urological Surgeons
BASA	British Automatic Sprinkler Association	**BAV**	Bureau Aardappelverbouw
BASAF	British and South African Forum	**BAWA**	British Amateur Wrestling Association
BASAM	British Association of Grain, Seed, Feed and Agricultural Merchants	**BAWE**	British Association of Women Executives
		BAWLA	British Amateur Weight Lifting Association
BASC	British Aerial Standards Council	**BAWRA**	British Australian Wool Realisation Association
BASCOL	Bauxite Alumina Study Company Ltd (Ghana)	**BAYS**	British Association of Young Scientists
BAsD	Banque Asiatique de Développement	**BAYWA**	Bayerische Warenvermittlung Landwirtschaftlicher Genossenschaften
BASE	British Association Service for the Elderly		
BASE	Bureau Africain des Sciences de l'Éducation (Zaire)	**BBA**	Biologische Bundesanstalt
		BBA	British Backgammon Association
BASEEFA	British Approvals Service for Electrical Equipment in Flammable Atmospheres	**BBA**	British Bankers' Association
		BBA	British Bee-Keepers Association
BASES	British Anti-Smoking Education Society	**BBA**	British Bobsleigh Association
BASF	Badische Anilin und Soda-Fabrik	**BBAA**	Bureau Belge des Assureurs Automobiles
BASI	British Association of Ski Instructors	**BBAC**	British Balloon and Airship Club
BASLC	British Association of Sports Ground and Landscape Contractors Ltd	**BBB**	Bedrijfslaboratorium voor Grondonderzoek
BASM	British Association of Sport and Medicine	**BBBA**	British Bird Breeders' Association
BASMA	Boot and Shoe Manufacturers' Association and Leather Trades Protection Society	**BBBC**	British Boxing Board of Control
		BBC	British Broadcasting Corporation
BASMM	British Association of Sewing Machine Manufacturers	**BBCC**	British Bottle Collectors Club
		BBCF	British Bacon Curers' Federation
BASO	British Association for Surgical Oncology	**BBCMA**	British Baby Carriage Manufacturers Association
BASOMED	Basutoland Socio-Medical Services		
BASP	British Association for Social Psychiatry	**BBCS**	British Beer-mat Collectors Society
BASR	Bureau of Applied Social Research (U.S.A.)	**BBCS**	British Butterfly Conservation Society
BASRA	British Amateur Scientific Research Association	**BBFC**	British Board of Film Censors
		BBFI	Baptist Bible Fellowship International (U.S.A.)
BASRM	British Association of Synthetic Rubber Manufacturers	**BBG**	Algemene Nederlandse Bond van Binnenlandse Groothandelaren in Groente en Fruit
BASS	Belgian Archives for the Social Sciences		
BASS	British Association of Ship Suppliers		
BASSA	British Airline Stewards and Stewardesses Association	**BBGA**	British Broiler Growers Association
		BBGOA	Boletin Bibliográfico de Geofísica y Oceanografía Americanas (Mexico)
BASW	British Association of Social Workers		
BAT	British-American Tobacco Company	**BBI**	British Bottlers Institute
BAT	Bureau de l'Assistance Technique (*see* TAB)	**BBIRA**	British Baking Industries' Research Association (*now* FMBRA)
BATA	Bakery Allied Traders Association		
BATD	British Association of Teachers of Dancing	**BBKA**	British Beekeepers' Association
BATMA	Bookbinding and Allied Trades Management Association	**BBKC**	British Bee-keeping Centre
		BBL	British Bridge League
BATO	British Association of Tourist Officers	**BBLO**	Belgische Bond voor Lichamelijke Opvoeding
BATU	Brotherhood of Asian Trade Unionists (Philippines)	**BBM**	Algemene Nederlandse Bond van Bierhandelaren en Mineraalwaterfabrikanten

BBMA	British Bath Manufacturers' Association
BBMA	British Brush Manufacturers Association
BBMA	British Button Manufacturers' Association
BBMA	Building Board Manufacturers' Association of Great Britain
BBMRA	British Brush Manufacturers Research Association
BBMS	British Battery Makers Society
BBO	British Ballet Organisation
BBO	Gesamtverband Büromaschinen, Büromöbel und Organisationsmittel
BBPHA	British Poultry Breeders and Hatcheries Association
BBR	Belgische Beroepsvereniging van Reisbureaus
BBRS	Blair Bell Research Society
BBRU	Bituminous Binder Research Unit (South Africa)
BBS	Bartó Béla Szövetség
BBS	British Archaeological Association
BBS	British Biophysical Society
BBS	British Bryological Society
BBS	British Button Society
BBSA	British Blind and Shutter Association
BBSATRA	British Boot, Shoe and Allied Trades Research Association
BBSI	British Boot and Shoe Institution
BBSR	Bermuda Biological Station for Research
BBTA	British Bureau of Television Advertising
BBTA	Bund Baugewerblich Tätiger Architekten
BCA	British Carton Association
BCA	British Casino Association
BCA	British Casting Association
BCA	British Chicken Association
BCA	British Chiropractors Association
BCA	British College of Accountancy
BCA	British Confectioners' Association
BCAB	British Computer Association for the Blind
BCAC	British Conference on Automation and Computation
BCAI	British Columbia Artificial Insemination Centre
BCAL	British Caledonian Airways Ltd
BCAR	British Council for Aid to Refugees
BCAS	British Compressed Air Society
BCB	British Consultants Bureau
BCB	Bureau Congolais des Bois
BCC	Banque Commerciale Congolaise
BCC	British Caravanners Club
BCC	British Colour Council
BCC	British Communications Corporation
BCC	British Copyright Council
BCC	British Council of Churches
BCC	British Cryogenic Council
BCC	Bureau Central de Compensation
BCCCUS	British Commonwealth Chamber of Commerce in the United States
BCCF	British Cast Concrete Federation
BCCG	British Cooperative Clinical Group
BCD	Banque Camerounaise de Développement
BCD	British Crop Driers, Ltd
BCD	Bureau du Commerce et du Développement (*of* UNCTAD)
BCDTA	British Chemical and Dyestuffs Traders Association
BCE	Board of Customs and Excise
BCEAE	Banque Centrale des États de l'Afrique Équatoriale et du Cameroun
BCEAO	Banque Centrale des États de l'Afrique de l'Ouest
BCECA	British Chemical Engineering Contractors Association
BCECC	British and Central-European Chamber of Commerce
BCEL	British Commonwealth Ex-Services League
BCEMA	British Combustion Equipment Manufacturers Association
BCEOM	Bureau Central d'Études pour les Équipements d'Outre-Mer
BCeramRA	British Ceramic Research Association
BCF	Bacon Curers Federation
BCF	British Chess Federation
BCF	British Concrete Federation
BCF	British Cycling Federation
BCFA	British-China Friendship Association
BCFGA	British Columbia Fruit Growers' Association
BCFL	British Czechoslovak Friendship League
BCFS	British Columbia Forestry Society
BCFTE	British Commonwealth Forest Translation Exchange
BCGA	British Compressed Gases Association

BCGA	British Cotton Growing Association	**BCMN**	Bureau Central de Mesures Nucléaires (Belgium)
BCGLO	British Commonwealth Geographical Liaison Office	**BCN**	Biblioteca del Congreso de la Nación (Argentina)
BCHC	British Crane Hire Corporation	**BCOB**	Bond van Christelijke Ondernemers in het Bakkersbedrijf
BCHFA	British-Canadian Holstein Friesian Association		
BCHS	British Canadian Holstein Society	**BCOG**	British College of Obstetricians and Gynaecologists
BCI	Bedrijfsgroep Chemische Industrie		
BCI	Bonsai Clubs International (U.S.A.)	**BCORA**	British Colliery Owners' Research Association
BCI	Bureau Consultatif Interorganisations	**BCPA**	British Commonwealth Pacific Airlines
BCIA	British Columbia Institute of Agrologists	**BCPA**	British Concrete Pumping Association
BCIA	British Cooking Industry Association	**BCPA**	British Copyright Protection Association
BCIE	Banco Centroamericano de Integración Económica (Honduras)	**BCPC**	British Crop Protection Council
BCINA	British Commonwealth International Newsfilm Agency	**BCPIT**	British Council for the Promotion of International Trade
BCIPPA	British Cast Iron Pressure Pipe Association	**BCPMA**	British Chemical Plant Manufacturers Association (*now* PPA)
BCIRA	British Cast Iron Research Association	**BCPMMA**	British Ceramic Plant and Machinery Manufacturers Association
BCIRA	British Cotton Industries Research Association (*now* British Cotton, Silk and Man-made Fibres Association)	**BCPO**	British Commonwealth Producers' Organisation
BCIS	Bureau Central International de Séismologie	**BCPPC**	British Christian Pen Pal Club
BCISC	British Chemical Industry Safety Council (*now* CISHEC)	**BCPR**	Belgisch Centrum voor Public Relations
		BCR	Bituminous Coal Research (U.S.A.)
BCIT	British Columbia Institute of Technology	**BCR**	Bureau of Commercial Research
BCIU	Business Council for International Understanding (U.S.A.)	**BCR**	Bureau Communautaire de Référence
BCK	Belgisch Centrum voor Kwaliteitszorg	**BCRA**	British Carbonization Research Association
BCLMA	British Columbia Lumber Manufacturers' Association	**BCRA**	British Cave Research Association
		BCRA	British Ceramic Research Association
BCM	Banque Centrale du Bali	**BCRA**	British Coke Research Association
BCMA	British Caramel Manufacturers Association	**BCRC**	British Columbia Research Council
BCMA	British Carpet Manufacturers Association	**BCRD**	British Council for the Rehabilitation of the Disabled
BCMA	British Chip Board Manufacturers' Association	**BCRG**	Banque Centrale de la Republique de Guinée
BCMA	British Closure Manufacturers Association	**BCRU**	British Committee on Radiological Units
BCMA	British Colour Makers Association	**BCRUM**	British Committee on Radiation Units and Measurements
BCMA	British Columbia Medical Association		
BCMA	British Council of Maintenance Associations	**BCS**	Bond van Christelijke Slagerspatroons
BCMA	British Country Music Association	**BCS**	British Cardiac Society
BCMA	Bureau Commun du Machinisme Agricole (*now* BCMEA) (France)	**BCS**	British Cartographic Society
		BCS	British Ceramic Society
BCMEA	Bureau Commun du Machinisme et de l'Équipement Agricole	**BCS**	British Computer Society
		BCS	British Crossbow Society
		BCSA	British College Sports Association
BCMF	British Ceramic Manufacturers Federation	**BCSA**	British Constructional Steelwork Association

BCSH	British Committee for Standards in Haematology
BCSIR	Bangladesh Council of Scientific and Industrial Research
BCSO	British Commonwealth Scientific Office (U.S.A.)
BCTA	British Canadian Trade Association
BCTC	British Ceramic Tile Council
BCTP	British Continental Trade Press
BCU	Banco Central del Uruguay
BCU	British Canoe Union
BCU	British Commonwealth Union
BCURA	British Coal Utilization Research Association
BCVA	British Cattle Veterinary Association
BCVA	British Columbia Veterinary Association
BCWA	British Cotton Waste Association
BCWIU of A	Bakery and Confectionery Workers International Union of America
BCWLF	British Commonwealth Weightlifting Federation
BCWMA	British Clock and Watch Manufacturers Association
BCZ	Belgische Centrale Zuivelcommissie
BCZV	Bond van Cöoperatieve Zuivelverkoopverenigingen
BDA	British Deaf Association
BDA	British Dental Association
BDA	British Diabetic Association
BDA	British Dietetic Association
BDA	British Domestic Appliances, Ltd
BDA	British Dyslexia Association
BDA	Bund Deutscher Architekten
BDA	Bundesvereinigung der Deutschen Arbeitgeberverbände
BDAC	Bureau of Drug Abuse Control (U.S.A.)
BDB	Bibliotéca del Bibliotecário (Argentina)
BDB	Bund Deutscher Baumeister, Architekten und Ingenieure
BDB	Bundesverband der Deutschen Bürstenindustrie
BDB	Bund Deutscher Baumschulen
BDC	Book Development Council
BDC	Bureau International de Documentation des Chemins de Fer
BDCC	British Defence Coordinating Committee
BDD	Banque Dahoméenne de Développement
BDD	Bund Deutscher Detektive
BDDA	British Deaf and Dumb Association
BDDRG	British Deep-Drawing Research Group
BDDSA	British Deaf Amateur Sports Association
BDDV	Bund Deutscher Dolmetscherverbände
BDE	Bundesverband Deutscher Einsenbahnen
BDEAC	Banque de Développement des États de l'Afrique Centrale
BDET	Banque de Développement Économique de Tunisie
BDF	Banque de France
BDF	Bundesverband des Deutschen Güterfernverkehrs
BDFA	British Dairy Farmers' Association
BDFA	Bundesverband der Finanz- und Anlageberater
BDFG	Bundesverband des Deutschen Farbengrosshandels
BDFI	Bund Deutscher Fliesengeschäfte
BDG	Bund Deutscher Grafik-Designer
BDH	British Drug Houses, Ltd
BDHA	British Dental Hygienists Association
BDI	Bundesverband der Deutschen Industrie
BDI	Bureau of Dairy Industry (U.S.A.)
BDIA	Bund Deutscher Innenarchitekten
BDIC	Bibliothèque de Documentation Internationale Contemporaine
BDK	Bundesvervand Deutscher Kosmetikerinnen
BDL	Bund der Deutschen Landjugend im Deutschen Bauernverband
BDL	Bundesverband Deutscher Lederhändler
BDLA	Bund Deutscher Landschaftsarchitekten
BDLI	Bundesverband der Deutschen Luft- und Raumfahrtindustrie
BDM	Banque de Développement du Mali
BDMA	British Disinfectant Manufacturers Association
BDMAA	British Direct Mail Advertising Association
BDMH	Bundesverband des Deutschen Musikinstrumentenhersteller
BDN	Bundesverband des Deutschen Güternahverkehrs
BDO	Bund Deutscher Orgelbaumeister
BDP	Bundesverband des Deutschen Personenverkehrsgewerbes
BDP	Bundesverband Deutscher Pflanzenzüchter

BDPA	British Disposable Products Association	**BEA**	British European Airways
BDPA	Bureau pour le Développement de la Production Agricole	**BEAB**	British Electrical Approvals Board
		BEAC	Banque des États de l'Afrique Centrale, Paris
BDPh	Bund Deutscher Philatelisten	**BEAC**	British European Airways Corporation
BDRA	British Drag Racing Association	**BEAIRA**	British Electrical and Allied Industries Research Association
BDRN	Banque de Développement de la République du Niger	**BEAMA**	British Electrical and Allied Manufacturers Association
BDS	British Deer Society		
BDS	British Display Society	**BEAS**	British Educational Administration Society
BDS	Bund Deutscher Sekretärinnen	**BEC**	British Employers' Confederation (*now* CBI)
BDS	Bundesverband der Deutschen Schrottwirtschaft	**BEC**	British Evangelical Council
		BEC	Bureau Européen du Café
BDS	Bundesverband Deutscher Stahlhandel	**BECC**	British Empire Cancer Campaign
BDSA	British Dental Students' Association	**BECC**	Bureau d'Études Coopérative et Communautaires
BDSC	British Deaf Sports Council		
BdSW	Bundesverband der Selbstbedienungs-Warenhäuser	**BECCR**	British Empire Cancer Campaign for Research (*now* CRC)
BDT	Banque de Développement du Tchad	**BECEB**	Bedrijfs-Economisch Centrum voor de Elektrotechnische Bedrijfstak
BDTA	British Dental Trade Association		
BDTA	Bundesverband Deutscher Tabakwaren-Grosshändler und Automatenaufsteller	**BECETEL**	Centre Belge d'Études Technologiques sur Tuyauteries et Accessoires
BDU	Bund Deutscher Unternehmensberater	**BECGC**	British Empire and Commonwealth Games Council
BDÜ	Bundesverband der Dolmetscher und Übersetzer	**BECGF**	British Empire and Commonwealth Games Federation
BDV	Bundesverband Deutscher Volks- und Betriebswirte	**BECMA**	British Electro-Ceramic Manufacturers Association
BDV	Bundesverband der Versandschlachtereien	**BECOIJ**	Bureau Européen de Coordination des Organisations Internationales de Jeunesse
BDV	Bundesverband Deutscher Vorzugsmilcherzeuger	**BECSM**	British Electrical Conduit Systems Manufacturers (*now* BESA)
BDVB	Bundesverband Deutscher Volks- und Betriebswirte	**BECWLC**	British Empire and Commonwealth Weight Lifting Council
BDVI	Bund der Öffentlich Bestellten Vermessungsingenieure	**BEDA**	British Electrical Development Association
BDVT	Bund Deutscher Verkaufsforderer und Verkaufstrainer	**BEDA**	Bureau Européen des Designers Associés
		BEDEK	Israel Aircraft Industries
BDW	Bund Deutscher Werbeberater	**BEDFPU**	Brigada de Estudos da Defesa Fitossanitária dos Produtos Ultramarinos (Portugal)
BDWB	Bundesverband Deutscher Wirtschaftsberater	**BEDSE**	Bureau d'Étude et de Documentation sur la Santé des Étudiants (Italy)
BDZ	Bundesverband der Deutschen Zahnärzte		
BdZ	Bundesverband der Zigarrenindustrie	**BEE**	Bureau Européen d'Environnement
BDZV	Bundesverband Deutscher Zeitungsverleger	**BEEA**	British Educational Equipment Association
BEA	British Egg Association	**BEEP**	Bureau Européen de l'Education Populaire
BEA	British Electrical Authority (now CEA)	**BEF**	British Employees Federation
BEA	British Engineers' Association	**BEF**	British Equestrian Federation
BEA	British Epilepsy Association	**BEFMC**	British Educational Furniture Manufacturers Council
BEA	British Esperanto Association		

BEG	Brush Export Group
BEGEBI	Bureau d'Études et de Gestion des Élevages Bovines Intensifs
BEGS	British and European Geranium Society
BEHA	British Export Houses Association
BEI	Banque Européenne d'Investissement
BEIA	Bureau d'Éducation Ibéro-Américain
BEIC	Bureau Européen d'Informations Charbonnières
BEICIP	Bureau d'Études des Industrielles et de Coopération de l'Institut Français du Pétrole
BEIS	British Egg Information Service (formerly NEIS)
BEJE	Bureau Européen de la Jeunesse et de l'Enfance
BELF	Bundesministerium für Ernährung, Landwirtschaft und Forsten
BELGA	Agence Télégraphique Belge de Presse
BELRA	British Empire Leprosy Relief Association
BELVAC	Société Belge de Vacuologie et de Vacuotechnique
BEMA	British Essence Manufacturers' Association
BEMAC	British Export Marketing Advisory Committee
BEMB	British Egg Marketing Board
BEMSA	British Eastern Merchant Shippers Association
BEN	Bureau d'Études Nucléaires (Belgium)
BENA	British (Empire) Naturalists Association
BENELUX	Belgium, Netherlands, Luxembourg Union
BEO	Bureau d'Études Océanographiques
BEPA	British Egg Products Association
BEpA	British Epilepsy Association
BEPC	British Electric Power Convention
BEPI	Bureau d'Études et de Participations Industrielles (Morocco)
BEPQ	Bureau of Entomology and Plant Quarantine (U.S.A.)
BEPTOM	Bureau d'Études des Postes et Télécommunications d'Outre Mer
BERC	Basic Education Research Centre, Nairobi (Kenya)
BERCO	British Electric Resistance Company
BES	British Ecological Society
BES	British Endodontic Society
BES	Brooklyn Entomological Society (U.S.A.)
BESA	British Electrical Systems Association
BESA	British Engineering Standards Association (*now* BSI)
BESA	British Esperanto Scientific Association
BESL	British Empire Service League (Canada)
BESO	British Executive Service Overseas
BESONU	Bureau des Affaires Économiques et Sociales des Nations Unies, Beirut
BEST	Bureau d'Études de Standardisation et de Technique en Arboriculture Fruitère (*ceased*)
BET	British Electric Traction Company
BETA	Bureau for Education Technology and Administration (U.S.A.)
BETA	Business Equipment Trade Association
BETAA	British Export Trade Advertising Association
BETMA	Bureau Professionnel d'Études Techniques des Marchés Agricoles
BETRO	British Export Trade Research Organisation
BETURE	Bureau d'Études Techniques pour l'Urbanisme et l'Équipement
BEU	Benelux Economic Union
BEUC	Bureau Européen des Unions de Consommateurs
BEVA	British Equine Veterinary Association
BEVETAB	National Beroepsvereniging van Importeurs, Handelaars, Commissionairs, Makelaars en Agenten in Tabakken in Bladeren in België
BEVIA	Verband von Vieh-, Fleisch- und Fleischwarenimporteuren
BEVIFA	Vereninging der Belgische Vismeelfabrikanten
BEWAC	British West Indian Corporation
BEWEDIT	Belgische Comité voor Weverij en Diverse Textielindustrieën
BF	Banque de France
BF	Bibliotekarforeningen
BFA	British Fellmongers Association
BFA	British Film Authority
BFA	Bundestelle für Aussenhandelsinformation
BFAC	British Federation of Aesthetics and Cosmetology
BFACM	Banque Française de l'Agriculture et du Crédit Mutuel
BFAK	Bundesforschungsanstalt für Kleintierzucht
BFB	Bibliotheksforum Bayern
BFB	Bundesanstalt für Bodenforschung
BFBB	British Federation of Brass Bands

BFBN	Bond van Fabrikanten van Betonwaren in Nederland	**BFMF**	British Federation of Music Festivals
		BFMF	British Footwear Manufacturers Federation
BFBPM	British Federation of Business and Professional Women	**BFMIRA**	British Food Manufacturing Industries Research Association
BFBS	British Forces Broadcasting Service	**BFMP**	British Federation of Master Printers (*now* BPIF)
BFBS	British and Foreign Bible Society		
BFC	British Falconers' Club	**BFMSA**	British Firework Manufacturers Safety Association
BFC	Bureau International de Film pour les Chemins de Fer	**BFN**	Vereniging van Beroepsfotografen in Nederland
BFCA	British Federation of Commodity Associations	**BFPA**	British Film Producers' Association
BFCE	Banque Français du Commerce Extérieur	**BFPC**	British Farm Produce Council
BFCS	British Friesian Cattle Society	**BFPSA**	British Fire Protection Systems Association Ltd
BFE	Bedrijfsfederatie der Voortbrengers en Verdelers van Electriciteit in België	**BFQ**	Bibliotèque Fonds Quetelet (Belgium)
BFE	Bundesfachverband Edelmetallerzeugnisse und Verwandte Industrien	**BFR**	Banque Fédérative Rurale
		BFS	British Fuchsia Society
BFE	Bundesstelle für Entwicklungshilfe	**BFSA**	British Fire Services Association
BFEBS	British Far Eastern Broadcasting Service	**BFSLYC**	British Federation of Sand and Land Yacht Clubs
BFEC	British Food Export Council		
BFES	British Families Education Service	**BFSS**	British Field Sports Society
BFF	British Fishing Federation	**BFT**	Bundesverband Freier Tankstellen und Unabhängiger Deutscher Mineralölhändler
BFF	Bundesverband der Deutschen Fischindustrie und des Fischgrosshandels	**BFTA**	British Fur Trade Alliance
BFFA	British Film Fund Agency	**BFTU**	Bahamas Federation of Trade Unions
BFFC	British Federation of Folk Clubs	**BFUW**	British Federation of University Women
BFFF	British Frozen Foods Federation	**BFW**	Bread for the World (U.S.A.)
BFHMF	British Felt Hat Manufacturers Federation	**BFWA**	Bundesfachverband Wasseraufbereitung
BFI	British Film Institute	**BGA**	British Gaming Association
BFI	Verband der Schweizerischen Beutel- und Flexodruck-Industrie	**BGA**	British Gliding Association
		BGA	British Grit Association
BFIA	British Flower Industry Association	**BGA**	Bundesverband des Deutschen Gross- und Aussenhandels
BFID	Brancheforeningen af Farmaceutiske Industrivirksomheder i Danmark		
		BGA	Irish Sugar Beet Growers' Association
BFSIL	Búnadarfélag Islands	**BGB**	Booksellers Association of Great Britain and Ireland
BFISS	British Federation of Iron and Steel Stockholders		
		BGC	British Gas Council
BFJD	Bundesverband Freier Juristen Deutschlands	**BGC**	British Glues and Chemicals Ltd
BFL	Bahamas Federation of Labour	**BGCG**	British Guiana Consolidated Goldfields Ltd
BFM	British Furniture Manufacturers Federated Associations	**BGD**	Banque Gabonaise de Développement
BFMA	British Farm Mechanization Association	**BGD**	Bureau voor Gemeenschappelijke Diensten
BFMA	British Floorcovering Manufacturers Association	**BGF**	Banana Growers Federation (Australia)
		BGF	Schweizerischer Verband der Berufs- und Geschäftsfrauen
BFMA	Building Materials Factors Association		
BFMC	British Friction Materials Council	**BGGA**	British Golf Greenkeepers Association

BGGRA	British Gelatine and Glue Research Association	**BHMA**	British Herbal Medicine Association
BGH	Beroepsvereniging der Promoteurs voor Huisvesting en Ruimtelijke Ordening	**BHMEA**	British Hard Metal Export Association
BGIRA	British Glass Industry Research Association	**BHMRA**	British Hydromechanics Research Association
BGL	Bundesverband Garten- und Landschaftsbau	**BHNHE**	Bureau of Human Nutrition and Home Economics (U.S.A.)
BGMA	British Gear Manufacturers' Association	**BHPC**	British Hardware Promotion Council Ltd
BGMA	British Glucose Manufacturers Association	**BHRA**	British Hotels and Restaurants Association (*now* BHRCA)
BGN	Board on Geographic Names (U.S.A.)		
BGR	Board of Greenkeeping Research (*now* STRI)	**BHRA**	British Hydromechanics Research Association
BGRB	British Greyhound Racing Board	**BHRCA**	British Hotels, Restaurants and Caterers Association
BGRF	British Greyhound Racing Federation		
BGRG	British Geomorphological Research Group	**BHS**	British Herpetological Society
BGS	Bilgreinasambandid	**BHS**	British Horse Society
BGS	British Gladiolus Society	**BHSA**	British Heavy Steel Association
BGS	British Goat Society	**BHTA**	British Herring Trade Association
BGS	British Grassland Society	**BHV**	Bergshandteringens Vänner
BGV	Bergischer Geschichtsverein	**BI**	Befrienders International
BGW	Bundesverband der Deutschen Gas- und Wasserwirtschaft	**BIA**	Braille Institute of America
		BIA	British Institute of Acupuncture
BGWF	British Granite and Whinstone Federation	**BIA**	British Insurance Association
BGZL	Bundesverband der Rein Gewerblichen Zahntechnischen Laboratorien	**BIA**	British Ironfounders Association
		BIA	British Island Airways Ltd
BHA	British Homoeopathic Association	**BIAA**	British Industrial Advertising Association (*now* BIMA)
BHA	British Horse Association		
BHA	British Humanist Association	**BIAC**	Bioinstrumentation Advisory Council (U.S.A.) (*of* AIBS)
BHA	British Hypnotherapy Association		
BHAFRA	British Hat and Allied Feltmakers Research Association	**BIAC**	British Institute of Agricultural Consultants
		BIAC	Business and Industry Advisory Committee to OECD
BHCF	British Hire Cruiser Federation		
BHCSA	British Hospitals Contributory Schemes Association	**BIAD**	Bureau International d'Anthropologie Différentielle
BHE	Bureau of Home Economics (U.S.A.)	**BIAE**	British Institute of Adult Education
BHF	British Hardware Federation	**BIALL**	British and Irish Association of Law Librarians
BHG	Bundesverband Holzgrosshandel		
BHGA	British Hang Gliding Association	**BIAO**	Banque Internationale pour l'Afrique Occidentale
BHI	British Horological Institute		
BHI	Bureau Hydrographique International	**BIAP**	Bureau International d'Audiophonologie
BHKH	Bundesverband des Holz- und Kunstoffverarbeitenden	**BIAS**	Belgian International Air Services
		BIAS	Brooklyn Institute of Arts and Sciences (U.S.A.)
BHL	Bensinhandlernes Landsforbund		
BHL	British Housewives League	**BIATA**	British Independent Air Transport Association
BHM	Bandalag Háskólamanna		
BHMA	British Hacksaw Makers Association	**BIBA**	British Insurance Brokers' Association
BHMA	British Hard Metal Association	**BIBF**	British and Irish Basketball Federation

BIBM	Bureau International du Béton Manufacture
BIBOA	Fédération Internationale des Associations de l'Industrie, de l'Artisanat et du Commerce des Diamants, Perles, Pierres Précieuses, de Bijouterie, Orfèvrerie, Joaillerie, Horlogerie
BIBRA	British Industrial Biological Research Association
BIBW	Belgisch Instituut voor Bestuurswetenschappen
BIC	Baha'i International Community
BIC	Biodeterioration Information Centre
BIC	British Importers Confederation
BIC	Bureau International de la Chaussure et du Cuir
BIC	Bureau International du Cinéma
BIC	Bureau International des Containers
BICA	Bizonal International Control Administration
BICC	British Insulated Callender's Cables Ltd
BICC	Bureau International des Chambres de Commerce (France)
BICE	Banque Internationale pour la Coopération Économique
BICE	Bureau International Catholique de l'Enfance
BICEMA	British Internal Combustion Engine Manufacturers' Association
BICEP	British Industrial Collaborative Exponential Programme
BICERA	British Internal Combustion Engine Research Association
BICERI	British Internal Combustion Engine Research Institute
BICI	Banque Internationale pour le Commerce et l'Industrie
BICIA-HV	Banque Internationale pour le Commerce l'Industrie et de l'Agriculture de la Haute-Volta
BICI-CONGO	Banque Internationale pour le Commerce et l'Industrie- Congo
BICO	Bureau International d'Information et de Coopération des Éditeurs de Musique
BICS	Bangkok Institute for Child Study (Thailand)
BICS	Banque Industrielle et Commerciale (France)
BICS	British Institute of Cleaning Science
BICTA	British Investment Casters Technical Association
BID	Banque Interaméricaine de Développement
BIDC	Bureau Interafricain de Développement et du Coopération
BIDE	Bangladesh Institute of Development Economics
BIDE	Bureau Internationale de Documentation Éducative
BIDI	Banque Ivoirienne de Développement Industriel (Ivory Coast)
BIDIF	Bureau International de Documentation et d'Information des Festivals (France)
BIDS	Bangladesh Institute of Development Studies
BIE	British Institute of Embalmers
BIE	Bundesverband Industrieller Einkauf
BIE	Bureau International d'Éducation
BIE	Bureau International des Expositions
BIE	Bureau Ivoirien d'Engineering
BIEM	Bureau International de l'Édition Mécanique
BIEM	Bureau International des Sociétés Gérant les Droits d'Enregistrement et de Reproduction Mécanique
BIES	Bureau Interprofessionnel d'Études Statistiques Sucrières
BIET	British Institute of Engineering Technology
BIF	British Industries Fair
BIFA	British Industrial Film Association
BIFAC	British Isles Federation of Agricultural Co-operatives
BIFEDSA	Building Industries Federation, South Africa
BIFMA	British Industrial Floor Machine Association
BIFU	Banking Insurance and Finance Union
BIG	Bois Industriels du Gabon
BIG	Bund der Ingenieure des Gartenbaues
BIGA	Bundesamt für Industrie, Gewerbe und Arbeit (Switzerland)
BIH	Bureau International de l'Heure
BIHA	British Ice Hockey Association
BIHFS	British Institute of Hardwood Flooring Specialists
BIICC	Bureau International d'Information des Chambres de Commerce
BIICL	British Institute of International and Comparative Law
BIID	British Institute for Interior Design
BILA	British Insurance Law Association
BILC	Bureau for International Language Coordination

BILD	Bureau International de Liaison et de Documentation (Germany)
BIM	British Institute of Management
BIM	British Insulin Manufacturers
BIMA	British Industrial Marketing Association
BIMAS	Bimbingan Masyarakat (Indonesia)
BIMCAM	British Industrial Measuring and Control Apparatus Manufacturers' Association
BIMCO	Baltic and International Maritime Conference (Denmark)
BIML	Bureau International de Métrologie Légale (*of* OIML)
BIMR	Bureau International de Mécanique des Roches
BIMSOC	British Institute of Management Secretariat for Overseas Countries
BIN	Belgisch Instituut voor Normalisatie
BIN	Bureau of Information on Nickel
BINA	Bureau International des Normes de l'Automobile
BINAME	Biblioteca Nacional de Medicina (Uruguay)
BINC	Building Industries' National Council
BINGO	Business International Non-Governmental Organisation
BINOP	Institut National d'Étude du Travail et d'Orientation Professionnelle
BIO	Biomedical Information Processing Organisation (U.S.A.)
BIO	Bureau Interorganisations pour les Systèmes d'Information et les Activités Connexes
BIOS	British Institute of Organ Studies
BIOS	British Intelligence Objectives Sub-Committee
BIOSIS	Bio-Sciences Information Service of Biological Abstracts (U.S.A.)
BIOT	British Indian Ocean Territory
BIOTROP	Seameo Regional Center for Tropical Biology (Indonesia)
BIP	Banco Industrial del Perù
BIP	Banco Internacional de Pagos
BIP	British Industrial Plastics Ltd
BIP	Bureau Interprofessionnel du Pruneau (France) (*now* BNIP)
BIP	Union Belge des Installateurs Professionnels d'Antennes
BIPA	Bond van Importeurs van Pharmaceutische Artikelen
BIPAR	Bureau International des Producteurs d'Assurances et de Réassurances
BIPAVER	Bureau International Permanent des Associations des Vendeurs et Rechapeurs de Pneumatiques
BIPCA	Bureau International Permanent de Chimie Analytique pour les Matières Destinées à l'Alimentation de l'Homme et des Animaux
BIPE	Bureau d'Information et de Prévisions Économiques
BIPM	Bureau International des Poids et Mesures
BIPO	British Institute of Public Opinion
BIPP	British Institute of Practical Psychology
BIR	British Institute of Radiology
BIR	Bureau of Industrial Relations (U.S.A.)
BIR	Bureau International de la Récupération
BIRA	Belgisch Instituut voor Regeltechniek en Automatisatie
BIRC	British Industry Roads Campaign
BIRD	Banque Internationale pour la Reconstruction et le Développement (U.S.A.)
BIRE	British Institution of Radio Engineers
BIREME	Biblioteca Regional de Medicina (Uruguay)
BIRF	Banco Internacional de Reconstrucción y Fomento
BIRF	Brewing Industry Research Foundation (U.K.)
BIRISPT	Bureau International de Recherche sur les Implications Socials du Progrès Technique
BIRMO	British Infra-Red Manufacturers Organization
BIRPI	Bureaux Internationaux Réunis pour la Protection de la Propriété Intellectuelle
BIRS	British Institute of Recorded Sound
BIRS	Bureau International de Recherches sur la Sauvagine
BIRSH	Bureau of Information and Research on Student Health (Italy)
BIRU	Basic Ideology Research Unit (U.K.)
BIS	Bank for International Settlement (Switzerland)
BIS	British Ichthyological Society
BIS	British Information Services
BIS	British Interplanetary Society
BIS	British Iris Society
BIS	Bureau Interafricain des Sols (*now* BISER)

BIS	Bureau International du Scoutisme
BISA	Banco Industrial S.A. (Bolivia)
BISAKTA	British Iron and Steel and Kindred Trades Association
BISCOFA	Schweizerischer Verband der Biscuits- und Confiseriefabrikanten
BISEC	Board of Intermediate and Secondary Education (Pakistan)
BISER	Bureau Interafricain des Sols et de l'Économie Rurale (Central Africa)
BISF	British Iron and Steel Federation
BISFA	British Industrial and Scientific Film Association
BISFA	Bureau International pour la Standardisation des Fibres Artificielles (Switzerland)
BISI	British Iron and Steel Institute
BISITS	British Industrial and Scientific International Translation Service
BISPA	British Independent Steel Producers' Association
BISRA	British Iron and Steel Research Association
BISW	Befrienders International–Samaritans Worldwide
BIT	Bureau International du Travail (Switzerland)
BITA	British Industrial Truck Association
BITD	Bureau International des Tarifs Douaniers
BITEJ	Bureau International pour le Tourisme et les Échanges de la Jeunesse
BITS	Birla Institute of Technology and Science
BITS	Bureau International du Tourisme Social
BITU	Bustamante Industrial Trade Union (West Indies)
BIU	Bermuda Industrial Union
BIU	British Import Union (Denmark)
BIU	Bureau International des Universités
BIV	Belgisch Instituut voor Verpakking
BIW	Bund der Ingenieure des Weinbaues
BIWF	British-Israel World Federation
BIWS	Bureau of International Whaling Statistics
BIZ	Bank für Internationalen Zahlungsausgleich
BJA	British Jewellers Association
BJA	British Judo Association
BJCB	British Joint Communications Board (*now* BJCEB)
BJCC	British Junior Chambers of Commerce

BJCEB	British Joint Communications and Electronics Board
BJCG	British Joint Corrosion Group
BJSM	British Joint Services Mission (U.S.A.)
BJTRA	British Jute Trades Research Association
BJU	Bundesverband Junger Unternehmer
BKA	British Karate Association
BKEC	British Knitting Export Council
BKFA	British Kidney Fund Association
BKFA	British Kite Flyers Association
BKLF	Baker-og Konditormestrenes Landsförening
BKMV	Belgische Kamer der Medische Voetverzorgers
BKPA	British Kidney Patient Association
BKR	British Kendo Renmei
BKS	Bildende Kunstneres Styre
BKSK	Bundesverband Kunstoff- und Schwergewebekonfektion
BKSTS	British Kinematograph, Sound and Television Society
BKT	Bedrijfskadertraining
BKV	Belgische Kunststoffen Vereniging
BKVTF	Belgische Kamer van Vertalers, Tolken en Filologen
BL	British Legion
BLA	British Legal Association
BLAC	British Light Aviation Centre
BLACC	British and Latin American Chamber of Commerce
BLAISE	British Library Automated Information Service
BLASA	Bantu Library Association of South Africa
BLB	Brancheforeningen for Danske Leverandører af Butiksinventar
BLBS	Bundesverband der Lehrer an Beruflichen Schulen
BLC	British Lighting Council
BLE	Budhana Ligo Esperantista (Belgium)
BLESMA	British Limbless Ex-Servicemen's Association
BLEU	Belgisch-Luxemburgse Economische Unie
BLF	Brancheforeningen for Leverandører til Frisørstanden
BLF	British Leather Federation
BLF	British Lubricants Federation

BLFAE	Bureau de Liaison France-Afrique-Europe
BLGA	Bayerische Landesgewerbeanstalt
BLH	British Legion Headquarters
BLHA	British Linen Hire Association
BLIC	Bureau de Liaison des Industries du Caoutchouc de la Communauté Économique Européenne
BLIROL	Bureau de Liaison d'Information Religieuse pour l'Océan Indien
BLL	British Library Lending Division
BLL	Bund für Lebensmittelrecht und Lebensmittelkunde
BLMA	British Lead Manufacturers Association
BLMAS	Bible Lands Missions' Aid Society
BLMC	British Leyland Motor Corporation
BLMF	British Lawnmower Manufacturers Federation
BLMRA	British Leather Manufacturers Research Association
BLO	Bureau Landelijke Opbouw (Suriname)
BLOF	British Lace Operatives Federation
BLOWS	British Library of Wildlife Sounds
BLPES	British Library of Political and Economic Science
BLPS	British Landrace Pig Society
BLR	Bundesverband der Luftfahrtzbehör- und Raketenindustrie
BLRA	British Launderers Research Association
BLRA	British Leprosy Relief Association
BLS	Bureau of Labour Statistics (U.S.A.)
BLSGMA	British Lamp Blown Scientific Glassware Manufacturers Association
BLV	Bayerischer Landwirtschaftsverlag
BLVVG	Belgisch-Luxemburgse Vakgroep Vloeibaar Gas
BLWA	British Laboratory Ware Association
BMA	Bible Memory Association International (U.S.A.)
BMA	British Manufacturers' Association
BMA	British Medical Association
BMA	Bundesverband der Möbelgrosshändler und Austlieferungslager
BMAA	British Marine Aquarists Association
BMB	Baltic Marine Biologists (Sweden)
BMBA	British Motor Boat Association

BMBW	Bundesministerium für Bildung und Wissenschaft
BMC	Banque de Madagascar et des Comores
BMC	British Match Corporation
BMC	British Metal Corporation
BMC	British Motor Corporation (now BLMC)
BMC	British Mountaineering Council
BMCC	British Metal Castings Council
BMCD	Banque Malienne de Crédit et de Dépôts
BMCRC	British Motor Cycle Racing Club
BMDC	Biomedicinska Dokumentationscentralen
BMEC	British Marine Equipment Council
BMEF	British Mechanical Engineering Federation
BMEG	Building Materials Export Group
BMELF	Bundesministerium für Ernährung, Landwirtschaft und Forsten
BMF	British Motels Federation
BMF	British Motorcyclists Federation
BMF	Bundesverband Montagebau und Fertighäuser
BMFF	British Man-Made Fibres Federation
BMFSA	British Metal Finishing Suppliers Association
BMG	British Measures Group
BMI	Battelle Memorial Institute (U.S.A.)
BML	Föreningen Bekämpningsmedels-Leverantörer
BMLA	British Maritime Law Association
BMLF	Bundesministerium für Land- und Forstwirtschaft (Austria)
BMLS	British Matchbox Label Society
BMM	Association Benelux des Conseils en Marques et Modèles
BMMA	British Mantle Manufacturers Association
BMMMA	British Mat and Matting Manufacturers Association
BMP	Bricklayers, Masons and Plasterers International Union of America
BMP	National Council of Building Material Producers
BMPA	British Medical Pilots Association
BMPA	British Metalworking Plant Makers Association
BMPMA	British Metalworking Plant Makers Association
BMR	Bundesverband der Maschinenringe (Germany)

BMRA	British Manufacturers Representatives Association (South Africa)	**BNCD**	Banque Nationale Centrafricaine de Dépôts
BMRA	British Medical Representatives Association	**BNCI**	Banque National pour le Commerce et l'Industrie (Belgium)
BMRC	British Medical Research Council	**BNC-ICC**	British National Committee of the International Chamber of Commerce
BMS	Birmingham Metallurgical Society	**BNCM**	Bibliothèque Nationale du Conservatoire de Musique
BMS	British Mycological Society		
BMSA	British Medical Students Association	**BNCM**	British National Committee on Materials
BMSA	British Metal Sinterings Association	**BNCNDT**	British National Committee for Non-Destructive Testing
BMSE	Baltic Mercantile and Shipping Exchange		
BMSGMA	British Maize Starch and Glucose Manufacturers Association	**BNCOE**	British National Committee on Ocean Engineering
BMSMA	British Modified Starch Manufacturers Association	**BNCOR**	British National Committee for Oceanographic Research
BMSS	British Model Soldier Society	**BNCS**	British National Carnation Society
BMSSOA	British Motor and Sailing Ship Owners Association	**BNCS**	British Numerical Control Society
		BNCSAA	British National Committee on Surface Active Agents
BMTA	British Mining Tools Association		
BMTA	British Motor Trade Association	**BNCSR**	British National Committee for Scientific Radio
BMTFA	British Malleable Tube Fittings Association		
BMTI	Belgische Maatschappij van Technische Ingenieurs	**BNCWO**	Belgisch Nationaal Comité voor Wetenschappelijkes
BMV	Bundesmarktverband für Vieh und Fleisch	**BNDA**	Banque Nationale de Développement Agricole (Guinée, Ivory Coast)
BMW	Bayerische Motoren Werke		
BMWF	Bundesministerium für Wissenschaftliche Forschung	**BNDC**	Banque Nationale de Développement Congo
		BNDC	British Nuclear Design and Construction Ltd
BMWT	Vereniging van Fabrikanten van en Handelaren in Bouwmachines, Mijn- en Wegenbouwmachines en Transportmiddelen	**BNDD**	Bureau of Narcotics and Dangerous Drugs (U.S.A.)
		BNDE	National Development Bank (Brazil)
		BNDO	Bureau National des Données Océaniques
BMZ	Baumusterzentrale (Austria)	**BNDS**	Banque Nationale de Développement du Sénégal
BNA	Bond van Nederlandsche Architecten		
BNA	British Nursing Association	**BNEC**	British National Export Council (*now* BOTB)
BNA	Maatschappij tot Bevordering der Bouwkunst Bond van Nederlandsche Architecten	**BNEC**	British Nuclear Energy Council
		BNES	British Nuclear Energy Society
BNA	Bureau de la Nutrition Animale	**BNETD**	Bureau National d'Études Techniques de Développement (Ivory Coast)
BNAC	British North American Committee		
BNAE	Bureau de Normalisation de l'Aeronautique et de l'Espace	**BNF**	British Nuclear Forum
		BNF	British Nutrition Foundation, Ltd
BNatK	Bundesnotarkammer	**BNFL**	British National Fuels Ltd
BNAU	Bulgarian National Agrarian Union		
BNB	Bond van Nederlandse Bandfabrikanten	**BNFL**	British Nuclear Fuels Ltd
BNB	British National Bibliography	**BNFMF**	British Non-Ferrous Metals Federation
BNBC	British National Book Centre	**BNFMRA**	British Non-Ferrous Metals Research Association
BNCC	Banco Nacional de Crédito Cooperativo (Brazil)		
BNCC	British National Committee for Chemistry	**BNFMS**	British Bureau of Non-Ferrous Metal Statistics

BNFSA	British Non-Ferrous Smelters' Association
BNG	Bayerische Numismatische Gesellschaft
BNGA	British Nursery Goods Association
BNHPS	Belfast Natural History and Philosophical Society
BNHS	British Natural Hygiene Society
BNI	Beroepsvereniging van Nederlandse Interieurarchitekten
BNIA	Bureau National Interprofessionnel de l'Armagnac
BNIC	Bureau National Interprofessionnel du Cognac
BNICEVCP	Bureau National Interprofessionnel des Calvados et Eaux-de-Vie de Cidre et de Poire
BNIP	Bureau National Interprofessionel du Pruneau (France) (*formerly* BIP)
BNIRA	British Nautical Instrument Trade Association
BNL	Banca Nationale del Lavoro
BNL	Brookhaven National Laboratory (U.S.A.)
BNMA	British Non-wovens Manufacturers Association
BNOA	British Naturopathic and Osteopathic Association
BNOC	British National Oil Corporation
BNOC	British National Opera Company
BNOSP	Banco Nacional de Obras y Servicios Públicos (Mexico)
BNotK	Bundesnotarkammer
BNRS	British National Radio School
BNS	Bond van Nederlandsche Schilderspatroons
BNS	Bond van Nederlandse Stedebouwkundigen
BNS	British Numismatic Society
BNSA	Bethlehem Natural Science Association (U.S.A.)
BNT	Bond van Nederlandse Tuin-en Landschaps-architecten
BNTA	British Numismatic Trade Association
BNV	Belgische Natuurkundige Vereniging
BNX	British Nuclear Export Executive (*ceased*)
BOA	Bank of Alexandria (Egypt)
BOA	Boliviana de Aviación
BOA	British Olympic Association
BOA	British Optical Association
BOA	British Orthopaedic Association
BOA	British Osteopathic Association
BOAC	British Overseas Airways Corporation (*now* BAOD)
BOAD	Banque Ouest-Africaine de Développement (Togo)
BOAG	British Overseas Aid Group
BOBA	British Overseas Banks Association
BOBMA	British Oil-Burners Manufacturers' Association
BOC	British Ornithologists' Club
BOC	British Oxygen Company
BOCA	Building Officials and Code Administrators International (U.S.A.)
BOCM	British Oil and Cake Mills Ltd
BODC	Barclays Overseas Development Corporation
BODEPA	Bond van Detaillisten in de Parfumeriehandel
BOEC	British Oil Equipment Credits, Ltd
BOF	British Orienteering Federation
BOF	British Overseas Fairs Ltd
BÖG	Bund Österreichischer Gebrauchsgraphiker
BOGA	British Onion Growers Association
BOGETA	Bond van Grossiers in Electrotechnische Artikelen
BOGFEMA	British Oil and Gas Firing Equipment Manufacturers Association
BOHS	British Occupational Hygiene Society
BÖIA	Bund Österreicherischer Innenarchitekten
BOIL	British Overhead Irrigation Ltd
BOLA	Betting Office Licensees Association
BOLSA	Bank of London and South America
BOMA	British Overseas Mining Association
BONEFO	Bond van Nederlandse Fotodetailhandelaren
BÖP	Berufsverband Österreichischer Psychologen
BOP	Bureau of Operations and Programming (UNDP)
BOPR	Bureau d'Organisation des Programmes Ruraux (Congo)
BORAD	British Oxygen Research and Development Association
BORM	Bureau of Raw Materials for American Vegetable oils and Fats Industries
BOS	British Origami Society
BOS	British Orthoptic Society
BOSS	Bureau of State Security (South Africa)
BOSTID	Board on Science and Technology for International Development (U.S.A.)

BOT	Board of Trade (*now* DTI)
BOTAC	British Overseas Trade Advisory Council (*now* DTI)
BOTB	British Overseas Trade Board
BOTU	Board of Trade Unit
BOU	British Ornithologists' Union
BOV	Belgische Ornithologische Vereniging
BOVA	Nederlandse Bond van Varkenshandelaren
BOVAG	Bond van Automobiel-, Garage- en Aanwerwante Bedrijven
BOVAK	Bond van Kermisbedrijfhouders
BOVAL	Bond van Agrarische Loonbedrijven in Nederland
BOVEE	Nederlandse Bond voor Veehandelaren
BOWI-SPORT	Bond van Winkeliers in Sportartikelen
BPA	Berufsverband der Praktischen Ärzte und Ärzte für Allgemeinmedizin Deutschlands
BPA	Biological Photographic Association (U.S.A.)
BPA	British Paediatric Association
BPA	British Parachute Association Ltd
BPA	British Philatelic Association
BPA	British Ploughing Association
BPA	British Pyrotechnists' Association
BPAA	British Poster Advertising Association
BPAO	Société des Pétroles BP d'Afrique Occidentale
BPAS	British Pregnancy Advisory Service
BPBF	British Paper Box Federation
BPBHA	British Poultry Breeders and Hatcheries Association
BPBIF	British Paper and Board Industry Federation
BPBIRA	British Paper and Board Industry Research Association (*now* PIRA)
BPBMA	British Paper and Board Makers' Association
BPC	Black Peoples Convention
BPC	British Productivity Council
BPCA	British Pest Control Association
BPCA	British Pro-chiropractic Association
BPCF	British Postal Chess Federation
BPCF	British Precast Concrete Federation
BPCRA	British Professional Cycle Racing Association
BPE	Bedrijfschap voor Pluimvee en Eieren
BPEAR	Bureau for the Placement and Education of African Refugees (*of* OAU)
BPEEA	British Postal Equipment Engineering Association
BPEG	British Photographic Export Group
BPF	Borst-och Penselfabrikantföreningen
BPF	British Plastics Federation
BPF	British Poultry Federation
BPF	British Polio Fellowship
BPF	British Property Federation
BPGMA	British Pressure Gauge Manufacturers Association
BPGS	British Pelargonium and Geranium Society
BPHS	British Percheron Horse Society
BPHS	British Polled Hereford Society
BPI	Belgisch Petroleum- Instituut
BPI	British Phonographic Industry
BPIA	British Photographic Importers Association
BPICA	Bureau Permanent International des Constructeurs d'Automobiles
BPICM	Bureau Permanent International des Constructeurs de Motorcyles (France)
BPICS	British Production and Inventory Control Society
BPIF	British Printing Industries Federation
BPITT	Bureau Permanent International de la Tsétsé et de la Trypanosomiase
BPL	Bedrijfspensioenfonds voor de Landbouw
BPL	British Physical Laboratories Ltd
BPL	Bundesverband Personal- Leasing
BPMA	British Photographic Manufacturers Association
BPMA	British Poultry Meat Association
BPMA	British Premium Manufacturers Association
BPMA	British Printing Machinery Association
BPMA	British Pump Manufacturers' Association
BPMF	British Postgraduate Medical Federation
BPMF	British Pottery Manufacturers Federation (*now* BCMF)
BPMMA	British Paper Machinery Makers Association
BPMTG	British Puppet and Model Theatre Guild
BPNMA	British Plain Net Manufacturers Association
BPO	Union Tarifaire Balkan Proche- Orient (Bulgaria)
BPOC	British Post Office Corporation

BPPB	Balai Penjelidikan Perkebunan Besar (Indonesia)	**BRANZ**	Building Research Association of New Zealand
BPPB	Banque de Paris et Pays-Bas	**BRASTACS**	Bradford Scientific, Technical and Commercial Service
BPPMA	British Power-Press Manufacturers' Association	**BRB**	British Railways Board
BPPPG	Balai Penjelidikan Perusahaan Gula (Indonesia)	**BRC**	British Rabbit Council
		BRC	British Record Centre
BPRA	British Book Publishers' Representatives' Association	**BRCA**	British Roller Canary Association
BPRI	British Polarographic Research Institute	**BRCMA**	British Radio Cabinet Manufacturers Association
BPS	British Paper Stock Merchants Association, Ltd	**BRCS**	British Railways Catering Service
		BRCS	British Red Cross Society
BPS	British Pharmacological Society	**BRDA**	British Racing Drivers Association
BPS	British Photobiology Society	**BRDB**	British Rubber Development Board
BPS	British Phrenological Society	**BRDC**	British Racing Drivers' Club
BPS	British Postmark Society	**BRDC**	British Research and Development Corporation
BPS	British Printing Society		
BPS	British Psychological Society	**BRDG**	Bituminous Development Group
BPSA	British Pharmaceutical Students Association	**BRE**	Building Research Establishment
BpT	Bundesverband Praktischer Tierärzte	**BREDA**	Bureau Régional pour l'Éducation en Afrique (*of* UNESCO)
BPV	Buitenlandse Persvereniging in Nederland		
BQSF	British Quarrying and Slag Federation	**BREE-DANIA**	Export Board for Breeding Cattle (Denmark)
BR	Betongvaruindustrins Riksförbund		
BRA	Bee Research Association	**BREG**	British Rivet Export Group
BRA	Beef Research Association (*now* MLC)	**BREMA**	British Radio Equipment Manufacturers Association
BRA	British Radiesthesia Association		
BRA	British Records Association	**BRF**	Brewing Research Foundation
BRA	British Refrigeration Association (*now* BRACA)	**BRF**	British Road Federation
		BRFA	British-Romanian Friendship Association
BRA	British Resorts Association	**BRFFI**	Biochemical Research Foundation of the Franklin Institute (U.S.A.)
BRA	British Rheumatic Association		
BRA	British Rivet Association	**BRGM**	Bureau de Recherches Géologiques et Minières
BRAB	Building Research Advisory Board, National Research Council (U.S.A.)		
		BRI	Banque des Règlements Internationaux
BRACA	British Refrigeration and Air Conditioning Association	**BRIC**	Bloodstock and Racehorse Industries Confederation
BRACODI	Société des Brasseries de la Côte- d'Ivoire	**BRICERAM**	Société Centrafricaine de Briques et Céramiques
BRAEC	Bureau de Recherche et d'Action Économiques	**BRIMAFEX**	British Manufacturers of Malleable Tube Fittings Export Group
BRAK	Bundesrechtsanwaltskammer	**BRIMEC**	British Mechanical Engineering Confederation
BRALUP	Bureau of Resource Assessment and Land Use Planning (Tanzania)		
		BRINCO	British Newfoundland Development Corporation
BRAMA	British Rubber and Resin Adhesive Manufacturers Association		
		BRINEX	British Newfoundland Exploration
BRANIGER	Brasseries et Boissons Gazeuses du Niger	**BritIRE**	British Institution of Radio Engineers

BRL	Butterwick Research Laboratories	**BSA**	Bund Schweizer Architekten
BRMA	British Resin Manufacturers Association	**BSAA**	British School of Archaeology at Athens
BRMA	British Rubber Manufacturers Association	**BSAA**	British South American Airways Corporation (BOAC)
BRMA	Bureau de Recherches Minières de l'Algérie	**BSAC**	British Society of Antimicrobial Chemotherapy
BRMCA	British Ready Mixed Concrete Association		
BRMF	British Rainwear Manufacturers Federation	**BSAC**	British Sub-Aqua Club
BRP	Bureau de Recherches de Pétrole	**BSAF**	Berufsverband der Schweizer Augenoptiker mit Höherer Fachschulausbildung
BRPF	Bertrand Russell Peace Foundation		
BRPM	Bureau de Recherches et de Participations Minières (Morocco)	**BSAF**	British Sulphate of Ammonia Federation
		BSALS	British Society of Agricultural Labour Science
BRPRA	British Rubber Producers Research Association		
		BSANZ	Bibliographical Society of Australia and New Zealand
BRRA	British Rayon Research Association		
BRRA	British Refractories Research Association	**BSAP**	British Association of Animal Production
BRRAMA	British Rubber and Resin Adhesive Manufacturers' Association	**BSATA**	Ballast, Sand and Allied Trades Association
		BSAVA	British Small Animal Veterinary Association
BRRI	Bangladesh Rice Research Institute	**BSB**	Bangladesh Shilpa Bank
BRRI	Building and Road Research Institute (Ghana)	**BSB**	British Sugar Bureau
BRS	British Record Society	**BSBA**	British Starter Battery Association
BRS	Building Research Station	**BSBC**	British Social Biology Council
BRS	Burma Research Society	**BSBI**	Botanical Society of the British Isles
BRSCC	British Racing and Sports Car Club	**BSBSPA**	British Sugar Beet Seed Producers Association
BRTA	British Racing Toboggan Association		
BRTA	British Regional Television Association	**BSC**	Bibliographical Society of Canada
BRTA	British Reinforcement Textiles Association	**BSC**	Biological Stain Commission (U.S.A.)
BRTA	British Road Tar Association	**BSC**	British Safety Council
BRTDC	British Recorded Tape Development Committee	**BSC**	British Shippers Council
		BSC	British Shoe Corporation
BRTS	British Roll Turners Trade Society	**BSC**	British Society of Commerce
BRU	Bilharzia Research Unit (South Africa)	**BSC**	British Steel Corporation
BRUFMA	British Rigid Urethane Foam Manufacturers Association	**BSC**	British Sugar Corporation
		BSC	British Sulphur Corporation
BRVMA	British Radio Valve Manufacturers Association	**BSCA**	British Sulphate of Copper Association (Export) Ltd
BS	Bekloedningsindustriens Sammensluting	**BSCA**	Bureau of Security and Consular Affairs (U.S.A.)
BS	Biometric Society (U.S.A.)		
BSA	Bibliographical Society of America	**BSCC**	British Society for Clinical Cytology
BSA	Birmingham Small Arms Co.	**BSCC**	British Steelmakers Creep Committee
BSA	British Shipbreakers Association	**BSCC**	British Swedish Chamber of Commerce in Sweden
BSA	British Society of Aesthetics		
BSA	British Society of Audiology	**BSCC**	British-Swiss Chamber of Commerce in Switzerland
BSA	British Sociological Association		
BSA	British Speleological Association	**BSCC**	British Synchronous Clock Conference
BSA	Building Societies Association	**BSCD**	British Ski Club Disabled

BSCP	Biological Sciences Communication Project (U.S.A.)	**BSIRA**	British Scientific Instrument Research Association (*now* SIRA)
BSCRA	British Steel Castings Research Association (*now* SCRATA)	**BSIU**	British Society for International Understanding
BSCS	Biological Sciences Curriculum Study (U.S.A.)	**BSJA**	British Schools Judo Association
BSD	British Society of Dowsers	**BSJA**	British Show Jumping Association
BSDA	British Spinners and Doublers Association	**BSK**	Berghof Stiftung für Konfliktforschung
BSDB	British Society for Developmental Biology	**BSL**	Botanical Society of London
BSDE	British Society of Digestive Endoscopy	**BSL**	Bundesverband Spedition und Lageri
BSE	British Shipbuilding Exports	**BSMA**	British Secondary Metals Association
BSEA	British Steel Export Association	**BSMA**	British Skate Makers Association
BSEM	British Society of Electronic Music	**BSMGP**	British Society of Master Glass Painters
BSES	British Schools Exploring Society	**BSMMA**	British Sugar Machinery Manufacturers Association
BSF	British Shipping Federation (*now* GCBS)	**BSMSP**	Bernoulli Society for Mathematical Statistics and Probability
BSF	British Slag Federation		
BSF	British Society of Flavourists	**BSNDT**	British Society for Non-Destructive Testing
BSF	British Softball Federation	**BSOEA**	British Stationery and Office Equipment Association
BSF	British Stone Federation		
BSFA	British Sanitary Fireclay Association	**BSOPF**	British Stationery and Office Products Federation
BSFA	British Science Fiction Association		
BSFA	British Steel Founders Association	**BSP**	British Society of Phenomenology
BSFS	British Soviet Friendship Society	**BSP**	Bureau Sanitaire Panaméricain
BSFW	Bureau of Sport Fisheries and Wildlife (U.S.A.)	**BSPA**	Basic Slag Producers Association
		BSPA	British Speedway Promoters Association
BSG	British Society of Gastroenterology	**BSPA**	British Sports Photographers Association
BSG	Bund Schweizerischer Garten- und Landschafts-architekten	**BSPG**	Binnenschiffahrts-Berufsgenossenschaft
		BSPMA	British Sewage Plant Manufacturers Association
BSH	British Society of Haematology		
BSH	British Society of Hypnotherapists	**BSPP**	Burmese Socialist Program Party
BSHP	British Society of the History of Pharmacy	**BSPS**	British Show Pony Society
BSHS	British Society for the History of Science	**BSPS**	British Society for the Philosophy of Science
BSI	British Societies Institute	**BSR**	Bund Schweizerischer Reklameberater und Werbeagenturen
BSI	British Society for Immunology		
BSI	British Standards Institution	**BSRA**	British Ship Research Association
BSIA	British Security Industry Association Ltd	**BSRA**	British Society for Research on Ageing
BSIB	Boy Scouts International Bureau	**BSRA**	British Sound Recording Association
BSIB	British Society for International Bibliography (*now* ASLIB)	**BSRA**	British Sugar Refiners' Association
		BSRAE	British Society for Research in Agricultural Engineering
BSIC	British Ski Instruction Council		
BSIHE	British Society for International Health Education (*now* SHE)	**BSRC**	British Sporting Rifle Club
		BSRD	British Society of Restorative Dentistry
BSIP	Birbal Sahni Institute of Palaeobotany (India)	**BSRI**	Brewing Scientific Research Institute (Japan)
BSIR	Board for Scientific and Industrial Research (Israel)	**BSRIA**	Building Services Research and Information Association

BSS	Berufsverband der Sozialarbeiter	**BTCMPI**	British Technical Council of the Motor and Petroleum Industries
BSS	British Sailors Society	**BTCS**	British Transport Catering Service
BSS	British Sheep Society	**BTCV**	British Trust for Conservation Volunteers
BSSM	British Society for Strain Measurement	**BTD**	Banque Togolaise de Développement
BSSBG	British Society for Social and Behavioural Gerontology	**BTDB**	British Transport Docks Board
BSSG	British Society of Scientific Glassblowers	**BTDR**	Banque Tanzanienne de Développement Rural
BSSMS	British Society for the Study of Mental Subnormality	**BTE**	Böripari Tudományos Egyesület
BSSO	British Society for the Study of Orthodontics	**BTE**	Bundesverband des Deutschen Textil-Einzelhandels
BSSPD	British Society for the Study of Prosthetic Dentistry	**BTEA**	British Textile Employers Association
BSSR	Bureau of Social Science Research	**BTEMA**	British Tanning Extract Manufacturers Association
BSSRS	British Society for Social Responsibility in Science	**BTF**	British Tarpaviors Federation Ltd
BSSS	British Society of Soil Science	**BTF**	British Trampoline Federation
BSSSA	British Surgical Support Suppliers Association	**BTF**	British Trawlers Federation (*now* BFF)
		BTF	British Turkey Federation
BSSSC	Baltic Sea Salmon Standing Committee	**BTF**	Bundesverband Freier Tankstellen und Unabhängiger Deutscher Mineralölhändler
BST	Byggstandardiseringen	
BSTA	British Surgical Trades Association	**BTG**	British Toymakers' Guild
BStBK	Bundessteuerberaterkammer	**BTG**	Bundesverband des Deutschen Tankstellen und Garagengewerbes
BSTC	British Student Travel Centre	
BSTF	British Student Tuberculosis Foundation	**BTGV**	Belgische Technische Gieterijvereniging
BSW	Botanical Society of Washington (U.S.A.)	**BTH**	British Thomson-Houston Company Ltd
BSWB	Boy Scouts World Bureau (*now* WSB)	**BTHA**	British Travel and Holidays Association (*now* BTA)
BSWIA	British Steel Wire Industries Association	
BTA	Billiards Trade Association	**BTI**	Bundesverband der Tabakwaren- Importeure
BTA	Blood Transfusion Association (U.S.A.)	**BTIA**	British Tape Industry Association
BTA	British Tourist Authority (*formerly* British Travel Association)	**BTIA**	British Tar Industry Association
		BTIPR	Boyce Thompson Institute for Plant Research (U.S.A.)
BTA	British Trade Association of New Zealand	**BTL**	Bell Telephone Laboratories (U.S.A.)
BTA	British Tugowners Association	**BTMA**	British Textile Machinery Association
BTAO	Bureau of Technical Assistance Operations (UNO)	**BTMA**	British Theatre Museum Association
		BTMA	British Toy Manufacturers Association
BTASA	Book Trade Association of South Africa	**BTMA**	British Typewriter Manufacturers' Association
BTBA	British Tenpin Bowling Association	
BTBA	British Twinning and Bilingual Association	**BTN**	Bydogoskie Towarzystwo Naukowe
BTBMF	British Tin Box Manufacturers Association	**BTO**	Boeren-en Tuinders Onderlinge
BTC	British Textile Confederation	**BTO**	British Trust for Ornithology
BTC	British Transport Commission	**BTO**	Brussels Trade Organization (Belgium)
BTCC	Board of Transportation Commissioners of Canada	**BTOF**	Federation of British Trawler Officers
		BTOG	British Transport Officers Guild
BTCD	Banque Tchadienne de Crédit et de Dépôts	**BTPS**	Bâtiments et Travaux Publics Sénégalaise

BTR	British Telecommunications Research Ltd	**BVA**	British Radio Valve Manufacturers Association
BTRA	Bombay Textile Research Association (India)		
BTS	British Temperance Society	**BVA**	British Veterinary Association
BTS	British Transplantation Society	**BVA**	British Vigilance Association
BTS	British Trolleybus Society	**BVAB**	Bedrijfsvereniging voor het Agrarisch Bedrijf
BTS	Burma Translation Society	**BVB**	Belgische Vereniging der Banken
BTSA	British Tensional Strapping Association	**BVB**	Belgische Vereniging voor de Bedrijfspers
BTTA	British Thoracic and Tuberculosis Association	**BVB**	Beroepsvereniging voor Binnenhuisarchitekten
BTUC	Bahamas Trade Union Congress	**BvB**	Bond van Bontbedrijven
BU	British Union of Great Britain and Ireland	**BVB**	Bundesverband des Bodenlegerhandwerks
BUA	British United Airways	**BVB**	Bundesverband der Büromaschinen-Importeure
BUAF	British United Air Ferries		
BUAS	British Universities Association of Slavists	**BVD**	Belgische Vereniging der Detectives
BUAV	British Union for the Abolition of Vivisection	**BVD**	Belgische Vereniging voor Dokumentatie
BUFC	British Universities Film Council	**BVDB**	Börsenverein des Deutscher Büchhandels
BUFO	British Union of Family Organisations	**BVDL**	Bundesverband Deutscher Leibeserzieher
BUFOFI	Bundesforschung für Fischerie	**BVEM**	Belgische Vereniging voor Elektronen-Mikroskopie
BUFORA	British Unidentified Flying Objects Research Association	**BVFA**	Bundesverband Feuerlöschgeräte und Anlagen-Industrie
BUIC	Bureau Universitaire d'Information sur les Carrières	**BVG**	Nederlandse Bond voor het Glasbewerkings-, Glazeniers- en Glas-in Loodbedrijf
BUIRA	British Universities Industrial Relations Association	**BVG**	Svenska Byggvarugrossistföreningen
BUMICO	Bureau Minier Congolais	**BVI**	Bundesverband Deutscher Investment-Gesellschaften
BUNAC	British Universities North American Club	**BVK**	Bond van Kleermakerspatroons in Nederland
BUOC	British Union Oil Company	**BVK**	Bundesverband Deutscher Versicherungs-kaufleute
BUP	British United Press		
BUPA	British United Provident Association	**BVL**	Bergverkenes Landssammenslutning
BURISA	British Urban and Regional Information Systems Association	**BVLJ**	Belgische Vereniging van Landbouw-journalisten
BURO	Bureau Universitaire de Recherche Operationnelle (France)	**BVLT**	Belgische Vereniging van Laboratorium-technologen
BUS	Bureau Universitaire de Statistique et de Documentation Scolaire et Professionnelle	**BVM**	Bundesverband Deutscher Marktforscher
		BVMA	British Valve Manufacturers' Association
BUSA	British Universities Society of Arts	**BVMB**	Bundesvereinigung Mittelständischer Bau-unternehmunger
BUSDOM	Bureau Shell d'Outre-Mer		
BUSF	British Universities' Sports Federation	**BVÖ**	Berufsverband Bildender Künstler Österreichs
BUSTA	British Universities Student Travel Association	**BVÖ**	Bergmännischer Verband Österreichs
BUTYRA	Centrale Suisse de Ravitaillement en Beurre	**BVÖ**	Technisch-Wissenschaftlicher Verein 'Berg-männischer Verband Österreichs'
BUVOHA	Vereningen Bureau voor Handelsinlichtingen		
BV	Betonvereniging	**BVOP**	Belgisch-Luxemburgse Vereniging van de Ondernemingspers
BVA	Berufsverband der Augenärzte Deutschlands		
BVA	Bond van Adverteerders	**BvP**	Bond van Platenhandelaren

BVP	British Volunteer Programme
BVPA	Bundesverband der Pressebild-Agenturen, Bilderdienste und Bildarchive
BvPA	Bundesverband der Pressedienste und -agenturen
BVPG	Belgische Vakgroep voor Petroleumgassen
BVR	Belgische Vereniging van de Rubberindustrie
BVS	Bundesverband Öffenlich Bestellter und Vereidigter Sachverständiger
BVSM	Belgische Vereniging tot Studie, Beproefing en Gebruik der Materialen
BVTA	Bundesarbeitsgemeinschaft der Vereinigungen der Teer- und Asphalt-makadamherstellenden Firmen
BVUIH	Belgisch Vereniging van Uit- en Invoerhan-delaars
BVV	Belgische Vereniging voor Verlamden
BVVB	Belgische Vereniging der Voedingsbedrijven met Bijhuizen
BVVK	Beroepsvereniging der Vis Groothandelaars-Verzenders van de Kust
BVVO	Beroepsvereniging Verzekerings-ondernemingen
BVZ	Belgische Vereniging der Ziekenhuizen
BWA	Baptist World Alliance
BWA	British Waterfowl Association
BWA	British Waterworks Association
BWB	British Waterways Board
BWC	Baltic World Conference (U.S.A.)
BWCC	British Weed Control Council
BWCMG	British Watch and Clock Makers Guild
BWETPA	British Water and Effluent Treatment Plant Association
BWF	Belgische Wegenfederatie
BWF	British Whiting Federation
BWF	British Wool Federation
BWG	Braunschweigische Wissenschaftliche Gesellschaft
BWIA	British West Indies Airways
BWISA	British West Indies Sugar Association
BWK	Bund der Wasser- und Kulturbauingenieure
BWMA	British Woodwork Manufacturers' Association
BWMB	British Wool Marketing Board
BWPA	British Waste Paper Association
BWPA	British Women Pilots' Association

BWPA	British Wood Preserving Association
BWPA	British Wood Pulp Association
BWPUC	British Waste Paper Utilization Council
BWRA	British Welding Research Association
BWRE	Biological Warfare Research Establishment
BWRRA	British Wire Rod Rollers' Association
BWS	British Water Colour Society
BWSF	British Water Ski Federation
BWSTMA	British Welded Steel Tube Manufacturers Association
BWTA	British Women's Temperance Association
BWTA	British Wood Turners Association
BWV	Bundesverband Werkverkehr und Verlader
BWVS	Bundeswirtschaftsvereinigung Sport-schiffahrt
BWWA	British Waterworks Association
BYBA	British Youth Band Association
BYNA	British Young Naturalists Association
BZ	Bedrijfschap voor Zuivel (Dairy Produce Corporation) (Netherlands)
BZB	Verband der Deutschen Bauzubehörindustrie

C

CA	Chambre d'Agriculture (France)
CAA	Canadian Authors' Association
CAA	Caribbean Archives Association
CAA	Catholic Art Association (U.S.A.)
CAA	Central African Airways
CAA	Centro Azucarero Argentino
CAA	Christian Adventure Association
CAA	Civil Aeronautics Administration (U.S.A.)
CAA	Civil Aviation Authority
CAA	Collectors of American Art (U.S.A.)
CAA	Commonwealth Association of Architects (U.K.)
CAA	Community Aid Abroad (Australia)
CAA	Conseil Africain de l'Arachide
CAA	Cost Accountants' Association
CAAA	Canadian Association of Advertising Agencies

CAAB	Canadian Advertising Advisory Board	**CABMA**	Canadian Association of British Manufacturers and Agencies
CAABU	Council for the Advancement of Arab-British Understanding	**CABO**	Council of American Building Officials
CAAC	Civil Aviation Administration of China	**CABRA**	Copper and Brass Research Association (U.S.A.)
CAACTD	Comité Asesor sobre la Aplicación de la Ciencia y la Tecnologia al Desarrollo (*of* UNO)	**CAC**	Canterbury Agricultural College, Lincoln (N.Z.)
CAAE	Canadian Association for Adult Education	**CAC**	Colonial Advisory Council
CAAEO	Commission des Affaires d'Aise et d'Extrême-Orient de la Chambre de Commerce Internationale	**CAC**	Comité Administratif de Coordination (ECOSOC)
		CAC	Consumers Advisory Council (U.S.A.)
CAAIM	Coopérative Agricole d'Approvisionnement des Agriculteurs de le Marche	**CAC**	Consumers Association of Canada
CAAK	Civil Aviation Administration of Korea	**CACA**	Canadian Agricultural Chemicals Association
CAANS	Canadian Association for the Advancement of Netherlandic Studies	**CACA**	Cement and Concrete Association
		CACAS	Civil Aviation Council of the Arab States
CAARC	Commonwealth Advisory Aeronautical Research Council	**CACC**	Civil Aviation Communications Centre
CAARM	Confederación de Asociaciones Algodoneras de la República Mexicana	**CACCI**	Confederation of Asian Chambers of Commerce and Industry (Philippines)
CAAS	Canadian Association of African Studies	**CACDS**	Commonwealth Advisory Committee on Defence Science
CAAS	Canadian Association for American Studies	**CACE**	Central Advisory Council for Education
CAAS	Ceylon Association for the Advancement of Science	**CACEF**	Centre d'Action Culturelle de la Communauté d'Expression Française
CAASA	Centre Africain d'Application de Statistique Agricole (of FAO) (Nigeria)	**CACEP**	Société Camerounaise de Commercialisation et d'Exportation de Produits
CAAV	Central Association of Agricultural Valuers	**CACEPA**	Centre d'Actions Concertées des Entreprises de Produits Alimentaire
CAAV	Civil Aviation Administration of Vietnam	**CACEX**	Carteira de Comercio Exterior (Brazil)
CAB	Canadian Association of Broadcasters	**CACI**	Catholic Alumni Clubs International (U.S.A.)
CAB	Citizens Advice Bureau	**CACI**	Civil Aviation Chaplains International
CAB	Civil Aeronautics Board (U.S.A.)	**CACIA**	Compagnie d'Agriculture de Commerce et d'Industrie d'Afrique (Guinée)
CAB	Comité des Assurers Belges		
CAB	Commonwealth Agricultural Bureaux (*formerly* IAB)	**CACIP**	Central American Co-operative Corn Improvement Project
CAB	Compagnie Africaine des Bois (Ivory Coast)	**CACIP**	Confederación Argentina de Comercio de la Industria y de la Producción
CABA	Connecticut Artificial Breeding Association (U.S.A.)	**CACIRA**	Chambre Syndicale des Constructeurs d'Appareils de Contrôle Industriel et de Régulation Automatique
CABEI	Central American Bank for Economic Integration		
CABEI	Intergovernmental Committee on the River Plate Basin (Uruguay)	**CACJ**	Comité de Asuntos Constitucionales y Jurídicos (FAO)
CABET	Canadian Association of Business Education Teachers	**CACL**	Canadian Association of Children's Libraries
CABIN	Campaign Against Building Industry Nationalization	**CACM**	Central American Common Market
		CACMI	Comité Africain pour la Coordination des Moyens d'Information
CABM	Commonwealth of Australia Bureau of Meteorology	**CACOM**	Central American Common Market

CACP	Chambre des Agences-Conseils en Publicité (Belgium)	**CAEES**	Centre Algérien d'Expansion Économique et Social
CACR	Council for Agricultural and Chemurgic Research (U.S.A.)	**CAEF**	Comité des Associations Européennes de Fonderie
CACRMA	Caisse Autonome Centrale de Retraites Mutuelles Agricoles	**CAEI**	Compagnie Africaine d'Équipement Industriel (Ivory Coast)
CACTAL	Conference on the Application of Science and Technology to Latin America	**CAEJ**	Communauté des Associations d'Éditeurs de Journaux de la CEE
CACTM	Central Advisory Council of Training for the Ministry	**CAEM**	Campo Agrícola Experimental de Mexicali
CACUL	Canadian Society of College and University Libraries	**CAEM**	Conseil d'Assistance Économique Mutuelle (U.S.S.R.)
CAD	Centralforeningen af Autoreparatører i Danmark	**CAEMC**	Comité d'Associations Européennes de Médecins Catholiques
CAD	Comité Agricole Départmental	**CAEND**	Centro Argentino de Ensayo no Destructivos de Materiales (Argentine)
CAD	Comité d'Aide au Développement *of* OCDE	**CAEPC**	Comisión Asesora Europea sobre Pesca Continental
CADA	Campaign Against Drug Addiction		
CADAFE	Compania Anonima de Administración y Fomento Eléctrico (Venezuela)	**CAEPE**	Centre d'Assemblage et d'Essais des Propulseurs et des Engins
CADAL	Compagnie Africaine Forestière et des Allumettes	**CAES**	Canadian Agricultural Economics Society
CADAUMA	Coopérative Agricole d'Achat et d'Utilisation de Matériel Agricole de l'Aveyron	**CAES**	Central Association of Experiment Stations (Indonesia)
CADEB	Confederación Americana de Empleados Bancarios	**CAES**	Chiba Prefecture Agricultural Experiment Station (Japan)
CADEC	Christian Action for Development in the Caribbean (Antigua)	**CAESPCI**	Central Association of Experimental Stations for Perennial Crops in Indonesia
CADEF	Centro Argentino de Estudios Forestales	**CAEU**	Council of Arab Economic Unity
CADER	Consejo Argentino de Estudios sobre la Reproducción	**CAEVR**	Comité d'Action École et Vie Rurale
CADES	Centro Argentino de Estudios Sociológicos	**CAF**	Central African Federation
CADIA	Centro Argentino de Ingenieros Agrónomos	**CAF**	Comptoir Agricole Français
CADICEC	Association des Cadres et Dirigeants Chrétiens des Entreprises au Congo et au Rwanda-Burundi	**CAF**	Confédération Africaine de Football
		CAF	Conseil de l'Agriculture Française
CADIF	Cámara Argentina de la Industria Frigorífica	**CAF**	Corporación Andina de Fomento (Colombia)
CADIPPE	Comité d'Action pour le Développement de l'Interessement du Personnel à la Productivité des Entreprises	**CAFA**	Chambre Agricole Franco-Allemande
		CAFAC	Commission Africaine de l'Aviation Civile
CADO	Central Air Documents Office (U.S.A.)	**CAFADE**	Comisión Nacional Administración del Fondo de Apoyo al Desarrollo Económico (Argentina)
CADU	Chilalo Agricultural Development Unit (Ethiopia)		
CAE	Compagnie Européenne d'Automatisme Électronique	**CAFAL**	Compagnie Africaine Forestière et des Allumettes
CAEA	Central American Economics Association	**CAFC**	Compagnie Agricole et Forestière du Cameroun
CAEC	Committee of the Acta Endocrinologica Countries	**CAFCO**	Caisse d'Allocations Familiales des Sociétés Coopératives de Consommation et de Production de la Suisse Romande
CAEC	County Agricultural Executive Committee	**CAFCO**	Compagnie Africaine de Commerce et de Commission

CAFE	Compañia Americana de Fomento Económico
CAFEA-ICC	Commission on Asian and Far Eastern Affairs of the International Chamber of Commerce
CAFESA	Compañía Costarricense del Café
CAFI	Commercial Advisory Foundation in Indonesia
CAFIC	Combined Allied Forces Information Centre
CAFMNA	Compound Animal Feedingstuffs Manufacturers National Association
CAFMS	Central American Federation of Medical Students
CAFOD	Catholic Fund for Overseas Development
CAFPTA	Comisión Aministradora del Fondo para la Promoción de la Tecnología Agropecuaria (Argentina)
CAFRAD	Centre Africain de Formation et de Recherches Administratives pour le Développement (Morocco)
CAFTA	Central American Free Trade Association
CAFTA	Comisión Administradora para el Fondo de Tecnologia Agropecuaria (Argentina)
CAFTEX	Compagnie Africaine de Textile (Ivory Coast)
CAFUM	Companhia de Fumigaçoes de Moçambique
CAG	Canadian Association of Geographers
CAG	Comparative Administrative Group of the American Society for Public Administration
CAGAC	Civil Aviation General Administration of China
CAH	Compagnie Africaine d'Hôtellerie (Congo)
CAHN	Cooperative Agricole Haute Normand
CAI	Canadian Aeronautical Institute
CAI	Club Alpino Italiano
CAI	Consumers Association of Ireland
CAIA	Céntro Argentine de Ingeniéros Agrónomos
CAIA	Congreso Argentino de la Industria Aceitera
CAIC	Caribbean Association of Industry and Commerce
CAIC	Compagnie d'Agriculture d'Industrie et de Commerce (Madagascar)
CAIFOM	Caisse de la France d'Outre-Mer
CAIM	Compagnie Agricole et Industrielle de Madagascar
CAIM	Syndicat National des Créateurs d'Architectes Intérieures et de Modèles
CAIMO	Comité Asesor de Investigaciones Meteorólogicas Oceánicas (*of* WMO)
CAIR	Comité d'Action Interallié de la Résistance
CAIRM	Comité Asesor sobre Investigaciones de los Recursos Marinos (*of* FAO)
CAIRU	Colonial Agricultural Insecticides Research Unit
CAIS	Canadian Association for Information Science
CAIS	Central American Integration Scheme
CAITA	Compagnie Agricole et Industrielle des Tabacs Africains
CAJ	Internationale Christliche Arbeiterjugend
CAJP	Clubes Agricolas Juveniles del Perú
CAL	Centro di Azione Latina
CAL	China Airlines Ltd
CAL	Cocoa Association of London
CALA	Christiana Area Land Authority (West Indies)
CALANS	Caribbean and Latin American News Service
CALB	Confédération Africano-Levantine de Billard
CALCOFI	California Cooperative Oceanic Fisheries Investigations (U.S.A.)
CALG	Compagnie des Landes de Gascogne
CALL	Canadian Association of Law Libraries
CALNU	Cooperativa Agropecuaria Limitada Norte Uruguayo
CALO	Coopérative Agricole Lainière de l'Ouest
CALPA	Canadian Air Line Pilots Association
CALQ	Centro Académico "Luiz de Queiróz" (Brazil)
CALS	Canadian Association of Library Schools
CAM	Cercle Archaeologique de Mons
CAM	Commission for Agricultural Meteorology (WMO)
CAM	Committee for Aquatic Microbiology (U.N.)
CAM	Commonwealth Association of Museums
CAMAA	Comptoir Africain de Matériel Abidjan (Ivory Coast)
CAMACOL	Cámara Colombiana de la Construcción
CAMAD	Société Camerounaise de Produits Alimentaires et Diététiques
CAMAG	Société Camerounaise de Grands Magasins
CAMARCA	Caisse Mutuelle Autonome de Retraites Complémentaires Agricoles
CAMBOIS	Société Camerounaise des Bois

CAMC	Canadian Association of Management Consultants	**CANJ**	Ceramic Association of New Jersey (U.S.A.)
		CANSG	Civil Aviation Navigational Services Group
CAMC	Corporación Argentina de Productores Avícolas	**CANSM**	Caisse Autonome Nationale de la Sécurité dans les Mines
CAMDA	Car and Motorcycle Drivers Association	**CANTIER-MACCHI-NE**	Associazione Commercianti Importatori Macchine da Cantiere ed Affini
CAMDEV	Cameroons Development Corporation		
CAME	Conference of Allied Ministers of Education		
CAME	Consejo de Ayuda Mutua Económica (Cuba)	**CANTV**	Compania Anonima Nacional Telefonos de Venezuela
CAMEC	Compagnie Africaine de Métaux et de Produits Chimiques (Dahomey)	**CANUSPA**	Canada, Australia, New Zealand and United States Parents Association
CAMECO	Catholic Media Council (Germany)		
CAMEP	Société Camerounaise d'Études et de Promotion pour l'Afrique	**CANWEG**	Canadian National Committee of the World Energy Conference
CAMES	Conseil Africaine et Malgache pour l'Enseignement Supérieur	**CANYS**	Ceramic Association of New York State (U.S.A.)
CAMESA	Canadian Military Electronics Standards Agency	**CAO**	Canadian Association of Optometricists
		CAOBISCO	Association d'Industries de Produits Sucrés de la CEE
CAMGOC	Gulf Oil Company of Cameroon		
CAMI	Cameroon Motors Industries	**CAOPRI**	Central Arecanut and Oil Palm Research Institute (India)
CAMIG	Companhia Agricola de Minas Gerais (Brazil)	**CAORB**	Civil Aviation Operational Research Branch
CAMIRA	Comité d'Application des Méthodes Isotopiques aux Recherches Agronomiques (Belgium)	**CAOSO**	Coopérative Agricole Ovine du Sud-Ouest
		CAOT	Canadian Association of Occupational Therapy
CAMJA	Comisión Nacional de Apoyo al Movimiento Juvenil Agrario (Uruguay)	**CAP**	Canadian Association of Physicists
CAML	Canadian Association of Music Libraries	**CAP**	Central Agricultural Producers
CAMOA	Société Camerounaise d'Oxygène et d'Acétylène	**CAP**	Centres d'Alevinage Principaux (Zaire)
		CAP	Committee on Agricultural Policies (of ECE)
CAMRA	Campaign for the Revitalisation of Ale	**CAP**	Commonwealth Association of Planners
CAMROC	Cambridge Radio Observatory Committee (U.S.A.)	**CAP**	Compagnie Africaine d'Armement à la Pêche
		CAP	Compagnie d'Agences de Publicité
CAMS	Council for Asian Manpower Studies (Philippines)	**CAP**	Cooperative Agricole de Productie (Roumania)
CAMSI	Canadian Association of Medical Students and Interns	**CAPA**	Canadian Association of Purchasing Agents
		CAPA	Comisión Asesora de Politica Agraria (Venezuela)
CAMT	Cámara Argentina Maderas Terciadas		
CANA	Cooperative Agricole la Noelle, Ancenis	**CAPA**	Compagnie Africaine de Produits Alimentaires
CANAI	Comitato Artistico Nazionale Acconciatori Italiani	**CAPA**	Selección y Comercio de la Patata de Siembra
		CAPAC	Composers' Authors' and Publishers Association of Canada
CANCEE	Canadian National Committee for Earthquake Engineering		
		CAPAR	Centre d'Animation et de Promotion Agricole et Rurale
CANCIRCO	Cancer International Research Cooperative		
CANEFA	Comisión Asesora Nacional de Erradicación de la Fiebre Aftosa (Argentina)	**CAPC**	Central African Power Corporation
		CAPC	Comité Ampliado del Programa y de la Coordinación (UNDP)
CANGO	Committee for Air Navigation and Ground Organization		
		CAPE	Centre Africain de Promotion Économique

CAPEB	Confédération de l'Artisanat et des Petites Entreprises du Bâtiment	**CARASE**	Centre Algérien de la Recherche Agronomique, Sociologique et Économique
CAPEF	Coopérative Agricole des Producteurs d'Endives de France	**CARAVA**	Christian Association for Radio and Audio-Visual Aid (India)
CAPEL	Centre pour l'Accroissement de la Productivité des Entreprises Laitières	**CARBAP**	Confederación de Asociaciones Rurales de Buenos Aires y La Lampa (Argentina)
CAPEM	Comité d'Aménagement et du Plan d'Équipement de la Moselle	**CARC**	Central Asian Research Centre (U.K.)
CAPER	Caisse d'Accession à la Propriété et à l'Exploitation Rurales (Algeria)	**CARCLO**	Confederación de Asociaciones Rurales del Centro y Litoral Oeste (Argentina)
CAPERAS	Comité Argentino para el Estudio de la Regiones Aridas y Semiáridas	**CARD**	Campaign Against Racial Discrimination
CAPI	Comisión de Administración Pública Internacional	**CARD**	Center for Agricultural and Rural Development (U.S.A.)
CAPIA	Cámara Argentina de Productores Industriales Avícolas	**CARDAN**	Centre d'Analyse et de Recherche Documentaires pour l'Afrique Noire
CAPIEL	Common Market Association for Switchgear and Control Devices	**CARDE**	Canadian Armament Research and Development Establishment
CAPIM	Consortium Africain de Produits Industriels et Ménagers (Ivory Coast)	**CARE**	Cooperative for American Relief for Everywhere
CAPITB	Chemical and Allied Products Industry Training Board	**CAREF**	Centre Algérien de Recherches et Expérimentations Forestières
CAPL	Canadian Association of Public Libraries	**CARENA**	Compagnie Abidjanaise de Réparations Navales et de Travaux Industriels (Ivory Coast)
CAPL	Coastal Anti-Pollution League	**CARF**	Canadian Advertising Research Foundation
CAPMA	Caisse d'Assurance et de Prévoyance Mutuelle des Agriculteurs	**CARIBANK**	Caribbean Development Bank
CAPMS	Central Agency for Public Mobilisation and Statistics (Egypt)	**CARIC**	Compagnie Africaine de Représentations Industrielles et Commerciales (Congo, Gabon, Ivory Coast)
CAPRAL	Compagnie Africaine de Preparations Alimentaires (Ivory Coast)	**CARICOM**	Caribbean Community
CAPS	Centro de Adiestramiento para Promotores Sociales de la Universidad Rafael Landivar (Guatemala)	**CARIFTA**	Caribbean Free Trade Association
		CARIPLO	Cassa di Risparmio delle Province Lombarde
CAPS	Confédération Agricole des Producteurs de Plantes Saccharifères	**CARIRI**	Caribbean Industrial Research Institute (Trinidad)
CAPSES	Cooperativa Aragonesa de Productores de Semillas Selectas	**CARIRI-TIS**	Caribbean Industrial Research Institute. Technical Information Service
CAPSOME	Comité d'Action des Producteurs et Stockeurs d'Oléagineux pour les Marchés Extérieurs	**CARIS**	Current Agricultural Research Information System (of FAO)
CAR	Canadian Association of Radiologists	**CARIS-FORM**	Caribbean Institute for Social Formation
CAR	Central African Republic	**CARISOV**	Caribische Institut voor Social Vorming
CAR	Centre of African Studies	**CARITAS INTER-NATIO-NALIS**	Conférence Internationale des Charités Catholiques
CAR	Comité Agricole Régional		
CAR	Corporación Autóctona Regional de la Sabana de Bogota y de los Valles de Ullate y Chinquinquirá (Colombia)	**CARO**	Société de Fabrication de Carrelages et Revêtements au Cameroun
CARAC	Civil Aviation Radio Advisory Committee	**CARPA**	Caribbean Psychiatric Association

CARPAS	Comisión Asesora Regional de Pesca para el Atlántico Sud-occidental (FAO)	**CASME**	Commonwealth Association of Science and Mathematics Educators
CARS	Canadian Arthritis and Rheumatism Society	**CASMT**	Central Association of Science and Mathematics Teachers (U.S.A.)
CARS	Central Agricultural Research Station (Somalia)	**CASRO**	Commission d'Achat de la Suisse Romande
CARTG	Canadian Amateur Radio Teletype Group	**CASRSS**	Centre of Advanced Study and Research in Social Sciences (Bangladesh)
CARVOLT	Société de Cartoucherie Voltaïque	**CASSIS**	Communications and Social Science Information Service
CAS	Caribbean Air Services		
CAS	Club Alpin Suisse	**CAST**	Centre d'Actualisation Scientifique et Technique
CAS	Commission for Atmospheric Sciences (WMO)	**CAST**	Confédération Africaine des Syndicats Libres
CAS	Committee on Atlantic Studies (U.S.A.)	**CAST**	Consolidated African Selection Trust (Ghana)
CAS	Conciliation and Arbitration Service	**CAST-**	Conference of Ministers of African Member
CASA	Canadian Amateur Swimming Association	**AFRICA**	States Responsible for the Application of Science and Technology to Development
CASA	Canadian Automatic Sprinkler Association		
CASA	Contemporary Art Society of Australia	**CASTALA**	Conference of Ministers of Latin American Member States Responsible for the Application of Science and Technology to Development
CASANZ	Clean Air Society of Australia and New Zealand		
CASBO	Conference of American Small Business Organisations	**CASTARAB**	Conference of Ministers of Arab Member States Responsible for the Application of Science and Technology to Development
CASC	Caisse d'Assurances des Coopératives Suisse de Consommation	**CASTASIA**	Conference of Ministers of Asian Member States Responsible for the Application of Science and Technology to Development
CASC	Committee on African Studies in Canada		
CASCC	Canadian Agricultural Services Co-ordinating Committee	**CASU**	Co-operative Association of Suez Canal Users
CASDS	Centre for Advanced Study in the Developmental Sciences	**CASVAL**	Coopérative d'Approvisionnement des Syndicats Viticoles et Agricoles du Loire à Orléans
CASE	Committee on Academic Science and Engineering (U.S.A.)		
CASE	Confederation for the Advancement of State Education	**CAT**	Comité de l'Assistance Technique de l'O.N.U. (UNO)
CASEC	Confederation of Associations of Specialist Engineering Contractors	**CAT**	Compagnie Africaine de Transformation (Togo)
CASHA	Centre Africain des Sciences Humaines Appliquées	**CAT**	Compagnie Africaine de Transports
CASI	Canadian Aeronautics and Space Institute	**CATA**	Compagnie Africaine de Transports Automobiles
CASI	Commission Aéronautique Sportive Internationale	**CATC**	Commonwealth Air Transport Commission
CASLE	Commonwealth Association of Surveying and Land Engineering	**CATC**	Confédération Africaine des Travailleurs Croyants (Upper Volta)
CASL-HV	Confédération Africaine des Syndicats Libres de la Haute Volta	**CATCA**	Canadian Air Traffic Control Association
CASLF	Comité d'Action pour la Sauvegarde des Libertés Forestières	**CATCC**	Canadian Association of Textile Colourists and Chemists
CASLIS	Canadian Association of Special Libraries and Information Services	**CATECO**	Société Camerounaise d'Automobile de Technique et du Commerce

CATED	Centre d'Assistance Technique et de Documentation du Bâtiment et des Travaux Publique	**CBA**	Chambre Belge de l'Affichage et Média Connexes
CATEL	Compagnie Africaine de Télévision (Ivory Coast)	**CBA**	Concrete Block Association
CATET	Centro Argentino de Técnicos en Estudios del Trabajo	**CBA**	Council for British Archaeology
		CBABG	Commonwealth Bureau of Animal Breeding and Genetics
CATEX	Société Centrafricaine des Textiles pour l'Exportation	**CBAE**	Commonwealth Bureau of Agricultural Economics
CATG	Chinese Agricultural Technical Group (Vietnam)	**CBAH**	Commonwealth Bureau of Animal Health
CATI	Centres Administratifs et Techniques Interdépartementaux	**CBAMC**	Chambre Belge de l'Affichage et Média Connexes
CATIE	Centro Agrónomico Tropical de Investigación y Enseñanza (Costa Rica)	**CBAN**	Commonwealth Bureau of Animal Nutrition
		CBAT	Central Bureau for Astronomical Telegrams (Denmark)
CATM	Chinese Agricultural Technical Mission to Vietnam (*now* CATG)	**CBAT**	Centro de Biología Aquática Tropical (Portugal)
CATP	Compagnie Africaine de Travaux Publics (Ivory Coast)	**CBB**	Centrale Besturenbond v. Zuivelorganisaties in Nederland
CATPA	Comité d'Action Technique contre la Pollution Atmosphérique	**CBB**	Confédération des Betteraviers Belges
		CBB	Confédération des Brasseries de Belgique
CATRA	Cutlery and Allied Trades Research Association	**CBBA**	Comissão Brasileira de Bibliotecarios Agrícolas
CATRF	Central Africa Tea Research Foundation (Malawi)	**CBC**	Canadian Broadcasting Corporation
		CBC	Chad Basin Commission
CATU	Ceramic and Allied Trades Union	**CBC**	Société Commerciale des Bois du Cameroun
CAV	Cámara Agricola de Venezuela	**CBCC**	Canada-British Columbia Consultative Board
CAV	Ceskoslovenská Akademie Ved		
CAVEDINA	Cámara Venezolana de Industriales de Arroz	**CBCC**	Chemical-Biological Co-ordination Centre (U.S.A)
CAVI	Centre Audio-Visuel International	**CBCISS**	Centro Brasileiro de Cooperação e Intercambio de Serviços Sociais
CAVIC	Corporación Agroeconómica, Viticola, Industrial y Comercial (Argentina)	**CBCS**	Commonwealth Bureau of Census and Statistics (Australia)
CAVINEX	Société Camerounaise d'Exploitation Vinicole	**CBCSM**	Council of British Ceramic Sanitaryware Manufacturers
CAVN	Comité d'Aménagement de la Vallée du Niari	**CBD**	Centralforeningen af Benzinforhandlere i Danmark
CAVO	Centralgenossenschaft für Alkoholfreie Verwertung von Obstprodukten (Switzerland)	**CBD**	Comité Belge de la Distribution
		CBD	Corporación Boliviana de Desarrollo
CAVV	Coöperatieve Aan- en Verkoop Vereniging	**CBD**	International Council of Ballroom Dancing
CAVY	Coopérative Agricole et Viticole du Département de l'Yonne	**CBDIC**	Centre Belge de Documentation et d'Information de la Construction
CAWC	Central Advisory Water Committee	**CBDST**	Commonwealth Bureau of Dairy Science and Technology
CAZF	Comité des Agrumes de la Zone Franc		
CAZ	Ceskoslovenská Akademie Ved Zemedelských	**CBE**	Council of Biology Editors (U.S.A.)
CAZRI	Central Arid Zone Research Institute (India)	**CBEA**	Centro Brazileiro de Estatísticas Agropecuárias
CBA	Caribbean Atlantic Airways		

CBEFEN	Comité Belge des Expositions et des Foires et d'Expansion Nationale	**CBPBG**	Commonwealth Bureau of Plant Breeding and Genetics
CBEMA	Canadian Business Equipment Manufacturers Association	**CBPC**	Canadian Book Publishers Council
CBEN	Comisión Boliviana de Energia Nuclear	**CBPC**	Chambre Belge de la Publicité Cinématographique
CBEVE	Central Bureau for Educational Visits and Exchanges	**CBPDC**	Canadian Book and Periodical Development Council
CBF	Corporación Boliviana de Fomento	**CBPE**	Centro Brasileiro de Pesquisas Educacionais
CBG	Chambre Belge des Graphistes	**CBPF**	Centro Brasileiro de Pesquisas Fisicas
CBG	Compagnie des Bauxites de Guinée	**CBPFC**	Commonwealth Bureau of Pastures and Field Crops
CBH	Commonwealth Bureau of Helminthology		
CBHPC	Commonwealth Bureau of Horticulture and Plantation Crops	**CBPM**	Chambre Belge des Pédicures Médicaux
		CBQ	Centre Belge pour la Gestion de la Qualité
CBI	Comisión Ballenera Internacional	**CBR**	Centraal Bureau voor de Rijwielhandel
CBI	Confederation of British Industry	**CBR**	Consejo de Bienestar Rural (Venezuela)
CBJO	Co-ordinating Board of Jewish Organizations for Consultation with the Economic and Social Council of the United Nations	**CBRA**	Chemical Biological Radiological Agency (U.S.A.)
		CBRB	Centraal Bureau voor de Rijn- en Binnenvaart
CBK	Centraal Brouwerij Kantoor		
CBL	Centraal Bureau Levensmiddelenbedrijf	**CBRI**	Central Bee Research Institute (India)
CBL	Cercle Belge de la Librairie	**CBRI**	Central Building Research Institute (India)
CBL	Commission Centrale Belge du Lait	**CBRP**	Centre Belge des Relations Publiques
CBLIA	Centro Belgo-Luxembourgeois d'Information de l'Acier	**CBRS**	Coffee Board Research Station (India)
		CBS	Centraal Bureau Slachtveeverzekeringen
CBLT	Commission du Bassin du Lac Tchad	**CBS**	Centraal Bureau voor Schimmelcultures
CBM	Centrale Bond van Meubelfabrikanten	**CBS**	Central Bureau voor de Statistiek
CBM	Centre Technique et Scientifique de la Brasserie, Malterie et des Industries Connexes (Belgium)	**CBS**	Československá Botanicá Spoleenost
		CBS	Columbia Broadcasting System (U.S.A.)
		CBS	Commonwealth Bureau of Soils
CBMC	Communauté de Travail des Brasseurs du Marché Commun	**CBSN**	Centraal Bureau voor de Schapenfokkerij in Nederland
CBMPE	Council of British Manufacturers of Petroleum Equipment	**CBSN**	Christelijke Bond van Schoenwinkeliers
CBN	Commission on Biochemical Nomenclature	**CBT**	Centre Belge de Traductions
CBNM	Central Bureau for Nuclear Measurements (of Euratom)	**CBT**	Commission du Bassin du Tchad
		CBTB	Nederlandse Christelijke Boeren- en Tuindersbond
CBO	Conference of Baltic Oceanographers		
CBOB	Christelijke Bond van Ondernemers in de Binnenwaart	**CBTIP**	Chambre Belge des Traducteurs, Interprètes et Philologues
		CBV	Centraal Bureau voor de Veilingen
CBOI	Centro Biológico del Océano Indico	**CBV**	Central Bureau voor de Varkensfokkerij in Nederland
CBPAE	Centro Brasileiro de Pesquisas Agrícolas em Elano		
		CBV	Coopérative Suisse pour l'Approvisionnement en Bétail de Boucherie et en Viande
CBPAH	Council for British Plastics in Agriculture and Horticulture		
CBPAV	Chambre Belge des Publicités Audio-Visuelles	**CBVN**	Centraal Bureau voor de Varkensfokkerij in Nederland

CC	Caribbean Commission	CCAQ	Consultative Committee on Administrative Questions (*of* UNO)
CC	Commission de Climatologie (de l'OMM)	CCASTD	Comité Consultatif sur l'Application de la Science et de la Technique au Développement (*of* UNO)
CCA	Canadian Chemical Association		
CCA	Canadian Construction Association		
CCA	Cement and Concrete Association	CCAT	Comité de Coordination de l'Assistance Technique (de l'ONU)
CCA	Chamber of Commerce of the Americas		
CCA	Chemical Corps Association Inc. (U.S.A.)	CCAVMA	Caisse Centrale d'Assurance Vieillesse Mutuelle Agricole
CCA	Commonwealth Correspondents' Association		
		CCB	Compagnie Camerounaise des Boissons
CCA	Compagnie Commerciale Africaine (Ivory Coast)	CCB	Coöperative Centrale Boerenleenbank
		CCBAT	Comité Central Belge de l'Achèvement Textile
CCA	Conférence Chrétienne d'Asie Orientale		
CCA	Consejo de Cooperación Aduanera (Belgium)	CCBB	Comité Central de la Bonneterie Belge
CCA	Copper Conductors Association	CCBDA	Canadian Copper and Brass Development Association
CCAA	Conseil de Coordination des Associations Aéroportuaires (Switzerland)		
		CCBET	Comité Central Belge de Textile l'Ennoblissement
CCAAP	Central Committee for the Architectural Advisory Panels		
		CCBM	Copper Cylinder and Boiler Manufacturers' Association
CCAAP	Comisión Consultiva en Asuntos Administrativos y de Presupuesto (UN)		
		CCBN	Central Council for British Naturism
CCAB	Canadian Circulation Audit Board	CCBSA	Central Council of Bank Staff Associations
CCAC	Compagnie Commerciale de l'Afrique Centrale	CCBV	Comité Professionnel des Coopératives des Pays du Marché Commun pour le Bétail et la Viande
CCACU	Central Co-ordinating Allocation Committee for University Project Research (South Africa)		
		CCC	Canadian Chamber of Commerce
		CCC	Caribbean Conference of Churches
CCAF	Comité Central des Armateurs de France	CCC	Caribbean Conservation Corporation
CCAF	Compagnie Agricole et Forestière	CCC	Caribbean Consumer Committee (Jamaica)
CCAFMA	Caisse Centrale d'Allocations Familiales Mutuelles Agricoles	CCC	Caribbean Council of Churches
		CCC	Central Council of Co-operatives (Czechoslovakia)
CCAHC	Central Council for Agricultural and Horticultural Co-operation		
		CCC	Centrale Cultuurtechnische Commissie
CCAI	Chambre de Commerce, d'Agriculture et l'Industrie de Bamako (Mali)	CCC	Club Cricket Conference
		CCC	Commodity Credit Corporation (U.S.A.)
CCAM	Canadian Congress of Applied Mechanics	CCC	Conseil de Coopération Culturelle (*of* CE)
CCAMAA	Caisse Centrale d'Assurances Mutuelles Agricoles contre des Accidents	CCC	Council for the Care of Churches
CCAMAG	Caisse Centrale d'Assurances Mutuelles Agricoles contre la Grêle	CCC	Customs Co-operation Council (Belgium)
		CCCA	Cocoa, Chocolate and Confectionery Alliance
CCAMAI	Caisse Centrale d'Assurances Mutuelles Agricoles contre l'Incendie		
		CCCA	Comité Consultivo en Cuestiones Administrativas (UNO)
CCAMAMB	Caisse Centrale d'Assurances Mutuelles Agricoles contre la Mortalité du Bétail		
		CCCAM	Centro de Cooperación Científica de Asia Meridional (India)
CCAO	Chambre de Compensation de l'Afrique de l'Ouest (Senegal)		
CCAP	Citizens' Crusade Against Poverty (U.S.A.)	CCCAS	Centro de Cooperación Científica de Asia Sudoriental (Thailand)
CCAP	Culture Centre of Algae and Protozoa		

CCCB	Comissáo de Comércio do Cacau da Bahia (Brazil)	**CCEB**	Conseil Canadien des Écoles de Bibliothécaires
CCCBR	Central Council of Church Bell Ringers	**CCEE**	Consilium Conferentiarum Episcopalium Europae
CCCCN	Comissão Coordenadora da Criacao do Cavalo Nacional (Brazil)	**CCEI**	Comité Consultatif Économique et Industriel auprès de l'OCDE
CCCE	Caisse Centrale de Coopération Économique	**CCEIC**	Comité de Cooperación Económica del Istmo Centroamericana
CCCET	Comité Catholique de Coordination pour l'Envoi de Techniciens (Belgium)	**CCEN**	Chilian Nuclear Energy Commission
CCCFE	Comité Consultatif de Coordination du Financement à moyen terme des Exportations	**CCEP**	Commission Consultative des Études Postales (de l'Union Postale Universelle)
CCCI	Compagnie du Congo pour le Commerce et l'Industrie	**CCEPI**	Commission Consultative Européenne pour les Pêches dans les Eaux Intérieures
CCCI	Conseil Canadien pour la Coopération Internationale	**CCERO**	Centre d'Études de Recherche Operationelle (Belgium)
CCCLP	Confederación Centroamericana y del Caribe de Levantamiento de Pesas	**CCES**	Conseil Consultatif Économique et Social de l'Union Économique (Belgium)
CCCN	Caribbean Christian Communications Network	**CCESP**	Centre County Engineers' Society of Pennsylvania (U.S.A.)
CCCR	Co-ordinating Committee for Cancer Research	**CCETI**	Commission Consultative des Employés et des Travailleurs Intellectuels (de l'OIT)
CCCS	Colonial, Commonwealth and Continental Church Society	**CCETSW**	Central Council for Education and Training in Social Work
CCCD	Centrale Contrôle Dienst	**CCEUREA**	Centre Coopératif d'Expansion et d'Utilisation Rationnelles d'Équipement Agricole
CCD	Conseil de Coopération Douanière (Belgium)		
CCDA	Commercial Chemical Development Association (U.S.A.)	**CCF**	Centrale Cultuurfondsen (Indonesia)
CCDC	Capital City Development Corporation (Malawi)	**CCF**	Co-operative Commonwealth Federation Montreal (Canada)
CCDG	Société Commerciale du Gabon	**CCF**	Crédit Commercial de France
CCDP	Comisión Centroamericana de Desarrollo Pesquero (Salvador)	**CCFA**	Cancer Cytology Foundation of America
		CCFA	Caribbean Cane Farmers Association
CCDP	Compagnie Camerounaise de Dépôts Pétroliers	**CCFD**	Comité Catholique contre la Faim et pour le Développement
CCDR	Compagnie Camerounaise de Développement Regional	**CCFOM**	Caisse Centrale de la France d'Outre-Mer
		CCFPI	Comité Consultatif de la Fonction Publique Internationale
CCDS	Canadian Council on Social Development		
CCDVT	Caisse Centrale de Dépôts et Virements de Titres	**CCGA**	Compagnie de Constructions Générales en Afrique
CCE	Comite de Cooperación Económica del Istmo Centroamericano	**CCGB**	Cycling Council of Great Britain
		CCGS	Corpus Christi Geological Society (U.S.A.)
CCE	Conseil des Communes d'Europe	**CCHA**	Compagnie Commerciale Hollando-Africaine
CCEA	Commonwealth Council for Educational Administration		
		CCHE	Central Council for Health Education
CCEAC	Comité de Coopération Économique de l'Amérique Centrale	**CCHO**	Comité Consultatif d'Hydrologie Opérationnelle (*of* WMO)
CCEAE	Conférence des Chefs d'État de l'Afrique Équatoriale	**CCI**	Central Campesina Independienti (Mexico)
		CCI	Chambre de Commerce Internationale

CCI	Comités Consultatifs Internationaux
CCI	Compagnie Camerounaise Industrielle
CCI	Cotton Council International (U.S.A.)
CCIA	Camera di Commercio, Industria e Agricoltura di Rieti
CCIA	Commission of the Churches on International Affairs (Switzerland)
CCIA	Comité Cientifico de Investigaciones Antárticas (ICSU)
CCIA	Comptoir Commercial et Industriel Afrique
CCIAESC	Coffee Commission of the Inter-American Economic and Social Council (U.S.A.)
CCIC	Canadian Council for International Co-operation
CCIC	Centre Catholique International pour l'Unesco
CCIC	Comité Catholique International de Coordination Auprès de l'Unesco
CCIC	Comité Consultatif International du Coton
CCICMS	Council for the Co-ordination of International Congresses of Medicine
CCIDD	Canterbury College Industrial Development Department (N.Z.)
CCIEM	Catholic Committee for Intra-European Migration
CCIF	Comité Consultatif International Téléphonique
CCIL	Canadian Co-operative Implements Ltd
CCIM	Chambre de Commerce et d'Industrie de la Martinique
CCIO	Comité Cientificao de Investigaciones Oceánicas
CCIP	Chambre de Compensation Internationale des Produits de Base (UNCTAD)
CCIP	Commission du Commerce International des Produits de Base
CCIR	Catholic Council for International Relations
CCIR	Chambre de Commerce et l'Industrie de la Réunion
CCIR	Comité Consultative International des Radio-communications
CCIS	Compagnie Commerciale Industrielle du Sénégal
CCIT	Comité Consultatif International Télégraphique
CCITT	International Consultative Telegraph and Telephone Committee (of ITU)

CCITU	Coordinating Committee of Independent Trade Unions
CCIVS	Co-ordinating Committee for International Voluntary Service
CCIW	Canada Centre for Inland Waters
CCJ	Comité Européen de Coopération Juridique
CCJO	Consultative Council of Jewish Organisations
CCL	Caribbean Congress of Labour
CCL	Comité Central de la Laine
CCL	Conseil International de Continuation et de Liaison du Congrès Mondial des Forces de Paix
CCLA	Committee on Co-operation in Latin America
CCLF	Club des Congrès de Langue Française
CCLIL	Fédération Française de la Filature de Laine Cardée et Autres Fibres
CCLM	Committee on Constitutional and Legal Matters (FAO)
CCLN	Committee for Computerized Library Networks (NLISN)
CCMA	Caisse Centrale des Mutuelles Agricoles (France)
CCMA	Canadian Council of Management Association
CCMA	Cotton Canvas Manufacturers Association
CCMC	Committee of Common Market Constructors (Belgium)
CCMIE	Comité Catholique pour les Migrations Intra-européennes
CCMRG	Commonwealth Committee on Mineral Resources and Geology
CCMS	Committee on the Challenges of Modern Society (of NATO)
CCMW	Churches Committee on Migrant Workers (Switzerland)
CCNDT	Canadian Council for Non-Destructive Technology
CCNR	Central Commission for the Navigation of the Rhine
CCNR	Consultative Committee for Nuclear Research (of Council of Europe)
CCNSC	Cancer Chemotherapy National Service Center (U.S.A.)
CCNUD	Cycle de la Coopération des Nations Unies pour le Développement
CCNY	Carnegie Corporation of New York
CCOC	Comité de Coordination des Organisations des Consommateurs

CCODP	Canadian Catholic Organization for Development and Peace	**CCR**	Center for Conflict Resolution (U.S.A.)
CCOP/SOP-AC	Committee for the Coordination of Joint Prospecting for Mineral Resources in South Pacific Offshore Areas (*of* ECAFE)	**CCR**	Commission Centrale pour la Navigation du Rhin
		CCRA	Canadian Research Centre for Anthropology
CCOPA	Alentefo Co-ordinating Committee for Public Works (Portugal)	**CCRB**	Coöperatieve Centrale Raiffeisen-Bank
		CCRI	Central Coffee Research Institute (India)
CCOTACAL	Conseil Coordinateur des Organisations des Travailleurs Agricoles et des Paysans d'Amérique Latine	**CCRI**	Comité Consultatif de Recherche en Informatique
		CCRMO	Comité Consultatif de la Recherche Météorologique Océanique (WMO)
CCP	Chinese Communist Party		
CCP	Comité Cafetalero del Perú	**CCRN**	Centre Commun de Recherches Nucléaires
CCP	Committee on Commodity Problems (FAO)	**CCRP**	Corporación Centro Regional de Población (Colombia)
CCP	Confederación Científica Panamericana (Argentina)	**CCRRM**	Comité Consultatif de la Recherche sur les Ressources de la Mer (FAO)
CCP	Conférence Chrétienne pour la Paix	**CCRS**	Central Coconut Research Station (India)
CCPA	Centrale Cooperative des Productions Animales	**CCRST**	Comité Consultatif de la Recherche Scientifique et Technique
CCPE	Canadian Council of Professional Engineers		
CCPES	Canadian Council of Professional Engineers and Scientists	**CCRTD**	Committee for Coordination of Cathode Ray Tube Development
		CCS	Canadian Cancer Society
CCPF	Comité Central de la Propriété Forestière de la CEE	**CCS**	Canadian Ceramic Society
		CCS	Comptoir Commercial du Sénégal
CCPF	Comité de Coordination de la Production Fruitère	**CCS**	Corporation of Secretaries
CCPIT	China Committee for the Promotion of International Trade	**CCS**	Council of Communication Societies (U.S.A.)
		CCSA	Canadian Committee on Sugar Analysis
CCPMA	Caisse Centrale de Prévoyance Mutuelle Agricole	**CCSA**	Comité Chétien de Service en Algérie
CCPMNO	Comité de Coordination des Ports Méditerranéens Nord-Occidental	**CCSATU**	Coordinating Council of South African Trade Unions
		CCSD	Canadian Council on Social Development
CCPMO	Consultative Council of Professional Management Organisations	**CCSL**	Confédération Congolaise des Syndicats Libres
CCPO	Comité Central Permanent de l'Opium (Switzerland)	**CCSM**	Confederation Chrétienne des Syndicats Malgaches
CCPP	Caisse Commune des Pensions du Personnel des Nations Unies	**CCSM**	Czechoslovak Committee for Scientific Management
CCPR	Central Council for Physical Recreation		
CCPR	Cooperativa de Cafeteros de Puerto Rico	**CCSMA**	Caisse Centrale de Secours Mutuels Agricoles
CCPS	Commission Permanente du Pacifique Sud	**CCSR**	Canadian Consortium for Social Research
CCPS	Consultative Committee for Postal Studies (*of* UPU)	**CCSVI**	Comité de Coordination du Service Volontaire International
CCPW	Catholic Council for Polish Welfare		
CCQA	Comité Consultatif pour les Questions Administratives	**CCT**	Confederación Centroamericana de Trabajadores
		CCT	Confederación Costarricense del Trabago
CCQAB	Comité Consultative pour les Questions Administratives et Budgétaires (UN)	**CCT**	Consejo Centroamericana de Turismo

CCTA	Centrale Chemisch-Technische Afdeling (Indonesia)	**CDDA**	Conseil Départemental de Développement Agricole
CCTA	Committee for Technical Co-operation in Africa South of the Sahara	**CDDC**	Comisión de Documentación Científica (Argentina)
CCTAN	Confederación de Campesinos y Trabajadores Agrícolas de Nicaragua	**CDE**	Coal Development Establishment
CCTI	Conseil Central du Tourisme International	**CDF**	Capital Development Fund (UNO)
CCTS	Comité de Coordination des Télécommunications par Satellites (Switzerland)	**CDFC**	Commonwealth Development Finance Corporation
		CDG	Carl Duisberg-Gesellschaft
CCTU	Comité de Coordination des Télécommunications (*of* CNET)	**CDH**	Centralvereinigung Deutscher Handelsvertreter- und Handelsmakler Verbände
CCUN	Collegiate Council for the United States	**CDHAR**	Comités Départementaux de l'Habitat et de l'Aménagement Rural
CCURR	Canadian Council on Urban and Regional Research	**CDHR**	Comité Départemental de l'Habitat Rural
CCUS	Chamber of Commerce of the United States	**CDI**	Centraal Diergeneeskunde Instituut
CCVM	Centrale Commissie voor Melk Hygiene	**CDI**	Centre de Diffusion de l'Innovation (*of* ANVAR)
CCWM	Congregational Council for World Mission		
CCWU	Clerical and Commercial Workers Union (Guyana)	**CDI**	Centro de Documentação e Informação (Brazil)
CD	Commission du Danube	**CDI**	Commission du Droit International
CD	Cultuurtechnische Dienst	**CDICP**	Centrul de Documentare al Industriei Chimice si Petroliere (Romania)
CDA	Canadian Dental Association		
CDA	Centro de Documentação Agrária (Mozambique)	**CDIL**	Centro de Documentare Tehnica (Romania)
		CDISA	Centre de Documentation et d'Information de la Société des Africanistes
CDA	Compañia Dominicana de Aviación		
CDA	Copper Development Association	**CDIU**	Centrale Dienst voor de In- en Uitvoer
CDAE	Centre de Desarrollo Agrario del Ebro	**CDIUPA**	Centre de Documentation des Industries Utilisatrices de Produits Agricoles
CDAF	Compagnie des Dirigeants d'Approvisionnement et Acheteurs de France	**CDJA**	Cercle Départemental des Jeunes Agriculteurs
CDB	Caribbean Development Bank (Barbados)	**CDL**	County and Democratic League (Australia)
CDB	Cyprus Development Bank	**CDLDK**	Comité de Liaison des Kinésithérapeutes de la CEE
CDC	Cameroon's Development Corporation		
CDC	Canadian Development Corporation	**CDMI**	Centre de Documentation de Musique Internationale
CDC	China Development Corporation		
CDC	Colonial *later* Commonwealth Development Corporation	**CDNPA**	Canadian Dairy Newspaper Publishers Association
CDC	Comisión de Documentación Científica (Argentina)	**CDP**	Compagnie Camerounaise de Dépôts Petroliers
CDC	Commonwealth Development Corporation	**CDPPP**	Centre for Development Planning, Projections and Policies (*of* UNO)
CDCR	Centre for Documentation and Communication Research (U.S.A.)	**CDPT**	Centrul de Documentare şi Propagandă Tehnică (Romania)
CDCTM	Centro de Documentación Científica y Tecnica de Mexico	**CDR**	Centre for Development Research (Denmark)
CDCU	Centro de Documentação Científica Ultramarina (Portugal)	**CDR**	Centre de Documentation Rurale

CDRA	Committee of Directors of Research Associations
CDRB	Canadian Research Defence Board
CDRF	Canadian Dental Research Foundation
CDRI	Central Drug Research Institute (India)
CDS	Centre de Documentation Sidérurgique
CDSH	Centre de Documentation Sciences Humaines
CDSO	Commonwealth Defence Science Organisation
CDSP	Compagnie de Dirigeants de Services du Personnel (Belgium)
CDSVF	Comité de Défense Scientifique du Vin Français
CDTC	Confederation Dahoméenne des Travailleurs Croyants
CDU	Christlich-Demokratische Union Deutschlands (East Germany)
CDU	Christlich-Demokratische Union (West Germany)
CDUCE	Christian Democratic Union of Central Europe
CDUD	Christian Democratic Union of Germany
CDVM	Club Dirigenti Vendite e Marketing
CDVPA	Comité Départemental de la Vulgarisation et du Progrès Agricole
CDVTPR	Centre de Documentation du Verre Textile et des Plastiques Renforcés
CE	Conseil Économique
CE	Conseil d'État
CE	Council of Europe
CEA	Canadian Electrical Association
CEA	Central Electricity Authority (*formerly* BEA)
CEA	Centre d'Économique Alpine
CEA	Centre des Études Andines (France)
CEA	Centre d'Étude et Arbitrage de Droit Européen
CEA	Centro de Estudos Agrícolas (Brazil)
CEA	Cinematograph Exhibitors Association of Great Britain and Ireland
CEA	Comité Européen des Assurances
CEA	Commission Économique des Nations Unies pour l'Afrique
CEA	Commission de l'Énergie Atomique (*of* U.N.)
CEA	Commodity Exchange Authority (U.S.A.)
CEA	Communauté Européenne de l'Accordéon
CEA	Compañia Ecuatoriana de Aviación
CEA	Confederación de Educadores Americanos (Mexico)
CEA	Confédération Européenne de l'Agriculture (Switzerland)
CEAA	Centre Européen d'Aviation Agricole
CEAA	Council of European-American Associations
CEABH	Centre Eurafricain de Biologie Humaine
CEAC	Centro de Estudos de Antropología Cultural (Portugal)
CEAC	Commission Européenne de l'Aviation Civile
CEAC	Committee for European Airspace Coordination (*of* NATO)
CEAC	Confédération Européenne des Anciens Combattants
CEACRO	Comisión de Energía Atómica de Costa Rica
CEACS	Centre for East Asian Cultural Studies (Japan)
CEAEN	Centre d'Études pour les Applications de l'Énergie Nucléaire
CEAEO	Commission Économique pour l'Asie et l'Extrême-Orient (Thailand)
CEAF	Comité Européen des Associations de Fonderies
CEAI	Cercle d'Échanges Artistiques Internationaux
CEAL	Comité Europe-Amérique Latine (Belgium)
CEAL	Commission Économique pour l'Amérique Latin (Chile)
CEALDO	Comité de Expertos en Ajustes por Lugar de Destino Oficial (UNO)
CEALO	Comisión Económica para Asia y Lejano Oriente (U.S.A.)
CEAMP	Centrale d'Équipement Agricole et de Modernisation du Paysannat
CEANAR	Commission on Education in Agriculture and Natural Resources (U.S.A.)
CEAO	Commission Économique des Nations Unies pour l'Asie Occidentale
CEAO	Communauté Économique de l'Afrique de l'Ouest
CEAO	Confédération des Etudiants d'Afrique Occidentale
CEAS	Centro Erboristico Appenninico Sperimentale
CEAS	Cooperative Educational Abstracting Service (*of* IBE)

CEAT	Centre d'Études Aérodynamiques de Toulouse
CEB	Central Electricity Board
CEB	Central Electricity Board (Malaysia)
CEB	Comité Européen du Béton
CEB	Comité Européen des Constructeurs de Brûleurs
CEB	Confédération Européenne de Billard
CEBAC	Comisión Especial BrasileñoArgentina de Cooperación
CEBANOR	Comité Régional d'Expansion Économique de la Basse-Normandie
CEBAP	Centro de Estudios de Bosques Andino-Patagónicos (Argentina)
CEBEA	Centre Emile Bernheim pour l'Étude des Affaires (Belgium)
CEBECO	Nationale Coöperatieve Aan- en Verkoopvereniging voor Land- en Tuinbouw
CEBEDAIR	Centrale Belge d'Études et de Documentation de l'Air
CEBEDEAU	Centre Belge d'Étude et de Documentation des Eaux
CEBELA	Centro Brasileiro de Estudos Latino-Americanos
CEBELCOR	Centre Belge de l'Étude de la Corrosion
CEBERENA	Centre Belge de Recherches Navales
CEBETID	Comité Belge du Tissage et des Industries Textiles Diverses
CEBI	Comité Européen des Bureaux d'Ingénierie
CEBJ	Commission of Editors of Biochemical Journals
CEBLS	Council of EEC Builders of Large Ships
CEBOSINE	Centrale Bond van Scheepsbouwmeesters in Nederland
CEBRACO	Centro Brasileiro de Informação de Cobre
CEBRAP	Centro Brasileiro de Análise e Planejamento
CEBS	Centro de Estudios del Bosque Subtropical, La Plata (Argentina)
CEBSO	Comité d'Expansion Économique Bordeaux Sud-Ouest
CEBSP	Centre d'Étude Belge de Publicité
CEBTP	Centre Expérimental de Recherches et d'Études du Bâtiment et des Travaux Publics (Algeria)
CEBUCO	Centraal Bureau voor Courantenpubliciteit van de Nederlandse Dagbladpers
CEBV	Communauté Économique du Bétail et de la Viande (Africa)
CEC	Catholic Education Council
CEC	Centre for Economic Cooperation (UN)
CEC	Centre d'Études du Commerce
CEC	Centre Européen de la Culture
CEC	Clothing Export Council of Great Britain
CEC	Commission of the European Communities
CEC	Commonwealth Economic Committee (*formerly* IEC)
CEC	Commonwealth Education Cooperation
CEC	Conference of European Churches
CEC	Conseil Européen de l'Enseignement par Correspondance
CEC	Consejo Economico Centroamericana (*of* CACM)
CEC	Co-ordinating European Council for the Development of Performance Tests for Lubricants and Engine Fuels
CEC	Council for Education in the Commonwealth
CEC	Council for Exceptional Children (U.S.A.)
CECA	Carbonisation et Charbons Actifs SA
CECA	Communauté Européenne du Charbon et de l'Acier
CECA	Council on Economic and Cultural Affairs, Inc (*now* ADC) (U.S.A.)
CECA	Cyprus Employers Consultative Organisation
CECAF	FAO Fishery Committee for the Eastern Central Atlantic
CECA-GADIS	Compagnie d'Exploitations Commerciales Africaines–Société Gabonaise de Distribution
CECAL	Comité Européen de Coopération avec l'Amérique Latine
CECAL	Commission Episcopale de Coopération Apostolique Canada-Amérique Latine
CECAS	Conference of East and Central African States
CECAT	Centre for Agricultural Education and Co-operation (Italy)
CECATI	Centros de Capacitación para el Trabajo Industrial (Mexico)
CECB	Conseil Européen du Cuir Brut
CECC	Commonwealth Economic Consultative Council
CECC	Communaté Européenne des Coopératives de Consummateurs

CECC	Communauté Européenne de Crédit Communal
CECC	Compagnie d'Élevage et de Cultures du Cameroun
CECCB	Chambres des Experts-Comptable et des Comptables de Belgique
CECE	Centre d'Étude et Exploitation des Calculateurs Électroniques (Belgium)
CECE	Comisión Especial para la Formulación de Nuevas Medidas de Cooperación Económica Internacional
CECE	Committee for European Construction Equipment
CECEC	Communauté Européenne Culturelle des Étudiants en Chimie
CECED	Conseil Européen de la Construction Électro-Domestique
CECF	Commission Européenne des Communes Forestières et Communes de Montagne
CECG	Confédération Européenne du Commerce de la Chaussure en Gros (Belgium)
CECH	Comité Européen de la Culture du Houblon
CECI	Centre d'Étude de Cooperation Internationale (Canada)
CECI	Centre Européen du Commerce International
CECI	Centre Européen de Coopération Internationale (France)
CECIMO	Comité Européen de Cooperation des Industries de la Machine-Outil (Belgium)
CECINE	Centro de Ensino de Ciencias do Nordeste (Brazil)
CECIOS	European Council of International Committee of Scientific Management
CECIP	Comité Européen des Constructeurs d'Instruments de Pesage
CECIRNA	Centro de Coordinación de Investigaciones de Recursos Naturales y su Aplicacion (Argentina)
CECL	Comité Européen de Contrôle Laitier
CECLA	Commission Especiale de Coordinación Latinoamericana
CECLB	Comité Européen de Contrôle Laitier-Beurrier
CECLES	Conseil Européen pour la Construction de Lanceurs d'Engins Spatiaux
CECM	Commission pour l'Étude de la Construction Métallique (Belgium)
CECMA	Comité Européen des Constructeurs de Matériel Aéraulique
CECMAS	Centre d'Études des Communications de Masse
CECOAAP	Peruvian Sugar Cooperatives Association
CECOCO	Chuo Boeki Goshi Kaisha (Central Commercial Co) (Japan)
CECODE	Centre Européen du Commerce de Détail
CECODEC	Conseil Européen des Constructeurs de Cuisine
CECOM	Central European Mass Communication Research Documentation Centre (Poland)
CECOMAF	Comité Européen des Constructeurs de Matériel Frigorifique
CECORA	Central de Cooperatives de Reforma Agraria (Colombia)
CECPA	Comité Européen du Commerce des Produits Amylacés et Dérivés
CECPI	Commission Européenne Consultative pour les Pêches dans les Eaux Intérieures
CECPRA	Centre d'Études de la Commission Permanente du Risque Atomique
CECRI	Central Electrochemical Research Institute (India)
CECT	Comité Européen de la Chaudronnerie et de la Tôlerie
CECTAL	Centre for the Application of Science and Technology to the Development of Latin America
CECTK	Committee for Electro-Chemical Thermodynamics and Kinetics (Belgium)
CED	Centro de Esploro Kaj Dokumentado pri la Monda Lingvo-Problemo (U.K.)
CED	Committee for Economic Development (U.S.A.)
CEDA	Caisse d'Équipement pour le Développement de l'Algérie
CEDA	Canadian Electrical Distributors Association
CEDA	Centre for Economic Development and Administration (Nepal)
CEDA	Centre d'Édition et de Diffusion Africaines (Ivory Coast)
CEDA	Committee for the Economic Development of Australia
CEDAF	Centre for African Studies and Documentation (Belgium)
CEDAG	Centre d'Études et de Diffusion de l'Agriculture de Groupe
CEDAM	Casa Editrice Dott. Antonio Milani

CEDAMEL Centre d'Études et de Distribution des Appareils et du Matériel de l'Enseignement Linguistique

CEDAOM Centre d'Étude et de Documentation pour l'Afrique et l'Outre-Mer

CEDAP Centro de Desarrollo de Administracion Pública (Guatemala)

CEDDA Centre for Experiment Design and Data Analysis (*of* NOAA)

CEDE Centro de Estudios sobre Desarrollo Económico, Universidad de los Andes (Colombia)

CEDEAO Communauté Économique et Douanière de l'Afrique de l'Ouest

CEDEC Centre Européen de Documentation et de Compensation

CEDEFOP Centre Européen pour le Développement de la Formation Professionelle

CEDEG Centre Européen de Documentation et d'Études Gérontologiques (Belgium)

CEDEP Centre Européen d'Éducation Permanente (France)

CEDES Centre d'Étude du Développement Économique et Social (Morocco).

CEDES Corps Européen de Développement Économique et Social (Belgium)

CEDESA African Economic and Social Documentation Centre (Belgium)

CEDESE Communauté Européenne des Étudiants

CEDEV Centre d'Étude des Pays en Développement (Belgium)

CEDH Convention Européenne des Droits de l'Homme

CEDI Centre Européen de Documentation et d'Information

CEDIA Centro de Estudio, Documentación e Información de Africa (Spain)

CEDIA Centre d'Études pour l'Extension des Débouchés Industriels de l'Agriculture

CEDIAS Centre d'Études, de Documentation, d'Information et d'Action Sociales

CEDIC Comité Européen des Ingénieurs-Conseils du Marché Commun

CEDICE Centre d'Éducation et d'Information pour la Communauté Européenne

CEDIF Compagnie Européenne pour le Développement Industriel et Financier (Belgium)

CEDIGAZ Centre International d'Information sur le Gaz Naturel et tous Hydrocarbures Gazeux

CEDIM Centre d'Études de Droit International Médical

CEDIM Comité Européen des Fédérations Nationales de la Maroquinerie, Articles de Voyages et Industries Connexes

CEDIMAR Centro de Documentación e Información en Ciencias del Mar

CEDIMEX Centrafricaine de Distribution-Importation-Exportation

CEDIMON Centre Européen pour le Développement Industriel et la Mise en Valeur de l'Outre-Mer

CEDIP Centro de Estudos de Dinamica Populacional (Brazil)

CEDJ Centre d'Étude de la Délinquance Juvénile (Belgium)

CEDLA Centre d'Études et de Documentation Legislatives Africaines

CEDO Centre for Educational Development Overseas

CEDOC Centre Belge de Documentation et d'Information de la Construction

CEDOC Centro de Documentación Científica (Argentine)

CEDOCOS Centre de Documentation sur les Combustibles Solides (Belgium)

CEDOM Centre of Documentation and Teaching Materials (Peru)

CEDOPI Centre d'Études Documentaires de Propriété Industrielle

CEDORES Centre de Documentation et de Recherche Sociales (Belgium)

CEDP Centre d'Études et de Documentation Paléontologique

CEDR Comité Européen de Droit Rural

CEDRAL Comité Européen pour le Développement des Relations avec l'Amérique Latine

CEDRASE-MI Centre de Documentation et de Recherches sur l'Asie du Sud-Est et le Monde Insulindien

CEDRIC Centre d'Études de Documentation et de Recherches pour l'Industrie du Chauffage, du Conditionnement d'Air et des Branches Connexes

CEDSA Centro de Documentación del Sector Agrario (Peru)

CEDTT Committee for Economic Development of Trinidad and Tobago

CEDUS	Centre d'Études et de Documentation pour l'Utilisation du Sucre	**CEESA**	Conference of European Engineering Students Associations
CEDVAR	Centre National d'Études, de Documentation, de Vulgarisation Technique de l'Artisanat Rural	**CEET**	Compagnie Énergie Électrique du Togo
		CEF	Campaign for Earth Federation (Malta)
		CEF	Central European Federalists
CEE	Centro de Estudios Educativos (Mexico)	**CEF**	Commission Européenne des Forêts (Italy)
CEE	Commission Économique pour l'Europe	**CEF**	Conservation des Eaux et Forêts
CEE	Commission Internationale de Réglementation en veu de l'Approbation de l'Équipement Électrique	**CEFA**	Comité Europeo de Fabricantes de Azúcar (France)
CEE	Communauté Économique Européenne	**CEFAC**	Centre de Formations des Assistants Techniques du Commerce et des Consultants Commerciaux
CEEA	Centro de Estudos de Economia Agraria		
CEEA	Centro de Estudios para Empresas Agrícolas (Chile)	**CEFACD**	Comité Européen des Fabricants d'Appareils de Chauffage et de Cuisine Domestiques
CEEA	Communauté Européenne de l'Énergie Atomique (Euratom)	**CEFB**	Centre d'Études des Fontes de Bâtiment
CEEBA	Centre d'Études Ethnologiques de Bandundu (Zaire)	**CEFCTU**	Central European Federation of Christian Trade Unions
CEEC	Catholic International Education Office	**CEFD**	Centro de Estudios de Filosofica del Derecho (Venezuela)
CEEC	Commission Episcopale pour l'École Catholique (Libya)	**CEFIC**	Centre Européen des Fédérations de l'Industrie Chimique
CEEC	Committee of European Economic Co-operation	**CEFRACOR**	Centre Français de la Corrosion
CEECO	Comité d'Expansion Économique du Centre-Ouest	**CEFRES**	Centre Européen Féminin de Recherche sur l'Évolution de la Société (France)
CEED	Centro de Estudios Económicos y Demográficos (Mexico)	**CEFS**	Comité Européen des Fabricants de Sucre
		CEFTRI	Central Food Technological Research Institute (India)
CEEDIA	Centre d'Études pour l'Extension des Débouchés Industriels de l'Agriculture	**CEFV**	Centro de Estudios del Futuro de Venezuela
CEEGFP	Centre d'Études d'Économie et de Gestion de la Forêt Privée	**CEFYM**	Central European Federal Youth Movement (now CEF)
CEEH	Centre Européen d'Écologie Humaine (Switzerland)	**CEG**	Centre d'Études de Gramat (of DTAT)
CEEIM	Centre Européen d'Étude et d'Information sur les Sociétés Multinationales	**CEGAP**	European Committee of Landscape Architects
CEEMA	Centro de Ensenanza y Experimentación de la Maquinaria Agrícola (Argentina)	**CEGAT**	Centro de Estudios Ganaderos de Areas Tropicales (Argentina)
CEEMAT	Centre d'Études et d'Expérimentation du Machinisme Agricole Tropical	**CEGB**	Central Electricity Generating Board
		CEGEP	Collège d'Enseignement Générale et Professionel (Canada)
CEEP	Centre Européen de l'Entreprise Publique	**CEGET**	Centre d'Études de Géographie Tropicale
CEEP	Centre Européen d'Études de Population	**CEGOC**	Centro de Estudos de Gestão e Organizacão Cientifica (Portugal)
CEEP	Confédération Européenne d'Études de Phytopharmacie	**CEGOS**	Commission d'Études Générales de l'Organisation Scientifique
CEEPPA	Centre d'Études Économiques pour les Produits Agricoles	**CEGROB**	Communauté Européenne des Associations du Commerce de Gros de Bière des Pays Membres de la CEE
CEERI	Central Electronics Engineering Research Institute (India)		

CEH	Conférence Européenne des Horaires des Trains de Voyageurs	**CELA**	Committee for Exports to Latin America (*of* BNEC)
CEHILA	Comisió de Estudios de Historia de la Iglesia en America Latino	**CELAC**	Comité d'Études et de Liaison des Amendements Calcaires
CEHO	Compagnie Centrafricaine d'Exploitation Hôtelière	**CELADE**	Centro Latino-americano de Demografíca
CEHP	Comité Européen de l'Hospitalisation Privée	**CELADEC**	Commissão Evangelica Latinoamericana de Educação Crista
CEI	Centre d'Études Industrielles (Switzerland)	**CELAM**	Conseil Episcopal Latino-Americain
CEI	Comitato Elettrotecnico Italiano	**CELAME**	Comité de Liaison et d'Action des Syndicats Médicaux Européens
CEI	Commission Électrotechnique Internationale		
CEI	Commission Europe de l'IOMTR	**CELAP**	Centro Latinoamericano de Población y Familia (Chile)
CEI	Committee for Environmental Information (UN)	**CELATS**	Centro Latinoamericano de Trabajo Social
CEI	Council of Engineering Institutions	**CELC**	Commonwealth Education Liaison Committee
CEIA	Centre d'Entr'aide Intellectuelle Africaine		
CEIA	Comité Especial de Investigaciones Antárticas	**CELCA**	Centro Latinoamericano de Crédito Agrícola (Mexico)
CEIA	Coopérative d'Élevage et d'Insémination Artificielle	**CELE**	Centre Européen pour Loisir et l'Éducation (Czechoslovakia)
CEIB	Centrul Experimental pentru Ingrasaminte Bacteriene (Roumania)	**CELE**	Centro Coordinamento Elettronica
		CELF	Centre d'Études Littéraires Francophones (France)
CEIB	Confédération Européenne des Industries du Bois	**CELIB**	Comité d'Études et de Liaison des Intérêts Bretons
CEIC	Conseil Économique International du Cuir	**CELIBRIDE**	Comité de Liaison des Pays Membres de la CEE pour les Industries des Broderies, Dentelles et Rideaux
CEICN	Centre Européen d'Information pour la Conservation de la Nature		
CEIE	Centre d'Études et d'Information sur l'Enseignement	**CELIMAC**	Comité Européen de Liaison des Industries de la Machine à Coudre
CEIF	Council of European Industrial Federations	**CELME**	Centro Sperimentale Lavorazione Metalli
CEIM	Centre d'Études Industrielles du Maghreb (Morocco)	**CELMIC**	Comité Européen de Liaison des Médecins Interprètes de Conférences
CEIP	Carnegie Endowment for International Peace (U.S.A.)	**CELNUCO**	Comité Européen de Liaison des Négociants et Utilisateurs de Combustibles
CEIPA	Comité d'Études et d'Informations sur les Produits Agricoles	**CELOJ**	Scouts' Esperanto League
		CELOS	Centrum voor Landbouwkundig Onderzoek in Suriname
CEIR	Comité Européen de l'Industrie de la Robinetterie		
CEIST	Centro Europeo Informazione Scientifiche e Tecniche (Italy)	**CELPA**	Centro Espacial de Lanzamientos para la Prospección Atmosferica (Argentine)
CEITJA	Centre d'Étude Internationale sur le Travail des Jeunes dans l'Agriculture	**CELPUF**	Comité d'Études de Liaison du Patronat de L'Union Française
CEJ	Campagne Européenne de la Jeunesse	**CELTE**	Constructeurs Européens de Locomotives Thermiques et Électriques
CEJH	Communauté Européenne des Jeunes de l'Horticulture	**CELU**	Commonwealth Education Liaison Unit
		CELU	Confederation of Ethiopian Labour Unions
CEKOM	Central European Mass Communication Research Documentation Centre	**CEM**	Centre d'Essais de la Méditerranée
CEL	Committee on Engineering Laws (U.S.A.)	**CEM**	Christian Education Movement

CEM	Conférence Européen des Horaires des Trains de Merchandises	**CEMO**	Commission Économique pour le Moyen-Orient (UNO)
CEM	Council of European Municipalities	**CEMP**	Centre d'Étude des Matières Plastiques
CEM	Council of European Municipalities	**CEMP**	Centre d'Études et de Mesure de la Productivité
CEM	Croisade d'Evangélisation Mondiale		
CEMA	Canadian Electrical Manufacturers Association	**CEMS**	Compagnie des Experts Maritimes du Sénégal
CEMA	Catering Equipment Manufacturers Association	**CEMT**	Compagnie des Experts Maritimes du Togo
CEMA	Centre d'Études et de Modernisation Agricoles	**CEMT**	Conférence Européenne des Ministres des Transports
CEMA	Comité pour l'Étude des Maladies et de l'Alimentation du Bétail (Belgium)	**CEMU**	Centro Sperimentale per le Macchine Utensili
CEMA	Comité Européen des Groupements de Constructeurs de Machines Agricoles	**CEMUBAC**	Centre Médical de l'Université de Bruxelles au Congo
CEMA	Council for Economic Mutual Assistance (*Soviet Bloc*)	**CEN**	Centre d'Études Énergie Nucléaire (Belgium)
		CEN	Centro de Energia Nuclear (Brazil)
CEMAC	Committee of European Associations of Manufacturers of Active Electronic Components (*now merged into* CEMEC)	**CEN**	Comité Européen de Normalisation
		CENA	Centre d'Études Nord-Africaines
		CENA	Centre d'Experimentation de la Navigation Aérienne
CEMAG	Centre d'Étude de la Mécanisation en Agriculture de Gembloux (Belgium)	**CENAG**	Centre des Chefs d'Entreprises Agricoles (*now* CENECA)
CEMAP	Commission Européenne des Méthodes d'Analyse des Pesticides	**CENAMI**	Centro Nacional de Ayuda a Mexicanos Indigenas
CEMAT	Società per la Construzione e l'Esercizio dei Mezzi Ausiliari del Transporte	**CENAPEC**	National Centre for Promotion of Co-operative Enterprises (Ivory Coast)
CEMATEX	Comité Européen des Constructeurs de Matérial Textile (Switzerland)	**CENATRA**	Centre National d'Assistance Technique et de Recherche Appliquée (Belgium)
CEMBS	Committee for European Marine Biological Symposia	**CENCER**	Association of Certification (of CEN)
CEMBU-REAU	European Cement Association	**CENCI**	Centro de Estadisticas Nacionales y Comercio International del Uruguay
CEMD	Compagnie des Experts Maritimes du Dahomey	**CENCOS**	Centro Nacional de Comunicación Social (Mexico)
CEMDOC	Centro Multinacional de Documentación Científica sobre Geología, Geofisica de Colombia	**CENCRA**	Centro Nacional de Capicitacão em Reforma Agrária (Brazil)
		CENDES	Centro de Desarrollo Industrial del Ecuador
CEME	Centro Italiano per Studio delle Relazioni Economiche e dei Mercati Esteri	**CENDHR-RA**	Centre for the Development of Human Resources in Rural Asia (Philippines)
CEMEC	Committee of European Associations of Manufacturers of Electronic Components	**CENDIE**	Centro Nacional de Documentación e Información Educativa (Argentina)
CEMI	Conseil Européen pour le Marketing Industriel	**CENDIM**	Centro Nacional de Documentación e Información en Medicina y Ciencias de la Salud (Uruguay)
CEMLA	Centro de Estudios Monetarios Latinoamericanos (Mexico)	**CENDIP**	Centro Nacional de Documentación e Información Pedagógica (Colombia)
CEMM	Compagnie des Experts Maritimes de Madagascar	**CENDOC**	Centro Nacional de Documentación (Colombia)

CENECA	Centre National des Expositions et Concours Agricoles (*formerly* CENAG)
CENECO	Centre d'Entraînement à l'Économie
CENEL	Comité Européen de Coordination des Normes Électrotechniques
CENELCOM	Comité Européen de Coordination des Normes Électrotechniques des États Membres de la CEE
CENELEC	European Organization for Electrotechnical Standardisation
CENET	Centro Nacional de Electronica y Telecommunicaciones
CENFAM - RDP	Centro Nazionale per la Fisica della Atmosfera e la Meteorologia
CENFAR	Centre d'Études Nucléaires de Fontenay-aux-Roses
CENG	Centre d'Études Nucléaires de Grenoble
CENICIT	Centro Nacional de Información Científica y Técnica (Venezuela)
CENID	Centro Nacional de Información y Documentación (Chile)
CENIDE	National Centre for Educational Development and Research (Spain)
CENIM	Centro Nacional de Informação Científica en Microbiologia (Brazil)
CENIM	Centro Nacional de Investigaciones Metalúrgicas
CENIP	Centro Nacional de Productividad (Peru)
CENIS	Center for International Studies (U.S.A.)
CENITAL	Centro Nacional de Inseminación Artificial (Colombia)
CENPAR	Centre National de Promotion de l'Artisanat Rural
CENPHA	Centro Nacional de Pesquisas Habitacionais (Brazil)
CENPLA	Centro de Estudos, Pesquisa e Planejamento, (Brazil)
CENRA	Centro Nacional de Capacitación en Reforma Agraria (Peru)
CENS	Centre d'Étude Nucléaires de Saclay
CENSA	Committee of European and Japanese National Shipowners' Associations
CENTA	Centro Nacional de Tecnificación Agrícola (Salvador)
CENTA	Centro Nacional de Tecnologia Alimentaria (Peru)
CENTA	Combined Edible Nut Trade Association
CENTEX- BEL	Centre Scientifique et Technique de l'Industrie Textile Belge
CENTI	Centre pour le Traitement de l'Informatique
CENTO	Central Treaty Organisation (Turkey)
CENTRA- BOIS	Société Centrafricaine de Travaux du Bois
CENTRA- MINE	Compagnie Centrafricaine des Mines
CENTRI- FAN	Centre d'Institut Français d'Afrique Noire
CENTRO- COOP	Uniunea Centrala a Cooperativelor de Consum
CENTRO- MIN	Empresa Minera del Centro del Perú
CENYC	Council of European National Youth Committees
CEOA	Central European Operating Agency
CEOBOL	Centro de Documentación (Bolivia)
CEOC	Centre d'Études de l'Orient Contemporain
CEOC	Colloque Européen des Organismes de Contrôle
CEOP	Communauté Européenne des Organisations de Publicitaires
CEP	Centre d'Études des Matières Plastiques (Belgium)
CEP	European Committee for Plant Protection Research
CEPA	Centre d'Études des Problèmes Agricoles
CEPA	Cercle d'Études de la Productivité Agricole
CEPA	Comisión Económica para Africa (UNO)
CEPA	Comité d'Experts pour les Ajustements (UNO)
CEPA	Commission d'Études Pratiques d'Aviation
CEPA	Consumers Education and Protective Association International
CEPAC	Confédération Européenne de l'Industrie des Pâtes, Papiers et Cartons
CEPACC	Chemical Education Planning and Coordinating Committee (of American Chemical Society)
CEPADES	Centro Paraguayo de Estudios de Desarrollo Económico y Social
CEPAL	Comisión Económica para América Latina (UN)
CEPAL	Cooperativa Esportazione Produtti Agricoli
CEPALO	Comisión Económica para Asia y el Lejano Oriente (UNO)

CEPAO	Comisión Económica de las Naciones Unidas para el Asia Occidental	**CEPHR**	Comité d'Étude pour la Promotion de l'Habitat Rural
CEPAS	Centro di Educazione Professionale per Assistenti Sociali	**CEPIS**	Pan American Sanitary Engineering and Environmental Sciences Center (Peru)
CEPC	Central European Pipeline Committee	**CEPL**	Conférence Européenne des Pouvoirs Locaux
CEPC	Comité Élargi du Programme et de la Coordination (UNDP)	**CEPLA**	Comisión de Estudios para la Promoción de la Lana Argentina
CEPC	Comité Européen pour les Problèmes Criminels	**CEPLA**	Comité Espãnol de Plásticos en Agricultura
CEPCEO	Comité d'Étude des Producteurs de Charbon d'Europe Occidentale	**CEPLAC**	Comissão Executiva do Plano de Recuperação Econômico-Rural da Lavoura Cacaueira (Brazil)
CEPCH	Confederación de Empleados Particulares de Chile	**CEPLAN**	Centro de Estudios de Planificación Nacional (Chile)
CEPCIECC	Comisión Ejecutiva Permanente Consejo Interamericano para la Educación, la Ciencia y la Cultura	**CEPOI**	Centre d'Études des Pays de l'Océan Indien
		CEPOM	Centre d'Études des Problèmes d'Outre Mer
CEPCIES	Comisión Ejecutiva Permanente del Consejo Interamericano Economico y Social	**CEPRIG**	Centre de Perfectionnement pour la Recherche Industrielle et sa Gestion
CEPDAC	Comité d'Études pour la Défense et l'Amélioration des Cultures	**CEPRO**	Centre d'Étude des Problèmes Humains du Travail
CEPDECC-LA	Comisión Especial de Programación y Desarrollo de la Educación, la Ciencia y la Cultura en America Latina (U.S.A.)	**CEPS**	Central Europe Pipeline System (*of* NATO)
		CEPS	Centro de Estudos e Pesquisas de Sociologia (Brazil)
CEPE	Centre d'Études Phytosociologiques et Écologiques	**CEPSA**	Compania Española de Petroleos, S.A.
		CEPSE	Centre d'Études Politiques et Sociales Européennes
CEPE	Comisión Económica para Europa	**CEPSE**	Centre d'Execution des Programmes Sociaux et Economiques (Zaire)
CEPEC	Centro de Pesquisas do Cacau (Brazil)		
CEPEC	Committee of European Associations of Manufacturers of Passive Electronic Components	**CEPSI**	Centre d'Études des Problèmes Sociaux Indigènes (Zaire)
		CEPT	Centro de Estudos de Pedologia Tropical (Portugal)
CEPEM	Centre d'Études Européen pour les Problèmes de l'Environnement Marin	**CEPT**	Conférence Européenne des Administrations des Postes et des Télécommunications
CEPEP	Centro Paraguayo de Estudios de Población		
CEPEPA	Comité Économique de la Prune d'Ente et du Pruneau d'Agen	**CEPVDVM**	Centre d'Etude des Problèmes Viticoles et de Defense des Vins Meridionaux
CEPERN	Centro Panamericano de Entrenamiento para Evaluación de Recursos Naturales (Brazil)	**CERA**	Centre d'Etudes et de Recherches sur l'Aquiculture (Belgium)
CEPES	Centro de Estudios Políticos, Económicos y Sociales (Argentina)	**CERA**	Centre d'Etudes des Religions Africaines (Zaire)
CEPES	European Centre for Higher Education (Roumania)	**CERA**	Centre d'Etudes du Risque Atomique (Switzerland)
CEPES	European Committee for Economic and Social Development	**CERA**	Civil Engineering Research Association (*now* CIRIA)
CEPFAR	Centre Européen pour la Promotion et la Formation en Milieu Agricole et Rural	**CERAC**	Centre d'Etudes pour le Ruralisme et l'Aménagement des Campagnes
CEPGL	Communauté Économique des Pays des Grand Lacs	**CERAC**	Comité d'Expansion Régionale et d'Aménagement de la Champagne

CERAFER	Centre National d'Études Techniques et de Recherches Technologiques pour l'Agriculture, les Forêts et l'Équipement Rural (*formerly* CREGR)
CERAG	Centre d'Études Regionales Antilles-Guyane
CERAME-UNIE	Common Market Liaison Bureau for the Ceramic Industries (Belgium)
CERAT	Centre d'Étude et de Recherche sur l'Administration Économique et l'Aménagement du Territoire
CERBE	Centrum voor Rationele Bedrijfsvoering Zuidhollandse Eilanden
CERBOM	Centre d'Études et de Recherches de Biologie et d'Océanographie Médicale
CERC	Centre d'Études des Revenus et des Coûts
CERC	Civil Engineering Research Council
CERC	Comité Européen des Représentants de Commerce Group CEE
CERCA	Centre d'Enseignement Rural par Correspondance d'Angers
CERCA	Centre d'Études et de Recherches Catalanes des Archives
CERCA	Commonwealth and Empire Radio for Civil Aviation
CERCA	Compagnie pour l'Étude et la Réalisation de Combustibles Atomiques
CERCHAR	Centre d'Études et Recherches des Charbonnages de France
CERCI	Compagnie d'Études et de Réalisations de Cybérnetique Industrielle
CERCLE	Centre d'Études et de Recherches sur les Collectivités Locales en Europe (France)
CERCOL	Centre de Recherches Techniques et Scientifiques des Conserves de Légumes (Belgium)
CERDAC	Centro Regional de Documentación para el Desarrollo Agrícola de América Central (Costa Rico)
CERDAS	Centre for the Co-ordination of Social Science Research and Documentation in Africa South of the Sahara (Zaire)
CERE	Centre d'Études et de Recherches de Environnement (Belgium)
CERE	Comité Européen pour les Relations Economiques
CEREA	Centre National de Recherches pour l'Étude des Animaux Nuisibles ou Utiles à l'Agriculture (Belgium)
CEREA	Comisión Especial de Representantes de Entidades Agropecuarias (Argentina)
CEREBE	Centre de Recherche sur le Bien-être
CEREC	Centre Européen de Recherches Économiques et Commerciales
CEREFA	Comision Ejecutiva de Repoblacíon Educación Forestal Agropecuaria (Cuba)
CEREGE	Centre de Recherches en Économie et Gestion des Entreprises (Belgium)
CEREN	Centre d'Études Régionales sur l'Économie de l'Énergie
CERER	Comité d'Études et de Recherches Économiques Rurales
CERES	Centre d'Assais et de Recherches d'Engins Spéciaux
CERES	Centre d'Études et de Recherches Économiques et Sociales (Tunis)
CERES	Centre de Recherches Socio-Religieuses (Burundi)
CERES	Comité d'Études Régionales Économiques et Sociales
CERES	Controlled Environment Research Laboratory (*of* CSIRO) (Australia)
CERESIS	Centro Regional de Sismologia para América del Sur (Peru)
CERF	Centre d'Études et de Recherches en Fonderies (Belgium)
CERI	Central Education Research Institute (Korea)
CERI	Centre for Educational Research and Innovation (*of* OECD)
CERI	Centre d'Étude des Relations Internationals
CERIA	Centre d'Enseignement et de Recherches des Industries Alimentaires et Chimiques (Belgium)
CERIC	Consortium d'Études et de Réalisations Industrielles et Commerciales (Dahomey)
CERIS	Centro de Estatistica Religiosa e Investigacões Socias (Brazil)
CERK	Centre d'Études et de Recherches de Kara (Togo)
CERL	Central Electricity Research Laboratories
CERLAL	Centro Regional para el Formento del Libro en la América Latina (Colombia)
CERMA	Centre d'Études et de Recherches du Machinisme Agricole
CERMAP	Centre d'Études Mathématiques pour la Planification

CERMO	Centre d'Études et de Recherches de la Machine-Outil	**CESA**	Cooperative Educational Service Agency (U.S.A.)
CERN	Organisation Européenne pour le Recherche Nucléaire (*formerly* Conseil)	**CESAMP**	Group of Experts on the Scientific Aspects of Marine Pollution
CEROS	Centre Européen d'Observation par Sondages	**CESAP**	Commission Économique et Sociale des Nations Unies pour l'Asie et le Pacifique
CERP	Centre d'Études et de Recherches Psycho-techniques	**CESB**	Centre d'Enseignement Supérieur de Brazzaville
CERP	Centre Européen des Relations Publiques	**CESC**	European Confederation of Christian Trade Unions
CERPER	Empresa Pública de Certificaciones Pesqueras del Perú	**CESCJ**	Conseil Européen des Services Communautaires Juifs
CERPHOS	Centre d'Études et de Recherches des Phosphates Minéraux	**CESD**	Centre Européen pour la Formation de Statisticiens-Économistes pour les Pays en Voie de Développement
CERQUA	Centre de Développement des Certifications des Qualités Agricoles et Alimentaires	**CESDA**	Confederation of European Soft Drinks Associations
CERS	Centre d'Études et de Recherches Scientifiques	**CESE**	Centre d'Études de la Socio-Économie
CERS	Centre Européen de Recherches Spatiales	**CESE**	Comisión Ecuménica de Servicio, (Brazil)
CERSE	Centre National d'Études et de Recherches Socio-Économiques (Belgium)	**CESE**	Council for Environmental Science and Engineering
CERT	Comité de Roubaix-Tourcoing d'Études et d'Actions Économiques et Sociales	**CESERFO**	Centro Studi e Ricerche Fondiarie.
CERT	Comptoir d'Etudes Radio Techniques	**CESH**	Centre d'Études de Sciences Humaines (Zaire)
CERTS	Centre d'Études et Recherches en Technologie Spatiale	**CESI**	Centre for Economic and Social Information (*of* UNO)
CERTSM	Centre d'Études et de Recherches Techniques Sous-Marines	**CESIC**	Catholic European Study and Information Centre (France)
CERUSS	Comité Permanent International des Techniques et de l'Urbanisme Souterrains et Spatials	**CESIGU**	Comité pour l'Élaboration d'un Système Informatique de Gestion Universitaire (Canada)
CERVA	Consortium Européen de Réalisation et de Vente d'Avions	**CESII**	Centro de Sociologia Industrial e do Trabalho (Brazil)
CERVL	Centre d'Étude et de Recherche sur la Vie Locale	**CESIN**	Centro Economico Scambi Italo-Nipponici
CES	Centre for Environmental Studies	**CESL**	Camp Evans Signals Laboratory (U.S.A.)
CES	Centre d'Études Sociologiques	**CESL**	Conseil Européen de la Jeunesse Syndicale
CES	Comité Économique et Social (of CEE)	**CESLAMD**	Comité de Liaison des Secrétariats Latino-Américaines des Moyens de Diffusion
CES	Confédération Européenne des Syndicats		
CES	Conference of European Statisticians (UN)	**CESMAD**	Association des Transporteurs Routiers Internationaux Tschécoslovaques
CES	Conseil Économique et Social		
CESA	Canadian Engineering Standards Association	**CESO**	Canadian Executive Services Overseas
CESA	Central Ecuatoriana de Servicios Agraria	**CESO**	Centrum voor de Studie van het Onderwijs in Veranderende Maatschappijen
CESA	Centre d'Études Sociales Africaines (Zaire)	**CESO**	Concorde Engines Support Organisation Ltd
CESA	Comité Européen des Syndicats de l'Alimentation du Tabac et de l'Industrie Hôtelière dans la Communauté	**CESO**	Council of Engineers and Scientists Organisations (U.S.A.)

CESP	European Confederation of National Unions Associations and Professional Sections of Pediatricians (Belgium)	**CETIS**	European Atomic Energy Community Scientific Data-processing Centre
CESPAP	Comisión Económica y Social para Asia y el Pacifico (UN)	**CETISA**	Compañia Española de Editoriales Tecnológicas Internacionales
CESPQ	Compañia Ecuatoriana de Sal y Productos Químicos	**CETMA**	Centre d'Ethno-technologie en Milieux Aquatiques
CESR	Canadian Electronic Sales Representatives	**CETMA**	Centre d'Études Techniques Ménagères et Agricoles
CESSE	Council of Engineering and Scientific Society Executives (U.S.A.)	**CETO**	Centre for Educational Television Overseas
CESSTW	Center for the Economic and Social Study of the Third World (Mexico)	**CETOP**	Comité Européen des Transmissions Oléohydrauliques et Pneumatiques
CESTA	Conference on Education and Scientific and Technical Training in Relation to Development in Africa	**CETOPES**	Centre d'Études des Techniciens de l'Organisation Professionnelle
CESTI	Centre d'Études des Sciences et Techniques de l'Information (Dakar)	**CETP**	Confédération Européenne pour la Thérapie Physique
CET	Centre Européen de Traduction	**CETRA**	Compagnie Équatoriale de Travaux (Gabon)
CET	Commission Européenne du Tourisme	**CETRAMET**	Compagnie Équatoriale pour la Transformation des Métaux en République Centrafricaine
CET	Council for Educational Technology for the United Kingdom		
CETA	Centres d'Études Techniques Agricoles	**CETRAMET - CONGO**	Compagnie Équatoriale pour la Transformation des Métaux au Congo
CETA	Centro des Estudos Technicos de Automación	**CETS**	Centre Européen de Technologie Spatiale
CETA	Conference des Églises de toute l'Afrique	**CETSAS**	Centre d'Études Transdisciplinaires (Sociologie, Anthropologie, Sémiologie)
CETAM	Centre d'Etudes Techniques Agricoles Ménager	**CETT**	Centro de Entreamiento para Tecnicos en Telecommunicaciónes (Venezuela)
CETCA	Centre d'Enseignement Technique du Crédit Agricole	**CETT**	Compagnie Européenne de Télétransmissions
CETEHOR	Centre Technique de l'Industrie Horlogère	**CEU**	Constructional Engineering Union (*now* AUEW)
CETEM	Centre d'Enseignement des Techniques d'Étude de Marché	**CEUCA**	Centro de Estudios Universitarios Colombo-Americanos
CETEPA	Centre Professionnel Technique d'Études de la Pollution Atmosphérique	**CEUCA**	Customs and Economic Union of Central Africa
CETEX	Committee on Extra-Terrestrial Exploration	**CEUCORS**	Centre Européen de Coordination de Recherche et de Documentation en Sciences Sociales
CETF	Centre d'Études des Techniques Forestières		
CETHEDEC	Centre d'Études Théoretique de la Détection et des Communications	**CEUR**	Centro de Estudios Urbanos y Regionales (Argentina)
CETIE	Centre Technique International de l'Embouteillage	**CEUSA**	Committee for Exports to the United States of America (*now* BOTB)
CETIEF	Centre Technique des Industries de l'Estampage	**CEV**	Coöperatieve Eierveiling van de ABTB
		CEVECO	Centrale Organisatie van Veeafzet- en Vleesverwerkings-coöperaties
CETIL	Committee of Experts for the Transfer of Information between Community Languages (EEC)	**CEVOI**	Comptoir d'Exportation de Vanille de l'Océan Indien (Madagascar)
		CEWC	Council for Education in World Citizenship
CETIOM	Centre Technique Interprofessionnel des Oléagineux Metropolitains	**CEXIM**	Carteira de Exportação e Importação (Brazil) (*replaced by* CACEX)

CEXO	Société des Caoutchoucs d'Extrême-Orient (Viet-Nam)
CEZ	Centre Européen pour la Formation Professionnelle dans l'Assurance (Switzerland)
CEZA	Comité Européen de Zoologie Agricole
CEZMS	Church of England Zenana Missionary Society
CEZOO	Centre de Recherches Zoologiques Appliquées (Belgium)
CF	Comité des Forêts
CF	Commonwealth Fund (U.S.A.)
CF	Sveriges Civilingenjörsförbund
CFA	Canadian Federation of Agriculture
CFA	Canadian Forestry Association
CFA	Comité Français des Aérosols
CFA	Committee on Food Aid Policies and Programmes (FAO/WFP)
CFA	Commission des Forêts pour l'Afrique (FAO)
CFA	Commonwealth Forestry Association
CFA	Communauté Financière Africaine
CFA	Compagnie Forestière Africaine
CFA	Comptoir Français de l'Azote
CFA	Confédération Française de l'Artisanat
CFA	Confédération Française de l'Aviculture
CFA	Conférence des Femmes Africaines
CFA	Corporación Frutícola Argentina
CFA	Council of Ironfoundry Associations
CFA	Credit Foncier d'Afrique
CFAE	Centre de Formation en Aérodynamique Expérimentale (Belgium)
CFAE	Council for Financial Aid to Education (U.S.A.)
CFAL	Commission des Forêts pour l'Amérique Latine
CFAL	Current Food Additives Legislation (U.S.A.)
CFAN	Commission Forestière pour l'Amérique du Nord (FAO)
CFAO	Chief Fire Officers Association
CFAO	Compagnie Française de l'Afrique Occidentale
CFAP	Canadian Foundation for the Advancement of Pharmacy
CFAP	Commission des Forêts pour l'Asie et la Région du Pacifique

CFAT	Carnegie Foundation for the Advancement of Teaching (U.S.A.)
CFB	Commonwealth Forestry Bureau
CFB	Conselho Federal de Biblioteconomia (Brazil)
CFBS	Canadian Federation of Biological Sciences
CFC	Compagnie Forestière du Congo
CFCA	Confédération Française de la Coopération Agricole
CFCAM	Caisse Forestière de Crédit Agricole Mutuel et de Garantie Incendie Forestière
CFCB	Compagnie Française de Crédit et de Banque
CFCCA	Centre de Formation des Cadres pour Coopératives Agricoles (Rwanda)
CFCE	Conseil des Fédérations Commerciales d'Europe (*now* OIC)
CFCO	Chemin de Fer Congo-Océan
CFCPC	Comité des Fruits à Cidre et des Productions Cidricoles (France)
CFD	Christlicher Friedendienst
CFDA	Council of Fashion Designers of America
CFDC	Canadian Film Development Corporation
CFDC	Cane Farming Development Corporation (Guyana)
CFDC	Centre Français de Droit Comparé
CFDT	Compagnie Française pour le Développement des Fibres Textiles
CFDT	Confédération Française Démocratique de Travail
CFE	Comision Federal de Electricidad (Mexico)
CFE	Confédération de Groupements de Conseils Fiscaux des Pays de la Communauté Économique Européenne (Confédération Fiscale Européenne)
CFEI	Centre de Formation et d'Échanges Internationaux
CFEM	Comité pour une Fédération Européenne et Mondiale
CFEM	Compagnie Française d'Entreprises Métalliques
CFEP	Centre Français de Protection de l'Enfance
CFEU	Conseil Français pour l'Europe Unie
CFF	Chemins de Fer Fédéraux Suisse
CFF	Crédit Foncier de France
CFFA	Commonwealth Families and Friendship Association
CFG	Compagnie Forestière du Gabon

CFGE	California Fruit Growers Exchange (U.S.A.)	CFPI	Central Family Planning Institute (India)
CFGG	Compagnie Forestière du Golfe de Guinée	CFPI	Centro de Fomento y Productividad Industrial (Guatemala)
CFH	International Information Centre of the Swiss Watchmaking Industry	CFPI	Commission de la Fonction Publique Internationale
CFHA	Colorado Forestry and Horticulture Association (U.S.A.)	CFPO	Commission des Forêts pour le Proche-Orient
CFI	Commonwealth Forestry Institute (*formerly* IFI)	CFPPT	Centre de Formation et de Perfectionnement des Planteurs de Tabac
CFI	Consejo Federal de Inversiones (Argentina)	CFRAI	Comité Français des Relations Agricoles Internationales
CFI	Corporación Financiera Internacional		
CFI	Council of the Forest Industries of British Columbia	CFRI	Central Fuel Research Institute (India)
		CFRT	Colorado Foundation for Research in Tuberculosis (U.S.A.)
CFIA	Comisión de Fomento e Investigaciones Agrícolas (Chile)	CFRTI	Centre Français de Renseignements Techniques Industriels
CFIE	Conseil des Fédérations Industrielles d'Europe	CFRZ	Centre Fédéral de Recherches Zootechniques (Switzerland)
CFK	Christliche Friedenskonferenz (Czechoslovakia)	CFS	Comptoir Français des Superphosphates
CFLF	Comptoir des Filasses de Lin Françaises	CFSG	Compagnie Forestière du Sud-Gabon
CFL	Confektionsfabrikanternes Landsforbund	CFSI	Comité Français de la Semoulerie Industrielle
CFLA	Comisión Forestal Latinoamericana	CFSL	Central Forensic Science Laboratory
CFM	Council of Foreign Ministers	CFSTI	Clearinghouse for Federal Scientific and Technical Information (U.S.A.) (*now* NTIS)
CFME	Compagnie Franco-Malgache d'Entreprises		
CFMU	Compagnie Française des Minerais d'Uranium	CFTC	Commonwealth Fund for Technical Cooperation
CFMVA	Centre de Formation de Moniteurs et de Vulgarisateurs Agricoles	CFTC	Confédération Française des Travailleurs Chrétiens
CFN	Corporación Financiera Nacional (Colombia)	CFTF	Centre Technique Forestier Tropical (France)
		CFTH	Compagnie Française Thomson-Houston
CFNA	Comisión Forestal Norteamericana (FAO)	CFTRI	Central Food Technological Research Institute (India)
CFNCL	Comité Fédératif National de Contrôle Laitier	CFTV	Centre de Formation de Techniciens de Vulgarisation
CFNFMPR	Centre Familial National pour la Formation Ménagère et Professionnelle Rurale	CFV	Corporación Venezolana de Fomento
CFNI	Caribbean Food and Nutrition Institute	CFWCC	Children and Families World Community Chest
CFP	Canadian Forest Products	CFZV	Centrala Farmaseutica Zoo-Veterinara (Roumania)
CFP	Compagnie Français des Pétroles		
CFP	Confédération Française de la Photographie	CGA	Canadian Gas Association
CFPC	Centre Chrétien des Patrons et Dirigeants d'Entreprise Français	CGA	Confédération Générale de l'Agriculture
		CGA	Conseil Général de l'Agriculture
CFPC	Centre Français du Patronat Chrétien	CGA	Country Gentlemen's Association
CFPD	Compagnie Française Powell Duffryn	CGA	Cyprus Geographical Association
CFPFL	Confédération Française des Producteurs de Fruits et Légumes (*formerly* CNPFL)	CGAD	Confédération Générale de l'Alimentation en Détail
CFPFLC	Confédération Française des Producteurs de Fruits, Légumes et Champignons	CGADIP	Compagnie Gazière d'Afrique et de Distribution de Primagaz

CGAF	Confédération Générale des Architectes Français	**CGLS**	Confederazione Generale dei Lavoratori della Somalia
CGAF	Confédération Générale de l'Artisanat Français	**CGLV**	Breeders' Plant Licence Administration Fund
CGAP	Comité Général d'Action Paysanne	**CGM**	Compagnie Générale de Madagascar
CGB	Commonwealth Geographical Bureau (Sri Lanka)	**CGMA**	Casein Glue Manufacturers Association
CGB	Confédération Générale des Planteurs de Betteraves	**CGMA**	Compressed Gas Manufacturers' Association (U.S.A.)
CGBE	Christliche Gewerkschaft Bergbau und Energie	**CGMW**	Commission for the Geological Map of the World
CGC	Commonwealth Games Council	**CGOT**	Compagnie Générale des Oléagineux Tropicaux
CGC	Confédération Générale des Cadres	**CGP**	Commissariat Général au Plan
CGCA	Confédération Générale des Coopératives Agricoles (France) (*now* CFCA)	**CGP**	Commissariat Général à la Productivité
CGCI	Confédération Générale du Commerce et de l'Industrie	**CGPB**	Confederação General dos Pescadores do Brasil
CGCRI	Central Glass and Ceramics Research Institute, Calcutta (India)	**CGPB**	Confédération Générale des Planteurs de Betteraves
CGCT	Compagnie Générale de Constructions Téléphoniques	**CGPCC**	Confédération Générale des Planteurs de Chicorée à Café
CGD	Christliche Gewerkschaftbund Deutschland	**CGPEL**	Confédération Générale des Producteurs de Fruits et Légumes
CGE	Confederación General Económica (Argentina)	**CGPLBIR**	Confédération Générale des Producteurs de Lait de Brebis et des Industriels de Roquefort
CGE	Confédération Générale l'Épargne	**CGPM**	Conférence Générale des Poids et Mesures
CGEA	Confédération Générale Économique Algérienne	**CGPM**	Conseil Général des Pêches pour la Méditerrannée (FAO)
CGEC	Confederación General de Empleados de Comercio (Argentina)	**CGPME**	Confédération Générale des Petites et Moyennes Entreprises
CGECI	Compagnie Générale d'Électricité de Côte-d'Ivoire	**CGPP**	Confederazione Generale dei Produttori di Patate
CGER	Centre de Gestion et d'Économie Rurale	**CGPPT**	Confédération Générale des Producteurs de Pommes de Terre
CGF	Commonwealth Games Federation	**CGPS**	Canadian Government Purchasing Service
CGFPI	Consultative Group on Food Production and Investment in Developing Countries (FAO etc.)	**CGPT**	Confédération Générale des Paysans Travailleurs
CGFTL	Confédération Générale des Filateurs et Tisseurs de Lin	**CGRA**	China and Glass Retailers Association
		CGRA	Consortium Général des Recherches Aéronautiques
CGGP	Conference Group on German Politics	**CGRB**	Capital Gains Research Bureau
CGI	Comitato Glaciologico Italiano	**CGRB**	Combinatie Groningen v. Rationele Bedrijfsvoering
CGI	Congrès Géologique International	**CGRI**	Central Glass and Ceramic Research Institute (India)
CGIAR	Consultative Group on International Agricultural Research (FAO *etc*).	**CGS**	Canadian Geographical Society
CGIC	Comité Général Interprofessionnel Chanvrier	**CGSB**	Canadian Government Specifications Board
CGIL	Confederazione Generale Italiana Lavora	**CGSI**	Confédération Générale des Syndicats Indépendants
CGLI	City and Guilds of London Institute		

CGSLB	Centrale Générale des Syndicats Libéraux de Belgique
CGT	Centro de Geografía Tropical (Ecuador)
CGT	Commissariat Général au Tourisme
CGT	Compagnie Générale Transatlantique
CGT	Confédération Générale du Travail
CGTA	General Confederation of African Workers
CGTB	Canadian Government Travel Bureau
CGTFB	Confederación General de Trabajadores Fabriles de Bolivia
CGT-FO	Confédération Générale du Travail Force Ouvrière
CGTL	Confédération Générale du Travail du Luxembourg
CGTREO	Compagnie Générale de Travaux de Recherches et d'Exploitation Océaniques
CGU	Confederación General Universitaria (Brazil)
CGV	Confédération Générale de la Vieillesse
CGV	Confédération Générale des Vignerons
CGVCO	Confédération Générale des Vignerons du Centre-Ouest
CGVM	Confédération Générale des Vignerons du Midi
CGVSO	Confédération Générale des Vignerons du Sud-Ouest
CGWB	Canadian Government Wheat Board
CHA	Caribbean Hotel Association
CHA	Catholic Hospital Association (U.S.A.)
CHA	Chest and Heart Association
CHAC	Catholic Hospital Association of Canada
CHACONA	Chantier de Construction Navale
CHAFREC	Chambre Syndicate Française de l'Enseignement Privé par Correspondance
CHAIDIS	Chaine Africaine d'Importation, de Distribution et d'Exportation
CHAIS	Consumer Hazards Analysis Information Service
CHAMCOM	Chambre de Commerce d'Agriculture et de l'Industrie de la République du Tchad
CHANCOM	Channel Committee (of NATO)
CHAPA	Committee on the History of American Public Address
CHB	Central Housing Board (Kenya)
CHE	Comité Hygiène et Eau
CHEA	Centre des Hautes Études Administratives
CHEAM	Centre de Hautes Études Administratives sur l'Afrique et l'Asie Modernes
CHEAR	Council on Higher Education in the American Republics
CHEC	Commonwealth Human Ecology Council
CHENOP	Companhia Hidro-Eléctrica do Norte de Portugal
CHIA	Canadian Hovercraft Industries Association
CHIDRAL	Central Hidroelectrica del Rio Anchicaya, Limitada (Colombia)
CHISS	Centre Haitien d'Investigation en Sciences Sociales (Haiti)
CHOBISCO	Chambre Syndicale des Grossiers en Confiserie Chocolaterie, Biscuits et Autres Dérivés du Sucre (Belgium)
CHOCO-SUISSE	Union des Fabricants Suisses de Chocolat
CHR	Centralforeningen af Hotelvœrter og Restauratører i Danmark
CHS	Canadian Hydrographic Service
CI	Commonwealth Institute
CIA	Central Intelligence Agency (U.S.A.)
CIA	Centre d'Insémination Artificielle
CIA	Centre International des Antiparasitaires
CIA	Centro de Inseminación Artificial (Porto Rico)
CIA	Centro de Investigaciones Agronómicas (Venezuela)
CIA	Chemical Industries Association
CIA	Cigar Institute of America
CIA	Collegium Internationale Allergologicum
CIA	Comisión Internacional del Alamo (of FAO)
CIA	Comisión Internacional del Arroz (Thailand)
CIA	Comité International d'Auschwitz
CIA	Commonwealth Industries Association
CIA	Confederación Intercooperativa Agropecuaria (Argentina)
CIA	Confédération Internationale des Accordéonistes
CIA	Confédération Nationale Belge du Commerce Indépendant de l'Alimentation
CIA	Conseil International des Archives
CIAA	Centre International d'Aviation Agricole
CIAA	Comité International d'Assistance Aéroportuaire

CIAA	Commission des Industries Agricoles et Alimentaires de l'Union des Industries de la CEE	**CIAO**	Compagnie Industrielle Agricole Oubangui (Zaire)
CIAA	Comptoir Industriel et Agricole Abidjan (Ivory Coast)	**CIAO**	Conference Internationale des Africanistes de l'Ouest
CIAA	Confédération Internationale des Associations d'Artistes	**CIAP**	Centre d'Information Agricole des Planteurs
		CIAP	Centre d'Information de l'Aviation Privée
CIAB	Centro de Investigaciones Agrícolas de El Bajio (Mexico)	**CIAP**	Centro de Investigaciones en Administracion Pública (Argentina)
CIAB	Conseil International des Agences Bénévoles	**CIAP**	Comité Interamericano de la Alianza para el Progreso (OAS)
CIAC	Centrale Ivoirienne d'Achats et de Crédit	**CIAP**	Commission Internationale des Arts et Traditions Populaires
CIAC	Compagnie des Industries Africaines du Caoutchouc	**CIAP**	Compagnie Ivoirienne d'Armement à la Pêche
CIACAM	Compagnie Industrielle d'Automobiles du Cameroun	**CIAPAG**	Confédération Internationale des Anciens Prisonniers de Guerre
CIACOL	Compañia de Ingenieros Agrónomos de Colombia	**CIAPESC**	Companhia Amazónica de Pesca (Brazil)
CIADEC	Confédération Internationale des Associations d'Anciens des Élèves de l'Enseignement Commercial Supérieur	**CIAPG**	Confédération Internationale des Anciens Prisonniers de Guerre
CIADI	Centro Internacional de Arreglo de Diferencias Relativas a Inversiones	**CIAPY**	Centro de Investigacion Agricolas de la Peninsula de Yucatan (Mexico)
CIAECO-SOC	Consejo Interamericano Economico y Social	**CIAQ**	Centre d'Insémination Artificielle du Québec (Canada)
CIAFMA	Centre International de l'Actualité Fantastique et Magique	**CIARA**	Fundación para la Capacitación e Investigación Aplicada a la Reforma Agraria (Venezuela)
CIAGA	Confederación Interamericana de Ganaderos	**CIAS**	Centro de Investigación y Acción Social (Colombia)
CIAI	Comité International d'Aide aux Intellectuels	**CIAS**	Centro de Investigaciones Administrativas y Sociales (Venezuela)
CIAI	Conférence International des Associations d'Ingénieurs	**CIAS**	Centro de Investigaciones Agrícolas de Sinaloa (Mexico)
CIAL	Communauté Internationale des Associations de la Librairie	**CIAS**	Comité International d'Information et d'Action Sociale
CIAL	Council International des Auteurs Littéraires	**CIAS**	Comité Investigación Agua Subterránea (Argentina)
CIALA	Inter-Faculty Centre for African Anthropology and Linguistics (Zaire)	**CIAS**	Conference of Independent African States
CIALS	Confédération Intérnationale des Arts, des Lettres et des Sciences	**CIAS**	Consejo Inter-americano de Seguridad
CIAM	Colegio de Ingenieros Agrónomos de México	**CIASA**	Compania Internacional Aerea S.A. (Ecuador)
CIAM	Congrès Internationaux d'Architecture Moderne	**CIASC**	Confédération Interaméricaine d'Action Sociale Catholique
CIAMAC	International Conference of Associations of Amputees and Veterans	**CIASE**	Centro de Investigaciones Agrícolas del Sureste (Mexico)
CIAME	Commission Interministerielle pour les Appareils de Mesures Électriques et Électroniques	**CIAT**	Centro Interamericano de Administradores Tributarios
CIANE	Centro de Investigaciones Agrícolas del Noreste (Mexico)	**CIAT**	Centro Internacional por Agricultura Tropical (Colombia)

CIAT	Comisión Interamericana del Atún Tropical	CIC	Capital Issues Committee
CIAT	Comité des Industries de l'Achèvement Textile des Pays de la CEE	CIC	Caribbean Investment Corporation
		CIC	Centre International de Calcul (Switzerland)
CIATE	Cooperativa Industrial Agrícola Tropical Ecuatoriana	CIC	Chemical Institute of Canada
		CIC	Cinema International Corporation
CIATF	Comité International des Associations Techniques de Fonderie	CIC	Cobalt Information Centre
		CIC	Collège Internationale des Chirurgiens
CIATO	Centre Internationale d'Alcoologie/Toxicomanies	CIC	Comité International des Camps (of UIRD)
CIB	Centre Interaméricain de Biostatistique	CIC	Comité International de la Conserve
CIB	Centro Internacional Bibliografico	CIC	Comité International de Coordination pour l'Initiation à la Science et le Développement des Activités Scientifiques Extra-scolaires
CIB	Centro de Investigaciones Básicas (Mexico)		
CIB	Comité Interprofessionnel Bananier	CIC	Commission Internationale du Châtaignier (of FAO)
CIB	Communauté International Baha'ie		
CIB	Conseil Interfédéral du Bois	CIC	Compagnie Immobilière du Congo
CIB	Conseil International du Blé	CIC	Confédération Internationale des Cadres
CIB	International Council for Building Research Studies and Documentation	CIC	Confédération Internationale de la Coiffure
		CIC	Confédération Internationale de Défense du Cheval
CIB	International Timber Committee		
CIB	Société Congolaise Industrielle des Bois	CIC	Conférence Internationale du Crédit
CIBA	Ciba Foundation (for promotion of International Co-operation in Medical and Chemical Research)	CIC	Conseil International de la Chasse
		CIC	Conseil International des Compositeurs
		CIC	Council for International Contact
CIBAL	International Centre for Sources of Balkan History (Bulgaria)	CICA	Canadian Institute of Chartered Accountants
CIBC	Commonwealth Institute of Biological Control (West Indies)	CICA	Centro Interamericano de Ciêncas Administrativas
CIBC	Confédération Internationale de la Boucherie et de la Charcuterie	CICA	Centro de Investigaçao Cientifica Algodoeira (Portuguese W. Africa)
CIBE	Confédération Internationale des Betteraviers Européens	CICA	Comité International Catholique des Aveugles
CIBEP	Section des Six Pays du Commerce International de Bulbes à Fleurs et de Plantes Ornementales	CICA	Comité Internationale de la Crise Alimentaire
		CICA	Comité International de la Croisade des Aveugles
CIBER	Inter-African Centre for Information and Liaison in Rural Welfare	CICA	Commerciale Italiane Cooperative Agricole
CIBJO	Confédération Internationale de la Bijouterie, Joaillerie, Orfèvrerie, des Diamants, Perles et Pierres	CICA	Conférence Internationale des Contrôles d'Assurances des États Africains, Français et Malgache
CIBM	Centro de Investigación de Biología Marina (Argentina)	CICA	Confédération Internationale du Crédit Agricole
CIBRA	Comercio e Indústria de Produtos Agrícolas do Brasil	CICAA	Comisión Internacional para la Conservación del Atún del Atlántico
CIBRAZEM	Companhia Brasileira de Armazenamento (Brazil)	CICAE	Centre International des Cinémas d'Art et d'Essai
CIBS	Chartered Institution of Building Services	CICAF	Compagnie Industrielle des Combustibles Atomiques Frittes
CIBS	Conferencia Interamericana de Bienestar Social		

CICAF	International Committee for the Cinema and the Figurative Arts	**CICEIPB**	Comité Intérimaire de Coordination des Échanges Internationaux de Produits de Base
CICAJ	Centre International de Coordination de l'Assistance Juridique	**CICELPA**	Centro de Investigación de Celulosa y Papel (Argentina)
CICAM	Société Cotonnière Industrielle du Cameroun	**CICEP**	*See* CICYP
CICAP	Centre Interamericano de Capacitación en Administración Pública (Argentina)	**CICF**	Chambre des Ingénieurs-Conseils de France
CICAP	Consejo Internacional para la Colaboración en los Análisis de Plaguicidas	**CICF**	Confédération Internationale des Cadres Fonctionnaires
CICAR	Corporación Industrial Comercial Agropecuaria (Argentina)	**CICG**	Centre International du Commerce de Gros
CICAR	International Co-ordination Group for the Co-operative Investigations of the Caribbean and Adjacent Regions (FAO)	**CICG**	Centre International de Conférences Genève
		CICG	Conference Internationale Catholique du Guidisme
CICATI	Division of the Exchange and Coordination of International Technical Assistance (Brazil)	**CICH**	Centro de Información Científica y Humanística (Mexico)
CICATUR	Centro Interamericano de Capacitación Turistica (Argentina)	**CICH**	Comité Internationale de la Culture de Houblon
CICB	Chambre des Ingénieurs-Conseils de Belgique	**CICH**	Confederación Internacional Católica de Hospitales
CICB	Conférence Permanente Internationale des Centres du Bâtiment	**CICHE**	Computer Information Centre for Highway Engineering (South Africa) (*now* CICTRAN)
CICB	Société Royale Chambre des Ingénieurs Conseils de Belgique	**CICI**	Centre Industriel Centrafricaino-Israélien
CICC	Compagnie Immobilière et Commerciale du Cameroun	**CICIAMS**	Comité International Catholique des Infirmières et Assistantes Médico-Sociales
CICC	Conférence Internationale de Charitiés Catholiques	**CICIG**	Commissione Italiana del Comitato Internazionale di Geofisica
CICC	International Center for Comparative Criminology (Canada)	**CICIH**	Confédération Internationale Catholique des Institutions Hospitalières
CICCA	Centre International de Coordination pour la Célébration des Anniversaires	**CICILS**	Confédération Internationale du Commerce et des Industries des Légumes Secs
CICCH	Centre International Chrétien de la Construction d'Habilitation	**CICJ**	Comité International pour la Coopération des Journalistes
CICD	Collegium Internationale Chirugiae Digestivae	**CICLA**	Comité Internacional de Coordinación para el Combate de la Langosta Centro América
CICE	Centre International de Calcul Électronique (UNO)	**CICLA**	International Committee for Locust Control
		CICM	Centro de Investigación de Ciencias Marinas (Colombia)
CICE	Centre International de Culturisme en Europe	**CICM**	Commission Internationale Catholique pour les Migrations
CICE	Centre Ivoirien du Commerce Extérieur		
CICE	Centro de Investigaciones en Ciencias de la Educación (Argentina)	**CICOLAC**	Compañia Colombiana de Alimentos Lácteos
		CICOP	Catholic Inter-American Cooperation Program
CICE	Comité de l'Industrie Cinématographique Européenne	**CICOTE-PHAR**	Centre Technique International de Coordination Pharmaceutique
CICE	Compagnie Industrielle des Céramiques Électroniques	**CICP**	Comité Internacional para le Cooperación des los Periodistas
CICE	Information Centre of the European Railways (Italy)	**CICP**	Confédération Internationale du Crédit Populaire

CICPE	Comité d'Initiative pour le Congrès du Peuple Européen
CICPLA	Commission d'Information et de Coopération des Journalistes d'Amérique Latine
CICPLB	Comité International pour le Contrôle de la Productivité Laitière du Bétail
CICR	Comité Internationale de la Croix-Rouge
CICRA	Centre International pour la Coopération des Recherches en Agriculture (France)
CICRC	Commission Internationale contre le Régime Concentrationnaire
CICRED	Comité Internationale de Coopération des Recherches Nationales en Démographie (UN)
CICRIS	Co-operative Industrial and Commercial Reference and Information Service
CICS	Centre International de la Construction Scolaire
CICS	Commission Internationale Catholique de la Santé
CICS	Committee for Index Cards for Standards (*of* IOS)
CICSO	Centre International Culturel Social et Pedagogique de l'Université Libre de Bruxelles
CICT	Commission on International Commodity Trade (UNCTAD)
CICT	Conseil International du Cinéma et de la Télévision
CICTA	Commission Internationale pour la Conservation des Thonidés de l'Atlantique
CICTRAN	Computer Information Centre for Transportation (South Africa)
CICYP	Consejo Interamericano de Comercio y Producción
CICYT	Inter-American Committee on Science and Technology (U.S.A.)
CID	Centre d'Information et de Documentation du Congo et du Ruanda-Urundi
CID	Centre for Information and Documentation (EURATOM)
CID	Centre International pour le Développement (Switzerland)
CID	Centre International de Documentation des Producteurs de Scories Thomas (Belgium)
CID	Centro de Informacion y Documentacion
CID	Centro de Investigaciones para el Desarrollo (Colombia)
CID	Centro de Investigacion Documentaria (Argentina)
CID	Comité International du Dachau
CID	Comité International des Dérivés Tensioactifs
CID	Comité International de la Détergence
CIDA	Canadian International Development Agency
CIDA	Centre d'Information de Documentation et de l'Alimentation
CIDA	Centre International de Développement de l'Aluminium
CIDA	Centre International de Documentation Arachnologique
CIDA	Comité Interamericano de Desarrollo Agricola
CIDA	Comité Intergouvernemental du Droit d'Auteur
CIDA	Confederazione Italiana dei Dirigenti di Azienda
CIDA	Inter-American Centre for Archives Development (Argentina)
CIDADEC	Confédération Internationale des Associations d'Experts et de Conseils
CIDAECA	Comité International pour le Développement des Activités Éducatives et Culturelles en Afrique
CIDAL	Centro de Información y Documentación para América Latina
CIDALC	Comité International pour la Diffusion des Arts et des Lettres par le Cinéma
CIDAS	Centre d'Information et Documentation pour l'Agriculture et la Sylviculture (Roumania)
CIDAT	Centre d'Informatique Appliquée au Développement et à l'Agriculture Tropicale (Belgium)
CIDB	Chemie-Information und Dokumentation Berlin
CIDB	International Council for Building Documentation
CIDC	Comité International de Droit Comparé
CIDD	Conseil International de la Danse
CIDE	Centre Ibéroamericain de Documentation Européenne
CIDE	Centro de Información y Documentación Económica
CIDE	Centro de Investigación y Desarrollo de la Educación, Santiago (Chile)

CIDE	Comisión de Inversiones y Desarrollo Económico (Uruguay)	**CIDSE**	Coopération Internationale pour le Développement Socio-économique
CIDE	Commission Intersyndicale des Deshydrateurs Européennes	**CIDSP**	Centrule de Informare şi Documentare in Ştiinţe Sociale şi Politice (Roumania)
CIDE	Conseil International pour le Droit de l'Environnement	**CIDSS**	Comité International pour la Documentation des Sciences Sociales
CIDEA	Consejo Interamericano de Educación Alimenticia (Venezuela)	**CIDST**	Committee for Scientific and Technical Information and Documentation
CIDEC	Comité Interaméricain de la Culture (U.S.A.)	**CIDU**	Centro Interdisciplinario de Desarrollo Urbana y Regional (Chile)
CIDEC	Conseil Internationale pour le Développement du Cuivre	**CIE**	Cartographie des Invertébrés Européens
CIDECT	Comité Internationale pour le Développement et l'Étude de la Construction Tubulaire	**CIE**	Centre International de l'Enfance
		CIE	Centre International de l'Environnement
CIDEM	Inter-American Music Council	**CIE**	Centro de Investigaciones Económicas (Argentina, Colombia, Mexico)
CIDEP	Centre International de Documentation et d'Études Pétrolières	**CIE**	Comité Interafricain de Statistiques
CIDES	Centre de Investigación para el Desarrolo Economico Social (Argentina)	**CIE**	Comité International des Échanges
		CIE	Comité Interaméricain d'Éducation (U.S.A.)
CIDESA	Centre International de Documentation Economique et Social Africaine (Belgium)	**CIE**	Comissão Inter-Africana de Estatistica
		CIE	Commission Internationale de l'Éclairage
CIDESCO	Comité International d'Esthetique et de Cosmetologie	**CIE**	Commonwealth Institute of Entomology
		CIE	Compagnie Ivoirienne des Étiquettes
CIDH	Comisión Interamericana de Derechos Humanos (U.S.A.)	**CIE**	Consejo Interamericano de Escultismo (Costa Rico)
CIDHEC	Centre Intergouvernemental de Documentation sur l'Habitat et l'Environnement pour les Pays de la Commission Économique pour l'Europe des Nations Unies	**CIE**	Coras Iompair Eireann (Transport Organisation of Ireland)
		CIEA	Centre International de l'Élévage pour l'Afrique
CIDI	Centre International de Documentation et d'Information	**CIEA**	Centre International d'Études Agricoles
CIDIA	Centro Interamericano de Documentacióne e Información Agrícola (Costa Rico)	**CIEA**	Ceylonese Importers and Exporters Association
		CIEC	Centre International des Engrais Chimiques
CIDIA	Consejo Inter-Americano de Educación Alimenticia	**CIEC**	Centre International d'Études Criminologiques
CIDIAT	Centro Interamericano de Desarrollo Integral de Aguas y Tierras (Venezuela)	**CIEC**	Commission International de l'État Civil
CIDIC	Comité Interprofessionnel de Développement de l'Industrie Chevaline	**CIEC**	Confédération Interaméricaine d'Éducation Catholique
CIDITVA	Centre International de Documentation de l'Inspection Techniques des Véhicules Automobiles	**CIEC**	Conference on International Economic Cooperation
CIDOC	Centro Intercultural de Documentacion (Mexico)	**CIEC**	Conseil Internationale des Employeurs du Commerce (*now* OIC)
CIDP	Centre International de Documentation Parlementaire (Switzerland)	**CIECC**	Consejo Interamericano para la Educación, la Ciencia y la Cultura
CIDR	Compagnie International de Développement Rural	**CIECD**	Council for International Economic Cooperation and Development

CIECF	Commission Internationale Européenne des Communes Forestières et Communes de Montagne	**CIEPS**	Conseil International de l'Éducation Physique et Sportive
CIECMM	Comisión Internacional para la Exploración Cientifica del Mar Mediterráneo	**CIER**	Centro Interamericano de Educación Rural
CIEE	Consejo Internacional de Educación para la Enseñanza	**CIER**	Comisión de Integración Electrica Regional (Uruguay)
CIEF	Centre Interaméricain de Formation en Statistique Économique et Financière	**CIER**	Conseil International des Économies Régionales
CIEF	Centro de Investigaciones y Estudios Familiares	**CIERE**	Centre International d'Études et de Recherches Européennes
CIEH	Comité Interafricain d'Études Hydrauliques	**CIERIE**	Compagnie Ivoirienne d'Études et de Réalisations Informatiques et Économiques
CIEH	Comité Inter États des Études Hydrauliques (Senegal)	**CIERP**	Centre Intersyndical d'Études et de Recherches sur la Productivité (France)
CIEHV	Conseil International pour l'Éducation des Handicapés de la Vue	**CIERSES**	Centre International d'Études et de Recherches en Socio-Économie de la Santé (Fondation Royaumont)
CIEIA	Centro Internazionale per degli Studi sull Irrigazione	**CIES**	Centre International d'Enseignement de la Statistique
CIEL	Centre International d'Études Latines	**CIES**	Comité International des Entreprises à Succursales
CIEL	Commercial Importadora Exportadora S.A. (Canary Islands)	**CIES**	Comité Inter-Unions de l'Enseignement des Sciences
CIEM	Conseil International pour l'Exploration de la Mer	**CIES**	Commission Internationale pour l'Exploration Scientifique de la Mer Méditerrannée
CIEMA	Centre International des Études de la Musique Ancienne	**CIES**	Comparative and International Education Society (U.S.A.)
CIEN	Comisao Interamericano de Energia Nuclear	**CIES**	Consejo Interamericano Económico y Social
CIENCE	Commission Internationale d'Études de Normalisation Comptable Économique	**CIES**	Council for International Exchange of Scholars (U.S.A.)
CIENES	Centro Interamericano de Ensenanza de Estadistica (Chile)	**CIESEF**	Centre Interaméricaine d'Enseignement de Statistique Économique et Financière
CIENTAL	Centro de Investigaciones y Estudios Internacionales para la América Latina (Ecuador)	**CIESJ**	Centre International d'Enseignement Supérieur de Journalisme
CIEO	Catholic International Education Office	**CIESMM**	Commission Internationale pour l'Exploration Scientifique de la Mer Méditerranée
CIEP	Centre International d'Études Pédagogiques (France)		
CIEP	Consorcio dos Industriais de Equipaduento Pesado	**CIESPAL**	Centro Internacional de Estudios Superiores de Periodismo para América Latina (Ecuador)
CIEPA	Comité International de l'Éducation de Plein Air	**CIEST**	Centre International d'Études Supérieures de Tourisme
CIEPC	Commission Internationale d'Études de la Police de Circulation	**CIETA**	Calcutta Import and Export Trade Association (India)
CIEPI	Comité Interprofessionnel Européen des Professions Intellectuelles	**CIETA**	Centre International d'Étude des Textiles Anciens
CIEPRC	Confédération Internationale des Instituts Catholiques d'Éducation des Adultes Ruraux	**CIETAP**	Comité Interprofessionnel d'Études des Techniques Agricoles et Pesticides

CIETB	Centre Intercontinental d'Études de Techniques Biologiques
CIETT	Confédération Internationale des Entreprises de Travail Temporaire
CIEU	Centre Interdisciplinaire d'Études Urbaines
CIEU	Centro de Investigaciones Económicas (Chile)
CIEURP	Conférence Internationale pour l'Enseignement Universitaire des Relations Publiques
CIF	Commission Interaméricaine des Femmes
CIF	Confédération Internationale des Fonctionnaires
CIF	Conseil International des Femmes
CIF	Cork Industry Federation
CIF	Cultural Integration Fellowship (U.S.A.)
CIFA	Comité International de Recherche et d'Étude de Facteurs de l'Ambiance
CIFA	Committee for Inland Fisheries of Africa (FAO)
CIFA	Consociazione Italiani Federazioni Autotrasporti
CIFC	Council for the Investigation of Fertility Control
CIFCA	Centro Internacional de Formación de Ciencias Ambientales para Paises de Habla Española
CIFCA	Confédération Internationale des Installateurs d'Équipement de Réfrigération et de Conditionnement d'Air
CIFE	Central Institute of Fisheries Education (India)
CIFE	Centre International de Formation Européenne
CIFE	Comision Interministerial de Fomento Económico (Peru)
CIFE	Comité International du Film Ethnographique
CIFE	Conseil des Fédérations Industrielles d'Europe
CIFE	Conseil International du Film d'Enseignement
CIFEFTA	Council of the Industrial Federations·of EFTA
CIFEJ	Centre International du Film pour l'Enfance et la Jeunesse
CIFES	Comité International du Film Ethnographique et Sociologique
CIFF	Centro Incremento Frutticoltura Ferraresa
CIFI	Collegio Ingegneri Ferrovieri Italiani
CIFI	Consorzio Industriali Fotomeccanici Italiani
CIFOS	Compagnie Immobilière et Foncière du Sénégal
CIFRES	Centre International de Formation, de Recherches et d'Études Séricicoles (France)
CIFRI	Central Inland Fisheries Research Institute (India)
CIFT	Central Institute of Fisheries Technology (India)
CIFT	Committee on Invisibles and Financing Related to Trade (UNSTAD)
CIFTA	Comité International des Fédérations Théâtrales d'Amateurs de Langue Française
CIG	Comité Intergouvernemental Nations Unies/FAO
CIG	Comité International de Géophysique
CIG	Conférence Internationale du Goudron pour Routes
CIG	Intergovernmental Committee on the Establishment of a Free-trade Area (*of* OEEC)
CIGA	Centro de Investigaciones de Grasas y Aceites (Argentina)
CIGA	Compagnia Italian dei Grandi Alberghi
CIGAS	Cambridge Intercollegiate Graduate Application Scheme
CIGB	Commission International des Grand Barrages de la Conférence Mondiale de l'Énergie
CIGC	Comité Interprofessionnel du Gruyère du Comte
CIGDL	Chambre Immobilière du Grand-Duché de Luxembourg
CIGE	Centre Ivoirien de Gestion des Entreprises
CIGP	Conférence Internationale sur la Guerre Politique
CIGR	Commission Internationale du Génie Rurale
CIGRE	Conférence Internationale des Grands Réseaux Électriques
CIGS	Centre International de Gérontologie Sociale
CIHA	Comité Internationale d'Histoire de l'Art
CIHAN	Centraal Instituut ter Bevordering v. d. Buitenlandse Handel
CIHEAM	Centre International des Hautes Études Agronomique Méditerranéennes

CIHM	Commission Internationale d'Histoire Maritime
CIHM	Commission Internationale d'Histoire Militaire
CII	Centro Internacional de la Infancia
CII	Chartered Insurance Institute
CII	Compagnie Internationale pour l'Information
CII	Confederation of Irish Industry
CII	Conseil International des Infirmières
CII	Council of International Investigators (U.S.A.)
CIIA	Canadian Institute of International Affairs
CIIA	Commission Internationale des Industries Agricoles et Alimentaires
CIIC	Centre d'Information de l'Industrie des Chaux et Ciments
CIIC	Centro Internacional de Investigaciones sobre el Cáncer
CIID	Centro Internacional de Investigaciones para el Desarrollo (Canada)
CIID	Commission International des Irrigations et du Drainage
CIIG	Construction Industry Information Group
CIIM	Centre International d'Information de la Mutualité
CIINTE	Centralny Instytut Informacji Naukowo-Technicznej i Ekonomicznej (Poland)
CIIR	Catholic Institute for International Relations
CIITC	Confédération Internationale des Industries Techniques du Cinéma
CIJ	Commission International de Juristes
CIJ	Cour International de Justice
CIL	Christliche Internationale von Arbeiter der Lebensmittel- und Tabakindustrie und des Gastgewerbes
CIL	Comité International de la Lumière
CIL	Comité Interprofessionel du Logement
CIL	Confédération Nationale du Secteur Immobilier et du Logement (Belgium)
CILA	Centro Interamericano de Libros Academicos (Mexico)
CILAM	Compagnie Ivoirienne de Location Automobile et de Matériel
CILAS	Compagnie Industrielle des Lasers
CILB	Comité de l'Industrie Lainière Belge
CILB	Comité Interprofessional du Lait de Brebis

CILB	Commission International de Lutte Biologique contre les Ennemis des Cultures (*now* OILB)
CILC	Confédération Internationale du Lin et du Chanvre (France)
CILECT	Centre International de Liaison des Écoles de Cinéma et de Télévision
CILF	Conseil International de la Langue Française
CILG	CIRIA Information Liaison Group
CILO	Centraal Instituut voor Landbouwkundig Onderzoek
CILOPGO	Comité International de Liaison des Gynécologues et Obstétriciens
CILPE	Conférence Internationale de Liaison entre Producteurs d'Énergie Électrique
CILSS	Comité Permanent Inter-États de Lutte contre la Sécheresse dans le Sahel
CILT	Centre for Information on Language Teaching
CIM	Canadian Institute of Mining and Metallurgy
CIM	Carte Internationale du Monde
CIM	Centro Internacional del Medio Ambiente
CIM	China Inland Mission
CIM	Comisión Interamericana de Mujeres
CIM	Commission for Industry and Manpower
CIM	Congrès International des Fabrications Mécaniques
CIM	Congrès Islamique Mondial
CIM	Conseil International de la Musique
CIM	Consejo International de Mujeres
CIM	Convention Internationale Concernant le Transport des Merchandises par Chemins de Fer
CIM	Cooperative Investigations in the Mediterranean
CIMA	Centre Interdisciplinaire d'Étude du Milieu Naturel et de l'Aménagement Rural
CIMA	Compagnie Industrielle de Miroiterie Africaine (Cameroons, Congo)
CIMA	Compagnie International des Machines Agricoles
CIMAC	Congrès International des Machines à Combustion
CIMAF	Centro de Cooperação dos Industriais de Máquinas-Ferramentas (Portugal)
CIMAFOR	Comité Interprofessionnel du Machinisme Forestier

CIMAL	Centre d'Information Mondiale Anti-lèpre
CIMAO	Ciments de l'Afrique de l'Ouest (Ghana, Ivory Coast, Togo)
CIMAP	Commission Internationale des Méthodes d'Analyse des Pesticides
CIMAS	Conférence Internationale de la Mutualité et des Assurances Sociales
CIMCEE	Comité des Industries de la Moutarde de la CEE
CIMCLG	Construction Industry Metric Change Liaison Group
CIME	Centro de Investigación de Metodos y Tecnicas para Pequenos y Medianas Empresas (Argentine)
CIME	Comitato Intergovernativo per le Migrazioni Europee
CIME	Compagnie Industrielle des Métaux Électroniques
CIME	Conseil International des Moyens du Film d'Enseignement
CIME	Council of Industry for Management Education
CIMEA	Comité International des Mouvements d'Enfants et d'Adolescents
CIMEC	Comité des Industries de la Mesure Électrique et Électronique de la Communauté (*of* EEC)
CIMENCAM	Société des Cimenteries du Cameroun
CIMES	Concours International du Meilleur Enregistrement Sonore
CIMI	Centre of Industrial Microbiological Investigations (Argentina)
CIMM	Canadian Institute of Mining and Metallurgy
CIMMYT	International Centre for Corn and Wheat Improvement (Mexico)
CIMO	Club Européen des Importateurs de Fruits et Légumes d'Outre-Mer
CIMO	Commission for Instruments and Methods of Observation
CIMP	Commission Internationale de la Météorologie Polaire
CIMP	Conseil International de la Musique Populaire
CIMPM	Comité International de Médecine et de Pharmacie Militaires
CIMPO	Central Indian Medicinal Plants Organisation
CIMRST	Comité Interministeriel de la Recherche Scientifique et Technique
CIMS	Centro de Investigaciones Motivacionales y Sociales (Argentina)
CIMSCEE	Comité des Industries des Mayonnaises et Sauces Condimentaires de la CEE
CIMT	Compagnie Industrielle de Matériel de Transport (France)
CIMTAC	Committee for International Marine Telecommunications and Aviation Co-ordination
CINTEL	Cinema-Television Ltd
CIMTOGO	Société des Ciments du Togo
CIMTP	Congrès Internationaux de Médecine Tropicale et de Paludisme
CIN	Commission Internationale de Numismatique
CINA	Centralinstitutet för Nordisk Asienforskning
CINA	International Commission for Air Navigation
CINAB	Comité des Instituts Nationaux des Agents en Brevets
CINAV	Commission Internationale de la Nomenclature Anatomique Vétérinaire
CINCC	Coal Industry National Consultative Council
CINCHAN	Allied Commander-in-Chief Channel
CINCWIO	Steering Committee on Cooperative Investigations in the North and Central Western Indian Ocean
CINDA	Centre Inter-Universitaire pour le Développement des Andes (Chile)
CINE	Council on International Nontheatrical Events (U.S.A.)
CINECA	Co-operative Investigations of the Northern Part of the Eastern Central Atlantic (FAO)
CINFR	Central Institute for Nutrition and Food Research (Netherlands)
CING	Commission Internationale des Neiges et Glaces
CINOA	Confédération Internationale des Négociants en Oeuvres d'Art
CINP	Collegium Internationale Neuro-Psychopharmacologicum (Germany)
CINS	CENTO Institute of Nuclear Science
CINS	Collegium Internationale Activitatis Nervosae Superioris (Italy)
CINTECA	Centro de Información Tecnica Cafetalera (Brazil)
CINTER-FOR	Centro Interamericano de Investigación y Documentación sobre Formación Profesional (Uruguay)
CINU	Centre d'Information des Nations Unies
CINVA	Inter-American Housing and Planning Centre (Colombia)

CIO	Centar za Industrijsko Oblikovanje
CIO	Comité International Olympique
CIO	Commission Internationale d'Optique
CIO	Congress of Industrial Organisations (U.S.A.)
CIOA	Centro Italiano Assidatori Anodici
CIOFF	Comité International des Organisateurs de Festivals de Folklore
CIOIC	Commission Intérimaire de l'Organisation Internationale du Commerce
CIOMR	Comité Interallié des Officiers Médecins de Réserve
CIOMS	Council for International Organization of Medical Sciences
CIOPORA	Communauté Internationale des Obtenteurs de Plantes Ornementales de Reproduction Asexuée
CIOR	Confédération Interalliée des Officiers de Réserve
CIOS	Centro Italiano di Orientamento Sociale
CIOS	Comité International de l'Organisation Scientifique
CIOSL	Confederación Internacional de Organizaciones Sindicales Libres
CIOSTA	Comité International d'Organisation Scientifique du Travail en Agriculture
CIOT	Compagnie Industrielle d'Ouvrages en Textiles (Central Africa)
CIOTF	Conseil International des Organismes de Travailleuses Familiales
CIP	Cartel International de la Paix
CIP	Centre International de Paris
CIP	Centro Internacional de la Papa (Peru)
CIP	Centro de Investigaciones Pesqueras (Venezuela)
CIP	Collège International de Podologie
CIP	Comité International de Photobiologie
CIP	Commission Internationale du Peuplier
CIP	Commission Internationale de Phytopharmacie
CIP	Comptoir Ivorien des Papiers
CIP	Confédération Internationale des Parents
CIP	Council of Iron Producers
CIPA	Chartered Institute of Patent Agents
CIPA	Comité Interamericano Permanente Anti-Acridiano
CIPA	Comité Interamericano de Protección Agricola (Argentina)
CIPA	Comité International des Plastiques en Agriculture
CIPA	Council on International and Public Affairs (U.S.A.)
CIPAC	Collaborative International Pesticides Analytic Council Ltd
CIPACI	Société Commerciale et Industrielle des Produits Animaux en Côte d'Ivoire
CIPAIM	Cellule d'Intervention contre la Pollution dans les Alpes-Maritimes
CIPAM	Centro de Investigaciones de Plantas y Animales Medicinales (Mexico)
CIPAN	Commission Internationale des Pêcheries de l'Atlantique Nord-Ouest
CIPASE	Commission Internationale des Pêches pour l'Atlantique Sud-Est
CIPASH	Committee on International Programs in Atmospheric Sciences and Hydrology (U.S.A.)
CIPASO	Comisión Internacional de Pesquerías del Atlántico Sudoriental
CIPAT	Conseil International sur les Problèmes de l'Alcoolisme et des Toxicomanies
CIPBC	Centre National Interprofessionnel des Produits de Basse-Cour
CIPC	Centraal Instituut v. Physisch-Chemische Constanten
CIPC	Comité International Permanent de la Conserve
CIPCC	Comité International Permanent du Carbon Carburant
CIPCE	Information and Publicity Centre of the European Railways
CIPCI	Conseil International des Practiciens du Plan Comptable International
CIPCRO	Comité Intersecretarial sobre Programas Científicos Relacionados con la Oceanografica
CIPE	Centro Interamericana de Promoción de Exportaciones (Colombia)
CIPE	Collège International de Phonologie Expérimentale
CIPE	Comitato Inter-ministeriale per la Programmazione Economica
CIPE	Conseil International de la Préparation a l'Enseignement

CIPE	Consejo Internacional de la Película de Enseñanza	**CIPQ**	Centre International de Promotion de la Qualité
CIPEA	Centre International pour l'Élévage en Afrique	**CIPR**	Commission Internationale pour la Protection contre les Radiations
CIPEA	Comité International pour l'Étude des Argiles (*now* AIPEA)	**CIPRA**	Cast Iron Pipe Research Association (U.S.A.)
CIPEC	Conseil Intergouvernmental des Pays Exportateurs de Cuivre	**CIPRA**	Commission Internationale pour la Protection des Régions Alpines
CIPEMAT	Centre International pour l'Étude de la Marionnette Traditionnelle	**CIPROVA**	Comité Interprofessionnel pour la Promotion des Ventes des Produits Agricoles et Alimentaires
CIPEPC	Commission Internationale Permanente d'Études de la Police de la Circulation	**CIPS**	Canadian Information Processing Society
CIPEXI	Compagnie Ivoirienne de Promotion pour l'Exportation et l'Importation	**CIPS**	Comité Interprofessionnel des Productions Saccharifères
CIPF	Confédération Internationale du Commerce des Pailles, Fourrages et Dérivés	**CIPS**	Confédération Internationale de la Pêche Sportive
CIPFA	Chartered Institute of Public Finance and Accountancy	**CIPSH**	Conseil International de la Philosophie et des Sciences Humaines
CIPFE	Comité d'Initiative pour le Parti Fédéraliste Européen	**CIPSO**	Compagnie Industrielles de Plastiques Semi-Ouvres
CIPHP	Comisión Internacional de Pesquerias del Hipogloso del Pacífico	**CIPSRO**	Conseil Intersecrétariats des Programmes Scientifiques Relatifs à l'Océanographie
CIPI	Comité Interministériel de Politique Industrielle	**CIQ**	Confoederatio Internationalis ad Qualitates Plantarum Edulium Perquirendas
CIPIST	Centre International pour l'Information Scientifique et Technique	**CIQPEP**	*See* CIQ
CIPL	Comité International Permanent de Linguistes	**CIR**	Commission for Industrial Relations
		CIR	Commission International du Riz
CIPM	Comité International des Poids et Mesures	**CIRA**	Cast Iron Research Association
CIPM	Council for International Progress in Management (U.S.A.)	**CIRA**	Centre International de Recherches sur l'Anarchisme
CIPMME	Comité Intergovernemental Provisoire des Mouvements Migratories de l'Europe	**CIRA**	Centro Interamericano de Reforma Agraria (Colombia)
CIPO	Comité International pour la Protection des Oiseaux	**CIRA**	Centro Italiano Radiatori Alluminio
		CIRA	Commission Internationale pour la Réglementation des Ascenseurs et Monte-charges
CIPO	Corporación Industrial de Productos Oleaginosos (Argentina)		
CIPOL	Centre International de Publications Oecumiques des Liturgies	**CIRA**	Confederation of Industrial Research Associations
CIPP	Comisión Internacional de Problemas Pesqueros (*Apostolatus maris*)	**CIRA**	COSPAR International Reference Atmosphere
CIPP	Conseil Indo-Pacifiques des Pêches (*of* FAO)	**CIRB**	Centre International de Recherche Biologique
CIPPAS	Comité International Provisoire de Prévention Acridienne au Soudan Français	**CIRB**	Centre International de Recherches sur le Bilinguisme (Canada)
CIPPN	Commission Internationale des Pêcheries du Pacifique Nord	**CIRC**	Centre International de Recherche sur le Cancer
CIPPT	Centre International de Perfectionnement Professionnel et Technique	**CIRC**	Comité International de Réglementation du Caoutchouc

CIRCCE	Confédération Internationale de la Représentation Commerciale de la Communauté Européenne
CIRCF	Comité International de la Rayonne et des Fibres Synthétiques
CIRCOM	Centre International de Recherches sur les Communautés Coopératives Rurales
CIRDEC	Centre International de Recherche et de Documentation en Éducation Continue
CIRDI	Centre International pour le Règlement des Différends Relatifs aux Investissements
CIRDOM	Centre Interuniversitaire de Recherche et de Documentation sur les Migrations
CIRE	Confederación Internacional de Remolacheros Europeos
CIREC	Centre International de Recherches et d'Études Chréiologiques
CIRED	Centre International de Recherche sur l'Environnement et le Développement (France)
CIRES	Centre Ivoirien de Recherches Économiques et Sociales (Ivory Coast)
CIRET	Centre for International Research on Economic Tendency
CIRF	Centre International d'Information et de Recherche sur la Formation Professionnelle
CIRF	Corn Industries Research Foundation (U.S.A.)
CIRFED	Centre International de Recherche et de Formation en vue du Devéloppement Harmonisé
CIRFP	Centre International d'Information et de Recherche sur la Formation Policière
CIRFS	Comité International de la Rayonne et des Fibres Synthétiques
CIRIA	Construction Industry Research and Information Association
CIRIEC	Centre International de Recherches et d'Information sur l'Économie Collective
CIRIOL	Comitato Italiano di Rappresentanza Internazionale per l'Organizzazione del Lavoro
CIRIT	Comité Interprofessionel de Renovation de l'Industrie Textile
CIRM	Centre International Radio-Médical
CIRM	Comité International de Radio-Maritime
CIRP	Collège International pour l'Étude Scientifique des Techniques de Production Mécanique
CIRPHO	Cercle International de Recherches Philosophiques par Ordinateur
CIRR	Center on International Race Relations (U.S.A.)
CIRSA	Comité International Regional de Sanidad Agropecuaria (Latin America)
CIRSEA	Compagnia Italiana Ricerche Sviluppo Equipaggiamenti
CIRU	Colonial Insecticide Research Unit
CIRZ	Centro Italiano di Ricerche Zooeconomiche
CIS	Centre Interafricain de Sylviculture
CIS	Centre International d'Information de Sécurité et d'Hygiéne du Travail
CIS	Centre International des Stages
CIS	Centre International de Synthèse
CIS	Centro de Investigaciones Sociales (Colombia)
CIS	Centro Italiano di Sessuologia
CIS	Chartered Institute of Secretaries
CIS	Compagnie Ivoirienne de Sciages
CIS	Conference of Internationally-Minded Schools
CIS	Cranbrook Institute of Science (U.S.A.)
CIS	International Occupational Safety and Health Information Centre
CISA	Canadian Industrial Safety Association
CISA	Centro Italiano Studi Aziendali
CISA	Commission Internationale pour le Sauvetage Alpin
CISA	Confédération Internationale des Syndicats Arabes
CISA	Congresos Internacionales SA (Spain)
CISAC	Confédération Internationale des Sociétés d'Auteurs et Compositeurs
CISAE	Congrès International des Sciences Anthropologiques et Ethnologiques
CISAF	Conseil International des Services d'Aide Familiale
CISAI	Comité International de Soutien aux Antifascistes Ibériques
CISAL	Italian Confederation of Autonomous Labour Unions
CISAVIA	Civil Service Aviation Association
CISBH	Comité International de Standardisation en Biologie Humaine
CISC	Canadian Institute of Steel Construction

CISC	Confédération Internationale des Syndicats Chrétiens	**CISNAL**	Confederazione Italiana dei Sindacati Nazionali dei Lavoratori
CISC	Conférence Internationale du Scoutisme Catholique	**CISO**	Comité International des Sciences Onomastiques
CISCE	Comité International pour la Sécurité et la Coopération Européennes	**CISOR**	Centro de Investigaciones Sociales y Sociorreligiosas (Venezuela)
CISCO	Centro Italiano Studi Containers	**CISP**	Centro Italiano Smalti Porcellanati
CISCOD	Civil Service and Cooperation Office for Developing Countries (Belgium)	**CISP**	Comitato Italiano per lo Studio dei Probleme della Popolazione
CISCS	Centre International Scolaire de Correspondance Sonore Solidarité avec la Jeunesse Algérienne	**CISPM**	Confédération Internationale des Sociétés Populaires de Musique
CISDEN	Centro Italiano di Studi di Diritto dell'Energia Nucleare	**CISPP**	Centro Italiano di Studi e Programmazioni per la Pesca
CISE	Centro Informazioni Studi ed Esperienze	**CISPR**	Comité International Spécial des Perturbations Radiophoniques
CISEPA	Centro de Investigaciones Sociales, Económicas, Politicas y Antropologicas (Peru)	**CISR**	Center for International Systems Research (U.S.A.)
CISF	Centro Internazionale Studi Famiglia	**CISR**	Conférence Internationale de Sociologie Religieuse
CISF	Confédération Internationale des Sages-Femmes	**CISRC**	Computer and Information Science Research Center, Ohio (U.S.A)
CISGO	Commonwealth Interchange Study Group Operations	**CISRS**	Christian Institute for the Study of Religion and Society (India)
CISH	Comité International des Sciences Historiques	**CISS**	Comité Permanente Interamericano de Seguro Social (Mexico)
CISHEC	Chemical Industry Safety and Health Council (*of* CIA)	**CISS**	Conférence Interaméricaine de Securité Sociale
CISIC	Centro Internazionale Sociale Istituzione Clero	**CISS**	Conférence Internationale de Service Social
CISIP	Centro Internazionale Studi Irrigazione a Pioggia	**CISS**	Comité International des Sports Silencieux
		CISS	Conseil International des Sciences Sociales
CISIR	Ceylon Institute of Scientific and Industrial Research	**CISSB**	Civil Service Selection Board
CISJA	Comité International de Solidarité avec la Jeunesse Algérienne	**CISV**	Children's International Summer Villages
		CISWO	Coal Industry Social Welfare Organisation
CISL	Confédération Internationale des Syndicats Libres	**CIT**	Carnegie Institute of Technology (U.S.A.)
CISL	Confederazione Italiana Sindacati Lavoratori	**CIT**	Centre International du Tabac
		CIT	Chartered Institute of Transport
CISLE	Centre International des Syndicalistes Libres en Exil	**CIT**	Comité International de Télévision
CISL-ORE	Organisation Régionale Européenne de la CISL	**CIT**	Comité International des Transports par Chemins de Fer
CISM	Centre International des Sciences Mécaniques	**CIT**	Comité International Tzigane
		CIT	Conseil International des Tanneurs
CISM	Conseil International du Sport Militaire	**CIT**	Consejo Internacional del Trigo
CISMEDI	Comité International de Soutien pour la Sauvegarde et la Mise en Valeur de la Mer Méditerranée	**CITA**	Confédération Interaméricaine de Transport Aérien
		CITA	Confédération Internationale des Ingénieurs et Techniciens de l'Agriculture

ITA	Conférence Internationale des Trains Spéciaux d'Agences de Voyages	CITTA	Confédération Internationale des Fabricants de Tapis et de Tissus d'Ameublement
ITA	Consejo Interamericano de Archiveros	CIU	Chlorella International Union
ITAB	Compagnie Industrielle des Tabacs de Madagascar	CIUC	Consejo Internacional de Uniones Científicas
ITAM	Centre International de la Tapisserie Ancienne et Moderne	CIUFFAS	Comitato Italiano Utilizzatori Filati di Fibre Artificali e Sintetiche
ITB	Construction Industry Training Board	CIUMR	Commission Internationale des Unités et Mesures Radiologiques
ITC	Canadian Institute of Timber Construction	CIUPST	Commission Interunions de la Physique Solaire et Terrestre (U.S.A.)
ITC	Caribbean Interim Tourism Committee		
ITC	Comisión de Investigaciones Técnicas y Científicas (of OUA)	CIUS	Conseil International des Unions Scientifiques
ITC	Confédération Internationale des Industries Techniques du Cinéma	CIUSS	Catholic International Union for Social Service
ITCE	Comité International de Thermodynamique et de Cinétique Électrochimiques	CIUTI	Conférence Internationale Permanente de Directeurs d'Instituts Universitaires pour la Formation de Traducteurs et d'Interprètes
ITEC	Compagnie de l'Industrie Textile Cotonnière		
ITEC	Compagnie pour l'Information et les Techniques Électroniques de Contrôle	CIV	Centro de Investigaciones Veterinarias (Venezuela)
ITEF	Centro de Investigaciones de Tecnologia de Frutas y Hortalizas (Argentina)	CIV	Christelijke Internationale van Arbeiders in Voedings-, Tabak- en Hotelbedrijven
ITEFA	Instituto de Investigaciones Científicas y Técnicas de las Fuerzas Armadas (Argentina)	CIV	Commission Internationale du Verre
		CIV	Convention Internationale sur le Transport des Voyageurs et des Bagages
ITEJA	Comité International Technique d'Experts Juridiques Aériens	CIV	Coöperatieve Centrale Landbouw In-en Verkoopvereniging
ITEL	Comision Interamericana de Telecomunicaciones (U.S.A)	CIVAM	Centre d'Information et de Vulgarisation Agricole et Ménager
ITEN	Comité International de Teinture et du Nettoyage	CIVAS	Comité Interprofessionnel des Vins d'Anjou-Saumur
ITEPA	Centre Interprofessional Technique d'Études de la Pollution Atmosphérique	CIVB	Comité Interprofessionnel des Vins de Bergerac
ITI	Confédération Internationale des Travailleurs Intellectuels		
ITLA	Cámara Industrial Textil Lanera (Argentina)	CIVB	Comité Interprofessionnel des Vins de Bordeaux
ITLO	Centrum voor Informatieverwerking op het Gebied van Tropische Landbouw en Ontwikkeling (Belgium)	CIVC	Comité Interprofessionnel des Vins de Champagne
ITP	Conseil International des Télécommunications de Presse	CIVCP	Comité Interprofessionnel des Vins des Côtes de Provence
ITPPM	Confédération des Industries de Traitement des Produits des Pêches Maritimes	CIVCR	Comité Interprofessionnel des Vins des Côtes-du-Rhône
ITR	Compagnie Ivoirienne de Transports Routiers	CIVDN	Comité Interprofessionnel des Vins Doux Naturels
ITS	Commission Internationale Technique de Sucrerie	CIVEM	Constructions Ivoiriennes Électromécaniques
		CIVG	Comité Interprofessionnel des Vins de Gaillac
ITT	Commission Interaméricaine du Thon Tropical (FAO)	CIVI	Central Institute for Industrial Development (Netherlands)

CIVIJU	Association des Producteurs de Cidre, Vins, Jus de Fruits et des Embouteilleurs de Jus de Fruits (Belgium)	**CLAH**	Conference on Latin American History (U.S.A.)
CIVINEX	Société Ivoirienne d'Exploitation Vinicole	**CLAHCE**	Comité de Liaison des Associations Hôtelières de la Communauté Européenne
CIVO	Centraal Instituut voor Voedingsonderzoek (Netherlands)	**CLAID**	Comision Latino Americano de Irigacion y Drenaje
CIVPN	Comité Interprofessionnel des Vins du Pays Nantais	**CLAIET**	Comité de Liaison des Associations Internationales d'Entreprises Touristiques
CIVT	Comité Interprofessionel des Vins de Touraine	**CLAIRA**	Chalk Lime and Allied Industries Research Association (*now* WHRA)
CIVV	Centro Ittiologico Valli Venete	**CLAM**	Comité de Liaison pour l'Agrumiculture Méditeranéenne
CIVV	Commission Internationale Vol à Voile		
CIW	Carnegie Institute of Washington (U.S.A.)	**CLAMOP**	Centre Latino-Américain d'Opinion Publique
CIWLT	Comité Permanent des Syndicats de Travailleurs de la Compagnie International des Wagon-Lits et du Tourisme	**CLAO**	Consejo Latinoamericano de Oceanografica
		CLAPCS	Centro Latinamericano de Pesquisas en Ciencias Sociais (Brazil)
CJA	Conseil de la Jeunesse d'Afrique	**CLAPN**	Comité Latinoamericano de Parques Nacionales
CJCC	Commonwealth Joint Communications Committee		
CJD	Centre des Jeunes Dirigeants d'Entreprise	**CLAPTUR**	Corporation Latino-Americaine des Journalists Spécialisés en Tourisme
CJM	Congrès Jurif Mondial	**CLAQ**	Centro Latinoamericano de Quimica
CJP	Centre des Jeunes Patrons	**CLAR**	Confederacion Latino Americana de Religiosos (Colombia)
CKB	Christelijke Kruideniers Bond		
CKH	Centrale Kamer van Handelsbevordering	**CLARA**	Comite Latinoamericano para las Regiones Aridas
CKVR	Československý Komitét pro Vedecke Rízeni	**CLARCFE**	Consejo Latino Americano de Radiación Cósmica y Fisica del Espacio
CLA	Canadian Library Association		
CLA	Circolo dei Librai Antiquari	**CLARTE**	Centre de Liaison des Activités Régionales, Touristiques et Économiques
CLA	Confederación Lanera Argentina		
CLA	Country Landowners' Association	**CLAS**	Center for Latin American Studies (U.S.A.)
CLAB	Centre Latino-Americano de Ciencias Biologicas	**CLASA**	Confederación Latinoamericana de Sociedades de Anestesiología
CLACE	Centro Latinoamericano de Coordinación de Estudios (Brazil)	**CLASC**	Confederación Latino-Americaine des Syndicats Chrétiens
CLACE	Latin American Committee of Commercial Trade	**CLASP**	Consortium of Local Authorities in Wales
		CLASS	Current Literature Alerting Search Service (U.S.A.)
CLACSO	Consejo Latinoamericano de Ciencias Sociales (Argentina)		
		CLAT	Central Latinoamericana de Trabajodores
CLAD	Centro Latinoamericano de Administración para el Desarrollo (Venezuela)	**CLATE**	Confederación Latino-Americano de Trabajores Estatales (Argentina)
CLADEA	Consejo Latinoamericano de Escuelas de Administración	**CLATEC**	Comisión Latinoamericana de Trabajadores de la Educación
CLADES	Centro Latino Americano de Documentación Economica y Social (Chile)	**CLAT-RAMM**	Coordinación Latinoamericana de Trabajadores Metallúrgicos y Mineros
CLAF	Centro Latino-Americano de Fisica (Brazil)	**CLAW**	Consortium of Local Authorities in Wales
CLAF	Commission Latino-Américaine des Forêts		
CLAFE	Consejo Latino Americano de Física del Espacio (Mexico)	**CLC**	Caribbean Labour Congress
		CLC	Commonwealth Liaison Committee

CLCA	Comité de Liaison de la Construction Automobile pour les Pays de la CEE	CLPFF	Charles Lathrop Pack Forestry Foundation (U.S.A.)
CLCCR	Comité de Liaison de la Construction de Carrosseries et de Remorques	CLRI	Central Leather Research Institute (India)
CLEA	Centro Latinoamericano de Educación de Adultos (Chile)	CLTC	Confederación Latinoamericana de Trabajadores de Communicaciones
CLEAPSE	Consortium of Local Education Authorities for the Provision of Science Equipment	CLTEA	Council for Library Training in East Africa (Uganda)
CLEAR	Criminal Law Education and Research Center (U.S.A.)	CLTRI	Central Leprosy Teaching and Research Institute (India)
CLEC	Comité de Liaison de l'Engineering Chimique Français	CLV	Coöperatieve Landbouwvereniging
		CM	Chambre des Métiers
CLECAT	Comité de Liaison Européen des Commissionnaires et Auxiliaires de Transports du Marché Commun	CMA	Cable Makers' Association
		CMA	Canadian Manufacturers Association
		CMA	Canadian Medical Association
CLEIC	Comité de Liaison et d'Étude de l'Industrie de la Chaussure de la CEE	CMA	Catering Managers Association of Great Britain and Northern Ireland
CLEJFL	Centre de Liaison et d'Étude pour les Jus de Fruits et de Légumes (France)	CMA	Centre de Transport International par Véhicules Automobiles (Yugoslavia)
CLENE	Continuing Library Education Network and Exchange (U.S.A.)	CMA	Chocolate Manufacturers Association of the United States
CLEPA	Comité de Liaison de la Construction d'Équipements et de Pièces d'Automobiles	CMA	Commonwealth Magistrates Association
		CMA	Confédération Mondiale de l'Accordéon
CLF	Comité Linier de France	CMA	Congrès Mondial de l'Alimentation
CLIA	Cruise Lines International Association (U.S.A.)	CMA	Coopératives Marocaines Agricoles
		CMA	Crédit Mutuel Agricole
CLIF	Comité Latinoamericano de Investigaciones Forestales (Chile)	CMAA	Cigar Manufacturers Association of America
		CMAA	Cocoa Merchants Association of America
CLIMM	Commission de Liaison Inter-Nations Mars et Mercure	CMAA	Crane Manufacturers Association of America
CLIMMAR	Centre de Liaison International des Marchands de Machines Agricoles et Réparateurs	CMAAO	Confederation of Medical Associations in Asia and Oceania
CLIS	Clearinghouse for Library and Information Sciences (of ERIC)	CMAB	Centro Médico Argentino-Británico
		CMACP	Conseil Mondial pour l'Assemblée Constituante des Peuples
CLITAM	Centre de Liaison des Industries de Traitement des Algues Marines de la CEE	CMAE	Commission de Météorologie Aéronautique (de l'OMM)
CLITRAVI	Centre de Liaison des Industries Transformatrices de Viandes de la CEE	CMAg	Commission de Météorologie Agricole (de l'OMM)
CLMR	Central Laboratory, South Manchuria Railway Company	CMAO	Consejo Mundial de Artes y Oficios
CLO	Central Agricultural Organisation (Netherlands)	CMAR	Comité Maghrebin d'Assurances et de Réassurance (Morocco)
CLO	Centrum Landbouwkundig Onderzoek (Belgium)	CMAS	Confédération Mondiale des Activités Subaquatiques
CLOING	Comité de Liaison des Organisations Internationales Non-Gouvernementales	CMAV	Coalition Mondiale pour l'Abolition de la Vivisection
CLP	Club der Luftfahrtpublizisten (Austria)	CMBES	Canadian Medical and Biological Engineering Society

CMC	California Advisory Commission on Marine and Coastal Resources (U.S.A.)	**CMFRI**	Central Marine Fisheries Research Institute (India)
CMC	Canadian Marconi Company	**CMG**	Commission on Marine Geology (*of* IUGS)
CMC	Catholic Media Council	**CMH**	Commission de Météorologie Hydrologique (de l'OMM)
CMC	Collective Measures Committee of the United Nations	**CMHA**	Canadian Mental Health Association
CMC	Commission Médicale Chrétienne	**CMI**	Comité Maritime International
CMC	Consejo Monetario Centroamericano (Guatemala)	**CMI**	Commission Mixte Internationale pour les Expériences Relatives à la Protection des Lignes de Télécommunication et des Canalisation Souterraines
CMC	Coöperatieve Melk Centrale		
CMC	Groupement des Producteurs de Carreaux Céramiques du Marché Commun	**CMI**	Commonwealth Mycological Institute
CMCA	Constructions Métalliques du Centrafrique	**CMI**	Consejo Mundial de Iglesias
CMCA	Cycle and Motor Cycle Association	**CMIA**	Coal Mining Institute of America
CMCE	Comité Ministériel de Coordination Économique (Belgium)	**CMIDOM**	Centre Militaire d'Information et de Documentation sur l'Outre-Mer
CMCES	Comité Ministériel de Coordination Économique et Sociale	**CMIEB**	Centre Mondiale d'Information sur l'Éducation Bilingue
CMCF	Campagne Mondiale contre la Faim (*of* FAO)	**CMIRNU**	Centre Mondial d'Informations et de Recherches Appliquées aux Nuisances Urbaines (France)
CMCH	Campaña Mundial contra el Hambre (*of* FAO)	**CMITU**	Centre Mondial d'Informations Techniques et d'Urbanisme (Bulgaria)
CMCPT	Comité Maghrebin de Coordination des Postes et Télécommunications	**CMIU**	Cigar Makers International Union (U.S.A.)
CMCR	Compagnie Maritime des Chargeurs Réunis	**CMJP**	Centre Marocain des Jeunes Patrons et des Cadres Dirigeants
CMCSA	Canadian Manufacturers of Chemical Specialities Association	**CMM**	Commission de Météorologie Maritime (de l'OMM)
CMCW	Christian Mission to the Communist World	**CMMA**	Crane Manufacturers Association of America
CMD	Centralföreningen af Malermestre i Danmark	**CMN**	Comisia pentru Ocrotirea Monumentelor Naturii (Commission for the Protection of Natural Monuments) (Roumania)
CMD	Centrale Melkcontrôle Dienst		
CMDC	Central Milk Distributive Committee		
CME	Compagnie Mauritanienne d'Entreprises	**CMN**	Compagnie Malienne de Navigation
CME	Conférence Mondiale de l'Énergie	**CMO**	Centrale Melkhandelaren Organisatie
CMEA	Council for Middle Eastern Affairs (U.S.A.)	**CMOPE**	World Confederation of Organisations of the Teaching Profession
CMEA	Council for Mutual Economic Assistance (U.S.S.R.)	**CMP**	Christian Movement for Peace
CMEH	Council on Medication and Hospitals (U.S.A.)	**CMP**	Conseil Mondial de la Paix
		CMPA	Chinchilla Pelt Marketing Association
CMERI	Central Mechanical Engineering Research Institute, Durgapur (India)	**CMPAA**	Certified Milk Producers Association of America
CMET	Comité Maghrebin de l'Emploi et du Travail (Morocco)	**CMPCO**	Comité Mixta sobre Programas Científicos Relacionados con la Oceanografica
CMET	Council on Middle East Trade	**CMPE**	Comité Medical Permanent Européen
CMF	Cement Makers Federation	**CMPO**	Calcutta Metropolitan Planning Organisation (India)
CMF	Coal Merchants Federation of Great Britain		

CMR	Chrétiens dans le Monde Rural	CNAB	Confédération Nationale de Administrateurs de Biens
CMRA	Chemical Marketing Research Association (U.S.A.)	CNAD	Conference of National Armaments Directors
CMRC	Colonial Medical Research Committee	CNAE	Commisão Nacional de Actividades Especiais (Brazil)
CMREF	U.S. Committee on Marine Research, Education and Facilities	CNAF	Confédération Nationale de l'Aviculture Française
CMRI	Colonial Microbiological Research Unit (West Indies)	CNAG	Centro Nacional de Agricultura y Ganadería (Honduras)
CMRS	Central Mining Research Station (India)	CNAG	Commission Nationale d'Amélioration Génétique
CMRSS	Conseil Méditerranéen de Recherches en Sciences Sociales	CNALCM	Comité National d'Action et de Liaison des Classes Moyennes
CMS	Catholic Missionary Society	CNAM	Confédération Nationale de l'Artisanat et des Métiers
CMS	Church Missionary Society	CNAN	Compagnie Nationale Algérienne de Navigation
CMS	Commission de Météorologie Synoptique (de l'OMM)	CNAPT	Ceylon National Association for the Prevention of Tuberculosis
CMS	Corps Mondial de Secours	CNAR	Confédération Nationale pour l'Aménagement Rural
CMSCI	Council of Mechanical Speciality Contracting Industries (U.S.A.)	CNAR	Confédération Nationale des Artisans Ruraux
CMSER	Commission on Marine Science, Engineering and Resources	CNASA	Centre Nationale d'Aménagements des Structures Agricoles
CMT	Comité Maghrebin du Tourism (Tunisia)	CNASEA	Centre National pour l'Aménagement des Structures des Exploitations Agricoles
CMT	Confédération Mondiale du Travail	CNAT	Confédération Nord-Africaine des Transports (Morocco)
CMT	Construction Métallique Tropicale	CNAV	Christlinationaler Angestelltenverband der Schweiz
CMTC	Commission Maghrebine des Transports et Communications (Tunisia)	CNAVMA	Caisse Nationale d'Assurance Vieillesse Mutuelle Agricole
CMTI	Central Machine Tool Institute (India)	CNB	Centraal Normalisatie Bureau
CMTR	Compagnie Malienne de Transports Routiers	CNB	Comité National Belge
CMTT	Commission Mixte pour les Transmissions Télévisuelles	CNB	Confédération Nationale de la Boulangerie et Boulangerie Pâtisserie
CMV	Christlicher Metallarbeiterverband Deutschlands	CNB	Confédération Nord-Américaine de Billard (U.S.A.)
CNA	Central Neuropsychiatric Association (U.S.A.)	CNBE	Comité National Belge de l'Éclairage
CNA	Comissão Nacional de Alimentacão (Brazil)	CNBF	Centre National des Blés de Force
CNA	Comisión Nacional del Arroz (Ecuador)	CNBF	Centre National des Bureaux de Fret
CNA	Comissão Nacional de Avicultura (Brazil)	CNBF	Confédération Nationale de la Boucherie Française
CNA	Compagnie Nationale d'Assurance et de Réassurances (Ivory Coast)	CNBOS	Comité National Belge de l'Organisation Scientifique
CNA	Confédération Nationale de l'Artisanat	CNBT	Conseil National de la Blanchisserie et de la Teinturerie
CNA	Consejo Nacional Agrario (Peru)		
CNA	Corporación Nacional de Abastecimientos (Peru)		
CNAA	Comité National d'Action Agricole		
CNAA	Corporation Nationale de l'Agriculture et de l'Alimentation		
CNAA	Council for National Academic Awards		

CNBVSL	Confédération Nationale Belge des Industries et du Commerce des Vins, Spiritueux et Liqueurs	**CND**	Comptoir National du Diamant (Central Africa)
CNC	Comisión Nacional del Cacao (Ecuador)	**CNDC**	Comisión Nacional de Desarrollo Comunal (Peru)
CNC	Compagnie Nouvelle de Cadres	**CNDE**	Consejo Nacional de Desarrollo Económico (Peru)
CNC	Confederación Nacional Campesina (Mexico)	**CNDEP**	Conseil National des Détectives et Enquêteurs Privés
CNC	Confédération Nationale de la Construction (Belgium)	**CNDES**	Centre National de Documentation Économique et Sociale (Algeria)
CNC	Conseil National de Commerce	**CNDH**	Centre National de Documentation Horticole
CNC	Conseil National du Crédit	**CNDP**	Centre National de Documentation Pédagogique
CNC	Consejo Nacional Campesino (Costa Rica)		
CNC	Conselho Nacional de Cooperativismo (Brazil)	**CNDST**	Centre National Belge de Documentation Scientifique et Technique
CNC	Consorzio Nazionale Canapa	**CNDV**	Confédération Nationale des Distilleries Vinicoles
CNCA	Caisse Nationale de Crédit Agricole		
CNCA	Centre National de la Coopération Agricole	**CNE**	Centro Nacional de Economía (Nicaragua)
CNCA	Conselho Nacional Consultivo da Agricultura (Brazil)	**CNE**	Confédération Nationale de l'Élévage
		CNE	Conséjo Nacional de Educación (Bolivia)
CNCAF	Conseil National de la Coopération Agricole Française	**CNE**	Consejo Nacional de la Energía (Venezuela)
CNCATA	Centre National Coopératif Agricole de Traitements Antiparasitaires	**CNEA**	Comisión Nacional de Energía Atomica Argentina
CNCC	Confédération Nationale du Commerce Charbonnier	**CNEAF**	Comité National des Exploitants Agricoles Forestiers
CNCCEF	Comité National des Conseillers du Commerce Extérieur de la France	**CNEAF**	Confédération Nationale des Experts Agricoles et Fonciers
CNCCMM	Chambre Nationale des Constructeurs de Caravanes et de Maisons Mobiles	**CNEAT**	Centre National d'Études d'Agronomie Tropicale
CNCD	Confederazione Nazionale dei Coltivatori Diretti	**CNECB**	Collège National des Experts Compatables de Belgique
CNCE	Centre National du Commerce Extérieur	**CNEEJA**	Centre National d'Études Économiques et Juridiques Agricoles
CNCER	Centre National d'Économie Rurale		
CNCF	Confédération Nationale de la Charcuterie de France	**CNEEMA**	Centre National d'Études et d'Experimentation de Machinisme Agricole
CNCIA	Confédération Nationale des Commerces et Industries de l'Alimentation	**CNEF**	Cámara Nacional de Exploitación Forestal (Bolivia)
CNCM	Confédération Nationale du Crédit Mutuel	**CNEF**	Compagnie Nationale des Experts Forestiers
CNCrA	Caisse Nationale de Crédit Agricole	**CNEIA**	Comité National d'Expansion pour l'Industrie Aéronautique
CNCT	Consejo Nacional de Ciencia y Tecnologia (Mexico)	**CNEIL**	Centre National d'Études et d'Initiatives du Logement
CNCV	Confederación Nacional de Cooperativas de Venezuela	**CNEL**	Chambre Nationale Syndicale des Experts du Grand-Duché de Luxembourg
CNCV	Confédération Nationale des Coopératives Vinicoles	**CNEN**	Comision Nacional de Energia Nuclear (Mexico)
CND	Campaign for Nuclear Disarmament	**CNEN**	Comitato Nazionale per l'Energia Nucleare

CNENA	Centro Nacional de Energia Nuclear na Agricultura (Brazil)
CNEP	Comptoir National d'Escompte de Paris
CNEPA	Centro Nacional de Ensino e Pesquisas Agronomicas (Brazil)
CNEPDA	Comité National d'Étude des Problèmes du Développement Agricole
CNER	Campanha Nacional de Educaçao Rural (Brazil)
CNER	Centre National des Études Rurales
CNER	Conseil National des Économies Régionales
CNERA	Centre National d'Études et des Recherches Aéronautiques (Belgium)
CNERAD	Centre National pour l'Étude, la Recherche et l'Application du Développement
CNERIA	Centre National d'Études et de Recherches des Industries Agricoles
CNERNA	Centre National de Coordination des Études et Recherches sur la Nutrition Animale
CNES	Centre National d'Études Spatiales
CNET	Centre National d'Études des Télécommunications
CNETEA	Centre National d'Études Techniques et Économiques de l'Artisanat
CNEXO	Centre National pour l'Exploitation des Océans
CNF	Compagnie du Niger Français
CNFC	Centre National de Formation Coopérative (Cameroon)
CNFP	Consejo Nacional de Fomento Pesquero (Venezuela)
CNFR	Confédération Nationale de la Famille Rurale
CNFRA	Centre National Française de la Recherche Antarctique
CNFRO	Comité National Française de Recherche Océanique
CNG	Christlichnationaler Gewerkschaftbund der Schweiz
CNG	Confederación Nacional Ganadara (Mexico)
CNHR	Comité National de l'Habitat Rural
CNHRAC	Confédération Nationale pour l'Habitat Rural et l'Aménagement des Campagnes
CNI	Confederaçao Nacional das Industrias (Brazil)
CNI	Consiglio Nazionale degli Ingegneri

CNIA	Centro Nacional de Investigaciones Agropecuarias (Argentina, Colombia, Dominica, Salvador)
CNIA	Comité National Interprofessionnel de l'Amande
CNIA	Conseil National Interprofessionnel de l'Aviculture
CNIA	Consejo Nacional de Investigaciones Agricolas (Venezuela)
CNIB	Canadian National Institute for the Blind
CNIB	Confédération Nationale des Industries du Bois
CNIC	Centro Nacional de Investigaciones de Café (Colombia)
CNIC	Centro Nacional de Investigaciones Científicas (Cuba)
CNICI	Consejo Nacional de Investigaciones Científicas y Técnicas (Argentina, Uruguay)
CNICT	Consejo Nacional de Investigaciones Científicas y Técnicas
CNICTEI	Comité National Italien de Coopération Technique et Économique Internationale
CNIE	Comision Nacional de Investigaciones Especiales (Argentine)
CNIEC	China National Import and Export Corporation
CNIEL	Centre National Interprofessionnel d'Économie Laitière
CNIF	Conseil National des Ingénieurs Français
CNIH	Cámara Nacional de la Industria Hulera (Mexico)
CNIH	Comité National Interprofessionnel de l'Horticulture Florale et Ornementale et des Pépinières non Forestières
CNIH	Comité National Interprofessionnel du Houblon
CNIL	Comité National Interprofessionnel de la Laine
CNIOS	Comitato Nazionale Italiana per l'Organizzazione Scientifica del Lavoro
CNIP	Centre National des Indépendants et Paysans
CNIPA	Committee of National Institutes of Patent Agents (Netherlands)
CNIPBC	Comité National Interprofessionnel des Produits de Basse-Cour
CNIPT	Comité National Interprofessionnel de la Pomme de Terre
CNIR	Centre National Interprofessionnel du Rhum

CNIT	Cámara Nacional de la Industria de Transformación (Mexico)	**CNPF**	Conseil National du Patronat Français
CNIT	Centre National des Industries et des Techniques	**CNPFL**	Confédération Nationale des Producteurs de Fruits et Légumes (*now* CFPFL)
CNJA	Centre National des Jeunes Agriculteurs	**CNPFP**	Comité National de Propagande en Faveur du Pain
CNJPHP	Cercle National des Jeunes Producteurs de l'Horticulture et des Pépiniéres	**CNPFV**	Comité National de Propagande en Faveur du Vin
CNKi	Comité National du Kivu (Zaire)	**CNPI**	Comisión Nacional de Productividad Industrial
CNL	Commonwealth National Library, Canberra (Australia)	**CNPIO**	Commisão Nacional Portuguesa para Investigação
CNL	Confédération Nationale Laitiére	**CNPL**	Comissão Nacional da Pecuária do Leite (Brazil)
CNLA	Centre Nationale de Lutte Antiparasitaire		
CNLA	Council of National Library Associations (U.S.A.)	**CNPPLF**	Comité National de Propagande des Produits Laitiers Français
CNLSB	Ceylon National Library Services Board	**CNPRST**	Centre National de Planification de la Recherche Scientifique et Technologique
CNMA	Comitato Nazionale di Meccanica Agraria		
CNMB	Central Nuclear Measurements Bureau	**CNPS**	Confédération Nationale des Produits du Sol et Dérivés
CNMCCA	Confédération Nationale de la Mutualité, du Crédit et de la Coopération Agricoles	**CNPS**	Conseil National de la Politique Scientifique (Belgium)
CNME	Caisse Nationale des Marchés de l'État		
CNMI	Camera Nazionale della Moda Italiana	**CNPSEPC**	Confédération Nationale des Produits du Sol Engrais et Produits Connexes
CNMI	Comité National de la Meunerie Industrielle	**CNPV**	Comité National des Producteurs de Viande
CNO	Comisión Nacional del Olivo (Mexico)	**CNPVE-VAOC**	Confédération Nationale des Producteurs de Vins et Eaux-de-Vie de Vin à Appellations d'Origine Contrôlées
CNO	Council of National Organisations		
CNOF	Comité National de l'Organisation Française		
CNOP	Conseil National de l'Orde des Pharmaciens	**CNR**	Conseil National de la Récupération (Switzerland)
CNOPAR	Confédération Nationale des Organismes de Promotion Agricole et Rurale		
		CNR	Consiglio Nazionale delle Ricerche
CNOS	Comitato Nazionale per l'Organizzazione Scientifica	**CNRA**	Centre National de Recherches Agronomiques
CNOSA	Centro Nazionale Organizzazione Scientifica in Agricoltura (Italy)	**CNRA**	Consejo Nacional de Reforma Agraria (Bolivia)
CNOV	Comité National des Producteurs d'Oeufs à Couver et des Volailles dites d'Un Jour	**CNRC**	Centro Nacional de Radiación Cosmica (Argentine)
CNP	Comitato Nazionale per la Produttività	**CNRET**	Centre for Natural Resources, Energy and Transport (UN)
CNP	Comité National des Prix		
CNP	Consejo Nacional de Producción	**CNRF**	Centre National de Recherches Forestières
CNP	Corporation Nationale Paysanne	**CNRM**	Centre National de Recherches Métallurgiques (Belgium)
CNPA	Centro Nazionale de Patología Animal (Peru)		
CNPA	Comissão Nacional de Politica Agraria (Brazil)	**CNRN**	Comitato Nazionale per le Richerche Nucleari
CNPAR	Centre National de Progrès Agricole et Rural	**CNRS**	Centre National de la Recherche Scientifique
CNPCC	Confédération Nationale des Planteurs de Chicorée à Café	**CNRSH**	Centre Nigérien de Recherches en Sciences Humaines (Nigeria)
CNPE	Consejo Nacional de Planificación Económica (Guatemala, Salvador)	**CNRZ**	Centre National de Recherches Zootechniques

CNS	Cyprus Numismatic Society
CNSD	Confédération Nationale des Syndicats Dentaires
CNSM	National Confederation of Trade Unions of Mali (Africa)
CNSO	Confederación Nacional de Sindicatos Obreros (Chile)
CNT	Comisión Nacional del Trigo (Ecuador)
CNT	Confederación Nacional de Trabajadores (Chile)
CNTA	Comptoir National Technique Agricole
CNTC	Confederação Nacional dos Trabalhadores no Comércio (Brazil)
CNTG	Confédération Nationale des Travailleurs Guinéens
CNTI	Confederação Nacional dos Trabalhadores na Industria (Brazil)
CNTR	Compagnie Nationale des Transports Routiers (Central Africa)
CNTS	Confédération Nationale des Travailleurs Sénégalais
CNTUC	Ceylon National Trade Union Confederation
CNUCED	Centre du Commerce International
CNUCED	Conference des Nations Unies pour le Commerce et le Développement
CNUDCI	Commission des Nations Unies pour le Droit Commercial International
CNUDMI	Comisión de las Naciones Unidas para el Derecho Mercantil Internacional
CNUIP	Commission des Nations Unies pour l'Inde et le Pakistan
CNUURC	Commission des Nations Unies pour l'Unification et le Relèvement de la Corée
CNV	Christelijk Nationaal Vakverbond in Nederlands
CNVF	Comité National des Vins de France
CNVPA	Conseil National de la Vulgarisation du Progrès Agricole
CNVS	Confédération Nationale des Industries et Commerces en Gros des Vins, Cidres, Sirops, Spiritueux et Liqueurs de France
CO	Caribbean Organisation
COA	Commissie ter Bevordering v. h. Kweken en het Onderzoek v. Nieuwe Aardappelrassen
COAER	Union Costruttori Apparecchiature ed Impianti Aeraulici (Italy) (of ANIMA)
COAG	Committee on Agriculture (FAO)
COAL	National Committee on Arid Lands (U.S.A.) (of AAAS)
COAS	Council of the Organization of American States
COB	Centre Océanologique de Bretagne (CNEXO)
COBA	Central Ohio Breeding Association (U.S.A.)
COBAE	Comissão Brasiliera de Atividades Espaciais
COBAL	Companhia Brasileira de Alimentos
COBAM	Confection-Bonneterie Africaine et Malgache
COBCCEE	Comité des Organisations de la Boucherie-Charcuterie de la CEE
COBECEP	Comité Belge des Constructeurs d'Équipement Pétrolier
COBECHAR	Comptoir Belge des Charbons
COBELDA	Compagnie Belge d'Électronique et d'Automation
COBELPA	Association des Fabricants de Pâtes, Papiers et Cartons de Belgique
COBICA	Campanhia Brasileira de Industrialização da Castanha do Caju
COBOEN	Comisión Boliviana de Energía Nuclear (Bolivia)
COBRAG	Companhia Brasileira de Agricultura
COBRASA	Companhia Brasileira de Silos e Armazens
COBRECAF	Compagnie Bretonne de Cargos Frigorifiques
COBSA	Computer Service Bureaux Association
COBSI	Committee on Biological Sciences Information (U.S.A.)
COC	Commission Officielle de Contrôle (des semences et plants)
COC	Compagnie Ouest-Cameroun
COCAAP	Comisión Centroamericana de Autoridades Portuarias
COCADA	Compagnie des Commerçants Africains du Dahomey
COCAP	Comissão Coordenadora da Alianca para o Progresso (Brazil)
COCAST	Council for Overseas Colleges of Arts, Science and Technology
COCC	Confederación de Obreros y Campesinos Cristianos (Costa Rica)
COCCEE	Comité des Organisations Commerciales des Pays de la Communauté Économique Européenne
COCDYC	Conservative and Christian Democratic Youth Community

COCEAN	Compagnie d'Études et d'Exploitation des Techniques Océans
COCEI	Compagnie Centrale d'Études Industrielles
COCEMA	Comité des Constructeurs Européen de Matériel Alimentaire
COCERAL	Comité du Commerce des Céréales et des Aliments du Bétail de la CEE
COCESNA	Corporación Centroamericana de Servicios de Navegación Aerea (Guatemala)
COCI	Consortium des Agrumes et Plantes à Parfum de Côte-d'Ivoire
COCI	Consortium on Chemical Information
COCOBRO	Coördinatie van Cultuur en Onderzoek van Broodgraan
COCODI	Compagnie de Commerce de la Côte-d'Ivoire
COCOES	Comité de Coordination des Enquêtes Statistiques
COCOM	Consultative Group Cooperation Committee
COCOM	Coordinating Committee for East-West-Trade Policy (International)
COCOR	Commission de Coordination pour la Nomenclature des Produits Sidérurgiques (*of* ECSC)
COCOS	Co-ordinating Committee for Manufacturers of Static Converters in the Common Market Countries
COCOSEER	Co-ordinating Committee on Slavic and East European Library Services
COCSA	Compañia Organizadora del Consumo, S.A.
COCTA	Committee on Conceptual and Terminological Analysis (*of* International Political Science Association)
COD	Committee of Direction of Fruit Marketing (Australia)
CODAL	Comptoir Industriel de Produits Alimentaires (Madagascar)
CODATA	Committee on Data for Science and Technology (*of* ICSU)
CODAZR	Committee on Desert and Arid Zones Research (U.S.A)
CODE-AGRO	Amazonas Agricultural Development Company (Brazil)
CODECA	Corporation for Economic Development in the Caribbean
CODEL	Coordination in Development Inc. (U.S.A.)
CODEMAC	Comité des Déménageurs du Marché Commun
CODENA	Comité de Liaison des Entreprises de Démolition Navale de la CEE
CODENA	Council for the Development of the North-East of Brazil
CODEPAR	Companhia de Desenvolvimento Econômico do Paraná (Brazil)
CODESA	Consejo de Desarrollo de Salta (Argentina)
CODESRIA	Council for the Development of Economic and Social Research in Africa (Senegal)
CODESUL	Council for the Development of the Extreme South (Brazil)
CODETAF	Compagnie d'Étancheité Africaine en Côte d'Ivoire
CODE-VINTEC	Compagnie pour le Développement Industriel et Technique
CODEXAL	Conseil Européen di 'Codex Alimentarius'
CODIA	Comité de Industrialización de Algas (Argentina)
CODIA	Comité pour l'Organisation et le Développement des Investissements Intellectuels en Afrique et à Madagascar
CODIA	Council of Defense and Space Industry Associations (U.S.A)
CODIFAC	Comité de Développement d'Industrie de la Chaussure et des Articles Chaussants
CODIMA	Société Commerciale de Diffusion de Marques (Ivory Coast)
CODIPLAM	Comissão de Divulgação do Plano Global para a Amazonia (Brazil)
CODISUCO	Compania Distribuidora de Subsistenci, Conasupo (Mexico)
CODZR	Committee on Desert and Arid Zone Research (U.S.A.)
COE	Confederation of Employee Organisations
COE	Conseil Oecuménique des Églises
COEB	Conseil d'Orientation Économique du Bas Saint-Laurent (Canada)
COEC	Comité Central d'Océanographie et d'Étude des Côtes
COESA	Committee on Extension to the Standard Atmosphere (U.S.A)
COF	Comité Olympique Française
COFA	Commonwealth and Overseas Families Association
COFA	Comptoir Français Agricole
COFACE	Comité des Organisations Familiales auprès des Communautés Européennes (Belgium)

COFACE	Compagnie Française d'Assurance pour le Commerce Extérieur
COFACICO	Entreprises Financières Cinématographiques et Commerciales (Congo)
COFAG	Comité des Fabricants d'Acide Glutamique de la Communauté Économique Européenne
COFALEC	Comité des Fabricants de Levure de Panification de la CEE
COFAMA	Comptoir Franco-Africaine de Matériaux
COFAP	Comité Française des Applications du Pyrèthre
COFAZ	Compagnie Française de l'Azote
COFCA	Coffee and Cacao Institute of the Philippines
COFEB	Comité d'Études des Associations de Fabricants de Baignoires en Fonte Émaillée dans la CEE
COFI	Committee of Fisheries (*of* FAO)
COFI	Council of Forest Industries of British Columbia
COFIAGRO	Corporación Financiera de Fomento Agropecuario y Exportaciones (Colombia)
COFIBOIS	Nouvelle Compagnie Forestière et Industrielle du Bois (Congo)
COFICA	Compagnie pour le Financement de l'Industrie, du Commerce et de l'Agriculture
COFIEC	Compania Financiera, Ecuador
COFIFA	Compagnie Financière France-Afrique
COFIMPA	Compagnie Francaise Industrielle et Minière du Pacifique
COFINAN-CIERA	Corporación Financiera Colombiana
COFIREP	Compagnie Financière de Recherches Pétrolières
COFLA	Comisión Forestal Latinoamericana (Chile)
COFNA	Comisión Forestal Norteamericana (Mexico)
COFO	Committee on Forestry (FAO)
COFORGA	Compagnie Forestière Gabonaise
COFORIC	Compagnie Forestière et Industrielle du Congo
COFRAL	Comité Français Agricole de Liaison pour le Développement International
COFRAMET	Compagnie Franco-Américane des Métaux et Minérals
COFRAN-IMEX	Compagnie Française pour l'Exportation et l'Importation des Animaux Reproducteurs
COFRATEL	Compagnie Française des Téléphones
COFREDA	Compagnie pour Favoriser la Recherche et l'Élargissement des Débouchés Agricoles
COFREND	Comité Française pour l'Étude des Essais Non Destructifs
COFRUCI	Coopérative Agricole de Production Bananière et Fruitière de Côte-d'Ivoire
COG	Committee on Oceanography and GARP (*of* SCOR)
COGEGA	Comité Général de la Coopération Agricole des Pays de la CEE
COGEI	Comitato dei Geografi Italiani
COGEI	Compagnie de Gestion d'Investissements Internationaux
COGENE	Committee on Genetic Experimentation (Germany)
COGEO-DATA	Committee on Storage, Automatic Processing and Retrieval of Geological Data (Germany)
COGEQUIN	Confédération Générale de la Quincaillerie
COGERAF	Compagnie Générale d'Études et Recherches pour l'Afrique
COGE-TEXIM	Compagnie Générale Togolais d'Export-Import
COGIP	Compagnie Générale Ivoirienne de Piles Électriques
COGRA	Compañía Colombiana de Grasas
CoGroWa	Commissie Grondwaterleidingsbedrijven
COHATA	Compagnie Haitienne de Transports Aériens
COHSE	Confederation of Health Service Employees
COI	Central Office of Information
COI	Commission Internationale des Oeufs
COI	Commission Océanographique Intergouvernementale Permanente
COI	Conseil Oléicole International
COID	Council of Industrial Design
COID	Council on International Development
COIDIEA	Conseil des Organisations Internationales Directement Intéressées à l'Enfance et à l'Adolescence
COIF	Control of Intensive Farming
COINS	Committee on Improvement of National Statistics (*of* IASI)
COIPM	Comité International Permanent pour la Recherche sur la Préservation des Matériaux en Milieu Marin (*of* OECD)
COISM	Conseil des Organisations Internationales des Sciences Médicales

COJEV	Comité des Organisations de Jeunesses Européennes Volontaires
COJO	Conference of Jewish Organisations
COLAC	Comité Latinoamericano de Manejo de Cuencas de Torrentes
COLAC	Confederación Latinoamericana de Cooperativas de Ahorro y Crédito
COLACOT	Confederación Latinoamericana de Cooperativos de Trabajadores
COLA-TRADE	Comisión Latinoamericana de Trabajadores de la Energía
COLBAV	Colegio de Biblioteconomas y Archivistes de Venezuela
COLCIEN-CIAS	Fondo Colombiano para Investigaciones Cientificas
COLDI-GRASAS	Sociedad Colombiana de Industriales de Grasas Vegetales (Colombia)
COLFIN	Compañia Colombiana de Financiamiento
COLGRO	Verband Schweizerischer Grossisten der Kolonialwarenbranche
COLIME	Comité de Liaison des Industries Métalliques Européennes
COLIMO	Comité de Liaison de l'Industrie du Motorcycle des Pays de la CEE
COLIPA	Comité de Liaison des Syndicats Européens de l'Industrie de la Parfumerie et des Cosmétiques (Belgium)
COLIPED	Commission de Liaison des Pièces et Équipements de Deux Roues
COLN	Commissie Onderzoek Landbouwwaterhuishouding Nederland
COLOMBEX	Compañia Colombiana de Comercio Exterior
COLP	Comité Latino Americano de Parques Nacionales y de Vida Silvestre
COLTA-BACO	Compañia Colombiana de Tabaco
COLUMA	Comité Français de Lutte contre les Mauvaises Herbes
COM	Centraal Orgaan voor Melkhygiene
COMACH	Confederación Maritima de Chile
COMACI	Société de Commission et d'Approvisionnement de la Côte d'Ivoire
COMAF	Comité des Constructeurs de Matériel Frigorifique de la CEE
COMAFR-IQUE	Société Ivoirienne d'Expansion Commerciale
COMAGRI-COLA	Associazione Nationale Commercianti di Prodotti per l'Agricoltura
COMAL	Compagnie Commerciale Camerounaise de l'Alumine et de l'Aliuminium
COMALFA	Comptoir Maghrebin de l'Alfa (Algeria)
COMALFI	Sociedad Colombiana de Control de Malezas y Fisiologia Vegetal
COMAMIDI	Associazione Italiana dei Commercianti e degli Utilizzatori de Amidi, Fecole e Prodotti Derivati
COMANOR	Comité Maghrebin de Normalisation (Morocco)
COMAPI	Comité d'Action pour l'Isolation et l'Insonorisation
COMARAN	Compagnie Maritime de l'Afrique Noire
COMASCI	Société Commerciale d'Applications Scientifiques (Belgium)
COMATEX	Compagnie Malienne des Textiles
COMAUBEL	Chambre Syndicale du Commerce Automobile de Belgique
COMAU-NAV	Compagnie Mauritano-Algérienne de Navigation Maritime
COMBOFLA	Comité Boliviano de Fomento Lanero
COM-CORDE	Comisión Coordinadora para el Desarrollo Económico (Uruguay)
COMDA	Canadian Office Machine Dealers Association
COMDEV	Commonwealth Development Finance Company
COME-CAFCO	Commerciale Européenne de Cafés et Cacaos
COMECON	Council for Mutual Economic Aid (U.S.S.R.)
COMEPA	Comité Européen de Liaison du Commerce de Gros des Papiers et Cartons (Belgium)
COMES	Communauté Européenne des Écrivains
COMET	Collegium Medicorum Theatri (U.S.A)
COMET	Comité d'Organisation des Manifestations Économiques et Touristiques
COMET	Council of Middle East Trade
COMETEC-GAZ	Comité d'Etudes Economiques de l'Industrie du Gaz (Belgium)
COM-EURO-CAFE	Union des Cafetiers-Limonadiers de la Communauté Economique Européenne
COMEX	Commonwealth Expedition
COMEX	Compagnie Maritime d'Expertises
COMEX	Compagnie Mauritanienne d'Explosifs
COMEXAZ	Comité de Mexico y Aztlan
COMEXO	Committee for Oceanic Exploration

142

COMIAO	Compagnie Commerciale et Industrielle de l'Afrique de l'Ouest
COMIBOL	Corporación Minera de Bolivia
COMICORD	Association des Fabricants de Cordages et de Ficelles de la Communauté Économique Européenne (now EUROCORD)
COMIFA	Commission Internationale pour l'Étude Scientifique de la Famille
COMILOG	Compagnie Minière de l'Ogooué (Gabon)
COMIN-FORM	Information Bureau of Communist Parties and Workers
COMINOA	Comptoir des Mines et des Grands Travaux de l'Ouest Africain
COMIPHOS	Compagnie Minière et Phosphatière
COMISCO	Committee of International Socialist Conferences
COMI-TEXTIL	Comité de Coordination des Industries Textiles de la CEE
COMLA	Commonwealth Library Association (Jamaica)
COMPESCA	Companhia Brasileira de Pesca
COMPLAN	Comissão de Planejamento, Coordenação e Desenvolvimento Social e Econômico e Produtividade (Brazil)
COMPLES	Coopération Méditerranéenne pour l'Énergie Solaire
COMSAT	Communications Satellite Corporation (U.S.A.)
COMSER	Commission on Marine Science and Engineering Research (of UNO)
COMTELCA	Comision Tecnica de la Telecomunicaciónes de Centroamericana (of CEMA)
COMUF	Compagnie des Mines d'Uranium de Franceville (Gabon)
COMUR-HEX	Société pour la Conversion de l'Uranium en Métal et en Hexafluorure
COMUVIR	Institut d'Études Internationales de la Communication sur l'Environnement (France)
CONAC	Comisión Nacional de Acción Comunitaria (Uruguay)
CONACAJP	Comité Nacional de Clubes Agrícolas Juveniles Perú
CONACYT	Consejo Nacional de Ciencia y Tecnología (Argentina)
CONADE	Consejo Nacional de Desarrollo (Argentina)
CONADEP	Consejo Nacional de Desarrollo y Planificacion (Haiti)
CONA-HOTU	Corporación Nacional de Hoteles y Turismo (Venezuela)
CONAMAG	Comité Nacional de Mercadeo Agropecuario (Venezuela)
CONAP	Corporación Nacional de Abastecimientos del Perú
CONAPAC	Companhia Nacional de Produtos Alimenticios Cearenses (Brazil)
CONAPLAN	Consejo Nacional de Planificacion y Coordinación Economica (Salvador)
CONAREX	Consortium Africain de Réalisation et Exploitation (Dahomey)
CONARG	Consejo Nacional de Registros Genealógicos (Nicaragua)
CONART	Consejo Nacional de Radiodifusion y Television
CONASE	Consejo Nacional de Seguridad (Argentina)
CONASUPO	National Service for Popular Food Supply (Mexico)
CONATRAL	Congreso Nacional de Trabajadores Libres (Dominica)
CONAVI.	Confederación Nacional de Viñateros (Argentina)
CONAVI	Consejo Nacional de la Vivienda (Bolivia)
CONCA	Comité Nacional de Comercialización de Arroz (Bolivia)
CON-CACAF	Confédération d'Amérique du Nord, d'Amérique Centrale et des Caraïbes de Football (Guatemala)
CONCAMIN	Confederación de Cámaras Industriales de los Estados Unidos Mexicanos
CONCA-NACO	Confederación de Cámaras Nacionales de Comercio (Mexico)
CONCAWE	Oil Companies International Study Group for Conservation of Clean Air and Water in Europe
CONCEX	Conselho Nacional de Comércio Exterior (Brazil)
CONCP	Conferência das Organizações Nacionais deas Colónias Portuguesas
CONDAL	Comisión Nacional del Algodón (Ecuador)
CONDECA	Consejo de Defensa Centroamericana (Guatemala)
CONEP	Consejo Nacional de Empresa Privada (Panama)
CONES	Consejo Nacional Económico e Social (Argentina)

CONESCAL	Centro Regional de Construcciones Escolares para América Latina (Mexico)
CONESCAR	Convenio de Cooperación Tecnica, Estadistica y Cartografia (Peru)
CONET	Consejo Nacional de Educación Técnica (Argentina)
CONEX	Conservation and Extension Service (Rhodesia)
CONFAPI	Confederazione Italiana Piccola e Media Industria
CONFECA-MARAS	Confederación Colombiana de Cámaras de Comercio
CONFEDI-LIZIA	Confederazione Italiana della Proprietà Edilizia
CONFETRA	Confederazione Generale del Traffico e dei Trasporti
CONFIN	Consejo de Fomento e Investigación Agrícola (Chile)
CONFI-TARMA	Confederazione Nazionale degli Armatori Liberi
CONGITA	Confédération Général Italienne de la Technique Agricole
CONGO-BOIS	Compagnie Congolaise des Bois
CONGO-MECA	Société Congolaise de Mécanographie
CONGU	Council of National Golf Unions
CONI	Comitato Olimpico Nacionale Italiano
CONIA	Consejo Nacional de Investigaciones Agrícoles (Venezuela)
CONICIT	Consejo Nacional de Investigaciones Científicas y Tecnológicas (Venezuela)
CONIDA	Comisión Nacional de Investigación y Desarrollo Aeroespacial (Peru)
CONIE	Comisión Nacional de Investigación de Espacio
CONIN-AGRO	Confederación Intercooperativa Agropecuaria (Argentina)
CONITAL	Consorzio Italiano Allevatori
CONPROBA	Consorcio de Productores Bananeros (Ecuador)
CONSAL	Conference of South-East Asian Librarians
CONSENA	Consejo de Seguridad Nacional (Uruguay)
CONSOR-PESCA	Consorzio Nazionale fra Cooperative Pescatori ed Affini
CONSTRU-NAVES	Asociación de Constructores Navales Españoles
CONSUEL	Comité National pour la Securité des Usagers de l'Électricité
CONTAG	Confederação Nacional de Trabalhadores na Agricultura (Brazil)
CONTAC	Conference on the Atlantic Community (U.S.A.)
CONTEC	Confederação Nacional dos Trabalhadores nas Empresas de Crédito (Brazil)
CONTEL	Conselho Nacional de Telecomuniçãcoes (Brazil)
CONTU	Commission on New Technological uses of Copyrighted Works (U.S.A.)
CONVELE	Consejo Venezolano de la Leche (Venezuela)
COONA-COVEN	Confederación Nacional de Cooperativas de Venezuela
COOP	Co-opérative pour le Développement des Oléagineux
COOPEFOR	Société Coopérative Forestière d'Administration et de Gestion
COOPEN-AGRO	Cooperativa Nacional de Mercadeo Agropecuario Limitada (Colombia)
COOPLAIN-IERE	Coopérative Lainière de l'Île de France
COORD-COM	Coordinating Committee of South-East Asian Senior Officials on Transport and Communications (Malaysia)
COP	Contactgroep Opvoering Productiviteit
COPA	Comité des Organisations Professionnelles Agricoles de la CEE
COPA	Compania Panama de Aviación
COPAC	Comité Mixte pour la Promotion de l'Aide aux Coopératives (FAO)
COPAC	Committee on Pollution Abatement and Control (U.S.A.)
COPAC	Joint Committee for the Promotion of Aid to Cooperatives (FAO)
COPACA	Congresos Panamericanos de Carreteras
COPACAR	Corporación Paraguaya de Carnes
COPACE	Comité des Pêches pour l'Atlantique Centre-Est (FAO)
COPACEL	Confédération Française de l'Industrie des Papiers, Cartons et Celluloses
COPAL	Cocoa Producers Alliance (Nigeria)
COPANT	Comisión Panamericana de Normas Técnicas (Argentina)
COPARCO	Société Congolaise de Perfumerie et Cosmetiques

COPAR-MEX	Confederación Patronal de la República Mexicana	**CORA**	Confederación Odontológica Regional Andina
COPARROZ	Cooperativa de Productores de Arroz de Tacuarembó (Uruguay)	**CORA**	Corporación de la Reforma Agraria (Chile)
COPE	Committee on Political Education (U.S.A.)	**CORAL**	Corporation of Coastal Cotton Growers (Colombia)
COPE	Compagnie Orientale des Pétroles d'Égypte	**CORC**	Central Organisation for Rural Cooperatives (Iran)
COPEC	Conference of Politics, Economics and Christianity	**CORD**	Collegium Orbis Radiobiologiae Docentium (France)
COPECIAL	Comité Permanent des Congrès Internationaux pour l'Apostolat des Laïcs	**CORDE**	Corporación Dominicana de Expresas Estatalas
COPEL	Companhia Paranaense de Energia Elétrica (Brazil)	**CORDI-PLAN**	Central Office of Co-ordination and Planning (Africa)
COPERE	Cómite de Programación Económica y de Reconstrucción (Chile)	**CORE**	Center for Operations Research and Econometrics (Belgium)
COPERS	Commission Préparatoire Européenne de Recherches Spatiales (*now* ESRO)	**CORE**	Congress of Racial Equality (U.S.A.)
COPETAO	Compagnie des Pétroles Total Afrique Ouest	**CORE**	CSIR Committee on Research Expenditure (South Africa)
COPICA	Comité de Propagande pour les Industries et les Commerces Agricoles et Alimentaires	**CORECI**	Compagnie de Régulation et de Contrôle Industriel
COPLAN	Development Planning Commission (Brazil)	**COREM**	Conférences Régionales de Métiers
COPLAN-ARH	Comisión del Plan Nacional de Aprovechamiento de los Recursos Hidráulicos (Venezuela)	**COREMO**	Comité Revolucionario de Mocambique
		CORESTA	Centre de Coopération pour les Recherches Scientifiques Relatives du Tabac
COPMEC	Comité des Petites et Moyennes Entreprises Commerciales des Pays de la CEE	**CORFO**	Corporación de Fomento de la Producción (Chile)
COPOL	Council of Polytechnic Librarians	**CORGI**	Confederation for the Registration of Gas Installers
COPOR-CHAD	Coopérative des Transporteurs Tchadiens	**CORIP**	Comité de Recherches de l'Industrie Pharmaceutique (Belgium)
COPPSO	Conference of Professional and Public Service Organisations	**CORMA**	Corporación Chilena de la Mandera
COPR	Centre for Overseas Pest Research	**COROI**	Comptoir de Commerce et de Représentation pour l'Océan Indien
COPRAI	Comissaõ de Productivadade da Asociaçaõ Industrial Portugesa	**CORPAC**	Corporación Peruana de Aeropuertos y Aviación Commercial
COPRAM	Companhia Progresso do Amapa (Brazil)		
COPRAQ	Cooperative Programme of Research on Aquaculture (FAO)	**CORPO-FRUT**	Corporación de Productores de Frutas de Río Negro (Argentina)
COPRED	Consortium on Peace Research, Education and Development (U.S.A.)	**CORPO-SANA**	Corporación de Obras Sanitarias (Paraguay)
COPRIN	Comision de Productividad Precios e Ingresos (Venezuela)	**CORS**	Canadian Operational Research Society
COPRODE	Consejo Provincial de Desarrollo (Argentina)	**CORSAG**	Corporación Santiagueña de Ganaderos (Argentina)
COPROMA	Compagnie des Produits du Mali		
COPTAL	Comité Permanente Técnico para Asuntos del Asuntos del Trabajo, Latinoamerica	**CORSI**	Operational Research Society of India
		CORSO	Council of Relief Services Overseas (New Zealand)
COPUOS	UN Committee on the Peaceful Uses of Outer Space	**CORT**	Council of Repertory Theatres
COR	The Club of Rome	**COSA**	Cámaras Oficiales Sindicales Agrarias

CoSAMC	Commission for Special Applications of Meteorology and Climatology (WMO)	**COSUPI**	Comissão Supervisora do Plano dos Institutos (Brazil)
COSATA	Co-operative Supply Association of Tanzania	**COSVN**	Central Office for South Vietnam
COSATE	Commission Syndicale Technique (*of* OEA)	**COSWA**	Conference on Science and World Affairs
COSATI	Committee on Science and Technology Information (U.S.A.)	**COT**	Centrale Organisatie in de Tweewielerbranche
COSBA	Computer Services and Bureaux Association	**COTAL**	Confederación de Organizaciones Turísticas de la América Latina
COSEBI	Corporación de Servicios Bibliotecarios (Puerto Rico)	**COTC**	Canadian Overseas Telecommunications Corporation
COSEC	Coordinating Secretariat of National Unions of Students (Netherlands)	**COTEMA**	Compagnie Technique Mauritanienne
COSEM	Co-operative Seed Corn Society of Tunis	**COTIRC**	Comisión Técnica Interprovincial del Río Colorado (Argentina)
COSEMCO	Comité des Semences du Marché Commun (Belgium)	**COTOA**	Compagnie Textile de l'Ouest Africain (Senegal)
COSENA	Compagnie Sénégalaise de Navigation	**COTOMIB**	Compagnie Togolaise des Mines du Benin
COSERV	National Council for Community Services to International Visitors (U.S.A.)	**COTONCO**	Compagnie Cotonnière Congolaise
COSETAM	Compagnie Sénégalaise pour tous Appareillages Mécaniques	**COTON-FRAN**	Société Cotonnière Franco Tchadienne
COSIMEX	Compagnie Sénégalaise d'Importation et d'Exportation	**COTON-TCHAD**	Société Cotonnière du Tchad
COSIPA	Companhia Siderúgica Paulista (Brazil)	**COTRAM**	Union des Constructeurs de Matériel de Travaux Publics et de Manutention
CoSIRA	Council for Small Industries in Rural Areas	**COTRAMA**	Société Civile Coopérative d'Études des Transports et de Manutention
COSMA	Associazione Costruttori Macchine per Cucire	**COTRIJUI**	Cooperativa Regional Triticula Serra Ltda of Ijui (Brazil)
COSPAR	Committee on Space Research (Netherlands)	**COTRINAG**	Comissão de Organização de Triticultura Nacional e Armazenamento Geral (Brazil)
COSPIT	Centro Orientamento Studi e Propaganda Irrigua		
COSPUP	Committee on Science and Public Policy (*of* NAS) (U.S.A.)	**COTT**	Central Organization for Technical Training (South Africa)
COSRIMS	Committee on Research in the Mathematical Sciences (*of* NAS) (U.S.A.)	**COTTI**	Commission du Traitement et de la Transmission de l'Information
COSSEC	Cambridge, Oxford and Southern School Examinations Council	**COVAS**	Coöperatieve Vereniging voor de Afzet van Suikerbieten
COST	Committee for Overseas Science and Technology	**COVECO**	Centrale Organisatie van Veeafzet- en Vleesverwerkings-coöperaties
COST	Committee on Science and Technology (India)	**COVEG**	Stichting Centraal Orgaan voor de Voedings- en Genotmiddelenbranche
COST	Coopération Européenne dans la Domaine de la Recherche Scientifique et Technique	**COVENAL**	Corporación Venezolana de Aluminio
COSTED	Committee on Science and Technology in Developing Countries (*of* ICSU)	**COVEN-EXTA**	Cooperativa Venezolana de Exportadores de Tabaco
COSTI	National Centre of Scientific and Technical Information (Israel)	**COVENIN**	Comisión Venzolana de Normas Industriales
		COVENTA	Cooperativa Venezolana de Tabacaleros
COSTIC	Comité Scientifique et Technique de l'Industrie du Chauffage, de la Ventilation et du Conditionnement d'Air	**COVEPRO**	Cooperativa Venezolana de Productores
		COVINCA	Corporación Venezolana de la Industria Naval CA

COVINEX	Société Congolaise d'Exploitation Vinicole
COVODIAM	Compagnie Voltaïque de Distribution Automobile et de Matériel
COVON	Coöperatieve Vereniging van Ondernemers in het Natuursteenbedrijf
COVOS	Groupes d'Études sur les Consequences des Vols Stratosphériques
COWA	Council for Old World Archaeology (U.S.A.)
CoWaBo	Commissie inzake Wateronttrekking aan de Bodem
COWAR	Committee on Water Research (International)
COWT	Council of World Tensions (Switzerland)
CP	Centralkommitén for Produktivitetsfragor
CP	Convention Patronale de l'Industrie Horlogère Suisse
CPA	California Pharmaceutical Association (U.S.A.)
CPA	Canadian Pacific Airlines
CPA	Canadian Pharmaceutical Association
CPA	Canadian Postmasters Association
CPA	Canadian Psychological Association
CPA	Canvas Products Association International (U.S.A.)
CPA	Centre de Perfectionnement dans d'Administration des Affaires
CPA	Centre de Préparation aux Affaires
CPA	Chick Producers Association
CPA	Cocoa Producers Alliance (West Africa)
CPA	Commonwealth Parliamentary Association
CPA	Comité Permanent Agricole (of BIT)
CPA	Contractors' Plant Association
CPA	Cour Permanente d'Arbitrage (Netherlands)
CPAC	International Collaborative Pesticides Analytical Committee
CPACO	Comité de Pesca de la FAO para el Atlántico Centro-Oriental
CPANE	Comisión de Pesquerías del Atlántico Nordeste
CPANE	Commission des Pêches de l'Atlantique Nord-Est
CPANT	Comité Panamericano de Normas Técnicas (Uruguay)
CPAS	Church Pastoral Aid Society
CPB	Centraal Planbureau
CPBP	Comisión Protectora de Bibliotecas Populares (Argentina)
CPBP	Comité Professionnel du Butane et du Propane
CPC	Christian Peace Conference
CPC	Coffee Promotion Council Ltd
CPC	Colonial Products Council
CPC	Committee for Programme and Coordination (ECOSOC)
CPC	Compagnie des Potasses du Congo
CPC	Conservative Political Centre
CPCA	Comite des Pêches Continentales pour l'Afrique (FAO)
CPCAS	Commission Permanente de Coordination des Associations Spécialisées (of FNSEA)
CPCC	Conference Permanente des Chambres de Commerce et l'Industrie de la CEE
CPCEA	Caisse de Prévoyance des Cadres d'Exploitations Agricoles
CPCERMPS	Comisión Permanente para la Conservación y Exploitación de los Recursos Maritimos del Pacífico Sur
CPCI	Centre de Perfectionnement Pratique des Cadres Commerciaux dans l'Industrie
CPCIZ	Comité Permanent du Congrès International de Zoölogie
CPCM	Comité Permanent Consultatif du Maghreb
CPDL	Canadian Patents and Development Ltd
CPDP	Comité Professionnel du Pétrole
CPE	Comité de Politique Économique (de l'OCDE)
CPE	Congrès du Peuple Européen
CPED	Commission de la Participation des Églises au Développement (Switzerland)
CPEPA	Comité de la Prune d'Ente et du Pruneau d'Agen
CPEQ	Corporation of Professional Engineers of Quebec (Canada)
CPES	Centro Paraguayo de Estudios Sociologicos
CPF	Coopération Pharmaceutique Française
CPF	Cooperative Productive Federation
CPFS	Council for the Promotion of Field Studies
CPG	Bureau of Conference Planning and General Services (UNESCO)
CPGA	Comité Professionnel des Galeries d'Art
CPGPA	Caisse Professionnelle de Garantie des Producteurs Agricoles

CPHA	Canadian Public Health Association	**CPPC**	Copper Promotion Producers Committee (*now* CIDEC)
CPHERI	Central Public Health Engineering Research Institute (India)	**CPPCC**	Chinese People's Political Consultative Conference
CPI	Cinchona Products Institute (U.S.A.)	**CPPPD**	Centre de la Planification, des Projections et des Politiques Relatives au Développement (UN)
CPI	Commission Permanente Internationale de l'Acetylène, de la Soudure Autogène et des Industries qui s'y Rattachent		
CPI	Commission Phytosanitaire Interafricaine	**CPPS**	Comisión Permanente para la Exploitatación y Conservación de las Riquezas Marítimas del Pacífico Sur
CPI	Communist Party of India		
CPI	Conseil Phytosanitaire Interafricain	**CPRA**	Chinese Public Relations Association
CPI	Crop Protection Institute (U.S.A.)	**CPRE**	Council for the Preservation of Rural England
CPI	Stichting Coöperatief Pluimveefokkers Instituut		
CPIE	Centre de l'Information Européenne	**CPREA**	Canadian Peace Research and Education Association
CPIP	Consejo de Pesca Indo-Pacífico	**CPRI**	Canadian Peace Research Institute
CPITUS	Comité Permanent International des Techniques et de l'Urbanisme Souterrains	**CPRI**	Central Potato Research Institute (India)
CPIUS	Comité Permanent Internacional de Tecnicos y de Urbanismo Subterráneo	**CPRM**	Companhia de Pesquisas de Recursos Minerais (Brazil)
CPIV	Comité Permanent International du Vinaigre (Marché Commun)	**CPRM**	Companhia Portuguesa Radio Marconi
		CPRS	Canadian Public Relations Society
CPJI	Cour Permanente de Justice Internationale	**CPRU**	Colonial Pesticides Research Unit (East Africa)
CPL	Centre Paritaire du Logement		
CPL	Colonial Products Laboratory (*now* TPL)	**CPRW**	Council for the Preservation of Rural Wales
CPM	Comisión del Pacífico Meridional	**CPS**	Commission du Pacifique Sud
CPM	Corporación Pro-Crusada Mundial	**CPS**	Committee for Penicillin Sensitivity
CPME	Conseil Parlementaire du Mouvement Européen	**CPSA**	Canadian Political Science Association
		CPSA	Civil and Public Services Association
CPN	Communistische Partij van Nederland	**CPSA**	Clay Pigeon Shooting Association
CPNA	Commission Paritaire Nationale pour les Entreprises Agricoles	**CPSC**	Consumer Products Safety Commission (U.S.A.)
CPNCEP	Chambre Professionnelle Nationale des Conseillers de l'Économie Privée	**CPTB**	Clay Products Technical Bureau
CPNT	Comité Panamericano de Normas Técnicas (Argentina)	**CPSP**	Comisión Permanente para el Sur del Pacifico
		CPT	Confederación Paraguaya de Trabajadores
CPNU	Conférence des Plénipotentiaires	**CPT**	Confederation of British Road Passenger Transport
CPO	Centrum voor Plantenfysiologisch Onderzoek		
		CPTC	China Productivity and Trade Centre
CPO	Commonwealth Producers Organisation	**CPTE**	Comité Permanent des Transports Européens
CPOI	Comisión de Pesca para el Océano Indico	**CPU**	Commonwealth Press Union
CPOM	Centro de Preclasificación Océanica de México	**CPUSTAL**	Congrès Permanent de l'Unité Syndicale des Travailleurs d'Amérique Latine
CPP	Convention Peoples Party (Ghana)	**CPV**	Centrale Proefstations Vereniging
CPPA	Canadian Pulp and Paper Association	**CPWC**	Central Peoples Workers Council (Burma)
CPPB	Comité de Problemos de Productos Básicos (FAO)	**CPWD**	Central Public Works Department (India)
		CQBF	County Quality Bacon Federation

CQCJ	Comité des Questions Constitutionnelles et Juridiques (FAO)
CQEE	Conseil du Québec de l'Enfance Exceptionnelle
CQPPA	Council of Quality Pig Producers Associations
CQRI	Centre Québécois de Relations Internationales
CRA	Canadian Rheumatism Association
CRA	Centres de Recherches Agronomiques
CRA	Centres de la Recherche Appliquée (Zaire)
CRA	China Research Associates
CRA	Confederaciones Rurales Argentinas
CRAAM	Centro de Radio-Astronomia e Astrofisica Universidade Mackenzie (Brazil)
CRAC	Careers Research and Advisory Centre
CRACCUS	Comité Régional de l'Afrique Centrale pour la Conservation et l'Utilisation des Sols
CRAE	Centre de Recherches Agronomiques de l'État (Belgium)
CRAF	Centre de Recherches Africaines
CRAF	Comité Régional d'Arboriculture Fruitière du Bassin Parisien
CRAM	Centre de Recherches sur les Atomes et les Molécules (Canada)
CRAM	Collectivités Rurales Autochones Modernisées à Madagascar
CRAPE	Centre de Recherches Anthropologiques Préhistoriques et Ethnographiques (Algeria)
CRAR	Committee for the Recovery of Archeological Remains (U.S.A.)
CRAS	Centre for Radiobiology and Radiation Protection (Netherlands)
CRATEMA	Centro di Ricerca e di Assistenza Tecnica e Mercantile alle Aziende
CRAV	Comisión de la Reforma Agraria y la Vivienda (Peru)
CRB	Confederação Rural Brasileira
CRBM	Centre Régional de Biologie Marine
CRC	Cancer Research Campaign
CRC	Centre de Recherches Techniques et Scientifiques Industries de la Tannerie, de la Chaussure, de la Pantoufle et des autres Industries Transformatrices du Cuir (Belgium)
CRC	Cotton Research Corporation (*formerly* ECGC)
CRC	Cuba Resource Centre (U.S.A.)
CRCA	Caisse Régionale de Crédit Agricole
CRCA	Comissao Reguladora do Comércio de Arroz (Portugal)
CRCAM	Caisse Régionale de Crédit Agricole Mutuel
CRCC	Canadian Red Cross Committee
CRCP	Costa Rican Cocoa Products Co
CRD	Centre de Recherches et de Documentation de l'Association Universelle pour l'Esperanto
CRDE	Centre de Recherches en Développement Économique (Canada)
CRDF	Conseil de la Recherche et du Développement Forestiers (Canada)
CRDI	Centre de Recherches pour le Développement International (Canada)
CRDLP	Centre for Research and Documentation of the Language Problem
CRDS	Centre de Recherches et de Documentation du Sénégal
CRDTO	Regional Documentation Centre for Oral Tradition (Niger)
CRE	Coal Research Establishment
CRE	Commercial Relations Export Department
CRE	Standing Conference of Rectors and Vice-Chancellors of the European Universities (Switzerland)
CREA	Centre de Recherches et d'Études Agricoles
CREA	Centro Regional de Educatión de Adultos (Venezuela)
CREA	Committee on the Relation of Electricity to Agriculture (U.S.A.)
CREA	Consorcio Regional de Experimentación Agrícola (Argentina)
CREA	Coopérative Régionale d'Équipement Agricole
CREACUS	Comité Régional de l'Afrique Orientale pour la Conservation et l'Utilisation du Sol
CREAI	Carteira de Credito Agricola e Industrial (Brazil)
CREAQ	Commission Royale d'Enquête sur l'Agriculture au Québec (Canada)
CRECIT	Centre de Recherches Essais et Contrôles Scientifiques pour l'Industrie Textile (Belgium)
CRED	Center for Research on Economic Development (U.S.A.)

CREDE	Regional Economic Research and Documentation Centre (Togo)	**CRFM**	Comité de Coordination de la Recherche Forestiére Méditeranéenne
CREDIFF	Centre de Recherches pour la Diffusion du Français	**CRG**	Cave Research Group of Great Britain
CREDILA	Centre de Recherches d'Études et de Documentation sur les Institutions et la Législation Africaines (Senegal)	**CRI**	Caribbean Research Institute
		CRI	Cement Research Institute (India)
		CRI	Central Research Institute (India)
CREDO	Centre for Curriculum Renewal and Educational Development Overseas	**CRI**	Croce Rossa Italiana
		CRI	Children's Relief International
CREDOC	Centre de Recherches et de Documentation sur la Consommation	**CRI**	Coconut Research Institute (Ceylon)
		CRIA	Caisse de Retraite Interenterprises Agricoles
CREDOP	Centre de Recherche d'Étude et de Documentation en Publicité (Belgium)	**CRIA**	Centre de Recherches sur les Trypanosomiases Animales (Central Africa)
CREEA	Comité Régional d'Expansion Économique de l'Auvergne	**CRIC**	Centre National de Recherches Scientifiques et Techniques pour l'Industrie Cimentière (Belgium)
CREEGIM	Conseil Régional d'Expansion Économique de la Gaspérie et des Îles-de-la-Madeleine (Canada)	**CRIC**	Centre de Recherches Industrielles sur Contrats
CREFAL	Centro Regional de Alfabetización Functional en las Zonas Rurale de America Latina (Mexico)	**CRIC**	Commercial Radio International Committee
		CRID	Centre pour la Recherche Interdisciplinaire sur le Développement (Belgium)
CREGR	Centre de Recherches et d'Expérimentation de Génie Rurale (France) (*now* CERAFER)	**CRIDAOL**	Centro Regional de Investigación y Desarrollo Agraria de Galicia
CRENO	Conférénce des Régions de l'Europe du Nord-Ouest	**CRIDE**	Centre de Recherches Interdisciplinaires pour le Développement de l'Éducation (Zaire)
CREO	Centre de Recherches et d'Études Océanographiques	**CRIDE**	Centre de Recherches Interdisciplinaires Droit-Economie (Belgium)
CREPS	Centre Régional d'Éducation Physique et Sportive	**CRIEL**	Comité Interprofessionnel des Eaux-de-vie du Languedoc
CREPS	Compagnie de Recherches et d'Exploitation de Pétrole du Sahara	**CRIEPI**	Central Research Institute of the Electrical Power Industry (Japan)
CRERMA	Conseillers Régionaux d'Étude de la Rentabilité du Machinisme Agricole	**CRIF**	Centre de Recherches Scientifiques et Techniques de l'Industrie des Fabrications Métalliques (Belgium)
CRES	Centre de Recherches Économiques et Sociales	**CRIG**	Cocoa Research Institute of Ghana
CRESA	Centre de Recherches Economiques et Sociales Appliquées	**CRILC**	Canadian Research Institute of Launderers and Cleaners
CRESHS	Centre de Recherches en Sciences Humaines et Sociales (Haiti)	**CRIN**	Cacao Research Institute of Nigeria
CRESM	Centre de Recherches et d'Études sur les Sociétés Musulmanes	**CRIPE**	Centre de Recherches et Techniques pour l'Industrie des Produits Explosifs (Belgium)
CRESR	Centre Régional d'Études Socio-Religieuses	**CRISP**	Centre de Recherche et d'Information Sociopolitiques (Belgium)
CREST	Committee on Reactor Safety Technology (*of* ENEA)	**CRIT**	Co-ordinating Centre for Regional Information Training, Nairobi (Kenya)
CRET	Commission Régionale Européenne de Tourisme	**CRL**	Chemical Research Laboratory
CRF	Calendar Reform Foundation (U.S.A.)	**CRLC**	Coopérative Régionale Lainière du Centre
CRFEA	Christian Rural Fellowship of East Africa	**CRM**	Compagnie Radio-Maritime

CRME	Committee on Research in Medical Economics (U.S.A.)	**CRWRC**	Christian Reformed World Relief Committee (U.S.A.)
CRMS	Centro Ricerche Malattie della Selvaggina	**CRYM**	Comisión Reguladora de la Producíon y Comercio de la Yerba Mate (Argentina)
CRO	Commissie voor Rassenonderzoek van Groenvoedergewassen	**CSA**	Canadian Standards Association
CRO	Commonwealth Relations Office	**CSA**	Caribbean Studies Association (U.S.A.)
CROACUS	Comité Régional de l'Afrique Occidentale pour la Conservation et l'Utilisation du Sol	**CSA**	Centralförbundet för Socialt Arbete
		CSA	Ceskoslovenské Aerolinie
CROC	Confederación Revolucionaria de Obreros y Campesinos (Mexico)	**CSA**	Chambre Syndicale de l'Amiante
		CSA	Civil Service Assembly (Canada and U.S.A.)
CROSSA	Centre Régional Opérationnel de Surveillance et de Sauvetage pour l'Atlantique	**CSA**	Confederate States of America
		CSA	Conseil Supérieur de l'Agriculture
CROSSMA	Centre Régional Operationnel de Surveillance et de Sauvetage pour la Manche	**CSA**	Scientific Council for Africa South of the Sahara
CRP	C. Rudolf Poensgen Stiftung zur Förderung von Führungskraften in der Wirtschaft e V.	**CSAA**	Canadian Sociology and Anthropology Association
CRPAO	Comisión Regional de Pesca para el Africa Occidental	**CSAA**	Child Study Association of America
		CSAA	Confédération Sud-Americaine d'Athlétisme
CRPL	Central Radio Propagation Laboratory (U.S.A.)	**CSAA**	South American Athletic Confederation
CRPQF	Comissao Reguladora dos Productos Químicos e Farmacéuticos (Portugal)	**CSAC**	Alliance Cocoa Scientific Advisory Committee
CRR	Centre de Recherches Routières (Belgium)	**CSAF**	Centro di Sperimentazione Agricola e Forestale
CRRAG	Countryside Recreation Research Advisory Group	**CSAGI**	Comité Spécial de l'Année Géophysique Spécial (International)
CRRI	Central Rice Research Institute (India)		
CRRI	Central Road Research Institute (India)	**CSAI**	Italian Automobile Sporting Commission
CRRL	Central Reference and Research Library (Ghana)	**CSAP**	Canadian Society of Animal Production
		CSAR	Compagnie Sénégalaise d'Assurances et de Réassurances
CRRS	Central Rainlands Research Station (Sudan)		
CRS	Cereals Research Station	**CSATM**	Confédération Sud-américaine de Tennis de Table (Uruguay)
CRSD	Co-operative Research and Service Division (U.S.A.)	**CSB**	Confédération Sud-Américaine de Billard
CRSIM	Centre de Recherches Scientifiques, Industrielles et Maritimes	**CSBNTP**	Chambre Syndicale Belge des Négociants en Timbres Poste
CRSV	Centre de Recherches Science et Vie	**CSBP**	Chambre Syndicale des Banques Populaires de France
CRSVI	Conférence Régionale du Service Volontaire International		
CRT	Confederación Revolucionaria de Trabajodores (Mexico)	**CSBVF**	Chambre Syndicale de la Boulonnerie et de la Visserie Forgées
CRU	Centre de Recherche d'Urbanisme	**CSC**	Chambre Syndicale Nationale des Industries de la Conserve
CRUESI	Centre de Recherches pour l'Utilisation de l'Eau Salée en Irrigation (Tunisia)	**CSC**	Civil Service Commission
CRUTAC	Centro Rural Universitario de Treinamento e de Acao Comunitaria (Brazil)	**CSC**	Commercial Solvents Corporation (U.S.A.)
		CSC	Commonwealth Science Council
CRWPC	Canadian Radio Wave Propagation Committee	**CSC**	Confédération des Syndicats Chrétiens (Belgium)

CSC	Confédération des Syndicats Chrétiens de la Suisse	**CSEU**	Confederation of Shipbuilding and Engineering Unions
CSCA	Chambre Syndicale des Constructeurs d'Automobiles	**CSF**	Coil Spring Federation
		CSF	Comité des Salines de France
CSCA	Consejo Superior de los Colegios de Arquitectos de España	**CSF**	Confederación Sudamericana de Fútbol
		CSFA	Canadian Scientific Film Association
CSCAW	Catholic Study Circle for Animal Welfare	**CSFA**	Confédération des Sociétés Françaises d'Architectes
CSCE	Canadian Society for Chemical Engineering		
CSCE	Canadian Society for Civil Engineering	**CSFE**	Canadian Society of Forest Engineers
CSCE	Conference on Security and Co-operation in Europe (*of* NATO)	**CSFIFF**	Chambre Syndicale Française des Industriels Fondeurs de Fromage
CSCF	Cast Stone and Concrete Federation	**CSFN**	Centro Siciliano di Fisica Nucleare
CSChE	Canadian Society for Chemical Engineering	**CSFRA**	Coil Spring Federation Research Organisation
CSCM	Commission Syndicale Consultative Mixte *auprès de* l'OCDE	**CSFSBA**	Chambre Syndicale des Fabricants de Supports en Béton Armé Destinés aux Canalisations Aériennes
CSCN	Chambre Syndicale des Constructeurs de Navires et de Machines Marines		
CSC-OCDE	Commission Syndicale Consultative *auprès de* l'OCDE	**CSFTI**	Committee on Southern Forest Tree Improvement (U.S.A.)
CSCR	Central Society for Clinical Research (U.S.A.)	**CSGA**	Canadian Seed Growers Association
		CSGB	Cartophilic Society of Great Britain
CSCS	Commonwealth Students Children Society	**CSGS**	Československá Gerontologická Společnost
CSD	Commonwealth Society for the Deaf	**CSH**	Chambre Suisse de l'Horlogerie
CSD	FAO's Consultative Sub-Committee on Surplus Disposal	**CSHB**	Chambre Syndicale de l'Horticulture Belge
		CSI	Cartel des Syndicats Independants des Services Publics (Belgium)
CSDHA	Centre for Social Development and Humanitarian Affairs (UN)		
		CSI	Chartered Surveyors Institution
CSDPP	Chambre Syndicale de la Distribution des Produits Pétroliers	**CSI**	Cinémathèque Scientifique Internationale
		CSI	Commission Séricicole Internationale
CSE	Centre de Sociologie Européenne	**CSI**	Commission Sportive International
CSE	Conférence Spatiale Européenne	**CSIC**	Consejo Superior de Investigaciónes Cientificas
CSE	Conférence des Statisticiens Européens		
CSEABC	Chambre Syndicale des Entreprises Artisanales du Bâtiment	**CSICC**	Canadian Steel Industries Construction Council
CSEB	Chambre Syndicale des Électriciens Belges	**CSID**	Centro de Servicios de Información y Documentación (Mexico)
CSEDB	Chambre Syndicale des Entrepreneurs de Déménagements Belgique		
		CSII	Centre for the Study of Industrial Innovation
CSEERI	Comité Scientifique pour l'Étude des Effets des Radiations Ionisantes (International)	**CSIJ**	Comité Sportif International de la Jeunesse
CSEI	Chambre Syndicale des Esthéticiens Industriels	**CSIO**	Central Scientific Instruments Organisation (India)
CSEM	Centre Séismologique Européo-Méditerranéen	**CSIR**	Council for Scientific and Industrial Research (Ghana, India etc.)
CSEMP	Chambre Syndicale des Emballages en Matières Plastiques	**CSIRO**	Commonwealth Scientific and Industrial Research Organisation (Australia)
CSESS	Cooperative State Experiment Station Service (U.S.A.)	**CSIRT**	Comité Scientifique International de Recherches sur les Trypanosomiases

CSIS	Center for Strategic and International Studies (U.S.A.)
CSIS	Comisia de Stat pentru Incercarea Soiurilor (Roumania)
CSIT	Comité Sportif International du Travail
CSJC	Chartered Societies Joint Committee
CSK	Comité Spécial du Katanga (Zaire)
CSL	Commonwealth Serum Laboratories (Australia)
CSL	Compagnie Sénégalaise des Lubrificants
CSLATP	Canadian Society of Landscape Architects and Town Planners
CSLO	Canadian Scientific Liaison Office
CSLT	Canadian Society of Laboratory Technologists
CSM	Commission Synoptic Meteorology (Technical Commission of the World Meteorological Organisation)
CSM	Compagnie Sénégalaise de Métallurgie
CSM	Centrale Suikermaatschappij
CSMA	Caisse de Secours Mutuels Agricoles
CSMA	Chemical Specialities Manufacturers Association (U.S.A.)
CSMCRI	Central Salt and Marine Chemicals Research Institute (India)
CSME	Canadian Society for Mechanical Engineers
CSME	Confédération Syndicale Mondiale des Enseignants
CSMF	Confédération des Syndicats Médicaux Français
CSMFRA	Cotton Silk and Man-Made Fibres Research Association (*formerly* Shirley Institute)
CSMG	Československa Společnost pro Mineralogii a Geologii
CSN	Confédération des Syndicats Nationaux
CSN	Conseil Supérieur du Notariat
CSNA	Commonwealth Society of North America (U.S.A.)
CSNC	Chambre Syndicale des Constructeurs de Navires et de Machines Marines
CSNCRA	Chambre Syndicale Nationale du Commerce et de la Réparation de l'Automobile
CSNDP	Chambre Syndicale Nationale des Agencies Privées de Recherches et Mandataires en Obtention de Renseignements et de Preuves
CSNEIMB	Chambre Syndicale des Entrepreneurs d'Installations de Magasins et Bureaux et Activités Annexes
CSNESA	Chambre Syndicale Nationale des Électriciens et Spécialistes de l'Automobile
CSNFEI	Chambre Syndicale Nationale des Fabricants d'Encres d'Imprimerie
CSNHP	Chambre Syndicale Nationale des Entreprises et Industries de l'Hygiène Publique
CSNISE	Chambre Syndicale Nationale des Installateurs de Stands et d'Expositions
CSNL	Chambre Syndicale Nationale de la Literie
CSNRD	Consortium for the Study of Nigerian Rural Development (U.S.A.)
CSNRRM	Chambre Syndicale Nationale des Rectifieurs et Reconstructeurs de Moteurs
CSO	Central Statistical Office
CSO	Centre de Sociologie des Organisations
CSOP	Commission to Study the Organization of Peace (U.S.A.)
CSP	Chartered Society of Physio-Therapy
CSP	Chambre Syndicale de la Phytopharmacie
CSP	Council on Scientific Policy
CSPAA	Conseil de Solidarité des Pays Afro-Asiatiques
CSPB	Comité Spécial du Programme Biologique International
CSPBI	Comité Spécial du Programme Biologique International
CSPCA	Canadian Society for the Prevention of Cruelty to Animals
CSPE	Comité Scientifique pour les Problèmes de l'Environnement (*of* ICSU)
CSPECVM	Chambre Syndicale Patronale des Enseignants de la Conduite des Véhicules à Moteur
CSPEFF	Chambre Syndicale des Producteurs et Exportateurs de Films Français
CSPFLC	Confédération Nationale des Producteurs de Fruits, Légumes et Champignons
CSPI	Citizen's Committee on Infant Nutrition (U.S.A.)
CSPP	Centro di Studi sui Problemi Portuali
CSPT	Compagnie Sénégalaise des Phosphates de Taiba
CSPU	Communist Party of the Soviet Union

CSQC	Ceylon Society for Quality Control
CSR	Circolo Speleologico Romano
CSR	Conférence Suisse de Sécurité dans le Trafic Routier
CSR	Cykel– och Sporthandlarnas Riksförbund
CSRA	Comité Scientifique pour les Recherches Antarctiques (ICSU)
CSRO	Comité Scientifique pour les Recherches Océaniques (ICSU)
CSROH	Revolucniho Odborového Hnuti
CSRS	Centre Suisse de Recherches Scientifiques en Côte d'Ivoire
CSRS	Cooperative State Research Service (U.S.A.)
CSRSOM	Conseil Supérieur des Recherches Sociologiques Outre-Mer
CSS	Commodity Stabilisation Service (U.S.A.)
CSS	Compagnie Sucrière Sénégalaise
CSS	Zentralverband Schweizerischer Schneidermeister
CSSA	Cactus and Succulent Society of America
CSSA	Civil Science Systems Administration (U.S.A.)
CSSA	Conseil Supérieur pour le Sport en Afrique (Cameroons)
CSSA	Crop Science Society of America
CSSE	Compagnie Sénégalaise du Sud-Est
CSSE	Conference of State Sanitary Engineers (U.S.A.)
CSSF	Chambre Syndicale de la Sérigraphie Française
CSSF	Chambre Syndicale de la Sidérurgie Française
CSSIMS	Central States Society of Industrial Medicine and Surgery (U.S.A.)
CSSP	Committee of Scientific Society Presidents (U.S.A.)
CSSPPA	Caisse de Stabilisation et de Soutien des Prix des Productions Agricoles (Ivory Coast)
CSSR	Centro Studi Sociologia Religiosa
CSSRC	Colonial Social Sciences Research Committee (U.K.)
CSSRO	Chambre Syndicale des Soies et Rayonnes Ouvrées
CSSS	Canadian Soil Science Society
CSTA	Canadian Society of Technical Agriculturists
CSTA	Canterbury Science Teachers' Association (N.Z.)
CSTA	Consejo Sindical de Trabajadores Andinos
CSTAL	Confederación Sindical de los Trabajadores de América Latina
CSTB	Centre Scientifique et Technique du Bâtiment
CSTC	Centre Scientifique et Technique de la Construction (Belgium)
CSTC	Consejo Sindical de Trabajadores del Caribe
CSTFTAB	Confederación Sindical de Trabajadores Ferroviarios, Ramas Anexas y Transportes Aéreos de Bolivia
CSTI	Council of Science and Technology Institutes
CSTM	Calcutta School of Tropical Medicine (India)
CSTM	Centro Studi Terzo Mondo
CSTM	Compagnie Sénégalaise pour la Transformation des Métaux
CSTP	Committee for Scientific and Technical Personnel (*of* OECD)
CSTR	*see* STRC
CSU	Confédération des Syndicats Unitiés de Belgique
CSUCA	Consejo Superior Universitario Centroamericano
CSUK	Chamber of Shipping of the United Kingdom (*now merged into* GCBS)
CSURF	Colorado State University Research Foundation (U.S.A.)
CSV	Centraal Stikstof Verkoopkantoor
CSVTS	Ceskoslovenská Vĕdecko-Technická Společnost
CSW	Christlicher Studenten-Weltbund
CT	Conseil de Tutelle (Trusteeship Council of UNO)
CTA	Camping Trade Association of Great Britain
CTA	Canadian Tuberculosis Association
CTA	Caribbean Travel Association
CTA	Chain Testers' Association of Great Britain
CTA	Channel Tunnel Association
CTA	Collegio dei Tecnici dell'Acciaio
CTA	Commercial Travellers' Association
CTAF	Comité des Transporteurs Aériens Français
CTAL	Confederación de Trabajadores de América Latina
CTAMBJO	Syndicat National des Cadres, Techniciens, et Agents de Maîtrise de la Bijouterie, Joaillerie Orfèvrerie et des Activités qui s'y Rattachent
CTAT	Centre Technique d'Agriculture Tropicale

CTAVI	Centre Technique Audio Visuel International
CTB	Centre Technique du Bois
CTB	Commonwealth Telecommunications Board
CTBLV	Christlicher Textil-, Bekleidungs- und Lederarbeiter-Verband
CTC	Central Training Council
CTC	Centre Technique de Conserves des Produits Agricoles
CTC	Centre Technique du Cuir
CTC	Confederación de Trabajadores de Colombia
CTC	Cuban Confederation of Workers
CTCA	Commission for Technical Cooperation in Africa (*of* OAU, *now* STRC)
CTCA	Confédération des Travailleurs d'Amérique Centrale (Honduras)
CTCB	Centre Technique du Cuir Brut
CTCB	Confederación de Trabajadores de Comercio de Bolivia
CTCD	Centre Technique pour le Contrôle de la Descendance
CTCE	Comité de Thermodynamique et de Cinétique Électrochimiques (Belgium)
CTCEE	Comisão Tecnica de Cooperacae Economic Externa (Portugal)
CTCI	Classic Thunderbird Club International (U.S.A.)
CTCRA	Comité Technique de Cooperation et Réalisations Agricoles (*now* IFCT) (France)
CTCRI	Central Tuber Crops Research Institute (India)
CTCSG	Centre Technique de la Canne et du Sucre de la Guadeloupe
CTCSM	Centre Technique de la Canne du Sucre de la Martinique
CTEI	Centro Tropical de Enseñanza e Investigación (Costa Rica)
CTETOC	Council for Technical Education and Training for Overseas Countries
CTF	Catholic Teachers Federation
CTF	Coffee Trade Federation
CTF	Comité de Tourisme et des Fêtes
CTFL	Centre Technique des Fruits et Légumes
CTFM	Comité des Transports Ferroviares du Maghreb
CTFMA	Copper Tube Fittings Manufacturers Association
CTFT	Centre Technique Forestier Tropical (Ivory Coast)
CTGA	Ceylon Tea Growers Association
CTI	Centraal Technisch Instituut TNO
CTI	Confédération des Travailleurs Intellectuels
CTI	Container Transport International (U.S.A.)
CTIB	Centre Technique de l'Industrie du Bois (Belgium)
CTIC	Comisiones Técnicas Inter-Crea (Argentina)
CTIF	Centre Techniques des Industries de la Fonderie
CTIF	Comité Technique International de Prévention et Extinction du Feu
CTIFL	Centre Technique Interprofessionnel des Fruits et Légumes
CTIOM	Centre Technique Interprofessionnel des Oléagineux Métropolitains
CTIP	Compagnia Tecnica Industrie Petrole
CTM	Confederación de Trabajadores de Mexico
CTM	Conférence Technique Mondiale
CTMA	Centre Technique du Machinisme Agricole
CTMB	Canal Transport Marketing Board
CTMC	Compagnie pour la Transformation des Métaux au Cameroun
CTNE	Compania Telefonica Nacional de Espana
CTNRC	Centre for Thai National Reference Collections
CTNSS	Centre for Thai National Standard Specifications
CTO	Central Tractor Organisation (India)
CTO	Comité Technique de l'Olivier
CTP	Centre Technique de l'Industrie des Papiers, Cartons et Celluloses
CTP	Confederación de Trabajadores del Peru
CTPA	Continental Tournaments Players Association (France)
CTPL	Commission Technique et de Promotion des Laitiers
CTPS	Permanent Technical Committee for Plant Breeding (France)
CTPTA	Centro Tropical de Pesquisas e Tecnologia de Alimentos (Brazil)
CTRA	Coal Tar Research Association
CTRC	Caribbean Tourism Research Centre (Barbados)
CTRI	Catholic Tape Recorders International (U.S.A.)

CTRI	Central Tobacco Research Institute (India)	**CUMM**	Council of Underground Machinery Manufacturers
CTRI	Central Tobacco Research Institute, Rustenburg (S. Africa)	**CUNA**	Credit Union National Association (U.S.A.)
CTRL	Cotton Technological Research Laboratory (India)	**CUNY**	City University of New York (U.S.A.)
		CUPE	Canadian Union of Public Employees
CTRM	Compagnie de Transports Routiers et de Messageries	**CUPM**	Committee on Undergraduate Program in Mathematics (U.S.A.)
CTRP	Confederación de Trabajadores de la Républica de Panama	**CUPRA**	Confederazione Unitaria della Produzione Agricola
CTRU	Colonial Termite Research Unit (Nigeria)	**CURAC**	Coal Utilization Research Advisory Committee (Australia)
CTS	Committee on the Teaching of Science (*of* ICSU)	**CURB**	Campaign on the Use and Restriction of Barbiturates
CTSA	Crucible and Tool Steel Association	**CURE**	Citizens United for Racial Equality (U.S.A.)
CTSCCV	Centre Technique de la Salaison de la Charcuterie et des Conserves de Viande	**CUREI**	Centre Universitaire de Recherche Européenne et Internationale
CTT	Centrum voor Tuinbouwtechniek	**CURS**	University Scientific Research Centre (Morocco)
CTT	Irish Export Promotion Organisation		
CTU	Conservative Trade Unionists	**CUS**	Conférence Universitaire Suisse
CTUF	Ceylon Trade Union Federation	**CUSA**	Council for United States Aid (China)
CTUY	Confederation of Trade Unions of Yugoslavia	**CUSO**	Canadian University Service Overseas
CTVM	Centre for Tropical Veterinary Medicine	**CUSRPG**	Canada-United States Regional Planning Group (*of* NATO)
CTV	Confederación de Trabajadores de Venezuela	**CUSURDI**	Council of United States Universities for Rural Development in India
CUA	Department of Cultural Activities (UNESCO)	**CUSUS-WASH**	Council of U.S. Universities for Soil and Water Development in Arid and Sub-humid Areas
CUB	Confederación Universitaria Boliviana		
CUC	Canterbury University College, Christchurch (N.Z.)	**CUT**	Comité de l'Unité Togolaise
		CUT	Cooperative Union of Tanganyika
CUC	Coal Utilization Council	**CUTAL**	Confédération Unique des Travailleurs de l'Amérique Latine
CUC	Computers Users' Committee (UNDP)		
CUCES	Centre Universitaire de Coopération Économique et Sociale	**CUTCH**	Central Unica de Trabajadores de Chile
CUEA	Consejo de la Unidad Económica Arabe	**CV-AV**	International Commission CV-AV Catholic Movement for Children
CUEBS	Commission on Undergraduate Education in the Biological Sciences (*of* AIBS)	**CVB**	Centraal Veevoederbureau in Nederland
CUF	Catholicarum Universitatum Foederatio	**CVC**	Corporación Autónima Regional del Valle del Cauca (Colombia)
CUF	Companhia União Fabril (Portugal)		
CUKT	Carnegie United Kingdom Trust	**CVD**	Veterinary Department, South Cameroons
CULPAVAL	Cultivadores de Patata Valdivia	**CVF**	Corporación Venezolana de Fomento
CUMA	Canadian Urethane Manufacturers Association	**CVG**	Corporación Venezolana de Guayana
		CVI	Centraal Veevoeder Instituut
CUMA	Coopérative d'Utilisation de Matériel Agricole	**CVJM**	Weltbund der Christlichen Vereine Junger Männer
CUMATEX	Associazione Nazionale Rappresentanti Commercianti Macchine e Accessori per l'Industria Tessile, Maglierie e per Cucire	**CVJR**	Centre de Voyages de la Jeunesse Rurale
		CVLB	Christelijke Veenkoloniale Landbouwbond

CVM	Controlestation voor Melkproducten
CVM	Corporación Autónima Regional de los Valles de Magdalena y Sinú (Colombia)
CVMA	Canadian Veterinary Medical Association
CVNW	Centrale Vereniging van Nederlandse Wijnhandelaren
CVP	Christelijk Volkspartij (Belgium)
CVP	Corporación Venezolana del Petróleo
CVPCEE	Comité des Ventes Publiques de Cuirs et Peaux Verts des Pays de la CEE
CVRS	Centre Voltaique de la Recherche Scientifique (Haute-Volta)
CVSM	Central-Verband Schweizerischer Mobeltransporteurs
CVT	Centrale Vakgroep Tuinbouw van de Belgische Boerenbond
CVT	Committee on Vacuum Techniques (U.S.A.)
CVTM	Compagnie Voltaïque pour la Transformation des Métaux
CVV	Coöperatieve Veeafzetvereniging v. Noord- en Zuid-Holland
CVV	Coöperatieve Venlose Veiling Vereniging
CWA	Country Women's Association (Australia)
CWAEC	County War Agricultural Executive Committee
CWB	Canadian Wheat Board
CWB	Commonwealth Writers of Britain
CWC	Canadian Welfare Council
CWC	Catering Wages Commission
CWC	Ceylon Workers Congress
CWC	Comenius World Council (U.S.A.)
CWC	Commonwealth of World Citizens
CWCC	Childrens World Community Chest
CWDC	Canadian Wood Development Council
CWDE	Centre for World Development Education
CWDWD	Committee for World Development and World Disarmament (U.S.A.)
CWE	Co-operative Wholesale Establishment (Sri Lanka *etc.*)
CWF	Commonwealth Weightlifting Federation
CWGC	Commonwealth War Graves Commission
CWINC	Central Waterways, Irrigation and Navigation Commission (India)
CWINRS	Central Waterpower, Irrigation and Navigation Research Station (India)
CWL	Catholic Women's League

CWM	Caribbean Workers' Movement
CWM	Council for World Mission
CWME	Commission on World Mission and Evangelism of the World Council of Churches
CWOIH	Conference of World Organisations Interested in the Handicapped
CWP	Coordinating Working Party on Atlantic Fishery Statistics (FAO)
CWPC	Central Water and Power Commission (India)
CWPRS	Central Water and Power Research Station (India)
CWRA	Canadian Water Resources Association
CWRL	Citrus Wastage Research Laboratory (Australia)
CWS	Church World Service (U.S.A.)
CWS	Co-operative Wholesale Society
CWU	Chemical Workers' Union
CWU	Church Women United
CWU	Congress of World Unity (U.S.A.)
CWWA	Coloured Workers Welfare Association
CWY	Canada World Youth
CYAC	Commonwealth Youth Affairs Council
CYATCA	Cyprus Air Traffic Controllers Association
CYEC	Commonwealth Youth Exchange
CYM	Commonwealth Youth Movement
CYSA	Community Youth Service Association
CYTA	Cyprus Telecommunications Authority
CZC	Centrale Zuivelcommissie
CZL	Contrôlestation voor Zuivelproducten
CZPA	Comisia de Zonare a Produselor Agricole (Roumania)

D

DA	Dansk Agronomforening
DA	Directio Administrativa (Roumania)
DAAD	Deutscher Akademischer Austauschdienst
DAAE	Dansk Andels Aegexport
DAC	Development Assistance Committee (*of* OECD)

DACA	Institute for the Development of Agricultural Cooperation in Asia (Japan)	**DAMDA**	Dairy Appliance Manufacturers and Distributors Association
DAD	Department Administratiewe Dienste (South Africa)	**DANA**	Andelsslagteriernes Konserveseksport
DADA	Designers and Art Directors Association	**DANATOM**	Danish Association for Industrial Development of Atomic Energy
DADJ	Den Almindelige Danske Jordemoderforening	**DANBIF**	Danske Boghandleres Importørforening
DAEP	Directorate of Aircraft Equipment Production	**DANE**	Departamento Administrativo Nacional de Estadística (Colombia)
DAEP	Division of Atomic Energy Production	**DANFIP**	Dansk Føderation for Informationbehandling og Virksomhedsstyring
DAER	Departmento Autônomo de Estradas do Rodagem (Brazil)	**DANHORS**	Danish Farmers Export Union
DAF	Danmarks Automobil-Forhandler-Forening	**DANIDA**	Danish International Development Agency
DAF	Dansk Annoncør-Forening	**DANPATA-TAS**	Danske Kartoffelavleres og Kartoffeleksportørers Faellesorganisation
DAF	Dansk Arbejdsgiverforening	**DANR**	Department of Agriculture and Natural Resources (Philippines)
DAFECO	Direction des Affaires Extérieures et de la Coopération d'Électricité de France	**DANRIC**	Department of Agriculture and Natural Resources Information Council (Philippines)
DaFFO	Dansk Forening til Fremme af Opfindelser	**DAP**	Servicio de Divulgación Agrícola de Panamá
DAFS	Department of Agriculture and Fisheries for Scotland	**DAPD**	Directorate of Aircraft Production Development
DAG	Deutsche Angestellten Gewerkschaft	**DAPIS**	Danish Agricultural Products Information Service
DAG	Development Assistance Group (U.S.A. etc.)		
DAGA	Deutsche Arbeitsgemeinschaft für Akustik	**DAR**	Daughters of the American Revolution
DAGK	Deutschen Arbeitsgemeinschaft Kybernetic	**DARA**	Deutsche Arbeitsgemeinschaft für Rechenanlagen
DAGV	Deutsche Arbeitsgemeinschaft Vakuum		
DAGV	Deutscher Automaten-Grosshandels-Verband	**DAS**	Dansk Akustisk Selskab
DAH	Danmarks Aktive Handelsrejsende	**DAS**	Dansk Anaesthesiologisk Selskab
DAHOTEX	Société Dahomey-Texas du Pétrole	**DAS**	Den Danske Arktiske Station
DAI	Deutscher Architekten- und Ingenieur-Verband	**DASA**	Defense Atomic Support Agency (U.S.A.)
DAIS	District Agricultural Improvement Stations (China)	**DASA**	Dental Association of South Africa
		DASC	Department of Agriculture, Southern Cameroons
DAK	Deutsche Atomkommission Geschaftsfuhrung (of BMWF)	**DASIAC**	Defense Atomic Support Agency Information and Analysis Centre (U.S.A.)
DAKOFO	Danske Korn-Og-Foderstof-Im-Og Eksportorers Faellesorganisation	**DASP**	Departmento Administrativo do Servico Público (Brazil)
DAKS	Danske Automobil Komponentfabrikkers Sammenslutning	**DASUCH**	Department of Social Action, University of Chile
DAL	Danske Arkitekters Landforbund	**DATA**	Derivation and Tabulation Associates (U.S.A.)
DAL	Deutscher Arbeitsring für Lärmebekämpfung		
DALA	Departmento de Asuntos Latinoamericanos (Cuba)	**DATA**	Draughtmen's and Allied Technicians Associations (U.K.) (now AUEW)
DALIA	Distribuidora Argentina Libro Ibero-Americano	**DATAR**	Délégation à l'Aménagement du Territoire et à l'Action Régionale
DALPA	Danish Air Line Pilots Association	**DAtF**	Deutsches Atomforum

DATO	Discover America Travel Organisation (U.S.A.)	**DCRA**	Dyers and Cleaners Research Association
		DCRO	Dyers and Cleaners Research Organization
DATUM	Dokumentions und Ausbildungszentrum für Theorie und Methode der Regionalforschung	**DCSM**	Danish Council for Scientific Management
DAV	Deutscher Alpenverein	**DD**	Data for Development International Association
DAV	Deutscher Altphilologenverband	**DDA**	Dominion Department of Agriculture (Canada)
DAV	Deutscher Anwaltverein		
DAV	Deutscher Apotheker-Verein	**DDB**	Deutscher Dolmetscherbund
DAW	Deutsche Akademie der Wissenschaften zu Berlin	**DDBF**	Den Dansk Bagerstands Foellesorganisation
		DDC	Diamond Distributors Centrafrique
DAW	Deutscher Arbeitskreis Wasserforschung	**DDC**	U.S. Defense Documentation Centre
DB	Danmarks Biblioteksforening	**DdD**	Den Danske Dyrlægeforening
DB	Dansk Blomsterhandlerforening	**DDF**	Dental Documentary Foundation (Belgium)
DBB	Deutscher Beamtenbund	**DDG**	Deutsche Dendrologische Gesellschaft
DBD	Democratic Peasant's Party of Germany	**DDG**	Deutsche Dermatologische Gesellschaft
DBE	Development Bank of Ethiopia	**DDGSR**	Division of the Director-General of Scientific Research
DBF	Den Danske Boghandlerforening		
DBfk	Deutscher Berufsverband für Krankenpflege	**DDR**	Deutsche Demokratische Republik
DBI	Landsforening Dansk Betonvare-Industri	**DDS**	Dansk Dermatologisk Selskab
DBIU	Dominion Board of Insurance Underwriters (Canada)	**DE**	Dansk Erhvervsfrugtavl
		DEA	Department of Economic Affairs
DBIV	Deutsche Braunkohlen-Industrieverein	**DEAIC**	Dirección de Educación Artesanal, Industrial y Comercial (Venezuela)
DBR	Division of Building Research (Canada)		
DBS	Deutsche Berufsverband der Sozialarbeiter und Sozialpädagogen	**DEBEG**	Deutsche Betriebsgesellschaft für Dratlose Telegraphie
DBV	Deutscher Bäderverband	**DEBRIV**	Deutscher Braunkohlen-Industrie-Verein
DBV	Deutscher Bauernverband	**DEC**	Dollar Exports Council
DBV	Deutscher Betonverein	**DECAT**	Departamento de Conservación y Asistencia Técnica del Ministerio de Agricultura (Chile)
DBV	Deutscher Bibliotheksverband		
DBV	Deutsche Binnentankreedervereinigung	**DECEE**	Dirección de Estadística, Catastro y Estudios Económicos (Peru)
DBV	Deutscher Büchereiverband		
DCB	Decimal Currency Board	**DECHEMA**	Deutsche Gesellschaft für Chemisches Apparatewesen
DCCC	Domestic Coal Consumers' Council	**DECP**	Division de la Coordination Économique et du Plan (Morocco)
DCF	Fédération Nationale des Directeurs Commerciaux de France		
		DECSA	Departmento de Conservación de Suelos y Agua (Chile)
DCG	Democracia Cristiana Guatemalteca		
DChIV	Deutscher Chemie-Ingenieur-Verband	**DEF**	Danske Elværkers Forening
DCI	Directorate of Chemical Inspection	**DEF**	Directia Economiei Forestiere (Roumania)
DCIOO	Import Opportunities Office for Developing Countries	**DEG**	Danske Erhvervsgartnerforening
		DEG	Deutsche Entomologische Gesellschaft
DCIS	Delaware Country Institute of Science (U.S.A.)	**DEG**	Deutsche Exlibris-Gesellschaft
DCL	Distillers Co., Ltd	**DEG**	Direction des Études Générales (Morocco)
DCPE	Dominion Council of Professional Engineers (Canada)	**DEGEBO**	Deutsche Forschungsgesellschaft für Bodenmechanik

DEGUSSA	Deutsche Gold- und Silber Scheideanstalt
DEH	Danske Ejendomshandlerforening
DEHOGA	Deutscher Hotel- und Gaststättenverband
DEHR	Direction de l'Hydraulique et de l'Équipement Rural (Algeria)
DEIP	Division de Exploraciones e Introducción de Plantas (Argentina)
DELCO	Sierra Leone Development Company
DELIMCO	German Liberian Mining Company
DEMBA	Demarara Bauxite Company (Guyana)
DEMKO	Dansk Elektrische Materialkontrol
DEMYC	Democratic Youth Community (Germany)
DENACAL	Departamento Nacional de Acueductos y Alacantarillados (Nicaragua)
DENAGEO	Departamento Nacional de Geología (Bolivia)
DEP	Département Fédéral de l'Économie Publique (Switzerland)
DEP	Department of Employment and Productivity
DEPCA	International Study Group for the Detection and Prevention of Cancer
DEPO	Nederlandse Vereniging van Detailhandelaren in Pootaardappelen
DEPP	Société Dahoméenne d'Antreposage de Produits Pétroliers
DER	Deutscher Erfinderring
DERE	Dounreay Experimental Reactor Establishment (Scotland)
DEREL-VANS	Département d'Enseignement et de Recherche Langues Vivantes aux Non-Spécialistes
DERL	Defence Electronics Research Laboratory, Hyderabad (India)
DES	Department of Education and Science
DESAL	Centro para el Desarrollo Económico y Social de América Latina, Santiago (Chile)
DESIDOC	Defence Scientific Information and Documentation Centre (India)
DETA	Divisão de Exploração dos Transportes Aéreos (Mozambique)
DETEX	Stichting Detailhandel in Textielgoederen
DETI	Drents Economisch Technologisch Instituut
DEUA	Diesel Engine Users' Association
DEULA	Deutsche Landmaschinenschulen
DEV	Deutscher Erfinderverband
DEV	Directia Economiei Vînatului (Roumania)

DEVCO	Committee for Standardisation in the Developing Countries (of ISO)
DEZAPA	Algemene Nederlandse Bond van Detailhandelaren in Zaden en Aanverwante Artikelen
DF	Danske Fysioterapeuter
DF	Landsforeningen Dansk Frugtavl
DFBO	Deutsche Forschungsgesellschaft für Blechverarbeitung und Oberflächenbehandlung
DFCK	Development Finance Company of Kenya Ltd
DFCU	Development Finance Co. of Uganda
DFD	Democratic Women's Federation of Germany
DFD	Département Fédéral des Finances et des Douanes (Switzerland)
DFDS	Det Forenede Dampskibs-Selskab
DFF	Dansk Fotografisk Forening
DFF	Den Danske Forlaeggerforening
DFG	Deutschen Forschungsgemeinschaft
DFH	Danmarks Farmaceutiske Højskole
DFGH	Danske Fotogrossisters Handelsforening
DFIK	Dansk Forening for Industriel Kvalitetskontrol
DFK	Dansk Flaskegas Komité
DFK	Dansk Forening for Kvalitetsstyring
DFL	Deutsche Forschungsanstalt für Luftfahrt
DFOM	Départements Français d'Outre-Mer
DFR	Deutscher Fernschulrat
DFR	Diplomerade Företagsekonomers Rijksförbund
DFRA	Drop Forging Research Association
DFRC	Distillers Feed Research Council (U.S.A.)
DFV	Deutsche Feuerwehrverband
DFV	Deutscher Fischereiverband
DFVLR	Deutsche Forschungs- und Versuchsanstalt für Luft- und Raumfahrt
DFWR	Deutscher Forstwirtschaftsrat
DG	Deutsche Gesellschaft für Galvanotechnik
DGA	Deutsche Gesellschaft für Anaesthesia
DGA	Direction Générale de l'Agriculture
DGA	Durum Growers Association of the United States
DGAA	Dirección General de Asuntos Agrarios (Guatemala)

DGAB	Direction de la Gestion Administrative et du Budget (UNDP)		**DGFP**	Dirección General de Fomento Pecuario (Ecuador)
DGAE	Deutsche Gesellschaft für Angewandte Entomologie		**DGFPS**	Deutsche Gesellschaft für Psychologie
DGAO	Deutsche Gesellschaft für Angewandt Optik		**DGfZ**	Deutsche Gesellschaft für Züchtungskunde
DGAP	Deutsche Gesellschaft für Auswärtige Politik		**DGG**	Deutsche Gartenbau-Gesellschaft
DGAW	Deutsche Gesellschaft für Anästhesie und Wiederbelebung		**DGG**	Deutsche Geologische Gesellschaft
			DGG	Deutsche Glastechniche Gesellschaft
DGB	Deutsche Gesellschaft für Betriebswirtschaft		**DGG**	Dirección General de Ganadería (Salvador)
DGB	Deutscher Gewerkschaftbund		**DGGM**	Dirección General de Geografica y Meteorología (Mexico)
DGBAS	Directorate General of Budgets, Accounts and Statistics (Formosa)		**DGGR**	Direction Générale du Génie et de l'Hydraulique Agricole
DGBW	Deutsche Gesellschaft für Bewasserungswirtschaft		**DGGTOT**	Directia Generala Geo-Topografica si de Organizare a Teritoriului (Roumania)
DGD	Deutsche Gesellschaft für Dokumentation		**DGH**	Deutscher Grosshändlerverband für Heizungs-, Lüftungs- und Klimadedarf
DGE	Deutsche Gesellschaft Endokrinologie		**DGHM**	Deutsche Gesellschaft für Hygiene und Mikrobiologie
DGE	Deutsche Gesellschaft für Ernährung			
DGE	Directia Generala de Exploatare		**DGIA**	Dirección General de Investigaciones Agrícolas (Salvador)
DGEA	Dirección General de Extensión Agropecuaria (Ecuador)		**DGIEA**	Dirección General de Investigación y Extensión Agrícola (Guatemala)
DGEC	Dirección General de Estadistica y Censos (Nicaragua)		**DGIFLC**	Directia Generala de Imbunatatiri Funciare si Constructii Agricole (Roumania)
DGEF	Direction Générale des Eaux et Forêts			
DGEG	Deutsche Gesellschaft für Erd- und Grundbau		**DGK**	Deutsche Geodätische Kommission
DGemG	Deutsche Gemmologische Gesellschaft		**DGK**	Deutsche Gesellschaft für Kybernetik
DGF	Dansk Geologisk Forening		**DGLR**	Deutsche Gesellschaft f. Luft- und Raumfahrt
DGF	Deutsche Gesellschaft für Fettwissenschaft		**DGLRM**	Deutsche Gesellschaft für Luft- und Raumfahrtmedizin
DGF	Deutsche Gesellschaft für Flugwissenschaften		**DGM**	Deutsche Gesellschaft für Metallkunde
DGfA	Deutsche Gesellschaft für Amerikastudien		**DGMA**	German Society for Measuring Technique and Automation
DGfA	Deutsche Gesellschaft für Arbeitschutze			
DGFA	Dirección General de Fomento Agrícola (Argentine)		**DGMK**	Deutsche Gesellschaft für Mineralölwissenschaft und Kohlechemie
DGfB	Deutsche Gesellschaft für Betriebswirtschaft		**DGMKG**	Deutsche Gesellschaft für Mund-, Kiefer- und Gesichtschirurgie
DGfBUI	Deutsche Gesellschaft für Bluttransfusion und Immunohaematologie		**DGMS**	Deutsche Gesellschaft für Medizinische Soziologie
DGfdB	Deutsche Gesellschaft für das Badewesen		**DGMU**	Dirección General de Meteorología del Uruguay
DGfH	Deutsche Gesellschaft für Hochschulkunde			
DGFH	Deutsche Gesellschaft für Holzforschung		**DGN**	Dirección General de Normas (Mexico)
DGfH	Deutsche Gesellschaft für Hopfenforschung		**DGN**	Direccion de Geológia de la Nación (Argentina)
DGFI	Deutsches Geodätisches Forschungsinstitut			
DGFK	Deutsche Gesellschaft für Friedens- und Konfliktforschung		**DGON**	Deutsche Gesellschaft für Ortung und Navigation
DGfK	Deutsche Gesellschaft für Kartographie		**DGOR**	Deutsche Gesellschaft für Operations Research
DGFP	Deutsche Gesellschaft für Personalführung			

DGOT	Deutsche Gesellschaft für Orthopädie und Traumatologie	**DGU**	Deutsche Gesellschaft für Unternehmensforschung
DGP	Deutsche Gesellschaft für Parasitologie	**DGV**	Deutscher Genossenschaftsverband
DGP	Deutsche Gesellschaft für Parodontologie	**DGV**	Deutscher Germanistenverband
DGP	Deutsche Gesellschaft für Photogrammetrie	**DGV**	Deutscher Giessereiverband
DGPA	Dirección General de Planificación y Administración (Panama)	**DGV**	Deutsche Gesellschaft für Völkerkunde
		DGV	Deutsche Gesellschaft für Volkskunde
DGPA	Directia Generala a Productiei Animale (Roumania)	**DGV**	Deutsche Graphologische Vereinigung
		DGVN	Deutsche Gesellschaft für die Vereinten Nationen
DGPH	Deutsche Gesellschaft für Photographie		
DGPM	Direction de la Géologie et de la Prospection Minière (Ivory Coast)	**DGZMK**	Deutsche Gesellschaft für Zahn-, Mund- und Kieferheilkunde
DGPN	Deutsche Gesellschaft für Psychiatrie und Nervenheilkunde	**DGZFP**	Deutsche Gesellschaft für Zerstörungsfreie Prüfverfahren
DGPPA	Dirección General de la Pequeña Propiedad Agricola (Mexico)	**DH**	Deutsche Heilpraktikerschaft
		D & HAA	Dock and Harbour Authorities Association
DGPT	Deutsche Gesellschaft für Psychotherapie und Tiefenpsychologie	**DHEW**	Departments of Health, Education and Welfare (U.S.A.)
DGPV	Directia Generala a Productiei Vegetale (Roumania)	**DHG**	Deutsche Hämophiliegesellschaft
		DHG	Dungekalk- Hauptgemeinschaft
DGQ	Deutsche Gesellschaft für Qualität	**DHI**	Decennie Hydrologique Internationale
DGR	Deutsche Gesellschaft für Rehabilitation	**DHI**	Deutsches Hydrographisches Institut
DGRA	Dirección General de Reforma Agraria (Panama)	**DHIA**	Dairy Herd Improvement Association (U.S.A.)
DGRH	Dirección General de Recursos Hidráulicos (Ecuador)	**DHMV**	Deutscher Holzmastenverband
DGRN	Dirección General de Recursos Naturales (Honduras)	**DHR**	International Commission for the Hydrology of the River Rhine Basin
DGRR	Deutsche Gesellschaft für Raketentechnik und Raumfahrt	**DHSS**	Department of Health and Social Security
		DHV	Deutscher Handels- und Industrieangestelltenverband
DGRST	Délégation Générale à la Recherche Scientifique et Technique		
		DHV	Deutscher Hugenottenverein
DGRV	Deutscher Genossenschafts- und Raiffeisenverband	**DIA**	Danske Interieur Arkitekter
		DIA	Departmento de Investigación Agropecuaria (Colombia)
DGS	Directia Generala Silvica (Roumania)		
DGS	Deutsche Gesellschaft für Sozialmedizin	**DIA**	Design and Industries Association
DGSF	Deutsche Gesellschaft für Sexualforschung	**DIAA**	Direction des Industries Agricoles et Alimentaires
DGSMT	Directio Generala a Statiunilor de Masini si Tractoare (Roumania)		
		DIAL	Danske Indendørs Arkitekters Landsforbund
DGSNM	Dirección General del Servicio Nacional Meteorológico (Argentina)	**DIB**	Deutsches Institut für Betriebswirtschaft
		DIBEVO	Landelijke Organisatie Dibevo
DGSP	Deutsche Gesellschaft für Soziale Psychiatrie in der Bundesrepublik Deutschland	**DICE**	Dairy and Ice Cream Equipment Association
		DICORE	División de Conservación de Recursos (Chile)
DGSV	Dirección General de Sanidad Vegetal (Mexico)		
DGTS	Directio Generala Tehnica Stiintifica (Roumania)	**DICSA**	División de Investigacion de Conservación de Suelos y Aguas (Porto Rico)

DID	Drainage and Irrigation Department (Malaysia)	DIZ	Deutsches Institut für Zeitgeschichte
DID	Verband Deutscher Industrie-Designer	DJP	Départment Fédéral de Justice et Police (Switzerland)
DIDA	Dirección de Inspección y Defensa Agraria (Peru)	DJT	Deutscher Juristentag
		DJV	Deutsche Journalistenverband
DIDEFA	División de Defensa Agropecuaria (Chile)	DKB	Deutscher Konditorenbund
DIE	Danish Institute for the International Exchange of Scientific and Literary Publications	DKF	Dansk Kiropraktorforening
		DKF	Danske Konsummoelkmejeriers Foellesreproesentation
DIEESE	Departamento Intersindical de Estatısticas e Estudos Sócio-Econõmicos (Brazil)	DKG	Deutsche Kautschukgesellschaft
DIELCI	Diffusion Électrique de la Côte-d'Ivoire	DKG	Deutsche Keramische Gesellschaft
DIF	Dansk Ingeniørforening	DKG	Deutsche Krankenhausgesellschaft
DIF	Deutsches Institut zur Förderung des Industriellen Führungsnachwuches	DKI	Deutsches Kunststoff Institut
		DKI	Deutsches Kupferinstitut
DIFCA	La Diffusion du Caoutchouc	DKM	Dansk Kulturhistorisk Museumsforening
DIFPOA	Divisão de Inspeção e Fiscalização de Produtos de Origem Animal (Brazil)	DK-U	Dansk Køreloerer-Union
		DKV	Deutscher Kaltetechnisher Verein
DIGAP	Direct Investigation Group Aerial Phenomena	DL	Deutscher Lehrerband
		DL	Foreningen af Danske Landskabsarkitekter
DIHT	Deutscher Industrie- und Handelstag	DLCO-EA	Desert Locust Control Organization for Eastern Africa
DIICA	Departamento Técnico Interamericano de Cooperación Agrícola (Chile)		
		DLF	Dagligvaruleverantörers Förbund
DILAPSA	Distribuidora Latinoamericana de Publicaciones (Chile)	DLF	Danmarks Loererforening
DILF	Danske Indkøbschefers Landsforening	DLF	Foreningen af Danske Lysreklame Fabrikanter
DIMES	Distribution de Matériel Électrique au Sénégal	DLF	Danske Landboforeningers Froforskning
DIMO	Danske Interne Medicineres Organisation	DLG	Deutsche Landwirtschafts-Gesellschaft
DIN	Deutsche Industrie Norm	DLH	Deutsche Lufthansa AG
DINFIA	Dirección Nacional de Fabricaciones e Investigaciones Aeronáuticas (Argentina)	DLIS	Desert Locust Information Service (FAO)
		DLV	Deutsche Lehrmittelverband
DIPAN	Directoria da Produçao Animal (Brazil)	DMB	Deutscher Museumsbund
DIPROA	División de Producción Agropecuaria (Chile)	DMDS	Deutsche Gesellschaft für Medizinische Dokumentation und Statistik
DIPUVEN	Distribuidora de Publicaciones Venezolanas		
DIQUIVEN-JA	Distribuidora Química Venezolana	DME	Directorate of Mechanical Engineering
		DMF	Danske Mineralbandsfabrikanters
DISCS	Domestic International Sales Corporations (U.S.A.)	DMF	Dansk Møbeltransport Forening
		DMG	Deutsche Mineralogische Gesellschaft
DISI	Dairy Industries Society International (U.S.A.)	DMG	Deutsche Morgenländische Gesellschaft
		DMG	Deutsche Mozart-Gesellschaft
DISTRI-PRESS	Fédération Internationale des Distributeurs de Presse	DMG	Foreningen af Danske Manufaktur-Grossiter
		DMI	Danske Meteorologiske Institut
DITB	Distributive Industry Training Board	DMIAA	Diamond Manufacturers and Importers Association of America
DIVENAZ	Distribuidora Venezolana de Azúcares		
DIW	Deutsches Institut für Wirtschaftforschung	DMN	Direction de la Météorologie Nationale

DMpF	Dansk Musikpœdagogisk Forening	**DNT**	Det Norske Travselskap
DMS	Danmarks Mejeritekniske Selskab	**DNTF**	De Norske Teatres Forening
DMS	Dansk Medicinsk Selskab	**DNV**	Deutscher Nautischer Verein
DMV	Deutsche Marketing Vereinigung	**DNV**	De Norske Veterinœrforening
DMV	Deutscher Markscheiderverein	**DOAT**	Direction des Opérations de l'Assistance Technique (*of* UN)
DMV	Deutscher Marmorverband		
DMV	Deutsche Mathematikervereinigung	**DOBETA**	Domestic Oil Burning Equipment Testing Association
DMV	Deutscher Musikverleger Verband		
DNA	Deutsche Normenausschuss	**DOC**	Dépôts Océan Congo
DNB	Dirección Nacional del Banano (Ecuador)	**DOCA**	Automatic Documentation Section (*of* CETIS)
DNB	Vereniging 'De Nederlandse Baksteen-industrie'	**DOCAPES-CA**	Grémio dos Armadores da Pesca de Arrasto
DNDR	Dirección Nacional de Desarrollo (Bolivia)	**DOD**	Deutsches Ozeanographisches Datenzentrum
DNER	National Department of Public Roads (Brazil)		
		DoE	Department of the Environment
DNF	Den Norske Forsikringsforening	**DØF**	Danske Økonomers Forening
DNFB	De Norske Blikemballagefabrikers Forening	**DOF**	Dansk Ornithologisk Forening
DNFF	Den Norske Fagpresses Forening	**DOG**	Deutsche Ornithologen-Gesellschaft
DNGE	Dirección Nacional de Granos y Elevadores (Argentina)	**DOI**	Department of Industry
		DOMO	Dispensing Opticians Manufacturing Organisation
DNH	Den Norske Husflidsforening		
DNH	Udgiverselskab for Danmarks Nyeste Historie	**DOP**	Direction des Opérations et de la Programmation (UNDP
DNIBR	Danish National Institute of Building Research	**DORDEC**	Domestic Refrigeration Development Committee
DNJ	Det Norske Justervesen	**DOREMA**	Société Européenne de Documentation, de Recherche et de Marketing
DNL	Det Norske Luftartselkap		
DNM	Det Norske Myrselskap	**DORS**	Danish Operations Research Society
DNO	Danske Nervelaegers Organisation	**DOS**	Dansk Oto-laryngologisk Selskab
DNOCS	Departamento Nacional de Obras contra as Sêcas (Brazil)	**DOSCO**	Dominion Steel and Coal Corporation (Canada)
DNOS	Departamento Nacional de Obras de Saneamento (Brazil)	**DOSME**	Direccion de Obra Social y Ministerio de Educacion (Argentine)
DNP	Departamento Nacional de Planeación (Colombia)	**DOT**	Department of Transport (Canada)
		DOZ	Deutsches Olympia Zentrum
DNPM	Departamento Nacionál de Producaçao Mineral (Brazil)	**DP**	Danske Psykologforening
DNPV	Departamento Nacional de Produção Vegetal (Brazil)	**DPA**	Deutsche Press Agentur
		DPAG	Dangerous Pathogens Advisory Group
DNPVN	Departamento Nacional de Portos e Vias Navegáveis (Brazil)	**DPC**	Defence Planning Committee (NATO)
		DPCP	Department of Prices and Consumer Protection
DNR	Deutsche Naturschutzring		
DNR	Den Norske Reisebyråforening	**DPEA**	Departamento de Pesquisa e Experimentaçao Agropecuarias (Brazil)
DNSE	Dirección Nacionál del Servicio Estadístico (Argentina)		
		DPF	Dansk Pilotforening
DNSL	De Norske Saltfisekspørters Landsforening	**DPF**	Départment Politique Fédéral (Switzerland)

DPF	Directia Plan Financiar (Roumania)		**DRTE**	Defence Research Telecommunications Establishment (Canada)
DPG	Deutsche Physikalische Gesellschaft			
DPG	Deutsche Physiologische Gesellschaft		**DRV**	Deutscher Raiffeisenverband
DPhG	Deutsche Pharmakologische Gesellschaft		**DRV**	Deutscher Reifenhändlerverband
DPhV	Deutscher Philologen-Verband		**DRV**	Deutscher Reisebüroverband
DPI	Department of Public Information (UNO)		**DRWAW**	Distillery, Rectifying, Wine and Allied Workers International Union of America
DPK	Deutsche Pappelkommission		**DS**	Danmarks Sprogloererforening
DPK	Deutsche Pudel-Klub		**DS**	Dansk Standardiseringsråd
DPMA	Data Processing Management Association		**DSA**	Direction des Services Agricoles
DPOM	Directia Planificarii si Organizarii Muncii (Roumania)		**DSA**	Duodecimal Society of America
DPP	Directia Propagandei si Presei (Roumania)		**DSB**	Dachverband der Schweizerischen Bekleidungsindustrie
DPRG	Deutsche Public-Relations-Gesellschaft		**DSB**	Deutscher Sauna-Bund
DPRK	Dansk Public Relations Klub		**DSB**	Danish State Railways
DPRK	Democratic Peoples Republic of Korea		**DSB**	Deutsche Schaustellerbund
DPS	Dansk Pediatrisk Selskab		**DSB**	Drug Supervisory Body (Switzerland)
DPS	Dansk Psykiatrisk Selskab		**DSBy**	Dansk Selskab for Bygningsstatik
DPV	Dansk Patent-og Varemaerkekonsulent-forening		**DSE**	Deutsche Stiftung für Entwicklungsländer
DPV	Deutsche Verein zur Erforschung Palästina-Verein		**DSF**	Danske Salgslederes Foellesråd
			DSF	Dansk Skattevidenskabelig Forening
DPWV	Deutscher Paritaetischer Wohlfahrts-verbande		**DSF**	German-Soviet Friendship Society
			DSF	Dansk Fysiurgisk Selskab
DRB	Danske Reklamebureauers Brancheforening		**DSF**	Dansk Skibshandlerforening
DRB	Defence Research Board (Canada)		**DSF**	Dansk Socialrådgiverforening
DRF	Dansk Rationaliserings Forening		**DSI**	Dairy Society International (U.S.A.)
DRG	Deutsche Rheologische Gesellschaft		**DSI**	General Directorate of State Hydraulic Works (Turkey)
DRG	Deutsche Röntgengesellschaft—Gesellschaft für Medizinische Radiologie, Strahlenbiologie und Nuklearmedizin		**DSIM**	Dansk Selskab for Intern Medicin
			DSIR	Department of Scientific and Industrial Research
DRI	Denver Research Institute (U.S.A.)			
DRNR	Dirección de Recursos Naturales Renovables (Venezuela)		**DSIS**	Development Support Information Service (UN)
DRO	Danske Røntgendiagnostikeres Organisation		**DSKV**	Den Danske Sammenslutning af Konsulentev i Virksomhedsledelse
DROGA	Schweizerischer Verband Angestellter Drogisten		**DSL**	Danske Slagtermestres Landsforening
			DSO	Dansk Selskab for Optometri
DRP	Development Resources Panel (UNDP)		**DSOM**	Dansk Selskab for Oldtids-og Middelalder-forskning
DRPC	Defence Research Policy Committee		**DSP**	Democratic Socialist Party (Japan)
DRPLC	Département des Recherches des Plantations Lever au Congo		**DSpÄB**	Deutscher Sportärzebund
			DSR	Dansk Sygeplejeråd
DRS	Dansk Radiologisk Selskab		**DSRF**	Dansk Salgs-og Reklameforbund
DRTC	Documentation Research and Training Centre, Bangalore (India)		**DSSV**	Deutschschweizerischer Sprachverein
			DST	Deutscher Städtetag

DStB	Deutscher Städtbund
DStG	Deutsche Statistische Gesellschaft
DStGB	Deutscher Städte-und Gemeindebund
DSTO	Defence Sciences and Technology Organization (Australia)
DSTS	Dansk Selskab for Teoretisk Statistik
DSTV	Deutscher Stahlbauverband
DSV	Direction des Services Vétérinaires
DT	Deutsche Tierarzteschaft
DTAT	Direction Technique des Armaments Terrestres
DTB	Danmarks Tekniske Bibliotek
DTC	Department of Technical Co-operation
DTC	Départment des Transports et Communications et de l'Énergie (Switzerland)
DTF	Domestic Textiles Federation
DTF	Dairy Trade Federation
DTH	Danmarks Tekniske Højskole
DTI	Dansk Textil Institut
DTI	Department of Trade and Industry
DTICA	Departamento Tecnico Interamericano de Cooperación Agricola (Chile)
DTL	Dansk Teknisk Litteraturselskab
DTL	Dansk Teknisk Loereforening
DTO	Dansk Teknisk Oplysningstjeneste
DTREO	Départment des Travaux, Recherches et Exploitation Océaniques
DTRI	Dairy Training and Research Institute (Philippines)
DTU	Dansk Textil Union
DTV	Deutscher Transport- Versicherungs-Verband
DUGG	Deutsche Union für Geodäsie und Geophysik
DUW	Dijksdienst voor de Uitvoering van Werken
DVA	Deutsche Versicherungs Akademie
DVB	Deutscher Bäderverband
DVB	Deutscher Buchereiverband
DVC	Damodar Valley Corporation (India)
DVFA	Deutsche Vereinigung für Finanzanalyse und Anlageberatung
DVFB	Deutscher Vieh- und Fleischhandelsbund
DVFFA	Deutscher Verland Forstlicher Forschungsanstalten
DVfVW	Deutscher Verein für Versicherungswissenschaft
DVG	Deutsche Volkswirtschaftliche Gesellschaft
DVGW	Deutscher Verein van Gas- und Wasserfachmännern
DVKJ	Deutsche Vereinigung für Kinder- und Jugendpsychiatrie
DVL	Deutsche Versuchsanstalt für Luftfahrt
DVM	Deutsche Verband für Materialprüfung
DVMF	Dansk Vulkanisør- Mester-Forening
DVMLG	Deutsche Vereinigung für Mathematische Logik und Grundlagenforschung der Exakten Wissenschaften
DVOH	Deutsche Verband für Oberflachenveredlung und Härtung
DVPW	Deutsche Vereinigung für Politische Wissenschaft
DVS	Deutscher Verband für Schweisstechnik
DVT	Deutscher Verband Technisch-Wissenschaftlicher Vereine
DVTA	Deutscher Verband Technischer Assistentinnen und Assistenten
DVTWV	Deutscher Verband Technisch-Wissenschaftlicher Verbands
DVV	Deutscher Verzinkerei Verband
DVW	Deutscher Verein für Vermessungswesen
DVWG	Deutsche Verkehrswissenschaftliche Gesellschaft
DVWW	Deutscher Verband für Wasserwirtschaft
DWG	Deutsche Weltwirt-schaftliche Gesellschaft
DWG	Deutsche Werbewissenschaftliche Gesellschaft
DWK	Deutsche Wissenschaftliche Kommission für Meersforschung
DWK	Deutsches Woll-Komitee
DWP	Verband Deutscher Werbefilmproduzenten
DWT	Deutsche Gesellschaft für Wehrtechnik
DWV	Deutsche Waren-Vertriebsgesellschaft
DWV	Deutscher Wäscherei Verband
DWV	Deutscher Weinbauverband
DZB	Development Bank of Zambia
DZF	Deutsche Zentrale für Fremdenverkehr
DZG	Deutsche Zoologische Gesellschaft
DZK	Deutsches Zentralkomitee zur Bekämpfung der Tuberkulose
DZL	Deutsche Zentralinstitut für Lehrmittel
DZT	Deutsche Zentrale für Tourismus

DZVHA	Deutscher Zentralverein Homöopathischer Ärzte
DZW	Deutsche Dokumentations Zentrale Wasser

E

EA	Elektriska Arbetsgivareföreningen
EAA	East African Airways Corporation
EAA	Electrical Appliance Association
EAA	European Accounting Association
EAA	European Athletic Association
EAAA	European Association of Advertising Agencies
EAAC	East African Academy (Kenya)
EAAC	East African Airways Corporation
EAAC	European Agricultural Aviation Centre
EAAC	European Association of Audiophonological Centres (France)
EAACI	European Academy of Allergology and Clinical Immunology
EAAFRO	East African Agricultural and Forestry Research Organisation
EAAP	European Association of Animal Production (Italy)
EAAS	East Anglian Aviation Society
EABA	European Amateur Boxing Association
EAC	East African Community
EAC	Electro-Agricultural Centre, Kenilworth
EAC	Engineering Advisory Council
EAC	Études Agricoles par Correspondance
EAC	European Agency for Cooperation
EAC	European Banks Advisory Committee
EACA	European Association of Charter Airlines (Netherlands)
EACC	East Asia Christian Conference
EACC	European Association of Audiophonological Centres (France)
EACE	Euro-American Cultural Exchange
EACN	European Air Chemistry Network
EACR	European Association for Cancer Research
EACRP	European American Committee on Reactor Physics (of ENEA)

EACSO	East African Common Services Organisation
EADA	East African Dental Association
EADB	East African Development Bank
EADD	East African Development Division (of ODM)
EAE	Eastern Association of Electro-encephalographers (U.S.A.)
EAEC	East African Examinations Council
EAEC	East African Extract Corporation
EAEC	European Atomic Energy Community (Euratom)
EAEE	Evangelische Arbeitsgemeinschaft für Erwachsenenbildung in Europa
EAEG	European Association of Exploration Geophysicists
EAEM	Escola de Agronomica Eliseu Maciel (Brazil)
EAENF	Engineering and Allied Employers' National Federation (now EEF)
EAES	European Atomic Energy Society
EAF	Elektrokemiske Arbeidsgiverforening
EAF	Employment Agents' Federation of Great Britain
EAFFRO	East African Freshwater Fishery Research Organisation
EAFRO	East African Fisheries Research Organisation
EAG	Europäische Atomgemeinschaft (Belgium)
EAG	European-Atlantic Group
EAGGF	European Agricultural Guidance and Guarantee Fund
EAHC	East African High Commission
EAHRA	East African Railways and Harbours Administration
EAHTMA	Engineers' and Allied Hand Tool Makers' Association
EAHY	European Architectural Heritage Year
EAIMB	East Africa Industries Management Board
EAIMR	East African Institute for Medical Research (Tanzania)
EAIRB	East African Industrial Research Board
EAIRO	East African Industrial Research Organization
EAK	Cyprus Farmers Union
EALA	East African Library Association
EALB	East African Literature Bureau (Tanzania)

EALRC	East African Leprosy Research Centre (Uganda)
EALS	East African Literature Service
EAMA	États Africains et Malgache Associés
EAMC	European Airlines Montparnasse Committee
EAMD	East African Meteorological Department
EAMDA	European Alliance of Muscular Dystrophy Associations
EAMF	European Association of Music Festivals
EAMFRO	East African Marine Fisheries Research Organisation
EAMFS	European Association for Maxillo-Facial Surgery
EAMRC	East African Medical Research Council (Tanzania)
EAMTC	European Association of Management Training Centres (*now* EFMD)
EAMU	East African Malaria Unit
EAMVBD	East African Institute of Malaria and Vector-Borne Diseases (Tanzania)
EAN	Engineering Association of Nashville (U.S.A.)
EANA	European Alliance of News Agencies
EANDC	European American Nuclear Data Committee (*of* ENEA)
EANHS	East African National Health Service
EANHS	East Africa Natural History Society
EANRRC	East African National Resources Research Council (Kenya)
EAO	Egyptian Agricultural Organization
EAPA	European Asphalt Pavement Association
EAPAC	Eggs Authority Producer Advisory Committee
EAPCO	East African Pesticides Control Organization
EAPH	East Africa Publishing House (Kenya)
EAPM	European Association for Personnel Management
EAPR	European Association for Potato Research (Netherlands)
EAPT	East African Posts and Telecommunications
EAR	European Association of Radiology
EARAC	East Anglian Regional Advisory Council
EARB	European Airlines Research Bureau (*now* AEA)
EARCCUS	East African Regional Committee for the Conservation and Utilisation of the Soil
EARDHE	European Association for Research and Development in Higher Education
EARI	Engineer Agency for Resources Inventories (U.S.A.)
EARIC	East African Research Information Centre
EAROPH	Eastern Regional Organisation for Planning and Housing (India)
EARS	Eldoret Agricultural Research Station (Kenya)
EAS	Europese Associaties voor Samenwerking
EASA	Engineers Association of South Africa
EASB	East African Settlement Board
EASD	European Association for the Study of Diabetes
EASE	European Association for Special Education (Sweden)
EASHP	European Association of Senior Hospital Physicians
EASL	East African School of Librarianship
EASL	European Association for the Study of the Liver (Germany)
EASS	Editura Agro-Silvica de Stat (Roumania)
EAT	Entreprise Africaine de Travaux
EAT	Europäische Association für Thermographie
EATA	East Asia Travel Association
EATCS	European Association for Theoretical Computer Science
EATEC	East African Tanning Extract Company
EATIC	Corporation East African Tuberculosis Investigation Centre (Kenya)
EATITU	East African Tractor and Implement Testing Unit
EATJP	European Association for the Trade in Jute Products
EATP	European Association for Textile Polyolefins
EATPHHSA	European Association of Training Programmes in Hospital and Health Service Administration
EATRO	East African Trypanosomiasis Research Organisation
EATU	Eastern African Telecommunications Union
EAVRI	East African Virus Research Institute (Uganda)
EAVRO	East African Veterinary Research Organisation

EAWAG	Eidgenössischen Anstalt für Wasserversorgung, Abwasserreinigung und Gewässerschutz (Switzerland)	**ECAC**	European Civil Aviation Conference
EBA	English Bowling Association	**ECAFE**	Economic Commission for Asia and the Far East (Thailand) (*now* ESCAP)
EBAD	École des Bibliothécaires, Archivistes et Documentalistes (Senegal)	**ECAM**	Employers Consultative Association of Malawi
EBAE	European Bureau of Adult Education	**ECAM**	Enseignement Catholique au Maroc (Morocco)
EBBA	English Basket Ball Association	**ECARBICA**	East and Central African Regional Branch of the International Council on Archives
EBBS	European Brain and Behaviour Society		
EBC	European Bibliographical Centre—Clio Press	**ECAS**	Electrical Contractors' Association of Scotland
EBC	European Billiards Confederation	**ECAT**	École Coloniale d'Agriculture de Tunis
EBC	European Brewery Convention	**ECAT**	Emergency Committee for American Trade
EBES	Sociétés Réunies d'Énergie du Bassin de l'Escaut (Belgium)	**ECB**	European Coordination Bureau for International Youth Organisations
EBF	European Baptist Federation		
EBIAMS	Executive Board of the International Association of Microbiological Societies	**ECBA**	European Community Biologists Association
		ECBIYO	European Coordination Bureau for International Youth Organizations
EBIC	EFTA Brewing Industry Council		
EBIC	European Banks International Company (Belgium)	**ECBO**	European Cell Biology Organisation
		ECC	English Ceramic Circle
EBL	European Bridge League	**ECC**	European Cultural Centre (Switzerland)
EBM	Estación de Biologia Marina (Chile)	**ECCA**	East Caribbean Currency Authority
EBM	Wirtschaftsverband Eisen, Blech und Metall-Verarbeitende	**ECCA**	European Coil Coating Association
		ECCASA	Empresa de Curtidos Centro Americana, S.A.
EBNI	Electricity Board for Northern Ireland		
EB & RA	Engineer Buyers' and Representatives' Association	**ECCC**	Ecology Centre Communications Council (U.S.A.)
EBSA	Estuarine and Brackish-Water Sciences Association (U.S.A.)	**ECCLA**	European Committee for Cooperation with Latin America
EBU	European Boxing Union	**ECCM**	Eastern Caribbean Common Market
EBU	English Bridge Union	**ECCP**	European Committee on Crime Problems
EBU	European Broadcasting Union (Switzerland)	**ECCS**	European Union of Christian-Democratic and Conservative Students
EBYC	European Bureau for Youth and Childhood		
ECA	Economic Commission for Africa (UN)	**ECCU**	English Cross Country Union
ECA	Economic Co-operation Administration (*later* MSA) (U.S.A.)	**ECE**	Economic Commission for Europe
		ECE	Export Council for Europe
ECA	Educational Centres Association	**ECEA**	Economic Community of Eastern Africa
ECA	Electrical Contractors Association	**ECEM**	Études et Construction Électro-Mécaniques et Médicales
ECA	Entreprise de Centre Afrique (Haute-Volta)		
ECA	Empresa de Comercio Agrícola de Chile	**ECEPLAN**	Escritório Central de Planejamento e Contrôle (Brasil)
ECA	Europe China Association		
ECA	European Camac Association	**ECF**	Eastern Counties Farmers
ECA	European Confederation of Agriculture (*formerly* ICA) (Switzerland)	**ECF**	European Commission on Forestry and Forest Products (*of* FAO)
ECA	European Congress of Accountants	**ECFA**	European Committee for Future Activities

ECFCI	European Centre of Federations of the Chemical Industry	**ECMWF**	European Centre for Medium-Range Weather Forecasting
ECFFP	European Commission on Forestry and Forest Products	**ECNR**	European Council for Nuclear Research
		ECO	European Coal Organisation (UNO)
ECFI	East Caribbean Farm Institute	**ECOCEN**	Economic Cooperation Centre for the Asian and Pacific Region (Thailand)
ECFMS	Educational Council for Foreign Medical Students		
		ECOLOS	Ecological Coalition on the Law of the Sea
ECFTU	European Confederation of Free Trade Unions in the Community	**ECOM**	Centro de Computadoras del Gobierno de Chile
ECGC	Empire Cotton Growing Corporation (U.K.) (*now CRC*)	**ECOP**	Extension Committee on Organisation and Policy (U.S.A.)
ECGD	Export Credits Guarantee Department	**ECOPEMAR**	Empresa Conservera de Pescados y Mariscos (Cuba)
ECICW	European Centre of the International Council of Women		
		ECO-PETROL	Empresa Colombiana de Petróleos (Colombia)
ECIS	European Community Information Service		
ECITO	European Central Inland Transport Organisation.	**ECOR**	Engineering Committee on Oceanic Resources
ECITS	Ente Conzorziale Interprovinciale Toscano Sementi	**ECOROPA**	European Ecology Group
		ECOSAL	Equipo de Conferencias Sindicales de América Latina
ECIWA	European Committee of Importers and Wholesaler Grocers Associations		
		ECOSEC	European Cooperation Space Environment Committee
ECJCS	European Council of Jewish Community Services		
		ECOSOC	Economic and Social Council of the United Nations
ECLA	Economic Commission for Latin America (U.N.)		
		ECOSOC for OAS	Economic and Social Council for the Organization of American States
ECLE	European Centre for Leisure and Education		
ECLF	Centre Européen pour Loisir et l'Éducation	**ECOTAL**	Equipo de Conferencias de Trabajadores de America Latina
ECLM	Economic Community for Livestock and Meat (Africa)		
		ECOWAS	Economic Community of West African States
ECLOF	Ecumenical Church Loan Fund		
ECMA	European Carton Makers Association	**ECP**	European Confederation for Plant Protection Research
ECMA	European Computer Manufacturers Association		
		ECPA	Expert Committee on Post Adjustments (UNO)
ECMBR	European Committee on Milk-Butterfat Recording		
		ECPC	Enlarged Committee for Programme and Coordination (UNDP)
ECMC	Electric Cable Makers Confederation		
ECMC	European Container Manufacturers' Committee	**ECPD**	Engineers' Council for Professional Development, (U.S.A.)
ECME	Economic Commission for the Middle East (UNO).	**ECPE**	European Centre for Public Enterprises
		ECPR	European Consortium for Political Research
ECMF	Electric Cable Makers' Federation	**ECPS**	English Connemara Pony Society
ECMMR	European College of Marketing and Marketing Research (U.K.)	**ECRIB**	European Commissary Resale Items Board
		ECRL	Eastern Caribbean Regional Library
ECMRA	European Chemical Marketing Research Association	**ECRO**	European Chemoreception Research Organization
		ECSA	European Computing Services Association
ECMT	European Conference of Ministers of Transport	**ECSC**	European Coal and Steel Community

ECSIM	European Centre of Study and Information on Multinational Corporations	**EDITEAST**	Association of Editors in the South-East Asian Region (Indonesia)
ECSWTR	European Centre for Social Welfare Training and Research (Austria)	**EDITERRA**	European Association of Earth Science Editors
ECTA	Eastern Caribbean Tourist Association (Antigua)	**EDM**	Société Énergie du Mali
		EDMA	European Direct Marketing Association
ECTA	Electrical Contractors' Trading Association	**EDPAA**	International EDP Auditors Association (U.S.A.)
ECTCI	Entreprise Commerciale et de Transports en Côte d'Ivoire	**EDRA**	Environmental Design Research Association (U.S.A.)
ECU	European Chiropractors Union		
ECU	European Credit Union	**EDS**	Environmental Data Service (U.S.A.)
ECUSAT	Ecumenical Satellite Commission	**EDS**	Étudiants Démocrates Européens
ECWA	Economic Commission for Western Asia (*of* UN)	**EDS**	European Democrat Students
		EDTA	European Dialysis and Transplant Association
ECWA	Economic Community of West Africa		
EDA	British Electrical Development Association (*sometimes abbreviated* BEDA)	**EDUCOM**	Interuniversity Communications Council (U.S.A.)
EDA	Educational Development Association	**EDV**	Eisendrahtvereinigung
EDA	English Draughts Association	**EEA**	Dirección de Economia y Estadística Agropecuaria (Venezuela)
EDA	Essential Oil Association of the United States		
EDA	European Demolition Association	**EEA**	Electronic Engineering Association
EDA	European Disposables Association	**EEA**	Estación Experimental de Agricultura (Bolivia)
EDAC	Electronics Development Analysis Centre (Korea)	**EEA**	European Evangelical Alliance
EDANA	European Disposables and Nonwovens Association	**EEAT**	Estación Experimental Agrícola de Tucumán (Argentina)
EDB	Economic Development Board (Singapore)	**EEB**	Eastern Electricity Board
EDC	Economic Development Committee (*of* NEDC)	**EEB**	European Environmental Bureau (Belgium)
EDCC	Environmental Dispute Coordination Commission (Japan)	**EEBP**	Estaçao Experimentál de Biologia e Piscicultura (Brazil)
EDCCI	Economic Development Committee for the Chemical Industry	**EEC**	English Electric Company Ltd
		EEC	European Economic Community
EDE	Etablissements d'Utilité Agricole d'Élevage	**EECA**	European Electronic Component Manufacturers Association
EDEKA	Purchasing Cooperative of German Merchants	**EECE**	Emergency Economic Commission for Europe
EDF	Economic Development Foundation (Philippines)	**EECI**	Énergie Électrique de la Côte-d'Ivoire
		EED	European Enterprises Development Company
EDF	Électricité de France. Direction Générale		
EDF	European Development Fund	**EEDC**	Electronics Economic Development Committee (*of* NEDC)
EDHASA	Editora y Distribuidora Hispano Americana S.A.	**EEF**	Eisenhower Exchange Fellowships (U.S.A.)
EDI	Economic Development Institute (Nigeria)	**EEF**	Engineering Employers' Federation
EDI	Entraide pour le Développement Intégral	**EEG**	Electroencephalographic Society
EDICA	Egyptian Documentation and Information Centre for Agriculture	**EEG**	Essence Export Group
		EEG	Europese Economische Gemeenschap

EEI	Edison Electric Institute (U.S.A.)
EEM	Eastern European Mission (U.S.A.)
EEMO	Exposition Européenne de la Machine Outil
EEMS	European Environmental Mutagen Society
EEOA	Compagnie des Eaux et Électricité de l'Ouest Africaine
EEOC	Equal Employment Opportunity Commission (U.S.A.)
EER	European Economic Recovery Committee (UNO)
EERI	Environmental and Ecological Research Institute (Thailand)
EETC	East Europe Trades Council
EETPU	Electrical, Electronic, Telecommunications and Plumbing Union
EETS	Early English Text Society
EEUA	Engineering Equipment Users Association
EEVC	English Electric Valve Company
EEW	Erfassung der Europäischen Wirbellosen
E & F	Eaux et Forêts (France)
EF	Engineering Foundation (U.S.A.)
EFA	École Française d'Afrique
EFA	Empire Forestry Association
EFA	European Federation of Agricultural Workers in the Community
EFA	European Finance Association
EFAA	English Field Archery Association
EFACI	Société d'Exploitations Forestières et Agricoles de la Côte-d'Ivoire
EFAPI	Euromarket Federation of Animal Protein Importers
EFBA	Entreprise Forestière des Bois Africains (Ivory Coast)
EFBACA	Entreprise Forestière de Bois Africains Centrafrique
EFBTE	Eastern Federation of Building Trades' Employers
EFC	Entreprise Forestiere Camerounaise
EFC	European Federation of Corrosion
EFC	European Forestry Commission
EFCC	European Federation of Conference Cities
EFCE	European Federation of Chemical Engineering
EFCEM	European Federation of Catering Equipment Manufacturers
EFCS	European Federation of Cytology Societies
EFCT	European Federation of Conference Towns
EFCTC	European Federation of Connective Tissue Clubs
EFDA	European Federation of Data Processing Associations
EFDSS	English Folk Dance and Song Society
EFEMA	Association des Fabricants Européens d'Emulsifiants Alimentaires
EFEO	European Flight Engineers Organization
EFF	Elektronikfabrikantforeningen
EFF	European Furniture Federation
EFGA	English Farmers Growers Association
EFI	Ekonomiska Forskningsinstitutet (Sweden)
EFI	Electronic Forum for Industry
EFIL	European Federation for Intercultural Learning
EFJC	Europäische Foderation Junger Chore
EFLA	Educational Film Library Association (U.S.A.)
EFLRY	European Federation of Liberal and Radical Youth
EFM	European Federalist Movement
EFMA	European Financial Marketing Association
EFMD	European Foundation for Management Development
EFMK	European Federation of Masseurs-Kinesitherapeutes
EFNEP	Expanded Food and Nutrition Education Program (U.S.A.)
EFNMS	European Federation of National Maintenance Societies
EFP	European Federation of Purchasing
EFPB	Employers Federation of Papermakers and Boardmakers (*of* BPBIF)
EFPMB	Employers' Federation of Papermakers and Boardmakers (*now* BPBIF)
EFPS	European Federation of Productivity Services
EFPW	European Federation for the Protection of Waters
EFS	Europäische Forschungsgemeinschaft für Stahlradiatoren (*now* EURORAD)
EFSC	European Federation of Soroptimist Clubs
EFSS	Emergency Food Supply Scheme (WFP)
EFTA	European Free Trade Association
EFTA	European Technological Forecasting Association
EFTAMALT	EFTA Malting Industry Association

EFTAPA	EFTA Plastics Association (*now* Society of Plastic Associations in Europe)
EFTA-TUC	Trade Union Committee for the European Free Trade Area
EFTC	Electrical Fair Trading Council
EFU	Europäische Frauenunion
EFVA	Education Foundation for Visual Aids
EG	Engineers' Guild
EGA	Électricité et Gaz d'Algérie
EGA	Entreprise Générale Atlantique
EGA	Europese Gemeenschap voor Atomenergie (Belgium)
EGB	Eastern Gas Board
EGCI	Export Group for the Constructional Industries
EGCM	Entreprise Gabonaise de Constructions Métalliques
EGCS	English Guernsey Cattle Society
EGGA	European General Galvanizers Association
EGGMA	European Gas Control Manufacturers' Association (*now* AFECOGAZ)
EGIG	Expédition Glaciologique Internationale au Groenland (U.K.)
EGK	Europäische Güterzugfahrplankonferenz
EGKS	Europäische Gemeinschaft für Kohle und Stahl
EGM	European Glass Container Manufacturers' Committee
EGOA	Europäische Gesellschaft für Osteo-Arthrologie
EGOS	European Group for Organization Studies
EGOTI	Egyptian General Organization for Trade and Industry
EGPA	Egyptian General Petroleum Authority
EGRSA	Edible Gelatin Research Society of America
EGS	European Geophysical Society
EGSC	Eastern Group Supply Council
EGSL	European Group for the Study of Lysosomes
EGTO	Egyptian General Trade Organisation
EGU	English Golf Union
EGZ	Europäische Gesellschaft für Zusammenarbeit
EH	International Institute of Human Economy
EHB	Europäisches Hopfenbaubüro
EHC	European Hotel Corporation
EHCC	European Hops Culture Committee
EHGC	European Hop Growers Convention
EHL	Elektriska Hushållsapparatleverantörer
EHL	Entente des Hôpitaux Luxembourgeois
EHSC	European Home Study Council
EIAC	Electronics Industries Association of Canada
EIA	Engineering Industries Association
EIAS	Institut Européen Inter-Universitaire de l'Action Sociale
EIASM	European Institute for Advanced Studies in Management (Belgium)
EIB	Economisch Instituut voor de Bouwnij-verheid
EIB	Europäische Investitionsbank
EIB	European International Business Association
EIBA	Electrical Industries Benevolent Association
EIBIS	Engineering in Britain Information Services
EIBM	Escuéla Interamericana de Bibliotecología (Colombia)
EIC	Engineering Institute of Canada
EICA	East India Cotton Association
EICF	European Investment Casters Federation
EIECC	Inter-American Council for Education, Science and Culture
EIEI	General Directorate of Electrical Surveys Administration (Turkey)
EIFAC	European Inland Fisheries Advisory Commission (*of* FAO)
EIFEL	European Group for the Ardennes and the Eifel
EIFI	Electrical Industries Federation of Ireland
EIGA	Engineering Industry Group Apprenticeship
EIJC	Engineering Institutions Joint Council
EIJHE	East Indian Jute and Hessian Exchange
EIL	British Association of the Experiment in International Living
EIL	Elektroinstallatorenes Landsforbund
EIN	Escuéla Industriál de la Nación (Argentina)
EIO	Economische Voorlichtingsdienst
EIO	Elektriska Installatörganisationen
EIOI	Expedición Internacional al Océano Indico
EIP	Association Mondiale pour l'École Instrument de Paix
EIPC	European Institute of Printed Circuits
EIRC	Équipes Internationales de Renaissance Chrétienne

EIRENE	International Christian Service for Peace	**ELEP**	European Federation of Anti-Leprosy Associations (*now* ILEP)
EIRMA	European Industrial Research Management Association (France)	**ELF**	Eritrean Liberation Front
EIS	Educational Institute of Scotland	**ELF**	Esperanto-Ligo Filatelista
EIS	Elektroniikkainsinöörien Seura	**ELF**	European Landworkers' Federation
EIS	European Invertebrate Survey	**ELFA**	Electric Light Fittings Association
EISCAT	European Incoherent Scatter Organisation	**ELFO**	Elektroinstallatørernes Landsforening
EISW	Inter-University European Institute on Social Welfare	**ELGA**	European Liaison Group for Agriculture
		ELIC	Electric Lamp Industry Council
EIT	European Institute for Trans-National Studies in Group and Organisational Development	**ELIF**	Sveriges Elektroindustriförening
		ELKEPA	Ellenikon Kentron Paragogikotitos
EITB	Engineering Industry Training Board	**ELLA**	European Long Lines Agency (of NATO)
EIU	Economic Intelligence Unit	**ELMA**	Electric Lamp Manufacturers' Association
EIVT	European Institute for Vocational Training	**ELMAF**	Emballages Légers Métalliques Africains
EJC	Engineers Joint Council (U.S.A.)	**ELMIA**	European Agricultural and Industrial Fair (Sweden)
EJCS	English Jersey Cattle Society		
EJCSC	European Joint Committee of Scientific Cooperation (*of* CE)	**ELMO**	European Laundry and Dry Cleaning Machinery Manufacturers Organisation
		ELPA	Automobile Association of Greece
EJMA	English Joinery Manufacturers' Association	**ELPA**	Eléveurs Limousin Plein Air
EKESO	Europees Korps voor Ekonomische en Sociale Ontwikkeling (Belgium)	**ELRA**	European Leisure and Recreation Association
EKI	Instituto por Esperanto en Komerco kaj Industrio (Netherlands)	**ELSE**	European Life Science Editors
		ELU	English Lacrosse Union
EKRIS	Enosis Katastimatarchon Radiofonon & Illektrikon Syskevon	**ELWCHG**	European Labor and Working Class History Group (U.S.A.)
EKS	Etaireia Kypriakon Spoudon (Cyprus)		
EKSG	Europese Kolen en Staal Gemeenschap	**EM**	European Movement
EL	Entreprenørenes Landssammenslutning	**EMA**	Empreza de Mecanisaçao Agricola (Brazil)
ELA	Elicottero Lavoro Aereo	**EMA**	Entertainment Managers Association of Great Britain and Ireland
ELANE	Electronics Association for the North East		
		EMA	Evangelical Missionary Alliance
ELB	Environment Liaison Board (NGO)	**EMA**	Evaporated Milk Association (U.S.A.)
ELBS	English Language Book Society	**EMA**	European Monetary Agreement
ELC	Environment Leisure Centre (Kenya)	**EMAA**	European Mastic Asphalt Association
ELDO	European Launcher Development Organisation	**EMAB**	Enterprise Malienne du Bois
		EMAC	Educational Media Association of Canada
ELDOK	Elektronisk Dokumentationsog Patentforening	**EMACO**	Electromedicinsk Apparat Compagni
		EMAIA	Electrical Meter and Allied Industries Association (Australia)
ELEC	English Language Education Council (Japan)		
ELEC	English Language Exploratory Committee (Japan)	**EMAP**	European Marketing and Advertising Press
		EMARC	Escola Média de Agricultura da Região Cacaueira (Brazil)
ELEC	European League for Economic Co-operation		
		EMA-UK	European Marketing Association United Kingdom
ELEOUR-GIKI	Central Cooperative Union of Olive and Olive Oil Producers of Greece		
		EMB	Europäischer Metallgewerkschaftsbund

EMBAL-GROS	Chambre Syndicale des Négociants en Papiers d'Emballage et Cartons en Gros (Belgium)
EMBC	European Molecular Biology Conference
EMBO	European Molecular Biology Organisation
EMBRAER	Empresa Brasileira de Aeronautica
EMBRATEL	Empresa Brasileira Telecomunicacoes
EMBRATER	Empresa Brasileira de Assisténcia Técnica e Extensão Rural
EMC	Enterprise Minière et Chimique
EMC	European Medicum Collegium
EMC	European Marketing Council
EMCAPA	Empresa Capixaba de Pesquisa Agropecuaria (Brazil)
EMCC	European Municipal Credit Community
EMCCC	European Military Communications Coordinating Committee (*of* NATO)
EMCF	European Monetary Cooperation Fund
EMF	European Management Forum
EMF	European Metalworkers Federation
EMF	European Motel Federation
EMGI	Ethiopian Mapping and Geography Institute
EMI	Electrical and Musical Industries Ltd
EMIC	Environmental Mutagen Information Centre (U.S.A.)
EMP	Ethnikon Metsovion Polytechneion
EMPA	Eidgenössische Materialprüfungsanstalt (Switzerland)
EMPA	European Maritime Pilots Association
EMPAGRI	Empresas Agricolas C.A.Ltda (Costa Rica)
EMPCO	English Metal Powder Company
EMRB	European Marketing Research Board
EMRLS	East Midlands Regional Library Service
EMS	Econometric Society (U.S.A.)
EMS	Environmental Mutagen Society (U.S.A.)
EMSA	Electron Microscope Society of America
EMSA	Entreprenadmaskinleverantörernas Samarbetsorgan
EMSS	Elisha Mitchell Scientific Society (U.S.A.)
EMTA	Electro Medical Trade Association
EMU	European Economic and Monetary Union
EMV	Europäischer Möbel-Verband
ENA	École Nationale d'Administration
ENA	École Nationale d'Agriculture
ENA	Émaillerie Nouvelle Afrique

ENA	European Neurosciences Association
ENAA	École Nationale d'Agriculture d'Alger
ENAF	École Nationale Agronomique Féminine
ENAF	Empresa Nacional de Fundiciones (Bolivia)
ENAG	Escuela Nacional de Agricultura y Ganadería (Nicaragua)
ENAL	Ente Nazionale Assistenza Lavoratori
ENAMI	Empresa Nacional de Minería (Chile)
ENAP	Empresa Nacional de Petróleos (Chile)
ENAP	Escuela Nacional de Administración Pública
ENAPI	Ente Nazionale Artigianato e Piccole Industrie
ENASA	Empresa Nacional de Autocamiones SA (Spain)
ENAT	Entreprise Africaine de Travaux (Ivory Coast)
ENBC	Eastern Nigeria Broadcasting Corporation
ENC	École Nationale de la Coopération (Tunisia)
ENC	Ente Nazionale Circhi
ENCA	European Naval Communications Agency (*of* NATO)
ENCASCO	Empresa Nacional Calvo Sotelo
ENCB	Escuela Nacional de Ciencias Biológicas
ENCC	Ente Nazionale per la Cellulose e per la Carta
ENCK	Eerste Nederlandse Coöperatieve Kunstmestfabriek
ENCOE	British National Committee on Ocean Engineering
ENCONA	Environmental Coalition for North America
ENCOTEL	Empresa Nacional de Correos y Telegrafos (Argentina)
ENDC	Eastern Nigeria Development Corporation
ENDC	Eighteen-Nation Disarmament Committee
ENDE	Empresa Nacional de Electricidad (Bolivia)
ENDESA	Hydrology Division of the National Electricity Company of Chile
ENDEV	Development Finance Co. (Eastern Nigeria)
ENDS	Empresa Nacional de Semillas (Chile)
ENEA	European Nuclear Energy Agency (OECD)
ENEF	École Nationale des Eaux et Forêts
ENEF	English New Education Fellowship
ENELCAM	Énergie Électrique du Cameroun
ENEL	Ente Nazionale per l'Energia Elettrica
ENEMA	École Nationale d'Enseignement Ménager Agricole, à Rennes

ENERCA	Énergie Centrafricaine
ENERGAS	Empresa Nacional de Gas (Spain)
ENEX	Engineering Export Association of New Zealand
ENFA	École Nationale Féminine d'Agronomie
ENFPPM	École Nationale de Formation et de Perfectionnement de Patrons de Pêche et de Mécaniciens
ENG	European Nursing Group
ENGACO	Entreprises Gabonaises de Constructions
ENGR	École Nationale du Génie Rural
ENGREF	École Nationale du Génie Rural, des Eaux et des Forêts
ENH	École Nationale des Haras
ENH	École Nationale d'Horticulture
ENHER	Empresa Nacional Hidroelectuca del Ribagorzana
ENMS	European Nuclear Medicine Society
ENI	Ente Nazionale Idrocarburi
ENIA	École Nationale des Industries Agricoles et Alimentaire
ENISA	École Nationale d'Ingénieurs Spécialisés en Agriculture
ENIT	Ente Nazionale Italiano Turismo
ENITA	École Nationale des Ingénieurs de Travaux Agricoles
ENNICO	Entreprise Nigérienne de Confiserie
ENO	Comité Hellénique de Normalisation
ENPI	Ente Nazionale Prevenzione Infortuni
ENPS	École Nationale de Promotion Sociale (Madagascar)
ENRC	European Nuclear Research Centre
ENREA	École Nationale de Radiotechnique et d'Électricité Appliquée
ENRI	Electronic Navigation Research Institute (Japan)
ENS	European Nuclear Society
ENSA	École Nationale Supérieure Agronomique
ENSAE	École Nationale de la Statistique et de l'Administration Economique
ENSAJF	École Nationale Supérieure d'Agronomie pour Jeunes Filles
ENSAN	École Nationale Supérieure Agronomique de Nancy
ENSAT	L'École Nationale Supérieure Agronomique de Toulouse
ENSEME	Entreprise Sénégalaise des Mousses et Plastiques
ENSH	École Nationale Supérieure d'Horticulture
ENSIAA	École Nationale Supérieure des Industries Agricoles et Alimentaires
ENSMIC	École Nationale Supérieure de Meunerie et des Industries Céréalières
ENSP	École Nationale de la Santé Publique
ENSPM	École Nationale Supérieure du Pétrole et des Moteurs
ENSSAA	École Nationale Supérieure des Sciences Agronomiques Appliquées
ENTEL	Empresa Nacional de Telecomunicaciónes (Bolivia, etc.)
ENUSA	Empresa Nacional del Urano SA
ENV	Écoles Nationales Vétérinaires
EOA	English Orienteering Association
EOARDC	European Office of the U.S. Air Research and Development Command
EOC	Equal Opportunities Commission
EODA	Eastern Ontario Development Association (Canada)
EOKA	National Organisation of Cypriot Combatants
EOM	Ellinikos Organismos Marketing
EONR	European Organisation for Nuclear Research
EOQC	European Organization for Quality Control
EORTC	European Organisation for Research on Treatment of Cancer
EOS	Egyptian Organization for Standardization
EOS	European Orthodontic Society
EO-WCL	European Organisation of the World Confederation of Labour
EP	European Parliament
EPA	Environmental Protection Agency (U.S.A.)
EPA	European Productivity Agency (of OECD)
EPACCI	Economic Planning and Advisory Council for the Construction Industries
EPADC	East Pakistan Agricultural Development Corporation
EPARD	East Pakistan Academy for Rural Development
EPASA	Electron Probe Analysis Society of America
EPC	Economic Policy Committee (*of* OECD)
EPC	Export Publicity Council

EPCA	Economic Planning and Coordination Authority (Hawaii)	**EPUL**	École Polytechnique de l'Université de Lausanne
EPCA	European Petrochemical Association	**EPWAPDA**	East Pakistan Water and Power Development Authority
EPD	Eidgenössisches Politisches Department (Switzerland)	**EQUAPAC**	International Cooperative Expedition EQUAPAC
EPDC	Electric Power Development Corporation (Japan)	**ERA**	École Régionale d'Agriculture
EPEA	Electrical Power Engineers' Association	**ERA**	Electrical Research Association
EPF	École Polytechnique Fédérale (Switzerland)	**ERA**	European Recreation Association
EPF	European Packaging Federation	**ERA**	European Rotogravure Association
EPFCL	Esso Pakistan Fertilizer Co. Ltd	**ERAP**	Entreprise de Recherches et d'Activités Pétrolières
EPFL	École Polytechnique Fédérale de Lausanne (Switzerland)	**ERB**	Educational Records Bureau (U.S.A.)
EPFTR	Expert Panel for the Facilitation of Tuna Research (FAO)	**ERC**	Economic Research Council
		ERC	Empire Rheumatism Council
EPG	European Press Group	**ERC**	Regional Conference for Europe (FAO)
EPHE	École Pratique des Hautes Études	**ERCHCW**	European Regional Clearing House for Community Work
EPIC	Electronic Properties Information Centre (U.S.A.)	**ERCO**	Electrical Reduction Company of Canada
EPIC	Export Payment Insurance Corporation (Australia)	**ERDA**	Electrical and Radio Development Association (N.S. Wales)
EPIDC	East Pakistan Industrial Development Council	**ERDA**	European Research and Development Agency
EPLA	East Pakistan Library Association	**ERDC**	Eastern Region Development Corporation (Nigeria)
EPLF	Eritrean Popular Liberation Front		
EPLMRA	European Pharmaceutical Marketing Research Foundation	**ERDC**	European Research and Development Committee
EPNS	English Place-Name Society	**ERDE**	Electronics and Radar Development Establishment, Bangalore (India)
EPOA	European Property Owners Association	**ERDO**	European Research and Development Organization
EPOC	Eastern Pacific Ocean Conference		
EPOS	Europees Pedagogisch Secretariat	**ERERCA**	Énergie Centrafricaine
EPP	European People's Party	**ERFA**	European Radio Frequency Administration (of NATO)
EPPMA	Expanded Polystyrene Product Manufacturers Association		
EPPMP	European Power Press Manufacturers Panel	**ERGOM**	European Research Group on Management
EPPO	European and Mediterranean Plant Protection Organisation (France.)	**ERIC**	Educational Resources Information Center (U.S.A.)
EPS	European Physical Society	**ERIRUP**	European Research Institute for Regional and Urban Planning
EPS	Experimental Psychology Society		
EPSEP	Empresa Pública de Servicios Pesqueros	**ERIW**	European Research Institute for Welding
EPTA	Expanded Programme of Technical Assistance (UNO)	**ERO**	European Regional Organization (of ICFTU)
		EROPA	Eastern Regional Organization for Public Administration (Philippines)
EPU	Economic Planning Unit (Malaysia)		
EPU	European Payments Union	**ERP**	European Recovery Programme (UNO)
EPU	European Picture Union	**ERPDB**	Eastern Regional Production Development Board (Nigeria)
EPU	European Press Photo Agencies Union		

ERPTUAC	European Recovery Programme Trade Unions Advisory Committee	**ESB**	Export Services Branch (*of* BOT)
ERRL	Eastern Regional Research Laboratory (U.S.A.)	**ESBA**	English Schools Badminton Association
		ESBBA	English Schools Basket Ball Association
ERS	Economic Research Service (U.S.A.)	**ESBP**	European Society for Biochemical Pharmacology
ERU	English Rugby Union	**ESC**	Economic and Social Committee (*of* EEC)
ERVA	Erhversvaskeriernes Brancheforening	**ESC**	Entomological Society of Canada
ES	Econometric Society (U.S.A.)	**ESC**	European National Shippers' Councils
ESA	École Supérieure d'Agriculture et de Viticulture d'Angers (Belgium)	**ESC**	European Space Conference
		ESCA	East of Scotland College of Agriculture
ESA	Ecological Society of America	**ESCA**	English Schools Cricket Association
ESA	Electrolysis Society of America	**ESCAP**	Economic and Social Commission for Asia and the Pacific (UN)
ESA	Employment Services Agency		
ESA	Engineers and Scientists of America	**ESC**	European National Shippers' Councils
ESA	Entomological Society of America	**ESCC**	Engineering Standards Co-ordinating Committee
ESA	Ethnological Society of America		
ESA	European Schoolmagazine Association	**ESCES**	Experimental Satellite Communication Earth Centre (India)
ESA	European Space Association		
ESAA	École Supérieure d'Agriculture d'Angers	**ESCI**	European Society for Clinical Investigation
ESAA	English Schools Athletic Association	**ESCO**	European Sterility and Conception Organization
ESAAT	École Supérieure d'Application d'Agriculture Tropicale		
		ESCOFAR	Eastern Counties Farmers Ltd
ESAB	Elektriska Svetsningsaktiebolaget	**ESCOM**	Electricity Supply Commission (S.Africa)
ESABR	European Society of Animal Blood Research	**ESCOP**	Experiment Station Committee on Organization and Policy (U.S.A.)
ESACG	École Supérieure d'Application des Corps		
ESALQ	Escola Superior de Agricultura "Luiz de Queiroz" (Brazil)	**ESCOR**	Economic and Social Committee for Overseas Research
ESAN	Graduate School of Business Administration (Peru)	**ESCOW**	Engineering and Scientific Committee on Water (New Zealand)
ESANZ	Economic Society of Australia and New Zealand	**ESCSP**	European Society of Corporate and Strategic Planners
		ESDAC	European Space Data Centre
ESAP	Egyptian Society of Animal Production	**ESDEN**	Ethnikos Syndesmos Diplomatouchon Ellinidon Nosokomon
ESAP	Escuela Superior de Administración Pública (Colombia)		
		ESDP	European Social Development Programme
ESAPAC	Escuela Superior de Administracion Publica America Central	**ESDR**	European Society for Dermatological Research
ESARDA	European Safeguards Research and Development Association	**ESEE**	European Society for Engineering Education
ESARIPO	Industrial Property Organization of English-speaking African Countries (Cameroons)	**ESEF**	Electrotyping and Stereotyping Employers' Federation
ESAURP	Escola Superior de Agricultura da Universidade Rural de Pernambuco (Brazil)	**ESEF**	European Society for Engineering Education
		ESF	Egyptologiska Sällskapet i Finland
ESAV	Escola Superior de Agricultura e Veterinaria (Brazil)	**ESF**	European Science Foundation
		ESF	European Social Fund
ESB	Economic Stabilisation Board (China)	**ESFA**	English Schools Football Association
ESB	European Settlement Board	**ESG**	Engineers and Scientists Guild (U.S.A.)

ESGA	English Schools Gymnastics Association	ESRIN	European Space Research Institute
ESGE	European Society of Gastrointestinal Endoscopy	ESRO	European Space Research Organisation
ESH	European Society of Haematology	ESRS	European Society for Rural Sociology
ESIC	Environmental Science Information Center (NOAA)	ESRU	English Schools Rugby Union (*now* RFSU)
		ESS	Eastern Searoad Service (Australia)
ESIP	Engineering Societies International Publications Committee	ESS	Eastern Surgical Society (U.S.A.)
ESJ	Entomological Society of Japan	ESSA	Electricity Supply Association of Australia
ESLAB	European Space Laboratory	ESSA	English Schools Swimming Association
ESLI	Esperanto Sak-Ligo Internacia	ESSA	Environmental Science Services Administration (U.S.A.)
ESLO	European Satellite Launcher Organisation	ESSCIRC	European Solid State Circuits Conference
ESM	European Society for Microcirculation	ESSFA	Essens Fabrikant Foreningen
ESMA	Electrical Sign Manufacturers' Association	ESSRA	Economic and Social Science Research Association
ESMOC	European Solar Meeting Organizing Committee	ESTA	European Security Transport Association
ESN	European Society of Nematologists	ESTA	European String Teachers Association
ESNA	European Society of Nuclear Methods in Agriculture	ESTEC	European Space Research and Technology Centre
ESNE	Engineering Societies of New England (U.S.A.)	ESTI	European Space Technology Institute
		ESTL	European Space Tribology Laboratory
ESNZ	Entomological Society of New Zealand	ESTRA	English Speaking Tape Respondents Association
ESO	European Southern Observatory		
ESOC	European Space Operations Centre	ESTRACK	European Satellite Tracking, Telemetry and Telecommand Network
ESOMAR	European Society for Opinion and Marketing Research	ESU	English Speaking Union
ESONEC	European Standard of Nuclear Electronics Committee	ESVA	English Schools Volleyball Association
		ETA	Basque Homeland and Liberty (Spain)
ESP	European Society of Pathology	ETA	European Tallying Association
ESPB	European Student Press Bureau	ETA	European Taxpayers Association
ESPE	European Society for Paediatric Endocrinology	ETA	European Teacher's Association
		ETA	European Thermographic Association
ESPI	Ente Siciliano per la Promozione Industriale	ETA	European Tugowners Association
ESPN	European Society for Pediatric Nephrology	ETAF	École d'Enseignement Technique Féminin
ESPR	European Society for Paediatric Research	ETAP	Expanded Technical Assistance Programme (U.S.A.)
ESR	Europa Saaten Dienst	ETB	English Tourist Board
ESRA	Economische en Sociale Raad van Advies der Benelux Economische Unie	ETC	European Tea Committee
		ETC	European Tourist Conference
ESRANGE	European Space Launching Range	ETC	European Translating Centre
ESRC	European Science Research Council	ETC	European Travel Commission
ESRF	Economic and Scientific Research Foundation (India)	ETDS	Electric Transport Development Society
		ETE	Epitőipari Tudományos Egyesület
ESRI	Economic and Social Research Institute (Eire)	ETE	Experimental Tunnelling Establishment
ESRI	European Systems Research Institute (Belgium)	ETFA	European Technological Forecasting Association

ETH	Eidgenössische Technische Hochschule (Switzerland)
ETIC	English-Teaching Information Centre
ETIF	Economisch-Technologisch Instituut Friesland
ETIO	Economisch-Technologisch Instituut Overijssel
ETIU	Economisch-Technologisch Instituut Utrecht
ETIYRA	El Toro International Yacht Racing Association (U.S.A.)
ETJC	Engineering Trades Joint Council
ETL	Elintarviketeollisuusliitto
ETMA	English Timber Merchants' Association
ETO	European Transportation Organisation
ETP	European Training Programme in Brain and Behaviour Research
ETPM	Société Entrepose pour les Travaux Pétroliers Maritimes
ETPO	European Trade Promotion Organisations Conference
ETRAC	Educational Television and Radio Association of Canada
ETS	Electrodepositors' Technical Society
ETTA	English Table Tennis Association
ETTU	European Table Tennis Union
ETTUC	European Teacher Trade Union Committee
ETUC	European Trade Union Confederation
ETWA	English Tiddlywink Association
EUBCA	Escuela Universitaria de Bibliotecnologia y Ciencias Afines (Uruguay)
EUBL	Europa Unuigo de Blindaj Laboruloj
EUBS	European Undersea Bio-medical Society
EUBW	European Union for Blind Workers
EUCA	Fédération Européenne des Associations de Torrefacteurs du Café
EUCARPIA	European Association for Research on Plant Breeding (Netherlands)
EUCDA	Europäische Union Christlich Demokratischer Arbeitsnehmer
EUCEPA	European Liaison Committee for Pulp and Paper
EUCHEM	European Chemical Congress
EUCHEMAP	European Committee of Chemical Plant Manufacturers
EUCO	Association de l'Industrie Européenne du Coco

EUD	European Union of Dental Medicine Practitioners
EUDICE	Association Européenne pour le Développement de l'Information et la Connaissance de l'Environnement
EUF	European Union of Federalists (France)
EUFMD	European Commission for the Control of Foot and Mouth Disease
EUFODA	European Foodstuffs Distributors Association
EUFTW	European Union of Film and Television Workers
EUGROPA	Union des Distributeurs de Papiers et Cartons de la CEE
EUHOFA	Association Européenne des Directeurs d'Écoles Hôtelières
EULABANK	Banco Euro-Latinoamericano
EULAR	European League Against Rheumatism
EULEP	European Late Effects Project Group
EUM	Entr' aide Universitaire Mondiale
EUMABOIS	European Committee of Woodworking Machinery Manufacturers
EUMA-PRINT	European Committee of Associations of Printing and Paper Converting Machinery Manufacturers
EUMOTIV	European Association for Study of Economic, Commercial and Industrial Motivation
EUPA	European Union for the Protection of Animals
EUR	Europäische Union der Rechtspfleger
EURABIA	European Coordinating Committee of Friendship Societies with the Arab World
EURAFREP	Société de Recherches et Exploitation de Pétrole (Mauritania)
EURAG	European Federation for the Welfare of the Elderly
EURAS	European Anodisers Association
EURATOM	Organisation Atomique Européenne
EUREL	Association Européenne pour les Réserves Libres
EUREL	Convention of National Societies of Electrical Engineers of Western Europe
EUREMAIL	Conférence Permanente de l'Industrie Européenne de Produits Émaillés
EURES	European Group for Research on Spatial Problems

EURES European Reticulo-Endothelial Society

EURESCO Conseil de Coopération Culturelle Européenne

EURIM European Conference on the Contribution of Users to Planning and Policy Making for Information Systems and Networks

EURIMA European Insulation Manufacturers Association

EURINCAD Fédération Européenne des Indépendants et des Cadres

EURO Association of European Operational Research Societies

EUROAVIA Association of European Aeronautical and Astronautical Students

EURO-BITUME European Bitumen Association

EUROBOIS European Group of Woodworking Journals

EUROCAE European Organisation for Civil Aviation Electronics

EUROCEAN European Oceanographic Association

EUROCEN-TRES Foundation for European Language and Educational Centres

EURO-CHEMIC European Company for the Chemical Processing of Irradiated Fuels

EUROCOM Union Européenne des Négociants en Combustibles

EUROCOMP European Computing Congress

EUROCON-TROL European Organisation for the Safety of Air Navigation

EURO-COOP Union Européenne des Centrales de Production et de Gros des Sociétés Coopératives de Consommation

EUROCOP-COST European Cooperation and Coordination in the Field of Scientific and Technical Research

EUROCORD Fédération des Industries de Corderie-Ficellerie de l'Europe Occidentale

EURO-COTON EEC Committee for the Cotton and Allied Textile Industries

EURODATA Eurodata Foundation

EURO-DIDAC Association Européenne de Fabricants et de Revendeurs de Matériel Didactique

EURODOC Joint Documentation Service of ESRO, EUROSPACE and the European Organisation for the Development and Construction of Space Vehicle Launchers

EURO-FEDAG European Federation of Agricultural Workers

EURO-FEDAL European Federation of Workers in Food and Allied Industries (*of* EO-WCL)

EURO-FEDOP European Federation of Employees in Public Service

EUROFER European Confederation of Iron and Steel Industries

EUROFEU European Committee of the Manufacturers of Fire Engines and Apparatus

EUROFIMA Société Européenne pour le Financement de Matériel Ferroviaire

EUROFI-NANCE Union Internationale d'Analyse Économique et Financière

EURO-FINAS Association of European Finance Houses

EUROFUEL Société Européenne de Fabrication de Combustibles à Base d'Uranium pour Reacteurs à Eau Légère

EURO-GLACES Association of the Ice Cream Industries of the EEC

EUROGRAF Group of Federations of Graphics Industries in the EEC

EURO-GRAM Société Européenne de Recherches et d'Études Programmées

EURO-GROPA Union des Distributeurs de Papiers et Cartons

EURO-HKG European High Temperature Nuclear Power Stations Society

EUROLIBRI Association Européenne d'Éditeurs Juridiques et Économiques

EUROMAI-SIERS Groupement des Associations des Maïsiers de la CEE

EUROMALT Comité de Travail des Malteries de la CEE

EUROMAP European Committee of Machinery Manufacturers for the Plastics and Rubber Industries

EURO-MECH European Mechanics Colloquia

EURO-MICRO European Association of Microprocessor Users

EUROMINE European Federation of the Mining Timber Associations

EUROMOT European Committee of Internal Combustion Engine Manufacturers' Association

EURONET European Network for Scientific and Technical Information

EUROP European Railway Wagon Pool

EUROPA-DRESS European Association of Direct Mail Houses

EURO-PECHE Association des Organisations Nationales d'Entreprises de Pêche de la CEE

EUROPHOT Association Européenne des Photographes Professionels

EUROPHY-SICS European Physics Congress

EURO-PRESSE-FAMILIA Association Européenne des Éditeurs de la Presse Périodique d'Information Féminine ou Familiale

EURO-PRESS-JUNIOR Association Européenne des Éditeurs de Publications pour la Jeunesse

EUROPUMP European Committee of Pump Manufacturers

EURORAD European Association of Manufacturers of Steel-Panelled Radiators

EUROSAC Fédération Européenne des Fabricants de Sacs en Papier a grande Contenance

EURO-SPACE European Industrial Space Study Group

EURO-STRUCT-PRESS European Association of Publishers in the Field of Building and Design

EUROTEST European Association of Testing Institutions

EUROTOX Comité Européen Permanent de Recherches sur la Protection des Populations contre les Risques de Toxicité à Long Terme

EUROVENT European Committee of Manufacturers of Air Handling Equipment

EURO-VISION Union Européenne de Radio-Diffusion

EURP European Union of Public Relations

EUSA Evangelical Union of South America (U.K.)

EUSAFEC Eastern United States Agricultural and Food Export Council

EUSAMA European Shock Absorber Manufacturers Association

EUSEC Conférènce des Représentants de Sociétés d'Ingénieurs de l'Europe Occidentale et des États-Unis d'Amérique

EUSIDIC European Association of Scientific Information Dissemination Centres

EUSIREF European Network of Scientific Information Referral Centres

EUTO European Union of Tourism Executives

EUTOR European Association for Technical Orthopaedics and Orthopaedic Rehabilitation

EUTRA-PLAST Committee of Western European Plastics Converters Federations

EUW European Union of Women

EuWiD Europäischer Wirtschaftsdienst

EUYCD European Union of Young Christian Democrats

EV Erdöl-Vereiningung (Switzerland)

EVA Electric Vehicle Association of Great Britain

EVA English Vineyards Association

EVA English Volleyball Association

EVAF European Association for Industrial Marketing Research

EVD Eidgenössiches Volkswirtschaftsdepartement (Switzerland)

EVD Veterinary Department, Eastern Region (Nigeria)

EVEM Institute Européen de Vente et de Marketing (Belgium)

EVI Ex-Volunteers International

EVKI Europäische Vereinigung der Keramik-Industrie

EVMAC-MEX Ejecutivos de Ventas y Mercadotecnia de México

EVO Algemene Verladers-en Eigen Vervoerders Organisatie

EVP Europäische Volkspartei (Belgium)

EVS Erfinder-und Patentinhaber-Verband der Schweiz

EVSE Enosis Viomichanon Sporelaiourgon Ellados

EVT Europäische Vereinigung für Tierzucht

EWA Europäisches Währungsabkommen

EWAA European Wrought Aluminium Association

EWAC European Wheat Aneuploid Co-operative

EWF Electrical Wholesalers' Federation

EWG Europäische Wirtschaftsgemeinschaft

EWGAE European Working Group on Acoustic Emission

EWONA Educational Welfare Officers National Association

EWRC European Weed Research Council (*now* EWRS)

EWRS European Weed Research Society

EWSF European Work Study Federation (*now* EFPS)

EXBOA Export Buying Offices Association

EXIMBANK Banco de Exportación e Importacion del Gobierno de los Estados Unidos de Norte América

EXP	Exchange of Persons Service (*of* UNESCO)
EXPAINSO	Société de Développement du Sud-Ouest
EXPAN-ENTRE	Société pour l'Expansion Économique de la Région du Centre
EXTEL	Exchange Telegraph Co., Ltd
EYC	European Youth Campaign
EZS	Elektrotehniška Zveza Slovenije
EZU	Europäische Zahlungs-Union

F

FA	Forretningsbankenes Arbeidsgiverforening
FAA	Federación Agraria Argentina
FAA	U.S. Federal Aviation Agency
FAA	Foundation for American Agriculture
FAAPF	Federación Argentina de Asociaciones de Productores Forestales
FAAVCA	Federación de Asociaciones de Agencias de Viajes de Centro América
FAB	Fédération Nationale des Auto-Écoles Professionnelles de Belgique
FAB	Fédération Royale des Sociétés d'Architectes de Belgique
FABC	Federation of Asian Bishops Conferences
FABES	Vereniging van Fabrikanten van Beton-straatstenen
FABI	Fédération Royale des Associations Belges d'Ingénieurs
FABRI-METAL	Fédération des Entreprises de l'Industrie des Fabrications Métalliques (Belgium)
FAC	Confédération Africaine de Football
FAC	Fonds d'Aide et de Cooperation Technique et Économique
FACA	Federación Argentina de Cooperativas Agrarias
FACA	Fédération Algérienne de la Coopération Agricole
FACC	Federación Argentina de Cooperativas de Consumo
FACFF	Fédération des Associations de Communes Forestières Françaises
FACIM	Fondation pour l'Action Culturelle Internationale en Montagne

FACOPHAR	Syndicat National de la Fabrication et du Commerce des Produits à Usage Pharmaceutique et Parapharmaceutique
FACP	Food and Agriculture Council, Pakistan
FACREA	Federación Argentina de Consorcios Regionales de Experimentación Agrícola (*now* AACREA)
FACS	Federation of American Controlled Shipping
FACS	Fédération des Amis des Chemins de Fer Secondaires
FACSS	Federation of Analytical Chemistry and Spectroscopy (U.S.A.)
FACT	Fertilisers and Chemicals Travancore (India)
FACTS	Federation of Australian Commercial Television Stations
FACTU	Föreningen Svensk Fachpress
FAD	Fonds Africain de Développement (Ivory Coast)
FAE	Federación de Amigos de la Enseñanza
FAE	Federation of Arab Engineers
FAEAB	Federação das Associações dos Engenheiros Agrónomos do Brasil
FAECF	Fédération des Associations Européennes des Constructeurs de Fenêtres
FAEP	Federation of Association of Periodical Publishers (*of* EEC)
FAF	Finska Antikvariatforeningen
FAGAM	Groep Fabrieken van Gasmeters
FAGEC	Fédération d'Associations et Groupements pour les Études Corses
FAGS	Federation of Astronomical and Geophysical Services (ICSU)
FAGT	Federation of Agricultural Group Traders
FAH	Fédération Arabe d'Haltérophilie
FAH	Forschungsinstitut für Absatz und Handel (Switzerland)
FAI	Fédération Abolitionniste Internationale
FAI	Fédération Aéronautique Internationale
FAI	Federazione Apicoltori Italiani
FAI	Federazione Autorimesse Italiane
FAI	Federazione Autotrasportatori Italiani
FAI	Fertiliser Association of India
FAI	Football Association of Ireland
FAIAT	Federazione delle Associazioni Italiane Alberghi e Turismo
FAIB	Fédération des Associations Internationales Établies en Belgique

FAIC	Federation of Australian Investment Clubs	**FAOE**	Federation of African Organisations of Engineers
FAIMA	Federación Argentina de la Industria de la Madera y Afines	**FAPA**	Federation of Asian Pharmaceutical Associations
FAIR	Federation of Afro-Asian Insurers and Reinsurers	**FAPAL**	Groep Fabrieken van Aktieve en Passieve Elektronische Bouwelementen
FAIR	Union Professionnelle des Fabricants et Importateurs de Matériel Électronique (Belgium)	**FAPEB**	Fédération des Artisans et des Petites Entreprises du Bâtiment
FAIRT	Suomen Kansainvälisten Muuttokuljetusliikkeiden Liitto	**FAPES**	Fundacion Argentina para la Promocion del Desarrollo Económico y Social
FAITA	Federación de Asociaciones Industriales Textiles del Algodón (Mexico)	**FAPESP**	Fundaçâo de Amparo à Pesquisa do Estado de São Paulo (Brazil)
FAMA	Fachverband Messen und Ausstellungen	**FAPTA**	Fédération Suisse des Associations des Planteurs de Tabac
FAMA	Federal Agricultural Marketing Authority (Malaysia)	**FAR**	Federal Department of Agricultural Research (Nigeria)
FAMA	Foundation for Mutual Assistance in Africa South of the Sahara	**FAR**	Foreign Area Research Co-ordination Group (U.S.A.)
FAMAB	Fachverband Messe- und Ausstellungsbau	**FAR**	Föreningen Auktoriserade Revisorer
FAMED	Vereinigung Schweizerischer Fabriken der Medizinischen Technik	**FAR**	Foundation of Applied Research (U.S.A.)
FAMEM	Federation of Associations of Mine Equipment Manufacturers	**FAREC**	Unione Fabbricanti Apparecchi di Riscaldamento e Cucine
FAMEX	Foreningen af Danske Mælkekonservesfabrikker med Landbrugsministeriel Autorisation til Fremstilling af Mælkekonserves for Export	**FARGRO**	Farmers' and Growers' Industries, Ltd
		FARM	Filipino Agrarian Reform Movement
		FARM-UNIONE	Associazione Nazionale dell' Industria Farmaceutica Italiana
FAMHEM	Federation of Associations of Materials Handling Equipment Manufacturers	**FARN**	Fuerzas Armadas de la Resistencia Nacional (El Salvador)
FAMHM	Federation of Associations of Material Handling Manufacters	**FARON**	Fabrieken van Röntgen en Andere Elektromedische Apparatuur in Nederland
FAMHW	Federation of Associations of Mental Health Workers (*now* FMHW)	**FAS**	European Federation of Associations of Industrial Safety and Medical Officers
FAMID	Foreningen af Mineralvandsfabrikanter i Danmark	**FAS**	Federation of American Scientists
FAMPA	Ferro Alloys and Metals Producers Association	**FAS**	Fédération des Architectes Suisses
		FAS	Foreign Agricultural Service (U.S.A.)
FAMSA	African Medical Students Association	**FAS**	Verband Schweizerischer Fachgeschäfte für Arzt- und Spitalbedarf
FAN	Federación Agraria Nacional (Costa Rica)		
FANAL	Federación Agraria Nacional (Colombia)	**FASA**	Federación Argentina de Sindicatos Agrarios
FANCIF	Fondo Antárquico National para la Capacitación e Investigación Forestal (Argentina)	**FASA**	Federación Argentina de Sociedades Apícolas
FANOA	Fédération des Appellations et Noms d'Origine Agricole	**FASASA**	Fonds d'Action Sociale pour l'Aménagement des Structures Agricoles
		FASC	Federation of Asian Shippers Council
FANS	Federation of Asian Nutrition Societies	**FASE**	Fédération des Sociétés d'Acoustique Européennes
FAO	Food and Agriculture Organisation (UNO)		
FAOB	Federation of Asian and Oceanian Biochemists	**FASEB**	Federation of American Scientists for Experimental Biology

FASFID	Fédération des Associations et Sociétés Françaises d'Ingénieurs Diplômés	**FBA**	Federation of British Audio
FASII	Federation of Associations of Small Industries in India	**FBA**	Freshwater Biological Association
		FBAS	Federation of British Aquatic Societies
FASNUDS	Fondo Fiduciario de las Naciones Unidas para el Desarrollo Social	**FBBDO**	Fibre Building Board Development Organization
FASNUPPD	Fonds d'Affectation Spéciale des Nations Unies pour la Planification et des Projections en Matière de Développement	**FBBF**	Fibre Building Board Federation
		FBBM	Federation of Building Block Manufacturers (*now* CBA)
FASOMG	Fédération Avicole du Sud-Ouest et du Midi Garonnais	**FBCA**	Federation of British Cremation Authorities
FASS	Federation of Associations of Specialists and Sub-contractors	**FBCAEI**	Federation of Builders Contractors and Allied Employers of Ireland
FASST	Federation of Americans Supporting Science and Technology	**FBCE**	Fellowship of British Christian Esperantists
		FBCM	Federation of British Carpet Manufacturers (*now merged into* BCMA)
FAST	Federazione delle Associazioni Scientifiche e Tecniche	**FBCN**	Fundação Brasileira para e Conservação da Natureza
FAT	Fonds Arabo-Africain d'Assistance Technique (Egypt)	**FBEP**	Fédération Belge d'Éducation Physique
FAT	Föreningen Auktoriserade Translatorer	**FBFM**	Federation of British Film Makers
FAT	Forschungsvereinigung Automobiltechnik	**FBG**	Fachverband Bürobedarf für Grossverbraucher
FATA	Fondo Assicurativo tra Agricoltori	**FBG**	Federation of British Growers
FATIPEC	Fédération des Associations de Techniciens des Industries des Peintures et Encres d'Imprimerie de l'Europe Continentale	**FBH**	Fachgruppe für Brückenbau und Hochbau
		FBH	Fédération Belge des Horticoles Semences
FATIS	Food and Agriculture Technical Information Service (*of* OECD)	**FBHTM**	Federation of British Hand Tool Manufacturers
FATME	Fabbrica Apparecchiature Telefoniche e Materiale Elettrico	**FBI**	Federal Bureau of Investigation (U.S.A.)
		FBI	Federation of British Industries (*now* CBI)
FATRE	Federación Argentina de Trabajadores Rurales y Estibadores	**FBI**	Fonds du Bien-Être Indigène (Belgium)
FATS	Federation of Arab Teachers Syndicates	**FBM**	Fachvereinigung der Bunt- und Metallpapierfabriken
FATTA	Federation of Arab Travel Agents' Associations	**FBMA**	Finnish Boat and Motor Association
FAVAD	Vereniging van Fabrikanten van Zwakalcoholhoudende en Alcoholvrije Dranken	**FBMA**	Union Suisse des Entreprises de Forge, du Bois, du Métal et de la Machine Agricole
		FBMSG	Federation of British Manufacturers Sports and Games
FAVF	Fédération des Associations Viticoles de France	**FBMV**	Federación Boliviana de Médicos Veterinarios
FAW	Fachverband Aussenwerbung	**FBPP**	Federation of Plant Pathologists
FAWA	Federation of Asian Women's Associations	**FBPS**	Forest and Bird Protection Society of New Zealand
FAWC	Federation of African Women's Clubs	**FBR**	Forskningsbiblioteksrådet
FAWCO	Federation of American Women's Clubs Overseas	**FBR**	Foundation for Business Responsibilities
FB	Federation of Bakers	**FBRAM**	Federation of British Rubber and Allied Manufacturers
FBA	Farm Buildings Association	**FBSC**	Federation of British Scooter Clubs
FBA	Federation of British Astrologers	**FBTRC**	Federation of British Tape Recording Clubs

FBU	Fire Brigades Union
FBUA	Franco-British Union of Architects
FBUI	Federation of British Umbrella Industries
FBVA	Forstliche Bundesversuchsanstalt (Austria)
FBVL	Fonds ter Bevordering van de Veredeling van Landbouwgewassen
FBW	Forschungsgemeinschaft Bauen und Wohnen
FCA	Farm Credit Administration, (U.S.A.)
FCA	Foncière de la Côte d'Afrique
FCAA	Federación de Cooperativas Arroceras Argentinas
FCAATSI	Federal Council for the Advancement of Aborigines and Torres Strait Islanders (Australia)
FCACV	Federación de Cooperativas de Ahorro y Crédito de Venezuela
FCAM	Fédération Cotonnière d'Afrique Francophone et de Madagascar
FCAT	Société Franco-Centrafricaine des Tabacs
FCB	Fédération Nationale des Coopératives Agricoles de Transformation de la Betterave Industrielle
FCBA	Friesland Cattle Breeders' Association of South Africa
FCBM	Federation of Clinker Block Manufacturers
FCC	Federal Communications Commission (U.S.A.)
FCCA	Christian Federation of Craftsmen and Apprentices (Luxembourg)
FCCAM	Fédération Centrale du Crédit Agricole Mutuel
FCCC	Federación de Cámaras de Comercio del Istmo Centroamericano (Salvador)
FCCC	Federation of Commonwealth Chambers of Commerce
FCCD	Foundation for Cultural Cooperation and Development (France)
FCCST	Federal Co-ordinating Council for Science, Engineering and Technology (U.S.A.)
FCDA	Federal Civil Defense Administration (U.S.A.)
FCDC	Fertilizer and Chemical Development Council (Israel)
FCDE	Federation of Clothing Designers
FCE	Femmes Chefs d'Entreprises Mondiales
FCEC	Federation of Civil Engineering Contractors

FCECA	Fishery Committee for the Eastern Central Atlantic
FCEP	Christian Federation of Employees and Civil Servants (Luxembourg)
FCEV	Fédération des Clubs Européens de Formules IV
FCF	Footwear Components Federation
FCI	Factors Chain International (Netherlands)
FCI	Fédération Cynologique Internationale
FCI	Fertiliser Corporation of India
FCI	Fundación Cientifica Internacional
FCIA	Foreign Credit Insurance Association (U.S.A.)
FCJ	Fédération Internationale des Journalistes Catholiques
FCK	Central Organisation of Farmers' Co-operatives (Hungary)
FCL	Federación Campesina Latino Americana (Venezuela)
FCLA	Fisheries Council for Latin America
FCMI	Federation of Coated Macadam Industries
FCML	Christian Federation of Luxembourg Metalworkers
FCMRF	Fédération des Centres Musicaux Ruraux de France
FCO	Farmers Central Organization
FCOBC	Christian Federation of Building and Quarry Workers (Luxembourg)
FCOMF	Fédération des Coopératives Oléicoles du Midi de la France
FCOUL	Christian Federation of Luxembourg Factory Workers
FCPSP	Christian Federation of Public Service Workers (Luxembourg)
FCR	Association des Fabriques de Chaudières et Radiateurs (Switzerland)
FCRE	Foundation for Cotton Research and Education (U.S.A.)
FCRIMS	Freight Committee of the Rubber Industry of Malaysia and Singapore
FCS	Farm Cooperative Service (U.S.A.)
FCS	Federation of Concrete Specialists
FCST	Federal Council for Science and Technology (U.S.A.)
FCTA	Fédération Suisse des Travailleurs du Commerce des Transports et de l'Alimentation

FCTPAS	Christian Federation of Social Insurance Pensioners	**FDJ**	Free German Youth
		FDK	Fachverband Deutsche Klavierindistrie
FCTU	Federation of Associations of Catholic Trade Unionists	**FDLA**	Democratic Front for the Liberation of Angola
FCTV	Federación de Cooperativas de Transporte de Venezuela	**FDM**	Fachverband des Deutschen Maschinen- und Werkzeug-Grosshandels
FCV	Federación de Campesinos de Venezuela	**FDMO**	Fund for the Development of Manpower (Portugal)
FCWV	Federatie van de Katholieke en Protestants-Christelijke Werkgeversverbonden	**FDO**	Federatie van Nederlandse Danslerarenorganisaties
FCX	Farmers Cooperative Exchange (U.S.A.)		
FDA	Food Distribution Administration (U.S.A.)	**FDO**	Fédération Départementale Ovine
FDA	Food and Drug Administration (U.S.A.)	**FDO**	Foreningen af Danske Osteproducenter
FDA	Freier Deutscher Autorenverband	**FDP**	Freie Demokratische Partie (W. Germany)
FDAR	Federal Department of Agricultural Research (Nigeria)	**FDS**	Fachverband der Deutschen Schulmöbelindustrie
FDB	Faellesforeningen for Danmarks Brugsforeninger	**FDSEA**	Fédération Départementale des Syndicats d'Exploitants Agricoles
FDBR	Fachverband Dampfkessel-, Behälter- und Rohrleitungsbau	**FDT**	Fachverband des Deutschen Tapethandels
		FDVR	Federal Department of Veterinary Research (Nigeria)
FDC	Federation of Dredging Contractors		
FDC	Fiji Development Co.	**FDW**	Fachverband Film- und Diapositiv-Werbung
FDC	Foreningen af Dansk Civiløkonomer	**FEA**	Federation of European Aerosol Associations (Switzerland)
FDC	Furniture Development Council (*now* FIRA)		
FDCETA	Fédération Départementale des Centres d'Études Techniques Agricoles	**FEA**	Fédération Internationale pour l'Éducation Artistique
FDD	Fondation Documentaire Dentaire (Belgium)	**FEAAF**	Fédération Européenne des Associations d'Analystes Financiers
FDD	Fundación Dominicana de Desarrollo (Dominica)	**FEACO**	Fédération Européenne des Associations de Conseils en Organisation
FDE	Fachverband Deutscher Eisenwaren- und Hausrathändler	**FEAICSMT**	Fédération Européenne des Associations d'Ingénieurs et Chefs de Services de Sécurité et des Médecins du Travail (*now* FAS)
FDES	Fonds de Développement Économique et Social		
FDF	Fachverband Deutscher Floristen	**FEAL**	Fédération Nationale des Groupements de Labels Agricoles
FDF	Footwear Distributors Federation	**FEAM**	Fédération Européenne des Associations de Mécanographes
FDFR	Federal Department of Forestry Research (Nigeria)		
FDFU	Federation of Documentary Film Units	**FEANF**	Fédération des Étudiants d'Afrique Noire Française
FDGB	Freier Deutscher Gewerkschaftsbund	**FEANI**	European Federation of National Associations of Engineers
FDGB	Confederation of Free German Trade Unions		
FDGPA	Fédération Départementale des Groupements de Productivité Agricole	**FEAO**	Federation of European American Organisations
FDI	Fédération Dentaire Internationale	**FEB**	Fédération des Éditeurs Belges
FDIC	UK Food and Drink Industries Council	**FEB**	Fédération des Entreprises de Belgique
FDIF	Fédération Democratique Internationale des Femmes	**FEB**	Fédération des Expéditeurs de Belgique
FDIM	Federación Democrática Internacional de Mujeres	**FEBAB**	Federaçao Brasiliera de Associaçoes de Bibliotecários

FEBECA	Fédération Belge du Commerce Alimentaire
FEBELBOIS	Fédération Belge des Industriels du Bois
FEBELCAR	Fédération Belge de la Carrosserie et des Métiers Connexes
FEBEL-HOUT	Belgische Federatie der Houtnijveraars
FEBELQUIN	Fédération Belge des Quincailliers
FEBELTEX	Fédération de l'Industrie Textile Belge
FEBEVO	Federatie van de Belgische Voedingshandel
FEBIAC	Chambre Syndicale des Constructeurs d'Automobiles et de Motocycles de Belgique et Fédération Belge des Industries de l'Automobile et du Cycle "Réunies"
FEBIC	Fédération Belge de l'Industrie de la Chaussure
FEBO	Fund for Experimental Concrete Research (Netherlands)
FEBS	Federation of European Biochemical Societies
FEC	Far Eastern Commission (U.S.A.)
FEC	Far East Conference (U.S.A.)
FEC	Foundation for Environmental Conservation (Switzerland)
FEC	Fondation Européenne de la Culture
FECAICA	Federación de Cámaras y Associaciones Industriales de Centroamérica (Costa Rico)
FECAMCO	Federación de Cámaras de Comercio del Istmo Centroamericano (Panama)
FECAUBEL	Fédération des Concessionnaires de l'Automobile de Belgique
FECB	Foreign Exchange Control Board
FECC	Federación Campesina Cristiana Costarricences
FECEP	Fédération Européenne des Constructeurs d'Équipement Pétrolier
FECESI-TLIH	Federación Central de Sindicatos de Trabajadores Libres de Honduras
FECETRAG	Federación Central de Trabajadores de Guatemala
FECHIMIE	Fédération des Industries Chimiques de Belgique
FECOL-TRACOM	Federación Colombiana de Trabajadores
FECOM	Fonds Européen de Coopération Monétaire
FECOVE	Federación de Cooperativas de Consumo de Venezuela
FECOVI	Fédération Nationale des Fabricants de Conserves de Viandes
FECS	Fédération Européenne des Fabricants de Céramiques Sanitaires
FED	European Development Fund
FEDAAS	Federación Española de Asociaciones de Asitentes Sociales
FEDAC	Fédération Européenne des Anciens Combattants
FEDAR-LINEA	Associazione Italiana dell' Armamento di Linea
FEDAS	Federación Española de Actividades Subacuáticas
FEDC	Federation of Engineering Design Companies
FEDEAGRO	Federación Nacional de Asociaciones de Productores Agropecuarios (Venezuela)
FEDE-ARROZ	Federación Nacional de Arrozeros (Colombia)
FEDE-CACAO	Federación Nacional de Cacaoteros (Colombia)
FEDECAM-ARAS	Federación Venezolana de Cámeras y Asociaciones de Comercio y Producción
FEDECAME	Fédération des Planteurs de Café Amérique
FEDECHAR	Fédération Charbonnière de Belgique
FEDECOM-LEGNO	Federazione Nazionale dei Commercianti del Legno e del Sughero
FEDEGAN	Federación Colombiana de Ganaderos (Colombia)
FEDEL	Fédération Française des Syndicats d'Éleveurs de Chevaux de Selle
FEDEMAR	Fédération Belge des Exploitants Forestiers et Marchands de Bois de Mine et Papeterie
FEDE-METAL	Federación Metalúrgica Colombiana
FEDEMOA	Federación Mexicana de Organizaciones Agrícolas
FEDEMOL	Federación Nacional de Molineros de Trigo (Colombia)
FEDENAGA	Federación Nacionale de Ganaderos (Venezuela)
FEDENTEL	Fédération Nationale des Dentelles, Tulles, Broderies, Guipures et Passementeries
FEDE-PALMA	Federación Nacional de Cultivadores de Palma Africana
FEDEPAS	Federación Nacional de Fabricantes de Pastas Alimenticias (Colombia)
FEDE-POMTER	Fédération Nationale des Syndicats de Négociants en Pommes de Terre et Légumes en Gros

FEDERA Fédération des Sociétés Commerciales Pharmaceutiques Belges

FEDERA-BOIS Fédération Nationale des Négociants en Bois (Belgium)

FEDERA-CAFE Federación Nacional de Cafeteros (Colombia)

FEDER-AGENTI Federazione Nazionale Agenti Raccomandatori Marittimi, Agenti Aerei e Pubblici Mediatori Marittimi

FEDERAG-RONOMI Federazione Nazionale Dottori in Scienze Agrarie

FEDERAL-GODON Federación Nacional de Algodoneros (Colombia)

FEDER-CON-SORZI Federazione Italiana dei Consorzi Agrari

FEDEREC Fédération Nationale des Syndicats des Industries et Commerces de la Récupération

FEDEREL Fédération des Rélamineurs du Fer et de l'Acier de la Communauté Européenne

FEDER-FIORI Federazione Nazionale Fioristi

FEDERFISA Federazione Nazionale tra Fabbricanti ed Esportatori Italiani di Fisarmoniche ed Altri Strumenti Musicali

FEDER-GROS-SISTI Federazione Nazionale del Commercio Alimentare all'Ingrosso

FEDER-HOUT Nationale Federatie van Houthandelaars (Belgium)

FEDER-LEGNO Federazione Italiana delle Industrie del Legno, del Sughero e dell' Arredamento

FEDERMA-GAZZINI Federazione Italiana Magazzini Generali

FEDERMAR Fédération Maritime de la Côte-d'Ivoire

FEDER-MECCA-NICA Federazione Sindacale dell'Industria Metalmeccanica

FEDER-NATURA Federazione Nazionale Pro Natura

FEDER-OLIO Federazione Nazionale del Commercio Oleario

FEDER-OTTICA Federazione Nazionale dei Titolari di Esercizi di Ottica Optometrica Foto-Ottica

FEDER-PESCA Federazione Nazionale delle Imprese di Pesca

FEDERPOL Federazione Nazionale degli Istitut di Polizia Privata

FEDER-SARTI Federazione Nazionale Sarti e Sarte d'Italia

FEDER-TERME Federazione Nazionale delle Industrie Idro-Termali

FEDERVINI Federazione Italiana Industriali Produttroni Esportatori ed Importatori di Vini, Acquaviti, Liquori, Sciroppi, Aceti ed Affini

FEDES Federazione Europea dei Fabbricanti di Sachetti di Carta

FEDESPEDI Federazione Nazionale Spedizionieri

FEDETAB Fédération Belgo Luxembourgeoise du Tabac

FEDETRAM Federazione Nazionale Aziende Municipalizzate di Trasporto

FEDEX-PORT Federazione Italiana dei Consorzi Agrari

FEDHOTEL Fédération Nationale de l'Hôtellerie Belge

FEDIA Fédération des Ingénieurs Agronomes de Belgique

FEDICA Fédération des Associations de l'Industrie et du Commerce de l'Automobile (Belgium)

FEDICER Fédération des Industries Céramiques de Belgique et du Luxembourg

FEDIL Fédération des Industries Luxembourgeois

FEDIMA European Federation of Manufacturers of Bakers' and Confectioners' Ingredients and Additives

FEDIOL Fédération de l'Industrie de l'Huilerie de la CEE

FEDIPAC Fédération Nationale des Distributeurs de Produits Alimentaires et de Grande Consommation

FEDIVER Fédération de l'Industrie du Verre (Belgium)

FEDO FACT Engineering and Design Organization (India)

FEDOLIVE Fédération de l'Industrie de l'Huile d'Olive de la CEE

FEDOM Fonds Européen de Développement Outre-mer

FEDS Foreign Economic Development Service (U.S.A.)

FEE Federation of Employers of Ethiopia

FEECA Fédération Européenne pour l'Éducation Catholique des Adultes

FEFAC Fédération Européenne des Fabricants d'Aliments Composés pour Animaux (Belgium)

FEFANA Fédération Européenne des Fabricants d'Adjuvants pour la Nutrition Animale

FEFCEB Fédération Européenne des Fabricants de Caisses et Emballages en Bois

FEFCO	Fédération Européenne des Fabricants de Carton Ondulé
FEFPEB	Fédération Européenne des Fabricants de Caisses et Emballages en Bois
FEG	Föderation Europäischer Gewässerschutz
FEGAP	Fédération Européenne de la Ganterie de Peau
FEGARBEL	Fédération des Garagistes de Belgique
FEGARLUX	Fédération des Garagistes-Réparateurs du Grand-Duché de Luxembourg
FEGAZLIQ	Fédération Nationale des Centres de Liaison Régionaux de Concessionaires de Gaz Liquefiés
FEGOZI	Federatie Goud en Zilver
FEGRAB	Fédération des Industries Graphiques de Belgique
FEGRO	European Federation for the Wholesale Watch Trade
FEHA	Foreningen af Fabrikanter og Importører af Elektriske
FEHAN	Groep Fabrieken van Elektrische Huishoudelijke Apparaten in Nederland
FEHCOVIL	Federación Hondureña de Cooperativas de Vivienda (Honduras)
FEI	Federación Endodóncica Iberoamericana
FEI	Fédération Équestre Internationale
FEIA	Flight Engineers International Association (U.S.A.)
FEIC	Fédération Européenne de l'Industrie du Contreplaque
FEICA	Fédération Européenne des Industries de Colles et Adhésifs
FEICADE	Federación de Instituciones Centroamericanas de Desarrollo (Guatemala)
FEICRO	Federation of European Industrial Co-operative Research Organizations
FEIEA	Federation of European Industrial Editors' Associations
FEIM	Fédération Européenne des Importateurs de Machines de Bureau
FEIM	Fundación para las Encuentras Internacionales en las Montanas
FEITC	Fédération Européenne des Industries Techniques du Cinéma
FEJLR	Fédération Européenne des Jeunesses Libérales et Radicales
FEKO	Federatie van Kleinhandelsorganisaties

FELAC	Federación Latinoamericana de Consultores
FELACEX	Federación Latinoamericana y del Caribe de Asociaciones de Exportadores
FELA-TRABS	Federación Latinoamericana de Trabajadores Bancarios y de Seguros
FELATURS	Federación Latinoamericana de Turismo Social
FELCRA	Federal Land Consolidation and Rehabilitation Authority (Malaysia)
FELDA	Federal Land Development Authority (Malaysia)
FELEBAN	Federación Latinoamericana de Bancos (Colombia)
FEM	Fédération Européenne de la Manutention
FEM	Fédération Européenne des Metallurgistes
FEM	Fédération Européenne des Motels
FE-MA	Fédération Nationale des Unions Professionnelles de Négociants en Matériaux de Construction de Belgique
FEMAR	Fondação de Estudos do Mar
FEMAS	Far East Merchants Association (U.S.A.)
FEMC	Fédération Européenne des Médecins de Collectivités
FEMCA	Federación de Estudiantes de Medicina Centroamericanos
FEMIB	Fédération Européenne des Syndicats de Fabricants de Menuiseries Industrielles de Bâtiment
FEMIBE	Fédération Mondiale des Dirigeants des Instituts de Beauté et de l'Esthétique (Belgium)
FEMIPI	Fédération Européenne des Mandataires de l'Industrie en Propriété Industrielle
FEMK	Fédération Européenne des Masseurs-Kinésithérapeutes Praticiens en Physiothérapie
FEMO	Fédération del'Enseignement Moyen Officiel du Degré (Belgium)
FEMOSI	Fédération Mondiale des Syndicats d'Industries
FEMPI	European Federation of Agents of Industry in Industrial Property
FEMSA	Fabrica Espanola Magnetos, S.A.
FEMUSI	Federación Mundial de Sindicatos de Industrias
FEN	Federation de l'Éducation Nationale
FENA	Fédération Européenne du Négoce de l'Ameublement

FENACEM	Fédération Nationale du Commerce de l'Équipement Ménager
FENACOA	Federación Nacional de Cooperativas Agropecuarias (Uruguay)
FENACOAC	Federación Nacional de Cooperativas de Ahorro y Crédito de Guatemala
FENADAG	Fédération Nationale des Détaillants en Alimentation Générale (Belgium)
FENAGH	Federación Nacional de Agricoltores y Ganaderos de Honduras
FENAL	Federazione Esercenti Latterie e Derivati del Latte
FENALCE	Federación Nacional de Cultivadores de Cereales (Colombia)
FENALCO	Federación Nacional de Comerciantes (Colombia)
FENARUM	Fédération Nationale des Producteurs de Rhum
FENASI-BANCOL	Federación Nacional de Sindicatos Bancarios Colombianos
FENA-SYCOA	Fédération Nationale des Syndicats du Commerce Ouest-Africain
FENASYDA	Fédération Nationale des Syndicats de la Distribution des Équipements et Outillages pour l'Automobile et Activités Annexes
FENAVIAN	Fédération Nationale des Fabricants de Produits et Conserves de Viandes
FENAVINO	Fédération Nationale de la Viticulture Nouvelle
FENCO	Foundation of Canada Engineering Corporation
FENEC	Federación Nicaraguense Educación Católica
FENECAFE	Federación Nacional de Cooperativas Cafetaleras (Ecuador)
FENEDEX	Federatie voor de Nederlandse Export
FENEMA	Fédération des Négociants de Machines Agricoles (Luxembourg)
FENETEC	Fédération des Syndicats de Négociants Techniques
FENEWOL	Federatie Nederlandse Wolindustrie
FENEX	Federatie van Nederlandse Expediteursorganisaties
FENFIRO	Fédération Nationale des Groupements de Femelles Prolifiques issues de Béliers Finnois ou Romanov
FENIOF	Federazione Nazionale Imprese Onoranze Funebri

FENIT	Federazione Nazionale Imprese Trasporti
FENNO-BOARD	Finnish Wallboard Industry Association
FENSIL	Federación Nacional Sindical Libre (Guatemala)
FENU	Fonds d'Équipement des Nations Unies
FENUDE	Fondo Especial de las Naciones Unidas para el Desarrollo Económico
FEO	Fishmeal Exporters Organization
FEO	Flora Europea Organisation
FEODT	Fédération Européenne des Organisations des Détaillants en Tabacs
FEOF	Foreign Exchange Operations Fund (Laos)
FEOGA	Fonds Européen d'Orientation et de Garantie Agricole
FEOTC	Federal Exporters Oversea Transport Committee (UK-Continent Trade) (Australia)
FEP	Federación Española de Pesca
FEPA	Fédération de l'Enseignement Privé Agricole
FEPA	Fédération Européenne des Fabricants de Produits Abrasifs
FEPAFAR-BIO	Fédération Panaméricaine de Pharmacie et de Biochimie
FEPAFEM	Pan-American Federation of Associations of Medical Schools (Colombia)
FEPE	Fédération Européenne pour la Protection des Eaux
FEPE	Fédération Européenne de la Publicité Extérieure
FEPEM	Federation of European Petroleum Equipment Manufacturers
FEPF	Fédération Européenne des Industries de Porcelaine et de Faïence de Table et d'Ornementation
FEPRABEL	Fédération des Producteurs d'Assurances de Belgique
FEPRANAL	Federación Nacional del Sector Privado para la Acción Comunal (Colombia)
FEPRINCO	Federación de la Producción, la Industria y el Comercio (Paraguay)
FER	Federation of Engine Re-manufacturers
FERA	Föreningen för Elektricitetens Rationella Användning
FERC	Regional Conference for Asia and the Far East (FAO)
FERE	Federación Espanola de Religiosos de Enseñanza

FERE	Fondation Égyptologique Reine Elisabeth (Belgium)	**FEUGRES**	Fédération Européenne des Fabricants de Tuyaux en Grès
FERES	Fédération Internationale des Instituts Catholiques de Recherches Socio-Religieuses	**FEUPF**	Fédération Européenne des Unions Professionelles de Fleuristes
FEROPA	Fédération Européenne des Syndicats de Panneaux de Fibres	**FEVC**	Fédération Européenne des Villes de Congrès (Belgium)
FERPI	Federazione Relazioni Pubbliche Italiana	**FEVE**	Fédération Européenne du Verre d'Emballage
FES	Fédération des Éditeurs Suisses	**FEVE**	Ferrocarriles de Via Estrecha
FESAC	Fondation de l'Enseignement Supérieur en Afrique Centrale	**FEVIR**	Federation of European Veterinarians in Industry and Research
FeSAPI	Federazione Sindacati Avvocati e Procuratori Italiani	**FEZ**	Fédération des Entreprises du Zaire
FESPF	Fédération Européenne des Syndicats de Fabricants de Parquets	**FEZ**	Fédération Européenne de Zootechnie
FESIC	Far East Seed Improvement Conference	**FF**	Finlands Fysioterapeutförbund
FESITRANH	Federación Sindical de Trabajadores Nacionales de Honduras	**FFA**	Federation of Financial Associations (Korea)
FESIW	Far East Seed Improvement Workshop	**FFA**	Flygtekniska Försöksanstalten
FESPA	Federation of European Screen Printers Associations	**FFA**	Fédération Française d'Athlétisme
		FFA	Föreningen för Arbetarskydd
FESPO	Federation of European Science Policy Organizations	**FFA**	Foundation for Foreign Affairs (U.S.A.)
		FFA	Future Farmers of America (U.S.A.)
FESSCAP	Fédération d'Étudiants Sociaux-Chrétiens d'Amérique Centrale et Panama	**FFAC**	Société Fiduciaire France Afrique (Cameroons, Congo)
FEST	Foundation for Education, Science and Technology (South Africa)	**FFAEAF**	Fédération Française des Associations d'Élevages d'Animaux à Fourrure
FESTAL	Fédération Syndicale du Teillage Agricole du Lin	**FFAG**	Fiduciare France-Afrique-Gabon
		FFAS	Fiduciare France-Afrique-Sénégal
FESYP	Fédération Européenne des Syndicats de Fabricants de Panneaux de Particules	**FFC**	Fédération Française de Cuniculiculture
		FFC	Finlands Fachföreningars Centralförbund
FETA	Fire Extinguisher Trades Association	**FFCAA**	Fédération Française des Coopératives Agricoles d'Approvisionnement
FETAB	Federación Dominicana de Cooperativas Agropecuarias y del Tabaco	**FFCAC**	Fédération Française des Coopératives Agricoles de Céréales
FETANOR	Fédération des Industries du Blanchiment, de la Teinture et des Apprêts de la Région du Nord	**FFCAT**	Fédération Française des Commissionnaires et Auxiliaires de Transport, Commissionnaires en Douane, Transitaires, Agents Maritimes et Aériens
FETIBALC	Federation of Workers in the Banana Industry of Latin America and the Caribbean	**FFCB**	Federal Farm Credit Board (U.S.A.)
FETAP	Fédération Européenne des Transports Aériens Privés	**FFCFLH**	Fédération Française de la Coopération Fruitière, Légumière et Horticole
FETRA	Fédération des Industries Transformatrices de Papier et de Carton (Belgium)	**FFCFP**	Fédération Française de Cadres de la Fonction Publique
FETRAN-JAS	Federación Nacional de Trabajadores Agropecuarios, Recursos Naturales Renovables, Jardineros y Similares (Venezuela)	**FFEA**	Fédération Française d'Économie Alpestre
		FFEM	Fédération Française d'Économie Montagnarde
FEUCA	Fédération des Étudiants Universitaires d'Amérique Centrale	**FFEPGV**	Fédération Française d'Éducation Physique et de Gymnastique

FFF	Farm Field Foundation, Washington (U.S.A.)
FFF	Fédération des Foires-Expositions de France
FFF	Finlands Farmaceutförbund
FFF	International Federations of Performers
FFFLCAF	Fédération Française de la Filature de Laine Cardée et Autres Fibres
FFH-AD	Freedom from Hunger—Action for Development
FFHC	Freedom From Hunger Campaign (of FAO)
FFI	Fachverband Faltschachtelindustrie
FFINTEL	Fédération Française des Importateurs Négociants-Transformateurs et Exportateurs de Laines
FFITP	Fédération Française des Industries Transformatrices des Plastiques
FFIVM	Fédération Française des Industries du Vêtement Masculin
FFJP	International Federation of Fruit-Juice Producers
FFLA	Federal Farm Loan Association (U.S.A.)
FFMC	Federal Farm Mortgage Corporation (U.S.A.)
FFMI	Fédération Française du Matériel d'Incendie
FFMIN	Fédération Française des Marches d'Intérêt National
FFMKR	Fédération Française des Masseurs Kinésithérapeutes Rééducateurs
FFMW	Federation of Fresh Meat Wholesalers
FFNFPMAP	Fédération Familiale Nationale pour la Formation Professionnelle et Ménagère Agricole Privée
FFNUDS	Fondo Fiducairio de las Naciones Unidas para el Desarrollo Social
FFNUPPD	Fondo Fiduciario de las Naciones Unidas para Planificación y Proyecciones del Desarrollo
FFP	Fund for Peace (U.S.A.)
FFPE	Fédération de la Fonction Publique Européenne
FFPLB	Fédération Française des Producteurs de Lait de Brebis
FFPN	Française Frisonne Pie Noire (race bovine)
FFPRI	Forest and Forest Product Research Institute (Ghana)
FFRC	Food Freezer Refrigeration Council
FFRP	Fédération Française des Relations Publiques

FFRSA	Fondation pour Favoriser les Recherches Scientifiques (Belgium)
FFS	Föreningen för Samhällsplanering
FFSA	Fédération Française des Sociétés d'Assurances
FFSB	Fédération des Foires et Salons du Benelux
FFSE	Fédération Française des Sports Équestres
FFSL	Fédération Française des Syndicats de Librairies
FFSM	Fédération des Fondations pour la Santé Mondiale
FFSPBPV	Fédération Française des Syndicats de Producteurs de Bois et Plants de Vigne
FFSPIG	Fédération Française des Syndicats Patronaux de l'Imprimerie et des Industries Graphiques
FFSPN	Fédération des Sociétés de Protection de la Nature
FFSU	Fédération Française des Stations Uvales
FFTB	Fédération des Fabricants de Tuiles et de Briques de France
FFTC	Food and Fertilizer Technology Centre, Taipei (China)
FFTL	Fédération Française du Tissage de Laine et Autres Fibres
FFTRI	Fruit and Food Research Institute, Stellenbosch (South Africa)
FFTS	Fédération Française des Travailleurs Sociaux
FFU	Forskningsrådense Fellesutvag
FFZ	Fédération Française de Zootechnie
FGA	Fachgemeinschaft Antriebstechnik im VDMA
FGA	Fédération Générale de l'Agriculture (*of* CFTC)
FGAT	Fédération des Unions Professionnelles des Grossistes en Articles Tréfilés (Belgium)
FGB	Federation of Associations of Wholesale Dealers in Building Materials (Netherlands)
FGBI	Federation of Soroptimist Clubs of Great Britain and Ireland
FGBMFI	Full Gospel Business Men's Fellowship International (U.S.A.)
FGCA	Fédération Générale des Cadres de l'Agriculture
FGDS	Fédération de la Gauche Démocrate et Socialiste

FGEI	Fédération des Géomètres-Experts Indépendants (Belgium)	**FHPL**	Fédération Horticole Professionnelle Luxembourgeoise
FGF	Fachgruppe der Forstingenieure (Switzerland)	**FHR**	Fachvereinigung Hartpapierwaren und Rundgefässe
FGG	Fränkische Geographische Gesellschaft	**FHRF**	Finney-Howell Research Foundation (U.S.A.)
FGGM	Federation of Gelatine and Glue Manufacturers	**FHS**	Finlands Hundstambok
FGH	Forschungsgemeinschaft für Hochspannungs- und Hochstromtechnik	**FHTA**	Federated Home Timber Associations
FGHS	Vereniging van Fabrikanten en Groothandelaren in Sportbenodigheden	**FIA**	Federación Interamericana de Abogados
		FIA	Fédération des Industries Agricoles et Alimentaires (Belgium)
FGI	Fédération Graphique Internationale	**FIA**	Fédération Internationale des Aveugles
FGIL	Fédération Générale des Instituteurs Luxembourgeois	**FIA**	Fédération Internationale des Acteurs
		FIA	Fédération Internationale de l'Artisanat
FGL	Foreningen af Grossister i Landbrugsmaskiner	**FIA**	Fédération Internationale de l'Automobile
FGMEE	Fédération Nationale des Syndicats de Grossistes en Matériel Électrique et Électronique	**FIA**	Federation of Islamic Associations in the United States and Canada
		FIA	Fédération Nationale des Syndicats des Industries de l'Alimentation
FGMOPA	Fonds de Garantie Mutuelle et d'Orientation de la Production Agricole	**FIAA**	Fédération Internationale d'Athlétisme Amateur
FGÖD	Fachwissenschaftliche Gesellschaft Österreichischen Dentisten	**FIAB**	Federación Internacional de Asociaciones de Bibliotecarios
FGPE	Fédération Générale du Personnel Enseignant (Belgium)	**FIABCI**	Fédération Internationale des Administrateurs de Biens Conseils Immobiliers
FGR	Fachgemeinschaft Gusseieme Rohre		
FGS	Forschungsgesellschaft für das Strassenwesen im Österreich	**FIABGRAL**	Federação Internacional de Associacões de Bibliotecarios-Grupo Regional América Latina
FGT	Fachverband der Garagen-, Tankstellen- und Service-Stations-Unternehmungen (Austria)	**FIAC**	Fédération Interaméricaine des Automobile Clubs
FGTB	Fédération General du Travail de Belgique	**FIAC**	Fédération Internationale des Agences Catholiques de Presse
FGYA	Franco-German Youth Agency		
FH	Fédération Horlogère Suisse	**FIAC**	Fédération Internationale Amateur de Cyclisme
FH	Fédération Suisse des Associations de Fabricants d'Horlogerie	**FIAC**	Fédération Internationale de l'Artisanat de la Chaussure
FHA	Farmers' Home Administration (U.S.A.)		
FHA	Federal Housing Administration (U.S.A.)	**FIACC**	Five International Associations Co-ordinating Committee
FHA	Félag Husgagnarkitekta		
FHA	Future Homemakers of America	**FIAD**	Fédération Internationale des Associations des Distributeurs de Films
FHD	Foreningen af Herreekviperingshandlere i Danmark	**FIADEJ**	Fédération Internationale des Associations de Directeurs et d'Éditeurs de Journaux
FHF	Federation of Hardware Factors		
FhG	Fraunhofer-Gesellschaft zur Förderung der Angewandten Forschung	**FIAEM**	Fédération Internationale des Associations des Étudiants en Médecine
FHI	Fédération Haltérophile Internationale	**FIAF**	Fédération Internationale des Archives du Film
FHI	Félag Húsgagna-og Innanhússarkitekta		
FHKI	Federation of Hong Kong Industries		

FIAI	Fédération Internationale des Associations d'Instituteurs	**FIAT**	Field Information Agency, Technical (U.S.A.)
FIAJ	Fédération Internationale des Auberges de la Jeunesse	**FIATA**	Fédération Internationale des Associations de Transitaires et Assimilés
FIAJF	Fédération Internationale des Amies de la Jeune Fille	**FIATC**	Fédération Internationale des Associations Touristiques de Cheminots
FIALEC	Federazione Italiana fra le Associazioni Laureati in Economia e Commercio	**FIATE**	Fédération Internationale des Associations de Travailleurs Évangéliques
FIAM	Fédération Internationale des Associations de Mécanographes	**FIAV**	Fédération Internationale des Agences de Voyagers
FIAMC	Fédération Internationale des Associations des Médecins Catholiques	**FIAV**	Fédération Internationale des Artistes de Variétés
FIANEI	Fédération Internationale des Associations Nationales d'Élèves Ingénieurs	**FIAV**	Fédération Internationale des Associations de Vexillologie
FIANET	Fédération Internationale des Associations Nationales d'Exploitants de Téléphériques, Funiculaires et autres Transports par Câbles pour Voyageurs	**FIAVET**	Federazione Italiana dello Associazioni degli Uffici Viaggio e Turismo
		FIB	Fédération Française de l'Industrie du Béton
FIAP	Fédération Internationale des Architectes Paysagistes	**FIB**	Fédération des Industries Belges
		FIB	Federation of Insurance Brokers
FIAP	Federazione Italiana Autotrasportatori Professionali	**FIB**	Fédération Internationale de Boules
FIAP	Fédération Internationale de l'Art Photographique	**FIBA**	Fédération Internationale de Baseball
FIAP	Fédération Internationale des Associations Pédagogiques	**FIBA**	Fédération Internationale de Basket-Ball Amateur
FIAP	Fédération Internationale des Attachés de Presse	**FIBEP**	Fédération Internationale des Bureaux d'Extraits de Presse
FIAPA	Fédération Internationale des Associations de Chefs de Publicité d'Annonceurs	**FIBEPA**	Fachverband für Imprägnierte und Beschichtete Papiere
FIAPE	Fédération des Associations de la Presse d'Église	**FIBMA**	National Federation of Ironmongers and Builders Merchants Staff Associations
FIAPF	Fédération Internationale des Associations de Producteurs de Films	**FIBP**	Federazione Italiana delle Biblioteche Popolari
FIAPS	Fédération Internationale des Associations de Professeurs des Sciences	**FIBT**	Fédération Internationale de Bobsleigh et de Tobogganing
FIAR	Vereniging van Fabrikanten, Importeurs en Agenten op Electronicagebied	**FIBTP**	Fédération Internationale du Bâtiment et des Travaux Publics
FIARBC	Federal Interagency River Basin Committee (U.S.A.)	**FIBV**	Fédération Internationale des Bourses de Valeurs
FIARO	Federazione Italiana Associazioni Regionali Ospedaliere	**FIC**	Fédération de l'Industrie Cimentière (Belgium)
FIARP	Federación Interamericana de Asociaciones de Relaciones Públicas	**FIC**	Fédération Internationale de Canoë
		FIC	Fédération Internationale des Enterprises de Couverture
FIARVEP	Federazione Italiana Agenti Rappresentanti, Viaggiatori e Piazzisti	**FIC**	Federazione Italiana Caccia
		FIC	Foundation for International Cooperation
FIAT	Fabbrica Italiana Automobile Torino	**FICA**	Fédération Internationale des Cheminots Antialcooliques
FIAT	Fédération Internationale des Associations de Thanatopraxie	**FICAC**	Fédération Internationale des Coloniaux et Anciens Coloniaux

FICAE	Federación Latinoamericana del Cariba de Asociaciones de Exportadores (Venezuela)	**FIDA**	Federación Internacional de Abogadas (Chile)
FICB	Federal Intermediate Credit Bank (U.S.A.)	**FIDA**	Federal Industrial Development Authority (Malaysia)
FICC	Fédération des Industries Complémentaires de la Construction	**FIDA**	Federation of Industrial Development Associations
FICC	Fédération Internationale de Chimie Clinique	**FIDA**	Federazione Italiana Dettaglianti dell'Alimentazione
FICC	Fédération Internationale de Camping et de Caravanning	**FIDA**	Nederlandse Vereniging van Fabrikanten, Importeurs en Detaillisten van Audiologische Apparatuur
FICC	Fédération Internationale de Ciné-clubs		
FICCI	Federation of the Indian Chambers of Commerce and Industry	**FIDAC**	Fédération Interalliée des Anciens Combattants
FICCIA	Fédération Internationale des Cadres de la Chimie et des Industries Annexes	**FIDAE**	Federazione Istituti Dipendenti della Autorità Ecclesiastica
FICE	Fédération Internationale des Communautés d'Enfants	**FIDAF**	Federación Internacional de Asociaciones de Ferreteros y Almacenistas de Hierros
FICEMA	Fédération Internationale des Centres d'Entraînement aux Méthodes d'Éducation Active	**FIDAL**	Federación Internacional del Algodón (Mexico)
FICEP	Fédération Internationale Catholique d'Éducation Physique	**FIDAP**	Federazione Italiana delle Aziende di Pulimento
FICIC	Fédération Internationale du Commerce et des Industries de Camping	**FIDAQ**	Fédération Internationale des Associations de Quincailliers et de Fer
FICJF	Fédération Internationale des Conseils Juridiques et Fiscaux	**FIDAS**	Fondation Internationale d'Art Sacré
FICM	Fédération Internationale des Cadres des Mines	**FIDE**	Fédération de l'Industrie Dentaire en Europe
		FIDE	Fédération Internationale pour le Droit Européen
FICOB	Fédération des Industries et du Commerce des Équipements de Bureau et d'Informatique	**FIDE**	Fédération Internationale des Échecs
FICP	Fédération Internationale des Clubs de Publicité	**FIDEGEP**	Fédération Interalliée des Évadés de Guerre et des Passeurs
FICP	Fédération Internationale du Cyclisme Professionnel	**FIDEM**	Fédération Internationale des Éditeurs de Médailles
FICPH	Fédération Internationale de Commerçants des Produits Horticoles	**FIDES**	Federación Interamericana de Empresos de Seguros
FICS	Fédération Internationale des Chasseurs de Sons	**FIDES**	Fonds d'Investissement pour le Développement Économique et Social (of UNO)
FICSA	Federation of International Civil Servants Associations		
FICSAS	Federation of Institutions Concerned with the Study of the Adriatic Sea (Yugoslavia)	**FIDH**	Fédération Internationale des Droits de l'Homme
FICT	Fédération Internationale de Centres Touristiques	**FIDI**	Fédération Internationale des Déménageurs Internationaux
FICUR	Fédération Interprofessionnelle de la Congélation Ultrarapide	**FIDIA**	Fédération Internationale des Intellectuels Aveugles
FID	Fédération Internationale du Diabète	**FIDIC**	Fédération Internationale des Industries du Cinema de Film Étroit
FID	Fédération Internationale de Documentation	**FIDIC**	Fédération Internationale des Ingénieurs-Conseils
FIDA	Federación Interamericana del Algodon		

IDIIDS Fédération Internationale des Docteurs-Ingénieurs et Ingénieurs-Docteurs-ès-Sciences

IDJC Fédération Internationale des Directeurs de Journaux Catholiques

IDO Film Industry Defence Organisation

IDOM Fonds d'Investissement et de Développement Économique des Départements d'Outre-Mer

IDOR Fibre Building Board Development Organization Ltd

IDS Falkland Islands Dependencies Survey

IDUBEL Union des Filatures Belges de Fibres Dures

IDUROP Fédération des Fabricants de Ficelles et Cordages de l'Europe Occidentale (*now* EUROCORD)

IDUROP Vereinigung der Westeuropäischen Seil- und Tauwerk-Fabrikanten

IE Fédération Internationale d'Escrime

IEA Fédération Internationale des Experts en Automobile

IEC Fédération Internationale des Associations d'Études Classiques

IEC Fédération Internationale Européenne de la Construction

IEC Fellowship of Independent Evangelical Churches

IED Fédération Internationale des Étudiants en Droit

IEDC Faculté Internationale pour l'Enseignement de Droit Comparé

IEDO Federazione Italiana Exercizi Dettaglianti Ortofrutticoli

IEEBTP Fédération Internationale des Entrepreneurs Européens de Bâtiment et de Travaux Publics

IEESA Fédération Internationale des Électriciens, Électroniciens et Spécialistes de l'Automobile

IEF Fédération Internationale pour l'Economie Familiale

IEFF Fédération Internationale de Football Féminin

IEG Federazione Italiani Editori Giornali

IEJ Fédération Internationale des Éditeurs de Journaux et Publications

IEL Foundation of Latin-American Economic Research

IELS Foreign Information Exchange for Life Scientists (U.S.A.)

FIEM Fédération Internationale de l'Enseignement Ménager

FIEM Fonds International d'Entr'aide Musicale

FIEN Forum Italiano dell' Energia Nucleare

FIEO Federation of Indian Export Organizations

FIEP Fédération Internationale des Écoles de Parents et d'Éducateurs

FIEP Fédération Internationale d'Éducation Physique

FIEP Fédération Internationale des Étudiants en Pharmacie

FIERP Federazione Italiana Esperti Relazioni Pubbliche

FIESP Fédération Internationale des Étudiants en Sciences Politiques

FIET Fédération Internationale des Employés et des Techniciens

FIEU Fonds International d'Échanges Universitaires (de la Conférence Internationale des Étudiants)

FIEV Fédération des Industries des Équipements pour Véhicles

FIF Félag Islenzkra Ferdaskrifstofa

FIF Félag Islenzkra Flugumferdarstjora

FIFA Fédération Internationale du Film d'Art

FIFA Fédération Internationale de Football Association

FIFARMA Federación Latinoamericana de la Industria Farmaceutica (Argentina)

FIFAS Fédération des Industries Françaises d'Articles de Sports

FIFCJ Fédération Internationale des Femmes des Carrières Juridiques

FIFCLC Fédération Internationale de Femmes de Carrières Libérales et Commerciales

FIFDU Fédération Internationale des Femmes Diplômées des Universités

FIFE Fédération Internationale des Associations de Fabricants de Produits d'Entretien

FIFRA Federal Insecticide, Fungicide and Rodenticide Act (U.S.A.)

FIFSP Fédération Internationale des Fonctionnaires Supérieurs de Police

FIG Fédération Internationale des Géomètres

FIG Fédération Internationale de Gymnastique

FIGA Fretted Instrument Guild of America

FIGADI Financière Gabonais de Développement Immobilier

FIGAWA	Technische Vereinigung der Firmen im Gas- und Wasserfach	**FIJC**	Fédération Internationale de la Jeunesse Catholique
FIGAZ	Fédération de l'Industrie du Gaz (Belgium)	**FIJET**	Fédération Internationale des Journalistes et Écrivains du Tourisme
FIGED	Fédération Internationale des Grandes Entreprises de Distribution	**FIJL**	Fédération International des Journalistes Libres
FIGIEFA	Fédération Internationale des Grossistes et Importateurs et Exportateurs en Fournitures Automobiles	**FIJM**	Fédération Internationale des Jeunesses Musicales
FIGISC	Federazione Italiana Gestori Impianti Stradali Carburanti	**FIJPAA**	Fédération Internationale des Journalistes Professionnels de l'Aéronautique et de l'Astronautique
FIGO	Fédération Internationale de Gynécologie et d'Obstetrique	**FIJU**	Fédération Internationale des Producteurs de Jus de Fruits
FIH	Fédération Internationale de Handball	**FIL**	Fédération Internationale de Laiterie
FIH	Fédération Internationale de l'Harmonica	**FIL**	Federación Internacional del Luge
FIH	Fédération Internationale de Hockey sur Gazon	**FILA**	Federation of Indian Library Associations
FIH	Fédération Internationale des Hôpitaux	**FILA**	Fédération Internationale de Lutte Amateur
FIHC	Fédération Internationale Haltérophile et Culturiste	**FILA**	Föreningen Importörer av Lantbruksmaskiner
FIHC	Fédération Internationale des Hommes Catholiques	**FILB**	Fédération des Industries Lourdes du Bois
FIHU	Fédération Internationale de l'Habitation et de l'Urbanisme	**FILDIR**	Fédération Internationale Libre des Déportés et Internes de la Résistance
FIHUAT	Fédération Internationale de l'Habitation et de l'Urbanisme et de l'Aménagement du Territoire	**FILISBEL**	Syndicat Belge des Canalisations Électriques
		FILLM	Fédération Internationale des Langues et Littératures Modernes
FII	Federation of Irish Industries, Ltd	**FILT**	Fédération Internationale de Lawn Tennis
FII	Felag Islenzkra Idnrekenda	**FIM**	Fédération Internationale Motocycliste
FIIC	Fédération Interaméricaine de l'Industrie de la Construction	**FIM**	Fédération Internationale des Musiciens
FIICPI	Fédération Internationale Ingénieurs-conseils en Propriété	**FIM**	Finnish Institute of Management
		FIMA	Federazione Italiana Mercanti d'Arte
FIIG	Fédération des Institutions Internationales Semi-officielles et Privées Etablies à Genève	**FIMA**	Feria Técnica Internacional de la Maquinaria Agricola
FIIM	Fédération Internationale de l'Industrie du Médicament	**FIMAA**	Federazione Italiana Mediatori e Agenti di Affari
FIIM	Fédération Internationale des Ingénieurs Municipaux	**FIMARC**	Fédération Internationale des Mouvements d'Adultes Ruraux Catholiques
FIIP	Fédération Internationale de l'Industrie Phonographique	**FIMCAP**	Fédération Internationale des Mouvements de Jeunesse Catholique Paroissiales
FIIR	Federal Institute of Industrial Research (Nigeria)	**FIMCEE**	Fédération Internationale des Marbriers de la CEE
FIIRO	Federal Institute of Industrial Research Oshodi (Nigeria)	**FIME**	Fédération Internationale des Maisons de l'Europe
FIJ	Fédération Internationale des Journalistes	**FIMEM**	Fédération Internationale des Mouvements d'École Moderne
FIJ	Fédération Internationale de Judo	**FIMF**	Federación Internacional de Medicina Fisica
FIJA	Fédération Internationale des Journalistes Agricoles	**FIMITIC**	Fédération Internationale des Mutilés et Invalides du Travail et des Invalides Civils

FIMK	Fédération Internationale des Masseurs-Kinésithérapiques Practiciens et Physiothérapie	**FIOCC**	Fédération Internationale des Ouvriers de la Chaussure et du Cuir
FIMM	Fédération des Importeurs de la Métallurgie et de la Mécanique	**FIOCES**	Fédération Internationale des Organisations de Correspondances et d'Échanges Scolaires
FIMOC	Fédération Internationale des Mouvements Ouvriers Chrétiens	**FIODS**	International Federation of the Organisation of Blood Donors
FIMOP	Chambre Syndicale Belge des Fabricants et Importateurs de Matériel de Transmission Oléo-Hydraulique et Pneumatique	**FIOM**	Fédération Internationale des Ouvriers Métallurgistes
FIMP	Fédération Internationale de Médecine Physique	**FIOPI**	Federaçao Interamericana de Organizaçoes des Profissionais da Imprensa
FIMPR	Fédération Internationale de Médecine Physique et Réadaptation	**FIOPP**	Federación Interamericana de Organizaciones de Periodistas Profesionales
FIMS	Fédération Internationale Médecine Sportive	**FIORH**	Fédération Internationale pour l'Organisation de Rencontres pour Handicapés
FIMTM	Fédération des Industries Mécaniques et Transformatrices des Métaux	**FIOST**	Fédération Internationale des Organisations Syndicales du Personnel des Transports
FIMU	Federación Internacional de Mujeres Universitarias	**FIOW**	First International Organisation of Welcome
FIN	Fédération des Industries Nautiques	**FIP**	Federación Internacional de Periodistas
FIN	Futures Information Network (U.S.A.)	**FIP**	Fédération International Pharmaceutique
FINA	Fédération Internationale de Natation Amateur	**FIP**	Fédération Internationale de Philatélie
FINAM	Financial Agricultural Company for the South (Italy)	**FIP**	Fédération Internationale des Phonothèques
		FIP	Fédération Internationale des Piétons
FINAT	Fédération Internationale des Fabricants et Transformateurs d'Adhésifs et Thermo-Collants sur Papiers et autres Supports	**FIP**	Fédération Internationale de Podologie
		FIP	Fédération Internationale de la Précontrainte
		FIP	Federazione Italiana della Pubblicità
FINATA	Fédération Internationale des Associations de Transporteurs et Assimilés	**FIP**	Félag Islenzkra Prentidnadarins
FINCEC	Fédération des Syndicats de Cadres et Agents de Maîtrise de l'Importation et du Négoce des Combustibles et de l'Exploitation de Chauffage	**FIPA**	Fédération Internationale de la Presse Agricole
		FIPA	Fédération Internationale des Producteurs Agricoles
		FIPA	Federazione Italiana Periti Agrari
FINEFTA	Finland — European Free Trade Association	**FIPACE**	Fédération Internationale des Producteurs Autoconsommateurs Industriels d'Électricité
FINN-BOARD	Finnish Board Mills Association	**FIPAD**	Fondation Internationale pour un Autre Développement
FINNBRO-KER	Finlands Skeppsmäklareförbund	**FIPAGO**	Fédération Internationale des Fabricants de Papiers Gommes
FINNCELL	Finska Cellulosaföreningen		
FINNMET-AL	Suomen Metalliteollisuusyhdstys	**FIPAL**	Fondation Internationale pour le Progrès de L'Alimentation
FINNPAP	Finnish Paper Mills' Association	**FIPC**	Fédération Internationale des Pharmaciens Catholiques
FINS	Fishing Industry News Service (Australia)		
FINUMA	Fabrique Ivoirienne de Nuoc Mam	**FIPCO**	Fédération Internationale pour la Philatélie Constructive
FIO	Food Investigation Organisation		
FIO	Fédération Internationale d'Oléicultur	**FIPDU**	Fédération Internationale des Femmes Diplômées des Universités

FIPE	Federazione Italiana Pubblici Esercizi	**FIRI**	Fishing Industry Research Institute (S. Africa)
FIPESO	Fédération Internationale des Professeurs de l'Enseignement Secondaire Officiel	**FIRM**	Fédération Internationale des Rectifieurs et Reconstructeurs de Moteurs
FIPET	Federación Interamericana de Periodistas y Escritores de Turismo	**FIRMS**	Fonds d'Intervention et de Régularisation du Marché du Sucre
FIPF	Fédération Internationale des Professeurs de Français	**FIRN**	Foreningen af Importorer af Raavarer til Naeringsmiddelindustrien (Denmark)
FIPG	Fédération de l'Industrie du Petit Granit	**FIRP**	Federazione Italiana Relazioni Pubbliche
FIPGV	Fédération Internationale de la Presse Gastronomique et Vinicole	**FIRP**	Fondation Internationale pour la Recherche dans le Domaine de la Publicité
FIPIF	Finnish Plastics Industry Federation	**FIRS**	Fédération Internationale de Roller-Skating
FIPJF	Fédération Internationale des Producteurs de Jus de Fruits	**FIRST**	Federal Information Research Science and Technology Network (*of* COSATI)
FIPLV	Fédération Internationale des Professeurs de Langues Vivantes	**FIS**	Fédération Internationale du Commerce des Semences
FIPM	Fédération Internationale de Psychothérapie Médicale	**FIS**	Fédération Internationale de Sauvetage
FIPMEC	Fédération Internationale des Petites et Moyennes Entreprises Commerciales	**FIS**	Fédération Internationale de Ski
		FIS	Fédération Internationale des Settlements
FIPMI	Fédération Internationale des Petites et Moyennes Entreprises Industrielles	**FIS**	Federazione Italiana Sementi
FIPO	Fédération Internationale de la Presse Orientale	**FIS**	Federazione Italiana della Strada
		FIS	Félag Íslenzka Stórkaupmanna
FIPOI	Fondation des Immeubles pour les Organisations Internationales	**FIS**	Fondation Internationale pour la Science (UNESCO)
FIPP	Fédération Internationale Pénale et Pénitentiare	**FIS**	Fondation Internationale Scientifique
		FISA	Federation of Insurance Staffs Associations
FIPP	Fédération Internationale de la Presse Périodique	**FISA**	Fédération Internationale des Semaines d'Art
FIPP	Fédération Internationale pour la Protection des Populations	**FISA**	Fédération Internationale des Sociétés Aérophilatéliques
FIPRA	Fédération Internationale de la Presse Agricole	**FISA**	Fédération Internationale des Sociétés d'Aviron
FIPREGA	Fédération Internationale de la Presse Gastronomique, Vinicole et Touristique	**FISAG**	Federación Interamericana de Sociedades de Autores y Compositores
FIPRESCI	Fédération Internationale de la Presse Cinématographique	**FISAIC**	Fédération Internationale des Sociétés Artistiques et Intellectuelles de Cheminots
FIPTP	Fédération Internationale de la Presse Technique et Périodique	**FISB**	Fédération Internationale de Ski-bob
		FISC	Federation Internationale des Chasseurs du Son
FIR	Fédération Internationale des Résistants	**FISC**	Foundation for International Scientific Co-ordination
FIRA	Fédération Internationale de Rugby Amateur	**FISC**	Fund for International Student Cooperation
FIRA	Furniture Industry Research Association (*formerly FDC*)	**FISCA**	Fédération Internationale des Syndicats Chrétiens de l'Agriculture
FIRAC	Fédération Internationale des Radio Amateurs Cheminots	**FISCC**	Fruit Industry Sugar Concession Committee (Australia)
FIREC	Fédération Internationale des Rédacteurs en Chef		

FISCETCV Fédération Internationale des Syndicats Chrétiens d'Employés Techniciens, Cadres et Voyageurs

FISCM Fédération Internationale des Syndicats Chrétiens de la Métallurgie

FISCOA Fédération Internationale des Syndicats Chrétiens d'Ouvriers Agricoles

FISCOBB Fédération Internationale des Syndicats Chrétiens d'Ouvriers du Bâtiment et du Bois

FISCTTH Fédération Internationale des Syndicats Chrétiens des Travailleurs du Textile et de l'Habillement

FISD Fédération Internationale de Sténographie et de Dactylographie

FISE Fédération Internationale des Sociétés d'Électroencéphalographie

FISE Fédération Internationale Syndicate de l'Enseignement

FISE Fonds International de Secours à l'Enfance (*of* UNO)

FISEC Fédération Internationale Sportive de l'Enseignement Catholique

FISEM Fédération Internationale des Sociétés d'Écrivains Médecins

FISGV Federazione Internazionale della Stampa Gastronomica e Vinicola

FISH Fédération Internationale des Sociétés Magiques

FISH Forskningsinstitutet vid Svensk Handelshogskolan

FISITA Fédération Internationale des Sociétés d'Ingénieurs et de Techniciens de l'Automobile

FISP Fédération Internationale des Sociétés de Philosophie

FISPIU Federazione Italiana Servizi Pubblici Igiene Urbana

FISS Fédération Internationale de Sauvetage et de Secourisme

FIST Fédération de l'Industrie Suisse du Tabac

FISTAV Fédération Internationale des Syndicats des Travailleurs de l'Audio-Visuel

FISU Fédération Internationale du Sport Universitaire

FIT Fédération Internationale des Traducteurs

FIT Federazione Italiana Tabaccai

FITA Fédération Internationale des Techniciens Agronomes

FITA Fédération Internationale de Tir à l'Arc

FITAC Fédération Interaméricaine du Touring et des Automobile-Clubs

FITAP Fédération Internationale des Transports Aériens Privés

FITB Fédération Internationale des Techniciens de la Bonneterie

FITBB Fédération Internationale des Travailleurs du Bâtiment et du Bois

FITC Fédération Internationale du Thermalisme et du Climatisme

FITCA Fédération Internationale des Transports Commerciaux par Automobiles

FITCC-OROC Fédération Internationale de Tai Chi Chuan Orient-Occident (France)

FITCE Fédération des Ingénieurs des Télé-communications de la Communauté Européenne

FITCH Federación Industrial Ferroviaria de Chile

FITCM Federación Internacional de Trabajadores de la Construcción y la Madera

FITCRE Fédération Internationale des Travailleurs Chrétiens Refugiés et Émigrés

FITE Federación Interamericana de Trabajores del Espectáculo

FITEC Fédération Internationale du Thermalisme et du Climatisme

FITH Fédération Internationale des Travailleurs de l'Habillement

FITIM Federación Internacional de Trabajadores de las Industrias Metalurgicas

FITIM Société de Filature et de Tissage de Madagascar

FITITHC Fédération Internationale des Travailleurs des Industries du Textile de l'Habillement et du Cuir

FITITV Federación Interamericana de Trabajadores de la Industria Textil y del Vestuario (Peru)

FITP Fédération Internationale des Travailleurs du Pétrole

FITPAS Federación Internacional de los Trabajadores de las Plantaciones, Agricolas y Similares

FITPASC Fédération Internationale des Travailleurs des Plantations, de l'Agriculture et des Secteurs Connexes

FITPC Fédération Internationale des Travailleurs du Pétrole et de la Chimie

FITPQ Federación Internacional de Trabajadores Petroleros y Químicos

FITS	Fédération Internationale du Tourisme Social
FITT	Fédération Internationale de Tennis de Table
FITT	Fédération International des Travailleurs de la Terre
FIUC	Fédération Internationale des Universités Catholiques
FIV	Fédération de l'Industrie du Verre
FIVA	Fédération Internationale des Voitures Anciennes
FIVA	Federazione Italiana Venditori Ambulanti e Giornalai
FIVB	Fédération Internationale de Volleyball
FIVU	Federación Internacional de Vivienda y Urbanismo
FIVZ	Fédération Internationale Vétérinaire de Zootechnie
FIYTO	Federation of International Youth Travel Organisations
FJCEE	Fédération des Jeunes Chefs d'Entreprises d'Europe
FJF	Finlands Journalistförbund
FJK	Flyjournalisternas Klubb
FKCO	Finlands Kennel Centralorgan
FKE	Federation of Kenya Employers
FKH	Forschungskommission für Hochspannungsfragen (Switzerland)
FKI	Fachvereinigung der Deutschen Kartonagen-Industrie
FKI	Förderungs für Konsumenten-Information (Switzerland)
FKM	Forschungskuratorium Maschinenbau
FKS	Vereniging van Handelaren in Fourage-, Kunstmest-, Hooi-, Stro en Ruwvoeders
FKTG	Fernseh- und Kinotechnische Gesellschaft
FKTU	Federation of Korean Trade Unions
FKV	Fachgruppe der Kultur- und Vermessungsingenieure (Switzerland)
FLAA	Federación Latino Americana de Agrimensores (Uruguay)
FLACSO	Latin American School of Sociology (Chile)
FLAP	Federación Latinoamericana de Parasitologia
FLAPF	Federación Latinoamericana de Productores de Fonograms y Videograms
FLATE-VECU	Federación Latinoamericana de Trabajadores del Textil, Vestido, Calzado, Cuero y Conexos
FLATGRA-PA	Federación Latinoamericana de Trabajadores Gráficos, Papeleros y Afines
FLATICOM	Federación Latinoamerica de Trabajordes de la Industria de la Construcción y la Madera
FLATREP	Comité Pro-Federación Latinoamericana de Trabajadores del Espectaculo Publico
FLATT	Federación Latinoamericana de Trabajadores del Transporte
FLATVECU	Federación Latinoamericana de Trabajadores del Textil, Vestido, Calzado, Cuero y Conexos
FLB	Federal Land Bank (U.S.A)
FLDA	Federal Land Development Authority (Malaysia)
FLEC	Federatie van Land-en Tuinbouwwerktuigen Exploiterende Coöperaties
FLECE	Federación Libre de Escuelas de Ciencias de la Empresa
FLF	Finlands Läkarforbund
FLGEB	Fédération des Livres Généalogiques de l'Espèce Bovine
FLGEC	Fédération des Livres Généalogiques de l'Espèce Chevaline
FLGEP	Fédération des Livres Généalogiques de l'Espèce Porcine
FLI	Fédération Lainière Internationale
FLIDEPEC	Federation of Liberal and Democratic Parties in the European Community
FLING	Guinea National Independence Liberation Front
FLIRT	Federal Librarians Round Table of the American Library Association
FLM	Fédération Luthérienne Mondiale
FLN	Front de Libération Nationale (Algeria)
FLOAG	Front for the Liberation of the Occupied Arabian Gulf
FLOSY	Front for the Liberation of Occupied South Yemen
FLP	Forest Products Laboratory (U.S.A)
FLQ	Front de Libération du Québec (Canada)
FLRFA	Federation of Land Reform Farmers Association (Philippines)
FLS	Finska Läkaresällskapet
FLT	Fachverband Landwirtschaftlicher Trocknungswerke
FLTA	French Lawn Tennis Association

FLTPR	Federación Libre de los Trabajadores de Puerto Rico	**FMF**	Food Manufacturers Federation
FLUG	Flugfelag Islands	**FMFR**	Fédération Mondiale des Femmes Rurales
FM	Félag Menntaskólakennara	**FMH**	Foederatio Medicorum Helveticorum (Switzerland)
FM	Fraternité Mondiale	**FMH**	Verbindung der Schweizer Ärzte
FMA	Farm Management Association	**FMHW**	Federation of Mental Health Workers
FMA	Federation of Management Associations	**FMI**	Federation of Malta Industries
FMA	Fertilizer Manufacturers' Association	**FMI**	Fonds Monétaire Internationale
FMA	Food Machinery Association (*now* PPA)	**FMIG**	Food Manufacturers Industrial Group
FMAC	Fédération Mondiale des Anciens Combattants	**FMJC**	Federation Mundial de Juventud Catolica
FMAEM	Federazione Nazionale Aziende Elettriche Municipalizzate	**FMJD**	Fédération Mondiale de la Jeunesse Démocratique
FMAM	Fédération Mondiale des Amis de Musées	**FMJFC**	Fédération Mondiale des Jeunesses Feminines Catholiques
FMANU	Fédération Mondiale des Associations pour les Nations Unies	**FMJLR**	Fédération Mondiale des Jeunesses Libérales et Radicales
FMATH	Fédération Mondiale de Travailleurs des Industries Alimentaires, du Tabac et Hôtelière	**FMM**	Fédération Mondiale de la Métallurgie (Belgium)
FMB	Federation of Master Builders	**FMMB**	Fédération des Chambres Syndicales des Métaux
FMBRA	Flour Milling and Baking Research Association	**FMME**	Fund for Multinational Management (U.S.A.)
FMBSA	Farmers' and Manufacturers' Beet Sugar Association (U.S.A.)	**FMN**	Fédération Mondiale de Neurologie
FMC	Fatstock Marketing Corporation, Ltd	**FMN**	Fédération Motocycliste Nationale
FMC	Federal Maritime Commission (U.S.A.)	**FMO**	Federation of Manufacturing Opticians
FMC	Section des Fleuristes du Marché Commun de la Fédération Européenne des Unions Professionnelles de Fleuristes	**FMO**	Fédération Professionnelle Agricole pour la Main-d'Oeuvre Saisonnière
FMC	Finnish Management Council	**FMOB**	Federation of Master Organ Builders
FMCB	Fédération Mondiale des Organisations de Construction et du Bois	**FMOI**	Fédération Mondiale des Organisations d'Ingénieurs
FMCE	Federación Mundial Cristiana de Estudiantes	**FMPA**	Fédérations Mondiale pour la Protection des Animaux
FMCE	Federation of Manufacturers of Construction Equipment (*now* FMCEC)	**FMPE**	Federation of Master Process Engravers (*now* GRF)
FMCEC	Federation of Manufacturers of Construction Equipment and Cranes	**FMPTE**	Federation of Municipal Passenger Transport Employers
FMCP	Federation of Manufacturers of Contractors' Plant	**FMRA**	Fertilizer Manufacturers' Research Association (New Zealand)
FMCU	Federación Mundial de Ciudades Unidas (France)	**FMS**	Fédération Mondiale des Sourds
FMD	Foreningen af Markedsanalyse-Instittuter i Danmark	**FMSE**	Federation of Medium and Small Employers
FME	Federatie Metaal- en Electrotechnische Industrie	**FMSI**	Federazione Medicosportiva Italiano
FMF	Fachverband Moderne Fremdspracken	**FMSM**	Fédération Mondiale pour la Santé Mentale
FMF	Fédération des Médecins de France	**FMT**	Federation of Merchant Tailors of Great Britain, Inc.
		FMTA	Farm Machinery and Tractor Trade Association of New South Wales

FMTA	Fédération Mondiale de Travailleurs Agricoles	**FNAS**	Fédération Nationale des Chambres Syndicales des Grossistes en Équipements Sanitaires, Chauffage et Canalisation
FMTCM	Federación Mundial de Trabajadores de la Construcción y la Madere	**FNASAVPA**	Fédération Nationale des Associations des Salariés de l'Agriculture pour la Vulgarisation du Progrès Agricole
FMTH	Federación Mundial de Trabajadores Agricoles	**FNASSEM**	Fédération Nationale de Sauvegarde des Sites et Ensembles Monumentaux
FMTNM	Fédération Mondiale des Travailleurs Non Manuels	**FNB**	Fédération Nationale du Bois
FMTS	Fédération Mondiale des Travailleurs Scientifiques	**FNB**	Fédération Nationale des Boissons
FMVI	Fachverband Metallwaren- und Verwandte Industrien	**FNB**	Fédération Nationale Bovine
		FNB	Food and Nutrition Board (U.S.A.)
FMVJ	Fédération Mondiale des Villes Jumelées	**FNBB**	Fédération Nationale Belge de la Blanchisserie
FNAAPDAV	Fédération Nationale des Associations Agricoles pour le Développement de l'Assurance-Vie	**FNBC**	Fédération Nationale des Bibliothèques Catholiques (Belgium)
FNAARC	Federazione Nazionale fra le Associazioni Agenti e Rappresentanti di Commercio	**FNBTR**	Fédération Nationale Belge des Transporteurs Routiers
FNAB	Fédération Nationale des Artisans du Bâtiment et des Branches Professionnelles Annexes	**FNC**	Federación Nacional de Cafeteros (Colombia)
FNAC	Fédération Nationale des Agents Commerciaux	**FNC**	Federación Nacional del Campesino (Bolivia)
		FNC	Fédération Nationale Chevaline
FNACE	Fédération Nationale des Agents sous Contrat de l'État (Zaire)	**FNC**	Fédération Nationale de la Coiffure
		FNC	Fédération Nationale des Cressiculteurs
FNAEM	Federatione Nazionale Aziende Elletriche Municipalizzate	**FNCA**	Fédération Nationale de la Coopération Agricole (*now* CFNA)
FNAFO	Fédération Nationale de l'Agriculture Force Ouvrière	**FNCA**	Fédération Nationale des Coopératives Apicoles
FNAH	Fonds National de l'Amélioration de l'Habitat	**FNCA**	Fédération Nationale des Coopératives Artisanales de France et d'Outre-Mer
FNAIM	Fédération Nationale des Agents Immobiliers et Mandataires en Vente de Fonds de Commerce	**FNCA**	Fédération Nationale du Crédit Agricole
		FNCAA	Fédération Nationale des Coopératives Agricoles d'Approvisionnement (*now* SYNERVA)
FNAMAC	Fédération Nationale Artisanale des Métiers d'Art et de Création du Bijou et de l'Horlogerie	**FNCAC**	Fédération Nationale des Coopératives Agricoles de Céréales
FNAMGAV	Federazione Nazionale Aziende Municipalizzate Gas, Acqua, Varie	**FNCAFLPT**	Fédération Nationale des Coopératives Agricoles de Fruits, Légumes et Pommes de Terre (France) (*now* FFCFLH)
FNAMI	Fonds National Assurance-Maladie-Invalidité	**FNCAM**	Fédération Nationale du Crédit Agricole Mutuel
FNAMS	Fédération Nationale des Agriculteurs Multiplicateurs de Semences	**FNCASEF**	Fédération Nationale des Cooperatives Agricoles de Semences Fourragères
FNAO	Fédération Nationale des Commerces de l'Antiquité, de l'Occasion et des Objets de Collection	**FNCAST**	Fédération Nationale de la Coopération Agricole Scientifique et Technique
FNAP	Fédération Nationale des Agences de Presse	**FNCATBI**	Fédération Nationale des Coopératives Agricoles de Transformation de la Betterave Industrielle
FNARER	Fédération Nationale des Associations Régionales d'Économie Rurale		

FNCATS Fédération Nationale de la Coopération Agricole Technique et Scientifique

FNCAUMA Fédération Nationale des Coopératives d'Achat et d'Utilisation de Matériel Agricole

FNCAv Fédération Nationale de la Coopération Avicole

FNCB Fédération Nationale des Coopératives Agricoles de Transformation de la Betterave Industrielle

FNCB Fédération Nationale des Commercants en Bestiaux de France

FNCBPV Fédération Nationale du Commerce du Betáil, Porcs et Viande (Belgium)

FNCBV Fédération Nationale de la Coopération Bétail et Viande

FNCC Fédération Nationale de Conserveries Coopératives

FNCC Fédération Nationale des Coopératives de Céréales

FNCC Fédération Nationale des Coopératives Chrétiennes

FNCC Fédération Nationale des Coopératives Cidricoles

FNCC Fédération Nationale des Coopératives de Consommation

FNCC Fondo Nacional del Café y del Cacao (Venezuela)

FNCCIB Fédération Nationale des Chambres de Commerce et d'Industrie de Belgique

FNCCRE Fédération Nationale des Collectivités Concédantes de Régies Électriques

FNCERO Fédération Nationale des Comités Économiques Régionaux

FNCERVO Fédération Nationale des Comités Économiques Régionaux de la Volaille

FNCETA Fédération Nationale des Centres d'Études Techniques Agricoles

FNCFI Federazione Nazionale Commercianti Filatelici Italiani

FNCFP Fédération Nationale des Coopératives Agricoles de Fruits, Primeurs, Fleurs et Autres Produits Agricoles

FNCG Fédération Nationale des Centres de Gestion

FNCG Fédération Nationale du Commerce des Grains

FNCH Fédération Nationale des Coopératives d'Huilerie

FNCHR Fédération Nationale des Coopératives d'Habitat Rural

FNCIA Fédération Nationale des Coopératives d'Insémination Artificielle

FNCIB Fédération Nationale des Chambres Immobilières de Belgique

FNCIVAMA Fédération Nationale des Centres d'Information et de Vulgarisation Agricoles et Ménagères Agricoles

FNCL Fédération Nationale des Coopératives Lainières

FNCL Fédération Nationale des Coopératives Laitières

FNCL Fédération Nationale des Coopératives Linières

FNCO Federazione Nazionale dei Collegi delle Ostetriche

FNCP Federación Nacional de Cooperativas de Producción (Venezuela)

FNCP Fédération Nationale des Centres de Préformation

FNCP Fédération Nationale des Constructeurs Promoteurs

FNCPA Fédération Nationale des Syndicats de Conserveurs de Produits Agricoles

FNCPBV Fédération Nationale des Coopératives de Producteurs de Bétail et de Viande

FNCPSA Fédération Nationale des Coopératives de Producteurs de Sel de l'Atlantique

FNCPV Fédération Nationale des Cooperatives de Producteurs de Viande

FNCPVRT Fédération Nationale des Coopératives de Production et de Vente des Raisins de Table

FNCR Fédération Nationale des Coopératives Rizicoles

FNCRA Fédération Nationale des Comités Régionaux de Propagande et l'Expansion de Produits Agricoles

FNCrA Fédération Nationale du Crédit Agricole

FNCRP Fédération Nationale des Comités Régionaux de Propagande

FNCSD Fédération Nationale des Chambres Syndicales Dentaires (Belgium)

FNCSM Fédération Nationale des Chambres Syndicales de Médecins

FNCSO Fédération Nationale des Coopératives de Stockage d'Oléagineux

FNCTB Fédération Nationale des Coopératives Agricoles de Transformation de la Betterave

FNCTSA Fédération Nationale de la Coopération Technique Scientifique Agricole

FNCTTFEL National Federation of Railwaymen, Transport Workers, Civil Servants and Employees of Luxembourg

FNCUMA Fédération Nationale des Coopératives d'Achat et d'Utilisation de Matériel Agricole

FNCV Federación Nacional de Cooperatives de Vivienda (Venezuela)

FNCV Fédération Nationale des Coopératives Vinicoles

FNDAB Fédération Nationale de Défense de l'Agriculture Biologique

FNDCV Fédération Nationale des Distilleries Coopératives Vinicoles

FNDE Fondo Nacional de Desarrollo Económico (Peru)

FNDF Fédération Nationale des Distributeurs de Films

FNDPL Fédération Nationale des Détaillants en Produits Laitiers

FNEAA Fédération Nationale des Exploitants d'Autobus et Autocars

FNEAF Fédération Nationale des Éleveurs d'Animaux à Fourrure

FNEB Fédération Nationale des Fabricants de Caisses et Emballages en Bois de France

FNEC Fédération Nationale des Éleveurs de Chèvres

FNECC Fédération Nationale des Employés Commerciaux et Cadres (Zaire)

FNED Fédération Nationale des Étudiants en Droits et en Sciences Politiques

FNEE Fédération Nationale de l'Équipement Electrique

FNEEGA Fédération Nationale de l'Énergie Électrique et du Gaz d'Algérie

FNEF Fédération Nationale des Étalonniers de France

FNENF Fédération Nationale des Entrepreneurs de Nettoyage de France

FNETA Fédération Nationale des Entrepreneurs de Travaux Agricoles de France

FNF Fédération Nationale de la Fourrure

FNFC Fédération Nationale des Fabricants de Cravates

FNFC First National Finance Corporation

FNFF Fédération Nationale des Fleuristes de France

FNFHFTM Federation of Needle, Fish Hook and Fishing Tackle Makers

FNFMBC Fédération Nationale des Fabricants de Menuiseries, Charpentes et Bâtiments Industrialisés

FNFPVEI Fédération Nationale des Fabricants de Peintures, Vernis et Encres d'Imprimerie

FNFR Fédération Nationale de la Famille Rurale

FNFR Fédération Nationale des Foyers Ruraux

FNFT Fédération Nationale des Fabricants-Transformateurs de l'Industrie Cotonnière

FNG Fédération Nationale du Genêt

FNGAA Fédération Nationale des Groupements Agricoles d'Approvisionnement

FNGDSB Fédération Nationale des Groupements de Défense Sanitaire du Bétail

FNGFS Fédération Nationale des Graines Fourragères de Semence

FNGH Fédération Nationale de l'Horlogerie en Gros

FNGPA Fédération Nationale des Groupements de Productivité Agricole

FNGPC Fédération Nationale des Groupements de Protection des Cultures

FNGPPTP Fédération Nationale des Groupements et Producteurs de Pommes de Terre de Primeur

FNGRA Fédération Nationale des Groupements Agricoles d'Approvisionnement

FNGSP Fédération Nationale des Graines de Semences Potagères, de Fleurs, Semi-Fourragères, Betteraves Fourragères, Haricots, Pois et Fèves de Semences

FNGVPA Fédération Nationale des Groupements de Vulgarisation et du Progrès Agricole

FNHG Fédération Nationale de l'Horlogerie en Gros

FNHMID Fédération Nationale des Huileries Métropolitaines et Industries Dérivées

FNHPV Fédération Nationale des Herbagers et Producteurs de Viande

FNHR Fédération Nationale de l'Habitat Rural

FNHRATR Fédération Nationale de l'Habitat Rural et de l'Aménagement du Territoire Rural

FNI Fédération Naturiste Internationale

FNIA Fondo Nacional de Investigaciones Agropecuarias (Venezuela)

FNIB Fédération Nationale des Infirmières Belges

FNIC Fédération Nationale des Industries du Corset

FNIC Food and Nutrition Information and Educational Resources Center (U.S.A.)

FNICG Fédération Nationale de l'Industrie des Corps Gras

FNICGV Fédération Nationale des Industries et Commerces en Gros des Viandes

FNIE Fédération Nationale des Industries Électroniques

FNIE Fédération Nationale de l'Industrie des Engrais

FNIEBI Fédération Nationale des Installateurs-Électriciens du Bâtiment et de l'Industrie

FNIEF Federazione Nazionale Insegnanti Educazione Fisica

FNIH Fédération Nationale de l'Industrie Hôtelière de France et d'Outre-Mer

FNIL Federação Nacional dos Industriais de Lanifícios (Portugal)

FNIL Fédération Nationale des Syndicats d'Industriels Laitiers

FNIM Federação Nacional dos Industriais de Moagem (Portugal)

FNIMME Fédération Nationale des Importateurs de la Métallurgie, de la Mécanique et de l'Électronique

FNINF Fédération Nationale Interprofessionnelle de la Noix Française (of CNPFL)

FNIPVEICF Fédération Nationale des Industries des Peintures, Vernis, Encres d'Imprimerie et Couleurs Fines

FNISM Federazione Nazionale Insegnanti Scuole Medie

FNITCE Fédération Nationale des Ingénieurs, Techniciens, Cadres et Employés

FNJAP Fédération Nationale des "Jeunes Alliances Paysannes"

FNLA National Front for the Liberation of Angola

FNLG Fédération Nationale des Livres Zootechniques

FNLVPT Fédération Nationale des Loueurs de Voitures de Place à Taximètre

FNMA Fédération Nationale de la Mutualité Agricole

FNMBC Fédération Nationale des Négociants en Gros en Bonneterie, Mercerie, Chaussures et Négoces Connexes de France

FNMCCA Fédération Nationale de la Mutualité du Crédit et de la Coopération Agricoles

FNMF Fédération Nationale de la Marbrerie Funéraire

FNMIP Fédération Nationale des Malades, Infirmes et Paralysés

FNMTTB Fédération Nationale des Maîtres Tailleurs et Tailleuses de Belgique

FNMV Federation Nationale des Entreprises de Miroiterie-Vitrerie

FNNBEB Fédération Nationale des Négociants en Bières et Eaux de Boisson (Belgium)

FNNMC Fédération Nationale des Négociants en Matériaux de Construction

FNO Fédération Nationale Ovine

FNOA Fédération Nationale des Organisations Agricoles

FNOCPAB Fédération Nationale des Organismes de Contrôle des Performances des Animaux de Boucherie

FNOFPCCA Fédération Nationale des Organismes de Formation et de Promotion des Conseillers et Cadres de l'Agriculture

FNOGA Fédération Nationale des Organismes de Gestion Agricole

FNOM Federazione Nazionale degli Ordini dei Medici

FNOMER Fédération Nationale des Organismes de Migration et d'Établissement Ruraux

FNOMI Fédération Nationale des Organismes de Migrations Intérieures

FNOOMM Federazione Nazionale degli Ordeni dei Medici

FNOP Federatie van Nederlandse Organisaties voor het Personenvervoer

FNOSAD Fédération Nationale des Organisations Sanitaires Apicoles Départementales

FNOSS Fédération Nationale des Organismes de Sécurité Sociale

FNOVI Federazione Nazionale degli Ordini dei Veterinari Italiani

FNP Fédération Nationale de la Pisciculture

FNP Fédération Nationale Porcine

FNPA Fédération Nationale de la Propriété Agricole

FNPBRF Fédération Nationale des Producteurs de Bois et Reboiseurs Français

FNPC Fédération Nationale des Producteurs de Chanvre

FNPECSF Fédération Nationale des Propriétaires et Éleveurs du Cheval de Selle et de Sport Français

FNPF	Fédération Nationale de la Pisciculture Française
FNPF	Fédération Nationale des Producteurs de Fraises
FNPF	Fédération Nationale des Producteurs de Fruits
FNPFB	Fédération Nationale des Entrepreneurs de Pompes Funèbres de Belgique
FNPFC	Fédération Nationale des Producteurs de Fruits à Cidre
FNPHP	Fédération Nationale des Producteurs de l'Horticulture et des Pépinières
FNPL	Fédération Nationale des Producteurs de Lait
FNPL	Fédération Nationale des Producteurs de Légumes
FNPLL	Fédération Nationale des Producteurs de Lavande et de Lavandin
FNPP	Federation Nationale de la Photographie Professionnelle (Belgium)
FNPPPT	Fédération Nationale Producteurs de Plantes de Pommes de Terre
FNPPTC	Fédération Nationale des Producteurs de Pommes de Terre de Consommation (*now* FNPTC)
FNPPTI	Fédération Nationale des Producteurs de Pommes de Terre Industrielles
FNPRCM	Fédération Nationale des Producteurs de Reinette Canada de Montagne
FNPRT	Fédération Nationale des Producteurs de Raisins de Table
FNPSA	Fédération Nationale de Producteurs de Sel de l'Atlantique
FNPSM	Fédération Nationale des Producteurs de Semences de Maïs
FNPT	Federaçao Nacional dos Productores de Trigo (Portugal)
FNPT	Fédération Nationale des Planteurs de Tabac
FNPT	Fédération Nationale des Producteurs de Topinambours
FNPT	Fédération Nationale des Producteurs de Truffes
FNPTC	Fédération Nationale des Groupements de Producteurs de Pommes de Terre de Consommation
FNPVCC	Fédération Nationale des Producteurs de Vins de Consommation Courante
FNPVDQS	Fédération Nationale des Producteurs de Qualité Supérieure
FNRC	Food and Nutrition Research Centre (Philippines)
FNRS	Fonds National de la Recherche Scientifique (Belgium)
FNS	Fédération Nationale des Scieries (Belgium)
FNSA	Fédération Nationale Sanitaire Apicole (*now* FNOSAD)
FNSA	Fédération Nationale des Sinistrés Agricoles
FNSA	Fédération Nationale des Syndicats Agricoles (Belgium)
FNSACC	Fédération Nationale des Syndicats Agricoles des Cultivateurs de Champignons
FNSAFER	Fédération Nationale des Sociétés d'Aménagement Foncier et d'Établissement Rural
FNSAGA	Fédération Nationale des Syndicats d'Agents Généraux
FNSBS	Fonda Nacional de Salud y Bienestar Social (Peru)
FNSCC	Fédération Nationale des Sociétés Coopératives de Commerçants
FNSCCF	Fédération Nationale des Syndicats de Confituriers et Conserveurs de Fruits
FNSDPL	Fédération Nationale des Syndicats de Détaillants en Produits Laitiers
FNSEA	Fédération Nationale des Syndicats d'Exploitants Agricoles
FNSECSF	Fédération Nationale des Syndicats d'Éleveurs de Chevaux de Selle Français
FNSELC	Fédération Nationale des Syndicats d'Éleveurs de Lapins de Chair
FNSFPA	Fédération Nationale des Syndicats de Fabricants de Pâtes Alimentaires
FNSHEE	Fédération Nationale des Syndicats d'Herbagers, Emboucheurs et Engraisseurs
FNSI	Federazione Nazionale della Stampa Italiana
FNSIA	Fédération Nationale des Syndicats des Industries de l'Alimentation
FNSIAA	Fédération Nationale des Syndicats des Industries de l'Alimentation Animale
FNSIC	Fédération Nationale des Syndicats d'Ingénieurs et de Cadres
FNSICA	Fédération Nationale des Sociétés d'Intérêt Collectif Agricole
FNSICAE	Fédération Nationale des Sociétés d'Intérêt Collectif Agricole d'Électricité
FNSIL	Fédération Nationale des Syndicats d'Industriels Laitiers

FNSIOT	Fédération Nationale des Syndicats d'Initiative et Offices de Tourisme	**FNUDC**	Fondo de las Naciones Unidas para el Desarrollo de la Capitalización
FNSITC-EOAA	Fédération Nationale des Syndicats d'Ingénieurs, Techniciens, Cadres Administratifs et Employés des Organisations Agricoles de l'Agriculture	**FNUDIO**	Fonds des Nations Unies pour le Développement de l'Irian Occidental
FNSOAI	Fédération Nationale des Syndicats Ouvriers Agricoles Indépendants	**FNUMAB**	Fédération Nationale Unifiée des Maîtres-Artisans du Bâtiment
FNSP	Fédération Nationale des Sapeurs-Pompiers Français	**FNUNF**	Fédération Nationale pour l'Utilisation Naturelle des Fruits
FNSPF	Fédération Nationale des Sociétés Photographiques de France	**FNUPA**	Fédération Nationale des Unions Professionnelles Agricoles (Belgium)
FNSPFS	Fédération Nationale des Syndicats de Propriétaires Forestiers Sylviculteurs	**FNUR**	Fonds des Nations Unies pour les Réfugiés
FNSPP-TCQC	Fédération Nationale des Syndicats des Producteurs de Pommes de Terre de Consommation de Qualité Contrôlée	**FNVPA**	Fonds National de la Vulgarisation et du Progrès Agricoles
FNSPV	Fédération Nationale des Syndicats de Pépiniéristes Viticulteurs	**FNZ**	Koninklijk Nederlandse Zuivelbond
		FOA	U.S. Foreign Operations Administration
FNSSN	Fédération des Sociétés de Sciences Naturelles	**FOAD**	Fédération des Organisations Agricoles Diverses
FNSUTL	Fédération Nationale des Syndicats Utilisateurs et Transformateurs de Lait (now FNSIL)	**FOB**	Federatie van Onderlinge Brandwaarborg-maatschappij in Nederland
FNT	Federación Nacional de Tabacaleros (Colombia)	**FOBB**	Fédération Suisse des Ouvriers sur Bois et du Bâtiment
		FOBFO	Federation of British Fire Organisations
FNTA	Fédération Nationale des Transporteurs Auxiliaires	**FOBID**	Federatie van Organisaties op het Gebied van Bibliotheek-Informatie-, en Dokumentatie-wezen
FNTA	National Federation of Sugar Workers (Cuba)	**FOCAP**	Fédération Odontologique d'Amérique Centrale et du Panama
FNTAF	Fédération Nationale des Travailleurs de l'Agriculture et des Forêts de France et d'Outremer	**FOCOL**	Federation of Coin-Operated Launderettes
FNTAL	Fédération Nationale du Teillage Agricole du Lin	**FOCWA**	Nederlandse Vereniging van Ondernemers in het Carosseriebedrijf
FNTCA	Fédération Nationale des Techniciens et Cadres de l'Agriculture (CGA)	**FOE**	Friends of the Earth (U.S.A.)
FNTDP	Fédération Nationale des Transports de Denrées Périssables et Assimilés	**FOEGIN**	Vereniging voor Fabrieken op Electrotechnisch Gebied in Nederland
FNTM	Federação Nacional dos Trabalhadores Marítimos (Brazil)	**FOESSA**	Fundación Fomento de Estudios Sociales y de Sociología Aplicada
FNTP	Federação Nacional dos Productores de Trigo (Portugal)	**FOEXP**	Export Expansion Group (Brazil)
FNTP	Fédération Nationale des Transformateurs de Papier	**FOFATUSA**	Federation of Free African Trade Unions of South Africa
FNTR	Fédération Nationale des Transports Routiers	**FOFI**	Federazione degli Ordini dei Farmacisti Italiani
		FOFTA	Fédération Odontologique de France et des Territoires Associés
FNUAP	Fonds des Nations Unies pour les Activités en Matière de Population	**FOGA**	Fonds d'Orientation de Garantie Agricole (de la C.E.E.)
		FOGRA	Deutsche Gesellschaft für Forschung im Graphischen Gewerbe
		FOGRA	Forschungsgesellschaft für Druck- und Reproduktiontechnik

FOLA	Federaçion Odontologica Latino-Americana (Argentina)
FOM	Federatie Organisaties in de Machinehandel
FOM	Stichting voor Fundamenteel Onderzoek der Materie
FOMH	Fédération Suisse des Ouvriers sur Métaux et Horlogers
FOMIZ	Federation des Ouvriers des Mines du Zaire
FOMO	Federatie van het Officieel Middelbaar Onderwijs van de Hogere Graad van België
FOMRE	Stichting Fundamenteel Onderzoek der Materie met Röntgen- en Electronenstralen
FONADE	Fondo Nacional para el Desarrollo (Colombia)
FONADER	Fonds National de Développement Rural (Cameroons)
FONAIAP	Fondo National de Investigaciones Agropecuarias (Venezuela)
FONASBA	Federation of National Associations of Ship Brokers and Agents
FONUBEL	Forum Nucléaire Belge
FONUR	Fondo de las Naciones Unidas para los Refugiados
FOPERDA	Père Damien Foundation
FOPRA	Federation of Private Residents Associations
FOPS	Federation of Playgoers Societies
FOPSA	Federation of Productivity Services Associations
FORALAC	Société Forestière Agricole, Industrielle et Commerciale en Afrique Équatoriale
FORATOM	Forum Atomique Européen
FOREAMI	Fonds Reine Elizabeth pour l'Assistance Médicale aux Indigènes (Belgium)
FOREX	International Association of Exchange Dealers
FORMA	Fonds d'Orientation et de Régularisation des Marchés Agricoles
FORPPA	Fondo de Ordenacion y Regulacion de Productos y Precios Agrarios
FORS	Fondation pour la Recherche Sociale
FORTRA	Federation of Radio and Television Retailers Association
FOS	Fisheries Organisation Society
FOS	Foreniging för Orientaliska Studier
FOSKOR	Phosphate Development Corporation (South Africa)
FOSS	Föreningen Ostra Sveriges Skogsarbeten
FOTIM	Fotobranchens Importørforening
FPA	Family Planning Association
FPA	Fédération de la Propriété Agricole
FPA	Film Production Association of Great Britain
FPA	Fire Protection Association
FPA	Foreign Press Association
FPA	Foyers de Progrès Agricole
FPAA	Federación Panamericana de Asociaciones de Arquitectos
FPAI	Family Planning Association of India
FPAP	Family Planning Association of Pakistan
FPBAI	Federation of Publishers' and Booksellers' Association in India
FPC	Federation of Painting Contractors Ltd. (*now* NFPDC)
FPC	Flowers Publicity Council
FPC	Fondation pour la Protection des Consommateurs (Switzerland)
FPC	United States Federal Power Commission
FPCEA	Fibreboard Packing Case Employers Association
FPCMA	Fibreboard Packing Case Manufacturers Association
FPCS	Farm Planning Computer Service
FPDA	Finnish Plywood Development Association
FPE	Fédération Professionnelle des Producteurs et Distributeurs d'Électricité de Belgique
FPF	Finska Pappersingeniörsföreningen
FPGAUS	Federated Pecan Growers Associations of the United States
FPI	Fédération Prohibitionniste Internationale
FPM	Fachverband Pulver-Metallurgie
FPPB	Family Planning and Population Board (Singapore)
FPPE	Fédération du Prêt à Porter Feminin
FPPTE	Federation of Public Passenger Transport Employers
FPRC	Flying Personnel Research Committee
FPRI	Forest Products Research Institute (Ghana, Philippines)
FPRL	Forest Products Research Laboratory
FPRS	Forest Products Research Society (U.S.A.)
FPS	Fauna Preservation Society
FPS	Federation of Personnel Services of Great Britain
FPS	Koninklijke Vereniging 'Het Friesch Paardenstamboek'

FPVPC	Federation of Paint and Varnish Production Clubs (U.S.A.)	**FRMPP**	Fédération Romande des Maîtres Plâtriers-Peintres
FR	Fotohandlarnas Riksförbund	**FRO**	Fire Research Organisation *see* JFRO
FRA	Federación Rural Boliviana	**FROLINAT**	Front de Libération Nationale Tschadienne
FRAME	Fund for the Replacement of Animals in Medical Experiments	**FROLIZI**	Front for the Liberation of Zimbabwe
FRANA	Groupement des Fabricants et Représentants des Adjuvants en Nutrition Animale (Belgium)	**FRP**	Fédération Romande de Publicité (Switzerland)
		FRR	Foreningen af Registrerede Revisorer
FRAP	Frente de Acción Popular (Chile)	**FRS**	Federal Reserve System (U.S.A.)
FRB	Federal Reserve Board (U.S.A.)	**FRS**	Fruit Research Station (DSIR) (N.Z.)
FRB	Fédération Routière Belge	**FRS**	Schweizerischer Strassenverkehrsverband
FRB	Fisheries Research Board of Canada	**FRSEB**	Fédération Régionale des Syndicats des Éleveurs de Brebis
FRB	Frente de la Revolución Boliviana		
FRC	File Research Council	**FRSKGD**	Fauna Research Section of the Kenya Game Department
FRD	Fédération Romande des Détaillants	**FRUBO**	Nederlandse Bond van Grossiers in Zuidvruchten
FRD	Forbrugerrådet		
FRE	Fédération Romande des Écoles de Conduite	**FRUCOM**	Fédération Européenne des Importateurs de Fruits Secs, Conserves, Épices et Miels
FREC	Forestry Research and Education Centre (Sudan)	**FRV**	Fédération Romande des Vignerons (Switzerland)
FRED	Fund for Rural Economic Development (Canada)	**FRV**	Félag Rådgjafarverkfroedinga
FREJULI	Frente Justicialista do Liberacion (Argentina)	**FRW**	Federation of Rural Workers
FRELIMO	Mozambique Liberation Front	**FS**	Fachverband für Strahlenschutz (Switzerland)
FRG	Federal Republic of Germany		
FRH	Fédération pour le Respect de l'Homme et de l'Humanité	**FS**	Forest Service (U.S.A.)
FRHB	Federation of Registered House-builders	**FSA**	Farm Security Administration (U.S.A.)
FRI	Fédération Romande Immobilière (Switzerland)	**FSA**	Fédération Suisse des Avocats
		FSA	Federazione Svizzera degli Avvocati
FRI	Food Research Institute (U.S.A.)	**FSA**	Föreningen Sveriges Arbetsterapeuter
FRI	Foreningen af Rådgivende Ingeniører	**FSAA**	Family Service Association of America
FRI	Forest Research Institute (India)	**FSAC**	Folia Scientifica Africae Centralis
FRIA	Compagnie Internationale pour la Fabrication de l'Aluminium (Africa)	**FSAD**	Foreningen af Sygehusadministratores i Danmark
FRICO	Friesche Coöperatieve Zuivel-Export Vereniging	**FSAI**	Fédération Suisse des Architectes Indépendants
FRIDA	Fund for Research and Investment for the Development of Africa Ltd (U.K.)	**FSASR**	Fédération des Sociétés d'Agriculture de la Suisse Romande
FRISA	Fuel Research Institute of South Africa	**FSAV**	Fédération Suisse des Agences de Voyages
FRITALUX	Union Économique France, Italie, Benelux	**FSB**	Fachverband Schweizerischer Betonvorfabrikanten
FRL	Fisheries Research Laboratory Marine Department (N.Z.)		
FRM	Fédération Romande des Maîtres Marbriers	**FSB**	Fédération Spéléologique de Belgique
FRM	Fédération Romande des Maîtres Menuisiers Ébenistes, Fabricants de Meubles, Charpentiers et Parqueteurs (Switzerland)	**FSC**	Fédération Suisse des Consommateurs
		FSCC	Federal Surplus Commodities Corporation (U.S.A.)

FSCRH	Fédération Suisse des Cafetiers, Restaurateurs et Hôteliers	**FSP**	Popular Socialist Front (Portugal)
FSE	Fédération des Sociétés Suisses d'Employés	**FSPD**	Fachverband Schweizerischer Privat-Detektive
FSE	Fonds Social Européen	**FSPSP**	Fédération Suisse du Personnel des Services Publics
FSF	Fédération Suisse du Franchising	**FSR**	Foreningen af Statsautoriserede Revisorer
FSF	Federazione Svissera dei Fisioterapisti Diplomati	**FSRA**	Federal Sewage Research Association (U.S.A.)
FSF	Finlands Sjuksköterskeförbund	**FSRP**	Forum Suisse des Relations Publiques
FSF	Flight Safety Foundation (U.S.A.)	**FSS**	Fédération Suisse des Sélectionneurs
FSFA	Federation of Specialised Film Associations	**FSS**	Föreningen Sveriges Skrivmaterielleveran-törer
FSFF	Finlands Svenska Författareföreningen		
FSFRL	Far Seas Fisheries Research Laboratory	**FSSA**	Fertilizer Society of South Africa
FSG	Föreningen Svenska Glasstillverkare	**FST**	Federatie Steen-, Cement-, Glas- en Keramische Industrie
FSGD	Federation of Sports Goods Distributors		
FSI	Fachverband Schneidwarenindustrie	**FSTAL**	Fédération Syndicale du Teillage Agricole du Lin
FSI	Fédération Spirite Internationale		
FSI	Föreningen Sveriges Industrifornonodenhets-leverantörer	**FSTL**	Föreningen Svenska Tradgärds- och Land-skapsarkitekter
FSI	International Society of Fire Service In-structors	**FSUEO**	Fédération des Syndicats Unis des Employés et Ouvriers du Liban
FSK	Fachverband Schaumkunstoffe im GKV	**FSWA**	Federation of Sewage Works Associations (U.S.A.)
FSK	Finlands Svenska Kommunförbund		
FSK	Finlands Svenska Köpmannaförbund	**FSWU**	Federation of Sudanese Workers Unions
FSK	Schweizerischer Fachverband für Sand und Kies	**FTA**	Federation of Trade Associations
		FTA	Fördergesellschaft Technischer Ausbus
FSLJ	Föreningen Skogs- och Lantbruksjournalister	**FTA**	Freight Trade Associations Ltd
FSLTT	Fédération des Syndicats Libres des Travailleurs de la Terre	**FTC**	Federal Trade Commission (U.S.A.)
		FTESA	Foundry Trades Equipment and Supplies Association
FSM	Fédération Sephardite Mondiale		
FSM	Fédération Syndicale Mondiale	**FTF**	Fibre Trade Federation
FSMG	Vereniging van Fabrikanten van Stempels, Matrijzen, Mallen en Andere Speciale Gereedschappen	**FTG**	Forschungsgemeinschaft für Technisches Glas
		FTGB	Federatie Textiel Groothandelsbonden
FSMGB	Federation of Small Mines of Great Britain	**FTMA**	Federated Textile Managers Associations
FSMT	Fédération Suisse des Marchands de Tabacs	**FTO**	Fruit Traffic Organisation
FSN	Fachverband Schweizerischer Neonfirmen	**FTPR**	Federación del Trabajo de Puerto Rico
FSN	Federatie van Schoenwinkeliersverenigingen	**FTPS**	Food Trades Protection Society
FSNRIC	Federation Syndicate Nationale de la Répre-sentation Commerciale	**FTS**	Fédération Internationale de Sauvetage
		FTSKO	Federation of Textile Societies and Kindred Organisations
FSNT	Federazione Svizzera dei Negozianti in Tabacchi	**FTU**	Federation of Trade Unions (Hong Kong)
FSP	Fédération Suisse des Physiothérapeutes	**FTUN**	Federación de Transportadores Unidos Nicaraguense
FSP	Foreningen Sveriges Plastfabrikanter		
FSP	Foundation for the Peoples of the South Pacific	**FUAAV**	Fédération Universelle des Associations d'Agencies de Voyages

FUACE	Fédération Universelle des Associations Chrétiennes d'Étudiants
FUCUA	Federation of University Conservative and Unionist Associations
FUDECO	Fundación para el Desarrollo de la Región Centro-Occidental de Venezuela
FUE	Federated Union of Employers (Eire)
FUEN	Federal Union of European Nationalities
FUEV	Föderalistische Union Europäischer Volksgruppen
FUGB	Federation of Ukrainians in Great Britain
FULREAC	Fondation de l'Université de Liège pour les Recherches Scientifiques en Afrique Centrale
FUMOA	Société des Fûts Métalliques de l'Ouest Africain
FUNBEG	Brazilian Foundation for the Development of Science Teaching
FUND	International Monetary Fund
FUNDA-COMUN	Fundación para el Desarrollo de la Comunidad
FUNDAR	Fundación para el Desarrollo Regional
FUNDWI	Fund of the United Nations for the Development of West Irian
FUNK	Front Uni National du Kampuchea (Cambodia)
FUNU	Force d'Urgence des Nations Unies
FUPAC	Federación de Universidades Privadas de America Central (Guatemala)
FUPADE	Fundación Panamericana de Desarrollo (U.S.A.)
FURC	Fonds pour l'Utilisation Rationelle des Combustibles
FUS	Fruit-Union Suisse
FUW	Farmers Union of Wales
FVAV	Fédération Vaudoise des Sociétés d'Agriculture et de Viticulture (Switzerland)
FVB	Fabrikanten-Verband für Beleuchtungskörper
FVCQFRA	Fruit and Vegetable Canning and Quick Freezing Research Association (U.K.) (now FVPRA)
FVG	Fachverband für das Güterbeförderungsgewerbe Österreiche
FVH	Föreningen för Vattenhygien
FVK	Landelijke Vereniging van Kaashandelaren
FVL	Fachverband Lichtwerbung

FVM	Föreningen Svenska Verktygmaskintillverkare
FVNH	Federatief Verbond Nederlandse Houtindustrie
FVPRA	Fruit and Vegetable Preservation Research Association (formerly FVCQFRA)
FVR	Federal Department of Veterinary Research (Nigeria)
FVTDV	Groep der Fabrikanten en Vertegenwoordigers van Toevoegingsmiddelen voor de Dierlijke Voeding
FWA	Farmers and World Affairs (U.S.A.)
FWCC	Friends World Committee for Consultation
FWEA	International Federation of Workers Educational Associations
FWHF	Federation of World Health Foundations
FWID	Federation of Wholesale and Industrial Distributors
FWMB	Federation of Wholesale and Multiple Bakers (now FB)
FWO	Federation of Wholesale Organisations (now FWID)
FWPCA	Federal Water Pollution Control Administration (U.S.A.)
FWQA	Federal Water Quality Administration (later WQO of EPA) (U.S.A.)
FWRMGB	Federation of Wire Rope Manufacturers of Great Britain
FYDEP	Empresa Nacional de Fomento y Desarrollo Económico del Petén (Guatemala)
FYF	Finlands Yrkeskvinnors Förbund
FZD	Finanz- und Zolldepartement (Switzerland)
FZG	Federation of Zoological Societies of Great Britain and Northern Ireland
FZLE	Federatie der Zelfstandige Landmeters-Experten (Belgium)
FZY	Federation of Zionist Youth

G

GA	General Assembly of the United Nations
GA	Gemmological Association
GA	Geographical Association

GA	Grafiska Arbetsgivareförbundet	**GAMM**	Gesellschaft f. Angewandt Mathematik und Mechanik
GA	Gypsum Association (U.S.A.)		
GAAM	Ghana Association for the Advancement of Management	**GAMS**	Groupement pour l'Avancement des Méthodes Spectroscopiques et Physicochimiques d'Analyse
GABA	Nederlandse Vereniging van Bedrijven in de Gemengde Branche (Glas, Aardewerk en Bijbehorende Artikelen)	**GAMTA**	General Aviation Manufacturers and Traders Association
GABIM	La Gabonaise Immobilière	**GANEFO**	Federation of the Games of the New Emerging Forces (Indonesia)
GABOA	Société Gabonaise d'Oxygène et d'Acétylène	**GANVAM**	Grupo Autonomo Nacional de Vendedores de Automobiles, Camiones y Motorcicletas del Sindicato Nacional del Metal
GABOMA	Société Gabonaise des Grands Magasins		
GABONAP	Société Gabonaise de Diffusion d'Appareils Électriques	**GAPAN**	Guild of Air Pilots and Navigators
GABONEX	Société Gabonaise d'Exploitation Vinicole	**GAPAVE**	Groupement des Associations de Propriétaires d'Appareils à Vapeur et Électriques
GACIFAL	Groupe Consultatif de la Recherche et de l'Enseignement Forestier pour l'Amérique Latine		
		GAPINDO	Perkumpulan Koperasi Gabungan Pembelian Importir Indonesia
GAD	Groupe Africaine de Distribution	**GAPMB**	Ghana Agricultural Produce Marketing Board
GAD	Groupe d'Aide au Développement		
GADEF	Groupement des Associations Dentaires Francophones	**GARB**	Garment and Allied Industries Requirements Board
GAE	Groupements Agricoles d'Exploitation	**GARP**	Global Atmospheric Research Programme (Switzerland)
GAEC	Groupements Agricoles d'Exploitation en Commun		
GAF	Glasmästeribranchens Arbetsgivareförbund	**GAS**	General Aviation Services (Canada)
GAF	Gulvbeloegningsbranchens Arbejdsgiverforening	**GAS**	Group Autonomous Specialised Working Party (*of* CCITT)
GAFICA	Grupo Asesor de la FAO para la Integración Económica Centroamericana (Guatemala)	**GASC**	German-American Securities Corporation
		GASGA	Group for Assistance on Storage of Grains in Africa
GAFTA	Grain and Feed Trade Association		
GAGB	Gemmological Association of Great Britain	**GAT**	Groupement Africain des Travaux au Cameroun
GAI	Guild of Architectural Ironmongers		
GAIF	General Arab Insurance Federation (Egypt)	**GATA**	Glass and Allied Trades Association
GAIF	General Assembly of International Sports Federations	**GATCO**	Guild of Air Traffic Control Officers
		GATR-AMAR	Société Gabonaise de Transports Maritimes
GAILL	Groupement des Allergologistes et Immunologistes de Langues Latines		
GAJ	Guild of Agricultural Journalists	**GATT**	General Agreement on Tariffs and Trade (Switzerland)
GALA	Grupo de Acústicos Latinoamericanos	**GAUFCC**	General Assembly of Unitarian and Free Christian Churches
GALF	Groupement des Acousticiens de Langue Française		
GALIAF	Société Gaz Liquéfiés d'Afrique	**GAUK**	Gamekeepers Association of the United Kingdom
GAM	Groupement des Aciers Moulés (Belgium)	**GAV**	Gemeinschaftsausschuss Verzinken
GAMA	Guitar and Accessory Manufacturers Association of America	**GAWI**	Gesellschaft für Abwicklung Wirtschaftlicher Angelegenheiten
GAMI	Groupement pour l'Avancement de la Mécanique Industrielle	**GAZ-EUROUD**	Comité Européen des Fabricants d'Appareils et de Machines de Soudage aux Gaz

GBAEV	Gesellschaft für Biologische Anthropologie, Eugenik und Verhaltenforschung
GBARC	Great Britain Aeronautical Research Committee
GBDL	Gesellschaft für Bibliothekswesen und Dokumentation des Landbaues
GBDO	Guild of British Dispensing Opticians
GBF	Grafiske Bedrifters Felleskontor
GBI	Gesamtverband Besteckindustrie
GBNE	Guild of British Newspaper Editors
GBO	Groepering van de Vloer- en Muurbekledingsondernemigen (Belgium)
GBO	Groupement Belge des Omnipraticiens
GBRS	Groupe Belge de Recherche Sous-Marine
GBS	Groupement des Unions Professionnelles Belges de Médecins
GCA	Groep Fabrieken van Apparaten voor de Chemische Industrie
GCB	Greyhound Consultative Body
GCBA	Guernsey Cattle Breeders' Association
GCBS	General Council of British Shipping
GCDP	Grupo Coordinador do Desenvolvimento da Pesca (Brazil)
GCDRA	Green Crop Driers Research Association
GCE-CEE	Groupement des Caisses d'Épargne de la CEE
GCFI	Gulf and Caribbean Fisheries Institute
GCHQ	Government Communications Headquarters
GCI	Génie Climatique International
GCIAI	Grupo Consultivo sobre Investigación Agricola International (FAO etc.)
GCIC	Groupement Cinématographique International de Conciliation
GCPAI	Groupe Consultatif de la Production Alimentaire et de Investissement (FAO)
GCPAIA	Grupo Consultivo sobre Producción Alimentaria e Inversiones Agrícolas (FAO)
GCRAI	Groupe Consultatif de la Recherche Agricole Internationale (FAO etc.)
GCRI	Glasshouse Crops Research Institute
GCRO	General Council and Registrar of Osteopaths
GCS	Game Conservation Society (U.S.A.)
GCT	Groupe Consultatif Technique (UNO)
GCW	Gesellschaft der Chirurgen in Wien (Austria)
GDAPS	Grémio dos Armadores da Pesca da Sardinha (Portugal)
GdB	Gesellschaft des Bauwesens
GDBA	Genossenschaft Deutscher Bühnen-Angehörigen
GDBH	Gesellschaft Deutscher Berg- und Hüttenleute
GDCh	Gesellschaft Deutscher Chemiker
GDDA	General Desert Development Authority (Egypt)
GDE	Gemeinschaft Deutscher Einkaufskontore des Nahrungsmittelgrosshandels
GDF	Gaz de France
GDG	Gemeinschaft Deutscher Gross-Messen
GDL	Gemeinschaft Deutscher Lehrerverbände
GDL	Gesamtverband des Deutschen Leder-Gross- und -Aussenhandels
GDM	Gesamtverband Deutscher Metallgiessereien
GDM	Gesamtverband Deutscher Musikfachgeschäfte
GDMB	Gesellschaft Deutscher Metallhütten- und Bergleute
GDNÄ	Gesellschaft Deutscher Naturforscher und Arzte
GDO	Gesellschaft der Orgelfreunde
GDPF	Groupement des Directeurs Publicitaires de France
GDR	German Democratic Republic
GDS	Gesamtverband Deutscher Spielwaren-exporteure
GDSI	Global Development Studies Institute (U.S.A.)
GEA	Ghana Employers Association
GEA	Global Education Associates (U.S.A.)
GEAE	Groupement Européen des Ardennes et de l'Eifel
GEAMR	Groupement Européen des Associations des Maisons de Réforme
GEB	General Education Board (U.S.A.)
GEBCO	General Bathymetric Chart of the Oceans
GEBECOMA	Groupement Belge des Constructeurs de Matériel Aérospatial
GEBO	Golventreprenörernas Branschorganisation
GEBRAM	Gespreksgroep Fabrikanten van Brand-weervoertuigen, -Apparaten en-Material
GEC	General Electric Company, Ltd
GECA	Groupe Européen de Chimiothérapie Anticancéreuse

GECA	Groupement National d'Exploitation des Conserves Agricoles (France)
GECICAM	Entreprise de Génie Civil et Construction au Cameroun
GECITEX	Groupement Européen de Coordination d'Industries Textiles Diverses (France)
GECOMIN	General Congolese Ore Company
GECUS	Groupe d'Études et de Coordination de l'Urbanisme Souterrain
GEDAG	Gesamtverband Deutscher Angestellten-Gewerkschaften
GEDIP	Grupo Executivo do Desenvolimento da Industria de Pesca
GEDRT	Groupe Européen d'Échange d'Experience sur la Direction de la Recherche Textile
GEEDA	Groundnut Extractions Export Development Association (India)
GEER	Groupement d'Étude pour l'Équipement Rural
GEERS	Groupe d'Études Européen des Recherches Spatiales
GEFACS	Groupement des Fabricants d'Appareils Sanitaires en Céramique de la CEE
GEFAP	Groupement Européen des Associations Nationales de Fabricants de Pesticides
GEFCO	Griqualand Exploration and Finance Company
GEFIU	Gesellschaft für Finanzwirtschaft in der Unternehmensführung
GEIA	Executive Group for the Automotive Industry (Brazil)
GELNA	Groupe d'Études sur la Littérature Néo-Africaine
GELTSPAP	Group of Experts on Long-Term Scientific Policy and Planning (UNESCO)
GEMAS	Groupement Européen des Maisons d'Alimentation et d'Approvisionnement à Succursales
GEMEC	Grupo de Estudio para el Mejoramiento de la Ensenanza de las Ciencias en Honduras
GEMP	Groupe d'Études et de Mesures de la Productivité (*of* AFAP)
GEMS	Gilevi Exploration and Mining Syndicate (Tanzania)
GEN	Group of European Nutritionists (Switzerland)
GENCO	Société Générale de Construction au Cameroun
GENECO	Genootschap van Nederlandse Componisten
GENEMA	Groupement d'Exportation des Navires et Engins de Mer et Acier
GENICIAT	Genie Civil en Afrique Tropicale (Ivory Coast)
GEOAR	General Egyptian Organization for Aquatic Resources
GEOBOL	Servicio Geológico de Bolivia
GEP	Groupement Intersyndical pour l'Equipement des Industries du Pétrole, du Gaz Naturel et de la Pétrochimie
GEPA	Gulf-European Freight Association (U.S.A.)
GEPHA	Bundesverband des Genossenschaftlichen Pharmazeutischen Grosshandels in Deutschland
GEPLACEA	Grupo de los Paises Latinoamericanos y del Caribe Exportadores del Azucar
GEPLASE	Grupo de Estudos para o Plantio da Seringueira (Brazil)
GEPS	Groupe d'Études des Protéines de Soja
GER	Group of European Radiotherapists
GER	Groupement des Entreprises de Revêtements de Sols et Murs (Belgium)
GERCA	Grupo Executivo de Racionalizaçao da Cafeicultura (Brazil)
GERDAT	Groupement d'Études et de Recherches pour le Développement de l'Agronomie Tropicale
GERDEC	Groupe d'Études et de Recherches pour le Développement Culturel
GERDES	Groupe d'Études et de Recherches pour le Développement des Sciences Sociales
GEREC	Groupement pour l'Étude et la Réalisation d'Ensembles Contrôle-Commande
GERIP	Groupe d'Études et de Recherches des Infirmiers Psychiatriques
GERSPPA	Group d'Études et de Recherches pour les Solutions aux Problèmes des Personnes Âgées
GES	Gesellschaft für Electronische Systemforschung
GESAMP	Joint Group of Experts on the Scientific Aspects of Marine Pollution
GESEM	Groupement Européen des Sources d'Eaux Minérales Naturelles
GEVES	Groupe d'Étude et de Contrôle des Variétés et des Semences
GEVL	Groupement International d'Étude pour l'Exploitation des Voitures-Lits en Europe
GEW	Gewerkschaft Erziehung und Wissenschaft

GEWINA	Genootschap voor Geschiedenis der Geneeskunde, Wiskunde, Natuurwetenschappen en Techniek
GfA	Gesellschaft für Arzneipflanzenforschung
GFA	Groupement Foncier Africain
GFA	Groupement Français d'Assurances
GFB	Gemeinschaft Fachärztlicher Berufsverbände
GFB	Schweizerische Gesellschaft für Bauforschung
GFC	Groep Fabrikanten van Compressoren
GFCI	Groupement Foncier de la Côte-d'Ivoire
GFCM	General Fisheries Council for the Mediterranean (FAO)
GFDNA	Grain and Feed Dealers National Association (U.S.A.)
GfdS	Gesellschaft für Deutsche Sprache
GFF	Gesellschaft zur Förderung der Forschung (Switzerland)
GFFC	Groupement Français des Fabricants de Carton
GFI	Glas Forsknings Institutet
GfK	Gesellschaft für Kernforschung
GfK	Gesellschaft für Konsum-, Markt- und Absatzforschung
GFM	Gesellschaft f. Marktforschung
GFM	Schweizerische Gesellschaft für Marktforschung
GFP	Gesellschaft zur Förderung der Photographie
GFPE	Gesellschaft für Praktische Energiekunde
GFPF	Gesellschaft zur Förderung Pädagogischer Forschung
GFSAEPCS	Groupement Fédératif des Syndicats et Associations d'Éleveurs et Propriétaires de Chevaux de Sang
GFTU	General Federation of Trade Unions
GFU	Gemeinschaft Freier Unternahmensberater
GfW	Gesellschaft für Wehrkunde
GFWC	General Federation of Womens Clubs
GFZFF	Gesellschaft zur Förderung von Zukunfts- und Friedensforschung
GGB	Gesellschaft für die Geschichte und Bibliographie des Brauwesens
GGC	Groupe Spécialisé du Génie Chimique (Switzerland)
GGPO	Gesellschaft f. d. Geschichte des Protestantismus in Österreich
GGRA	Gelatine and Glue Research Association (*now merged with* BFMIRA)
GGW	Groep Gereedschapswerktuigen van de Vereniging van Metaalindustrieën
GHA	Gartneriets og Hagebrukets Arbeidsgiverforening
GhLM	Ghaqda Letteraja Maltija
GHM	Groep Houtbewerkingsmachines
GHP	Groep Fabrikanten van Hydraulische et Pneumatische
GI	Gesellschaft für Informatik
GI	Gideons International (U.S.A.)
GIA	Gemmological Institute of America
GIA	Groupement Ivoirien d'Assurances
GIAC	Groupement des Industries Agricoles, Alimentaires et de Grande Consommation
GIAM	Conference on Global Impacts of Applied Microbiology
GIANA	Groupement International des Analystes de l'Alimentation
GIAP	State Institute for the Nitrogen Industry (U.S.S.R.)
GIASTA	Groupement International pour l'Avancement des Sciences et Techniques Alimentaires
GIAT	Groupement d'Industries Atomiques
GIBAIR	Gibraltar Airways Ltd
GIC	Glass Industry Club (Belgium)
GIC	Guilde Internationale des Cöopératrices
GICAM	Groupement Interprofessionnel pour l'Étude et le Coordination des Intérêts Économiques du Cameroun
GICRD	Groupe International de Coopération et de Recherche en Documentation
GIDA	Groupement Interprofessionel des Entreprises du Dahomey
GIDAVI	Groupement Interprofessionnel pour la Défense et l'Amélioration des Vins de Consommation Courante
GIDNT	Glówny Instytut Dokumentacji Naukowo-Technicznej
GIDOTOM	Groupement Interprofessionnel pour le Développement de la Product des Oléagineux dans les Territoires d'Outre-Mer
GIF	Grafiska Industriförbundet
GIFAM	Groupement des Industries Françaises des Appareils d'Équipement Ménager
GIFAP	Groupement International des Associations Nationales de Fabricants de Pesticides

GIFAS	Groupement des Industries Françaises Aéronautiques et Spatiales
GIFCO	Gruppo Italiano Fabbricanti Cartone Ondulato
GIFPA	Groupement Interprofessionnel des Fleurs et Plantes Aromatiques
GIIGNL	Groupe International des Importateurs de Gaz Naturel Liquéfié
GIIN	Groupe Intersyndical de l'Industrie Nucléaire
GIIP	Groupement International de l'Industrie Pharmaceutique des Pays de la Communauté Économique Européenne
GILS	Grémio dos Industriais de Lanifícios do Sul (Portugal)
GIM	Gruppe Internationale Möbelspediteure
GIMCI	Groupement des Industries de la Métallurgie en Côte-d'Ivoire
GIMEE	Groupement Syndical des Industries de Matériels d'Équipement Électrique
GIMMOM	Groupement des Industries Minières et Métallurgiques d'Outre-Mer
GIMPA	Ghana Institute of Management and Public Administration
GIMRADA	U.S. Army Geodesy, Intelligence and Mapping Research and Development Agency
GINA	Gaufretterie Industrielle Africaine
GINTEX	Groupement International des Comités Nationaux de l'Étiquetage pour l'Entretien des Textiles
GIOM	Groupement Interprofessionnel des Oléagineux Métropolitains
GIPCEL	Groupement des Industries du Polyurethane Cellulaire
GIPEC	Groupe d'Études International pour Utilizations de Profils Creux dans la Construction (Switzerland)
GIPFA	Groupement Interprofessionnel des Plantes à Parfum et Aromatiques
GIPME	Global Investigation of Pollution in the Marine Environment (FAO)
GIPP	Gremio dos Industriais de Panificação do Porto
GIQOM	Groupement Intersyndical de la Quincaillerie, de l'Outillage et du Ménage
GIRA	Groupement de l'Industrie de la Radio et de l'Électricité (Belgium)
GIRCA	Groupement Interprofessionnel pour l'Étude et de Développement de l'Économie Centrafricaine
GIRCETAPE	Groupement Interrégional des Centres d'Études Techniques Agricoles pour les Problèmes d'Entreprise
GIREP	Group International pour la Recherche sur l'Enseignement des Sciences Physiques
GIRGV	Groupe International des Ressources Génétiques Végétales
GIRP	Groupement International de la Répartition Pharmaceutique des Pays de la Communauté Européenne
GIRPIA	Groupements Interprofessionnels de Répartition des Produits Indispensables à l'Agriculture
GIRS	Groupement International pour la Recherche Scientifique en Stomatologie
GISA	Vereniging van Groothandelaren in Sanitaire Artikelen
GISECA	Groupement Ivoirien des Sociétés d'Exportation et Coopératives Agricoles
GISL	Groupement des Industries Sidérurgiques Luxembourgeoises
GISRA	Guyana Institute for Social Research and Action
GITA	Grémio dos Industriais de Transportes em Automóveis (Portugal)
GITB	Gas Industry Training Board
GITCE	Gecaga Institute of Tropical Comparative Endocrinology (Kenya)
GITO	Groupement Interprofessionnel des Entreprises du Togo
GIU	General Importers' Union (Malta)
GKC	Gesellschaft Deutscher Kosmetik-Chemiker
GKE	Geodéziai és Kartográfiai Egyesület
GKF	Beroepsvereniging van Interieurarchitecten
GKN	Gemeenschappelijke Kerneenergiecentrale in Nederland
GKSS	Gesellschaft für Kernenergieverwertung in Schiffbau und Schiffahrt
GKT	Groep Kranen en Transportinrichtingen (Netherlands)
GKV	Gesamtverband Kunststoffverarbeitende Industrie
GL	Glassmestrenes Landsforening
GLC	Greater London Council
GLECS	Groupe Linguistique d'Études Chamito-sémitiques
GLFC	Great Lakes Fishery Commission (U.S.A.)
GLINT	Gospel Literature International

GLM	Gesellschaft für Lehr- und Lernmethoden (Switzerland)
GLP-AACR	Gibraltar Labour Party and Association for the Advancement of Civil Rights
GLSM	Gruppen Luftteknik inom Sveriges Mekanförbund
GLV	Graphische Lehr- und Versuchsanstalt (Austria)
GMA	Greek Management Association
GMAA	Gold Mining Association of America
GMBA	Gibraltar Master Bakers' Association
GMBS	Verband Schweizerischer Grossisten der Mercerie, Bonneterie und Strickgarne
GMC	General Medical Council
GMD	Gesellschaft für Mathematik und Datenverarbeitung
GMEA	Groupement Médicale d'Études sur l'Alcoolisme
GMI	Grupo Mudanzas Internationales
GMITPM	Gorgas Memorial Institute of Tropical and Preventive Medicine (U.S.A.)
GMSC	General Medical Services Council
GMT	Société Générale des Moulins du Togo
GMV	Groep Fabrieken van Machines voor de Voedings- en Genotmiddelenindustrie
GMWU	National Union of General and Municipal Workers
GNA	Groupement National d'Achat
GNAPO	Groupement National d'Achat des Produits Oléagineux
GNAPRCAR	Groupement National des Associations Professionnelles Régionales des Commissionnaires Affrêteurs-Routiers
GNAS	Grand National Archery Society
GNAVT	Grémio Nacional das Agências de Viajens e Turismo
GNB	Groupement National Bulbicole
GNCB	Groupement National du Cuir Brut (Belgium)
GNEL	Grémio Nacional des Editores e Livreiros (Portugal)
GNEPLC	Groupement National des Éleveurs Professionnels de Lapins de Chair
GNERFEA	Groupement National des Éleveurs "Reine de France" et Essaims d'Abeilles
GNESLRP	Groupement National Éleveurs Selectionneurs de Lapins de Race Pure
GNET	Gremio Nacional dos Exportadores de Têxteis
GNF	Grémio Nacional das Farmácias (Portugal)
GNIAA	Groupement National des Industries de l'Alimentation Animale
GNIBC	Groupement National Interprofessionnel de la Betterave, de la Canne et des Industries Productrices de Sucre et d'Alcool
GNIC	Grémio Nacional dos Industriais de Calçado (Portugal)
GNICTMP	Grémio Nacional dos Industriais de Composição e Transformação de Matérias Plásticas (Portugal)
GNIFC	Groupement National Interprofessionnel des Fruits à Cidre
GNIJR	Groupement National Interprofessionnel des Jus de Raisins et Dérivés
GNIL	Groupement National Interprofessionnel Linier
GNIMFVA	Grémio Nacional dos Industriais de Montagem e Fabricação de Veículos Automóveis (Portugal)
GNIN	Groupement National des Importateurs et du Négoce de Laine (Belgium)
GNIPTIT	Groupement National Interprofessionnel de la Pomme de Terre Industrielle et des Industries de Transformation
GNIS	Groupement National Interprofessionnel de Production et d'Utilisation des Semences Graines et Plantes
GNIT	Gremio Nacional dos Industriais de Tomate
GNIT	Groupement National Interprofessionnel du Topinambour
GNITC	Groupement National de l'Industrie de la Terre Cuite (Belgium)
GNOE	Groupement du Nursing de l'Ouest Européen (Belgium)
GNTC	Ghana National Trading Corporation
GNV	Gesellschaft für Nukleare Verfahrenstechnik
GODB	Gal Oya Development Board (Sri Lanka)
GOETO	Grand Order of European Tour Organizers (France)
GOGECA	Comité Générale de la Coopération Agricole de la CEE
GOMAC	Groupement des Opticiens du Marché Commun
GOMP	Groupement Outre-Mer Pharmaceutique (Ivory Coast)

GOPR	Groupement pour l'Opération de Productivité Rizicole (Madagascar)	**GRAIN-UNION**	Société Commerciale de l'Union Générale des Coopératives Agricoles de Céréales
GOSPLAN	Central Planning Agency of the Union of Soviet Socialist Republics	**GRAM-ACOP**	Grain Marketing Cooperative of the Philippines
GOVPF	Groupement Obligatoire des Viticulteurs et Producteurs de Fruits (Tunisia)	**GRAO**	Group Régional de l'Afrique de l'Ouest
GPA	Groupement de Pharmaciens d'Afrique	**GRAPO**	First of October Anti-Fascist Revolutionary Group (Spain)
GPA	Groupement de Productivité Agricole	**GRB**	Gas Research Board
GPB	Groupement Professionnel des Bitumes	**GRCA**	Glassfibre Reinforcements Cement Association
GPBN	Groupement Pharmaceutique Benin-Niger		
GPC	Groupe Spécialisé des Ponts et Charpentes (Switzerland)	**GRCETA**	Groupement Régional de Centre d'Études Techniques Agricoles
GPC	Groupements de Producteurs de Ciment (Belgium)	**GRD**	Groupe des Ressources pour le Développement (UNDP)
GPDA	Gypsum Plasterboard Development Association	**GRDP**	Groupement National des Transporteurs Routiers de Denrées et Produits Périssables
GPDA	Gypsum Products Development Association	**GREM**	Groupement Romand pour l'Étude du Marché et du Marketing (Switzerland)
GPE	Guided Projectile Establishment		
GPECC	Groupement Professionnel des Exportateurs de Café et de Cacao (Ivory Coast)	**GREMA-DEIRAS**	Grémio dos Exportadores de Madeiras (Portugal)
GPEI	Gabungan Perusahaan Ekspor Indonesia	**GREPR**	Groupe de Recherches et d'Études pour la Promotion Rurale
GPIN	Groupement Professionnel de l'Industrie Nucléaire (Belgium)	**GRF**	Graphic Reproduction Federation
GPLS	Groupement Professionnel des Commercants et Industriels Libanais du Sénégal	**GRF**	Grassland Research Foundation (U.S.A.)
		GRG	Groupe Spécialisé des Ingénieurs du Génie Rural et Géomètres (Switzerland)
GPMA	Grocery Products Manufacturers Association (Canada)	**GRG**	International Committee on General Relativity and Gravitation
GPO	Association Générale des Producteurs d'Oléagineux	**GRI**	Grassland Research Institute
GPO-PIA	Government Printing Office and Printing Industry of America	**GRI**	Groupe de Recherches Ionosphériques
		GROFOR	Deutscher Verband des Grosshandels mit Oelen, Fetten und Oelrohstoffen
GPPEPA	Groupement des Producteurs de la Prune d'Ente et du Pruneau d'Agen	**GRONTMIJ**	Grondverbetering- en Ontiginningsmaat-schappij (Netherlands)
GPRA	Algerian Provisional Government	**GROPACA**	Chambre Syndicale des Grossistes en Papiers et Cartons pour Écriture et Impression (Belgium)
GPRA	Gesellschaft Public Relations Agenturen		
GPRMC	Groupement des Plastiques Renforcés du Marché Commun	**GROPO**	Nederlandse Vereniging voor de Binnenlandse Groothandel in Pootaardappelen
GPV	Gesellschaft Pro Vindonissa (Switzerland)		
GPV	Groep Fabrieken van Pompen voor Vloeistoffen	**GROUP-AROMA**	Syndicat National des Fabricants et Importateurs d'Huiles Essentielles et Produits Aromatiques Naturels
GPV	Schweizerischer Glas- und Prozellanhandels-Verband	**GROUP-ISOL**	Group of Producers of Mineral Insulating Material for Electrotechnical Use (of EEC)
GR	Génie Rurale (Direction du)	**GRPA**	Guyana Rice Producers Association
GRA	Game Research Association	**GRTU**	General Retailers and Traders Union (Malta)
GRAE	Gouvernement Révolutionnaise de l'Angola en Exil	**GRUNK**	Cambodian National Union Government

GRUR	Deutsche Vereinigung für Gewerblichen Rechtsschutz und Urheberrecht
GS	Glassbransjens Servicekontor
GSA	Genetics Society of America
GSA	Geological Society of America
GSA	Groupe Spécialisé de l'Architecture (Switzerland)
GSC	Geographical Society of Chicago (U.S.A.)
GSF	Groupe Spécialisé des Ingénieurs Forestiers (Switzerland)
GSF	Schweizerische Genossenschaft f. Schlacht-vieh u. Fleischversorgung
GSFC	Gujarat State Fertilizers Company (India)
GSG	Grosshandelszentralverband für Spielwaren und Geschenkartikel
GSIS	Group for the Standardisation of Information Services (U.S.A.)
GSK	Gesellschaft für Schweizerische Kunst-geschichte
GSL	Geological Society of London
GSL	Gesellschaft Schweizerischer Landwirte
GSL	Vereniging "De Gezamenlijke Steenkolen-mijnen in Limburg"
GSM	Geological Survey of Great Britain and Museum of Practical Geology
GSMAMP	Groupement Suisse des Marchands d'Aciers Spéciaux, Métaux et Plastique
GSN	Groupement des Soufflantes Nucléaires
GSNMS	Groupement des Syndicats Nationaux de Médecins Spécialisés
GSP	Geographical Society of Philadelphia (U.S.A.)
GSRTST	German Society for Rocket Technology and Space Travel
GSSOS	Groupement des Sociétiés Scientifiques Odonto-Stomatologiques
GST	Gesellschaft Schweizerischer Tierärtze
GSZ	Gesellschaft Schweizerische Zeichenlehrer
GTA	Graduate Teachers' Association (Malta)
GTA	Groupement Togolais d'Assurance
GTC	Ghana Tobacco Company
GTCS	Groupe de Travail Intergouvernmental du Contrôle ou de la Surveillance (UNO)
GTE	Gépipari Tudományos Egyesület
GTICM	Grupo de Trabajo Intergubernamental sobre Contaminación de los Mares (IMCO)
GTIV	Grupo de Trabajo Intergubernamental sobre Vigilancia o Supervisión (UNO)
GTM	Groep Textielmachines van de Vereniging van Metaal-Industrieën
GTN	Gdańskie Towarzystwo Naukowe
GTS	Gesellschaft für Tribologie und Schmierungs-technik
GTUC	Grenada Trade Union Council
GTUC	Guyana Trades Union Council
GTW	Gesellschaft der Tierärzte in Wien (Austria)
GTZ	Deutsche Gesellschaft für Technische Zusammenarbeit
GUIMAG	Société Guinéenne de Grands Magasins
GUINELEC	Société Guinéenne d'Installations Électriques
GULP	Grenada United Labour Party
GUMR	Groupement des Utilisateurs de Matériaux Réfractaires (Belgium)
GUPCO	Gulf of Suez Petroleum Company
GUS	Great Universal Stores
GUVU	Gesellschaft für Ursachenforschung bei Verkehrsunfällen
GVA	Groupement de Vulgarisation Agricole
GVAM	Groupement de Vulgarisation Agricole et Ménagère
GVC	Gesellschaft Verfahrenstechnik und Chemieingenieurwesen
GVK	Gesellschaft f. Vergleichende Kunstfor-schung (Austria)
GVM	Groep Fabrieken van Verbrandingsmotoren
GVMA	Groupement de Vulgarisation Ménagère Agricole
GVN	Grafische Vormgevers Nederland
GvR	Genootschap voor Reclame
GVS	Grosshandelsverband Schreib-, Papierwaren und Bürobedarf
GVT	Forschungs-Gesellschaft Verfahrens-Technik
GWA	Gesellschaft Werbeagenturen
GWDB	Ground Water Development Bureau (Taiwan)
GWI	Gaswärme Institut
GWK	Gesellschaft zur Wiederaufarbeitung von Kernbrennstoffen
GWU	Gambia Workers Union
GWU	General Workers Union (Malta)
GYMES	Great Yarmouth Mediterranean Herring Exporters Association

H

HA	Historical Association
HA	Hydraulic Association
HAA	Helicopter Association of America
HAC	Horticultural Advisory Council for England and Wales
HAES	Hawaii Agricultural Experiment Station
HAF	Haandverkernes Arbeidsgiverforening
HAFRA	British Hat and Allied Feltmakers Research Association
HAG	Hauptarbeitsgemeinschaft des Landmaschinen-Handels und -Handwerks
HAGB	Helicopter Association of Great Britain (*now incorp. in* RAeS)
HAGD	Hauptvereinigung des Ambulanten Gewerbes und der Schausteller in Deutschland
HAIG	Helsinki Agreements Implementation Group (Belgium)
HAIL	Hague Academy of International Law (Netherlands)
HAKA	Verband der Deutschen Herren- und Knaben-Oberbekleidungsindustrie
HAKAF	Vereniging van Groothandelaren in Katoen-en Kunstzijdeafvallen
HAL	Holland American Line
HAO	Handelns Arbetsgivareorganisation
HAPM	Hollands-Amerikaanse Plantage Maat-schappij
HAPS	Historic Aircraft Preservation Society Ltd
HAS	Hawaiian Academy of Science
HAS	Vereniging van Leveranciers van Huishoudelijke Artikelen, Speelgoederen, Houtwaren en Soortgelijke Artikelen
HASA	Editorial Hispanoamericana S.A. (Argentina)
HASI	Hubbard Association of Scientologists International
HASL	U.S. Atomic Energy Commission. Health and Safety Laboratory
HATCA	Hungarian Air Traffic Controllers Association

HATRA	Hosiery and Allied Trades Research Association
HBAA	Human Betterment Association of America
HBC	Hudson's Bay Company (Canada)
HBF	House Builders Federation
HBI	Vereniging van Handelaren in Plantenziekten-Bestrijdingsmiddelen en Landbouw-Insecticiden
HBS	Hawaiian Botanical Society
HBTI	Harcourt Butler Technological Institute (India)
HCAR	Higher Committee for Agrarian Reform (Egypt)
HCB	Huileries du Congo Belge
HCC	Hyderabad Commercial Corporation (India)
HCCC	Hyderabad Co-operative Commercial Corporation (India)
HCGB	Hover Club of Great Britain
HCITB	Hotel and Catering Industry Training Board
HCNN	Hoofdcommissie voor de Normalisatie in Nederland
HCPRU	Hot Climate Physiological Research Unit (Nigeria)
HCR	Haut-Commissaire des Nations Unies pour les Réfugiés
HCS	Harvey Cushing Society (U.S.A.)
HCSA	Hospital Consultants and Specialists Association
HDE	Hauptgemeinschaft des Deutschen Einzelhandels
HDF	Hauptverband Deutscher Filmtheater
HDGA	Hot Dip Galvanisers Association
HDH	Hauptverband der Deutschen Holzindustrie und Verwandter Industriezweige
HDP	Hauptverband für Zucht und Prüfung Deutscher Pferde
HDRA	Henry Doubleday Research Association
HDRI	Hannah Dairy Research Institute (Scotland)
HDS	Hauptverband der Deutschen Schuhindustrie
HEA	Heating Engineering Association
HEA	Horticultural Education Association
HEAA	Home Economics Association of Australia
HEC	École des Hautes Études Commerciales
HEIX	Home Economics Information Exchange of FAO
HELORS	Hellenic Operational Research Society (Greece)

HELPIS	Higher Education Learning Programmes Information Service
HEPCC	Heavy Electrical Plant Consultative Council
HEPI	Haute École Populaire Internationale (Denmark)
HERA	High Energy Reaction Analysis Group (Switzerland)
HERR-AMEX	Fabricantes Exportadores de Herramientas Manuales
HES	Hawaiian Entomological Society
HETMA	Heavy Edge Tool Manufacturers' Association
HEVAC	Heating, Ventilating and Air Conditioning Manufacturers Association
HEW	United States Department of Health, Education and Welfare
HFFF	Hungarian Freedom Fighters Federation
HFI	Hemmens Forskningsinstitut
HFI	Hjúkrunarfelag Íslands (Icelandic Nurses Association)
HFIAW	International Association of Heat and Frost Insulators and Asbestos Workers
HFMA	Health Food Manufacturers Association
HFO	De Danske Handelsforeningers Foelles-Organisation
HFRO	Hill Farming Research Organisation (Scotland)
HFS	Hrvatski Filatelistički Savez
HFSJG	Scientific Stations of Jungfraujoch and Gornergrat (Switzerland)
HFWF	Hired Farm Working Force (U.S.A.)
HGA	Hop Growers of America
HGGA	Heraldische-Genealogische Gesellschaft 'Adler' (Austria)
HGHSC	Home Grown Herbage Seeds Committee
HGTAC	Home Grown Timber Advisory Committee
HGTMC	Home Grown Timber Marketing Corporation
HGTPJC	Home Grown Threshed Peas Joint Committee
HGV	Hohenzollischer Geschichtsverein
HHG	Heinrich Heine-Gesellschaft
HHI	Harness Horse International (U.S.A.)
HI	Hotline International (U.S.A.)
HIA	Hawaiian Irrigation Authority
HIA	Horological Institute of America

HIAS	Hebrew Immigration Aid Society (U.S.A.)
HIB	Herring Industry Board
HIBIN	Vereniging van Handelaren in Bouwmaterialen in Nederland
HICS	Holt International Children's Service Inc.
HIDB	Highlands and Islands Development Board
HIE	Hibernation Information Exchange
HIID	Harvard Institute for International Development (U.S.A.)
HIK	Statens Handels-och Industrikommission
HIOW	Hoger Institut v. Opvoedkundige Wetenschappen (Belgium)
HISWA	Nederlandse Vereniging voor Handel en Industrie op het Gebied van Scheepbouw en Watersport
HIVOS	Humanistic Institute for Co-operation with Developing Countries (Netherlands)
HKCEC	Hong Kong Catholic Education Council
HKI	Fachverband Heiz- und Kochgeräte-Industrie
HKMA	Hong Kong Management Association
HLA	Hawaii Library Association
HLCF	Holy Land Conservation Fund (U.S.A.)
HLSRS	High Level Sisal Research Station (E. Africa)
HLUSA	Honeywell Large Systems Users Association (Europe)
HMA	Hellenic Marketing Association
HMBI	His *or* Her Majesty's Borstal Institution
HMC	Horticultural Marketing Council
HMDS	Her Majesty's Diplomatic Service
HMNFE	Her Majesty's Norfolk Flax Establishment
HMOCS	Her Majesty's Overseas Civil Service
HMPA	Hawaii Macadamia Producers Association
HMSO	Her Majesty's Stationery Office
HMU-CMS	Harmonie Mondiale Universelle-Conseil Mondiale du Service (U.K.)
HMvL	Hollandsche Mij. van Landbouw
HNGNA	Hellenic National Graduate Nurses Association (Greece)
HO	Hovedorganisationen af Mesterforeninger i Byggefagene i Danmark
HO	U.S. Hydrographic Office
HOA	Huileries de l'Ouest Africain
HOC	Holland Organizing Centre (Netherlands)
HOG	Hermann-Oberth-Gesellschaft

HORECA	International Union of National Associations of Hotel, Restaurant and Café Keepers
HORECAF	Nederlandse Bond van Werkgevers in Hotel-, Restaurant-, Café- en Aanverwante Bedrijven
HORESCA	Fédération Nationale des Hôteliers, Restaurateurs et Cafetiers du Grande-Duché de Luxembourg
HORU	Home Office Research Unit
HOTAFRIC	Société de Développement Hôtelier et Touristique de l'Afrique de l'Ouest (Ivory Coast)
HPCA	Hiroshima Peace Center Associates (U.S.A.)
HPF	Horace Plunkett Foundation for Co-operative Studies
HPRS	Hellenic Public Relations Society (Greece)
HPRS	Houghton Poultry Research Station
HPV	Hauptverband der Papier, Pappe und Kunstoffe Verarbeitenden Industrie
HRAF	Human Relations Area Files (U.S.A.)
HRB	Highway Research Board (U.S.A.)
HRCC	Humanities Research Council of Canada
HRI	Horticultural Research International
HRIS	Highway Research Information Service (of AAHSO)
HRN	Hotelli- ja Ravintolaneuvosto
HRS	Hop Research Station (DSIR) (N.Z.)
HRS	Hydraulics Research Station
HRTK	Hoger Rijksinstituut voor Textiel en Kunststoffen (Belgium)
HRU	Hydrologic Research Unit (of NERC)
HSAC	Hebridean Spinners Advisory Committee
HSA-UWC	Holy Spirit Association for the Unification of World Christianity
HSBA	Herdwick Sheep Breeders Association
HSFK	Hessische Stiftung für Friedens- und Konfliktsforschung
HSIU	Haile Selassie I University Library (Ethiopia)
HSMHA	Health Services and Mental Health Administration (U.S.A.)
HSNY	Horticultural Society of New York (U.S.A.)
HSPA	Hawaiian Sugar Planters' Association
HSQ	Historical Society of Queensland (Australia)
HSRC	Human Sciences Research Council (South Africa)
HSRD	National Center for Health Services Research and Development (U.S.A.)

HSS	History of Science Society (U.S.A.)
HSSA	High Speed Steel Association
HST	Hawaiian Sugar Technologists
HTA	Horticultural Trades Association
HTC	Holland-Tanganyika Compagnie
HTG	Hafenbautechnische Gesellschaft
HTG	Hemtextilgrossisterna
HTLDC	Hsinchu Tidal Land Development Planning Commission (Taiwan)
HTMA	Hawaii Territorial Medical Association
HTMAEW	Home Timber Merchants Association of England and Wales
HTRP	Humid Tropics Research Programme (of UNESCO)
HUK	Verband der Haftpflicht-, Unfall- und Kraftverkehrs- Versicherer
HULTIS	Hull Technical Interloan Scheme
HUMRRO	Human Resources Research Office
HVCA	Heating and Ventilating Contractors' Association
HVG	Hüttentechnische Vereinigung der Deutschen Glasindustrie
HVRA	Hawaiian Volcano Research Association
HVRA	Heating and Ventilating Research Association (now BSRIA)
HWMV	Schweizerischer Hartweizenmüller-Verband
HWWA	Hamburgisches Weltwirtschaftsarchiv
HYPECO	Hybrid Poultry Breeding Corporation (Belgium-Netherlands)

I

IA	Institute of Actuaries
IAA	Institut Agricole d'Algérie
IAA	Instituto do Açúcar e do Alcool (Brazil)
IAA	Institute of Automobile Assessors
IAA	Instituto Antártica Argentino
IAA	International Academy of Astronautics
IAA	International Allergy Association (U.S.A.)
IAA	International Acetylene Association
IAA	International Actuarial Association
IAA	International Advertising Association

IAA	International Aerosol Association
IAA	International Apple Association (U.S.A.)
IAA	International Association for Aerobiology
IAA	International Association of Allergology (U.S.A.)
IAA	International Association of Art-Painting, Sculpture, Graphic Art
IAA	International Association of Astacology
IAAA	Irish Association of Advertising Agencies
IAAALD	Inter-American Association of Agricultural Librarians and Documentalists (Costa Rica)
IAAAM	International Association for Aquatic Animal Medicine
IAAB	Inter-American Association of Broadcasters
IAABO	International Association of Approved Basketball Officials
IAAC	International Agricultural Aviation Centre
IAAC	International Antarctic Analysis Centre
IAAC	International Association of Art Critics
IAACC	Inter-Allied Aeronautical Commission of Control
IAACR	Instituto Agrario Argentino de Cultura Rural
IAAE	Institution of Automotive and Aeronautical Engineers (Australia) (now SAE-Australasia)
IAAE	International Association of Agricultural Economists
IAAE	Israel Association of Agricultural Engineering
IAAEE	International Association for the Advancement of Ethnology and Eugenics
IAAER	International Association for the Advancement of Educational Research
IAAF	International Amateur Athletic Federation
IAAI	International Airports Authority of India
IAAI	International Association of Arson Investigators
IAAJ	International Association of Agricultural Journalists
IAALD	International Association of Agricultural Librarians and Documentalists
IAAM	International Association of Automotive Modelers
IAAO	International Association of Assessing Officers (U.S.A.)
IAAP	International Association for Analytical Psychology
IAAP	International Association of Applied Psychology
IAAPA	International Association of Amusement Parks and Attractions (U.S.A.)
IAAPEA	International Association Against Painful Experiments on Animals
IAARC	International Administrative Aeronautical Radio Conference
IAAS	Incorporated Association of Architects and Surveyors
IAAS	International Association of Agricultural Students
IAATM	International Association for Accident and Traffic Medicine (Sweden)
IAB	ICSU Abstracting Board
IAB	Imperial Agricultural Bureaux (UK) (now CAB)
IAB	Industrial Advisory Board
IAB	Institut Agricole de Beauvais (Oise)
IAB	International Aquatic Board
IAB	Internationale Akademie für Bäderkunde und Bädertechnik
IAB	Internationale Akademie für Bader-, Sport-, und Freizeitbau
IAB	International Council of Scientific Unions Abstracting Board
IABA	International Amateur Boxing Association
IABA	International Association of Aircraft Brokers and Agents
IABC	International Association of Business Communicators (U.S.A.)
IABE	Ibero-American Bureau of Education (Spain)
IABE	Internacia Asocio de Bankistoj Esperantistaj
IABG	International Association of Botanic Gardens
IABLA	Inter-American Bibliographical and Library Association
IABO	International Association of Biblicists and Orientalists
IABO	International Association for Biological Oceanography
IABS	International Advisory Committee for Biological Standardization
IABSE	International Association for Bridge and Structural Engineering
IABSOIW	International Association of Bridge, Structural and Ornamental Iron Workers
IAC	Indian Airlines Corporation

IAC	Industries Assistance Commission (Australia)	**IACD**	International Association of Clothing Designers
IAC	Institute of Administration and Commerce of South Africa	**IACDT**	International Advisory Committee for Documentation and Terminology
IAC	Inter Afrique Charters	**IACED**	Inter-African Advisory Committee on Control of Epizootic Diseases (*now* IACAHP)
IAC	International Advisory Committee on Research in the Natural Sciences (UNESCO)		
IAC	International Aerological Commission	**IACES**	International Air Cushion Engineering Society
IAC	Internationaal Agrarisch Centrum (Netherlands)	**IACFO**	Asociación Internacional para las Ciencias Fisicas del Océano
IAC	International Artists Cooperation	**IACI**	Inter-American Children's Institute
IAC	International Athletes Club	**IACI**	Inter-American Copyright Institute
IACA	Inter-American College Association	**IACIT**	International Association of Conference Interpreters and Translators
IACA	International Air Carrier Association (U.S.A.)		
IACA	International Air Charter Association (Switzerland)	**IACL**	International Academy of Comparative Law
		IACL	International Association of Criminal Law
IACA	International Association of Consulting Actuaries	**IACM**	International Association of Circulation Managers
IACAHP	Inter-African Advisory Committee for Animal Health and Production (*formerly* IACED) (Kenya)	**IACME**	International Association of Crafts and Small and Medium-sized Enterprises
		IACO	Inter-African Coffee Organisation
IACB	Inter-Agency Consultative Board	**IACODLA**	International Advisory Committee on Documentation, Libraries and Archives (UNESCO)
IACB	International Advisory Committee on Bibliography		
IACB	International Association of Convention Bureaux (U.S.A.)	**IACOMS**	International Advisory Committee on Marine Sciences
IACBC	International Advisory Committee on Biological Control	**IACP**	International Association of Chiefs of Police
		IACP	International Association for Child Psychiatry
IACBDT	International Advisory Committee on Bibliography, Documentation and Terminology	**IACP**	International Association of Computer Programmers (U.S.A.)
IACC	Instituto Argentino de Control de la Calidad	**IACPAP**	International Association for Child Psychiatry and Allied Professions
IACC	International Agricultural Coordination Commission	**IACPP**	International Association for Cross-Cultural Psychology
IACC	International Association for Cereal Chemistry (Austria)	**IACS**	Indian Association for the Cultivation of Science
IACC	International Association of Congress Centres	**IACS**	International Academy of Christian Sociologists
IACCHE	Inter-American Confederation of Chemical Engineering	**IACS**	International Association of Classification Societies
IACCI	International Association of Credit Card Investigators	**IACS**	International Association of Counselling Services (U.S.A.)
IACCP	Inter-American Council for Commerce and Production	**IACSAC**	Inter-American Catholic Social Action Confederation
IACCP	International Association for Cross-Cultural Psychology	**IACSS**	Inter-American Conference of Social Security

IACVB	International Association of Convention and Visitors Bureaux		**IAEA**	Institute of Asian Economic Affairs (Japan) (*now* IDE)
IACVF	International Association of Cancer Victims and Friends		**IAEA**	Inter-American Educational Association
IACW	Inter-American Commission of Women		**IAEA**	International Agricultural Exchange Association (Denmark)
IAD	Instituto Agrario Dominicano		**IAEA**	International Atomic Energy Agency
IADA	Internationale Arbeitsgemeinschaft der Archiv-, Bibliotheks- und Graphik-restauratoren		**IAEC**	International Association of Environmental Coordinators
IADB	Inter-American Defense Board		**IAECO-SOC**	Inter-American Economic and Social Council
IADB	Interamerican Development Bank		**IAEE**	International Association for Earthquake Engineering
IADC	Inter-American Defense College			
IADC	International Association of Dentistry for Children		**IAEF**	Internacia Asocio de la Esperantistaj Feruojistoj
IADC	International Association of Dredging Companies		**IAEG**	International Association of Engineering Geology
IADC	International Association of Drilling Contractors		**IAEI**	International Association of Electrical Inspectors
IADF	Inter-American Association for Democracy and Freedom		**IAEL**	International Association of Electrical Leagues
IADIS	Irish Association for Documentation and Information Services		**IAEO**	Internationale Atoménergie Organisation
			IAES	Institute of Aeronautical Sciences
IADIWU	International Association for the Development of International and World Universities		**IAESC**	Inter-American Economic and Social Council
IADL	International Association of Democratic Lawyers		**IAESP**	Institúto Agronómico de Estado de Sao Paulo (Brazil)
IADLA	International Association for the Development of Documentation, Libraries and Archives in Africa		**IAESTE**	International Association for the Exchange of Students for Technical Experience
IADO	Instituto Argentino de Oceanografica		**IAEVG**	International Association for Educational and Vocational Guidance
IADO	Instituto Agroindustrial de Oleaginosos (Argentina)		**IAEVI**	International Association for Educational and Vocational Information
IADO	Iran Agriculture Development Organization		**IAEWP**	International Association of Educators for World Peace
IADP	Intensive Agricultural District Programme (India)		**IAF**	Inter-American Foundation
IADPE	Institut Asiatique pour le Développement et la Planification Économique (Thailand)		**IAF**	International Abolitionist Federation
			IAF	International Association Futuribles
IADR	International Association for Dental Research		**IAF**	International Astronautical Federation
IADS	International Agricultural Development Service (U.S.A.)		**IAF**	International Automobile Federation
IADS	International Association of Dental Students		**IAFC**	Inter-American Freight Conference
IADS	International Association of Department Stores		**IAFC**	International Association of Fire Chiefs (U.S.A.)
IAE	Institut d'Administration des Entreprises		**IAFD**	International Association of Food Distribution
IAE	Institute of Automobile Engineers		**IAFE**	International Association of Fairs and Expositions
IAEA	Indian Adult Education Association			

IAFEI	International Association of Financial Executives Institutes
IAFF	International Art Film Federation
IAFF	International Association of Fire Fighters
IAFMM	International Association of Fish Meal Manufacturers
IAFP	Instítúto de Anatomia y Fisiologia Patólogicas (Argentina)
IAFP	International Association of Financial Planners (U.S.A.)
IAFS	International Association of Family Sociology
IAFS	International Association of Forensic Sciences
IAFWNO	Inter-American Federation of Working Newspaperman's Organisations
IAG	IFIP Administrative Data Processing Group
IAG	Institute of American Genealogy
IAG	International Administrative Data Processing Group (of IFIP)
IAG	International Association of Geodesy
IAG	International Association of Gerontology
IAG	Internationale Arbeitsgemeinschaft f.d. Unterrichtsfilm
IAGA	Instituto Argentino de Grasas y Aceites
IAGA	International Association of Geomagnetism and Aeronomy
IAGB & I	Ileostomy Association of Great Britain and Ireland
IAGC	International Academy of Gynecological Cytology
IAGC	International Association on Geochemistry and Cosmochemistry
IAGFA	International Association of Government Fair Agencies
IAGFCC	International Association of Game, Fish and Conservation Commissioners
IAGLO	International Association of Governmental Labour Officials
IAGLP	International Association of Great Lakes Ports (Canada)
IAGLR	International Association for Great Lakes Research
IAGOD	International Association on the Genesis of Ore Deposits
IAGRE	Institution of Agricultural Engineers
IAH	International Association of Hydrogeologists

IAH	International Association of Hydrology
IAHA	Inter-American Hotel Association
IAHA	International Arabian Horse Association (U.S.A.)
IAHA	International Association of Historians of Asia
IAHB	International Association of Human Biologists
IAHCSM	International Association of Hospital Central Service Management
IAHE	International Association for Hydrogen Energy
IAHIC	International Association of Home Improvement Council
IAHM	Incorporated Association of Headmasters
IAHP	International Association of Horticultural Producers
IAHR	International Association for the History of Religions
IAHR	International Association for Hydraulic Research
IAHS	International Academy of History of Science
IAHS	International Association for Housing Science
IAHS	International Association of Hydrological Sciences
IAHU	International Association of Health Underwriters
IAI	International African Institute (U.K.)
IAI	Institute for International Collaboration in Agriculture and Forestry (Czechoslovakia)
IAI	International Anthropological Institute
IAI	International Apple Institute (U.S.A.)
IAI	International Association for Identification
IAI	Israel Aviation Industries
IAI	Istituto Affari Internazionali
IAI	International Automotive Institute (Monaco)
IAIABC	International Association of Industrial Accident Boards and Commissions
IAIAS	Inter-American Institute of Agricultural Sciences
IAIC	International Association of Insurance Counsel (U.S.A.)
IAICM	International Association of Ice Cream Manufacturers
IAIDEC	Instituto Argentino de la Industria y Exportación de Carnes

IAIGC	Inter-Arab Investment Guarantee Corporation (Kuwait)	**IAM**	International Afro-American Museum (U.S.A.)
IAII	Inter-American Indian Institute (*of* OAS)	**IAM**	International Association of Machinists and Aerospace Workers
IAIP	International Association of Independent Producers	**IAM**	International Association of Meteorology
IAIP	International Association of Individual Psychology	**IAM**	Internationale Arbeitsgemeinschaft für Müllforschung
IAIR	International Association of Industrial Radiation	**IAMA**	Incorporated Advertising Managers Association
IAIS	Industrial Aerodynamics Information Service (*of* BHMRA)	**IAMA**	International Abstaining Motorists Association
IAJC	Inter-American Juridical Committee	**IAMA**	Irish Association of Municipal Authorities
IAJE	Internacio Asocio de Juristoj-Esperantistoj	**IAMAM**	International Association of Museums of Arms and Military History
IAJRC	International Association of Jazz Record Collectors (U.S.A.)	**IAMAP**	International Association of Meteorology and Atmospheric Physics
IAK	Internationales Auschwitz-Komitee	**IAMAT**	International Association for Medical Assistance to Travellers
IAKS	Internationalen Arbeitskreis Sportstättenbau	**IAMB**	International Association of Macrobiologists
IAL	Imperial Arts League	**IAMB**	International Association of Microbiologists
IAL	Institut Archeologique du Luxembourg	**IAMB**	Irish Association of Master Bakers
IAL	International Arbitration League	**IAMBE**	International Association for Medicine and Biology of Environment
IAL	International Association of Laryngectomees	**IAMCA**	International Association of Milk Control Agencies
IAL	International Association of Theoretical and Applied Limnology	**IAMCR**	International Association for Mass Communication Research
IAL	Irish Academy of Letters	**IAMD**	International Association of Managing Directors (U.S.A.)
IALA	International African Law Association	**IAMFE**	International Association on Mechanisation of Field Experiments
IALA	International Association of Lighthouse Authorities	**IAMFES**	International Association of Milk, Food and Environmental Sanitarians (U.S.A.)
IALA	International Auxiliary Language Association	**IAMG**	International Association for Mathematical Geology
IALB	Internationalen Arbeitskreises Landwirtschaftlicher Berater	**IAML**	International Association of Music Libraries
IALCRF	International Association for Liberal Christianity and Religious Freedom	**IAMLT**	International Association of Medical Laboratory Technologists
IALI	International Association of Labour Inspection	**IAMM**	International Association of Medical Museums
IALL	International Association for Labor Legislation (U.S.A.)	**IAMO**	Inter-American Municipal Organisation
IALL	International Association of Law Libraries	**IAMR**	Institute of Applied Manpower Research (India)
IALP	International Association of Logopedics and Phoniatrics (U.S.A.)	**IAMRC**	International Antarctic Meteorological Research Centre
IALS	International Agency Liaison Service (*of* FAO)	**IAMS**	International Association of Microbiological Societies
IALS	International Association of Legal Science		
IAM	Institute of Administrative Management		
IAM	Institute of Advanced Motorists		
IAM	Institute of Aviation Medicine		

IAMS	International Association for Mission Studies
IAMS	International Association of Municipal Statisticians
IAMV	Internationaler Anti-Militarischer Verein
IAMWF	Inter-American Mine Workers Federation
IAN	Institúto Agrario Nacional (Venezuela etc.)
IAN	Institúto Agrónomico de Norte (Brazil)
IAN	Internationale des Amis de la Nature
IANC	Instituto de Asuntas Nucleares de Colombia
IANC	International Airline Navigators Council
IANC	International Anatomical Nomenclature Committee
IANEC	Inter-American Nuclear Energy Commission
IANSA	Industria Azucarera Nacional (Chile)
IAO	International Association of Orthodontics (U.S.A.)
IAO	Internationale Arbeitsorganisation
IAOL	International Association of Orientalist Librarians
IAOO	Irish Agricultural Officers Organisation
IAOPA	International Council of Aircraft Owner and Pilot Associations
IAOS	International Association of Oral Surgeons
IAOS	Irish Agricultural Organisation Society
IAP	Institute of Australian Photographers
IAP	Instituto Argentino del Petróleo
IAP	International Academy of Pathology
IAP	International Academy of Poets
IAP	International Academy of Proctology
IAP	International Association of Psychotechnics
IAPA	Inter-American Press Association
IAPB	International Association for the Prevention of Blindness
IAPC	International Association for Pollution Control
IAPCO	International Association of Professional Congress Organisers
IAPES	International Association of Personnel in Employment Security
IAPESGW	International Association of Physical Education and Sports for Girls and Women
IAPH	International Association of Ports and Harbours
IAPHC	International Association of Printing House Craftsmen
IAPI	Institute of Advertising Practitioners in Ireland
IAPI	Institute of American Poultry Industries
IAPI	Institúto Argentino de Promoción del Intercambio
IAPIP	International Association for the Protection of Industrial Property
IAPL	International Association for Penal Law
IAPMO	International Association of Plumbing and Mechanical Officials
IAPN	International Association of Professional Numismatists
IAPO	International Association of Physical Oceanography
IAPP	Indian Association for Plant Physiology
IAPP	International Association for Plant Physiology
IAPP	International Association of Police Professors (U.S.A.)
IAPP	International Association of Prevention Programs (U.S.A.)
IAPPLT	Inter-American Program for Linguistics and Language Teaching
IAPPW	International Association of Pupil Personnel Workers (U.S.A.)
IAPR	International Association for Pattern Recognition (U.S.A.)
IAPS	International Academy of Political Science (*Ceased*)
IAPS	International Affiliation of Planning Societies
IAPS	International Association of Pipe Smokers Clubs
IAPS	International Association on the Properties of Steam
IAPSC	Inter-African Phytosanitary Commission (U.K.)
IAPSO	International Association for the Physical Sciences of the Ocean
IAPT	International Association for Plant Taxonomy
IAPTA	International Allied Printing Trades Association
IAPW	International Association of Personnel Women
IAQ	International Academy for Quality
IAQR	Indian Association for Quality and Reliability
IAQR	International Association on Quarternary Research

IAR	International Authority for the Ruhr	**IASA**	International Association of Schools in Advertising
IARA	Inter-Allied Reparation Agency		
IARA	International Association of Rebekah Assemblies	**IASA**	International Association of Sound Archives
		IASAA	International Agricultural Students Association of the Americas
IArb	Institute of Arbitrators		
IARC	International Agency for Research on Cancer (*of* WHO)	**IASB**	International Aircraft Standard Bureau
		IASC	International Accounting Standards Committee (*of* ICCAP)
IARC	International Amateur Radio Club		
IARCB	International Asian Research Conference Board	**IASC**	Inter-American Safety Council (U.S.A.)
		IASC	International Association of Seed Crushers
IARCS	Institut Asiatique de Recherche sur les Constructions Scolaires (Sri Lanka)	**IASC**	International Association for Statistical Computing
IARF	International Association for Liberal Christianity and Religious Freedom	**IASF**	International Atlantic Salmon Foundation
		IASH	International Association of Scientific Hydrology
IARI	Indian Agricultural Research Institute		
IARIGAI	International Association of Research Institutes for the Graphic Arts Industry	**IASI**	Inter-American Statistical Institute
		IASIA	International Association of Schools and Institutes of Administration
IARIW	International Association for Research in Income and Wealth		
		IASL	Inter-American School of Librarianship (Colombia)
IARM	Instituto Argentino de Racionalización de Materiales		
		IASL	International Association of School Librarianship
IARMI	International Association of Rattan Manufacturers and Importers		
		IASL	International Association for the Study of the Liver
IARP	Indian Association for Radiation Protection		
IARR	International Association for Radiation Research	**IASLIC**	Indian Association of Special Libraries and Information Centres
IARS	Institute of Agricultural Research Statistics (India)	**IASM**	Instituto per l'Assistenzo alla Sviluppo del Mezzogiorno
IARS	International Anesthesis Research Society	**IASMAL**	International Academy of Social and Moral Sciences, Arts and Letters
IARU	International Amateur Radio Union		
IARUS	International Association for Regional and Urban Statistics	**IASP**	International Association of Scholarly Publishers
IARW	International Association of Refrigerated Warehouses	**IASP**	International Association for Social Progress
		IASP	International Association of Space Philatelists
IAS	Association Internationale de Sémiotique		
IAS	Institute of Andean Studies (U.S.A.)	**IASP**	International Association for the Study of Pain
IAS	Institute of the Aeronautical Sciences (U.S.A.)		
		IASP	International Association for Suicide Prevention
IAS	International Association of Sedimentologists (IUGS)		
		IASPEI	International Association of Seismology and Physics of the Earth's Interior
IAS	International Association of Seismology and of Physics of the Earth's Interior		
		IASPM	International Association of Scientific Paper Makers
IAS	International Association of Siderographers		
IAS	International Audiovisual Society	**IASRA**	International Arthur Schnitzler Research Association (U.S.A.)
IAS	Irish Archaeological Society		
IASA	International Air Safety Association	**IASPS**	International Association for Statistics in Physical Sciences

IASS	International Association of Security Services (U.S.A.)	**IATR**	International Association for Tamil Research (Malaysia)
IASS	International Association for Semiotic Studies	**IATR**	International Association of Teachers of Russian
IASS	International Association for Shell Structures	**IATSW**	Indian Association of Trained Social Workers
IASS	International Association of Survey Statisticians	**IATTC**	Inter-American Tropical Tuna Commission
IASSMD	International Association for the Scientific Study of Mental Deficiency	**IATU**	Inter-American Telecommunications Union
IASSW	International Association of Schools of Social Work	**IATUL**	International Association of Technical University Libraries
IASTED	International Association of Science and Technology for Development	**IAU**	International Academic Union
		IAU	International Association of Universities
IASV	Internationale Arbeitsgemeinschaft von Sortimenter Vereinigungen	**IAU**	International Astronomical Union
IAT	Institute of Animal Technicians	**IAUP**	International Association of University Presidents
IAT	International Association for Time-Keeping	**IAUPE**	International Association of University Professors of English
IATA	Instituto de Agroquimica y Tecnologia de Alimentos	**IAUPL**	International Association of University Professors and Lecturers
IATA	International Air Transport Association	**IAUR**	Instituto de Antibióticos da Universidade do Recife (Brazil)
IATA	International Amateur Theatre Association		
IATAL	International Association of Theoretical and Applied Limnology	**IAV**	International Association of Volcanology
		IAVC	International Audio-Visual Centre
IATC	International Association of Tool Craftsmen	**IAVCEI**	International Association of Volcanology and Chemistry of the Earth's Interior
IATE	International Association of Television Editors	**IAVFH**	International Association of Veterinary Food Hygiene
IATE	International Association for Temperance Education	**IAVG**	International Association for Vocational Guidance
IATEFL	International Association of Teachers of English as a Foreign Language	**IAVI**	International Association of Voice Identification
IATEM	Instituto Agrotécnico Económico de Misiones (Argentina)	**IAVRS**	International Audiovisual Resource Service
IATFIS	Inter-Agency Task Force on Information Exchange and Transfer of Technology (IOB)	**IAVTC**	International Audio-Visual Technical Centre (Belgium)
IATL	International Academy of Trial Lawyers	**IAW**	International Alliance of Women
IATL	International Association of Theological Libraries	**IAWA**	Incorporated Advertising Managers Association
IATLIS	Indian Association of Teachers of Library Science	**IAWA**	Independent American Whiskey Association
IATM	International Association for Testing Materials	**IAWA**	International Association of Wood Anatomists
IATM	International Association of Tour Managers	**IAWC**	International Association of Whaling Corporations
IATM	International Association of Transport Museums	**IAWCC**	International Association of Wall and Ceiling Contractors (U.S.A.)
IATME	International Association of Terrestrial Magnetism and Electricity	**IAWHPJ**	International Association of Women and Home Page Journalists
IATO	International Association of Theatre Public Organization	**IAWL**	International Association for Water Law

IAWM	Industrial Association of Wales and Monmouthshire
IAWMC	International Association of Workers for Maladjusted Children
IAWP	International Association of Women Police
IAWPR	International Association on Water Pollution Research
IAWR	Internationale Arbeitsgemeinschaft der Wasserwerke im Rheineinzugsgebiet
IAWRT	International Association of Women in Radio and Television
IAWS	International Academy of Wood Science
IAWS	Irish Agricultural Wholesale Society
IAYM	International Association of Youth Magistrates
IAZ	Instituto de Agricultura y Zootecnia (Peru)
IB	Instituut voor Bodemvruchtbaarheid
IB	Institute of Bankers
IBA	Independent Broadcasting Authority
IBA	Institute of British Architects
IBA	International Banker Association
IBA	International Bar Association
IBA	International Bauxite Association
IBA	International Biographical Association
IBA	International Bookstall Contractors Association
IBA	International Bridge Academy
IBAA	Independent Bankers Association of America
IBAA	Investment Bankers' Association of America
IBAB	Institut Belge pour l'Amélioration de la Betterave
IBAE	Institution of British Agricultural Engineers
IBAH	Inter-African Bureau for Animal Health (*now* IBAR)
IBAHP	Inter-African Bureau for Animal Health and Production (*formerly* IBED) (Kenya)
IBAM	Institute of Business Administration and Management (Japan)
IBAM	Instituto Brasileiro de Administraçao Municipal
IBAN	Institut Belge pour l'Alimentation et la Nutrition
IBANA	Institut de Biologie Appliquée à la Nutrition et l'Alimentation
IBAP	Internationales Büro für Audiophonologie
IBAP	Intervention Board for Agricultural Produce

IBAR	Interafrican Bureau for Animal Resources
IBB	Institute of British Bakers
IBB	International Bowling Board
IBB	International Brotherhood of Bookbinders
IBBC	Instituut voor Bouwmaterialen en Bouwconstructies
IBBD	Instítuto Brasileiro de Bibliografia e Documentaçao
IBBH	Internationaler Bund der Bau- und Holzarbeiter
IBBYP	International Board on Books for Young People (Switzerland)
IBC	Instituto Brasileiro do Café
IBC	Instítuto Bacteriológico de Chile
IBC	International Biographical Centre (U.K.)
IBC	International Biotoxicological Centre, World Life Research Institute (U.S.A.)
IBC	International Boundary Commission (U.S.A.)
IBCA	International Braille Chess Association
IBCA	International Bureau for Cultural Activities (*of* COSEC)
IBBD	Instituto Brasileiro de Bibliografia e Documentacao
IBCA	Instituto Boliviano de Cultivos Andinos
IBCAM	Institute of British Carriage and Automobile Manufacturers
IBCC	International Building Classification Committee (Netherlands)
IBCC	International Business Communications Centers (U.S.A.)
IB-CC	International Business Contact Club
IBCE	International Bureau for Cultural Exchange
IBCG	Internationaler Bund der Christlichen Gewerkschaften
IBCGTB	Internationaler Bund der Christlichen Gewerkschaften im Textil- und Bekleidungswerbe
IBCHBV	Internationaler Bund Christlicher Holz- und Bauarbeiterverbände
IBCIN	International Biologisch Contact- en Informatie-bureau voor Nederland
IBCS	International Bureau of Commercial Statistics
IBD	Incorporated Institute of British Decorators and Interior Designers
IBD	International Bureau for Declarations of Death

IBDA	Instituto Brasileiro de Direito Agrário
IBDC	Institut Belge de Droit Comparé
IBDF	Instituto Brasileiro de Desenvolvimento Florestal
IBE	Institute Belge de l'Emballage
IBE	Institute of British Engineers
IBE	International Bureau of Education
IBE	International Bureau for Epilepsy
IBEAS	Instituto Boliviano de Estudio y Accion Social
IBEC	International Bank for Economic Cooperation
IBEC	International Basic Economy Corporation (U.S.A.)
IBECC	Brazilian Institute of Education, Science and Culture
IBED	Inter-African Bureau of Epizootic Diseases (*now* IBAHP)
IBEE	International Builders Exchange Executives (U.S.A.)
IBEG	International Book Export Group
IBEG	Internationaler Bund der Erziehungsgemeinschaften
IBELCO	Institut Belge de Coopération Technique
IBERSOM	Institut Belge pour l'Encouragement de la Recherche Scientifique Outre-Mer
IBERTO	Société Industrielle et Commerciale Ibéro-Togolaise
IBEW	International Brotherhood of Electrical Workers
IBF	Institute of British Foundrymen
IBF	International Badminton Federation
IBF	International Balut Federation
IBFCC	International Border Fancy Canary Club
IBFD	Instituto Brasileiro de Direito Financeiro
IBFD	International Bureau of Fiscal Documentation
IBFG	Internationaler Bund Freier Gewerkschaften
IBFI	International Business Forms Industries (U.S.A.)
IBFMP	International Bureau of the Federations of Master Printers
IBFO	International Brotherhood of Fireman and Oilers
IBG	Incorporated Brewers' Guild
IBG	Institute of British Geographers
IBG	Internationales Büro für Gebirgsmechanik
IBGE	Instituto Brasileiro de Geografia e Estatistica
IBHP	Institut Belge des Hautes Pressions
IBI	Institut International des Châteaux Historiques
IBI	Intergovernmental Bureau for Informatics (Italy)
IBI	International Broadcast Institute
IBI	Internationales Burgen Institut
IBICC	Incorporated British Institute of Certified Carpenters
IBICT	Instituto Brasileiro de Informação en Ciencia e Tecnologia
IBIS	International Book Information Services, Inc.
IBIT	Instituto Brasileiro para Investigaçao da Tuberculose
IBK	Institute of Bookkeepers
IBK	Internationale Beleuchtungs-Kommission
IBL	Institute of British Launderers
IBL	Instytut Badawczy Lesnictwa
IBLA	Institut des Belles-Lettres Arabes (Tunis)
IBLA	Inter-American Bibliographical and Library Association
IBLC	Institut Belgo-Luxembourgeois du Change
IBM	Indian Bureau of Mines
IBM	International Brotherhood of Magicians (U.S.A.)
IBM	International Business Machines Corporation
IBMA	International Bar Managers Association
IBME	Institúto de Biológia y Medicína Experimental (Argentina)
IBMR	International Bureau for Mechanical Reproduction
IBN	Institut Belge de Normalisation
IBNS	International Bank Note Society
IBO	International Baccalaureate Office (Switzerland)
IBO	Instituut voor Bosbouwkundig Onderzoek
IBO	Internationale Bouworde
IBOA	Irish Bank Officials' Association
IBOB	International Brotherhood of Old Bastards
IBOPC	Instituto Brasileiro de Oftalmologia e Prevencao da Cegueira
IBP	Institut Belge du Pétrole
IBP	Institute of British Photographers

IBP	Institute for Business Planning	**IBST**	Institute of British Surgical Technicians
IBP	Instituto Boliviano del Petroleo	**IBT**	International Brotherhood of Teamsters, Chauffeurs, Warehousemen and Helpers of America
IBP	Instituto Brasileiro de Potasa		
IBP	International Biological Programme		
IBP	Internationaler Bund der Privatangestellten	**IBTA**	International Baton Twirling Association of America and Abroad
IBPA	International Bridge Press Association		
IBPC	Institut Biologique Physico-Chimique	**IBTA**	International Business Travel Association
IBPCS	International Bureau for Physico-Chemical Standards	**IBTE**	Imperial Board of Telecommunications (Ethiopia)
IBPGR	International Board for Plant Genetic Resources (FAO etc.)	**IBTE**	International Bureau of Technical Education
		IBTT	International Bureau for Technical Training
IBPI	International Bureau for Plant Taxonomy and Nomenclature (Netherlands)	**IBTS**	International Beer Testing Society
		IBTTA	International Bridge and Tunnel-Turnpike Association (U.S.A.)
IBPR	International Board for Plant Genetic Resources	**IBU**	International Broadcasting Union
IBPT	Instituto de Biologia e Pesquisas Tecnológicas (Portugal)	**IBU**	Internationale Bürgermeister-Union
		IBUPL	International Bureau for the Unification of Penal Law
IBRA	Institut Belge de Régulation et Automatisme		
IBRA	Instituto Brasileiro de Administração	**IBUPU**	International Bureau of the Universal Postal Union
IBRA	Instituto Brasileiro de Reforma Agraria		
IBRA	International Bee Research Association	**IBVEA**	International Bureau of Veterinary Educational Aids (Australia)
IBRA	International Bible Reading Association		
IBRADES	Instituto Brasileiro de Desenvolvimento	**IBVL**	Instituut voor Bewaring en Verwerking van Landbouwprodukten
IBRAPE	Industria Brasileira de Produtos Electronicos e Electricos	**IBVT**	Instituut voor Bewaring en Verwerking van Tuinbouwproducten
IBRAR	Instituto Brasileiro de Reforma Agrária Regional	**IBW**	Instituut voor Bestuurwetenschappen
IBRC	International Bird Rescue Center (U.S.A.)	**IBWC**	International Boundary and Water Commission (USA-Mexico)
IBRD	International Bank for Reconstruction and Development	**IBWM**	International Bureau of Weights and Measures
IBRE	Instituto Brasileiro de Economia	**IBWS**	International Bureau of Whaling Statistics
IBRI	Instituto Brasileiro de Relações Internacionais	**IC**	Islamic Congress
IBRO	International Brain Research Organisation	**ICA**	Common Market Group of the International Confederation of Agricultural Credit
IBS	Institut Belge de la Soudre		
IBS	Institute of Bankers in Scotland	**ICA**	Fédération Internationale Chrétienne des Travailleurs de l'Alimentation, du Tabac et de l'Hôtellerie
IBS	Instituut voor Biologisch en Scheikundig Onderzoek van Landbouwgewassen		
IBS	International Broadcasters Society	**ICA**	Imprimerie Centrale d'Afrique
IBSA	Institut Belge des Sciences Administratives	**ICA**	Industria y Comercio de Alimentación
IBSCC	International Bureau for the Suppression of Counterfeit Coins	**ICA**	Information Centre for Aeronautics (India)
		ICA	Institut Culturel Africain
IBSFC	International Baltic Sea Fishery Commission	**ICA**	Institute of Company Accountants
IBSL	Internationaler Bund der Schuh- und Lederarbeiter	**ICA**	Institute of Contemporary Art
		ICA	Instituto Colombiano Agropêcuario
IBSL	Internationales Berufs-Sekretariat der Lehrer	**ICA**	Instituto Colombiano de Antropología

ICA	Institutul de Cercetari Alimentare (Roumania)	**ICAES**	International Congress of Anthropological and Ethnological Sciences
ICA	Inter-Cultural Cooperation Association	**ICAF**	International Committee on Aeronautical Fatigue
ICA	Intergovernmental Council for Automatic Data Processing	**ICAFI**	International Commission of Agriculture and Food Industries
ICA	International Caribbean Airways	**ICAI**	Instituto Católico de Artes e Industrias (Spain)
ICA	International Cartographic Association		
ICA	International Chefs Association	**ICAI**	International Commission for Agricultural Industries
ICA	International Chiropractors Association		
ICA	International Claim Association	**ICAI**	International Committee for Aid to Intellectuals
ICA	International Commission on Acoustics		
ICA	International Communications Association	**ICAITI**	Instituto Centro Americano de Investigación y Tecnologia Industrial (Guatemala)
ICA	International Control Agency		
ICA	International Co-operation Administration (U.S.A.) (*now* AID)	**ICALU**	International Confederation of Arab Labour Unions
ICA	International Co-operative Alliance	**ICAM**	Institut Culturel Africain, Malgache et Mauricien
ICA	International Council for Archives		
ICA	Jewish Colonization Association (Israel)	**ICAM**	Institute of Corn and Agricultural Merchants (U.K.) *now* BASAM
ICA	United States International Cooperation Administration	**ICAMAS**	International Centre for Advance Mediterranean Agronomic Studies
ICAA	International Civil Airport Association		
ICAA	International Confederation of Artists Associations	**ICAME**	International Centre for the Advancement of Management Education (U.S.A.)
ICAA	International Council on Alcohol and Addictions	**ICAN**	International College of Applied Nutrition (U.S.A.)
ICAAN	International Committee on Avian Anatomical Nomenclature	**ICAN**	International Commission on Air Navigation
		ICANA	Instituto Cultural Argentina Norte-Americano
ICAB	Industries Camerounaises des Annexes du Bâtiment	**ICAO**	International Civil Aviation Organisation
ICAB	International Council against Bullfighting	**ICAP**	Instituto Centroamericano de Administración Publica
ICAC	Independent Commission Against Corruption (Hong Kong)	**ICAP**	Inter-American Committee on the Alliance for Progress
ICAC	International Civil Aviation Committee		
ICAC	International Confederation for Agricultural Credit	**ICAP**	International Committee of Architectural Photogrammetry
ICAC	International Cotton Advisory Committee	**ICAPE**	International Chemical and Petroleum Engineering Exhibition
ICAD	Inter-American Committee for Agricultural Development	**ICAPF**	Instituto Centroamericano de Población y Familia (Guatemala)
ICAE	International Commission of Agricultural Engineering		
ICAE	International Commission on Atmospheric Electricity	**ICAR**	Indian Council of Agricultural Research
		ICAR	Institutul de Cercetari Agronomice al Romîniei
ICAE	International Conference of Agricultural Economists		
ICAE	International Council for Adult Education	**ICARDA**	International Centre for Agricultural Research in the Dry Areas (Middle East)
ICAES	Instituto Centroamericano de Estudios Sociales (Costa Rico)	**ICARE**	Instituto Chileno de Administración Racional de Empresas (Chile)

ICARE	International Center for the Advancement of Research and Education (Italy)	**ICC**	Association Internationale de Chimie Céréalière
ICARES	Institut International Catholique de Recherches Sociales	**ICC**	Imprimerie Commerciale du Cameroun
ICARMO	International Council of the Architects of Historical Monuments	**ICC**	International Cello Centre
		ICC	International Chamber of Commerce
ICAS	Interdepartmental Committee for Atmospheric Science (U.S.A.)	**ICC**	International Children's Centre, Paris
		ICC	International Climatological Commission
ICAS	International Council of Aeronautical Sciences	**ICC**	International Computing Centre (Switzerland)
ICASALS	International Centre for Arid and Semi-arid Land Studies (U.S.A.)	**ICC**	International Congregational Council
		ICC	International Cooperation Council
ICASE	Central American Institute of Educational Administration and Supervision	**ICC**	International Coordinating Committee for the Presentation of Science and the Development of Scientific Out-of-School Activities (Belgium)
ICASE	International Council of Associations for Science Education		
ICASSI	International Committee for Adlerian Summer Schools and Institutes	**ICC**	International Corrosion Council
		ICC	International Creative Centre (Switzerland)
ICAT	International Committee on Autogenic Therapy	**ICC**	International Cricket Conference
		ICCA	Industrie Cotonnière Centrafricaine
ICATO	Iranian Civil Aviation Training Organization	**ICCA**	Instituto Centroamericano de Ciencias Agricolas
ICATS	International Centre of Advanced Tourism Studies (*of* IUOTO)	**ICCA**	Intercontinental Corrugated Case Association
ICATU	International Confederation of Arab Trade Unions	**ICCA**	International Committee on Co-ordination for Agriculture
ICAW	International Conference on Automation in Warehousing	**ICCA**	International Congress and Convention Association
ICB	Indian Coffee Board		
ICB	Industrial Co-ordination Bureau	**ICCAD**	International Centre for Computer-Aided Design (Italy)
ICB	International Christian Broadcasters		
ICB	International Container Bureau	**ICCAIA**	International Coordinating Council of Aerospace Industries Associations
ICB	International Convention Bureau (Belgium)		
ICBA	International Community of Booksellers Associations	**ICCAM**	International Committee of Children's and Adolescent's Movements
ICBB	International Commission for Bee Botany	**ICCAP**	International Coordinating Committee for the Accountancy Profession (*now* IFA)
ICBBA	International Cornish Bantam Breeders Association	**ICCAS**	International Conference on Computer Applications in the Automation of Shipyard Operation and Ship Design
ICBD	International Council of Ballroom Dancing		
ICBL	International Conference on the Biology of Lipids	**ICCAT**	International Commission for the Conservation of Atlantic Tunas
ICBN	International Committee on Bacteriological Nomenclature (*now* ICNB)	**ICCB**	Institúto Cultural Colombo-Británico
		ICCB	International Catholic Child Bureau
ICBO	International Conference of Building Officials	**ICCBC**	International Committee for Colorado Beetle Control
ICBP	International Committee for Bird Preservation		
		ICCC	Indian Central Coconut Committee
ICBY	International Council on Books for Young People	**ICCC**	Inter-Council Co-ordination Committee (France)

ICCC	International Centre for Comparative Criminology	**ICCP**	International Council for Children's Play
ICCC	International Conference of Catholic Charities	**ICCR**	Indian Council for Cultural Relations
		ICCRA	Associazione Nazionale Importatori Carni Congelate, Refrigerate ed Affini
ICCC	International Conference Centers Consultants (Belgium)	**ICCRA**	Investigaciones Cooperatives en el Mar Caribe y Regiones Adjacentes (FAO)
ICCC	International Conference on Computer Communication	**ICCREA**	Istituto di Credito delle Casse Rurali e Artigiane
ICCC	International Conference on Co-ordination Chemistry	**ICCS**	International Catholic Conference of Scouting
ICCC	International Congresses on the Communication of Culture through Architecture, Arts and Mass Media	**ICCS**	International Centre of Criminological Studies
		ICCS	International Commission for Control and Supervision
ICCC	International Council of Christian Churches		
ICCD	Institute of Chocolate and Confectionery Distributors	**ICCS**	International Container and Chassis Services (Belgium)
ICCE	Instituto Colombiano de Construcciones Escolares	**ICCSTI**	Inter-Departmental Co-ordinating Committee for Scientific and Technical Information
ICCE	International Council of Commerce Employers	**ICCTA**	International Consultative Council of Travel Agents
ICCE	International Council for Correspondence Education	**ICCU**	International Cross-Country Union
		ICCW	Indian Council for Child Welfare
ICCEE	International Classification Commission for Electrical Engineering	**ICD**	International Centre for Development (Africa)
ICCF	International Committee on Canned Food	**ICD**	International Committee of Dermatology
ICCF	International Correspondence Chess Federation	**ICDA**	International Catholic Deaf Association
ICCH	International Commodity Clearing House	**ICDA**	International Coalition for Developing Action
ICCH	International Conference on Computers and the Humanities	**ICDC**	Indian Cotton Development Council
ICCICA	Interim Co-ordinating Committee on International Commodity Arrangements (U.S.A.)	**ICDC**	Industrial and Commercial Development Corporation
		ICDCS	Interstate Permanent Committee for Drought Control in the Sahelian Zone
ICCJ	International Committee for Co-operation of Journalists	**ICDECAA**	International Committee for the Development of Educational and Cultural Activities in Africa
ICCJ	International Council of Christians and Jews		
ICCL	International Committee of Comparative Law	**ICDO**	International Civil Defence Organisation
ICCLA	International Centre for the Co-ordination of Legal Assistance	**ICDP**	International Confederation for Disarmament and Peace
ICCO	International Carpet Classification Organization	**ICE**	Institut Italien pour le Commerce Extérieur
ICCO	International Cocoa Organization	**ICE**	Institute of Ceramic Engineers (U.S.A.)
ICCO	International Council of Containership Operators	**ICE**	Institution of Civil Engineers
		ICE	Instituto Costarricense de Electricidad
ICCP	Institutul de Cercetari pentru Cultura Porumbului (Roumania)	**ICE**	International Centre for the Environment
		ICE	International Cultural Exchange
ICCP	International Commission on Cloud Physics	**ICE**	IOMTR Committee for Europe

ICE	Istituto Nazionale per il Commercio con l'Estero	ICET	International Council on Education for Teaching
ICEA	Institut Canadien d'Éducation des Adultes	ICETEX	Instituto Colombiano de Especializacion Tecnica en el Exterior (Colombia)
ICEA	International Childbirth Education Association (U.S.A.)	ICETK	International Committee of Electrochemical Thermodynamics and Kinetics
ICEATCA	Icelandic Air Traffic Controllers Association	ICETT	Industrial Council for Educational and Training Technology
ICEBY	International Conference for the Education of Blind Youth	ICEVH	International Council for Education of the Visually Handicapped
ICECOOP	Chilean Institute for Cooperative Education	ICF	Ice Cream Federation
ICECU	Instituto Centroamericano de Extensión y Cultura (Costa Rica)	ICF	Institutul de Cercetari Forestiere (Roumania)
ICED	International Council for Educational Development (U.S.A.)	ICF	International Canoe Federation
ICED	International Council on Environmental Design	ICF	International Casting Federation
ICED	International Cryogenic Engineering Committee	ICF	International Cheerleading Foundation (U.S.A.)
ICED	International Council for Educational Development	ICF	International Congress on Fracture
ICEF	International Childrens Emergency Fund	ICF	International Consultants Foundation (U.S.A.)
ICEF	International Committee for Research and Study on Environmental Factors	ICF	International Cultural Foundation
ICEF	International Committee for Ethnographic Films	ICF	International Federation of Chemical and General Workers Unions
ICEF	International Conference on Environmental Future	ICF	Société des Ingénieurs Civils de France
ICEF	International Council for Educational Films	ICFA	International Cystic Fibrosis Association (now ICF(M)A)
ICEI	Institute of Civil Engineers of Ireland	ICFC	Industrial and Commercial Finance Corporation
ICEL	Instituto Colombiano de Energía Eléctrica	ICFC	International Centre of Films for Children
ICEL	International Committee on English in the Liturgy	ICFCYP	International Centre of Films for Children and Young People
ICEL	International Council of Environmental Law	ICFES	Instituto Colombiana para el Fomento de la Educación Superior
ICEM	Institutul de Cercetari Metalurgice (Roumania)	ICFG	International Cold Forging Group
ICEM	Inter-governmental Committee for European Migration	ICF(M)A	International Cystic Fibrosis (Mucoviscidosis) Association
ICEM	International Council for Educational Media	ICFOST	International Committee for Food Science Technology
ICEMIN	Institutul de Cercetări Miniere (Roumania)	ICFPW	International Confederation of Former Prisoners of War
ICER	Institute for Central European Research (U.S.A.)	ICFTA	International Committee of Foundry Technical Associations
ICER	Information Centre of the European Railways	ICFTU	International Confederation of Free Trade Unions
ICES	International Council for the Exploration of the Sea	ICFTU-ARO	Asian Regional Organisation of ICFTU
ICESA	International Conference on Environment Sensing and Assessment	ICFTU-ORIT	Inter-American Regional Organisation of Workers of the ICFTU
ICET	International Centre for Economy and Technology (Belgium)		

ICFU	International Council on the Future of the University
ICFW	International Christian Federation of Food, Drink, Tobacco and Hotelworkers
ICG	International Commission on Glass
ICG	International Congress of Genetics
ICG	International Geophysical Committee
ICG	Inter-Union Commission on Geodynamics
ICGA	International Carnival Glass Association
ICGA	International Classic Guitar Association
ICGEL	International Crushing and Grinding Equipment Ltd
ICGI	International Council of Goodwill Industries
ICGS	International Catholic Girls Society
ICHC	International Committee for Horticultural Congresses
ICHCA	International Cargo Handling Co-ordination Association
ICHDA	International Cooperative Housing Development Association (U.S.A.)
ICHE	International Councils on Higher Education
I Chem E	Institution of Chemical Engineers
ICHEO	Inter-University Council for Higher Education Overseas
ICHHS	International Council of Home-Help Services
ICHMT	International Centre for Heat and Mass Transfer (Yugoslavia)
ICHPER	International Council on Health, Physical Education and Recreation
ICHR	Indian Council for Historical Research
ICHS	Interafrican Committee for Hydraulic Studies
ICHS	International Committee of Historical Sciences
ICHS	International Council of Home-Help Services
ICHT	International Committee on Haemostasis and Thrombosis
ICHV	Institutul de Cercetari Horti-Viticole (Roumania)
ICI	Imperial Chemical Industries
ICI	Inküpscentralemas Aktiebolag
ICI	Instituto de Colonización e Immigración (Colombia)
ICI	Inter-American Co-operative Institute (Panama)
ICI	Inter-American Copyright Institute (Brazil)
ICI	International Commission on Illumination
ICI	Istituto Cotoniero Italiana
ICIA	International Centre of Information on Antibiotics (Belgium)
ICIA	International Credit Insurance Association
ICIA	International Crop Improvement Association
ICIANZ	Imperial Chemical Industries of Australia and New Zealand
ICIB	Indian Commercial Information Bureau
ICIB	International Council for Building Research, Studies and Documentation
ICICI	Industrial Credit and Investment Corporation of India
ICID	International Commission on Irrigation and Drainage (India)
ICIDCA	Instituto Cubano de Investigaciones de los Derivados de la Caña de Azúcar
ICIE	International Centre for Industry and the Environment
ICIF	International Co-operative Insurance Federation
ICIFI	International Council of Infant Food Industries
ICIP	Instituto Colombiano de la Investigación Pedagógica
ICIPE	Informateur Centre International de Propagation du Jeu d'Échecs (France)
ICIPE	International Centre of Insect Physiology and Ecology (Kenya)
ICIPU	Istituto di Credito per le Imprese di Pubblica Utilità
ICIRA	Instituto de Capacitación e Investigación en Reforma Agraria (Chile)
ICIREPAT	Committee for International Cooperation in Information Retrieval among Examining Patent Offices
ICIS	International Conference on Ion Sources
ICIT	Instituto Cubano de Investigaciones Tecnológicas (Cuba)
ICITA	International Chain of Industrial and Technical Advertising Agencies
ICITA	International Co-operative Investigations of the Tropical Atlantic
ICITO	Interim Committee of the International Trade Organisation
ICIV	Instituto Cooperativo Interamericano de la Vivienda (Guatemala)
ICIW	International Confederation of Professional and Intellectual Workers

ICJ	International Commission of Jurists	ICMR	Indian Council of Medical Research
ICJ	International Court of Justice	ICMRD	International Center for Marine Resource Development
ICJA	International Criminal Justice Association (U.S.A.)	ICMREF	Interagency Committee on Marine Science, Research, Engineering and Facilities (U.S.A.)
ICJW	International Council of Jewish Women	ICMRT	International Center for Medical Research and Training (of NIH) (U.S.A.)
ICL	International Computers Limited		
ICL	Irish Central Library for Students	ICMS	International Commission on Mushroom Science
ICLA	International Committee on Laboratory Animals	ICMSA	Irish Creamery Milk Suppliers Association
ICLA	International Comparative Literature Association	ICMSF	International Commission on Microbiological Specifications for Foods
ICLA	Investigadores de Cafe de Latino America	ICN	International Chemical and Nuclear Corporation
ICLARM	International Center for Living Aquatic Resources Management (Philippines)	ICN	International Council of Nurses
ICLG	International and Comparative Librarianship Group (of LA)	ICNAF	International Commission for the Northwest Atlantic Fisheries
ICLM	International Christian Leprosy Mission	ICNACO	Investigaciones Cooperativas en la Parte Norte del Atlantico Centro-Oriental (FAO)
ICLY	International Council on Lethal Yellowing	ICNATVAS	International Council of the National Academy of Television Arts and Sciences
ICM	International Confederation of Midwives		
ICMA	Institute of Cost and Management Accountants	ICNB	International Committee on Nomenclature of Bacteria
ICMA	International Center of Medieval Art	ICNDT	International Committee for Non-Destructive Testing
ICMA	International Christian Maritime Association	ICNND	Interdepartmental Committee on Nutrition for National Defense (U.S.A.)
ICMA	International Circulation Managers Association (U.S.A.)		
ICMA	International City Managers' Association	ICNT	International Committee for Natural Therapeutics
ICMA	International Congresses for Modern Architecture	ICNV	International Committee for the Nomenclature of Viruses
ICMAR	Institut International de Culture Maritime	ICO	Conference of International Catholic Organizations
ICMC	International Catholic Migration Commission		
ICMC	International Circulation Managers Commission	ICO	Intergovernmental Commission on Oceanography
ICMC	International Congress on Metallic Corrosion	ICO	International Chemistry Office
ICMEA	Institutul de Cercetari pentru Mecanizarea si Electrificarea Agriculturii (Roumania)	ICO	International Coffee Organisation
		ICO	International Commission on Oceanography
ICMF	Indian Cotton Mills Federation	ICO	International Commission on Optics
ICMI	International Commission of Mathematical Instruction	ICO	International Congress of Otolaryngology
		ICOA	International Castor Oil Association (U.S.A.)
ICMICA	International Catholic Movement for Intellectual and Cultural Affairs	ICOBA	International Confederation of Book Actors
ICMLT	International Congress of Medical Laboratory Technologists	ICOC	Indian Central Oilseeds Committee
		ICODA	Industrie Cotonnière du Dahomey
ICMMP	International Committee of Military Medicine and Pharmacy	ICODES	Instituto Colombiano de Desarrollo Social
ICMPH	International Centre of Medical and Psychological Hypnosis (Italy)	ICODI	Société des Impressions sur Tissus de Côte-d'Ivoire

ICOFA	International Scientific Commission on the Family
ICOFTA	Indian Council of Foreign Trade
ICOGRADA	International Council of Graphic Design Associations
ICOHM	International Committee on Occupational Mental Health
ICOHTEC	International Cooperation in History of Technology Committee
ICOLD	International Commission on Large Dams of the World Power Conference
ICOLPE	Instituto Colombiano de Pedagogia
ICOM	International Council of Museums
ICOME	International Committee on Microbial Ecology
ICOMI	Industria et Commercio de Minerios (Brazil)
ICOMIA	International Council of Marine Industry Associations
ICOMON	Conseil International des Monuments
ICOMOS	International Council of Monuments and Sites
ICON	Inter-Institutional Committee on Nutrition (U.S.A.)
ICON	Investment Company of Nigeria
ICONTEC	Instituto Colombiano de Normas Tecnicas
ICOO	Iraqi Company for Oil Operations
ICOP	Instituto Colombiano de Opinión Pública
ICOPA	International Conference of Police Associations
ICOPA	International Congress on Parasitology
ICOPRAPA	International Conference of Peace Researchers and Peace Activities
ICOR	Intergovernmental Conference on Oceanic Research
ICOS	International Committee of Onomastic Sciences
ICOSA	International Council of Seamen's Agencies (U.S.A.)
ICOSO	International Committee for Outer Space Onomastics
ICOTAF	Industrie Cotonnière Africaine
ICOU	Organisation Internationale des Unions de Consommateurs
ICP	International Committee for Learning by Participation
ICP	International Commission for Palynology
ICP	International Council of Psychologists
ICP	International Institute of Cellular and Molecular Pathology (Belgium)
ICP	Investment Corporation of Pakistan
ICPA	International Commission for the Prevention of Alcoholism
ICPA	International Co-operative Petroleum Association
ICPC	International Cable Protection Committee
ICPCE	International Great Plains Conference of Entomologists
ICPDP	International Committee for Pollution Damage to Plants
ICPFR	International Committee on Physical Fitness Research
ICPHS	International Council for Philosophy and Humanistic Studies
ICPI	Instituto Colombiano de Planeación Integral
ICPIGP	Internationale Chrétienne Professionelle pour les Industries Graphiques et Papetières
ICPM	International Commission for Plant Raw Materials
ICPM	International Committee on Polar Meteorology
ICPO	International Criminal Police Organisation
ICPP	International Conference on the Internal and External Protection of Pipes
ICPR	Indian Council of Peace Research
ICPRP	International Commission for the Protection of the Rhine Pollution
ICPS	Institute of Cost and Production Surveyors
ICPS	International Conference on the Properties of Steam
ICPS	International Congress of Photographic Science
ICPS	Trade Unions International of Chemical Oil and Allied Workers
ICPTO	International China Painting Teachers Organization (U.S.A.)
ICPU	International Catholic Press Union
ICR	Institute of Cultural Research
ICR	International Congress of Radiology
ICR	International Council for Reprography
ICRA	Instituto Costaricense de Defensa Agraria
ICRA	International Catholic Rural Association
ICRA	International Centre for Research in Accounting (U.K.)
ICRA	Irish Civil Rights Association

ICRB	International Center for Research on Bilingualism (Canada)	**ICSB**	International Committee on Systematic Bacteriology (*of* IAMS)
ICRC	Indian Cancer Research Centre	**ICSC**	Indian Central Sugarcane Committee
ICRC	International Committee of the Red Cross	**ICSC**	Interim Communications Satellite Commission (*of* INTELSAT)
ICRCP	International Centre for Relief to Civilian Population	**ICSC**	International Civil Service Commission
ICRDB	International Cancer Research Data Bank (U.S.A.)	**ICSC**	International Council of Shopping Centers (U.S.A.)
ICRE	International Centre for Remedial Education	**ICSC**	Inter-ocean Canal Study Commission (U.S.A.)
ICRE	International Commission on Radiological Education and Information	**ICSCHM**	International Commission for a History of the Scientific and Cultural Development of Mankind
ICREP	Instituto Chileno de Relaciones Publicas		
ICRH	International Congress on Religious History	**ICSDW**	International Council of Social Democratic Women *now* Socialist Internationalist Women
ICRICE	International Centre of Research and Information on Collective Economy (Belgium)		
ICRISAT	International Crop Research Institute for the Semi-Arid Tropics (India)	**ICSEAF**	International Commission for the Southeast Atlantic Fisheries
ICRM	Instituto Cubano de Recursos Minerales	**ICSEB**	International Congress of Systematic and Evolutionary Biology
ICRO	International Cell Research Organisation		
ICRP	International Commission on Radiation Protection	**ICSEM**	International Centre of Studies on Early Music
ICRPMA	International Committee for Recording the Productivity of Milk Animals	**ICSEMS**	International Commission for the Scientific Exploration of the Mediterranean Sea
ICRS	International Commission on Radium Standards	**ICSHB**	International Committee for Standardisation in Human Biology
ICRSC	International Council for Research in the Sociology of Cooperation	**ICSH**	International Congress Services Holland
ICRU	International Commission on Radiation Units and Measurements	**ICSI**	International Commission of Snow and Ice (*of* IASH)
ICS	Indian Chemical Society	**ICSID**	International Centre for Settlement of Investment Disputes
ICS	Institute of Caribbean Science (Puerto Rico)		
ICS	Institute of Chartered Shipbrokers	**ICSID**	International Council of Societies of Industrial Design
ICS	International Chamber of Shipping		
ICS	International Clarinet Society	**ICSM**	International Committee of Scientific Management
ICS	International Conrad Society (U.S.A.)		
ICS	International Crocodilian Society (U.S.A.)	**ICSMA**	International Conference on Strength of Metals and Alloys
ICS	International College of Surgeons (U.S.A.)		
ICS	International Correspondence Schools (U.S.A.)	**ICSOM**	International Conference of Symphony and Opera Musicians
ICSA	International Civil Service Agency	**ICSP**	International Council of Societies of Pathology
ICSA	International Correspondence Society of Allergists (U.S.A.)	**ICSPE**	International Council of Sport and Physical Education
ICSA	International Council for Scientific Agriculture	**ICSPFT**	International Committee for the Standardisation of Physical Fitness Tests
ICSAB	International Civil Service Advisory Board	**ICSPHR**	International Centre of Studies for the Protection of Human Rights (U.S.A.)
ICSB	International Centre of School-Building		

ICSPRO	Inter-Secretariat Committee on Scientific Programmes Relating to Oceanography	**ICTAA**	Imperial College of Tropical Agriculture Association
ICSPS	International Council for Science Policy Studies	**ICTB**	International Customs Tariffs Bureau
ICSS	Instituto Colombiano de Seguros Sociales	**ICTC**	Indian Central Tobacco Committee
ICSS	International Center for Strategic Studies (U.S.A.)	**ICTC**	International Cooperative Training Centre (U.S.A.)
ICSS	International Committee for Shell Structures (*now* IASS)	**ICTF**	International Cocoa Trades Federation
		ICTF	International Conference on Thin Films
ICSSD	International Committee for Social Sciences Documentation	**ICTMM**	International Congresses on Tropical Medicine and Malaria
ICSSID	International Committee for Social Science Information and Documentation	**ICTR**	International Centre of Theatre Research (France)
ICSSR	Indian Council of Social Science Research	**ICTS**	International Catholic Truth Society
ICSSW	International Committee of Schools for Social Work	**ICTS**	International Congress on Transplantation
		ICTT	Internacional del Personal de los Servicios de Correos, Télegrafos y Teléfonos
ICST	Imperial College of Science and Technology, London	**ICTTC**	International Consultative Telegraph and Telephone Committee
ICSTI	International Centre for Scientific and Technical Information (USSR)	**ICTU**	Irish Congress of Trade Unions
ICSTO	International Civil Service Training Organization	**ICU**	Institut pour la Coopération Universitaire
		ICU	International Chemistry Union
ICSU	International Council of Scientific Unions	**ICUAE**	International Congress of University Adult Education
ICSUAB	International Council of Scientific Unions Abstracting Board	**ICUE**	International Committee on the University Emergency
ICSUIA	Instituto de Ciencias Sociales de la Universidad Iberoamericana (Mexico)	**ICUEPR**	International Conference on University Education for Public Relations
ICSV	Internationale Christlich-Soziale Vereinigung (Belgium)	**ICUMSA**	International Commission for Uniform Methods of Sugar Analysis
ICSW	International Council on Social Welfare	**ICUP**	International Catholic Union of the Press
ICSWOA	International Centre for Scientific Work Organisation in Agriculture	**ICUS**	International Conference on the Unity of the Sciences
ICT	Institute of Clay Technology	**ICUSS**	International Council for the United Services to Seamen
ICT	International Computers and Tabulators, Ltd	**ICV**	International Commission of Viticulture
ICT	International Council of Tanners	**ICVA**	International Council of Voluntary Agencies
ICTA	Imperial College of Tropical Agriculture (West Indies)	**ICVAN**	International Committee on Veterinary Anatomical Nomenclature (Austria)
ICTA	Institute of Agricultural Science and Technology (Guatemala)	**ICVD**	Internationale Christelijke Vredesdient
ICTA	International Centre for the Typographic Arts (Germany)	**ICVG**	International Council for the Study of Viruses and Virus Diseases of Grapevine
ICTA	International Confederation of Technical Agriculturists	**ICW**	Institute of Clayworkers
ICTA	International Confederation for Thermal Analysis	**ICW**	Institute of Clerks of Works of Great Britain
		ICW	Instituut voor Cultuurtechniek en Waterhuishouding
ICTA	International Council for Travel Agents		
ICTA	Ivory Coast Travel Agency	**ICW**	Inter-American Commission of Women

ICW	International Chemical Workers Union (U.S.A.)	IDAF	International Defence and Aid Fund for Southern Africa
ICW	International Council for Women	IDAMI	Istituto di Documentazione della Associazione Meccanica Italiana
ICWA	Indian Council of World Affairs		
ICWA	Institute of Cost and Works Accountants (now ICMA)	IDATEX	Industrie Dahoméenne du Textile
		IDB	Industrial Development Board (Sri Lanka)
ICWA	International Coil Winding Association	IDB	Insurance Development Bureau (Sweden)
ICWES	International Conference of Women Engineers and Scientists	IDB	Inter-American Development Bank
		IDB	International Peace Bureau (Switzerland)
ICWG	International Co-operative Womens Guild	IDBI	Industrial Development Bank of India
ICWM	International Committee of Weights and Measures	IDBP	Industrial Development Bank of Pakistan
		IDBRA	International Drivers Behaviour Research Association
ICWP	International Council of Women Psychologists	IDBT	Industrial Development Bank of Turkey
ICWS	International Co-operative Wholesale Society	IDC	Industrial Development Corporation (South Africa, Trinidad and Tobago)
ICWU	International Chemical Workers Union		
ICY	International Christian Youth	IDC	International Dairy Committee
ICYE	International Council for the International Christian Youth Exchange	IDC	International Dance Council
		IDC	International Documentation Centre (Sweden)
ICYF	International Catholic Youth Federation		
ICZ	Institutul de Cercetari Zootehnice (Roumania)	IDC	International Dermatological Committee
		IDCA	Industrial Design Council of Australia
ICZN	International Commission for Zoological Nomenclature	IDCAS	Industrial Development Centre for Arab States
IDA	Industrial Diamond Association of America	IDCHEC	Intergovernmental Documentation Centre on Housing and Environment of the Countries of the United Nations Economic Commission for Europe
IDA	International Defenders of Animals (U.S.A.)		
IDA	International Development Action (Australia)		
IDA	International Development Association	IDD	Industrielle Designere Danmark
IDA	International Diplomatic Academy (U.S.A.)	IDDE	Instituto para el Desarrollo de la Dirección de Empresas (Uruguay)
IDA	International Discotheque Association		
IDA	International Doll Association	IDDRG	International Deep Drawing Research Group
IDA	International Drummers Association	IDDS	International Dairy Development Scheme
IDA	Irish Dental Association	IDE	Institut Danois des Échanges Internationaux de Publications Scientifiques et Littéraires
IDA	Irish Drug Association		
IDAA	International Doctors in Alcoholics Anonymous (U.S.A.)	IDE	Institut de Développement Économique (de la Banque Mondiale)
IDAAN	Instituto de Acueductos y Alcantarillados Nacionales (Panama)	IDE	Institute of Developing Economies (Japan) (formerly IAEA)
IDAC	Import Duties Advisory Committee	IDEA	Instituto para el Desarrollo de Ejecutivos en la Argentina
IDACA	Institute for the Development of Agricultural Cooperation in Asia (Japan)		
		IDEA	Instituto de Estudios Africanos
IDACE	Association des Industries des Aliments Diététiques de la Communauté Économique Européenne	IDEA	International Downtown Executives Association (U.S.A.)
IDAF	Institutet f. Distribution-Ekonomisk och Administrativ Forskning	IDEAS	Institutional Development Economic Affairs Service Inc. (U.S.A.)

IDEF	Institut International de Droit des Pays d'Expression Française	**IDMA**	International Dancing Masters' Association (*now* IDTA)
IDEMA	Instituto de Mercadeo Agropecuario (Colombia)	**IDMA**	International Doll Makers Association
IDEP	Institut Africain de Développement Économique et de Planification	**IDO**	International Dental Organisation
		IDOC	International Documentation and Communication Centre (Italy)
IDER	Instituto Dominicano de Educación Rural	**IDOC**	International Documentation on the Contemporary Church (Association) (U.S.A.)
IDERPC	Institut de Développement Économique de la République Populaire du Congo		
IDERT	Institut d'Enseignement et de Recherches Tropicales	**IDOE**	International Decade of Ocean Exploration (U.S.A.)
IDES	Instituto de Desarrollo Económico y Social (Argentina)	**IDORT**	Instituto de Organizacão Racional do Trabalho (Brazil)
IDET	Institut pour le Développement Économique et Technique	**IDP**	Institute of Data Processing
		IDR	International Dental Relief
IDEVI	Instituto de Desarrollo del Valle Inferior del Río Negro (Argentina)	**IDRA**	International Desert Racing Association
		IDRC	International Development Research Centre (Canada)
IDEX	Ivoirienne de Distribution et d'Exportation		
IDF	International Dairy Federation	**IDREM**	Institut Européen de Documentation et de Recherche sur les Maladies
IDF	Institut pour le Développement Forestier		
IDF	International Democratic Fellowship	**IDRF**	International Disaster Relief Force
IDF	International Dental Federation	**IDS**	Industrieverband Deutscher Schmieden
IDF	International Diabetes Federation	**IDS**	Institute of Development Studies, University of Sussex
IDFA	Interessengemeinschaft Deutscher Fachmessen und Ausstellungsstädte		
		IDS	International Development Services
IDFF	Internationale Demokratische Frauenföderation	**IDSA**	Indian Dairy Science Association
		IDSA	Industrial Designers Society of America
IDHA	International District Heating Association (U.S.A.)	**IDSA**	International Development Service of America
IDHE	Institute of Domestic Heating Engineers	**IDSO**	International Diamond Security Organization
IDI	Institut de Droit International	**IDT**	Institutul de Documentare Technica (Roumania)
IDIA	Industrial Design Institute of Australia		
IDIB	Industrial Diamond Information Bureau	**IDTA**	International Dance Teachers' Association
IDICIT	Instituto de Documentación y Información Científica y Técnica (Cuba)	**IDU**	International Dendrology Union
		IDV	Interessengemeinschaft Deutscher Versandbier-Grosshändler
IDICT	Instituto de Documentación e Información Científica y Técnica (Cuba)		
		IdW	Institut der Wirtschaftsprüfer in Deutschland
IDIS	International Dairy Industries Society	**IE**	Institute of Engineers
IDIT	Institut du Droit International des Transports	**I of E**	Institute of Export
IdK	Internationaler der Kriegsdienstgegner	**IE**	Institution of Electronics
IDLIS	International Desert Locust Information Service	**IEA**	Institut Économique Agricole (Belgium)
		IEA	Institute of Economic Affairs
IDLSG	International Drycleaners and Launderers Study Group	**IEA**	Institute of Engineers, Australia
		IEA	Instituto de Experimentaciones Agropecuarias (Argentina)
IDMA	International Diamond Manufacturers Association	**IEA**	International Association for the Evaluation of Educational Achievement

IEA	International Economic Association	**IEDR**	Institute of Economic Development and Research (Philippines)
IEA	International Electrical Association		
IEA	International Energy Agency	**IEE**	Institute of Explosives Engineers
IEA	International Entomological Association	**IEE**	Institution of Electrical Engineers
IEA	International Epidemiolgical Association	**IEEE**	Institute of Electrical and Electronic Engineers (U.S.A.)
IEA	International Ergonomics Association		
IEA	International Executives Association	**IEEE**	Instituto Español del Envase y Embalaje
IEA	Irish Exporters Association	**IEEFI**	Institut Européen pour l'Étude des Fibres Industrielles
IEAAC	Institut d'Études Agronomiques d'Afrique Centrale		
IEAB	Internacia Esperanto-Asocio de Bibliotekistoj	**IEETE**	Institution of Electrical and Electronics Technician Engineers
IEAG	Instituto Ecuatoriano de Antropologiá y Geografíca	**IEF**	Instituto Ecuatoriano del Folklore
		IEF	International Eye Foundation
IEAJ	International Esperanto Association of Jurists	**IEF**	International Ecumenical Fellowship
IEAV	Internationaler Eisenbahn Alkoholgegner Verband	**IEFC**	International Emergency Food Committee (FAO)
		IEG	Immunopathology Exchange Group
IEAZ	Instituto Experimental de Agricultura Zootécnica	**IEGSP**	Union Intercommunale pour l'Étude et la Gestion des Services Publics à Caractère Industrial et Communal
IEB	Institúto de Estudos Brasilieros		
IEB	International Education Board	**IEHEI**	Institut Européen des Hautes Études Internationales (France)
IEB	International Energy Bank		
IEC	Imperial Economic Committee (*now* CEC)	**IEI**	Industrial Education International
IEC	Institut d'Études Centrafricaines	**IEI**	Institute of Electrical Inspectors (Australia)
IEC	International Edsal Club	**IEI**	Institution of Engineering Inspection
IEC	International Egg Commission	**IEI**	International Esperanto Institute
IEC	International Electrotechnical Committee	**IEIAS**	Institut Européen Interuniversitaire de l'Action Sociale (Belgium)
IEC	International Energy Cooperative Inc. (U.S.A.)		
		IEIC	Institution of Engineers-in-Charge
IEC	International Extension College (U.K.)	**IEIP**	Institut Européen des Industries de la Pectine (Belgium)
IEC	Israel Electric Corporation		
IECA	Imperial Ethiopian College of Agriculture	**IEISW**	Inter-University European Institute on Social Welfare
IECAMA	Imperial Ethiopian College of Agriculture and Mechanical Arts	**IEKA**	Internacia Esperanto-Klubo Automobilista
IECIC	International Engineering and Construction Industries Council (U.S.A.)	**IEKV**	Internationale Eisenbahn-Kongress-Vereinigung
		IEMCS	Industrial Estates Management Corporation for Scotland
IECN	Instituto Ecuatoriano de Ciencias Naturales		
IED	Institut d'Études du Développement (Switzerland)	**IEME**	Instituto Español de Moneda Extranjera
		IEMVPT	Institut d'Élevage et de Médecine Vétérinaire des Pays Tropicaux
IED	Institution of Engineering Designers		
IED	International Education Development	**IEO**	Instituto Español de Oceanografíca
IEDA	Institut d'Études du Développement Africain	**IEP**	International Economic Publishers (U.S.A.)
IEDD	Institution of Engineering Draughtsmen and Designers	**IEPA**	International Economic Policy Association (U.S.A.)
IEDES	Institut d'Étude de Développement Économique et Social	**IEPAL**	Instituto de Estudios Políticos para América Latina

IEPC	NAS Committee for International Environmental Programs (U.S.A.)	**IEV**	Institúto Experimental de Veterinária (Brazil)
		IEY	International Education Year
IER	Institute for Economic Research (Iran)	**IFA**	Industries et Forêts Africaines (Cameroons, Central Africa, Congo)
IER	Institute of Engineering Research California (U.S.A.)	**IFA**	Institut for Atomenergi
IER	Organization for International Economic Relations (U.N.)	**IFA**	Institut Français de l'Alcool
		IFA	Instituto de Fomento Algodonero (Colombia)
IERAC	Instituto Ecuatoriano de Reforma Agraria y Colonización	**IFA**	International Federation of Accountants
		IFA	International Federation of Actors
IERE	Institution of Electronic and Radio Engineers	**IFA**	International Federation on Ageing
IERE	International Electrical Research Exchange	**IFA**	International Federation of Airworthiness
IEREGEM	Institut Équatorial de Recherches et d'Études Géologiques et Minières	**IFA**	International Florists Association
		IFA	International Footprint Association
IERF	Industrial Educational and Research Foundation (*now* FBR)	**IFA**	International Franchise Association
		IFA	International Frisbee Association
IERH	Instituto Ecuatoriano de Recursos Hidráulicos	**IFA**	International Fertility Association
		IFA	International Filariasis Association
IERS	Institut d'Études et de Recherches Sociales (Iran)	**IFA**	International Fiscal Association
IERS	International Educational Reporting Service (IBE)	**IFABC**	International Federation of Audit Bureaux of Circulations
IES	Illuminating Engineering Society	**IFAC**	Institut Français d'Action Coopérative
IES	Illuminating Engineering Society (U.S.A.)	**IFAC**	Institut Français de Recherches Fruitières Outre-Mer
IES	Illuminating Engineering Societies of Australia	**IFAC**	Institut des Fruits et Agrumes Coloniaux
IES	Institute of European Studies (U.S.A.)	**IFAC**	International Federation of Advertising Clubs
IES	Institution of Engineers and Shipbuilders in Scotland	**IFAC**	International Federation of Automatic Control
IESA	Institut Français des Sciences Administratives	**IFAD**	International Fund for Agricultural Development
IESA	Instituto Español del Envase y Embalaje	**IFAE**	Interamerican Federation for Adult Education
IESA	International Society for Electrosleep and Electroanaesthesia	**IFAJ**	International Federation of Agricultural Journalists
IESC	International Executive Service Corps (U.S.A.)	**IfAL**	Institut für Ausländische Landwirtschaft, Berlin
IESNEC	Institution of Engineers and Shipbuilders of the North-East Coast	**IFALPA**	International Federation of Air Line Pilots Associations
IESRI	Institut Européen d'Études et de Relations Intercommunales (Switzerland)	**IFALS**	International Federation of Arts, Letters and Sciences
IESS	Institution of Engineers and Shipbuilders in Scotland	**IFAN**	Institut Français d'Afrique Noire
IESSA	Institute of Economic Studies and Social Action, Manila (Philippines)	**IFAN**	International Federation for the Application of Standards
IESTIS	Instituto Ecuatoriano de Sociología y Técnica, Transculturación, Integración e Investigación Social	**IFAP**	Industrie Africaine de Filets de Pêche
IESTO	Institut d'Études Supérieures des Techniques d'Organisation	**IFAP**	International Federation of Agricultural Producers

FAPP	International Federation of the Associations of Pharmaceutical Physicians	**IFCC**	International Federation of Children's Communities
FARHU	Instituto para a Formación y Aprovechamiento de Recursos Humanos (Panama)	**IFCC**	International Federation of Clinical Chemistry
		IFCCA	International Federation of Community Centre Associations
FAS	International Federation of Aquarium Societies	**IFCCTE**	International Federation of Commercial, Clerical and Technical Employees
FAT	Institut Français d'Amérique Tropicale (*of* ORSTOM)	**IFCE**	Institut Française des Combustibles et de l'Énergie
FATCA	International Federation of Air Traffic Controllers Associations	**IFCE**	International Federation of Consulting Engineers
FATCC	International Federation of Associations of Textile Chemists and Colourists	**IFCI**	Industrial Finance Corporation of India
FATE	International Federation of Airworthiness Technology and Engineering (*now* IFA)	**IFCJ**	International Federation of Catholic Journalists
FATSEA	International Federation of Air Traffic Safety Electronic Associations	**IFCM**	International Federation of Christian Metalworker's Unions
FATU	International Federation of Arab Trade Unions	**IFCMU**	International Federation of Christian Miner's Unions
FAW	International Fund for Animal Welfare	**IFCO**	International Fan Club Organization
FAWPCA	International Federation of Asian and Western Pacific Contractors' Associations	**IFCO**	International Fisheries Cooperative Organization
FB	International Federation of the Blind	**IFCO**	Interreligious Foundation for Community Organization (U.S.A.)
FB	International Film Bureau		
FBA	International Fire Buff Associations	**IFCP**	International Federation of Catholic Pharmacists
FBB	International Federation of Body Builders		
FBBF	Imported Fibre Building Board Federation	**IFCT**	Industrial Finance Corporation of Thailand
FBPW	International Federation of Business and Professional Women (*now* FBBF)	**IFCT**	Institut Française de Coopération Technique
		IFCTU	International Federation of Christian Trade Unions
FBSO	International Federation of Boat Show Organisers	**IFCTUBWW**	International Federation of Christian Trade Unions of Building and Woodworkers
FBWW	International Federation of Building and Wood Workers	**IFCTUGPI**	International Federation of Christian Trade Unions of Graphical and Paper Industries
FC	Institut Français du Caoutchouc	**IFCTUSET-MSCT**	International Federation of Christian Trade Unions of Salaried Employees, Technicians, Managerial Staff and Commercial Travellers
FC	International Finance Corporation (U.S.A.)		
FC	International Fisheries Commission		
FCA	International Federation of Catholic Alumnae	**IFCTUTCW**	International Federation of Christian Trade Unions of Textile and Clothing Workers
FCATI	International Federation of Cotton and Allied Textile Industries	**IFCU**	International Federation of Catholic Universities
FCAWU	International Federation of Christian Agricultural Workers' Unions	**IFCUAW**	International Federation of Christian Unions of Agricultural Workers
FCB	International Federation for Cell Biology		
FCC	Institut Français du Café, du Cacao et d'Autres Plantes Stimulantes	**IFD**	Institute of Food Distribution
		IFD	International Federation for Documentation
FCC	International Federation of Camping and Caravanning	**IFD**	Internationale Federation des Dachdeckerhandwerks

IFDA	International Federation of Data Processing Associations	**IFFF**	Internationale Frauenliga für Frieden und Freiheit
IFDA	International Food Service Distributors Association	**IFFJ**	International Federation of Free Journalists of Central and Eastern Europe and Baltic and Balkan Countries
IFDA	International Foundation for Development Alternatives (Switzerland)	**IFFJP**	International Federation of Fruit Juice Producers
IFDA	International Franchised Dealers Association	**IFFPA**	International Federation of Film Producers' Associations
IFDES	Institut Français d'Études Stratégiques		
IFDIB	International Festivals Documentation and Information Bureau (France)	**IFFS**	International Federation of Film Societies
IFE	Asociación de Investigación Técnica de la Industria Papelera Española	**IFFS**	International Fellowship of Former Scouts and Guides
IFE	Institut für Technische Forschung und Entwicklung (Austria)	**IFFTU**	International Federation of Free Teachers' Unions
IFE	Institute of Fire Engineers	**IFG**	Institúto de Fisiograpia y Geológica (Argentina)
IFEC	Institut Français de l'Emballage et du Conditionnement	**IFGA**	International Federation of Grocer's Associations
IFEC	Institut Français des Experts Comptables	**IFGB**	Institute of Foresters of Great Britain
IFEES	International Federation of Electro-Encephalographic Societies	**IFGO**	International Federation of Gynecology and Obstetrics
IFEF	International Federation of Esperantist Railwaymen	**IFGVP**	International Federation of Gastronomical, Vinicultural and Touristic Press
IFEI	Institut Français d'Esthétique Industrielle	**IFHE**	International Federation of Home Economics
IFEIA	Instituto Franco-Ecuatoriano de Investigaciónes Agronómicas	**IFHE**	International Federation of Hospital Engineers
IFEMS	International Federation of Electron Microscope Societies	**IFHP**	International Federation for Housing and Planning
IFEO	International Federation of Eugenic Organizations	**IFHPSM**	International Federation for Hygiene, Preventive Medicine and Social Medicine
IFEP	Danish Electronics Reliability Institute	**IFHTM**	International Federation for the Heat Treatment of Materials
IFER	Fédération Internationale des Sociétés de Publicité Ferroviaire	**IFI**	Imperial Forestry Institute, Oxford (*now* CFI)
IFER	Internationale Föderation des Eisenbahn-Reklame- Gesellschaften (Switzerland)	**IFI**	Information for Industry Ltd. (U.S.A.)
IFES	International Fellowship of Evangelical Students	**IFI**	International Federation of Interior Designers
IFEW	Inter-American Federation of Entertainment Workers	**IFI**	Internationale Föderation Innenarchitekten
IFF	Industriens Forskningsforening	**IFI**	International Foundation for Independence (U.S.A.)
IFF	Industrifarmaceutforeningen	**IFI**	Israel Furniture Industry
IFF	Institute for the Future (U.S.A.)	**IFIA**	International Federation of Inventors' Associations
IFF	International Flying Farmers (U.S.A.)		
IFFA	Institut f. Forstliche Arbeitswissenschaft	**IFIA**	Instituto Forestal de Industrialización y Administración (Argentina)
IFFA	Institut Français de la Fièvre Aphteuse		
IFFA	International Federation of Film Archives	**IFIA**	International Federation of Ironmongers and Iron Merchants Associations
IFFA	International Frozen Food Association		
IFFCO	Indian Farmers Fertilizer Co-operative	**IFIA**	International Fence Industry Association

IFIAS	International Federation of Institutes for Advanced Study	**IFLS**	International Federation of Law Students
IFIDA	International Film Importers and Distributors of America	**IFM**	International Falcon Movement
		IFM	Institute of Fisheries Management
IFIE	Instituto Forestal de Investigaciones y Experiencias	**IFMA**	International Federation of Margarine Associations
IFIF	Internationale Föderation von Industriegewerkschaften und Fabrik-arbeiterverbänden	**IFMA**	International Foodservice Manufacturers Association (U.S.A.)
		IFMA	International Food Manufacturers Association (U.S.A.)
IFIG	Internationales Forschungs- und Informationszentrum für Gemeinwirtschaft	**IFMA**	Irish Flour Millers Association
IFIP	International Federation for Information Processing	**IFMAP**	Irish Federation of Musicians and Associated Professions
IFIP	International Project in the Field of Food Irradiation	**IFMBE**	International Federation for Medical and Biological Engineering
IFIPS	International Federation of Information Processing Societies	**IFMC**	International Folk Music Council
		IFME	International Federation for Medical Electronics (*now* IFMBE)
IFIS	International Food Information Service		
IFITU	Indian Federation of Independent Trade Unions	**IFME**	International Federation of Municipal Engineers
IFIWA	International Federation of Importers and Wholesale Grocers' Associations	**IFMMS**	International Federation of Mining and Metallurgical Students
IFJ	International Federation of Journalists	**IFMP**	International Federation for Medical Psychotherapy
IFJU	International Federation of Fruit Juice Producers	**IFMSA**	International Federation of Medical Student Associations
IFK	Industrieverband Füllhalter und Kugelschreiber	**IFM-SEI**	International Falcon Movement—Socialist Educational International
IFKAB	Internationale Federatie van Katholieke Arbeiders Bewegingen	**IFMI**	Irish Federation of Marine Industries
IFKM	Internationale Föderation für Kurzschrift und Maschinenschreiben	**IFMW**	International Federation of Mazdaznan Women
IFKT	International Federation of Knitting Technologists	**IFNAES**	International Federation of the National Associations of Engineering Students
IFL	Icelandic Federation of Labour	**IFNSA**	International Federation of the National Standardizing Association
IFL	Institute of Fluorescent Lighting		
IFL	Institutet för Företagsledning	**IFO**	Institut für Wirtschaftforschung
IFL	International Federation of Lithographers, Process Workers and Kindred Trades	**IFO**	Institute for Fermentation (Japan)
		IFO	International Farmers Organization
IFL	International Friendship League	**IFOAM**	International Federation of Organic Agriculture Movements
IFLA	International Federation of Landscape Architects	**IFOCAP**	Institut de Formation pour des Cadres Paysans
IFLA	International Federation of Library Associations	**IFOFSAG**	International Fellowship of Former Scouts and Guides
IFLAIC	Instituto Forestal Latino-americano de Investigación y Capacitación	**IFOG**	International Federation of Olive Growers
IFLFF	Internationale Frauenliga für Frieden und Freiheit	**IFOP**	Institut Français d'Opinion Publique
IFLS	Institut Français de Libre Service	**IFOP**	Instituto de Fomento Pesquero, Santiago (Chile)

IFOR	International Fellowship of Reconciliation	**IFPRI**	International Food Policy Research Institute
IFORS	International Federation of Operational Research Societies	**IFPS**	International Federation of Philosophical Societies
IFORVU	International Federation of Recreational Vehicle Users	**IFPTO**	International Federation of Popular Travel Organisations
IFOS	International Federation of Oto-Rhino-Laryngological Societies	**IFPW**	International Federation of Petroleum Workers
IFOSA	International Federation of Stationers Associations	**IFPWA**	International Federation of Public Warehousing Associations
IFOTES	International Federation for Services of Emergency Telephonic Help	**IFR**	Indian Famine Relief
		IFR	Internationaler Frauenrat
IFP	Institut Français du Pétrole	**IFRA**	INCA-FIEJ Research Association
IFP	Institut Français de Polémologie	**IFRA**	International Fund-Raising Association (U.S.A.)
IFP	International Federation of Purchasing		
IFPA	Information Film Producers of America	**IFRB**	International Frequency Registration Board
IFPA	Industrial Fire Protection Association of Great Britain	**IFRC**	International Fusion Research Council
		IFRF	International Flame Research Foundation
IFPA	Inter-American Federation of Personnel Administration	**IFRPD**	Institute of Food Research and Product Development (Thailand)
IFPA	International Fire Photographers Association	**IFRU**	Institut Français du Royaume-Uni
IFPAAW	International Federation of Plantation, Agricultural and Allied Workers	**IFRW**	International Federation of Resistance Workers
IFPCS	International Federation of Unions of Employees in Public and Civil Services	**IFS**	International Federation of Settlements and Neighbourhood Centres
IFPCW	International Federation of Petroleum and Chemical Workers	**IFS**	International Federation of Surveyors
		IFS	International Film Seminars
IFPE	International Federation for Parent Education	**IFS**	International Foundation for Science (UNESCO)
IFPI	International Federation of the Phonographic Industry	**IFSA**	Institut Français des Sciences Administratives
IFPLAA	Internationale Föderation der Plantagen, Land- und anverwandten Arbeiter	**IFSCC**	International Federation of Societies of Cosmetic Chemists
IFPLVB	Internationale Föderation der Plantagen- und Landarbeiter und Verwandter Berufsgruppen	**IFSDA**	International Federation of Stamp Dealers's Associations
IFPM	International Federation of Physical Medicine	**IFSDP**	International Federation of the Socialist and Democratic Press
IFPMA	International Federation of Pharmaceutical Manufacturers Associations	**IFSEA**	International Federation of Scientific Editors' Associations
IFPMM	International Federation of Purchasing and Materials Management	**IFSEM**	International Federation of Societies for Electron Microscopy
IFPNT	International Federation of Practitioners of Natural Therapeutics	**IFSMA**	International Federation of Ship Master Associations
IFPRA	Inter-American Federation of Public Relations Associations	**IFSMU**	Irish Free State Medical Union
IFPRA	International Federation of Park and Recreation Administration	**IFSNC**	International Federation of Settlements and Neighbourhood Centres
IFPRI	International Food Policy Research Institute (USA)	**IFSP**	International Federation of Societies of Philosophy

IFSPO	International Federation of Senior Police Officers	**IFWRI**	Institute of Furniture Warehousing and Removal Industry
IFST	Institute of Food Science and Technology	**IFWTA**	International Federation of Workers Travel Associations
IFST	International Federation of Shorthand and Typewriting	**IFYC**	International Federation of Young Co-operators
IFSTA	International Fire Service Training Association	**IFYE**	International Farm Youth Exchange
IFTO	International Federation of Tour Operators	**IFYGL**	International Field Year for the Great Lakes (U.S.A.)
IFSW	International Federation of Social Workers		
IFT	Institute of Food Technologists (U.S.A.)	**IGA**	Inspection Générale de l'Agriculture
IFT	International Federation of Translators	**IGA**	Interessen-Gemeinschaft Aerosole
IFTA	Institut Français des Transports Aériens	**IGA**	International Geneva Association (U.S.A.)
IFTA	International Federation of Teachers' Associations	**IGA**	International Geographical Association
IFTA	International Federation of Thanatopraxis	**IGA**	International Gold Association
IFTA	International Fine Technics Association	**IGA**	Irish Gas Board
IFTC	International Federation of Thermalism and Climatism	**IGAEA**	International Graphic Arts Education Association (U.S.A.)
IFTC	International Film and Television Council	**IGAM**	Internationale Gesellschaft für Allgemein-medizin
IFTF	International Fur Trade Federation	**IGAP**	Internationale Gesellschaft für Ärztliche Psychotherapie
IFTOMM	International Federation for the Theory of Machines and Mechanisms	**IGAS**	International Graphic Arts Society (U.S.A.)
IFTR	International Federation for Theatre Research	**IGAS**	International Graphoanalysis Society (U.S.A.)
IFTUTW	International Federation of Trade Unions of Transport Workers	**IGB**	Internationaler Genossenschaftsbund
		IGC	International Garden Centres
IFTW	International Federation of Tobacco Workers	**IGC**	International Garden Club
		IGC	International Geological Congress
IFTWA	International Federation of Textile Workers Associations	**IGC**	International Geophysical Committee
		IGC	International Grassland Congress
IFU	Internationale Fruchtsaft-Union	**IGC**	UN/FAO Intergovernmental Committee
IFUC	Interprovincial Farm Union Council (Canada)	**IGCA**	Industrial Gas Cleaning Association
IFUNO	Indian Federation of United Nations Associations	**IGCC**	Intergovernmental Copyright Committee
		IGCR	Instituto Geográfico de Costa Rica
IFUW	International Federation of University Women	**IGCR**	Inter-Governmental Committee on Refugees
		IGE	Institution of Gas Engineers
IFVA	International Federation of Variety Artistes	**IGE**	International Guiding Eyes (U.S.A.)
IFVV	Internationale Federatie van Vakorganisaties van Vervoerspersoneel	**IGEME**	Ihracati Geliştirme Etüd Merkezi (Export Promotion Research Centre) (Turkey)
IFW	International Federation of Wargaming	**IGER**	Institut Nationale de Gestion et d'Économie Rurale
IFWA	International Federation for Weeks of Art		
IFWEA	International Federation of Workers Educational Associations	**IGF**	International Genetics Federation
		IGF	International Graphical Federation
IFWHA	International Federation of Women's Hockey Associations	**IGF**	International Gymnastic Federation
IFWL	International Federation of Women Lawyers	**IGFA**	International Game Fish Association

IGFAP	International Gesellschaft für Analytische Psychologie	**IGU**	International Geographical Union
IGFRI	Indian Grassland and Fodder Institute	**IGU**	Internationale Gewerbeunion
IGGA	International Grooving and Grinding Association	**IGV**	Internationaler Gemeindeverband
		IGWF	International Garment Workers' Federation
IGGI	Inter-Governmental Group on Indonesia	**IGY**	International Geophysical Year
IGI	Industrial Graphics International	**IHA**	International Hahnemannian Association (U.S.A.)
IGI	International Wallpaper Manufacturers Association	**IHA**	International Horse Association
IGL	Institut Gramme de Liège (Belgium)	**IHA**	International Hotel Association
IGM	Instítúto Geográfico Militar (Argentina)	**IHA**	International House Association
IGM	Internationale Gesellschaft für Moorfor- schung	**IHA**	Irish Hardware Association
IGMAA	International Gas Model Airplane Associa- tion (U.S.A.)	**IHAIO**	International Historical Association of the Indian Ocean
IGMB	Instituut voor Graan, Meel en Brood	**IHATIS**	International Hides and Allied Trades Improvement Society
IGMG	Internationale Gustav Mahler Gesellschaft	**IHB**	International Hydrographic Bureau
IGMW	Internationale Gesellschaft f. Musikwissen- schaft	**IHB**	Internationale Hopfenbaubüro
		IHBS	International Hajji Baba Society
IGN	Institut Géographique National	**IHC**	Industrieele Handelscombinatie
IGN	Instituto Geográfica Nacional (Peru)	**IHC**	Intercontinental Hotels Association
IGN	Instituto Geológico Nacional (Colombia)	**IHC**	International Help for Children
IGNM	Internationale Gesellschaft für Neue Musik	**IHCA**	International Hebrew Christian Alliance
IGO	Inter-Governmental Organisation	**IHD**	Institute of Human Development (U.S.A.)
IGOSS	Integrated Global Ocean Station System	**IHD**	International Hydrological Decade
IGP	Grossistforeningen for Isenkram- Glas- og Porceloensbranschen	**IHE**	Institution of Highway Engineers
		IHEA	Institut des Hautes Études Agraires
IGP	Instituto Geofisico del Perú	**IHEA**	International Health Evaluation Association
IGP	International Guild of Prestidigitators	**IHEB**	International Heat Economy Bureau
IGPAI	Inspeção-Geral dos Produtes Agricolas e Industrias (Portugal)	**IHEDREA**	Institut des Hautes Études de Droit Rural et d'Économie Agricole
IGR	International Guild of Prestidigitators (U.S.A.)	**IHES**	Illinois Horticultural Experiment Station (U.S.A.)
IGROF	Internationale Rorschach-Gesellschaft	**IHEU**	International Humanist and Ethical Union
IGRS	Irish Genealogical Research Society	**IHF**	International Hockey Federation
IGS	Irish Graphical Society	**IHF**	International Hospital Federation
IGS	International Geranium Society	**IHFA**	Industrial Hygiene Foundation of America
IGSA	International Golf Sponsors Association	**IHFBC**	International High Frequency Broadcasting Conference
IGSP	Internationale Gesellschaft der Schrift- psychologie	**IHFPA**	Instituto de Higiene y Fomento de la Producción Animal (Chile)
IGSS	International Graduate Summer School in Librarianship and Information Service	**IHGB**	Instítúto Histórico e Geográfico Braziliero
IGTYF	International Good Templar Youth Federation	**IHGC**	International Hop Growers Convention
IGU	International Gas Union	**IHGS**	Institute of Heraldic and Genealogical Studies

IHHA	International Halfway House Association (U.S.A.)
IHI	Internationales Hilfskomitee für Intellektuelle
IHK	Internationale Handelskammer
IHL	International Hockey League
IHL	International Homeopathic League
IHLADI	Instituto Hispano-Luso-Americano de Derecho Internacional
IHMB	Industrie des Huiles Minérales de Belgique
IHMEE	International Hotel and Motel Educational Exposition
IHO	International Health Organisation
IHO	International Hydrographic Organisation
IHP	Intergovernmental Council of the International Hydrological Programme
IHR	Institute of Historical Research, London
IHRB	International Hockey Rules Board
IHRMA	Irish Hotel and Restaurant Managers' Association
IHS	Institute of Human Sciences (U.S.A.)
IHS	International Haemophilia Society
IHS	International Hydrofoil Society
IHSA	Inversiones Huascaran Soc. Anon (Peru)
IHVE	The Institution of Heating and Ventilating Engineers
II	Ikebana International
IIA	Institut International d'Anthropologie
IIA	Instituto de Investigaciones Agropecuarias (Chile)
IIA	International Illawarra Association
IIA	International Institute for Africa
IIA	International Institute of Agriculture (*now* FAO)
IIAA	Institute of Inter-American Affairs
IIAA	Instituto International de Asuntos Ambientales
IIAA	Instituto de Investigação Agronomica de Angola
IIAG	Institut für Angewandt Geodäsie
IIAI	Indian Institution of Art in Industry
IIAL	International Institute of Arts and Letters
IIALM	International Institute of Adult Literacy Methods, Tehran (Iran)
IIAM	Institut de la Recherche Agronomique Mozambique
IIAP	Institut International d'Administration Publique
IIAR	International Institute of Ammonia Refrigeration (U.S.A.)
IIAS	Indian Institute of Asian Studies
IIAS	Inter-American Institute of Agricultural Sciences
IIAS	International Institute of Administrative Sciences (Belgium)
IIASA	International Institute for Applied Systems Analysis (Austria)
IIB	Institut International des Brevets
IIB	International Investment Bank
IIBD & ID	Incorporated Institute of British Decorators and Interior Designers
IIBEM	Indian Institute of Biochemistry and Experimental Medicine
IIC	India International Centre
IIC	Institúto de Ingeneiros de Chile
IIC	International Institute of Communications (Italy)
IIC	International Institute of Communications (U.K.)
IIC	International Institute for the Conservation of Historic and Artistic Works (U.K.)
IIC	International Institute for Cotton (U.S.A.)
IICA	Institute of Instrumentation and Control, Australia
IICA	Instituto Interamericano de Ciencias Agricolas de la OEA (Costa Rica)
IICA	Instituto Internacional de las Cajas de Ahorro
IICA	Instituto Internacional de Ciencias Administrativas
IICA	Instituto de Investigacão Cientifica de Angola
IICAF	Institute for International Collaboration in Agriculture and Forestry (Czechoslovakia)
IICAT	Investigación Internacional Cooperativa del Atlántico Tropical
IICC	International Institute for Study and Research in the Field of Commercial Competition (Belgium)
IICCSE	International Information Centre for Computers in Secondary Education (U.K.)
IICE	Institut International des Caisses d'Épargne
IICI	Institut International de Coopération Intellectuelle

IICM	Instituto de Investigação Científica de Moçambique	**IIEO**	International Islamic Economic Organisation
IICS	Institut International de Chimie Solvay	**IIEP**	International Institute for Educational Planning
IICT	Institúto de Investigaciónes Científicas y Tecnologícas (Argentina)	**IIES**	Institut International d'Études Sociales (Switzerland)
IICY	International Independent Christian Youth	**IIES**	International Institute for Environmental Studies
IICY	International Investment Corporation for Yugoslavia	**IIF**	Institut International du Froid
IIDA	Institut Interaméricain de Droit d'Auteur	**IIFA**	International Institute of Films on Art
IIDARA	Instituto Iberoamericano de Derecho Agrario y Reforma Agraria (Venezuela)	**IIFCOOP**	Instituto Interamericano de Financiamienta Cooperativo (Chile)
IIDC	Instituto de Investigaciones Económicas (Mexico)	**IIFP**	Institut International des Finances Publiques (Belgium)
IIDH	Institut International de Droit Humanitaire	**IIFT**	Indian Institute of Foreign Trade
IIDP	Institut International du Droit Public	**IIGBM**	Institut International de Génie Biomédical
IIDU	Istituto Internazionale di Diritto Umanitario (Italy)	**IIGEAG**	Instituto de Investigaciones Geologicas Edafologicas y Agrobiologicas de Galicia
IIE	Institut Interaméricain de l'Enfance	**IIHA**	International Institute of the Hylean Amazon
IIE	Institut International de l'Environnement	**IIHF**	International Ice Hockey Federation
IIE	Institut International d'Embryologie	**IIHL**	International Institute of Humanitarian Law (Italy)
IIE	Institut International d'Étiopathie (France)		
IIE	Institut International de l'Épargne	**III**	Institut Isostatique International
IIE	Institution Internationale d'Esperanto	**III**	Instituto Interamericano Indigenista (Mexico)
IIE	Instituto Interamericano de Estadistica (U.S.A.)	**III**	Inter-American Indian Institute
IIE	Instituto Interamericano de Estadistica	**III**	International Institute of Interpreters (U.S.A.)
IIE	Instituto Internacional de Estadística	**III**	Internationales Institut für Industrieplanung (Austria)
IIEA	International Institute of Environmental Affairs	**III**	Istituto Italiano Imballaggio
IIEB	Institut International d'Études Bancaires	**IIIA**	Israeli Institute of International Affairs
IIEC	European Institute of Environmental Cybernetics	**IIIC**	International Institute for Intellectual Co-operation
IIEC	Istituto Internazionale di Educazione Cinematografica	**IIIC**	International Irrigation Information Centre (Israel)
IIED	International Institute for Environment and Development	**IIIHS**	International Institute of Integral Human Sciences (Canada)
IIEE	Institut International d'Études sur l'Éducation (Belgium)	**IIJP**	Institúto de Investigaciónes Juridico-Politicas (Argentina)
IIEIC	International Institute Examinations Inquiry Committee	**IIL**	Institute of International Law (Netherlands)
		IIL	Instituto Italo-Latinamericano
IIEJ	Instituto Interamericano de Estudios Juridicos Internacionales	**IIL**	Insurance Institute of London
		IILA	Istituto Italo-Latino-Americano
IIEL	Institut International d'Études Ligures	**IILC**	Internationaal Instituut voor Landaanwinning en Cultuurtechniek
IIEL	Instituto Internacional de Estudios Laborales (Switzerland)		
IIEM	Indian Institute of Experimental Medicine	**IILI**	Institut International de Littérature Ibéro-Américaine

IILS	International Institute for Labour Studies (*of* ILO)	**IIR**	Deutsches Institut für Interne Revision
IIM	Indian Institute of Management	**IIR**	Institute of International Relations (Trinidad and Tobago)
IIM	Indian Institute of Metals	**IIR**	International Institute for Refrigeration
IIM	Institute of Industrial Managers	**IIRA**	International Industrial Relations Association
IIM	Institúto de Investigaciónes Microquimícas (Argentina)	**IIRB**	Institut International de Recherches Betteravières (Belgium)
IIMC	Institut International de Musicologie Comparée	**IIRE**	International Institute for Resource Economics (U.S.A.)
IIMC	International Institute of Municipal Clerks (U.S.A.)	**IIRG**	Institut International de Recherches Gra-phologiques
IIMP	Institúto de Investigaciónes de Materias Primas (Chile)	**IIRI**	International Industrial Relations Institute
IIMT	International Institute for the Management of Technology (Italy)	**IIRR**	International Institute for Rice Research (Philippines)
IIMT	International Institute of Milling Technology (U.K.)	**IIRR**	International Institute of Rural Reconstruc-tion (U.S.A.)
IIN	Institúto Indigenista Nacional (Guatemala)	**IIRS**	Institute for Industrial Research and Stan-dards (Eire)
IIN	Instituto Interamericano del Niño	**IIS**	Indian Institute of Science
IIN	Istituto Italiano di Navigazione	**IIS**	Institut International de la Soudure
IINA	International Islamic News Agency	**IIS**	Institut International de Statistique
IINS	Interuniversity Institute of Nuclear Sciences (Belgium)	**IIS**	Institute of Industrial Supervisors (*now* ISM)
IIO	International Islamic Organization	**IIS**	Institute of Information Scientists
IIOE	International Indian Ocean Expedition	**IIS**	Institute for Intercultural Studies (U.S.A.)
IIOST	Institut International d'Organisation Scien-tifique du Travail (Switzerland)	**IIS**	Instituut voor Internationale Studien (Netherlands)
IIP	Indian Institute of Packaging	**IIS**	International Institute of Sociology
IIP	Indian Institute of Petroleum	**IIS**	Internationales Institut der Sparkassen
IIP	Institut International de la Presse	**IIS**	Irish Institute of Secretaries
IIP	Institute of Incorporated Photographers	**IISA**	Institut International des Sciences Administratives (Belgium)
IIP	International Institute of Philosophy	**IISBR**	International Institute of Sugar Beet Researchers (Belgium)
IIP	Israel Institute of Petroleum		
IIP	Israel Institute of Productivity	**IISCO**	Indian Iron and Steel Company
IIPA	Indian Institute of Public Administration	**IISE**	International Institute of Social Economics (U.K.)
IIPA	Institute of Incorporated Practitioners in Advertising	**IISEE**	International Institute of Seismology and Earthquake Engineering (Japan)
IIPE	Institut International de Planification de l'Éducation	**IISG**	International Instituut voor Sociale Geschiedenis
IIPE	Institution of Incorporated Plant Engineers	**IISHI**	Institut International des Sciences Humaines Intégrales (Canada)
IIPER	International Institution of Production Engineering Research	**IISI**	International Iron and Steel Institute (Belgium)
IIPF	International Institute for Public Finance		
IIPS	International Institute for Population Studies (India)	**IISL**	International Institute of Space Law
IIPU	Istituto Italiano di Paleontologia Umana	**IISL**	Istituto Internazionale di Studi Liguri

IISN	Institut Interuniversitaire des Sciences Nucléaires (Belgium)	**IJGD**	Germany Voluntary Service
IISO	Institution of Industrial Safety Officers	**IJI**	International Juridical Institute
IISPS	International Institute of Social and Political Science (Switzerland)	**IJIRA**	Indian Jute Industry's Research Association
		IJK	Internationale Juristen-Kommission
IISR	Indian Institute of Sugar-cane Research	**IJMA**	Indian Jute Mills Association
IISR	Institute for International Social Research (U.S.A.)	**IJMARI**	Indian Jute Mills Association Research Institute
IISR	International Institution of Submarine Research	**IJNPS**	Instituto Joaquim Nabuco de Pesquisas Sociais (Brazil)
IISRP	International Institute of Synthetic Rubber Producers (U.S.A.)	**IJO**	International Juridical Organisation for Developing Countries
IISS	International Institute for the Science of Sintering	**IJWU**	International Jewelry Workers Union
IISS	International Institute for Strategic Studies	**IKAPI**	Ikatan Penerbit Indonesia
IISSP	Institut International des Sciences Sociales et Politiques	**IKAR**	Internationale Kommission für Alpines Rettungswesen
IIST	Institut International des Sciences Théoriques	**IKBK**	Internationales Katholisches Bureau für das Kind
IISWM	Institute of Iron and Steel Wire Manufacturers	**IKD**	Internationale Kommission der Detektivverbände
IIT	Indian Institute of Technology	**IKEWM**	Internationales Komitee zur Ermittlung der Wirtschaftlichkeit von Milchtieren
IIT	Institut Interafricain du Travail		
IIT	Institut International du Tapis	**IKG**	International Gift Commission
IIT	Institut International du Théâtre	**IKG**	Internationale Kommission für Glas
IIT	Institute of Industrial Technicians	**IKI**	Internationales Kali-Institut
IIT	Instituto de Investigaciones Tecnológicas (Colombia)	**IKJ**	Internationales Kuratorium für das Jugendbuch
IIT	International Investment Trust (Africa)	**IKMB**	Internationale Katholische Mittelstandsbewegung
IITA	International Institute of Tropical Agriculture (Nigeria)	**IKN**	Internationale Kommission für Numismatik
IITS	International Institute of Theoretical Sciences	**IKOFA**	International Exhibition of Groceries and Fine Foods (Germany)
IIUPL	International Institute for the Unification of Public Law	**IKPE**	Interministerielles Komitee für Entwicklungshilfe (Austria)
IIVRS	International Institute for Vital Registration and Statistics	**IKPO**	Internationale Kriminalpolizeiliche Organisation
IIVW	Internationales Institut für Verwaltungswissenschaften	**IKRK**	Internationales Komitee von Roten Kreuz
IIW	International Inner Wheel (U.K.)	**IKS**	Interkantonale Kontrolstelle für Heilmittel (Switzerland)
IIW	International Institute of Welding	**IKS**	Internationales Kautschukbüro, Sektion Schweiz
IJA	International Jugglers Association		
IJAN	Internationale des Jeunes Amis de la Nature	**IKSJ**	Internationale Katholische Studierende Jugend
IJC	International Joint Commission (Canada)		
IJCIC	International Jewish Committee on Interreligious Consultations	**IKUE**	Internacia Katolika Unuigo Esperantista
		IKUP	Internationale Katholischen Union der Presse
IJF	International Judo Federation	**IKV**	Internationale Kartographische Vereinigung
IJG	Contactcentrum Fabrikanten Ijzerwaren en Gereedschappen	**IKV**	Internationaler Krankenhausverband

IKVSA	Internationale Katholische Vereinigung für Soziale Arbeit
IKW	Industrieverband Körperpflege- und Wasch-mittel
IL	Institute of Linguists
IL	L'Internationale Libérale
ILA	Institute of Landscape Architects
ILA	International Laundry Association
ILA	International Law Association
ILA	International Leprosy Association
ILA	International Longshoremen's Association
ILAA	International Legal Aid Association
ILAA	International Literary and Artistic Association
ILAB	International League of Antiquarian Booksellers
ILACDE	Instituto Latinoamericano de Cooperación y Desarrollo (Venezuela)
ILACO	International Land Development Consultants (Netherlands)
ILACPS	Instituto Latinoamericano de Ciencias Políticas y Sociales
ILAFA	Instituto Latinoamericano del Fierro y el Acero (Chile)
ILAFIR	Instituto Latinoamericano de Fisiología y Reproducción
ILAI	Italian-Latin American Institute
ILAMA	International Life-Saving Appliance Manufacturers Association
ILAP	Institute Latinoamericano del Plastico
ILAPES	Instituto Latinoamericano de Planificación Económica y Social
ILAR	Institute of Laboratory Animal Resources (U.S.A.)
ILAR	International League against Rheumatism
ILARI	Instituto Latinoamericano de Relaciones In-ternacionales
ILAS	Institute of Latin American Studies (U.S.A.)
ILAT	Instituto Latinoamericano de Tetro
ILATES	Instituto Latinoamericano de Estudios Sociales "Humberto Valdez" (Venezuela)
ILB	Instituut voor Landbouwbedrijfsgebouwen
ILB	International Labour Board (U.S.A.)
ILB	International Liaison Bureau
ILC	Industrial Liaison Centres
ILC	International Labelling Centre
ILC	International Law Commission
ILCA	Centro Internacional de Ganadería de Africa
ILCA	International Lightning Class Association
ILCA	International Livestock Centre for Africa (Ethiopia)
ILCE	Instituto Latinoamericano de Cinematografica Educativa (Mexico)
ILCE	Instituto Latinoamericano de la Comunicación Educativa
ILCMP	International Liaison Committee on Medical Physics
ILCOP	International Liaison Committee of Organizations for Peace
ILCORK	International Liaison Committee for Research on Korea (Korea)
ILDA	International Lutheran Deaf Association
ILDIS	Instituto Latinoamericano de Investigaciones Sociales (Chile)
ILE	Institution of Locomotive Engineers
ILEA	Inner London Education Authority
ILEC	Institut de Liaisons et d'Études des Industries de Consommation
ILEF	International League of Esperantist Amateur Photographers, Cinephotographers and Tape-Recording
ILEI	Internacia Ligo de Esperantistaj Instruistoj
ILEP	International Federation of Anti-Leprosy Associations
ILEPES	Instituto Latinoamericano de Planificación Economica y Social (Chile)
ILERA	International League of Esperantist Radio Amateurs
ILERI	Institut Libre d'Étude des Relations In-ternationales
ILESA	Institute of Lighting Engineers of South Africa
ILET	Instituto Latinoamericano de Estudios Trans-nationales (Mexico)
ILF	Industrial Leathers Federation
ILF	International Landworkers' Federation
ILF	Intreprindere de Lucrari Forestiere (Roumania)
ILFI	International Labour Film Institute
ILGO	Irish Local Government Officials Union

ILGPNWU	International Leather Goods, Plastic and Novelty Workers Union (U.S.A.)
ILGWU	International Ladies' Garment Workers Union (U.S.A.)
ILHR	International League for Human Rights
ILI	Inter-African Labour Institute
ILIC	International Library Information Center (U.S.A.)
ILID	Institut für Landwirtschaftliche Information und Dokumentation
ILLA	Irish Ladies Lacrosse Association
ILLL	International Lutheran Laymen's League
ILM	Internationaler Landmaschinenmarkt
ILMA	Instituto Latinoamericano de Mercadeo Agrícola
ILMAC	International Congress and Fair for Laboratory, Measuring and Automation Techniques in Chemistry
ILO	Instituut voor Landhouwhuishoudkundig Onderzoek
ILO	International Labour Office
ILO	International Labour Organisation
ILOB	Instituut voor Landbouwkundig Onderzoek van Biochemische Producten
ILocoE	Institution of Locomotive Engineers
ILP	Independent Labour Party
ILPA	International Labor Press Association (U.S.A.)
ILPES	Instituto Latinoamericano de Planificación Económica y Social
ILPH	International League for the Protection of Horses
ILPNR	International League for the Protection of Native Races (U.S.A.)
ILR	Independent Local Radio
ILR	Instituut voor Landbouwtechniek en Rationalisatie
ILRAD	International Laboratory for Research on Animal Diseases (Kenya)
ILRCO-CSA	International Red Locust Control Organization for Central and Southern Africa
ILRI	Indian Lac Research Institute
ILRI	International Institute for Land Reclamation and Improvement (Netherlands)
ILRM	International League for the Rights of Man
ILS	Incorporated Law Society
ILS	International Latitude Service

ILS	International Limnological Society (ICSU)
ILS	International Lunar Society
ILS	Irish Literary Society
ILSA	Inspection des Lois Sociales en Agriculture
ILSC	International Learning Systems Corporation
ILSGB	International Language Society of Great Britain
ILSI	International Life Sciences Institute
ILSMH	International League of Societies for the Mentally Handicapped
ILTAM	Institute for Literature and Mass Artistic Techniques
ILTF	International Lawn Tennis Federation
ILTTA	International Light Tackle Tournament Association
ILU	International Legal Union
ILWU	International Longshoremen's and Warehousemen's Union
ILZRO	International Lead Zinc Research Organisation
ILZSG	International Lead Zinc Research Organisation (U.S.A.)
IM	Institute of Marketing
IM	Svenska Leverantöföreningen för Instrument och Mätteknik
IMA	Industrial Marketing Association
IMA	Institute for Mediterranean Affairs (U.S.A.)
IMA	Institutional Management Association
IMA	Instituto de Matemática Aplicada (Argentina)
IMA	International Management Association
IMA	International Milling Association
IMA	International Mineralogical Association
IMA	International Music Association
IMA	International Mycological Association
IMA	International Mycophagist Association
IMA	Irish Medical Association
IMA	Stjornunarfélag (Icelandic Management Association)
IMA	Schweizerisches Institut für Landmaschinenwesen und Landarbeitstechnik
IMAA	International Maine-Anjou Association (U.S.A.)
IMAB	Comité Européen Importateurs de Machines à Bois

IMAC	International Movement of Apostolate Children	IMCS	Pax Romana, International Movement of Catholic Students
IMACE	Association des Industries Margarinières des Pays de la CEE	IMCYC	Instituto Mexicano del Cemento y del Concreto
IMACS	International Association for Mathematics and Computers in Simulation	IMDA	International Magic Dealers Association
		IMDA	International Mail Dealers Association
IMAG	Instituut voor Mechanisatie, Arbeid en Gebouwen	IMDBI	Industrial and Mining Development Bank of Iran
IMAG	Internationaler Messe und Ausstellungsdienst GmbH	IMDT	International Institute for Music, Dance and Theatre in the Audio-visual Media
IMAJ	International Management Association of Japan	IME	Institut Mondial de l'Environnement
		IME	Institute of Makers of Explosives (U.S.A.)
IMAPEC	Industries Mauritaniennes de Pêche	IME	Instituto de Médicos Especialistas (Brazil)
IMarE	Institute of Marine Engineers	IME	International Medical Exchange
IMARPE	Instituto del Mar del Perú	IMEA	Institut d'Études Métallurgiques et Électroniques Appliquées (Switzerland)
IMASLA	International Muslim Academy of Sciences, Letters and Arts	IMEA	Incorporated Municipal Electrical Association
IMAT	Istituto di Microbiologia Agraria e Tecnica	IMechE	Institution of Mechanical Engineers
IMATEC	Société Internationale de Matériel Technique (Senegal)	IMEDE	Institut pour l'Étude des Méthodes de Direction de l'Entreprise (Switzerland)
IMAU	International Movement for Atlantic Union	IMEKO	International Measurement Conference
IMB	Internationaler Metallarbeiterbund	IMENUR	Institut Mondial des Cités Unies pour l'Environnement et l'Urbanisme (France)
IMBEX	International Mens and Boys Exhibition		
IMBM	Institute of Municipal Building Management	IMER	Institute for Marine Environmental Research
IMC	Industrial Marketing Council	IMERNAR	Istituto Mexicano de Recursos Naturales Renovables (Mexico)
IMC	Institute of Management Consultants		
IMC	Institute of Measurement Control	IMES	Instituto Mexicano de Estudios Sociológicos
IMC	Institute of Medicine of Chicago (U.S.A.)	IMESCIAL	Institut Mondial des Structures Communales et d'Information sur l'Administration Locale (France)
IMC	International Mailbag Club		
IMC	International Maritime Committee		
IMC	International Materials Conference	IMet	Institute of Metals
IMC	International Micrographic Congress	IMEXGRA	Chambre Syndicale pour le Commerce d'Importation et d'Exportation de Graines et Aliments pour le Bétail (Belgium)
IMC	International Mineral and Chemical Corporation (U.S.A.)		
IMC	International Missionary Council	IMF	International Marketing Federation
IMC	International Music Council	IMF	International Metal Workers' Federation
IMCA	International Motor Contest Association (U.S.A.)	IMF	International Metaphysical Festivals Inc. (Hawaii)
		IMF	International Monetary Fund
IMCAR	International Movement of Catholic Agricultural and Rural Youth (Belgium)	IMF	International Motorcycle Federation
		IMF	International Myomassethics Federation
IMCE	International Meeting of Cataloguing Experts	IMFURP	International Movement for Fraternal Union among Races and Peoples
IMCO	Inter-Governmental Maritime Consultative Organisation (U.S.A.)		
		IMG	Industrial Marketing Group
IMCOS	International Meteorological Consultant Service	IMG	International Mosel-Gesellschaft

IMH	Institute of Materials Handling		**IMPA**	International Museum Photographers Association (U.S.A.)
IMI	Imperial Metal Industries		**IMPA**	International Myopia Prevention Association (U.S.A.)
IMI	Imperial Mycological Institute (U.K.) (*now* CMI)		**IMPA**	International Personnel Management Association (U.S.A.)
IMI	Institute of the Motor Industry		**IMPBA**	International Model Power Boat Association (U.S.A.)
IMI	International Maintenance Institute (U.S.A.)		**IMPGA**	Institut de Météorologie et de Physique du Globe d'Algérie
IMI	International Masonry Institute (U.S.A.)			
IMI	International Metaphysical Institute (U.K.)		**IMPHOS**	Institut Mondial du Phosphate (France)
IMI	Irish Management Institute		**IMPHQA**	Institut Mondial pour la Protection de la Haute Qualité Alimentaire
IMIA	Instituto Mexicano de Informacion Avícola			
IMIA	International Machinery Insurers Association		**IMPI**	International Microwave Power Institute (U.S.A.)
IMIE	Instituto Mexicano de Investigaciones Económicas		**IMPORT-PESCA**	Associazione Nazionale Importatori Grossisti Prodotti Ittici Freschi e Congelati
IMIF	International Maritime Industry Forum		**IMPRECO**	Société des Impressions du Congo
IMinE	Institution of Mining Engineers		**IMPREGA**	Imprimerie Gabonaise
IMINOCO	Iranian Marine International Oil Company		**IMPROMER**	Société Ivoirienne d'Importation de Produits de la Mer
IMIQ	Instituto Mexicano de Ingenieros Químicos			
IMIT	Instituto Mexicano de Investigaciones Tecnológicas		**IMPS**	International Plastic Modelers Society
IMIT	Institute of Musical Instrument Technology		**IMRA**	Industrial Marketing Research Association
IMLO	Internationale Maatschappij v. Land-bouwkundige Ontwikkeling		**IMRA**	International Mission Radio Association (U.S.A.)
IMLS	Institute of Medical Laboratory Sciences		**IMRAMN**	International Meeting on Radio Aids to Marine Navigation
IMM	Institute of Mining and Metallurgy			
IMMK	Interkultura Monda Movado Kommunomej		**IMRC**	International Marine Radio Committee
IMMOA	International Mercantile Marine Officers Association		**IMRNR**	Instituto Mexicano de Recursos Naturales Renovables
IMMRAN	International Meeting of Marine Radio Aids to Navigation		**IMS**	Industrial Management Society (U.S.A.)
IMMS	International Material Management Society (U.S.A.)		**IMS**	Institute of Mathematical Statistics (U.S.A.)
			IMS	Institute of Manpower Studies
IMO	Inter-American Municipal Organisation		**IMS**	Institute of Mental Subnormality
IMO	International Meteorological Organisation		**IMS**	International Meditation Society
IMOB	Industrie van Minerale Oliën van België		**IMS**	International Musicological Society
IMOS	Interallied Military Organization 'Sphinx'		**IMSA**	International Motor Sports Association
IMP	Ideas Marketing Pool Ltd		**IMSA**	International Municipal Signal Association (U.S.A.)
IMPA	Institute for Improvement of Sugar Production (Mexico)			
IMPA	International Maritime Pilots Association		**IMSM**	Institute of Marketing and Sales Management
IMPA	International Marketing Public Relations and Advertising Consultants (U.S.A.)		**IMTA**	Imported Meat Trade Association
			IMTech	Institute of Metallurgical Technicians
IMPA	International Master Printers Association		**IMTG**	Internationale Moor und Torf-Gesellschaft
IMPA	International Motor Press Association		**IMTI**	Instituto del Minifundio y de las Tierras Indivisas (Argentina)
IMPA	International Movement for Peace Action		**IMTPA**	Institut de Médecine Tropicale Princesse Astrid (Belgium)

IMU	International Mailers Association (U.S.A.)
IMU	International Mathematical Union
IMU	International Molders' and Allied Workers' Union
IMun & CyE	Institute of Municipal and County Engineers
I Mun E	Institution of Municipal Engineers
IMV	Internationaler Milchwirtschaftverband
IMVS	Institute of Medical and Veterinary Science (Australia)
IMW	International Map of the World
IMWIC	International Maize and Wheat Improvement Centre (Mexico)
IMWOO	Instituut voor Maatschappij-Wetenschappelijk Onderzoek in de Ont-wikkelingslanden
IMWU	International Molders' and Allied Workers' Union
IMZ	Internationales Musikzentrum
IMZA	Association Professionnelle des Importateurs et Exportateurs Belges de Semences Fourragères
INA	Institut National Agronomique
INA	Instituto Nacional de Abastecimientos (Colombia)
INA	Instituto Nacional Agrario (Honduras)
INA	Instituto Nacional de Aprendizaje (Costa Rica)
INA	Institution of Naval Architects
INA	International Newsreel and News Film Association
INA	Ironfounders National Association
INA	Verenigung van Fabrikanten en Importeurs van Naaimachines
INAC	Istituto Nazionale per le Applicazioni del Calcolo
INACAP	Instituto Nacional de Capacitación Professional (Chile)
INACH	Instituto Antartico Chileno (Chile)
INACOL	Institut National pour l'Amélioration des Conserves de Légumes (Belgium)
INACP	Institut de Nutrition pour l'Amérique Centrale et Panama (Guatemala)
INAD	Instituto Nacional de Administracion para el Desarrollo (Guatemala)
INADES	Institut Africain pour le Développement Économique et Social
INAE	International Newspaper Advertising Executives

INAEICM	Institut Nationale Agricole d'Études et d'Initiatives Coopératives et Mutualistes
INAGRISA	Iniciativas Agrícolas, S.A.
INAH	Instituto Nacional de Anthrolopogia e Historia (Mexico)
INAIL	Instituto Nazionale per l'Assicurazione contro gli Infortuni sul Lavoro
INAIR	Internacional de Aviación SA (Panama)
INAL	Indian National Agricultural Library
INALI	Instituto Nacional de Limnología (Argentina)
INAM	Institut National d'Assurance contre la Maladie
INANDES	Instituto Andino de Estudios Sociales (Peru)
INANTIC	Instituto Nacional de Normas Tecnicas Industriales y Certificacion (Peru)
INAOV	Institut National des Appellations d'Origine des Vins et Eaux-de-Vie
INAP	Instituto Nacional de Acción Poblacional e Investigación (Chile)
INAPA	Instituto Nacional de Aquas Potables y Alcantarillados (Dominica)
INAPG	Institut National Agronomique Paris-Grignon
INARC	Institut Nord-Africain de Recherches Cotonnières
INARCH	Istituto Nazionale di Architettura
INAS	Institut Nationale d'Administration Scolaire et Universitaire
INASA	Industrias Nacionales Agrícolas (Nicaragua)
INAT	Institut National d'Assistance Technique (Belgium)
INATEIA	Istituto Nazionale di Assistenza Tecnico-Economica per Imprenditori Agricoli
INB	Institut National du Bois
INBA	Instituto Nacional de Bellas Artes (Mexico)
INBA	Instituto Nacional de Biología Animal (Bolivia & Peru)
INBH	Institut National Belge du Houblon
INBOLCA	Instituto Boliviano del Café
INC	Instituto Nacional de Colonización (Ecuador, Spain, Uruguay)
INC	Instituto Nicaraguense del Café
INC	International Nickel Company
INC	International Numismatic Commission
INC	Ironfounders National Confederation
INCA	Institut National de Crédit Agricole (Belgium)

INCA	Istituto Nazionale Confederale di Assistenza	**INDAL**	Indian Aluminium Co.
INCA	International Newspaper and Colour Association (Switzerland)	**INDC**	International Nuclear Data Committee (*of* IAEA)
INCAE	Instituto Centroamericano de Administracion de Empresas	**INDE**	Instituto Nacional de Electrificación (Guatemala)
INCAP	Instituto de Nutrición de Centroamérica y Panamá	**INDEC**	Independent Nuclear Disarmament Election Committee
INCB	International Narcotics Control Board	**INDECO**	Industrial Development Corporation (Zambia)
INCE	Instituto Nacional de Cooperación Educativa (Venezuela)	**INDER**	Instituto Nacional de Deportes, Educación Fisica y Recreación (Cuba)
INCEI	Instituto Nacional de Comercio Exterior e Interior (Nicaragua)	**INDERENA**	Instituto para el Desarrollo de los Recursos Naturales (Colombia)
INCIBA	Instituto Nacional de Cultura y Bellas Artes (Venezuela)	**INDESIT**	Industria Elettrodomestici Italiana
INCIDI	International Institute of Differing Civilisations	**INDIS**	Industrial Information System (*of* UNIDO)
INCIE	Instituto Nacional de las Ciencias de Educación, Barcelona	**INDITEC-NOR**	Instituto Nacional de Investigaciones Tecnologicas y Normalización (Chile)
INCOLDA	Instituto Colombiano de Administración	**INDRHI**	Instituto Nacional de Recursos Hidráulicos (Dominica)
INCOMAS	International Conference on Marketing Systems for Developing Countries	**INDUAR-ROZ**	Federación de Industriales del Arroz (Colombia)
INCOME	Industriale Cotonicola Meridionale	**INDUN-ARES**	Servicio Comercial y Técnico de Industrias Auxiliares de la Construcción Naval
INCOMEX	Instituto Colombiano de Comercio Exterior	**INE**	Instituto Nacional de Estadística
INCOMI	Indústria e Comércio de Minerios S.A. (Brazil)	**INEA**	Istituto Nazionale di Economia Agraria
INCOOP	Instituto Nacional de Cooperativas (Peru)	**INEA**	International Electronics Association
INCOR	Indian National Committee on Oceanic Research	**INEAC**	Institut National pour l'Étude Agronomique du Congo (Belgium)
INCOR	Intergovernmental Conference on Oceanographic Research	**INEC**	Institut Européen de Cancérologie
INCOR	Israeli National Committee for Oceanographic Research	**INEC**	Institut Européen d'Écologie et de Cancérologie (Belgium)
INCORA	Instituto Colombiano de la Reforma Agraria	**INEC**	Institut Européen des Industries de la Gomme de Caroube (Belgium)
INCOSPAR	Indian National Committee for Space Research	**INEC**	Instituto Nacional para el Mejoramiento de la Enseñanza de las Ciencias (Argentina)
INCP	Instítúto Nacionál de Ciência Politica (Brazil)	**INECAFE**	Instituto Ecuatoriano del Café
INCRA	International Copper Research Association	**INED**	Institut National d'Études Démographiques
INCREF	International Children's Rescue Fund	**INEDECA**	Industria Ecuatoriana Elaboradora de Cacao
INCUBAR	Asociación Colombiana de Incubadores	**INEDES**	Instituto Ecuatoriano de Planificación para el Desarrollo
INDA	Instituto Nacional do Desenvolvimento Agrário (Brazil)	**INEMO**	Chambre Syndicale des Importateurs et Négociants en Machines-Outils et Outillages de Belgique
INDA	International Nonwovens and Disposables Association		
INDAC	Integral Nuclear Data Centre (U.S.A.)	**INEN**	Instituto National de Energia Nuclear (Guatemala)
INDACY	Industrie Dahoméenne du Cycle		
INDAG	Industrial and Agricultural Co. Ltd (Nigeria)	**INEOA**	International Narcotic Enforcement Officers Association

INEP	Institut National d'Études Politiques (Zaire)
INEP	Instituto Nacional de Estudos e Pesquisas Educacionais (Brazil)
INERA	Institut National pour l'Étude et la Recherche Agronomique (Zaire)
INERHI	Instituto Ecuatoriano de Recursos Hidráulicos
INERM	Institut National d'Études Rurales Montagnardes à Grenoble
INETOP	Institut National de l'Enseignement Technique et d'Orientation Professionnelle
INF	Institúto Nacionál de Farmacologia (Brazil)
INF	International Naturist Federation
INFCO	Information Committee of ISO
INFEDOP	International Federation of Christian Trade Unions of Employees in Public Service and PTT
INFI	Instituto Nacional de Fomento Tabacalero (Colombia)
INFIC	International Network of Feed Information Centres (FAO)
INFIR	Istituto Nazionale per il Finanziamento della Ricostruzione
INFN	Istituto Nazionale de Fisico Nucleare
INFO	International Fortean Organization
INFONAC	Instituto de Fomento Nacional (Nicaragua)
INFOP	Instituto de Fomento de la Producción (Guatemala)
INFOR-EUROP	Press Information and Public Relations Service of Common Market Enterprises
INFORFILM	International Information Film Service
INFORM	International Reference Organization in Forensic Medicine and Sciences
INFOTERM	International Information Centre for Terminology (Austria)
ING	Instituto Nacional de Geografíca (Brazil)
INGC	Istituto Nazionale di Genetica per la Cerealicoltura
INGE	Instituto Nacional de Granos y Elevadores (Argentina)
INGO	International Non Governmental Organisation
INGRAF	Instituut for Grafisk Forskning
INGYO	International Non-Governmental Youth Organizations
INHADAH	Industrie d'Habillement du Dahomey
INI	Instituto Nacional Indigenista (Mexico)

INIA	Instituto Nacional de Investigaciones Agrícolas (Mexico)
INIA	Institúto Nacional de Investigaciones Agronómicas
INIAP	Instituto Nacional de Investigaciones Agropecuarias (Ecuador)
INIBP	Instituto Nacional de Investigaciones Biológico
INIC	Instituto Nacional de Imigraçao e Colonizaçâo (Brazil)
INIC	Instituto Nacional de la Investigación Científica (Mexico)
INIC	Instituto Nacional de Investigaciones Científicas (Paraquay)
INICHAR	Institut National de l'Industrie Charbonnière (Belgium)
INIDCYA	Institute for the Intellectual Development of Children and Young Adults (Iran)
INIF	Industria Nacional de Insecticidas e Fertilizantes (Brazil)
INII	Instituto Nacional de Investigacão Industrial (Portugal)
INIP	Instituto Nacional per l'Incremento della Produttività
INIP	Instituto Nacional de Investigaciones Pecuarias (Mexico)
INIRO	Indonesisch Instituut voor Rubber Onderzoek
INIS	International Nuclear Information System (Austria)
INITO	Société Initiative Togolaise
INL	Institut National du Logement
INLA	International Nuclear Law Association
INLD	Instituto Nacional do Livro e do Disco (Mozambique)
INLE	Instituto Nacional del Libro Espanol
INM	Instituto Nacional do Mate (Brazil)
INMA	Institut National de Médecine Agricole
INMARSAT	International Organization for Maritime Telecommunications by Satellites
INMAS	Institute of Nuclear Medicine and Allied Sciences (India)
INMV	Instituto Nacional de Medicina Veterinaria (Cuba)
INN	Instituto Nacional de la Nutrición (Argentina, Colombia, Ecuador, Venezuela)
INO	Irish Nurses Association
INOC	Iraq National Oil Company

INODEP	Institut Oecuménique pour le Développement des Peuples (Switzerland)	**INRE**	Instituto Nacionale de Reforma Económica (Cuba)
INOE	Internacia Naturista Organizo Esperantista	**INRF**	Institut National de Recherches Forestières (Tunis)
INORCOL	Instituto de Normas Colombiana		
INOS	Instituto Nacional de Obras Sanitarias (Venezuela)	**INRH**	Instituto Nacional de Recursos Hidráulicos (Cuba)
INOTEX	Industrie Nouvelle Textile (Cameroons)	**INRN**	Instituto Nacional de Racionalización y Normalización
INP	Institute of National Planning (Egypt)		
INP	Instituto Nacional de Pinho (Brazil)	**INRS**	Institut National de Recherche Scientifique (Rwanda, Togo)
INP	Instituto Nacional de Planificación (Peru)		
INP	Instituto Nacional de la Productividad (Argentina)	**INRS**	Institut National de Recherche et de Securité pour la Prévention des Accidents du Travail et de Maladies Professionelles
INPA	Institute Nacional de Pesquisas de Amazónia (Brazil)	**INRT**	Instituto Nacional de Racionalización del Trabajo
INPA	International Newspaper Promotion Association	**INRV**	Institut National de Recherche Vétérinaire (Belgium)
INPABO	Instituto Paranaense de Botanica	**INS**	Institut National de Sécurité
INPADOC	International Patent Documentation Centre, Vienna (Austria)	**INS**	International News Service
		INSA	Institut National des Sciences Appliquées
INPAR	Institut National de Promotion Agricole de Rennes	**INSA**	International Shipowners' Association
INPC	Irish National Productivity Committee	**INSAFOP**	Instituto Salvadoreño de Fomento de la Producción
INPE	Instituto Nacional de Pesca del Ecuador	**INSDOC**	Indian National Scientific Documentation Centre
INPFC	International North Pacific Fisheries Commission		
INPI	Institut National de la Propriété Industrielle	**INSEA**	Institut National de Statistiques et d'Économie Appliquée (Morocco)
INPI	Instituto Nacional de Promoción Industrial (Peru)	**INSEA**	International Society for Education through Art (France)
INPPSS	Instituto Nacional para le Producción de Semillas Selectas	**INSEAD**	Institut Européen d'Administration des Affaires
INPROA	Instituto de Promoción Agraria (Chile)	**INSEE**	Institut National de la Statistique et des Études Économiques
INPS	Institut National de la Prévoyance Sociale		
INQUA	Internationale Quartärvereinigung	**INSERM**	Institut National de la Santé et de la Recherche Médicale
INR	Institut National Belge de Radio-diffusion (Belgium)	**INSFOPAL**	Instituto Nacional de Fomento Municipal (Colombia)
INR	Institut National de Radio-diffusion (Greece)	**INSJ**	Institute for Nuclear Study (Japan)
INRA	Institut National de la Recherche Agronomique	**INSPEC**	Information Service in Physics, Electrotechnology and Control (*of* IEE)
INRA	Instituto Nacional de Reforma Agraria (Cuba)	**INSTAB**	Information Service on Toxicity and Biodegradability (*of* WPRL)
INRAT	Institut National de le Recherche Agronomique de Tunisie	**InstBE**	Institution of British Engineers
		InstE	Institution of Electronics
INRDG	Institut National de Recherche et de Documentation de Guinée	**InstMC**	Institute of Measurement and Control
		InstM	Institute of Metals
INRDP	Institut National de Recherche et de Documentation Pédagogiques, Paris	**INSTN**	Institut National des Sciences et Techniques Nucléaires

InstPLA	Institute of Public Loss Assessors
INSTOP	Institut National Scientifique et Technique d'Océanographie et de Pêche (Tunisia)
InstPC	Institute of Public Cleansing
InstR	Institute of Refrigeration
InstRA	Institute of Registered Architects
InstTA	Institute of Traffic Administration
INT	Institúto Nacionál de Tecnologia (Brazil)
INT	Istituto Nazionale Trasporti
INTA	Instituto Nacional de Technologia Agropecuaria (Argentina)
INTA	Instituto Nacional de Tecnica Aerospacial
INTA	Instituto Nacional de Transformación Agrária (Guatemala)
INTA	International New Thought Alliance
INTAL	Institute for Latin American Integration
INTAMEL	International Association of Metropolitan City Libraries
INTAPUC	Association Internationale du Nettoiement
INTASAF-CON	International Tanker Safety Conference
INTD	Institut National des Techniques de la Documentation
INTE	Instituto de Investigación Técnica (Chile)
INTEC	Comité de Investigaciones Tecnológicas de Corfo (Chile)
INTECNOR	Instituto Nacional de Tecnologia y Normalizacion (Paraguay)
INTECOL	International Association for Ecology (ICSU)
INTECOM	International Council for Technical Communication
INTELCAM	Société des Télécommunications Internationales du Cameroun
INTELCI	Télécommunications Internationales de la Côte-d'Ivoire
INTELCO	Office des Télécommunications Internationales du Congo
INTELSAT	International Telecommunications Satellite Consortium
INTEM	Inter-American Institute of Music Education
INTERAN	International Conference on the Analysis of Geological Materials
INTER-ASMA	Association Internationale d'Asthmologie
INTER-BRANT	Union Intercommunale des Centrales Électriques du Brabant (Belgium)
INTER-CENTRE	International Centre for the Terminology of the Social Sciences (Switzerland)
INTERCON-TAINER	International Company for Transport by Transcontainers
INTER-COOP	International Agricultural Cooperative Society (Netherlands)
INTER-COSMOS	Council on International Cooperation in Research and Uses of Outer Space
INTER-EXPO	Committee of Organisers of National Participations in International Economic Displays
INTERFAST	International Industrial Fastener Engineering Exhibition and Conference
INTERFILM	International Inter-Church Film Centre
INTER-FINISH	International Union for Electrodeposition and Surface Finishing
INTER-FORST	International Exposition of the Technology of Forestry and Forest Industries (Germany)
INTER-FRIGO	International Railway-owned Company for Refrigerated Transport
INTER-GASTRA	International Trade Fair for the Hotel and Catering Industry
INTERGU	Société Internationale pour le Droit d'Auteur
INTER-HYBRID	Association Intercontinentale du Mais Hybride
INTER-KAMA	Internationaler Kongress mit Ausstellung f. Messtechnik und Automatik
INTER-LAINE	Comité des Industries Lainières de la CEE
INTERLAIT	Société Interprofessionnelle de Lait
INTERMAG	International Association of Television Political Magazines
INTERMET	International Association for Metropolitan Research and Development
INTER-METAL	Organization for Cooperation in the Field of Heavy Metallurgy (Hungary)
INTERPHIL	International Conference for the Study of Promotion of Philanthropy
INTER-PHOTO	Fédération Internationale des Négociants en Photo et Cinéma
INTERPOL	International Criminal Police Organisation
INTEROPS	Commission pour la Coopération Multilatérale dans l'Observation des Satellites Artificiels de la Terre
INTER-PLAN	International Group for Studies in National Planning
INTER-PROPO	Sociedade de Propaganda Internacional de Produtos Portugeses

INTERSHOE	International Federation of the Independent Shoe Trade	**INVA**	Industri Vaskerienes Forbund
INTER-STENO	International Federation of Shorthand and Typewriting	**INVE**	Instituto Nacional de Viviendas Ecónomicas (Uruguay)
INTER-SU	Bureau de Liaison des Sanatoriums Universitaires et de Protection Antituberculeuse des Étudiants	**INVEMA**	Asociación de Investigación Industrial de la Maquina-Herramienta
INTER-TANKO	International Tanker Owners' Association	**INVESTI**	Instituto Venezolano de Investigaciones Tecnológicas e Industriales
INTERTEL	International Legion of Intelligence (U.S.A.)	**INVI**	Instituto Nacional de la Vivienda (Dominica)
INTERTEL	International Television Federation	**INVSL**	Indian National Veterinary Science Library
INTERVER-SITAS	World Association of Experiments in Post-Secondary Education	**INVU**	Instituto Nacional de Vivienda y Urbanismo (Costa Rica)
INTERVICO	Inter-American Organization of Cooperative Housing Technical Service Organizations (Colombia)	**INVUFLEC**	Institut National de Vulgarisation des Fruits, Légumes et Champignons
INTER-WOO-LABS	International Association of Wool Textile Laboratories	**IO**	Institut Océanographique
		IOA	Institute of Acoustics
INTERZUM	International Fair of Accessories and Materials for Woodworking and Furniture	**IOA**	International OMEGA Association (U.S.A.)
		IOA	International Ostomy Association
INTI	Instituto Nacional de Tecnologia Industrial (Argentina)	**IOAHPR**	International Organisation for the Advancement of High Pressure Research
INTO	Irish National Teachers Organisation	**IOAP**	International Office for Audiophonology
INTOSAI	International Organisation of Supreme Audit Institutions	**IOAT**	International Organisation Against Trachoma
INTRADE	International Trade Development Organisation	**IOB**	Institute of Brewing
		IOB	Institute of Bankers
INTRANED	Internationale Transport Agenturen 'Nederland'	**IOB**	Institute of Bookkeepers
		IOB	Institute of Builders
INTRATA	International Trading and Credit Company of Tanganyika Ltd	**IOB**	Inter-Organization Board for Information Systems and Related Activities (UN)
INTROP	Information Centre of Tropical Plant Protection (Germany)	**IOBB**	International Organization of Biotechnology and Bioengineering
INTSH	Institut National Tchadien pour les Sciences Humaines (Chad)	**IOBC**	Indian Ocean Biological Centre
		IOBC	International Organisation for Biological Control of Noxious Animals and Plants
INTSHU	Institut Togolais des Sciences Humaines	**IOBI**	Institute of Bankers in Ireland
INTSOY	International Soybean Program (Puerto Rico)	**IOBS**	Institute of Bankers in Scotland
		IOC	Indian Oil Corporation
INTUC	Indian National Trade Union Congress	**IOC**	Institute of Chemistry
INU	Institute Nazionale di Urbanistica	**IOC**	Instituto Oswaldo Cruz (Brazil)
INUA	Instituto Nazionale di Ultracustica	**IOC**	Intergovernmental Oceanographic Commission
INucE	Institution of Nuclear Engineers		
INUTOM	Institut Universitaire des Territoires d'Outremer (Belgium)	**IOC**	International Olympic Committee
		IOC	International Organising Committee of World Mining Congresses
INV	Institut National du Verre (Belgium)	**IOC**	International Ornithological Congress
INV	Instituto Nacional de Vitivinicultura (Argentina)	**IOCA**	Independent Oil Compounders Association (U.S.A.)

IOCARIBE	IOC Association for the Caribbean and Adjacent Regions	**IOMP**	International Organisation for Medical Physics
IOCC	International Office of Cocoa and Chocolate	**IOMTR**	International Office for Motor Trades and Repairs
IOCHS	International Organisation for Cultivating Human Spirit (*now* OISCA-INT)	**ION**	Institute of Navigation (U.S.A.)
IOCU	International Organization of Consumers Unions	**IOOC**	International Olive Oil Council (Spain)
		IOOF	Independent Order of Oddfellows
IOCV	International Organisation of Citrus Virologists	**IOOL**	International Optometric and Optical League
IOD	International Institute for Organizational and Social Development (Belgium)	**IOOTS**	International Organisation of Old Testament Scholars
IÖD	Internationale Öffentlichen Dienste	**IOP**	Institute of Packaging
IODE	Imperial Order of Daughters of the Empire (Canada)	**IOP**	Institute of Physics
		IOP	Institute of Petroleum
IOE	Indian Ocean Expedition	**IOP**	Institute of Plumbing
IOE	Institute for the Officialization of Esperanto (Yugoslavia)	**IOP**	Institute of Printing
		IOP	International Organisation of Palaeobotany
IOE	International Office of Epizootics	**IOP**	Institute of Pyramidology
IOE	International Organisation of Employers	**IOPAB**	International Organisation for Pure and Applied Biophysics
IOED	International Office of Epizootic Diseases	**IOPB**	International Organization of Plant Biosystematists
IOF	Institute of Fuel		
IOF	International Oceanographic Foundation	**IOPEC**	International Oil Pollution Exhibition and Conference
IOF	Internationale Orientierungslauf		
IOFC	Indian Ocean Fisheries Commission	**IOPH**	International Office of Public Health
IOFI	International Organisation of the Flavor Industry	**IOQ**	Institute of Quarrying
		IOR	Institute for Operational Research
IOGT	International Order of Good Templars (International Supreme Lodge)	**IORD**	International Organisation for Rural Development
IOI	International Ocean Institute (Malta)	**IORS**	International Orders Research Society
IOI	International Ozone Institute (U.S.A.)	**IORS**	Operations Research Society of Ireland
IOIE	International Organisation of Industrial Employers	**IOS**	Institute of Oceanographic Sciences
		IOS	Institute of Statisticians
IOJ	Institute of Journalists	**IOS**	International Offshore Services (U.K.)
IOJ	International Organisation of Journalists	**IOS**	International Organisation for Succulent Plant Study
IOK	International Order of Kabbalists (U.K.)		
IOK	Internationales Olympisches Komitee	**IOS**	Iraqi Organisation for Standardization
IOKSZ	Union of Handicrafts Co-operatives (Hungary)	**IOSA**	International Oil Scouts Association
IOL	Institute of Librarians (India)	**IOSA**	Incorporated Oil Seed Association
IOL	International Old Lacers (U.S.A.)	**IOSA**	Irish Offshore Services Association
IOM	Institute of Metals	**IOSHD**	International Organization for the Study of Human Development
IOM	Institute of Office Management (*now* IAM)		
IOMA	International Oxygen Manufacturers Association	**IOSOT**	International Organisation for the Study of the Old Testament
IOMC	International Organisation for Medical Co-operation	**IOST**	International Organization of Study Tours for Teachers (Belgium)

IOSTA	Institut d'Organisation Scientifique du Travail en Agriculture	**IPAE**	Instituto Peruano de Administración de Empresas (Peru)
IOSTT	International Organization of Scenographers and Theatre Technicians	**IPAFRIC**	Inter-Pêches Afrique (Senegal)
IOT	Institute of Transport	**IPAI**	International Primary Aluminium Institute (U.K.)
IOTA	Institute of Traffic Administration	**IPAM**	Institut Pédagogique Africain et Malgache
IOTA	Institut d'Ophthalmologie Tropicale de l'Afrique Occidentale	**IPAR**	Institut de Pédagogie Appliqué à Vocation Rurale
IOV	Instituto Oceanográfico de Valparaiso (Chile)	**IPARA**	International Publishers Advertising Representatives Association
IOVST	International Organisation for Vacuum Science and Technology	**IPART**	Institute of Photographic Apparatus Repair Technicians
IOW	Institute of Welding	**IPB**	International Peace Bureau (Switzerland)
IOZV	Internationale Organisation für Zivilverteidigung	**IPBA**	India, Pakistan and Bangladesh Association (U.K.)
IPA	Industrie des Pêches Algériennes	**IPBA**	Irish Paper Box Association
IPA	Institut Pédagogique Africain	**IPBAM**	International Permanent Bureau of Automobile Manufacturers
IPA	Institut de Préparation aux Affaires	**IPBF**	International Pony Breeders Federation
IPA	Institute of Practitioners in Advertising	**IPBMM**	International Permanent Bureau of Motor Manufacturers
IPA	Institute of Public Administration (Eire)		
IPA	Institute of Public Affairs (Australia)	**IPC**	Institute of Philippine Culture
IPA	Instituto de Pesquisas Agronómicas (Brazil)	**IPC**	Instituto Panameña de Café
IPA	International Paediatric Association	**IPC**	Inter-African Phytosanitary Commission (U.K.)
IPA	International Paleontological Association	**IPC**	International People's College in Denmark
IPA	International Peace Academy	**IPC**	International Photographic Council
IPA	International Peach Academy	**IPC**	International Poplar Commission
IPA	International Phonetic Association	**IPC**	International Potato Centre, Lima
IPA	International Pinball Association	**IPC**	Iraq Petroleum Company
IPA	International Platform Association	**IPC**	International Prison Commission
IPA	International Playground Association	**IPC**	International Publishing Corporation
IPA	International Police Association	**IPCA**	Industrial Pest Control Association (*now* BPCA)
IPA	International Psycho-Analytical Association		
IPA	International Publishers Association	**IPCA**	International Petroleum Co-operative Alliance
IPAA	Independent Petroleum Association of America	**IPCA**	International Postcard Collectors Association
IPAA	International Prisoners' Aid Association	**IPCCIOS**	Conseil Régional Indo-Pacifique (*of* CIOS)
IPAA	International Psycho-Analytical Association	**IPCIAA**	*See* IPCRSIAA
IPAC	Independent Petroleum Association of Canada	**IPCL**	India Petrochemicals Ltd
IPAC	Institut Polytechnique de l'Afrique Centrale	**IPCL**	Institut du Pétrole, des Carburants et Lubrifiants
IPAC	International Peace Academy Committee (U.S.A.)	**IPCR**	Institute for Physical and Chemical Research (Japan)
IPACA	Industria Papelera Centroamericana (Honduras)		
IPACK	International Packaging Material Suppliers Association		

IPCRSIAA	Institut Professionnel de Contrôle et de Recherches Scientifiques des Industries de l'Alimentation Animale (France)
IPCS	Institution of Professional Civil Servants
IPD	Institut Panafricain pour le Développement
IPD	Institut Prumyslového Designu
IPD	Institute of Professional Designers
IPDA	International Periodical Distributors Association (U.S.A.)
IPE	Incorporated Plant Engineers
IPE	Institute of Production Engineers
IPE	Instituto Português de Embalagem
IPEAAD	Instituto de Pesquisas e Experimentação Agropecuárias da Amazônia Ocidental (Brazil)
IPEACO	Instituto de Pesquisas e Experimentação Agropecuárias do Centro-Oeste (Brazil)
IPEACS	Instituto de Pesquisas e Experimentação Agropecuárias do Centro Sul (Brazil)
IPEAL	Instituto de Pesquisas e Experimentação Agropecuárias do Leste (Brazil)
IPEAME	Instituto do Pesquisas e Experimentação Agropecuárias do Meridional (Brazil)
IPEAN	Instituto de Pesquisas e Esperimentação Agropecuárias do Norte (Brazil)
IPEANE	Instituto de Pesquisas e Experimentação Agropecuárias do Nordeste (Brazil)
IPEAS	Instituto de Pesquisas e Experimentação Agropecuárias do Sul (Brazil)
IPEL	International Pipeline Engineering Ltd (Canada)
IPEONGC	Institute of Petroleum Exploration Oil and Natural Gas Commission (India)
IPEP	International Permanent Exhibition of Publications (Yugoslavia)
IPEPO	Instituto para la Propaganda Exterior de los Productos del Olivar
IPEX	International Printing Machinery and Allied Trades' Exhibition
IPF	International Pen Friends (Ireland)
IPF	International Pharmaceutical Federation
IPF	Irish Printing Federation
IPFC	Indo-Pacific Fisheries Council (Thailand)
IPFE	Instituto Peruano de Fomento Educativo
IPFEO	Institut des Producteurs de Ferro-alliages d'Europe Occidentale
IPG	Independent Publishers Guild
IPG	Industrial Policy Group
IPGC	Instituto de Pesca del Golfo de Mexico y el Caribe
IPGH	Pan-American Institute of Geography and History
IPGSA	International Plant Growth Substance Association
IPH	International Association of Paper Historians
IPHC	International Pacific Halibut Commission
IPHE	Institution of Public Health Engineers
IPHF	Illinois Poultry and Hatchery Federation (U.S.A.)
IPI	Institute of Patentees and Inventors
IPI	Institute of Professional Investigators
IPI	International Press Institute
IPIA	Institutul de Patologia si Igiena Animala (Roumania)
IPIA	International Patent and Trademark Association
IPIECA	International Petroleum Industry Environmental Conservation Association
IPIRA	Indian Plywood Industries Research Association
IPIRI	Indian Plywood Industries Research Institute
IPK	Interessengemeinschaft für Pharmazeutische und Kosmetische Produkte (Switzerland)
IPKO	International Information Centre on Peace-keeping Operation (France)
IPLA	Institut Pastoral d'Amérique Latine (Chile)
IPM	Institute of Personnel Management
IPMA	International Personnel Management Association
IPMER	Institute of Post-Graduate Medical Education and Research (India)
IPMS	International Plastic Modellers Society
IPMS	International Polar Motion Service
IPNA	International Pediatric Nephrology Association
IPNCB	Institut des Parcs Nationaux du Congo Belge
IPO	Institut voor Plantenziektenkundig Onderzoek
IPO	Istituto per l'Oriente
IPO	International Progress Organization
IPOEE	Institution of Post Office Electrical Engineers
IPPA	Indo-Pacific Prehistory Association
IPPA	International Pentecostal Press Association

IPPA	International Prisoners Aid Association
IPPA	Irish Professional Photographers Association
IPPC	Industrial Promotion and Productivity Centre (Nepal)
IPPEC	Inventaire Permanent des Périodiques Étrangères en Cours. Direction des Bibliothèques
IPPF	International Penal and Penitentiary Foundation
IPPF	International Planned Parenthood Federation
IPPS	Institute of Physics and the Physical Society
IPPTA	Indian Pulp and Paper Technical Association
IPR	Institute of Pacific Relations (U.S.A.)
IPR	Institute of Population Registration
IPR	Institute of Psychophysical Research
IPR	Institute of Public Relations
IPRA	Indian Painting Research Association
IPRA	Institute of Park Recreation Administration
IPRA	International Peace Research Association
IPRA	International Public Relations Association
IPRAO	Institut de Prêvoyance et de Retraite de l'Afrique Occidentale
IPREIG	Institut Professional de Recherches et d'Études des Industries Graphiques
IPRE	Institute of Practical Radio Engineers (*now* Incorporated Practitioners in Radio and Electronics)
IPRO	International Pallet Recycling Organisation
IProd E	Institution of Production Engineers
IPRS	International Confederation for Plastic and Reconstructive Surgery
IPS	Incorporated Phonographic Society
IPS	Institute of Professional Salesmen
IPS	Instituut voor Pluimveeteelt
IPS	International Confederation for Plastic Surgery
IPS	International Peat Society
IPS	International Primatological Society
IPSA	Independent Postal System of America
IPSA	International Passenger Ship Association (U.S.A.)
IPSA	International Police and Security Association
IPSA	International Political Science Association
IPSC	International Pacific Salmon Committee
IPSCI	Industrial Promotion Services en Côte d'Ivoire
IPSF	International Pharmaceutical Students Federation
IPSFC	International Pacific Salmon Fisheries Commission (Canada)
IPSI	International Political Science Institute (U.S.A.)
IPSOA	Istituto Post-universitario per lo Studio dell'Organizzazione Aziendale
IPSRA	International Professional Ski Racers' Association
IPSSG	International Printers Supply Salesmen's Guild (U.S.A.)
IPST	Israel Programme for Scientific Translations
IPT	Institúto de Pesquisas Tecnológicas (Brazil)
IPTA	International Patent and Trademark Association
IPTC	International Press Telecommunications Committee
IPTEA	Internacia Postista Kaj Telekunikista Esperanto- Asocio
IPTPA	International Professional Tennis Players' Association
IPTT	Internationale du Personnel des Postes, Télégraphes et Téléphones
IPU	International Paleontological Union
IPU	International Peasant Union
IPU	International Population Union
IPU	Inter-Parliamentary Union (Switzerland)
IPVS	International Pig Veterinary Society
IPVU	Instituto Paraguayo de Vivienda y Urbanismo
IPW	Institüt für Internationale Politik un Wirtschaft
IQ	Institute of Quarrying
IQ	International Quorum of Motion Picture Producers
IQA	InstUtúto de Químico Agricola (Brazil)
IQB	Institúto Químico Biológico (Brazil)
IQC	International Quality Centre (*of* EOQC)
IQCA	Irish Quality Control Association
IQPS	Institute of Qualified Private Secretaries
IQS	Institute of Quantity Surveyors
IQSY	International Year of the Quiet Sun
IRA	Institute of Registered Architects
IRA	International Racquetball Association
IRA	International Reading Association

IRA	International Recreation Association (U.S.A.) (*now* WLRA)	**IRC**	International Rainwear Council
		IRC	International Red Cross
IRA	International Rodeo Association	**IRC**	International Rescue Committee
IRA	International Rubber Association	**IRC**	International Research Council
IRA	Irish Republican Army	**IRC**	International Resources Office
IRAA	Independent Refiners Association of America	**IRC**	International Rice Commission
IRABA	Institut de Recherche Appliquée du Beton Armé	**IRCA**	Institut de Recherches sur le Caoutchouc en Afrique
IRABOIS	Institut de Recherches Appliques au Bois	**IRCA**	Institution de Retraites Complémentaires Agricoles
IRAC	Instituto de Reforma Agraria y Colonización (Peru)	**IRCA**	International Railway Congress Association
IRAC	Interdepartment Radio Advisory Committee (U.S.A.)	**IRCAM**	Institut de Recherches Scientifiques (Cameroons)
IRAC	International Records Administration Conference. U.S. National Archives	**IRCAM**	Institute for Research and Acoustic/Musical Co-ordination (France)
IRAD	Institut de Recherches Appliquées du Dahomey	**IRCC**	Instrument Repair and Calibration Centre (Thailand)
IRAD	Institute for Research on Animal Diseases (*of* ARC)	**IRCE**	Istituto Nazionale per le Relazioni Culturali con l'Estero
IRADES	Istituto Ricerche Applicate, Documentazione e Studi	**IRCHA**	Institut National de Recherche Chimique Appliquée
IRAG	Centre International de Recherche des Aptitudes à la Gestion	**IRCI**	Institut de Recherches sur le Caoutchouc en Indochine
IRAM	Institut de Recherches Agronomiques de Madagascar	**IRCIHE**	International Referral Centre for Information Handling Equipment (Yugoslavia)
IRAM	Institut de Recherches et d'Application de Méthodes de Développement	**IRCN**	Institut de Recherches de la Construction Navale
IRAM	Instituto Argentino de Racionalización de Materiales	**IRCOBI**	Comité International de Recherche sur la Biocinétique des Chocs
IRAM	International Reformed Agency for Migration	**IRCT**	Institut Recherche Coloniale Tropicale
IRAMM	Institut de Recherche et d'Action contre la Misère Mondiale	**IRCT**	Institut de Recherches du Coton et des Textiles Exotiques
IRANDOC	Iranian Documentation Centre	**IRDA**	Industrial Research and Development Authority
IRANORM	Instituto Nacional de Racionalización y Normalización	**IRDC**	International Rubber Development Committee (*now* IRRDB)
IRAP	Organisation Internationale pour l'Avancement de la Recherche aux Hautes Pressions	**IREA**	Institut de Recherches de l'Économie Alimentaire
IRAS	Industriforbundets Rasjonaliseringskontor	**IREC**	International Rotary Engine Club (U.S.A.)
IRASA	International Radio Air Safety Association	**IREC**	Irrigation Research and Extension Advisory Committee (Australia)
IRAT	Institut de Recherches Agronomiques Tropicales et des Cultures Vivrières	**IREDA**	International Radio and Electrical Distributors Association
IRATRA	Instituto Nacional de Racionalización del Trabajo	**IREE**	Institute of Radio and Electronic Engineers (Australia)
IRB	Institute of Radiation Breeding (Japan)		
IRB	Instituto de Reeseguros do Brasil	**IREP**	Institut de Recherche Économique et de Planification
IRB	Irish Republican Brotherhood		

IRES	Institut de Recherches Économiques et Sociales (Zaire)
IRES	Instituto de Reinserción Social
IRESD	Institut Régional pour l'Enseignement Supérieur et le Développement (Singapore)
IRESP	Institut de Recherches Économique, Sociales et Politiques (Belgium)
IREX	International Research and Exchanges Board
IRF	International Re-education Foundation (U.S.A.)
IRF	International Reform Federation
IRF	International Road Federation
IRF	International Rowing Federation
IRFA	Imprimerie Reliure Franco-Africaine (Ivory Coast)
IRFAA	International Rescue and First Aid Association
IRFED	Institut Internationale de Recherches et de Formation en Vue du Développement Harmonisé
IRFIS	Istituto Regionale per il Finanziamento alle Industrie in Sicilia
IRFV	Internationaler Regenmantelfabrikantenverband
IRG	Internationale des Résistants à la Guerre
IRGCP	International Research Group for Carcinoembryonic Proteins
IRGOM	International Research Groups on Management
IRHA	International Rural Housing Association
IRHD	Internationaler Rat der Hauspflegedienste
IRHO	Institut de Recherches pour les Huiles de Palme et Oléagineux
IRI	Institut des Relations Internationales (Belgium)
IRI	Institution of the Rubber Industry
IRI	Inveresk Research International (Scotland)
IRI	Istituto per la Ricostruzione Industriale
IRIA	Indian Rubber Industries Association
IRIA	Institut Recherche d'Information et d'Automatique
IRIA	Instituto Regional de Investigaciones del Algodón (Salvador)
IRIA	Ivoirienne de Représentation Industrielle et Automobile
IRIEC	Institut de Recherche en Informatique et en Économie
IRIFIP	International Research Institute for Immigration and Emigration Politics
IRIJ	Institut de Recherche d'Informatique Juridique
IRIPS	Instituto di Ricerche e di Interventi Psico-Sociali
IRIS	Industrial Research and Information Services
IRL	Information Retrieval Ltd
IRL	Institute of Rural Life at Home and Overseas
IRL	Internationaler Ring für Landarbeit
IRLA	International Religious Liberty Association
IRLCO-CSA	International Red Locust Control Organisation for Central and Southern Africa
IRLCS	International Red Locust Control Service (*now* IRLCO-CSA)
IRM	Institut Suisse de Recherches Ménagères
IRMA	International Rehabilitation Medicine Association
IRMB	Institut Royal Météorologique de Belgique
IRMC	International Radio-Maritime Committee
IRMRA	Indian Rubber Manufacturers' Research Association
IRNU	Institut de Recherche des Nations Unies pour le Développement Social
IRO	International Refugees Organisation
IROPCO	Iranian Offshore Petroleum Company
IRPA	International Radiation Protection Association
IRPA	Irrigation Pump Administration (Philippines)
IRPTC	International Register of Potentially Toxic Chemicals (Switzerland)
IRQPC	International Rubber Quality and Packing Conferences
IRR	Institute of Race Relations
IRRA	Industrial Relations Research Association (U.S.A.)
IRRB	International Rubber Research Board (*now* IRRDB)
IRRDB	International Rubber Research and Development Board
IRRI	Institut Royal des Relations Internationales (Belgium)
IRRI	International Rice Research Institute
IRRT	International Relations Round Table
IRS	Institut de Recherches Sahariennes
IRS	Instituut voor Rationele Suikerproductie

RS	International Referral System (Kenya)	IRYDA	Instituto Nacional de Reforma Desarrollo Agrario
RS	International Rorschach Society	IRZA	Institut de Recherches sur la Zone Aride en Arabia Saoudite
RS	Irrigation Research Station (N.Z.)		
RSA	Istituto di Ricerca Sulle Acque	IS	Industrial Society
RSAC	Institut pour la Recherche Scientifique en Afrique Centrale	ISA	Indian Society of Advertisers
		ISA	Industrie Siderurgiche Associate (Italy)
RSC	Institut de Recherches Scientifiques au Congo	ISA	Instrument Society of America
RSCL	International Research Society for Children's Literature	ISA	International Schools Association
		ISA	International Settlement Authority
RSE	Institution of Railway Signal Engineers	ISA	International Sign Association Inc. (U.S.A.)
RSEN	International Rehabilitation - Special Education Network	ISA	International Silk Association
		ISA	International Sociological Association
RSF	Inland Revenue Staff Federation	ISA	International Studies Association (U.S.A.)
RSFC	International Rayon and Synthetic Fibres Committee	ISAB	Institute for the Study of Animal Behaviour
		ISABR	International Society for Animal Blood Group Research
RSG	International Rubber Study Group		
RSIA	Institut pour l'Encouragement de la Recherche Scientifique dans l'Industrie et l'Agriculture (Belgium)	ISABU	Institut des Sciences Agronomiques du Burundi (Zaire)
		ISAC	International Scientific Agricultural Council
RSID	Institut de Recherches de la Sidérurgie	ISAC	International Security Affairs Committee (U.S.A.)
RSM	Institut de Recherches Scientifiques de Madagascar		
		ISAC	Interuniversity South-East Asia Committee (U.S.A.)
RSP	Irish Republican Socialist Party		
RSUR	Institut de Recherche en Sociologie Urbaine et Rurale	ISAD	Information Science and Automation Division (ALA)
RT	Institute of Reprographic Technology	ISADA	Industries et Savonneries du Dahomey
RT	Institut de Reboisement de Tunis	ISAE	Indian Society of Agricultural Economics
RTAC	International Round Table for the Advancement of Counselling	ISAE	Internacia Scienca Asocio Esperantista
		ISAGA	International Simulation and Gaming Association
RTC	International Road Tar Conference		
RTE	Institute of Road Transport Engineers	ISAHM	International Society for Animal and Human Mycology
RTO	Institut de Recherche Scientifique au Togo		
RTO	International Radio and Television Organisation	ISAKE	Internacia Societo de Arkitektoj kaj Konstruistoj Esperantistoj
		ISAL	Iglesia y Sociedad en América Latina
RTS	International Radio and Television Society (U.S.A.)	ISALPA	Incorporated Society of Auctioneers and Landed Property Agents (now ISVA)
RTU	International Railway Temperance Union		
RU	International Raiffeisen Union	ISAP	Instituto Superior de Administración Publica (Argentina)
RU	International Relief Union		
RU	International Road Transport Union	ISAP	South American Petroleum Institute
RV	Internationale Rat für Vogelschutz	ISAPA	International Screen Advertising Producers' Association (U.S.A.)
RVAM	Istituto per le Richerche e le Informazioni di Mercato e la Valorizzazione della Produzione Agricola	ISAR	Institut des Sciences Agronomiques du Rwanda (Zaire)
		ISAR	International Society for Astrological Research
RWC	International Registry of World Citizens		

ISAS	Istituto di Scienze Ammistrative e Socio-Economiche	**ISCLT**	International Society for Clinical Laboratory Technology
ISAS	International Screen Advertising Services	**ISCM**	International Society for Contemporary Music
ISAW	International Society of Aviation Writers		
ISB	Institute of Scientific Business	**ISCM**	International Society of Cybernetic Medicine
ISB	Institut für Selbstbedienung	**ISCMA**	International Superphosphate and Compound Manufacturers Association
ISB	International Society of Biometeorology		
ISB	Internationaler Studentenbund	**ISCOR**	South African Iron and Steel Industrial Corporation, Ltd
ISBA	Incorporated Society of British Advertisers	**ISCP**	International Society for Clinical Pathology
ISBB	International Society of Bioclimatology and Biometeorology	**ISCRP**	International Society of City and Regional Planners
ISBC	International Society of Bible Collectors	**ISCS**	International Scientific Co-operative Service
ISBE	International Society for Business Education (U.S.A.)	**ISCSC**	International Society for the Comparative Study of Civilizations
ISBGA	Irish Sugar Beet Growers Association	**ISCTC**	Inter-Service Components Technical Committee
ISBI	International Savings Banks Institute		
ISBO	Instituto de Sociología Boliviana	**ISCTP**	International Study Commission for Traffic Police
ISBP	International Society for Biochemical Pharmacology	**ISCTR**	International Scientific Committee for Trypanosomiasis Research
ISC	Interamerican Society of Cardiology		
ISC	Internationale Heinrich Schütz-Gesellschaft	**ISCUS**	Indo-Soviet Cultural Society (India)
ISC	International Seismological Centre (U.K.)	**ISCYRA**	International Star Class Yacht Racing Association (U.S.A.)
ISC	International Sericultural Commission	**ISD**	International Society for Development
ISC	International Society of Cardiology	**ISD**	International Society of Differentiation
ISC	International Society of Chemotherapy	**ISDB**	International Society of Developmental Biologists
ISC	International Society of Citriculture		
ISC	International Student Conference	**ISDIBER**	Instituto de Sociología y Desarrollo del Area Iberica
ISC	International Sugar Council	**ISDN**	Institute for the Study of Developing Nations (U.S.A.)
ISCA	International Senior Citizens Association		
ISCA	International Standards Co-ordination Association	**ISDRA**	International Sled Dog Racing Association
ISCAY	International Solidarity Committee with Algerian Youth	**ISDS**	International Sheep Dog Society
		ISE	Institution of Sales Engineers
ISCB	International Society for Cell Biology	**ISE**	Institution of Sanitary Engineers (*now* IPHE)
ISCD	International Society for Community Development	**ISE**	Institution of Structural Engineers
		ISE	International Society of Electrochemistry
ISCE	International Society of Christian Endeavour	**ISE**	Instituto per gli Studi di Economia
ISCEH	International Society for Clinical and Experimental Hypnosis	**ISEA**	Institut de Science Économique Appliquéé
ISCERG	International Society for Clinical Electroretinography	**ISEA-AN**	Institut de Science Économique Appliquée, Centre d'Afrique du Nord (Tunis)
ISCET	International Society of Certified Electronics Technicians	**ISEAS**	Institute of South-East Asian Studies (Singapore)
ISCFB	International Society of Cranio-Facial Biology	**ISEC**	International Securities and Exchange Commission
ISCL	US Coalition for Life (U.S.A.)	**ISEC**	International Solvent Extraction Conference

ISEAS	Institute of Southeast Asian Studies (Singapore)	ISGA	International Study Group of Aerogrammes
ISEC	International Statistics Educational Centre	ISGC	International Society of Guatemala Collectors
ISECSI	International Society for Educational, Cultural and Scientific Interchanges	ISGE	International Society of Gastroenterology
ISEK	International Society of Electrophysiological Kinesiology	ISGI	International Service for Geomagnetic Indices (Netherlands)
ISEP	International Society for Educational Planners	ISGML	International Study Group for Mathematics Learning
ISEP	International Statistical Ecology Programme	ISGO	International Society of Geographic Ophthalmology
ISER	Institut Supérieur d'Économie Rurale	ISGRCM	International Study Group for Research in Cardiac Metabolism
ISER	Institute of Social and Economic Research (West Indies)	ISGSH	International Study Group for Steroid Hormones
ISES	Institut des Sciences Économiques et Sociales (Switzerland)	ISH	International Society of Haematology
ISES	International Schools Examination Syndicate (*now* IBO)	ISH	International Society of Hypertension
		ISHAM	International Society of Human and Animal Mycology
ISES	International Ship Electric Service Association	ISHI	International Society for the History of Ideas
ISES	International Society of Explosives Specialists	ISHM	Institut des Sciences Humaines du Mali (Mali)
ISES	International Solar Energy Society	ISHM	International Society for Hybrid Microelectronics
ISETU	International Secretariat of Entertainment Trade Unions (Belgium)	ISHOBSS	International Society for the History of the Behavioral and Social Sciences
ISF	International Science Foundation	ISHRA	Iron and Steel Holding and Realisation Agency
ISF	International Shipping Federation Ltd		
ISF	International Society for Fat Research	ISHS	International Society for Horticultural Science
ISF	International Softball Federation	ISI	Indian Social Institute (India)
ISF	International Spiritualist Federation	ISI	Indian Standards Institution (India)
ISF	Svenska Ingenjörssamfundet	ISI	Indian Statistical Institute
ISFA	Institute of Shipping and Forwarding Agents	ISI	International Safety Institute (U.S.A.)
ISFA	International Scientific Film Association	ISI	Institute for Scientific Information (U.S.A.)
ISFADPM	International Society for the Abolition of Data Processing Machines	ISI	International Statistical Institute
ISFC	Institut Scientifique Franco-Canadienne (Canada)	ISI	Iron and Steel Institute
ISFC	International Scholarship Fund Committee	ISIA	International Snowmobile Industry Association (U.S.A.)
ISFL	Interessengemeinschaft Schweizerischer Foto-Kino-Lieferanten	ISIB	Inter-Services Ionospheric Bureau
ISFL	International Scientific Film Library	ISIC	Instituto Salvadoreño de Investigaciónes de Café
ISFNR	International Society for Folk-Narrative Research	ISIC	International Solvay Institute of Chemistry
ISFSC	International Society of Food Service Consultants	ISICIB	Centro Internazionale Bibliografico dell' Istituto di Studi sul Lavoro
ISG	Interessengemeinschaft der Schweizerischen Gärungsessig-Industrie	ISID	Research Institute of the Iron and Steel Industry (France)
ISG	Internationale Heinrich Schütz-Gesellschaft		

ISIG	Institute of Standards and Industrial Research (Ghana)	**ISLWF**	International Shoe and Leather Workers Federation
ISIG	Instituto di Sociologia Internazionale, Gorizia	**ISLWG**	International Shipping Legislation Working Group (*of* UNCTAD)
ISIL	Indian Society of International Law	**ISM**	Institute of Supervisory Management
ISIM	International Society of Internal Medicine	**ISMA**	Industrie Sénégalaise de Marbre et d'Agglomérés
ISIO	Institute for the Study of International Organisations	**ISMA**	Institute for the Study of Man in Africa (South Africa)
ISIP	Istituto Italiano di Polemologia e di Ricerche sui Conflitti	**ISMA**	International Shipmasters Association of the Great Lakes (U.S.A.)
ISIP	Internacianalna stalna izlozbo Publikacija (Yugoslavia)	**ISMA**	International Superphosphate Manufacturers Association (*now* ISCMA)
ISIR	Institute of Standards and Industrial Research (Ghana)	**ISMCM**	Institut Supérieur des Matériaux et de la Construction Mécanique
ISIR	International Society for Invertebrate Reproduction	**ISME**	Institute of Sheet Metal Engineering
ISIRI	Institute of Standards and Industrial Research of Iran	**ISME**	International Association for Music Education
ISIS	Indian School of International Studies (India)	**ISMEO**	Istituto Italiano per il Medio e l'Estremo Oriente
ISIS	Integrated Scientific Information System (Switzerland)	**ISMES**	Instituto Sperimentale Modelli e Structure
ISIS	International Student Information Service	**ISMEX**	International Shoe Machinery Exhibition
ISIS	Women's International Information and Communication Service	**ISMFE**	International Society of Soil Mechanics and Foundation Engineering
ISITB	Iron and Steel Industry Training Board	**ISMG**	International Scientific Management Group (*of* GARP)
ISIUA	Institut Supérieur et International d'Urbanisme Appliqué (Belgium)	**ISMGF**	International Stoke Mandeville Games Federation
ISIYM	International Society of Industrial Yarn Manufacturers (U.S.A.)	**ISMH**	International Society of Medical Hydrology
ISJP	International Society for Japanese Philately	**ISMM**	International Society of Mini- and Micro-Computers
ISK	International Seidenbau Kommission	**ISMOG**	Instituut voor Sociaal-Economische Studie van Minder Ontwikkelde Gebieden
ISKA	Internasjonalen for Stats-og Kommunalansatte	**ISMRC**	Inter-Services Metallurgical Research Council
ISKCON	International Society for Krishna Consciousness	**ISMUN**	International Student Movement for the United Nations
ISL	International Soccer League (U.S.A.)	**ISN**	International Society for Neurochemistry
ISL	International Society of Lymphology	**ISN**	International Society of Nephrology
ISLI	Istituto di Studi sul Lavoro	**ISNA**	Indian Science News Association
ISLA	Information Services on Latin America (U.S.A.)	**ISNA**	Instituto di Studi Nucleari per l'Agricoltura
ISLE	Institute of Sociology of Law for Europe (Belgium)	**ISNAR**	International Service for Agricultural Research (Germany)
ISLIC	Israel Society of Special Libraries and Information Centres	**ISNP**	International Society of Naturpathic Physicians
ISLTC	International Society of Leather Trades Chemists	**ISNVP**	International Society for Non Verbal Psychotherapy

ISO	International Self-service Organisation	**ISPE**	Istituto di Studi per la Programmazione Economica
ISO	International Shopfitting Organisation		
ISO	International Society of Organbuilders (Germany)	**ISPEMA**	Industrial Safety (Protective Equipment) Manufacturers Association
ISO	International Standardisation Organisation	**ISPLS**	International Society of Phonetic Sciences
ISO	International Sugar Organization	**ISPI**	Istituto per gli Studi di Politica Internazionale (Italy)
ISOCARP	International Society of City and Regional Planners	**ISPM**	International Society of Plant Morphologists (India)
ISOD	International Sports Organisation for the Disabled	**ISPMB**	International Society for the Protection of Mustangs and Burros
ISODARCO	International School on Disarmament and Research on Conflicts (Italy)	**ISPO**	International Society for Prosthetics and Orthotics
ISODOC	International Centre for Standards in Information and Documentation (*of* ISO)	**ISPP**	Indian Society for Plant Pathology
ISONET	International Standards Information Network	**ISPP**	International Society of Plant Pathology
		ISPP	International Society for Portuguese Philately
ISONEVO	Instituut voor Sociaal Onderzoek van het Nederlandse Volk	**ISPP**	Inter-Services Plastic Panel
		ISPP	International Society for Plant Pathology
ISORT	Interdisciplinary Student-Originated Research Training (U.S.A.)	**ISPROM**	Istituto di Studi e Programmi per il Mediterraneo
ISOSC	International Society for Soilless Culture	**ISPS**	Institutul de Studii si Proiectari Silvice (Roumania)
ISP	Incorporated Society of Planters (Malaysia)		
ISP	Institute of Sewage Purification	**ISPW**	International Society for the Psychology of Writing
ISP	Institute for the Study of Peace (U.S.A.)		
ISP	Interessengemeinschaft der Schweizerischen Parkettindustrie	**ISQA**	Israel Society for Quality Assurance
		ISR	Institute of Seaweed Research, Inveresk
ISP	International Society for Photogrammetry	**ISR**	Institute for Social Research (South Africa)
ISP	Internationale des Services Publiques	**ISR**	International Society of Radiology
ISPA	Institutul de Studii si Proiectari Agricole (Roumania)	**ISRA**	International Society for Research on Aggression
ISPA	International Screen Publicity Association	**ISRAIN**	Institut Supérieur de Recherche Appliquée pour les Industries Nucléaires (Belgium)
ISPA	International Small Printers' Association		
ISPA	International Society for the Protection of Animals	**ISRB**	Inter-Services Research Bureau
		ISRCA	Institute for Scientific Research in Central Africa
ISPA	International Sporting Press Association		
ISPA	International Squash Players Association	**ISRCDVS**	International Society for Research on Civilization Diseases and Vital Substances
ISPAS	International Society of Professional Ambulance Services (U.S.A.)	**ISRCSC**	Inter-Service Radio Components Standardization Committee
ISPCA	Ironmaking and Steelmaking Plant Contractors Association	**ISRD**	International Society for Rehabilitation of the Disabled
ISPCC	Irish Society for the Prevention of Cruelty to Children	**ISRF**	International Squash Rackets Federation
		ISRF	International Sugar Research Foundation (U.S.A.)
ISPE	Institute and Society of Practitioners in Electrolysis	**ISRFCTC**	Inter-Services Radio-Frequency Cables Technical Committee
ISPE	International Society of Planetarium Educators	**ISRM**	International Society for Rock Mechanics

ISRO	Indian Space Research Organisation	**ISSRS**	Institut de Service Social et de Recherches Sociales
ISRR	International Society for Rorschach Research	**ISSS**	International Society for Socialist Studies
ISRRA	International Standard Rex Rabbit Association	**ISSS**	International Society of Soil Science
ISRRT	International Society of Radiographers and Radiological Technicians	**ISSS**	International Society for the Study of Symbols (U.S.A.)
ISRS	Institute for Study of Religions and Society in Singapore and Malaysia	**ISST**	Institut des Sciences Sociales du Travail
ISRSA	International Synthetic Rubber Safety Association	**ISST**	Instituto Scientifico Sperimental dei Tabacchi
ISRU	International Scientific Radio Union	**ISST**	International Society for the Study of Time
ISS	Institute for Strategic Studies	**IST**	Institute of Science Technology
ISS	International Society for Sterology	**IST**	International Society on Toxinology
ISS	Institute of Social Studies (Netherlands)	**ISTA**	Indian Scientific Translators Association
ISS	International Schools Services (U.S.A.)	**ISTA**	International Seed Testing Association
ISS	International Seismological Summary	**ISTA**	International Sight-Seeing and Tours Association
ISS	International Social Service	**ISTA**	International Society for Technology Assessment
ISS	International Student Service (U.S.A.)	**ISTA**	International Special Tooling Association
ISS	International Sunshine Society	**ISTA**	International Statistiche Agrarinformationen
ISSA	International Ship Suppliers' Association	**ISTAT**	Istituto Nazionale di Statistica
ISSA	International Slurry Seal Association	**ISTC**	Institute of Scientific and Technical Communicators
ISSA	International Social Security Association		
ISSB	Inter-Service Security Board	**ISTC**	International Shade Tree Conference (U.S.A.)
ISSC	International Ship Structures Conference	**ISTC**	International Student Travel Conference
ISSC	International Social Science Council	**ISTC**	International Switching and Testing Centre (U.K.)
ISSCB	International Society for Sandwich Construction and Bonding	**ISTC**	Iron and Steel Trades Confederation
ISSCL	Social Service Institution for Housing for Workers (Italy)	**ISTCL**	International Scientific and Technical Committee on Laundering
ISSCT	International Society of Sugar Cane Technologists	**ISTD**	Imperial Society of Teachers of Dancing Incorporated
ISSER	Institute of Statistical, Social and Economic Research (Ghana)	**ISTD**	Institute for the Study and Treatment of Delinquency
ISSF	International Service of the Society of Friends/Quakers (U.S.A.)	**ISTD**	International Society of Tropical Dermatology
ISSI	International Social Science Institute (U.S.A.)	**ISTD**	Inter-Services Topographical Department
ISSMFE	International Society of Soil Mechanics and Foundation Engineering	**ISTE**	International Society of Tropical Ecology
ISSO	International Self-Service Organisation	**ISTF**	International Society of Tropical Foresters (U.S.A.)
ISSOCO	Istituto per lo Studio della Società Contemporanea	**ISTH**	International Society on Thrombosis and Haemostasis
ISSOL	International Society for the Study of the Origin of Life	**ISTPM**	Institute Scientifique et Technique des Pêches Maritimes
ISSP	Institute for Solid State Physics (Japan)	**ISTEA**	Iron and Steel Trades Employers' Association
ISSP	International Society of Sports Psychology		

ISTESU	International Secretariat for Teaching Educational Sciences in Universities	**ITA**	International Taxicab Association (U.S.A.)
ISTIC	Institute of Scientific and Technical Information of China	**ITA**	International Temperance Association
		ITA	International Tunnelling Association
ISTRA	Interplanetary Space Travel Research Association	**ITA**	Indian Tea Association
ISTRAK	International Strassenteer Konferenz	**ITA**	Institut Technique de l'Aviculture des Produits de Basse-cour et des Élevages de Petits Animaux (*formerly* ITEA)
ISTU	International Student Theatre Union	**ITA**	Institut de Transport Aérien
ISTUS	Internationalen Studienkommission für Motorlosen Flug	**ITA**	Institute of Traffic Administration
ISTVS	International Society for Terrain-Vehicle Systems	**ITA**	Institute of Travel Agents
		ITA	International Thermographers Association
ISU	International Council of Scientific Unions	**ITAA**	International Transactional Analysis Association
ISU	International Salvage Union	**ITAC**	Interagency Textile Administrative Committee (U.S.A.)
ISU	International Skating Union		
ISU	International Society of Urology	**ITAL**	Institute of Food Technology (Brazil)
ISUDO	International Symposium on Ultrasonic Diagnostics in Ophthalmology (Belgium)	**ITAL**	Instituut voor Toepassing van Atoomenergie in de Landbouw
ISUNAM	Instituto de Investigaciones Sociales (Mexico)	**ITALSIEL**	Società Italiana Sistemi Informativ Elettronica
ISUSE	International Secretariat for the University Study of Education	**ITAP**	Institut Technique des Administrations Publiques
ISV	Interessengemeinschaft Schweizerischer Verleger	**ITAU**	Compania Itaú des Transportes Acéros (Brazil)
ISVA	Incorporated Society of Valuers and Auctioneers	**ITAVI**	Institut Technique de l'Aviculture, des Productions de Basse-Cour et des Élevages de Petits Animaux
ISVE	Istituto di Studi per lo Sviluppo Economico		
ISVET	Istituto per gli Studi sullo Sviluppo ed il Progresso Tecnico	**ITAVI**	Servizio Telecommunicazioni e Meteorológico dell' Aeronautica
ISVR	Institute of Sound and Vibration Research	**ITB**	Agricultural, Horticultural and Forestry Industry Training Board
ISVS	International Secretariat for Voluntary Service	**ITB**	Institut Français de la Betterave Industrielle
ISVSK	Internationaler Ständiger Verband für Schiffahrt-Kongresse	**ITB**	International Time Bureau
ISW	Institute of Social Welfare	**ITB**	Internationaler Turnerbund
ISW	Interessengemeinschaft für den Schweizerischen Weinimport	**ITB**	Irish Tourist Board
		ITBA	International Toy Buff's Association
ISWA	International Science Writers Association	**ITBB**	Fédération Internationale des Travailleurs du Bâtiment et du Bois
ISWA	International Solid Wastes and Public Cleansing Association	**ITBLAV**	Internationale Textil-, Bekleidungs und Lederarbeiter Vereinigung
ISWC	International Secretariat of World Citizens		
ISWC	International Society for the Welfare of Cripples (*now* ISRD)	**ITBON**	Instituut v. Toegepast Biologisch Onderzoek in de Natuur (*now* RIN)
ISWM	Institute of Solid Wastes Management	**ITBTP**	Institut Technique du Bâtiment et des Travaux Publiques
ITA	Independent Television Authority	**ITC**	Imperial Tobacco Company
ITA	Institute of Transactional Analysis	**ITC**	Industrial Training Council
ITA	International Tape Association	**ITC**	Inter-American Travel Congresses

ITC	International Institute for Aerial Survey and Earth Sciences (Netherlands)
ITC	International Tar Conference
ITC	International Tea Committee
ITC	International Teletraffic Congress
ITC	International Textbook Company Ltd
ITC	International Tin Council
ITC	International Trade Centre
ITCA	Independent Television Companies Association
ITCA	Inter-American Technical Council of Archives
ITCA	International Typographic Composition Association
ITCAA	Institut Technique Coopératif des Aliments pour Animaux
ITCAS	International Training Centre for Aerial Survey
ITCC	International Technical Cooperation Centre (Israel)
ITCF	Institut Technique des Céréales et des Fourrages
ITCPN	International Technical Conference on Protection of Nature
ITCRA	International Textile Care and Rental Association
ITDC	International Trade Development Committee (U.S.A.)
ITDG	Intermediate Technology Development Group Ltd
ITE	Institute of Traffic Engineers (U.S.A.)
ITE	Internationale Évangélique Ouvrière
ITEA	Institut Technique de l'Élevage Avicole (France) (*now* ITA)
ITEA	International Esperanto Tourist Association
ITEB	Institut Technique d'Élevage Bovin
ITEC	International Total Energy Congress
ITECA	International Educational and Cultural Association
ITEMA	Industrie Textile du Mali
ITEO	International Trade and Employment Organisation
ITERG	Institut Technique d'Études et des Recherches des Corps Gras
ITESM	Instituto Tecnológico y de Estudios Superiores de Monterrey (Mexico)
ITF	Committee of Transport Workers Unions in the EEC
ITF	Institut Textile de France
ITF	Instrumenttekniska Föreningen
ITF	International Trampolining Federation
ITF	International Transport Workers' Federation
ITFCA	International Track and Field Coaches Association
ITG	Institut Technique du Gruyère
ITG	International Tabakwissenschaftliche Gesellschaft
ITG	International Trumpet Guild
ITGWF	International Textile and Garment Workers Federation
ITGWU	Irish Transport and General Workers Union
ITI	Indian Telephone Industries
ITI	Institute for Technical Interchange (Hawaii)
ITI	International Technical Institute of Flight Engineers
ITI	International Technology Institute (U.S.A.)
ITI	International Theatre Institute
ITI	International Thrift Institute
ITI	Irish Timber Industries Ltd
ITIC	International Tsunami Information Centre (Hawaii)
ITICA	Chambre Syndicale Nationale d'Isolation Thermique, de l'Insonorisation et de la Correction Acoustique
ITIPAT	Institut pour la Technologie et l'Industrialisation des Produits Agricoles Tropicaux (Ivory Coast)
ITIS	Industrial Technical Information Service (Singapore)
ITIS	Insect Toxicologists Information Service (Netherlands)
ITK	Internationale Teerkonferenz
ITM	Instituto di Tecnologia Meccanica
ITMA	Institute of Trade Mark Agents
ITMEB	International Tea Market Expansion Board
ITMRC	International Travel Market Research Council
ITN	Independent Television News Ltd
ITO	Indian Tourist Office
ITO	International Trade Organisation
ITOCY	Industrie Togolaise du Cycle et du Cyclomoter

ITOVIC	Institut Technique de l'Élevage Ovin et Caprin
ITP	Institut Technique de la Pomme de Terre
ITP	Institut Technique du Porc
ITPA	Institut Technique de Pratique Agricole
ITPA	Irish Trade Protection Association
ITRC	Industrial Toxicology Research Centre (India)
ITRC	International Tin Research Council
ITS	Instituut voor Toegepaste Sociologie
ITS	International Technogeographical Society
ITS	International Thespian Society
ITS	International Tracing Service
ITS	International Trade Secretariats' Co-ordinating Committee
ITSC	International Telephone Service Centres
ITSG	International Tin Study Group
ITT	Instituto Torcuato di Tella, Buenos Aires (Argentina)
ITT	Industrie Textile Togolaise
ITT	Instituut voor Tuinbouwtechniek
ITTC	International Telegraph and Telephone Corporation
ITTC	International Towing Tank Conference
ITTCC	International Teachers Trade Union Cooperative Committee
ITTF	International Table Tennis Federation
ITTTA	International Technical Tropical Timber Association
ITU	International Telecommunications Union
ITU	International Temperance Union
ITU	International Typographical Union
ITV	Institut Technique du Vin
ITV	Instituto Técnico Vocacional (Guatemala)
ITVTP	Internationale Tierärztliche Vereinigung für Tierproduktion
ITVV	Internationaler Transport-Versicherungs-Verband
ITZN	International Trust for Zoological Nomenclature
IU	Interlingue Union
IU	International Environmental Protection Union
IUA	International Union of Advertising
IUA	International Union Against Alcoholism
IUA	International Union of Architects
IUA	International Union of Arts
IUAA	International Union of Advertisers Associations
IUAA	International Union of Alpine Associations
IUAC	International Union Against Cancer
IUADM	International Union of Associations of Doctor-Motorists
IUAES	International Union of Anthropological and Ethnological Sciences
IUAI	International Union of Aviation Insurers
IUAJ	International Union of Agricultural Journalists
IUAO	International Union for Applied Ornithology
IUAPPA	International Union of Air Pollution Prevention Associations
IUAS	International Union of Agricultural Sciences
IUAT	International Union against Tuberculosis
IUB	International Union of Biochemistry
IUB	International Universities' Bureau
IUBS	International Union of Biological Sciences
IUBS	International Union of Building Societies
IUC	International Union of Chemistry
IUC	Inter-University Council for Higher Education Overseas
IUC	International University Contact for Management Education
IUCAF	Inter-Union Committee for Frequency Allocations for Radio Astronomy and Space Science
IUCE	International Union of Cinematograph Exhibitors
IUCI	International Union on the Ionosphere
IUCM	Inter-Union Commission for Studies of the Moon
IUCN	International Union for Conservation of Nature and Natural Resources
IUCOG	Inter-Union Commission on Geodynamics
IUCr	International Union of Crystallography
IUCRM	Inter-Union Commission on Radio Meteorology
IUCS	Inter-Union Commission on Spectroscopy
IUCST	Inter-Union Commission on Science Teaching
IUCSTP	Inter-Union Commission on Solar-Terrestrial Physics
IUCSTR	Inter-Union Commission on Solar and Terrestrial Relationships

IUCW	International Union for Child Welfare
IUDW & C	Irish Union of Distributive Workers and Clerks
IUDZG	International Union of Directors of Zoological Gardens
IUE	International Union of Electrical Workers
IUE	International Union for Electro-heat
IUEC	International Union of Elevator Constructors
IUEC	Inter-Universitare Efficiency Commissie
IUEE	Institut Universitaire d'Études Européennes (Switzerland)
IUEF	International University Exchange Fund
IUF	International Union of Food and Allied Workers' Association
IUFDT	International Union of Food, Drink and Tobacco Workers' Associations
IUFO	International Union of Family Organisations
IUFOST	International Union of Food Science and Technology
IUFRO	International Union of Forest Research Organisations
IUFTAV	Internationale Union der Forschung, Technik und Anwendung des Vakuums
IUGB	International Union of Game Biologists
IUGG	International Union of Geodesy and Geophysics
IUGS	International Union of Geological Sciences
IUHE	International Union for Health Education
IUHEI	Institut Universitaire de Hautes Études Internationales (Switzerland)
IUHPS	International Union of the History and Philosophy of Science
IUHR	International Union of Hotel, Restaurant and Bar Workers
IUHS	International Union of History of Sciences
IUI	Industriens Utredningsinstitut
IUI	International Union of Interpreters
IUIS	International Union of Immunological Societies
IUJCD	Internationale Union Junger Christlicher Demokraten
IUKP	Internationale Union der Katholischen Presse
IUL	International Union der Gewerkschaften der Lebens- und Genussmittelarbeiter Gewerkschaften
IULA	International Union of Local Authorities
IULCS	International Union of Leather Chemists Societies
IULCW	International Union of Liberal Christian Women
IULEC	Inter-University Labour Education Committee (U.S.A.)
IULIA	International Union of Life Insurance Agents
IUMI	International Union of Marine Insurance
IUMMSW	International Union of Mine, Mill and Smelter Workers
IUMS	International Union for Moral and Social Action
IUMSWA	Industrial Union of Marine and Shipbuilding Workers of America
IUNS	International Union of Nutritional Sciences
IUNT	Instituto Uruguayo de Normas Tecnicas
IUOE	International Union of Operating Engineers
IUOTO	International Union of Official Travel Organizations
IUP	Irish University Press
IUPA	International Union of Practitioners in Advertising
IUPAB	International Union of Pure and Applied Biophysics
IUPAC	International Union of Pure and Applied Chemistry
IUPAP	International Union of Pure and Applied Physics
IUPERJ	Instituto Universitário de Pesquisas do Rio de Janeiro (Brazil)
IUPGWA	International Union of United Plant Guard Workers of America
IUPHAR	International Union of Pharmacology
IUPIP	International Union for the Protection of Industrial Property
IUPM	International Union for Protecting Public Morality
IUPN	International Union for the Protection of Nature
IUPS	International Union of Physiological Sciences
IUPS	International Union of Psychological Science
IUPW	International Union of Petroleum Workers (U.S.A.)
IUR	International Union of Railways
IUR	International University of Radiophonics (France)
IURN	Institut Unifié de Recherches Nucléaires

IURP	Imprensa da Universidade Rural de Pernambuco (Brazil)		**IVBH**	Internationale Vereinigung für Brückenbau und Hochbau
IUS	International Union of Students		**IVBS**	Industriele Vereniging tot Bevordering van de Stralingsveiligheid
IUSA	International Underwater Spearfishing Association		**IVC**	Industrievereinigung Chemiefaser
IUSDT	International Union of Social Democratic Teachers		**IVC**	Permanent Committee for the International Veterinary Congresses
IUSF	International Union of Societies of Foresters		**IVCC**	Institut des Vins de Consommation Courante
IUSP	International Union of Scientific Psychology		**IVCLG**	Internationaler Verband Christlicher Landarbeitergewerkschaften
IUSS	International Union for Social Studies			
IUSSI	International Union for Study of Social Insects		**IVD**	Industrievereinigung Chemiefaser
			IVE	Institute of Vitreous Enamellers
IUSSP	International Union for the Scientific Study of Population		**IVE**	Instituto Veterinario Ecuatoriano
			IVE	Internationale Vereinigung des Eisenwaren- und Eisenhändlerverbände
IUSY	International Union of Socialist Youth			
IUT	International Union against Tuberculosis		**IVEL**	Instituto Veterinario Ecuatoriano del Litoral
IUTAM	International Union of Theoretical and Applied Mechanics		**IVF**	Industrieverband Friseurbedarf
			IVF	Institutet för Verkstadsteknisk Forskning
IUTCT	International Union for Thermal Medicine and Climatothalassotherapy		**IVFGR**	Internationale Vereinigung für Gewerblichen Rechtsschultz
IUVAA	Internationale Unie van Verenigingen van Artsen-Automobilisten		**IVFT**	Instituut voor Veterinaire Farmacologie en Toxicologie der Rijksuniversiteit, Utrecht
IUVDT	International Union against the Venereal Diseases and the Treponematoses		**IVFZ**	International Veterinary Federation of Zootechnics
IUVSTA	International Union for Vacuum Science, Technique and Applications		**IVG**	Internationale Vereinigung für Germanische Sprach- und Literaturwissenschaft
IUWA	International Union of Women Architects		**IVGWP**	Internationaler Verband der Gastronomie- und Weinbau-Presse
IUWDS	International Ursigrams and World Days Service			
			IVH	Industrieverband für Heimtierbedarf
IUYCD	International Union of Young Christian Democrats		**IVH**	Internationale Vereinigung des Handwerks
			IVHW	Internationaler Verband für Hauswirtschaft
IVA	Ingenjörsvetenskapsakademien		**IVIC**	Instituto Venozolano de Investigaciones Cientificas
IVA	Institúto de Vacuna Antivariolosa (Bolivia)			
IVA	Internationale Vereinigung der Anschlussgeleisse-Benützer		**IVIO**	Instituut voor Individueel Onderwijs
			IVIP	Internationale Vereinigung f. Individual-psychologie
IVA	Swedish Academy of Engineering Sciences			
IVAAP	International Veterinary Association for Animal Production		**IVITA**	Instituto Veterinario de Investigaciones Tropicales y de Altura (Peru)
IVAC	Instituto Venezolano de Acción Comunitaria		**IVJH**	Internationale Vereinigung für Jugendhilfe
			IVK	Institutet för Växtforskning och Kyallagring (Sweden)
IVAKV	Internationale Vereinigung Aerztlicher Kraftfahrer-Verbände			
IVANK	Internationale Veterinär- Anatomische Nomenklatur- Kommission		**IVKDF**	Institut von Karman de Dynamique des Fluides (Belgium)
IVBA	International Volley-Ball Association (*now* IVBF)		**IVKM**	Internationaler Verband der Katholischen Mädchenschutzvereine
IVBF	International Volleyball Federation		**IVKMH**	International Vereinigung der Klein- und Mittelbetriebe des Handels

IVKMI	Internationale Vereinigung der Klein- und Mittelbetriebe der Industrie	**IVSP**	Internationale Vereinigung für Selbstmord-prophylaxe
IVL	Institutet för Vatten-och Luftvardsforskning	**IVSS**	Internationale Vereinigung für Soziale Sicherheit
IVL	Instituut voor Veredeling van Land-bouwgewassen	**IVSU**	International Veterinary Students Union
IVL	Internationale Vereinigung der Lehrerver-bände	**IVT**	Industrieverband Textil (Switzerland)
IVL	Internationale Vereinigung für Theoretische und Angewandte Limnologie	**IVT**	Instituut voor de Veredeling van Tuin-bouwgewassen
IVLD	Internationale Vereinigung der Organisationen von Lebensmittel-Detaillisten	**IVT**	International Association of Textile Purchasing Societies
IVMB	Internationale Vereinigung der Musikbibliotheken	**IVT**	International Visual Theatre Research Community
IVN	Internationale Vereniging voor Nederlandistiek	**IVT**	Internationaler Verband der Tarifeure
IVO	Instituut voor Veeteelkundig Onderzoek T.N.O.	**IVU**	Instituto Veterinario Uruguay
		IVU	International Vegetarian Union
IVOIRAGRI	Société Ivoirienne d'Exploitation Agricole	**IVV**	Internationale Vereinigung für Vegetations-kunde
IVOIRAL	Compagnie Ivoirienne de l'Aluminium	**IVWO**	International Vine and Wine Office
IVOIRAP	Société Ivoirienne de Diffusion d'Appareils Électriques	**IVWSR**	Internationaler Verband für Wohnungs-wesen, Städtebau und Raumordnung
IVOLCY	Industrie Voltaïque de Cycle et du Cyclomoteur	**IWA**	Institute of World Affairs (U.S.A.)
IVP	Industrie des Vernis et Peintures, Mastics, Encres d'Imprimerie et Couleurs d'Art	**IWA**	International Wheat Agreement
IVP	Instituto Venezolano de Petroquimica	**IWA**	International Women's Auxiliary to the Veterinary Profession
IvP	Instituut voor Plantenveredeling	**IWAHMA**	Industrial Warm Air Heater Manufacturers Association
IvP	Instituut voor Pluimveeteelt	**IWBP**	Integration with Great Britain Party (Gibraltar)
IVP	Instituut voor Visserijprodukten	**IWC**	International Commission on Whaling
IVPC	Internationaler Verband der Petroleum- und Chemie-arbeiter	**IWC**	International Wheat Council (U.K.)
IVPO	Internationale Vereniging voor Plattelandont-wikkeling	**IWCA**	International World Calendar Association
		IWCC	International Wrought Copper Council
IVR	Internationale Vereinigung für Rechts- und Sozialphilosophie	**IWCS**	International Wood Collectors Society
		IWDS	International World Days Service
IVR	Internationale Vereinigung des Rheinschiffs-registers	**IWE**	Institution of Water Engineers (*now* IWES)
		IWES	Institution of Water Engineers and Scientists
IVRI	Indian Veterinary Research Institute	**IWF**	International Weightlifting Federation
IVRO	Instituut voor Rassenonderzoek van Land-bouwgewassen	**IWF**	Internationaler Währungsfonds
		IWFA	International Women's Fishing Association
IVS	International Voluntary Service	**IWFS**	International Wine and Food Society
IVS	Internationale Verbindung für Schalen-tragwerke	**IWG**	International Writers Guild
		IWG	Internationale Werbegesellschaft
IVSA	International Veterinary Students Association	**IWGC**	Imperial War Graves Commission
IVSB	Industrieverband Schneidwaren und Bestecke	**IWGIA**	International Work Group for Indigenous Affairs

IWGM	Intergovernmental Working Group on Monitoring or Surveillance (UNO)
IWGMP	Intergovernmental Working Group on Marine Pollution (IMCO)
IWHS	Institute of Works and Highways Superintendents
IWIM	Institut für Wissenschaftsinformation in der Medizin
IWIS	Instituut TNO voor Wiskunde, Informatieverwerking en Statistiek
IWIU	Insurance Workers International Union
IWL	Institut für Gewerbliche Wasserwirtschaft und Luftreinhaltung
IWLA	Izaak Walton League of America (U.S.A.)
IWM	Institution of Works Managers
IWO	Institute for Works Order (U.S.A.)
IWO	International Wine Office
IWOCA	Instituut voor Wetenschappelijk Onderzoek in Centraal Africa
IWOSC	International Working-Group on Soilless Culture
IWP	Indicative World Plan for Agricultural Development (FAO)
IWPA	International Word Processing Association
IWPC	Institute of Water Pollution Control
IWRA	International Water Resources Association (U.S.A.)
IWRB	International Wildfowl Research Bureau
IWRI	International Wildfowl Research Institute
IWRMA	Irish Wholesale Ryegrass Machiners Association
IWRPF	International Waste Rubber and Plastic Federation
IWRS	International Wood Research Society
IWS	Industrial Welfare Society (*now* IS)
IWS	Institute of Water Study
IWS	Institute of Wood Science
IWS	International Wool Secretariat
IWSA	International Water-Supply Association
IWSA	International Workers Sport Association
IWSAW	Institute for Women's Studies in the Arab World (Lebanon)
IWSc	Institute of Wood Science
IWSC	International Weed Science Council
IWSG	International Wool Study Group
IWSI	Irish Work Study Institute
IWSP	Institute of Work Study Practitioners

IWTA	Inland Water Transport Authority (Pakistan)
IWTO	International Wool Textile Organisation
IWV	Internationale Warenhaus-Vereinigung
IWW	Industrial Workers of the World (U.S.A.)
IWWA	International Wild Waterfowl Conservation Association
IWY	International Women's Year (UN)
IWYF	International World Youth Friendship
IYC	International Year of the Child
IYCS	International Young Christian Students
IYF	International Youth Federation for Environmental Studies and Conservation
IYHF	International Youth Hostel Federation
IYRU	International Yacht Racing Union
IZD	Internationaler Zivildienst
IZS	Internationale Zentralstelle für Schulbau

J

JA	Jordbrukets Arbeidsgiverforening
JAALD	Japanese Association of Agricultural Librarians and Documentalists
JABC	Japan Audit Bureau of Circulation
JAC	Jeunesse Agricole Catholique
JAC	Jeunesse Agricole Chrétienne
JACA	Japan Air Cleaning Association
JACARI	Joint Action Committee Against Racial Interference
JACF	Jeunesse Agricole Catholique Féminine
JAEC	Japanese Atomic Energy Commission
JAEC	Joint Atomic Energy Committee (U.S.A.)
JAERI	Japan Atomic Energy Research Institute
JAES	Japan Atomic Energy Society
JAFC	Japan Atomic Fuel Corporation
JAIEG	Joint Atomic Information Exchange Group
JAIF	Japan Atomic Industrial Forum
JAIMS	Japan-America Institute of Management Science
JAIS	Japan Aircraft Industry Society
JAL	Japan Air Lines Company
JALMA	Japan Leprosy Mission for Asia

JAMA	Japan Automobile Manufacturers Association	**JCBMI**	Joint Committee for the British Monumental Industry
JAMC	Japan Aircraft Manufacturing Corporation	**JCBSF**	Joint Commission for Black Sea Fisheries
JAMINTEL	Jamaica International Telecommunications Ltd	**JCEA**	Junta de Control de Energía Atómica (Peru)
JAMSAT	Japan Radio Amateur Satellite Corporation	**JCEC**	Joint Communication Electronics Committee (U.S.A.)
JAMSTEC	Japan Marine Science and Technology Centre	**JCEPF**	Fédération des Jeunes Chambres Économiques des Pays Utilisant le Français dans leurs Relations Communes
JAMTS	Japan Association of Motor Trade and Service	**JCET**	Joint Committee on Educational Television (U.S.A.)
JAPCo	Japan Atomic Power Company		
JAPEX	Japan Petroleum Exploration Company	**JCFA**	Japan Chemical Fibres Association
JAPIA	Japan Auto Parts Industries Association	**JCHARS**	Joint Commission on High Altitude Research Stations (Switzerland)
JARDOR	Comité Français pour les Jardins et l'Horticulture	**JCI**	Jaycees International (U.S.A.)
JARI	Japanese Association of Railway Industries	**JCI**	Junior Chamber International
JARI	Jute Agricultural Research Institute (India)	**JCIA**	Japan Camera Industry
JARL	Japan Amateur Radio League	**JCLA**	Joint Council of Language Associations
JARTS	Japan Railway Technical Service	**JCM**	Junta Consultiva Mixta
JAS	Jamaica Agricultural Society	**JCMF**	Jednota Ceskoslovenských Matematikua Fysiku
JAS	Jewish Agricultural Society (U.S.A.)		
JAS	Jysk Arkæologisk Selskab	**JCP**	Japan Communist Party
JAST	Jamaican Association of Sugar Technologists	**JCPI**	Japan Cotton Promotion Institute
JAT	Jugoslovenski Aerotransport	**JCPS**	Joint Center for Political Studies (U.S.A.)
JAT	Junta de Asistencia (*see* TAB)	**JCR**	Junta for Revolutionary Coordination (Argentina)
JATCC	Joint Aviation Telecommunications Co-ordination Committee	**JCRR**	Joint Commission (Chinese-American) on Rural Reconstruction (China)
JAVIC	Japan Audio-Visual Information Centre	**JCS**	Joint Commonwealth Societies
JAWS	Japan Animal Welfare Society (U.K.)	**JCSTR**	Joint Commission on Solar and Terrestrial Relationships
JBC	Jamaica Broadcasting Corporation		
JBC	Japanese Broadcasting Corporation	**JCUDI**	Japan Computer Usage Development Institute
JBHCPIUA	Journeymen Barbers, Hairdressers, Cosmetologists and Proprietors' International Union of America	**JCULS**	Joint Committee on the Union List of Serials (U.S.A.)
JBMA	John Burroughs Memorial Association (U.S.A.)	**JDA**	Japan Defence Agency
		JDA	Japan Domestic Airlines
JBPA	Japan Book Publishers Association	**JDB**	Japan Development Bank
JBCSA	Joint British Committee for Stress Analysis	**JDCE**	Jeunes Démocrates Chrétiens Européens
JBTB	Jongeren Boeren-en Tuindersbond	**JDREMC**	Joint Departmental Radio and Electronics Measurements Committee
JCADR	Japan Centre for Area Development		
JCAE	Joint Committee on Atomic Energy (U.S.A.)	**JEAC**	Junta de Exportaçao do Algodao Colonial (Portugal)
JCAM	Joint Commission on Atomic Masses		
JCAPI	Junta Consultiva de Administración Publica Internacional	**JEC**	Junta de Exportaçao dos Cereais (Portugese)
JCAR	Joint Commission of Applied Radioactivity	**JECC**	Japan Electronic Industry Development Association

JECC	Joint Egyptian Cotton Committee
JECI	Jeunesse Étudiante Catholique Internationale
JECI	Jeunesse Étudiante Chrétienne Internationale
JECMA	Japan Export Clothing Makers Association
JEF	Jeunesses Européennes Fédéralistes
JEIA	Joint Export-Import Agency (U.K. & U.S.A.)
JEL	Jeunesses Européennes Libérales
JENER	Joint Establishment for Nuclear Energy Research (Netherlands & Norway)
JEOL	Japan Electron Optics Laboratory
JERC	Japan Economic Research Centre
JERI	Japan Economics Research Institute
JERS	Japan Ergonomics Research Society
JES	Japanese Electroplating Society
JESA	Japanese Engineering Standards Association
JESC	Japanese Engineering Standards Committee
JESC	Joint Electronics Standardisation Committee
JETEC	Joint Electron Tube Engineering Council (U.S.A.)
JETRO	Japanese External Trade Recovery Organisation
JF	Jordbrukets Förskningsrad
JFC	Jugend für Christus
JFCC	Japanese Federation of Culture Collections of Microorganisms
JFEA	Japan Federation of Employers Associations
JFM	Jeunesses Fédéralistes Mondiales
JFPS	Japan Fire Prevention Society
JFRCA	Japanese Fisheries Resources Conservation Association
JFRO	Joint Fire Research Organisation of DSIR and Fire Officers Committee
JFRO	Joint Fisheries Research Organisation (Zambia & Malawi)
JFTC	Joint Fur Trade Committee
JGC	Jugoslovenski Gradjevinski Centar
JHDA	Junior Hospital Doctors Association
JHEA	Junta de Historia Eclesiástica (Argentina)
JIB	Joint Intelligence Bureau
JIBA	Japanese Institute of Business
JIC	Joint Industrial Council
JIC	Joint Iron Council
JICI	Jeunesse Indépendante Chrétienne Internationale

JICNARS	Joint Industry Committee for National Readership Surveys
JICST	Japan Information Centre of Science and Technology
JICTAR	Joint Industry Committee for Television Advertising Research
JID	Junta Interamericana de Defensa
JIDA	Japan Industrial Designers Association
JIDC	Jamaica Industrial Development Corporation
JIE	Junior Institution of Engineers
JIEA	Japan Industrial Explosives Association
JIFA	Japanese Institute for Foreign Affairs
JIFE	Junta Internacional de Fiscalización de Estupefacientes
JIMA	Japan Industrial Management Association
JIMTOF	Japan International Machine Tool Fair
JINR	Joint Institute for Nuclear Research
JIOA	Joint Intelligence Objectives Agency
JIS	Jamaica Information Service
JISC	Japan Industrial Standards Committee
JITPA	Japanese International Trade Promotion Association
JIU	Junta de Investigaçao de Ultramer (Portugal)
JKA	Jugoslavenski Komitet za Aerosole
JKFC	Japan-Republic of Korea Joint Fisheries Commission
JLA	Japanese Library Association
JLA	Jordan Library Association
JLP	Jamaica Labour Party
JMA	Jamaica Manufacturer's Association
JMA	Japan Management Association
JMA	Japan Meteorological Agency
JMG	Järnmanufakturgrossisternas Förening
JMI	Japan Management Institute
JMIA	Japan Mining Industry Association
JMIF	Japan Motor Industrial Federation
JMMA	Japan Materials Management Association
JMRP	Joint Meteorological Radio Propagation Sub-Committee
JMTBA	Japan Machine Tool-Builders Association
JNA	Junta Nacional del Algodón (Argentina)
JNAU	Jawaharlal Nehru Agricultural University (India)
JNC	Junta Nacional de Carnes (Argentina)
JNG	Junta Nacional de Granos (Argentina)

JNP	Junta Nacional de Planeamiento (Bolivia)	**JSC**	Japan Science Council
JNPC	Junta Nacional de Planificación y Coordinación (Dominica)	**JSCAACR**	Joint Committee for Revision of the Anglo-American Cataloguing Rules
JNPCE	Junta Nacional de Planificación y Coordinación Económica (Ecuador)	**JSD**	Jugoslovensko Statističko Društvo
		JSEA	Japan Ship Exporters Association
JNPP	Junta Nacional dos Produtos Pecuários (Portugal)	**JSEE**	Japanese Society for Engineering Education
		JSEM	Japan Society for Electron Microscopy
JNS	Japan Nuclear Society	**JSFC**	Japanese-Soviet Fisheries Commission for the Northwest Pacific
JNSDA	Japan Nuclear Ship Development Agency		
JNTA	Japan National Tourist Association	**JSIA**	Japan Software Industry Association
JNTO	Japan National Tourist Organization	**JSLE**	Japan Society of Lubrication Engineers
JNV	Junta Nacional de la Vivienda (Peru)	**JSLS**	Japan Society of Library Science
JOC	Jeunesse Ouvrière Chrétienne Internationale	**JSMDA**	Japan Ship Machinery Development Association
JOC	Joint Organizing Committee for GARP		
JODC	Japanese Oceanographic Data Centre	**JSME**	Japanese Society of Mechanical Engineers
JONSIS	Joint North Sea Information Service	**JSMEA**	Japan Ship Machinery Export Association
JPA	Jamaica Press Association	**JSP**	Japanese Socialist Party
JPC	Japan Productivity Centre	**JSPB**	United Nations Joint Staff Pension Board
JPC	Juventud para Cristo	**JSPF**	United Nations Joint Staff Pension Fund
JPDC	Japan Petroleum Development Corporation	**JSPS**	Japanese Society for the Promotion of Science
JPI	Japan Packaging Institute		
JPIA	Japan Plastics Industry Association	**JSQC**	Japan Society for Quality Control
JPMO	Jersey Potato Marketing Organisation	**JSSF**	Japanese Society of Scientific Fisheries
JPRG	Japan Peace Research Group	**JSWB**	Java Suiker Werkgevers Bond
JPRS	Joint Publications Research Service (U.S.A.)	**JSZS**	Japanese Society of Zootechnical Science
JPT	Japan Publications Trading Company	**JTAC**	Joint Technical Advisory Committee (U.S.A.)
JRA	Japanese Red Army		
JRB	Joint Radio Board (U.S.A.)	**JTC**	Japan Tobacco Corporation
JRDA	Jeunesse du Rassemblement Démocratique Africain	**JTES**	Japan Techno-Economics Society
		JTRL	Jute Technological Research Laboratory (India)
JRDC	Japan Research and Development Corporation	**JTRU**	Joint-Services Tropical Research Unit (Australia)
JREA	Japanese Railway Engineering Association		
JRIA	Japan Radioisotope Association	**JTUAC**	Joint Trade Union Advisory Committee
JRIA	Japan Rocket Industry Association	**JU**	Jeunesse Universelle
JRIA	Japan Rubber Industry Association	**JUCSPA**	Joint University Council for Social and Public Administration
JRP	Jeunesse Rurale Protestante		
JRR	Jeunesse Révolutionnaire Rwagasore (Burundi)	**JUDCA**	Juventud Democrata Cristiana de America
		JUDRAL	Democratic Revolutionary Youth of Latin America
JRSMA	Japan Rolling Stock Manufacturers Association		
		JUF	Jordbruksare-Ungdomen Forbunds
JSA	Jesuit Seismological Association (U.S.A.)	**JUKL**	Jugoslovensko Udruženje Kontrolora Letenja
JSAE	Japan Society of Automotive Engineering		
JSAP	Japan Society of Applied Physics	**JUMA**	Jugoslovensko Udruženje za Marketing
JSAWC	Joint Services Amphibious Warfare Centre	**JUMV**	Jugoslovensko Društvo za Motore i Vozila

JUN	Jordbrukets Upplysningsnamand
JUNAL	Junta Nacional de Algodão (Brazil)
JUNIC	Joint United Nations Information Committee
JUS	Jugoslavenski Zavod za Standardizaciju
JUS	Jurist-och Samhällsvetareförbundet
JUSE	Japanese Union of Scientists and Engineers
JUSK	Jugoslovenski Savez Organizacija za Unapredenje Kvaliteta i Pouzdanosti
JUSMAG	Joint United States Military Advisory Group
JUSMAP	Joint United States Military Advisory and Planning Group
JUSTIS	Japan-United States of America Textile Information Service
JUTIBELIN	Association Belge du Lin, Chanvre, Jute de Fibres et Produits Apparentés Naturels et Synthétiques
JUVENTO	Mouvement de la Jeunesse Togolaise
JVA	Jordan Valley Authority (Israel)
JWCA	Japan Watch and Clock Association
JWDS	Japan Work Design Society
JWEF	Joinery and Woodwork Employers' Federation
JWPAC	Joint Waste Paper Advisory Council
JWS	Japan Welding Society

K

KÄB	Kneippärztebund
KAC	Kuwait Airways Corporation
KADU	Kenya African Democratic Union
KAF	Konfeksjonsfabrikkenes Arbeids-giverforening
KAFAB	Verband Schweizerischer Kartonfabrikanten
KAL	Suomen Kuorma-Autoliitto
KAMEDO	Swedish Organizing Committee for Disaster Medicine
KANTAFU	Kenya African National Traders and Farmers Union
KANU	Kenya African Nationalists Union
KANUPP	Karachi Nuclear Power Project
KANZEKO	Kahama Nzega Co-operative Union (Tanzania)

KAPMO	Kent Apple and Pear Marketing Organisation
KARNA	Kweekbedrijf v. Aardappelrassen d. Nederlandse Aardappelmeelindustrie
KAS	Kentucky Academy of Science
KASEF	Katholisches Sekretariat für Europäische Fragen
KASKA	Koninklijke Academie voor Schoone Kunsten Antwerpene
KATY	Kemikalialan Tukkukauppiasyhdistys
KAU	Kenya African Union
KAVB	Koninklijke Algemene Vereniging voor Bloembollencultuur
KBBM	Koninklijke Belgische Bosbouwmaatschappij
KBF	Kommunale Bibliotekarers Forening
KBKI	Indonesian Democratic Labour Organization
KBM	Katholieke Bond Metallbewerkingsbedrijven
KBV	Nederlandse Katholieke Bond van Vervoers-personaal
KBVE	Koninklijke Belgische Vereniging der Elektrotechnici
KBVT	Koninklijke Belgische Vereniging voor Tand-heelkunde
KCC	Kenya Cooperative Creameries
KCI	Key Club International (U.S.A.)
KCNA	Korean Central News Agency
KDB	Kenya Dairy Board
KDF	København Detailhandlerforening
KDFC	Korea Development Finance Corporation
KDI	Korea Development Institute
KDI	Kwaliteitsdienst van de Industrie
KDS	Khuzistan Development Service
KDT	Kammer der Technik der Deutschen Demokratischen Republik
KDVS	Det Kongelige Danske Videnskabernes Selskab (Royal Danish Academy of Science and Letters)
KEDI	Korean Education Development Institute
KEIDAN-REN	Federation of Economic Organisation (Japan)
KEK	Konferenz Europäischer Kirchen
KELI	Kristina Esperantista Ligo Internacia
KEMA	Keuring van Electrotechnische Materialen
KES	Kvakera Esperantista Societo
KES	Kwaliteitsbureau voor te Exporteren Schapen
KESC	Karachi Electric Supply Corporation

KEST	Studiengesellschaft zur Förderung der Kernenergiewertung in Schiffbau und Schiffahrt	**KLF**	Kjøttbransjens Landsforbund
		KLIAU	Korea Land Improvement Association Union
KF	Kooperativa Forbundet	**KLM**	Koninklijke Luchtvaart Maatschappij
KFA	Kammer für Aussenhandel der Deutschen Demokratischen Republik	**KLSS**	Korean Library Science Society
		KLTV	Katholieke Vereniging van Land- en Tuin-bouwonderwijzers
KFA	Kenya Farmers Association		
KFL	Kenya Federation of Labour	**KLY**	Konttorikoneliikkeiden Yhdistys
KFL	Kosmetikkfabrikkenes Landsforening	**KMA**	Swedish Control Institution for Dairy Products and Eggs
KFW	Kreditanstalt für Wiederaufbau		
KGB	Komitet Gosudarstvennoi Bezopasnosti (Committee of State Security) (U.S.S.R.)	**KMB**	Katholieke Bond Metaalbewerkingsbedrijven
		KMBA	Koninklijke Maatschappij voor Bouwmeesters van Antwerpen
KHVS	Kunsthandelsverband der Schweiz		
KIA	Kenya Institute of Administration	**KMC**	Kenya Meat Commission
KIB	Arbeitskreis der beim Gesamtverband Kun-stoffverarbeitende Industrie Registrierten Selbstandigen Kunstoff-Ingenieure und-Berater	**KMF**	Kontormaskin- och Kontorsmöbelhandlar-nas Förening
		KML	Kauppamallastamojen Liitto
		KMO	Koulujen Musiikinopettajat
KIF	Knitting Industries Federation	**KNAG**	Koninklijk Nederlands Aardrijkskundig Genootschap
KIF	Konfektionsindustriföreningen		
KIF	Kvarnindustriföreningen	**KNAK**	Kongelik Norsk Automobilklubb
KIFP	Korean Institute for Family Planning	**KNAN**	Koninklijke Nederlandse Akademie voor Naturwetenschappen
KIIB	Koninklijk Instituut voor Internationale Betrekkingen (Belgium)	**KNAW**	Royal Netherlands Academy of Sciences and Letters
KIM	Kenya Institute of Management	**KNBB**	Katholieke Nederlandse Boerinnenbond
KIO	Kenya Information Office	**KNBTB**	Katholieke Nederlandse Boeren- en Tuinders-bond
KIO	Kring Industriële Ontwerpers		
KIRBS	Korean Institute for Research in the Behavioural Sciences	**KNBV**	Koninklijke Nederlandse Brand-weervereniging
KISA	Korean International Steel Associates	**KNCCI**	Kenya National Chamber of Commerce and Industry
KISOSZ	Kiskereskedók Országos Szervezete		
KIST	Korean Institute of Science and Technology	**KNCU**	Kilimanjaro Native Cooperation Union Ltd
KIT	Koninklijk Instituut voor de Tropen	**KNCV**	Koninklijke Nederlandse Centrale Vereniging tot Bestrijding der Tuberculose
KIV	Karten Industrie Verlags Verband		
KIVI	Koninklijk Instituut van Ingenieurs	**KNCV**	Koninklijke Nederlandse Chemische Vereniging
KIWA	Keuringsinstituut voor Waterleidingsar-tikelen	**KNDP**	Kamerun National Democratic Party
KJV	Kartell Juedischer Verbindungen in Great Britain	**KNGMG**	Koninklijk Nederlands Geologisch Mijn-bouwkundig Genootschap
KKL	Kommunale Kinematografers Landsforbund	**KNHM**	Royal Netherlands Land Development and Reclamation Society
KLA	Kingdom of Libya Airlines		
KLA	Korean Library Association	**KNJBTB**	Katholieke Nederlandse Jonge Boeren- en Tuindersbond
KLA	Kungl. Lantbruksakademien	**KNLC**	Koninklijk Nederlands Landbouw Comité
KLBV	Verband der Konzertlokalbesitzer und aller Veranstalter Österreichs	**KNMG**	Koninklijke Nederlandsche Maatschappij tot Bevordering der Geneeskunst

KNMvD	Koninklijke Nederlandse Maatschappij voor Diergeneeskunde
KNMI	Koninklijke Nederlandse Meteorologisch Instituut
KNNP	Katholieke Nederlandse Nieuwsblad Pers
KNNV	Royal Netherlands Association of Natural History
KNPC	Kuwait National Petroleum Company
KNRV	Koninklijke Nederlandse Redersvereniging
KNSM	Koninklijke Nederlandse Stoomboot Maatschappij
KNTV	Koninklijke Nederlandse Toonkunstenaars-Vereniging
KNUB	Koninklijke Nederlandsche Uitgeversbond
KNUST	Kwame Nkrumah University of Science and Technology (Ghana)
KNVD	Koninklijk Nederlands Verbond van Drukkerijen
KNVL	Koninklijke Nederlandse Vereniging voor Luchtvaart
KNVTO	Koninklijke Nederlandse Vereniging van Transport-Ondernemingen
KNVvL	Koninklijke Nederlandse Vereniging voor Luchtvaart
KNZ	Koninklijke Nederlandse Zuivelbond
KOL	Kuvaamataidon Opettajan Liitto
KONPAPP	Kontors-och Pappersvaruleverantörernas Förening
KORDI	Korean Ocean Research and Development Institute
KORSTIC	Korean Scientific and Technological Information Centre
KOSLO	Konferenz Schweizerischer Lehrerorganisationen
KOTRA	Korea Trade Promotion Corporation
KOUDPRO-FIEL	Vereniging van Handelaren in Koudgevormde Profielen
KOV	Katholieke Onderwijzers Verbond
KOWACO	Korea Water Resources Development Corporation
KPC	Korea Productivity Centre
KPCU	Kenyan Planters' Co-operative Union
KPD	Kommunistische Partei Deutschlands
KPDR	Korean People's Democratic Republic
KPJN	Katholieke Plattelands Jongeren Nederland
KPNO	Kitt Peak National Observatory (U.S.A.)

KRAB	Kamer van Reclame-Adviesbureaus (Belgium)
KRIB	Kamer van Raadgevend Ingenieurs van België
KRIPA	Korean Research Institute of Public Administration
KRL	Vereniging Katoen, Rayon-, Linnen- en Jute-Industrie
KRO	Koustnärernas Rijksorganisation
KROM	Scandinavian Association for Penal Reform (Norway)
KRW	Vereinigung der Kessel- und Radiatoren-Werke (Switzerland)
KSA	Eidgenossisches Kommission für die Sicherheit von Atomlagen (Switzerland)
KSJ	Internationale Katholische Studierende Jugend
KSLA	Kungliga Skogs- och Lantbruksakademien
KSO	Klaedegrossisternes og Skraedderfagets Oplysningsudvalg
KSOS	Central Sultana-Raisins Co-operative Organisation (Greece)
KSS	Eidgenossisches Kommission zur Stahlenschutz (Switzerland)
KTBL	Kuratorium für Technik und Bauwesen in der Landwirtschaft
KTCCA	Kotwali Thana Central Cooperative Association (Bangladesh)
KTDA	Kenya Tea Development Authority
KTDC	Kenya Tourist Development Corporation
KTE	Kozlekedéstományi Egyesület
KTF	Kemisk-Tekniska Leverantörförbundet
KTG	Kerntechnische Gesellschaft im Deutschen Atomforum
KTGA	Kenya Tea Growers Association
KTH	Kungl. Tekniska Högskolan (Sweden)
KTIBF	Cyprus Turkish Trade Union Federation
KTL	Kuratorium f. Technik in der Landwirtschaft
KTN	Kieleckie Towarzystwo Naukowe
KTS	Kerntechnische Sektion der Schweizerischen Vereinigung für Atomenergie
KTV	Kaffee- und Teeverband (Austria)
KULSAA	Karachi University Library Science Alumni Association
KUNC	Kamerun United National Congress
KURRI	Kyoto University Research Reactor Institute (Japan)

KUVV	Katholieke Unie van Verpleegkunden en Verzorgenden
KVA	Koninklijke Vlaamse Academie voor Wetenschappen, Letteren en Schone Kunsten van België
KVARN	Sveriges Kvarnyrkesförbund
KVBG	Koninklijke Vereniging der Belgische Gasvaklieden
KvF	Svenska Kraftverksföreningen
KVHAA	Kungliga Vitterhets Historie och Antikvitets Akademien
KVIV	Koninklijke Vlaamse Ingenieursvereniging
KVL	Den Kongelige Veterinaer-og Landbohojskole
KVNT	Koninklijke Vereniging 'Het Nederlandse Trekpaard'
KVO	Katholieke Vervoeders Organisatie
KVO	Koninklijke Verbond van Ondernemers in het Kleine en Middelgrote Bedrijf
KVOB	Katholieke Vereniging van Ondernemers in het Bakkersbedijf
KVOB	Katholieke Vereniging van Ondernemers in het Bloembollenbedrijf
KVP	Katholieke Volkspartij
KVS	Kansanvalistusseura
KVWM	Katholieke Vereniging van Werkgevers in het Metaalindustrie
KWP	Korean Workers Party
KWV	Ko-operative Wijnbouwers Vereniging van Zuid-Afrika
KYDEP	Home Products Handling Administration (Greece)

L

LA	Library Association
LAA	Library Association of Australia
LAA	Libyan Arab Airlines
LAAD	Latin American Agribusiness Development Corporation
LAAS-CNRS	Laboratoire d'Automatique et de ses Applications Spatiales du CNRS
LAB	Laboratory Animals Bureau
LAB	Library Association of Barbados

LAB	Lloyd Aero Boliviano
LABAZ	Société Belge de l'Azote et des Produits Chimiques du Marly, Division Pharmaceutique
LABOR-ELEC	Laboratoire de l'Industrie Électrique (Belgium)
LABORIA	Laboratoire de Recherche en Informatique et en Automatique
LACAP	Latin-American Cooperative Acquisitions Project
LACFFP	Latin-American Commission on Forestry and Forestry Products
LACI	London Association of Conference Interpreters
LACSA	Lineas Aereas Costaricenses SA
LACSAB	Local Authorities Conditions of Service Advisory Board
LADE	Lineas Aereas del Estado (Argentine)
LANDSIR-LAC	Liverpool and District Scientific, Industrial and Research Library Advisory Council
LAE	London Association of Engineers
LAECC	Laïcat et Communauté Chrétienne (Switzerland)
LAFC	Latin American Forestry Commission
LAFTA	Latin American Free Trade Association
LAFU	Ladies Amateur Fencing Union
LAGB	Linguistic Association of Great Britain
LAGE	Lineas Aereas Guinea Ecuatorial
LaH	Landssammenslutningen af Hospitalslaboranter
LAI	Library Association of Ireland
LAI	Linee Aeree Italiane
LAIC	Les Argiles Industrielles du Cameroun
LAIICS	Latin American Institute for Information and Computer Sciences (Chile)
LAMA	Latin American Museological Association
LAMA	Locomotive and Allied Manufacturers Association
LAMCO	Liberian, American-Swedish Minerals Co.
LAMDA	London Academy of Music and Dramatic Art
LAMP	Latin American Market Planning (Centre) (U.S.A.)
LAMPA	Lampleverantörernas Förening
LAMSAC	Local Authorities Management Services and Computer Committee
LAN	Linea Aera Nacional (Chile)

LANAP	Latin American Natural Areas Program	**LAWG**	Latin American Working Group (Canada)
LANICA	Lineas Aereas de Nicaragua	**LBC**	Les Bois du Congo
LANSA	Lineas Aereas Nacionales S.A. (Peru)	**LBF**	Lantbruksförbundets Byggnadsförening
LAOSA	Librarianship and Archives Old Students Association	**LBIDI**	Liberian Bank for Industrial Development and Investment
LAP	Lineas Aereas Paraguayas	**LC**	Lärarnas Centralförbund
LAPCO	Lavan Petroleum Company (Iran)	**LC**	Lutheran Council of Great Britain
LAR	Landskapsarkitekternas Riksforbund	**LCA-GB**	Lightweight Cycle Association of Great Britain
LARC	Association for Library Automation Research Communications (U.S.A.)	**LCBC**	Lake Chad Basin Commission
LARC	Libyan-American Reconstruction Commission	**LCF**	Laboratoire Central de Fitopatologia (Argentina)
LARO	Latin American Regional Office (FAO)	**LCF**	Labour Co-operative Farms (Bulgaria)
LAS	Land Agents' Society	**LCGB**	Locomotive Club of Great Britain
LAS	Library Association of Singapore	**LCGIL**	Libera Confederazione Generale Italiana dei Lavoratori
LAS	League of Arab States		
LASA	Laboratory Animals Science Association	**LCI**	Library for Cultural Initiation (Spain)
LASA	Latin American Shipowners Association	**LCIGB**	Locomotive and Carriage Institution of Great Britain and Eire
LASA	Latin American Studies Association (U.S.A.)	**LCP**	League of Coloured People
LASAS	Secretariado Latinoamericano para Asistencia Universitaria	**LCT**	Laboratoire Central de Télécommunications
LASCA	Los Angeles State and County Arboretum (U.S.A.)	**LCWIO**	Liaison Committee of Women's International Organisation
LASCO	Latin American Unesco Science Co-operation Office	**LDA**	Lead Development Association
LASEDECO	Land Settlement and Development Corporation (Philippines)	**LDFPA**	Laboratorio da Defesa Fitossanitária dos Produtos Armazenados (Portugal)
LASIM	Los Angeles Society of Internal Medicine (U.S.A.)	**LDOS**	Lord's Day Observance Society
LASL	Los Alamos Scientific Laboratory (U.S.A.)	**LDP**	Landsforeningen af Danske Plantehandlere
		LDP	Liberal-Democratic Party (Japan)
LASMO	London and Scottish Marine Oil	**LDPD**	Liberal Democratic Party of Germany
LASPAU	Latin American Scholarship Program of American Universities	**LDRTA**	Long Distance Road Transport Association of Australia
LASRA	Leather and Shoe Research Association (N.Z.)	**LDV**	Landsforeningen Danske Vognmoend
LASSI	Latin American Secretariat of the Socialist International	**LEA**	Ligue des États Arabes (Egypt)
		LEA	Local Education Authority
LAT	Liga Argentina contra la Tuberculosis	**LEAP**	Loan and Educational Aid Programme (Nigeria)
LATICI	Latin American Technical Institute for Cooperative Integration (Puerto Rico)	**LEASEU-ROPE**	European Federation of Equipment Leasing Company Associations
LATT	Library Association of Trinidad and Tobago	**LEAT**	International Institute of Legal, Economic and Administration Terminology (France)
LAV	Landmaschinen- und Ackerschlepper-Vereinigung	**LEC**	Liberia Electricity Corporation
LAV	Lineas Aeropostal Venezolana	**LECE**	Ligue Européenne de Co-opération Économique
LAWASIA	Law Association for Asia and the Western Pacific (Australasia)	**LECT**	League for the Exchange of Commonwealth Teachers

LEDU	Local Enterprise Development Unit (N. Ireland)	**LI**	Ligue Internationale de la Représentation Commerciale (Switzerland)
LEF	Landbouw Egalisatie Fonds	**LIA**	Lead Industries Association (U.S.A.)
LEF	Lantbruksakademiens Kommitté for Ekonomisk Forskning	**LIA**	Leather Industries of America
LEGACOOP	Lega Nazionale delle Cooperative e Mutue	**LIA**	Lebanese International Airways
LEGPA	Laboratory of Engineering and Applied Physics	**LIA**	Ligue Internationale d'Arbitrage
LEI	Landbouw Economisch Instituut	**LIAT**	Leeward Islands Air Transport Services
LEI	Landsforeningen for Elektroteknisk Industri	**LIB**	Landbrugsmaskin- Importørernes Brancheforening
LEKNAS	National Institute of Economic and Social Research (Indonesia)	**LIBA**	Long Island Biological Association (U.S.A.)
LEMIT	Laboratorio de Ensayo de Materiales e Investigaciones Tecnológicas (Argentina)	**LIBE**	Ligo Internacia de Blindaj Esperantistoj
		LIBER	Ligue des Bibliothèques Européennes de Recherche
LEN	Ligue Européenne de Natation	**LICA**	Ligue Internationale contre le Racisme et l'Antisémitisme
LENA	Laboratorio Energia Nucleare Applicata		
LEND	Linguia e Nuova Didattica	**LICCD**	Ligue Internationale contre la Concurrence Déloyale
LEO	Lyons Electronic Office	**LICOSA**	Libreria Commissionaria Sansoni
LEPOR	Long-term and Expanded Programme of Oceanic Exploration and Research	**LICOTRA**	L'Essor Ivoirien de Construction et de Travaux Publics
LEPRA	British Leprosy Relief Association	**LIDC**	Lead Industries Development Council
LES	Licensing Executives Society International	**LIDE**	Liga de Activación de la Región del Delta (Argentina)
LET	Laboratoire Électrotechnique de Tokyo		
LETATA	Light Edge Tool and Allied Trades Association	**LIDH**	Ligue Internationale des Droits de l'Homme
LEY	Liberal European Youth	**LIDIA**	Liaison Internationale des Industries Alimentaires
LFEM	Laboratoire Fédéral d'Essai des Matériaux (Switzerland)	**LIEN**	Ligue Internationale pour l'Éducation Nouvelle
LFF	Land- und Forstwirtschaftlicher Forschungsrat e.v. Bonn	**LIF**	Lighting Industry Federation
		LIF	Läkemedelsindustriföreningen
LFI	Laxforskningsinstitutet	**LIFE**	League for International Food Education (U.S.A.)
LFL	Landøkonomisk Forsøgslaboratorium		
LFLRASP	Lifwynn Foundation for Laboratory Research in Analytical and Social Psychiatry (U.S.A.)	**LIFMA**	Leather Importers, Factors and Merchants Association
		LIFPL	Ligue Internationale de Femmes pour la Paix et la Liberté
LFTD	Stichting Landbouw Fysisch-Technische Dienst	**LIGNUM**	Schweizerische Arbeitsgemeinschaft für das Holz
LGC	Laboratory of the Government Chemist		
LGEB	Local Government Examinations Board	**LIHG**	Ligue Internationale de Hockey sur Glace
LGTA	Ligue Générale des Travailleurs de l'Angola	**LIHS**	Long Island Horticultural Society (U.S.A.)
LGTB	Local Government Training Board	**LIL**	Laboratoire International de la Lune
LGU	Ladies Golf Union	**LILA**	Ligue Internationale de la Librairie Ancienne
LHF	Landbo- og Husmandsforeningernes	**LIM**	Groupement des Laboratoires Internationaux de Recherche et d'Industrie du Médicament
LHI	Lefthanders International		
LHI	Ligue Homeopathique Internationale	**LIMEP**	Internationale des Mères et des Éducatrices pour la Paix
LI	Liberal International (World Liberal Union)		

LIMEX	L'Ivoirienne d'Import-Export
LIMPL	Liga Internacional de Mujeres pro Paz y Libertad
LINOSCO	Libraries of North Staffordshire in Co-operation
LIO	Laboratorium voor Insekticidenonderzoek
LIP	London International Press
LIPA	Ligue Panafricaine contre le Tribalisme, le Sectarianisme, et le Racisme
LIPI	Indonesian Institute of Sciences
LIRA	Lambeg Industrial Research Association
LIRA	Linen Industry Research Association (Eire)
LIRAR	Les Ingénieurs Radio Réunis
LIRI	Leather Industries Research Institute (S. Africa)
LIRMA	Laboratoire International de Recherche sur les Maladies des Animaux
LIS	Light Industries Services (Singapore)
LISC	Lions International Stamp Club
LIST	Library Information Service for Teesside
LiTG	Lichttechnische Gesellschaft
LITINT	Literacy International
LIVI	Lämpöinsinööriyhdistys
LJK	Liikeenjohdon Konsultit
LJUSA	Ljusarmaturleverantorerna
LK	Liiketyönantajain Keskusliitto
LKD	Leverantörföreningen Kontors- och Datautrustning
LKP	Liberaalinen Kansanpuolue (Finland)
LKTP	Lembaga Kemajuan Tanah Persekutuan (Malaysia)
LLA	Lebanese Library Association
LLEPO	Ligue Luxembourgeoise pour l'Étude et la Protection des Oiseaux
LLH	Leverantörföreningen for Lek- och Hobbyartikler
LLLI	La Leche League International
LLS	Limburgsch Landbouw Syndicaat
LLSBA	Leicester Longwool Sheep Breeders Association
LMA	Linoleum Manufacturers Association
LMAGB	Locomotive Manufacturers' Association of Great Britain
LMC	Liga Maritima de Chile
LME	London Metal Exchange
LME	Telefonaktiebolaget L.M.Ericsson
LMHI	Liga Medicorum Homeopathica Internationalis
LMS	London Mathematical Society
LMS	Riksföreningen för Lärarna i Moderna Språk
LNB	Landsforbundet Norsk Brukskunst
LNBEE	Laboratoire National Belge d'Électrothermie et d'Électrochimie
LO	Landorganisasjonen i Norge
LO	Landorganisationen i Danmark
LO	Landorganisationen i Sverige
LOAS	Loyal Order of Ancient Shepherds
LOB	Landelijke Organisatie van Bedrijfspluimveehouders
LOBB	Vereniging Landbouwkundig Overleg Bemestings Beleid
LOBE	Landelijke Organisatie van Bedrijfseendenhouders
LOF	Landelijke Organisatie van Fokkers
LOFA	Leisure and Outdoor Furniture Association
LOG	Landbrukets Emballasjeforretning og Gartnernes Felleskjop
LOK	Landelijke Organisatie van Kuikenmesters
LONRHO	London and Rhodesian Mining and Land Co.
LOP	Landelijke Organisatie van Piepkuikenfokkers
LORCS	League of Red Cross Societies
LOS	Landelijke Organisatie van Pluimveeselecteurs
LOT	Polskie Linie Lotnieze
LOV	Landelijke Organisatie van Vermeerderaars
LPA	Leather Producers Association for England, Scotland and Wales
LPA	Local Planning Authority
LPAB	Nederlandse Bond van Logies-, Pension- en Aanverwante Bedrijven
LPAC	Launching Programmes Advisory Committee
LPMB	Lunar and Planetary Missions Board (NASA)
LPMC	Liberian Produce Marketing Corporation
LPO	Ligue Française pour la Protection des Oiseaux
LPT	Landsforeningen af Praktiserende Tandteknikere i Danmark
LPV	Laboratorio de Patologia Veterinaria (Portuguese)

LQFE	Laboratório Quimico Farmacêutico de Exército (Brazil)
LR	Lärarnas Riksförbund
LRA	Lace Research Association
LRCS	League of Red Cross Societies
LRDE	Technical Information Centre of the Electronics and Radar Development Establishment (India)
LRF	Lantbrukarnas Riksförbund
LRP	Society for Long Range Planning
LSA	Land Settlement Association
LSAA	Linen Supply Association of America
LSCR	Ligue des Sociétés de la Croix-Rouge
LSE	London School of Economics
LSHA	Louisiana State Horticultural Association (U.S.A.)
LSHTM	London School of Hygiene and Tropical Medicine
LSL	Loervare- og Sportsartikkelfabrikantenes Landsforening
LSMB	Lint and Seed Marketing Board, Tanzania
LSMI	Lake Superior Mining Institute (U.S.A.)
LSNSW	Linnean Society of New South Wales
LSNY	Linnean Society of New York (U.S.A.)
LSPN	Ligue Suisse pour la Protection de la Nature
LSRH	Laboratoire Suisse de Recherches Horlogères
LSV	Landelijke Specialisten Vereniging
LT	Lantbrukssallskapets Tidskriftsaktiebolag
LTA	Lawn Tennis Association
LTB	Katholieke Land-en Tuinbouwbond
LTC	Les Transports au Congo
LTF	Lithographic Technical Foundation (U.S.A.)
LTF	Lufttraffikkledelsens Forening
LTIB	Lead Technical Information Bureau
LTJ	Land-en Tuinbouw Jongeren
LTN	Lódzkie Towarzystwo Naukowe
LTP	Library Technology Project. American Library Association
LTRS	Low-Temperature Research Station, Cambridge (*Ceased*)
LTS	Lysteknisk Selskab
LTY	Lääketeollisuuyhistys
LU	Ligue Universelle
LUCCO	Land Utilisation Coordination Committee (Cyprus)

LUF	Ligue Universelle de Francs-Maçons
LUFORO	London Unidentified Flying Objects Research Organisation
LUFS	Land Use and Forest Resource Survey of Taiwan
LUT	Loge Unie des Théosophes
LUXAIR	Société Anonyme Luxembourgeoise de Navigation Aérienne
LUXATOM	Syndicat Luxembourgeois pour l'Industrie Nucléaire
LVCC	Landelijk Verbond der Christelijke Coöperatieven (Belgium)
LVFS	Lake Victoria Fisheries Service (Kenya)
LVM	Limburgse Vinyl Maatschappij (Belgium)
LVMEB	Landelijke Vereniging der Meesters Elektriekers van België
LWF	Lutheran World Federation
LWIU	Leather Workers International Union of America
LWMEL	Leonard Wood Memorial for the Eradication of Leprosy (U.S.A.)
LWS	Landbouw Winter Scholen
LYMEC	Liberal Youth Movement of the European Community
LZT	Beurs voor Landbouw Zuivel en Techniek

M

MA	Mathematical Association
MA	Metric Association (U.S.A.)
MAA	Maison de l'Agriculture Algérienne
MAA	Manitoba Association of Architects (Canada)
MAA	Manufacturers Agents Association of Great Britain and Ireland
MAA	Mathematical Association of America
MAA	Medical Artists Association of Great Britain
MAA	Medieval Academy of America
MAA	Motor Agents' Association
MAAC	Mastic Asphalt Advisory Council
MAAGB	Medical Artists Association of Great Britain

MAB	International Co-ordinating Council of the Programme on Man and the Biosphere
MAB	Man and the Biosphere Programme
MAB	Menswear Association of Britain Ltd
MABI	Groep Nederlandse Fabrikanten van Magazijn-, Archief- en Bibliotheekinrichtingen
MAC	Massey Agricultural College, Palmerston North (N.Z.)
MAC	Ministerio de Agricultura y Cria (Venezuela)
MACC	Manufacture d'Armes et de Cartouches Congolaises
MACI	Ministerio de Agricultura, Comercio e Industria (Panama)
MACOMA	Matériaux de Construction de Madagascar
MACS	Maharashtra Association for the Cultivation of Science (India)
MADEPA	Movimiento Apolítico de Productores Agropecuarios (Uruguay)
MAE	Magyar Agrártudományic Egyesület
MAE	Manchester Association of Engineers
MAE	Medical Association of Eire
MAER	Ministry of Agriculture, Eastern Region (Nigeria)
MAF	Motorbranschens Arbetsgivareförbund
MAFA	Maison des Agriculteurs Français d'Algérie
MAFF	Ministry of Agriculture, Fisheries and Food
MAFRIMA	Manufacture Centrafricaine de Matelasserie
MAG	Medical Association of Georgia (U.S.A.)
MAGATE	Mercados, Silos y Frigoríficos del Distrito Federal (Venezuela)
MAGB	Microfilm Association of Great Britain
MAGLI-CALZE	Associazione Italiana Produttori Maglierie e Calzetterie
MAHISSA	Maices Hibridos y Semillas, S.A.
MAILL-EUROP	Comité des Industries de la Maille des Pays de la CEE
MALAS	Midwest Association for Latin American Studies (U.S.A.)
MALIGAZ	Société Malienne des Gaz Industriels
MALRY	Malayan Leprosy Relief Association
MAMBO	Mediterranean Association for Marine Biology and Oceanology (Italy)
MAN	Mouvement pour un Alternatif Nonviolent (France)
MANA	Music Advisers National Association
MANI	Ministry of Agriculture of Northern Ireland
MANR	Ministry of Agriculture and Natural Resources (Nigeria)
MANTIS	Manchester Technical Information Service
MANU	Makedonska Akademija na Naukite i Umetnostite
MANU	Moçambique African National Union
MAOTE	Magyar Általános Orvosok Tudományos Egyesülete
MAP	Management Association of the Philippines
MAPI	Machinery and Allied Products Institute (U.S.A.)
MAPRIAL	International Association of Professors of Russian Language and Literature
MAPU	Movimiento de Acción Popular Unida (Chile)
MAPW	Medical Association for the Prevention of War
MAR	Mouvement d'Action Rurale
MARC	Monitoring and Assessment Research Centre
MARC-OGAZ	Union des Industries Gaziéres des Pays du Marché Commun (Belgium)
MARDB	Mountain Agricultural Resources Development Bureau (Taiwan)
MARDI	Malaysian Agricultural Research and Development Institute
MARINCO	Marketing International Consultants
MARKFED	Punjab State Co-operative Supply and Marketing Federation (India)
MARU	Middle American Research Unit
MAS	Military Agency for Standardization (of NATO)
MASA International	Mail Advertising Service Association International (U.S.A.)
MASI	Molinera Argentina Sociedad Industrial
MAT	Magyar Allerológiai Társaság
MAT	Magyar Aluminiumipari Troszt
MATA	Museums Association of Tropical Africa
MATE	Méréstechnikai és Automatizálási Tudományos Egyesület
MATFORM	Syndicat des Constructeurs Français de Matériel pour la Transformation des Matières Plastiques et du Caoutchouc
MATRA	Mauritanienne de Transit Transport Representation Assurances
MAURELEC	Société Mauritanienne d'Eau et d'Électricité
MAURINAP	Société Mauritanienne de Diffusion d'Appareils Électriques

MAVEC	Materiae Vegetabiles (Netherlands)	**MCP**	Mouvement Chrétien pour la Paix
MAVIS	Maize Virus Information Service (U.S.A.)	**MCPS**	Mechanical Copyright Protection Society
MAVOCI	Manufacture Voltaïque de Cigarettes	**MCS**	Malaysian Civil Service
MAWEV	Verband der Maschinen- und Werkzeughändler (Austria)	**MCS**	Mechanical Cultivation Services (Greece)
		MCS	Military College of Science
MAWR	Ministry of Agriculture Western Region (Nigeria)	**MCST**	Manchester College of Science and Technology
MBA	Marine Biological Association of the United Kingdom	**MCSU**	Melkcontrolestation Utrecht
		MCT	Missão de Combate as Tripanosomiasis (Portugese)
MBAA	Master Brewers Association of America		
MBAUK	Marine Biological Association of the United Kingdom	**MCTA**	Mild Coffee Trade Association (E. Africa)
		MCWA	Massey College Wool Association (N.Z.)
MBG	Mission Biologique du Gabon	**MDA**	Maize Development Association
MBIA	Malting Barley Improvement Association (U.S.A.)	**MDA**	Malt Distillers Association of Scotland
MBL	Marine Biological Laboratory (U.S.A.)	**MDAA**	Muscular Dystrophy Associations of America, Inc.
MBMA	Master Boiler Makers' Association (U.S.A.)	**MDB**	Movimento Democrático Brasileiro
MBS	Mutual Broadcasting System (U.S.A.)	**MDC**	Malawi Development Corporation
MBT	Magyar Biologiai Társaság	**MDC**	Mwanachi Development Corporation (Tanzania)
MBW	Movement for a Better World (Italy)		
MC	Department of Mass Communication (France)	**MDF**	Les Meubles de France (Ivory Coast)
		MDIS	Ministry of Industrial and Scientific Development (France)
MCA	Malaysian-Chinese Association		
MCA	Malaysian Commercial Association (U.K.)	**MDP**	Portugese Democratic Movement
MCA	Management Consultants Association	**MDPA**	Mines Domaniales de Potasse d'Alsace
MCA	Manufacturing Chemists' Association of the United States	**MDRA**	Mouvement Démocratique du Renouveau Algérien
MCAA	Mechanical Contractors Association of America	**MDS**	Minnesota Dermatologic Society (U.S.A.)
		ME	Mouvement Européen
MCAC	Marché Commun de l'Amérique Centrale	**MEA**	Marketing Executives Association of Belgium
MCB	Management Center do Brasil	**MEA**	Middle East Airlines Company
MCBSF	Mixed Commission for Black Sea Fisheries (FAO)	**MEAN**	Mission d'Étude et d'Aménagement du Niger (Nigeria)
MCC	Marylebone Cricket Club		
MCC	Mennonite Central Committee (U.S.A.)	**MEAU**	Missão de Estudos Agrónomicos do Ultramar
MCCA	Conference of the Methodist Church in the Caribbean and the Americas	**MEAUP**	Missão de Estudos Apícolas do Ultramar Português
MCCA	Mercado Común Centroamericano		
MCCO	Mercado Común del Caribe Oriental	**MEBPA**	Missão de Estudos Broceanólogicas e de Pesca de Angola
MCE	Mercado Común Europeo	**MEC**	Mercato Europeo Comune
MCF	Movement for Colonial Freedom	**MECAN-**	Société Africaine d'Emballages Métalliques
MCFTU	Mauritius Confederation of Free Trade Unions	**EMBAL**	(Ivory Coast)
		MECAS	Middle East Centre for Arab Studies
MCIE	Midland Counties Institution of Engineers	**MECCA**	Missionary and Ecumenical Council of the Church Assembly
MCP	Malaysian Communist Party		

MECNY	Municipal Engineers of the City of New York	**MEPRA**	Misión de Estúdios de Patológia Regionál Argentina
MEDD	Middle East Development Service (*of* ODM)	**MEPW**	Ministry of Economic Planning, Western Region (Nigeria)
MEDIA-CULT	International Institute for Audio-Visual Communication and Cultural Development (Austria)	**MERALCO**	Manila Electric Company (Philippines)
MEDICA EURO-PRESS	Comité Permanent de la Presse Médicale Européenne	**MERIP**	Middle East Research and Information Project (U.S.A.)
MEDICO	A service of CARE	**MERL**	Mechanical Engineering Research Laboratory (*now* NEL)
MEDIF	Medicinalimportorforening	**MERML**	Mid-Eastern Medical Regional Library Program (U.S.A.)
MEE	Magyar Electrotechnikai Egyesület		
MEEC	Middle East Economic Committee	**MERNU**	Missão de Estudo do Rendimento Nacional do Ultramar
MEECI	Mechanical and Electrical Engineering Construction Industry	**MERRA**	Middle East Relief and Rehabilitation Administration
MEEU	Missão de Estudos Económicos do Ultramar		
MEF	Maskinentreprenorenes Forbund	**MERU**	Maharishi European Research University
MEF	Mauritius Employers Federation	**MERU**	Mechanical Engineering Research Unit (S. Africa)
MEFA	Foreningen af Danske Medicinfabrikker	**MES**	Malaysian Economic Society
MEFTA	Metalworking Industries in EFTA	**MESA**	Middle East Studies Association of North America
MEG	Max-Eyth-Gesellschaft für Agrartechnik		
MEG	Münchner Entomologische Gesellschaft	**MESA**	United States Mining Enforcement and Safety Administration
MEGJR	Mitteleuropäischer Guttempler- Jugendrat	**MESAN**	Mouvement d'Évolution Sociale d'Afrique Noir
MEIU	Medical Education and Information Unit, Spastics Society	**MESCO**	Middle East Science Co-operation Office (UNESCO)
MEKOG	N.V. Maatschappij tot Exploitatie van Kooksovengassen		
MEL	Musika Esperanta Ligo	**MESPF**	Malaysian Estates Staff Provident Fund
MELA	Middle East Librarians Association (U.S.A.)	**MESR**	Mysore Engineering Research Station (India)
MEM	Mondpaca Esperantista Movada	**MESS**	Türkiye Madenî Eşya Sanayicileri Sendikai
MEMA	Marine Engine and Equipment Manufacturers' Association	**META**	Model Engineering Trade Association
MEMO	Association Internationale pour l'Enseignement des Langues Vivantes par les Méthodes Modernes	**MÉTE**	Magyar Élelmezésipari Tudományos Egyesület
		METO	Middle East Treaty Organisation
MENOFER	Fédération des Unions Professionnelles des Distributeurs de Métaux Non-Ferreux et Appareils Sanitaires (Belgium)	**METRO**	Metropolitan Reference and Research Library Organization, New York
		METU	Middle East Technical University (Turkey)
MENS	Middle East Neurosurgical Society	**MEWAC**	Mediterranean Europe, West Africa Conference
MEOCAM	Mouvement d'Étudiants de l'Organisation Commune Africaine, Malagache et Mauricienne	**MEXE**	Military Engineering Experimental Establishment
MEP	Movimento Electoral del Pueblo (Venezuela)	**MEZU**	Missão de Estudos Zoológicos do Ultramar
MEPA	Missão de Estudos de Pesca de Angola	**MFA**	Motor Factors Association
MEPC	Marine Environment Protection Committee (IMCO)	**MFAL**	Marginal Farmers and Landless Labourers Agency (India)
MEPP	Société Mauritanienne d'Entreposage de Produits Pétroliers	**MFALDA**	Marginal Farmers and Agricultural Labourers Development Agency (India)

MFAR	Maison Familiale d'Apprentissage Rural
MFC	Movimiento Familiar Cristiano (Uruguay)
MFD	Mennonietischer Freiwilligen Dienst
MFE	Magyar Fogorvosok Egyesülete
MFE	Mouvement Fédéraliste Européen
MFECS	Mediterranean Far East Container Service
MFI	Malmö Flygindustri
MFMI	Men for Missions International (U.S.A.)
MFNO	Midland Federation of Newspaper Owners
MFP	Marematlou Freedom Party (Lesotho)
MFP	Ministry of Fuel and Power
MFPA	Mouth and Foot Painting Artists
MFPB	Malta Federation of Professional Bodies
MFR	Mouvement Familial Rural (France) (*now* CMR)
MFRA	Multiple Food Retailers Association
MFT	Magyar Földrajzi Társaság
MFT	Svensk Föreningen för Medicinsk Fysik och Teknik
MGA	Ministerio de Ganadería y Agricultura (Uruguay)
MGA	Missão Geográfica de Angola
MGA	Mushroom Growers Association
MGE	Magyar Geofizikusok Egyesület
MGE	Mouvement Gauche Européenne
MGF	Musikkgrossistenes Förening
MGFHU	Missão de Geografia Física e Humana do Ultramar
MGM	Missao Geografica de Moçambique
MGMI	Mining, Geological and Metallurgical Institute of India
MGMS	Manchester Geological and Mining Society
MH	Musiklärarnas Riksförening
MHA	Manila Hemp Association
MHA	Mental Health Administration (U.S.A.)
MHEA	Mechanical Handling Engineers Association
MHEDA	Material Handling Equipment Distributors Association (U.S.A.)
MHLG	Ministry of Housing and Local Government
MHN	Museo Histórico Nacionál (Argentina)
MHRA	Modern Humanities Research Association
MHS	Malta Heraldic Society
MHS	Malta Historical Society
MHS	Massachusetts Horticultural Society (U.S.A.)

MHT	Magyar Hidrológiai Társaság
MIA	Malleable Ironfounders' Association
MIA	Manitoba Institute of Agrologists (Canada)
MIA	Murrumbidgee Irrigation Area (Australia)
MIAA	Missão de Inquéritos Agrícolas de Angola
MIAM	Fédération Nationale du Matériel Industriel, Agricole et Ménager en Bois
MIAMSI	Mouvement International d'Apostolat des Milieux Sociaux Indépendants
MIAP	Mouvement International d'Action pour la Paix
MIATCO	Mid-America International Agri-Trade Council
MIB	Metal Information Bureau
MIC	Magnesium Industry Council
MIC	Malayan-Indian Congress
MICC	Malaysian International Chamber of Commerce
MICUMA	Société des Mines de Cuivre de Mauritanie
MIDADE	Mouvement International d'Apostolat des Enfants
MIDADEN	Movimiento Internacional de Apostolado de los Niños
MIDEC	Middle East Industrial Development Projects Corporation
MIDFC	Malaysian Industrial Development Finance Co.
MIDS	Madras Institute of Development Studies (India)
MIE	Mouvement pour l'Indépendance de l'Europe
MIEC	Pax Romana, Mouvement International des Étudiants Catholiques
MIF	Miners' International Federation
MIFERMA	Société des Mines de Fer de Mauritanie
MIFU	Margarine-Industriens Foelles-Udvalg
MIGB	Millinery Institute of Great Britain
MII	Muslim Intellectuals' International (Pakistan)
MIIC	Mouvement International des Intellectuels Catholiques
MIJARC	Mouvement International de la Jeunesse Agricole et Rurale Catholique
MIL	Maanmittausinsinöörien Liitto
MILC	Midwest Interlibrary Centre (U.S.A.)
MIM	Malaysian Institute of Management
MIMAF	Musicians International Mutual Aid Fund (France)

MIMC	Marconi International Marine Communication Company	**MIV**	Milchindustrie-Verband
MIME	Midland Institute of Mining Engineers	**MJA**	Movimiento de la Juventud Agraria (Uruguay)
MINESLA	Conference of Ministers of Education and those Responsible for the Promotion of Science and Technology in Relation to Development in Latin America and the Caribbean	**MJSZ**	Magyar Jogasz Svövetség
		MKA	Mezhdunarodnyj Kooperativnyj Alians
		MKE	Magyar Könyvtärosek Egyesülete
		MKFE	Magyarországi Nemzetközi Közúti Fuvarozók Egyesülete
MINETRAS	Syndicat des Constructeurs de Matériels pour Mines et Travaux Souterrains	**MKL**	Maatalouskeskusten Liitto
MINRA	Miniature International Racing Association (U.S.A.)	**MKSZ**	Magyar Képzomüvészek Szövetsége
		MLA	Malta Library Association
MIPE	Moscow Institute of Power Engineering	**MLA**	Modern Language Association (U.S.A.)
MIPI	Madjelis ilmu pengetahaun Indonesia	**MLAF**	Mainostajien Liitto Annonsörernas
MIPN	Mouvement Italien pour la Protection de la Nature	**MLAGB**	Muzzle Loaders' Association of Great Britain
		MLC	Meat and Livestock Commission
MIR	Mouvement International de la Réconciliation	**MLEU**	Mouvement Libéral pour l'Europe Unie
		MLV	Ministerie van Landbouw en Visserij
MIRA	Motor Industry Research Association	**MMA**	Meter Manufacturers Association
MIRF	Myopia International Research Foundation (U.S.A.)	**MMB**	Milk Marketing Board
		MMFITB	Man-made Fibres Producing Industry Training Board
MIRINZ	Meat Industry Research Institute, New Zealand	**MMI**	Foreninger af Mobelarkitekter og Indretningsarkitekter i Danmark
MIRT	Meteorological Institute for Research and Training (Egypt)		
		MMM	Mouvement Militant Mauricien
MIS	Milieu Information Service (U.S.A.)	**MMM**	Mouvement Mondial des Mères
MIS	Mining Institute of Scotland	**MMP**	International Organization of Masters, Mates and Pilots
MISLIC	Mid-Staffordshire Libraries in Co-operation		
MISO	Mostra Internazionale Scambi Occidente	**MMPS**	Commission Médico-Pédagogique et Psycho-Sociale (of BICE)
MISR	Macaulay Institute for Soil Research		
MISR	Makerere Institute of Social Research (Uganda)	**MMRA**	Maritime Marshland Rehabilitation Administration (Canada)
		MMS	Moravian Missionary Society
MISR	Malawi Institute of Social Research	**MMSA**	Mercantile Marine Service Association
MIT	Massachusetts Institute of Technology (U.S.A.)	**MMSA**	Mining and Metallurgical Society of America
MITA	Schweizerischer Verband des Mineral- und Tafelwasserhandels	**MMSC**	Mediterranean Marine Sorting Centre
		MMTC	Marine Mineral Technology Center (U.S.A.)
MITEX	Federatie van Middenstandsorganisaties in de Textildetailhandel	**MMTC**	Minerals and Metals Trading Corporation of India Ltd
MITI	Japanese Ministry of International Trade and Industry	**MMTC**	Mouvement Mondial des Travailleurs Chrétiens
MITI	Ministry for International Trade and Industry (Japan)	**MNA**	Mouvement National Algérien
		MNBA	Multinational Business Association (U.S.A.)
MITRA	Management Institute for Training and Research in Asia	**MNC-L**	Mouvement National Congolais-Lumumba
MIU	Microalgae International Union	**MNCP**	Mbandzeni National Convention Party (Swaziland)
MIV	Melk-Inkoop-Vereniging		

MNE	Mouvement National pour la Défense et le Développement d'Épargne	**MOTESZ**	Magyar Orvostudományi Társásagok és Egyesületek Szovetsege
MNF	Millers' National Federation (U.S.A.)	**MOTOR-AGRIC**	Agricultural Mechanisation Organization (Ivory Coast)
MNHN	Museo Nacional de Historia Natural (Uruguay)	**MPA**	Magazine Publishers Association (U.S.A.)
MNLF	Moro National Liberation Front (Philippines)	**MPA**	Marketing and Promotion Association
MNUOM	Mision de las Naciones Unidas en el Oriente Medio	**MPA**	Master Photographers Association of Great Britain
MOA	Ministry of Aviation	**MPA**	Music Publishers Association of the United States
MOAC	Ministry of Agriculture and Cooperatives (Thailand)	**MPAA**	Motion Picture Association of America
MOC	Melkhygiënisch Onderzoek Centrum	**MPAGB**	Modern Pentathlon Association of Great Britain
MOCHI	Moniteur du Commerce International		
MOD	Ministry of Overseas Development	**MPAU**	Mahatma Phule Agricultural University (India)
MODEF	Mouvement de Défense des Exploitations Agricoles Familiales	**MPBP**	Metal Polishers, Buffers, Platers and Helpers International Union (U.S.A.)
MODUR	Movimiento de Unidad Ruralista (Uruguay)	**MPBW**	Ministry of Public Building and Works
MOE	Ministry of Education	**MPCA**	Manpower Citizens' Association (Guyana)
MOEA	Ministry of Economic Affairs (Taiwan)	**MPCRI**	Management Promotion Council of the Ryukyu Islands
MOF	Ministry of Food (later MAFF)		
MOH	Ministry of Health	**MPF**	Metallurgical Plantmakers Federation
MOI	Ministry of Information (now COI)	**MPG**	Max-Planck-Gesellschaft zur Förderung der Wissenschaften
MOJMRP	Meteorological Office, Joint Meteorological Radio Propagation Sub-Committee	**MPI**	Meeting Planners International (U.S.A.)
MOK	Mezhpravitelstvennaia Okeanograficheskaia Komissiia	**MPI**	Middle Path International (Buddhism)
MOM	Musée Océanographique de Monaco	**MPIAS**	Max Planck Institute for the Advancement of Science (Germany)
MONOTAR	Mouvement National des Travailleurs Agricoles Ruraux	**MPJ**	Mouvement Panafricain de la Jeunesse
MONUMO	Mission de l'Organisation des Nations Unies au Moyen-Orient	**MPLA**	Popular Movement for the Liberation of Angola
MOPC	Ministerio de Obras Publicas y Comuni- caciones (Paraguay)	**MPM**	Milli Prodüktivite Merkezi (National Productivity Centre) (Turkey)
MORI	Market and Opinion Research International	**MPNI**	Ministry of Pensions and National Insurance
MOS	Malta Ornithological Society	**MPPF**	Malaysian Planters Provident Fund
MOS	Ministry of Supply	**MPRP**	Mongolian Peoples Revolutionary Party
MOSICP	Movimiento Sindical Cristiano del Perú	**MPS**	Mouvement Populaire Sénégalais
MOSID	Ministry of Supply Inspection Department	**MPU**	Medical Practitioners Union
MOSSAD	Israeli Secret Service	**MRA**	Misiones Rurales Argentinas
MOSST	Ministry of State for Science and Technology (Canada)	**MRA**	Moral Re-Armament (International)
MOST	Ministry of Science and Technology (Korea)	**MRAP**	Mouvement contre le Racisme, l'An- tisémitisme et pour la Paix
MOSZK	Central Union of Hungarian Co-operative Societies	**MRC**	Medical Research Council
		MRCC	Mineral Resources Consultative Committee
MOT	Ministry of Transport	**MRCI**	Medical Research Council of Ireland
MOTCP	Ministry of Town and County Planning	**MRD**	Microbiological Research Department

MRE	Malaysian Rubber Exchange	**MSJ**	Meteorological Society of Japan
MRELB	Malaysian Rubber Exchange and Licensing Board	**MSP**	Association Suisse des Marchands de Papier Peints
MRf	Malaremästarnas Riksförening i Sverige	**MSRA**	Multiple Shoe Retailers' Association
MRF	Motorbranschens Riksförbund	**MSRI**	Malaysian Sociological Research Institute
MRFB	Malaysian Rubber Fund Board	**MSSGB**	Motion Study Society of Great Britain
MRG	Minority Rights Group	**MSSL**	Mullard Space Science Laboratory
MRI	Malt Research Institute (U.S.A.)	**MSSP**	International Association of Marble, Slate and Stone Polishers, Rubbers and Sawyers etc. (U.S.A.)
MRI	Marine Research Institute, Djakarta		
MRIS	Maritime Research Information Service (*of* NAS) (U.S.A.)	**MSSRC**	Mediterranean Social Sciences Research Council
MRJC	Mouvement Rural de la Jeunesse Catholique	**MSSVD**	Medical Society for the Study of Venereal Diseases
MRJCF	Fédération du Mouvement Rural de Jeunesse Chrétienne Féminine		
		MSWEG	Mild Steel Wire Export Group
MRL	Ministère de la Reconstruction et du Logement	**MTA**	Magyar Tudományos Akadémia
		MTA	Mica Trades Association
MRP	Mouvement Républican Populaire	**MTA**	Mineral Research and Exploration Institute of Turkey
MRPP	Maoists of the Movement for the Reorganisation of the Portugese Proletariat		
		MTA	Mobel- og Trearbeidings- industriens Arbeidsgiverforening
MRRDB	Malaysian Rubber Research and Development Board		
		MTCA	Ministry of Transport and Civil Aviation
MRS	Market Research Society	**MTCF**	Multilateral Technical Cooperation Fund (*of* CENTO)
MRTA	Marketing Research Trade Association (U.S.A.)		
		MTES	Müszaki és Természettudomány Egyesületek Szövetsége
MS	Movement for Survival		
MSA	Malaysia-Singapore Airlines Ltd	**MTF**	Materialteknisk Forening
MSA	Mellan-och Sydsvenska Skogbrukets Arbetsstudier	**MTHL**	Metalliteollisuudenharjoittajain Liitto
		MTI	Meinatoeknafélag Islands
MSA	Motor Schools Association of Great Britain	**MTI**	Metal Treating Institute (U.S.A.)
MSA	Mouvement Socialiste Africain	**MTIN**	Ministry of Trade and Industry, Northern Region (Nigeria)
MSA	Mutualité Sociale Agricole		
MSA	Mutual Security Agency (U.S.A.)	**MTIRA**	Machine Tool Industry Research Association
MSA	Mycological Society of America	**MTIW**	Ministry of Trade and Industry, Western Region (Nigeria)
MSC	Manpower Services Commission		
MSC	Mediterranean Sub-Commission (Silva Mediterranea) (*of* FAO)	**MTK**	Maataloustuottajain Keskusliitto
		MTL	Mainostoimistojen Liitto
MSC	Meteorological Service of Canada	**MTMA-UK**	Methods-Time Measurement Association of the United Kingdom
MSC	Mikrobiologická Spolecnost Ceskoslovenská		
MSEUE	Mouvement Socialiste pour les États-Unis d'Europe	**MTOA**	Manufacture de Tabacs de l'Ouest Africain
		MTP	Manufacture Togolaise des Plastiques
MSF	Multiple Shops Federation	**MTPS**	Syndicat National des Industries d'Équipement
MSHG	Nederlandse Vereniging van Agenten in Metaalwaren, Sanitaire, Huishoudelijke en Aanverwante Artikelen en Galanterieën		
		MTS	Marine Technology Society
MSI	Movimento Sociale Italiano		
MSIRI	Mauritius Sugar Industry Research Institute	**MTTA**	Machine Tools Trades' Association

MTU	Motoren- und Turbinen-Union
MTUC	Malay Trade Union Conference
MUBA	Schweizer Mustermesse in Basel
MUCIA	Midwest Universities Consortium for International Activities (U.S.A.)
MUCM	Mouvement Universel pour Confédération Mondiale
MUDRA	Training and Research Centre for the Performing Arts (Belgium)
MUF	Malta Union of Farmers
MUFM	Mouvement Universel pour une Fédération Mondiale
MUNT	Magyar Urológusok és Nephrológusok Társasága
MUP	Malta Union of Pharmacists
MURA	Midwestern Universities Research Association (U.S.A.)
MURS	Mouvement Universel de la Responsabilité Scientifique
MUT	Magyar Urbanisztikai Társaság
MUT	Malta Union of Teachers
MUZ	Institute for International Collaboration in Agriculture and Forestry (Czechoslovakia)
MVA	Missouri Valley Authority (U.S.A.)
MVDA	Motor Vehicle Dismantlers Association of Great Britain
MVL	Mekaniske Verksteders Landsforening
MVS	Mennonite Voluntary Service (Germany)
MVSofSA	Mine Ventilation Society of South Africa
MWG	Montanwissenschaftliche Gesellschaft der DDR
MWIA	Medical Women's International Association
MWTCo	Marconi's Wireless Telegraph Co. Ltd
MWV	Mineralölwirtschaftsverband
MY	Muoviyhdistys
MZS	Office Hongrois de Normalisation
MZV	Mineralöl Zentralverband

N

NA	Nordisk Amatørteaterrad
NAA	National Academy of Arbitrators (U.S.A.)

NAA	National Aeronautic Association (U.S.A.)
NAA	National Arborist Association (U.S.A.)
NAA	National Automobile Association (U.S.A.)
NAA	Nederlandse Aardappel-Associatie
NAAA	National Alliance of Athletic Associations
NAAB	National Association of Artificial Breeders (U.S.A.)
NAABC	National Association of American Business Clubs
NAABI	National Association of Alcoholic Beverage Importers (U.S.A.)
NAAC	National Association of Agricultural Contractors
NAAC	National Association of Archery Coaches
NAACIE	National Association of Agricultural, Commercial and Industrial Employees (Guyana)
NAACP	National Association for the Advancement of Coloured Peoples (U.S.A.)
NAAF	Norges Astma-og Allergiforbund
NAAF	North-African Air Force
NAAFI	Navy, Army and Air Force Institutes
NAAG	North American Advisory Group (*of* BOTB)
NAALD	Nigerian Association of Agricultural Librarians and Documentalists
NAAMSA	National Association of Automobile Manufacturers of South Africa
NAAO	North Africa Area Office (*of* UNICEF)
NAAP	National Association of Advertising Publishers (U.S.A.)
NAAR	National Association of Advertising Representatives
NAAS	National Agricultural Advisory Service (*now* ADAS)
NAAS	National Association of Art Services (U.S.A.)
NAATS	National Association of Air Traffic Specialists (U.S.A.)
NAAW	National Association of Amateur Winemakers
NAB	National Assistance Board
NAB	National Association of Broadcasters (U.S.A.)
NAB	National Association of Bookmakers, Ltd
NABAC	National Association of Bank Auditors and Comptrollers (U.S.A.)
NABB	Nationale Associatie des Compatables de Belgique
NABBA	National Amateur Body Building Association

NABC	National Association of Boys' Clubs
NABC	National Association of Building Centres
NABE	National Association of Business Economists (U.S.A.)
NABE	National Association for Business Education (*now amalgamated with* BACIE)
NABET	National Association of Broadcast Employees and Technicians (U.S.A.)
NABF	Norsk Antikvarbokhandlerforening
NABM	National Association of Biscuit Manufacturers
NABM	National Association of British Manufacturers (*now* CBI)
NABMA	National Association of British Market Authorities
NABP	National Associations of Boards of Pharmacy (U.S.A.)
NABS	National Advertising Benevolent Society
NABT	National Association of Biological Teachers (U.S.A.)
NABU	Vereniging van Nederlandse Aannemers met Belangen in het Buitland
NAC	National Agricultural Centre, Kenilworth
NAC	National Airways Corporation (South Africa)
NAC	National Amusements Council
NAC	National Anglers Council
NAC	National Archives Council
NAC	National Association of Choirs
NAC	Nederlandse Akkerbouw Centrale
NAC	North American Committee of NGOs for Environment
NACA	National Advisory Committee for Aeronautics (U.S.A.) (*now* NASA)
NACA	National Agricultural Chemicals Association (U.S.A.)
NACA	National Athletic and Cycling Association
NACAA	National Association of Country Agricultural Agents (U.S.A.)
NACAB	National Agricultural Centre Advisory Board
NACAE	National Advisory Council on Art Education
NACAM	National Association of Corn and Agricultural Merchants
NACAR	National Advisory Committee on Aeronautical Research (S. Africa)
NACAS	National Advisory Committee on Agricultural Services (Canada)
NACCAM	National Co-ordinating Committee for Aviation Meteorology
NACCG	National Association of Crankshaft and Cylinder Grinders (*now* FER)
NACCU	National Association of Canadian Credit Unions
NACCW	National Advisory Centre of Careers for Women
NACD	National Association of Chemical Distributors (U.S.A.)
NACD	National Association for Community Development (U.S.A.)
NACDS	National Association of Chain Drug Stores (U.S.A.)
NACE	National Advisory Committee on Electronics (India)
NACE	National Association of Corrosion Engineers (U.S.A.)
NACEBO	Nationale Centrale voor Metaal-, Hout- en Bouwvakondernemingen
NACEIC	National Advisory Council on Education for Industry and Commerce
NACF	National Agricultural Cooperative Federation (Korea)
NACF	National Association of Church Furnishers
NACFRC	North Atlantic Coastal Fisheries Research Centre
NACILA	National Council of Indian Library Associations (*now* FILA)
NACLA	North American Congress on Latin America (U.S.A.)
NACM	National Association of Charcoal Manufacturers
NACM	National Association for Cider Makers
NACM	National Association of Colliery Managers
NACM	National Association of Cotton Manufacturers (U.S.A.)
NACO	National Agricultural Company (Tanzania)
NACO	National Agricultural Credit Office (Vietnam)
NACO	National Association of Caravan Owners
NACO	National Association of Cooperative Officials
NACOA	National Advisory Committee on the Oceans and Atmosphere (U.S.A.)
NACO-BROUW	National Comité voor Brouwgerst
NACODS	National Association of Colliery Overmen, Deputies and Shotfirers

NaCoVo	National Comité van Voederbouw	**NAECOE**	National Academy of Engineering, Committee on Ocean Engineering (U.S.A.)
NACP	National Association of Creamery Proprietors and Wholesale Dairymen Inc.	**NAEDS**	National Association of Engravers and Diestampers
NACPCC	National Advisory Committee for Pig Carcass Competitions	**NAEE**	National Association of Environmental Education
NACRO	National Association for the Care and Resettlement of Offenders	**NAEGA**	North American Grain Export Association
NACT	National Association of Careers Teachers	**NAET**	National Association of Creamery Proprietors and Wholesale Dairymen
NACT	National Association of Cycle Traders	**NAF**	Nederlands Atoomforum
NACTA	National Association of Colleges and Teachers of Agriculture (U.S.A.)	**NAF**	Norske Annonsørers Förening
NACTST	National Advisory Council on the Training and Supply of Teachers	**NAF**	Norsk Arbeitsgiverförening
NAD	National Association of the Deaf	**NAF**	Norges Apotekerförening
NAD	National Academy of Design (U.S.A.)	**NAF**	Norsk Arbeidgiverförening
NADA	National Association of Drama Advisers	**NAFAS**	National Association of Flower Arrangement Societies of Great Britain
NADA	National Automobile Dealers Association (U.S.A.)	**NAFC**	National Anti-fluoridation Campaign
NADC	Northern Region Agricultural Development Centre (Thailand)	**NAFC**	National Association of Food Chains (U.S.A.)
NADECO	National Development Company (Ghana)	**NAFC**	North-American Forestry Commission (*of* FAO)
NADEE	National Association of Divisional Executives for Education	**NAFC**	North-East Atlantic Fisheries Commission (U.K.)
NADEEC	NATO Air Defence Electronic Environment Committee	**NAFCO**	National Agricultural and Food Corporation (Tanzania)
NADEFCOL	Defense College (*of* NATO)	**NAFCO**	National Airways and Finance Corporation (South Africa)
NADFAS	National Association of Decorative and Fine Art Societies	**NAFD**	National Association of Funeral Directors
NADFS	National Association of Drop Forgers and Stampers	**NAFEKAV**	Nationale Federatie der Kleinhandelaars in Algemene Voedingswaren (Belgium)
NADGE	NATO Air Defence Ground Environment System Organization	**NAFEP**	National Association of Frozen Egg Packers
NADJ	National Association of Disc Jockeys	**NAFEC**	National Aviation Facilities Experimental Center (U.S.A.)
NADL	National Animal Disease Laboratory (Japan)	**NAFF**	National Association for Freedom
NADPAS	National Association of Discharged Prisoners' Aid Societies, Inc.	**NAFFP**	National Association of Frozen Food Producers (*now* UKAFFP)
NAE	National Academy of Engineering (U.S.A.)	**NAFHE**	National Association of Further and Higher Education
NAE	National Association of Exhibitors	**NAFO**	National Association of Fire Officers
NAEA	National Association of Estate Agents	**NAFRC**	National Atlantic Fisheries Research Center (*of* NMFS) (U.S.A.)
NAEB	National Association of Educational Broadcasters (U.S.A.)	**NAFSA**	National Association of Foreign Student Advisers (USA)
NAEC	National Aeronautical Establishment, Canada	**NAFSA**	National Fire Services Association of Great Britain
NAEC	National Agricultural Engineering Corporation (China)	**NAFTA**	North Atlantic Free Trade Area
NAEC	National Association of Exhibition Contractors	**NAFTRAC**	National Foreign Trade Council (U.S.A.)

NAFWR	National Association of Furniture Warehousemen and Removers, Ltd
NAG	National Association of Goldsmiths of Great Britain and Ireland
NAG	National Association of Grooms
NAG	National Association of Groundsmen
NAG	Nederlands Akoestisch Genootschap
NAG	Nederlands Architecten Genootschap
NAGARD	NATO Advisory Group for Aeronautical Research and Development
NAGC	National Association of Gifted Children
NAGM	National Association of Glove Manufacturers
NAGS	National Allotments and Gardens Society
NAGS	National Association of Hospital Management Committee Group Secretaries
NAH	Ministry of Animal Health, Northern Region (Nigeria)
NAHA	National Association of Health Authorities
NAHA	North American Highway Association
NAHA	Norwegian-American Historical Association
NAHBO	National Association of Hospital Broadcasting Organisations
NAHI	Nederlands Agronomisch Historisch Instituut
NAHRI	National Animal Husbandry Research Institute (Denmark)
NAHRO	National Association of Housing and Redevelopment Officials (U.S.A.)
NAHS	National Association of Health Stores
NAHSE	National Association of Health Services Executives (U.S.A.)
NAHSO	National Association of Hospital Supplies Officers
NAHT	National Association of Head Teachers
NAI	Nordiska Afrikaninstitutet (Sweden)
NAIBD	National Association of Industries for the Blind and Disabled
NAIC	National Association of Investment Clubs
NAIC	National Astronomy and Ionosphere Center (U.S.A.)
NAIDA	National Agricultural and Industrial Development Association (Eire)
NAIDM	National Association of Insecticide and Disinfectant Manufacturers (U.S.A.)
NAIF	National Association for Irish Freedom
NAIG	Nippon Atomic Industry Group (Japan)

NAII	National Association of Ice Industries (U.S.A.)
NAIL	Neurotics Anonymous International Liaison Inc. (U.S.A.)
NAIPRC	Netherlands Automatic Information Processing Research Centre
NAIRO	National Association of Intergroup Relations Officials (U.S.A.)
NAISS	National Association of Iron and Steel Stockholders
NAIWC	National Association of Inland Waterway Carriers
NAIY	National Association of Indian Youth (U.K.)
NAK	Nederlandse Algemene Keuringsdienst voor Landbouwzaden en Aardappelpootgoed
NAKB	Nederlandse Algemene Keuringsdienst voor Boomkwekerijgewassen
NAKG	Nederlandse Algemene Keuringsdienst voor Groente en Bloemzaden
NAKS	Nederlandse Algemene Keuringsdienst voor Siergewassen
NAL	National Aeronautical Laboratory (India)
NAL	National Air Lines (U.S.A.)
NAL	Norske Arkitekters Landsforbund
NAL	Norske Avisers Landforbund
NAL	National Agricultural Library (U.S.A.)
NALA	National Association of Language Advisers
NALBSC	National Association of Licensed Bingo and Social Clubs
NALC	National Association of Local Councils
NALCC	National Automatic Laundry Cleaning Council
NALCD	National Agricultural Library and Centre for Documentation (Hungary)
NALGO	National and Local Government Officers Association
NALHM	National Association of Licensed House Managers
NALI	National Association of the Laundry Industry
NALM	National Association of Lift Makers
NALO	National Association of Launderette Owners
NALSAT	National Association of Land Settlement Association Tenants
NALSO	National Association of Labour Student Organisations

NAM	National Association of Manufacturers (U.S.A.)	**NAOP**	National Association of Operative Plasterers
NAM	Nederlandsche Aardolie Maatschappij	**NAP**	Niger Agricultural Project (Nigeria)
NAMA	North American Mycological Association	**NAP**	Northern Agricultural Producers
NAMARCO	National Marketing Corporation (Philippines)	**NAPA**	National Association of Park Administrators
		NAPAEO	National Association of Principal Agricultural Education Officers
NAMB	National Agricultural Marketing Board (Canada, Zambia)	**NAPB**	National Agricultural Products Board (Tanzania)
NAMB	National Association of Master Bakers, Confectioners and Caterers	**NAPB**	Nederlandse Aannemersbond en Patroonsbond voor de Bouwbedrijven in Nederland
NAMC	Mananga Agricultural Management Centre (*of* CDC)	**NAPC**	National Association of Parish Councils (*now* NALC)
NAMC	Nihon Aeroplane Manufacturing Company (Japan)	**NAPCA**	National Air Pollution Control Administration (*of* HEW) (U.S.A.)
NAMCW	National Association for Maternal Child Welfare	**NAPCA**	National Association of Pipe Coating Applicators (U.S.A.)
NAME	National Association of Marine Enginebuilders	**NAPD**	National Association of Pharmaceutical Distributors
NAME	National Association of Marine Engineers of Canada	**NAPE**	National Association of Port Employers
		NAPE	National Association of Power Engineers (U.S.A.)
NAMG	National Association of Multiple Grocers		
NAMH	National Association for Mental Health	**NAPF**	National Association of Pension Funds
NAMI	National Association of Malleable Ironfounders	**NAPGC**	National Association of Public Golf Courses
		NAPIM	National Association of Printing Ink Manufacturers (U.S.A.)
NAMM	National Association of Margarine Manufacturers (U.S.A.)	**NAPL**	National Association of Photo-Lithographers (U.S.A.)
NAMM	National Association of Master Masons		
NAMMC	Natural Asphalt Mine-Owners' and Manufacturers' Council	**NAPM**	National Association of Paper Merchants
NAMMO	NATO Multi-Role Combat Aircraft Development and Production Management Organization	**NAPM**	National Association of Purchasing Management (U.S.A.)
		NAPO	National Association of Probation Officers
NAMO	National Association of Marketing Officers (U.S.A.)	**NAPO**	National Association of Property Owners
		NAPP	National Association of Poultry Packers
NAMPUS	National Association of Master Plumbers of the United States	**NAPR**	National Association of Pram Retailers
NAMRU	United States Naval Medical Research Unit	**NAPRE**	National Association of Practical Refrigerating Engineers (U.S.A.)
NAMSO	NATO Maintenance and Supply Organisation	**NAPS**	National Association of Personal Secretaries Ltd
NANFM	National Association of Non-Ferrous Scrap Metal Merchants	**NAPT**	National Association for the Prevention of Tuberculosis (*now* CHA)
NANP	National Association of Naturopathic Physicians (U.S.A.)	**NAPTW**	National Association of Pet Trade Wholesalers
NANU	National Association of Non-Unionists	**NAPV**	National Association of Prison Visitors
NANTIS	Nottingham and Nottinghamshire Technical Information Service	**NAQP**	National Association of Quick Printers (U.S.A.)
NAO	National Accordion Association		
NAOE	National Association for Outdoor Education	**NAR**	Nordisk Amatørteaterrad

NARACC	National Association of Refrigeration and Air Conditioning Contractors
NARAS	National Academy of Recording Arts and Sciences (U.S.A.)
NARBA	North American Regional Broadcasting Agreement
NARC	National Association for Retarded Children (U.S.A.)
NARCOM	North American Research Group on Management
NARE	National Association of Remedial Education
NARF	National Association of Retail Furnishers
NARG	Norfolk Archaeological Retrieval Group
NARGN	National Association of Retail Grocers of Norway
NARGUS	National Association of Retail Grocers of the United States
NARI	Natal Agricultural Research Institute (S.Africa)
NARI	National Agricultural Research Institute (Japan)
NARI	National Association of Recycling Industries (U.S.A.)
NARIC	National Rice and Corn Corporation (Philippines)
NARO	North American Regional Office (*of* FAO)
NARR	National Association of Radiator Repairers
NARRA	National Resettlement and Rehabilitation Administration (Philippines)
NARS	National Archives and Records Service (U.S.A.)
NARSIS	National Association for Road Safety Instruction in Schools
NARST	National Association for Research in Science Teaching (U.S.A.)
NARTB	National Association of Radio and Television Broadcasters (U.S.A.)
NARTEL	North Atlantic Radio Telephone Committee
NARTM	National Association of Rope and Twine Merchants
NAS	National Academy of Sciences (U.S.A.)
NAS	National Adoption Society
NAS	National Association of Schoolmasters
NAS	National Association of Shopfitters
NAS	National Audubon Society (U.S.A.)
NAS	Noise Abatement Society
NAS	Norges Akademikersamband
NASA	National Settlement Authority (Libya)
NASA	U.S. National Aeronautics and Space Administration
NASA	Nigerian Anthropological and Sociological Association
NASAB	National Association of Shippers Advisory Boards (U.S.A.)
NASBA	National Automobile Safety Belt Association
NASC	National Aeronautics and Space Council (U.S.A.)
NASC	National Association of Scaffolding Contractors
NASC	National Association of Student Councils (U.S.A.)
NASCO	National Academy of Sciences Committee on Oceanography (U.S.A.)
NASCO	National Agricultural Supply Company (U.S.A.)
NASD	National Amalgamated Stevedores and Dockers
NASD	National Association of Securities Dealers (U.S.A.)
NASDEC	National Assets and Services Development Export Consortium
NASDU	National Amalgamated Stevedores and Dockers Union
NASEES	National Association for Soviet and East European Studies (Scotland)
NASEN	National Association of State Enrolled Nurses
NASH	National Association of Specimen Hunters
NASIS	National Association for State Information Systems (U.S.A.)
NASMAR	National Association of Sack Merchants and Reclaimers Ltd
NASPM	National Association of Seed Potato Merchants
NASRF	National Association of Shoe Repair Factories
NASS	National Association of Steel Stockholders
NASSS	National Association for the Support of Small Schools
NASU	National Adult School Union
NASU	National Association of State Universities (U.S.A.)
NASW	National Association of Science Writers (U.S.A.)

NASW	National Association of Social Workers (U.S.A.)	**NATTKE**	National Association of Theatrical, Television and Kine Employees
NASWM	National Association of Scottish Woollen Manufacturers	**NATTS**	National Association of Trade and Technical Schools (U.S.A.)
NAT	Nämnden för Avkommeundersökning av Tjurar	**NAUA**	National Automobile Underwriters' Association (U.S.A.)
NATA	National Association of Testing Authorities (Australia)	**NAUI**	National Association of Underwater Instructions (U.S.A.)
NATAS	National Academy of Television Arts and Sciences (U.S.A.)	**NAV**	Nederlandse Aerosole Vereniging
		NAV	Nederlandse Anesthesisten
NATCC	National Air Transport Coordinating Committee (U.S.A.)	**NAV**	Nederlandse Anthropogenetische Vereniging
NATD	National Association of Teachers of Dancing	**NAVAC**	National Audio-Visual Aids Centre
NATD	National Association of Tobacco Distributors (U.S.A.)	**NAVAS**	Nederlandse Aannemers Vereniging van Afbouw-en Stukadoorswerken
NATD	National Association of Tool Dealers	**NaVAST**	Nationaal Verbond der Aannemers-Schrijnwerkers en Timmerlieden
NATE	National Association for the Teaching of English	**NAVEG**	Nederlandse Agentenvereniging op Verlichtings- en Electrotechnisch Gebied
NATEC	Naval Air Technical Evaluation Centre	**NAVEMHA**	Nationaal Verbond der Melk- en Zuivelhandelaars van België
NATESA	National Alliance of Television and Electronic Service Associations (U.S.A.)	**NAVETEX**	Nationaal Verbond der Textieldetaillanten (Belgium)
NATEX	National Textile Industries Corporation Ltd (Tanzania)	**NAVEWA**	Nationale Vereniging der Waterleidingbedrijven (Belgium)
NATFHE	National Association of Teachers of Further and Higher Education	**NAVF**	Norges Almenvitenskapelige Forskningsråd
NATGA	National Amateur Tobacco Growers' Association	**NAVH**	National Association of Voluntary Hostels
		NAVIGA	European Model Ships Federation
NATKE	National Association of Theatrical and Kine Employees	**NAVL**	National Anti-Vaccination League
		NAVS	National Anti-Vivisection Society
NATMH	National Association of Teachers of the Mentally Handicapped	**NAVSA**	Syndicat National de Vente et Services Automatiques
NATN	National Association of Theatre Nurses	**NAWAFA**	North Atlantic Westbound Freight Association
NATO	National Association of Temperance Officials	**NAWAPA**	North American Water and Power Alliance
NATO	National Association of Tenants Organizations (Eire)	**NAWB**	National Association of Wine and Beer-makers
NATO	North Atlantic Treaty Organisation	**NAWB**	National Association of Workshops for the Blind Incorporated
NATR	National Association of Tenants and Residents	**NAWC**	National Association of Women's Clubs
NATR	National Association of Toy Retailers	**NAWCH**	National Association for the Welfare of Children in Hospital
NATRFD	National Association of Television and Radio Firm Directors (U.S.A.)	**NAWDC**	National Association of Waste Disposal Contractors Ltd
NATS	National Air Traffic Services	**NAWDOFF**	National Association of Wholesale Distributors of Frozen Foods
NATS	Nordisk Avisteknisk Samarbetsnämnd	**NAWF**	North American Wildlife Foundation (U.S.A.)
NATSOPA	National Society of Operative Printers, Graphical and Media Personnel		

NAWG	National Association of Wheat Growers (U.S.A.)
NAWICS	National Anglo-West Indian Conservative Society
NAWM	National Association of Wool Manufacturers (U.S.A.)
NAWND	National Association of Wholesale Newspaper Distributors
NAWP	National Association of Women Pharmacists
NAWPM	National Association of Wholesale Paint Merchants
NAWTCH	National Association for the Welfare of Children in Hospital
NAWU	National Agricultural Workers Union (U.S.A.)
NAYC	National Association of Young Cricketers
NAYC	National Association of Youth Clubs
NAYO	National Association of Youth Orchestras
NAYSO	National Association of Youth Service Officers
NB	Norges Byforbund
NBA	National Benzole and Allied Products Association
NBA	National Brassfoundry Association
NBAA	National Business Aircraft Association
NBAHMF	National Building and Allied Hardware Manufacturers Federation
NBB	Nederlandse Boekverkopersbond
NBB	Nederlandse Bond van Bouwondernemers
NBBE	National Board for Bakery Education
NBBFP	Nationale Bond der Belgische Filmproducenten
NBBS	Nederlands Bureau voor Buitenlandse Studentenbetrekkingen
NBBZ	Nederlandse Bond van Bad- en Zweminrichtingen
NBC	National Book Council (*now* NBL)
NBC	National Broadcasting Corporation (U.S.A.)
NBC	Nordens Bondeorganisationers Centralråd
NBCK	Nederlandse Bond van Copieerders en Klein-Offsetdrukkers
NBCS	Nederlandse Bond van Christelijke Schilderpatroons
NBDC	National Broadcasting Development Committee
NBER	National Bureau of Economic Research (U.S.A.)
NBF	National Bedding Federation
NBF	Norsk Bibliotekforening
NBF	Norges Bilbransjeforbund
NBF	Norsk Botanisk Forening
NBF	Norsk Brannvern Forening
NBFBV	Nationale Belgische Federatie der Baanvervoerders
NBFU	National Bureau of Fire Underwriters (U.S.A.)
NBIRN	National Bureau of Industrial Research, Nanking (China)
NBKV	Nederlandse Bond van Konijnenfokkersverenigingen
NBL	National Book League
NBL	Norsk Bibliotekarlag
NBL	Norsk Blomsterdyrkerlag
NBLC	Nederlands Bibliotheek en Lektuur Centrum
NBM	Nederlandse Bond van Makelaars in Onroerende Goederen
NBNI	Nasionale Bounavorsingsinstituut (South Africa)
NBO	Nordic Housing Companies Organization
NBOV	Nederlandse Banketbakkers Ondernemers Vereniging
NBPI	National Board for Prices and Incomes
NBPS	Nederlandse Bond van Patroons in het Steen-, Houtgraniet- en Kunststeenbedrijf
NBR	National Board of Roads and Water (Finland)
NBR	Norske Bedriftavisers Redaktørklubb
NBRI	National Building Research Institute (South Africa)
NBS	National Broadcasting Service (New Zealand)
NBS	National Bureau of Standards (U.S.A.)
NBS	Norsk Biokjemisk Selskap
NBS	Norske Bonde- og Småbrukarlag
NBSS	National Bible Society of Scotland
NBSS	National British Softball Society
NBTPI	National Book Trade Provident Institution
NBU	Nordiska Bankmanaunionen
NBvA	Nederlandse Bond van Assurantie-Agenten
NC	Norsk Cementforening
NCA	National Canners Association (U.S.A.)
NCA	National Coal Association (U.S.A.)

NCA	National Coffee Association of USA	**NCBRM**	Nederlandse Christelijke Bond van Rijwiel-en Motorhandelaren
NCA	National Council for Alcoholism		
NCA	National Council of Aviculture	**NCBT**	Nationale Confederatie van de Belgische Textielreiniging
NCA	National Cranberry Association (U.S.A.)		
NCA	National Cricket Association	**NCBTB**	Nederlandse Christelijke Boeren- en Tuindersbond
NCAA	National Children Adoption Association		
NCAB	National Citizen's Advice Bureaux	**NCC**	National Caravan Council
NCAB	National College der Accountants van België	**NCC**	National Climatic Center (NOAA)
		NCC	National Consumer Council
NCABC	National Citizens' Advice Bureaux Committee	**NCC**	National Cotton Council of America
		NCC	National Council of Churches in New Zealand
NCACC	National Civil Aviation Consultative Committee		
NCAE	National College of Agricultural Engineering	**NCCA**	Inter-Scandinavian Committee on Consumer Matters (Norway)
NCAEG	National Confederation of American Ethnic Groups (U.S.A.)	**NCCA**	National Club Cricket Association
		NCCA	National Cotton Council of America
NCAER	National Council of Applied Economic Research (India)	**NCCAT**	National Committee for Clear Air Turbulence (U.S.A.)
NCAFMW	National Council of Associations of Fresh Meat Wholesalers	**NCCD**	National Council on Crime and Delinquency (U.S.A.)
NCAI	National Congress of American Indians		
NCAI	National Council of American Importers	**NCCE**	Northern Counties Co-operative Enterprise (Northern Ireland)
NCAIE	National Council of the Arts in Education (U.S.A.)	**NCCEE**	Netherlands Committee for the Common Market
NCAPC	National Center for Air Pollution Control (*of* DHEW) (U.S.A.)	**NCCFN**	National Coordinating Committee on Food and Nutrition (Philippines)
NCAR	National Centre for Atmospheric Research (New Zealand)	**NCCI**	National Committee for Commonwealth Immigrants
NCAR	National Centre for Atmospheric Research (U.S.A.)	**NCCIA**	North Carolina Crop Improvement Association Inc. (U.S.A.)
NCARB	National Council of Architectural Registration Boards (U.S.A.)	**NCCK**	National Christian Council of Kenya
		NCCK	Nederlandse Club voor Chefkoks
NCASI	National Council of the Paper Industry for Air and Stream Improvement (U.S.A.)	**NCCL**	National Council of Canadian Labour
		NCCL	National Council for Civil Liberties
NCAVAE	National Committee for Audio-visual Aids in Education	**NCCM**	National Council of Catholic Men
NCAW	National Council for Animal Welfare	**NCCM**	National Council of Concentrate Manufacturers
NCB	National Coal Board		
NCB	Nationale Confederatie van het Bouwbedrijf (Belgium)	**NCCOP**	National Corporation for the Care of Old People
NCB	Nederlandse Consumentenbond	**NCCT**	National Council for Civic Theatres
NCB	Nordic Copyright Bureau	**NCCV**	Nederlandse Cacao en Cacaoproducten Vereniging
NCB	Stichting Nederlandse Centrale voor het Begrafenisbedrijf		
		NCCW	National Council of Catholic Women
NCBA	National Cattle Breeders' Association	**NCD**	Netherlands Centrum van Directeuren
NCBA	National Chinchilla Breeders of America	**NCDB**	National Development Credit Agency (Tanzania)
NCBMP	National Council of Building Material Producers	**NCDB**	Nederlandse Christelijke Drogistenbond

NCDC	National Cooperative Development Association (India)	**NCIP**	Comision Nacional de Productividad Industrial
NCDL	National Canine Defence League	**NCIT**	National Council on Inland Transport
NCDS	National Community Development Service (U.S.A.)	**NCITD**	National Committee for International Trade Documentation (U.S.A.)
NCEA	National Catholic Education Association (U.S.A.)	**NCL**	National Carriers Limited
		NCL	National Central Library
NCEA	North Central Electric Association (U.S.A.)	**NCL**	National Chemical Laboratory (India)
NCEC	National Christian Education Council	**NCLB**	Nederlandse Christelijke Landarbeidersbond
NCERT	National Council of Educational Research and Training (India)	**NCLC**	National Council of Labour Colleges
NCES	National Center for Educational Statistics (U.S.A.)	**NCLIS**	National Commission on Libraries and Information Science (U.S.A.)
NCET	National Council for Educational Technology	**NCM**	National College of Music
		NCMA	National Contract Management Association (U.S.A.)
NCF	National Clayware Federation	**NCMB**	Nigerian Cocoa Marketing Board
NCF	Norges Colonialgrossisters Forbund	**NCMB**	Nordic Council for Marine Biology
NCFC	National Council of Farmer Cooperatives (U.S.A.)	**NCME**	National Council on Measurement in Education (U.S.A.)
NCFM	American National Commission on Food Marketing	**NCMH**	National Committee for Mental Hygiene (U.S.A.)
NCFR	National Council on Family Relations (U.S.A.)	**NCMRED**	National Council on Marine Resources and Engineering Development (U.S.A.)
NCFS	National Conference of Friendly Societies	**NCMV**	Nationaal Christelijk Middenstandsverbond (Belgium)
NCGG	National Committee for Geodesy and Geophysics (Pakistan)	**NCNA**	New China News Agency
NCGGO	National Centrum voor Grasland- en Groenvoederonderzoek	**NCNC**	National Council for Nigeria and the Cameroons
NCGT	National Council of Geography Teachers (U.S.A.)	**NCNL**	Nasionale Chemiese Navorsingslaboratorium (South Africa)
NCGV	Nationaal Centrum voor de Geestelijke Volksgezondheid	**NCOA**	National Council on the Ageing (U.S.A.)
		NCOI	National Council for the Omnibus Industry
NCHEE	National Council for Home Economics Education	**NCOR**	National Committee for Oceanographic Research (Pakistan)
NCHP	Nederlandse Centrale van Hoger Personeel	**NCOS**	Netherlands Christelijk Ondernemersverbond voor het Schildersbedrijf
NCHPTWA	National Clearing House for Periodical Abstracts Service (U.S.A.)	**NCOV**	Nederlands Christelijk Ondernemersverband
NCHS	National Center for Health Statistics (U.S.A.)	**NCPA**	National Cottonseed Products Association (U.S.A.)
NCHSO	National Committee of Hungarian Students Organization	**NCPJ**	Nederlandse Christelijke Plattelands Jongeren Bond
NCHV	Nederlandse Vereniging van Christelijke Handelsreizigers en Handelsagenten	**NCPJB**	Nederlandse Christelijke Plattelands Jongeren Bond
NCIA	National Cavity Insulation Association	**NCPL**	National Centre for Programmed Learning
NCIC	National Cancer Institute of Canada	**NCPTA**	National Confederation of Parent Teacher Associations
NCIH	National Conference on Industrial Hydraulics (U.S.A.)		

NCPUA	National Committee on Pesticide Use in Agriculture (Canada)
NCQR	National Council for Quality and Reliability
NCR	Nationale Coöperatieve Raad
NCRAC	National Community Relations Advisory Council (U.S.A.)
NCRD	National Council for Research and Development (Israel)
NCRL	National Chemical Research Laboratory (S.Africa)
NCRP	National Committee on Radiation Protection (U.S.A.)
NCRR	National Center for Resource Recovery (U.S.A.)
NCRT	National College of Rubber Technology
NCRV	Nederlandsche Christelijke Radio Vereniging
NCS	National Chrysanthemum Society
NCSA	National Crushed Stone Association (U.S.A.)
NCSAW	National Catholic Society for Animal Welfare (U.S.A.)
NCSC	National Council on Schoolhouse Construction (U.S.A.)
NCSE	National Council for Special Education
NCSI	National Council for Stream Improvement (U.S.A.)
NCSPS	National Committee for Support of the Public Schools (U.S.A.)
NCSR	National Council for Social Research (S.Africa)
NCSS	National Cactus and Succulent Society
NCSS	National Center for Social Statistics (U.S.A.)
NCSS	National Council for the Social Studies (U.S.A.)
NCSS	National Council of Social Service, Inc.
NCSTTO	National Council for the Supply and Training of Teachers Overseas
NCT	National Chamber of Trade
NCTA	National Cable Television Association (U.S.A.)
NCTA	National Council for Technological Awards
NCTAEP	National Committee on Technology, Automation and Economic Progress
NCTD	National College of Teachers of the Deaf
NCTET	National Council for Teacher Education and Training
NCTF	National Check Traders' Federation
NCTJ	National Council for the Training of Journalists
NCTL	National Commercial Temperance League
NCTM	National Council of Teachers of Mathematics (U.S.A.)
NCTYL	National College for the Training of Youth Leaders
NCU	National Cyclists' Union
NCUA	U.S. National Credit Union Administration
NCUMC	National Council for the Unmarried Mother and her Child
NCUR	National Committee for Utilities Radio (U.S.A.)
NCVA	National Centre for Voluntary Action (U.S.A.)
NCVCCO	National Council of Voluntary Child Care Organisations
NCW	National Council of Women of Great Britain
NCW	Nederlands Christelijk Werkgeversbond
NCWA	National Children's Wear Association
NCWC	National Catholic Welfare Conference (U.S.A.)
NCWCC	North Central Weed Control Committee (U.S.A.)
NCWM	National Conference on Weights and Measures (U.S.A.)
NCWTD	National Centrum voor Wetenschappelijke en Technische Documentatie (Belgium)
NCYA	National Catholic Youth Association
NCZ	Nationale Coöperatieve Zuivelverkoopcentrale
NDA	National Dairymens' Association
NDA	National Development Association
NDAC	Nuclear Defence Affairs Committee (NATO)
NDAGB	National Darts Association of Great Britain
NDALTP	Nationale Dienst voor Afzet van Land-en Tuinbouwproduktion
NDBI	National Dairymen's Benevolent Institution
NDC	National Dairy Council (U.S.A.)
NDC	National Development Corporation (Tanzania)
NDC	NATO Defence College
NDC	Norsk Designcentrum
NDCS	National Deaf Children's Society
NDEA	National Defence Education Act (U.S.A.)
NDEA	National Display Equipment Association

NDF	National Development Foundation (South Africa)
NDF	Norges Drosjeeier-Forbund
NDFA	National Drama Festivals Association
NDFS	National Deposit Friendly Society
NDFTA	National Dried Fruit Trade Association
NDHF	Norges Dame- og Herrefrisørmestres Forbund
NDL	National Diet Library (Japan)
NDMB	National Defense Mediation Board (U.S.A.)
NDMF	National Development and Management Foundation (South Africa)
NDOA	National Dog Owners' Association
NDP	Vereniging De Nederlandse Dagbladpers
NDPA	National Dairy Producers' Association
NDPD	National Democratic Party of Germany
NDPKC	National Domestic Poultry Keepers Council
NDPS	National Data Processing Service
NDRC	National Defence Research Committee (U.S.A.)
NDRI	National Dairy Research Institute (India)
NDS	National Dahlia Society
NDSB	Narcotic Drugs Supervisory Body (*of* UN)
NDV	Netherlands Dendrological Society
NEA	National Education Association (U.K. and U.S.A.)
NEA	Nuclear Energy Agency (OECD)
NEACT	New England Association of Chemistry Teachers (U.S.A.)
NEADEC	Near East Animal Production and Health Development Centre (Lebanon)
NEAFC	North East Atlantic Fisheries Commission
NEAHI	Near East Animal Health Institute
NEAVB	National Employers Association of Vehicle Builders
NEB	National Economic Board (Korea)
NEB	National Electricity Board of the States of Malaysia
NEB	Nederlandse Eiercontrôle Bureau
NEBA	Nederlandse Katholieke Bond van Beroeps-Assurantiebezorgers
NEBF	National Farm Bureau Federation (U.S.A.)
NEBSS	National Examinations Board in Supervisory Studies
NEBUPZA	Nederlands Bureau voor de Uitvoer van Granen, Zaden en Peulvruchten
NEBUTA	Nederlands Bureau voor Technische Hulp
NEC	National Economic Council (Pakistan or Philippines)
NECA	Nigerian Employers Consultative Association
NECC	Near East Council of Churches
NECCTA	National Educational Closed Circuit Television Association
NECIES	North-East Coast Institution of Engineers and Shipbuilders
NECOB-ETRA	Nederlandse Christelijke Ondernemersbond Electrotechniek en Radio
NECSR	North East Coast Ship Repairers
NECTA	National Electrical Contractors Trading Association
NED	Nederlandse Emigratiedienst
NEDA	National Electronics Development Association (New Zealand)
NEDACO	Vereniging Nederlandse Dakpannenfabrikanten Corporatie
NEDC	National Economic Development Council
NEDC	North-East Development Council
NedCBTB	Nederlandse Christelijke Boeren-en Tuindersbond
NEDECO	Nederlands Ingenieursbureau voor Buitenlandse Werken
NEDELSA	Nederlandse Fabrieken van Electrische Schakelapparatuur
NEDERF	Nederlandse Stichting ter Voorbereiding en Uitvoering van het Erfgewassenproject
NEDER-GRES	Nederlandse Vereniging van Gresbuizenfabrikanten
NEDO	National Economic Development Office (*of* NEDC)
NEEB	North-East Engineering Bureau
NEEB	North Eastern Electricity Board
NEEC	National Export Expansion Council (U.S.A.)
NEERI	National Electrical Engineering Research Institute (South Africa)
NEETU	National Engineering and Electrical Trades Union
NEF	Norges Eiendomsmeglerforbund
NEF	New Education Fellowship (International)
NEF	Norsk Elektroteknisk Forening
NEFA	North East Frontier Agency (India)
NEFATO	Vereniging van Nederlandse Fabrikanten van Voedertoevoegingen

NEFC	Near East Forestry Commission	**NERC**	National Electronics Research Council (*now* NEL)
NEFRS	Near East Forest Rangers' School		
NEFSG	Northeastern Forest Soils Group (U.S.A. & Canada)	**NERC**	National English Rabbit Club
		NERC	Natural Environment Research Council
NEFTIC	Northeastern Forest Tree Improvement Conference (U.S.A.)	**NERC**	Regional Conference for the Near East (FAO)
NEFYTO	Nederlandse Stichting voor Fytofarmacie	**NERO**	Near East Regional Office (*of* FAO)
NEGB	North Eastern Gas Board	**NERRS**	New England Röntgen Ray Society (U.S.A.)
NEGI	National Federation of Engineering and General Ironfounders	**NES**	National Extension Service (India)
NEI	Nederlandsch Economisch Instituut	**NESBIC**	Netherlands Students Bureau for International Cooperation
NEI	Nouvelles Équipes Internationales	**NESC**	Nuclear Engineering and Science Conference
NEIMME	North of England Institute of Mining and Mechanical Engineers	**NET**	Vereniging Nederlandse Eigen-Textieldruckers
NEIS	National Egg Information Service (*now* BEIS)	**NETAC**	Nuclear Energy Trade Associations Conference
NEL	National Electronics Council (*formerly* NERC)	**NEV**	Nederlandsche Entomologische Vereniging
		NEVAC	Nederlandse Vacuumvereniging
NEL	National Engineering Laboratory	**NEVEC**	Nederlandse Economische Vereniging voor de Confectie-Industrie
NELSAT	National Association of Land Settlement Association Tenants		
NEMA	National Electrical Manufacturers (U.S.A.)	**NEVEHAC**	Nederlandse Vereniging van Handelaren in Chemicaliën
NEMEC	Nederlandse Fabrieken van Elektrische en Elektronische Meeten Regelapparatuur	**NEVEM**	Nederlandse Vereniging voor Physical Distribution en Material Management
NEMI	North European Management Institute (Norway)	**NEVEMA**	Nederlandse Vereniging van Matrassenfabrikanten
NEMKO	Norges Elektriske Materiellkontrol	**NEVEPA**	Vereniging van Nederlandse Papierzakken-Fabrikanten
NEMO	National Egg Marketing Organisation		
NEMOG	Groep Nederlandse Fabrieken van Elektrische Motoren en Generatoren	**NEVESUCO**	Nederlandse Vereniging voor de Suikerwerk- en Chocoladeverwerkende Industrie
NEN	Stichting Nederlands Normalisatie-Instituut	**NEVEXPO**	Nederlandse Vereniging van Exporteurs van Pootaardappelen
NEODA	National Edible Oil Distributors Association		
NEOS	New England Ophthalmological Society (U.S.A.)	**NEVI**	Nederlands Vlasinstituut
		NEVIE	Nederlandse Vereniging voor Inkoop-Efficiency
NEPA	Northeastern Pennsylvania Artificial Breeding Cooperative (U.S.A.)	**NEVIM**	Nederlandse Vereniging voor International Meubeltransport
NEPAL	National Egg Packers Association		
NEPP	National Egg and Poultry Promotion	**NEVO**	Nederlandse Volksdansvereniging
NEPPCO	Northeastern Poultry Producers Council (U.S.A.)	**NEVOK**	Nederlandse Vereniging van Ondernemers in het Kappersbedrift
NEPRA	National Egg Producers Retail Association	**NEVON**	Nederlandse Vereniging van Ondernemers in het Natuursteenbedrijf
NEPRO-PHARM	Nederlandse Vereninging van Fabrikanten van Pharmaceutische Producten	**NEVRA**	Nederlandse Vereniging van Groothandelaren in Rioleringsartikelen
NERATU	Groep Nederlandse Fabrieken van Radio-, Televisie- en Muziekapparatuur	**NEWO**	Nederlandse Electrotechnische Winkeliers Organisatie
NERBA	New England Road Builders' Association	**NEZC**	New England Zoological Club (U.S.A.)

NFA	National Federation of Anglers	**NFCU**	National Federation of Claimants Unions
NFA	National Farmers Association (Eire)	**NFCU**	National Federation of Construction Unions
NFA	National Fertilizer Association (U.S.A.)	**NFD**	National Federation of Drapers and Allied Trades, Ltd (Eire)
NFA	Norsk Forening for Automatisering		
NFAC	National Federation of Aerial Contractors Ltd	**NFDC**	National Federation of Demolition Contractors
NFAC	National Food and Agriculture Council (Philippines)	**NFDC**	National Fertilizer Development Centre (U.S.A.)
NFAIS	National Federation of Abstracting and Indexing Services (U.S.A.)	**NFDSP**	National Forum on Deafness and Speech Pathology (U.S.A.)
NFB	National Federation of the Blind of the United Kingdom	**NFE**	Nederlandse Vereniging van Fokkers van Edelpelsdieren
NFBB	Norsk Forening for Bolig-og Byplanlegging	**NFEA**	National Federated Electrical Association
NFBBB	Nationale Federatie Beroepsverenigingen van Aannemers van Begrafenissen van België	**NFEC**	National Foundation for Environmental Control (U.S.A.)
NFBC	National Film Board of Canada	**NFEGI**	National Federation of Engineering and General Ironfounders
NFBCa	National Film Bureau of Canada		
NFBF	Nationale Federatie van de Beroepsfotografie	**NFER**	National Foundation for Educational Research in England and Wales
NFBPM	National Federation of Builders and Plumbers Merchants	**NFETM**	National Federation of Engineers' Tool Manufacturers
NFBS	Committee for Co-operation between the Nordic Research Libraries	**NFF**	National Federation of Fishmongers
		NFF	National Froebel Foundation
NFBSS	National Federation of Bakery Students' Societies	**NFF**	Norges Farmaceutiske Förening
		NFF	Norges Farvehandlerforbund
NFBTE	National Federation of Building Trades Employers	**NFF**	Norske Fiskeredskapfabrikanters Förening
NFBTO	National Federation of Building Trade Operatives	**NFF**	Norges Fotografforbund
		NFF	Norske Forskningsbibliotekars Förening
NFC	National Freight Corporation	**NFF**	Norsk Fruktgrossisters Forbund
NFCA	National Federation of Community Associations	**NFF**	Norske Fysioterapeuters Forbund
		NFFA	National Frozen Food Association (U.S.A.)
NFCA	National Foster Care Association	**NFFC**	National Film Finance Corporation
NFCC	National Farm Chemurgic Council (U.S.A.)	**NFFF**	National Federation of Fish Friers
NFCDA	National Federation of Civil Defence Associations of Great Britain and the Commonwealth	**NFFMR**	Nordisk Förening för Medicinsk Radiologi (Finland)
NFCG	National Federation of Consumer Groups	**NFFPT**	National Federation of Fruit and Potato Trades, Ltd
NFCGA	National Federation of Constructional Glass Associations	**NFFQO**	National Federation of Freestone Quarry Owners
NFCI	National Federation of Clay Industries	**NFFTU**	National Federation of Furniture Trade Unions
NFCS	National Federation of Construction Supervisors		
NFCSIT	National Federation of Cold Storage and Ice Trades	**NFG**	Nordwestdeutsche Futtersaatbaugesellschaft
		NFGC	National Federation of Grain Cooperatives (U.S.A.)
NFCTA	National Federation of Corn Trade Associations (*now* GAFTA)	**NFGS**	National Federation of Gramophone Societies
NFCTC	National Foundry Craft Training Centre		

NFHO	National Federation of Homophile Organisations
NFHS	National Federation of Housing Societies
NFI	National Federation of Ironmongers (*now* BHF)
NFI	National Fisheries Institute (U.S.A.)
NFI	Naturfreunde-Internationale
NFIK	Norsk Forening for Industriell Kvalitetskontroll (Norway)
NFIKB	Nationale Federatie der Immobilienkamers van België
NFIM	Norges Forbund for Internasjonale Møbeltransporter
NFIMA	Non-Ferrous Ingot Metal Institute (U.S.A.)
NFIP	National Foundation for Infantile Paralysis (U.S.A.)
NFIR	National Federation of Indian Railwaymen
NFISM	National Federation of Iron and Steel Merchants
NFJM	National Foundation for Junior Museums (U.S.A.)
NFKHNB	Nationale Federatie der Kamers voor Handel en Nijverheid van België
NFL	Norske Fotoimportørers Landsforbund
NFLA	National Farm Loan Association (U.S.A.)
NFLSVN	National Front for the Liberation of South Vietnam
NFLV	National Federation of Licensed Victuallers
NFMA	National Fireplace Makers Association
NFMP	National Federation of Master Painters and Decorators of England and Wales
NFMPS	National Federation of Master Printers in Scotland
NFMR	National Foundation for Metabolic Research (U.S.A.)
NFMR	Norsk Forening for Medicinsk Radiologi
NFMS	National Federation of Music Societies
NFMSLCE	National Federation of Master Steeplejacks and Lightning Conductor Engineers
NFMTA	National Federation of Meat Traders Associations
NFMWC	National Federation of Master Window Cleaners
NFNL	Nationale Fisiese Navorsingslaboratorium (South Africa)
NFO	National Freight Organization (U.S.A.)
NFO	Nederlandse Federatie van Onderwijsvakorganisaties
NFO	Nederlandse Fruittelersorganisatie
NFOAPA	National Federation of Old Age Pensioners Associations
NFOO	National Federation of Owner Occupiers Associations
NFP	Nederlandse Federatie voor de Handel in Pootaardappelen
NFPA	National Fire Protection Association (U.S.A.)
NFPA	National Foster Parents Association
NFPA	National Flaxseed Processors Association (U.S.A.)
NFPC	National Federation of Plastering Contractors
NFPDC	National Federation of Painting and Decorating Contractors
NFPDHE	National Federation of Plumbers and Domestic Heating Engineers
NFPHC	National Federation of Permanent Holiday Camps, Ltd
NFPO	National Federation of Property Owners
NFPTA	National Federation of Parent Teacher Associations (*now* NCPTA)
NFPW	National Federation of Professional Workers
NFR	Statens Naturvetenskapliga Forskningsråd
NFRC	National Federation of Roofing Contractors
NFRI	National Food Research Institute (South Africa)
NFRN	National Federation of Retail Newsagents, Booksellers and Stationers
NFRR	Norsk Forening af Rådgivende Rasjonaliseringsfirmaer
NFS	Norsk Fysisk Selskap
NFSA	National Federation of Sea Anglers
NFSA	National Fire Services Association (*now* BFSA)
NFSAIS	National Federation of Science Abstracting and Indexing Services (U.S.A.)
NFSH	National Federation of Spiritual Healers
NFSO	National Federation of Site Operators
NFSWMM	National Federation of Scale and Weighing Machine Manufacturers
NFT	National Federation of Textiles (U.S.A.)
NFTA	National Federation of Taxicab Associations
NFTA	National Fillings Trades Associations

NFTC	National Foreign Trade Council (U.S.A.)	**NGPR**	Nederlands Genootschap voor Public Relations
NFTF	Norges Kvalitetstekmiske Forening		
NFTMS	National Federation of Terrazzo-Mosaic Specialists	**NGRC**	National Greyhound Racing Club
		NGRH	Nationale Groepering van Ruwe Huiden
NFU	National Farmers' Union	**NGRI**	National Geophysical Research Institute (India)
NFUDCL	National Farmers Union Development Co., Ltd		
		NGRS	National Greyhound Racing Society of Great Britain (*now* NGRC)
NFUS	National Farmers Union of Scotland		
NFVB	Nederlandse Federatie van Verenigingen van Bedrijfspluimveehouders	**NGS**	National Geographic Society (U.S.A.)
		NGSDC	National Geophysical and Solar-Terrestrial Data Center (NOAA)
NFVL	National Federatie van Verenigingen van Laboratorium-assistenten (Belgium)		
		NGSF	Norges Glass-og Stentøihandleres Forbund
NFVT	National Federation of Vehicle Trades	**NGSI**	National Geographical Society of India
NFWB	Nederlandse Federatie van Werkgevers-Organisaties in het Bontbedrijf	**NGT**	National Guild of Telephonists
		NGTE	National Gas Turbine Establishment
NFWG	National Federation of Wholesale Grocers and Provision Merchants	**NGTM**	National Guild of Transport Managers
		NGU	Norges Geologiske Undersökelse
NFWIR	National Federation of Women's Institutes of Rhodesia	**NGUT**	National Group of Unit Trusts
		NGV	Nederlandse Geologische Vereniging
NFWI	National Federation of Women's Institutes	**NGV**	Nederlands Genootschap van Vertalers
NFWPM	National Federation of Wholesale Poultry Merchants	**NGZ**	Naturforschende Gesellschaft in Zürich
		NH	Norges Herredsforbund
NFYFC	National Federation of Young Farmers' Clubs	**NHA**	National Hairdressers' Association
		NHA	National Horse Association of Great Britain
NGA	National Graphical Association	**NHA**	National Housewives Association
NGAA	Natural Gasoline Association of America	**NHBRC**	National House-Builders Registration Council
NGB	National Garden Bureau (U.S.A.)		
NGB	Naturforschende Gesellschaft in Bern	**NHC**	National Health Council (U.S.A.)
NGC	National Guild of Co-operators	**NHC**	Nederlandse Hardevezelconventie
NGC	Nederlands Graancentrum	**NHDAA**	National Home Demonstration Agents Association (U.S.A.)
NGCAA	National Golf Clubs Advisory Association		
NGEA	National Gastroenterological Association (U.S.A.)	**NHF**	National Hairdressers Federation
		NHF	Norges Handelstands Forbund
NGF	National Grocers Federation	**NHG**	Neue Helvetische Gesellschaft
NGF	Norges Grossistforbund	**NHG**	Natuurhistorisch Genootschap im Limburg
NGF	Norsk Gartnerforbund	**NHG**	Nederlands Historisch Genootschap
NGI	Norsk Gerontologisk Institutt	**NHG**	Nederlands Huisarten Genootschap
NGIZ	Nederlandsch Genootschap voor Internationale Zaken	**NHGA**	National Hang Gliding Association
		NHIC	National Home Improvement Council
NGL	Nederlands Genootschap van Leraren	**NHIF**	Norske Håndverks- og Industribedrifters Forbund
NGL	Norsk Galvano-Teknisk Landsforening		
NGL	Norsk Grafisk Leverandørforening		
NGMB	Nigeria Groundnuts Marketing Board	**NHK**	Japan Broadcasting Corporation
NGO	Non-Governmental Organizations	**NHM**	Nederlandse Heidemaatschappij
NGO/OPI	Executive Committee of Non-Governmental Organizations Associated with the United Nations Office of Public Information	**NHMRCA**	National Health and Medical Research Council of Australia

NHOS	National House Owners Society	**NIBIN**	Netherlands Instituut voor Beleids-Informatie
NHPLO	NATO Hawk Production and Logistics Organization	**NIBS**	Nippon Institute for Biological Science (Japan)
NHR	Nederlandse Huishoudraad	**NIC**	National Illumination Committee of Great Britain
NHRF	Norsk Hotell- og Restaurantforbund		
NHRV	Nederlandse Handelsreizigers en Handelsagent-Vereniging	**NICAMAR**	Compañía Nicaraguense Mercantil e Industrial de Ultramar
NHS	National Health Service	**NICAP**	National Investigations Committee on Aerial Phenomena (U.S.A.)
NHS	Nordiska Handelsarbetsgivare-Föreningarnas Samarbetskommité	**NICB**	National Industrial Conference Board (U.S.A.)
NHSB	National Highway Safety Bureau (U.S.A.)	**NICD**	National Institute of Cleaning and Dyeing (U.S.A.)
NHSS	National Home Study Council (U.S.A.)		
NHTPC	National Housing and Town Planning Council	**NICD**	National Institute of Community Development (India)
NI	Numismatics International (U.S.A.)	**NICD**	National Institute of Communicable Diseases (India)
NIA	National Irrigation Administration (Philippines)	**NICE**	National Institute of Ceramic Engineers (U.S.A.)
NIAA	National Institute of Animal Agriculture (U.S.A.)	**NICEC**	National Institute of Careers, Education and Counselling
NIAB	National Institute of Agricultural Botany	**NICEIC**	National Inspection Council for Electrical Installation Contracting
NIAE	National Institute of Adult Education		
NIAE	National Institute of Agricultural Engineering	**NICEM**	National Information Centre for Educational Media (U.S.A.)
NIAESS	National Institute of Agricultural Engineering Scottish Station	**NICHA**	Northern Ireland Chest and Heart Association
NIAG	NATO Industrial Advisory Group	**NICHD**	National Institute for Child Health and Human Development (of NIH)
NIAH	National Institute of Animal Health (Japan)		
NIAI	National Institute of Animal Industry (Japan)	**NICIA**	Northern Ireland Coal Importers Association
NIAID	National Institute of Allergy and Infectious Diseases (of NIH) (U.S.A.)	**NICSO**	NATA Integrated Communications System Organization
NIAM	Nederlands Instituut Agrarisch Markton-derzoek	**NICSS**	Northern Ireland Council of Social Services
NIAMAC	Chambre Nationale des Négociants en Gros et Agents Généraux en Machines de Fabrication, Matériel d'Émouteillage, d'Emballage et de Conditionnement pour Toutes Industries (Belgium)	**NICSSE**	National Information Centre for Social Science Education (Australia)
		NID	National Institute of Design (India)
		NIDA	National Institute of Development Administration (Thailand)
NIAMD	National Institute of Arthritis and Metabolic Diseases (of NIH) (U.S.A.)	**NIDB**	Nigerian Industrial Development Bank
NIAS	National Institute of Agricultural Sciences (Japan)	**NIDC**	Nepal Industrial Development Corporation
NIB	Nordic Investment Bank (Finland)	**NIDC**	Northern Ireland Development Council
NIBE	Nederlands Instituut voor het Bank- en Effectenbedrijf	**NIDER**	Netherlands Institute for Documentation and Registration
NIBEM	Nationaal Instituut voor Brouwgerst, Mout en Bier	**NIDFA**	National Independent Drama Festivals Association
NIBID	National Investment Bank for Industrial Development (Greece)	**NIDI**	Nederlands Interuniversitair Demografisch Instituut

NIDIG	Netherlands Instituut van Directeuren en Ingenieurs van Gemeentewerken
NIDO	Nationaal Instituut voor Diergeneeskundige Onderzoek (Belgium)
NIDOC	National Information and Documentation Centre (Egypt)
NIECE	Nigerian International Educational and Cultural Exchange Centre
NIEF	National Ironfounding Employers Federation
NIESR	National Institute of Economic and Social Research
NIF	Nordic Institute of Folklore (Finland)
NIF	Nordiska Institutet for Fargforskning
NIF	Norske Ingeniörforening (Norway)
NIFES	National Industrial Fuel Efficiency Service
NIFOR	National Information Office, Poona (India)
NIFOR	Nigerian Institute for Oil Palm Research
NIGC	National Insurance and Guarantee Corporation
NIGERCAP	Société Nigérienne de Diffusion d'Appareils Électriques
NIGERLEC	Société Nigérienne d'Électricité
NIGER-TOUR	Société Nigérienne pour le Développement du Tourisme et de l'Hôtellerie
NIGGECIBA	Société Nigérienne de Génie Civil et Bâtiment
NIGMS	National Institute of General Medical Services (of NIH)
NIGP	National Institute of Governmental Purchasing (U.S.A.)
NIH	National Institute of Hardware
NIH	National Institutes of Health (of HEW) (U.S.A.)
NIHAE	National Institute of Health Administration and Education (India)
NIHJ	National Institutes of Health, Japan
NII	Netherlands Industrial Institute
NIIP	National Institute of Industrial Psychology
NIIR	National Institute of Industrial Research (Nigeria)
NIJSI	Vereniging de Nederlandse Ijzer- en Staal-producerende Industrie
NIL	Nederlands Instituut voor Lastechniek
NIL	Norske Interiørarkitekters Landsforening
NILCO	National Instituut voor de Landbouwstudie in Congo
NILFO	Norsk Innkjøpslederforbund

NILI	Nederlands Instituut voor Landbouwkundige Ingenieurs
NILN	Navorsingsinstituut vir die Leernywerheid (South Africa)
NILU	Norsk Institutt for Luftforskning
NIM	National Institute of Metallurgy (South Africa)
NIMA	Nederlands Instituut voor Marketing
NIMA	Northern Ireland Ministry of Agriculture
NIMAWO	Nederlands Instituut voor Maatschapplijk Werk Onderzoek
NIMD	National Institute of Management Development (Egypt)
NIMH	National Institute of Medical Health (U.S.A.)
NIMH	National Institute of Medical Herbalists
NIMH	National Institute of Mental Health (of NIH) (U.S.A.)
NIMO	Nederlands Instituut voor Maatschappelijke Opbouw
NIMR	National Institute for Medical Research
NIMRA	National Industrial Materials Recovery Association
NINB	National Institute of Neurology and Blindness
NINDB	National Institute of Neurological Diseases and Blindness (U.S.A.)
NINDS	U.S. National Institute of Neurological Diseases and Strokes
NIO	National Institute of Oceanography
NIOC	National Iranian Oil Company
NIOM	Nordisk Institut for Odontologisk Materialprøvning
NIOPR	Nigerian Institute for Oil Palm Research
NIOSH	National Institute for Occupational Safety and Health (U.S.A.)
NIOZ	Nederlands Instituut voor Onderzoek der Zee
NIP	National Institute of Psychology (Iran)
NIP	Nederlands Instituut van Psycholegen
NIPA	National Institute of Public Administration (Pakistan, Zambia)
NIPDOK	Nippon Dokumentesyon Kyokai
NIPG	Nederlands Instituut voor Praeventieve Geneeskunde
NIPH	National Institute of Poultry Husbandry
NIPL	Nederlands Instituut voor Personeelsleiding
NIPO	Nederlands Instituut voor de Publieke Opinie en het Marktonderzoek

NIPR	National Institute for Personnel Research (South Africa)	**NITR**	Nigerian Institute of Trypanosomiasis Research
NIR	Belgisch Nationaal Instituut voor Radio-Omroep	**NIV**	Nederlands Instituut voor Volksvoeding
		NIVA	Norsk Institutt for Vannforskning
NIRC	National Industrial Relations Court	**NIVAG**	Nederlands Instituut van Aannemers Groot-bedrijf
NIRD	National Institute for Research in Dairying		
NIRI	National Information Research Institute (U.S.A.)	**NIVB**	Navorsingsinstituut vir die Visserybedryf (South Africa)
NIRIA	Nederlandse Ingenieursvereniging	**NIVE**	Netherlands Institute for Efficiency
NIRNS	National Institute for Research in Nuclear Science	**NIVNO**	Nasionale Instituut vir Vuurpylnavorsing en -ontwikkeling (South Africa)
NIRO	Nederlandsche Indisch Instituut voor Rub-beronderzoek	**NIVRA**	Nederlands Instituut van Registeraccoun-tants
NIRR	National Institute for Road Research (South Africa)	**NIVV**	Nederlands Instituut voor Vredesvraag-stukken
NIRRD	National Institute for Rocket Research and Development (South Africa)	**NIWO**	Stichting Nederlandsche Internationale Wegvervoer Organisatie
NIRS	National Institute of Radiological Sciences (Japan)	**NIWR**	National Institute for Water Research (South Africa)
NIRT	National Iranian Radio and Television	**NIWU**	National Industrial Workers Union (U.S.A.)
NIS	Nordiska Ingenjörssamfundet	**NIZO**	Nederlandsche Instituut voor Zuivelon-derzoek
NISCON	National Industrial Safety Conference (*of* ROSPA)		
		NJ	Norsk Journalistlag
NISC	National Industrial Space Committee	**NJ**	Norges Juristforbund
NISEE	National Information Service for Earthquake Engineering (U.S.A.)	**NJA**	National Jewellers' Association
		NJAC	National Joint Advisory Council
NISER	Nigerian Institute for Social and Economic Research	**NJBG**	Nederlandse Jeugdbond ter Bestudering van de Geschiedenis
NISI	National Institute of Sciences of India	**NJC**	National Joint Council for Local Authorities' Administrative, Professional, Technical and Clerical Services
NISRA	National Industrial Salvage and Recovery Association		
NIST	National Institute of Science and Technology (Philippines)	**NJCBI**	National Joint Council for the Building Industry Administrative Council
NISTEX	National Industrial Safety Trade Exhibition (*of* ROSPA)	**NJCC**	National Joint Consultative Committee of Architects, Quantity Surveyors and Builders
NISO	National Industrial Safety Organisation	**NJCEI**	National Joint Council for the Exhibition Industry
NISW	National Institute for Social Work		
NISWT	National Institute for Social Work Training	**NJF**	Nordic Federation of Journalists
		NJF	Nordiske Jordbrugsforskeres Förening
NITA	Nicophilic Institute of Tobacco Antiquarians	**NJHF**	Norges Jernvarehandleres Forbund
NITCs	National Information Transfer Centres	**NJIC**	National Joint Industrial Council for Gas Industry
NITEX	Société Nigérienne des Textiles		
NITHO	Nederlands Instituut voor Toegepast Huishoudkundig Onderzoek	**NJLS**	Norges Jordskriftedommer- og Landmåler-samband
NITO	Norges Ingeniorörganisasjon	**NJN**	Nederlandse Jeugdbond voor Natuurstudie
NITR	National Institute for Telecommunications Research (South Africa)	**NJPA**	New Jersey Pharmaceutical Association (U.S.A.)

JSHS	New Jersey State Horticultural Society (U.S.A.)	**NLA**	National Lime Association (U.S.A.)
		NLA	Nigerian Library Association
JSPE	New Jersey Society of Professional Engineers (U.S.A.)	**NLB**	National Library for the Blind
		NLC	National Liberal Club
JU	Nordiska Järnvägsmanna-Unionen	**NLC**	National Liberation Council (Ghana)
JV	Nederlandse Juristen-Vereniging	**NLCA**	Norwegian Lutheran Church of America
JV	Nederlandse Vereniging van Journalisten	**NLCIF**	National Light Castings Ironfounders' Federation
KA	Nordiska Kontaktorganet för Atomenergifragor		
		NLF	National Liberal Federation
KB	Nederlandse Kermisbond	**NLF**	National Liberation Front (South Vietnam)
KB	Nordiska Kommittén för Byggbestammelser	**NLF**	Norges Lastebileier-Forbund
KE	Nordiskt Kollegium för Ekologi	**NLF**	Norske Litotrykkeriers Forening
KF	Norges Kjott og Flesksentral	**NLH**	Norges Landbrukshogskole
KF	Norsk Kiropraktor Forening	**NLHE**	National Laboratory for Higher Education (U.S.A.)
KF	Norsk Kommunalteknisk Forening		
KF	Norsk Korrosjonsteknisk Forening	**NLL**	National Lending Library for Science and Technology
KG	Nordiska Kommissionen för Geodesi		
KI	Norges Kjemiske Industrigruppe	**NLM**	National Library of Medicine (U.S.A.)
KI	Növényvédelmi Kutató Intézet	**NLM**	Nederlandse Luchtvaart Maatschappij
KI	Vereniging de Nederlandse Koeltechnische Industrie	**NLMA**	National Lumber Manufacturers Association (U.S.A.)
KIM	Nederlands Kali-import Mij	**NLMC**	National Labour Management Council
KJ	Nordiska Kontaktorganet för Jordbruks-forskning	**NLMGB**	National Liberation Movement of Guinea-Bissau
KK	Nordiska Kulturkommisionen	**NLNE**	National League of Nursing Education (U.S.A.)
KK	Nordkalottkommittén		
KL	Norges Kooperative Landsforening	**NLO**	National Liberal Organisation
KLB	Noord-Nederlandse Cooperatieve Eierhandel	**NLOGF**	National Lubricating Oil and Grease Federation
KLF	Norges Kolonial- og Landhandelforbund		
KOV	Nederlands Katholiek Ondernemers Verbond	**NLPGA**	National LP-Gas Association (U.S.A.)
KP	Norges Kommunistiske Parti	**NLR**	National Lucht en Ruimtevaartlaboratorium
KS	Nederlandse Kastelenstichting	**NLRB**	National Labour Relations Board (U.S.A.)
KS	Norsk Keramisk Selskap	**NLRY**	Nordic Liberal and Radical Youth (Sweden)
KS	Norsk Khemisk Selskap	**NLS**	Nordiska Läraorganisationernas Samrad
KT	Nordiska Kommittén för Trafiksäkerhets-forskning	**NLSB**	National Land Survey Board (Sweden)
		NLTF	Norsk Landbruksteknisk Forening
KTF	Nordiska Kommittén för Transport-ekonomisk Forskning	**NLU**	Naturvåordsverkets Limnologiska Under-sökning
KTF	Norges Kvalitetstekniske Forening	**NLVF**	Norges Landbruksvitenskapelige Forskningsrad (Norway)
KV	Nederlands Katholiek Vakverbond		
KV	Nordiska Kommittén för Vägtrafiklagstiftung	**NLYL**	National League of Young Liberals
KVT	Nederlandsche Katholieke Vereniging van Ondernemers in de Textielhandel	**NM**	Norsk Musikerforbund
		NMA	National Medical Association (U.S.A.)
KWV	Nederlands Katholiek Werkgevers Verband	**NMAB**	Natural Materials Advisory Board of the National Academy of Sciences (U.S.A.)
L	Norsk Lektorlag		

NMAC	National Medical Audiovisual Center (U.S.A.)	**NMSSA**	Nato Maintenance Supply Services Agency
NMBLA	North Midland Branch of the Library Association	**NMTAS**	National Milk Testing and Advisory Service
NMBS	Nationale Maatschappij e Belgische Spoorwegen	**NMTBA**	National Machine Tool Builders' Association (U.S.A.)
NM–BYGG	Scandinavian Committee on Materials Research and Testing, Subcommittee on Building	**NMTF**	National Market Traders Federation
		NMTFA	National Master Tile Fixers' Association
		NMTS	National Milk Testing Service (U.S.A.)
NMC	National Marketing Council	**NMV**	Nederlandse Malacologische Vereniging
NMC	National Mastitis Council (USA)	**NMWA**	National Mineral Wool Association (U.S.A.)
NMCA	National Meat Canners Association (U.S.A.)	**NNA**	Nigerian National Alliance
NMDC	National Mineral Development Corporation (India)	**NNA**	Norwegian Nurses Association
		NNBOB	Nieuwe Nederlandse Bond van Ondernemers in het Bouwbedrijf
NMERI	National Mechanical Engineering Research Institute (South Africa)	**NNC**	Noord-Nederlandse Co-operatieve
NMF	Norges Markedføringsforbund	**NNDC**	New Nigeria Development Company
NMF	Norsk Meteorologforening	**NNDP**	Nigerian National Democratic Party
NMFS	National Marine Fisheries Service (*of* NOAA) (U.S.A.)	**NNF**	Norsk Nopatisk Forening
		NNF	Northern Nurses Federation (Sweden)
NMGC	National Marriage Guidance Council	**NNGA**	Northern Nut Growers Association (U.S.A.)
NMHC	National Materials Handling Centre	**NNI**	Netherlands Normalisatie-Instituut
NMHF	Norges Musikkhandlerforbund	**NNIL**	Northern Nigeria Investments Ltd
NMHRA	National Mobile Homes Residents Association	**NNLC**	Ngwane National Liberatory Congress (Swaziland)
NMIA	National Meteorological Institute of Athens (Greece)	**NNML**	Norske Naturhistoriske Museers Landsforbund
NMK	Norse Marconi Kompani	**NNP**	Vereniging 'De Nederlandse Nieuwsbladpers'
NMKL	Nordisk Metodik-Komité for Levnedsmidler	**NNPA**	National Newspaper Publishers Association (U.S.A.)
NML	National Federation of Norwegian Milk Producers	**NNRC**	Neutral Nations Repatriation Commission
NML	National Metallurgical Laboratory (India)	**NNRI**	National Nutrition Research Institute (South Africa)
NML	Norske Melkeprodusenters Landsforbund	**NNRO**	Norske Nasjonalkomite for Rasjonell Organisasjon
NML	Norske Murmestres Landsforening		
NMLF	Norsk Maling- og Lakkteknisk Forening	**NNV**	Nederlandse Natuurkundige Vereniging
NMLL	Norsk Musikklaereres Landsforbund	**NNV**	Norges Naturvernforband
NMMA	National Macaroni Manufacturers' Association (U.S.A.)	**NOAA**	National Oceanic and Atmospheric Administration (U.S.A.)
NMOC	National Marketing Organisation Committee	**NOAACP**	National Organization of African, Asian and Caribbean People
NMPA	National Marine Paint Association	**NOB**	Nationale Organisatie voor het Beroeps-goederenvervoer Wegtransport
NMPC	National Milk Publicity Council		
NMPF	National Milk Producers Federation (U.S.A.)	**NOBIN**	Stichting Nederlands Orgaan voor de Bevordering van de Informatie-verzorging
NMS	National Malaria Society (U.S.A.)		
NMS	Norske Meieriers Salgs Sentral	**NOCI**	Nederlandse Organisatie voor Chemische Informatie
NMS	Norwegian Dairies Sales Centre		
NMSS	National Multiple Sclerosis Society (U.S.A.)	**NOCIL**	National Organic Chemical Industries (India)

NOCOCA	Nouvelle Confiserie Camerounaise
NODA	National Operatic and Dramatic Association
NODC	National Oceanographic Data Centre (U.S.A.)
NOEM	Netherlands Oil and Gas Equipment Manufacturers
NOF	Nordisk Odontologisk Forening
NOFAKI	Norges Farmasoytisk-Kjemiske Industriforening
NOFI	National Oil Fuel Institute (U.S.A.)
NOFM	Nederlandse Overzeese Financierings-Maatschappij
NOFTIG	Nordic Association of Applied Geophysics (Sweden)
NÖG	Nationalökonomische Gesellschaft (Austria)
NOG	Nederlandse Oogheelkundig Gezelschap
NOGA	Nederlandse Organisatie van Glasassuradeuren
NoHaKa	Nederlandse Organisatie van Handelaren in de Kantoormachinebranche
NOIC	National Oceanographic Instrumentation Board (U.S.A.)
NOIL	Naval Ordnance Inspection Laboratory
NOISE	National Organization to Ensure a Sound-controlled Environment (U.S.A.)
NOJFU	Nordiska Järnvägars Forsknings-och Utvecklingsråd
NOK	Nordisk Okonomisk Kvaegavl
NOKIL	Norske Kinoleverandørers Landsforbund
NOKYO	Union of Agricultural Cooperatives (Japan)
NOL	Nederlandse Organisatie van Loonconfectionnairs
NOLPE	National Organisation on Legal Problems of Education (U.S.A.)
NOMA	National Office Management Association (U.S.A.)
NOMI	Norges Medisinalindustris Felleskontor
NOMOFO	Norske Motoroverhalings-verksteders Forbund
NONAS	Negros Occidental National Agricultural School (Philippines)
NOP	Nederlandse Organisatie van Pluimveehouders
NOPA	National Office Products Association (U.S.A.)
NOPHN	National Organisation for Public Health Nursing (U.S.A.)
NOPPMB	Nigeria Oil Palm Produce Marketing Board
NOPWC	National Old Peoples Welfare Council
NORAD	North American Air Defence
NORAD	Norwegian Agency for International Development
NORC	National Opinion Research Centre (U.S.A.)
NORCOFEL	Normalisation et Commercialisation des Fruits et Légumes (International)
NORDAF	Northern Federation of Advertisers Association (Sweden)
NORDEK	Organisation for Nordic Economic Cooperation
NORDEL	Organ för Nordiskt Elkraftsamarbete
NORDINFO	Nordic Council for Scientific Information and Research Libraries (Finland)
NORD-FORSK	Nordiska Forskningsdelegationen
NORD-FORSK	Nordiska Samarbets-organisationen för Teknisk-Naturvetens-kaplig Forskning
NORDGU	Nordic Council of the International Good Templar Youth Federation
NORDICOM	Nordic Documentation Centre for Mass Communication Research
NORDITA	Nordisk Institut för Teoretisk Atomfysik
NORD-PACK	International Packaging Fair
NORDPLAN	Nordic Institute for Social Planning
NORDPLAN	Nordic Institute for Urban and Regional Planning
NORDREFO	Nordiska Arbetsgruppen för Regionalpolitisk Forskning
NORG	Nederlandse Organisatie voor de Radio Groothandel
NORM	National Optimism Revival Movement
NORS	Norwegian Operational Research Society
NORSAM	Nordic Organization for the Care of the Old
NORVEN	Comisión Venezolana de Normas Industriales
NORWAID	Norwegian Aid Society for Refugees and International Development
NOS	Joint Board for the Nordic Research Councils in the National Sciences
NOSA	National Occupational Safety Association (South Africa)
NOSALF	Scandinavian Association for Research on Latin America
NOS-M	Nordiska Samarbertsnämnden för Medicinsk Forskning

NOSO	Norsk Sosionomforbund
NOSOCO	Nouvelle Société Commerciale Sénégalaise
NOSON-TRAM	Nouvelle Société Nationale des Transports Mauritaniens
NOT	Naczelna Organizacja Techniczna w Polsce
NOTBA	National Opthalmic Treatment Board Association
NOTU	Nederlandse Organisatie van Tijdschrift Uitgevers
NOU	Nederlandse Ornithologische Unie
NOV	Nederlandse Orthopaedische Vereniging
NOVA-TRANS	Société Nouvelle d'Exploitation de Transports Combinés
NOVIB	Netherlands Organization for International Development Corporation
NOVO	Nederlandse Organisatie van Oliehandelaren
NOVOK	Nederlandse Organisatie van Olie- en Kolenhandelaren
NOW	National Organization for Women (U.S.A.)
NOWEA	Nordwestdeutsche Ausstellungs-Gesellschaft
NP	Norsk Presseforbund
NPA	National Packaging Association (Australia)
NPA	National Parks Association (U.S.A.)
NPA	National Petroleum Association (U.S.A.)
NPA	National Pigeon Association
NPA	National Planning Association (U.S.A.)
NPA	National Production Authority (U.S.A.)
NPA	Newspaper Publishers Association
NPAC	National Project in Agricultural Communication (U.S.A.)
NPACI	National Production Advisory Council on Industry (U.S.A.)
NPAV	Nederlandse Patholoog Anatomen Vereniging
NPBA	National Pig Breeders' Association
NPC	National Parks Commission
NPC	National Patent Council (U.S.A.)
NPC	National Peace Council
NPC	National Peach Council (U.S.A.)
NPC	National Peanut Council (U.S.A.)
NPC	National Petroleum Council (U.S.A.)
NPC	National Pharmaceutical Council (U.S.A.)
NPC	National Potato Council (U.S.A.)
NPC	NATO Parliamentarians' Conference
NPC	Northern Peoples Congress (Nigeria)

NPCA	National Pest Control Association (U.S.A.)
NPCC	National Projects Construction Corporation (India)
NPD	Nationaldemokratische Partei Deutschlands
NPD	Nuclear Physics Division (*of* SRC)
NPDMC	National Property Development and Management Company (Tanzania)
NPF	Nederlandse Pluimvee Federatie
NPF	Norske Patentingeniørers Forening
NPF	Norsk Plastforening
NPF	Norsk Psykologforening
NPFA	National Playing Fields Association
NPFC	Northwest Pacific Fisheries Commission
NPFI	National Plant Food Institute
NPFSC	North Pacific Fur Seal Commission
NPG	Nuclear Planning Group (NATO)
NPI	Norsk Produktivitetsinstitut
NPIP	National Poultry Improvement Plant (U.S.A.)
NPL	National Physical Laboratory
NPL	Nederlandse Vereniging voor Produktieleiding
NPL	Norske Pelsskinneksportørers
NPL	Norske Papirhandlers Landsforbund
NPL	Norsk Planteskolelag
NPO	Nederlandse Pluimvee Organisatie
NPPF	National Poultry Producers Federation (U.S.A.)
NPPTB	National Pig Progeny Testing Board
NPRA	National Petroleum Refiners Association
NPRCG	Nuclear Public Relations Contact Group (Italy)
NPRFCA	National Petroleum Radio Frequency Co-ordinating Association (U.S.A.)
NPRL	National Physical Research Laboratory (South Africa)
NPRS	Norske Public Relations Klubb
NPS	National Philatelic Society
NPS	National Pony Society
NPTA	National Paper Trade Association (U.S.A.)
NPU	National Pharmaceutical Union
NPV	Nederlandse Planteziektenkundige Vereniging
NPVLA	National Paint, Varnish and Lacquer Association (U.S.A.)

NPWA	National Pure Water Association
NQBA	National Quality Bacon Association
NRA	National Reclamation Association (U.S.A.)
NRA	National Recreation Association (U.S.A.)
NRA	National Renderers Association (Italy)
NRA	National Rifle Association
NRA	National Rounders Association
NRAC	National Research Advisory Council (New Zealand)
NRAC	National Rural Advisory Council (Australia)
NRAO	National Radio Astronomy Observatory (U.S.A.)
NRB	Natural Resources Board (Rhodesia)
NRC	National Redemption Council (Ghana)
NRC	National Reformation Council (Sierra Leone)
NRC	National Research Council (Canada etc.)
NRC	National Research Council (U.S.A.)
NRC	Niger River Commission
NRCA	Natural Resources Council of America
NRCC	National Republican Congressional Committee (U.S.A.)
NRCD	National Reprographic Centre for Documentation
NRCP	National Research Council of the Philippines
NRCST	National Referral Center for Science and Technology (Library of Congress) (U.S.A.)
NRDB	Natural Rubber Development Association (Malaysia)
NRDC	National Research Development Corporation
NRESA	National Rural and Environmental Studies Association (*now* NAEE)
NRF	Norske Radiofabrikanters Forbund
NRF	Norges Rutebileierforbund
NRFF	National Research Foundation for Fertility (U.S.A.)
NRHA	National Roller Hockey Association
NRHC	National Rivers and Harbours Congress (U.S.A.)
NRIC	National Reserves Investigation Committee
NRIMS	National Research Institute for Mathematical Sciences (South Africa)
NRIND	National Research Institute for Nutritional Diseases (South Africa)
NRIO	National Research Institute for Oceanology (South Africa)
NRIOD	National Research Institute for Occupational Diseases (South Africa)
NRK	Norsk Rikskringkasting
NRL	Naval Research Laboratory (U.S.A.)
NRL	Nelson Research Laboratory
NRL	Norske Radio/TV-handleres Landsforbund
NRL	Norske Rørleggerbedrifters Landsforening
NRL	Nutrition Research Laboratory (India)
NRLA	Nordic Research Librarians' Association
NRLB	Northern Regional Library Bureau
NRLCC	Nordic Research Libraries' Committee of Co-operation
NRLM	National Research Laboratory of Metrology (Japan)
NRLO	National Agricultural Project Administration (U.S.A.)
NRLO	Nationale Raad voor Landbouwkundig Onderzoek
NRLSI	National Reference Library of Science and Invention
NRMA	National Roads and Motorists Association (Australia)
NRMC	National Records Management Council (U.S.A.)
NRPRA	Natural Rubber Producers Research Association
NRPTAA	National Road Passenger Transport Ambulance Association
NRRA	Northern Regional Research Laboratory (U.S.A.)
NRRD	Natural Resources Research Division (*of* UNESCO)
NRS	Nederlandsche Rundvee Stamboek
NRSA	National Rural Studies Association (*now* NRESA)
NRU	Nederlandsche Radio-Unie
NS	Natural Sciences, Department of UNESCO
NS	Newcomen Society
NSA	National Sawmilling Association
NSA	National Sheep Association
NSA	National Shellfisheries Association (U.S.A.)
NSA	National Skating Association of Great Britain
NSA	National Slag Association (U.S.A.)
NSA	Nederlands Studenten Akkoord
NSA	Norsk Svineavlslag

NSA	Norwegian Gerontological Society
NSAA	National Sulphuric Acid Association
NSAC	National Society for Autistic Children
NSACS	National Society for Abolition of Cruel Sports
NSAE	National Society for Art Education
NSAS	National Smoke Abatement Society
NSB	Norwegian State Railways
NSBA	National Sheep Breeders' Association (*now* NSA)
NSBA	National Silica Brickmakers' Association
NSC	National Safety Council (U.S.A.)
NSC	National Security Council (U.S.A.)
NSC	National Seeds Corporation (India)
NSC	National Sporting Club
NSC	Nutrition Society of Canada
NSCA	National Safety Council of Australia
NSCA	National Society for Clean Air
NSCN	National Society of Children's Nurseries
NSCR	National Society for Cancer Relief
NSDAP	Nationalsozialistiche Deutsche Arbeiterpartie
NSDB	National Science Development Board (Philippines)
NSDC	National Space Development Centre (Japan)
NSDF	National Social Democratic Front (South Vietnam)
NSDO	National Seed Development Organisation
NSE	National Society of Epileptics
NSE	Nottingham Society of Engineers
NSEI	Norsk Selskap for Elektronisk Informasjonsbehandling
NSES	National Society of Electrotypers and Stereotypers
NSF	National Science Foundation (U.S.A.)
NSF	Nederlandse Sport Federatie
NSF	Nordens Skogsägareorganisationers Forbund
NSF	Norske Sivilokonomers Forening
NSF	Norsk Skuespillerforbund
NSF	Norsk Sykepleierforbund
NSFF	Norsk Selskap for Fotografi
NSFGA	Nova Scotia Fruit Growers Association (Canada)
NSFGB	National Ski Federation of Great Britain
NSFRC	National Soil and Fertiliser Research Committee (U.S.A.)
NSG	Norsk Sau- og Geitalslag
NSG	Nouvelle Société du Gabon
NSGA	National Sand and Gravel Association (U.S.A.)
NSGPMA	National Salt Glazed Pipe Manufacturers' Association
NSGT	Non-Self Governing Territories
NSH	Nouvelle Société Helvétique
NSHC	North Sea Hydrographic Commission
NSHEB	North of Scotland Hydro-Electric Board
NSI	National Sugar Institute (India)
NSI	Neytandasamtökin (Consumers Union of Iceland)
NSI	Norsk Senter for Informatik
NSIA	National Security Industrial Association (U.S.A.)
NSIC	National Small Industries Corporation (Tanzania)
NSICC	North Sea International Chart Commission
NSKO	Nationaal Secretariaat van het Katholiek Onderwijs
NSL	National Sporting League
NSL	Norske Skofabrikkers Landssammenslutning
NSLF	Norske Sporveiers og Lokalbaners Forening
NSMF	Norske Sykkel- og Mopedfabrikanters Forening
NSMHC	National Society for Mentally Handicapped Children
NSMP	National Society of Master Patternmakers
NSMR	National Society for Medical Research (U.S.A.)
NSNS	National Society of Non-Smokers
NSO	Nederlandse Sigarenwinkeliers-Organisatie
NSOA	Nouvelles Savonneries de l'Ouest Africain
NSODCC	North Sumatra Oil Development Corporation (Japan)
NSP	National Society of Painters
NSP	Nederlandse Sport Pers
NSP	Nylands Svenska Lantbruksproducentförbund
NSPA	Nova Scotia Pharmaceutical Association (Canada)
NSPB	National Society for the Prevention of Blindness (U.S.A.)

NSPCC	National Society for Prevention of Cruelty to Children
NSPE	National Society of Professional Engineers (U.S.A.)
NSPI	National Society for Programmed Instruction (U.S.A.)
NSPS	National Sweet Pea Society
NSPI	National Society for Performance and Instruction (U.S.A.)
NSPRI	Nigerian Stored Products Research Institute
NSPWSND	National Society of Provincial Wholesale Sunday Newspaper Distributors
NSR	Nederlandse Studenten Raad
NSR	Nordiska Skogsarbets-studieernas
NSRA	National Smallbore Rifle Association
NSRA	Nuclear Safety Research Association (Japan)
NSRB	National Security Resources Board (U.S.A.)
NSRC	National Shoe Retailers' Council
NSRDC	National Space Science Data Center (U.S.A.)
NSRF	Norges Statsautoriserte Revisorers Forening
NSRF	Nova Scotia Research Foundation (Canada)
NSRG	Northern Science Research Group (Canada)
NSRI	Nelspruit Subtropical Research Institute (South Africa)
NSS	National Society of Stenotypists
NSS	National Speleological Society (U.S.A.)
NSS	Nordisk Kommittén för Samordning av Elektriska Säkerhetsfragor
NSSA	National School Sailing Association
NSSE	National Society for the Study of Education (U.S.A.)
NSSL	National Seed Storage Laboratory (U.S.A.)
NSTA	National Science Teachers' Association (U.S.A.)
NSTC	National Shade Tree Conference (U.S.A.)
NSTU	Nova Scotia Teachers Union
NSVV	Nederlandse Stichting voor Verlichtings-kunde
NSWMA	National Soybean Crop Improvement Council (U.S.A.)
NT	Nederlands Textielinstituut
NTA	National Technical Association (U.S.A.)
NTA	National Trolleybus Association
NTA	National Tuberculosis Association (U.S.A.)
NTC	National Lending Library and the American National Translations Centre
NTC	Nigerian Tobacco Company
NTDA	National Trade Development Association
NTDA	National Tyre Distributors Association
NTDRA	National Tire Dealers and Retreaders Association (U.S.A.)
NTEA	National Tax Equality Association (U.S.A.)
NTEC	National Traction Engine Club
NTETA	National Traction Engine and Tractor Association
NTF	Nationalföreningen för Trafiksakerhetens Främjande
NTF	Norske Tannlaegeforening
NTFC	National Television Film Council (U.S.A.)
NTFI	Norsk Tekstil Forsknings Instituut
NTG	Nachrichten-Technische Gesellschaft im VDE
NTG	Nederlandse Tandheelkundig Genootschap
NTH	Norges Tekniske Hogskole
NTHF	Norske Turisthotellers Forening
NTI	Norsk Treteknisk Institutt
NTIAM	National Swedish Testing Institute for Agricultural Machinery
NTIS	National Technical Information Service (U.S.A.) (*formerly* CFSTI)
NTNF	Norges Teknisk-Naturvitenskapelige Forskningsråd
NTO	Nederlandse Tegelhandelaren-Organisatie
NTOG	National Tourist Organisation of Greece
NTPC	National Technical Planning Committee (Sudan)
NTPS	National Turf Protection Society
NTR	Nordiska Trafiksakerhetsrådet
NTR	Nordiska Träskyddsrädet
NTRL	National Telecommunications Research Laboratory (South Africa)
NTS	Nederlandsche Televisie Stichting
NTS	Nordiska Tidningsutgivarnas Samarbets-nämnd
NTS	Norske Trevarefabrikkers Servicekontor
NTSAC	New Technical and Scientific Activities Committee (*of* IEEE)
NTSB	National Transportation Safety Board (U.S.A.)
NTSC	National Television Systems Committee (U.S.A.)
NTSK	Nordiska Tele-Satelit Kommitten

NTT	Nippon Telegraph and Telephone Public Corporation (Japan)	**NUI**	National University of Ireland
NTTF	Norsk Tekstil Teknisk Forbund	**NUIW**	National Union of Insurance Workers
NTTK	Nordisk Turisttrafik-Kommitte	**NUJ**	National Union of Journalists
NTU	National Taiwan University (China)	**NULC**	National Union of Liberal Clubs
NTUC	Nigerian Trade Union Congress	**NULMW**	National Union of Lock and Metal Workers
NTUC	Nyasaland Trade Union Congress	**NULO**	National Union of Labour Organisers
NTZ	Nederlandse Vereniging voor de Teelt van en de Handel in Tuinbouwzaden	**NULV**	National Union of Licensed Victuallers
NUAAW	National Union of Agricultural and Allied Workers	**NULWAT**	National Union of Leather Workers and Allied Trades
NUAB	Italian National Union against Blasphemy	**NUM**	National Union of Manufacturers
NUAT	Nordisk Union for Alkoholfri Trafik	**NUM**	National Union of Mineworkers
NUAW	National Union of Agricultural Workers	**NUMA**	National Underwater and Marine Agency (U.S.A.)
NUBE	National Union of Bank Employees		
NUBSO	National Union of Boot and Shoe Operatives (*now* NUFLAT)	**NUMAB**	Nederlandsche Unie van Metaalgieterijen en Aanwerwante Bedrijven
NUCLEX	International Nuclear Industrial Fair and Technical Meetings	**NUMAS**	National Union of Manufacturers Advisory Service, Ltd
NUCO	National Union of Co-operative Officials (*now* NACO)	**NuMOV**	Nah- und Mittelost-Verein
		NUPBPW	National Union of Printing, Bookbinding and Paper Workers
NUCR	Nouvelle Union Corporative des Résineux	**NUPE**	National Union of Public Employees
NUCUA	National Union of Conservative and Unionist Associations	**NUR**	National Union of Railwaymen
		NURA	National Union of Ratepayers Associations
NUDBTW	National Union of Dyers, Bleachers and Textile Workers	**NURC**	National Union of Retail Confectioners (*now* RCA)
NUEA	National University Extension Association (U.S.A.)	**NURT**	National Union of Retail Tobacconists
		NUS	National Union of Seamen
NUF	Norges Urmakerforbund	**NUS**	National Union of Students of the United Kingdom
NUFAG	Northern Union of Farmers' Groups (Thailand)	**NUSAS**	National Union of South African Students
NUFCW	National Union of Funeral and Cemetery Workers	**NUSMW-CHDE**	National Union of Sheet Metal Workers Coppersmiths, Heating and Domestic Engineers
NUFFIC	Netherlands University Foundation for International Co-operation		
NUFLAT	National Union of the Footwear, Leather and Allied Trades	**NUSS**	National Union of School Students
		NUSS	National Union of Small Shopkeepers
NUFSO	National Union of Funeral Service Operators	**NUSUK**	National Union of Students of the United Kingdom
NUFTIC	Nuclear Fuels Technology Information Center (*of* ORNL) (U.S.A.)	**NUT**	National Union of Teachers
NUFTO	National Union of Furniture Trade Operatives	**NUTA**	National Union of Tanganyika Workers
		NUTAE	Nuffield Unit of Tropical Animal Ecology (East Africa)
NUGMW	National Union of General and Municipal Workers	**NUTG**	National Union of Townswomen's Guilds
NUGSAT	National Union of Gold, Silver and Allied Trades	**NUTGW**	National Union of Tailors and Garment Workers
NUHW	National Union of Hosiery Workers	**NUTI**	Nationale Unie der Technische Ingenieurs (Belgium)

NUTN	National Union of Trained Nurses
NUTS	National Union of Track Statisticians
NUU	Nordic Union of Young Conservatives
NUVB	National Union of Vehicle Builders
NUVO	Nederlandse Unie van Opticiens
NUVU	Nederlandse Unie van Ondernemers in het Uitvaartverzorgingsbedrijf
NUWA	National Unemployed Workers Association
NUWDAT	National Union of Wallcoverings, Decorative and Allied Trades
NUWWE	National Union of Water Works Employees
NVA	Nederlandsche Vereniging van Antiquaren
NVA	Nederlandse Vereniging van Assurantie-bezorgers
NVALA	National Viewers and Listeners Association
NVB	Nederlandse Vereniging voor Biochemie
NVBA	Nederlandse Vereniging van Bedrijfs-archivarissen
NVBB	Nationale Vereniging voor Beveiliging tegen Brand
NVBF	Nordiska Vetenskapliga Bibliotekarieför-bundet
NVBL	Nederlandse Vereniging ter Bevordering van het Levensverzekeringswezen
NVBV	Nationaal Verbond van Belgische Verpleeg-sters
NVC	Nederlands Verpakkingscentrum
NVC	Nederlands Vrouwen Comité
NVD	Nederlandse Vereniging van Diëtisten
NVE	Nederlandse Vereniging voor Ergonomie
NVEV	Nederlandse Vrouwen Electriciteits-vereniging
NVEW	Nederlandse Vereniging van Electrotechnische Werkgevers
NVF	National Vitamin Foundation (U.S.A.)
NVF	Nederlandse Vereniging van Fruitteelers
NVF	Norske Vaskeriers Forening
NVF	Norske Ventilasjons-entreprenores Forening
NVFF	Nederlandse Vereniging voor Fysiologie en Farmacologie
NVFK	Nederlandse Vereniging-Federatie voor Kunststoffen
NVFL	Nederlandse Vereniging van Fabrikanten van Landbouwwerktuigen
NVG	Nederlandse Vereniging voor Geodesie
NVG	Nederlandse Vereniging voor Gerontologie
NVG	Nederlandse Vereniging voor Gezinscrediet
NVGA	National Vocational Guidance Association (U.S.A.)
NVGD	Nederlandsche Vereniging van Gramofoonplaten-handelaren
NVGI	Nederlandse Vereniging van Gramofoonplaten Importeurs en Fabrikanten
NVGZ	Nederlandsche Vereniging van Grind- en Zandhandelaren
NVHT	Nederlandse Vereniging voor Herpetologie en Terrariumkunde "Lacerta"
NVIB	Nederlandse Vereniging voor de Industriële Bakkerij
NVJ	Nederlandse Vereniging van Journalisten
NVK	Nederlandse Vereniging van Keuken- en Voedingdeskundigen
NVKL	Nederlandse Vereniging van Ondernemingen op het Gebied van de Koudetechniek en Luchtbehandeling
NVL	Nederlandse Vereniging voor Lastechniek
NVLG	Nederlandse Vereniging van Leveranciers van Grootkeukenapparatuur
NVLP	Nederlandse Vereniging van Lucht- en Ruimtevaart-Publicisten
NVM	Nederlandse Vuilafvoer Maatschappij
NVMA	National Veterinary Medical Association
NVMW	Nederlandse Vereniging van Maatschappelijk Werkers
NVNB	Nederlandse Vereniging van Nachtveiligheids-diensten en Bewakingsbedrijven
NVNI	Nasionale Voedingnavorsingsinstituut (South Africa)
NVOB	Nederlandse Vereniging van Ondernemers op Brandbeveil Gebied
NVOS	Nederlandse Vereniging voor Orthodontische Studie
NVOZ	Nederlandse Vereniging van Ongevallen- en Ziektenverzekeraars
NVP	Nederlandse Vereniging voor Personeelbeleid
NVPH	Nederlandsche Vereniging van Postzegelhan-delaren
NVR	Nederlandse Vereniging van Rubber-fabrikanten
NVR	Nederlandse Vereniging voor Ruimtevaart
NVRD	Nederlandse Vereniging van Radio en TV Detailhandelaren
NVRD	Nederlandse Vereniging van Reinigings-directeuren

NVRL	Nederlandse Vereniging van Radiologisch Laboraten
NVRS	National Vegetable Research Station
NVRSA	National Vegetable Research Station Association
NVS	Nederlandse Vereniging van Schoolmeubelfabrikanten
NVS	Nederlandse Vereniging voor Stralingshygiene
NVS	National Vegetable Society
NVSH	Nederlandse Vereniging voor Sexuele Hervorming
NVSKPT	National Verbond der Syndikale Kamer der Praktici in de Tandheelkunde
NVT	Nederlandse Vereniging van Toneelkunstenaars
NVTL	Nederlandse Vereniging Techniek in de Landbouw
NVTO	Nederlandse Vereniging voor Tekenonderwijs
NVTS	Nederlandse Vereniging van Technici op Scheepvartgebied
NVUA	Nederlands Vereniging van Universiteits Artsen
NVV	Nationaal Verbond der Vlaswevers (Belgium)
NVV	Nederlands Verbond van Vakverenigingen
NVVA	Nederlandse Vereniging van Automobielassuradeuren
NVVB	Nationale Vereniging voor Beveiliging tegen Brand (Belgium)
NVvGT	Nederlandse Vereniging van Gieterijtechnici
NVvIJ	Nederlandse Vereniging van Handelaren in Ijzerwaren
NVVK	Nederlandse Vereniging voor Koeltechniek
NVVL	Nederlandse Vereniging voor Luchttransport
NVvL	Nederlandse Vereniging voor Luchtvaarttechniek
NVvN	Nederlandse Vereniging van Neurochirurgen
NVVT	Nederlandse Vereniging van Verftechnici
NVvV	Nederlandse Vereniging voor Vlaggenkunde
NVVW	Nederlandse Vereniging tot Verbetering van het Welsumer
NVvW	Nederlandse Vereniging van Wiskundeleraren
NVWB	Nederlandse Vereniging van Wegenbouwers
NVWE	Nederlandse Vereniging van Electrotechnische Werkgevers
NVWFT	Nederlandse Vereniging voor de Wetenschappelijke
NVWH	Nederlandse Vereniging van Werkgevers in het Heibedrijf
NWA	North West Airlines (U.S.A.)
NWC	New World Coalition (U.S.A.)
NWCA	National Women Citizens Association
NWCC	National Weed Committee of Canada
NWDA	National Wholesale Druggist Association (U.S.A.)
NWEB	North Western Electricity Board
NWF	National Wildlife Federation (U.S.A.)
NWF	Norske Wallboard-fabrikkers Forening
NWGA	National Wholesale Grocers Alliance
NWGA	National Wool Growers Association (U.S.A.)
NWGA	National Wool Growers Association (South Africa)
NWGB	North Western Gas Board
NWIC	National Wheat Improvement Committee (U.S.A.)
NWKV	Nasionale Wolkwekersvereniging van Suid-Afrika
NWMA	National Wool Marketing Corporation (U.S.A.)
NWPC	Nordic Wood Preservation Council
NWPO	Northwest Pacific Oceanographers
NWRC	National Weather Records Center (of ESSA) (U.S.A.)
NWRLS	North Western Regional Library System
NW&SCA	National Water and Soil Conservation Organisation (New Zealand)
NWTEC	National Wool Textile Export Corporation
NWU	National Worker Union (Jamaica)
NYAM	New York Academy of Medicine
NYAS	New York Academy of Sciences
NYES	New York Entomological Society
NYHA	National Yacht Harbour Association
NYHA	New York Heart Association
NYL	Norges Yrkeslaererlag
NYLC	National Young Life Campaign
NYSE	New York Stock Exchange
NYSEM	New York Society of Electron Microscopists
NYSPA	New York State Pharmaceutical Association
NYSSIM	New York State Society of Industrial Medicine

NYT	Landsforeningen Norske Yrkestegners
NYTC	National Youth Temperance Council
NYUIMS	New York University Institute of Mathematical Sciences
NYZS	New York Zoological Society
NZAB	New Zealand Association of Bacteriologists
NZAEI	New Zealand Agricultural Engineering Institute
NZAPMB	New Zealand Apple and Pear Marketing Board
NZASc	New Zealand Association of Scientists
NZB	Netherlands Dairy Bureau
NZBC	New Zealand Broadcasting Corporation
NZBS	New Zealand Broadcasting Service
NZBTO	New Zealand Book Trade Organization
NZCER	New Zealand Council for Educational Research
NZDA	New Zealand Department of Agriculture
NZDA	New Zealand Dietetic Association
NZDCS	New Zealand Department of Census and Statistics
NZDLS	New Zealand Department of Lands and Survey
NZDSIR	New Zealand Department of Scientific and Industrial Research
NZEI	New Zealand Electronics Institute
NZES	New Zealand Ecological Society
NZFL	New Zealand Federation of Labour
NZFMRA	New Zealand Fertilizer Manufacturers Research Association
NZFP	New Zealand Forest Products Ltd
NZFRI	New Zealand Forest Research Institute
NZFS	New Zealand Forest Service
NZGA	New Zealand Grassland Association
NZGenS	New Zealand Genetical Society
NZGS	New Zealand Geographical Society
NZIA	New Zealand Institute of Architects
NZIAS	New Zealand Institute of Agricultural Science
NZIC	New Zealand Institute of Chemistry
NZIE	New Zealand Institution of Engineers
NZIER	New Zealand Institute of Economic Research
NZIF	New Zealand Institute of Foresters
NZIIA	New Zealand Institute of International Affairs

NZIM	New Zealand Institute of Management
NZIMP	New Zealand Institute of Medical Photography
NZInstW	New Zealand Institute of Welding
NZIRE	New Zealand Institute of Refrigeration Engineers
NZJCB	New Zealand Joint Communications Board
NZLA	New Zealand Library Association
NZMS	New Zealand Meteorological Service
NZNAC	New Zealand National Airways Corporation
NZNCOR	New Zealand National Committee on Oceanic Research
NZNRAC	New Zealand National Research Advisory Council
NZOI	New Zealand Oceanographic Institute
NZPOA	New Zealand Purchasing Officers Association
NZR	Vereniging Nationale Ziekenhuisraad
NZSA	New Zealand Society of Accountants
NZSA	New Zealand Statistical Association
NZSAP	New Zealand Society of Animal Production
NZSCA	New Zealand Soil Conservation Association
NZSI	New Zealand Standards Institute
NZSLO	New Zealand Scientific Liaison Office
NZSSS	New Zealand Society of Soil Science
NZVA	New Zealand Veterinary Association
NZWCC	New Zealand Weed Control Conference
NZWIRI	New Zealand Wool Industries Research Institute

O

OAA	Ontario Association of Architects (Canada)
OAA	Organisation des Nations Unies pour l'Alimentation et l'Agriculture
OAA	Orient Airlines Association (Philippines)
OAAA	Outdoor Advertising Association of Australia Inc.
ÖAAB	Österreichischer Arbeiten- und Angestelltenbund
OAAC	Outdoor Advertising Association of Canada

OAAPS	Organisation for Afro-Asian Peoples Solidarity	**OBAA**	Oil Burning Apparatus Association
OAAS	Ontario Association of Agricultural Societies (Canada)	**OBAE**	Office des Bois de l'Afrique Équatoriale (Gabon)
OAC	Oceanic Affairs Committee	**OBAP**	Office Belge pour l'Accroissement de la Productivité
OAC	Ontario Agricultural College (Canada)	**OBCE**	Office Belge du Commerce Extérieur
OAC	Outdoor Advertising Council	**OBEA**	Office Belge de l'Économie et de l'Agriculture
OACI	Organisation de l'Aviation Civile Internationale	**OBI**	Office du Baccalauréat International
OAD	Offices Agricoles Départementaux (supprimés)	**OBRA**	Overseas Broadcasting Representatives Association
ÖAeV	Österreichische Äerosol-Vereinigung	**OBSA**	Organización Boliviana de Sanidad Agropecuaria
OAF	Oljeselskapenes Arbeidgiverforening	**OCA**	Organización de Cooperativas de América
OAGB	Osteopathic Association of Great Britain	**OCAA**	Office Central des Associations Agricoles du Finistère et des Côtes-du-Nord
OAH	Organization of American Historians		
OAIA	Organisation des Agences d'Information d'Asie	**OCAM**	Organisation Commune Africaine et Mauricienne (*formerly* UAMCE)
ÖAL	Österreichischer Arbeitsring für Lärmbekämpfung	**OCAMM**	Organisation Commune Africaine, Malgache et Mauricienne
OAMA	Oil Appliance Manufacturers Association	**OCAS**	Organization of Central American States
OAMCAF	African and Malagasy Coffee Organisation	**OCAW**	Oil, Chemical and Atomic workers International Union (U.S.A.)
OAMCE	Organisation Africaine et Malgache de Coopération Économique (*now* OCAM)	**OCB**	Organisation Camerounaise de la Banane
OAMJTB	Organisation pour l'Afrique des Mouvements de Jeunesse et du Travail Bénévole	**OCBN**	Organisation Commune Benin-Niger des Chemins de Fer et des Transports
OAMPI	Office Africain et Malgache de la Propriété Industrielle	**OCCA**	Oil and Colour Chemists Association
		OCCGE	Organisation de Coopération contre les Grandes Endémies
OANA	Organisation of Asian News Agencies		
OAP	Office Algérien de Publicité	**OCCGEAC**	Organisation de Co-ordination et de Coopération pour la Lutte Contre des Grandes Endémies en Afrique Centrale (*now* OCEAC)
OAP	Organisation Asiatique de la Productivité		
OAPEC	Organization of Arab Petroleum Exporting Countries	**OCCMP**	Office Centrafricain de Commercialisation des Pierres et Métaux Précieux
OAPEP	Organisation Arabe des Pays Exportateurs de Pétrole (Kuwait)	**OCDE**	Organisation de Cooperation et de Développement Économique (*formerly* OEEC)
OAPI	Organisation Africaine de la Propriété Intellectuelle (Cameroon)		
OAS	Organization of American States	**OCDN**	Dahomey-Niger Common Organisation
OAS	Ohio Academy of Science (U.S.A.)	**OCE**	Office de Commercialisation et d'Exportation (Morocco)
OAU	Organisation of African Unity		
ÖAV	Österreichischer Alpenverein	**OCEAC**	Organisation de Coordination pour la Lutte Contre des Endémies en Afrique Centrale
ÖAV	Österreichischer Apothekerverband	**OCEC**	Oficio Central de Educación Católicos (Chile)
ÖAV	Österreichische Arbeitsgemeinschaft für Volksgesundheit		
OAW	Österreichische Akademie der Wissenschaften	**OCFF**	Ordre des Conseils Fiscaux de France et d'Outre-Mer
		OCFT	Office du Chemin de Fer Transcamerounais
OB	Ordnance Board	**ÖCG**	Österreichische Computer Gesellschaft

OCH	Office Congolais de l'Habitat	**OCTRF**	Ontario Cancer Treatment and Research Foundation (Canada)
OCI	Oficina Central de Información (Venezuela)	**OCUFA**	Ontario Confederation of University Faculty Associations (Canada)
OCIBU	Office des Cultures Industrielles du Burundi	**OCW**	Opzoekingscentrum voor de Wegenbouw (Belgium)
OCIC	Office Catholique International du Cinéma		
OCIC	Office Chérifien Interprofessionel des Céréales	**OD**	Office of Distribution (U.S.A.)
OCIMF	Oil Companies International Marine Forum	**ODA**	Official Development Assistance (*of* OECD)
OCIPE	Office Catholique d'Information sur les Problèmes Européens	**ODA**	Ontario Dental Association (Canada)
OCIRU	Office des Cafés Indigènes du Rwanda et Burundi	**ODA**	Overseas Development Administration
		ODAMAP	Office Dahoméen des Manutentions Por-tuaires
OCLA	Organisation Commune de Lutte Anti-Acridienne (*now* OCLALAV)	**ODBA**	Oregon Dairy Breeders Association (U.S.A.)
OCLAE	Organizacion Continental Latino-Americana de Estudiantes	**ODC**	Overseas Development Council (U.S.A.)
OCLALAV	Organisation Commune de Lutte Antiacridienne et de Lutte Antiaviaire (Senegal)	**ODCA**	Organización Demócrata Cristiana de América
		ODCBA	Oxford and District Cattle Breeders Association
OCLAV	Organisation Commune de Lutte Anti-Avaire (Africa) *now* OCLALAV	**ODECA**	Organización de Estados Centramericanos
OCM	Ordo Constantini Magni	**ODEF**	Office National de Développement et d'Exploitation des Ressources Forestières (Togo)
OCMA	Oil Companies' Material Association		
OCMI	Organisation Consultative Maritime Inter-gouvernementale	**ODEPA**	Oficina de Planificación Agrícola (Chile)
		ODEPA	Organizacion Deportiva Panamericana
OCP	Offices des Céréales Panifiables (Syria)	**ÖDG**	Österreichische Dermatologische Gesellschaft
OCPCA	Oil and Chemical Plant Constructors Association		
		ODI	Open Door International for the Economic Emancipation of the Woman Worker
OCPLACS	Ontario Co-operative Program in Latin American and Caribbean Studies (Canada)	**ODI**	Organisation Interaméricaine de Défense
OCRA	Office Commercial du Ravitaillement et de l'Agriculture (Belgium)	**ODI**	Overseas Development Institute
		ODM	Ministry of Overseas Development (*incorp. former* Department of Technical Co-operation)
OCRA	Office de Coopération Radiophonique		
OCRPI	Office Central de Répartition des Produits In-dustriels		
		ODSA	Overseas Development Service Association
OCRS	Organisation Commune des Régions Sahariennes	**ODSBA**	Oxford Down Sheep Breeders Association
		ODTA	Organisation for the Development of African Tourism
OCRTA	Office du Chemin de Fer Transgabonais		
OCS	Organ de Contrôle des Stupéfiants (UNO)	**ODUCAL**	Organización de Universidades Católicas de América Latina
OCT	Associated Overseas Countries and Territories	**ÖDV**	Österreichische Detektiv-Verband
OCT	Office du Commerce de la Tunisie	**OEA**	Organisation of European Aluminium-Smelters
OCTI	Office Central des Transports Internationaux par Chemins de Fer	**OEA**	Organización de los Estados Americanos
OCTPC	Organization for Cooperation of Socialist Countries in the domain of Tele- and Postal Communications (U.S.S.R.)	**OEAS**	Organisation Europäischer Aluminium Schmelzhutten
		OEB	Ondervakgroep Export van Bloembollen

OEBC	Organisation Européenne de Biologie Cellulaire	**OESO**	Organisatie voor Economische Samenwerking en Ontwikkeling
OEBI	Oficina de Estadísticas Balleneras Internacionales	**OETB**	Offshore Energy Technology Board
OEBM	Organisation Européenne de Biologie Moléculaire	**OEUFSJT**	Organisation Européenne des Unions de Foyers et Services pour les Jeunes Travailleurs
OECA	Organisation des États Centro–Américains	**OEVA**	Office de l'Expérimentation et de la Vulgarisation Agricoles (Tunisia)
OECD	Organisation for Economic Co-operation and Development (*formerly* OEEC)	**OEWS**	Oesterreichische Stickstoffwerke AG, Linz (Austria)
OECE	Organisation Européenne de Coopération Économique (*now* OECD)	**OFA**	Office Arabe de Presse et de Documentation (Syria)
OECEI	Oficina de Estudio para la Colaboración Económica Internacional (Argentina)	**OFALAC**	Office Algérien d'Action Économique et Touristique
OECL	Ordre des Experts Comptables Luxembourgeois	**OFAR**	Office of Foreign Agricultural Relations (U.S.A.)
OECL	Organisation Européenne des Industries de la Conserve de Légumes	**OFBEC**	Office Franco-Britannique d'Études et de Commerce
OE – CMT	Organisation Européenne de la Confédération Mondiale du Travail	**OFC**	Overseas Food Corporation
OECQ	Organisation Européenne pour le Contrôle de la Qualité	**OFCA**	Organisation des Fabricants de Produits Cellulosiques Alimentaires de la CEE
OEEC	Organisation for European Economic Co-operation (*now* OECD)	**OFCF**	Overseas Farmers Co-operative Federation Ltd
OEEPE	Organisation Européenne d'Études Photogrammétriques Expérimentales	**OFE**	Organization de Flora Europaea
OEF	Organisation of Employers Federations and Employers in Developing Countries	**OFEROM**	Office Central des Chemins de Fer d'Outre-Mer
OEFLEI	Verband Österreichischer Fleischervereinigungen	**OFESAUTO**	Oficina Española de Aseguradores de Automoviles
OEHI	Organisai Exportir Hasilbumi Indonesia	**OFFINTAC**	Offshore Installations Technical Advisory Committee
OEI	Oficina de Educación Ibero-americana	**OFFRO**	Office of Foreign Relief and Rehabilitation Operations (U.S.A.)
OEI	Organisation Européenne d'Information	**ÖFG**	Österreichische Forschungsgesellschaft für Philatelie und Postgeschichte
OEICCF	Organisation Européenne des Industries des Confitures et Conserves de Fruits	**OFI**	Orientation à la Fonction Internationale
ÖEKV	Österreichischer Energiekonsumenten-Verband	**OFIAMT**	Office Fédéral de l'Industrie, des Arts et Métiers et du Travail (Switzerland)
OEMOLK	Österreichischer Molkerei- und Käsereiverband	**OFICEMA**	Oficina Central Maritima
		OFIGAN	Oficina Nacional de Ganadería (Costa Rica)
OEPP	Organisation Européenne et Méditerranéenne pour la Protection des Plantes	**OFIPLAN**	Oficina de Planificación (Costa Rica)
OER	Office Européen de Radiodiffusion	**OFITEC**	Office Tunisien de l'Expansion Commerciale et du Tourisme
OERS	Organisation des États Riverains du Sénégal (*now* OMVS)	**OFITOMEP**	Office International de Reseignements des Fabricants de Toiles Métalliques pour Papeteries
OERS	Organisation Européenne de Recherches Spatiales	**ÖFLEI**	Verband Österreichischer Fleischervereinigungen
OERTC	Organisation Européenne de Recherche sur le Traitement du Cancer	**OFNACOM**	Office National du Commerce (Congo)

OFR	Oliebranchens Foellesreproesentation	OIAC	Organisation Inter-Africaine du Café
OFRS	Office Français de Recherches Sous-Marines	ÖIAG	Österreichische Industrie-Verwaltungs A.G.
OFT	Oljeeldningstekniska Föreningen	ÖIAV	Österreichischer Ingenieur- und Architekten-Verein
OFTEL	Office Technique des Éleveurs		
OG	Organisation Gestosis (Switzerland)	ÖIB	Österreichischer Imkerbund
OGABI	Omnium Gabonais de Développement Immobilier	OIC	International Coffee Organization
		OIC	Organisation Interaméricaine du Café
ÖGB	Österreicher Gewerkschaftbund	OIC	Organisation Internationale Catholique
ÖGDB	Österreichische Gesellschaft für Dokumentation und Bibliographie	OIC	Organisation Internationale du Commerce
		OICC	Office International du Cacao et du Chocolat
ÖGDI	Österreichischer Gesellschaft für Dokumentation und Information	OICI	Oficina Internacional Católica de la Infancia
		OICI	Omnium Immobilier de Côte-d'Ivoire
ÖGE	Österreichische Gesellschaft für Ernährungsforschung	OICI	Organización Interamericana de Cooperación Intermunicipal
ÖGEA	Organisation & Gestion de l'Entreprise Agricole	OICM	Office Intercantonal de Contrôle des Médicaments (Switzerland)
ÖGEFA	Österreichische Gesellschaft für Arbeitstechnik und Betriebsrationalisierung	OICM	Organisation Internationale pour la Coopération Médicale
ÖGEW	Österreichische Gesellschaft für Erdölwissenschaften	OICMA	Organisation Internationale pour le Contrôle Criquet Migrateur Africain
ÖGF	Oslo Geofysikeres Forening	OICNM	Organisation Intergouvernementale Consultative de la Navigation Maritime
ÖGfM	Österreichische Gesellschaft für Musik		
ÖGFT	Österreichische Gesellschaft für Weltraumforschung und Flugkörpertechnik	OICRF	Office International du Cadastre et Régime Foncier
ÖGG	Österreichische Geographische Gesellschaft	OICS	Institute of Colonial Studies
ÖGH	Österreichische Gesellschaft für Holzforschung	OICS	Organe International de Contrôle des Stupéfiants
ÖGHMP	Österreichische Gesellschaft für Hygiene, Mikrobiologie und Praventivmedizin	OIE	Organisation Internationale des Employeurs
		OIE	Office International des Epizootics
ÖGI	Österreichische Gesellschaft für Informatik	OIEA	Office International pour l'Enseignement Agricole
ÖGI	Österreichische Giesserei-Institut	OIEA	Organismo Internacional de Energia Atómica
ÖGP	Österreichische Gesellschaft für Politikwissenschaft	OIEC	Office International de l'Enseignement Catholique
ÖGRR	Oesterreichische Gesellschaft f. Raumforschung und Raumplanung	OIEC	Organisation Internationale d'Échanges Culturelles
ÖGS	Österreichische Gesellschaft für Strassenwesen	OIEP	Office International d'Échange de Produits
ÖGSI	Österreichische Gesellschaft für Statistik und Informatik	OIETA	Office Inter-États du Tourisme Africain
		ÖIF	Österreichisches Institut für Formgebung
OHA	Ontario Horticultural Association (Canada)	ÖIFR	Österreichisches Institut fur Raumplanung
OHE	Office of Health Economics	OIG	Organisation Intergouvernementale
OHEG	Austrian Hard Cheese Export Company	OIJ	Organisation Internationale des Journalists
ÖHFI	Österreichisches Holzforschungsinstitut	OILB	Organisation Internationale de Lutte Biologique contre les Animaux et les Plantes Nuisibles
OHI	Organisation Hydrographique Internationale		
ÖHKV	Österreichischer Heilbäder- und Kurorteverband		

OIML	Organisation Internationale de Métrologie Légale
OIN	Organisation Internationale de Normalisation
OINA	Oyster Institute of North America
OING	Organisations Internationales Non-Gouvernementales
OIP	Organisation Internationale de la Paléobotanique
OIP	Organización Internacional de Periodistas
OIP	Société Belge d'Optique et d'Instruments de Précision
OIPA	Organisation Internationale pour la Protection des Oeuvres d'Art
OIPC	Organización Internacional de Policia Criminal
OIPC	Organisation Internationale de Protection Civile
OIPEEC	Organisation Internationale pour l'Étude de l'Endurance des Câbles
OIPN	Office International pour la Protection de la Nature
OIPQA	Oficina Internacional Permanente de Quimica Analítica para los Alimentos Humanos y Animales
ÖIR	Österreichisches Institut für Raumplanung
OIR	Inter-American Radio Office
OIR	Organisation Internationale pour les Réfugiés
OIRP	Organisation Internationale de Régies Paléobotanique
OIRSA	Organismo Internacional Regional de Sanidad Agropecuaria (Central America)
OIRT	Organisation Internationale de Radiodiffusion et Télévision
OIS	Office of Investigatory Services (U.S.A.)
OIS	Organisation Internationale du Sucre
OISA	Office of International Scientific Affairs (U.S.A.)
OISCA – INT	Organisation for Industrial, Spiritual and Cultural Advancement International
OISE	Ontario Institute for Studies in Education (Canada)
OISS	Organización Iberoamericana de Seguridad Social
OISTT	International Organization of Scenographers and Theatre Technicians
OISTV	Organisation Internationale pour la Science et la Technique du Vide

OIT	Organisation International du Travail
OITAF	Organizzazione Internationale dei Transporti a Fune
OITRA	Organizacion Internacional de Trabajadores de Radio y Television de las Americas
OIUC	Organización Internacional de las Uniones de Consumidores
OIV	Office International du Vin
ÖIV	Österreichisches Institut für Verpackungswesen
OIVST	Organisation Internationale pour la Science et la Technique du Vide
OJIF	Ordre des Jurisconsultes Internationaux de France
OJU	Oceania Judo Union (Australia)
OK	Oljekonsumenternas Förbund
OK	Oppikoulunopettajien Keskusjärjestö
ÖKEV	Österreicherischer Klub für Englische Vorstehkunde
OKISZ	National Handicrafts Co-operative Society (Hungary)
ÖKL	Österreichisches Kuratorium für Landtechnik
OKL	Osuuspankkien Keskusliitto
ÖKV	Österreichischer Krankenflegeverband
ÖKW	Österreichisches Kuratorium für Wirtschaftlichkeit
OL	Office of Labour (U.S.A.)
OL	Ovnstøperienes Landforening
OLADE	Latin American Energy Organization
OLAP	Organizacion Latino-Americaine para Promocion de los Ciegos y Deficientes Visuales
OLAS	Organización Latinoamericana de Solidaridad (Cuba)
OLAVU	Organización Latinoamericana del Vino y de la Uva
OLC	Overseas Liaison Committee of American Council on Education
OLCP – EA	Organisation de Lutte Contre le Criquet Pèlerin dans l'Est Africain
ÖLMA	Östschweizerisch Land- und Milchwirtschaftliche Austellung
OLML	Our Lady's Missionary League
ÖLV	Österreichischer Lehrerverband
OMA	Oilskin Manufacturers Association of Great Britain Ltd

OMA	Overall Manufacturers Association of Great Britain	**OMS International**	Oriental Missionary Society International
OMA	Overseas Mining Association	**OMVA**	Office de Mise en Valeur Agricole (Morocco)
OMAAEEC	Organisation Mondiale des Anciens et Anciennes Élèves de l'Enseignement Catholique	**OMVS**	Organisation pour la Mise en Valeur du Fleuve Sénégal
OMAI	Organisation Mondiale Agudas Israel	**OMVVM**	Office de Mise en Valeur de la Vallée de la Medjerda (Tunisia)
OMASD	Office of Management Appraisal and Systems Development (U.S.A.)	**OMW**	Oberrheinische Mineralölwerke GmbH
OMBKE	Országos Magyar Bányászati és Kohaszati Egyesület	**ÖN**	Österreichisches Normungsinstitut
OMBVI	Office Malien du Bétail et de la Viande	**ONA**	Overseas National Airways (U.S.A.)
OMC	Organisation Mondiale du Commerce (UNO)	**ONAA**	Office National Anti-Acridien
OMCI	Organisation Intergouvernementale Consultative de la Navigation Maritime	**ONAF**	Office National des Forêts (Congo)
		ONAH	Office National des Hydrocarbures (Guinée)
OMECOMS	Organisation pour le Mécanographie la Compatibilité et la Secretariat (Ivory Coast)	**ONAREST**	Office National de la Recherche Scientifique et Technique (Cameroon)
OMEF	Office Machines and Equipment Federation	**ÖNB**	Österreichische Nationalbibliothek
OMEP	Organisation Mondiale pour l'Éducation Préscolaire	**ONBG**	Office National des Bois du Gabon
		ONCA	Office National de Commercialisation Agricole (Gabon)
OMF	Office of Marketing Facilities (U.S.A.)	**ONCAD**	Office National de Coopération et d'Assistance pour le Développement (Sénégal)
OMFP	Officine Meccan. Ferroviarie Pistoiesi		
OMG	Österreichische Mathematische Gesellschaft		
OMG	Österreichische Mineralogische Gesellschaft	**ONCPA**	Office Nationale de Commercialisation des Produits Agricoles (Central Africa, Congo)
OMGE	Organisation Mondiale de Gastro-Entérologie	**OND**	Office National des Diamants (Central Africa)
OMİPE	Office Mondial d'Information sur les Problèmes d'Environnement	**ONDAH**	Office National des Débouchés Agricoles et Horticoles (Belgium)
OMIS	Organisation Mondiale de l'Image et du Son	**ONDEPA**	Organización Nacional de Profesionales Agropecuarios (Colombia)
OMKDK	Országos Müszaki Könyvtár és Dokumentációs Központ, Budapest	**ONERA**	Office National d'Études et de Recherches Aéronautiques
OMM	Organisation Météorologique Mondiale	**ONERN**	Oficina Nacional de Evaluacion de Recursos Naturales (Peru)
OMMSA	Organisation of Museums, Monuments and Sites in Africa (Ghana)	**ONF**	Office National des Forêts (France, Central Africa)
ÖMOLK	Österreichischer Molkerei- und Käsereiverband		
		ONG	Organisations Non Gouvernementales
OMPA	Organizacion para el Mejoramiento de la Produccion Azucarera (Cuba)	**ÖNG**	Österreichische Gesellschaft für Nuclearmedizin
OMPE	Organisation Mondiale de la Profession Enseignante	**ONGC**	Oil and Natural Gas Commission (India)
		ONGT	Organisation Non-Gouvernementale de Portée Transnationale
OMPI	Organisation Mondiale de la Propriété Intellectuelle	**ONHA**	Office National de l'Huilerie d'Abèche (Tchad)
OMPSA	Organisation Mondiale pour la Protection Sociale des Aveugles	**ONI**	Office National d'Immigration
		ONI	Office National des Irrigations (Morocco)
OMS	Office of Marketing Services (U.S.A.)	**ONIA**	Office National Industriel de l'Azote (*now* EMC)
OMS	Organisation Mondiale de la Santé		

ONIB	Office National Interprofessionnel du Blé
ONIBEV	Office National Interprofessionnel du Bétail et des Viandes
ONIC	Office National Interprofessionnel des Céréales
ONISEP	Office National d'Information sur les Enseignements et les Professions
ONL	Office National du Lait et de ses Dérivés
ONM	Office National Météorologique
ONMR	Office National de la Modernisation Rurale (Morocco)
ÖNORM	Österreichischer Normenausschuss
ONR	Office of Naval Research (U.S.A.)
ONRA	National Office of Agrarian Reform (Algeria)
ONRAP	Oficina Nacional de Racionalizacion y Capacitacion de la Administracion Publica (Peru)
ONRD	Office National de la Recherche et du Développement (Zaire)
ONRI	Orde van Nederlandse Raadgevende Ingenieurs
ONS	Oriental Numismatic Society
ONSS	Office National de la Sécurité Sociale (Belgium)
ONU	Organisation des Nations Unies
ONUC	Organisation des Nations Unies au Congo
ONUDI	Organización de las Naciones Unidas para el Desarrollo Industrial
ONUDI	Organisation des Nations Unies pour le Développement Industriel
ONULP	Ontario New Universities Library Project (Canada)
ONUST	Organisme des Nations Unies Chargé de la Surveillance de la Trève (en Palestine)
OOA	Orde van Organisatiekundigen en-Adviseurs
OOMOTO	Universal Love and Brotherhood Association (Japan)
OOPS	Organismo de Obras Públicas y Socorro de las Naciones Unidas para los Refugiados de Palestina en el Cercano Oriente
OPA	Office of Price Administration (U.S.A.)
OPAC	Office des Produits Agricoles de Coster-mansville (Zaire)
OPAK	Office des Produits Agricoles du Kivu (Zaire)
ÖPAK	Österreichische Patentanwaltskammer
OPAM	Office des Produits Agricoles du Mali

OPANAL	Organisme pour l'Interdiction des Armes Nucléaires en Amérique Latine (Mexico)
OPAS	Office des Produits Agricoles de Stanleyville (Zaire)
OPAS	Operational Assistance
OPAT	Office des Produits Agricoles du Togo
OPC	Overseas Press Club of America
OPCD	Organisation pour la Planification de la Coopération au Développement
OPE	Omilos Pedagogikon Erevnon Kyprou
OPEC	Organization of Petroleum Exporting Countries
OPEG	OEEC Petroleum Emergency Group
OPEI	Office National de Promotion d'Entreprise Ivoirienne
OPEIU	Office and Professional Employees International Union (U.S.A.)
OPEM	Office National pour la Promotion de l'Exportation (Petites et Moyennes Entreprises)
OPEP	Organisation des Pays Exportateurs de Pétrole
OPEV	Office de Promotion de l'Entreprise Voltaïque
ÖPEV	Österreichischer Patentinhaber- und Erfinderverband
OPEX	UN Programme for the Provision of Operational Executive and Administrative Personnel
ÖPG	Österreichische Physikalische Gesellschaft
OPGC	Oil Palm Growers Council (Malaysia)
OPIC	Organización Internacional Permanente de la Carne
OPIC	Overseas Private Investment Corporation (U.S.A.)
OPICBA	Office Professionnal des Industries et Commerces du Bois et de l'Ameublement
OPMA	Overseas Press and Media Association
OPOSA	Organizacion de la Patata del Pirineo Occidental
OPPEM	Organizacion para la Protección de las Plantas en Europa y en al Mediterráneo
OPPI	Organisation of Pharmaceutical Producers of India
ÖPRG	Österreichische Public-Relations-Gesellschaft
OPRS	Oil Palm Research Station (*Now* WAIFOR)
OPS	Organisation Panaméricaine de la Santé

OPTULA	Oikeuspoliittinen Tutkimuslaitos	**ORIT**	Organización Regional Interamericana de Trabajadores
OPUS	Office des Publications Scientifiques de Langue Française	**ORLEIS**	Office Régional Laïque d'Éducation par l'Image et par le Son
OPVN	Office des Produits Vivriers du Niger	**ORNAMO**	Association of Finnish Designers
ÖPWZ	Österreichisches Zentrum für Wirtschaft-lichkeit	**ORNL**	Oak Ridge National Laboratory (U.S.A.)
ÖPZ	Österreichisches Produktivitäts-Zentrum (Austria)	**ORRRC**	Outdoor Recreation Resources Review Commission (Australia)
ORA	Office des Renseignements Agricoles	**ORS**	Operational Research Society
ORA	Organisation Régionale Asienne (*of* CISL)	**ORSA**	Operations Research Society of America
ORAF	Organisation Régionale Africaine de la CISL	**ORSI**	Operations Research Society of India
ÖRAK	Osterreichischer Rechtsanwaltkammertag	**ORSI**	Operations Research Society of Ireland
ORAMEI	Oeuvre Reine Astrid de la Mère et de l'Enfant Indigènes (Zaire)	**ORSIS**	Operations Research Society of Israel
		ORSJ	Operations Research Society of Japan
ORANA	Organisme de Recherches sur l'Alimentation et la Nutrition Africaine	**ORSTOM**	Office de la Recherche Scientifique et Technique d'Outre-Mer
ORAP	Organisation Régionale de l'Orient pour l'Administration Publique	**ORT**	Organisation – Reconstruction – Travail, Union Mondiale
ORB	Observatoire Royal de Belgique	**ORTF**	Office de la Radiodiffusion-Télévision Française (*formerly* RTF)
ORB	Operational Research Branch (U.S.A.)		
ORCA	Ocean Resources Conservation Association	**ORTHO-BANDA**	Vereniging tot het Behartigen van de Belangen van de Nederlandse Orthopedisten en Bandagisten
ORCA	Organisme Européen de Recherches sur la Carie		
ORCD	Organisation for Regional Co-operation and Development (Iran, Pakistan, Turkey)	**ORTHOMA**	Nederlandse Bond van Orthopaedisch Maat-schoenmakers
ORD	Organisme Régional de Développement du Nord Mossi (Upper Volta)	**ORTPA**	Oven-Ready Turkey Producers' Association
		ORTS	Office de la Radiodiffusion et Télévision Sénégalaise
ORDINEX	International Organisation of Experts	**OS**	Office of Supply (U.S.A.)
ORE	Organisation Régionale Européenne de la CISL	**OSA**	Optical Society of America
ORE	Ornitologia Rondo Esperantlingva	**OSA**	Organic Soil Association of Southern Africa
ORE	Union Internationale des Chemins de Fer: Office de Recherches et d'Essais	**OSAS**	Overseas Service Aid Scheme
		OSCAS	Office of Statistical Coordination and Standards (Philippines)
OREALC	Oficina Regional de Educación para América Latina y el Caribe (Chile)	**OSCE**	Office Statistique des Communautés Européennes
OREAM	Organisation d'Études d'Aires Métropolitains		
ORES	European Society for Opinion Surveys and Market Research (Denmark)	**OSCO**	Oil Service Company of Iran
		OSE	Union Mondiale pour la Protection de la Santé des Populations Juives et Oeuvres de Secours aux Enfants
ORESCO	Overseas Research Council		
ORF	Ontario Research Foundation (Canada)		
ÖRF	Österreichischer Rundfunk	**OSEC**	Office Suisse d'Expansion Commerciale
ORGALIME	Organisme de Liaison des Industries Métalli-ques et Électriques Européennes	**OSFAS**	Overseas Students Fee Awards Scheme (*of* ODA)
OR(I)C	Oceanographic Research (International) Committee	**ÖSGK**	Österreichische Studiengesellschaft für Kybernetik
ORINS	Oak Ridge Institute of Nuclear Studies (U.S.A.)	**OSHE**	Office pour le Soutien de l'Habitat Économique (Ivory Coast)

OSHR	Organisme Spécialisé d'Habitat Rural	**OTAN**	Organisation du Traité de l'Atlantique-Nord (NATO)
OSIC	International Offshore Suppliers Information Centre	**OTAN**	Organisation of Tropical American Nematologists (Porto Rico)
OSIC	Overseas Spinning Investment Company Ltd.	**OTASE**	Organisation du Traité pour la Défense Collective de l'Asie du Sud-Est
OSIS	Office of Science Information Service (U.S.A.)	**OTC**	Organisation for Trade Co-operation
OSJD	Organisation for the Collaboration of Railways (Poland)	**OTCA**	Overseas Technical Cooperation Agency (Japan)
OSL	International Order of Saint Luke the Physician	**OTI**	Organisación de la Televisión Iberoamericana
OSLAM	Organización de Seminarios Latinoamericanos	**OTI**	Organizzazione Tecnica Internazionale
OSNZ	Ornithological Society of New Zealand	**OTIPI**	Associazione Italiana delle Agenzie di Pubblicità a Servizio Completo
OSO	Offshire Supplies Office		
OSPA	Organisation Sanitaire Pan-Américaine	**OTIU**	Overseas Technical Information Unit
OSPAAL	Organisation de Solidarité des Peuples d'Afrique, d'Asie et d'Amérique Latine (Cuba)	**OTK**	Co-operative Wholesale Association (Finland)
OSR	Organisation for Seientific Research (Indonesia)	**OTL**	Organización de la Televisión Iberoamericana (Mexico)
OSRB	Overseas Services Resettlement Bureau	**OTPN**	Opolskie Towarzystwo Przyjaciól Nauk
OSRO	Office for the Sahelian Relief Operation (FAO)	**OTR**	Office des Transports par Route (Belgium)
OSRD	Office of Scientific Research and Development (U.S.A.)	**OTRACO**	Office d'Exploitation des Transports Coloniaux (Zaire)
OSSA	Office of Space Science and Applications (*of* NASA)	**OTRAN**	Ocean Test Ranges and Instrumentation Conference (Honolulu)
OSShD	Organisation pour la Collaboration des Chemins de Fer	**OTS**	Office of Technical Services (U.S.A.)
OST	Organisation Scientifique du Travail	**OTS**	Organization for Tropical Studies (Costa Rica)
OSTAC	Ocean Science and Technology Advisory Committee (*of* NSIA)	**OTU**	Office of Technology Utilization (*of* NASA)
OSTI	Office for Scientific and Technical Information (*formerly* D.S.I.R.)	**OTUA**	Office Technique pour l'Utilisation de l'Acier
OSTIV	Organisation Scientifique et Technique Internationale du Vol à Voile	**OTUS**	Office Tunisien de Standardisation
OSTP	Office of Scientific and Technical Personnel (OECD)	**ÖTVV**	Österreichischer Transport-Versicherungs-Verband
OSTS	Official Seed Testing Station	**OUA**	Organisation de l'Unité Africaine
OSUK	Ophthalmological Societies of the United Kingdom	**OUAAT**	Organisation Universelle d'Associations d'Agents de Tourisme
OSWEP	Overseas Student Welfare Expansion Programme (British Council)	**OV**	Optometristen Vereniging
		ÖVA	Gesellschaft für den Volkskundeatlas in Österreich
OSZH	National Co-operative Credit Institute (Hungary)	**OVAC**	Overseas Visual Aid Centre
OTA	World Touring and Automobile Organization	**ÖVE**	Österreichischer Verband für Elektrotechnik
OTAAI	Oficina Técnica de Asuntos Agrícolas Internacionales (Venezuela)	**OVEIP**	Organisatie Verenigde Exporteurs van Indonesische Producten
		ÖVFG	Österreichischer Verband für Flüssiggas
		ÖVG	Österreichische Verkehrswissenschaftliche Gesellschaft
		OVM	Onderlinge Verzekeringsmaatschappij

ÖVP	Österreichische Volkspartei
OVRIJ	Organisatie van Rand-en IJsselmeervissers
ÖVS	Österreichischer Verband für Strahlenschutz
OVSL	Organisation Voltäique des Syndicats Libres
ÖVZ	Österreichisches Verpackungszentrum
OWAEC	Organization for West African Economic Co-operation
ÖWG	Österreichische Werbegesellschaft
OWRC	Ontario Water Resources Commission (Canada)
OWRT	Office of Water Research and Technology (U.S.A.)
ÖWWV	Österreicherischer Wasserwirtschaftsverband
OXEXPORT	Landbrugets Kvaeg- og Kødsalg
OXFAM	Oxford Committee for Famine Relief
ÖZEPA	Österreichische Vereinigung der Zellstoff- und Papierchemiker und Techniker
OZONE	International Bureau of Atmospheric Ozone

P

PA	Paintmakers' Association of Great Britain
PA	Direction de la Production Agricole
PA	Parapsychological Association (U.S.A.)
PA	Publishers' Association
PAA	Potato Association of America
PAA	Population Association of America
PAAA	Pan American Association of Anatomy
PAAAC	Pan-American Agricultural Aviation Centre
PAABS	Pan American Association of Biochemical Societies
PAAT	Programa Ampliado de Asistencia Técnica (see ETAP)
PAC	Packaging Association of Canada
PAC	Pan American Highway Congresses
PAC	Permanent Agricultural Committee (of ILO)
PACB	Pan-American Coffee Bureau
PACCIOS	Conseil Régional Panaméricain (of CIOS)
PACCS	Pan American Cancer Cytology Society
PACD	Presidential Arm on Community Development (Philippines)

PACDIS	Pacific Area Communicable Disease Information Service (Philippines)
PACE	Philippine Association of Civil Engineers
PACEHOPE	Fachverband der Papier-, Zellulose-, Holzstoff- und Pappenindustrie Österreichs
PACES	Political Action Committee for Engineers and Scientists (U.S.A.).
PACRA	Pottery and Ceramics Research Association (N.Z.)
PACS	Primary Agricultural Credit Societies (India)
PACT	Private Agencies Collaboration Together (U.S.A.)
PADF	Pan American Development Foundation
PADOG	Plan d'Aménagement et d'Organisation Générale de la Région Parisienne.
PAEC	Pakistan Atomic Energy Commission
PAF	Papirindustriens Arbeidsgiverforening
PAF	Petroleumbranschens Arbetsgivareförbund
PAFA	Pan-American Festival Association
PAFC	Philippine-American Financial Commission
PAFIE	Pacific Asian Federation of Industrial Engineering
PAFLU	Philippine Association of Free Labour Unions
PAFMECA	Pan African Freedom Movement of East and Central Africa
PAFMECSA	Pan-African Freedom Movement for East, Central and Southern Africa (now OAU)
PAG	Protein-Calorie Advisory Group of the United Nations System
PAGB	Poultry and Egg Producers Association of Great Britain Ltd
PAGB	Proprietary Association of Great Britain
PAGC	Port Area Grain Committee
PAGENACI	Participation Générale Africaine de la Côte-d'Ivoire
PAHEF	Pan American Health and Education Foundation (U.S.A.)
PARC	Pacific-Asia Resources Center (Japan)
PAHMC	Pan-American Homeopathic Medical Congress
PAHO	Pan American Health Organization
PAID	Pan-African Institute for Development
PAIGC	African Party for the Independence of Portugese Guinea and Cape Verde
PAIGH	Pan-American Institute of Geography and History

PAIMEG	Pan-American Institute of Mining Engineering and Geology	**PAPF**	Philippine Association for Permanent Forests
PAINT	Primera Asociación Internacional de Noticieros y Television	**PAPMAD**	Papeteries de Madagascar
		PARCA	Pan American Railway Congress Association
PAIS	Public Affairs Information Service (U.S.A.)	**PARD**	Pakistan Academy for Rural Development
PAJU	Pan-African Union of Journalists	**PARIBAS**	Compagnie Financière de Paris et des Pays-Bas
PAK	Panhellenic Liberation Movement (Greece)		
PAL	Philippine Air Lines	**PARL**	Prince Albert Radar Laboratory (Canada)
PAL	Pioneer Air Lines (U.S.A.)	**PAREX**	European Programme of Cooperative Research in the Social Studies of Science
PALCO	Pan-American Liaison Committee of Women's Organizations		
		PARME-HUTU	Parti du Mouvement de l'Émancipation Hutu (Rwanda)
PALSS	Physical and Life Sciences Society (South Africa)	**PASA**	Pacific American Steamship Association
PAM	Programme Alimentaire Mondial	**PASA**	Pacific Asian Studies Association
PAMA	Pan-American Medical Association	**PASA**	Powder Activated Tools Association
PAMEE	Philippine Association of Mechanical and Electrical Engineers	**PASB**	Pan-American Sanitary Bureau
		PASEGES	Panellinios Synomospondia Enoseon Georgikon Synetairismon
PAMET-RADA	Parsons and Marine Engineering Turbine Research and Developing Association		
		PASLIB	Pakistan Association of Special Libraries
PAMM	British Ceramic Plant and Machinery Manufacturers Association	**PASM**	Pan African Student Movement
		PASO	Pan-American Sanitary Organisation
PAN	Polish Academy of Sciences	**PASO**	Pan American Sports Organisation
PANA	Philippine Association of National Advertisers	**PASTIC**	Pakistan Scientific and Technological Information Centre
PANA	Pan-African Information Agency	**PATA**	Pacific Area Travel Association (U.S.A.)
PANAC	Plantations Association of Nigeria and the Cameroons	**PATA**	Proprietary Articles Trade Association
PANACH	Panafrican Chemical Industries (Ivory Coast)	**PATCO**	Professional Air Traffic Controllers Organisation (U.S.A.)
PANAFTEL	Panafrican Union of Telecommunications	**PATRA**	Printing and Allied Trades' Research Association
PANAGRA	Panorama Agrícola Nacional de los Países Latinoamericanos (Mexico)	**PAU**	Pan-American Union
		PAUJ	Pan African Union of Journalists
PANAM	Pan American World Airways	**PAV**	Programme d'Assistance Volontaire (WMO)
PANASA	Productos Alimentacios Nacionales (Costa Rica)	**PAVE**	Philippine Association for Vocational Education
PANPA	Pacific Area Newspaper Production Association	**PA of W**	Pentecostal Assemblies of the World (U.S.A.)
PANPESAS	Panamerican Confederation of Weightlifting	**PAW**	Proefstation voor Akker- en Weidebouw
PANSDOC	Pakistan National Scientific Documentation Centre	**PAWC**	Pan African Workers Congress
		PAYM	Pan African Youth Movement
PAOA	Pan-American Odontological Association	**PBCP**	Political Bureau of the Communist Party
PAP	People's Action Party (Singapore)	**PBEC**	Pacific Basin Economic Council (Australia)
PAP	Polska Agencja Prasowa	**PBF**	Papirindustrielle Bedrifters Forbund
PAPBC	Pharmaceutical Association of the Province of British Columbia (Canada)	**PBFL**	Planning for Better Family Living (FAO)
PAPC	Public Agricultural Production Corporation (Sudan)	**PBI**	Pan Britannica Industries Ltd
		PBI	Programa Biológico Internacional

PBM	Proefstation voor de Nederlandse Brouw-en Moutindustrie	**PCIZC**	Permanent Committee of International Zoological Congresses
PBO	Publiekrechtelijke Bedrijfsorganisatie (Netherlands)	**PCJC**	Pakistan Central Jute Committee
		PCMA	Professional Convention Management Association (U.S.A.)
PBU	Pali Buddhist Union		
PBWG	Pakistan Bibliographical Working Group	**PCN**	Partido Conservador de Nicaragua
PCA	Parochial Clergy Association	**PCOB**	Permanent Central Opium Board (Switzerland)
PCA	Permanent Court of Arbitration (Netherlands)		
		PCSAS	Policy Committee for Scientific Agricultural Societies (U.S.A.)
PCA	Production Credit Association (U.S.A.)		
PCAC	Poultry Costings Advisory Council	**PCSIR**	Pakistan Council of Scientific and Industrial Research
PCACT	Programa de Cultivos Alimenticios del Centro de Turrialba (Costa Rica)		
		PCSP	Permanent Commission of the Conference on the Use and Conservation of the Marine Resources of the South Pacific
PCARR	Philippines Council for Agricultural Resources and Research		
PCB	Nederlandse Bond van Protestants-Christelijke Beroepsgoederenvervoeders	**PCVM**	Research Association of British Paint, Colour and Varnish Manufacturers
PCBO	Protestants-Christelijke Bond voor Onderwijzend Personeel	**PCWPC**	Permanent Committee of the World Petroleum Congress
PCBS	Permanent Committee on Biological Standards	**PD**	Plantenziektenkundige Dienst
		PDA	Democratic Party of Angola
PCC	Palestine Conciliation Commission	**PDA**	Panhellenic Dental Association
PCC	Philippine Cotton Corporation	**PDAF**	Taiwan Provincial Department of Agriculture and Forestry
PCCC	Pakistan Central Cotton Committee		
PCCEMRSP	Permanent Commission for the Conservation and Exploitation of the Maritime Resources of the South Pacific	**PDC**	Parti Démocratique Chrétien (Burundi)
		PDC	Parti Démocratique Congolais
		PDCA	Purebred Dairy Cattle Association (U.S.A.)
PCCMCA	Programa Cooperativo Centroamericano para el Mejoramiento de Cultivos Alimenticios (Mexico)	**PDCI**	Parti Démocratique de la Côte d'Ivoire
		PDFLP	Popular Democratic Front for the Liberation of Palestine
PCEA	Programma Cooperativo de Experimentación Agropecuaria (*now* SIPA) (Peru)	**PDG**	Parti Démocratique de Guinée
		PDIN	Indonesian National Scientific Documentation Centre
PCEM	Parliamentary Council of the European Movement		
		PDIUM	Partito Democratico Italiano di Unità Monarchica
PCF	Parti Communiste Français		
PCGN	Permanent Committee on Geographical Names	**PDPA**	Bureau pour le Développement de la Production Agricole Outre-Mer
PCI	Italian Communist Party	**PDRSY**	People's Democratic Republic of South Yemen
PCI	Population Council of India		
PCI	Press Council of India	**PDRY**	People's Democratic Republic of Yemen
PCI	Prospectors Club International (U.S.A.)	**PDSA**	People's Dispensary for Sick Animals
PCIFC	Permanent Commission of the International Fisheries Convention	**PDTS**	Powell Duffryn Technical Services
		PE	Parlement Européen
PCII	Potato Chip Institute International (U.S.A.)	**PEA**	Physical Education Association of Great Britain and Northern Ireland
PCIJ	Permanent Court of International Justice		
PCIM	Programa Cooperativo de Investigaciones de Maiz (Peru)	**PEAB**	Professional Engineers' Appointments Bureau

PEAT	Programme Élargi d'Assistance Technique des Nations Unies
PECAM	Pêcheries Camerounaises
PECI	Plastiques et Elastomères de la Côte-d'Ivoire
PEDAEP	Projet d'Expérimentation et de Démonstration en Arboriculture, Élevage et Pâturage (Tunis)
PEEAFE	Panellinios Enosis Emporikon Antiprosopon Pharmakon Exoterikou
PEF	Palestine Exploration Fund (U.K.)
PEFC	Paper Exporters Freight Committee
PEFU	Panel of Experts on Fish Utilization (FAO)
PEIA	Poultry and Egg Institute of America
PEKSI	Persatuan Exportir Indonesia
PEN	Fédération Internationale des Pen Clubs
PEN	Poets, Playwrights, Essayists and Novelists
PENB	Poultry and Egg National Board (U.S.A.)
PEO	Programme Evaluation Organization (India)
PEON	Commission pour la Production d'Électricité d'Origine Nucléaire
PEP	Political and Economic Planning
PEPSU	Patiala and East Punjab States Union
PERA	Production Engineering Research Association of Great Britain
PERI	Pakistan Economic Research Institute
PERULAC	Compañia Peruana de Alimentos Lácteos, S.A.
PES	Société Plastique et Elastomère du Sénégal
PESA	Progressive English Speaking Association (Israel)
PESGB	Petroleum Exploration Society of Great Britain
PEST	Pressure for Economic and Social Toryism
PET	Panellinois Enosis Technikon
PETROPAR	Société de Participations Pétrolières (Mauritania)
PETT	Project – Engineers and Technologists for Tomorrow
PFA	Professional Footballers' Association
PFA	Provincial Forestry Administration (Taiwan)
PFB	Provincial Food Bureau (Taiwan)
PFBCA	Pennsylvania Farm Bureau Cooperative Association (U.S.A.)
PFEL	Pacific Far East Line (U.S.A.)
PFI	Papirindustriens Forskningsinstitutt

PFIOFO	Percy FitzPatrick Institute of Ornithology (South Africa)
PFLOAG	Popular Front for the Liberation of Oman and the Arabian Gulf
PFLP	Peoples Front for the Liberation of Palestine
PFM	Political Freedom Movement
PFN	Partido Frente Nacional (Costa Rico)
PFPA	Pitch Fibre Pipe Association of Great Britain
PFPUT	Pension Fund Property Unit Trust
PFRA	Prairie Farm Rehabilitation Act (Canada)
PFU	Partie Féministe Unifié
PFW	Proefstation voor de Fruitteelt, Wilhelminadorp
PGA	Professional Golfers Association
PGAH	Pineapple Growers Association of Hawaii
PGA – NOC	Permanent General Assembly of National Olympic Committees
PGBI	Protein Grain Products International (U.S.A.)
PGL	Papirgrossistenes Landsforening
PGMTT	Professional Group on Microwave Theory and Techniques (U.S.A.)
PGRO	Pea Growers Research Organisation (*now* Process Growers Research Organisation)
PGV	Proefstation voor de Groenteteelt in de Volle Grond
PHBGB	Poll Hereford Breeders of Great Britain
PHCA	Pig Health Control Association
PHCI	Société Plantations et Huileries de Côte-d'Ivoire
PHI	Conseil Intergouvernemental du Programme Hydrologique International
PHILASAG	Philippine Association of Agriculturists
PHILCOA	Philippine Coconut Administration
PHIL-COMAN	Philippines Council of Management
PHILCUSA	Philippine Council for U.S.Aid
PHILSUGIN	Philippine Sugar Institute
PHOTO-KINA	World Fair of Photography
PHS	Personhistoriska Samfundet
PHSA	Provincial Hospital Services Association
PHYTO-PHAR	Groupement des Fabricants Belges de Produits Belges de Produits de Phytopharmacie

PI	The Plastics Institute
PIA	Pakistan International Airlines
PIA	Pharmaceutical Industries Association in EFTA
PIA	Photographic Importers Association
PIA	Pilots International Association
PIA	Plastics Institute of America
PIA	Plastics Institute of Australia
PIA	Program Implementation Agency (Philippines)
PIAC	Programa de Integración de las Naciones Unidas para la América Central
PIANC	Permanent International Association of Navigation Congresses
PIARC	Permanent International Association of Road Congresses
PIAWA	Printing Industry and Allied Workers' Union (Guyana)
PIB	Petroleum Information Bureau
PIBAC	Permanent International Bureau of Analytical Chemistry of Human and Animal Food
PIBR	Pig Industry Board of Rhodesia
PICA	Palestine Jewish Colonization Association
PICA	Private Investment Company for Asia
PICAA	Permanent International Committee of Agricultural Associations
PICAO	Provisional International Civil Aviation Organisation
PICC	Provisional International Computation Centre
PICEA	Private Information Center on Eastern Arabia (Belgium)
PICG	Programme International de Corrélation Géologique
PICGC	Permanent International Committee for Genetic Congresses
PICIC	Pakistan Industrial Credit and Investment Corporation
PICM	Permanent International Committee of Mothers
PICMME	Provisional Intergovernmental Committee for the Movement of Migrants from Europe
PICOP	Paper Industries Corporation of the Philippines
PICPA	Philippine Institute of Certified Public Accountants
PICS	Publishers Information Card Services
PICUTPC	Permanent and International Committee of Underground Town Planning and Construction
PICV	Permanent International Commission of Viticulture
PID	Partido Institucional Democrático (Guatemala)
PIDA	Pig Industry Development Authority (*now* MLC)
PIDC	Pakistan Industrial Development Corporation
PIDE	Pakistan Institute of Development Economics
PIDR	Programa Interamericano para el Desarrollo Rural (Costa Rico)
PIF	British Paper and Board Industry Federation
PIFC	Pakistan Industrial Finance Corporation
PIIF	Pakistan International Industrial Fair
PIIP	Programa Interamericano de Información Popular (Costa Rico)
PIJR	Programa Interamericano para la Juventud Rural (Costa Rico)
PIL	Pest Infestation Laboratory
PILCAM	Société Camerounaise de Fabrication de Piles Électriques
PILOT	Panel on Instrumentation for Large Optical Telescopes
PILS	Pacific Information and Library Services (Hawaii)
PIM	Plan Indicatif Mondial pour le Développement Agricole (FAO)
PIMC	Pineapple Industry Marketing Corporation (Malaysia)
PIME	Pontificial Foreign Mission Institute (Italy)
PIMEC	Programa Interamericano para Mejorar la Enseñanza de las Ciencias (*of* OEA)
PINA	Potash Institute of North America
PINA	Programa Integrado de Nutrición Aplicada (Colombia)
PINAC	Permanent International Association of Navigation Congresses
PINAPA	Panel on Interactions between the Neutral and Ionized Part of the Ionosphere
PINGW	Panstwowy Instytut Naukowy Gospodarstwa Wiejskiego w Pulawach
PINSTECH	Pakistan Institute of Nuclear Science and Technology

PINTEC	Plastics Institute National Technical Conference
PINZ	Plastics Institute of New Zealand
PIOSA	Pan-Indian Ocean Science Association
PIPA	Pacific Industrial Property Association
PIRA	Research Association for the Paper and Board, Printing and Packaging Industries
PIRI	Paint Industries Research Institute (S. Africa)
PIRRCOM	Project for the Intensification of Regional Research on Cotton, Oilseeds and Millets (India)
PIRSA	Psychological Institute of the Republic of South Africa
PISPESCA	Asociación Colombiana de Piscicultura y Pesca
PITA	Pacific International Trapshooting Association (U.S.A.)
PITAC	Pakistan Industrial Technical Assistance Centre
PITB	Petroleum Industry Training Board
PIWR	Panstowy Instytut Wydawnictw Rolniczych
PJA	Pakistan Jute Association
PJGN	Plattelands Jongeren Gemeenschap Nederland
PJMA	Pakistan Jute Mills Association
PKL	Plast- och Kemikalieleverantörers Förening
PKTF	Printing and Kindred Trades Federation
PKV	Verband der Privaten Krankenversicherung
PL	Parlamento Latino-Americano (Peru)
PLA	Pakistan Library Association
PLA	Palestine Liberation Army
PLA	Philippine Library Association
PLA	Port of London Authority
PLA	Private Libraries Association
PLANASEM	Plano Nacional de Sementes (Brazil)
PLANATES	Plano Nacional de Assistência Técnica a Suinicultura (Brazil)
PLANAVE	Plano Nacional de Avicultura (Brazil)
PLANER	Plano Nacional de Extensão Rural (Brazil)
PLASCO	Latin American School of Social Sciences (Chile)
PLAST-AFRIC	Société Africaine de Transformation de Matières Plastiques (Haute-Volta)
PLATO	Programmed Learning Automatic Teaching Organisation (U.S.A.)
PLDT	Philippine Long Distant Telephone Company
PLGS	Partito Liberale dei Giovani Somali
PLI	Partido Liberal Independiente (Nicaragua)
PLI	Partito Liberale Italiano
PLN	Partido Liberacion Nacional (Costa Rico)
PLN	Partido Liberal Nacionalista (Nicaragua)
PLO	Palestine Liberation Organization
PLP	Parti pour la Liberté et le Progrés (Belgium)
PLR	Partido Liberal Radical (Paraguay)
PLRA	Patronto de Leprosos de la Repúblic Argentina
PLRE	Partido Liberal Radical Ecuatoriano
PLRG	Public Libraries Research Group
PLSA	Pacific Law and Society Association (U.S.A.)
PLUNA	Primeras Lineas Uruguayas de Navigación Aerea
PLUVA	Stichting voor Onderzoek van Pluimvee en Varkens
PMA	Pakistan Medical Association
PMA	Programa Mundial de Alimentos
PMA	Production and Marketing Administration (U.S.A.)
PMAC	Pharmaceutical Manufacturers Association of Canada
PMAC	Purchasing Management Association of Canada
PMAEA	Port Management Association of Eastern Africa
PMATA	Paint Manufacturers and Allied Trades Association
PMBC	Plywood Manufacturers of British Columbia
PME	Petites et Moyennes Entreprises
PMEG	Perforated Metal Experimental Group
PMFC	Pacific Marine Fisheries Commission
PMH	Pari Mutuel sur les Hippodromes
PMIP	Pan-Malaysian Islamic Party
PMSD	Parti Mauricien Social Democrate
PMU	Missionary Union of Priests, Brothers, Nuns
PMU	Pari Mutuel Urbain
PMV	Pro Mundi Vita. International Research and Information Centre (Belgium)
PN	Produktivitetsnämnden
PNB	Philippine National Bank
PNCA	Programa Nacional de Capacitación Agropecuaria (Colombia)

PNDC	Programa Nacional de Desarrollo de la Comunidad (Guatemala)
PNEU	Parents National Education Union
PNEUROP	European Committee of Manufacturers of Compressed Air Equipment
PNM	People's National Movement (Trinidad and Tobago)
PNOC	Philippine National Oil Company
PNP	Partido Nuevo Progresista (Puerto Rico)
PNP	People's National Party (Jamaica)
PNTA	Pakistan National Tuberculosis Association
PNUD	Programme des Nations Unies pour le Développement
PNUE	Programme des Nations Unies pour l'Environnement
PNUMA	Programa de las Naciones Unidas para el Medio Ambiente
PNYME	Papir- és Nyomdaipari Műszaki Egyesület
POAAPS	Permanent Organisation for Afro-Asian Peoples Solidarity
POC	Stichting Provinciale Onderzoekcentra
POED	Post Office Engineering Department
POEM	Palm Oil Estates Managers (Africa)
POEU	Post Office Engineering Union
POGO	Polar Orbiting Geophysical Observatory (U.S.A.)
POKE	Panellinios Organosis Kinimatografikon Epicheirision
POMAG	Société de Grands Magasins de Pointe-Noir (Congo)
POMSA	Post Office Management Staffs Association
POOL	Ad hoc Group of Experts on Pollution of the Ocean Originating on Land (IOC)
POPLAB	International Program of Laboratories for Population Statistics
PORIS	Post Office Radio Interference Station
PORLA	Palm Oil Registration and Licensing Authority (Malaysia)
POSL	Parti Ouvrier Socialiste Luxembourgeois
POSMAS	Panellinios Osmospondia Somateion Mesiton Astikon Symbaseon
POUNC	Post Office Users' National Council
POUR	President's Organization for Unemployment Relief (U.S.A.)
POWU	Post Office Workers Union
PP	Periphery Press (Norway)

PPA	Pakistan Press Association
PPA	Peat Producers Association of Great Britain and Ireland
PPA	Periodical Publishers Association
PPA	Process Plant Association
PPA	Progressive People's Alliance (Gambia)
PPAB	Programme and Policy Advisory Board (FAO)
PPBF	Pan-American Pharmaceutical and Biochemical Federation
PPCS	Primary Producers Co-operative Society (N.Z.)
PPD	Partido Popular Democrático (Puerto Rico)
PPD	Provinciale Planologische Diensten
PPDA	Produce Prepackaging Development Association, Ltd
PPE	Parti Populaire Européen (Belgium)
PPI	Pakistan Press International
PPI	Pickle Packers International (U.S.A.)
PPIP	Philippine Poultry Improvement Plan
PPM	Parti du Peuple Mauritanien
PPMA	Produce Packaging and Marketing Association
PPMC	People to People Music Committee (U.S.A.)
PPMC	Produce Prepackaging Machinery Co.
PPN	Parti Progressiste Nigérien
PPP	People's Political Party (St Vincent)
PPP	People's Progressive Party (Gambia, Guyana, Malaysia)
PPPRF	Pan Pacific Public Relations Federation
PPR	Press and Public Relations Ltd.
PPRIC	Pulp and Paper Research Institute of Canada
PPS	Parti Popular Socialista (Mexico, El Salvador)
PPS	Partido Popular Salvadoreño
PPSA	Pan-Pacific Surgical Association
PPSEAWA	Pan Pacific and Southeast Asia Women's Association
PPT	Parti Progressiste Tschadien
PPU	Peace Pledge Union
PPV	Fachverband der Papier und Pappe Verarbeitenden Industrie (Austria)
PQAA	Province of Quebec Association of Architects (Canada)
PRA	Paint Research Association

PRA	Parti du Regroupement Africaine
PRA	Partido Revolucionario Auténtico (Bolivia)
PRA	Personnel Research Association (U.S.A.)
PRA	Prairie Rail Authority (Canada)
PRAC	Pyrethrum Research Advisory Committee (Kenya)
PRAI	Planning Research and Action Institute, Lucknow (India)
PRAIS	Pesticide Residue Analysis Information Service
PRATRA	Philippines Relief and Trade Rehabilitation Administration
PRB	Partido de la Revolución Boliviana
PRC	People's Republic of China
PRD	Partido Revolucionario Dominicano
PRD	Polytechnic Research and Development Co. (U.S.A.)
PRE	Fédération Européenne des Fabricants de Produits Réfractaires
PRE	Programme de Reconstruction Européenne
PRF	Petroleumhandelns Riksförbund
PRI	Partido Republicano Italiano
PRI	Partido Revolucionario Institucional (Mexico)
PRI	Performance Registry International (U.S.A.)
PRI	Prévention Routière Internationale
PRI	Public Relations Institute of Ireland
PRIH	Pineapple Research Institute of Hawaii
PRII	Public Relations Institute of Ireland
PSIL	Philippine Society of International Law
PRIMI-FANO	Commission pour les Enfants Privés de Milieu Familial Normal (of BICE)
PRIN	Partido Revolucionario de Izquierda Nacionalista (Bolivia)
PRINZ	Public Relations Institute of New Zealand
PRIO	International Peace Research Institute in Oslo
PRISA	Public Relations Institute of South Africa
PRISCO	Price Stabilisation Corporation (Philippines)
PRL	Prairie Research Laboratory Canada.
PRM	Parti du Regroupement Mauritanienne
PRO	Public Record Office
PROA	Plantations Réunies de l'Ouest Africain
PROAGRO	Comisión Nacional de Promoción Agropecuario (Argentina)
PROCH-IMAD	Société des Produits Chimiques de Madagascar
PRODAC	Production Advisers' Consortium
PROD-AROM	Syndicat National des Fabricants de Produits Aromatiques
PRODEHA	Protestants-Christelijke Bond van Detaillisten in Luxe en Huishoudellijke Artikelen
PRODES	Productores de Semillas, S.A.
PRODISEGE	Syndicat Professionnel des Producteurs d'Énergie et des Services Publics Autonomes
PROHUZA	Centre d'Études et d'Information des Problèmes Humains dans les Zones Arides
PROLUMA	Produits Lubrificants de Madagascar
PROM-ARCA	Schweizerische Gesellschaft der Konsumgüterindustrie
PROMSTRA	Production Methods and Stress Research Association (Netherlands)
PRONADI	Chambre Syndicale Belge des Fabricants et Distributeurs de Produits Naturels et Diététiques
PRONASE	National Seed Production Agency (Mexico)
PRONENCA	Programa Nacional de Educación Nutricional y Complementación Alimentaria (Colombia)
PROPASI	Productores de Patata de Siembra
PROTAAL	Proyecto Cooperativo de Investigacion sobre Tecnologia Agropecuario en América Latina
PROTERRA	Programa de Redistribuição de Terras e de Estimulos a Agro-industria do Norte e do Nordeste (Brazil)
PROVO	Stichting Proefbedrijf Voedselbestraling
PRP	People's Revolutionary Party (Vietnam)
PRRM	Philippine Rural Reconstruction Movement
PRS	Groupement National des Papetiers Répartiteurs Spécialisés
PRS	Paint Research Station
PRS	Protestant Reformation Society
PRSA	Public Relations Society of America
PRSC	Partido Revolucionario Social Cristiano (Dominica)
PRSP	Public Relations Society of the Philippines
PRTA	Public Road Transport Association
PRUCIS	Philippine Rural Community Improvement Society
PS	Parapsychological Society (U.S.A.)
PS	Physical Society

PSA	Pacific Science Association (Hawaii)	**PTA**	Physikalisch-Technische Anstalt zu Braunschweig
PSA	Pacific Seedsmens Association (U.S.A.)		
PSA	Pakistan Sociological Association	**PTA**	Polskie Towarzystwo Astronautyczne
PSA	Parti Solidaire Africain (Zaire)	**PTA**	Primary Tungsten Association
PSA	Photographic Society of America	**PTA**	Printing Trades Alliance
PSA	Poultry Stock Association (*now* BPBHA)	**PTAiN**	Polskie Towarzystwo Archeologiczne i Numizmatyczne
PSAC	President's Science Advisory Service (U.S.A.)		
PSAE	Philippine Society of Agricultural Engineers	**PTAS**	Productivity and Technical Assistance Secretariat
PSAU	Plan de Suministros Alimentarios de Urgencia (WFP)	**PTB**	Physikalisch-Technische Bundesanstalt
PSC	Pacific Science Council	**PTB**	Polskie Towarzystwo Biometryczne
PSC	Partie Social Chrétien (Belgium)	**PTBBiMF**	Polskie Towarzystwo Balneologii, Bioklimatologii i Medycyny Fizykalnej
PSC	Peulvruchten Studie Combinatie		
PSD	Parti Social Démocrate de Madagascar et des Comores	**PTBR**	Polskie Towarzystwo Badan Radiacyjnych im Marii Sktodowskiej-Curie
PSD	Parti Socialiste Démocratique (Morocco)	**PTC**	Polskie Towarzystwo Chemiczne
PSD	Partido Social Demócrata (Bolivia)	**PTCh**	Polskie Towarzystwo Chemiczne
PSDI	Partito Socialista Democratico Italiano	**PTCR**	Patent, Trademark and Copyright Research Institute (U.S.A.)
PSDIS	Partito Socialista Democratico Independente Sanmarinese (San Marino)		
		PTD	Polskie Towarzystwo Dermatologiczne
PSFC	International Pacific Salmon Fisheries Commission	**PTDL**	Polskie Towarzystwo Diagnostyki Laboratoryjnej
PSFG	Permanent Service on the Fluctuations of Glaciers of IUGG	**PTE**	Polskie Towarzystwo Entomologiczne
		PTEK	Polskie Towarzystwo Ekonomiczne
PSFN	Polskie Stowarzyszenie Filmu Naukowego	**PTF**	Papirindustriens Tekniske Forening
PSI	Partito Socialista Italiano	**PTF**	Polskie Towarzystwo Farmakologiczne
PSI	Pharmaceutical Society of Ireland	**PTF**	Polskie Towarzystwo Filologiczne
PSI	Public Services International	**PTFarm**	Polskie Towarzystwo Farmaceutyczne
PSIDC	Punjab State Industrial Development Corporation (India)	**PTG**	Polskie Towarzystwo Geograficzne
		PTG	Polskie Towarzystwo Geologiczne
PSIP	Poultry Stock Improvement Plan	**PTGWO**	Philippine Transport and General Workers Organisations
PSIUP	Partito Socialista Italiano di Unità Proletaria		
PSMSL	Permanent Service for Mean Sea Level (*of* IAPO)	**PTH**	Polskie Towarzystwo Historyczne
		PTHiC	Polskie Towarzystwo Histochemików i Cytochemików
PSNI	Pharmaceutical Society of Northern Ireland		
PSP	Pacifistich Socialistiche Partij (Netherlands)	**PTI**	Press Trust of India
PSQC	Philippine Society for Quality Control	**PTIDG**	Presentation of Technical Information Discussion Group
PSSA	Pharmaceutical Society of South Africa	**PTIO**	Pesticides Technical Information Office (Canada)
PSSA	Photogrammetric Society of South Africa		
PSSC	Philippine Social Science Council	**PTJ**	Polskie Towarzystwo Jezykoznawcze
PSSG	International Printers Supply Salesmen's Guild (U.S.A.)	**PTK**	Pienteollisuuden Keskusliitto
		PTL	Polskie Towarzystwo Logopedyczne
PSU	Parti Socialiste Unifié	**PTL**	Polskie Towarzystwo Ludoznawcze
PSU	Partito Socialista Unitario	**PTN**	Polskie Towarzystwo Nautologiczne
PSWO	Picture and Sound World Organisation	**PTN**	Polskie Towarzystwo Neurologiczne

PTO	Polskie Towarzystwo Okulistyczne
PTO	Polskie Towarzystwo Onkologiczne
PTO	Polskie Towarzystwo Orientalistyczne
PTOiTr	Polskie Towarzystwo Ortopedyczne i Traumatologiczne
PTOM	Pays et Territoires d'Outremer (of EEC)
PTP	Polskie Towarzystwo Pediatryczne
PTP	Polskie Towarzystwo Psychologiczne
PTR	Physikalisch-Technische Reichsanstalt
PTR	Polskie Towarzystwo Religioznawcze
PTS	Polskie Towarzystwo Semiotyczne
PTT	International Federation of Christian Trade Unions of Employers in Public Service and PTT
PTT	Postes, Télégraphes, Téléphones
PTTI	Postal, Telegraph and Telephone International
PTU	Plumbing Trades Union
PTZ	Polskie Towarzystwo Zootechniczne
PTZool	Polskie Towarzystwo Zoologiczne
PUA	Pacific Union Association
PUAS	Postal Union of the Americas and Spain
PUC	Public Utilities Committee (ECE)
PUCHE	Potchefstroom University for Christian Higher Education (South Africa)
PUCR	Partido Unión Cívico Revolucionaria (Costa Rico)
PUDINE	Programa Universitario de Desenvolvimento Industrial do Nordeste (Brazil)
PUDOC	Centrum voor Landbouwpublikaties en Landbouwdocumentatie, Wageningen
PUN	Partido Unión Nacional (Costa Rico)
PUP	People's United Party (British Honduras)
PUWP	Polish United Workers Party
PV	Protection des Végétaux
PVB	Provinciale Veevoederbureau
PVC	Provinciale Voedselcommissaris
PVDA	Partij van de Arbeit (Netherlands)
PVFM	Planification pour une Vie Familiale Meilleure (FAO)
PVGA	Processed Vegetable Growers Association
PVTA	Philippine Virginia Tobacco Administration
PVV	Partij voom Vrijheid en Vooruitgang (Belgium)
PWC	Peasants' Work Co-operatives (Yugoslavia)

PWC	Peoples World Convention
PWCA	Peoples World Constituent Assembly
PWCB	Provincial Water Conservancy Bureau (Taiwan)
PWFA	Petroleum Workers Federation of Aruba
PWIF	Plantation Worker's International Federation
PWLB	Public Works Loan Board
PWPMA	Philippine Welding Products Manufacturers Association
PWU	Provision Wholesalers Union (Malta)
PZITB	Polski Zwiazek Inzynierów Techników Budownictwa
PZITS	Polskie Zrzeszenie Inzynierów i Techników Sanitarnych

Q

QANTAS	Queensland and Northern Territory Aerial Services, Ltd (Australia)
QCGA	Queensland Cane Growers' Association (Australia)
QCGC	Queensland Cane Growers' Council (Australia)
QEA	Qantas Empire Airways (Australia)
QIMA	Queensland Institute of Municipal Administration
QMFCI	Quarter-Master Food and Container Institute (U.S.A.)
QSPP	Quebec Society for the Protection of Plants (Canada)
QUANA	Authorized Newsagents Association of Queensland
QUI	Queen's University of Ireland

R

RAA	Royal Academy of Arts
RAAD	Rijks Zuivel-Agrarische Afvalwaterdienst
RAAF	Royal Australian Air Force

RAAG	Research Association of Applied Geometry (Japan)	**RAM**	Royal Academy of Music
		RAMAC	Radio Marine Associated Companies
RAAM	Refineria Argentina de Aceites Minerales	**RAMNAC**	Radio Aids to Marine Navigation Application Committee
RAAS	Racial Adjustment Action Society		
RAB	Rationalisatie v. d. Arbeidstechniek in de Bosbouw	**RAOB**	Royal Antediluvian Order of Buffaloes
		RAOU	Royal Australasian Ornithologists Unions
RABDF	Royal Association of British Dairy Farmers	**RAP**	Rhodesian Action Party
RABFM	Research Association of British Flour Millers (*now* FMBRA)	**RAPRA**	Rubber and Plastics Research Association of Great Britain (*formerly* RABRM)
RABI	Royal Agricultural Benevolent Institution	**RARC**	Ruakura Agricultural Research Centre (New Zealand)
RABPCVM	Research Association of British Paint, Colour and Varnish Manufacturers (*now* PRA)		
		RARDE	Royal Armament Research and Development Establishment
RABRM	Research Association of British Rubber Manufacturers (*now* RAPRA)		
		RAS	Royal Asiatic Society
RAC	Royal Automobile Club	**RAS**	Royal Astronomical Society
RACP	Royal Australian College of Physicians	**RASB**	Royal Asiatic Society of Bengal
RACS	Royal Australian College of Surgeons	**RAS of C**	Royal Agricultural Society of the Commonwealth
RACSA	Radio Aeronautica de Cuba		
RAD	Royal Academy of Dancing	**RASC**	Royal Astronomical Society of Canada
RADA	Royal Academy of Dramatic Art	**RASE**	Royal Agricultural Society of England
RADC	Rome Air Development Centre (U.S.A.)	**RASK**	Royal Agricultural Society of Kenya
RADD	Royal Association in Aid of the Deaf and Dumb	**RASU**	Rangoon Arts and Science University
		RATEKSA	Radiobranchens Tekniske og Kommercielle Sammenslutning
RAE	Radiodifusion Argentina al Exterior		
RAE	Royal Aircraft Establishment	**RATP**	Régie Autonome des Transports Parisiens
RAeS	Royal Aeronautical Society	**RAU**	République Arabe Unie
RAF	Redernes Arbeidsgiverforening	**RAW**	Rationalisierungs-Ausschusses der Deutschen Wirtschaft
RAF	Reklameatelierenes Forening		
RAF	Rörledningsfirmornas Arbetsgivareförbund	**RBA**	Royal Society of British Artists
RAFA	Royal Air Forces Association	**RBAI**	Royal Belfast Academical Institution
RAFE	Regional Office for Asia and the Far East (FAO)	**RBS**	Royal Botanical Society
		RBS	Royal Society of British Sculptors
RAFES	Royal Air Force Educational Service	**RBV**	Rohrleitungsbauverband
RAFR	Regional Office for Africa (FAO)	**RC**	Rijksconsultentschap
RAFSC	Royal Air Force Staff College	**RCA**	Race Course Association
RAGB	Refractories Association of Great Britain	**RCA**	Radio Corporation of America
RAGB	Restaurateurs Association of Great Britain	**RCA**	Reinforced Concrete Association
		RCA	Research Council of Alberta (Canada)
RAHS	Royal Australian Historical Society	**RCA**	Retail Confectioners Association
RAI	Nederlandse Vereniging de Rijwiel en Automobiel-Industrie	**RCA**	Royal Choral Society
		RCA	Royal College of Art
RAI	Radiotelevisione Italiana		
RAI	Royal Anthropological Institute	**RCAA**	Royal Canadian Academy of Arts
RAI	Royal Archaeological Institute	**RCAS**	Royal Central Asia Society
RAIA	Royal Australian Institute of Architects		
RAIC	Royal Architectural Institute of Canada	**RCCO**	Royal Canadian College of Organists

RCD	Regional Co-operation for Development (Iran, Palestine, Turkey)
RCE	Union Restaurants Collectifs Européens
RCEEA	Radio Communication and Electronic Engineering Association
RCGP	Royal College of General Practitioners
RCGS	Royal Canadian Geological Society
RCI	Recontres Creatives Internationales
RCI	Research and Control Instruments, Ltd
RCI	Royal Canadian Institute
RCIA	Retail Clerks International Association (U.S.A.)
RCIVS	Regional Conference on International Voluntary Service
RCK	Research Centrum Kalkzandsteen Industrie (Netherlands)
RCM	République des Citoyens du Monde
RCM	Royal College of Midwives
RCM	Royal College of Mines
RCM	Royal College of Music
RCMA	Rubber Cultuur Maatschappij 'Amsterdam'
RCMP	Royal Canadian Mounted Police
RCN	Reactor Centrum Nederland
RCN	Royal College of Nursing
RCO	Royal College of Organists
RCOG	Royal College of Obstetricians and Gynaecologists
RCP	Royal College of Physicians
RCPA	Rice and Corn Production Administration (Philippines)
RCPCC	Rice and Corn Production Coordinating Council (Philippines)
RCPI	Royal College of Physicians of Ireland
RCPS	Royal College of Physicians and Surgeons
RCRDC	Radio Components Research and Development Committee
RCRF	Society of Roman Ceramic Archaeologists (Switzerland)
RCS	Royal Choral Society
RCS	Royal Commonwealth Society
RCS	Royal College of Science
RCS	Royal College of Surgeons of England
RCSB	Royal Commonwealth Society for the Blind
RCSC	Radio Components Standardization Committee
RCSEd	Royal College of Surgeons of Edinburgh

RCSI	Royal College of Surgeons in Ireland
RCU	Rural Cooperative Unions (Iran)
RCVS	Royal College of Veterinary Surgeons
RDA	Rassemblement Démocratique Africain
RDA	République Démocratique Allemande
RDB	Research and Development Board (U.S.A.)
RDB	Ring Deutscher Bergingenieure
RDC	Universal Esperanto Association Research and Documentation Centre
RDCOT	Regional Documentation Centre for Oral Tradition (Niger)
RDM	Bundesverband Ring Deutscher Makler
RDOEI	Research and Development Organization for the Electrical Industry (India)
RDS	Research Defence Society
RDS	Royal Drawing Society
RDS	Royal Dublin Society
RDSO	Research Designs and Standards Organisation (India)
REA	Rural Electrification Administration (U.S.A)
REAF	Rutebileiernes Arbeidsgiverforening
REAL	Real-Aerovias do Brasil
REAP	Reinforcing Evangelists and Pastors (Japan)
REBIA	Regional Building Institute for Africa
REC	Rural Electrification Corporation (India)
RECA	Research and Education Centre (Japan)
RECE	Representación Cubana del Exilio (U.S.A.)
RECMF	Radio and Electronic Components Manufacturers' Association
RECOBAA	Office of the Government Commissioner for Foreign Agricultural Affairs (Netherlands)
REconS	Royal Economic Society
RECSAM	Regional Centre for Education in Science and Mathematics (Malaysia)
REDA	Ramo Editoriale degli Agricoltori
REE	Comité Européen de Reconstruction Économique Européenne
REFA	Real Estate Fund of America
REGABON	Radio Électricité Gabonaise
REHVA	Representatives of European Heating and Ventilating Associations
REI	Rat der Europäischen Industrieverbände
REIC	Radiation Effects Information Centre (U.S.A)
REKU	Raditoren- en Ketel-Unie

REL	Riksförbundet för Electrikfieringen pa Landsbygden
RELC	Regional English Language Centre (Malaysia)
REMC	Radio and Electronics Measurements Committee
REMP	Research Group for European Migration Problems
RENFE	Red Nacional de los Ferrocarriles Espanoles
RENVA	Rengørings-og Vagtselskabernes Arbejdsgiverforening
REOU	Radio and Electronic Officers Union
REPESA	Refineria de Petroleos de Escombreras, S.A.
RES	Royal Empire Society
RES	Royal Entomological Society of London
RESEDA	Réseau de Documentation en Économie Agricole
RETMA	Radio-Electronics-Television Manufacturers Association (U.S.A.)
REUR	Regional Office for Europe (FAO)
REVIMA	Société pour la Revision et l'Entretien du Materiel Aéronautique
RF	Radiobranchens Faellesrad
RFAC	Royal Fine Art Commission
RFC	Reconstruction Finance Corporation (U.S.A.)
RFCWA	Regional Fisheries Commission for Western Africa
RFFSA	Rede Ferroviaria Federal, S.A. (Brazil)
RFLW	Rijksfaculteit Landbouw-wetenschappen, Gent (Belgium)
RFS	Royal Forestry Society
RFSEW	Royal Forestry Society of England and Wales
RFSU	Rugby Football Schools Union
RFU	Rugby Football Union
RGA	Rubber Growers Association
RGAHS	Royal Guernsey Agricultural and Horticultural Society
RGD	Radio Gramophone Development Company
RGDATA	Retail Grocery, Dairy and Allied Trades Association (Eire)
RGE	Rat der Gemeinden Europas
RGO	Royal Greenwich Observatory
RGS	Royal Geographical Society
RGSA	Royal Geographical Society of Australasia
RGW	Rat für Gegenseitige Wirtschaftshilfe
RHA	Royal Hibernian Academy (Eire)
RHCSA	Regional Hospitals Consultants and Specialists Association
RHE	Road Haulage Executive
RHEL	Rutherford High Energy Laboratory, Chilton
RHI	Racial Harmony International (U.K.)
RHistS	Royal Historical Society
RHS	Royal Horticultural Society
RHS	Royal Humane Society
RHSI	Royal Horticultural Society of Ireland
RHSV	Royal Historical Society of Victoria (Canada)
RI	Rotary International
RI	Royal Institute of Painters in Water Colours
RI	Royal Institution of Great Britain
RIA	Railway Industry Association of Great Britain
RIA	Réunions Internationales d'Architects
RIA	Royal Irish Academy
RIAA	Record Industry Association of America
RIAC	Royal Irish Automobile Club
RIAI	Royal Institute of the Architects of Ireland
RIAM	Royal Irish Academy of Music
RIAS	Radio in American Sector (Germany)
RIAS	Research Institute for Animal Science, Irene (South Africa)
RIAS	Royal Incorporation of Architects in Scotland
RIB	Racing Information Bureau
RIB	Research Institute of Brewing (Japan)
RIB	Rural Industries Bureau (*now* COSIRA)
RIBA	Royal Institute of British Architects
RIBI	Rotary International in Great Britain and Ireland
RIC	Radio Industry Council
RIC	Research and Information Commission (*of* COSEC)
RIC	Rice Improvement Conference (of PDAF)
RIC	Royal Institute of Chemistry
RIC	Union Internationale des Voitures et Fourgons
RICA	Research Institute for Consumer Affairs
RICA	Réseau d'Information Agricole
RICASIP	Research Information Center and Advisory Service on Information Processing (U.S.A.)

RICE	Rice Information Cooperative Effort (Philippines)
RICM	Registre International Citoyens du Monde
RICOB	Rice and Corn Board (Philippines)
RICOCI	Représentations Industrielles et Commerciales de l'Ouest de la Côte-d'Ivoire
RICS	Royal Institution of Chartered Surveyors
RIDA	Rural Industrial Development Authority (Malaysia)
RIEC	Research Institute for Estate Crops (Indonesia)
RIF	Radgivende Ingeniorers Forening
RIGB	Royal Institution of Great Britain
RIHED	Regional Institute of Higher Education and Development (Singapore)
RIIA	Reuniones de Intercambio de Información Agropecuaria (Argentina)
RIIA	Royal Institute of International Affairs
RIL	Suomen Rakennusinsinöörien Förbund
RILC	Racing Industry Liaison Committee
RILDD	Research Institute of Launderers, Drycleaners and Dyers (N.Z.)
RILEM	Réunion Internationale des Laboratoires d'Essais et de Recherches sur les Matériaux et les Constructions
RIM	Rhodesian Institute of Management
RIMCU	Research Institute for Mindanao Culture (Philippines)
RIN	Rijksinstituut voor Natuurbeheer
RIN	Royal Institution of Navigation
RINA	Royal Institution of Naval Architects
RINAVI	Associazione Nazionale Industriali Riparatori Navali
RINORD	Consulting Engineers in the Nordic Countries
RIOP	Royal Institute of Oil Painters
RIP	Rijksinstituut voor Pluimveeteelt
RIPA	Royal Institution of Public Administration
RIPHH	Royal Institute of Public Health and Hygiene
RIPS	United Nations Regional Institute for Population Studies (Ghana)
RISCO	Rhodesian Iron and Steel Company
RISCOM	Rhodesian Iron and Steel Commission
RISPA	Research Institute of the Sumatra Planters Association (Indonesia)
RIT	Recherches et Industries Thérapeutiques (Belgium)

RITENA	Reunión Internacional de Técnicos de la Nutrición Animal
RIV	Regolamento Internazionale Veicoli (Union Internationale des Wagons)
RIVON	Rijksinstituut voor Veldbiologisch Onderzoek ten behoeve van het Natuurbehoud (*now* RIN)
RIZA	Rijksinstituut voor Zuivering van Afvalwater
RJAHS	Royal Jersey Agricultural and Horticultural Society
RJAS	*see* RJAHS
RKJB	Rooms-Katholieke Jonge Boerenstand
RKL	Rationalisierungs-Kuratorium für Landwirtschaft
RKTL	Reichskuratorium für Technik in der Landwirtschaft
RKW	Rationalisierungs-Kuratorium der Deutschen Wirtschaft
RL	Reproducørernes Landsforening
RLA	Rhodesia Library Association
RLAT	Regional Office for Latin America (FAO)
RLBWM	Regional Library Bureau, West Midlands
RLC	Rijkslandbouwconsultentschap
RLF	Riksforbündet Landsbygdens Folk
RLH	Swedish Farmers Flax and Hemp Growers Association
RLL	Radio-Leverandorenes Landsforbund
RLL	Radioliikkeiden Liitto
RLSS	Royal Life Saving Society
RLVD	Rijkslandbouwvoorlichtingsdienst
RLWS	Rijkslandbouwwinterscholen
RMA	Royal Musical Association
RMA	Rubber Manufacturers Association (U.S.A.)
RMAI	Radio Manufacturers' Association of India
RMBC	Regional Marine Biological Centre
RMC	Regional Meteorological Centre (WMO)
RMCC	Royal Military College of Canada
RMCS	Royal Military College of Science
RMetS	Royal Meteorological Society
RMIC	Research Materials Information Center (*of* ORNL) (U.S.A.)
RmP	Riksföreningen mot Polio
RMPA	Royal Medico-Psychological Association
RMR	Riksförbundet mot Reumatism
RMS	Royal Medical Society

RMS	Royal Meteorological Society
RMS	Royal Microscopical Society
RND	Rijksnijverheidsdienst
RNEA	Regional Office for the Near East (FAO)
RNET	Régie Nationale des Eaux du Togo
RNFU	Rhodesia National Farmers' Union
RNHU	Royal National Homing Union
RNIB	Royal National Institute for the Blind
RNID	Royal National Institute for the Deaf
RNLAF	Royal Netherlands Air Force
RNLI	Royal National Lifeboat Institution
RNMDSF	Royal National Mission to Deep Sea Fishermen
RNPL	Royal Naval Physiological Laboratory
RNRS	Royal National Rose Society
RNS	Royal Numismatic Society
RNSAS	Royal Netherlands Society for Agricultural Science
RNSS	Royal Naval Scientific Service
RNSTS	Royal Naval Supply and Transport Service
RNTP	Régie Nationale des Transports et des Travaux Publics
RNZAS	Royal Astronomical Society of New Zealand
RNZIH	Royal New Zealand Institute of Horticulture
ROA	Raad van Organisatie-Adviesbureaus
ROA	Racehorse Owners Association
ROC	Royal Observer Corps
ROCAP	Regional Office for Central America and Panama
ROE	Royal Observatory Edinburgh (Scotland)
ROMANA	Société d'Archéologie Romana
ROMTRANS	Association Roumaine pour Transports Routiers Internationaux
RORC	Royal Ocean Racing Club
ROSCM	Research Organisation of Ships Compositions Manufacturers
ROSCO	Road Operators Safety Council
ROSPA	Royal Society for the Prevention of Accidents
ROSTA	Regional Office for Science and Technology for Africa (UNESCO)
ROSTSCA	Regional Office for Science and Technology for South and Central Asia (UNESCO)
RP	Royal Society of Portrait Painters
RPAA	Regional Planning Association of America
RPC	Rijkspluimveeteeltconsulentschap
RPE	Rocket Propulsion Establishment
RPFLP	Revolutionary Popular Front (Lebanon)
RPMI	Roswell Park Memorial Institute (U.S.A.)
RPP	Republican People's Party (Turkey)
RPPITB	Rubber and Plastics Processing Industry Training Board
RPRA	Royal Pigeon Racing Association
RPRA	Rubber and Plastics Reclamation Association
RPS	Royal Philatelic Society
RPS	Royal Philharmonic Society
RPS	Royal Photographic Society
RPvZ	Rijksproefstation voor Zaadcontrôle
RR	Rörledningsfirmirnas Riksorganisation
RRCBC	Regional Research Centre of the British Caribbean (Trinidad)
RRCC	Redwood Region Conservation Council (U.S.A.)
RRE	Royal Radar Research Establishment
RRI	Rowett Research Institute (Scotland)
RRI	Rubber Research Institute (Malaysia)
RRIC	Rubber Research Institute of Ceylon
RRII	Rubber Research Institute of India
RRIN	Rubber Research Institute of Nigeria
RRIWB	River Research Institute, West Bengal
RRL	Radio Research Laboratory (Japan)
RRL	Regional Research Laboratory (India)
RRL	Road Research Laboratory
RRP	Republican Reliance Party (Turkey)
RS	Royal Society
RSA	Rancha Santa Ana Botanic Garden (U.S.A.)
RSA	Relay Services Association of Great Britain
RSA	Royal Scottish Academy
RSA	Royal Society of Arts
RSA	Royal Society of Australia
RSAC	Royal Scottish Automobile Club
RSAI	Royal Society of Antiquaries of Ireland
RSAS	Royal Sanitary Association of Scotland
RSAS	Royal Surgical Aid Society
RSASA	Royal South Australian Society of Arts
RSC	Royal Society of Canada
RSCM	Royal School of Church Music
RSD	Royal Society of Dublin
RSE	Royal Society of Edinburgh (Scotland)

RSF	Real Sociedad Fotográfica	**RTEB**	Radio Trades Examination Board
RSF	Riksförbundet Svensk Frukt	**RTEC**	Retail Trades Education Council
RSGB	Radio Society of Great Britain	**RTF**	Radiodiffusion et Télévision Française (*now* ORTF)
RSGS	Royal Scottish Geographical Society	**RTI**	Round Table International
RSH	Royal Society of Health	**RTIC**	Regional Technical Information Centres (*now* ILC)
RSI	Royal Sanitary Institute		
RSIC	Radiation Shielding Information Center (*of* ORNL) (U.S.A.)	**RTITB**	Road Transport Industry Training Board
		RTM	Radiodiffusion Télévision Marocaine
RSL	Royal Society of Literature	**RTMA**	Radio and Television Manufacturers Association (Canada or U.S.A.)
RSM	Royal School of Mines		
RSM	Royal Society of Medicine	**RTPB**	Radio Technical Planning Board (U.S.A.)
RSM	Royal Society of Musicians	**RTPI**	Royal Town Planning Institute
RSMA	Royal Society of Marine Artists	**RTRA**	Radio Electrical and Television Retailers Association
RSMD	Remote Sensing and Meteorological Applications Division (IAEA)		
		RTRO	Reclamation Trades Research Organisation
RSNA	Radiological Society of North America	**RTS**	Royal Television Society
RSNZ	Royal Society of New Zealand	**RTS**	Royal Toxophilite Society
RSPB	Royal Society for the Protection of Birds	**RTSA**	Retail Trading Standards Association
RSPCA	Royal Society for the Prevention of Cruelty to Animals	**RTT**	Radiodiffusion-Télévision Tunisienne
		RUA	Royal Ulster Academy
RSR	République Socialiste de Roumanie	**RUAA**	Royal Ulster Academy Association
RSS	Royal Statistical Society	**RUAS**	Royal Ulster Agricultural Society
RSSI	Royal Statistical Society of Ireland	**RUI**	Royal National University of Ireland
RSTMH	Royal Society of Tropical Medicine and Hygiene	**RUKBA**	Royal United Kingdom Beneficent Association
RSUA	Royal Society of Ulster Architects	**RUSI**	Royal United Service Institute for Defence Studies
RTA	Comité de Coordination de la Route Trans-africaine (Ethiopia)		
		RVC	Rijksveeteeltconsulentschap
RTA	Rhodesian Tobacco Association	**RVCI**	Royal Veterinary College of Ireland
RTA	Road Transport Association	**RVIA**	Royal Victoria Institute of Architects (Australia)
RTA	Rubber Trade Association of London		
RTAC	Regional Technical Aids Center (U.S.A.)	**RVP**	Rijksvoorlichtingsdienst voor de Pluimveeteelt
RTBI	National Association of Round Tables of Great Britain and Ireland		
		RVS	Reifengewerbe-Verband der Schweiz
RTC	Rijkstuinbouwconsulentschap	**RWAS**	Royal Welsh Agricultural Society
RTCEG	Rubber and Thermoplastic Cables Export Group	**RWE**	Rheinisch-Westfälisches Electrizitätswerk
		RWF	Radio Wholesalers Federation
RTCH	National Conference of Road Transport Clearing Houses	**RWS**	Royal Society of Painters in Water Colours
		RYA	Royal Yachting Association
RTCMA	Rubber and Thermoplastic Cable Manufacturers Association	**RZC**	Rijkszuivelconsulentschap
		RZSI	Royal Zoological Society of Ireland
RTE	Radio Telefis Eireann	**RZSS**	Royal Zoological Society of Scotland

S

SA	Salvation Army
SA	Skogbrukets Arbeidsgiverforening
SA	Sparebankenes Arbeidsgiverforening
SA	Svenska Agghandelsförbundet
SA	Svenska Akeriförbundet
SAA	Scottish Anglers Association
SAA	Scottish Archery Association
SAA	Schweizerische Astronautische Arbeits-gemeinschaft
SAA	Sociedád Argentina de Agronomia
SAA	Sociedad Argentina de Apicultores
SAA	Sociedád Argentina de Antropologia
SAA	South African Airways
SAA	Standards Association of Australia
SAA	Svenska Aerosolföreningen
SAAA	Scottish Amateur Athletic Association
SAAAS	South African Association for the Advancement of Science
SAAB	Svensk Aeroplan Aktiebolaget
SAACE	South African Association of Consulting Engineers
SAAD	Society for the Advancement of Anaesthesia in Dentistry
SAAEB	South African Atomic Energy Board
SAAEVA	Southern Association for Agricultural Engineering and Vocational Agriculture (U.S.A.)
SAAI	Specialty Advertising Association International (U.S.A.)
SAAMBR	South African Association for Marine Biological Research
SAANZ	Sociological Association of Australia and New Zealand
SAAO	South African Astronomical Observatory
SAARA	Sociedad de Amigos del Arbol de la República Argentina
SAARBS	South African Angora Ram Breeders' Society

SAARCI	Sindicato Autonomo Agenti Rappresentanti Commercio Industria
SAAT	Society of Architects and Associated Technicians
SAATC	Southern African Air Transport Council
SAAU	South African Agricultural Union
SAAU	Système d'Approvisionnement Alimentaire d'Urgence (WFP)
SAB	Schweizerische Arbeitsgemeinschaft der Bergbauern
SAB	Sociedád Argentina de Biologia
SAB	Sociedad Argentina de Botánica
SAB	Sociedád Arqueológica de Bolivia
SAB	Société Africaine des Bois
SAB	Société Africaine de Bonneterie (Ivory Coast)
SAB	Society of American Bacteriologists
SAB	Society of Applied Bacteriology
SAB	Stichting v. Aardappelbewaring
SAB	Sveriges Allmänna Biblioteksförening
SABA	Scottish Amateur Boxing Association
SABA	South African Brick Association
SABB	Société d'Arrimage des Battures de Beauport (Canada)
SABC	Scottish Association of Boys Clubs
SABC	Société des Brasseries du Cameroun
SABC	South African Broadcasting Corporation
SABCA	Société Anonyme Belge de Constructions Aéronautiques
SABCO	Society for the Areas of Biological and Chemical Overlap (Japan)
SABE	Société Africaine d'Exploitation des Brevets Eries
SABEA	Societa Alimentari Bevande e Affini
SABENA	Société Anonyme Belge d'Exploitation de la Navigation Aérienne
SABI	Société Africaine de Biscuiterie (Ivory Coast)
SABM	Société Africaine de Beton Manufacture
SABRA	Suid-Afrikaanse Bureau vir Rasse Aangeleenthede
SABRAO	Society for the Advancement of Breeding Researches in Asia and Oceania (Japan)
SABRE	Sociedad Alemã Brasileira de Refloresta-mento
SABS	South African Bureau of Standards

SABTS	South African Blood Transfusion Service
SAC	Schweizer Alpen Club
SAC	Scientific Advisory Committee (IAEA)
SAC	Sociedád de Agricultores de Colombia
SAC	Sociedád Agronómica de Chile
SAC	Sociedád Argentina de Criminologia
SAC	Société Africaine de Culture
SAC	Society for Analytical Chemistry
SAC	Society of Applied Cosmetology
SAC	Southern African Committee (U.S.A.)
SAC	State Advances Corporation (Australia)
SAC	Statistical Advisory Committee (FAO)
SACA	Societa per Azioni Costruzioni Aeronavali
SACA	Société Agricole de Côte d'Afrique (Ivory Coast)
SACA	Société Auxiliare de Commerce Africain (Mali)
SACA	South African Cricket Association
SACAC	South African Council for Automation and Computation
SACAF	Société Centrafricaine du Sac
SACAM	Société Auxiliaire Coopérative de Crédit Agricole Mutuel
SACANGO	Southern African Committee on Air Navigation and Ground Operation
SACAR	Société Abidjanaise de Carrelages (Ivory Coast)
SACCA	Servicio Agrónomico de los Cultivadores de Caña de Azúcar (Venezuela)
SACCB	Société Anonyme des Cultures au Congo Belge
SACDA	South African Copper Development Association
SACEM	Société des Auteurs, Compositeurs et Éditeurs de Musique
SACEM	Syndicat des Cadres et Agents de Maîtrise
SACEUR	Supreme Allied Commander Europe
SACFER	Société Africaine de Construction et de Fabrication d'Engins Roulants (Ivory Coast)
SACH	Sociedad Agronómica de Chile
SACHIA	Salone delle Tecniche Chimiche nell'Industria e nell'Agricoltura
SACHIM	Société des Amis de la Maison de la Chimie
SACI	Société Africaine de Commerce et d'Industrie (Ivory Coast)
SACIA	Société Africaine pour le Commerce l'Industrie et l'Agriculture
SACLANT	Supreme Allied Commander Atlantic
SACLANT-CEN	SACLANT Anti-Submarine Warfare Research Centre
SACLAT	Standing Advisory Committee on Local Authorities and the Theatre
SACM	Société Abidjanaise de Constructions Mécaniques (Ivory Coast)
SACM	Société Africaine de Constructions Métallurgiques
SACM	Société Alsacienne de Constructions Mécaniques
SACMA	Société Anonyme de Construction de Moteurs Aéronautiques
SACO	Société Africaine de Cacao (Ivory Coast)
SACO	Sveriges Akademikers Centralorganisation
SACOMAT	Société Africaine de Construction et Matériaux (Dahomey)
SACOS	Società Azionaria Centrali Ortofrutticole Siciliane
SACOTRA	Société Africaine de Consignation et de Transit (Dahomey)
SACPA	South African Cement Producers Association
SACRA	Société Africaine de Courtage et de Représentation d'Assurances (Ivory Coast)
SACS	Sakata Agricultural Co-operative Society (Japan)
SACS	Swedish Agro Co-operative Services
SACSEA	Supreme Allied Commander South East Asia
SACSIR	South African Council for Scientific and Industrial Research
SACSIT	Scottish Association of Cold Storage and Ice Trades
SACT	Section Administrative de la Coopération Technique (UNO)
SACT	Société Algérienne de Constructions Téléphoniques
SACTU	South African Congress of Trade Unions
SACTW	South African Council of Transport Workers
SACU	Sociedad de Avicultores y Cunicultores del Uruguay
SACU	Society for Anglo-Chinese Understanding
SACU	South African Cricket Union
SACUGS	South African Scientific Committee for the International Union of Geological Sciences
SAD	Scottish Association for the Deaf

SAD	Société Andine de Développement (Venezuela)	**SAE**	Society for the Advancement of Education (U.S.A.)
SAD	Spolecnost Antonína Dvoráka	**SAE**	Society of Automotive Engineers (U.S.A.)
SADA	Sociedad Argentina de Apicultores	**SAE**	Society of Automotive Engineers Australasia (*formerly* IAAE)
SADACI	Société Anonyme d'Applications de Chimie Industrielle (Belgium)	**SAE**	Sveriges Allmanna Exportförening
SADARET	Société Anglaise d'Études et de Réalisations d'Énergie et de Télécommunications	**SAEC**	Société Abidjanaise d'Expansion Chimique (Ivory Coast)
SADAS	Syllogos Architektonon Anotaton Scholon	**SAED**	Société Africaine d'Études et de Développement
SADC	Scottish Agricultural Development Council	**SAED**	Société d'Aménagement et d'Exploitation des Terres du Delta du Fleuve Sénégal
SADD	South African Development Division (*of* ODM)	**SAEGHT**	Société Africaine de Gestion Hôtelière et Touristique (Ivory Coast)
SADE	Società Adriatica di Ellettricità	**SAEL**	Sociedád Argentina de Estudios Lingúisticos
SADE	Société Alsacienne de Développement et d'Expansion	**SAEP**	Société Africaine d'Éditions et de Publicité
SADEL	Secretario Argentino de la Lano	**SAEPC**	Société Anonyme d'Explosifs et de Produits Chimiques
SADEP	Société Auxiliaire pour la Diffusion des Éditions de Productivité	**SAEST**	Society for the Advancement of Electrochemical Science and Technology (India)
SADER	Société Africaine de Déroulage des Déserts Rougier et Fils (Gabon)	**SAETA**	Sociedad Anonima Emisorars de Television y Anexos (Uruguay)
SADF	South African Defence Forces	**SAEWA**	South African Electrical Workers' Association
SADG	Société des Architectes Diplomés par le Gouvernment	**SAF**	Skibsfartens Arbeidsgiverforening
SADHEA	South African Dietetics and Home Economics Association	**SAF**	Skofabrikkenes Arbeidsgiverforening
SADI	Société Africaine de Développement Industriel	**SAF**	Société Africaine Forestière (Ivory Coast)
SADIA	Société Africaine de Diffusion Industrielle et Automobile (Ivory Coast)	**SAF**	Société des Agriculteurs de France
SADIA	Société Auxiliaire de l'Industrie de l'Azote	**SAF**	Société Anonyme Française
SADIAMIL	Société Africaine du Développement de l'Industrie Alimentaire du Millet et du Sorgho (Niger)	**SAF**	Société Astronomique de France
		SAF	Society of American Foresters
SADIM	Société Anonyme pour le Dévéloppement Immobilier de Monaco	**SAF**	South African Foundation
SADIO	Sociedad Argentina de Investigación Operativa	**SAF**	Sports Aid Foundation
		SAF	Svenska Aktiva Fastighetsmäklareförbundet
SADITA	Société Africaine d'Importation et de Distribution de Tabacs et Articles Divers (Ivory Coast)	**SAF**	Svenska Anestesiologisk Förening
		SAF	Svenska Antikvariatföreningen
		SAF	Svenska Arbetsgivareföreningen
SADMN	Sociedad Argentina de Medicina Nuclear	**SAF**	Syndicat Général des Affineurs de France
SADOI	Sociedad Argentina de Organización Industrial	**SAFA**	Scottish Amateur Football Association
		SAFA	Société d'Achat France-Afrique
SADP	Syndicat Agricole de Défense Paysanne	**SAFA**	Société Africaine Forestière et Agricole
SADRAC	South African Defence Research Advisory Committee	**SAFA**	Société Anon. Forestière et Agricole, Edea (French Cameroons)
		SAFA	South African Freedom Association
SADTC	SHAPE Air Defence Technical Centre	**SAFAA**	Société Française d'Appareils Automatiques

SAFAD	Swedish Agency for Administrative Development	**SAFTEL**	Société Africaine d'Électronique et de Télécommunications
SAFAL	Société Africaine de Fonderie d'Aluminium	**SAFTO**	South African Foreign Trade Organization
SAFAMI	Société Africaine de Fabrications Métalliques Industrielles (Ivory Coast)	**SAFUES**	South African Federation of University Engineering Students
SAFAR	Société Africaine de Fabrication des Automobiles Renault (Ivory Coast)	**SAFV**	Sociedad Argentina de Fisiología Vegetal
SAFB	Schweizerische Arbeitsgemeinschaft für Bevölkerungsfragen	**SAG**	Scandinavian Society of Geneticists
		SAG	Schweizerische Astronomische Gesellschaft
SAFBAIL	Société Africaine de Crédit Bail (Ivory Coast)	**SAG**	Secretaría de Agricultura y Ganadería (Mexico)
SAFCA	Société Africaine de Fabrication de Cahiers	**SAG**	Shell Aviation Guinée
SAFCO	Saudi Arabian Fertiliser Company	**SAG**	Société Agricole de Guinée
SAFCO	Société Africaine Colombani et Cie (Gabon)	**SAGA**	Schweizerische Akademische Gesellschaft der Anglisten
SAFCO	Société Afrique Commerce (Dahomey)	**SAGA**	Society of American Graphic Artists
SAFCO	Société Africaine de Conserveries (Ivory Coast)	**SAGB**	Schizophrenia Association of Great Britain
SAFCO	Standing Advisory Committee on Fisheries	**SAGB**	Spiritualist Association of Great Britain
SAFEL	Société Agricole de Fruits et Légumes	**SAGAGB**	Sand and Gravel Association of Great Britain
SAFER	Sociétés d'Aménagement Foncier et Établissement Rural	**SAGD**	Suid-Afrikaanse Geneeskundige Diens
SAFI	Sammenslutningen af Automobil-Fabrikanter og Importorer	**SAGE**	Syndicat National des Fabricants d'Articles Galvanisés et Étamés
SAFI	Société Africaine de Fabrication Industrielle	**SAGEC**	Société Africaine de Génie Rurale (Haute-Volta)
SAFICA	Société Africaine de Fabrication et d'Impression de Cahiers (Ivory Coast)	**SAGECCOM**	Société Africaine de Génie Civil et de Constructions Métalliques
SAFICO	Société Abidjanaise de Fournitures pour l'Industrie et les Constructions en Côte d'Ivoire	**SAGECO**	Société Abidjanaise de Gerance et d'Exploitation Commercial (Ivory Coast)
SAFID	Sammenslutningen af Frugtpulpfabrikanter-eksportrer i Danmark	**SAGEM**	Société d'Applications Générales d'Électricité et de Mécanique
SAFIE	Société Africaine d'Installations Électriques	**SAGROCOL**	Sociedad Agrológica Colombiana
SAFIZ	Società Anonima Forniture Impianti Zootecnici	**SAGS**	Schweizerische Akademische Gesellschaft der Slavisten
SAFM	Société Africaine de Fabrication Métallique (Ivory Coast)	**SAH**	Sociedad Argentina de Horticultura
SAFR	Schweizerische Arbeitsgemeinschaft für Raketentechnik	**SAH**	Sveriges Allmänna Hypoteksbank
		SAHM	Société Africaine des Halles Modernes
SAFRA	Société Africaine d'Assurances (Senegal)	**SAHR**	Society of Army Historical Research
SAFRIC	Société Africaine de Confection (Ivory Coast)	**SAHSA**	Servicio Aéreo de Honduras SA
		SAHT	Sallskapet for Agronomisk Hydroteknik
SAFRICA	Société Africaine d'Armement (Dahomey)	**SAI**	Scottish Agricultural Industries Ltd
SAFRICA	Société Africaine de Management (Ivory Coast)	**SAI**	Senior Advocates International (U.S.A.)
		SAI	Servicio Agricola Interamericana
SAFRINEX	Société Africaine d'Exploitation Vinicole	**SAI**	Società Anonima Italiana
SAFRIPA	Société Africaine de Parfumerie	**SAI**	Società Attori Italiani
SAFT	Société Africaine de Fabrication et de Transformation	**SAI**	Société Arabe d'Investissement (Saudi Arabia)

SAI	Society of Antiquaries of Ireland
SAI	Southeast Asia Institute (U.S.A.)
SAIA	South Australian Institute of Architects
SAIAA	South African Institute of Assayers and Analysts
SAIB	Société Africaine des Industries du Bâtiment
SAIC	Scottish Agricultural Improvement Council
SAICA	Société Agricole et Industrielle de la Côte d'Afrique
SAICCOR	South African Industrial Cellulose Corporation (Pty) Ltd
SAICE	South African Institute of Civil Engineers
SAIChem.E	South African Institution of Chemical Engineers
SAICI	Società Agricola Industriale della Cellulosa Italiana
SAICOS	Société Agricole Industrielle et Commerciale du Sénégal
SAIDC	South African Inventions Development Corporation
SAIE	Société Abidjanaise Import-Export (Ivory Coast)
SAIEE	South African Institute of Electrical Engineers
SAIET	Société Africaine d'Importation et d'Exportation Tchadienne
SAIF	Société Agricole d'Investissement Foncier
SAIF	South African Industrial Federation
SAIF	South African Institute of Foundrymen
SAIH	Société Africaine Immobilière et Hôtelière
SAII	Société Africaine d'Impressions Industrielles
SAILA	South African Indian Library Association
SAIM	Società Agraria Industriale Meridionale
SAIMech.E	South African Institution of Mechanical Engineers
SAIMM	South African Institute of Mining and Metallurgy
SAIMR	South African Institute for Medical Research
SAIO	Sociedad Argentina de Investigacion Operativa (Argentina)
SAIORG	Supreme Assembly of the International Order of Rainbow for Girls (U.S.A.)
SAIPA	South African Institute for Public Administration
SAIPA	Sociedad Argentina para la Investigación de Productos Aromaticos
SAIPE	South African Institute for Production Engineering
SAIRAC	South African Institute of Refrigeration and Air-conditioning
SAIRR	South African Institute of Race Relations
SAIS	School of Advanced International Studies, Johns Hopkins University (U.S.A.)
SAIS	Scientific Apparatus Information Service (U.S.A.)
SAIS	Sociedades Agrícoles de Interés Social (Peru)
SAIS	Società Agricola Italo Somalia
SAIS	South African Interplanetary Society
SAISSA	Scottish Amateur Ice Speed Skating Association
SAIT	Société Anonyme Internationale de Télégraphie Sans Fil (Belgium)
SAIT	South African Institute of Translators
SAIW	South African Institute of Welding
SAJ	Suomen Ammattijärjestö
SAJA	Société des Amateurs de Jardins Alpins
SAK	Kuwait Investment Company
SAK	Suomen Ammattiyhdistysten Keskusliitto
SAKF	Svenska Akustikkonsulenters Förening
SAKO	Suomen Ammattikoulunopettajien Liitto
SAL	Schweizerische Arbeitsgemeinschaft voor Logopädie
SAL	Société Astronomique de Liège
SAL	Sveriges Allmänna Lantbrukssallskap
SALA	South African Library Association
SALALM	Seminars on the Acquisition of Latin American Library Materials
SALCI	Société des Ananas de la Côte-d'Ivoire
SALF	Sveriges Agronom-och Lantbrukslärareforbund
SALINTO	Société des Salines du Togo
SALNR	South Africa Lombard Nature Reserve
SALP	Société Africaine de Librairie-Papeterie (Gabon)
SALP	South African Labour Party
SALS	South African Logopedic Society
SALT	Soviet-American Strategic Arms Limitation Talks
SAM	Sociedad Agronómica Mexicana
SAM	Société Africaine de Menuiserie (Ivory Coast)
SAM	Società Aerea Mediterrania

SAM	Society for the Advancement of Management (U.S.A.)
SAMA	Scientific Apparatus Makers of America
SAMA	Scottish Agricultural Machinery Association
SAMA	Scottish Association of Manufacturers Agents
SAMA	South African Museums Association
SAMAO	Société Auxiliare de Matériel pour l'Afrique Occidentale (Ivory Coast)
SAMB	Scottish Association of Master Bakers
SAMC	Scottish Association of Manufacturing Coppersmiths
SAMDA	Société Agricole Mutuelle d'Assurance
SAMDC	South African Medical and Dental Council
SAME	Society of American Military Engineers
SAMES	Société Anonyme de Machines Électro-statiques
SAMG	Sociedád Argentina de Mineria y Geologia
SAMH	Scottish Association for Mental Health
SAMI	Société Africaine de Matériel Industriel (Gabon Tchad)
SAMM	Société d'Applications des Machines Motrices
SAMOA	Société Agence Maritime de l'Ouest Africain (Ivory Coast)
SAMOGA	Société d'Aménagement de la Moyenne Garonne
SAMPA	Services d'Approvisionnement en Moyens de Production Agricole
SAMPE	Society of Aerospace Material and Process Engineers (U.S.A.)
SAMPM	Scottish Association of Milk Products Manufacturers
SAMRA	South African Market Research Association
SAMS	Société d'Application de Mécanisation des Semis
SAMS	South American Missionary Society
SAMSA	Silica and Moulding Sands Association
SAMTAS	Supervisory and Management Training Association of Singapore
SAN	Science Association of Nigeria
SANAA	Servicio Autonomo Nacional de Agua y Alcantarillado (Honduras)
SANAE	South African National Antarctic Expedition
SANAS	Service d'Alimentation et Nutrition Appliquée du Sénégal
SANB	South African National Bibliography
SANBRA	Sociedade Algodoeira do Nordeste Brasileiro
SANCA	South African National Council on Alcoholism and Drug Dependence
SANCAD	Scottish Association for National Certificate and Diplomas
SANCAR	South African National Committee for Antarctic Research
SANCC	South African National Consumers Council
SANCGASS	South African National Committee for Geomagnetism, Aeronomy and Space Sciences
SANCI	South African National Committee on Illumination
SANCOLD	South African National Committee on Large Dams
SANCOR	South African National Committee for Oceanographic Research
SANCOT	South African National Committee on Tunnelling
SANF	Société des Autoroutes du Nord de la France
SANLAM	Suid-Afrikaanse Nasionale Lewensassuransie-maatskappy
SANP	Sociedád de Anatomia Normal y Patológica (Argentina)
SANROC	South African Non-Racial Olympics Committee
SANTA	South African National Tuberculosis Association
SANU	Sudan African National Union
SANZ	Standards Association of New Zealand
SAO	Scottish Association of Opticians
SAONIC	Section Algérienne de l'Office National Inter-professionnel des Céréales
SAOS	Scottish Agricultural Organisation Society
SAOT	Scottish Association of Occupational Therapists
SAP	Nouvelle Société Africaine des Plastiques
SAP	Schweizerische Arztegesellschaft für Psychotherapie
SAP	Sociedad Agronómica de Panamá
SAP	Société Africaine des Peaux
SAP	Société Africaine de Pétroles
SAP	Sociedád Argentina de Pediatria
SAP	Société Africaine de Pneumatiques (Haute-Volta)
SAP	Société Agricole de Prévoyance

SAPA	Société d'Application de Peintures en Afrique (Congo)	**SAPS**	Servico de Alimentação da Previdencia Social (Brazil)
SAPA	South African Poultry Association	**SAPT**	Société Africaine de Photogrammetrie et de Topographie
SAPA	South African Press Association		
SAPA	South African Psychological Association	**SAPT**	Société d'Astronomie Populaire de Toulouse
SAPAC	Société Anonyme de Pêche, d'Armement et de Conservation	**SAPV**	Suid-Afrikaanse Pluimvee Vereniging
		SAQ	Schweizerische Arbeitsgemeinschaft f. Qualitätsbeforderung
SAPAL	Société Africaine de Produits Alimentaires		
SAPAR	Associazione Nazionale Sezioni Apparecchi per Pubbliche Attrazioni Ricreative	**SAR**	Secteurs d'Améliorations Rurales (Algeria)
		SAR	Société Africaine Radioélectrique
SAPAR	Société d'Appareillage Électrique	**SAR**	Société Africaine de Raffinage
SAPC	Société Africaine de Plomberie et Couverture	**SAR**	Société Africaine de Ravitaillement (Congo)
SAPCAM	Société Africaine de Produits Chimiques Agricoles et Ménagers	**SAR**	Société Africaine de Représentation (Haute-Volta)
SAPCS	Société Africaine des Produits Chimiques Shell (Ivory Coast)	**SAR**	Société Suisse d'Anesthésiologie et de Réanimation
SAPEB	Syndicat des Artisans et des Petites Entreprises du Bâtiment	**SAR**	Svenska Arkitekters Riksförbund
		SARA	Scottish Amateur Rowing Association
SAPEC	Syndicat des Fabricants d'Appareils de Production d'Eau Chaude par le Gaz	**SARA**	South African-Rhodesian Association
		SARAM	Société d'Applications Radioélectriques à l'Aéronautique et à la Marine
SAPECO	Société Africaine de Promotion Économique		
SAPEF	Société Africaine de Publicité et d'Éditions Fusionnées	**SARBICA**	South-East Asian Regional Branch of the International Council on Archives
SAPEGA	Société d'Approvisionnement et de Pêche du Gabon	**SARC**	South Asia Regional Council (U.S.A)
		SARCCUS	Southern African Regional Committee for the Conservation and Utilisation of the Soil
SAPELEC	Société Africaine des Piles Électriques (Ivory Coast)		
		SARCO	Saudi Arabian Refinery Company
SAPEM	Société d'Applications Pneumatiques Électriques et Méchaniques	**SAREC**	Swedish Agency for Research Cooperation with Developing Countries
SAPH	Société Africaine de Plantations d'Hévéas (Ivory Coast)	**SAREPA**	Société Africaine de Recherches et d'Études pour Aluminium
SAPHY-DATA	Systems for Acquisition, Transmission and Processing of Hydrological Data	**SARF**	South African Road Federation
		SARF	Sveriges Annons-och Reklambyraers Förbund
SAPI	Société Africaine de Pêche Industrielle		
SAPM	Scottish Association of Paint Manufacturers	**SARGAS**	Station Avicole de Recherches Génétiques Appliquées à la Sélection
SAPM	Syndicat pour l'Amélioration de la Production Mulassière	**SARL**	Sociedade Anónima de Responsabilidade Limitada (Portugal)
SAPN	Société Agricole et Pastorale du Niari (Zaire)		
SAPPI	South African Pulp and Paper Industries Ltd	**SARL**	Société à Responsabilité Limitée
SAPRI	Società per Azione Produttori Riso Italiana	**SARL**	South African Radio League
SAPRIM	Société Abidjanaise de Promotions Industrielles et Immobilières (Ivory Coast)	**SARMAG**	Société Africaine de Ravitaillement Maritime et d'Approvisionnements Généraux (Ivory Coast)
SAPROC	Société d'Achats de Produits du Cameroun		
SAPROCSY	Société Africaine de Produits Chimiques et de Synthèse (Ivory Coast)	**SARP**	Stowarzyszenie Architektow Polskich
		SARST	Société Auxiliare de la Recherche Scientifique et Technique
SAPROLAIT	Société Africaine de Produits Laitiers		

SARTEX	Schweizerische Arbeitsgemeinschaft für Textil-Kennzeichnung	**SAT**	Société Abidjanaise de Torrefaction (Ivory Coast)
SARTOC	South Africa Regional Tourism Council	**SAT**	Société Abidjanaise de Transport (Ivory Coast)
SARUPRI	Indonesian Plantation Workers Trade Union		
SARY	Suomen Autorengasyhdistys	**SAT**	Société Africaine de Transit
SAS	Scandinavian Airlines System	**SAT**	Société Anonyme de Télécommunications
SAS	Schweizerischer Arbeitsgeberverband für das Schneidergewerbe	**SAT**	Société Archéologique de Touraine
		SAT	Society of Acoustic Technology (*now* BAS)
SAS	Société Africaine des Silicates	**SATA**	Sociedade Acoriana de Transportes Aéreos
SAS	Société Astronomique de Suisse	**SATA**	Société Africaine de Transit et d'Affrètement (Congo, Gabon)
SAS	Svenska Akustikkonsulenters Förening		
SASA	Scottish Amateur Swimming Association	**SATA**	Société Anonyme de Transport Aérien (Switzerland)
SASA	Semilleros Argentinos S.A.		
SASA	South African Sugar Association	**SATA**	Student Air Travel Association
SASAC	South African Council for Automation and Computation	**SATAM**	Société Anonyme pour tous Appareillages Mécaniques
SASAP	South African Society of Animal Production	**SAT-AMIKA**	Association of French-Language Countries Nationless Esperantist Workers
SASCAR	South African Scientific Committee for Antarctic Research	**SATC**	Société Abidjanaise de Tissus et Confections (Ivory Coast)
SASCO	Singapore and Australia Shipping Company	**SATC**	Société d'Applications Techniques au Cameroun
SASCO	South Asia Science Cooperation Office (UNESCO)		
SASI	Southern Association of Science and Industry (U.S.A.)	**SATCOM**	U.S. National Academy of Sciences-National Academy of Engineering Committee on Scientific and Technical Communication
SASIF	Société Africaine de Soudages, Injections Forages	**SATE**	Swiss Association of Teachers of English
SASIF-CI	Société Africaine de Soudages, Forages de Côte-d'Ivoire	**SATEC**	Société d'Aide Technique et de Coopération (Senegal, Upper Volta)
SASIO	Field Science Co-operation Office for South Asia	**SATEC**	Société Africaine de Traitements Électrochimiques
SASK	Suid-Afrikaanse Seinkorp	**SATEC**	Société d'Assistance Technique et de Crédit
SASLIC	Surrey and Sussex Libraries in Co-operation	**SATEL**	Société Africaine des Techniques Électroniques (Dahomey)
SASLO	South African Scientific Liaison Office	**SATENA**	Servicio de Aeronavegación a Territorios Nacionales (Colombia)
SASMAL	South African Sugar Millers Association Ltd		
SASMI	Sindacato Autonomo Scuola Media Italiana	**SATERCO**	Société Anonyme de Terrassements et de Constructions (Belgium)
SASMIRA	Silk and Art Silk Mills Research Association (India)	**SATET**	Société Africaine de Travaux et d'Études Topographiques (Congo)
SASO	Saudi Arabia Standards Organization	**SATG**	Schweizerische Automobiltechnische Gesellschaft
SASO	South African Students Association		
SASOL	South African Coal, Oil and Gas Corporation	**SATI**	Société Anonyme de Transporte Isothermes (Belgium)
SASP	South African Society of Physiotherapy		
SASS	Société Académique des Slavistes Suisses	**SATI-CI**	Société Africaine de Transit et d'Affrètement (Ivory Coast)
SAST	Swiss Association for Space Technology	**SATK**	Suid-Afrikaanse Toeristekorporasie
SASTA	South African Sugarcane Technologists Association	**SATMACI**	Société d'Assistance Technique pour la Modernisation Agricole de la Côte d'Ivoire
SAT	Sennacieca Asocio Tutmonda		

SATMAR	South African Torbanite Mining and Refining Company	**SAYC**	Scottish Association of Youth Clubs
SATNUC	Société pour les Applications de l'Énergie Nucléaire	**SAYFC**	Scottish Association of Young Farmers' Clubs
SATO	South American Travel Organisation	**SBA**	Scottish Beekeepers' Association
SATOM	Société de Travaux d'Outre-Mer	**SBA**	Smaller Business Association
SATPN	Société Assistance Technique pour les Produits Nestlé (Switzerland)	**SBA**	Sociedade Brasileira de Agronomia
		SBAC	Société J. Bastos de l'Afrique Centrale
SATRA	Shoe and Allied Trades Research Association	**SBAC**	Society of British Aerospace Companies
SATRAM	Société Africaine de Travaux Maritimes et Fluviaux (Ivory Coast)	**SBARMO**	Scientific Ballooning and Radiations Monitoring Organization
		SBAT	Service Botanique et Agronomique de Tunisie
SATT	Société Africaine de Travaux et de Transports (Ivory Coast)	**SBAT**	Sociedade Brasiliera de Autores Tetrais
		SBB	Sociedade Botanica de Brasil
SATU	South African Typographical Union	**SBB**	Société Belge de Biologie
SAUK	Suid-Afrikaanse Uitsaaikorporasie	**SBBNF**	Ship and Boat Builders National Federation
SAUTE	Swiss Association of University Teachers of English	**SBC**	Sociedade Brasileira de Cartografia
SAUU	South African Underwater Union	**SBC**	Swedish Farmers Beet Growers Association
SAV	Schweizerischer Altphilogenverband	**SBCBC**	Société des Bitumes et Cut-backs du Cameroun
SAV	Schweizerischer Anwaltsverband		
SAV	Schweizerischer Apothekerverein	**SBCCPA**	Sociedade Brasileira de Criadores de Cães Pastores Alemães
SAV	Slovak Academy of Sciences	**SBCI**	Sociedade Brasileira de Cultura Inglêsa
SAVA	South African Veterinary Association	**SBCUK**	School Broadcasting Council for the United Kingdom
SAVA	Verband Schweizerischer Annoncen-Verwaltungen und Agenturen		
		SBD	Société Dahoméenne de Banque
SAVCONGO	Savonnerie du Congo	**SBE**	Sociedade Brasileira de Entomologia
SAVEC	Société Africaine de Vente et de Consignation (Ivory Coast)	**SBE**	Société Belge des Électriciens
		SBE	Société Belge d'Ergologie
SAVFAN	Standing Advisory Committee on Food and Nutrition (Caribbean)	**SBE**	Society of Business Economists
SAVI	Society for the Advancement of the Vegetable Industry (Philippines)	**SBEE**	Société Belge d'Études d'Expansion
		SBEF	Svenska Byggnadsentreprenörföreningen
SAVI	Suid-Afrikaanse Vertalersinstituut	**SBET**	Society of British Esperantist Teachers
SAVIA	Sociedad Agronomica Viveros Industriales Argentinos	**SBF**	Sociedade Brasileira de Floricultura
		SBF	Svenska Bageriförbund
SAVR	Special Army Volunteer Reserve	**SBF**	Svenska Bergsmannaföreningen
SAVS	Scottish Anti-Vivisection Society	**SBF**	Svenska Brandförsvarsföreningen
SAWA	Scottish Amateur Wrestling Association	**SBF**	Svenska Busstrafikförbundet
SAWA	Screen Advertising World Association	**SBF**	Sveriges Bildelsgrossisters Förening
SAWAU	South African Women's Agricultural Union	**SBF**	Sveriges Biografägareförbund
SAWEK	Suid-Afrikaanse Akademie vir Wetenskap en Kuns	**SBFV**	Schweizerischer Berufsfischerverband
		SBG	Schweizerische Botanische Gesellschaft
SAWGU	South African Wattle Growers Union	**SBG**	Sociedade Brasileira de Geologia
SAWMA	Soil and Water Management Association	**SBG**	Stichting Bevordering Galvanotechniek
SAWTRI	South African Wool Textile Research Institute	**SBGE**	Société Belge de Gasto-Entérologie

SBGI	Society of British Gas Industries	**SBS**	Sociedad Brasileira de Silvicultura
SBGW	Städtische Büchereien der Gemeinde Wien (Austria)	**SBS**	Svenska Bibliotekariesamfundet
		SBSA	Show and Breed Secretaries Association
SBHED	Sociedade Brasileira de Herbicides e Ervas Daninhas	**SBSA**	Standard Bank of South Africa
		SBSMP	Société Bernoulli pour la Statistique Mathématique et la Probabilité
SBHV	Schweizerischer Briefmarkenhändler-Verband		
		SBTC	Sino British Trade Council
SBI	Società Botanika Italiano	**SBU**	Schweizerische Butter-Union
SBI	Statens Byggeforskningsinstitut (Denmark)	**SBU**	Scottish Badminton Union
SBI	Swedish Farmers Distillers Association	**SBU**	Sociedades Biblicas Unidas
SBIA	Société Belge des Ingénieurs de l'Automobile	**SBU**	Sumitomo Bayer Urethane Co., Ltd (Japan)
SBIT	Société Belge des Ingénieurs Techniciens	**SBUAM**	Société Belge des Urbanistes et Architectes Modernistes
SBKV	Schweizerischer Bäcker-Konditorenmeister-Verband		
		SBV	Schweizerischer Bank Verein
SBL	Skibsbyggerienes Landsforening	**SBV**	Schweizerischer Baumeisterverband
SBL	Suomen Bensiinikauppiaitten Liitto	**SBV**	Schweizerischer Bergführerverband
SBLAM	Syndicat Belge de la Librairie Ancienne et Moderne	**SBV**	Schweizerischer Bootbauer-Verband
		SBV	Schweizerischer Brennstoffhändler-Verband
SBM	Sociedad Botánica de México	**SBV**	Schweizerischer Beirbrauerverein
SBM	Société Belge des Mécaniciens	**SBV**	Schweizerischer Buchdruckerverein
SBM	Société de Biologie de Montréal (Canada)	**SBV**	Schweizerischer Büchsemacher-Verband
SBME	Société Belge de Microscopie Électronique	**SBVV**	Schweizer Buchhändler und Verleger Verein
SBMV	Sociedade Brasileira de Medicina Veterinaria	**SBWA**	Standard Bank of West Africa
SBN	Schweizerischer Bund für Naturschutz	**SCA**	Scottish Canoe Association
SBNS	Society of British Neurological Surgeons	**SCA**	Scottish Chess Association
SBO	Stichting Bloedgroepen Onderzoek	**SCA**	Sociedad Científica Argentina
SBOT	Société Belge de Chirurgie Orthopédique et de Traumatologie	**SCA**	Société Centrale d'Apiculture
		SCA	Société Commerciale Africaine
SBP	Société Belge de Photogrammétrie	**SCA**	Society of Company and Commercial Accountants
SBP	Stowarzyszenie Bibliotekarzy Polskich		
SBPC	Sociedade Brasileira para o Progresso da Ciencia	**SCA**	Svenska Cellulose Aktiebolaget
		SCAAF	Société Centrale d'Approvisionnement des Agriculteurs de France
SBPIM	Society of British Printing Ink Manufacturers		
SBPM	Society of British Paint Manufacturers	**SCAAP**	Special Commonwealth African Assistance Plan
SBPR	Sociedad de Bibliotecarios de Puerto Rico		
SBR	Société Belge Radio-électrique	**SCAB**	Sociedad Cooperativa de Agrónomos de Bolivia
SBR	Society for Biological Rhythm (Porto Rico)		
SBR	Svenska Byggnadsingenjörers Riksförbund	**SCAB**	Société Centrale d'Architecture de Belgique
SBR	Sveriges Bensinhandlares Riksförbund	**SCAD**	Société Centrafricaine de Déroulage
SBREC	Sugar Beet Research and Education Committee	**SCADOA**	Service Commun d'Armements Desservant l'Ouest Africain
SBRF	Sveriges Bokförings-och Revisionsbyraers Förbund	**SCAEI**	Syndicat des Constructeurs d'Appareillage Électrique d'Installations
SBRS	Sheep Breeding Research Station (India)	**SCAF**	Compagnie des Scieries Africaines
SBS	Schweizerischer Berufsverband der Sozialarbeiter	**SCAF**	Société Centrale d'Aviculture de France

SCAFA	Société Centrafricaine d'Affrètement et d'Acconage
SCAFR	Société Centrale d'Aménagement Foncier Rural
SCAHUR	Société Congolaise d'Aménagement de l'Habitat Urbain et Rurale
SCALMS	Syndicat des Constructeurs d'Appareils de Levage, de Manutention et de Matériels de Stockage
SCALOM	Société Camerounaise de Location de Matériel et de Travaux Publics
SCAM	Société de Colonisation Agricole au Mayumbe (French West Africa)
SCAM	Sociétés Coopératives Agricoles Marocaines
SCAMAP	Syndicat des Cadres et Agents de Maîtrise de l'Aéroport de Paris
SCAMTRA	Société Camerounaise de Manutention, de Transport et de Transit
SCANAUS-TRAL	Scandinavian Australia Carriers Ltd (Norway)
SCANDOC	Scandinavian Documentation Centre
SCAP	Société Centrale d'Aquiculture et de Pêche
SCAPA	Society for Checking the Abuses of Public Advertising
SCAR	Scandinavian Council for Applied Research
SCAR	Scientific Committee on Antarctic Research (ICSU)
SCARA	Syndicat de Compagnies Assurant les Risques Automobiles (Belgium)
SCART	Syndicat de Constructeurs d'Appareils Radio-Récepteurs et Téléviseurs
SCASA	Servicio Cooperativo Agrícola Salvadoreño Americano
SCATS	Southern Counties Agricultural Trading Society
SCAUL	Standing Conference of African University Libraries
SCAULEA	Standing Conference of African University Libraries, Eastern Area
SCAULWA	Standing Conference of African University Libraries, Western Area
SCB	Sociedad Cubana de Botánica
SCB	Schweizerische Chemische Gesellschaft
SCB	Société Camerounaise de Banque
SCB	Société Chimique de Belgique
SCB	Société d'Étude et de Développement de la Culture Bananière (Ivory Coast)
SCB	Statistiska Centralbyran
SCBE	Société Canadienne des Brevets et d'Exploitation Limitée
SCBK	Société Congolaise des Brasseries Kronenbourg
SCBM	Société Camerounaise de Beton Manufacture
SCC	Scandinavian Clothing Council
SCC	Society of Cosmetic Chemists of Great Britain
SCC	Swedish Cooperative Centre
SCCAPE	Scottish Council for Commercial, Administrative and Professional Education
SCCE	Société Camerounaise de Conditionnement et d'Entreposage
SCCF	Société Centrale Canine de France
SCCH	Sociedad Científica de Chile
SCCS	Sociedad Colombiana de la Ciencia del Suelo
SCCU	Scottish Cross Country Union
SCE	Sociedad Colombiana de Economistas
SCEAM	Symposium des Conférences Épiscopates d'Afrique et de Madagascar
SCEAR	Scientific Committee on the Effects of Radiation (U.S.A.)
SCED	Société Centrafricaine d'Exploitation Diamantifère
SCEES	Société Central des Études et des Enquêtes Statistiques
SCEF	Société Camerounaise d'Exploitation Forestière
SCEFL	Société Camerounaise Équatoriale de Fabrication de Lubrifiants
SCEL	Société Coopérative d'Édition et de Librairie
SCEL	Standing Committee on Education in Librarianship
SCEP	Société Continentale d'Éditions et Périodiques
SCEPAG	Société pour le Conditionnement et l'Exportation des Produits Agricoles (Madagascar)
SCEPS	Strategic and Corporate Europlanners Society (Belgium)
SCET-International	Société Centrale pour l'Équipement du Territoire Internationale
SCETA	Société de Contrôle et d'Exploitation des Transport Auxiliaires
SCF	Société Chimique de France
SCF	Société de Comptabilité de France
SCF	Svenska Civilekonomföreningen

SCFCEF	Syndicat des Constructeurs Française de Condensateurs Électrique Fixes	**SCIDE**	Servicio Cooperativo Interamericano de Educación (Bolivia)
SCFMO	Syndicat des Constructeurs Français de Machines-Outils	**SCIDT**	Scottish Country Industries Development Trust
SCG	Schweïzerische Chemische Gesellschaft	**SCIEC**	Société Civile Immobilière des Entrepôts de Coton
SCGAF	Société Centrale de Gestion des Agriculteurs de France	**SCIEC**	Syndicat des Commerçants Importateurs et Exportateurs du Cameroun
SCGB	Ski Club of Great Britain	**SCIENCE**	Société des Consultants Indépendants et Neutres de la Communauté Européenne
SCGI	Société Congolaise de Gaz Industriels		
SCHE	Sociedad Chilena de Entomología	**SCIF**	Servicio Cooperativo Interamericano de Irrigación, Vías de Comunicación e Industrias (Peru)
SCHF	Sociedad Chilena de Física		
SCHG	Sociedad Chilena de Genética		
SCHHG	Sociedad Chilena de Historia y Geografía	**SCIFE**	Servicio Cooperativo Interamericano de Fomento Económico (Panama, Peru)
SCHHN	Sociedad Chilena de Historia Natural		
SCHI	Southern California Horticultural Institute (U.S.A.)	**SCIMA**	Syndicat des Constructeurs et Constructeurs-Installateurs de Matériel Aéraulique
SCHM	International Commission for a History of the Scientific and Cultural Development of Mankind	**SCIMO**	Société Commerciale et Industrielle pour la Métropole et Outre-Mer
		SCIMPEX	Syndicat des Commerçants Importateurs et Exportateurs (Ivory Coast, Mali, Mauritania, Niger, Senegal, Upper Volta)
SCHMC	Society of Catering and Hotel Management Consultants		
SCHN	Société Canadienne d'Histoire Naturelle	**SCIMPEXNI**	Syndicat des Commerçants Importateurs et Exportateurs du Niger
SCHNBT	Sociedad Chilena de Nutrición, Bromatología y Toxicología	**SCIMP-EXTO**	Syndicat des Commerçants Importateurs et Exportateurs de la République Togolaise
SCHP	Sociedad Chilena de Parasitología		
SCHPA	Sociedad Chilena de Producción Animal	**SCIMPOS**	Société Camerounaise d'Injection et de Modelage de Produits Organiques et Synthétiques
SCHQ	Sociedad Chilena de Química		
SCI	Sea Containers Inc.		
SCI	Service Civil Internationale	**SCIPA**	Servicio Cooperativo Inter-Americano de Producción de Alimentos
SCI	Société Camerounaise Industrielle		
SCI	Society of Chemical Industry	**SCIPAG**	Syndicat des Constructeurs de Machines pour les Industries du Papier, du Carton et des Arts Graphiques
SCI	Southern Cross International (U.K.)		
SCIA	Servicio Cooperativo Interamericano de Agricultura		
		SCIPLAC	Sciages et Placages Centrafricains
SCIA	Société Commerciale et Immobilière de l'Atlantique (Dahomey)	**SCIPS**	Servicio Cooperativo Interamericano Plan del Sur (Peru)
SCIBP	Special Committee for the International Biological Programme	**SCIR**	Syndicat Central d'Initiatives Rurales (France)
SCIC	Société Centrale Immobilière de la Caisse des Dépôts	**SCISP**	Servicio Cooperativo Interamericano de Salud Pública (Paraguay)
SCIC	Southern Corn Improvement Conference (U.S.A.)	**SCITS**	Servicio de Comercio de la Industria Textil Sedara
SCICA	Société Chimique et Industrielle Camerounaise	**SCIVU**	Scientific Council of the International Vegetarian Union
SCIDA	Servicio Cooperativo Interamericano de Agricultura (Guatemala)	**SCLP**	Scientists Committee on Loyalty Problems (U.S.A.)
		SCM	Société Camerounaise Michelin

SCM	Société Camerounaise de Minoterie
SCM	Société de Chirurgie de Montréal (Canada)
SCM	Sous-Commission de Coordination des Questions Forestières Méditerranéennes (*of* FAO)
SCM	Student Christian Movement of Great Britain and Ireland
SCMA	Service Cinématographique du Ministère de l'Agriculture
SCMA	Society of Cinema Managers of Great Britain and Ireland
SCMV	Schweizerischer Coiffeurmeister-Verband
SCNEA	Sealing Commission for the Northeast Atlantic
SCNR	Scientific Committee of National Representatives (*of* SHAPE)
SCNVYO	Standing Conference of National Voluntary Youth Organisations
SCNWA	Sealing Commission for the Northwest Atlantic
SCOA	Société Commerciale de l'Ouest Africain
SCOCLIS	Standing Conference of Co-operative Library Information Services
SCODI	Société des Conserves de Côte-d'Ivoire
SCOFET	Syndicat des Constructeurs de Fours et d'Équipements Thermiques
SCOLLUL	Standing Conference of Librarians of Libraries of the University of London
SCOLMA	Standing Conference on Library Materials on Africa
SCOM	Société Centrale d'Organisation et Méthodes
SCOMAD	Service de Contrôle du Conditionnement de Madagascar
SCONMEL	Standing Conference for Mediterranean Librarians
SCONUL	Standing Conference of National and University Libraries
SCOP	Société Coopératives Ouvrières de Production
SCOPE	Scientific Committee on Problems of the Environment (*of* ICSU)
SCOPE	Standing Committee on Professional Exchange (Denmark)
SCOR	Scientific Committee on Oceanic Research
SCOSTEP	Special Committee for Solar Terrestrial Physics (*of* ICSU)
SCOTA	Scottish Offshore Training Association
SCOTAPLL	Standing Conference on Theological and Philosophical Libraries in London

SCOW	Steel Company of Wales
SCP	Social Credit Party (Canada)
SCP	Sociedad Científica de Paraguay
SCP	Société Camerounaise des Peaux
SCP	Société du Canal de Provence et d'Aménagement de la Région Provençale
SCP	Syndicat des Constructeurs de Pompes
SCPA	Société Commerciale des Potasses d'Alsace
SCPA	Société Commerciale des Potasses et de l'Azote
SCPI	Structural Clay Products Institute (USA)
SCPR	Scottish Council of Physical Recreation
SCPR	Social and Community Planning Research
SCR	Society for Cultural Relations with the U.S.S.R.
SCR	Southern Council of Research (USA)
SCRA	Secteur Côtier des Recherches Agronomiques
SCRAL	Sociedad Cooperativa Rural Argentina Ltd.
SCRAM	Scottish Campaign to Resist the Atomic Menace
SCRATA	Steel Castings Research and Trade Association
SCRCC	Soil Conservation and Rivers Control Council (N.Z.)
SCRE	Scottish Council for Research in Education
SCRE	Syndicat des Constructeurs de Relais Électriques
SCREAM	Society for the Control and Registration of Estate Agents and Mortgage Brokers
SCREM	Syndicat National du Commerce Radio Télévision et de l'Équipement Ménager
SCRN	Sociedad Colombiana de Recursos Naturales
SCRP	Syndicat de la Crèmerie de la Région Parisienne
SCS	Société Camerounaise de Sacherie
SCS	Société Commerciale Sénégalaise
SCS	Society of Civil Servants
SCS	Soil Conservation Service (U.S.A.)
SCSA	Scottish Cold Storage Association
SCSA	Société Canadienne de Sociologie et d'Anthropologie
SCSA	Soil Conservation Society of America
SCSA	Statiunea Centrala pentru Sericicultura si Apicultura (Roumania)
SCSA	Supreme Council for Sports in Africa

SCSK	Shellfish Commission for the Skagerrak-Kattegat	**SDANA**	Section Dahoméenne de Nutrition et d'Alimentation Appliquée
SCSKU	Svaz Ceských Skaladatelu a Koncertních Umelcu	**SDAR**	Savez Drustava Arhivskih Radnika Jugoslavije
SCSS	Scottish Council of Social Service	**SDAT**	Sociedad Dásonómica de la América Tropical
SCT	Société Camerounaise du Tabac		
SCT	Société Cotonnière Transocéanique	**SDC**	Society of Dyers and Colourists
SCTA	Société Camerounais de Transport et d'Affrétement	**SDC**	Synthetic Diamond Company (Eire)
		SDCA	Society of Dyers and Colourists of Australia
SCTC	Société Commerciale Transocéanique des Conteneurs	**SDECE**	Service de Documentation Extérieure et de Contre-Espionnage
SCTHP	Syndicat des Constructeurs de Transmissions Hydrauliques et Pneumatiques	**SDEE**	Société Dahoméenne d'Électricité et d'Eau
		SDF	Svenska Dataföreningen
SCTN	Société Agricole pour le Contrôle de la Descendance des Taureaux de Race Normande	**SDFM**	Section Départementale des Fermiers et Métayers
		SDG	Schweizerische Diabetes Gesellschaft
SCTR	Standing Conference on Tele-communications Research	**SDGTE**	Société Dahoméenne des Grands Travaux de l'Est
SCTTAO	Société Commerciale de Transports Trans-atlantiques Afrique Occidentale	**SDHBS**	South Devon Herd Book Society
		SDI	Secours Dentaire International
SCTU	Security Council Truce Commission (Palestine)	**SDI**	Sociedad para el Desarrollo Internacional
SCU	Scottish Cricket Union	**SDI**	Società Dantesca Italiana
SCUA	Scottish Conservative and Unionist Association	**SDIA**	Soap and Detergent Industry Association
		SDIC	Société de Développement Industriel du Cameroun
SCUA	Suez Canal Users Association		
SCUAS	Standing Conference of University Appointments Services	**SDIG**	Société pour le Développement de l'Industrie du Gaz
SCUMRA	Société Centrale de l'Uranium et des Minerais et Métaux Radioactifs	**SDIT**	Service de Documentation et d'Information Techniques de l'Aéronautique
SCVANYO	Standing Conference of Voluntary Youth Organizations	**SDK**	Société de Kinésithérapie
		SDL	Syndicat des Distillateurs-Liquoristes de Belgique
SCVM	Service Central des Ventes du Mobilier de l'État		
SCVU	Svaz Ceských Výtvarných Umelcu	**SDLP**	Social and Democratic Labour Party (N. Ireland)
SCWR	Scientific Committee on Water Research (ICSU)	**SDMFAJ**	Savex Drustava Matematicara, Fizicara i Astronoma Jugoslavije
SCWS	Scottish Co-operative Wholesale Society	**SDN**	Société des Nations (replaced by UNO)
SCYA	Scottish Christian Youth Assembly	**SDP**	Swaziland Democratic Party
SCYCO-MIMPEX	Syndicat des Industries de l'Afrique Équatoriale	**SDPG**	Société Dahoméenne de Pointes Galvanisées
		SDR	Société de Développement Régional
SDA	Schweizerische Depeschenagentur	**SDRA**	Société pour le Développement de la Riviéra Africaine (Ivory Coast)
SDA	Sheep Development Association (*now* NSA)		
SDA	Société de l'Aérotrain	**SDS**	Servizio di Documentazione Spaziale
SDA	Syndicat de la Distillerie Agricole	**SDS**	Slavisticno Drustvo Slovenije
SDAI	Syndicat National de la Distribution pour l'Automobile et l'Industrie	**SDSTA**	Section Technique de l'Armée, Documentation Technique et Scientifique

SDT	Société Dahoméenne de Transports
SDT	Society of Dairy Technology
SDTIM	Society for the Development of Techniques in Industrial Marketing
SDTU	Sign and Display Trades Union
SDUK	Society for the Diffusion of Useful Knowledge
SDV	Schweizerischer Dachdeckermeister-Verband
SDV	Schweizerischer Detaillistenverband
SDV	Schweizerischer Drogisten-Verband
SDV	Stichting Doelmatig Verzinken
SE	Society of Engineers
SEA	Science and Education Administration (U.S.A.)
SEA	Shipbuilding Exports Association
SEA	Société Équatoriale d'Assurances
SEA	Société d'Électronique et d'Automatisme
SEA	Sociedad Entomológica Argentina
SEA	Société d'Études Ardennaises
SEA	Société d'Équipement pour l'Afrique (Gabon)
SEA	Stazione di Entomologia Agraria
SEAAC	South-East Asia Air Command
SEAC	Social and Economic Archives Centre
SEAC	South-East Asia Command
SEACEN	South-East Asian Central Banks
SEADAG	South-East Asia Development Advisory Group (U.S.A.)
SEADD	South-East Asia Development Division (*of* ODM)
SEAF	Sveriges El-och Elektronikagenters Förening
SEAFDEC	Southeast Asian Fisheries Development Centre
SEAG	Société d'Équipement pour l'Afrique-Gabon
SEAISI	South East Asia Iron and Steel Institute
SEALPA	South-East Asia Lumber Producers Association
SEAM	Servicio de Equipos Agricolas Mecanizados (Chile)
SEAMEO	Southeast Asian Ministers of Education Organisation
SEAMES	Southeast Asian Ministers of Education Secretariat
SEAN	Servicio Escolar de Alimentación y Nutrición
SEAN	Société d'Équipement pour l'Afrique-Niger
SEAP	South-East Asia Project (*of* IUCN)

SEAPAL	South East Asia and Pacific League against Rheumatism
SEAP-CENTRE	South East Asia Centre for the Promotion of Trade, Investments and Tourism (Japan)
SEARCA	Southeast Asian Regional Centre for Graduate Study and Research in Agriculture (Philippines)
SEARCC	South-East Asia Regional Computer Conference
SEARCF	Société d'Encouragement pour l'Amélioration des Races de Chevaux en France
SEARS	South and East Asian Regional Section (*of* IOBC)
SEAS	Centre for Southeast Asia Studies of Kyoto University (Japan)
SEAS	Scientific Exploration of the Atlantic Shelf
SEAS	SHARE European Association
SEAS	Société d'Équipement pour l'Afrique-Sénégal
SEASCO	Field Science Co-operation Office for South-East Asia
SEASSE	Southeast Asian Society of Soil Engineering (Thailand)
SEATAG	South East Asia Trade Advisory Group
SEATO	South-East Asia Treaty Organisation
SEAVOM	Société d'Études et d'Applications Video-Optique Mécanique
SEB	Sociedad Española de Bioquímica
SEB	Société Équatoriale des Bois (Gabon)
SEB	Société d'Exploitation des Briqueteries
SEB	Society for Economic Botany (U.S.A.)
SEB	Society for Experimental Biology
SEB	Southern Electricity Board
SEB	Syndicat des Éditeurs Belges
SEB	Syndicat des Exploitants de Bauxite
SEBA	Société Sénégalaise d'Exploitation des Bois Africains
SEBACAM	Société d'Études des Bauxites du Cameroun
SEBC	Societe d'Exploitation des Bois du Cameroun
SEBOGA	Société pour l'Expansion des Boissons Hygiéniques au Gabon
SEBT	South-Eastern Brick and Tile Federation
SEC	Société Européenne de Cardiologie
SEC	Société Européenne de Culture
SEC	State Electricity Commission of Victoria (Australia)

SECA	Société pour l'Expansion Commerciale Africaine (Togo)
SECA	Société d'Exploitation de Constructions Aéronautiques
SECA	Syndicat d'Études des Centrales Atomiques
SECAB	Secrétariat Exécutif de la Convention Andrés Bello (Peru)
SECAM	Société d'Exploitation des Cadres Maritimes
SECAM	Symposium of Episcopal Conferences of Africa and Madagascar
SECAN	Société d'Études et de Constructions Aéro-Navales
SECAP	Servicio Ecuatoria de Capacitación Profesional
SECARTYS	Servicio de Exportación de Electrónica
SECAS	Sociedad de Estudiantes de Ciencias Agronómicas Salvadoreñas
SECB	Société Européenne de Construction de l'Avion Bregeut
SECCAN	Science and Engineering Clubs of Canada
SECEA	Servicio Comercial de la Industria Textil Algodonera
SECED	Society for Earthquake and Civil Engineering Dynamics
SECF	Société des Experts Comptables Français
SECEM	Sociedad Espanola Construcciones Electro-Mecanicas
SECMA	Société d'Exploitation Cinématographique Africaine
SECO	Bureau de Contrôle pour la Sécurité de la Construction en Belgique
SECOBRAH	Société d'Encouragement de la Culture des Orges de Brasserie et des Houblons en France
SECPANE	Servicio Cooperativo Peruano-Norteamericano de Educación
SECPIA	Société d'Étude Chimiques pour l'Industrie et l'Agriculture
SECS	Sociedad Española de Ciencia del Suelo
SECT	Société des Ecrivains de Cinéma et de Télévision
SECTAB	Section Spécialisée pour le Tabac du Comité des Organisations Professionnelles Agricoles de la CEE
SEDA	Société d'Éditions Documentaires Agricoles
SEDA	Société d'Études pour le Développement de l'Automatisme
SEDAGRI	Société d'Étude et de Développement Agricole

SEDAM	Société d'Études et de Développement des Aéroglisseurs Marins, Terrestres et Amphibies
SEDAR	Sociedad Española de Anestesiología y Reanimación
SEDEC	Société d'Édition, de Documentation Économique et Commerciale
SEDECOS	Secretaríado de Comunicación Social (Chile)
SEDEIS	Société d'Études et de Documentation Économiques Industrielles et Sociales
SEDERCAL	Société d'Équipement et de Développement Rural de la Nouvelle-Calédonie
SEDES	Société pour l'Étude et le Développement Économique et Social
SEDHA	Secretariat for Dental Health in Africa
SEDIA	Société d'Étude du Développement Industriel et Agricole (Algeria)
SEDIA	Société d'Études et de Distribution Inter-Africaines (Ivory Coast)
SEDIAC	Société pour l'Étude et le Développement de l'Industrie, de l'Agriculture et du Commerce (Upper Volta)
SEDIBRA	Syndicat National d'Étude et de Défense des Intérêts de la Brasserie Française
SEDIMA	Syndicat National des Entreprises de Service et Distribution du Machinisme Agricole
SEDIVER	Société Européenne d'Isolateurs en Verre
SEDNI	Syndicat des Entrepreneurs de Dragages de Navigation Intérieure
SEDOS	Servizio di Documentazione e Studi
SEDPA	Société d'Édition et de Diffusion de la Presse Agricole
SEE	Société des Électriciens, des Électroniciens et des Radioélectriciens
SEE	Société d'Études et d'Expansion (Belgium)
SEE	Society of Electronic Engineers (India)
SEE	Society for Environmental Education
SEE	Society of Environmental Engineers
SEEA	Société Européenne d'Énergie Atomique
SEEB	South Eastern Electricity Board
SEECA	South Eastern Electricity Commercial Association
SEECF	Société d'Encouragement à l'Élévage du Cheval Français
SEEF	Service des Études Économiques et Financières
SEEF	Society of Electronics Engineers, Finland

SEEG	Société d'Énergie et d'Eau du Gabon
SEEN	Syndicat d'Études de l'Énergie Nucléaire
SEEP	Sociedad Española para el Estudio de los Pastos
SEET	Société d'Études et d'Équipements Techniques
SEF	Shipbuilding Employers' Federation
SEF	Société Entomologique de France
SEF	Société d'Ethonographie Française
SEF	Svenska Elverksföreningen
SEF	Svenska Exlibrisföreningen
SEF	Syndicat des Exportateurs Suisses de Fromage
SEFA	Genossenschaft Schweizerischer Strassenemulsions-Fabrikanten
SEFA	Scottish Educational Film Association
SEFAC	Société d'Exploitation Forestière et Agricole du Cameroun
SEFE	Suomen Ekonomiliitto
SEFEL	Secrétariat Européen des Fabricants d'Emballages Métalliques Légers (Belgium)
SEFI	Société Européenne pour la Formation des Ingénieurs
SEFI	Syndicat des Entreprises Françaises de Travaux Publics a Vocation Internationale
SEFIC	Société d'Exploitations Forestières et Industrielles du Cameroun
SEFIPA	Société Européenne de Financement et de Participation
SEFRAN	Syndicat des Embouteilleurs de France
SEFT	Society for Education in Film and Television
SEG	Saatgut-Erzeuger-Gemeinschaft Schleswig-Holstein
SEG	Schweizerische Entomologische Gesellschaft
SEG	Société d'Exploitations Gabonaises
SEG	Society of Exploration Geophysicists (U.S.A.)
SEG	Sveriges Elgrossisters Förening
SEG	Verband Schweizerischer Eier- und Geflügel-verwertungs-Genossenschaften
SEGA	Société d'Études Gabonaises
SEGA	Société d'Exploitation de Gravières en Afrique
SEGAP	Société d'Études pour l'Exploitation des Calcaires, Gypses, Argiles et Pouzzolanes de Madagascar
SEGB	South Eastern Gas Board
SEGCA	Gladstone Association of Celtic Europeans and their Friends
SEGEC	Syndicat Nationale Eau – Gas – Électricité des Cadres et Techniciens
SEGENI	Société Générale Sénégalaise pour le Négoce et l'Industrie
SEGESA	Société d'Études Géographiques, Économiques, et Sociologiques Appliquées
SEGI	Société Exploitation de Granit Ivoirien
SEGOA	Société Sénégalaise d'Oxygène et d'Acetylène
SEGRAM	Société Équatoriale de Grands Magasins
SEGRANI	Société d'Étude pour la Création d'une Usine de Graines au Niger
SEH	Société Européenne d'Hematologie
SEI	Service d'Expérimentation et d'Information (*of* I.N.R.A.)
SEI	Società Editrice Internazionale (Italy)
SEI	Societas Ergophthalmologica Internationalis
SEI	Société Générale d'Entreprises Immobilières et de Investissements (Belgium)
SEI	Société Sénégalaise d'Entreprises Industrielles
SEI	Society for Environmental Improvement
SEI	Syndicat de l'Emballage Industriel
SEICI	Société d'Exportation et d'Importation de la Côte-d'Ivoire
SEIE	Société d'Études de l'Industrie de l'Engrenage
SEIFA	Società Esportazione Importazione Fertilizanti Azotati
SEIFSA	Steel and Engineering Industries Federation of South Africa
SEIMAD	Société d'Équipement Immobilier de Madagascar
SEIN	Société d'Électronique Industrielle et Nucléaire
SEIN	Société d'Encouragement pour l'Industrie Nationale
SEINA	Société Européenne d'Instruments Numériques et Analogiques
SEIO	Sociedad Española de Investigación Operativa
SEITA	Service d'Exploitation Industrielle des Tabacs (Tunisia)
SEIU	Service Employers International Union (U.S.A.)
SEKE	Synetairistike Enosis Kapnoparagogon Ellados

SEKV	Schweizerische Einkäufer-Vereinigung	**SENA**	Société d'Énergie Nucléaire Franco-Belge des Ardennes
SEL	Scout's Esperanto League		
SELA	Sistema Economicano Latinoamericano	**SENA**	Société d'Études Numismatiques et Archéologiques
SELAF	Société pour l'Étude des Langues Africains		
SELEC	Société d'Étude des Électrocompresseurs	**SENABI**	National Scientific and Technical Library and Documentation Services (South America)
SELF	Société d'Ergonomie de Langue Française	**SENAC**	Serviço Nacional de Aprendizagem Comercial (Brazil)
SELF	Syndicat des Écrivains de Langue Française		
SELNI	Società Elettronucleare Italiana	**SENAI**	Serviço Nacional de Aprendizagem Industrial (Brazil)
SELSA	Servicio de Luchas Sanitarias (Argentina)		
SEM	Schweizerischer Engros-Möbelfabrikantenverband	**SENALFA**	Servicio Nacional de Lucha contra la Fiebre Aftosa (Paraguay)
SEM	Secretariat for European Medicine (Belgium)	**SENAPET**	Servicio Nacional de Programación y Evaluación Técnica (of INTA) (Argentina)
SEM	Société d'Équipement de la Mauritanie		
SEM	Syndesmos Epistimonon Michanikon Kyprou	**SENAPI**	Servicio Nacional de Artesanías y Pequeñas Industrias (Panama)
SEMA	Société d'Économie et de Mathématiques Appliquées	**SENATI**	Servicio Nacional de Aprendizaje y Trabajo Industrial (Peru)
SEMA	Société d'Équipement de Materiel Aéronautique (Congo)	**SEND**	Scientists and Engineers for National Development (U.S.A.)
SEMA	Société Équipement du Mali	**SENE**	Servicio Nacional de Empleo (Panama)
SEMA	Storage Equipment Manufacturers' Association	**SENEGA-LAP**	Société Sénégalaise de Diffusion d'Appareils Électriques
SEMA	Spray Equipment Manufacturers Association	**SENELEC**	Société Sénégalaise de Distribution d'Énergie Électrique
SEMABLE	Secteur de Modernisation d'Agriculture, Blé (Chad)	**SENEPESCA**	Société Sénégalaise pour l'Expansion de la Pêche Côtière, Surgélation et Conditionnement des Aliments
SEME	Sociedad Española de Microscopía Electrónica		
SEMFA	Scottish Electrical Manufacturers' and Factors' Association	**SENETRA-NSFIL**	Société Sénégalaise de Transformation du Fil de Metal
SEMI	Société des Eaux Minérales Ivoiriennes	**SENFOR**	Servicio Nacional de Formación Profesional (Paraguay)
SEMI	Société d'Ébénisterie et de Menuiserie Ivoirienne	**SENICUA**	Servizio per gli Elenchi Nominativi dei Lavoratori e per i Contributi Unificati in Agricultura
SEMKO	Svenska Elecktriska Materielkontrollanstalten		
SEMO	Société Belgo-Française d'Énergie Nucléaire Mosane	**SENN**	Società Elettronucleare Nazionale
		SENTA	Société d'Études Nucléaires et de Techniques Nouvelles
SEMRAD	Syndicat des Industries de l'Électronique Médicale et de la Radiologie (France)	**SEOL**	Suomen Elokuvateatter-inomistajain Liitto
SEMRY	Société d'Expansion et de Modernisation de la Riziculture de Yagoua	**SEOL**	Suomen Erikois-Optikkojen Liitto
SEMT	Société d'Études de Machines Thermiques	**SEP**	Sociedad Entomológica del Perú
SEMY	Syndesmos Ergostasiarchon Michanikis Ypodimatopoias	**SEP**	Société Équatoriale Pharmaceutique
		SEP	Société Européenne de Planification à Long Terme
SEMZA	Association Professionnelle Belge des Négociants Préparateurs en Semences Agricoles	**SEP**	Stowarzyszenie Elektryków Polskich
SENA	Servicio Nacional de Aprendizaje (Colombia)	**SEPA**	Société d'Éditions et de Publications Agricoles

SEPAB	Section on Experimental Psychology and Animal Behaviour of the IUBS
SEPAM	Société d'Exploitation des Produits Animaux du Mali
SEPBA	Société d'Exploitation du Parc à Bois d'Abidjan (Ivory Coast)
SEPBC	Société d'Exploitation des Parcs à Bois du Cameroun
SEPC	Société d'Exploitation de Produits de Côte-d'Ivoire
SEPCAE	Société d'Engrais et Produits Chimiques d'Afrique Équatoriale
SEPCEM	Société d'Étude pour la Promotion de la Culture et l'Exploitation du Maïs au Cameroun
SEPCM	Société d'Engrais et de Produits Chimiques de Madagascar
SEPCO	Services Electronic Parts Co-ordinating Committee
SEPCR	Societas Europaea Physiologiae Clinicae Respiratoriae
SEPE	Secretariat pour l'Étude des Problèmes de l'Eau
SEPECAT	Société Européenne de Production de l'Avion École de Combat et d'Appui Tactique
SEPHAR	Section Internationale de Pharmacologie de l'Union Internationale de Sciences Physiologiques
SEPIA	Société d'Études et de Production Industrielle en Afrique
SEPIA	Société d'Études de Protection des Installations Atomiques
SEPM	Society of Economic Paleontologists and Mineralogists (U.S.A.)
SEPOM	Société d'Exploitation des Produits Oléagineux du Mali
SEPOR	Service des Programmes des Organismes de Recherche
SEPP	Société d'Entreposage de Produits Pétroliers (Congo)
SEPP	Société d'Étude de la Prévision et de la Planification (Switzerland)
SEPR	Société d'Étude de la Propulsion par Réaction
SEPT	Serviço de Estatistica da Previdencia e Trabalho (Brazil)
SEPT	Société d'Étude de Psychodrame Thérapeutique
SEQC	Sociedad Española de Quimicos Cosmeticos
SER	Service d'Économie Rurale (Luxemburg)
SER	Sociaal Economische Raad
SER	Svenska Elektroingenjörers Riksförening
SER	Sveriges Schaktentreprenörers Riksförbund
SERA	Socialist Environment and Resources Association
SERAI	Société d'Études de Recherches et d'Applications pour l'Industrie (Belgium)
SERAM	Service d'Études et de Recherches Antimalariennes (Zaire)
SERAS	Société d'Exploitation des Ressources Animales du Sénégal
SERC	Structural Engineering Research Centre (India)
SERC	Service d'Étude et de Recherches de la Circulation Routière (France)
SERCA	Société d'Exploitation de la République Centrafricaine
SERCE	Syndicat des Entrepreneurs de Réseaux, de Centrales et d'Équipement Industriel Électriques
SERCEL	Société d'Exploitation et de Recherches Électroniques
SERCOM	Station d'Essais et de Recherches de la Construction Métallique (Belgium)
SERCO-METAL	Servicio Técnico Comercial de Construcciones Metálicas y de Calderaria
SEREM	Sociedad Española de Radiología y Electrología Médicas y de Medicina Nuclear
SEREPCA	Société de Recherches et d'Exploitation des Pétroles du Cameroun
SERES	Société d'Études Rurales et Sociales
SERIA	Société d'Études et de Réalisations Industrielles d'Abidjan (Ivory Coast)
SERICC	Société d'Études et de Recherches pour l'Industrie et le Commerce Camerounais
SERL	Services Electronics Research Laboratory
SERLB	South Eastern Regional Library Bureau
SERM	Société d'Études et de Recherches Minières de Madagascar
SERMIS	Société d'Études et de Recherches Minières du Sénégal
SERMOTO	Servicio Técnico-Comercial de Fabricantes y Montadores de Motocicletas
SERNAUTO	Asociación Nacional de Fabricantes de Equipos y Componentes para Automoción
SERS	Société d'Étude et Recherche Sociologiques

SERT	Society of Electronic and Radio Technicians	**SETCI**	Société d'Extrusion et de Tissage de Côte-d'Ivoire
SERTAF	Services Techniques Africains Côte d'Ivoire	**SETCO**	Société d'Éditions Techniques Coloniales
SERTI	Société d'Études et de Réalisation pour le Traitement de l'Information	**SETEL**	Société Européenne pour l'Étude et l'Intégration des Systèmes Spatiaux
SERUG	Seminarie voor Toegepaste Economie bij de Rijksuniversiteit te Gent (Belgium)	**SETFP**	Syndicat de l'Extrusion et de la Transformation des Films Plastiques
SES	Scientific Exploration Society	**SETIAC**	Société des Éditions Techniques Industrielles, Agricoles et Commerciales
SES	Société Européenne de Semences (Belgium)		
SES	Solar Energy Society (U.S.A.)	**SETIS**	Société Européenne d'Étude et d'Intégration de Systèmes Spatiaux
SES	Studies and Expansion Society (Belgium)		
SES	Suomen Egyptologinen Seura	**SETRA-CONGO**	Société d'Études et des Travaux au Congo
SES	Swedish Engineers' Society (U.S.A.)		
SES	Swiss Entomological Society	**SETRAPEM**	Société Équatoriale de Travaux Pétroliers Maritimes (Gabon)
SESA	Social and Economic Statistics Administration (U.S.A.)	**SETU**	Société d'Études et de Travaux pour l'Uranium
SESA	Société d'Études des Systèmes d'Automation	**SEV**	Schweizerischer Elektrotechnischer Verein
SESA	Society for Experimental Stress Analysis (U.S.A.)	**SEV**	Soviet Ekonomitcheskoi Vzaimopomochtchi
SESD	Society of Experimental Station Directors (U.S.A.)	**SEV**	Syndesmos Ellinon Viomichanon
SESDA	Secretariat de Santé Dentaire de l'Afrique	**SEVIMA**	Société d'Exploitation de la Viande à Madagascar
SESEP	Société d'Études et de Soins pour les Enfants Poliomyélitiques	**SEVMA-CAM**	Société d'Exploitation et de Valorisation des Marbres, Cipolins et Aragonites à Madagascar
SESK	Verband Schweizerischer Schachtel-käsefabriken		
SESN	Società Elvetica di Scienze Naturali (Switzerland)	**SEVPEN**	Service de Vente des Publications de l'Éducation Nationale
SESO	Studiecentrum voor Economisch en Sociaal Onderzoek	**SEYCO**	Selección y Comercio de Patata
		SEZEB	Société d'Ethnozoologie et d'Ethnobotanique
SESPA	Scientists and Engineers for Social and Political Action (U.S.A.)	**SF**	Sagwerksförbundet
		SFA	Scientific Film Association
SESR	Société Européenne de Sociologie Rurale	**SFA**	Société Française d'Archéologie
SESSIA	Société d'Études, de Constructions de Souffleries Simulateurs et Instrumentation Aérodynamique	**SFA**	Société Française d'Astronautique (*Incorp. in* AAAF)
		SFA	Soroptimist Federation of the Americas
SESUAM	Société d'Études Sucrières en Afrique et à Madagascar	**SFA**	Syndicat Français des Adhésifs
		SFAF	Société Française des Analystes Financiers
SESUHV	Société d'Études Sucrières de Haute-Volta	**SFAJ**	Société Française d'Architecture de Jardins
SET	Serviço de Expansao do Trigo (Brazil)	**SFAK**	Selskabet for Analytisk Kemi
SET	Wirtschaftsverband Stahlbau und Energie-Technik	**SFAS**	Solid Fuel Advisory Service
		SFBIU	Scottish Farm Buildings Investigation Unit
SETADEC	Société d'Études pour l'Amélioration, le Développement et l'Équipement des Collectivités locales	**SFC**	Société Française de Céramique
		SFC	Société Française des Chrysanthèmistes
		SFC	Standing Federation Committee (West Indies)
SETAO	Société d'Études et de Travaux pour l'Afrique Occidentale	**SFCM**	Société Française de Commerce à Madagascar

SFD	Société Française du Dahlia
SFDA	Small Farmers Development Agency (India)
SFDAS	Société Française de Droit Aérien et Spatial
SFE	Société Financière Européenne
SFE	Société Française d'Égyptologie
SFE	Société Française des Électriciens
SFE	Société Française d'Électrologie Médicale
SFEA	Scottish Further Education Association
SFEA	Société Française d'Études Agricoles
SFEC	San Francisco Engineering Council (USA)
SFEC	Société de Fabrication d'Éléments Catalytiques
SFEDTP	Société Française d'Entreprises de Dragages et de Travaux Publics
SFENA	Société Française d'Équipements pour la Navigation Aérienne
SFER	Société Française d'Économie Rurale (France)
SFER	Société Française des Électriciens et Radio-électriciens
SFERB	Syndicat des Fabricants d'Émulsions Routières de Bitume
SFEV	Syndicat Française des Éleveurs de Visons
SFF	Society of Filipino Foresters
SFF	Svenska Folkbibliotekarie Förbundet
SFF	Svenska Fysioterapeutiska Föreningen
SFF	Sveriges Filatelist-Förbund
SFFCCP	Syndicat Français des Fournisseurs pour Coiffeurs et Coiffeurs Parfumeurs
SFFL	Svensk Förening för Foniatri och Logopedics
SFG	Société Française de Gynécologie
SFG	Studien- und Förderungsgesellschaft (Belgium)
SFGV	Schweizerischer Frauengewerbeverband
SFH	Samfundet för Hembygdsvard
SFH	Studiengesellschaft für Hochspannungs-anlagen
SFHM	Société Française d'Histoire de la Médecine
SFHOM	Société Française d'Histoire d'Outre-Mer
SFHR	Society for Film History Research
SFHV	Schweizerischer Fischhändler-Verband
SFI	Société Financière Internationale
SFI	Société Française des Amateurs d'Iris
SFIB	Syndicat National des Fabricants d'Ensembles de Information et des Machines de Bureau

SFICE	Syndicat des Industries de Pièces Détachées et Accessoires Radio-Électriques et Électroniques
SFIE	Syndicat des Fabricants d'Isolants pour l'Électricité
SFIG	Syndicat des Fabricants Industriels de Glaces, Sorbets et Crèmes Glacées
SFIM	Société de Fabrication d'Instruments de Mesure
SFIM	Svenska Forbundet for Internationaler Möbeltransporter
SFIO	Section Française Internationale Ouvrière
SFIT	Swiss Federal Institute of Technology
SFITV	Société Française des Ingénieurs Techniciens du Vide
SFL	Statens Forskningskommitté för Lant-mannagbyggnader
SFL	Suomen Farmaseuttiliitto
SFL	Svenska Facklärarförbundet
SFL	Sveriges Fotolevantörers Förbund
SFM	Sociedad Forestal Mexicana
SFM	Société Française de Mesothérapie
SFM	Société Française de Métallurgie
SFMA	Scottish Furniture Manufacturers Association
SFME	Société Française de Médecine Esthétique
SFME	Société Française de Microscopie Électronique
SFMGV	Schweizerischer Fahrrad- und Motorrad-Gewerbe-Verband
SFMI	Société Française de Moteurs à Induction
SFMS	Société Française de Médecine du Sport
SFMT	Scottish Federation of Merchant Tailors
SFMT	Société Française de Médecine du Trafic
SFMTA	Scottish Federation of Meat Traders Associations
SFN	Société Française de Numismatique
SFNI	Suikerfabrieknavorsingsinstituut (South Africa)
SFO	Société Française d'Ophthalmologie
SFOM	Société Financière pour les Pays d'Outre-Mer
SFOM	Société Française d'Optique et de Mécanique
SFOS	Société Française d'Organo-Synthèse
SFP	Société Française de Pédagogie
SFP	Société Française de Photogrammétrie
SFP	Société Française de Photographie

SFP	Société Française de Psychologie
SFPH	Svenska Föreningen för Psykisk Hälsovård
SFPMAC	Société Française de Physiologie et de Médecine Aéronautiques et Cosmonautiques
SFR	Skogsägareföreningarnas Riksförbund
SFR	Société Française Radioélectrique
SFR	Société Française des Roses
SFR	Svenska Fargeritekniska Riksförbundet
SFR	Svenska Försäkringsbolags Riksförbund
SFR	Sveriges Färghandlares Riksförbund
SFRP	Société Française de Radioprotection
SFS	Société Française de Sociologie
SFS	Suomen Standardisoimisliitto
SFS	Svenska Fornskriftsällskapet
SFSA	Scottish Federation of Sea Anglers
SFSA	Scottish Field Studies Association
SFSA	Steel Founders' Society of America
SFSR	Socialist Federation of Soviet Republics
SFT	Société Française des Télécommunications
SFT	Société Française des Thermiciens
SFT	Société Française des Traducteurs
SFT	Society of Feed Technologists
SFTA	Society of Film and Television Arts
SFTAS	Syndicat Français des Textiles Artificiels et Synthétiques
SFTM	Société Française de Transports Maritimes
SFTSA	Scottish Forest Tree Seed Association
SFTV	Verband Gewerbsmässiger Ferntransportunternehmer der Schweiz
SFU	Société Française des Urbanistes
SFV	Schweizerischer Feuerwehrverband
SFV	Schweizerischer Floristenverband
SFV	Schweizerischer Forstverein
SFV	Schweizerische Franchising-Vereinigung
SFV	Société Française du Vide
SFZ	Sozialwissenschaftliches Forschungszentrum
SG	Société Générale
SGA	Schweizerische Gesellschaft für Automatik
SGA	Society of Graphic Artists
SGACC	Sécrétariat Général à l'Aviation Civile et Commerciale
SGAE	Schweizerische Gesellschaft für Anthropologie und Ethnologie
SGAEI	Société Gabonaise d'Aménagement et d'Équipement Immobiliers
SGAG	Schweizerische Gesellschaft für Angewandte Geographie
SGAR	Schweizerische Gesellschaft für Anästhesiologie und Reanimation
SGB	Schweizerische Gesellschaft für Betriebswissenschaft
SGB	Schweizerischer Gewerkschaftsbund
SGB	Scottish Gas Board
SGB	Sociedad Geológica Boliviana
SGB	Sociedade Geográfica Brasileira
SGB	Société des Bois du Gabon
SGBI	Santa Gertrudis Breeders International (U.S.A.)
SGBS	Société Générale de Banques au Sénégal
SGC	Service Générale de Contrôle (Belgium)
SGC	Sociedad Geográfica de Colombia
SGCE	Syndicat Général de la Construction Électrique
SGCH	Sociedad de Genética de Chile
SGCH	Sociedad Geológica de Chile
SGCI	Schweizerische Gesellschaft für Chemische Industrie
SGCTMA	Syndicat Général des Constructeurs et Machines Agricoles
SGD	Stichting Gezondheidsdienst voor Dieren
SGE	Société Gabonaise d'Entreposage
SGE	Société Gabonaise d'Entreprises
SGEP	Syndicat Général de l'Enseignement Public
SGEVE	Synomospondia Geniki Epangelmation kai Viotechnon
SGF	Scottish Growers Federation
SGF	Société Géologique de France
SGF	Studiengemeinschaft für Fertigbau
SGF	Svensk Geotekniska Föreningen
SGF	Svenska Gasföreningen
SGF	Sveriges Gjuteritekniska Förening
SGF	Sveriges Summtekniska Förening
SGFF	Schweizerische Gesellschaft für Familienforschung
SGFF	Syndicat Général des Fondeurs de France et Industries Connexes
SGFHTF	Syndicat Général des Fabricants d'Huile et de Tourteaux de France
SGFT	Schweizerische Gesellschaft für Feintechnik

SGG	Schweizerische Geisteswissenschaftliche Gesellschaft
SGG	Schweizerische Geologische Gesellschaft
SGG	Schweizerische Genossenschaft für Gemüsebau
SGG	Schweizerische Graphologische Gesellschaft
SGgG	Schweizerische Geographische Gesellschaft
SGGG	Société Générale du Golfe de Guinée
SGGMN	Schweizerische Gesellschaft für Geschichte der Medizin und der Naturwissenschaften
SGH	Schweizerische Gesellschaft für Hämatologie
SGH	Schweizerische Gesellschaft für Höhlenforschung
SGHC	Société des Grands Hôtels du Cameroun
SGI	Servicio Geodésico Interamericano
SGI	Società Geologica Italiana
SGICF	Syndicat Général de l'Industrie Cotonnière Française
SGIEO	Sistema Global Integrado de Estaciones Oceánicas
SGIJ	Syndicat Général de l'Industrie du Jute
SGIPA	Syndicat Général de l'Industrie du Plastique Armé
SGIPR	Syndicat Général de l'Industrie des Plastiques Renforcés
SGIT	Savez Gradevinskih Inzenjera i Tehnicara Jugoslavije
SGK	Stichting Verkoopkantoor voor Gras- en Klavermeel
SGKC	Schweizerische Gesellschaft für Klinische Chemie
SGKV	Studiengesellschaft für den Kombinierten Verkehr
SGM	Service Géologique de Madagascar
SGM	Société Gabonaise de Mécanique
SGM	Society of General Microbiology
SGMB	Société Géologique et Minéralogique de Bretagne
SGN	Section de Génie Nucléaire de l'Association Suisse pour l'Énergie Atomique
SGN	Servicio Geológico Nacional (Colombia, Nicaragua, Salvador)
SGO	Schweizerische Gesellschaft für Onkologie
SGOEM	Schweizerische Gesellschaft für Optik und Elektronen-mikroskopie
SGOIP	Syndicat Général de l'Optique et des Instruments de Précision
SGOP	Syndicat Générale des Ouates et Pansements
SGP	Schweizerischer Gesellschaft für Personalfragen
SGP	Schweizerische Gesellschaft für Phlebologie
SGP	Schweizerische Gesellschaft für Psychiatrie
SGP	Schweizerische Gesellschaft für Psychologie
SGP	Sociedad Geológica del Perú
SGP	Stowarzyszenie Geodetów Polskich
SGP	Syndicat des Graphologues Professionnels
SGPF	Sveriges Glas- och Porslinshandlareförbund
SGPFBM	Syndicat Générale des Producteurs Fournisseurs de Bois aux Mines
SGPMR	Schweizerische Gesellschaft für Physikalische Medizin und Rheumatologie
SGPP	Schweizerische Gesellschaft für Praktische Psychologie
SGPSM	Schweizerischer Gesellschaft für Psychosomatische Médecin
SGR	Sveriges Golvhandlares Riksförbund
SGRB	Société Générale des Représentants de Belgique
SGSH	Société Générale Suisse d'Histoire
SGSPM	Schweizerische Gesellschaft für Sozial- und Präventivmedizin
SGSR	Society for General Systems Research (U.S.A.)
SGSS	Schweizerische Gesellschaft für Skandinavische Studien
SGSS	Società Generale Svizzera di Storia
SGSV	Schweizerische Gesellschaft für Statistik und Informatik
SGT	Schweizerische Galvano-technische Gesellschaft
SGT	Société des Garde-Temps (Switzerland)
SGT	Société Guinéenne de Transport
SGT	Society of Glass Technologists
SGTE	Société Générale de Techniques et d'Études
SGTK	Schweizerische Gesellschaft für Theaterkultur
SGTS	Scottish Gaelic Texts Society
SGU	Schweizerische Gesellschaft für Umweltschutz
SGU	Scottish Golf Union
SGU	Svenska Geologiska Undersökning
SGV	Schweizerischer Geflügelzuchtverband
SGV	Schweizerische Gesellschaft für Volkskunde

SGV	Schweizerischer Gewerbeverband	**SHS**	Suomen Hammaslääkäriseura
SGV-NOK	Ständige Generalversammlung der Nationalen Olympischen Komitees	**SHSHV**	Société des Huiles et Savons de Haute-Volta
SHA	Sociedäd de Historia Argentina	**SHSK**	Schweizerische Häutschäden-Kommission
SHA	Swiss Hotel Association	**SHSN**	Société Helvétique des Sciences Naturelles
SHAC	Société Havraise Africaine de Commerce (Ivory Coast)	**SHT**	Société des Hévéas de Tay-Ninh (Vietnam)
SHADA	Haitian-American Society for Agricultural Development	**SHTF**	Sveriges Handelsträdgardsmästareförbund
SHAL	Société d'Histoire et d'Archéologie de la Lorraine	**SHTM**	Société des Hôtelleries et du Tourisme du Mali
SHALTA	Skin, Hide and Leather Trades Association	**SHU**	Société Hippique Urbaine
SHAPE	Supreme Headquarters of the Allied Powers in Europe	**SHU**	Státni Hydrometeorologicky Ústáv
		SHV	Schweizer Hotelier-Verein
SHAS	Smallholders' Advisory Service (Malaysia and Sri Lanka)	**SHV**	Schweizerischer Hafnermeisterverband, Ofenbau- und Plattengeschäfte
SHAT	Sociedad Horticola para América Tropical (Costa Rico)	**SHV**	Schweizerischer Hebammen-Verband
SHCF	Saint Hubert Club de France	**SHY**	Suomen Henkilökuntalehtien Yhdistys
SHD	Scottish Home Department	**SHY**	Suomen Hypnoosiyhdistys
SHD	State Hydro-electric Department (New Zealand)	**SI**	Smithsonian Institution (U.S.A.)
		SI	Sveriges Industriförbund
SHE	Society for Health Education	**SIA**	Saskatchewan Institute of Agrologists (Canada)
SHF	Société Hippique Française		
SHF	Société Hydrotechnique de France	**SIA**	Schweizerischer Ingenieur- und Architekten-Verein
SHF	Sveriges Handelsagenters Förbund		
SHFL	Sveriges Hogre Flickskolors Lararförbund	**SIA**	Singapore International Airlines
SHG	Schweizerische Heraldische Gesellschaft	**SIA**	Société Immobilière Agricole
SHIC	Société Hôtelière et Immobilière du Congo	**SIA**	Société des Ingénieurs de l'Automobile
SHIO	Sveriges Hantverks- och Industriorganisation	**SIA**	Société Internationale d'Acupuncture
SHIV	Schweizerischer Handels- und In-dustrieverein	**SIA**	Société Interprofessionnelle de l'Aviculture et des Produits de Bassecour
		SIA	Société d'Investissements Africains
SHIV	Schweizerischer Holzindustrie-Verband	**SIA**	Société Ivoirienne d'Assurances
SHJPF	Société d'Horticulture et des Jardins Pop-ulaires de France	**SIA**	Société Suisse des Ingénieurs et des Architectes
SHK	Schweizerische Hochschulkonferenz	**SIA**	Society of Industrial Artists
SHL	Suomen Huonekalukauppiatten Liitto	**SIA**	Soroptimist International Association
SHN	Société des Huileries du Niger	**SIA**	Sprinkler Irrigation Association (U.S.A.)
SHNC	Société Hôtelière Nord-Cameroun	**SIAB**	Sociedad de Ingenieros Agrónomos de Bolivia
SHOM	Service Hydrographique et Océanographique de la Marine		
SHRH	Servicio Hidráulico de la República Haitiana	**SIAB**	Stiftung für Internationalen Austauch in den Bergen (France)
SHR	Société Hippique Rurale	**SIAC**	Secrétariat Inter-américain d'Action Catholique
SHRI	Scottish Horticultural Research Institute	**SIAC**	Secrétariat International des Artistes Catholi-ques
SHS	Scottish History Society		
SHS	Stowarzyszenie Historyków Sztuki	**SIAC**	Società Italiana Acciaierie Cornigliano
		SIA-CONGO	Société Industrielle et Agricole du Congo

SIAD	Societa Italiana Autori Drammatici
SIAD	Society of Industrial Artists and Designers
SIAEN	Sociedad Iberoamericana de Estudios Numismaticos
SIAEX	Société d'Achat d'Exportation
SIAF	Société des Ingénieurs Agronomes de France
SIAF	Società Italiana di Audiologia e Foniatria
SIAG	Société Industrielle et Automobile de Guinée
SIAM	Society for Industrial and Applied Mathematics (U.S.A.)
SIAMU	Secretariado Ibero-Americano de Municipios (Spain)
SIAN	Société Industrielle et Agricole du Niari (French Equatorial Africa)
SIAP	Sociedad Interamericana de Planificación
SIAP	Société Industriel d'Articles de Papeterie (Congo)
SIAP	Société Industrielle Africaine de Plastiques
SIAPA	Società Italo-Americana Prodotti Anti-Parassitari
SIAPAP	Société Industrielle et Agricole de la Pointe-à-Pitre (Guadeloupe)
SIAPE	Société Industrielle d'Acide Phosphorique et d'Engrais
SIAR	Société de la Surveillance Industrielle
SIAR	Stiftelsen Företagsadministrativ Forskning
SIAS	Scandinavian Institute of African Studies
SIAS	Small Industries Advisory Service (Rhodesia)
SIAS	Société Industrielle et Agricole de la Somme
SIAT	Société Industrielle et Agricole du Congo
SIATSA	Servicios para la Investigación Agricola Tropical (Honduras)
SIB	Shipbuilding Industry Board
SIB	Società Italiana di Biometria
SIB	Société Internationale de Biometrie
SIB	Société Ivoirienne de Banque
SIBAF	Société Industrielle des Bois Africains
SIBAG	Société d'Industries de Bois au Gabon
SIBC	Association Mondiale des Sociétés d'Anatomie Pathologique et de Biologie Clinique
SIBEV	Société Interprofessionnelle du Bétail et des Viandes
SIBMAS	Section Internationale des Bibliothèques et Musées des Arts du Spectacle (of FIAB)
SIBRAS	Société Industrielle de Brasseries du Sénégal
SIC	Schweizerischer Verband von Comestibles-Importeuren und -Händlern
SIC	Science Information Council (of NFS) (U.S.A.)
SIC	Société Immobilière du Cameroun
SIC	Société Industrielle des Cacaos (Cameroons)
SIC	Société Intercontinentale des Containers
SIC	Société Internationale de Cardiologie
SIC	Société Internationale de Chirurgie
SICA	Société Immobilière de la Côte d'Afrique
SICA	Société Industrielle de l'Est Camerounaise
SICA	Société d'Intérêt Collectif Agricole
SICA	Société Internationale de Coopératives Agricoles
SICA	Society of Industrial and Cost Accountants of Canada
SICAB	Société Industrielle Camerounaise de Bois
SICABAG	Société d'Intérêt Collectif Agricole de Guadeloupe
SICABAM	Société d'Intérêt Collectif Agricole de la Martinique
SICAE	Société d'Intérêt Collectif Agricole d'Électricité
SICAF	Société Industrielle de Couvertures Africaines
SICAF	Société Ivoirienne de Culture d'Ananas Frais
SICAG	Société Industrielle Commerciale et Agricole de Guinée
SICAHR	Société d'Intérêt Collectif d'Habitat Rural
SICAP	Servicio Interamericano de Cooperacion Agricola en Panamá
SICAP	Société Italo-Congolaise d'Armement et de Pêche
SICAPEB	Société d'Intérêt Collectif Agricole des Planteurs et Producteurs-Exportateurs de Bananes (Guadeloupe)
SICASSO	Société d'Intérêt Collectif Agricole des Sylviculteurs du Sud-Ouest
SICC	Shell International Chemical Company Ltd
SICC	Société Suisse des Ingénieurs en Chauffage et Climatisation
SICFA	Société Industrielle et Commerciale Franco-Africaine
SICH	Sociedad Internacional de la Ciencia Horticola
SICI	Société Immobilière et Commerciale Ivoirienne
SICIND	Società Incremento Cotonicolo Industriale nella Daunia

SICM	Secretariat International des Citoyens
SICM	Société Ivoirienne de Ciments et Matériaux
SICN	Société Industrielle de Combustible Nucléaire
SICN	Société Industrielle Commerciale Nigérienne
SICOC	Syndicat des Ingénieurs-Conseils en Organisation et Conseillers de Direction
SICOCAM	Société Industrielle et Commerciale du Cameroun
SICOD	Service Interconsulaire du Commerce et de la Distribution
SICOFEG	Société des Ingénieurs-Conseils de France en Génie Civil
SICOFEM	Société Ivoirienne de Confections Féminines et Masculines
SICOGERE	Société Ivoirienne de Copropriété et de Gérance
SICOGI	Société Ivoirienne de Construction et de Gestion Immobilière
SICOM	Società Italiana Costruzioni e Montaggi
SICOMAD	Société Industrielle de la Côte Ouest de Madagascar
SICOMED	Société Ivoirienne de Construction Médicale
SICOMI	Sociétés Immobilières pour le Commerce et l'Industrie
SICONIGER	Société Industrielle et Commerciale du Niger
SICORES	Société Internationale de Coopération pour Réalisations Économiques et Sociales
SICOT	Société Internationale de Chirurgie Orthopédique et de Traumatologie
SICOTP	Société Ivoirienne Commerciale Ouvrière de Travaux Publics et de Bâtiments
SICOTP	Société Ivoirienne de Construction et de Travaux Publics
SICOVAM	Société Interprofessionnelle pour la Compensation des Valeurs Mobilières (Organismes inter-banques)
SICOVO	Société Industrielle et Commerciale Voltaïque
SICRUS	Société Ivoirienne de Crustaces
SICS	Sociedad Internacional de las Ciencias del Suelo (Italy)
SICS	Société Internationale des Conseillers de Synthèse
SICT	Société Industrielle et Commerciale du Tchad
SID	Föreningen Svenska Industridesigner
SID	Society for International Development
SID	Society for Investigative Dermatology (U.S.A.)
SID	Verband Schweizer Industrial Designers
SIDA	Swedish International Development Authority
SIDADT	Société Industrielle pour le Développement Automobile au Dahomey et au Togo
SIDB	Société Industrielle des Bois (Congo)
SIDEA	Italian Society of Agricultural Economics
SIDEB	Société Ivoirienne de Distribution et d'Équipement de Bureaux
SIDEC	Stanford International Development Education Centre (U.S.A.)
SIDECO	Société Ivoirienne de Distribution Économique
SIDEFCOOP	Sociedad Interamericana para el Desarrollo del Financiamiento Cooperativo (Chile)
SIDELAF	Société Ivoirienne d'Électrification
SIDEPI	Seminario Internacional de Desarrollo Pesquero-Industrial (Peru)
SIDER-AFRIC	Centre d'Information et de Promotion des Produits Sidérurgiques et des Tubes d'Acier Français en Afrique
SIDERSA	Empresa Siderúrgica Boliviana
SIDES	Società Italiana di Dermatologia e Sifilografia
SIDEST	Société Indépendante de Documentation et d'Éditions Scientifiques et Techniques
SIDF	Société Ivoirienne de Développement et de Financement
SIDI	Société Ivoirienne de Développement Industriel
SIDIAMIL	International Company for the Development of Food Industries using Sorghum and Millet (Africa)
SIDITEX	Société Internationale pour le Développement de l'Industrie Textile (Cameroons)
SIDM	Società Italiana di Musicologia
SIDO	Société Interprofessionnelle de Oléagineux
SIDP	Seed Industry Development Programme (*of* FAO)
SIDS	Société Internationale de Défense Sociale
SIDS	Société Internationale de Droit Social
SIE	Servicios Industriales Especiales (UNIDO)
SIE	Società Italiana di Ergonomia
SIE	Société Internationale d'Électrochimie
SIE	Society of Industrial Engineers
SIEBEG	Société Ivoirienne d'Exploitation des Bois en Grumes

SIEC	Société Internationale pour l'Enseignement Commercial
SIECA	Secrétariat Permanent du Traité Général d'Intégration Économique de l'Amérique Centrale
SIECC	Société Internationale d'Étude des Cultures Comparées
SIECUS	Sex Information and Education Council of the U.S.
SIED	Société pour l'Importation et l'Exportation de Métaux Précieux au Dahomey
SIEDS	Società Italiana di Economia Demografia e Statistica
SIEF	Société Internationale d'Ethnographie et de Folklore
SIEHT	Société Ivoirienne d'Équipement Hôtelier et Touristique
SIELOR	Société Ivoirienne d'Emballages Métalliques
SIEMI	Société d'Importation et d'Exportation de Matériel Industriel (Cameroons, Central Africa)
SIEMPA	Syndicat des Importateurs-Exportateurs de Matières Premières Aromatiques
SIEN	Société Internationale d'Études Néroniennes
SIEPM	Société Internationale pour l'Étude de la Philosophie Médiévale
SIERE	Syndicat des Industries Électroniques de Reproduction et d'Enregistrement
SIERI	Société Ivoirienne d'Études et de Réalisations Industrielles
SIERS	Société Industrielle d'Études et Réalisations Scientifiques
SIES	Société Industrielle d'Engrais au Sénégal
SIES	Soils and Irrigation Extension Service (Australia)
SIESC	Secrétariat International des Enseignants Secondaires Catholiques
SIET	Société Internationale d'Écologie Tropicale
SIETA	Société Internationale d'Études et de Travaux en Afrique (Ivory Coast)
SIETHO	Société Ivoirienne d'Expansion Touristique et Hôtelière
SIEUSE	Secrétariat International de l'Enseignement Universitaire des Sciences de l'Éducation
SIEXI	Société Ivoirienne d'Exportation et d'Importation
SIF	Selskabets for Industriel Formgivning
SIF	Smøreolje Importørenes Forening
SIF	Società Italiana Fisica
SIFA	Société Industrielle pour la Fabrication des Antibiotiques
SIFB	Society of Industrial Furnace Builders
SIFCCA	Société Industrielle Forestière et Commerciale Camerounaise
SIFERCOM	Société Ivoirienne d'Entreprise et de Construction Métallique
SIFET	Società Italiana di Fotogrammetria e Topografia
SIFIDA	Société Internationale Financière pour les Investissements et le Développement en Afrique
SIFO	Società Italiana di Farmacia Ospedaleria
SIFPAF	Syndicat des Industriels Fabricants de Pâtes Alimentaires de France
SIFRA	Société Industrielle des Fruits Africains
SIFRIA	Société Immobilière de l'Aluminium (Africa)
SIG	Service d'Information Géologique
SIGA	Società Italiana di Genetica Agraria
SIGE	Società Italiana di Genetica e Eugenica
SIGE	Società Italiana Gestione Elicotteri
SIGE	Société Internationale de Gastro-Entérologie
SIGESO	Sub-committee, Intelligence German Electronics Signals Organisation
SIGEXA	Société Ivoirienne de Gestion et d'Exploitation Automobile
SIGI	Société Ivoirienne de Gestion Immobilière
SIGM	Società Italiana di Ginnastica Medica, Medicina Fisica e Riabilitazione
SIGMA	Société Industriale Générale de Mécanique Appliquée
SIGMA	Station Internationale de Géobotanique Méditerranéenne et Alpine
SIGP	Société Industrielle de la Grande Pêche
SIGRAG	Société Industrielle d'Exploitation des Granits Guinéens
SIGUE	Society for Developments in Guinea
SIH	Schweizerisches Institut für Hauswirtschaft
SIH	Société Internationale d'Hématologie
SIH	Société Ivoirienne d'Hôtellerie
SIHM	Société Internationale d'Histoire de la Médecine
SIHTCO	Société Ivoirienne Hôtelière et Touristique de la Comoé

SIIAEC	Secrétariat International des Ingénieurs, des Agronomes et des Cadres Économiques Catholiques	**SIMAR**	Société Industrielle de Machines Agricoles Rotatives (Switzerland)
SIIAS	Staten Island Institute of Arts and Sciences (U.S.A.)	**SIMAVIN**	Société d'Importation Africaine Vinicole
		SIMC	Société Internationale de Médecine Cybernétique
SIIC	Secrétariat International des Groupements Professionnels des Industries Chimiques des Pays de la CEE	**SIMC**	Société Internationale pour la Musique Contemporaine
SIK	Svenska Institutet för Könserveringsforskning	**SIMCA**	Société Industrielle de Mécanique et Carosserie
SIL	Sähköinsinööriliitto	**SIMCO**	Société Immobilière et de Constructions du Tchad
SIL	Secrétariat International de la Laine (IWS)	**SIMDER**	Syndicat National du Matériel de Dessin, Beaux-Arts, Reprographie
SIL	Service International des Latitudes		
SIL	Societas Internationalis Limnologiae Theoretica et Applicae	**SIMEA**	Società Italiana Meridionale Energia Atomica
SIL	Société Internationale de la Lèpre	**SIMEA**	Société Ivoirienne de Montage et d'Exploitation Automobile
SIL	Suomen Ilmailuliitto	**SIMECO**	Société Ivoirienne de Menuiserie, d'Ébénisterie et de Constructions Immobilières
SILAF	Società Italiana per Lavori Agricoli e Forestali		
SILCO	Société Ivoiro-Libanaise de Commerce	**SIMEI**	Société Ivoirienne de Matériaux Étanches et Isolants
SILF	Svenska Inköpsledores Förening		
SILIN	Société Interprofessionnelle des Graines et Huiles de Lin	**SIMEX**	Société Ivoirienne d'Importation et Exportation
SILP	Société Internationale de Linguistique Psychologique	**SIMG**	Societas Internationalis Medicinae Generalis
		SIMH	Société Internationale de Médecine Hydrologique
SILS	Société d'Investissements Libano-Sénégalaise		
SIM	Singapore Institute of Management	**SIMHA**	Société Internationale de Mycologie Humaine et Animale
SIM	Société Sénégalaise d'Investissements Maritimes		
		SIMI	Società Italiana Macchine Idrauliche
SIM	Société Internationale de la Moselle	**SIMI**	Società Italiana di Medicina Interna
SIM	Société Internationale de Musicologie	**SIML**	Società Italiana di Medicina del Lavoro
SIMA	Salon International de la Machine Agricole	**SIMMA**	Syndicat des Industries de Matériels de Manutention
SIMA	Scientific Instrument Manufacturers' Association of Great Britain		
		SIMO	Société Ivoirienne des Matériels d'Organisation
SIMA	Société d'Importation et d'Exportation Centrafricaine		
		SIMOCA	Société Industrielle du Moyen-Orient au Cameroun
SIMA	Société Industrielle de Matériel Agricole		
SIMA	Société Ivoirienne de Menuiserie et d'Ameublement	**SIMP**	Società Italiana di Medicina Psicosomatica
		SIMP	Società Italiana di Mineralogia e Petrologia
SIMAC	Société Immobilière d'Afrique Centrale	**SIMP**	Stowarzyszenie Inżynierów i Techników Polskich
SIMAC	Société Ivoirienne d'Importation de Matériaux de Construction		
SIMACO	Société Ivoirienne de Matériaux de Construction	**SIMPA**	Société Industrielle Moderne de Plastiques Africaines
SIMAFRUIT	Société Interprofessionnelle Maritime et Fruitière (Ivory Coast)	**SIMPEX**	Syndicat des Commerçants Importateurs et Exportateurs (Gabon, Ivory Coast)
SIMAQ	Syndicat des Nécogiants Importateurs Métropolitaines	**SIMPEXDA**	Syndicat des Importateurs et Exportateurs du Dahomey

SIMPL	Scientific, Industrial and Medical Photographic Laboratories	**SIP**	Società Italiana de Pediatria
SIMPOL	Société Ivoirienne de Mousse Polyester	**SIP**	Società Italiana di Psichiatria
		SIP	Société Inter-Américaine de Psychologie
SIMRA	Scientific Instruments Manufacturers' Research Association	**SIPA**	Servicio de Investigación y Promotión Agropecuaria (*formerly* SCIPA and PCEA) (Peru)
SIMS	Scandinavian Simulation Society		
SIMS	Società Italiana di Medicina Sociale	**SIPA**	Société Industrielle de Produits Africains
SIMS	Student's International Meditation Society (U.S.A.)	**SIPAI**	Sociedad Italo Peruana Agrícola Industrial (Peru)
SIMT	Società Italiana di Medicina del Traffico	**SIPAG**	Société Industrielle de Planification de Guinée
SIN	Schweizerisches Institut für Nuclearforschung	**SIPAG**	Syndicat National des Importateurs d'Équipements pour les Industries Papetières et Graphiques
SIN	Società Italiana di Neurochirurgia		
SIN	Society for International Numismatics (U.S.A.)	**SIPAI**	Società per l'Incremento della Produzione Avicola Italiana
SINA	Shellfish Institute of North America	**SIPAK**	Vereniging van Groothandelaren in Sisalpaktouw
SINA	Sociedad Ibérica de Nutrición Animal		
SINAGI	Sindicato Nazionale Giornalai d'Italia	**SIPARE**	Syndicat des Industries de Pièces Détachées et Accessoires Radio-Électriques et Électroniques
SINAMOS	Sistema Nacional de Apoyo a la Movilización Social (Peru)		
SINCATEX	Société Industrielle Camerounaise de Textiles	**SIPC**	Société Interprofessionnelle pour la Production des Cocons, Graines de Vers à Soie et de Soie Grège en France
SINCO	Société Internationale de Commerce (Cameroons)		
SINFAC	Syndicat Interprofessionnel des Fabricants d'Articles Manufacturés pour Chaussures	**SIPCAM**	Società Italiana Prodotti Chimici e per l'Agricoltura, Milano
SINFDOK	Swedish Council for Scientific Information and Documentation	**SIPE**	Société Internationale de Psychologie de l'Écriture
SINN	Société de Imprimerie Nationale du Niger	**SIPE**	Société Internationale de Psychopathologie de l'Expression
SINP	Saha Institute of Nuclear Physics (India)	**SIPEC**	Société Industrielle des Pêches du Cameroun
SINTEF	Selskap f. Industriell og Teknisk Forskning	**SIPECA**	Service d'Information Pastorale Européenne Catholique (Belgium)
SINTO	Sheffield Interchange Organisation		
SINTRA	Société Industrielle des Nouvelles Techniques Radioélectriques	**SIPEGA**	Société Industrielle des Pêches du Gabon
		SIPG	Société Internationale de Pathologie Géographique
SIO	Sisustusarkkitehdit		
SIOFA	Société Interprofessionnelle des Oléagineux Fluides Alimentaires	**SIPH**	Société Indochinoise de Plantation d'Hévéas (Vietnam)
SIOG	Società Italiana di Ostetricia e Ginecologia	**SIPI**	Scientists Institute for Public Information (U.S.A.)
SIOI	Sezione Italiana per l'Organizzazione Internazionale	**SIPMAD**	Société Industrielle de Pêche à Madagascar
SIOP	Société Internationale d'Oncologie Pédiatrique	**SIPOA**	Société Industrielle Pharmaceutique de l'Ouest Africain
SIOT	Società Italiana di Ortopedia e Traumatologia	**SIPP**	Society of Irish Plant Pathologists
		SIPRAG	Société Ivoirienne de Promotion Agricole
SIP	Sociedad Interamericana de Planificación (Porto Rico)	**SIPRC**	Society of Independent Public Relations Consultants
SIP	Sociedad Interamericana de Prensa	**SIPRI**	Stockholm International Peace Research Institute
SIP	Società Italiana di Parapsicologia		

SIPRT	Sociedad Internacional de Professionales de Radio y Televisión	**SIS**	Società Italiani di Statistica
SIPS	Società Internazionale di Psicologia della Acrittura	**SIS**	Società Italiana di Stomatologia
		SIS	Société Immobilière du Sénégal
		SIS	Société Internationale Scotiste
SIPS	Società Italiana per il Progresso delle Scienze	**SIS**	Special Industrial Services (of UNIDO)
SIPS	Società Italiana di Psicologia Scientifica	**SIS**	Sveriges Standardiseringskommission
SIPS	Société Industrielle de Papeterie au Sénégal	**SISCO**	Special Inter-Departmental Selection Committee (FAO)
SIR	Service International de Recherches (of CICR)	**SISCOMA**	Société Industrielle Sénégalaise de Constructions Mécaniques et de Matériels Agricoles
SIR	Società Italiana Resine		
SIR	Sociedad Internacional Rorschach	**SISF**	Società Italiana di Scienze Farmaceutiche
SIR	Société Ivoirienne de Raffinage	**SISGAC**	Scottish Industrial Safety Group Advisory Council
SIR	Svenska Inredningsarkitekters Riksförbund		
SIRA	Scientific Instrument Research Association	**SISH**	Société Internationale de la Science Horticole
SIRAID	Scientific Instrument Research Association Information and Data Service	**SISIR**	Singapore Institute for Standards and Industrial Research
SIRC	Socialist International Research Council	**SISMES**	Società Italiana di Statistica Medico-Sanitaria
SIRCA	Société Industrielle de République Centrafricaine	**SISP**	Schweizerische Interessengemeinschaft f. d. Schutz von Pflanzenneuheiten
SIRCE	Società per l'Incremento Rapporti Commerciali con l'Estero	**SISPA**	Società Italiana Studio e Prevenzione dell' Alcoolismo
SIREP	Société Internationale pour la Recherche et l'Exploitation du Pétrole (Tchad)	**SISS**	Secrétariat International des Syndicats du Spectacle
SIRI	Société Internationale pour la Réadaptation des Invalides	**SISS**	Società Italiana Serbatoi Speciali
SIRI	Sugar Industry Research Institute (Mauritius)	**SISS**	Société Internationale de la Science du Sol
SIRIP	Société Irano-Italienne de Pétrole	**SISTER**	Special Institutions for Scientific and Technological Education and Research
SIRM	Società Italiana di Radiologia Medica		
SIRM	Società Italiana Radio-Marittima	**SISV**	Secrétariat International du Service Volontaire
SIRM	Società Italiana per le Ricerche di Mercata		
SIRMCE	Société Internationale pour la Recherche sur les Maladies de Civilisation et l'Environnement	**SISV**	Società Italiana delle Scienze Veterinarie
		SISWO	Stichting Interuniversitair Instituut voor Sociaalwetenschappelijk Onderzoek
SIRMN	Società Italiana di Radiologia Medica e Medicina Nucleare	**SIT**	Samband Islenzkra Trygginafélaga
SIRNv	Société International de Recherches Neurovégétatives	**SIT**	Servicio de Información Técnica (Ecuador)
		SIT	Singapore Improvement Trust
		SIT	Société Interafricaine de Transport
SIRT	Société Internationale de la Radio et Télévision	**SIT**	Société Intercontinentale de Transactions
		SIT	Society of Instrument Technology (now IMC)
SIRT	Société Interprofessionnelle du Raison de Table	**SITA**	Société Internationale de Télécommunications Aéronautiques
SIRTC	Société Internationale de Recherche contre la Tuberculose et le Cancer	**SITA**	Students International Travel Association
SIRTI	Società Italiana Reti Telefoniche Interurbane	**SITAF**	Société Industrielle des Transports Automobiles Africains (Ivory Coast)
SIS	Samband Islenzkra Samvinnufélaga		
SIS	Secret Intelligence Service	**SITAM**	Société Industrielle des Tabacs Malgaches
SIS	Senologic International Society	**SITAO**	Société Immobilière et Touristique de l'Afrique de l'Ouest

SITB	Société Industrielle de Travaux de Bureaux
SITC	Swiss Insurance Training Centre
SITCA	Secretaria de Integración Turistica de Centroamérica (Nicaragua)
SITEL	Société Belge des Ingénieurs des Télécommunications et d'Électronique
SITELESC	Syndicat des Industries de Tubes Électroniques et Semiconducteurs
SITEMSH	Société Internationale de Traumatologie de Ski et de Médecine des Sports d'Hiver
SITH	Société Internationale de Technique Hydrothermale
SITI	Sezione Imprese Traslochi Internazionali
SITKom	Stowarzyszenie Inzynierów i Technikow Komunikacji
SITIM	Société Internationale des Techniques d'Imagerie Mentale
SITJ	Savez Inzenjera i Tehnicara Jugoslavije
SITLiD	Stowarzyszenie Inzynierów i Techników Leśnictwa i Drzewnictwa
SITMA	Société des Ingénieurs et Techniciens du Machinisme Agricole
SITO	Société Ivoirienne des Transports de l'Ouest
SITO	Stowarzyszenie Naukowo-Techniczne Inzynierów i Techników Ogrodnictwa
SITOFA	Société des Industries de Transformation des Oléagineux Fluides Alimentaires
SITP	Société Ivoirienne de Transports Publics
SITPC	Syndicat des Industries de la Transformation de la Pellicule Cellulosique
SITPChem	Stowarzyszenie Inzynierów i Techników Przemyslu Chemicznego
SITPH	Stowarzyszenie Inzynierów i Techników Przemyslu Hutniczego
SITPMB	Stowarzyszenie Inzynierów i Techników Przemyslu Materialow Budowlanych
SITPP	Stowarzyszenie Inzynierów i Techników Przemyslu Papierniczego
SITPRO	U.K. Committee for the Simplification of International Trade Procedures
SITR	Stowarzyszenie Naukowo-Techniczne Inzynierów i Techników Rolnictwa
SITRA	South India Textile Research Association
SITRAC	Société Industrielle de Transformation Centrafricaine
SITRAM	Société Industrielle de Transformation des Métaux (Central Africa)
SITS	Società Italiana Telecommunicazione Siemens
SITS	Société Internationale de Transfusion Sanguine
SITS	Syndicat Général des Industries pour le Traitement des Surfaces
SITT	Syndicat des Industries Téléphoniques et Télégraphiques
SITUMER	Société d'Ingénierie du Tunnel sous la Mer
SITVAR	Syndicat National des Industries Transformateurs de Vanille et des Elements Aromatiques Naturels au Chimiques
SITWM	Stowarzyszenie Inzynierów i Techników Wodnych i Melioracyjnych
SIU	Social Investigation Unit (of RSPCA)
SIU	Société Internationale d'Urologie
SIUNA	Seafarers International Union of North America
SIV	Schweizerischen Inserenten-Verband
SIV	Société Immobilière de la Volta
SIV	Société Sénégalaise pour l'Industrie du Vêtement
SIVA	Société Industrielle de Vêtements en Afrique
SIVAK	Société Ivoirienne Agricole et Industrielle du Kenaf
SIVEL	Société Ivoirienne d'Électricité
SIVENG	Société Ivoirienne d'Engrais
SIVETI	Société Ivoirienne de Vêtements sur Mesures Industrielles
SIVIE	Société Ivoirienne d'Installations Électriques
SIVIT	Société des Industries de la Viande du Tchad
SIVOA	Société Ivoirienne d'Oxygène et d'Acetylène
SIVOM	Société Ivoirienne d'Opérations Maritimes
SIW	Stichting Internationale Werkkampen
SJCM	Standing Joint Committee on Metrication
SJF	Svenska Journalistförbundet
SJF	Syndicat des Journalistes Français
SJIA	Saint Joan's International Alliance
SJK	Svenska Jordbrukskreditkassan
SJPA	Syndicat des Journalistes de la Presse Agricole
SJU	Schweizerische Journalisten Union
SJUF	Scandinavisk Jodisk Ungdomsforbund
SK	Schweizerische Käseunion
SK	Svenska Kartongfabrikantföreningen
SKAF	Sveriges Konst- och Antikhandlarförening

SKAG	Verband Schweizerischer Konzessionierter Automobilunternehmungen	**SLA**	Scottish Libraries Association
SKB	Schweizerischer Konsumentenbund	**SLA**	Sammenslutningen av Landbrukets Arbeids- giverforeningen
SKB	Svenska Kuvertfabrikanters Branschrad	**SLA**	Special Libraries Association (U.S.A.)
SKBT	Syndicale Kamer van de Belgische Tuinbouw	**SLA**	Svenska Lantarbetsgivareforeningen
SKCV	Schweizerischer Konditor- Confiseurmeisterverband	**SLAC**	Stanford Linear Accelerator Centre (U.S.A.)
SKF	Svenska Kylfirmors Förening	**SLAC**	Structures Lamellées d'Afrique Centrale
SKFB	Skandinaviska Kreatursförsäkringsbolaget	**SLACES**	Syndicat de la Librairie Ancienne et du Commerce de l'Estampe en Suisse
SKFB	Sveriges Köpmannaförbund	**SLAD**	Society of London Art Dealers
SKHS	Suomen Kirkkohistoriallinen Seura	**SLADE**	Society of Lithographic Artists, Designers, Engravers and Process Workers
SKK	Stichting Kernvootstuwing Koopvaardij- schepen	**SLAET**	Society of Licensed Aircraft Engineers and Technologists
SKKS	Suomen Kemian Seura		
SKI	Szöleszeti Kutató Intézet	**SLAIA**	Latin American Society of Agricultural Engineers
SKIF	Svenska Konsulterande Ingenjörers Förening	**SLAMS**	Syndicat des Constructeurs d'Appareils de Levage, de Manutention et de Matériels de Stockage
SKIV	Schweizerischer Kioskinhaber-Verband		
SKL	Suomen Kiinnteistönvälittäjäin Liitto		
SKL	Sveriges Kemisk-Tekniska Leveran- torförening	**SLAIP**	Sociedad Latinoamerica na de Investigación Pédiatrica
SKMV	Schweizerischer Kaminfegermeisterverband	**SLAMI**	Société Agricole Minière et Industrielle (Madagascar)
SKOGA	Airline of Peoples Democratic China		
SKOL	Suomen Konsulttitoimistojen Liitto	**SLAN**	Sociedad Latinoamericana de Nutrición (Venezuela)
SKR	Svenska Kemiingenjörers Riksförening		
SKS	Schweizerische Konferenz für Sichheit im Strassenverkehr	**SLAS**	Society for Latin American Studies
		SLC	Scandinavian Library Centre (Denmark)
SKS	Stiftung für Konsumentenschutz (Switzerland)	**SLC**	Svenska Lantbruksproducenternas Cen- tralförbund
SKS	Suomalaisten Kemistien Seura	**SLD**	Savez Lekarskih Drustava
SKS	Svenska Keramiska Sällskapet	**SLE**	Societas Linguistica Europaea (Germany)
SKT	Verband Schweizerischer Kammgarnweber, Tuch- und Decken-Fabrikanten	**SLEAT**	Society of Laundry Engineers and Allied Trades
SKTF	Sveriges Kvalitetstekniska Förening	**SLESR**	Société des Librairies de la Suisse Romande
SKTL	Suomen Kähertäjätyönantajaliitto	**SLF**	Scottish Landowners Federation
SKTY	Suomen Kunnallisteknillinen Yhdistys	**SLF**	Skandinaviska Lackteknikers Förbund
SKV	Schweizerischer Kaninchenzucht-Verband	**SLF**	Skolledarförbundet
SKV	Schweizerischer Kaufmännischer Verein	**SLF**	Svenska Laboratieassistent Föreningen
SKV	Schweizerischer Kochverband	**SLF**	Svenska Lantbrukstjänstemannaförbundet
SKV	Schweizerischer Reklame-Verband	**SLF**	Sveriges Lantmätareförening
SKVS	Svenska Konsulterande VVS-Ingenjörers Förening	**SLFP**	Sri Lanka Freedom Party
SKY	Suomen Kuljetwstaloudellinen Yhdistys	**SLFSP**	Sri Lanka Freedom Socialist Party
SL	Suomen Lääkintavoimistelijaliitto	**SLFV**	Schweizerischen Landfrauenverbandes
SL	Sveriges Lantbruksförbund	**SLFY**	Suomen Logopedis-Foniatrinen Yhdistys
SL	Sveriges Lararförbund	**SLG**	Schweizerische Lichttechnische Gesellschaft

SLH	Selskabet for Levnedsmiddelteknologi og -hygiene
SLICE	St. Louis Institute of Consulting Engineers (U.S.A.)
SLiR	Société de Linguistique Romane
SLIP	Sociedad Latinoamericana de Investigadores en Papas (Venezuela)
SLITUF	Sri Lanka Independent Trade Union Federation
SLL	Skotøy- og Loervareindustriens Leverandørforening
SLL	Suomen Lääkäriliitto
SLLA	Sierra Leone Library Association
SLLA	Sri Lanka Library Association
SLLW	Société de Langue et de Littérature Wallonnes (Belgium)
SLM	Sociedad Latinoamericana de Maiz
SLMH	Schweizerischer Verband des Schmiede-, Landmaschinen-, Metall- und Holzewerbes
SLO	Stichting Landbouwhuishoudkundig Onderzoek
SLOW	Steam Launch Operations of the World (U.S.A.)
SLPMB	Sierra Leone Produce Marketing Board
SLPP	Sierra Leone Peoples Party
SLR	Svenska Lantmännens Riksförbund
SLR	Sveriges Lassmedsmästares Riksförbund
SLR	Sveriges Leksakshandlares Riksförbund
SLRP	Society for Long Range Planning
SLS	Stephenson Locomotive Society
SLS	Svenska Läkarsällskapet
SLS	Svenska Litteratursällskapet i Finland
SLSA-GB	Surf Life Saving Association of Great Britain
SLST	Sierra Leone Selection Trust
SLTA	Scottish Lawn Tennis Association
SLTC	Society of Leather Technologists and Chemists
SLV	Schweizerischen Landwirtschaftlichen Verein
SLV	Schweizerischer Lehrerverein
SLV	Schweizerischer Lichtspieltheater-Verband
SLVL	Suomen Liike-ja Virkanaisten Liitto
SLY	Suomen Lintutieteellinen Yhistys
SMA	Servico Meteorológico de Angola
SMA	Singapore Manufacturers Association
SMA	Sheffield Metallurgical Association

SMA	Société Méditerrannéenne d'Acupuncture
SMA	Société des Missions Africaines (Canada)
SMA	Steel Merchants Association
SMA	Sugar Manufacturers' Association (Jamaica)
SMAE	Society of Model Aeronautical Engineers
SMAG	Société Meunière et Avicole
SMAK	Svensk Matpotatiskontroll
SMB	Sociedad Meteorológica de Bolivia
SMB	Société Mauritanienne de Banque
SMB	Société Mathématique de Belgique
SMB	Society of Missionaries of Bethlehem in Switzerland
SMBA	Scottish Marine Biological Association
SMBPA	Société Malienne de Biscuiterie et Pâtes Alimentaires
SMC	Schweizerischer Verkaufs- und Marketingleiter Club
SMC	Sealant Manufacturers Conference
SMC	Sociedad Mexicana de Cactalogía
SMC	Sveriges Möbelhandlares Centralförbund
SMCCL	Society of Municipal and County Chief Librarians
SMCS	Sociedad Mexicana de la Ciencia del Suelo
SMDN	Société Minière du Niger
SME	Sociedad Mexicana de Entomología
SMEC	Société Malienne d'Entreprises et de Constructions
SMECMA	Société Malienne d'Études et de Construction de Matériel Agricole
SMECOMA	Landbouwmechanisatiebedrijven
SMEG	Spring Makers' Export Group
SMF	Chambre Syndicale Nationale des Constructeurs et Constructeurs-Installateurs de Matériels et d'Équipements Frigorifiques
SMF	Sociedad Mexicana de Fitogenética
SMF	Sociedad Mexicana de Fitopatología
SMEI	Sales and Marketing Executives International (U.S.A.)
SMEPC	Société Suisse des Maîtres des Écoles Professionnelles Commerciales
SMER	Société Médicale Internationale d'Endoscopie et de Radio-Cinématographie
SMERT	Société Malienne de Fabrication d'Articles Métalliques
SMF	Société Météorologique de France
SMG	Schweizerische Mathematische Gesellschaft

SMG	Schweizerische Musikforschende Gesellschaft
SMGE	Sociedad Mexicana de Geografíca y Estadística
SMGI	Société Mauritanienne des Gaz Industriels
SMGS	Socialist Countries Convention on Transport of Goods by Rail
SMGV	Schweizerischer Maler- und Gipsermeister-Verband
SMHI	Sveriges Meteorologiska och Hydrologiska Institut
SMHN	Sociedad Mexicana de Historia Natural
SMI	Sindacato Musicisti Italiani
SMI	Sveriges Möbelindustriförbund
SMI	Syndicat National des Constructeurs de Maisons Individuelles
SMIA	Sheet Metal Industries Association
SMIC	Syndicat des Fabricants de Meubles Métalliques Industriels et Commerciaux
SMIE	Société Mauritanienne d'Importation et d'Exportation
SMIER	Société Médicale Internationale d'Endoscopie et de Radiocinématographie
SMIF	Sveriges Motorcykel- och Mopedimportöres Förbund
SMIPCTER	Société Médicale Internationale de Photo Cinématographie et Télévision Endoscopique et Radiocinématographie (*now* SMIER)
SMIS	Society for Management Information Systems (U.S.A.)
SMISB	Société Mauritanienne des Industries Secondaires du Bâtiment
SMISO	Systéme Mondial Intégré de Stations Océaniques
SMIVAC	Société de Mise en Valeur de la Corse
SML	Stichting Machinale Landbouw (Suriname)
SML	Suomen Museoliitto
SML	Suomen Matkailuliitto
SMM	Sucreries Marseillaises de Madagascar
SMM	Serviço Meteorológica de Moçambique
SMMB	Scottish Milk Marketing Board
SMMCZ	Sociedad Mexicana de Medicina y Cirugía Zootécnicas
SMMT	Society of Motor Manufacturers and Traders
SMMV	Schweizerischer Mechanikermeister-Verband
SMMY	Suomen Myynti- ja Mainosyhdistys
SMN	Serviço Meterológico Nacionál (Argentina)
SMN	Société des Mélasses du Niari (Zaire)
SMOL	Suomen Musiikinopettajain Liitto
SMOM	Sovrano Militaire Ordine di Malta
SMP	Sociedad Mexicana de Parasitología
SMP	Society of Mural Painters
SMP	Suomen Maaseudun Puloue
SMPA	Scottish Master Patternmakers Association
SMPC	Scottish Milk Publicity Council
SMPC	Société Marocaine des Produits Chimiques
SMPMA	Sausage and Meat Pie Manufacturers Association
SMPMF	Scottish Metal and Plumbers' Merchants' Federation
SMPS	Socialist Countries Convention on Transport of Passengers by Rail
SMPS	Society of Master Printers of Scotland
SMPTE	Society of Motion Picture and Television Engineers (U.S.A.)
SMPV	Schweizerischer Musikpädagogischer Verband
SMR	Svenska Mejeriernas Riksförening
SMR	Svenska Mekanisters Riksförening
SMRA	Scottish Milk Records Association
SMRA	Spring Manufacturers' Research Association (*now* SRA)
SMRC	Scottish Motor Racing Club
SMRC	Stoneham Museum and Research Centre (Kenya)
SMRE	Safety in Mines Research Establishment
SMRI	Sugar Milling Research Institute (South Africa)
SMS	Société Mathématique Suisse
SMS	Sullivant Moss Society (U.S.A.)
SMS	Suomen Maataloustieteellinen Seura
SMS	Sveriges Malarmästareförening
SMS	Syndicat National des Fabricants de Matériels de Soudage
SMSP	Société Médicale Suisse de Psychothérapie
SMSR	Société des Meuniers de la Suisse Romande
SMSW	State Medical Society of Wisconsin (U.S.A.)
SMT	Sammenslutningen af Maskinfabrikker for Troeindustrien
SMT	Statiunea de Masini si Tractoare (Roumania)
SMTA	Scottish Motor Trade Association
SMTF	Scottish Milk Trade Federation

SMTH	Société Mauritanienne de Tourisme et d'Hôtellerie
SMTL	Suomen Muoviteollisuusliitto
SMTS	Scottish Machinery Testing Station
SMTY	Suomen Materiaalitaloudellinen Yhdistys
SMU	Schweizerische Metall-Inion
SMU	Surinaamse Mijnwerkers Unie
SMUH	Secrétariat des Missions d'Urbanisme et d'Habitat
SMUJ	Savez Muzickih Umetnika Jugoslavije
SMUSE	Socialist Movement for the United States of Europe
SMUV	Schweizerischer Metall- und Uhrenarbeiterverband
SMV	Schweizerischer Markt-Verband
SMV	Schweizerischer Musikerverband
SN	Sveriges Naturvetareförbund
SNA	Sindicato Nacional dos Arquitectos
SNA	Sociedade Nacional de Agricultura (Brazil)
SNA	Société Nationale d'Acclimatation
SNA	Société Nationale d'Assurances et de Réassurances de la République de Guinée
SNA	Syndicat National d'Apiculture
SNAA	Servicio Nacional de Acueductos y Alcantarillado (Costa Rica)
SNAA	Syndicat National des Aviculteurs Agréés
SNABM	Syndicat National des Adjuvants pour Bétons et Mortiers
SNABV	Syndicat National des Agences et Bureaux de Voyages
SNACGP	Syndicat National des Armateurs de Chalutiers de Grande Pêche
SNACH	Sociedad Nacional de Agricultura de Chile
SNAD	Sindacato Nazionale Autori Drammatici
SNADAP	Syndicat National de la Domicile et des Actions Promotionnelles
SNAF	Société Nationale des Architectes de France
SNAFOP	Société Nationale pour le Développement Forestier (Dahomey)
SNAGE	Syndicat National des Affineurs de Gruyère et d'Emmental
SNAHDA	Société Nationale des Huileries du Dahomey
SNAI	Società Nazionale Agricola Industriale (Somalia)
SNAM	Società Nazionale Metanodotii
SNAM	Syndicat National des Articles Métalliques et de leurs Dérivés
SNAME	Society of Naval Architects and Marine Engineers (U.S.A.)
SNAP	Servicia Nacional de Agua Potable (Argentina)
SNAP	Société Industrielle des Nouvelles Applications des Matières Plastiques (Cameroons)
SNAP	Syndicat National des Agences de Publicité
SNAPO	Syndicate National de la Publicité par l'Objet
SNAQ	Syndicat National Angora Qualité
SNAS	Syndicat National du Commerce de Gros des Appareils Sanitaires, de Canalisation et de Chauffage
SNASA	Sociedad Nacional de Agricultura (Mexico)
SNASA	Syndicat National des Agents de Sociétés d'Auteurs
SNASDP	Syndicat National des Annuaires et Supports Divers de Publicité
SNASE	Sindacato Nazionale Autonomo Scuola Elementare
SNATPA	Syndicat National de l'Action Technique et Professionnelle Agricole
SNAV	Société Nouvelle des Ateliers de Venissieux
SNBATI	Syndicat National du Béton Armé et des Techniques Industrialisées
SNBBR	Section Nationale des Bailleurs de Baux Ruraux
SNBC	Syndicat National des Bouilleurs de Cru Producteurs de Fruits et Professions Connexes
SNBTF	Scottish National Building Trades Federation
SNC	Cameroon National Society
SNC	Société Nationale du Cameroun
SNC	Société Nationale de Colombiculture
SNC	Société Nationale de Construction
SNC	Société Nigérienne de Cimenterie
SNC	Société en Nom Collectif
SNC	Syndicat National des Cidriers et Fabricants d'Eau-de-Vie de Cidre
SNCA	Société Nationale de Construction Aéronautique
SNCAO	Syndicat National du Commerce de l'Antiquité et de l'Occasion
SNCAR	Syndicat National des Courtiers d'Assurances et de Réassurances
SNCB	Société Nationale des Chemins de Fer Belges

SNC-BOIS	Société Nationale du Cameroun – Bois
SNCDC	Syndicat National des Commerçants Détaillants en Confiserie
SNCEA	Syndicat National des Cadres d'Exploitations Agricoles (CGA)
SNCEOOA	Syndicat National des Cadres, Employés et Ouvriers des Organisations Agricoles (CGA)
SNCF	Sindacato Nazionale Commercianti di Francobolli
SNCF	Société Nationale des Chemins de Fer Français
SNCFA	Société Nationale des Chemins de Fer Algériens
SNCGEPVO	Syndicat National du Commerce en Gros des Equipements, Pièces pour Véhicules et Outillages
SNCI	Société National de Crédit à l'Industrie
SNCIMIP	Syndicat National des Constructeurs et Installateurs de Matériels Industriels en Plastiques
SNCM	Syndicat National des Chaînes Mécaniques
SNCP	Société Nigérienne de Collecte des Cuirs et Peaux
SNCP	Syndicat National du Commerce du Porc
SNCP	Syndicat National des Conseils en Publicité
SNCRP	Syndicat National des Conseils en Relations Publiques
SNCT	Société Nationale Centrafricaine de Travaux et de Transports
SNCTN	Syndicat National des Cadres et Techniciens du Notariat
SNCTR	Syndicat National du Commerce des Tubes et Raccords
SNCV	Société Nationale des Chemins de Fer Vicinaux
SND	Syndicat National du Décolletage
SNDE	Société Nationale de Distribution d'Eau (Congo)
SNDE	Syndicat National du Découpage et de l'Emboutissage
SNDF	Syndicat National des Déshydrateurs de France
SNDM	Syndicat National des Directeurs de Mutualité
SNDOPA	Syndicat National des Directeurs d'Organismes Professionnels Agricoles
SNDSDCA	Syndicat National des Directeurs et Sous-Directeurs de Coopératives Agricoles
SNE	Société Nationale des Eaux (Haute-Volta)
SNE	Société Nationale d'Énergie (Congo)
SNE	Syndicat National des Emballeurs
SNEA	Société Nationale d'Encouragement à l'Agriculture
SNEA	Société Nationale d'Exploitation Agricole (Central Africa)
SNEALC	Syndicat National d'Elevage et d'Amélioration du Lapin de Chair
SNEC	Société Nationale des Eaux du Cameroun
SNEC	Syndicat National de l'Exploitation d'Équipements Thermiques et de Génie Climatique
SNECIPA	Sindicato Nacional dos Empregados do Comercio e da Industria da Provincia de Angola
SNECMA	Société Nationale d'Étude et de Construction et Moteurs d'Aviation
SNED	Société Nationale d'Édition et de Diffusion (Algeria)
SNED	Syndicat National des Négociants Embouteilleurs et Distributeurs en Vins et Spiritueux de France
SNEF	Syndicat National des Entreprises du Froid et du Conditionnement de l'Air
SNEF	Syndicat National de l'Estampage et de la Forge
SNEFAC	Société Nouvelle d'Entreprises Franco-Africaines de Constructions (Congo)
SNEFCA	Syndicat National des Entreprises du Froid et du Conditionnement de l'Air
SNEFP	Syndicat National des Experts Forestiers Patentes
SNEI	Société Nouvelle d'Éditions Industrielle
SNEP	Société Nationale des Entreprises de Presse
SNEP	Syndicat National des Cadres de l'Enseignement Privé
SNEPA	Syndicat National de l'Édition Phonographique et Audiovisuelle
SNEPE	Société Nigérienne d'Étude pour la Production de l'Élevage
SNEPMA	Syndicat National de l'Enseignement Professionnel et Ménager Agricole
SNEPP	Syndicat National des Extrudeurs de Profilés Plastiques
SNES	Syndicat National des Enseignements de Second Degré
SNESup	Syndicat National de l'Enseignement Supérieur

SNET	Syndicat National de l'Enseignement Technique
SNETAP	Syndicat National de l'Enseignement Technique Agricole
SNETI	Syndicat National des Entrepeneurs de Travaux Immergés
SNETP	Syndical National des Enseignements Techniques et Professionelles
SNF	Svenska Naturskyddsföreningen
SNF	Svenska Numismatiska Föreningen
SNF	Syndicat National des Industries et Commerces de la Récupération de la Ferraille
SNFBM	Syndicat National des Fabricants de Boîtes, Emballages et Bouchages Métalliques
SNFBTE	Scottish National Federation of Building Trades Employers
SNFC	Société Nationale des Chemins de Fer Français
SNFCCM	Syndicat National des Fabricants de Crèmes et Conserves de Marrons
SNFEV	Syndicat Français des Éleveurs de Visons
SNFFS	Syndicat National des Fabricants de Fruits au Sirop
SNFL	Syndicat National des Fabricants de Liqueurs
SNFM	Section Nationale des Fermiers et des Métayers
SNFPA	Syndicat National des Fabricants de Produits Abrasifs
SNFPAS	Syndicat National des Fabricants de Produits Aromatiques de Synthèse
SNFQ	Syndicat National des Fabricants de Quincaillerie
SNFP	Syndicat National des Fabricants de Ressorts
SNFS	Syndicat National des Fabricants de Sirops
SNFS	Syndicat National des Fabricants de Sucre de France
SNFTRP	Syndicat National des Fabricants de Tuyaux et Raccords en Polyoléfines
SNFU	National Farmers' Union of Scotland
SNFV	Syndicat National des Fabricants de Vinaigres
SNG	Schweizerische Naturforschende Gesellschaft
SNG	Schweizerische Neurologische Gesellschaft
SNG	Schweizerische Numismatische Gesellschaft
SNGC	Stichting Nederlands Graancentrum
SNGM	Servicio Nacional de Geología y Minería (Ecuador)
SNGP	Syndicat National des Graphistes Publicitaires
SNGP	Syndicat National des Grossistes Distributeurs en Produits de Parfumerie et Accessoires de Toilette
SNGTN	Société Nationale des Grand Travaux du Niger
SNH	Société Nationale de l'Habitat (Central Africa)
SNHBM	Société Nationale des Habitations à Bon Marché (Belgium)
SNHF	Société Nationale d'Horticulture de France
SNHMV	Syndicat National des Hybrideurs et Métisseurs Viticoles
SNHTPC	Scottish National Housing and Town Planning Council
SNI	Société Nationale d'Investissements (Madagascar, Tunisia)
SNI	Studieselskapet for Norsk Industri
SNI	Syndicat National des Instituteurs et Institutrices
SNIA	Servicio Nacional de Investigaciones Agropecuarias (Panama)
SNIA	Sindacato Nazionale Istruzione Artistica
SNIAS	Société Nationale Industrielle Aérospatiale
SNIBB	Syndicat National des Instituts de Beauté
SNIC	Singapore National Institute of Chemistry
SNICL	Syndicat National de l'Industrie et du Commerce des Lubrifiants
SNIE	Syndicat National des Industries de l'Émail
SNIECV	Syndicat National des Industries Extractives pour la Céramique et la Verrerie
SNII	Serikat Nelajan Islam Indonesia
SNIL	Suomen Neuvottelevien Insinöörien Liitto
SNIM	Société Nationale Industrielle et Minière (Mauritania)
SNIMA	Service de Normalisation Industrielle Marocaine
SNIMaBI	Syndicat National des Importateurs de Matériels de Bureau et d'Informatique
SNIP	Syndicat National de l'Industrie Pharmaceutique
SNIP	Syndicat National Interprofessionnel de Porc
SNIPOT	Société Nationale Interprofessionnelle de la Pomme de Terre
SNIPV	Syndicat National de l'Industrie Pharmaceutique Vétérinaire

SNIR	Fédération Française des Syndicats Nationaux des Industries Radioélectriques et Électroniques	**SNPCRT**	Syndicat National de la Publicité Cinématographique, Radiophonique et Télévisée
SNIR	Syndicat National des Industries de la Robinetterie	**SNPD**	Syndicat National de la Publicité Directe
		SNPE	Société Nationale des Poudres et Explosifs
SNIRA	Syndicat National des Industries de Récupérations Animales	**SNPEN**	Syndicat National des Professeurs des Écoles Normales
SNIRI	Snickerifabrikernas Riksförbund	**SNPEP**	Syndicat National Professionnel des Engrais Phosphates
SNJ	Syndicat National des Journalistes		
SNL	Serviço Nacional de Lepra (Brazil)	**SNPF**	Syndicat National des Pédiatres Français
SNM	Sociedad Nacional de Minería (Chile)	**SNPF**	Syndicat National des Producteurs de Fraisiers
SNMA	Servicios Nacionales de Meteorologia y Aerofotografica (Peru)	**SNPI**	Servicio Nacional de Productividad Industrial (Spain)
SNMG	Syndicat National de la Mécanique Générale	**SNPIC**	Syndicat National des Professionnels de l'Information et de la Communication des Entreprises et Collectivités
SNMH	Servicio Nacional de Meteorología e Hidrología (Ecuador)		
SNMI	Syndicat National de la Mécanique Industrielle d'Usinage et de Constructions Spéciales	**SNPL**	Syndicat National des Pilots de Ligne
		SNPLV	Syndicat National de la Promotion et de la Publicité sur le Lieu de Vente
SNMM	Syndicat National des Constructeurs de Menuiserie, Murs-Rideaux et Cloisons Métalliques	**SNPMI**	Syndicat National des Producteurs de Mortiers Industriels
SNMM	Syndicat National du Mobilier Métallique	**SNPMT**	Syndicat National Professionnel des Médecins du Travail
SNMP	Syndicat National du Moulage et de la Transformation des Feuilles et Films Plastiques	**SNPN**	Société National de Protection de la Nature et d'Acclimatation de France
SNMRMA	Syndicat National des Marchands Réparateurs de Machines Agricoles	**SNPNC**	Syndicat National du Personnel Navigant Commercial
SNN	Syndicat National des Notaires	**SNPNH**	Syndicat National des Producteurs de Nouveautés Horticoles
SNO	Scottish National Orchestra Society		
SNOF	Société Nationale d'Oléiculture de France	**SNPOQ**	Syndicat National des Producteurs d'Oeufs de Qualité
SNOP	Secrétariat National de l'Opinion Publique Secrétariat Général de l'Episcopat Français	**SNPPA**	Syndicat National du Profilage des Produits Plats en Acier
SNP	Scottish National Party	**SNPPFOC**	Syndicat National des Producteurs de Plantes de Fraisiers Officiellement Contrôlés
SNPA	Serviço Nacional de Pesquisas Agrónomicas		
SNPA	Scottish Newspaper Proprietors Association	**SNPPM**	Syndicat National des Producteurs, Ramasseurs et Collecteurs de Plantes Médicinales, Aromatiques et Industrieiles
SNPa	Syndicat National de la Parfumerie (Belgium)		
SNPA	Syndicat National des Plastiques Alvéolaires	**SNPPT**	Société Nationale de la Petite Propriété Terrienne (Belgium)
SNPA	Société Nationale des Pétroles d'Aquitaine		
SNPA & ER	Service National de la Production Agricole et de l'Enseignement Rurale (Haiti)	**SNPRCI**	Syndicat National des Producteurs, Ramasseurs et Collecteurs de Plantes Médicinales, Aromatiques et Industrielles
SNPAMR	Syndicat National de la Presse Agricole et du Monde Rurale		
SNPBR	Section Nationale des Preneurs de Baux Ruraux	**SNPT**	Société Nationale de Promotion Touristique (Senegal)
SNPC	Secretaría Nacional de Planificación y Coordinación (Bolivia)	**SNPVAC**	Sindicato Nacional de Pessoal de Vôo da Aviação Civil (Portugal)

SNR	Society for Nautical Research
SNRA	Servicio Nacional de Reforma Agraria (Bolivia)
SNRC	Israel Atomic Energy Commission
SNRTM	Sydicat National de Revêtement et du Traitement des Métaux
SNRTMS	Syndicat National des Revêtements et Traitements des Métaux et Substrats
SNS	Sindicato Nazionale Scrittori
SNS	Société Nationale de Sidérurgie (Algeria)
SNS	Studieförbundet Näringsliv och Samhälle
SNSAF	Syndicat National des Spécialistes Apicoles de France
SNSC	Scottish National Ski Council
SNSE	Society of Nuclear Scientists and Engineers (U.S.A.)
SNSM	Sindicato Nazionale Scuola Media
SNSO-GATRA	Société Nouvelle Société Gabonaise de Travaux
SNSRC	Swedish Natural Science Research Council
SNST	Société Nationale pour la Vente des Scories Thomas
SNTA	Société Nigérienne de Transport Automobile
SNTA	Syndicat National des Transporteurs Aériens
SNTC	Sindicato Nacional de Transportes y Comunicaciones
SNTF	Syndicat National des Téléphériques et Téléskis de France
SNTFM	Société Nationale des Transports Ferroviaires
SNTL	Statui Nakladatelstvi Technicke Literatury (Czechoslovakia)
SNTN	Société Nationale des Transports Nigériens
SNTP	Société Nationale de Travaux Publics et Particuliers (Senegal)
SNTPC	Scottish National Town Planning Council
SNTRPCVR	Syndicat National des Fabricants de Tubes et Raccords en Polychlorure de Vinyle Rigide
SNTS	Studiorum Novi Testamenti Societas (U.K.)
SNTU	Société Nigérienne de Transport Urbain
SNTZ	Syndicat National des Travailleurs Zairois
SNUiF	Stichting Nederlandse Uienfederatie
SNV	Association Suisse de Normalisation
SNVF	Syndicat National des Vétérinaires Français
SNVPF	Syndicat National des Vétérinaires Praticiens Français

SNVV	Stichting voor de Nederlandse Vlasteelt en Vlasbewerking
SOAE	State Organization for Administration and Employment Affairs (Iran)
SOAEM	Société Ouest-Africaine d'Entreprises Maritimes
SOAH	Syndicat de l'Outillage Agricole et Horticole
SOAM	Société d'Oxygène et d'Acetylène de Madagascar
SOAS	School of Oriental and African Studies
SOB	Sociedade de Olericultura do Brasil
SOB	Swiss Official Board of Ballroom Dancing
SOBAMAD	Société Bananière de Madagascar
SOBEMAP	Société Belge d'Économie et de Mathématique Appliquée
SOBER	Sociedade Brasileira de Economistas Rurais
SOBEVECO	Société Ophthalmologique Belge des Verres de Contact
SOBIPO	Société Bretonne Interprofessionnelle de la Pomme de Terre
SOBOA	Société des Brasseries de l'Ouest Africain
SOBOCA	Société des Bois du Sud-Ouest Cameroun
SOBOCI	Société des Boissons Hygiéniques de la Côte-d'Ivoire
SOBRAGA	Société des Brasseries du Gabon
SOBRAMIL	Sociedade Brasileira de Mineraçao Ltda
SOC	Sveriges Oljeväxtodlares Centralförening
SOCABU	Société de Caoutchouc Butyl
SOCACI	Société Commerciale et Agricole de la Côte d'Ivoire
SOCACIG	Société Centrafricaine de Cigarettes
SOCAD	Société de Commercialisation et de Crédit Agricole du Dahomey
SOCADEM	Société Camerounaise d'Emballages Métalliques
SOCADEP	Société Camerounaise d'Édition et de Publicité
SOCADI	Société Centrafricaine de Diamant Industriel
SOCADIS	Société Camerounaise de Distribution
SOCAEM	Société Ouest Africaine d'Entreprises Maritimes
SOCAFER	Société Camerounaise de Plomberie et de Ferronnerie
SOCAGI	Société Centrafricaine des Gaz Industriels
SOCAHIT	Société Camerounaise Hotêlière, Immobilière et Touristique
SOCALTRA	Société Alsacienne d'Études et Travaux

SOCAM	Société Camerounaise de Menuiserie
SOCAM	Société Commerciale Africaine d'Importation (Ivory Coast)
SOCAMBO	Société Camerounaise Industrielle du Bois
SOCAMCO	Société Camerounaise de Conserveries
SOCAME	Société Camerounaise des Engrais
SOCAMETA	Société Camerounaise de Constructions Métalliques
SOCANA	Société Camerounaise de Navigation
SOCAPALM	Société Camerounaise des Palmeraies
SOCAPE	Société Camerounaise de Presse et d'Éditions
SOCAR	Société Cameroun d'Assurances et de Réassurances
SOCAREC	Société Africaine de Rectification
SOCAS	Société de Conserves Alimentaires du Sénégal
SOCASEP	Société Camerounaise de Sepultures et Transports Spéciaux
SOCATCI	Société des Caoutchoucs de Côte-d'Ivoire
SOCATEX	Société Africaine de Confection et de Bonneterie
SOCATRAL	Société Camerounaise de Transformation de l'Aluminium
SOCAVER	Société Camerounaise de Verrerie
SOCC	Super Ocean Carrier Conference (U.S.A.)
SOCCA	Société Camerounaise de Crédit Automobile
SOCEA	Société Charentaise d'Équipements Aéronautiques
SOCECO	Société Camerounaise d'Études et de Constructions
SOCEF	Société de Construction et d'Exploitation d'Installations Frigorifiques en Côte-d'Ivoire
SOCEPPAR	Sociedade Cerealista Exportadora de Produtos Paranaenses (Brazil)
SOCFI	Société d'Organisation de Congrès Français et Internationaux
SOCGPA	Seed, Oil, Cake and General Produce Association
SOCIAC	Singapore-Soviet Shipping Agency
SOCIACI	Société Commerciale et Industrielle Africaine de Côte d'Ivoire
SOCIAGRI	Société Ivoirienne d'Expansion Agricole
SOCICA	Société Cinématographique Africaine
SOCICADI	Société Dahoméenne de Promotion du Commerce et de l'Industrie
SOCICO	Société Immobilière et Commerciale du Congo
SOCIDIS	Société Ivoirienne d'Importation et de Distribution
SOCIGA	Société de Cigarettes du Gabon
SOCIM	Société Centrafricaine d'Investissements Immobiliers
SOCIM	Société de Constructions et l'Industries de la Mauritanie
SOCIMA	Société des Ciments du Mali
SOCIMEX	Société d'Importation et d'Exportation de l'Océan Indien (Madagascar)
SOCIPAR	Société Ivoirienne de Participation
SOCIPEC	Société Ivoirienne de Participations Économiques
SOCITR-ACAM	Société Camerounaise Interprofessionelle pour la Fourniture de Traverses et de Bois Débites au Transcamerounais
SOCIVER	Société Ivoirienne de Verrerie
SOCOBLE	Société Coopérative des Producteurs de Blé
SOCOBOIS	Société Congolaise des Bois
SOCOCIM	Société Ouest Africaine des Ciments
SOCOD-EBAS	Société Commerciale pour le Développement de la Basse-Sanaga
SOCODI	Société Congolaise de Disques
SOCOFFA	Société Commerciale et Financière Franco-Africaine
SOCOFIDE	Société Congolaise de Financement du Développement
SOCOFOR	Forestry Co-operative (Indo-China)
SOCOFRA	Société Commerciale Francais (Congo)
SOCOFR-ACIM	Société Commerciale Franco-Africaine des Ciments
SOCO-FROID	Société Congolaise de Conservation et de Congélation
SOCOL	Société de Construction d'Entreprises Générales (Belgium)
SOCOLOR	Sociedad Colombiana de Orquideología
SOCOMA	Société des Conserves du Mali
SOCOMAF	Société pour le Conditionnement de Maïs Français
SOCOMID	Société de Caution Mutuelle des Industries Diverses
SOCOPA	Société Co-opérative des Produits Agricoles (Zaire)
SOCOPRE	Société Sénégalaise de Commercialisation des Produits de l'Élevage
SOCOPRISE	Société Africaine d'Entreprises Industrielles et Immobilières (Congo)

SOCORAM	Société de Constructions Radio-Électriques du Mali
SOCOTEL	Société Mixte pour le Développement de la Technique de la Communication dans le Domaine des Télécommunications
SODACA	Société Dahoméenne de Crédit Automobile
SODACOP	Société Dahoméenne de Commerce et de Pêche
SODACRUS	Société Dahoméenne de Crustaces
SODAF	Société Dahoméenne d'Ananas et de Fruits
SODAFE	Société pour le Développement de l'Afrique Équatoriale
SODAIC	Société Dahoméenne pour le Développement de l'Industrie et du Commerce
SODAK	Société Dahoméenne Agricole et Industrielle du Kénaf
SODA-METRO	Société Dahoméenne de Messageries et de Transports Routiers
SODAMI	Société Dahoméenne de Minoterie
SODAPAR	Société Dahoméenne de Parfumerie
SODAPEC	Société Dahoméenne de Peintures et Colorants
SODAPLAS-TICA	Société Dahoméenne de Plastique
SODASEL	Société Dahoméenne de Sel
SODEAM	Société pour le Développement de l'Électricité en Afrique et à Madagascar
SODECAO	Société pour le Développement de Cacao (Cameroons)
SODECI	Société de Distribution d'Eau de la Côte-d'Ivoire
SODEFEL	Société pour le Développement de la Production des Fruits et Légumes (Ivory Coast)
SODEFOR	Société pour le Développement des Plantations Forestières (Ivory Coast)
SODEL	Société pour Développement des Applications de l'Électricité
SODELAC	Société Cotonnière du Tchad
SODELEC	Société d'Études de l'Économie de Consummation
SODEMI	Société pour le Développement Minier de la Côte d'Ivoire
SODEN-ICOB	Société de Développement Regional de la Vallée du Niari et de Jacob (Congo)
SODEPALM	Société d'État pour le Développement du Palmier à Huile (Ivory Coast)
SODEPAX	Exploratory Committee on Society, Development and Peace of the Roman Catholic Church and the World Council of Churches
SODEPRA	Société pour le Développement des Productions Animales (Ivory Coast)
SODERN	Société Anonyme d'Études et Réalisations Nucléaires
SODE-SUCRE	Société pour le Développement des Plantations de Cannes a Sucre, l'Industrialisation et la Commercialisation du Sucre
SODETAM	Société pour le Développement des Voyages et du Tourisme en Afrique et à Madagascar
SODETEG	Société d'Études Techniques et d'Entreprises Générales
SODETRAM	Société d'Études pour Réalisations en Outre-Mer
SODIACAM	Société de Distribution Alimentaire du Cameroun
SODIC	Société pour la Conversion et le Développement Industriels
SODIMA	Société de Diffusion des Marques
SODIMAF	Société de Distribution des Grandes Marques pour l'Afrique (Ivory Coast)
SODIMPEX	Société Commerciale d'Import-Export (Ivory Coast)
SODIP	Société pour la Diffusion de la Presse (Belgium)
SODIPHAC	Société de Diffusion Pharmaceutique en Afrique Centrale
SODOMEI	Japan Federation of Trade Unions
SODRE	Servicio Oficial de Difusion Radio-electrica (Uruguay)
SODT	Swiss Office for the Development of Trade
SOEC	Statistical Office of the European Communities
SOEKOR	Southern Oil Exploration Corporation (South Africa)
SOF	Société Ornithologiques de France
SOF	Sveriges Ornithologische Unie
SOF	Syndicat des Osiéristes Français
SOFACO	Société Africaine de Fabrication, de Formulation et de Conditionnement (Ivory Coast)
SOFAIGUI	Society for Development of Agricultural and Industrial Products of Guinea
SOFAMI	Société de Fabrication Métallique Ivoirienne
SOFBA	Société Française des Bois Africaine
SOFCA	Société Française de Compléments Alimentaires

SOFFO	Société Financière pour la France et les Pays Outre-Mer
SOFICAL	Société de Financement Industriel Commercial et Agricole
SOFICO	Société pour l'Exploitation des Fibres Locales (Zaire)
SOFIDAK	Société pour la Foire Internationale de Dakar
SOFIDECA	Société de Financement et de Développement de l'Économie Agricole
SOFIFA	Société Financière et Immobilière Franco-Africaine
SOFINA	Société Financière de Transports et d'Entreprises Industrielles (Belgium)
SOFIRAD	Société Financière de Radiodiffusion
SOFIRAN	Société Française des Pétroles d'Iran
SOFMA	Société Française de Matériels d'Armement
SOFRAMER	Société Française d'Achats pour l'Outre-Mer
SOFRA-TOME	Société Française d'Études et de Réalisation Nucléaires
SOFRATOP	Société Française de Travaux Topographiques et Photogrammétriques
SOFREAVIA	Société Française d'Études et de Réalisation d'Équipements Aéronautiques
SOFRECOM	Société Française d'Études et de Réalisations d'Équipements de Télécommunications
SOFREGAZ	Société Française d'Études Gaz
SOFRELEC	Société Française d'Études Électrique
SOFRE-MINES	Société Française d'Études Minière
SOFRESID	Société Française d'Études Sidérurgique
SOFREXAM	Société Française d'Exportation de Matériels Naval et Militaires
SOFRAVIN	Société Française des Vins (Senegal)
SOFRIGAL	Société des Frigorifiques du Sénégal
SOFRINA	Société Française pour l'Industrie en Afrique
SOG	Schweizerische Ophthalmologische Gesellschaft
SOGABOL	Société Gabonaise des Oléagineux
SOGACA	Société Gabonaise de Crédit Automobile
SOGACAM	Société Gabonaise de Cabotage Maritime et Fluvial
SOGACAR	Société Gabonaise de Carrières
SOGACEL	Société Gabonaise de Cellulose
SOGACHIM	Société Gabonaise de Chimie
SOGADA	Société Générale d'Approvisionnement du Dahomey
SOGAF-INEX	Société Gabonaise de Financement et d'Expansion
SOGAFRIC	Société Gabonaise Froid et Représentations Industrielles et Commerciales
SOGAMAR	Société Gabonaise de Marbre et Matériaux
SOGAME	Société Gabonaise de Matériel et d'Équipement
SOGAMIRE	Société Gabonaise de Miroiterie et Ébénisterie
SOGAPECI	Société Générale d'Armement et de Pêche de Côte-d'Ivoire
SOGAR-AREC	Société Gabonaise de Électrification et de Mécanique Générale
SOGARES	Société Gabonaise de Réalisations de Structures
SOGAS	Stichting Samenwerkende Organisaties van Detaillisten in Gasapparaten
SOGAT	Society of Graphical and Allied Trades
SOGATOL	Société Gabonaise de Toles et Produits Sidérurgiques
SOGATRAM	Société Gabonaise de Transport Maritime
SOGEC	Société Gabonaise d'Électrification et de Canalisation
SOGECOR	Société de Gestion et de Conseil en Organisation
SOGEDEM	Société Gabonaise d'Étude et de Développement Maritimes
SOGEF	Société de Gestion d'Entrepôts Frigorifiques en Côte d'Ivoire
SOGEL	Société Gabonaise d'Élevage
SOGELEM	Société Générale d'Électricité de Mauritanie
SOGEM	Société de Gestion Moderne
SOGEP	Société Générale d'Études et de Planification
SOGERCA	Société pour l'Entreprise de Réacteurs et de Centrales Atomiques
SOGESCI	Société Belge pour l'Application des Méthodes Scientifiques de Gestion
SOGES-ETRA	Société Sénégalaise de Bâtiments et Travaux Publics
SOGETA	Société Générale des Techniques Agricoles (Upper Volta)
SOGETHA	Société Génerale des Techniques Hydro-Agricoles (Tunis)
SOGET-OCAM	Société de Gestion pour le Tourisme au Cameroun
SOGETRA	Société Générale de Travaux (Belgium)
SOGETRAF	Société Générale de Travaux et de Représentations en Afrique (Ivory Coast)

SOGET-RANS	Société de Gestion pour le Tourisme au Cameroun
SOGEV	Société Générale du Vide
SOGIEXCI	Société Générale d'Importation et d'Exportation de Côte-d'Ivoire
SOGIP	Société Générale pour l'Industrialisation de la Pêche
SOGISMA	Société des Gaz Industriels de Madagascar
SOGREAH	Société Grenobloise d'Études et d'Application Hydrauliques
SOHIMA	Société Hôtelière et Immobilière de Madagascar
SOHORA	Société des Hôtels de la Riviéra Africaine (Ivory Coast)
SOHOTCI	Société Hôtelière et Touristique de Côte-d'Ivoire
SOIDAH	Société Industrielle d'Habillement du Dahomey
SOIDI	Société Ivoirienne de Distribution
SOIPAC	Società Italiana di Patologia Clinica
SOIVRE	Servicio Oficial de Inspección, Vigilancia y Regulación de la Exportaciones
SOK	Suomen Osuuskauppojen Keskuskunta
SOK	Svenska Organisations Konsulters Förening
SOKSI	Sentral Organisasi Karyawan Socialis Indonesia
SOL	Suomen Opettajain Liitto
SOLCA	Sociedad de Lucha contra el Cáncer (Ecuador)
SOLET	Società Orvietana Essiccazione e Lavorazione dei Tabacchi
SOLF	Sveriges Optikleverantöres Förening
SOLIBRA	Société de Limonaderies et Brasseries d'Afrique
SOLIDA-RIOS	Consejo de Fundaciones Americanas de Desarrollo (Guatemala)
SOLIMAC	Société Libano-Ivoirienne de Matériaux de Construction
SOM	Society of Metaphysicians
SOM	Society of Occupational Medicine
SOMA	Société Maritime de Madagascar
SOMACO	Société Nationale de Commerce (Madagascar)
SOMACOM	Société Maritime et Commerciale (Gabon)
SOMACOTP	Société Mauritanienne de Construction et de Travaux Publics

SOMACO-TRET	Société Mauritanienne de Commerce, de Transport, de Représentation et de Transit
SOMADEC	Société Mauritanienne de Développement et de Commerce
SOMAF	Société Marbrière Africaine
SOMAGA	Société Marseillaise du Gabon
SOMAIR	Société des Mines de l'Air
SOMALAC	Société Malgache Lac Alaotra-Malagasy Lake Alaotra Society (Madagascar)
SOMALIBO	Société Malienne de Boissons Gazeuses
SOMAP	Sociétés Marocaines de Prévoyance
SOMAP	Société Mauritanienne d'Armement et de Pêche
SOMAPA	Société Malienne de Parfumerie
SOMAREM	Société Nationale de Recherches et d'Exploitation des Ressources Minierès du Mali
SOMASAC	Société Malienne de Sacherie
SOMA-QUIRE	Société Mauritanienne de Quincaillerie et de Représentation
SOMAURAL	Société Mauritanienne des Allumettes
SOMDIAA	Société Multinationale de Développement pour les Industries Alimentaires et Agricoles
SOMEC	Société Mutuelle d'Études et de Coopération Industrielles
SOMECAF	Société d'Ateliers Mécaniques Africains
SOMECAF-RIQUE	Société pour la Mécanisation des Entreprises en Afrique
SOMEPI	Société Mauritanienne d'Études et de Promotion Industrielles
SOMET	Société Maroc Études
SOMETER	Société Mauritanienne d'Études Techniques et de Représentation
SOMFA	Soya Bean Meal Futures Association
SOMICOA	Société Maritime et Industrielle de la Côte Occidentale d'Afrique
SOMIEX	Société Malienne d'Importation et d'Exportation
SOMIMA	Société Minière de Mauritanie
SOMIP	Société Mauritanienne des Industries de la Pêche
SOMIREN	Società Minerali Radioattivi Energia Nucleare
SOMISA	Sociedad Mixta Siderurgia Argentina
SOMIVAC	Société pour la Mise en Valeur Agricole de la Corse

SOMMEP	Syndicat de l'Outillage à Main et des Machines Électro-Portatives
SONADER	Société Nationale pour Développement Rural (Dahomey)
SONABA	Société Nationale du Bâtiment (Tchad)
SONAC	Société Nationale de la Céramique Artisanale et Industrielle du Dahomey
SONACO	Société Nationale Agricole pour le Coton (Dahomey)
SONACO	Société Nationale de Commerce (Madagascar)
SONACO	Société Nationale de Conditionnement (Ivory Coast)
SONACOB	Société Nationale de Commercialisation des Bois et Dérivés (Algeria)
SONACOB	Société Nationale de Construction de Bâtiments (Senegal)
SONACOM	Société Nationale de Commerce (Togo)
SONACOME	Société Nationale des Construction Mécaniques
SONACOT	Société Nationale de Commercialisation du Tchad
SONADER	Société Nationale pour le Développement Rural du Dahomey
SONADIG	Société Nationale d'Investissements du Gabon
SONADIS	Société Nouvelle pour l'Approvisionnement et la Distribution au Sénégal
SONAFI	Société Nationale de Financement (Ivory Coast)
SONAFOR	Société Nationale des Forages (Senegal)
SONAFRIG	Société Nationale des Frigorifiques (Senegal)
SONAGA	Société Nationale de Garantie et d'Assistance au Commerce (Senegal)
SONAP	Sociedade Nacional de Petroleos
SONAP	Sociedad de Navigación Petrolera (Chile)
SONAP	Société Nationale des Articles de Papeterie (Central Africa)
SONAPH	Société Nationale pour le Développement de la Palmerale et des Huileries
SONARA	Société Nigérienne de Commercialisation de l'Arachide
SONAREM	Société Nationale de Recherches et d'Exploitations Minières (Algeria)
SONATAM	Société Nationale des Tabacs et Allumettes du Mali

SONATITE	Société Nationale des Travaux d'Infrastructure des Télécommunications (Algeria)
SONATRAB	Société Nationale de Transformation du Bois
SONATRAC	Société Nationale de Transit et de Consignation (Dahomey)
SONAT-RACH	Société Nationale de Transport de Carburant (Algeria)
SONATRAM	Société Nationale de Travaux Maritimes (Algeria)
SONEAB	Société Nationale d'Exploitation des Arachides de Bouche (Senegal)
SONEES	Société Nationale d'Exploitation des Eaux du Sénégal
SONEG	Société Nationale d'Entreprise Générale (Senegal)
SONEL	Société Nationale d'Élevage (Zaire)
SONELGAZ	Société Nationale de l'Électricité et du Gaz (Algeria)
SONEPI	Société Nationale d'Études et de Promotion Industrielle (Senegal)
SONEPRESS	Société Nationale d'Édition et de Presse (Haute-Volta)
SONERAN	Société Nigérienne d'Exploitation des Ressources Animales
SONETE	Sociedade Nacional de Estudos e Financiamento de Empreendimentos Ultramarinos (Portugal)
SONETRA	Société Nationale d'Entreprises et de Travaux Publics (Mali)
SONEXI	Société Nigérienne d'Exploitation Cinématographique
SONIBATP	Société Nigériènne de Bâtiment et de Travaux Publics
SONIC	Société Nationale des Industries de la Cellulose (Algeria)
SONICA	Société Nigérienne de Crédit Automobile
SONICAR	Société Nigérienne de Carrelage
SONIC-ERAM	Société Nigérienne de Produits Céramiques
SONIFAME	Société Nigérienne de Fabrications Métalliques
SONIMCO	Société Nationale d'Impression en Continu (Senegal)
SONIMEX	Société Nationale d'Importation et d'Exportation (Mauritania)
SONIPAL	Société Nigérienne pour la Production d'Allumettes

SONIPLA	Société Nigérienne de Plastique
SONIPRIM	Société Nigérienne de Primeurs
SONITAN	Société Nigérienne de Tannerie
SONITO	Société Nationale d'Intervention sur le Marché de la Tomate
SONITRA	Société Nationale Ivoirienne de Travaux
SONOCRAF	Société Nouvelle des Comptoirs Réunis d'Afrique
SONRA	Society of Newfoundland Radio Amateurs
SONUCI	Société Nigérienne d'Urbanisme et de Construction Immobilière
SOPAD	Société de Produits Alimentaires et Diététiques
SOPANI	Société de Parfumerie Nigérienne
SOPAO	Société de Pêche de l'Afrique Occidentale
SOPARMOD	Société des Parfums Modernes du Tchad
SOPARCO	Société Africaine de Parfumerie et de Conditionnement (Mali)
SOPECI	Société de Peinture en Côte-d'Ivoire
SOPECOBA	Société des Pêcheries Coloniales à la Baleine
SOPELEM	Société d'Optique, Précision, Électronique et Mécanique
SOPEMEA	Société pour le Perfectionnement des Matériels et Équipements Aérospatiaux
SOPESEA	Société des Pêcheries Sénégalaises de l'Atlantique
SOPEXA	Société pour la Promotion de l'Exportation des Produits Agricoles et Alimentaires
SOPIM	Société de Promotion Immobilière de la Côte-d'Ivoire
SOPIMA	Société des Piles de Madagascar
SOPIVOLTA	Société des Piles de Haute-Volta
SOPREP	Sociedade Portuguesa de Relacões Publicas
SOPRIA	Société d'Étude et de Financement pour la Promotion des Industries Agricoles et de l'Alimentation
SOPROD-AVCI	Société d'Études pour la Production de l'Avocat en Côte-d'Ivoire
SOPROGI	Société pour la Promotion et la Gestion Industrielle
SOR	Sectie Operationele Research
SOR	Society for Occupational Research (U.S.A.)
SOR	Sveriges Legitimerade Optikers Riksförbund
SORA	Svenska Operationsanalysföreningen
SORCA	Société de Recherche Operationelle et d'Économie Appliquée (Belgium)
SOREAS	Syndicat des Fabricants d'Organes et d'Équipement Aéronautiques et Spatiaux
SOREDIA	Société de Recherche et d'Exploitation Diamantiféres (French Equatorial Africa)
SOREFAME	Sociedades Reunidas Fabriacoes Metalicas (Portugal)
SOREMI	Société des Recherches et d'Exploitation Minières
SORIN	Società Richerche ed Impianti Nucleari
SORO	Special Operations Research Office, American University, Washington
SOS	International Federation of Bloodgivers Organisations
SOSAC	Société des Spécialités Agricoles et Chimiques (France)
SOSAP	Société Sénégalaise d'Armement à la Pêche
SOSATCO	Société Sénégalaise d'Assistance Technique et de Conseil de Gestion
SOSC	Smithsonian Oceanographic Sorting Centre (U.S.A.)
SOSECI	Société Sénégalaise pour le Commerce et l'Industrie
SOSECOD	Société Sénégalaise pour le Commerce et le Développement
SOSECODA	Société Sénégalaise de Courtages et d'Assurances
SOSEDECO	Société Sénégalaise pour le Développement Commercial
SOSEFIL	Société Sénégalaise de Filterie
SOSEG	Société Sénégalaise d'Amaillage et de Galvanisation
SOSETAM	Société Sénégalaise de Tannerie-Mégisserie
SOSETER	Société Sénégalaise de Terassements
SOSETRA-PROMER	Société Sénégalaise pour le Traitement des Produits de la Mer
SOSE-TRAUR	Société Sénégalaise de Travaux Urbains et Ruraux
SOSEX-CATRA	Société Sénégalaise d'Exploitation de Carrières et de Transports
SOSSI	Scouts on Stamps Society International (U.S.A.)
SOSU	Société Sucrière Voltaïque
SOSUCAM	Société Sucrière du Cameroun
SOSUMAV	Société Sucrière de la Mahavavy
SOSU-TCHAD	Société Sucrière du Tchad
SOTA	Société Coopérative pour l'Achat du Tabac (Switzerland)

SOTA	Société des Transports Africains	**SOVETIV**	Société de Vêtements Ivoiriens
SOTEGA	Société Industrielles Textile du Gabon	**SOVIAMAD**	Société des Viandes de Madagascar
SOTELEC	Société Mixte pour le Développement de la Technique des Télécommunications sur Cables	**SOVICA**	Société Voltaïque d'Intervention et de Coopération avec l'Agriculture
SOTEXCO	Société des Textiles du Congo	**SOVIMAS**	Société Voltaïque d'Importation Azar et Salam
SOTICI	Société de Transformation Industrielle de Côte-d'Ivoire	**SOVINCI**	Société des Vins de la Côte d'Ivoire
SOTOCA	Société Industrielle et Commerciale Togolaise du Café	**SOVINCO**	Société des Vins du Congo
		SOVOCA	Société Voltaïque de Crédit Automobile
SOTOCAM	Société de Topographie au Cameroun	**SOVOG**	Société Voltaïque de Groupage
SOTO-HOMA	Société Touristique et Hôtelière de Madagascar	**SOVOLCI**	Société Voltaïque de Commerce et d'Industrie
SOTOM	Société de Topographie de Madagascar	**SOVOLCOM**	Société Voltaïque de Commercialisation
SOTOMA	Société des Tabacs et Oléagineux de Madagascar	**SOVOL-PLAS**	Société Voltaïque de Plastique
SOTOMA	Société Togolaise de Marbrerie et Matériaux	**SOVOLSEM**	Société Voltaïque d'Entreprise de Surrurerie Menuiserie Métallique et Charpente
SOTOMAT-ERIAUX	Société Togolaise de Matériaux	**SOY**	Suomen Ostopäälliköiden Yhdistys
SOTOPLAN	Société Togolaise de Plantation	**SOXADA**	Société d'Oxygène et d'Acetylène du Dahomey
SOTOTRAC	Société Togolais de Transit et de Con-signation	**SP**	Commission Internationale de Phare du Cap Spartel
SOTRA	Société des Transports Abidjanais (Ivory Coast)	**SPA**	Föreninger Sveriges Praktiserande Arkitekter
SOTRABCI	Société de Travaux Publics et de Bâtiments Côte-d'Ivoire	**SPA**	Society of Public Analysts
		SPA	Screen Printing Association International
SOTRABO	Société de Transformation du Bois	**SPA**	Singapore People's Alliance
SOTRABOI	Société de Transformation des Bois Ivoiriens	**SPA**	Sociedade Portuguesa de Autores
SOTREC	Société des Tréfileries et Clouteries de la Côte-d'Ivoire	**SPA**	Society of St Peter Apostle for Native Clergy
SOTREF	Société Tropicale d'Exploitation Forestière (Cameroons, Ivory Coast)	**SPA**	Southern Pine Association (U.S.A.)
		SPA	Sumatra Planters Association (Indonesia)
SOTREP	Société Tchadienne de Réalisation et d'En-treprise de Pneumatiques	**SPA**	Syndicat de la Presse Agricole
SOTROPAL	Société Tropicale des Allumettes (Ivory Coast)	**SPA**	Systems and Procedures Association (U.S.A.)
SOTROPCO	Société Tropicale de Commerce	**SPAB**	Society for the Protection of Ancient Build-ings
SOTUC	Société de Transports Urbains du Cameroun	**SPAC**	Société Sénégalaise de Produits Alimentaires Congèles
SOV	Schweizerischer Obstverband		
SOV	Schweizerischer Optiker-Verband	**SPACEM**	Sociedad Puertorriquena de Autores, Com-positores y Editores Musicales
SOV	Schweizerischer Orientteppichhändler-Verband	**SPAEF**	Société des Pétroles d'Afriques Équatoriale Française
SOVEC	Société Voltaïque d'Étanchéité et de Carrelage	**SPAG**	Syndicat des Produits Alimentaires en Gros
		SPAI	Service Professionnel Agricole International (*of* APPCA)
SOVEG	Société Voltaïque d'Engineering et de Gestion	**SPAM**	Stowarzyszenie Polskich Artystów Muzyków
SOVETCO	Société pour la Vente de Thons Congèles (Ivory Coast)	**SPANA**	Society for the Protection of Animals in North Africa

SPANC	Society of St Peter the Apostle for Native Clergy
SPARMO	Solar Particle Altitude Radiation Monitoring Organisation
SPAS	Chambre Syndicale des Producteurs d'Aciers Fins et Spéciaux
SPASK	Service Provincial de l'Agriculture de Sud Kivu (Zaire)
SPATC	South Pacific Air Transport Council
SPATF	South Pacific Appropriate Technology Foundation (New Guinea)
SPB	Sociedad Peruana de Botánica
SPBA	Poultry and Egg Producers Association of Great Britain
SPBS	Scottish Plant Breeding Station
SPBW	Society for the Preservation of Beers from the Wood
SPC	Seed Production Committee
SPC	Sociedade Portuguesa de Commercialização
SPC	Société Française de Ceramique
SPC	South Pacific Commission (New Caledonia)
SPC	Swiss Publishers Corporation
SPCI	Société de Promotion Commerciale Ivoirienne
SPCI	Svenska Papers- och Cellulosaingeniörsföreningen
SPCN	Société de Produits Chimiques du Niger
SPD	Sozialdemokratische Partei Deutschlands
SPD	Svenska Privatdetektivförbundet
SPE	Society of Plastic Engineers (U.S.A.)
SPEA	Sales Promotion Executives Association (U.S.A.)
SPEA	Scottish Physical Education Association
SPEC	Society for Pollution and Environmental Control (Canada)
SPEC	South Pacific Bureau for Economic Cooperation (Fiji)
SPECI	Société de Presse et d'Édition de la Côte-d'Ivoire
SPECI-CHAMBRE	Chambre Syndicale des Fabricants et Concessionnaires de Spécialités Pharmaceutiques
SPEF	Scottish Plumbing Employers Federation
SPEF	Svenska Putsentreprenörföreningen
SPEIN	Syndicat Patronal des Entreprises et Industries du Niger
SPEL	Société Provisoire de l'Économique Laitière
SPEO	Société de Presse et d'Édition Ovine
SPEPE	Secrétariat Permanent pour l'Étude des Problèmes de l'Eau
SPER	Syndicat des Industries de Matériel Professionnel Électronique et Radioélectrique
SPF	Scottish Pharmaceutical Federation
SPF	Société Pomologique de France
SPF	Société Préhistorique Française
SPF	Svenska Pappershandlareföreningen
SPF	Svensk Pilotförening
SPF	Sveriges Papersindustriförbund
SPF	Sveriges Plastforbund
SPF	Sveriges Pomologiska Förening
SPFB	Chambre Syndicale des Producteurs de Fontes Brutes
SPFE	Society for the Preservation of the Fauna of the Empire
SPFF	Syndicat des Propriétaires Forestiers de France
SPFGBS	Syndicat des Producteurs Français des Graines de Betterave à Sucre
SPFV	Schweizerischer Pelz-Fachverband
SPG	Schweizerische Philosophische Gesellschaft
SPG	Schweizerische Physikalische Gesellschaft
SPG	Society for the Propagation of the Gospel in Foreign Parts
SPGB	Socialist Party of Great Britain
SPhV	Schweizerischer Photographenverband
SPI	Service Pédologique Inter-africain
SPI	Comité de Coordination des Secrétariats Professionnels Internationaux
SPI	Society of the Plastics Industry (USA)
SPI	Svenska Petroleum Institutet
SPIC	Society of the Plastics Industry of Canada
SPIC	Southern Petrochemical Industries Corporation (U.S.A.)
SPICA	Société Industrielle de Produits Chimiques et Aromatiques (Cameroons)
SPICRIM	Société pour la Participation Industrielle et Commerciale pour la Représentation Industrielle en Mauritanie
SPIDS	Syndicat Patronal des Industries de Dakar et du Sénégal
SPIE	Secrétariat Professionnel International de l'Enseignement
SPIEA	Syndicat Professionnel de l'Industrie des Engrais Azotés

SPIFDA	South Pacific Islands Fisheries Development Agency	**SPRL**	Society for the Promotion of Religion and Learning
SPIGED	Syndicat Professional des Industries des Goudrons et Dérivés	**SPRM**	Société des Plantations Réunies de Mimot (Vietnam)
SPIH	Syndicat des Producteurs Independants de Houblons	**SPRU**	Science Policy Research Unit
		SPS	Stichting Planbureau Suriname
SPIL	Society for the Promotion and Improvement of Libraries (India)	**SPSF**	Syndicat des Pisciculteurs-Salmoniculteurs de France
SPILS	Society for the Promotion of the Interests of Librarianship Students	**SPSL**	Society for the Protection of Science and Learning
SPIO	Spitzenorganisation der Filmwirtschaft	**SPSS**	Syndicat des Producteurs de Semences Sélectionnées
SPIRIM	Société Ivoirienne de Promotion et de Réalisations Immobilières	**SPSSI**	Society for the Psychological Study of Social Issues (U.S.A.)
SPKC	Small Pig Keepers' Council		
SPM	Société des Pétroles de Madagascar	**SPSSR**	Syndicat du Personnel Social des Services Sociaux Ruraux
SPMA	Sewage Plant Manufacturers Association		
SPMA	Society for Post-Medieval Archaeology	**SPT**	Brancheforeningen for Soebe- Parfumeri-, Toilet-og Kemisk-Tekniske Artikler
SPMF	Syndicat des Producteurs de Miel de France		
SPML	Sociedade Portuguesa de Medicina Laboratorial	**SPT**	Society of Photo-Technologists (U.S.A.)
		SPT	Sveriges Personaltidningsförening
SPN	Sociedade Portuguesa de Numismática	**SPTIY**	Suomen Puunteollisuss-insinöörien Yhdistys
SPNR	Society for the Promotion of Nature Reserves	**SPTL**	Society of Public Teachers of Law
SPO	Socialistische Partei Österreichs	**SPTL**	Suomen Pesuteollisuusliitto
SPOE	Society of Post Office Engineers	**SPTR**	Société des Plantations des Terres Rouge (Vietnam)
SPOFA	Leverantörföreningen för Sport- och Fritids-artiklar		
		SPUC	Society for the Protection of the Unborn Child
SPOOM	Syndicat des Producteurs d'Oléagineux d'Outre-mer	**SPUD**	Society for the Prevention of Unnecessary Damage (to Potatoes)
SPP	Swaziland Progressive Party		
SPPA	Serviço de Pesquisas de Patologia Animal (Brazil)	**SPUR**	Singapore Planning Urban Research Group
		SPURS	Special Program for Urban and Regional Studies of Developing Areas (U.S.A.)
SPQR	Senatus Populusque Romanus		
SPR	Sociedade Portuguesa de Reumatologia	**SPV**	Schweizerischer Pferdezuchtverband
SPR	Société Pédagogique de la Suisse Romande	**SPV**	Schweizerische Schlachtvieh Produ-zentenverband
SPR	Society for Psychical Research		
SPR	Studievereniging voor Psychical Research	**SPVEA**	Superintendência de Valorizaçao Económica da Amazonia
SPR	Sveriges Pälsdjursuppfodares Riksförbund	**SPY**	Suomen Paperi-Insinöörien Yhdistys
SPR	Sveriges Parfymhandlares Riksförbund	**SQI**	Sociedad de Quimica Industrial
SPR	Sveriges Public Relations Förening	**SQLA**	Scotch Quality Lamb Association
SPRC	Society for Prevention and Relief of Cancer	**SQM**	Sociedad Química de México
SPRDA	Solid Pipeline Research and Development Association (Canada)	**SQP**	Sociedad Química del Perú
		SR	Sagverkens Riksförbund
SPRF	Schweizer Public-Relations-Forum	**SRA**	Science Research Associates (U.S.A.)
SPRG	Schweizerische Public Relations Gesellschaft	**SRA**	Sociedad Rural Argentina
SPRI	Scott Polar Research Institute, Cambridge	**SRA**	Spring Research Association

SRA	Squash Rackets Association
SRAA	Société Royale d'Astronomie d'Anvers
SRAB	Société Royale des Beaux-Arts (Belgium)
SRAIN	Société de Représentations Automobiles et Industrielles au Niger
SRAPL	Société Romande d'Audiophonologie et de Pathologie du Langage
SRAT	Section Région d'Afrique Tropicale (*of* IOBC)
SRAT	Société de Recherches et d'Applications Techniques
SRB	Sociedad Rural Boliviana
SRB	Sociedade Rural Brasileira
SRB	Statens Rad for Byggnadsforskning
SRBB	Société Royale de Botanique de Belgique
SRBE	Société Royale Belge des Électriciens
SRBG	Société Royale Belge de Géographie
SRBII	Société Royale des Ingénieurs et des Industriels (Belgium)
SRBMD	Société Royale Belge de Médecine Dentaire
SRC	Science Research Council
SRC	Shri Ram Centre for Industrial Relations (India)
SRC	Social Research Centre (Cyprus, Hong Kong)
SRCC	Société Nationale pour la Renovation et le Développement de la Cacoyère et de Cafetière Togolaise
SRCI	Société Routière Colas de la Côte-d'Ivoire
SRCL	Service Rural de Culture et Loisirs
SRCMA	Steel Radiator and Convector Manufacturers' Association
SRCOA	Société Routière Colas de l'Ouest Africain
SRCRA	Shipowners Refrigerated Cargo Research Association
SRDA	Scottish Retail Drapers Association
SRDC	Shopfitting Research and Development Council
SRDE	Signals Research and Development Establishment (*of* MOS)
SREB	Southern Regional Educational Board (U.S.A.)
SREPB	Société Royale d'Économie Politique de Belgique
SRESA	Société de Recherche Économique et Sociologique en Agriculture
SRF	Svenska Reklambyra Forbundet
SRF	Svenska Resebyraföreningen
SRF	Sveriges Rationaliseringsförbund
SRF	Sveriges Redareförening
SRF	Syndicat des Riziculteurs de France
SRFB	Société Royale Forestière de Belgique
SRFCAM	Section de Recherches Forestières au Cameroun
SRG	Schweizerische Rundspruch Gesellschaft
SRGS	South Rhodesia Geological Survey
SRHE	Society for Research into Higher Education
SRI	Shri Ram Institute for Industrial Research (India)
SRI	Ski Retailers International (U.S.A.)
SRI	Stanford Research Institute (U.S.A.)
SRI	Sugar Research Institute (Australia)
SRIFIR	Shiram Institute for Industrial Research (India)
SRIS	Safety Research Information Service (U.S.A.)
SRIT	Section d'Études et Fabrications des Télécommunications
SRL	Science Reference Library (British Library)
SRL	Sveriges Radioleverantörer
SRL	Vereinigung der Stadt-, Regional- und Landesplaner
SRLR	Societatea Româna de Linguistica Romanica
SRM	International Spiritual Regeneration Movement (U.K.)
SRNA	Shipbuilders and Repairers National Association
SRP	Serengeti Research Project (Tanzania)
SRP	Society for Radiological Protection
SRPO	Science Resources Planning Office (U.S.A.)
SRPTA	Scottish Road Passenger Transport Association
SRR	Società Retorumantscha
SRR	Sveriges Radiohandlares Riksförbund
SRRC	Scottish Research Reactor Centre
SRRL	Southern Regional Research Laboratory (U.S.A.)
SRS	Service de la Recherche Sociologique (Switzerland)
SRS	Soil Research Station (New Zealand)
SRS	Svenska Revisoramfundet
SRSA	Scientific Research Society of America
SRTI	Société de Recherches Techniques et Industrielles

SRTPA	Syndicat des Redacteurs Techniques de la Presse Agricole	**SSFA**	Stainless Steel Fabricators' Association of Great Britain
SRU	Scottish Rugby Union	**SSFC**	Société Suisse des Fabriques de Cartonnages
SRUBLUK	Society for the Reinvigoration of Unremunerative Branch Lines in the United Kingdom	**SSFF**	Skogbrukets of Skogindustrienes Forsknings-forening
SRV	Schweizerischer Reklame-Verband	**SSFF**	Solid Smokeless Fuels Federation
SRZB	Société Royale Zoologique de Belgique	**SSFODF**	Syndicat des Spécialistes Français en Orthopédie Dento-Faciale
SS	Department of Social Sciences (UNESCO)	**SSG**	Schweizerische Sprachwissenschaftliche Gesellschaft
SS	Sveriges Slakteriförbund (Sweden)		
SSA	Forskningsstiftelsen Skogsarbeten	**SSGA**	Société Suisse de Géographie Appliquée
SSA	Seismological Society of America	**SSH**	Société Suisse des Hôteliers
SSA	Social Security Administration	**SSHA**	Social Science History Association (U.S.A.)
SSA	Società Svizzera degli Albergatori	**SSHA**	Société Scientifique d'Hygiène Alimentaire
SSA	Société Suisse Amerikanisten-Gesellschaft	**SSHB**	Society for the Study of Human Biology
SSA	Society of Scottish Artists	**SSHM**	Scottish Society for the History of Medicine
SSA	Svenska Sockerfabriks Aktiebolaget	**SSHMSN**	Société Suisse d'Histoire de la Médecine et des Sciences Naturelles
SSAFA	Soldiers' Sailors' and Airmen's Families Association	**SSHRC**	Social Sciences and Humanities Research Council (Canada)
SSAE	Société Suisse d'Anthropologie et d'Ethnologie	**SSI**	Service Social International
SSAO	Société Shell de l'Afrique Occidentale	**SSI**	Smart Set International (U.S.A.)
SSC	Société Suisse de Chimie	**SSI**	Stichting Sprenger Instituut
SSC	Société Suisse des Cuisiniers	**SSIA**	Scottish Society for Industrial Archaeology
SSCC	Société Suisse de Chimie Clinique	**SSIC**	Social Science Information Center (U.S.A.)
SSE	Société Suisse des Écrivains	**SSIC**	Società Svizzera degli Impresari-Costruttori
SSE	Société Suisse des Entrepreneurs	**SSIC**	Société Suisse des Industries Chimiques
SSE	Société Suisse d'Ethnologie	**SSIDA**	Steel Sheet Information and Development Association
SSEA	Société Suisse des Exploitants d'Autotaxis et de Voitures de Remise	**SSIE**	Smithsonian Science Information Exchange Inc. (USA)
SSEC	Secondary School Examinations Council		
SSEC	Social Science Education Consortium (U.S.A.)	**SSIF**	Sveriges Skogsindustriförbund
		SSIGE	Société Suisse de l'Industrie du Gaz et des Eaux
SSEC	Société Sucrière d'Études et de Construction, Tirlemont (Belgium)	**SSIL**	Société Suisse d'Industrie Laitière
SSEF	Sveriges Städentreprenörers Förbund	**SSIMF**	Società Svizzera dei Insegnanti di Matematica e Fisica
SSEPC	Société Sénégalaise d'Engrais et de Produits Chimiques	**SSIP**	Sozialwissenschaftlicher Studienkreis f. Internationale Probleme
SSF	Società Svizzera di Farmacia		
SSF	Stiftelsen Svensk Skeppsforskning	**SSISI**	Statistical and Social Inquiry Society of Ireland
SSF	Svensk Sjuksköterskeförening		
SSF	Svenska Slöjdföreningen	**SSIV**	Schweizerischer Spenglermeister- und In-stallateurverband
SSF	Svenska Stämpelfabrikantföreningen	**SSJ**	Savez Sindikata Jugoslavije
SSF	Sveriges Stenindustri Förbund	**SSL**	Suomen Sairaanhoitajaliitto
SSF	Sveriges Stuvareförbund	**SSL**	Société Suisse de Linguistique

SSL	Société Suisse des Liquoristes	**SSR**	Sveriges Radiohandlares Rijksförbund
SSL	Suomen Sanomalehtimiesten Liitto	**SSR**	Sveriges Skogsägareföreningars Riksförbund
SSLF	Sveriges Livsmedelshandlareförbund	**SSR**	Sveriges Skorstensfejaremästares Riksförbund
SSM	Societatea de Stiinte Matematice din RSR		
SSMA	Scottish Steel Makers' Association	**SSR**	Sveriges Snickeriföretageres Riksförbund
SSMAF	Société Suisse des Mensurations et Améliorations Foncières	**SSRA**	Scottish Seaweed Research Association
		SSRA	Scottish Squash Rackets Association
SSMC	Société Suisse des Maîtres Charpentiers	**SSRA**	Secteur Soudanais des Recherches Agronomiques
SSMD	Société Suisse des Maîtres de Dessin		
SSMG	Société Suisse des Maîtres de Gymnastique	**SSRB**	Soil Survey Research Board (*of* ARC)
SSMI	Société Suisse des Maîtres Imprimeurs	**SSRC**	Social Science Research Council (Philippines, U.K., U.S.A. etc)
SSMLL	Society for the Study of Mediaeval Languages and Literature		
		SSRCC	Social Science Research Council of Canada
SSMUTA	Sheet and Strip Metal Users' Technical Association	**SSRD**	Social Science Research and Development Corporation (U.S.A.)
SSN	Sociedad Silvícola Nacional (Cuba)	**SSRG**	Schweizerische Studiengesellschaft f. Rationellen Guterumschlag
SSN	Société Suisse de Numismatique		
SSNTA	Scottish Seed and Nursery Trade Association	**SSRI**	Social Science Research Institute (Hawaii)
SSO	Société Suisse d'Odonto-Stomatologie	**SSRS**	Society for Social Responsibility in Science (U.S.A.)
SSO	Société Suisse d'Oncologie		
SSOL	Suomen Silmäoptikkojen Liitto	**SSRT**	Société Sénégalaise de Réalisation Touristique
SSOME	Société Suisse d'Optique et de Microscopie Électronique	**SSS**	Société Suisse de Spéléologie
		SSS	Suomen Säätöteknillinen Seura
SSOMV	Schweizerischer Schuhmacher- und Orthopädieschuhmachermeister-Verband	**SSS**	Svenska Spannmalsföreningarnas Samorganisation
SSP	Schweizerische Gesellschaft für Psychologie	**SSSA**	Soil Science Society of America
SSP	Société Suisse de Philosophie	**SSSF**	Sodra Sveriges Skogagares Forbund
SSP	Société Suisse de Physique	**SSSH**	Société Suisse des Sciences Humaines
SSP	Société Suisse de Psychiatrie	**SSSI**	Soil Science Society of Ireland
SSPES	Société Suisse des Professeurs de l'Enseignement Secondaire	**SSSP**	Society for the Study of Social Problems (U.S.A.)
SSPH	Société Suisse de Pharmacie	**SSSWP**	Seismological Society of the South-West Pacific (New Zealand)
SSPL	Société Suisse des Patrons Lithographes		
SSPM	Société Suisse de Pédagogie Musicale	**SSTA**	Secondary School Teachers Association of Malta
SSPMP	Société Suisse des Professeurs de Mathématique et de Physique		
		SSTEF	Svenska Sagverks-och Trävaruexport-föreningen
SSPP	Scandinavian Society for Plant Physiology (Denmark)	**SSTL**	Suomen Sähkötukkuliikkeiden Liitto
SSPP	Society for the Study of Physiological Patterns	**SSTS**	Scandinavian Student Travel Service
		SSV	Schweizerischer Sachversicherungsverband
SSPR	Société Suisse de Public Relations	**SSV**	Schweizerischer Samenhändlerverband
SSPT	Société Sénégalaise des Phosphates de Thiès	**SSV**	Schweizerischer Schriftstellerverband
SSPWB	Scottish Society for the Protection of Wild Birds	**SSV**	Schweizerischer Spiegelglasverband
SSR	Société Suisse de Radiodiffusion	**SSV**	Schweizerischer Städteverband

SSVC	Società Svizzera dei Viaggiatori di Commercio
SSVC	Société Suisse des Voyageurs de Commerce
SSWEG	Stainless Steel Wire Experiment Group
SSZ	Société Suisse de Zoologie
SSZ	Society of Systematic Zoologists (U.S.A.)
ST	Société Théosophique (India)
ST	Svensk Trycheriföreningen
STA	Science and Technology Agency (Japan)
STA	Sociedad de Tecnicos de Automoción
STA	Société de Travail Aérien (Algeria)
STAA	Student Travel Association of Asia (Japan)
STACA	Servicio Tecnico Agricola Colombian Americano
STACO	Society of Telecommunications Administrative and Controlling Officers
STACRES	Standing Committee on Research and Statistics (FAO)
STAN	Servicio Técnico Agrícola de Nicaragua
STANAV-FORCHAN	NATO Standing Naval Force Channel
STANAV-FORLANT	NATO Standing Naval Force Atlantic
STAREC	Société Technique d'Application et de Recherche Électronique
STAS	Oficiul de Stat pentru Standarde (Roumania)
STATEC	Service Central de la Statistique et des Études Économiques (Luxembourg)
STAUK	Seed Trade Association of the United Kingdom
STAV	Stiftelsen for Administrativ Vidareutbildning
STB	Société Togolaise de Boissons
STC	Scandinavian Trade Centre
STC	SHAPE Technical Centre
STC	Stowarzyszenie Techników Cukrowników
STC	Sveriges Trä- och Byggvaruhandlares Centralförbund
STCAN	Service Technique des Constructions et Armes Navales
STCAU	Service Technique Central d'Aménagement et d'Urbanisme
STCI	Société de Transports de la Côte-d'Ivoire
STDV	Schweizerischer Textildetaillisten-Verband
STE	Société Togolaise d'Entreposage
STEC	Société Technique d'Entreprises Chimiques
STEC	Storage and Transport of Explosives Committee (India)
STECI	Société de Travaux d'Équipement de la Côte-d'Ivoire
STEE	Société Tchadienne d'Énergie Électrique
STEEP	Société Tchadienne d'Entreposage de Produits Pétroliers
STEF	Société des Transports et Entrepôts Frigorifiques
STEFO	Sveriges Tecknares och Formgivares Riksförbund
STEG	Société Tchadienne d'Entreprises Générales
STEL	Société de Traitements Électrolytiques et Électrothermiques
STELO	Stuenta Tutmonda Esperantista Ligo
STEMI	Société de Transports et Manutentions Industriels
STEN	Société Togolaise des Engrais
STEPC	Société Tropicale d'Engrais et de Produits Chimiques (Ivory Coast)
STET	Società Torinese Esercizi Telefonici
STF	Scandinavian Transport Workers Federation
STF	Skipsteknisk Forbund
STF	Svenska Taxiförbundet
STF	Svenska Teknologföreningen
STF	Sveriges Takpappfabrikanters Förening
STF	Sveriges Tandläkarförbund
STFI	Svenska Träforskingsinstitutet
STG	Schiffbautechnische Gesellschaft
STG	Suomen Taidegraafikot
STI	Société Tchadienne d'Investissement
STI	Statens Teknologiske Institutt
StiBoka	Stichting voor Bodemkartering
STICA	Servicio Técnico Inter-Americano de Cooperación Agrícola (Costa Rica)
STICPA	Société Tchadienne Industrielle et Commerciale de Produits Animale
STICUSA	Nederlandse Stichting voor Culturele Samenwerking met Suriname en de Nederlandse Antillen
STID	Scientific and Technical Information Division (of NASA) (U.S.A.)
STIL	Service Technique Interprofessionnel du Lait
STIMA	Société de Techniques Industrielles et Maritimes (Ivory Coast)
STIP	Science Teaching Improvement Programme (U.S.A.)

STIPEL	Società Telefonica Interregionale Piemontese e Lombarda	**STTIF**	Sveriges Tval-och Tvättmedelsindustriförening
STISEC	Scientific and Technological Information Services Enquiry Committee (New Zealand)	**STU**	Swedish Board for Technical Development
		STUC	Scottish Trade Union Congress
STKL	Suomen Turkiseläinten Kasvattajain Liitto	**STULM**	Stichting tot Uitvoering van Landbouw-Maatregelen
STL	Standard Telecommunication Laboratories		
STL	Suomen Teatteriliitto	**STUMOKA**	Studiekring voor Moderne Kantoortechniek
STL	Suomen Teollisuusliitto	**STUVA**	Studiengesellschaft für Interidische Verkehrarlagen
STL	Suomen Tukkukauppiaiden Liitto		
STLV	Schweizerischer Turnlehrer-Verein	**STV**	Schweizerischer Technischer Verband
STM	International Group of Scientific, Technical and Medical Publishers	**STV**	Schweizerischer Tonkünstlerverein
		STV	Schweizerischer Transport-Versicherungs-Verein
STMHV	Schweizerischer Taxi- und Mietwagenhalter-Verband	**SUACI**	Service d'Utilité Agricole a Compétence Interdépartementale (*of* CA)
STMSA	Scottish Timber Merchants and Sawmillers Association	**SUAD**	Services d'Utilité Agricole de Développement
STOCA	Société Togolaise de Crédit Automobile	**SUBAW**	Scottish Union of Bakers and Allied Workers
STONIC	Section Tunisienne de l'Office National Inter-professionnel des Céréales	**SUCEE**	Socialist Union of Central-Eastern Europe
		SUCESU	Sociedade de Usairios de Computadores Electronicos e Equipmentos Subsidiaros (Brazil)
STOP	Stowarzyszenie Techniczne Odlewników Polskich		
STOPA	Stichting Overname Pootaardappelen	**SUCO**	Service Universitaire Canadian Outre-Mer
STP	Société Togolaise des Plastiques	**SUCOMA**	Sugar Corporation of Malawi
STPC	Society of Technical Presentation and Communication	**SUCRP**	Société des Usines Chimiques Rhône-Poulenc
STPCM	Secrétariat Technique Permanent de la Conférence des Ministres de l'Éducation Nationale des États d'Expression Française d'Afrique et de Madagascar	**SUCSE**	Scottish Universities Council on Studies in Education
		SUDAM	Superintendência do Desenvolvimento da Amazônia (Brazil)
STPTC	Standard Tar Products Testing Committee	**SUDAP**	Superintendência da Agricultura e Produção (Brazil)
STR	Sveriges Tandteknikers Riksförbund		
STR	Sveriges Trafikbilägares Rijksorganisation	**SUDENE**	Superintendency for the Development of the North-East (Brazil)
STR	Sveriges Trähusfabrikers Riksförbund		
STRA	Scottish Textile Research Association	**SUDEPE**	Superintendency for Fisheries Development (Brazil)
STRC	Scientific, Technical and Research Commission (*of* OAU)	**SÜDV**	Schweizerischer Übersetzer- und Dolmetscherverband
STRI	Smithsonian Tropical Research Institute (Panama)	**SUE**	Sociedad Uruguaya de Entomología
STRI	Sports Turf Research Institute	**SUERF**	Société Universitaire Européenne de Recherches Financières
STRIM	Société Technique de Recherches Industrielles et Mécanique	**SUF**	Svenska Uppfinnareföreningen
STS	Société Textile Sénégalaise	**SUFJ**	Savez Udruzenja Folklorista Jugoslavije
STS	Suomen Teknillinen Seura	**SUHAF**	Sveriges Universitets- och Högskoleamanuensers Förbund
STSA	Science Technology and Society Association		
STSN	Società Toscana di Scienze Naturali	**SUKOL**	Suomen Kieltenopettajien Liitto
STTA	Service Technique des Télécommunications de l'Air	**SUM**	Servicio Universitario Mundial
		SUMOC	Superintendência da Moeda e Crédito (Brazil)

SUN	Spiritual Unity of Nations
SUN	Symbols, Units and Nomenclature Commission (*of* IUPAP)
SUNAB	National Superintendency of Supplies (Brazil)
SUNFED	Special United Nations Fund for Economic Development
SUNKLO	Suomen Näytelmäkirjailijaliitto
SUPARCO	Space and Upper Atmosphere Research Committee (Pakistan)
SUPLAN	Sub-secretaria de planejamento e orçamento Ministério da Agricultura Brazil
SURDD	Southern Utilisation Research and Development Division (U.S.A.)
SUS	Schweizerischer Verband des Seilbahnunternehmungen
SUS	Suomalais- Ugrilainen Seura
SUSTA	Scottish Union of Students Travel Association
SUT	Society for Underwater Technology
SUVA	Schweizerische Unfallversicherungs-Anstalt
SV	Stifterverband für die Deutsche Wissenschaft
SVA	Schweizerische Vereinigung für Altertumswissenschaft
SVA	Schweizerische Vereinigung für Atomenergie
SVAE	Schweizerischer Verband der Auto-Elektriker
SVAJ	Schweizerische Vereinigung der Agrarjournalisten
SVAM	Società per lo Sviluppo Agricolo del Mezzogiorno
SVB	Schweizerischer Verband für Berufsberatung
SVB	Speleologisch Verband van België
SVB	Stichting voor Bodemkartering
SVBF	Schweizerischer Verband für das Arbeitsstudium
SVBF	Schweizerischer Verband von Betriebsfachleuten
SVBL	Schweizerische Vereinigung zur Förderung der Betriebsberatung in der Landwirtschaft
SVC	Svejsecentralen
SVC	Svenska Västkustfiskarnas Centralförbund
SVCC	Schweizerischer Verein der Chemiker-Coloristen
SVCF	Schweizerischer Verband der Cementwarenfabrikanten
SVCN	Sociedad Venezolana de Ciencias Naturales
SVCP	Société Voltaïque des Cuirs et Peaux
SVCS	Sociedad Venezolana de la Ciencia del Suelo
SVD	Schweizerischer Drogisten-Verband
SVD	Schweizerische Vereinigung f. Dokumentation
SVDK	Schweizerischer Verband Diplomierter Krankenschwestern und Krankenpfleger
SVDP	Schweizerischer Verband Diplomierter Psychiatrieschwestern und -pfleger
SVE	Sociedad Venezolana de Entomologia
SVE	Society for Visual Education (U.S.A.)
SVEABUND	Svenska Väg-och Vattenbyggarnas Arbetsgivareförbund
SVEB	Schweizerische Vereinigung für Erwachsenenbildung
SVEFF	Sveriges Färgfabrikanters Förening
SVERTEX	Sveriges Textilindustriförbund
SVF	Schweizerischer Vereinigung von Färbereifachleuten
SVF	Stiftelsen för Värmeteknisk Forskning
SVF	Svenska Vägföreningen
SVF	Sveriges Varvsindustriförening
SVF	Sveriges Veterinärförbund
SVFJ	Schweizerische Vereinigung Freier Berufsjournalisten
SVG	Schweizerischer Fachverband für Gemeinschaftsverpflegung
SVG	Sociedad Venezolana de Geólogos
SVGP	Schweizerischer Verband der Gartenbauproduzenten
SVGU	Schweizerischer Verband der Glas- und Gebäudereinigungs- Unternehmer
SVGW	Schweizerischer Verein von Gas- und Wasserfachmännern
SVHA	Société Vaudoise d'Histoire et d'Archéologie
SVI	Vereinigung Schweizerisches Verpackungsinstitut
SVIA	Schweizerischer Verband der Ingenieur-Agronomen
SVIA	Sociedad Venezolana de Ingenieros Agrónomos
SVIAL	Schweizerischer Verband der Ingenieur-Agronomen und der Lebensmittel-ingenieure
SVIF	Sociedad Venezolana de Ingenieros Forestales
SVIH	Sociedad Venezolana de Ingeniería Hidráulica
SVIL	Schweizerische Vereinigung für Innerkolonisation und Industrielle Landwirtschaft

SVIM	Sociedad Venezolana de Minas y Metalurgicos
SVIMU	Associazione Italiana per lo Sviluppo della Ricerca nelle Macchine Utensili
SVIQ	Sociedad Venezolana de Ingenieros Químicos
SVIS	Schweizerischer Verband der Innendekorateure und Sattler
SVIT	Schweizerischer Verband der Immobilien-Treuhänder
SVK	Schweizerische Vereinigung für Kleintiermedizin
SVKAZ	Schweizerischer Verband Kantonal Approbrierter Zahnärzte
SVKS	Schweizerischer Verband der Klavierbauer und- Stimmer
SVKW	Schweizerischer Verband der Konfektions- und Wäsche-Industrie
SVL	Suomen Vähittäiskauppiasliitto
SVL	Suomen Valokuvaajain Liitto
SVLFC	Schweizerische Vereinigung der Lack- und Farbenchemiker
SVLP	St Vincent Labour Party
SVLR	Schweizerische Vereinigung für Luft- und Raumrecht
SVLT	Schweizerischer Verband für Landtechnik
SVM	Service Volontaire Mennonite (Germany)
SVM	Stichting voor Melkhygiëne
SVMF	Sveriges Vertygsmaskinaffärers Förening
SVMIU	Associazione Italiana per lo Svipuppo della Ricerca nelle Macchine Utensili
SVMT	Schweizerischer Verband für die Materialprüfungen der Technik
SVMY	Suomen Vene- ja Mootoriyhdistys
SVNLF	South Vietnamese National Liberation Front
SVO	Stiching voor Oliehoudende Zaden
SVO	Stichting voor Veevoedings Onderzoek
SVOB	Schweizerischer Verband der Orthopädisten und Bandagisten
SVOI	Staatsveeartsenijkundig Onderzoekings Instituut
SVOR	Schweizerische Vereinigung f. Operations Research
SVOT	Schweizer Verband der Orthopädie-Techniker
SVP	Schweizerischer Pedicure-Verband
SVP	Schweizerischer Verband Staatlich Anerkannter Physiotherapeuten
SVP	Sociedad Venezolana de Planificación
SVP	Stichting v. Plantenveredeling
SVP	Studiekring voor Plantenveredeling
SVPC	Société Voltaïque de Peintures
SVPC	Syndicat des Entreprises de Vente par Correspondance
SVPG	Schweizerisches Verband für Photo-Handel und -Gewerbe
SVPP	Schweizerisches Vereinigung für Para-psychologie
SVQ	Sociedad Venezolana de Quimica
SVR	Svenska Väg- och Vattenbyggares Riksförbund
SVS	Schweizerische Verein für Schweisstechnik
SVS	Société des Vétérinaires Suisses
SVS	Society of Visiting Scientists
SVSF	Sveriges Vetenskapliga Specialbiblioteks Förening
SVSN	Société Vaudoise des Sciences Naturelles (Switzerland)
SVST	Slovenská Vysoká Skola Technická
SVT	Schweizerische Vereinigung für Tierzucht
SVTM	Schweizerischer Verband der Tapezierermeister-Dekorateure und des Möbel-Detailhandels
SVVIA	Schweizerischer Verband der Versicherungs-Inspektoren und- Agenten
SVVK	Schweizerischer Verein für Vermessungs-wesen und Kulturtechnik
SVW	Schweizerischer Verband für Waldwirtschaft
SVWG	Schweizerische Verkehrswissenschaftliche Gesellschaft
SVWS	Schweizerischer Verband der Wirkerei- und Strickerei-Industrie
SVWT	Schweizerische Vereinigung für Weltraum-technik
SVY	Suomen Voimalaitosyhdistys
SVZ	Sociedád Veterinaria de Zootecnia de Espâna
SW	Samaritans Worldwide
SW	Seaboard World Airlines (U.S.A.)
SWA	Sozialwissenschaftliche Arbeitsgemeinschaft (Austria)
SWAFAC	South West Atlantic Fisheries Advisory Commission
SWANU	South West Africa National Union
SWANUF	South West Africa National United Front

SWAPO	South West Africa People's Organisation
SWB	Schweizerischer Werkbund
SWCRD	Soil and Water Conservation Research Division (U.S.A.)
SWDA	Scottish Wholesaler Druggists Association
SWEB	South Western Electricity Board
SWF	Svenska Wallboardföreningen
SWG	Society of Woman Geographers (U.S.A)
SWGA	Société des Exportateurs de Vins Suisse
SWGB	South Western Gas Board
SWHV	Schweizerischer Weinhändlerverband
SWIE	South Wales Institute of Engineers
SWIF	Svenska Wellpappindustriföreningen
SWIFT	Society for Worldwide Interbank Financial Telecommunications (Belgium)
SWIG	South-Western Irrigated Cotton Growers Association (U.S.A.)
SWIRECO	Southwestern Institute of Radio Engineers Conference and Electronics Show (U.S.A.)
SWKI	Schweizerischer Verein von Wärme- und Klimaingenieuren
SWLA	South Western Library Association (U.S.A.)
SWMA	Steel Wool Manufacturers' Association
SWO	Surinaamse Werknemers -Organisatie
SWOA	Scottish Woodland Owners Association
SWOV	Stichting Wetenschappelijk Onderzoek Veerkeersveiligheid
SWP	Stowarzyszenie Wtokienników Polskich
SWRLS	South Western Regional Library System
SWS	Sozialwissenschaftliche Studiengesellschaft
SWSF	Society for a World Service Federation (U.S.A.)
SWT	Scottish Wild Life Trust
SWTE	Society for Water Treatment and Examination (*now* IWES)
SWTEA	Scottish Woollen Trade Employers Association
SWTMA	Scottish Woollen Trade Mark Association
SWV	Schweizerischer Wasserwirtschaftsverband
SWV	Schweizerischer Webeblatt-Fabrikanten-Verband
SWV	Schweizerischer Wirtverein
SWWJ	Society of Women Writers and Journalists
SYBAZ	Syndicat du Bâtiment du Zaire
SYBELIC	Syndicat Belge d'Études et de Recherches Électroniques

SYBESCO	Syndicat Belge des Scories Thomas
SYBESI	Syndicat Belge pour le Séparation Isotopique
SYBETRA	Syndicat Belge d'Entreprises à l'Étranger
SYCEF	Syndicat des Constructeurs Français de Condensateurs
SYCOMEL	Syndicat National des Constructeurs Français de Matériel et Équipement Laitier Industriel
SYCOM-IMPEX	Syndicat des Commerçants Importateurs et Exportateurs (Central African Republique, Congo)
SYCOMOM	Syndicat des Constructeurs Belge de Machines-outils pour le Travail des Métaux
SYCOSER	Syndicat des Constructeurs et Constructeurs-Installateurs
SYFAC	Syndicat des Fabricants d'Aliments Composés pour l'Alimentation Animale
SYFACAR	Chambre des Fabricants des Négociants en Papiers d'Emballage et Cartons en Gros (Belgium)
SYFAMER	Syndicat National des Fabricants de Moteurs, Matériel Naval, Équipements de Bords et Remorques pour la Navigation
SYFODIA	Syndicat des Fabricants d'Outillage et de Produits à Base de Diamant
SYGECAM	Syndicat Général des Constructeurs d'Équipements pour la Chimie, les Matières Plastiques et le Caoutchouc, l'Alimentation et pour Industries Diverses
SYLAITEX	Syndicat du Commerce d'Exportation de Produits Laitiers et Avicoles
SYMA	Syndicat des Constructeurs de Machines pour l'Alimentation
SYMACAP	Syndicat des Constructeurs Français de Matériel pour le Caoutchouc et les Matières Plastiques
SYMACO	Syndicat des Constructeurs de Matériels de Conditionnement
SYMCA	Syndicat des Constructeurs de Machines et Appareils pour les Industries Chimiques et Industries de l'Alimentation
SYMCAP	Syndicat des Constructeurs Français de Matériel pour le Caoutchouc et les Matières Plastiques
SYMCO	Syndicat des Constructeurs de Matériels de Conditionnment
SYMAFO	Chambre Syndicale des Fabricants et Négociants en Machines et Fournitures pour Chassures (Belgium)

SYMATEX Syndicat des Constructeurs Belges de Machines Textiles

SYNABATI Syndicat National des Fabricants et Constructeurs de Bâtiments Industrialisés

SYNACID Syndicat National des Commerçants et Industriels Africains du Dahomey

SYNACO-BOIS Syndicat National des Constructeurs Français de Machines à Bois et Outillages Annexes

SYNAC-OMEX Syndicat National du Commerce Extérieur des Céréales

SYNAD Syndicat National des Producteurs de Béton Prêt à l'Emploi

SYNAFA Syndicat National des Fabricants d'Aliments pour les Animaux

SYNAGRA Syndicat National du Commerce des Céréales et Légumes Secs (Belgium)

SYNAME Syndicat National de la Mesure Électrique et Électronique

SYNAP Syndicat National des Attachés de Presse Professionnels

SYNAQ Syndicat National d'Amélioration de la Qualité pour les Coopératives Agricoles

SYNCOBEL Syndicale Kamer der Fabrikanten van Confectie van België

SYNCOPAC Syndicat National des Coopératives Préparant des Aliments Composés

SYNCOPEX Syndicat National des Coopératives Agricoles Exportatrices

SYNCOT Syndicat National du Commerce des Tourteaux sons et Issues

SYNDI-CALU Syndicat National des Fabricants d'Articles de Ménage en Aluminium

SYNDICH-AMPAGNE Chambre Syndicale des Agents Accrédités par les Maisons de Champagne de Marque

SYNDICUIR Syndicat Général des Cuirs et Dérivés (Belgium)

SYNDI-SCOTCH Chambre Syndicale des Agents Accrédités de Scotch Whisky (Belgium)

SYNDUS-TREF Syndicat des Industries de l'Afrique Équatoriale

SYNDUST-RICAM Syndicat des Industriels du Cameroun

SYNECOT Syndicat National des Fabricants d'Engrenages et Constructeurs d'Organes de Transmission

SYNERCAU Syndicat National d'Études de la Recherche pour les Coopératives Agricoles et Leurs Unions

SYNERVA Syndicat National d'Études de Revision et de Vulgarisation des Coopératives Agricoles

SYNPA Syndicat National des Producteurs d'Additifs Alimentaires

SYNTEC Chambre Syndicale des Sociétés d'Études et de Conseils

SYNTECAM Société Camerounaise pour la Fabrication des Tissus Synthétiques

SYPAL Syndicat National des Fabrikants et Fabricants Distributeurs de Palettes en Bois

SYR Sveriges Yrkesfruktodlares Riksförbund

SYSNA Société des Systemes d'Aides à la Navigation

SZBV Schweizer und Zürcher Buchhändlervereine

SZF Schweizerische Vereinigung für Zukunftforschung

SZG Schweizerische Zoologische Gesellschaft

SZH Schweizerische Zentrale für Handelsförderung

SZN Stazione Zoologica di Napoli

SZOT Magyar Szakszervezetek Országos Tanácsa

SZS Schweizerische Zentralstelle für Stahlbau

SZU Sociedad Zoológica del Uruguay

SZV Schweizerischer Saatzuchtverband

SZV Schweizerischer Zahntechnikerverband

SZV Schweizerischer Zeitungsverlegerverband

SZV Schweizerischer Zimmermeisterverband

SZVT Szervezési és Vezetési Tudományos Társaság

SZZV Schweizerischer Ziegenzuchtverband

T

TAA Technical Assistance Administration (UNDP)

TAA Trans-Australia Airlines

TAAF Terres Australes et Antarctiques Françaises

TAALS The American Association of Language Specialists

TAAS Telegraphic Agency of the Union of Socialist Soviet Republics

TAB Technical Assistance Board (UNDP)

TABA Timber Agents and Brokers Association of the United Kingdom

TABA	Société Agricole Tchadienne de Collecte et de Traitement des Tabacs	**TAT**	Transportes Aéreos de Timor
TABA	Transportes Aeras de Buenos Aires (Argentina)	**TAUN**	Technical Assistance of the United Nations
		TAVR	Territorial Army Voluntary Reserve
TAC	Tanganyika Agricultural Corporation (*now* NDC)	**TAZARA**	Tanzania-Zambia Railway Authority
		TBD	Türk Belediyecilik Dernegi
TAC	Technical Assistance Committee (UNO)	**TBE**	European Federation of Tile and Brick Manufacturers
TAC	Technische Advies Commissie van het NaCaBrouw	**TBMA**	Timber Building Manufacturers Association
TAC	Tobacco Advisory Committee	**TBPA**	Tenpin Bowling Proprieters Association
TAC	Trades Advisory Council	**TBTAK**	Scientific and Technical Research Council of Turkey
TACAC	Trans Atlantic Committee on Agricultural Change	**TC**	Taraxacum Club (Netherlands)
TAM	Technical Association of Malaysia	**TC**	Trusteeship Council (UNO)
TAMCO	Société de Transports. d'Automobile et de Mécanique au Congo	**TCA**	Tanners' Council of America
		TCA	Technical Co-operation Administration (U.S.A.)
TAMDA	Timber and Allied Materials Development Association (South Africa)	**TCA**	Trans-Canada Air Lines
TAMTU	Tanganyika Machinery Testing Unit	**TCC**	Transport and Communications Commission (UNO)
TAN	Transportes Aeros Nacionales (Honduras)		
TANCA	Technical Assistance to Non-Commonwealth Countries	**TCCA**	Textile Colour Card Association of the United States
TANU	Tanganyika African National Union	**TCCA**	Textile and Clothing Contractors Association
TAO	Technical Assistance Operations (UNDP)	**TCCB**	Test and County Cricket Board
TAP	Technical Advisory Panel (UNO)	**TCD**	Trinity College, Dublin
TAP	Technical Assistance Program (U.S.A.)	**TCEA**	Training Centre for Experimental Aerodynamics (Belgium)
TAP	Svenska Tapetfabrikanternas Förening		
TAP	Transportes Aéroes Portugueses	**TCGA**	Tanzania Coffee Growers Association
TAPA	Tanzania African Parents Association	**TChP**	Towarzystwo Chirurgów Polskich
TAPI	Tropical Agricultural Products Institute (Thailand)	**TCI**	Tall Clubs International (U.S.A.)
		TCI	Traffic Clubs International (U.S.A.)
TAROM	Transporturi Aeriene Rômine (Roumania)	**TCJCC**	Trades Councils' Joint Consultative Committee
TAPPI	Technical Association of the Pulp and Paper Association (U.S.A.)	**TCL**	Tanganyika Creameries Ltd
TARC	Tropical Agriculture Research Center (Japan)	**TCM**	Trustul Centrolelor Mecanice (Roumania)
		TCMA	Textile Commission Manufacturers Association
TARI	Taiwan Agricultural Research Institute (China)	**TCMA**	Telephone Cable Makers' Association
TAROM	Transporturi Aeriene Române	**TCMA**	Tufted Carpet Manufactures Association
TARS	Technical Assistance Recruitment Service (of UN)	**TCN**	Tekniska Nomenklaturcentralens
		TCO	Tjänstemannens Centralorganisation
TARS	Tropical African Regional Section (*of* IOBS)	**TCOT**	Transit Congo-Oubanqui-Tchad
TAS	Tennessee Academy of Science (U.S.A.)	**TCPA**	Town and Country Planning Association
TASMA	Tanganyika Sisal Marketing Board	**TCRC**	Tobacco Chemists Research Conference (U.S.A.)
TASPO	Thalacker Allgemeine Samen- u. Pflanzen Offerte	**TCS**	Technology Club of Syracuse (U.S.A.)

TCZB	Turkiye Cumhuriyeti Ziraat Bankasi (Turkey)
TDA	Textile Distributors' Association
TDA	Timber Development Association (U.S.A.)
TDB	Trade and Development Board (UNCTAD)
TDC	Tanganyika Development Corporation (*now* NDC)
TDC	Trade Development Council (Hong Kong)
TDFL	Tanzania Development Finance Company Ltd
TDK	Türk Dil Kurumu
TEA	Trans-European Airways (Belgium)
TEAM	The European-Atlantic Movement (U.K.)
TEAR	The Evangelical Alliance Relief Fund
TEBROC	Tehran Book Processing Centre (Iran)
TECA	Trans-Europa Compañia de Aviación SA
TECHNI-CHAR	Association pour le Perfectionnement Technique des Appareils Domestiques d'Utilisation du Charbon (Belgium)
TECHNI-COL	Association pour le Perfectionnement Technique des Appareils Domestiques d'Utilisation des Combustibles Liquides (Belgium)
TECHNO-CEAN	Société Technique pour l'Océanologie
TECHNO-NET	Asia Network for Industrial Technology Information and Extension (Singapore)
TECNI-BERIA	Asociación Española Empresas de Estudios y Proyectos
TECO	Tanzania Extract Company
TECO	Technical Cooperation Committee (*of* OECD)
TECTRO	Société de Techniques Tropicales
TED	International Association for Training, Education and Development
TEDCO	Thames Estuary Development Company
TEEM	Trans-Europ Express Marchandises
TEFO	Svenska Textilforskningsinstitutet
TEGEWA	Verband der Textilhilfsmittel-, Lederhilfsmittel-, Gerbstoff- und Waschrohstoff-Industrie
TEGMA	Terminal Elevator Grain Merchants Association (U.S.A.)
TEJA	Tutmonda Esperantista Jurnalistica Asocio
TEJO	Tutmonda Esperantista Junulara Organizo
TEK	Turkiya Elektrik Kurumu (Turkey)
TELI	Technisch-Literarische-Gesellschaft
TELIMALI	Télécommunications Internationales du Mali
TEMA	Telecommunication Engineering and Manufacturing Association
TEPCO	Tokyo Electric Power Company (Japan)
TEPCORN	Tobacco Export Promotion Council of Rhodesia and Nyasaland
TERG	Technical Education Resources Group
TESCO	Hungary's International Scientific Co-operation Bureau
TESOL	Teachers of English to Speakers of other Languages (U.S.A.)
TESSILABIT	Associazione Italiana degli Industriali dell' Abbigliamento
TESSIL-VARI	Associazione Nazionale Produttori Tessili Vari e del Cappello
TETOC	Technical Education and Training Organisation for Overseas Countries (*of* ODM)
TEVA	Tutmonda Esperanta Vegetara Asocio
TEXTEL	Trinidad and Tobago Telecommunications Company
TF	Textile Foundation (U.S.A.)
TFA	Taiwan Forest Administration (China)
TFA	Tanganyika Farmers Association
TFA	Texas Forestry Association (U.S.A.)
TFCRI	Tropical Fish Culture Research Institute (Malaysia)
TFDL	Technisch Fysische Dienst voor de Landbouw
TFF	Association of Technical Physicists (Sweden)
TFF	Tekniska Fysikers Förening
TFIF	Tekniska Foreningen i Finland
TFK	Transportforskningskommissionen
TFRI	Taiwan Fisheries Research Institute
TFRI	Transnational Family Research Institute (U.S.A.)
TFTDWU	Taiwan Federation of Textile and Dyeing Workers Union
TG	Theosophische Gesellschaft (India)
TGF	Tekstilgrossistenes Forbund
TGS	Texas Geographic Society (U.S.A.)
TGSA	Tropical Grassland Society of Australia
TGV	Schweizerischer Transportgewerbeverband
TGWU	Transport and General Workers' Union
THD	Türk Hemsireler Dernegi
THE	Technical Help for Exporters

THL	Teollisuudenharjoittajain Liitto	**TISK**	Türkiye Isveren Sendikalari Konfederasyonu
THRA	Tasmanian Historial Research Association	**TIT**	Tutományos Ismeretter-jesztö Társulat
THY	Turun Historiallinen Yhdistys	**TITUS**	Textile Information Treatment Users Service
THYT	Teollisuudenharjoittajain Yleinen Ryhmä	**TKD**	Türk Kütüphaneciler Dernegi
TI	Textile Institute	**TKI**	Tejgazdasági Kiserleti Intézet
TIA	Trans-International Airlines (U.S.A.)	**TKP**	Türkiye Komünist Partisi
TIAC	Travel Industry Association of Canada	**TL**	Trehusindustriens Landsforbund
TIB	Tanzania Investment Bank	**TL**	Trelasthandlernes Landsforbund
TIB	Transivoirienne des Bois	**TL**	Turistvognmoendenes Landsorganisation
TIBE	Société Travaux Isolation, Bâtiment Étanchéité	**TLA**	Thai Library Association
		TLP	Tasmania Labour Party
TIBEA	Société Travaux Isolation-Bâtiment Étanchéité-Afrique (Congo)	**TLDPC**	Tidal Land Development Planning Commission of the Executive Yuan (Taiwan)
TIBO	Träindustrins Branschorganisation	**TLIF**	Traktor- og Landbruksmaskin-Importörenes Forening
TIC	Tantalum Producers International Study Centre (Belgium)	**TLJW**	Stichting Technisch Landbouw Jongerenwerk
TIC	Timber Industries Confederation		
TICCI	Technical Information Centre for Chemical Industry, Bombay (India)	**TLS**	Tekniska Litteratursällskapet
		TM	Tiedotusmiehet
TICER	Temporary International Council for Educational Reconstruction	**TMA**	Trans-Mediterranean Airways (Lebanon)
		TMA	Trinidad Manufacturers Association
TIDA	Travel and Industrial Development Association	**TMA**	Turkish Management Association
TIDU	Technical Information and Documents Unit of D.S.I.R.	**TMAC**	Transmeridian Air Cargo Ltd
		TMAMA	Textile Machinery and Accessory Manufacturers Association
TIE	The Institute of Ecology (U.S.A.)	**TMB**	Tobacco Marketing Board (Rhodesia)
TiFC	Towarzystwo im Fryderyka Chopina	**TMHiZK**	Towarzystwo Milosyników Historii i Zabytków Krakowa
TIFR	Tata Institute of Fundamental Research, Bombay (India)		
TIG	Télécommunications Internationales Gabonaises	**TMIS**	Technical Meetings Information Service (U.S.A.)
TIIAL	The International Institute of Applied Linguistics	**TMJP**	Towarzystwo Milosyników Jezyka Polskiego
		TMMB	Türkiye Muhendisler ve Mimarlar Birligi
TIMCON	Timber Packaging and Pallet Confederation	**TMMOB**	Turk Mühendis ve Mimar Odalari Birligi
TIMS	Institute of Management Sciences (U.S.A.)	**TMO**	Toprak Mahsulleri Offisi
TINFO	Tieteellisen Informoinnin Neuvosto	**TMSA**	Telephone Manufacturers of South Africa
TINTUC	Trinidad and Tobago National Trade Union Congress	**TMSE**	Tobacco Manufacturers Standing Committee
		TMTE	Textilpari Müszaki és Tudományos Egyesület
TIP	Towarzystwo Internistów Polskich	**TNDC**	Thai National Documentation Centre
TIP	Turkish Labour Party	**TNI**	Transnational Institute (Netherlands)
TIPER	Tanzanian and Italian Petroleum Refining Co.	**TNIMA**	Tubman National Institute of Medical Arts (Liberia)
TIRC	Tobacco Industry Research Committee	**TNIP**	Transkei National Independence Party (South Africa)
TIRU	Traitement Industriel des Résidus Urbains		
TIS	Technical Information Service (Canada)	**TNO**	Organisatie v. Toegepast Natuurweten-schappelijk Onderzoek
TISCO	Tata Iron and Steel Company (India)		

TNOIK	Towarzystwo Naukowe Organizacji i Kierownictwa
TNT	Towarzystwo Naukowe w Toruniu
TOAG	Research Division on Agriculture and Forestry (Turkey)
TOBETON	Société Togolaise de Béton
TØF	Transportøkomisk Forening
TOFINSO	Société Toulousaine Financière et Industrielle du Sud-Ouest
TOGO-FRUIT	Société Nationale de Développement de la Culture Fruitière (Togo)
TOGOGAZ	Société Togolaise des Gaz Industriels
TOK	Türk Otomatik Kontrol Kurumu
TOPRAKSU	General Directorate of Spil Conservation and Irrigation (Turkey)
TOT	Telephone Organization of Thailand
TOURAC	Association Internationale Auxiliaire des Touring Clubs de l'Afrique Centrale
TOURIS-MAD	Société Hôtelière et Touristique de Madagascar
TPC	Taiwan Pineapple Association
TPDC	Tanzania Petroleum Development Corporation
TpF	Talepoedagogisk Forening
TPG	Trésorier Payeur Général
TPI	Tropical Products Institute (*formerly* CPL)
TPI	Royal Town Planning Institute
TPIS	Tropical Pesticides Information Service
TPL	Tanganyika Packers Ltd
TPLA	Turkish People's Liberation Army
TPRC	Thermophysical Properties Research Center (U.S.A.)
TPRC	Tropical Pesticides Research Unit, Porton Down
TPRI	Tropical Pesticides Research Institute
TPTPA	Table Poultry and Turkey Producers Association
TR	Teatrarnas Riksförbund
TR	Textilgrossisternas Riksförbund
TRA	Thoroughbred Racing Association (U.S.A.)
TRACO-GRAS	Association Belge des Transformateurs de Corps Gras Industriels
TRADA	Timber Research and Development Association
TRAFO	Transportmateriel-Foreningen
TRAMA-GRAS	Transformateurs de Matières Grasses
TRAMET	Groupement du Négoce International et du Traitement Industriel des Déchets Métalliques
TRANSCAP	Société Eurafricaine de Voyages, de Transit et de Camionnage Portuaire
TRANS-COFER	*see* INTERCONTAINER
TRANS-EQUAT	Société de Transit Equatorial (Cameroons)
TRANS-FRIA	Société de Transport et d'Approvisionnement de l'Aluminium (Africa)
TRBR	Tobacco Research Board of Rhodesia
TRC	Technical Reports Centre, Ministry of Technology
TRC	Trade Relations Council of the United States (U.S.A.)
TRDB	Tanzanian Rural Development Bank
TRANSUD	Société des Transports du Sud de Madagascar
TRC	Textile Research Council
TRDC	Tana River Development Company (Kenya)
TRE	Telecommunications Research Establishment
TRI	Tape Respondents International
TRI	Tea Research Institute (Sri Lanka)
TRI	Textile Research Institute (U.S.A.)
TRI	Tin Research Institute
TRI	Tribal Research Institute and Training Centre (India)
TRICOMAD	Société Industrielle des Tricotages de Madagascar
TRIDO	Table Ronde Internationale pour le Développement de l'Orientation
TRIEA	Tea Research Institute of East Africa
TRITURAF	Société Ivoirienne pour la Trituration de Graines Oléagineuses et le Raffinage d'Huiles Végétales
TRI-UN	Department of Trusteeship and Information from Non-Self-Governing Territories
TRRB	Trade Relations Research Bureau
TRRL	Transport and Road Research Laboratory
TRS	Tobacco Research Station (New Zealand)
TRS	Tree-Ring Society (U.S.A.)
TRT	Télécommunications Radioélectriques et Téléphoniques

TRT	Turkish Radio
TRTA	Traders Road Transport Association (*now* FTA)
TS	Theosophical Society (India)
TSBA	Trustee Savings Banks Association
TSC	Taiwan Sugar Corporation
TSE	Turk Standardlari Enstitusu
TSF	Compagnie Générale de Télégraphie Sans Fil
TSGA	Tanzania Sisal Growers Association
TSIA	Trading Stamp Institute of America
TSK	Tradgardsnäringens Standardiseringskommitté
TSKB	Turkiye Sinai Kalinma Bankasi, A.S.
TSPC	Tropical Stored Products Centre (*of* MOD)
TSSA	Transport Salaried Staffs' Association
TTA	Tanzania Tea Authority
TTA	Teknillisten Tieteiden Akademia
TTC	Tanzania Tourist Corporation
TTC	Transit Transports Camerounais
TTDC	Thana Training and Development Centre (Pakistan)
TTEC	Thai Technical and Economic Cooperation Office
TTF	Timber Trade Federation
TTFTU	Trinidad and Tobago Federation of Trade Unions
TTGA	Tanganyika Tea Growers' Association
TTIC	Taiwan Tea Improvement Committee
TTIS	Translation and Technical Information Services
TTK	Türk Tarih Kurumu
T & TPC	Trinidad and Tobago Management Development and Productivity Centre
TTWMB	Taiwan Tobacco and Wine Monopoly Bureau
TU	Svenska Tidningsutgivareföreningen
TUA	Tractor Users Association
TUAC	Trade Union Advisory Committee (*of* OECD)
TUBE	Union of Bookmakers Employees
TUBITAK	Turkish Science and Technology Research Council
TUC	Trades' Union Congress
TUCSA	Trades Union Council of South Africa
TUF	Tokyo University of Fisheries
TUFEC	Thailand-Unesco Fundamental Education Centre
TUFMAC	Uganda Fish Marketing Corporation
TUIAFPW	Trade Unions International of Agricultural, Forestry and Plantation Workers (Italy) (*formerly* TUIAFW)
TUIWC	Trade Union International of Workers in Commerce
TUP	Towarzystwo Urbanistów Polskich
TUPLAN	Textil Uruguaya de Productos de Lana
TÜRDOK	Turkish Scientific and Technical Documentation Centre
TURKIS	Turkish Trade Union Confederation
TURSAB	Türkiye Seyahat Acentalari Birligi
TUSM	World Federation of Ukrainian Student Organizations of Michnowsky
TÜV	Vereinigung der Technischen Uberwachungs-Vereine (Austria)
TVA	Tennessee Valley Authority (U.S.A.)
TVS	Technical Valuation Society (U.S.A.)
TVA	Teglverkenes Arbeidsgiver-forening
TVK	Toimihenkilö- ja Virkamiesjärjestöjen
TVVL	Nederlandse Technische Vereniging voor Verwarming en Luchtbehandeling
TWA	Trans-World Airlines (U.S.A.)
TWARO	Textile Workers Asian Regional Organisation
TWAU	Transvaal Women's Agricultural Union (South Africa)
TWICO	Tanzania Wood Industries Corporation
TWIF	Tug of War International Federation
TWIU	Tobacco Workers International Union (U.S.A.)
TWK	Polskie Towarzystwo Walki z Kalectwem
TWL	Nederlandse Technische Vereniging voor Verwarming en Luchtbehandeling
TWOZ	Commissie voor Toegepast Wetenschappelijk Onderzoek in de Zeevisserij (Belgium)
TWP	Committee for the Provision of Technical Assistance for the Welfare of the People (Thailand)
TWU	Tobacco Workers Union
TWUA	Transport Workers' Union of America
TZF	Technische Zentralstelle der Deutschen Forstwirtschaft

U

UA	Ulkomaankaupan Agenttiliitto
UA	Underwater Association
UAA	United Arab Airlines (Egypt)
UAA	Union des Avocats Arabes
UAAEE	United Arab Atomic Energy Establishment
UAB	Universities Appointments Board
UABS	Union of American Biological Societies
UAC	Unified Agricultural Co-operatives (Czechoslovakia)
UAC	United Africa Company
UACB	Union des Agglomérés di Ciment de Belgique
UACEE	Union de l'Artisanat de la CEE
UACO	United Africa Company
UACP	Union des Agences et Conseils en Publicité
UACS	Union des Associations Cinématographiques Suisses
UADI	Union Argentina de Asociaciones de Ingenieros
UADW	Universal Alliance of Diamond Workers
UAE	United Arab Emirates
UAEE	Union des Associations Européennes d'Etudiants
UAFA	Union Arabe du Fer et de l'Acier
UAG	Österreichische Arbeitsgemeinschaft für Ur- und Frühgeschichte
UAI	Union Académique Internationale
UAI	Union des Associations Internationales
UAI	Union Astronomique Internationale
UAIA	Union des Agences d'Information Africaines
UAJ	Udruzenje Anesteziologa Jugoslavije
UAL	United Air Lines, Inc. (U.S.A.)
UAM	Union Africaine et Malgache (now OCAM)
UAMBD	Union Africaine et Malgache des Banques pour le Développement
UAMCE	Union Africaine et Malgache de Coopération Économique (now OCAM)
UAMD	Union Africaine et Malgache de Défense

UAMPT	Union Africaine et Malgache des Postes et Télécommunications
UANA	Union of African News Agencies
UANA	Union de Natation Amateur des Amériques
UANC	United African National Council
UAOS	Ulster Agricultural Organisation Society (N. Ireland)
UAP	Union des Assurances de Paris
UAP	United Australia Party
UAP	Uniunea Artistilor Plastici din Republica Socialista România
UAPA	Union des Agences de Presse Africaines
UAPF	Union des Amateurs à la Pêche de France
UAPT	United Association for the Protection of Trade
UAR	Union Asiatique de Radiodiffusion (Japan)
UAR	United Arab Republic
UARAEE	United Arab Republic Atomic Energy Establishment
UARN	Union des Chambres Artisanales du Bâtiment
UAS	Union of African States
UAS	University of Agricultural Sciences (India)
UASIF	Union des Associations Scientifiques et Industrielles Françaises
UASTM	Universidad Agraria de la Selva de Tingo María (Peru)
UAT	Union Aéromaritime de Transport
UATI	Union des Associations Techniques Internationales
UAU	Universities Athletic Union
UAW	International Union of United Automobile, Aerospace and Agricultural Workers of America
UBA	Union Belge des Annonceurs
UBA	Union Belge de l'Automatique
UBA	Union of Burma Airways Board
UBAC	Union Bancaire en Afrique Centrale
UBAF	Union des Banques Arabes et Françaises
UBAH	Union des Branches Annexes de l'Horlogerie (Switzerland)
UBBS	University of Basutoland, Bechuanaland Protectorate and Swaziland
UBESA	Unión de Bananeros Ecuatorianos
UBF	Universal Buddhist Fellowship (U.S.A.)
UBFTG	Union Belge des Fabricants de Tôles Galvanisées

UBG	Union Belge des Géomètres-Experts Immobiliers	**UCCI**	Union Carbide Côte d'Ivoire
UBIC	Union Belge des Installateurs en Chauffage Central, Ventilation et Tuyauteries	**UCCMA**	Union des Caisses Centrales de la Mutualité Agricole
UBM	Union Balkanique Mathématique	**UCD**	University College, Dublin
UBOS	Union de la Bijouterie et de l'Orfèverie Suisse	**UCDEC**	Union Chrétienne Démocrate d'Europe Centrale
UBS	Union Belge des Sérigraphes	**UCECOM**	Uniunea Centrala a Cooperativelor Mestesugaresti (Roumania)
UBS	United Bible Societies	**UCEI**	Union des Centres d'Échanges Internationaux
UBT	Union Togolaise de Banque		
UBZI	Unie der Belgische Zuivelindustrie	**UCEPA**	Unidad de Comercio Exterior de Productos Agrícolas (Venezuela)
UCAAF	Union des Coopératives Agricoles et Alimentaires Françaises	**UCERC**	Union des Centres d'Études Rurales par Correspondance
UCADIA	Unión Centroamericana de Asociaciones de Ingenieros y Arquitectos (Costa Rico)	**UCF**	Union des Chausseurs Français
UCAE	Universities Council for Adult Education	**UCF**	Union Culturelle Française
UCAEYL	L'Union des Coopératives d'Élevage de l'Yonne-Loiret	**UCF**	Unions Chrétiennes Féminines
		UCF	United Cooperative Farmers, Inc. (U.S.A.)
UCAL	Union des Cinémathèques d'Amérique Latine (Mexico)	**UCF**	United Counties Farmers Ltd
UCAM	Universidad Nacional Autonoma de México	**UCFAF**	Union Centrale des Syndicats Agricoles de France
UCAP	United Coconut Association of the Philippines	**UCG**	University College, Galway
UCAR	University Corporation for Atmospheric Research (U.S.A.)	**UCH**	Union Nationale des Chambres Syndicates d'Entreprises en Génie Climatique
UCASEF	Union Nationale des Coopératives Agricoles de Semences Fourragères	**UCI**	Ufficio Centrale Italiano
UCAT	Universidad Católica de Chile	**UCI**	Union Canine Internationale
UCATT	Union of Construction, Allied Trades and Technicians	**UCI**	Union Cycliste Internationale
		UCIC	Unione Costruttori Impianti di Combustione
UCB	Uitvoer-Contrôle-Bureau	**UCICIS**	Union Costruttori Italiani Carrelli Industriali Semoventi ed Affini
UCB	Union Camerounaise des Brasseries		
UCB	Union Chimique Belge	**UCID**	Union Cristiana Imprenditori Dirigenti
UCB	Union Nationale des Coopératives Agricoles de Transformation de Betterave	**UCIDT**	União Cátolica de Industriais e Dirigentes de Trabalho
UCC	Union Corporative de la Couleur	**UCIFA**	Union Centralschweizerischer Cigarrenfabrikanten
UCC	Union de la Critique du Cinéma (Belgium)	**UCIIM**	Unione Cattolica Italiana Insegnanti Medi
UCC	University College, Cork	**UCIL**	Uranium Corporation of India
UCCA	Union Cotonnière Centrafricaine	**UCIMU**	Unione Costruttori Italiani Macchine Utensili
UCCA	Universities Central Council on Admissions	**UCINA**	Unione Nazionale Cantieri e Industrie Nautiche ed Affini
UCCAO	Union des Coopératives de Café Arabica de l'Ouest (Cameroons)	**UCIP**	Union Catholique Internationale de la Presse
UCCD	Union des Producteurs Belges de Chaux, Calcaires, Dolomies et Produits Connexes	**UCIP**	Union del Comercio la Industria y la Produccion (Argentina)
UCCE	Union des Capitales de la Communauté Européenne	**UCIS**	University Center for International Studies (U.S.A.)
UCCEGA	Union des Chambres de Commerce et Établissements Gestionnaires d'Aéroports	**UCISP**	Unione Costruttori Italiani Strumenti per Pesare

UCISS	Union Catholique Internationale de Service Social
UCJG	Alliance Universelle des Unions Chrétiennes de Jeunes Gens
UCL	Uganda Creameries Ltd
UCLA	University of California at Los Angeles (U.S.A.)
UCLAP	Union Catholique Latino-Américaine de la Presse (Uruguay)
UCLG	United Cement, Lime and Gypsum Workers International Union (U.S.A.)
UCMA	Unione Costruttori Macchine Alimentari
UCML	University of California Microwave Laboratory
UCMTF	Union des Constructeurs de Matériel Textile de France
UCNW	University College of North Wales, Bangor
UCOA	Union Chimique de l'Ouest-Africain (Guinée)
UCODIMA	Union Commerciale de Diffusion de Marques
UCODIS	Union pour le Commerce et la Distribution des Grandes Marques
UCOMA	Union des Commerçants Maliens
UCOMAF	Union Commerciale Africaine
UCOMESA	Unione Costruttori Macchine Edili, Stradali, Minerarie ed Affini
UCONAL	Unión de Cooperativas Nacionales (Colombia)
UCOPS	Universal Coterie of Pipe Smokers (U.S.A.)
UCOWR	Universities Council on Water Resources Research (U.S.A.)
UCPL	Union Centrale des Producteurs de Lait (Switzerland)
UCPTE	Union pour la Coordination de la Production et du Transport de l'Électricité (Austria)
UCR	Union Corporative des Résineux (France) (*now* UIR)
UCRIFER	Unione Costruttori e Riparatori Ferrotramviari
UCRL	University of California Radiation Laboratory
UCRM	University College of Rhodesia and Malawi
UCS	Union des Centrales Suisses d'Électricité
UCS	Union des Coopératives de Semences
UCSMB	Union des Carrières et Scieries de Marbres de Belgique
UCSWM	University College of South Wales and Monmouthshire
UCTA	United Commercial Travellers' Association of Great Britain and Ireland
UCTAT	Union des Co-opératives de Travaux Agricoles de Tunisie
UCTF	Union Culturelle et Technique de Langue Française
UCW	University College of Wales
UCWI	University College of the West Indies
UCWRE	Under-Water Counter-Measures and Weapons Research Establishment
UDA	Union des Annonceurs
UDACI	Unione Donne di Azione Cattolica Italiana
UDAO	Union Douanière de l'Afrique de l'Ouest (*now* CEAO)
UDC	Uganda Development Corporation
UDCEC	Unión Democrática Cristiana de Europa Central
UDD	Association pour l'Utilisation et la Diffusion de la Documentation
UDDIA	Union Démocratique de Défense des Intérêts Africains
UDE	Union Douanière Équatoriale (*formerly* UDEAC)
UDEAC	Union Douanière et Économique de l'Afrique Centrale (*now* UDE)
UDEAO	Union Douanière des États de l'Afrique de l'Ouest
UDEC	Union d'Entreprises de Constructions (Ivory Coast)
UDECEVER	Union Européenne des Détaillants en Céramique et Verrerie
UDEL	Union des Éditeurs de Littérature
UDELAV	Union pour la Défense de la Lavande et du Lavandin
UDEMAG	Union de Empleados Profesionales del Ministerio de Agricultura y Ganadería (Costa Rica)
UDENAMO	Uniao Democratica Nacional de Moçambique
UDEPAC	Union Professionnelle des Détaillants en Porcelain et Cristaux (Belgium)
UDI	Unione Donne Italiane
UDIAS	Union des Constructeurs et Importateurs d'Appareils Scientifiques, Médicaux et de Contrôle (Belgium)
UDP	Institut International pour l'Unification du Droit Privé

UDPO	Union pour la Défense des Peuples Opprimés (L'Internationale de la Liberté)
UDPT	Democratic Union of Togolese Peoples
UDS	Union des Dentistes et Stomatologistes de Belgique
UDSSD	Union des Sociétés Suisses de Développement
UDT	United Dominions Trust
UDUAL	Unión de Universidades de América Latina
UEA	Union Européenne de l'Ameublement
UEA	Universala Esperanto-Asocio (Netherlands)
UEAC	Union des États de l'Afrique Centrale (Chad)
UEBL	Union Économique Belgo-Luxembourgeoise
UEC	Union Européenne de la Carrosserie
UEC	Union Européenne des Experts Comptables Économiques et Financiers
UECB	Union Européenne des Commerces du Bétail
UECBV	Union Européenne du Commerce et de la Viande
UECGPT	Union Européenne du Commerce de Gros des Pommes de Terre
UECL	Union Européenne des Constructeurs de Logements
UECP	Union Européenne des Coupeurs de Poil pour Chapellerie et Filature
UECR	Union des Ententes et Communautés Rurales
UEDC	Union Européenne Démocrate Chrétienne
UEDE	Union Économique et Douanière Européenne
UEEB	Union des Exploitations Electriques de Belgique
UEF	Union Européenne des Fédéralistes
UEF	Union Européenne Feminine
UEFA	Union of European Football Associations
UEIC	United East India Company
UEIG	Union des Expéditeurs Internationaux de Grèce
UEJ	Union Européenne de Judo
UEJDC	Union Européenne des Jeunes Démocrates-Chrétiens
UEM	Union Évangélique Mondiale
UEMO	Union Européenne des Médecins Omnipracticiens
UEMOA	Union des Exposants de Machines et d'Outillage Agricoles
UEMS	Union Européenne de Médecine Sociale
UEMS	Union Européenne des Médecins Spécialistes
UENCPB	Union Européenne des Négociants en Cuirs et Peaux Bruts
UENDC	Union Européenne des Négociants Détaillants en Combustibles
UEO	Union de l'Europe Occidentale
UEPMD	Union Européenne des Practiciens en Médecine Dentaire
UEP	Union Européenne de Paiements
UEP	Union Européenne de Pédopsychiatres
UEPGH	Union Européenne des Portiers des Grandes Hôtels
UEPMD	Union Européenne de Practiciens de Médecine Dentaire
UER	Union Européenne de Radiodiffusion
UERP	Union Européenne de Relations Publiques
UESC	Union Européenne du Spectacle Cinématographique
UESEM	Union Européenne des Sources d'Eaux Minérales Naturelles du Marché Commun
UET	United Engineering Trustees (U.S.A.)
UETA	Union Européenne des Travailleurs Aveugles
UETDC	Union Européenne des Travailleurs Démocrates Chrétiens
UETU	Union Européenne des Théâtres Universitaires
UEVH	Union Européenne des Vélodromes d'Hiver
UEVP	Union Européenne des Vétérinaires Practiciens
UFAC	Union des Fabricants d'Aliments Composés
UFACD	Union des Fabricants d'Appareils de Cuisine et de Chauffage Domestique
UFALEX	Union des Exportateurs Français de Demi-produits en Aluminium
UFARAL	Union des Fournisseurs des Artisans de l'Alimentation (Belgium)
UFAW	Universities Federation for Animal Welfare
UFC	Université Fédérale du Cameroun
UFC	Union Fédérale de la Consommation
UFCAC	Union Féderale des Coopératives Agricoles de Céréales (France)
UFCE	Union Fédéraliste des Communautés Ethniques Européennes
UFDC	Union des Femmes Démocrates Chrétiennes (Switzerland)
UFE	Union des Groupements Professionnels de l'Industrie de la Féculerie de Pommes de Terre (of CEE)

UFEA	Union Française pour l'Équipement Agricole
UFEMAT	Union des Fédérations Nationales des Négociants en Matériaux de Construction de la CEE
UFER	Mouvement International pour l'Union Fraternelle entre les Races et les Peuples
UFESAS	Universal Fair and Exhibition Service Ltd
UFI	Union des Foires Internationales
UFIDEC	Union pour l'Information et la Défense des Consommateurs (Belgium)
UFIE	Union Française des Industries Exportatrices de Biens de Consommation
UFIPTE	Union Franco-Ibérique pour la Production et le Transport de l'Électricité
UFINAL	Union Financière pour le Développement des Industries Alimentaires
UFK	Universala Framasona Ligo (Belgium)
UFL	Underraettelser fraan Flygledningen
UFLC	Union Internationale des Femmes Libérales Chrétiennes
UFMAT	Union des Fédérations Nationales des Négociants en Matériaux de Construction de la CEE
UFNE	Unión Federalista de Nacionalidades Europeas
UFOD	Union Française des Organismes de Documentation
UFORA	Unidentified Flying Objects Research Association
UFP	United Federal Party (N. Rhodesia)
UFRGS	Federal University of Rio Grande do Sul (Brazil)
UFRO	International Union of Forest Research Organisations
UFSAM	Union Féminine Suisse des Arts et Métiers
UPSEB	Uttar Pradesh State Electricity Board (India)
UFSS	Union Française des Syndicats Séricicoles
UFT	Union des Fédérations de Transports
UFTA	United Farmers Trading Agency
UFTAA	Universal Federation of Travel Agents Associations
UFTF	Union des Fabricants de Tapis de France
UFU	Ulster Farmers' Union
UFUCH	Unión de Federaciones Universitarias de Chile
UFWOG	United Farm Workers' Organising Committee (U.S.A.)
UGAASA	Union General de Autores y Artistas de El Salvador
UGAF	Union des Groupements Apicoles Français
UGAL	Union des Groupements d'Achat de l'Alimentation (Belgium)
UGAT	Union Générale de l'Agriculture Tunisienne
UGB	Union Gabonaise de Banque
UGBF	Union Générale de la Brasserie Française
UGC	University Grants Committee
UGCAA	Union Générale des Coopératives Agricoles d'Approvisionnement
UGCAC	Union Générale des Coopératives Agricoles de Céréales
UGCAF	Union Générale des Coopératives Agricoles Françaises
UGEA	Union des Groupements pour l'Exploitation Agricole
UGEAN	Union Générale des Étudiants d'Afrique Noire
UGEAO	Union Générale des Étudiants d'Afrique Occidentale
UGECO-BAM	Union Générale des Coopératives Bananières du Mungo (Cameroons)
UGEL	Union der Genossenschaftlichen Einkaufs-organisationen für Lebensmittel
UGET	General Union of Tunisian Students
UGEXPO	Union Générale des Exposants de Matériels et de Produits Destinés à Agriculture (Belgium)
UGGI	Union Géodésique et Géophysique Internationale
UGI	Union Géographique Internationale
UGIMA	Unione Generale degli Industriali Apuani del Marmo ed Affini
UGLE	United Grand Lodge of England
UGOCM	Unión General de Obreros y Campesinos de México
UGOPJ	Union Générale des Oeuvres Pastorales pour la Jeunesse (Italy)
UGSA	Union Générale Sidérurgie Arabe
UGSBF	Union Générale des Syndicats de la Brasserie Française
UGSD	Union Générale des Syndicats du Dahomey
UGSR	Uniunea Generala a Sindicatelor din România
UGT	Unión General de Trabajadores de España
UGTAN	General Union of Workers of Black Africa

UGTD	Union Générale des Travailleurs du Dahomey		**UICB**	Union Internationale des Centres du Bâtiment
UGTM	Union Générale des Travailleurs du Maroc		**UICC**	Union Internationale Contre le Cancer
UGTT	Union Générale Tunisienne du Travail		**UICCIA**	Unione Italiana della Camere di Commercio, Industria, Artigianto, Agricoltura
UHA	Union der Hörgeräte-Akustiker			
UI	Utrikespolitiska Institutet		**UICF**	Unión Internacional de Ciencias Fisiológicas
UIA	Union Immobilière Africaine (Congo)		**UICG**	Unión Internacional de Ciencias Geológicas
UIA	Unión Industrial Argentina		**UICGF**	Union Internationale du Commerce en Gros de la Fleur
UIA	Union of International Associations			
UIA	Union Internationale contre l'Alcoolisme		**UICM**	Union Internationale Catholique des Classes Moyennes
UIA	Union Internationale Antiraciste		**UICN**	Union Internationale pour la Conservation de la Nature et de ses Ressources
UIA	Union Internationale des Architectes			
UIA	Union Internationale des Avocats		**UICPA**	Union Internationale de Chimie Pure et Appliquée
UIA	Union International des Travailleurs des Industries Alimentaires et Connexes		**UICR**	Union Internationale des Chauffeurs Routières
UIAA	Union Internationale des Associations d'Alpinisme		**UICT**	Union Internationale Contre la Tuberculose
			UID	Union Internationale Dendrologie
UIAA	Union Internationale des Associations d'Annonceurs		**UIDA**	Union Internationale des Arts
UIACM	Union Internationale des Automobile-Clubs Médicaux		**UIDA**	Union Internationale des Organisations de Détaillants de la Branche Alimentaire
UIAE	Union Industrielle pour l'Afrique		**UIDIS**	Union International de Interlinguistic Service
UIAF	Union Interprofessionnelle de l'Angora Français		**UIDJZ**	Union Internationale des Directeurs de Jardins Zoologiques
UIAMS	Union Internationale d'Action Morale et Sociale		**UIE**	Union Internationale des Éditeurs
UIAOM	Union Internationale des Agriculteurs de l'Outre-Mer		**UIE**	Union Internationale d'Électrothermie
			UIE	Union Internationale des Étudiants
UIAP	Union Intérféderale des Armateurs à la Pêche		**UIEA**	Union Internationale de Étudiants en Architecture
UIAPME	Union Internationale de l'Artisanat et des Petites et Moyennes Entreprises		**UIEC**	Union Industrielle et d'Entreprise pour le Congo
UIAT	Union Internationale des Syndicats des Industries de l'Alimentation et du Tabac		**UIEC**	Union Internationale de l'Exploitation Cinématographique
UIB	Union Internationale de la Boulangerie		**UIEIS**	Union Internationale pour l'Étude des Insectes Sociaux
UIB	Syndikale Unie der Immobiliënberoepen van België		**UIEO**	Union of International Engineering Organisations
UIBPA	Union Internationale de Biophysique Pure et Appliquée		**UIEOA**	Union Internationale des Études Orientales et Asiatiques
UIBWM	Trade Unions International of Workers of Building, Wood and Building Materials In-dustries		**UIEP**	Union Internationale des Entrepreneurs de Peinture
UIC	Union of Independent Companies		**UIES**	Union Internationale pour l'Éducation Sanitaire
UIC	Union Industrielle pour le Cameroun			
UIC	Union des Industries Chimiques		**UIES**	Union Internationale d'Études Sociales
UIC	Union Internationale des Chemins de Fer		**UIESP**	Union International pour l'Étude Scientifique de la Population
UICB	Unión Internacional de Ciencias Biológicas			

UIFA	Union Internationale des Femmes Architectes
UIFI	Union Internationale des Fabricants d'Imperméables
UIFL	Union Internationale des Fédérations de Détaillants en Produits Laitiers
UIFPA	Union Internacional de Fisica Pura y Aplicada
UIG	Union Industrielle de Gruyère
UIGA	Unione Italiana Giornalisti dell' Automobile
UIGDC	Unione Internazionale del Giovani Democratici Cristiani
UIGG	Unión Internacional de Geodesia y Geofisica
UIH	Union Internationale Hôtelière
UIHE	Union Internationale de l'Humanisme et de l'Éthique
UIHL	Union Internationale de l'Humanisme Laïque
UIHMSU	Union Internationale d'Hygiéne et de Médecine Scolaires et Universitaries
UIHP	Union Internationale de l'Hospitalisation
UIHPS	Union Internationale d'Histoire et de Philosophie des Sciences
UIHS	Union Internationale d'Histoire des Sciences
UIIG	Union Internationale de l'Industrie du Gaz
UIIRF	Union Internationale des Instituts de Recherches Forestières
UIJA	Union Internationale des Journalistes Agricoles
UIJDC	Union Internationale de Jeunesse Démocrate Chrétienne
UIJPLF	Union Internationales des Journalistes et de la Presse de Langue Française
UIJS	Union Internationale de la Jeunesse Socialiste
UIL	Unione Italiana del Lavoro
UILB	Union de l'Industrie Laitière Belge
UILC	Unione Italiana Lavoratori Chimici
UILE	Union Internationale pour la Liberté d'Enseignement
UILI	Union Internationale des Laboratoires Indépendants
UILJ	Union International pour les Livres de Jeunesse
UILM	Unione Italiana Lavoratori Metallurgici
UIM	Union Internationale des Métis
UIM	Union Internationale Motonautique
UIM	Union of International Motorboating
UIMC	Union Internationale des Services Médicaux des Chemins de Fer
UIMJ	Union Internationale des Maisons de Jeunesse (*of* FIJC)
UIMM	Union des Industries Métallurgiques et Minières
UIMP	Union Internationale pour la Protection de la Moralité Publique
UIMTCT	Union Internationale de Médecine Thermale et de Climatothalassothérapie
UIMV	Union Internationale des Miroitiers-Vitriers
UINF	Union Internationale de la Navigation Fluviale
UINL	Union Internationale du Notariat Latin
UIO	Union Internationale des Orientalistes
UIOA	International Union for Applied Ornithology
UIOF	Union Internationale des Organismes Familiaux
UIOIF	Unión Internacional de Organizaciones de Investigación Forestal
UION	Uniunea Internationala pentru Ocrotirea Naturii (Roumania)
UIOOPT	Union Internationale des Organisations Officielles de Propagande Touristique
UIOOT	Union Internationale des Organismes Officiels de Tourisme
UIORF	Union Internationale des Organisations de Recherches Forestières
UIP	Union Internationale d'Associations de Propriétaires de Wagons de Particuliers
UIP	Union Internationale de Patinage
UIP	Union Internationale Paysanne
UIP	Union Internationale des Professeurs et Maîtres de Conférences des Universités Techniques et Scientifiques et des Instituts Post-Universitaires de Perfectionnement Technique et Scientifique
UIP	Union Internationale de la Publicitaires
UIP	Union Interparlementaire
UIPC	Union Internationale de la Presse Catholique
UIPC	Unione Italiana per il Progresso della Cultura
UIPCA	Union Internationale de Chimie Pure et Appliquée
UIPCG	Union Internationale de la Pâtisserie, Confiserie, Glacerie
UIPDE	Union Internationale des Producteurs et Distributeurs d'Énergie Électrique

UIPE	Union Internationale de Protection de l'Enfance
UIPFB	Union Internationale de la Propriété Foncière Bâtie.
UIPGH	Union Internationale des Portiers des Grands Hôtels
UIPI	Unión Internacional de Proteccióna la Infancia
UIPM	Union Internationale de Pentathlon Moderne
UIPM	Union Internationale de la Press Médicale
UIPMB	Union Internationale de Pentathlon Moderne et Biathlon
UIPN	Union Internationale pour la Protection de la Nature
UIPPA	Union Internationale de Physique Pure et Appliquée
UIPPI	Union Internationale pour la Protection de la Propriété Industrielle
UIPVT	Union Internationale contre le Péril Vénérien et les Tréponematoses
UIQPA	Unión Internacional de Química Pura y Aplicada
UIR	Union Internationale de Radio-diffusion
UIR	Union Interprofessionnelle des Résineux
UIRD	Union Internationale de la Résistance et de la Déportation
UIS	Union Internationale de Secours
UISA	Union Internationale des Sciences Agronomiques
UISAE	Union Internationale des Sciences Anthropologiques et Ethnologiques
UISB	Union Internationale des Sciences Biologiques
UISE	Union Internationale de Secours aux Enfants
UISG	Union Internationale des Sciences Géologiques
UISG	Union Internationale des Supérieurs Générales
UISLAF	Unione Internationale dei Sindicati dei Lavoratori Agricoli e Forestali
UISM	Union Internationale des Syndicats des Mineurs
UISMM	Union Internationale des Syndicats des Industries Métallurgiques et Mécaniques
UISN	Union Internationale des Sciences de la Nutrition
UISP	Union Internationale des Sciences Physiologiques
UISP	Union Internationale des Sociétés de la Paix
UISPP	Union Internationale des Sciences Préhistoriques et Protohistoriques
UISPTT	Union Internationale Sportive des Postes, des Téléphones et des Télécommunications
UISTABP	Union Internacional de Sindicatos de Trabajadores de la Agricultura, de los Bosques y de las Plantaciones
UISTAFP	Union Internationale des Syndicats des Travailleurs de l'Agriculture, des Forêts et des Plantations
UISTAV	Union Internationale pour la Science, la Technique et les Applications du Vide
UISTC	Union Internationale des Syndicats des Travailleurs du Commerce
UISTICPS	Union Internationale des Syndicats des Travailleurs des Industries Chimiques, du Pétrole et Similaires
UIT	Union Internationale Contre la Tuberculose
UIT	Union Internationale des Télécommunications
UITA	Unión Internacional de Associaciones de Trabajadores de Alimentos y Ramos Afines
UITAM	Union Internationale de Mécanique Théorique et Appliquée
UITBB	Union Internationale des Syndicats des Travailleurs du Bâtiment, du Bois et des Matériaux de Construction
UITP	Union Internationale des Transports Publics
UITU	Union Internationale des Théâtres Universitaires
UIUSD	Union Internationale Universitaire Socialiste et Démocratique
UIV	Union Internationale des Villes et Pouvoirs Locaux
UIVB	Union Interprofessionnelle des Vins du Beaujolais
UJAF	Union de la Jeunesse Agricole de France
UJEF	Union des Journaux d'Entreprise de France
UJNR	United States-Japan Cooperative Program in Natural Resources
UKA	United Kingdom Alliance
UKAC	United Kingdom Automation Council
UKAEA	United Kingdom Atomic Energy Authority
UKAFFP	United Kingdom Association of Frozen Food Producers
UKAMBY	United Kingdom Association of Manufacturers of Bakers Yeast

UKAPE	United Kingdom Association of Professional Engineers	**UKSA**	United Kingdom Sponsoring Authority for the Exchange of Young Agriculturists
UKASA	United Kingdom Agricultural Students Association	**UKSATA**	United Kingdom South African Trade Association
UKASTA	United Kingdom Agricultural Suppliers and Trade Association	**UKSM**	United Kingdom Scientific Mission
UKCA	United Kingdom Coffee Association	**UKSMA**	United Kingdom Sugar Merchants' Association
UKCBDA	United Kingdom Carbon Block Distributors' Association	**UKWAL**	United Kingdom West African Line
UKCCFSR	U.K. Co-ordinating Committee for Food Science and Technology	**UL**	Universal League
		ULA	Uganda Library Association
UKCIS	United Kingdom Chemical Information Service	**ULABEL**	Union Professionelle des Loueurs de Voiteurs sans Chauffeur de Belgique
UKCOSA	United Kingdom Council for Overseas Student Affairs	**ULADE**	Unión Latino American del Embalaje
UKCSBS	United Kingdom Civil Service Benefit Society	**ULAJE**	Unión Latinoamericana de Juventudes Evangélicas
UKCSMA	United Kingdom Cutlery and Silverware Manufacturers Association	**ULAPC**	Union Latino-Américaine de la Presse Catholique
UKCTA	United Commercial Travellers Association of Great Britain and Ireland	**ULAST**	Unión Latino Americana de Sociedades de Tisiologia
UKDA	United Kingdom Dairy Association	**ULC**	Union Luxembourgeoise des Consommateurs
UKF	Unie van Kunstmestfabrieken		
UKFA	United Kingdom Fellmongers Association	**ULC**	United Labour Congress (Nigeria)
UKFFCA	United Kingdom Freight Forwarders Container Association	**ULF**	Universitetslärarförbundet
		ULI	Union pour la Langue Internationale Ido
UKGPA	United Kingdom Glycerine Producers Association	**ULICS**	University of London Institute of Computer Science
UKHS	United Kingdom Hovercraft Society	**ULT**	United Lodge of Theosophists
UKI	Uniono Katolik Idista	**ULTAB**	Brazilian Agricultural Workers Union
UKIAS	United Kingdom Immigrant Advisory Service	**ULU**	Union of Latin American Universities
UKISC	United Kingdom Industrial Space Committee	**UMA**	Ultrasonic Manufacturers Association (U.S.A.)
UKISES	United Kingdom Section of the International Solar Energy Society	**UMA**	Union Marocaine de l'Agriculture
		UMA	Unión de Mujeres Americana
UKJGA	United Kingdom Jute Goods Association	**UMA**	Universal Medical Assistance International Centre
UKMAN-ZRA	United Kingdom Manufacturers and New Zealand Representatives Association		
		UMA	Utenti Motori Agricoli
UKMMA	United Kingdom Metal Mining Association	**UMAA**	Union Mondiale des Anciennes Élèves de l'Assomption
UKOBA	United Kingdom Outboard Boating Association	**UMAEC**	Union Monétaire de l'Afrique Équatoriale et du Cameroun
UKOOA	United Kingdom Offshore Operators Association	**UMAH**	Union Mondiale d'Avancée Humaine
UKOP	United Kingdom Oil Pipelines	**UMAI**	Unión Mexicana de Asociaciones de Ingenieros
UKPA	United Kingdom Pilot's Association		
UKPTF	United Kingdom Provision Trade Federation	**UMARCO**	Union Maritime et Commerciale
UKRA	United Kingdom Reading Association	**UMARCO**	Union Maritime et Commerciale Cameroun
UKRAS	United Kingdom Railway Advisory Service	**UMB**	Union Médicale Balkanique

UMB	Union Mondiale de Billard
UMBC	United Malayan Banking Corporation
UMC	Upper Mantle Committee
UMCA	Unión Monetaria Centroamericana (Salvador)
UMCA	Universities Mission to Central Africa
UMCA	Uraba, Medellin and Central Airways Inc. (Columbia)
UMCC	United Maritime Consultative Council
UMDC	Union Mondiale Démocrate Chrétienne
UME	Unitas Malacologica Europaea
UMEA	Universala Medicina Esperanto Asocio
UMEC	Union Mondiale des Enseignants Catholiques
UMEJ	Union Mondiale des Étudiants Juifs
UMEMPS	Union of Middle East Mediterranean Paediatric Societies
UMFIA	Union Médicale Latine
UMHE	United Ministries in Higher Education (U.S.A.)
UMHP	Union Mondiale des Sociétés d'Histoire Pharmaceutique
UMI	Union Mundial pro Interlingua
UMI	Unione Matematica Italiana
UMIMA	Union Malienne d'Industries Maritimes
UMIMA	Union Mauritanienne d'Industries Maritimes
UMIST	University of Manchester Institute of Science and Technology
UMJL	Union Mondiale pour un Judaïsme Libéral
UMML	Union Médicale de la Méditerranée Latine
UMNO	United Malays' National Organisation
UMNS	Union Mondiale des Nationaux Socialistes
UMOA	Union Monétaire Ouest Africaine
UMOFC	Union Mondiale des Organisations Féminines Catholiques
UMOSBESL	Union Mondiale des Organisations Syndicales sur Base Économique et Sociale Libérale
UMOSEA	Union Mondiale des Organismes pour la Sauvegarde de l'Enfance et de l'Adolescence
UMP	Uganda Meat Packers Ltd
UMP	Upper Mantle Project
UMPB	Union Professionnelle des Maîtres Photograveurs Belges
UMPC	Uganda Milk Processing Company Ltd
UMPF	Union Mondiale de la Presse Féminine

UMPH	Union Mondiale des Sociétés d'Histoire Pharmaceutique
UMS	Union Maraîchère Suisse
UMS	Union des Meuniers Suisses
UMS	Union Suisse des Marchands Forains
UMS	University Mailing Service
UMSN	Union Mondiale de Ski Nautique
UMSR	Universal Movement for Scientific Responsibility
UMT	Union Marocaine du Travail
UMVF	Union Mondiale des Voix Françaises
UMWA	United Mine Workers of America
UN	*See* UNO
UNA	Union Nationale de l'Aviculture et des Productions Rattachées
UNA	Unione Nazionale dell' Avicoltura
UNA	United Nations Association
UNAA	United Nations Association of Australia
UNAAFR	Union Nationale des Associations d'Aides Familiales Rurales
UNACA	Unión Nacional de Astronomia y Ciencias Afines
UNACAFE	Unión Nacional Agrícola de Cafeteros (Mexico)
UNACAP	Union Nationale des Coopératives Apicoles
UNACAST	United Nations Advisory Committee on the Application of Science and Technology to Development
UNACC	United Nations Administrative Committee and Co-ordination
UNACI	Union Africaine pour le Commerce et l'Industrie en Côte-d'Ivoire
UNACIL	United Africa Commercial and Industrial Ltc
UNACOMA	Unione Nazionale Costruttori Macchine Agricole
UNACO-OPRL	Unión Nacional de Cooperatives (Costa Rica)
UNADA	United Nations Atomic Development Authority
UNADI	United Nations Asian Development Institu
UNAEC	United Nations Atomic Energy Commissic
UNAF	Union Nationale de l'Apiculture Française
UNAF	Union Nationale des Associations Familial
UNAFIMA	Union Nationale des Associations de Form tion et d'Information Mutualistes Agricoles
UNAFR	Union Nationale des Aides Familiales Rurales

UNAG	Verband Schweizerischer Zeitungsagenturen und Büchergrossisten	**UNCAC**	Union Nationale de Coopératives Agricoles Chanvrières
UNAGA	Unión Nacional de Asociaciones Ganaderas (Colombia)	**UNCAFL**	Union Nationale des Coopératives Agricoles de Fruits et Légumes
UNAIS	United Nations Association International Service	**UNCAMB**	Union Nationale des Coopératives Agricoles de Meunerie et de Meunerie-Boulangerie
UNALOR	Union Allumettière Équatoriale (Cameroons)	**UNCAMTC**	Union Nationale des Coopératives Agricoles de Meunerie et de Transformation des Céréales
UNAM	Union Nationale des Analystes Médicales (Belgium)		
UNAM	Universidad Nacional Autónoma de México	**UNCAP**	National Union of the Agricultural Production Cooperatives of Roumania
UNAP	Union Nationale des Artistes Professionnels des Arts Plastiques et Graphiques (Belgium)	**UNCARR**	Union Nationale des Comités d'Action Renovation Rurale
UNAP	Union Nationale des Attachés de Presse	**UNCASTD**	United Nations Advisory Committee on the Application of Science and Technology to Development
UNAPACE	Unione Nazionale Aziende Produttrici Auto-Consumatrici di Energia Elettrica		
UNAPHAL	Union Nationale des Pharmaciens Luxembourgeois	**UNCATA**	Union Nationale des Coopératives Agricoles des Traitements Antiparasitaires
UNASAD	Union Nationale des Associations Sanitaires Apicoles Départementales (France) (*now* FNOSAD)	**UNCC**	Union Nacional de Colegios Católicos (Dominican Republic)
		UNCC	Union Nigérienne de Crédit et de Coopération
UNASCA	Unione Nazionale Autoscuole e Studi di Consulenza Automobilistica	**UNCCP**	United Nations Conciliation Commission for Palestine
UNASCO	Uniao Nacional das Associacoes de Cooperativas (Argentina)	**UNCDC**	Union Nationale des Caves et Distilleries Coopératives
UNAT	Union Nationale des Associations de Tourisme	**UNCDCV**	Union Nationale des Caves et Distilleries Coopératives Vinicoles
UNAT	Unione Nazionale Artisti Teatrali	**UNCDF**	United Nations Capital Development Fund
UNATCA	Union Nationale des Associations de Techniciens du Conseil Agricole	**UNCEA**	Union Commerciale pour l'Europe et l'Afrique
UNAU	Unione Nazionale Assistenti Universitari	**UNCEF**	Union Nationale des Caisses d'Épargne de France
UNAULA	Universidad Autonoma Latinoamericana (Colombia)	**UNCEIA**	Union Nationale des Coopératives d'Élevage et d'Insémination Artificielle
UNA-USA	United Nations Association of the USA	**UNCEM**	Unione Nazionale Comuni ed Enti Montani
UNAVCA	Union Nationale des Associations de Vulgarisation et de Conseillers Agricoles	**UNCFI**	United Nations Commission for Indonesia
UNBSA	United Nations Bureau of Social Affairs		
UNBTAO	United Nations Bureau of Technical Assistance Operations	**UNCGABV**	Union Nationale des Coopératives et Groupements Agricoles de Bétail et de Viande
UNC	Union Nazionale Chinesiologi	**UNCHBP**	Centre for Housing, Building and Planning (UNO)
UNC	Union Suisse des Négociants en Combustibles	**UNCI**	Unione Nazionale Chimici Italiani
UNC	Unione Nazionale Consumatori	**UNCI**	United Nations Commission for Indonesia
UNC	Universidad Nacional de Colombia	**UNCIET**	Unione Nazionale Costruttori Impianti Elettrici e Telefonici
UNCAA	Union Nationale des Coopératives Agricoles d'Approvisionnement		
UNCAC	Union National des Coopératives Agricoles de Céréales	**UNCIO**	United Nations Conference on International Organisation

UNCIP	United Nations Commission for India-Pakistan	**UNEB**	Union Nationale des Industries Françaises de l'Emballage Utilisant le Bois
UNCITRAL	United Nations Commission on International Trade Law	**UNEBECE**	Association d'Utilisateurs et Négociants Belges de Combustibles
UNCL	Union Nationale des Cafetiers-Limonadiers	**UNEC**	Unión Nacional Educación Católica (Uruguay)
UNCL	Union Nationale des Coopératives Laitières	**UNEC**	Union Nationale des Établissements Catholiques (Upper Volta)
UNCLOTS	United Nations Conference on the Law of the Sea	**UNEC**	United Nations Education Conference
UNCLS	United Nations Conference on the Law of the Sea	**UNECA**	Union Européenne des Fondeurs et Fabricants de Corps Gras Animaux
UNCO	United Nations Civilian Operations Mission (Zaire)	**UNECA**	United Nations Economic Commission for Africa
UNCOK	United Nations Commission on Korea (*formerly* UNTCOK)	**UNECO-LAIT**	Union Européenne du Commerce Laitier
UNCP	United Nations Conference of Plenipotentiaries	**UNEDA**	United Nations Economic Development Administration
UNCSAI	Unione Nazionale Costruttori Serramenti in Alluminio e Leghe Pregiate	**UNEEPF**	Union Nationale des Éditeurs-Exportateurs de Publications Périodiques Françaises
UNCSAT	United Nations and Conference on the Application of Science and Technology for the Benefit of Less Developed Areas	**UNEESA**	Union Nationale des Étudiants de l'Enseignement Supérieur Agricole
UNCSCMP	Union Nationale des Chambres Syndicales de Charpente, Menuiserie et Parquets	**UNEF**	Union Nationale des Étudiants de France
		UNEF	United Nations Emergency Force
UNCSTD	United Nations Conference on Science and Technology for Development	**UNEGA**	Union Européenne des Fondeurs et Fabricants de Corps Gras Animaux
UNCTAD	United Nations Conference on Trade and Development	**UNELAM**	Movement for Evangelical Unity in Latin America (Uruguay)
UNCULTA	Unión Nacional de Cultivadores de Tabaco (Venezuela)	**UNEMAF**	Union des Employers Agricoles et Forestiers (Ivory Coast)
UNCURK	United Nations Commission for the Unification and Rehabilitation of Korea	**UNEMI**	Union Editori di Musica Italiani
		UNEMO	National Union of Mozambican Students
UNCVDC	Union Nationale des Coopératives Viticoles et Distilleries Coopératives	**UNEO**	United Nations Emergency Operation
		UNEP	Union Nationale des Éleveurs de Porcs
UNDA	International Catholic Association for Radio and Television	**UNEP**	United Nations Environmental Programme
		UNEPA	Unión Económica Patagónica (Argentina)
UNDAT	United Nations Multinational Interdisciplinary Advisory Teams	**UNESCO**	United Nations Educational, Scientific and Cultural Organisation
UNDCC	United Nations Development Cooperation Cycle	**UNESDA**	Union des Associations de Boissons Gazeuses des Pays Membres de la CEE
UNDD	United Nations Development Decade	**UNESEM**	Union Européenne des Sources d'Eaux Minérales du Marché Commun
UNDOF	United Nations Disengagement Observer Force	**UNESID**	Union de Empresas y Entidades Siderurgicas
UNDP	United Nations Development Programme	**UNESOB**	United Nations Economic and Social Office in Beirut
UNDRO	United Nations Disaster Relief Co-ordinator's Office	**UNETAS**	United Nations Emergency Technical Aid Service
UNEAP	Union Nationale de l'Enseignement Agricole Privé	**UNEUROP**	Association Économique Européenne

UNEXSO	International Underwater Explorers Society
UNFAO	United Nations Food and Agriculture Organisation
UNFB	United Nations Film Board
UNFDAC	United Nations Fund for Drug Abuse Control
UNFC	United Nations Food Conference
UNFICYP	United Nations Peacekeeping Force in Cyprus
UNFP	Union Nationale des Forces Populaires (Morocco)
UNFPA	United Nations Fund for Population Activities
UNFRFJ	Union Nationale des Foyers Ruraux de la Famille et des Jeunes
UNGA	United Nations General Assembly
UNGP	Union Nationale des Grandes Pharmacies
UNHCR	Office of the High Commissioner for Refugees (of UNO)
UNHHSF	United Nations Habitat and Human Settlements Foundation
UNHQ	United Nations Headquarters
UNI	Ente Nazionale Italiano di Unificazione
UNI	Union Nationale des Intellectuels
UNIA	Union Nationale des Industries Agricoles
UNIA	Union Nationale des Ingénieurs Agricoles
UNIADUS-EC	Union Internationale des Associations de Diplômés Universitaires en Sciences Économiques et Commerciales
UNIAPAC	Union Internationale des Associations Patronales Catholiques
UNIARTE	Unión Nacional de Industriales y Artesanos (Venezuela)
UNIATEC	Union Internationale des Associations Techniques Cinématographiques
UNIBA	Unione Nazionale Industrie Bigiotterie ed Affini
UNIBEV	Union Nationale Interprofessionnelle du Bétail et des Viandes
UNIBEX	Union des Brasseries Belges d'Exportation
UNIC	Union Nationale Interprofessionnelle du Cheval
UNIC	Unione Nazionale Industria Conciaria
UNIC	United Nations Information Centre
UNICA	Association of Universities and Research Institutes from the Caribbean
UNICA	Union Internationale du Cinéma d'Amateurs

UNICA	Universidad Nacional, Instituto Colombiano Agropecuario
UNICAF	Union d'Importationes Industrielles et Commerciales Africains
UNICAP	Unione Nazionale Italiana Collegi Associazioni Periti
UNICE	Union des Industries de la Communauté Européenne
UNICEF	United Nations International Children's Emergency Fund
UNICELPE	Association Européenne des Producteurs de Protéines Unicellulaires
UNICEM	Union Nationale Interprofessionnelle des Carrières et Matériaux de Construction
UNICEMA	Union Nationale des Industriels, Commerçants et Entrepreneurs de Mauritanie
UNICERE-ALES	Union Nationale Interprofessionnelle des Céréales
UNICETA	Union Nationale des Ingénieurs des Centres d'Études Techniques Agricoles
UNICHAD	Union Interprofessionelle du Tchad
UNICHAL	Union Internationale des Distributeurs de Chaleur
UNICHOCO	Union des Chambres Syndicales des Chocolatiers Confiseurs Fabricants Détaillants
UNICID	Union Nationale Interprofessionnelle Cidricole
UNICLIMA	Union Intersyndicale des Constructeurs de Matériel Aéraulique
UNICOCYM	Union Internationale du Commerce et de la Réparation du Cycle et du Motorcycle
UNICOLHV	Union Industrielle et Commerciale des Oléagineux de Haute-Volta
UNICOMA	Union des Coopératives du Morbihan et le Loire-Atlantique
UNICOMAT	Union Intersyndicale des Constructeurs de Matériel Aéraulique, Thermique et Frigorifique
UNICOMER	Union des Comptoirs d'Outre-Mer
UNICONGO	Union Patronale et Interprofessionnelle du Congo
UNICON-SERVE	Union Nationale Interprofessionnelle de la Conserve
UNICOOP	Union Coopérative de Viticulteurs Charentais
UNICUIR	Union Internationale des Négociants en Cuir

UNIDO	United Nations Industrial Development Organisation
UNIDROIT	International Institute for the Unification of Private Law
UNIEG	Unione Nazionale Industrie Editoriali e Grafiche
UNIEM	Union Nationale des Entrepreneurs-Menuisiers et Charpentiers (Belgium)
UNIEMA	Union des Industries et Entreprises de Mauritanie
UNIENSA	Union des Ingénieurs Diplomés des Écoles Nationales
UNIEP	Union Internationale des Entrepreneurs de Peinture
UNIFA	Union Nationale des Industries Français de l'Ameublement
UNIFE	Union des Industries Ferroviaires Européennes
UNIFICYP	Force de Maintien de la Paix des Nations-Unies à Chypre
UNIFIL	United Nations Interim Force in Lebanon
UNIFL	Union Nationale Interprofessionnelle des Fruits et Légumes
UNIFO-DENT	Union Professionnelle des Négociants en Fournitures Dentaires de Belgique
UNIFRUITS	Union Nationale Interprofessionnnelle des Fruits, Légumes et Pommes de Terre
UNIGABON	Union Interprofessionnelle Économique et Sociale du Gabon
UNIGRA	Union des Industries Graphiques et du Livre (Belgium)
UNIGRAINS	Union Financière pour le Développement de l'Économie Céréalière
UNIL	United Nordic Importers Ltd (Denmark)
UNILEC	Union Nationale Interprofessionnelle des Légumes de Conserve (France) (*now* ANILEC)
UNIM	Union Nationale des Industries de la Manu-tention dans les Ports Français
UNIMA	Union Internationale de Grands Magasins
UNIMA	Union Internationale de la Marionnette
UNIMA	Union Nazionale Imprese di Meccanizzazione Agricola
UNIMA	Union Internationale des Marionettes
UNIMES	Union des Importateurs-Exportateurs Sénégalaise
UNIMETAL	Union Nationale des Petites et Moyennes Entreprises du Métal (Belgium)
UNINAT	Union des Industries de Matériaux Naturels
UNIO	United Nations Information Organisation
UNIOM	Union Nationale Interprofessionnelle des Oléagineux Métropolitains
UNION	Union des Conseils Européens en Brevets
UNIONCHI-MICA	Unione Nazionale Piccole e Medie Industrie Chimiche ed Affini
UNION FLEURS	International Association of Flowers Wholesalers
UNION-LEGNO	Unione Nazionale Piccole e Medie Industrie del Legno
UNION-PLAST	Unione Nazionale Industrie Materie Plastiche
UNIONRISO	Unione Italiana dell'Industria Risiera
UNIP	Unión Interamericana de Padres de Familia
UNIP	United National Independent Party (Zambia)
UNIPAC	Union Industrielle des Fabricants de Papiers et Cartons
UNIPAR	Union de Participations de France et d'Outre-Mer
UNIPEDE	Union Internationale des Producteurs et Distributeurs d'Énergie Électrique
UNIPI	Unione Industriali Pastai Italiani
UNIPLPL	Union Nationale Interprofessionnelle de Propagande pour le Lait et les Produits Laitiers (France)
UNIPOL	Union des Industries de Produits Oléagineux
UNIPRO	Unione Nazionale delle Industrie di Profumeria Cosmesi, Saponi da Toilette e Affini
UNIPRO-LAIT	Union Nationale Interprofessionnelle des Produits Laitiers
UNIRIZ	Union Nationale Interprofessionnelle du Riz
UNIS	United Nations Information Service
UNIS	United Nations International School (U.S.A.)
UNISA	Union Nazionale Italiana Stampatori Acciaio
UNISCAN	British-Scandinavian Economic Committee
UNISCAT	United Nations Expert Committee on the Application of Science and Technology
UNISIST	World Science Information System (*of* ICSU-UNESCO)
UNISTOCK	Union Professionnelle des Stockeurs de Céréales dans la CEE
UNISYNDI	Union Intersyndicale d'Entreprises et d'In-dustries de l'Ouest Africain
UNIT	Union Nationale des Ingénieurs Techniciens (Belgium)

UNITA	Union for the Total Independence of Angola
UNITAB	Internationalen Union der Tabakspflanzer
UNITAN	Union de la Tannerie et de la Mégisserie Belge
UNITAP	United Nations Intermunicipal Technical Assistance Programme
UNITAR	United Nations Institute for Training and Research
UNITEC	Union Togolaise de Commerce
UNITEC	University Information Technology Corporation (U.S.A.)
UNITESA	Union Nazionale dell'Istruzione Tecnica e Professionale
UNITRA	Union pour l'Industrie et les Travaux Publics (Senegal)
UNIVCC	Union Nationale Intercoopérative des Vins de Consommation Courante
UNIVENCA	Unión Venezolana Criadores de Aves
UNIVIAN-DES	Union Nationale Interprofessionnelle des Viandes
UNIVIGNE	Union Nationale Interprofessionnelle de la Vigne
UNIVOL-AILLE	Union Nationale Interprofessionnelle de la Volaille
UNIVSERV	United Nations International Voluntary Service Fund
UNJSPB	United Nations Joint Staff Pension Board
UNKRA	United Nations Korean Reconstruction Agency
UNLC	United Nations Liaison Committee
UNLF	Uganda National Liberation Front
UNLG	Union Nationale des Livres Généalogiques
UNMC	United Nations Mediterranean Commission
UNME	Union Nationale des Maisons de l'Élevage
UNMEM	United Nations Middle East Mission
UNMFAR	Union Nationale des Maisons Familiales d'Apprentissage Rural
UNMOGIP	United Nations Military Observer Group in India and Pakistan
UNO	United Nations Organisation
UNOAI	Union Nationale des Ouvriers Agricoles Indépendants
UNOB	Union Nationale des Opticiens de Belgique
UNOC	United Nations Congo Operation
UNO-CARA-PEN	Union Internationale pour la Coopération Culturelle
UNOCCER	Union Nationale des Offices de Compatibilité et des Centres d'Économie Rurale
UNOE	Union Nationale des Oenologues
UNOH	Union Nationale des Ouvriers d'Haiti
UNOLE-ARIA	Associazione Nazionale dell' Industria Olearia
UNOOB	Union Nationale des Optométristes et Opticiens de Belgique
UNPA	United Nations Postal Administration
UNPADI	Unión Panamericana de Asociaciónes de Ingenieros
UNPAL	Unión Nacional de Productores de Aceite de Limón (Mexico)
UNPASA	Unión Nacional de Productores de Azúcar de Caña (Mexico)
UNPBF	Union Nationale des Producteurs Belges de Films
UNPC	United Nations Palestine Commission
UNPCC	United Nations Conciliation Commission for Palestine
UNPEG	Unión Nacional de Produtores y Exportadores de Garbanzo (Mexico)
UNPF	National Union of Popular Forces (Morocco)
UNPFA	United Nations Fund for Population Activities
UNPJF	Union Nationale des Producteurs et Distributeurs de Jus de Fruits et de Légumes (France)
UNPL	Union Nationale des Professions Libérales
UNPOC	United Nations Peace Observation Commission
UNPVF	Union Nationale des Peintres-Vitriers de France
UNRAE	Unione Nazionale Rappresentanti Autoveicoli Esteri
UNREF	United Nations Refugee Fund
UNREP	Union Nationale Rurale d'Éducation et de Promotion
UNRISD	United Nations Research Institute for Social Development
UNROD	United Nations Relief Operation, Dacca
UNRPR	United Nations Relief for Palestine Refugees
UNRRA	United Nations Relief and Rehabilitation Administration
UNRST	Union Nationale des Revêtements de Sol et du Tapis
UNRTD	United Nations Resources and Transport Division

UNRWA	United Nations Relief and Works Agency
UNRWA-PRNE	United Nations Relief and Works Agency for Palestine Refugees in the Near East
UNRWI	United Nations Representative for West Irian
UNSC	United Nations Security Council
UNSC	United Nations Social Commission
UNSCC	United Nations Standards Co-ordinating Committee
UNSCCUR	United Nations Scientific Conference on the Conservation and Utilisation of Resources
UNSCEAR	United Nations Scientific Committee on the Effects of Atomic Radiation
UNSCOB	United Nations Special Commission to the Balkans
UNSCOP	United Nations Special Commission on Palestine
UNSDD	United Nations Social Development Division
UNSDRI	United Nations Social Defence Research Institute (Italy)
UNSE	Union Nationale des Syndicats de l'Étang
UNSEPF	Union Nationale des Syndicats d'Entrepreneurs Paysagistes de France
UNSF	United Nations Special Fund
UNSFL	Union Nationale des Syndicats de Fabricants de Lunetterie
UNSOF	Union Nationale des Syndicats d'Opticiens de France
UNSTHV	Union Nationale des Syndicats des Travailleurs de la Haute Volta
UNSU	United Nations Study Unit
UNTAA	United Nations Technical Assistance Administration
UNTAB	United Nations Technical Assistance Board
UNTAM	United Nations Technical Assistance Mission
UNTC	Union Nationale des Travailleurs Congolais
UNTC	United Nations Trusteeship Council
UNTCOK	United Nations Temporary Commission on Korea (*now* UNCOK)
UNTEA	United Nations Temporary Executive Authority, West New Guinea
UNTEL	Union Nationale des Syndicats des Tissus Élastiques
UNTFDPP	United Nations Trust Fund for Development Planning and Projections
UNTFSD	United Nations Trust Fund for Social Development
UNTRA	Union of National Radio and Television Organisations of Africa
UNTS	Union Nationale des Travailleurs du Sénégal
UNTSO	United Nations Truce Supervision Organisation
UNTT	Union Nationale des Travailleurs Togolais
UNTT	United Nations Trust Territory
UNU	Uganda National Union
UNU	United Nations University
UNUCI	Unione Nazionale Ufficiali in Congedo d'Italia
UNV	United Nations Volunteers
UNWCC	United Nations War Crimes Commission
UNWG	United Nations Women's Guild
UNY	United Nations of Yoga
UNYOM	United Nations Yemen Observation Mission
UNZALPI	Universities of Nottingham and Zambia, Agricultural Labour Productivity Investigation
UOASE	Union des Organisations Agricoles du Sud-Est
UOF	Union Ovine de France
UOTAA	Universal Organisation of Travel Agents' Associations
UOVS	Universiteit van die Oranje Vrystaat (South Africa)
UP	Unione Petrolifera
UP	Union Pétrolière (Switzerland)
UP	Union des Propriétaires du Grand-Duché de Luxembourg
UPA	Unions Professionnelles Agricoles (Belgium)
UPA	Union of Angolan Peoples
UPA	Union Postale Arabe
UPA	United Printers Association
UPA	Utenti Pubblicità Associati
UPAB	Fédération des Unions Professionnelles Agricoles de Belgique
UPACCIM	Union des Ports Autonomes et des Chambres de Commerce et d'Industrie Maritimes
UPADI	Union Panamericana de Asociaciones de Ingenieros (Mexico)
UPAE	Union Postale des Amériques et de l'Espagne
UPAF	Union Postale Africaine
UPAFI	Union Professionnelle d'Agents, Fabricants et Importateurs Exclusifs d'Objets d'Art et de Cadeaux (Belgium

UPAJ	Union Panafricaine des Journalistes
UPAM	United Planters' Association of Malaya
UPAO	Union Postale de l'Asie et de l'Océanie
UPASI	United Planters' Association of Southern India
UPAU	Uttar Pradesh Agricultural University (India)
UPAV	Union Professionnelle Belge des Agences des Voyages
UPAVE	Unión de Productores de Azúcar de Venezuela
UPBAN	Union Professionnelle Belge des Approvisionneurs de Navires
UPBIF	Union Professionnelle Belge des Industriels du Froid
UPBMC	Union Professionnelle Belge des Médecins Ophtalmologistes
UPBOB	Union Professionnelle des Bandagistes et Orthopédistes de Belgique
UPBPP	Union Professionnelle Belge de la Police Privée
UPC	Union des Pelleteries et Confectionneurs en Fourrure
UPC	Union du Peuple Corse (Corsica)
UPCA	Union Professionnelle des Coopératives Agricoles (Belgium)
UPCA	University of the Philippines College of Agriculture
UPCIL	Union Interfédérale des Producteurs, des Coopératives et des Industriels Laitiers
UPCL	Union Professionnelle des Promoteurs de Logements et d'Aménagement du Territoire (Belgium)
UPDAL	Union Professionelle de Commerce de Gros des Produits Laitiers Indigènes et d'Importation autre que Beurre et Fromage (Belgium)
UPDBF	Union Professionnelle des Distributeurs Belges de Films
UPE	Union Parlementaire Européenne
UPE	Union de la Presse Étrangère en Belgique
UPDEA	Union of Producers, Conveyors and Distributors of Electric Power in African Countries, Madagascar and Mauritius (Ivory Coast)
UPEA	Union Professionnelle des Entreprises d'Assurances (Belgium)
UPEB	Unión de Países Exportadores de Banano (Philippines)
UPEFE	Union de la Presse Économique et Financière Européenne
UPET	Ufficio per la Esportazione Tabacco
UPETITA	Union Professionnelle des Entreprises de Travaux d'Isolation Thermique et Acoustique (Belgium)
UPETTC	Union Professionnelle des Exploitants de Taxis et de Taxis-Camionnettes
UPGA	United Progressive Grand Alliance (Nigeria)
UPGWA	International Union United Plant Guard Workers of America
UPHA	Utah Public Health Association
UPI	Union Syndicale des Professions Immobilières de Belgiques
UPI	United Press International
UPIA	Union Pharmaceutique Inter-Africaine
UPICV	Revolutionary Committee of the Cape Verde Islands People's Union
UPIGO	Union Professionnelle Internationale des Gynécologues et Obstétriciens
UPIL	Union des Pharmaciens d'Industrie Luxembourgeoise
UPIP	Union des Pharmaciens de l'Industrie Pharmaceutique (Belgium)
UPIR	Uttar Pradesh Irrigation Research Institute (India)
UPIU	United Paperworkers International Union
UPL	International Institute for the Unification of Private Law
UPLAC	Union des Producteurs de Levure-aliment de la CEE
UPLB	University of the Philippines Los Banos
UPN	Urad Pro Normalisaci (Czechoslovakia) (Standards Office)
UPNI	Unionist Party of Northern Ireland
UPOV	Union Internationale pour la Protection des Obtentions Végétales
UPOW	Union of Post Office Workers
UPP	United Peoples Party (Nigeria)
UPPB	Union de la Presse Périodique Belge
UPPIC	Union Syndicale Interprofessionnelle pour la Promotion de la Conserve
UPPN	Union Postale des Pays du Nord (Finland)
UPR	Union Professionnelle des Représentants de Commerce de Belgique
UPRF	Union Professionnelle Belge du Commerce des Fromages
UPROCA	Union Professionelle des Producteurs du Caoutchouc (Belgium)

UPRONA	Party for Unity and Progress (Burundi)	**URO**	Union des Remorquers de l'Océan
UPROTAB	Union Professionnelle Nationale des Importateurs Négociants, Commissionnaires, Courtiers et Agents en Tabacs en Feuilles en Belgique	**URPE**	Union for Radical Political Economics (U.S.A.)
		URPE	Union des Resistants pour une Europe Unie
UPS	Union Producteurs Suisses	**URSI**	Union Radio-Scientifique Internationale
UPS	Union Progressive Sénégalaise	**URSSAF**	Union pour le Recouvrement des Cortisations de la Sécurité Sociale et les Allocations Familiales
UPSA	Union Professionnelle Suisse de l'Automobile		
UPSTC	Uttar Pradesh State Textile Corporation (India)	**URTI**	Université Radiophonique et Télévisuelle Internationale
UPTC	Union Panafricaine des Travailleurs Croyants	**URTNA**	Union des Radiodiffusions et Télévisions Nationales d'Afrique
UPTD	Union Professionnelle des Teinuriers-Dégraisseurs (Belgium)	**URTU**	United Road Transport Union
		URW	United Rubber, Cork, Linoleum and Plastic Workers of America
UPTRI	Union Professionnelle Belge des Transporteurs Routiers Internationaux	**USAAPEB**	Union Syndicale Ardennaise des Artisans et Petites Entreprises du Bâtiment
UPU	Universal Postal Union		
UPW	Union of Post Office Workers	**USACASP**	Union des Sociétés d'Assurances et de Capitalisation par Actions du Secteur Privé
UQP	Universities and the Quest for Peace		
URANEX	Groupement d'Intérêt Économique pour la Commercialisation de l'Uranie	**USAEC**	United States Atomic Energy Commission
		USAFCRL	U.S. Air Force Cambridge Research Laboratories
URBAN-ICOM	Association Internationale Urbanisme et Commerce		
		USAI	Union Sud-Americana de Asociaciones de Ingenieros
URCAM	Union Régionale des Coopératives du Midi		
URCC	Union Régionale des Coopératives Cidricoles	**USAID**	United States Agency for International Development
URCCE	Union des Régions des Capitales de la Communauté Européenne	**USAIRE**	United States of America Aerospace Industries Representatives in Europe
URD	Union Republicana Democrata (Venezuela)		
		USAL	Union Suisse des Acheteurs de Lait
UREGER	Union pour la Recherche et l'Expansion de la Gestion et de l'Économie Rurale	**USAM**	Union Suisse des Arts et Métiers
		USAM	Union des Syndicats Autonomes de Madagascar
UREMG	Universidade Rural do Estado de Minas Gerais (Brazil)		
URF	Union des Services Routiers des Chemins de Fer Européens	**USAR**	Union des Syndicats Agricoles Romands (Switzerland)
URGA	Unión Recibidores de Granos y Anexos (Argentina)	**USARP**	United Nations Antarctic Research Programme
URGCI	Union Romande des Gérants et Courtiers en Immeubles	**USASI**	United States of America Standards Institute (now ANSI)
URI	Université Radiophonique et Télévisuelle Internationale	**USB**	Union Schweizerischer Briefumschlagfabriken
		USB	Union Sénégalaise de Banque
URISA	Urban and Regional Information Systems Association (U.S.A.)	**USBGN**	United States Board on Geographic Names
URJ	Union Romande de Journaux (Switzerland)	**USBM**	United States Bureau of Mines
		USBR	United States Bureau of Reclamation
URLAC	Union Régionale Laitière Agricole Coopératives	**USC**	Union Suisse des Coopératives de Consumation
URMA	Union Romande de Moulins Agricoles (Switzerland)	**USC**	Unione Svizzera dei Cartolai

USC	Universidad de San Carlos (Guatemala)
USCA	Union Syndicale des Courtiers en Assurances
USCAP	Union Syndicate des Cadres du Pétrole
USCAR	United States Civil Administration, Ryukyu Islands
USCAS	South American Union of Societies of Cardiology (Venezuela)
USCI	Union Suisse du Commerce et de l'Industrie
USCIGW	Union of Salt, Chemical and Industrial General Workers
USCL	United Society for Christian Literature
USCO	Union Steel Corporation (South Africa)
USCOLD	United States Committee on Large Dams
USCSC	United States Civil Service Commission
USCSC	United States Cuban Sugar Council
USCV	Union Scientifique Continentale du Verre
USDA	Union Suisse des Acheteurs
USDA	United States Department of Agriculture
USDAM	Union Suisse des Artistes Musiciens
USDAW	Union of Shop, Distributive and Allied Workers
USDC	Union Svizzera dei Compratori
USDC	United States Department of Commerce
USDI	United States Department of the Interior
USDIS	Union Suisse des Métiers de la Décoration d'Intérieure et de la Sellerie
USDL	United States Department of Labor
USELPA	Usinas Eletricas do Paranapanema (Brazil)
USEM	Confederación de Unions Sociales de Enpresarios Mexicanos
USF	Unione Svizzera dei Fotografi
USFB	Union Suisse des Fabricants de Boîtes de Montres
USFDA	United States Food and Drug Administration
USFGC	U.S. Feed Grains Council
USFHTF	L'Union Syndicate des Fabricants d'Huile et de Tourteaux de France
USFJ	Union Suisse des Fabricants de Jouets
USFLF	Union Syndicale des Fabricants de Limes de France
USFMC	Union Syndicale des Fabricants de Matières Colorantes et d'Hydrosulfites
USFO	Union Syndicale Française du Carton Ondulé
USFWS	United States Fish and Wildlife Service
USG	Union Suisse de la Glace Polie
USG	Union of Superiors-General (Italy)
USGA	United States Travel Service
USGOS	Union des Stockeurs de Graines Oléagineuses de Semences
USGPO	United States Government Printing Office
USGS	United States Geological Survey
USHF	L'Union Syndicale de l'Huilerie Française
USI	Union of Students in Ireland
USI	United Schools International
USIA	U.S. Information Agency
USIAS	Union Syndicale des Industries Aéronautiques et Spatiales (*now* GIFAS)
USIC	Union Sportive Internationale des Cheminots
USIC	Union Suisse des Industriels en Carrosserie
USIEM	Union des Syndicats d'Intérêt Économique de Madagascar
USIMA	Union Sénégalaise d'Industries Maritimes
USINEN	Société Ivoirienne d'Usinage
USINOR	Union Sidérurgique du Nord et de l'Est de la France
USIO	Union Syndicale Interprofessionnelle Oléicole
USIPA	Union des Syndicats des Industries des Produits Amylacés et de leurs Dérivés
USIRF	Union Syndicale des Industries Routières Françaises
USIS	United States Information Service
USITA	United States Independent Telephone Association
USITT	U.S. Institute for Theatre Technology
USJ	Union Suisse des Journalistes
USL	Union Suisse pour la Lumière
USL	United States Lines
USLSA	United States Livestock Sanitary Association
USLTA	United States Lawn Tennis Association
USLV	Union des Schweizerischen Lichtspieltheater-Verbände
USM	Union des Semouliers de Maïs
USMAP	Union Syndicale de la Maîtrise du Pétrole
USMB	Union Suisse des Marchands de Beurre
USMC	Union Suisse des Marchands de Chaussures
USMC	Union Suisse des Marchands de Cuir
USMC	United States Maritime Commission
USMCM	Union Suisse des Mécaniciens en Cycles et Motos
USMMASA	Union Scientifique Mondiale des Médecins Acupuncteurs et des Sociétés d'Acupuncture

USNCFID	United States National Committee for FID
USNEF	Union Syndicale National des Exploitations Frigorifiques
USNM	United States National Museum
USNSA	United States National Student Association
USNTCE-OOPA	Union des Syndicats Nationaux de Techniciens, Cadres, Employés et Ouvriers des Organisations Professionnelles Agricoles
USNTIS	United States National Technical Information Service
USOE	United States Office of Education
USOI	U.S. Office of Information
USOM	United States Overseas Mission (*now* AID)
USOO	United States Oceanographic Office
USP	Union Suisse des Papetiers
USP	Union Suisse des Photographes
USPA	Union Syndicale Panafricaine
USPC	United States Pharmacopoeial Convention
USPE	Utah Society of Professional Engineers
USPG	United Society for the Propagation of the Gospel
USPHS	United States Public Health Service
USPI	Unione della Stampa Periodica Italiana
USPM	Union des Syndicats Patronaux de Madagascar
USPMOM	Union des Sociétés de Pédiatre du Moyen-Orient et de la Méditerranée
USPO	United States Post Office
USR	Union Suisse des Industries Graphiques de Reproduction
USRM	Union Suisse des Reconstructeurs de Moteurs
USRT	Union Suisse des Installateurs Concessionnaires en Radio et Télévision
USS	Union Syndicale Suisse
USSASA	University Science Students Association of South Africa
USSCC	University Social Sciences Council Conference (East Africa)
USSEA	United States Scientific Export Association
USSI	Union des Sociétés Suisses d'Ingénieurs-Conseils
USSI	Unione Stampa Sportiva Italiana
USSM	Uniunea Societatilor de Stiinte Medicale din RSR
US-SPE	Union Syndicale- Service Public Européen (Belgium)
USSR	Union of Soviet Socialist Republics
UST	Union des Entreprises Suisses de Transports Publics
UST	Union of Speech Therapists
USTA	United States Trademark Association
USTC	United States Tariff Commission
USTD	University Science and Technology Division (*of* SRC)
USTEL	Union Syndicale du Tréfilage, Étirage et Laminage à Froid de l'Acier
USTIL	Syndicat National des Fabricants d'Utensiles Industriels de Laiterie
USTS	United States Travel Service
USTTA	United States Table Tennis Association
USUARIOS	Association of Maritime Transport Users in the Central American Isthmus (Guatemala)
USUCA	United Steelworkers Union of Central Africa
USUN	United States Mission to the United Nations
USVB	Union Syndicale Vétérinaire Belge
USVBA	United States Volleyball Association
USVC	Union Suisse des Fabricants de Vernis et de Couleurs
USWA	United Steelworkers of America
USWB	United States Weather Bureau
USWD	Undersurface Warfare Division
UT	Conférence Internationale pour l'Unité Technique des Chemins de Fer
UTA	Ulster Transport Authority
UTA	Union des Transports Aériens
UTAC	Union Technique de l'Automobile et du Cycle
UTAFRIQ	Union Trading Afrique tout pour l'Auto (Ivory Coast)
UTAL	Universidad de los Trabajadores de América Latina (Venezuela)
UTC	Union de Trabajadores de Colombia
UTCGA	Union Tunisienne de la Confédération Générale de l'Agriculture
UTCPT	Union Internationale des Organismes Touristiques et Culturels des Postes et des Télécommunications
UTDA	Ulster Tourist Development Association
UTE	Union Technique de l'Électricité
UTE	Usinas Electricas los Telefonos del Estado (Uruguay)
UTE	Universidad Técnica del Estado (Chile)

UTEHA	Unión Tipográfica Editorial Hispano Americana (Mexico)
UTEXI	Union Textile de Côte d'Ivoire
UTGC	Uganda Tea Growers Corporation
UTH	Union Touristique et Hôtelière
UTHI	Ukrainian Technical Husbandry Institute, New York (U.S.A.)
UTI	Unione Tabacchicoltori Italiani
UTI	Union Technique Interprofessionnelle des Fédérations
UTICA	Union Tunisienne de l'Industrie, du Commerce et de l'Artisant
UTIFAR	Unione Tecnica Italiana Farmacisti
UTIP	Union Technique Intersyndicale Pharmaceutique
UTM	Union Trading Monaco
UTMM	Union Technique des Constructeurs de Menuiserie Métallique (Belgium)
UTO	United Towns Organization (France)
UTO	Universal Tourism Organisation
UTOP	United Technological Organisations of the Philippines
UTPP	United Thai People's Party
UTPUR	Union des Transports Publics Urbains et Régionaux
UTRAMM-ICOL	Union de Trabajadores Metalurgicos y Mineros de Colombia
UTRAT-EXCO	Unión de Trabajadores Textiles de Colombia
UTS	Union Technique Suisse
UTU	Universidad del Trabajo del Uruguay
UTWA	United Textile Workers of America
UTZ	Union Nationale des Travailleurs Zairoises
UUUC	United Ulster Unionist Council
UVAT	Unie van Assurantietussenpersonen
UVCB	Union des Villes et Communes Belges
UVS	Union des Villes Suisses
UVT	Union Voltaïque de Transport
UVTP	Union des Usagers de Véhicules de Transport Privé
UWH/WCS	Universal World Harmony World Council of Service
UWI	University of the West Indies
UWIST	University of Wales Institute of Science and Technology
UWM	United World Mission (U.S.A.)
UWPC	United World Press Cooperative (U.S.A.)
UWT	Union of Women Teachers
UY	Universal Youth
UZD	Umetnostnozgodovinsko Drustvo Slovenije
UZRA	United Zionist Revisionists of America

V

VAA	Verband angestellter Akademiker der Chemischen Industrie
VAB	Voluntary Agencies Bureau
VABB	Vereniging van Archivarissen en Bibliothecarissen van België
VAC	Verbond van Nederlandse Fabrikanten van Asbestcementwaren
VAD	Directia Aprovizionarii si Desfacerii (Roumania)
VAD	Vereinigung von Afrikanisten in Deutschland
VAHA	Vereniging Fabrieken van Aluminium Huishoudelijke Artikelen
VAHVA	Vahinkovakuutusyhdistys
VAK	Verband der Aufbau- und Geräte-Industrie für Kommunalzwecke
VALA	National Viewers' and Listeners' Association
VALCO	Volta Aluminium Co. (Ghana)
VAM	Vereniging voor Algemene Machinehandel
VAN	Vereniging van Archivarissen in Nederland
VANDPF	Vietnam Alliance of National, Democratic and Popular Forces
VAÖ	Verband der Agrarjournalisten in Österreich
VAÖ	Verband der Antiquare Österreichs
VAP	Verband Schweizerischer Anschussgeleise- und Privatgüterwagenbesitzer
VAP	Voluntary Assistance Programme (WMO)
VAPI	Vereniging der Apotekers van de Pharmaceutische Industrie (Belgium)
VAR	Vereniging voor Agrarisch Recht
VARA	Vereniging v. Arbeiders Radio-Amateurs
VARIM	Vattenreningsgruppen inom Sveriges Mekanförbund
VASCA	Electronic Valve and Semi-conductor Manufacturers Association

VASF	Verband der Angestelten des Schweizer Fernsehens	**VBNA**	Vereniging ter Behartiging van den Nederlandschen Aardappelhandel
VASGB	Vasectomy Advancement Society of Great Britain	**VBNN**	Society for Nature Conservation in the Netherlands
VASP	Viacao Aérea Sao Paulo (Brazil)	**VBÖ**	Verband der Baustoffhändler Österreichs
VATE	Victorian Association for the Teaching of English (Australia)	**VBO**	Vereinigung für Bankbetriebsorganisation
		VBO	Vereniging Belge des Omnipraticiens
VATEVA	Vaatetuseollisuuden Keskusliitto	**VBP**	Vlaamse Bond van Postzegelverzamelaars
VAV	Svenska Vatten- och Avloppsverksföreningen	**VBRA**	Vehicle Builders and Repairers Association
VAVI	Vereninging voor de Aardappelverwerkende Industrie	**VBS**	Verbond der Belgische Beroepsverenigingen van Geneesheren-Specialisten
VBA	Vereniging der Belgische Aannemers van Werken van Burgerlijke Bouwkunde (Belgium)	**VBSG**	Vereniging van Belgische Steden en Gemeenten
VBAM	Vereniging der Belgische Aannemers van Montagewerk	**VbU**	Verband Bergbaulicher Unternehmen und Bergbauverwandter Organisationen
VBB	Veenkoloniale Boerenbond	**VBV**	Vereniging Band-, Vlecht- en Kantindustrie
VBB	Verein der Bibliothekare an Öffentlichen Büchereien	**VBV**	Vereniging voor Bedrijfsvoorlichting
		VBV	Vereinigung Beratender Betriebs- und Volkswirte
VbBV	Verband Beratender Betriebs- und Volkswirte, Wirtschaftsjuristen und Sachverstandiger	**VBVB**	Vereniging ter Bevordering van het Vlaamse Boekwezen
VBC	Vereningen Bedrijfsleven Curacao	**VBW**	Vereniging voor Bitumineuze Werken
VBE	Verband Bildung und Erziehung	**VBZ**	Verband der Lieferanten für Brandschutz, Zivilschutz und Erste Hilfe
VBI	Verband der Beleuchtungs-Industrie (Switzerland)	**VCC**	Veteran Car Club of Great Britain
VBI	Verein Beratender Ingenieure	**VCG**	Vereniging tot Behartiging v. d. Belangen v. Coöperatieve Grasdrogerijen
VBI	Vereniging van Blikverwerkende Industrieën	**VCI**	Variety Clubs International (U.S.A.)
VBK	Verband der Deutschen Bodenbelags-, Kunststoff- Folien- und Beschichtungs-Industrie	**VCI**	Verband der Chemischen Industrie
		VCL	Vereinigung Christlicher Lehrer an den Höheren Schulen Österreichs
VBKD	Verband Bildender Künstler Deutschlands, Sektion Gebrauchsgraphik	**VCN**	Vereniging van Classici in Nederland
VBKDDR	Verband Bildender Künstler Deutsche Demokratische Republik	**VCOAD**	Voluntary Committee on Overseas Aid and Development
VBLJ	Vereniging van Belgische Landbouw-journalisten	**VCOD**	Vereniging van Christelijke Ondernemers in de DHZ Detailhandel
VBMWG	Vereniging van de Belgische Medische Wetenschappelijke	**VCP**	Vêtements et Chemiserie de Paris (Ivory Coast)
VBN	Vereniging van Bedrijfsredacteuren in Nederland	**VCRS**	Verband Chemischer Reingungsanstalten der Schweiz
VBN	Vereniging voor Bedrijfsrestaurateurs in Nederland	**VCTA**	Victorian Commercial Teachers Association (Australia)
VBN	Vereniging van Betonmortelfabrikanten in Nederland	**VCTV**	Verbond der Coöperatieve Tuinbouwveilingen
		VCU	Vereniging van Christelijke Uitgevers
VBN	Vereniging van Boeren en Pluimveefokbedrijven in Nederland	**VCU**	Vereinigung Christlicher Unternehmer der Schweiz

VCUÖ	Verband Christlicher Unternehmer Österreichs		**VDG**	Verein Deutscher Giessereifachleute
			VDG	Vereinigung Deutsch Gewässerschutz
VCV	Vlaamse Chemische Vereniging (Belgium)		**VDH**	Verband Deutscher Häutehändler
VCW	Vereniging van Werkgevers in de Chemische Wasserijen en Ververijen		**VDH**	Verband Deutscher Heilbrunnen
			VDH	Verein Deutscher Holzeinfuhrhäuser
VD	Veeartsenijkundige Dienst		**VDI**	Verband der Importeure van Kraftfahrzeugen
VDA	Schweizerischer Verband Diplomieter Arztegehilfinnen		**VDI**	Verein Deutscher Ingenieure
VDA	Verband der Automobilindustrie		**VDID**	Verband Deutscher Industrie-Designer
VDA	Verband Deutscher Agrarjournalisten		**VDJ**	Deutscher Journalisten-Verband
VDA	Verband Deutscher Antiquare		**VDK**	Verband Deutscher Dokumentar- und Kurzfilmproduzenten
VdA	Verein Deutscher Archivare			
VDAI	Verband der Deutschen Automatenindustrie		**VDKF**	Verband Deutscher Kälte-Klima-Fachleute
VdB	Verband der Bautenschutzmittel-Industrie		**VDKF**	Verband Deutscher Kur- und Fremden- verkehrsfachleute
VDB	Verein Deutscher Bibliothekare		**VDL**	Verband Deutscher Akademiker für Land- wirtschaft, Ernährung und Landespflege
VDB	Verband Deutscher Badebetriebe			
VDB	Verband Deutscher Biologen		**VDL**	Verband Deutscher Diplomandwirte
VDB	Verein Deutscher Buchbindereien für Verlag und Industrie		**VDL**	Verband Deutscher Luftfahrttechniker
			VDL	Vereinigung Deutscher Landesschafzucht- verbände
VDBF	Verband der Briefumschlag- und Papierausstattungs-Fabriken			
			VdL	Verband der Lackindustrie
VDC	Verband Deutscher Fachschulchemiker		**VDLU**	Verband Deutscher Luftfahrt- Unternehmen
VDD	Industrieverband Bituminöse Dach- und Dichtungsbahnen		**VDLUFA**	Verband Deutscher Landwirtschaftlicher Untersuchungs- u. Forschungsanstalten
VDD	Verein Deutscher Dokumentare		**VDM**	Verband Deutscher Makler für Grundbesitz und Finanzierungen
VDD	Verband Deutscher Drogisten			
VdD	Verband der Druckfarbenindustrie		**VDM**	Verband der Deutschen Milchwirtschaft
VDD	Vereinigung der Drahtflechtereien		**VDM**	Verband Deutscher Mineralbrunnen
VdDB	Verein der Diplom-Bibliothekare an Wissen- schaftlichen Bibliotheken		**VDM**	Verband der Deutschen Möbelindustrie
			VdM	Verband der Mineralfarbenindustrie
VDDI	Verband Deutscher Diplom-Ingenieure		**VDMA**	Verein Deutscher Maschinenbauanstalten
VDDS	Vereinigung Diplomieter Kaufleute des Detailhandels der Schweiz		**VDMG**	Verband Deutscher Meteorologischer Gesellschaften
VDDW	Verband der Deutschen Wasserzählerin- dustrie		**VDMK**	Verband Deutscher Musikerzieher und Konzertierender Künstler
VDE	Verband Deutscher Elektrotechniker		**VDN**	Verband Deutscher Nähmaschinenhändler
VDEfa	Verein Deutscher Emailfachleute		**VDN**	Verband des Deutschen Nahrungsmitel- grosshandels
VDEh	Verein Deutscher Eisenhüttenleute			
VDEN	Vereniging van Directeuren van Electriciteits- bedrijven in Nederland		**VDP**	Verband Deutscher Papierfabriken
			VDP	Verband Deutscher Pradikätsweingüter
VDEW	Vereinigung Deutscher Elektrizitätswerke		**VDP**	Verband der Deutschen Parkett-Industrie
VDF	Verband der Deutschen Faserplattenindustrie und verwandter Betriebe		**VDPh**	Verband Deutscher Physiotherapeuten
			VDPI	Verband der Deutschen Photographischen Industrie
VDF	Verband Deutscher Feuerverzinkereien			
VDF	Verband der Deutschen Fruchtsaft-Industrie		**VDPI**	Verband Deutscher Post-Ingenieure
VDF	Verband Deutscher Flugleiter			

VdPÖ	Verband der Professoren Österreichs
VDPW	Verband der Patentwirtschaftler (Germany)
VDR	Verband Deutscher Realschullehrer
VDR	Verband Deutscher Reeder
VDRG	Verband Deutscher Rundfunk- und Fernseh-Fachgrosshändler
VDRI	Verein Deutscher Revisions-Ingenieure
VDRJ	Vereinigung Deutscher Reisejournalisten
VDRZ	Verband Deutscher Rechenzentren
VDS	Verband Deutscher Schiffswerften
VDS	Verband Deutscher Schulmuskerzieher
VDS	Verband Deutscher Studienschaften
VDS	Vereinigung Deutscher Sägewerksverbände
VDS	Verband Deutscher Schirmfachgeschäfte
VDSB	Verein Deutschschweizerischer Bienenfreunde
VDSI	Verein Deutscher Sicherheits-Ingenieure
VDSt	Verband Deutscher Stahlwarenhändler
VDT	Verband Deutscher Tapetenfabrikanten
VDT	Verband Deutscher Techniker
VDT	Verband des Deutschen Tischlerhandwerks
VdTUV	Vereinigung der Technischen Überwachungs-Vereine
VDU	Verband der Deutschen Uhrenindustrie
VDÜ	Verband Deutschsprachiger Übersetzer Literarischer und Wissenschaftlicher Werke
VDV	Verband Deutscher Vermessungsingenieure
VDV	Verband der Versandgeschäfte
VDVM	Verein Deutscher Versicherungsmakler
VdW	Verband der Deutschen Fruchtwein- und Fruchtschaumwein-Industrie
VDW	Verband Deutscher Weinexporteure
VdW	Verband der Waggonindustrie
VDW	Verband der Wellpappen-Industrie
VDW	Verein Deutscher Werkzeug-maschinenfabriken
VDWW	Vereinigung Deutscher Werks- und Wirtschaftsarchivare
VDZ	Verband Deutscher Zeitschriftenverleger
VDZ	Verein Deutscher Zementwerke
VDZ	Verband des Deutscher Zweiradhandels
VdZ	Vereinigung von Verbänden der Deutschen Zentralheizungswirtschaft
VDZI	Verband Deutscher Zahntechniker-Innungen
VEA	Nederlandse Vereniging voor Erkende Advertentiebureaux
VEA	Verband der Energie-Abnehmer
VEA	Vereinigung von Fabriken Elektrothermischer Apparate (Switzerland)
VEB	Vereniging Effectenbescherming
VEB	Vereniging der Electriciteitsbedrijven in België
VEB	Vereinigung Evangelischer Buchhändler
VEBIDAK	Vereniging van Bitumineuze Dakbedekkingsbedrijven
VEBO	Vereniging voor Brouwerij Onderzoek en Onderwijs
VEBUKU	Vereinigung der Buchantiquare und Kupferstichhändler der Schweiz
VECE	Coöperatieve Verkoopcentrale voor Eieren
VECO	Vereniging van op Coöperatieve Grondslag werkende Afzetorganisaties voor Zaaizaad en Pootgoed
VECOL	Empresa Colombiana de Productos Veterinarios
VECOR	Vanderbijl Engineering Corporation (South Africa)
VECTA	Vereniging van Ondernemers van Concertbureaux
VED	Verband der Exhibition-Designer
VED	Verkerks- und Energiewirtschaftsdepartement (Switzerland)
VEDAG	Verband Deutschschweizerischer Ärztegesellschaften
VEDC	Vitreous Enamel Development Council
VEDEWA	Vereinigung der Wasserversorgungsverbände und Gemeinden mit Wasserwerken
VEEN	Vereniging v. Exploitanten v. Electriciteitsbedrijven in Nederland
VEF	Vereniging van Emaillefabrieken
VEG	Bundesverband des Elektro-Grosshandels
VEG	Verband Österreichischer Elektro-Grosshändler
VEG	Vereniging van Exploitanten van Gasbedrijven
VEGA	Vegetable Growing Association of America
VEGAT	Verband Schweizerischer Garn- und Tricotveredler
VEGIN	Vereniging van Exploitanten van Gasbedrijven in Nederland
VEGROCOS	Nederlandse Vereniging van Groothandelaren in Cosmetica en Parfumerieën

VEHAVLAS	Vereniging der Handelaars in Vlasvezels
VEICB	Vereniging der Electrische Industriële Centrales van België
VEIMMAVO	Vereniging van Importeurs van en Handelaren in Machines voor de Zuivel-Dranken-Voedings- en Genotmiddelenindustrie
VEK	Veterana Esperentista Klubo (Germany)
VELEBI	Vereniging van Leraren in de Biologie
VELEDES	Schweizerischer Verband der Lebensmittel-Detaillisten
VELF	Verwaltung für Ernährung, Landwirtschaft und Forsten
VELINES	Vereniging van Leraren in Natuur- en Scheikunde
VEMI	Vereniging van Importeurs en Fabrikanten van en Groothandelaren in Melkwinning- en Bewaarapparatuur
VEMI	Vereniging van Muziekinstrumenten-handelaren
VENEAGRO	Venezolana de Exportaciones Agrícolas
VENEDAK	Vereniging van Nederlandse Dakrolfabrikanten
VENEFAB	Vereniging van Nederlandse Fabrikanten van Bestrijdingsmiddelen
VENEPAL	Venezolana de Pulpa y Papel
VENEXA	Vereniging van Nederlandse Exporteurs van Aardappelen
VENISS	Visual Education National Information Service for Schools
VENO	Verbond Algemene Exporthandel
VEÖ	Verband der Elektrizitätswerke Österreichisches
VEPAVE	Vereniging van Papierverwerkers
VERAS	Vereinigung Schweizerischer Asphaltunternehmungen
VERBISKO	Vereniging van Fabrikanten van Banket, Beschuit, Biscuit, Koek en Aanverwante Produkten
VEREM-ABEL	Groupement Belge des Vendeurs-Réparateurs de Tracteurs et Machines Agricoles
VERNOF	Vereniging van Nederlandse Fabrikanten van Eetbare Oliën en Vetten
VERTGLAS	Genossenschaft der Schweizerischen Glasgrosshändler
VERTRIKO	Vereniging van Tricot- en Kousenfabrikanten
VERVOER	Vereniging van Oesterkwekers en Exporteurs
VES	Voluntary Emergency Service
VESEIGA	Verband Schweizerischer Seidengarnfarbereien
VESKA	Verband Schweizerischer Krankenanstalten
VESKOF	Vereinigung Schweizerischer Kontrollfirmen f. Sämereien
VESTRA	Verband Schweizerischer Unternehmungen für Strassenbeläge
VETSALL	Veterinarians Alliance
VEV	Vereniging ter Bevordering van de Export van Vleeswaren en Vleesconserven
VEV	Vlaams Economische Verbond
VEWIN	Vereniging van Exploitanten van Waterleidingsbedrijven in Nederland
VF	Sveriges Verkstadsförening
VF	Vestlandske Fartybyggjarlag
VFB	Vereniging van Fabrikanten van Bakkerij-Installaties
VFDB	Vereinigung z. Förderung d. Deutschen Brandschutzes
VFFS	Verband der Freiberuflichen Fahrzeugsachverständigen
VFG	Verband fur Flüssiggas
VFG	Verein zur Förderung der Giesserei-Industrie
VFG	Versuchanstalt f. Getreideverwertung
VFI	Verkfroedingafélag Íslands
VFK	Vereniging v. Fourage-en Kunstmesthandelaren
VFK	Vereniging van Nederlandse Fabrieken van Ketels, Drukhouders en Tanks
VFM	Verband der Fahrrad- und Motorradindustrie
VFMA	Verband der Führungskräfte der Metall- und Electroindustrie
VFMG	Vereinigung der Freunde der Mineralogie und Geologie
VFN	Vereniging van Financieringsondernemingen in Nederland
VFP	Verband der Fellgrossisten und Pelzkonfektionäre
VFR	Verband der Radio Fernsch- und Elektro-Fachhandels Österreichs
VFW	Vereinigte Flugtechnische Werke
VGAA	Vegetable Growers' Association of America
VGAS	Verband Galvanischer Anstalten der Schweiz
VGB	Vereniging van Groothandelaren in Brandstoffen
VGB	Vereinigung der Grosskraftwerksbetreiber
VGCT	Verein für Gerberei-Chemie und -Technik

VGD	Vereniging van de Grote Distributie-ondernemingen van België
VGG	Verband der Hersteller von gewerblichen Geschirrspülmaschinen
VGHM	Vereniging voor de Groothandel in Huishoudelijke Artikelen en Metaalwaren
VGIG	Vereniging voor de Groothandel in Gasverwarmings- en Verbruikstoestellen en Andere Verwarmingstoestellen
VGL	Schweizerische Vereinigung für Gewasser-schutz und Lufthygiene
VGM	Verband Gross-Städtischer Milchver-sorgungsbetriebe
VGN	Verein für Geschichte der Stadt Nürnberg
VGN	Vereniging van Gasfabrikanten in Nederland
VGN	Vereniging Gereedschapsfabrieken in Nederland
VGN	Vereniging van Geschiedenisleraren in Nederland
VGP	Vereinigung von Grossiten für den Photohandel
VGRO	Vereniging van Grafische Reproductie On-dernemingen
VGS	Vereniging van Gespecialiseerde Schoolleveranciers
VGSW	Verein für Geschichte der Stadt Wien (Austria)
VGT	Nederlandse Vereniging van Groothan-delaren in Tandheelkundige Benodigdheden
VGT	Verband des Garagen- und Tankstellengewerbes
VGV	Vereniging van Gespecialiseerde Vloeren-bedrijven
VGW	Verband der Deutschen Gas- und Wasserwerke
VH	Versuchsanstalt der Hefeindustrie
VHF	Veterinaerhygienisk Forening
VHI	Verband der Deutschen Holzwerkstoff-Industrie
VHK	Verband der Hersteller von Konditoreihilf-stoffen
VHN	Vereniging van Houtimpregneerinrichtingen in Nederland
VHOK	Vereniging van Handelaren in Oude Kunst in Nederland
VHP	Nederlandse Verenninging voor de Handel in Pluimvee en Wild
VHPI	Verband der Schweizerischen Holzverpackungs- und Palettenindustrie
VHR	Vereniging voor de Handel in Rubber-artikelen
VHS	Vereniging Fabrieken van Hang- en Sluitwerk
VHTL	Verband der Handels-, Transport- und Lebensmittelarbeiter der Schweiz
VHV	Vereinigung der Holzhandelsverbände
VHVH	Nederlandse Vereniging van Handelaren in Verwarmings- en Huishoudelijke Apparaten
VHZ	Vereniging voor de Handel in Land-bouwzaaizaden
VHZMK	Vereinigung der Hochschullehre für Zahn-, Mund- und Kieferheilkunde
VIAR	Volcani Institute of Agricultural Research (Israel)
VIASA	Venezolana Internacional de Aviación, S.A.
VIB	Nederlandse Vereniging in het Isolatiebedrijf
VIB	Vereniging van Importeurs van Bouwmaterialen
VIB	Voedselvoorzienings in-en Verkoopbureau
VIBÖ	Vereinigung Industrieller Bauunter-nehmungen Österreichs
VICA	Vocational Industrial Clubs of America
VICORP	Virgin Islands Corporation
VID	Volunteers for International Development (U.S.A.)
VIE	Victorian Institute of Engineers (Australia)
VIF	Svenska Värmeisolermaterialfakrikanterna
VIF	Verband von Importeuren der Fisch- und Fischproduktenbranche
VIFKA	Vereniging van Importeurs en Fabrikanten van Kantoormachines
VIGE	Royal Institute of Agricultural Research (Greece)
VIGPA	Nederlandse Vereniging van Importeurs van en Groothandelaren in Glas, Porcelan en Aardewerk
VILF	Verband der Ingenieure des Lack- und Far-benfaches
VILLA	Ventes Immobilières de Logement et de Lotissements en Afrique (Congo)
VILS	Verband Schweizerischer Industrieliefaran-ten für Shrott
VIMAG	Vereniging van Importeurs van Machinegereedschappen voor de Metaalbewerking
VIMETAAL	Vereniging van Importeurs van Gereedschapswerktuigen

VIMHOUT	Vereniging van Importeurs van en Handelaren
VIMKO	Vereniging van Importeurs van Koelmachines en Koelkasten
VIMPOL	Vereniging v. Importeurs v. Landbouwwerktuigen
VIMPOLTU	Vereniging van Importeurs van en Groothandelaren in Land- en Tuinbouwmachines
VIMPOS-TAAL	Vereniging van Handelaren in Speciaalstaal
VIMTU	Vereniging v. Importeurs v. Tuinbouwwerktuigen
VIP	Verein der Industriefilmproduzenten
VIP	Vereniging Importeurs Pneumatische Werktuigen
VIP Teams	Visiting International Psychiatric Teams Inc. (U.S.A.)
VIPS	Vereinigung der Importeure Pharmazeutischer Spezialtäten (Switzerland)
VIR	Vereniging Informatie en Recherche-Bureauhouders
VIRO	Netherlands United Nations Association
VIS	Veterinary Investigation Service
VISACAM	Société des Viandes et Salaisons du Cameroun
VISTA	Volunteers in the Service of America
VITA	Volunteers for International Technical Assistance (U.S.A.)
VITAR	Veterinary Institute for Tropical and High Altitude Research (Peru)
VIV	Food Import Bureau (Holland)
VIV	Verband Schweizer Vieh-Importeure
VIV	Vereniging van Importeurs van Verbrandingsmotoren
VKD	Verband der Köche Deutschlands
VKE	Verband Kunstofferzeugende Industrie und Verwandt Gebiete
VKF	Vereniging van Kartonnagefabrikanten in Nederland
VKF	Vereinigung Schweizerischer Kabel-Fabriken
VKFA	Vereinigung Kantonaler Feuerversicherungsanstalten
VKG	Verband der Kraftfahrzeugteile
VKI	Groep Verwarmings- en Kookapparatenindustrie
VKI	Verband Kunststoff Verarbeitender Industriebetriebe der Schweiz
VKI	Vereniging Klei Industrie
VKIFD	Von Karman Institute for Fluid Dynamics (Belgium)
VKL	Vereniging van Kleuterschool Leveranciers
VKL	Vereniging van Katholieke Leraren "Sint-Bonaventura"
VKÖ	Verband der Köche Österreichs
VKS	Verband Kommunaler Städtereinigungsbetriebe
VLA	Vereniging Fabrieken van Luchttechnische Apparaten
VLB	Versuchs- und Lehranstalt für Brauerei in Berlin
VLET	Vereniging van Leveranciers van Electrotechnische
VLG	Vereniging van Leveranciers voor de Galvano-Techniek
VLGN	Verband Landwirtschaftlicher Genossenschaften der Nordwestschweiz
VLGZ	Verband Landwirtschaftlicher Genossenschaften der Zentralschweiz
VLHT	Vereniging van Laboratoriumhoudende Tandtechnici in Nederland
VLK	Verband der Landwirtschaftskammern
VLKB	Schweizerischer Verband der Lehrer an Kaufmännischen Berufsschulen
VLL	Nederlandse Vereniging van Leraren in Landbouw-Mechanica
VLM	Vereniging van Leveranciers van Merkspeelgoed
VLN	Vereniging tot Bevordering v. d. Landbouwtuigpaardfokkerij in Nederland
VLP	Schweizerische Vereinigung für Landesplanung
VLRP	Vitamin Laboratories of Roche Products (Australia)
VLSF	Verband der Lastwagen-Spediteure und Ferntransportunternehmer (Switzerland)
VKV	Vlaams Kinesitherapeutm Verbond
VLT	Vereniging van Loonveredilingsbedrijven voor de Textielindustrie
VLVB	Verband von Lieferanten Versilbenter Bestecke (Switzerland)
VLW	Bundesverband der Lehrer an Wirtschaftsschulen
VMAI	Veterinary Medical Association of Ireland
VMB	Vereniging van Metaalbeschermingsbedrijven
VMCC	Vintage Motor Cycle Club

VMD	Vereniging Milieudefensie	**VÖÄ**	Vereinigung Österreichischer Ärzte
VMF	Vieilles Maisons Françaises	**VÖAG**	Verband des Österreichischen Automatengewerbes
VMI	Vereniging van Metaal-Industrieën		
VMM	Volunteer Missionary Movement	**VÖB**	Verband Öffentlicher Banken
VMNICM	Vaikunth Mehta National Institute of Cooperative Management (India)	**VÖB**	Vereinigung Österreichischer Bibliothekare
		VÖCh	Verein Österreichischer Chemiker
VMÖ	Verband der Marktforscher Österreichs	**VOCOSS**	Voluntary Organisations Co-operating in Overseas Social Service
VMPA	Verband der Materialprüfungsämter		
VMR	Vereniging van Metalen-Ramenfabrikanten	**VOEST**	Vereinigte Österreichische Eisen – und Stahlwerke AG
VMS	Verband der Museen der Schweiz		
VMVM	Verbond der Middelgrote Verzekerings-maatschappijen	**VOF**	Verband der Fabrikanten von Technischen Ölen, Fetten und Verwandten Produkten
VNA	Vereniging van de Nederlandse Aardolie-Industrie	**VÖFVL**	Verband Österreichischer Flugsverkehrsleiter
		VOFyTOZ	Vereniging voor Studie en Onderzoek over Fytopatologie en Toegepaste Zoologie
VNA	Vietnamese News Agency		
VNCI	Vereniging van de Nederlandse Chemische Industrie	**VÖG**	Verein Österreichischer Giessereifachleute
		VÖI	Verband Österreichische Ingenieure
VNG	Verbond van de Nederlandse Groothandel	**VÖI**	Vereinigung Österreichischer Industrieller
VNG	Vereniging van Nederlandse Gemeenten	**VÖK**	Vereinigung Österreichischer Kunst-stoffverarbeiter
VNG	Vereniging van Nederlandse Grasdrogerijen		
VNGF	Vereniging van Kleuterschool Leveranciers	**VOLBRIC-ERAM**	Société Voltaïque de Briqueterie et de Céramique
VNK	Vereniging voor Japanse Kunst	**VOLG**	Verband Ostschweizerischer Landwirtschaft-icher Genossenschaften
VNK	Vereniging Nederlandse Kerftabakindustrie		
VNKI	Vereniging van Nederlandse Kolenimpor-teurs	**VOLINFLO**	Voluntary Action Information Flow
		VOLTAICA	Société Voltaïque pour l'Avancement de l'Industrie, du Commerce et de l'Agriculture
VNM	Vereniging Nederlandse Fabrieken van Melktransportkannen		
VNM	Vereniging Nederlandse Motorenrevisiebedrijven	**VOLTAP**	Société Voltaïque de Diffusion d'Appareils Électriques
		VOLTAVIN	Société des Vins de la Haute-Volta
VNMF	Vereniging van Nederlandse Mengvoederfabrikanten	**VOLTELEC**	Société Voltaïque d'Électricité
		VOLTEX	Société Voltaïque des Textiles
VNO	Verbond van Nederlandse Ondernemingen	**VOLTOA**	Société Voltaïque d'Oxygène et d'Acetylène
VNP	Vereninging van Nederlandsche Papierfabrikanten	**VOM**	Vereniging voor Oppervlaktetechnieken van Metalen
VNR	Vereniging van Nederlandse Reformhuizen		
VNRC	Vegetarian Nutritional Research Centre	**VÖN**	Verband der Österreichischen Neuphilologen
VNS	Verenigde Nederlandse Slijters	**VOO**	Vereniging voor Openbaar Onderwijs
VNU	Volontaires des Nations Unies	**VOP**	Stichting tot Bevordering van de Vakopleid-ing voor de Handel in Pluimvee, Wild en Tamme Konijnen
VNV	Vereniging van Nederlandse Verkeersvliegers		
VNV	Vereniging van Nederlandse Vleeswaren- en Vleesconservenfabrikanten	**VÖR**	Vereinigung des Österreichischen Rüben-bauerorganisationen
VNZ	Vereniging van Nederlandse Fabrikanten van Zuivelwerktuigen	**VORI**	Viticultural and Oenological Research Institute (South Africa)
VÖA	Verband Österreichischer Archivare	**VOSA**	Voluntary Overseas Service Association
VOA	Vereniging Ontwikkeling Arbeidstechniek	**VÖTC**	Verein Österreichischer Textilchemiker Coloristen
VOA	Vereniging voor Organisatieen Arbeidskunde		

VÖV	Verband Öffentlicher Verkehrsbetriebe
VOW	Vereniging van Ondernemers in Wand-bekleding
VÖWA	Verband Österreichischer Wirtschafts-akademiker
VÖZ	Verband Österreichischer Ziegelwerke
VÖZ	Verband Österreichischer Zeitungs-herausgeber
VÖZ	Verein Österreichischen Zementfabrikanten
VPA	Virginia Pharmaceutical Association
VPBS	Verband Papier, Bürobedarf und Schreibwaren in der Hauptgemeinschaft des Deutschen Einzelhandels
VPCA	Vereniging der Publiciteitschefs der Adver-teerders van België
VPCM	Vereniging van Protestants-Christelijke Metaalindustriëlen in Nederland
VPI	Nederlandse Vereniging van Producenten en Importeurs van Wegen- en Water-bouwmaterialen
VPI	Virginia Polytechnic Institute (U.S.A.)
VPLC	Vereniging v. Pluimveeselecteurs in Dienst v. Landbouwcoöperaties
VPM	Nederlandse Vereniging van Fabrikanten van Verbandstoffen, Pleisters en Maandverband
VPN	Verein für Psychiatric and Neurologie (Austria)
VPOD	Schweizerischer Verband des Personals Offentlicher Dienste
VPRI	Victorian Plant Research Institute (Australia)
VPRO	Vrijzinnig Protestantse Radio-Omroep
VPRP	Vietnam People's Revolutionary Party
VPS	Verband Privater Städtereinigungsbetriebe
VPSG	Verband Schweizerischer Papier- und Papierstoff- Fabrikanten
VRB	Vereniging van Religieus-Wetenschappelijke Bibliothecarissen
VRF	Verband der Radio, Fernseh- und Elektro-Fachhandels Österreichs
VRH	Verband der Reformwaren-Hersteller
VRKD	Verband Reisender Kaufleute Deutschlands
VRKÖ	Verband Reisender Kaufleute Österreichs
VRKS	Verband Reisender Kaufleute der Schweiz
VRM	Vereinigung der Regierungsbaumeister des Maschinenwesens "Motor"
VS	Verband Deutscher Schriftsteller
VSA	Föreningen Värmlands Skogarbetsstudier

VSA	Verband Schweizerischer Annoncen-Expeditionen
VSA	Vereinigung Schweizerischer Akkumulatorenfabrikanten
VSA	Vereinigung Schweizerischer Angestelltenverbände
VSA	Vereinigung Schweizerischer Archivare
VSAK	Verband Schweizer Antiquare und Kunsthändler
VSB	Schweizerischer Bierbrauerverein
VSB	Verband Schweizer Badekurorte
VSB	Verband Schweizerischer Baumschulbesitzer
VSB	Verband Schweizerischer Bücherexperten
VSB	Vereniging voor Strategische Beleidsvorming
VSB	Vereinigung Schweizerischer Bibliothekare
VSB	Vereinigung Schweizerischer Bohrfirmen
VSBF	Verband Schweizerischer Blechemballagen-Fabrikanten
VSBH	Verband Schweizerischer Baumaterial-Händler
VSBH	Verband Schweizerischer Baumwollabgang-Händler
VSBH	Vereinigung Schweizerischer Buchdruck-Hilfsarbeiter
VSBM	Verband Schweizerischer Baumaschinen – Fabrikanten und -Händler
VSBPF	Verband Schweizerischer Bürsten- und Pinselfabrikanten
VSBS	Verband Schweizerischer Bildhauer- und Steinmetzmeister
VSC	Verband Schweizerischer Carbesitzer
VSCC	Vintage Sports Car Club
VSCF	Verein Schweizerischer Cartonnage-Fabriken
VSchM	Verband Schweizerischer Müller
VSCI	Verband der Schweizerischer Carosserie-Industrie
VSCTU	Vereinigung Schweizerischer Chemischreinigungs- und Textilpflege-Unternehmen
VSD	Verband des Schweizerischen Darmhandels
VSD	Verband Schweizerischer Düngerhändler
VSE	Verband der Schweizerischen Edelstein-branche
VSE	Verband Schweizerischer Eisengiessereien
VSE	Verband Schweizerischer Eisenwarenhändler
VSE	Verband Schweizerischer Elektrizitätswerke

VSEF	Verband Schweizersicher Edelmetallwaren-Fabrikanten
VSEI	Verband Schweizerische Elektro-Installationsfirmen
VSEMK	Verband Schweizerischer Edelstahl-, Metall- und Kunststoffhändler
VSF	Värme- och Sanitetstekniska Föreningen i Finland
VSF	Verband Schweizerischer Seidenstoff-Fabrikanten
VSF	Vereinigung des Schweizerischen Farbenfachhandels
VSF	Vereinigung Schweizerischer Futtermittelfabrikanten
VSFAV	Verband Schweizerischer Film und AV-Produzenten
VSFBR	Verband Schweizerischer Fabrikanten van Besen aus Reisig
VSFE	Verband Schweizerischer Fabrikanten von Einbauküchen
VSFF	Verband Schweizerischer Fleischwaren-Fabrikanten
VSFK	Verein Schweizerischer Fabrikanten von Kunststoffpackungen
VSG	Verband Schweizerischer Gärtnermeister
VSG	Verband Schweizerischer Gaswerke
VSG	Verband Schweizerischer Gerbereien
VSG	Verband Schweizerischer Goldschmiede
VSG	Verband Schweizerischer Graphiker
VSG	Verband Schweizerischer Grastrocknungsbetriebe
VSG	Verband des Schweizerischen Spirituosengewerbes
VSG	Verein Schweizerischer Gymnasiallehrer
VSGF	Vereinigung Schweizerischer Gasherd-Fabrikanten
VSGH	Verband Schweizerischer Geflügelhalter
VSGI	Verband Schweizerischer Geflügel- und Wild-Importeure
VSGN	Vereinigung Schweizerischer Grosshandelsfirmen in Abfällen von Nichteisenmetallen
VSGP	Verband Schweizerischer Gemüseproduzenten
VSGT	Verband Schweizerischer Gummi- und Thermoplast-Industrieller
VSGU	Verband Schweizerischer Generalunternehmer
VSH	Verband Schweizerischer Hadernsortierwerke
VSH	Verband Schweizerischer Hartschotterwerke
VSH	Verband Schweizerischer Heuhandelsfirmen
VSH	Vereinigung Schweizerischer Hafermühlen
VSHF	Verband Schweizerischer Holzbearbeitungsmaschinen- und Werkzeug-Fabrikanten
VSHL	Verband Schweizerischer Heizungs- und Lüftungsfirmen
VSI	Bundesverband des Sanitär-Fachhandels
VSI	Verband Schmierfett-Industrie
VSI	Verband Schweizerischer Immobilienbureaux
VSI	Verband Schweizerischer Isolierfirmen
VSI	Verband Selbständiger Ingenieure
VSI	Vereinigung Schweizer Innenarchitekten
VSI	Vinnuveitandasamband Islands
VSIA	Verband Schweizerischer Industrie-Lieferanten für Altpapier
VSIEA	Vereinigung Schweizerischer Importeure Elektrischer Apparate
VSIG	Vereinigung des Schweizerischen Import- und Grosshandels
VSJE	Vereinigung Schweizerischer Juwelen- und Edelmetallbranchen
VSK	Verband Schweizerischer Konsumvereine
VSKB	Vereniging voor het Theologisch Bibliothecariaat
VSKE	Verband Schweizerischer Käseesporteure
VSKF	Verband Schweizerischer Kachelofenfabrikanten
VSKF	Verein Schweizerischer Kondensatoren-Fabrikanten
VSKI	Verband der Schweizerischen Keramischen Industrie
VSKM	Verband Schweizerischer Kundenmüller
VSL	Verband Schweizerischer Firmen für Linoleum und Spezialbodenbeläge
VSL	Verband Schweizerischer Lagerhäuser
VSL	Verband Schweizerischer Leinen-Industrieller
VSLB	Verein Schweizerischer Lithographiebesitzer
VSLF	Verband Schweizerischer Lack- und Farbenfabrikanten
VSLF	Vereinigung Schweizerischer Leichtbauplattenfabrikanten

VSLG	Verband Schweizerischer Grossisten für Linoleum und Spezialbodenbeläge
VSLR	Verband Schweizerischer Lichtpaus- und Reprografie-Betriebe
VSM	Verband Schweizerischer Marmor- und Granitwerke
VSM	Verein Schweizerischer Maschinen-Industrieller
VSM	Verband Schweizerischer Mineralquellen
VSM	Verein Schweizerischer Maschinen-Industrieller
VSM	Vereinigung Schweizerischer Modehäuser
VSM	Vereniging Fabrikanten van Stalen Kantooren Bedrijfsmeubelen
VSMB	Verband Schweizerischer Modellbaubetriebe
VSMBD	Verband Schweizerischer Mercerie- und Bonneterie-Detaillisten
VSMF	Vereinigung Schweizerischer Metallschutz-Firmen
VSMG	Verband Schweizerischer Metallgiessereien
VSMP	Verein Schweizerischer Mathematik- und Physiklehrer
VSMR	Verband Schweizerischer Motor-Revisionsbetriebe
VSMWH	Verband des Schweizerischen Maschinen- und Werkzeughandels
VSN	Vereinigung Schweizerischer Naturwissenschaftslehrer
VSN	Vereniging Smeerolieondernemingen Nederland
VSO	Voluntary Service Overseas
VSP	Verband Schweizerischer Papeteristen
VSP	Verband Schweizerischer Patentanwälte
VSP	Verband Schweizerischer Pferdemetzgereien
VSP	Verband Schweizerischer Pflasterermeister
VSP	Verein der Schweizer Presse
VSP	Vereinigung Schweizer Petroleum-Geologen und Ingenieure
VSPG	Verband Schweizerischer Papier-Grossisten
VSPPF	Verband Schweizerischer Papier- und Papierstoff-Fabrikanten
VSR	Verband Schweizerischer Rolladen-und Storenfabriken
VSR	Vereinigung Schweizerischer Reproduktionsbetriebe
VSR	Vereniging Fabrieken van Staalplaat Radiatoren
VSRD	Verband Schweizer Reform- und Diätfachgeschäfte
VSRT	Verband Schweizerischer Radio- und Televisionsfachgeschäfte
VSS	Verband Schweizerischer Schirmfabrikanten
VSS	Verband Schweizerischer Schmierölimporteurs
VSS	Verband Schweizerische Schuhindustrieller
VSS	Vereinigung Schweizerischer Strassenfachmänner
VSS	Verband Schweizerischer Studentenschaften
VSS	Vereinigung Schweizerischer Siebdruckereien
VSSB	Verband Schweizerischer Schloss- und Beschlägefabrikanten
VSSB	Verband Schweizerischer Schreib- und Büromaschinenhändler
VSSD	Verband Schweizerischer Spielwaren-Detaillisten
VSSF	Verband Schweizerischer Schallplatten-Fachgeschäfte
VSSF	Verband Schweizerischer Spielwarenfabrikanten
VSSJ	Verband Schweizer Sportjournalisten
VSSL	Verband Schweizerischer Schallplatten-Lieferanten
VSSM	Verband Schweizerischer Schreinermeister und Möbelfabrikanten
VSSÖ	Verband der Sportausrüster und Sportartikelerzeuger Österreichs
VSSTF	Verband Schweizerischer Sperrholz- und Tischlerplatten-Fabrikanten
VSSZ	Verein Schweizerischer Seidenzwirner
VST	Verband Schweizerischer Teigwarenfabrikanten
VST	Verband Schweizerischer Transportanstalten
VST	Verband Schweizerischer Transportunternehmungen des Öffentlichen Verkehrs
VST	Vereinigung Schweizerischer Teppichhändler
VST	Vereinigung Schweizerischer Tiefbauunternehmer
VSTF	Verein Schweizerischer Teppichfabrikanten
VSTG	Verband Schweizerischer Teppich-Grossisten
VSTG	Verband Schweizerischer Topfpflanzen- und Schnittblumengärtnereien
VSTH	Verband Schweizerischer Tabakhändler
VSTH	Verband Schweizerischer Technischer Händler

VSTH	Verband Schweizerischer Traubensaft-hersteller	**VUBI**	Verband Unabhängig Beratender Ingenieurfirmen
VSTI	Verein Schweizerischer Textilindustrieller	**VUC**	Victoria University College, Wellington (New Zealand)
VSTV	Verband der Schweizerischen Textil-Veredlungs-Industrie	**VUNB**	Vereniging van Uitgevers van Nederlands-talige Boeken
VSU	Verband Schweizerischer Uhrenfachgeschäfte	**VUPC**	Výskúmny Üstav Papiera a Celulózy
VSU	Verband Selbständiger Unternehmen der Nährmittelindustrie	**VUPP**	Výskúmny Üstav Prumysly Papírenského
		VUV	Výzkumný ústav Vodohosppodársky
VSV	Verband Schweizerischer Verkehrsvereine	**VVA**	Vee an Vlees Aankoopbureau
VSVF	Verband der Schweizer Versandmetzgereien und des Fleischhandels	**VVBADP**	Vlaamse Vereniging van Bibliotheek-, Archief- en Documentatiepersoneel
VSVM	Verband der Schweizer Versandmetzgereien	**VVBAP**	Vlaamse Vereniging van Bibliotheek- en Archiefpersoneel
VSVM	Vereinigung Schweizerischer Versicherungs-mathematiker	**VVD**	Volkspartij voor Vrijheid en Democratie (Netherlands)
VSVT	Verband Schweizerischer Vermessungs-techniker	**VVDF**	Vereniging van Drukinktfabrikanten
VSVVS	Vereinigung Schweiz Versuchs-und Ver-mittlungsstellen für Saatkartoffeln	**VVK**	Verband Vollpappe- Kartonagen
		VVK	Verein für Volkskunde (Austria)
VSW	Verband Schweizerischer Werbe-gesellschaften	**VvL**	Vereniging van Letterkundigen
VSWF	Vereinigung Schweizerischer Weisskalkfabrikanten	**VVMA**	Vereniging van Medische Analysten
		VVS	Kungliga Vetenskaps- och Vitterhets-Samhället i Göteborg
VSWK	Verband der Schweizerischen Waren- und Kaufhäuser	**VVS**	Svenska Rörgrossistförening
VSWM	Vereniging Fabrikanten van Stalen Woning-meubelen	**VVS**	Vereniging voor Statistiek
		VvU	Vereinigung von Unternehmerinnen
VSWS	Verband Schweizerischer Woll- und Seidenstoff-Fabrikanten	**VVV**	Vliegtuigeienaars- en Vlieëniersvereniging
VSZ	Verband Schweizerischer Zigarrenfabrikanten	**VVVF**	Vereniging van Vernis- en Verffakrikanten in Nederland
VSZKGF	Verein Schweizerischer Zement-, Kalk- und Gips-Fabrikanter	**VVVH**	Vereniging van Verfhandelaren in Nederland
		VVZM	Vereniging voor Zuivelindustrie en Melkhygiene
VSZS	Verband Schweizerischer Ziegel- und Steinfabrikanten	**VWA**	Bundesverband Deutscher Verwaltungs- und Wirtschafts-Akademien
VTCC	Verein der Textil-Chemiker und Coloristen	**VWA**	Vereinigung der Werbeleiter und Werbe-assistenten
VTCVG	Vereniging Technische Commissie Vloeibaar Gas	**VWF**	Verband der Wissenschaftler an Forschungs-instituten
VTFF	Verband Technischer Betriebe für Film- und Fernsehen	**VWFA**	Verband Unabhängiger Wirtschafts-, Finanz- und Anlageberater
VTG	Verband Schweizer Tierarzneimittel-grossisten	**VWI**	Vereniging van Weegwerktuig-Industrieën
VTO	Vereniging van Textielondernemingen in Nederland	**VWO**	Verbond van Wetenschappelijke Onder-zoekers
VTO	Vsemirnaja Turisticheskaja Organizatsija	**VWP**	Vietnam Workers' Party
		VZB	Vereniging van Zelfbedienings-Bedrijven
VTR	Verband Schweizerischer Unternehmungen für Tankreinigungen	**VZH**	Nederlandse Bond van Verzenhandelaren in Groenten en Fruit

VZI	Verband der Zigarettenpapier verarbeitenden Industrie
VZLS	Verband Zahntechnischer Laboratorien der Schweiz

W

WAA	Western Association of Africanists (U.S.A.)
WAAA	Women's Amateur Athletic Association
WAACCS	Western Australian Automobile Chamber of Commerce
WAAE	World Association for Adult Education
WAAER	World Association for the Advancement of Educational Research
WAALD	West African Association of Agricultural Librarians and Documentalists
WAAP	World Association for Animal Production
WAAS	World Academy of Art and Science
WAASP	World-Wide Association for Anomalous Scientific Phenomena
WAAVP	World Association for the Advancement of Veterinary Parasitology
WAC	Water Allocation Council (New Zealand)
WAC	West African Committee (U.K.)
WAC	Women's Advisory Committee of the British Standards Institution
WACA	Western Agricultural Chemicals Association (U.S.A.)
WACA	World Airlines Clubs Association
WACB	World Association for Christian Broadcasting
WACC	World Association for Christian Communication
WACH	West African Clearing House (Senegal)
WACL	World Anti-Communist League
WACMR	West African Council for Medical Research
WACO	World Air Cargo Organisation
WACP	West African College of Physicians (Ghana)
WACRAL	World Association of Christian Radio Amateurs and Listeners
WACRI	West African Cacao Research Institute, (Ghana)
WACU	West African Customs Union
WACY 2000	World Association for Celebrating Year 2000
WAD	World Association of Detectives (U.S.A.)
WADA	Wum Area Development Agency (Cameroons)
WADB	West African Development Bank (Togo)
WADC	Wright Air Development Centre (U.S.A.)
WADE	World Association of Document Examiners
WADVBS	World Association of Daily Vacation Bible Schools (U.S.A.)
WAE	World Association of Estonians (U.S.A.)
WAEC	War Agricultural Executive Committee
WAEC	West African Economic Community (Upper Volta)
WAEC	West African Examinations Council
WAEPA	Worldwide Assurance for Employees of Public Agencies (U.S.A.)
WAERSA	World Agricultural Economics and Rural Sociology Abstracts
WAFC	West African Fisheries Commissioner (FAO)
WAFRI	West-African Fisheries Research Institute
WAFRU	West African Fungicide Research Unit
WAGBI	Wildfowlers Association of Great Britain and Ireland
WAGGGS	World Association of Girl Guides and Girl Scouts
WAHO	World Arab Horse Organization
WAHS	West African Health Secretariat
WAIFOR	West African Institute for Oilpalm Research (*formerly* OPRS) (Nigeria)
WAIFTR	World Alliance for International Friendship through the Churches
WAIIC	Western State Agricultural and Industrial Investment Company (Nigeria)
WAISER	West African Institute of Social and Economic Research
WAITR	West African Institute for Trypanosomiasis Research
WAITRO	World Association of Industrial and Technological Research Organisations
WAJ	World Association of Judges
WAJAL	West African Joint Agency Ltd
WAL	Western Air Lines (U.S.A.)
WAL	World Association of Lawyers
WALA	West African Library Association
WAMRAC	World Association of Methodist Radio Amateurs and Clubs

WAMRU	West African Maize Research Unit
WAMS	World Association of Military Surgeons
WAMU	West African Monetary Union
WAOS	Welsh Agricultural Organisation Society
WAPDA	Water and Power Development Authority of West Pakistan
WAPET	West Australian Petroleum (Pty) Ltd.
WAPOR	World Association for Public Opinion Research
WAPMC	West African Postgraduate Medical College (Nigeria)
WAPT	Wild Animal Propagation Trust
WAPTT	World Association for Professional Training in Tourism
WARC	Women's Amateur Rowing Council
WARC	World Alliance of Reformed Churches
WARDA	West African Rice Development Association
WARI	Waite Agricultural Research Institute (Australia)
WARPATH	World Association to Remove Prejudice Against the Handicapped (U.S.A.)
WARRS	West African Rice Research Station
WAS	Washington Academy of Sciences (U.S.A.)
WAS	Witwatersrand Agricultural Society (South Africa)
WASA	West African Science Association
WASAL	Wisconsin Academy of Sciences, Arts and Letters
WASCO	National Water and Soil Conservation Organisation (New Zealand)
WASCU	World Association for the Senior Citizens Union (Switzerland)
WASID	Water and Soil Investigation Department (Pakistan)
WASP	World Association of Societies of Anatomic and Clinical Pathology
WASPRU	West African Stored Products Research Unit
WASU	West African Students Union
WAT	World Airport Technology (France)
WATA	World Association of Travel Agencies
WATBRU	West African Timber Borer Research Unit
WATTE	West African Tropical Testing Establishment
WAVA	World Association of Veterinary Anatomists
WAVE	World Association of Video-Makers and Editions
WAVFH	World Association of Veterinary Food Hygienists
WAVMI	World Association of Veterinary Microbiologists, Immunologists and Specialists in Infectious Diseases
WAVP	World Association of Veterinary Pathologists
WAWE	World Association of Women Executives
WAWF	World Association of World Federalists
WAY	World Alliance of Y.M.C.A's
WAY	World Assembly of Youth
WB	World Brotherhood
WBA	World Boxing Association
WBC	World Boxing Council
WBBG	Weltbund der Bibelgesellschaften
WBCA	Weltbewegung der Christlichen Arbeiter
WBC	World Business Council (U.S.A.)
WBDJ	Weltbund der Demokratischen Jugend
WBF	World Bridge Federation
WBG	Wiener Beethoven Gesellschaft
WBG	Wiener Bibliophilen-Gesellschaft
WBL	Nederlandse Vereniging tegen Water-, Bodem- en Luchtverontreiniging
WBMS	World Bureau of Metal Statistics (U.K.)
WBS	Wassmann Biological Society (U.S.A.)
WBS	Wellington Botanical Society (N.Z.)
WBSI	Western Behavioral Sciences Institute
WBV	Schweizerischer Weinbauverein
WCA	Women's Cricket Association
WCA	World Calendar Association
WCBA	Weltbewegung der Christlichen Arbeiter
WCC	World Cheerleader Council (U.S.A.)
WCC	World Council of Clergymen (U.S.A.)
WCC	World Council of Churches
WCC	World Crafts Council
WCCB	World Committee for Christian Broadcasting
WCCE	World Council of Christian Education
WCCESSA	World Council of Christian Education and Sunday School Associations
WCCI	World Council for Curriculum and Instruction (U.S.A.)
WCCS	World Chamber of Commerce Service (U.S.A.)
WCEMA	West Coast Electronic Manufacturers Association (U.S.A.)
WCEU	World's Christian Endeavour Union
WCF	World Congress of Faiths

WCFBA	World Catholic Federation for the Biblical Apostolate
WCL	World Confederation of Labour
WCMMF	World Congress of Man-Made Fibres
WCOTP	World Confederation of Organisations of the Teaching Profession (U.S.A.)
WCP	World Council of Peace
WCPA	World Constitution and Parliament Association (U.S.A.)
WCPS	World Confederation of Productivity Science
WCPT	World Confederation of Physical Therapy
WCPWC	World Council for the Peoples World Convention
WCRA	Weather Control Research Association (U.S.A.)
WCRA	Women's Cycle Racing Association
WCRP	World Conference of Religion for Peace
WCSC	World Correctional Service Center for Community and Social Concerns Inc. (U.S.A.)
WCWB	World Council for the Welfare of the Blind
WCYMSC	World Council of Young Men's Service Clubs
WDC	World Data Centre
WDK	Wirtschaftsverband der Deutschen Kautschukindustrie
WDM	World Development Movement (U.K.)
WDRC	World Data Referral Centre (France)
WdW	Weltbund der Weltföderalisten
WE	World Evangelism (U.S.A.)
WEA	Royal West of England Academy
WEA	Workers' Education Association
WEAA	Western European Airports Association
WEAAC	Western European Airports Association Conference
WEAAP	Western European Association for Aviation Psychology (Belgium)
WEBA	World Educational Broadcasting Assembly
WEC	World Energy Conference
WEC	World Engineering Conference
WEC	Worldwide Evangelisation Crusade
WECAFC	Western Central Atlantic Fishery Commission
WECo	Western Company (U.S.A.)
WECON	Western Electronics Show and Convention (U.S.A.)
WEDA	Wholesale Egg Distributors Association
WEDA	Wholesale Engineering Distributors Association
WEF	World Education Fellowship
WEF	World Evangelical Fellowship (Switzerland)
WEFC	West European Fisheries Conference
WEG	Wirtschaftsverband Erdölgewinnung
WEK	Weltweiter Evangelisations-Kreuzzug
WELG	Women's Ecumenical Liaison Group
WEM	Western European Metal Trades Employers Organizations
WEMA	Wirtschaftsverband Eisen-, Maschinen- und Apparatebau
WEPARM	Werkgroep Export Propaganda Agrarisch Reproductiemateriaal
WERC	World Environment and Resources Council
WES	Women's Engineering Society
WETUC	Workers Educational Trade Union Committee
WEU	Western European Union
WEXAS	World Expeditionary Association
WF	Wallboardfabrikkenes Felleskontor
WFA	War Food Administration (U.S.A.)
WFA	White Fish Authority
WFA	Women's Football Association
WFA	World Friendship Association (U.S.A.)
WFAA	Weltföderation Agrarischer Arbeiter
WFAC	World Federal Authority Committee
WFALW	Weltbund Freiheitlicher Arbeitnehmerverbände auf Liberaler Wirtschaftsgrundlage
WFAW	World Federation of Agricultural Workers
WFB	Weltrat für Bildung
WFB	World Federation of Buddists
WFBMA	Woven Fabric Belting Manufacturers Association
WFBW	World Federation of Building and Woodworkers Unions
WFC	World Food Congress (FAO)
WFC	World Food Council (UN)
WFCC	World Federation for Culture Collections
WFCLC	World Federation of Christian Life Communities
WFCS	World's Fair Collectors Society (U.S.A.)
WFCY	World Federation of Catholic Youth
WFCYWG	World Federation of Catholic Young Women and Girls

WFD	World Federation of the Deaf
WFDA	Wholesalers Floorcovering Distributors Association
WFDA	Wholesale Footwear Distributors Association
WFDY	World Federation of Democratic Youth
WFEA	World Federation of Education Associations
WFEO	World Federation of Engineering Organisations
WFF	World Friendship Federation
WFFL	World Federation of Free Latvians
WFFM	World Federation of Friends of Museums (Belgium)
WFFTH	World Federation of Workers in Food, Tobacco and Hotel Industries
WFGA	Women's Farm and Garden Association
WFH	Worldwide Federation of Healing (U.K.)
WFI	Wirtschaftsförderungsinstitut (Austria)
WFIJI	World Federation of International Juridical Institutions
WFIM	World Federation of Islamic Missions (Pakistan)
WFIS	Wagner Free Institute of Science (U.S.A.)
WFL	Women's Freedom League
WFLRY	World Federation of Liberal and Radical Youth
WFLTH	Weltföderation von Arbeiter in Lebensmittel, Tabak und Hotelindustrien
WFM	World Federation for the Metallurgic Industry
WFMH	World Federation for Mental Health
WFMW	World Federation of Methodist Women
WFN	World Federation of Neurology
WFNMB	World Federation of Nuclear Medicine and Biology (U.S.A.)
WFNS	World Federation of Neurosurgical Societies
WFOT	World Federation of Occupational Therapists
WFP	World Federation of Parasitologists
WFP	World Food Programme (Italy)
WFPA	World Federation for the Protection of Animals
WFPFFC	Worldwide Fairplay for Frogs Committee (U.S.A.)
WFPMM	World Federation of Proprietary Medicine Manufacturers
WFR	Weltfriedensrat
WFS	World Fertility Survey
WFS	World Food Security
WFS	World Future Society (U.S.A.)
WFSA	World Federation of Societies of Anaesthesiologists
WFSF	World Future Studies Federation
WFSW	World Federation of Scientific Workers
WFTU	World Federation of Teachers Unions
WFTU	World Federation of Trade Unions
WFUNA	World Federation of United Nations Associations
WFV	Werkfeuerwehrverband
WFVTH	Wereldfederatie van Arbeiders in Voedings-, Tabaks- en Hotelbedrijven
WFW	Weltföderation der Wissenschaftler
WFY	World Federalist Youth
WGA	Writers Guild of America
WGB	Weltgewerkschaftsbund
WGC	Womens Global Congress for International Friendship, Education and Culture
WGC	World Gospel Crusades (U.S.A.)
WGE	Wissenschaftliche Gesellschaft für Europarecht
WGfF	Westdeutsche Gesellschaft für Familienkunde
WGFSK	Wiener Gesellschaftzur Förderung der Schönen Künste (Austria)
WGGB	Writers Guild of Great Britain
WGM	World Gospel Mission (U.S.A.)
WGRA	Western Governmental Research Association
WHA	Wholesale Horticultural Association
WHGS	Wyoming Historical and Geological Society (U.S.A.)
WHO	World Health Organisation
WHOI	Woods Hole Oceanographic Institution (U.S.A.)
WHRA	Welwyn Hall Research Association (*formerly* CLAIRA and WIPRC)
WHRC	World Health Research Centre
WIA	Willow Importers' Association
WIA	Wool Importers Association
WIAB	Wistar Institute of Anatomy and Biology (U.S.A.)
WIAC	Women's International Art Club

WIACO	World Insulation Acoustics Congress Organization
WIBC	Women's International Bowling Congress (U.S.A.)
WIC	Water Information Centre (U.S.A.)
WIC	West Indian Committee (U.K.)
WICA	Witches International Craft Association (U.S.A.)
WICBC	West Indies Cricket Board of Control
WIDF	Women's International Democratic Federation
WIG	Verband Schweizerischer Wein-Importgrossisten
WIG	Weltverband der Industriegewerkschaften
WIIU	Workers International Industrial Union
WILCIC	Women's International Liaison Committee for International Cooperation Ye
WILPF	Women's International League for Peace and Freedom
WIM	Wirtschaftsvereinigung Industrielle Meerestechnik
WIM	Women in Management
WINBAN	Windward Islands Banana Association
WIO	Women's International ORT (Organisation-Reconstruction-Travail)
WIPO	World Intellectual Property Organisation
WIPOG	Wirtschaftspolitische Gesellschaft
WIPRC	Whiting and Industrial Powders Research Council (now WHRA)
WIRA	Wax Importers and Refiners Association (U.S.A.)
WIRA	Wool Industries Research Association
WIRF	Women's International Religious Fellowship (U.S.A.)
WIRFMD	Wellcome Institute for Research into Foot and Mouth Disease (E. Africa)
WIS	Wheat Information Service (Japan)
WISA	West Indies Sugar Association
WISC	West Indian Standing Conference
WISC	Women's Information and Study Centre
WISCO	West Indies Sugar Company
WISDA	Wirtschaftsgruppe Schweizerischer Dachpappenfabriken
WISI	World Information System on Informatics
WISICA	West Indies Sea Island Cotton Association
WIT	Winnebago International Travelers (U.S.A.)
WITB	Wool Industry Training Board
WIZ	Wissenschaftliches Informationzentrum
WIZO	Women's International Zionist Organisation
WJA	World Jazz Association (U.S.A.)
WJC	World Jewish Congress
WJCB	World Jersey Cattle Bureau
WJEC	Welsh Joint Education Committee
WJG	Wiener Juristische Gesellschaft (Austria)
WKFO	Weltunion der Katholischen Frauen-Organisationen
WKJ	Weltbund der Katholischen Jugend
WLA	Womens Land Army
WLDA	Wholesale Leather Distributors Association
WLF	Women's Liberal Federation
WLG	Witwatersrand Landbougenootskap (South Africa)
WLHB	Women's League of Health and Beauty
WLPSA	Wild Life Preservation Society of Australia
WLRA	World Leisure and Recreation Association (U.S.A.)
WLSA	Welsh Land Settlement Association
WLTBU	Watermen, Lightermen, Tugmen and Bargemen's Union
WLU	World Lebanese Union
WLUS	World Land Use Survey
WMA	Wellington Mathematical Association (N.Z.)
WMA	World Medical Association
WMC	World Methodist Council
WMCW	World Movement of Christian Workers
WMGB	West Midlands Gas Board
WMI	Wildlife Management Institute (U.S.A.)
WMM	World Movement of Mothers
WMMA	Woodworking Machinery Manufacturers Association
WMO	World Meteorological Organisation
WMOAS	Women's Migration and Oversea Appointments Society
WMPCE	World Meeting Planners Congress and Exposition
WMPL	World Mission Prayer League (U.S.A.)
WMR	World Medical Relief (U.S.A.)
WMS	World Magnetic Survey
WMWFG	World Movement for World Federal Government
WN	World Neighbours (U.S.A.)

WNNR	Wetenskaplike en Nywerheids-Navorsingsraad (South Africa)	**WPA**	World Parliament Association
WNR	World New Religion (U.S.A.)	**WPA**	World Pheasant Association
WOBA	Werkgroep Onderzoek Bestrijding Aardappelcystenaaltjes	**WPA**	Works Projects Administration (U.S.A.)
		WPA	World Presbyterian Alliance
WOBT	Welt-Organisation Bild und Ton	**WPADC**	West Pakistan Agricultural Development Corporation
WOCCU	World Council of Credit Unions	**WPBS**	Welsh Plant Breeding Station
WODA	World Dredging Association	**WPC**	World Peace Council
WODCON	World Dredging Conference	**WPC**	World Petroleum Congress
WOE	Women Overseas for Equality (Belgium)	**WPC**	World Power Conference
WOECE	World Organisation for Early Childhood Education	**WPCC**	Water Pollution Control Council (New Zealand)
WOFIWU	World Federation of Industrial Workers' Unions	**WPCF**	Water Pollution Control Federation (U.S.A.)
WOGSC	World Cybernetics and Systems Organisation	**WPF**	World Prohibition Federation
		WPFC	Commission for Fisheries Research in the West Pacific
WOHP	World Organization for Human Potential (U.S.A.)	**WPFL**	West Pakistan Federation of Labour
WOIEP	World Office of Information on Environmental Problems	**WPI**	World Press Institute (U.S.A.)
		WPIDC	West Pakistan Industrial Development Corporation
WOIH	Council of World Organizations Interested in the Handicapped (U.S.A.)	**WPK**	Wirtschaftsprüferkammer
WOM	Weltorganisation für Meteorologie	**WPLO**	West Pakistan Library Association
WOMAN	World Organization of Mothers of all Nations	**WPMA**	Wall Paper Merchants' Association of Great Britain
WOMPI	Women of the Motion Picture Industry International (U.S.A.)	**WPNA**	World Proof Numismatic Association (U.S.A.)
WONCA	World Organisation of National Colleges, Academies and Academic Associations of General Practitioners and Family Physicians	**WPO**	Water Programs Office (*of* EPA) (U.S.A.)
		WPO	World Packaging Organization
WONG	Netherlands Foundation for the Advancement of Research in New Guinea (*now* WOTRO)	**WPO**	World Ploughing Organization
		WPOA	Western Pacific Orthopaedic Association
		WPRA	Wallpaper, Paint and Wallcovering Retailers Association
WONPA	World Organisation of Negro Plastic Arts	**WPRA**	Waste Paper Recovery Association
WORMS	World Organisation for the Retention of Male Supremacy	**WPRL**	Water Pollution Research Laboratory
WOSIC	Watchmakers of Switzerland Information Bureau	**WPRS**	West Palaearctic Regional Section (*of* IOBC)
WOSUNA	Stichting Wetenschappelijk Onderzoek Suriname-Nederlandse Antillen (*now* WOTRO)	**WPS**	World Population Society (U.S.A.)
		WPSA	World's Poultry Science Association
		WPSMA	Welsh Plate and Steel Makers Association
WOTP	World Organisation of the Teaching Profession	**WPTLC**	World Peace Through Law Center (U.S.A.)
WOTRO	Stichting voor Wetenschappelijk Onderzoek van de Tropen (*formerly* WONG and WOSUNA)	**WPU**	Women's Protestant Union
		WPV	Weltpostverein
		WPY	World Population Year
WOWI	Women on Words and Images (U.S.A.)	**WQO**	Water Quality Office (*now* WPO of EPA) (U.S.A.)
WPA	Wisconsin Pharmaceutical Association (U.S.A.)	**WRA**	Water Research Association

WRAC	Women's Royal Army Corps		**WSLF**	Western Somalia Liberation Front
WRADAC	Water Research Association Distribution Analogue Centre		**WSO**	World Simulation Organisation
			WSRA	Women's Squash Rackets Association
WRAF	Women's Auxiliary Air Force		**WSS**	World Ship Society
WRB	Water Resources Board		**WSSI**	Weed Science Society of Indonesia
WRC	Water Research Centre		**WSSS**	Western Society of Soil Science (U.S.A.)
WRC	World Relief Commission (U.S.A.)		**WSTEC**	Western Samoa Trust Estates Corporation
WRCC	Wildlife Research Co-ordinating Committee (E. Africa)		**WTA**	World Transport Agency
			WTAA	World Trade Alliance Association
WRI	War Resister's International		**WTB**	Welttierschutzbund
WRK	Westdeutsche Rektorenkonferenze		**WTBA**	Water-Tube Boilermakers' Association
WRMA	Woollen Mills Research Association (N.Z.)		**WTCA**	World Trade Centres Association
WRNS	Women's Royal Naval Service		**WTD**	Wool Textile Delegation
WRO	Weed Research Organization		**WTG**	Welt-Tierärztegesellschaft
WRONZ	Wool Research Organization of New Zealand		**WTGS**	West Texas Geological Society (U.S.A.)
WRPC	Water Resources Planning Commission (Taiwan)		**WTI**	Wirtschaftlich-Technischer Informationsdienst (Austria)
WRPDB	Western Regional Production Development Board (Nigeria)		**WTIS**	World Trade Information Service (U.S.A.)
			WTLMF	Warszawskie Towarzystwo Lekarzy Medycyny Fizykalnej
WRRL	Western Regional Research Laboratory (U.S.A.)		**WTMA**	Welded Tool Manufacturers Association
WRRU	Water Resources Research Unit (Ghana)		**WTN**	Wroclawskie Towarzystwo Naukowe
WRSA	World Rabbit Science Association		**WTO**	World Tourism Organization
WRSIC	Water Resources Scientific Information Center (U.S.A.)		**WTP**	World Tape Pals
			WTRD	Water Treatment Research Division (South Africa)
WRU	Western Reserve University (U.S.A.)		**WTTA**	Wholesale Tobacco Trade Association of Great Britain and Northern Ireland
WRVS	Women's Royal Voluntary Service			
WRY	World Refugee Year		**WTUC**	World Trade Union Conference
WSA	World Service Authority		**WU**	Women's Union
WSAC	Water Space Amenity Committee		**WUA**	Workers' Unions' Association (Sudan)
WSAVA	World Small Animal Veterinary Association		**WUCT**	World Union of Catholic Teachers
WSB	World Scout Bureau		**WUCWO**	World Union of Catholic Women's Organisations
WSC	World Spiritual Council			
WSCF	World's Student Christian Federation		**WUF**	World Underwater Federation
WSCS	Western Society of Crop Science (U.S.A.)		**WUF**	World Union of Free Thinkers
WSE	Western Society of Engineers (U.S.A.)		**WUJS**	World Union of Jewish Students
WSE	World Society of Ekistics (Greece)		**WULTUO**	World Union of Liberal Trade Union Organisations
WSET	Writers and Scholars Educational Trust			
WSF	World Sephardic Federation		**WUM**	Women's Universal Movement (U.S.A.)
WSFS	World Science Fiction Society (U.K.)		**WUM**	World Union Movement
WSGF	Welsh Seed Growers Federation		**WUOSY**	World Union of Organisations for the Safeguard of Youth
WSISI	West of Scotland Iron and Steel Institute			
WSL	Warren Spring Laboratory		**WUPJ**	World Union for Progressive Judaïsm
WSL	Weldbund zum Schultze des Lebens		**WUPO**	World Union of Pythagorean Organisations

WUR	World University Roundtable	**WWML**	Wood, Wire and Metal Lathers' International Union
WURDD	Western Utilisation Research and Development Division (U.S.A.)	**WWSU**	World Water Ski Union
WUS	World University Service	**WWTA**	Woollen and Worsted Trades Association
WUSA	World University Service in Australia	**WWTF**	Woollen and Worsted Trades Federation
WUSL	Women's United Service League	**WWTT**	Worldwide Tapetalk (U.K.)
WVA	Wereld Verbond van de Arbeid	**WWW**	World Weather Watch (WMO)
WVA	Wirtschaftsverband Asbest	**WWWC**	World Without War Council
WUNS	World Union of National Socialists	**WYF**	World Youth Forum (U.S.A.)
WUUN	Women United for United Nations	**WYWCA**	World Young Women's Christian Association
WVA	World Veterinary Association	**WZO**	World Zionist Organisation (Israel)
WVAO	Wissenschaftliche Vereinigung für Augenoptik und Optometrie		
WVBH	Weltband der Bau- und Holzarbeiterorganisationen		
WVD	Wereldverbond van Diamantbewerkers		
WVF	World Veterans Federation		
WVGM	Wirtschaftliche Vereinigung Grosshandel Metallhalbfabrikate		

X

XR	External Relations Service (UNESCO)

WVHS	West Virginia Horticultural Society (U.S.A.)
WVL	Weltverband der Lehrer
WVLI	Wirtschaftsvereinigung der Lebensmittelindustrie
WVM	Wereldfederatie voor de Metaalindustrie
WVOP	Wereld Vakverbond van Onderwijzend Personeel

Y

WVPA	World Veterinary Poultry Association	**YARS**	Yugoslav Astronautical and Rocket Society
WVRSC	Wholesale Vegetable and Root Seeds Committee	**YASGB**	Youth Association of Synagogues in Great Britain
WVSMA	West Virginia State Medical Association (U.S.A.)	**YBDSA**	Yacht Brokers, Designers and Surveyors Association
WVSPA	West Virginia State Pharmaceutical Association (U.S.A.)	**YCF**	Yacimientos Carboniferos Fiscales (Argentine)
WVT	Weltvereinigung für Tierzucht	**YCS**	International Young Catholic Students
WVV	Wissenschaftlicher Verein für Verkehrswesen e.V.	**YCW**	International Young Christian Workers
WVZ	Wirtschaftliche Vereinigung Zucker	**YEA**	Yanhee Electricity Authority (Thailand)
WWABCC	World Wide Avon Bottle Collectors Club (U.S.A.)	**YEPWA**	Youth Environmental Programme for West Africa
WWC	World's Wristwrestling Championship (U.S.A.)	**YFC**	Young Farmers' Clubs
WWCC	Western Weed Control Conference (U.S.A.)	**YFC**	Youth for Christ, International (U.S.A.)
WWCTU	World's Woman's Christian Temperance Union	**YFCI**	Youth for Christ International
		YFCU	Young Farmers' Clubs of Ulster (N. Ireland)
WWF	World Wildlife Fund (*Adviser* IUCN)	**YGS**	Yorkshire Grassland Society
WWI	Werkgroep van Winkelinrichtingsbedrijven	**YHA**	Youth Hostels Association

YHANI	Youth Hostel Association of Northern Ireland
YMCA	The World Alliance of Young Men's Christian Associations
YMHA	World Federation of Young Men's Hebrew Associations and Jewish Community Centres
YMISIG	Young Mensa International Special Interest Group
YOL	Yleinen Ossuskauppojen Liitto
YPEM	Service of Productive Works of Macedonia
YPF	Yacimentos Petroliferos Fiscales (Argentina)
YPFB	Yacimientos Petroliferos Fiscales Bolivianos
YPSCE	Young People's Society for Christian Endeavour
YSKOR	Suid-Afrikaanse Yster en Staal Industriële Korporasie Beperk
YSSYEM	Service for the Completion and Maintenance of Works of Macedonia
YTP	Yeni Türkiye Partisi
YVFF	Young Volunteer Force Foundation
YWCA	Young Women's Christian Association
YWF	Young World Federalists
YWFD	Young World Food and Development (FAO)
YWPG	Young World Promotion Group (FAO)

Z

ZADCA	Zinc Alloy Die Casters' Association
ZAED	Zentralstelle f. Atomkernenergie Dokumentation
ZAMEFA	Metal Fabricators of Zambia
ZANLA	Zimbabwe African National Liberation Army
ZANU	Zimbabwe African National Union
ZAP	Zaaizaadvereniging Anna-Paulowna
ZAP	Zwiazek Polskich Artystów Plastyków
ZAPU	Zimbabwe African People's Union
ZASP	Union of Polish State Artists Abroad
ZAV	Zentralarbeitsgemeinschaft des Strassenverkehrsgewerbes
ZAW	Zentralausschuss der Werbewirtschaft
ZBHD	Zambia Broken Hill Development Co.

ZBI	Zentralverband Berufsständischer Ingenieurvereine
ZBZ	Zentrum Berlin für Zukunftsforschung
ZCCI	Zippy Collectors Club International (U.S.A.)
ZCI	Zambian Copper Investment Ltd
ZDA	Zinc Development Association
ZDB	Zentralverband des Deutschen Baugewerbes
ZDG	Zentralverband der Deutschen Geflügelwirtschaft
ZDH	Zentralverband des Deutschen Handwerks
ZDK	Zentralverband des Kraftfahrzeughandels
ZDV	Zentralverband des Deutschen Vulkaniseur-Handwerks
ZELLCHE-MING	Verein der Zellstoff- und Papier-Chemiker und Ingenieure
ZENKO	All-Japan Federation of Metal Miners Union
ZENRO	All-Japan Trade Union Congress
ZENSEN DOMEI	National Federation of Textile Industry Workers Unions (Japan)
ZENTEI	Japanese Postal Workers Union
ZEV	Zuivel-Export-Vereniging
ZFD	Zentralverband der Fusspfleger Deutschlands
ZFGBI	Zionist Federation of Great Britain and Ireland
ZFMA	Zip Fasteners Manufacturers Association (India)
ZFV	Deutsche Zentrale fur Fremdenverkehr
ZGA	Zambia Geographical Association
ZHI	Stichting v. d. Nederlandse Zelfstandige Handel en Industrie
ZHZ	Zuid-Hollandse Zuivelbond
ZI	Zonta International (U.S.A.)
ZIDA	Zentrum für Information und Dokumentation der Aussenwirtschaft
ZIID	Zentralinstitut für Information und Dokumentation
ZIMCO	Zambia Industrial and Mining Corporation
ZINCOM	Zambian Industrial and Commercial Association
ZINS	Zionist Information Service (U.S.A.)
ZIPRA	Zimbabwe People's Revolutionary Army
ZITS	Zveza Inzenirjev in Tehnikov SR Slovenije
ZIV	Zentrale Informationsstelle für Verkehr in der Deutschen Verkehrswissenschaftlichen
ZKB	Zuivel Kwaliteitscontrôle Bureau

ZKF	Zentralverband Karosserie- und Fahrzeug-technik	**ZSKBIP**	Zväz Slovenských Knihovnikov Bibliografov Informacných Pracovnikov
ZKP	Zwiazek Kompozytorów Polskich	**ZSN**	Zoological Stations of Naples
ZLA	Zambia Library Association	**ZTG**	Zentralverband des Tankstellen- und Garagengewerbes
ZLDI	Zentralstelle f. Luftfahrdokumentation und Information	**ZUPO**	Zimbabwe United Peoples Organization
ZMB	Zentrale f. Maikäfer- Bekampfungsaktionen	**ZUU**	Zemedelsky ústav Ucetnicko-sprayoredný (Czechoslovakia)
ZMP	Zentrale Markt- u. Presberichtstelle der Deutschen Landwirtschaft	**ZVA**	Zentralverband der Augenoptiker
ZMPD	Zrzesenie Miedzynarodowych Przewóznik ów Drogowych w Polsce	**ZVEI**	Zentralverband der Elektrotechnischen Industrie
ZNP	Zanzibar Nationalist Party	**ZVFIFU**	Zentralverband Forstindustrie und Forstunternehem
ZNTB	Zambia National Tourist Bureau	**ZVK**	Zentralverband des Kraftfahrzeughandwerks
ZNZ	Zuid-Nederlandse Zuivelbond	**ZVK**	Zentralverband Krankengymnastik
ZOA	Zentralverband der Organisationen des Automaten-Aufstell-Gewerbes	**ZVM**	Zentralverband Deutscher Mechaniker-Handwerke
ZOA	Zionist Organisation of America	**ZVR**	Zentralverband des Raumausstatter-handwerks
ZPC	Zaaizaad en Pootgoed Cooperatieve		
ZPDA	Zinc Pigment Development Association	**ZVSH**	Zentralverband Sanitär- und Heizungs-Technik
ZPHT	Zrzeszenie Polskich Hoteli Turystycznych	**ZVSHK**	Zentralverband Sanitär-, Heizungs- und Klimatechnik
ZPP	Zjednoczenie Przemyslu Piwowarskiego		
ZPPP	Zanzibar and Pemba Peoples Party	**ZVSM**	Zentralverband Schweizerischer Milchproduzenten
ZPTL	Zrzeszenie Polskich Towarzystw Lekarskich	**ZVSU**	Zentralverband Schweizerischer Uhrmacher
ZSA	Zululand Swaziland Association (U.K.)	**ZWO**	Nederlandse Organisatie voor Zuiverwetenschappelijk Onderzoek
ZSIG	Zürcherische Seidenindustrie-Gesellschaft		